The NIV

Interlinear Hebrew-English Old Testament

The NIV

Interlinear Hebrew-English Old Testament

Volume 2 / Joshua–2 Kings

Edited by
John R. Kohlenberger III

12/02

THE NIV INTERLINEAR HEBREW-ENGLISH OLD TESTAMENT, VOL. 2

Grand Rapids, Michigan

Library of Congress Cataloging in Publication Data (Revised)

Bible. O.T. Hebrew 1979.
The NIV interlinear Hebrew-English Old Testament.
Includes bibliographies.
CONTENTS: v. 1. Genesis–Deuteronomy.— v. 2. Joshua–II Kings.
1. Bible. O.T. Interlinear translations. English.
I. Kohlenberger, John R. II. Bible. O.T. English.
New International. 1979. III. Title.
BS715 1979 221.4′4 79-23008
ISBN 0-310-38880-5 (v. 1)
ISBN 0-310-38890-2 (v. 2)

Printed in the United States of America

CONTENTS

ACKNOWLEDGMENTS

The most difficult section to write in this work is the acknowledgments, for so many loving and helpful hands have aided in the making of this book. Although those listed below have made a special contribution, I am no less grateful or indebted to many others who are not mentioned here.

First, I must acknowledge two institutions omitted in the first volume: the New York International Bible Society, for granting permission to use their New International Version as the English text; and the Deutsche Bibelstiftung, for granting permission to use their *Biblia Hebraica Stuttgartensia* as the Hebrew text.

Next, I wish to extend thanks to Western Conservative Baptist Seminary for allowing a portion of this material to satisfy the requirements of my Masters product, and especially to Dr. Ronald Barclay Allen for the many helpful directions and comments in the development of Volume 2.

Great credit must go to Ron Walker and the people of SeTyp here in Portland for their work of setting the interlinear English text from my handwritten copy, and to Bernie Maron and the people of Auto-Graphics in Los Angeles for their work of setting the NIV text to conform to the margin. For their tedious labors of setting the Hebrew in place, special thanks go to John Hemmingsen, R. Burwell Davis, Rosalie Donais, and Linda Schley. And, for the tedious task of proof-reading, I wish to thank Paul Jesclard and John Hemmingsen.

Above all, again, I praise God for His encouragement through my family—wife Carolyn and daughter Sarah—who kept me going through the many difficulties and set-backs of this volume.

TO MY DAUGHTER
SARAH NATANYA

INTRODUCTION

In view of the complete introductions for the general reader and the student of Hebrew contained in the first volume of the *NIV Interlinear Hebrew-English Old Testament* (hereafter, Vol. 1), only such matters as pertain to the special problems of this volume will be discussed here. The reader is referred to pages ix-xxx of Vol. 1 for a discussion of the texts, translation techniques and characteristics, and usage of the volumes of this set.

The Contents and the Canons

As is clear from the table of contents, this set follows the Greek canonical order, adopted by most versions, rather than the Hebrew. This order was chosen because the work is based on the New International Version (NIV). Moreover, most Hebrew tools for the English reader or the beginning/intermediate student of Hebrew are also arranged according to the Greek order, such as the *Englishman's Hebrew and Chaldee Concordance of the Old Testament* (Grand Rapids: Zondervan, 1970) and the *Reader's Hebrew-English Lexicon of the Old Testament* (Grand Rapids: Zondervan, 1980), thus the NIVIHEOT will be more easily used in conjunction with them for having adopted this order.

When the contents of the two arrangements are compared, however, it is apparent that the NIVIHEOT also complements the Hebrew order in its larger divisions (see Table 1). Volume 1, Genesis to Deuteronomy, contained fully the Hebrew Torah. Volume 2, Joshua to 2 Kings, contains the Former Prophets with the addition of Ruth. Volume 3, 1 Chronicles to Song of Songs, will contain the Writings, but not including Ruth, Lamentations, and Daniel. Volume 4, Isaiah to Malachi, will contain the Latter Prophets with the addition of Lamentations and Daniel. Thus the order 1-2-4-3 approximates the divisions of the Hebrew canon, though not its internal order.

Table 1

GREEK CANONICAL ORDER

- I. THE PENTATEUCH
  - A. Genesis
  - B. Exodus
  - C. Leviticus
  - D. Numbers
  - E. Deuteronomy
- II. THE HISTORICAL BOOKS
  - A. Joshua
  - B. Judges
  - C. Ruth
  - D. 1 and 2 Samuel
  - E. 1 and 2 Kings
  - F. 1 and 2 Chronicles
  - G. Ezra
  - H. Nehemiah
  - I. Esther
- III. THE BOOKS OF POETRY AND WISDOM
  - A. Job
  - B. Psalms
  - C. Proverbs
  - D. Ecclesiastes
  - E. Song of Songs
- IV. THE PROPHETS
  - A. The Major Prophets
    1. Isaiah
    2. Jeremiah and Lamentations
    3. Ezekiel
    4. Daniel
  - B. The Minor Prophets
    1. Hosea
    2. Joel
    3. Amos
    4. Obadiah
    5. Jonah
    6. Micah
    7. Nahum
    8. Habakkuk
    9. Zephaniah
    10. Haggai
    11. Zechariah
    12. Malachi

HEBREW CANONICAL ORDER

- I. THE TORAH
  - A. Genesis
  - B. Exodus
  - C. Leviticus
  - D. Numbers
  - E. Deuteronomy
- II. THE PROPHETS
  - A. The Former Prophets
    1. Joshua
    2. Judges
    3. 1 and 2 Samuel
    4. 1 and 2 Kings
  - B. The Latter Prophets
    1. Isaiah
    2. Jeremiah
    3. Ezekiel
    4. The Twelve
       - a. Hosea
       - b. Joel
       - c. Amos
       - d. Obadiah
       - e. Jonah
       - f. Micah
       - g. Nahum
       - h. Habakkuk
       - i. Zephaniah
       - j. Haggai
       - k. Zechariah
       - l. Malachi
- III. THE WRITINGS
  - A. The Books of Truth
    1. Psalms
    2. Job
    3. Proverbs
  - B. The Scrolls
    1. Ruth
    2. Song of Songs
    3. Ecclesiastes
    4. Lamentations
    5. Esther
  - C. The Rest
    1. Daniel
    2. Ezra-Nehemiah
    3. 1 and 2 Chronicles

The Hebrew Text

As stated in Vol. 1 (pp. xvii–xix), the NIVIHEOT follows the Masoretic Text (MT) according to the Leningrad Codex B19a (L) as reproduced in the *Biblia Hebraica Stuttgartensia* (BHS). Most suggested emendations or corrections to this text in Vol. 1 involved simple spelling differences between L and the majority MT tradition. Only in seven places (Gen. 4:8; 47:21; Exod. 8:19[23]; 14:25; 20:18; 34:19; Deut. 32:43) were actual changes to the MT suggested in order to provide the textual base presumed by the NIV translation when this translation could not be considered simply an idiomatic rendering of the MT. Of these, only one reading (Gen. 4:8) was introduced into the text, and that in brackets.

The Hebrew text, other than the Pentateuch, though in remarkable condition for its antiquity, is not as well preserved. This resulted in a few more necessary suggestions for textual emendation, all handled in footnotes with the following exceptions:

Verses 36 and 37 of Joshua 21 are omitted in some texts, including L, probably because verses 35 and 37 end with the same word and verses 36 and 38 begin with the same word, thus making it quite easy to skip from 35 to 38. (See C. D. Ginsburg, *Introduction to the Massoretico-Critical Edition of the Hebrew Bible* [New York: KTAV, repr. 1966], pp. 178ff. for a full treatment.) The text of the verses missing in L are included in their proper place in a slightly reduced Hebrew type.

Judges 16:13b, present in some Septuagint manuscripts and adopted by most modern versions, is inserted into the text in brackets. The Hebrew is reproduced from the conjectured translation of the Septuagint contained in the textual apparatus of BHS. (See Ginsburg, pp. 176–77 for a full treatment.)

These two textual insertions were made to accommodate the interlinear text to that of the NIV. In all other cases, the MT was followed as the basis of the interlinear text, though this often required translating from the NIV footnotes rather than the text, especially in the textually difficult books of Samuel. Though seemingly numerous, all of these textual emendations of the NIV are very short and inconsequential and do not alter in any way the *teaching* of the Old Testament according to the MT.

Besides the excellent *Hebrew-English Lexicon* of Brown, Driver, and Briggs (Oxford: Oxford University Press, 1907) and Gesenius's *Hebrew Grammar* (Oxford: Oxford University Press, 2nd English ed. 1910), those interested in a more detailed treatment of textual difficulties and Hebrew idioms may consult the excellent commentaries available on this section of canon.

S. R. Driver's *Notes on the Hebrew Text of the Books of Samuel* (Oxford: Oxford University Press, 2nd ed. 1913, repr. by Alpha Publications, 1981) was indispensable in the preparation of this volume. It is an outstanding treatment of textual criticism, difficult Hebrew idioms, and grammatical idiosyncracies intended for the intermediate/advanced student of Hebrew and thoroughly footnoted in the *Lexicon* and *Grammar* mentioned above.

The Anchor Bible commentaries on *Judges* by Robert G. Boling (Garden City: Doubleday, 1975) and *Ruth* by E. F. Campbell, Jr. (Garden City: Doubleday, 1975) handle most textual and translational difficulties for the beginning/intermediate Hebraist as well as provide excellent cultural and historical materials and perceptive interpretive insights.

Standard for textual work are the volumes of the International Critical Commentary (Edinburgh: T & T Clark). Of this commentary, only the fine work on *Kings* by James A. Montgomery and Henry S. Gehman (1951) was used extensively in the preparation of this volume, though the reader is referred to the other books in this series in conjunction with the more up-to-date treatments mentioned above.

Comments On Volume One

Though few comments and reviews have been received on Vol. 1 to date, some criticisms of the translation and format chosen by the editor need response.

Perhaps the most questionable choice in translation was the exclusion of the definite article from a word in construct relation to a definite or proper noun (Vol. 1, p. xxiii). This bound word is certainly to be considered definite by its grammatical relationship to its governing noun (Gesenius, §127a), but as the article is not graphically present on the bound word it was decided not to represent it in translation. This is in keeping with part of the purpose of the interlinear translation, namely to provide an exacting word-for-word rendering of the Hebrew into English, regardless of how clumsy the resulting English may be (Vol. 1, p. xxii). Comparison with the NIV in the margin will show the definiteness of the word in construct to a definite noun.

Similarly, rendering collective singulars as singular instead of plural when no English collective exists, and rendering Hebrew idiomatic plurals expressive of a singular object as plurals (Vol. 1, p. xxii) may also confuse those who are not studying Hebrew formally or who do not read the introduction with understanding. Again, a purpose of the interlinear translation is to provide a grammatically consistent rendering to aid the student of Hebrew in recognizing person, number, and gender, though these designations may not communicate good sense in English (ibid.). Comparison with the NIV text should clear up any questions of the proper understanding of a collective or idiomatic plural grammatically represented in the interlinear translation.

Finally, the verse numbering of the Hebrew sometimes conflicts with the English. Usually, in such instances of discrepancy, a chapter begins in one version with the final verse of the previous chapter in the other (e.g., p. 220). Sometimes, however, the numbering is off by more than one verse (e.g., p. 346). A footnote identifies the one-verse discrepancy in the former case, while brackets are used in the latter to place the English numeration alongside the Hebrew. This choice was made in order to preserve the versification of both texts for the purpose of more convenient cross-reference to both Hebrew- and English-based tools.

וַיְהִי אַחֲרֵי מוֹת מֹשֶׁה עֶבֶד יְהוָה וַיֹּאמֶר יְהוָה
Yahweh then-he-said Yahweh servant-of Moses death-of after and-he-was (1:1)

אֶל־יְהוֹשֻׁעַ בִּן־ נוּן מְשָׁרֵת מֹשֶׁה לֵאמֹר׃ מֹשֶׁה עַבְדִּי
servant-of-me Moses (2) to-say Moses one-aiding-of Nun son-of Joshua to

מֵת וְעַתָּה קוּם עֲבֹר אֶת־ הַיַּרְדֵּן הַזֶּה אַתָּה וְכָל־
and-all-of you the-this the-Jordan *** cross! get-ready! so-now he-is-dead

הָעָם הַזֶּה אֶל־ הָאָרֶץ אֲשֶׁר אָנֹכִי נֹתֵן לָהֶם לִבְנֵי יִשְׂרָאֵל׃
Israel to-sons-of to-them giving I that the-land into the-this the-people

כָּל־ מָקוֹם אֲשֶׁר תִּדְרֹךְ כַּף־ רַגְלְכֶם בּוֹ לָכֶם
to-you on-him foot-of-you sole-of she-sets where place every-of (3)

נְתַתִּיו כַּאֲשֶׁר דִּבַּרְתִּי אֶל־ מֹשֶׁה׃ מֵהַמִּדְבָּר
from-the-desert (4) Moses to I-promised just-as I-will-give-him

וְהַלְּבָנוֹן הַזֶּה וְעַד־ הַנָּהָר הַגָּדוֹל נְהַר־ פְּרָת
Euphrates River-of the-great the-river even-to the-this and-the-Lebanon

כֹּל אֶרֶץ הַחִתִּים וְעַד־ הַיָּם הַגָּדוֹל מְבוֹא הַשָּׁמֶשׁ
the-sun setting-of the-Great the-Sea even-to the-Hittites country-of all-of

יִהְיֶה גְּבוּלְכֶם׃ לֹא־ יִתְיַצֵּב אִישׁ לְפָנֶיךָ כֹּל
all-of against-you man he-will-stand not (5) territory-of-you he-will-be

יְמֵי חַיֶּיךָ כַּאֲשֶׁר הָיִיתִי עִם־ מֹשֶׁה אֶהְיֶה עִמָּךְ לֹא
not with-you I-will-be Moses with I-was just-as lives-of-you days-of

אַרְפְּךָ וְלֹא אֶעֶזְבֶךָּ׃ חֲזַק וֶאֱמָץ
and-be-courageous! be-strong! (6) I-will-forsake-you and-not I-will-leave-you

כִּי אַתָּה תַּנְחִיל אֶת־ הָעָם הַזֶּה אֶת־ הָאָרֶץ אֲשֶׁר־
that the-land *** the-this the-people *** you-will-lead-to-inherit you for

נִשְׁבַּעְתִּי לַאֲבוֹתָם לָתֵת לָהֶם׃ רַק חֲזַק
be-strong! only (7) to-them to-give to-fathers-of-them I-swore

וֶאֱמַץ מְאֹד לִשְׁמֹר לַעֲשׂוֹת כְּכָל־ הַתּוֹרָה אֲשֶׁר
that the-law as-all-of to-obey to-be-careful very and-be-courageous!

צִוְּךָ מֹשֶׁה עַבְדִּי אַל־ תָּסוּר מִמֶּנּוּ יָמִין וּשְׂמֹאול לְמַעַן
so-that or-left right from-him you-turn not servant-of-me Moses he-gave-you

תַּשְׂכִּיל בְּכֹל אֲשֶׁר תֵּלֵךְ׃ לֹא־ יָמוּשׁ סֵפֶר הַתּוֹרָה
the-Law Book-of you-let-depart not (8) you-go where in-every you-may-succeed

הַזֶּה מִפִּיךָ וְהָגִיתָ בּוֹ יוֹמָם וָלַיְלָה לְמַעַן
so-that and-night by-day on-him but-you-meditate from-mouth-of-you the-this

תִּשְׁמֹר לַעֲשׂוֹת כְּכָל־ הַכָּתוּב בּוֹ כִּי־ אָז
then for in-him the-being-written as-all-of to-do you-may-be-careful

תַּצְלִיחַ אֶת־ דְּרָכֶךָ וְאָז תַּשְׂכִּיל׃ הֲלוֹא
not? (9) you-will-succeed and-then way-of-you *** you-will-prosper

The LORD Commands Joshua

1 After the death of Moses
the servant of the LORD,
the LORD said to Joshua son of
Nun, Moses' aide: 2"Moses my
servant is dead. Now then,
you and all these people, get
ready to cross the Jordan River
into the land I am about to
give to them—to the Israelites.
3I will give you every place
where you set your foot, as I
promised Moses. 4Your territory will extend from the
desert and from Lebanon to
the great river, the Euphrates—all the Hittite country—
and to the Great Sea[a] on the
west. 5No one will be able to
stand up against you all the
days of your life. As I was with
Moses, so I will be with you; I
will never leave you or forsake
you.
6"Be strong and courageous,
because you will lead these
people to inherit the land I
swore to their forefathers to
give them. 7Be strong and very
courageous. Be careful to obey
all the law my servant Moses
gave you; do not turn from it
to the right or to the left, that
you may be successful
wherever you go. 8Do not let
this Book of the Law depart
from your mouth; meditate on
it day and night, so that you
may be careful to do everything written in it. Then you
will be prosperous and successful. 9Have I not com-
manded you? Be strong and

[a]4 That is, the Mediterranean

צִוִּיתִיךָ חֲזַק וֶאֱמָץ אַל־ תַּעֲרֹץ וְאַל־
and-not you-be-terrified not and-be-courageous! be-strong! I-commanded-you

תֵּחָת כִּי עִמְּךָ יְהוָה אֱלֹהֶיךָ בְּכֹל אֲשֶׁר תֵּלֵךְ׃
you-go where in-every God-of-you Yahweh with-you for you-be-discouraged

וַיְצַו יְהוֹשֻׁעַ אֶת־ שֹׁטְרֵי הָעָם לֵאמֹר׃ עִבְרוּ
go! (11) to-say the-people being-officials-of *** Joshua so-he-commanded (10)

בְּקֶרֶב הַמַּחֲנֶה וְצַוּוּ אֶת־ הָעָם לֵאמֹר הָכִינוּ לָכֶם
for-you get-ready! to-say the-people *** and-tell! the-camp through-midst-of

צֵידָה כִּי בְּעוֹד שְׁלֹשֶׁת יָמִים אַתֶּם עֹבְרִים אֶת־ הַיַּרְדֵּן הַזֶּה
the-this the-Jordan *** ones-crossing you days three-of from-now for supply

לָבוֹא לָרֶשֶׁת אֶת־ הָאָרֶץ אֲשֶׁר יְהוָה אֱלֹהֵיכֶם נֹתֵן לָכֶם
to-you giving God-of-you Yahweh that the-land *** to-possess to-go-in

לְרִשְׁתָּהּ׃ וְלָרֻאוּבֵנִי וְלַגָּדִי וְלַחֲצִי
and-to-half-of and-to-the-Gadite but-to-the-Reubenite (12) to-possess-her

שֵׁבֶט הַמְנַשֶּׁה אָמַר יְהוֹשֻׁעַ לֵאמֹר׃ זָכוֹר אֶת־ הַדָּבָר
the-command *** to-remember (13) to-say Joshua he-said the-Manasseh tribe-of

אֲשֶׁר צִוָּה אֶתְכֶם מֹשֶׁה עֶבֶד־ יְהוָה לֵאמֹר יְהוָה אֱלֹהֵיכֶם מֵנִיחַ
giving-rest God-of-you Yahweh to-say Yahweh servant-of Moses you he-gave that

לָכֶם וְנָתַן לָכֶם אֶת־ הָאָרֶץ הַזֹּאת׃ נְשֵׁיכֶם
wives-of-you (14) the-this the-land *** to-you and-he-granted to-you

טַפְּכֶם וּמִקְנֵיכֶם יֵשְׁבוּ בָּאָרֶץ אֲשֶׁר נָתַן לָכֶם
to-you he-gave that in-the-land they-may-stay and-stocks-of-you child-of-you

מֹשֶׁה בְּעֵבֶר הַיַּרְדֵּן וְאַתֶּם תַּעַבְרוּ חֲמֻשִׁים לִפְנֵי
ahead-of ones-being-armed you-must-cross but-you the-Jordan on-east-of Moses

אֲחֵיכֶם כֹּל גִּבּוֹרֵי הַחַיִל וַעֲזַרְתֶּם אוֹתָם׃ עַד
until (15) them so-you-must-help the-fight men-of all-of brothers-of-you

אֲשֶׁר־ יָנִיחַ יְהוָה לַאֲחֵיכֶם כָּכֶם וְיָרְשׁוּ גַם־
also and-they-possess as-you to-brothers-of-you Yahweh he-gives-rest when

הֵמָּה אֶת־הָאָרֶץ אֲשֶׁר־ יְהוָה אֱלֹהֵיכֶם נֹתֵן לָהֶם וְשַׁבְתֶּם
then-you-may-go-back to-them giving God-of-you Yahweh that the-land *** they

לְאֶרֶץ יְרֻשַּׁתְכֶם וִירִשְׁתֶּם אוֹתָהּ אֲשֶׁר נָתַן לָכֶם
to-you he-gave which her and-you-may-occupy possession-of-you to-land-of

מֹשֶׁה עֶבֶד יְהוָה בְּעֵבֶר הַיַּרְדֵּן מִזְרַח הַשָּׁמֶשׁ׃
the-sun rise-of the-Jordan on-east-of Yahweh servant-of Moses

וַיַּעֲנוּ אֶת־ יְהוֹשֻׁעַ לֵאמֹר כֹּל אֲשֶׁר־ צִוִּיתָנוּ
you-commanded-us that all to-say Joshua *** then-they-answered (16)

נַעֲשֶׂה וְאֶל־ כָּל־ אֲשֶׁר תִּשְׁלָחֵנוּ נֵלֵךְ׃ כְּכֹל אֲשֶׁר־
that as-all (17) we-will-go you-send-us that everywhere and-to we-will-do

courageous. Do not be terrified; do not be discouraged,
for the LORD your God will be
with you wherever you go."
10So Joshua ordered the
officers of the people: 11"Go
through the camp and tell the
people, 'Get your supplies
ready. Three days from now
you will cross the Jordan here
to go in and take possession of
the land the LORD your God is
giving you for your own.' "
12But to the Reubenites, the
Gadites and the half-tribe of
Manasseh, Joshua said,
13"Remember the command
that Moses the servant of the
LORD gave you: 'The LORD your
God is giving you rest and has
granted you this land.' 14Your
wives, your children and your
livestock may stay in the land
that Moses gave you east of
the Jordan, but all your
fighting men, fully armed,
must cross over ahead of your
brothers. You are to help your
brothers 15until the LORD gives
them rest, as he has done for
you, and until they too have
taken possession of the land
that the LORD your God is giving them. After that, you may
go back and occupy your own
land, which Moses the servant
of the LORD gave you east of
the Jordan toward the sunrise."
16Then they answered
Joshua, "Whatever you have
commanded us we will do,
and wherever you send us we
will go. 17Just as we fully

שָׁמַעְנוּ אֶל־מֹשֶׁה כֵּן נִשְׁמַע אֵלֶיךָ רַק יִהְיֶה יְהוָה אֱלֹהֶיךָ
God-of-you Yahweh may-he-be only to-you we-will-obey so Moses to we-obeyed

עִמָּךְ כַּאֲשֶׁר הָיָה עִם־מֹשֶׁה׃ כָּל־אִישׁ אֲשֶׁר־יַמְרֶה אֶת־
*** he-rebels who man any-of (18) Moses with he-was just-as with-you

פִּיךָ וְלֹא־יִשְׁמַע אֶת־דְּבָרֶיךָ לְכֹל אֲשֶׁר־
that against-anything words-of-you *** he-obeys and-not word-of-you

תְּצַוֶּנּוּ יוּמָת רַק חֲזַק וֶאֱמָץ׃
and-be-courageous! be-strong! only he-will-die you-may-command-him

וַיִּשְׁלַח יְהוֹשֻׁעַ־בִּן־נוּן מִן־הַשִּׁטִּים שְׁנַיִם־אֲנָשִׁים מְרַגְּלִים
ones-spying men two the-Shittim from Nun son-of Joshua then-he-sent (2:1)

חֶרֶשׁ לֵאמֹר לְכוּ רְאוּ אֶת־הָאָרֶץ וְאֶת־יְרִיחוֹ וַיֵּלְכוּ
so-they-went Jericho and the-land *** look-over! go! to-say secretly

וַיָּבֹאוּ בֵּית־אִשָּׁה זוֹנָה וּשְׁמָהּ רָחָב
Rahab and-name-of-her prostitute woman house-of and-they-entered

וַיִּשְׁכְּבוּ־שָׁמָּה׃ וַיֵּאָמַר לְמֶלֶךְ יְרִיחוֹ לֵאמֹר הִנֵּה
see! to-say Jericho to-king-of and-he-was-told (2) at-there and-they-stayed

אֲנָשִׁים בָּאוּ הֵנָּה הַלַּיְלָה מִבְּנֵי יִשְׂרָאֵל לַחְפֹּר אֶת־הָאָרֶץ׃
the-land *** to-spy-out Israel from-sons-of the-night here they-came men

וַיִּשְׁלַח מֶלֶךְ יְרִיחוֹ אֶל־רָחָב לֵאמֹר הוֹצִיאִי הָאֲנָשִׁים
the-men bring-out! to-say Rahab to Jericho king-of so-he-sent (3)

הַבָּאִים אֵלַיִךְ אֲשֶׁר־בָּאוּ לְבֵיתֵךְ כִּי לַחְפֹּר אֶת־
*** to-spy-out for into-house-of-you they-entered who to-you the-ones-coming

כָּל־הָאָרֶץ בָּאוּ׃ וַתִּקַּח הָאִשָּׁה אֶת־שְׁנֵי הָאֲנָשִׁים
the-men two-of *** the-woman but-she-took (4) they-came the-land whole-of

וַתִּצְפְּנוֹ וַתֹּאמֶר ׀ כֵּן בָּאוּ אֵלַי הָאֲנָשִׁים וְלֹא יָדַעְתִּי
I-knew but-not the-men to-me they-came yes and-she-said and-she-hid-him

מֵאַיִן הֵמָּה׃ וַיְהִי הַשַּׁעַר לִסְגּוֹר בַּחֹשֶׁךְ וְהָאֲנָשִׁים
and-the-men at-the-dusk to-close the-gate and-he-was (5) they from-where

יָצָאוּ לֹא יָדַעְתִּי אָנָה הָלְכוּ הָאֲנָשִׁים רִדְפוּ מַהֵר אַחֲרֵיהֶם
after-them quickly go-after! the-men they-went to-where I-know not they-left

כִּי תַשִּׂיגוּם׃ וְהִיא הֶעֱלָתַם הַגָּגָה
to-the-roof she-took-up-them but-she (6) you-may-catch-them for

וַתִּטְמְנֵם בְּפִשְׁתֵּי הָעֵץ הָעֲרֻכוֹת לָהּ עַל־
on by-her the-ones-being-laid the-stalk under-flax-of and-she-hid-them

הַגָּג׃ וְהָאֲנָשִׁים רָדְפוּ אַחֲרֵיהֶם דֶּרֶךְ הַיַּרְדֵּן עַל
to the-Jordan road-of after-them they-pursued so-the-men (7) the-roof

הַמַּעְבְּרוֹת וְהַשַּׁעַר סָגָרוּ אַחֲרֵי כַּאֲשֶׁר יָצְאוּ
they-went-out just-as after they-closed and-the-gate the-fords

obeyed Moses, so we will obey
you. Only may the LORD your
God be with you as he was
with Moses. 18Whoever rebels
against your word and does
not obey your words, whatever you may command them,
will be put to death. Only be
strong and courageous!"

Rahab and the Spies

2 Then Joshua son of Nun
secretly sent two spies
from Shittim. "Go, look over
the land," he said, "especially
Jericho." So they went and entered the house of a prostitute[b]
named Rahab and stayed
there.
2The king of Jericho was
told, "Look! Some of the Israelites have come here tonight to
spy out the land." 3So the king
of Jericho sent this message to
Rahab, "Bring out the men
who came to you and entered
your house, because they have
come to spy out the whole
land."
4But the woman had taken
the two men and hidden
them. She said, "Yes, the men
came to me, but I did not
know where they had come
from. 5At dusk, when it was
time to close the city gate, the
men left. I don't know which
way they went. Go after them
quickly. You may catch up
with them." 6(But she had tak-
en them up to the roof and
hidden them under the stalks
of flax she had laid out on the
roof.) 7So the men set out in
pursuit of the spies on the
road that leads to the fords of
the Jordan, and as soon as the
pursuers had gone out, the
gate was shut.

[b]1 Or possibly *an innkeeper*

הָרֹדְפִים אַחֲרֵיהֶם׃ וְהֵמָּה טֶרֶם יִשְׁכָּבוּן וְהִיא
then-she they-lay-down before and-they (8) after-them the-ones-pursuing

עָלְתָה עֲלֵיהֶם עַל־ הַגָּג׃ וַתֹּאמֶר אֶל־ הָאֲנָשִׁים יָדַעְתִּי כִּי־
that I-know the-men to and-she-said (9) the-roof on to-them she-went-up

נָתַן יְהוָה לָכֶם אֶת־ הָאָרֶץ וְכִי־ נָפְלָה אֵימַתְכֶם עָלֵינוּ
on-us fear-of-you she-fell and-that the-land *** to-you Yahweh he-gave

וְכִי נָמֹגוּ כָּל־ יֹשְׁבֵי הָאָרֶץ מִפְּנֵיכֶם׃
because-of-you the-country ones-living-of all-of they-melt-in-fear and-that

כִּי שָׁמַעְנוּ אֵת אֲשֶׁר־ הוֹבִישׁ יְהוָה אֶת־ מֵי יַם־ סוּף
Reed Sea-of waters-of *** Yahweh he-dried-up how *** we-heard for (10)

מִפְּנֵיכֶם בְּצֵאתְכֶם מִמִּצְרָיִם וַאֲשֶׁר עֲשִׂיתֶם לִשְׁנֵי
to-two-of you-did and-what from-Egypt when-to-come-you from-before-you

מַלְכֵי הָאֱמֹרִי אֲשֶׁר בְּעֵבֶר הַיַּרְדֵּן לְסִיחֹן וּלְעוֹג אֲשֶׁר
whom and-to-Og to-Sihon the-Jordan on-east-of who the-Amorite kings-of

הֶחֱרַמְתֶּם אוֹתָם׃ וַנִּשְׁמַע וַיִּמַּס לְבָבֵנוּ וְלֹא־
and-not heart-of-us then-he-sank when-we-heard (11) them you-destroyed

קָמָה עוֹד רוּחַ בְּאִישׁ מִפְּנֵיכֶם כִּי יְהוָה אֱלֹהֵיכֶם
God-of-you Yahweh for because-of-you in-anyone courage any-more she-remained

הוּא אֱלֹהִים בַּשָּׁמַיִם מִמַּעַל וְעַל־ הָאָרֶץ מִתָּחַת׃ וְעַתָּה הִשָּׁבְעוּ־
swear! so-now (12) at-below the-earth and-on at-above in-the-heavens God he

נָא לִי בַּיהוָה כִּי־ עָשִׂיתִי עִמָּכֶם חָסֶד וַעֲשִׂיתֶם
that-you-will-show kindness to-you I-showed because by-Yahweh to-me now!

גַּם־ אַתֶּם עִם־ בֵּית אָבִי חֶסֶד וּנְתַתֶּם לִי אוֹת אֱמֶת׃
sure sign to-me and-you-give kindness father-of-me house-of to you also

וְהַחֲיִתֶם אֶת־ אָבִי וְאֶת־ אִמִּי וְאֶת־
and mother-of-me and father-of-me *** that-you-will-let-live (13)

אַחַי וְאֶת־ אַחְוֹתַי° וְאֵת כָּל־ אֲשֶׁר לָהֶם וְהִצַּלְתֶּם אֶת־
*** and-you-will-save to-them who all and sisters-of-me and brothers-of-me

נַפְשֹׁתֵינוּ מִמָּוֶת׃ וַיֹּאמְרוּ לָהּ הָאֲנָשִׁים נַפְשֵׁנוּ תַחְתֵּיכֶם
for-you life-of-us the-men to-her and-they-said (14) from-death lives-of-us

לָמוּת אִם לֹא תַגִּידוּ אֶת־ דְּבָרֵנוּ זֶה וְהָיָה בְּתֵת־
when-to-give then-he-will-be this deed-of-us *** you-tell not if to-die

יְהוָה לָנוּ אֶת־ הָאָרֶץ וְעָשִׂינוּ עִמְּךָ חֶסֶד וֶאֱמֶת׃
and-faithfully kindly with-you then-we-will-treat the-land *** to-us Yahweh

וַתּוֹרִדֵם בַּחֶבֶל בְּעַד הַחַלּוֹן כִּי בֵיתָהּ
house-of-her for the-window through by-the-rope so-she-let-down-them (15)

בְּקִיר הַחוֹמָה וּבַחוֹמָה הִיא יוֹשָׁבֶת׃ וַתֹּאמֶר לָהֶם
to-them now-she-said (16) living she and-in-the-wall the-wall in-city-of

°13 ק אחיותי

[8]Before the spies lay down
for the night, she went up on
the roof [9]and said to them, "I
know that the LORD has given
this land to you and that a
great fear of you has fallen on
us, so that all who live in this
country are melting in fear because of you. [10]We have heard
how the LORD dried up the
water of the Red Sea[c] for you
when you came out of Egypt,
and what you did to Sihon
and Og, the two kings of the
Amorites east of the Jordan,
whom you completely de-
stroyed.[d] [11]When we heard of
it, our hearts sank and everyone's courage failed because of
you, for the LORD your God is
God in heaven above and on
the earth below. [12]Now then,
please swear to me by the
LORD that you will show kindness to my family, because I
have shown kindness to you.
Give me a sure sign [13]that you
will spare the lives of my father and mother, my brothers
and sisters, and all who belong to them, and that you will
save us from death."
[14]"Our lives for your lives!"
the men assured her. "If you
don't tell what we are doing,
we will treat you kindly and
faithfully when the LORD gives
us the land."
[15]So she let them down by a
rope through the window, for
the house she lived in was part
of the city wall. [16]Now she had

[c]10 Hebrew *Yam Suph;* that is, Sea of Reeds
[d]10 The Hebrew term refers to the irrevocable giving over of things or persons to the LORD, often by totally destroying them.

הָהָרָה לֵּכוּ פֶּן־ יִפְגְּעוּ בָכֶם הָרֹדְפִים וְנַחְבֵּתֶם
and-you-hide-selves the-ones-pursuing to-you they-find so-not go! to-the-hill

שָׁמָּה שְׁלֹשֶׁת יָמִים עַד שׁוֹב הָרֹדְפִים וְאַחַר תֵּלְכוּ
you-go and-after the-ones-pursuing to-return until days three-of at-there

לְדַרְכְּכֶם׃ וַיֹּאמְרוּ אֵלֶיהָ הָאֲנָשִׁים נְקִיִּם אֲנַחְנוּ מִשְּׁבֻעָתֵךְ
from-oath-of-us we ones-free the-men to-her and-they-said (17) on-way-of-you

הַזֶּה אֲשֶׁר הִשְׁבַּעְתָּנוּ׃ הִנֵּה אֲנַחְנוּ בָאִים בָּאָרֶץ
into-the-land ones-entering we unless (18) you-made-swear-us that the-this

אֶת־ תִּקְוַת חוּט הַשָּׁנִי הַזֶּה תִּקְשְׁרִי בַּחַלּוֹן אֲשֶׁר הוֹרַדְתֵּנוּ
you-let-down-us that in-the-window you-tie this the-scarlet rope cord-of ***

בוֹ וְאֶת־ אָבִיךְ וְאֶת־ אִמֵּךְ וְאֶת־ אַחַיִךְ וְאֵת
and brother-of-you and mother-of-you and father-of-you and through-him

כָּל־ בֵּית אָבִיךְ תַּאַסְפִי אֵלַיִךְ הַבָּיְתָה׃
into-the-house with-you you-bring father-of-you house-of all-of

וְהָיָה כֹּל אֲשֶׁר־ יֵצֵא מִדַּלְתֵי בֵיתֵךְ ׀
house-of-you from-doors-of he-goes-out who anyone and-he-will-be (19)

הַחוּצָה דָּמוֹ בְרֹאשׁוֹ וַאֲנַחְנוּ נְקִיִּם
ones-not-responsible and-we on-head-of-him blood-of-him into-the-street

וְכֹל אֲשֶׁר יִהְיֶה אִתָּךְ בַּבַּיִת דָּמוֹ בְרֹאשֵׁנוּ אִם־
if on-head-of-us blood-of-him in-the-house with-you he-is who but-anyone

יָד תִּהְיֶה־ בּוֹ׃ וְאִם־ תַּגִּידִי אֶת־ דְּבָרֵנוּ זֶה וְהָיִינוּ
then-we-are this deed-of-us *** you-tell but-if (20) on-him she-lays hand

נְקִיִּם מִשְּׁבֻעָתֵךְ אֲשֶׁר הִשְׁבַּעְתָּנוּ׃ וַתֹּאמֶר
and-she-replied (21) you-made-swear-us that from-oath-of-you ones-released

כְּדִבְרֵיכֶם כֶּן־ הוּא וַתְּשַׁלְּחֵם וַיֵּלֵכוּ וַתִּקְשֹׁר
and-she-tied and-they-departed so-she-sent-away-them he so as-words-of-you

אֶת־ תִּקְוַת הַשָּׁנִי בַּחַלּוֹן׃ וַיֵּלְכוּ וַיָּבֹאוּ
then-they-went when-they-left (22) in-the-window the-scarlet cord-of ***

הָהָרָה וַיֵּשְׁבוּ שָׁם שְׁלֹשֶׁת יָמִים עַד־ שָׁבוּ
they-returned until days three-of there and-they-stayed into-the-hill

הָרֹדְפִים וַיְבַקְשׁוּ הָרֹדְפִים בְּכָל־ הַדֶּרֶךְ
the-road along-all-of the-ones-pursuing and-they-searched the-ones-pursuing

וְלֹא מָצָאוּ׃ וַיָּשֻׁבוּ שְׁנֵי הָאֲנָשִׁים
the-men two-of then-they-started-back (23) they-found but-not

וַיֵּרְדוּ מֵהָהָר וַיַּעַבְרוּ וַיָּבֹאוּ אֶל־ יְהוֹשֻׁעַ
Joshua to and-they-came and-they-forded from-the-hill and-they-went-down

בִּן־ נוּן וַיְסַפְּרוּ־ לוֹ אֵת כָּל־ הַמֹּצְאוֹת אוֹתָם׃
to-them the-things-happening all-of *** to-him and-they-told Nun son-of

said to them, "Go to the hills
so the pursuers will not find
you. Hide yourselves there
three days until they return,
and then go on your way."
17The men said to her, "This
oath you made us swear will
not be binding on us 18unless,
when we enter the land, you
have tied this scarlet cord in
the window through which
you let us down, and unless
you have brought your father
and mother, your brothers
and all your family into your
house. 19If anyone goes outside your house into the street,
his blood will be on his own
head; we will not be responsible. As for anyone who is in
the house with you, his blood
will be on our head if a hand
is laid on him. 20But if you tell
what we are doing, we will be
released from the oath you
made us swear."
21"Agreed," she replied. "Let
it be as you say." So she sent
them away and they departed.
And she tied the scarlet cord
in the window.
22When they left, they went
into the hills and stayed there
three days, until the pursuers
had searched all along the
road and returned without
finding them. 23Then the two
men started back. They went
down out of the hills, forded
the river and came to Joshua
son of Nun and told him
everything that had happened

וַיֹּאמְרוּ אֶל־יְהוֹשֻׁעַ כִּי־נָתַן יְהוָה בְּיָדֵנוּ אֶת־
*** into-hand-of-us Yahweh he-gave surely Joshua to and-they-said (24)

כָּל־הָאָרֶץ וְגַם־נָמֹגוּ כָּל־יֹשְׁבֵי הָאָרֶץ
the-land ones-living-of all-of they-melt-in-fear and-also the-land whole-of

מִפָּנֵינוּ׃ וַיַּשְׁכֵּם יְהוֹשֻׁעַ בַּבֹּקֶר וַיִּסְעוּ
and-they-set-out in-the-morning Joshua and-he-rose (3:1) because-of-us

מֵהַשִּׁטִּים וַיָּבֹאוּ עַד־הַיַּרְדֵּן הוּא וְכָל־בְּנֵי יִשְׂרָאֵל
Israel sons-of and-all-of he the-Jordan to and-they-went from-the-Shittim

וַיָּלִנוּ שָׁם טֶרֶם יַעֲבֹרוּ׃ וַיְהִי מִקְצֵה
at-end-of and-he-was (2) they-crossed-over before there and-they-camped

שְׁלֹשֶׁת יָמִים וַיַּעַבְרוּ הַשֹּׁטְרִים בְּקֶרֶב הַמַּחֲנֶה׃
the-camp through-midst-of the-being-officers then-they-went days three-of

וַיְצַוּוּ אֶת־הָעָם לֵאמֹר כִּרְאֹתְכֶם אֵת אֲרוֹן
ark-of *** when-to-see-you to-say the-people *** and-they-ordered (3)

בְּרִית־יְהוָה אֱלֹהֵיכֶם וְהַכֹּהֲנִים הַלְוִיִּם נֹשְׂאִים אֹתוֹ
him ones-carrying the-Levites and-the-priests God-of-you Yahweh covenant-of

וְאַתֶּם תִּסְעוּ מִמְּקוֹמְכֶם וַהֲלַכְתֶּם אַחֲרָיו׃ אַךְ ׀
but (4) after-him and-you-follow from-position-of-you you-move-out then-you

רָחוֹק יִהְיֶה בֵּינֵיכֶם וּבֵינָו כְּאַלְפַּיִם אַמָּה
cubit about-two-thousands and-between-him between-you he-must-be distance

בַּמִּדָּה אַל־תִּקְרְבוּ אֵלָיו לְמַעַן אֲשֶׁר־תֵּדְעוּ אֶת־הַדֶּרֶךְ
the-way *** you-will-know then so-that to-him you-go-near not by-the-measure

אֲשֶׁר תֵּלְכוּ־בָהּ כִּי לֹא עֲבַרְתֶּם בַּדֶּרֶךְ מִתְּמוֹל
on-yesterday on-the-way you-have-been not since on-her you-must-go which

שִׁלְשׁוֹם׃ וַיֹּאמֶר יְהוֹשֻׁעַ אֶל־הָעָם הִתְקַדָּשׁוּ כִּי מָחָר
tomorrow for consecrated-selves! the-people to Joshua then-he-told (5) before

יַעֲשֶׂה יְהוָה בְּקִרְבְּכֶם נִפְלָאוֹת׃ וַיֹּאמֶר יְהוֹשֻׁעַ
Joshua and-he-said (6) things-being-amazing in-among-you Yahweh he-will-do

אֶל־הַכֹּהֲנִים לֵאמֹר שְׂאוּ אֶת־אֲרוֹן הַבְּרִית וְעִבְרוּ
and-cross-over! the-covenant ark-of *** take-up! to-say the-priests to

לִפְנֵי הָעָם וַיִּשְׂאוּ אֶת־אֲרוֹן הַבְּרִית וַיֵּלְכוּ
and-they-went the-covenant ark-of *** so-they-took-up the-people ahead-of

לִפְנֵי הָעָם׃ וַיֹּאמֶר יְהוָה אֶל־יְהוֹשֻׁעַ הַיּוֹם הַזֶּה
the-this the-day Joshua to Yahweh and-he-said (7) the-people ahead-of

אָחֵל גַּדֶּלְךָ בְּעֵינֵי כָּל־יִשְׂרָאֵל אֲשֶׁר יֵדְעוּן כִּי
that they-may-know that Israel all-of in-eyes-of to-exalt-you I-will-begin

כַּאֲשֶׁר הָיִיתִי עִם־מֹשֶׁה אֶהְיֶה עִמָּךְ׃ וְאַתָּה תְּצַוֶּה אֶת־הַכֹּהֲנִים
the-priests *** you-tell now-you (8) with-you I-am Moses with I-was just-as

°4 ק ובינו

to them. 24They said to Joshua,
"The LORD has surely given
the whole land into our hands;
all the people are melting in
fear because of us."

Crossing the Jordan

3 Early in the morning
Joshua and all the Israelites set out from Shittim and
went to the Jordan, where
they camped before crossing
over. 2After three days the
officers went throughout the
camp, 3giving orders to the
people: "When you see the ark
of the covenant of the LORD
your God, and the priests, who
are Levites, carrying it, you
are to move out from your positions and follow it. 4Then
you will know which way to
go, since you have never been
this way before. But keep a
distance of about a thousand
yards[e] between you and the
ark; do not go near it."
5Then Joshua told the
people, "Consecrate your-
selves, for tomorrow the LORD
will do amazing things among
you."
6Joshua said to the priests,
"Take up the ark of the covenant and cross over ahead of
the people." So they took it up
and went ahead of them.
7And the LORD said to
Joshua, "Today I will begin to
exalt you in the eyes of all Israel, so they may know that I am
with you as I was with Moses.
8Tell the priests who carry the

[e]4 Hebrew *about two thousand cubits* (about 900 meters)

נֹשְׂאֵי אֲרוֹן־ הַבְּרִית לֵאמֹר כְּבֹאֲכֶם עַד־ קְצֵה
edge-of to when-to-reach-you to-say the-covenant ark-of ones-carrying-of

מֵי הַיַּרְדֵּן בַּיַּרְדֵּן תַּעֲמֹדוּ׃ (9) וַיֹּאמֶר יְהוֹשֻׁעַ אֶל־
to Joshua so-he-said (9) you-stand in-the-Jordan the-Jordan waters-of

בְּנֵי יִשְׂרָאֵל גֹּשׁוּ הֵנָּה וְשִׁמְעוּ אֶת־ דִּבְרֵי יְהוָה אֱלֹהֵיכֶם׃
God-of-you Yahweh words-of *** and-listen! here come! Israel sons-of

(10) וַיֹּאמֶר יְהוֹשֻׁעַ בְּזֹאת תֵּדְעוּן כִּי אֵל חַי בְּקִרְבְּכֶם
in-among-you living God that you-will-know by-this Joshua and-he-said (10)

וְהוֹרֵשׁ יוֹרִישׁ מִפְּנֵיכֶם אֶת־ הַכְּנַעֲנִי וְאֶת־
and the-Canaanite *** from-before-you he-will-drive-out and-to-drive-out

הַחִתִּי וְאֶת־ הַחִוִּי וְאֶת־ הַפְּרִזִּי וְאֶת־ הַגִּרְגָּשִׁי
the-Girgashite and the-Perizzite and the-Hivite and the-Hittite

וְהָאֱמֹרִי וְהַיְבוּסִי׃ (11) הִנֵּה אֲרוֹן הַבְּרִית אֲדוֹן
Lord-of the-covenant ark-of see! (11) and-the-Jebusite and-the-Amorite

כָּל־ הָאָרֶץ עֹבֵר לִפְנֵיכֶם בַּיַּרְדֵּן׃ (12) וְעַתָּה קְחוּ
choose! so-now (12) into-the-Jordan ahead-of-you going the-earth all-of

לָכֶם שְׁנֵי עָשָׂר אִישׁ מִשִּׁבְטֵי יִשְׂרָאֵל אִישׁ־אֶחָד אִישׁ־אֶחָד לַשָּׁבֶט׃
from-the-tribe one man one man Israel from-tribes-of man ten two-of for-you

(13) וְהָיָה כְּנוֹחַ כַּפּוֹת רַגְלֵי הַכֹּהֲנִים נֹשְׂאֵי
ones-carrying-of the-priests feet-of soles-of as-to-set and-he-will-be (13)

אֲרוֹן יְהוָה אֲדוֹן כָּל־ הָאָרֶץ בְּמֵי הַיַּרְדֵּן מֵי
waters-of the-Jordan in-waters-of the-earth all-of Lord-of Yahweh ark-of

הַיַּרְדֵּן יִכָּרֵתוּן הַמַּיִם הַיֹּרְדִים מִלְמָעְלָה
from-above the-ones-flowing-down the-waters they-will-be-cut-off the-Jordan

וְיַעַמְדוּ נֵד אֶחָד׃ (14) וַיְהִי בִּנְסֹעַ הָעָם
the-people when-to-set-out and-he-was (14) one heap and-they-will-stand-up

מֵאָהֳלֵיהֶם לַעֲבֹר אֶת־ הַיַּרְדֵּן וְהַכֹּהֲנִים נֹשְׂאֵי
ones-carrying-of and-the-priests the-Jordan *** to-cross from-tents-of-them

הָאָרוֹן הַבְּרִית לִפְנֵי הָעָם׃ (15) וּכְבוֹא נֹשְׂאֵי
ones-carrying-of and-as-to-reach (15) the-people ahead-of the-covenant the-ark

הָאָרוֹן עַד־ הַיַּרְדֵּן וְרַגְלֵי הַכֹּהֲנִים נֹשְׂאֵי הָאָרוֹן
the-ark ones-carrying-of the-priests and-feet-of the-Jordan to the-ark

נִטְבְּלוּ בִּקְצֵה הַמָּיִם וְהַיַּרְדֵּן מָלֵא עַל־ כָּל־
all-of to he-is-full now-the-Jordan the-waters on-edge-of they-touched

גְּדוֹתָיו כֹּל יְמֵי קָצִיר׃ (16) וַיַּעַמְדוּ הַמַּיִם
the-waters and-they-stopped (16) harvest days-of all-of banks-of-him

הַיֹּרְדִים מִלְמַעְלָה קָמוּ נֵד־ אֶחָד הַרְחֵק מְאֹד
very to-be-distant one heap they-piled-up from-above the-ones-flowing-down

ark of the covenant: 'When
you reach the edge of the Jordan's waters, go and stand in
the river.' "
9Joshua said to the Israelites,
"Come here and listen to the
words of the LORD your God.
10This is how you will know
that the living God is among
you, and that he will certainly
drive out before you the Canaanites, Hittites, Hivites,
Perizzites, Girgashites, Amorites and Jebusites. 11See, the
ark of the covenant of the Lord
of all the earth will go into the
Jordan ahead of you. 12Now
then, choose twelve men from
the tribes of Israel, one from
each tribe. 13And as soon as
the priests who carry the ark
of the LORD—the Lord of all the
earth—set foot in the Jordan,
the water flowing down-
stream will be cut off and
stand up in a heap."
14So when the people broke
camp to cross the Jordan, the
priests carrying the ark of the
covenant went ahead of them.
15Now the Jordan is at flood
stage all during harvest. Yet as
soon as the priests who carried
the ark reached the Jordan and
their feet touched the water's
edge, 16the water from up-
stream stopped flowing. It
piled up in a heap a great distance away, at a town called

[f]16 That is, the Dead Sea

בְּאָדָם הָעִיר אֲשֶׁר מִצַּד צָרְתָן וְהַיֹּרְדִים עַל
to and-the-ones-flowing-down Zarethan in-vicinity that the-town at-Adam

יָם הָעֲרָבָה יָם־ הַמֶּלַח תַּמּוּ נִכְרָתוּ
they-were-cut-off they-were-complete the-Salt Sea-of the-Arabah Sea-of

וְהָעָם עָבְרוּ נֶגֶד יְרִיחוֹ׃ וַיַּעַמְדוּ
and-they-stood (17) Jericho opposite they-crossed-over so-the-people

הַכֹּהֲנִים נֹשְׂאֵי הָאָרוֹן בְּרִית־ יְהוָה בֶּחָרָבָה
on-the-dry-ground Yahweh covenant-of the-ark ones-carrying-of the-priests

בְּתוֹךְ הַיַּרְדֵּן הָכֵן וְכָל־ יִשְׂרָאֵל עֹבְרִים
ones-passing-by Israel and-all-of to-be-firm the-Jordan in-middle-of

בֶּחָרָבָה עַד אֲשֶׁר־ תַּמּוּ כָּל־ הַגּוֹי לַעֲבֹר אֶת־
*** to-cross the-nation whole-of they-completed when until on-the-dry-ground

הַיַּרְדֵּן׃ וַיְהִי כַּאֲשֶׁר־ תַּמּוּ כָל־ הַגּוֹי
the-nation whole-of they-finished just-as and-he-was (4:1) the-Jordan

לַעֲבוֹר אֶת־ הַיַּרְדֵּן וַיֹּאמֶר יְהוָה אֶל־ יְהוֹשֻׁעַ לֵאמֹר׃ קְחוּ
choose! (2) to-say Joshua to Yahweh then-he-said the-Jordan *** to-cross

לָכֶם מִן־ הָעָם שְׁנֵים עָשָׂר אֲנָשִׁים אִישׁ־אֶחָד אִישׁ־אֶחָד מִשָּׁבֶט׃ וְצַוּוּ
and-tell! (3) from-tribe one man one man men ten two the-people from for-you

אוֹתָם לֵאמֹר שְׂאוּ־ לָכֶם מִזֶּה מִתּוֹךְ הַיַּרְדֵּן מִמַּצַּב
from-place-of the-Jordan in-middle-of from-here for-you take-up! to-say them

רַגְלֵי הַכֹּהֲנִים הָכִין שְׁתֵּים־עֶשְׂרֵה אֲבָנִים וְהַעֲבַרְתֶּם אוֹתָם עִמָּכֶם
with-you them and-you-carry-over stones ten two to-stand the-priests feet-of

וְהִנַּחְתֶּם אוֹתָם בַּמָּלוֹן אֲשֶׁר־ תָּלִינוּ בוֹ הַלָּיְלָה׃
the-night in-him you-stay where at-the-place them and-you-put-down

וַיִּקְרָא יְהוֹשֻׁעַ אֶל־ שְׁנֵים הֶעָשָׂר אִישׁ אֲשֶׁר הֵכִין
he-appointed whom man the-ten two together Joshua so-he-called (4)

מִבְּנֵי יִשְׂרָאֵל אִישׁ־אֶחָד אִישׁ־ אֶחָד מִשָּׁבֶט׃ וַיֹּאמֶר לָהֶם
to-them and-he-said (5) from-tribe one man one man Israel from-sons-of

יְהוֹשֻׁעַ עִבְרוּ לִפְנֵי אֲרוֹן יְהוָה אֱלֹהֵיכֶם אֶל־ תּוֹךְ הַיַּרְדֵּן
the-Jordan middle-of into God-of-you Yahweh ark-of before go-over! Joshua

וְהָרִימוּ לָכֶם אִישׁ אֶבֶן אַחַת עַל־ שִׁכְמוֹ לְמִסְפַּר שִׁבְטֵי
tribes-of by-number-of shoulder-of-him on one stone each to-you and-take-up!

בְנֵי־ יִשְׂרָאֵל׃ לְמַעַן תִּהְיֶה זֹאת אוֹת בְּקִרְבְּכֶם כִּי־ יִשְׁאָלוּן
they-ask when in-among-you sign this she-will-be so-that (6) Israel sons-of

בְּנֵיכֶם מָחָר לֵאמֹר מָה הָאֲבָנִים הָאֵלֶּה לָכֶם׃
to-you the-these the-stones what? to-say future children-of-you

וַאֲמַרְתֶּם לָהֶם אֲשֶׁר נִכְרְתוּ מֵימֵי הַיַּרְדֵּן
the-Jordan waters-of they-were-cut-off that to-them then-you-tell (7)

°16 ק מאדם

Adam in the vicinity of Zarethan, while the water flowing
down to the Sea of the Arabah
(the Salt Sea[f]) was completely
cut off. So the people crossed
over opposite Jericho. 17The
priests who carried the ark of
the covenant of the LORD stood
firm on dry ground in the
middle of the Jordan, while all
Israel passed by until the
whole nation had completed
the crossing on dry ground.

4 When the whole nation
had finished crossing the
Jordan, the LORD said to
Joshua, 2"Choose twelve men
from among the people, one
from each tribe, 3and tell them
to take up twelve stones from
the middle of the Jordan from
right where the priests stood
and to carry them over with
you and put them down at the
place where you stay tonight."
4So Joshua called together
the twelve men he had ap-
pointed from the Israelites,
one from each tribe, 5and said
to them, "Go over before the
ark of the LORD your God into
the middle of the Jordan. Each
of you is to take up a stone on
his shoulder, according to the
number of the tribes of the Israelites, 6to serve as a sign
among you. In the future,
when your children ask you,
'What do these stones mean?'
7tell them that the flow of the
Jordan was cut off before the

מִפְּנֵי אֲרוֹן בְּרִית־ יְהוָה בְּעָבְרוֹ בַּיַּרְדֵּן
over-the-Jordan when-to-cross-him Yahweh covenant-of ark-of from-before

נִכְרְתוּ מֵי הַיַּרְדֵּן וְהָיוּ הָאֲבָנִים הָאֵלֶּה
the-these the-stones now-they-must-be the-Jordan waters-of they-were-cut-off

לְזִכָּרוֹן לִבְנֵי יִשְׂרָאֵל עַד־עוֹלָם׃ וַיַּעֲשׂוּ־ כֵן בְּנֵי־ יִשְׂרָאֵל
Israel sons-of this so-they-did (8) forever to Israel to-sons-of as-memorial

כַּאֲשֶׁר צִוָּה יְהוֹשֻׁעַ וַיִּשְׂאוּ שְׁתֵּי־עֶשְׂרֵה אֲבָנִים מִתּוֹךְ
from-middle-of stones ten two-of and-they-took Joshua he-commanded just-as

הַיַּרְדֵּן כַּאֲשֶׁר דִּבֶּר יְהוָה אֶל־יְהוֹשֻׁעַ לְמִסְפַּר שִׁבְטֵי בְנֵי־
sons-of tribes-of by-number-of Joshua to Yahweh he-told just-as the-Jordan

יִשְׂרָאֵל וַיַּעֲבִרוּם עִמָּם אֶל־ הַמָּלוֹן וַיַּנִּחוּם
and-they-put-down-them the-camp to with-them and-they-carried-them Israel

שָׁם׃ וּשְׁתֵּים עֶשְׂרֵה אֲבָנִים הֵקִים יְהוֹשֻׁעַ בְּתוֹךְ הַיַּרְדֵּן תַּחַת
at the-Jordan in-middle-of Joshua he-set-up stones ten and-two (9) there

מַצַּב רַגְלֵי הַכֹּהֲנִים נֹשְׂאֵי אֲרוֹן הַבְּרִית וַיִּהְיוּ
and-they-are the-covenant ark-of ones-carrying-of the-priests feet-of spot-of

שָׁם עַד הַיּוֹם הַזֶּה׃ וְהַכֹּהֲנִים נֹשְׂאֵי הָאָרוֹן
the-ark ones-carrying-of now-the-priests (10) the-this the-day to there

עֹמְדִים בְּתוֹךְ הַיַּרְדֵּן עַד תֹּם כָּל־ הַדָּבָר
the-thing every-of to-be-done until the-Jordan in-middle-of ones-standing

אֲשֶׁר־ צִוָּה יְהוָה אֶת־יְהוֹשֻׁעַ לְדַבֵּר אֶל־ הָעָם כְּכֹל אֲשֶׁר־
that as-all the-people to to-speak Joshua *** Yahweh he-commanded that

צִוָּה מֹשֶׁה אֶת־ יְהוֹשֻׁעַ וַיְמַהֲרוּ הָעָם וַיַּעֲבֹרוּ׃
and-they-came-over the-people and-they-hurried Joshua *** Moses he-directed

וַיְהִי כַּאֲשֶׁר־ תַּם כָּל־ הָעָם לַעֲבוֹר
to-cross the-people all-of he-finished just-as and-he-was (11)

וַיַּעֲבֹר אֲרוֹן־ יְהוָה וְהַכֹּהֲנִים לִפְנֵי הָעָם׃
the-people in-front-of and-the-priests Yahweh ark-of then-he-came-over

וַיַּעַבְרוּ בְּנֵי־ רְאוּבֵן וּבְנֵי־ גָד וַחֲצִי
and-half-of Gad and-sons-of Reuben sons-of and-they-crossed-over (12)

שֵׁבֶט הַמְנַשֶּׁה חֲמֻשִׁים לִפְנֵי בְּנֵי יִשְׂרָאֵל כַּאֲשֶׁר
just-as Israel sons-of in-front-of ones-being-armed the-Manasseh tribe-of

דִּבֶּר אֲלֵיהֶם מֹשֶׁה׃ כְּאַרְבָּעִים אֶלֶף חֲלוּצֵי
ones-being-armed-of thousand about-forty (13) Moses to-them he-directed

הַצָּבָא עָבְרוּ לִפְנֵי יְהוָה לַמִּלְחָמָה אֶל עַרְבוֹת יְרִיחוֹ׃
Jericho plains-of to for-the-war Yahweh before they-crossed-over the-battle

בַּיּוֹם הַהוּא גִּדַּל יְהוָה אֶת־ יְהוֹשֻׁעַ בְּעֵינֵי כָּל־
all-of in-eyes-of Joshua *** Yahweh he-exalted the-that on-the-day (14)

ark of the covenant of the
LORD. When it crossed the Jordan, the waters of the Jordan
were cut off. These stones are
to be a memorial to the people
of Israel forever."
8 So the Israelites did as
Joshua commanded them.
They took twelve stones from
the middle of the Jordan, according to the number of the
tribes of the Israelites, as the
LORD had told Joshua; and
they carried them over with
them to their camp, where
they put them down. 9 Joshua
set up the twelve stones that
had been[g] in the middle of the
Jordan at the spot where the
priests who carried the ark of
the covenant had stood. And
they are there to this day.
10 Now the priests who carried the ark remained standing in the middle of the Jordan
until everything the LORD had
commanded Joshua was done
by the people, just as Moses
had directed Joshua. The
people hurried over, 11 and as
soon as all of them had
crossed, the ark of the LORD
and the priests came to the
other side while the people
watched. 12 The men of Reuben, Gad and the half-tribe of
Manasseh crossed over,
armed, in front of the Israelites, as Moses had directed
them. 13 About forty thousand
armed for battle crossed over
before the LORD to the plains
of Jericho for war.
14 That day the LORD exalted
Joshua in the sight of all Israel;

g9 Or Joshua also set up twelve stones

יִשְׂרָאֵל וַיִּרְאוּ אֹתוֹ כַּאֲשֶׁר יָרְאוּ אֶת־ מֹשֶׁה כָּל־ יְמֵי
days-of all-of Moses *** they-revered just-as him and-they-revered Israel

חַיָּיו׃ וַיֹּאמֶר יְהוָה אֶל־ יְהוֹשֻׁעַ לֵאמֹר׃ צַוֵּה אֶת־
*** command! (16) to-say Joshua to Yahweh then-he-said (15) lives-of-him

הַכֹּהֲנִים נֹשְׂאֵי אֲרוֹן הָעֵדוּת וְיַעֲלוּ מִן־
from so-they-come-up the-Testimony ark-of ones-carrying-of the-priests

הַיַּרְדֵּן׃ וַיְצַו יְהוֹשֻׁעַ אֶת־ הַכֹּהֲנִים לֵאמֹר עֲלוּ מִן־
from come-up! to-say the-priests *** Joshua so-he-commanded (17) the-Jordan

הַיַּרְדֵּן׃ וַיְהִי° בַּעֲלוֹת הַכֹּהֲנִים נֹשְׂאֵי אֲרוֹן
ark-of ones-carrying-of the-priests as-to-come-up and-he-was (18) the-Jordan

בְּרִית־ יְהוָה מִתּוֹךְ הַיַּרְדֵּן נִתְּקוּ כַּפּוֹת רַגְלֵי
feet-of soles-of they-moved the-Jordan from-middle-of Yahweh covenant-of

הַכֹּהֲנִים אֶל הֶחָרָבָה וַיָּשֻׁבוּ מֵי־ הַיַּרְדֵּן
the-Jordan waters-of and-they-returned the-dry-ground to the-priests

לִמְקוֹמָם וַיֵּלְכוּ כִתְמוֹל־ שִׁלְשׁוֹם עַל־ כָּל־ גְּדוֹתָיו׃
banks-of-him all-of to before as-yesterday and-they-ran to-place-of-them

וְהָעָם עָלוּ מִן־ הַיַּרְדֵּן בֶּעָשׂוֹר לַחֹדֶשׁ
of-the-month on-the-tenth the-Jordan from they-went-up so-the-people (19)

הָרִאשׁוֹן וַיַּחֲנוּ בַּגִּלְגָּל בִּקְצֵה מִזְרַח יְרִיחוֹ׃
Jericho eastern-of on-border-of at-the-Gilgal and-they-camped the-first

וְאֵת שְׁתֵּים עֶשְׂרֵה הָאֲבָנִים הָאֵלֶּה אֲשֶׁר לָקְחוּ מִן־ הַיַּרְדֵּן
the-Jordan from they-took that the-these the-stones ten two and (20)

הֵקִים יְהוֹשֻׁעַ בַּגִּלְגָּל׃ וַיֹּאמֶר אֶל־ בְּנֵי יִשְׂרָאֵל לֵאמֹר
to-say Israel sons-of to and-he-said (21) at-the-Gilgal Joshua he-set-up

אֲשֶׁר יִשְׁאָלוּן בְּנֵיכֶם מָחָר אֶת־ אֲבוֹתָם לֵאמֹר מָה
what? to-say fathers-of-them *** future descendants-of-you they-ask when

הָאֲבָנִים הָאֵלֶּה׃ וְהוֹדַעְתֶּם אֶת־ בְּנֵיכֶם לֵאמֹר
to-say descendants-of-you *** then-you-tell (22) the-these the-stones

בַּיַּבָּשָׁה עָבַר יִשְׂרָאֵל אֶת־ הַיַּרְדֵּן הַזֶּה׃ אֲשֶׁר־
for (23) the-this the-Jordan *** Israel he-crossed on-the-dry-ground

הוֹבִישׁ יְהוָה אֱלֹהֵיכֶם אֶת־ מֵי הַיַּרְדֵּן מִפְּנֵיכֶם עַד־
until from-before-you the-Jordan waters-of *** God-of-you Yahweh he-dried-up

עָבְרְכֶם כַּאֲשֶׁר עָשָׂה יְהוָה אֱלֹהֵיכֶם לְיַם־ סוּף אֲשֶׁר־
that Reed to-Sea-of God-of-you Yahweh he-did just-as to-cross-over-you

הוֹבִישׁ מִפָּנֵינוּ עַד־ עָבְרֵנוּ׃ לְמַעַן דַּעַת
to-know so-that (24) to-cross-over-us until from-before-us he-dried-up

כָּל־ עַמֵּי הָאָרֶץ אֶת־ יַד יְהוָה כִּי חֲזָקָה הִיא לְמַעַן
so-that she powerful that Yahweh hand-of *** the-earth peoples-of all-of

and they revered him all the
days of his life, just as they
had revered Moses.
15 Then the LORD said to
Joshua, 16 "Command the
priests carrying the ark of the
Testimony to come up out of
the Jordan."
17 So Joshua commanded the
priests, "Come up out of the
Jordan."
18 And the priests came up
out of the river carrying the
ark of the covenant of the
LORD. No sooner had they set
their feet on the dry ground
than the waters of the Jordan
returned to their place and ran
at flood stage as before.
19 On the tenth day of the
first month the people went
up from the Jordan and
camped at Gilgal on the eastern border of Jericho. 20 And
Joshua set up at Gilgal the
twelve stones they had taken
out of the Jordan. 21 He said to
the Israelites, "In the future
when your descendants ask
their fathers, 'What do these
stones mean?' 22 tell them, 'Israel crossed the Jordan on dry
ground.' 23 For the LORD your
God dried up the Jordan before you until you had crossed
over. The LORD your God did
to the Jordan just what he had
done to the Red Sea[h] when he
dried it up before us until we
had crossed over. 24 He did this
so that all the peoples of the
earth might know that the
hand of the LORD is powerful

[h]23 Hebrew *Yam Suph;* that is, Sea of Reeds

°18 ק כעלות

יְרָאתֶם אֶת־ יְהוָה אֱלֹהֵיכֶם כָּל־ הַיָּמִים׃ וַיְהִי
now-he-was (5:1) the-days all-of God-of-you Yahweh *** you-might-fear

כִּשְׁמֹעַ כָּל־ מַלְכֵי הָאֱמֹרִי אֲשֶׁר בְּעֵבֶר הַיַּרְדֵּן יָמָּה
to-west the-Jordan on-side-of that the-Amorite kings-of all-of when-to-hear

וְכָל־ מַלְכֵי הַכְּנַעֲנִי אֲשֶׁר עַל־ הַיָּם אֵת אֲשֶׁר־ הוֹבִישׁ
he-dried-up how *** the-sea along that the-Canaanite kings-of and-all-of

יְהוָה אֶת־ מֵי הַיַּרְדֵּן מִפְּנֵי בְנֵי־ יִשְׂרָאֵל עַד־
until Israel sons-of from-before the-Jordan waters-of *** Yahweh

עָבְרָנוּ° וַיִּמַּס לְבָבָם וְלֹא־ הָיָה בָם עוֹד
longer in-them he-was and-not heart-of-them then-he-sank to-cross-over-them

רוּחַ מִפְּנֵי בְּנֵי־ יִשְׂרָאֵל׃ בָּעֵת הַהִיא אָמַר יְהוָה
Yahweh he-said the-that at-the-time (2) Israel sons-of because-of courage

אֶל־יְהוֹשֻׁעַ עֲשֵׂה לְךָ חַרְבוֹת צֻרִים וְשׁוּב מֹל אֶת־ בְּנֵי־
sons-of *** circumcise! and-return! flints knives-of for-you make! Joshua to

יִשְׂרָאֵל שֵׁנִית׃ וַיַּעַשׂ־ לוֹ יְהוֹשֻׁעַ חַרְבוֹת צֻרִים וַיָּמָל
and-he-circumcised flints knives-of Joshua for-him so-he-made (3) again Israel

אֶת־ בְּנֵי יִשְׂרָאֵל אֶל־ גִּבְעַת הָעֲרָלוֹת׃ וְזֶה הַדָּבָר אֲשֶׁר־
that the-reason now-this (4) Haaraloth Gibeath at Israel sons-of ***

מָל יְהוֹשֻׁעַ כָּל־ הָעָם הַיֹּצֵא מִמִּצְרַיִם הַזְּכָרִים
the-males from-Egypt the-one-coming the-people all-of Joshua he-circumcised

כֹּל ׀ אַנְשֵׁי הַמִּלְחָמָה מֵתוּ בַמִּדְבָּר בַּדֶּרֶךְ
on-the-way in-the-desert they-died the-military men-of all-of

בְּצֵאתָם מִמִּצְרָיִם׃ כִּי־ מֻלִים הָיוּ
they-were ones-being-circumcised indeed (5) from-Egypt after-to-leave-them

כָּל־ הָעָם הַיֹּצְאִים וְכָל־ הָעָם הַיִּלֹּדִים
the-ones-born the-people but-all-of the-ones-coming-out the-people all-of

בַמִּדְבָּר בַּדֶּרֶךְ בְּצֵאתָם מִמִּצְרַיִם לֹא־
not from-Egypt when-to-come-out-them on-the-journey in-the-desert

מָלוּ׃ כִּי ׀ אַרְבָּעִים שָׁנָה הָלְכוּ בְנֵי־ יִשְׂרָאֵל
Israel sons-of they-moved-about year forty now (6) they-were-circumcised

בַּמִּדְבָּר עַד־ תֹּם כָּל־ הַגּוֹי אַנְשֵׁי הַמִּלְחָמָה
the-military men-of the-nation all-of to-die until in-the-desert

הַיֹּצְאִים מִמִּצְרַיִם אֲשֶׁר לֹא־ שָׁמְעוּ בְּקוֹל יְהוָה אֲשֶׁר
for Yahweh to-voice-of they-obeyed not since from-Egypt the-ones-coming

נִשְׁבַּע יְהוָה לָהֶם לְבִלְתִּי הַרְאוֹתָם אֶת־הָאָרֶץ אֲשֶׁר נִשְׁבַּע יְהוָה
Yahweh he-promised that the-land *** to-see-them not to-them Yahweh he-swore

לַאֲבוֹתָם לָתֶת לָנוּ אֶרֶץ זָבַת חָלָב וּדְבָשׁ׃ וְאֶת־
and (7) and-honey milk flowing-of land to-us to-give to-fathers-of-them

and so that you might always
fear the LORD your God."

Circumcision at Gilgal

5 Now when all the Amorite
kings west of the Jordan
and all the Canaanite kings
along the seacoast heard how
the LORD had dried up the Jordan before the Israelites until
we had crossed over, their
hearts sank and they no longer had the courage to face the
Israelites.
2At that time the LORD said
to Joshua, "Make flint knives
and circumcise the Israelites
again." 3So Joshua made flint
knives and circumcised the Israelites at Gibeath Haaraloth.[i]
4Now this is why he did so:
All those who came out of
Egypt—all the men of military
age—died in the desert on the
way after leaving Egypt. 5All
the people that came out had
been circumcised, but all the
people born in the desert during the journey from Egypt
had not. 6The Israelites had
moved about in the desert
forty years until all the men
who were of military age
when they left Egypt had died,
since they had not obeyed the
LORD. For the LORD had sworn
to them that they would not
see the land that he had solemnly promised their fathers
to give us, a land flowing with
milk and honey. 7So he raised

[i]3 *Gibeath Haaraloth* means *hill of foreskins.*

*1 The NIV here translates the *Ketbib* form; the interlinear translates the *Qere.*

°1 ק עברם

בְּנֵיהֶם הֵקִים תַּחְתָּם אֹתָם מָל יְהוֹשֻׁעַ כִּי־
for Joshua he-circumcised them in-place-of-them he-raised-up sons-of-them

עֲרֵלִים הָיוּ כִּי לֹא־ מָלוּ אוֹתָם בַּדָּרֶךְ׃
on-the-way them they-circumcised not for they-were ones-uncircumcised

וַיְהִי כַּאֲשֶׁר־ תַּמּוּ כָל־ הַגּוֹי לְהִמּוֹל
to-be-circumcised the-nation whole-of they-were-done just-as and-he-was (8)

וַיֵּשְׁבוּ תַחְתָּם בַּמַּחֲנֶה עַד חֲיוֹתָם׃
to-be-healed-them until in-the-camp in-place-of-them then-they-remained

וַיֹּאמֶר יְהוָה אֶל־ יְהוֹשֻׁעַ הַיּוֹם גַּלּוֹתִי אֶת־ חֶרְפַּת
reproach-of *** I-rolled-away the-day Joshua to Yahweh then-he-said (9)

מִצְרַיִם מֵעֲלֵיכֶם וַיִּקְרָא שֵׁם הַמָּקוֹם הַהוּא גִּלְגָּל עַד הַיּוֹם
the-day to Gilgal the-that the-place name-of so-he-called from-on-you Egypt

הַזֶּה׃ וַיַּחֲנוּ בְנֵי־ יִשְׂרָאֵל בַּגִּלְגָּל וַיַּעֲשׂוּ
and-they-celebrated at-the-Gilgal Israel sons-of so-they-camped (10) the-this

אֶת־ הַפֶּסַח בְּאַרְבָּעָה עָשָׂר יוֹם לַחֹדֶשׁ בָּעֶרֶב בְּעַרְבוֹת
on-plains-of in-the-evening of-the-month day ten on-four the-Passover ***

יְרִיחוֹ׃ וַיֹּאכְלוּ מֵעֲבוּר הָאָרֶץ מִמָּחֳרַת
on-day-after-of the-land from-produce-of and-they-ate (11) Jericho

הַפֶּסַח מַצּוֹת וְקָלוּי בְּעֶצֶם הַיּוֹם הַזֶּה׃
the-that the-day on-very-of and-roasted-grain unleavened-breads the-Passover

וַיִּשְׁבֹּת הַמָּן מִמָּחֳרָת בְּאָכְלָם מֵעֲבוּר
from-food-of when-to-eat-them on-day-after the-manna and-he-stopped (12)

הָאָרֶץ וְלֹא־ הָיָה עוֹד לִבְנֵי יִשְׂרָאֵל מָן וַיֹּאכְלוּ
but-they-ate manna Israel for-sons-of longer he-was so-not the-land

מִתְּבוּאַת אֶרֶץ כְּנַעַן בַּשָּׁנָה הַהִיא׃ וַיְהִי
now-he-was (13) the-that in-the-year Canaan land-of from-produce-of

בִּהְיוֹת יְהוֹשֻׁעַ בִּירִיחוֹ וַיִּשָּׂא עֵינָיו וַיַּרְא
and-he-saw eyes-of-him that-he-lifted near-Jericho Joshua when-to-be

וְהִנֵּה־ אִישׁ עֹמֵד לְנֶגְדּוֹ וְחַרְבּוֹ שְׁלוּפָה
being-drawn and-sword-of-him in-front-of-him standing man and-see!

בְּיָדוֹ וַיֵּלֶךְ יְהוֹשֻׁעַ אֵלָיו וַיֹּאמֶר לוֹ הֲלָנוּ אַתָּה
you for-us? to-him and-he-asked to-him Joshua and-he-went in-hand-of-him

אִם־ לְצָרֵינוּ׃ וַיֹּאמֶר ׀ לֹא כִּי אֲנִי שַׂר־ צְבָא־
army-of commander-of I but neither and-he-replied (14) for-enemies-of-us or

יְהוָה עַתָּה בָאתִי וַיִּפֹּל יְהוֹשֻׁעַ אֶל־ פָּנָיו אַרְצָה
to-ground faces-of-him on Joshua then-he-fell I-came now Yahweh

וַיִּשְׁתָּחוּ וַיֹּאמֶר לוֹ מָה אֲדֹנִי מְדַבֵּר אֶל־ עַבְדּוֹ׃
servant-of-him to speaking lord-of-me what? to-him and-he-asked and-he-revered

up their sons in their place,
and these were the ones
Joshua circumcised. They
were still uncircumcised because they had not been circumcised on the way. 8And after the whole nation had been
circumcised, they remained
where they were in camp until
they were healed.
9Then the LORD said to
Joshua, "Today I have rolled
away the reproach of Egypt
from you." So the place has
been called Gilgal[j] to this day.
10On the evening of the fourteenth day of the month,
while camped at Gilgal on the
plains of Jericho, the Israelites
celebrated the Passover. 11The
day after the Passover, that
very day, they ate some of the
produce of the land: unleavened bread and roasted grain.
12The manna stopped the day
after[k] they ate this food from
the land; there was no longer
any manna for the Israelites,
but that year they ate of the
produce of Canaan.

The Fall of Jericho

13Now when Joshua was
near Jericho, he looked up and
saw a man standing in front of
him with a drawn sword in
his hand. Joshua went up to
him and asked, "Are you for
us or for our enemies?"
14"Neither," he replied, "but
as commander of the army of
the LORD I have now come."
Then Joshua fell facedown to
the ground in reverence, and
asked him, "What message
does my Lord[l] have for his
servant?"

j9 *Gilgal* sounds like the Hebrew for *roll.*
k12 *Or the day* l14 *Or lord*

וַיֹּאמֶר שַׂר־ צְבָא יְהוָה אֶל־ יְהוֹשֻׁעַ שַׁל־
take-off! Joshua to Yahweh army-of commander-of and-he-replied (15)

נַעַלְךָ מֵעַל רַגְלֶךָ כִּי הַמָּקוֹם אֲשֶׁר אַתָּה עֹמֵד עָלָיו
on-him standing you where the-place for foot-of-you from-on sandal-of-you

קֹדֶשׁ הוּא וַיַּעַשׂ יְהוֹשֻׁעַ כֵּן׃ וִירִיחוֹ סֹגֶרֶת וּמְסֻגֶּרֶת
and-being-shut being-shut now-Jericho (6:1) this Joshua so-he-did he holy

מִפְּנֵי בְּנֵי יִשְׂרָאֵל אֵין יוֹצֵא וְאֵין בָּא׃
one-coming-in and-not one-going-out not Israel sons-of because-of

וַיֹּאמֶר יְהוָה אֶל־ יְהוֹשֻׁעַ רְאֵה נָתַתִּי בְיָדְךָ אֶת־
*** into-hand-of-you I-delivered see! Joshua to Yahweh then-he-said (2)

יְרִיחוֹ וְאֶת־ מַלְכָּהּ גִּבּוֹרֵי הֶחָיִל׃ וְסַבֹּתֶם אֶת־
*** now-you-march-around (3) the-fight men-of king-of-her and Jericho

הָעִיר כֹּל אַנְשֵׁי הַמִּלְחָמָה הַקֵּיף אֶת־ הָעִיר פַּעַם אֶחָת כֹּה
this one time the-city *** to-go-around the-armed men-of all-of the-city

תַעֲשֶׂה שֵׁשֶׁת יָמִים׃ וְשִׁבְעָה כֹהֲנִים יִשְׂאוּ שִׁבְעָה שׁוֹפְרוֹת
trumpets-of seven they-must-carry priests and-seven (4) days six-of you-do

הַיּוֹבְלִים לִפְנֵי הָאָרוֹן וּבַיּוֹם הַשְּׁבִיעִי
the-seventh and-on-the-day the-ark in-front-of the-horns-of-rams

תָּסֹבּוּ אֶת־ הָעִיר שֶׁבַע פְּעָמִים וְהַכֹּהֲנִים יִתְקְעוּ
they-must-blow and-the-priests times seven-of the-city *** you-march-around

בַּשּׁוֹפָרוֹת׃ וְהָיָה בִּמְשֹׁךְ ׀ בְּקֶרֶן הַיּוֹבֵל
the-ram on-horn-of when-to-blast and-he-will-be (5) on-the-trumpets

בְּשָׁמְעֲכֶם אֶת־ קוֹל הַשּׁוֹפָר יָרִיעוּ כָל־
all-of then-they-must-shout the-trumpet sound-of *** when-to-hear-you

הָעָם תְּרוּעָה גְדוֹלָה וְנָפְלָה חוֹמַת הָעִיר תַּחְתֶּיהָ
around-her the-city wall-of then-she-will-collapse loud shout the-people

וְעָלוּ הָעָם אִישׁ נֶגְדּוֹ׃ וַיִּקְרָא יְהוֹשֻׁעַ
Joshua so-he-called (6) straight-in-him each the-people and-they-will-go-up

בִּן־ נוּן אֶל־ הַכֹּהֲנִים וַיֹּאמֶר אֲלֵהֶם שְׂאוּ אֶת־ אֲרוֹן
ark-of *** take-up! to-them and-he-said the-priests to Nun son-of

הַבְּרִית וְשִׁבְעָה כֹהֲנִים יִשְׂאוּ שִׁבְעָה שׁוֹפְרוֹת
trumpets-of seven they-must-carry priests and-seven the-covenant

יוֹבְלִים לִפְנֵי אֲרוֹן יְהוָה׃ וַיֹּאמְרוּ אֶל־ הָעָם
the-people to and-he-ordered (7) Yahweh ark-of in-front-of horns-of-rams

עִבְרוּ וְסֹבּוּ אֶת־ הָעִיר וְהֶחָלוּץ יַעֲבֹר
he-must-go and-the-being-armed the-city *** and-march-around! advance!

לִפְנֵי אֲרוֹן יְהוָה׃ וַיְהִי כֶּאֱמֹר יְהוֹשֻׁעַ אֶל־ הָעָם
the-people to Joshua after-to-speak and-he-was (8) Yahweh ark-of ahead-of

15The commander of the
LORD's army replied, "Take off
your sandals, for the place
where you are standing is
holy." And Joshua did so.

6 Now Jericho was tightly
shut up because of the Israelites. No one went out and
no one came in.
2Then the LORD said to
Joshua, "See, I have delivered
Jericho into your hands, along
with its king and its fighting
men. 3March around the city
once with all the armed men.
Do this for six days. 4Have sev-
en priests carry trumpets of
rams' horns in front of the ark.
On the seventh day, march
around the city seven times,
with the priests blowing the
trumpets. 5When you hear
them sound a long blast on the
trumpets, have all the people
give a loud shout; then the
wall of the city will collapse
and the people will go up,
every man straight in."
6So Joshua son of Nun called
the priests and said to them,
"Take up the ark of the covenant of the LORD and have
seven priests carry trumpets
in front of it." 7And he ordered
the people, "Advance! March
around the city, with the
armed guard going ahead of
the ark of the LORD."
8When Joshua had spoken to

°5 ק כשמעכם
°7 ק ויאמר

וְשִׁבְעָה הַכֹּהֲנִים נֹשְׂאִים שִׁבְעָה שׁוֹפְרוֹת הַיּוֹבְלִים
the-horns-of-rams trumpets-of seven ones-carrying the-priests then-seven

לִפְנֵי יְהוָה עָבְרוּ וְתָקְעוּ בַּשּׁוֹפָרוֹת וַאֲרוֹן
and-ark-of on-the-trumpets and-they-blew they-went-forward Yahweh before

בְּרִית יְהוָה הֹלֵךְ אַחֲרֵיהֶם׃ וְהֶחָלוּץ הֹלֵךְ
marching and-the-being-armed (9) after-them following Yahweh covenant-of

לִפְנֵי הַכֹּהֲנִים תֹּקְעֻו הַשּׁוֹפָרוֹת וְהַמְאַסֵּף
and-the-guarding-rear the-trumpets ones-blowing-of the-priests ahead-of

הֹלֵךְ אַחֲרֵי הָאָרוֹן הָלוֹךְ וְתָקוֹעַ בַּשּׁוֹפָרוֹת׃ וְאֶת־
but (10) on-the-trumpets and-to-sound to-follow the-ark after following

הָעָם צִוָּה יְהוֹשֻׁעַ לֵאמֹר לֹא תָרִיעוּ וְלֹא־ תַשְׁמִיעוּ
you-raise and-not you-give-war-cry not to-say Joshua he-commanded the-people

אֶת־ קוֹלְכֶם וְלֹא־ יֵצֵא מִפִּיכֶם דָּבָר עַד יוֹם
day until word from-mouth-of-you he-must-go and-not voice-of-you ***

אָמְרִי אֲלֵיכֶם הָרִיעוּ וַהֲרֵיעֹתֶם׃ וַיַּסֵּב אֲרוֹן־
ark-of so-he-had-go-around (11) then-you-shout shout! to-you to-tell-me

יְהוָה אֶת־ הָעִיר הַקֵּף פַּעַם אֶחָת וַיָּבֹאוּ הַמַּחֲנֶה
the-camp then-they-returned one time to-circle the-city *** Yahweh

וַיָּלִינוּ בַּמַּחֲנֶה׃ וַיַּשְׁכֵּם יְהוֹשֻׁעַ בַּבֹּקֶר
in-the-morning Joshua and-he-got-up (12) in-the-camp and-they-spent-night

וַיִּשְׂאוּ הַכֹּהֲנִים אֶת־ אֲרוֹן יְהוָה׃ וְשִׁבְעָה הַכֹּהֲנִים
the-priests and-seven (13) Yahweh ark-of *** the-priests and-they-took-up

נֹשְׂאִים שִׁבְעָה שׁוֹפְרוֹת הַיֹּבְלִים לִפְנֵי אֲרוֹן יְהוָה
Yahweh ark-of before the-horns-of-rams trumpets-of seven ones-carrying

הֹלְכִים הָלוֹךְ וְתָקְעוּ בַּשּׁוֹפָרוֹת וְהֶחָלוּץ
and-the-being-armed on-the-trumpets and-they-blew to-go-forward ones-going

הֹלֵךְ לִפְנֵיהֶם וְהַמְאַסֵּף הֹלֵךְ אַחֲרֵי אֲרוֹן יְהוָה
Yahweh ark-of after following and-the-guarding-rear ahead-of-them going

הוֹלֵךְ וְתָקוֹעַ בַּשּׁוֹפָרוֹת׃ וַיָּסֹבּוּ אֶת־ הָעִיר
the-city *** so-they-marched-around (14) on-the-trumpets and-to-sound to-march

בַּיּוֹם הַשֵּׁנִי פַּעַם אַחַת וַיָּשֻׁבוּ הַמַּחֲנֶה כֹּה עָשׂוּ
they-did this the-camp and-they-returned one time the-second on-the-day

שֵׁשֶׁת יָמִים׃ וַיְהִי ׀ בַּיּוֹם הַשְּׁבִיעִי וַיַּשְׁכִּמוּ
that-they-got-up the-seventh on-the-day and-he-was (15) days six-of

כַּעֲלוֹת הַשַּׁחַר וַיָּסֹבּוּ אֶת־ הָעִיר כַּמִּשְׁפָּט
as-the-manner the-city *** and-they-marched-around the-daybreak as-to-come

הַזֶּה שֶׁבַע פְּעָמִים רַק בַּיּוֹם הַהוּא סָבְבוּ אֶת־ הָעִיר
the-city *** they-circled the-that on-the-day except times seven-of the-this

the people, the seven priests
carrying the seven trumpets
before the LORD went forward,
blowing their trumpets, and
the ark of the LORD's covenant
followed them. [9]The armed
guard marched ahead of the
priests who blew the trumpets, and the rear guard followed the ark. All this time the
trumpets were sounding. [10]But
Joshua had commanded the
people, "Do not give a war cry,
do not raise your voices, do
not say a word until the day I
tell you to shout. Then shout!"
[11]So he had the ark of the LORD
carried around the city, cir-
cling it once. Then the people
returned to camp and spent
the night there.
[12]Joshua got up early the
next morning and the priests
took up the ark of the LORD.
[13]The seven priests carrying
the seven trumpets went forward, marching before the ark
of the LORD and blowing the
trumpets. The armed men
went ahead of them and the
rear guard followed the ark of
the LORD, while the trumpets
kept sounding. [14]So on the
second day they marched
around the city once and returned to the camp. They did
this for six days.
[15]On the seventh day, they
got up at daybreak and
marched around the city sev-
en times in the same manner,
except that on that day they
circled the city seven times.

°9 ק תקעי
°13 ק הלוך

שֶׁבַע פְּעָמִים׃ וַיְהִי בַּפַּעַם הַשְּׁבִיעִית תָּקְעוּ
they-sounded the-seventh on-the-time and-he-was (16) times seven-of

הַכֹּהֲנִים בַּשּׁוֹפָרוֹת וַיֹּאמֶר יְהוֹשֻׁעַ אֶל־ הָעָם הָרִיעוּ
shout! the-people to Joshua and-he-commanded on-the-trumpets the-priests

כִּי־ נָתַן יְהוָה לָכֶם אֶת־ הָעִיר׃ וְהָיְתָה הָעִיר חֵרֶם הִיא
she devoted the-city and-she-is (17) the-city *** to-you Yahweh he-gave for

וְכָל־ אֲשֶׁר־ בָּהּ לַיהוָה רַק רָחָב הַזּוֹנָה תִּחְיֶה הִיא
she she-shall-live the-prostitute Rahab only to-Yahweh in-her that and-all

וְכָל־ אֲשֶׁר אִתָּהּ בַּבַּיִת כִּי הֶחְבְּאַתָה אֶת־הַמַּלְאָכִים אֲשֶׁר שָׁלָחְנוּ׃
we-sent whom the-spies *** she-hid for in-the-house with-her who and-all

וְרַק־ אַתֶּם שִׁמְרוּ מִן־ הַחֵרֶם פֶּן־
so-not the-devoted-thing from keep-away! you but-however (18)

תַּחֲרִימוּ וּלְקַחְתֶּם מִן־ הַחֵרֶם וְשַׂמְתֶּם
or-you-will-make the-devoted-thing from when-you-take you-bring-destruction

אֶת־ מַחֲנֵה יִשְׂרָאֵל לְחֵרֶם וַעֲכַרְתֶּם אוֹתוֹ׃ וְכֹל
and-all-of (19) him and-you-will-destroy for-destruction Israel camp-of ***

כֶּסֶף וְזָהָב וּכְלֵי נְחֹשֶׁת וּבַרְזֶל קֹדֶשׁ הוּא לַיהוָה
to-Yahweh he sacred and-iron bronze and-articles-of and-gold silver

אוֹצַר יְהוָה יָבוֹא׃ וַיָּרַע הָעָם
the-people and-he-shouted (20) he-must-go-in Yahweh treasury-of

וַיִּתְקְעוּ בַּשֹּׁפָרוֹת וַיְהִי כִשְׁמֹעַ הָעָם אֶת־
*** the-people when-to-hear and-he-was on-the-trumpets when-they-sounded

קוֹל הַשּׁוֹפָר וַיָּרִיעוּ הָעָם תְּרוּעָה גְדוֹלָה וַתִּפֹּל
then-she-collapsed loud shout the-people and-they-shouted the-trumpet sound-of

הַחוֹמָה תַּחְתֶּיהָ וַיַּעַל הָעָם הָעִירָה אִישׁ
each into-the-city the-people so-he-charged around-her the-wall

נֶגְדּוֹ וַיִּלְכְּדוּ אֶת־ הָעִיר׃ וַיַּחֲרִימוּ אֶת־כָּל־
all *** and-they-devoted (21) the-city *** and-they-took straight-in-him

אֲשֶׁר בָּעִיר מֵאִישׁ וְעַד־ אִשָּׁה מִנַּעַר וְעַד־ זָקֵן וְעַד
even-to old even-to from-young woman even-to from-man in-the-city that

שׁוֹר וָשֶׂה וַחֲמוֹר לְפִי־ חָרֶב׃ וְלִשְׁנַיִם הָאֲנָשִׁים
the-men and-to-two (22) sword with-edge-of and-donkey and-sheep cattle

הַמְרַגְּלִים אֶת־ הָאָרֶץ אָמַר יְהוֹשֻׁעַ בֹּאוּ בֵּית־ הָאִשָּׁה
the-woman house-of go-into! Joshua he-said the-land *** the-ones-spying

הַזּוֹנָה וְהוֹצִיאוּ מִשָּׁם אֶת־ הָאִשָּׁה וְאֶת־כָּל־אֲשֶׁר־ לָהּ
to-her who all and the-woman *** from-there and-bring-out! the-prostitute

כַּאֲשֶׁר נִשְׁבַּעְתֶּם לָהּ׃ וַיָּבֹאוּ הַנְּעָרִים
the-young-men so-they-went-in (23) with-her you-made-oath just-as

16 The seventh time around,
when the priests sounded the
trumpet blast, Joshua commanded the people, "Shout!
For the LORD has given you the
city! 17 The city and all that is in
it are to be devoted[m] to the
LORD. Only Rahab the prostitute[n] and all who are with her
in her house shall be spared,
because she hid the spies we
sent. 18 But keep away from the
devoted things, so that you
will not bring about your own
destruction by taking any of
them. Otherwise you will
make the camp of Israel liable
to destruction and bring disaster on it. 19 All the silver and
gold and the articles of bronze
and iron are sacred to the LORD
and must go into his treasury."
20 When the trumpets sounded, the people shouted, and at
the sound of the trumpet,
when the people gave a loud
shout, the wall collapsed; so
every man charged straight in,
and they took the city. 21 They
devoted the city to the LORD
and destroyed with the sword
every living thing in it—men
and women, young and old,
cattle, sheep and donkeys.
22 Joshua said to the two men
who had spied out the land,
"Go into the prostitute's house
and bring her out and all who
belong to her, in accordance
with your oath to her." 23 So
the young men who had done

[m]17 The Hebrew term refers to the irrevocable giving over of things or persons to the LORD, often by totally destroying them; also in verses 18 and 21.
[n]17 Or possibly *innkeeper;* also in verses 22 and 25

הַמְרַגְּלִים וַיֹּצִיאוּ אֶת־ רָחָב וְאֶת־ אָבִיהָ וְאֶת־
and father-of-her and Rahab *** and-they-brought-out the-ones-spying

אִמָּהּ וְאֶת־ אַחֶיהָ וְאֶת־כָּל־ אֲשֶׁר־ לָהּ וְאֵת כָּל־
entire-of and to-her who all and brothers-of-her and mother-of-her

מִשְׁפְּחוֹתֶיהָ הוֹצִיאוּ וַיַּנִּיחוּם מִחוּץ לְמַחֲנֵה יִשְׂרָאֵל׃
Israel of-camp-of outside and-they-put-them they-brought-out families-of-her

וְהָעִיר שָׂרְפוּ בָאֵשׁ וְכָל־ אֲשֶׁר־ בָּהּ רַק ׀ הַכֶּסֶף
the-silver but in-her that and-all in-the-fire they-burned then-the-city (24)

וְהַזָּהָב וּכְלֵי הַנְּחֹשֶׁת וְהַבַּרְזֶל נָתְנוּ אוֹצַר
treasury-of they-put and-the-iron the-bronze and-articles-of and-the-gold

בֵּית־ יְהוָה׃ וְאֶת־ רָחָב הַזּוֹנָה וְאֶת־ בֵּית אָבִיהָ
father-of-her house-of and the-prostitute Rahab but (25) Yahweh house-of

וְאֶת־כָּל־ אֲשֶׁר־ לָהּ הֶחֱיָה יְהוֹשֻׁעַ וַתֵּשֶׁב בְּקֶרֶב יִשְׂרָאֵל עַד
to Israel in-among and-she-lives Joshua he-spared to-her who all and

הַיּוֹם הַזֶּה כִּי הֶחְבִּיאָה אֶת־הַמַּלְאָכִים אֲשֶׁר־ שָׁלַח יְהוֹשֻׁעַ לְרַגֵּל
to-spy-out Joshua he-sent whom the-spies *** she-hid for the-this the-day

אֶת־יְרִיחוֹ׃ וַיַּשְׁבַּע יְהוֹשֻׁעַ בָּעֵת הַהִיא לֵאמֹר
to-say the-that at-the-time Joshua and-he-pronounced-oath (26) Jericho ***

אָרוּר הָאִישׁ לִפְנֵי יְהוָה אֲשֶׁר יָקוּם וּבָנָה אֶת־
*** and-he-rebuilds he-undertakes who Yahweh before the-man being-cursed

הָעִיר הַזֹּאת אֶת־ יְרִיחוֹ בִּבְכֹרוֹ יְיַסְּדֶנָּה
he-will-found-her with-firstborn-of-him Jericho *** the-this the-city

וּבִצְעִירוֹ יַצִּיב דְּלָתֶיהָ׃ וַיְהִי יְהוָה
Yahweh so-he-was (27) gates-of-her he-will-set-up and-with-youngest-of-him

אֶת־ יְהוֹשֻׁעַ וַיְהִי שָׁמְעוֹ בְּכָל־ הָאָרֶץ׃
the-land through-all-of fame-of-him and-he-spread Joshua with

וַיִּמְעֲלוּ בְנֵי־ יִשְׂרָאֵל מַעַל בַּחֵרֶם
with-the-devoted unfaithfulness Israel sons-of but-they-were-unfaithful (7:1)

וַיִּקַּח עָכָן בֶּן־ כַּרְמִי בֶן־ זַבְדִּי בֶן־ זֶרַח לְמַטֵּה יְהוּדָה
Judah of-tribe-of Zerah son-of Zabdi son-of Carmi son-of Achan and-he-took

מִן־ הַחֵרֶם וַיִּחַר־ אַף יְהוָה בִּבְנֵי יִשְׂרָאֵל׃
Israel against-sons-of Yahweh anger-of so-he-burned the-devoted-thing from

וַיִּשְׁלַח יְהוֹשֻׁעַ אֲנָשִׁים מִירִיחוֹ הָעַי אֲשֶׁר עִם־ בֵּית אָוֶן מִקֶּדֶם
to-east Aven Beth near which the-Ai from-Jericho men Joshua now-he-sent (2)

לְבֵית־ אֵל וַיֹּאמֶר אֲלֵיהֶם לֵאמֹר עֲלוּ וְרַגְּלוּ אֶת־ הָאָרֶץ
the-region *** and-spy-out! go-up! to-say to-them and-he-told El of-Beth

וַיַּעֲלוּ הָאֲנָשִׁים וַיְרַגְּלוּ אֶת־ הָעָי׃ וַיָּשֻׁבוּ
when-they-returned (3) the-Ai *** and-they-spied-out the-men so-they-went-up

the spying went in and
brought out Rahab, her father
and mother and brothers and
all who belonged to her. They
brought out her entire family
and put them in a place outside the camp of Israel.
24Then they burned the
whole city and everything in
it, but they put the silver and
gold and the articles of bronze
and iron into the treasury of
the LORD's house. 25But Joshua
spared Rahab the prostitute,
with her family and all who
belonged to her, because she
hid the men Joshua had sent
as spies to Jericho—and she
lives among the Israelites to
this day.
26At that time Joshua pronounced this solemn oath:
"Cursed before the LORD is the
man who undertakes to re-
build this city, Jericho:

"At the cost of his firstborn son
will he lay its foundations;
at the cost of his youngest
will he set up its gates."

27So the LORD was with
Joshua, and his fame spread
throughout the land.

Achan's Sin

7 But the Israelites acted unfaithfully in regard to the
devoted things[o]; Achan son of
Carmi, the son of Zimri,[p] the
son of Zerah, of the tribe of
Judah, took some of them. So
the LORD's anger burned
against Israel.
2Now Joshua sent men from
Jericho to Ai, which is near
Beth Aven to the east of Bethel, and told them, "Go up and
spy out the region." So the
men went up and spied out Ai.
3When they returned to

[o]1 The Hebrew term refers to the irrevocable giving over of things or persons to the LORD, often by totally destroying them; also in verses 11, 12, 13 and 15.
[p]1 See Septuagint and 1 Chronicles 2:6; Hebrew *Zabdi*; also in verses 17 and 18.

אֶל־יְהוֹשֻׁעַ וַיֹּאמְרוּ אֵלָיו אַל־יַעַל כָּל־הָעָם
the-people all-of he-must-go-up not to-him then-they-said Joshua to

כְּאַלְפַּיִם אִישׁ אוֹ כִּשְׁלֹשֶׁת אֲלָפִים אִישׁ יַעֲלוּ
they-should-go-up man thousands about-three-of or man about-two-thousands

וְיַכּוּ אֶת־הָעָי אַל־תְּיַגַּע־שָׁמָּה אֶת־כָּל־הָעָם
the-people all-of *** at-there you-weary not the-Ai *** and-they-will-take

כִּי מְעַט הֵמָּה׃ וַיַּעֲלוּ מִן־הָעָם שָׁמָּה כִּשְׁלֹשֶׁת
about-three-of to-there the-people from so-they-went-up (4) they few for

אֲלָפִים אִישׁ וַיָּנֻסוּ לִפְנֵי אַנְשֵׁי הָעָי׃ וַיַּכּוּ
and-they-killed (5) the-Ai men-of before but-they-were-routed man thousands

מֵהֶם אַנְשֵׁי הָעַי כִּשְׁלֹשִׁים וְשִׁשָּׁה אִישׁ וַיִּרְדְּפוּם לִפְנֵי
from and-they-chased-them man and-six about-thirty the-Ai men-of from-them

הַשַּׁעַר עַד־הַשְּׁבָרִים וַיַּכּוּם בַּמּוֹרָד
on-the-slope and-they-struck-them the-stone-quarries as-far-as the-city-gate

וַיִּמַּס לְבַב־הָעָם וַיְהִי לְמָיִם׃ וַיִּקְרַע
then-he-tore (6) like-waters and-he-became the-people heart-of and-he-melted

יְהוֹשֻׁעַ שִׂמְלֹתָיו וַיִּפֹּל עַל־פָּנָיו אַרְצָה לִפְנֵי אֲרוֹן
ark-of before to-ground faces-of-him on and-he-fell clothes-of-him Joshua

יְהוָה עַד־הָעֶרֶב הוּא וְזִקְנֵי יִשְׂרָאֵל וַיַּעֲלוּ עָפָר עַל־
on dust and-they-sprinkled Israel and-elders-of he the-evening till Yahweh

רֹאשָׁם׃ וַיֹּאמֶר יְהוֹשֻׁעַ אֲהָהּ אֲדֹנָי יְהוִה לָמָה הֵעֲבַרְתָּ
you-brought-across why? Yahweh Lord ah! Joshua and-he-said (7) head-of-them

הַעֲבִיר אֶת־הָעָם הַזֶּה אֶת־הַיַּרְדֵּן לָתֵת אֹתָנוּ
us to-deliver the-Jordan *** the-this the-people *** to-bring-across

בְּיַד הָאֱמֹרִי לְהַאֲבִידֵנוּ וְלוּ הוֹאַלְנוּ וַנֵּשֶׁב
and-we-stayed we-were-content if-only to-destroy-us the-Amorite into-hand-of

בְּעֵבֶר הַיַּרְדֵּן׃ בִּי אֲדֹנָי מָה אֹמַר אַחֲרֵי אֲשֶׁר הָפַךְ
he-turned that now can-I-say what? Lord oh! (8) the-Jordan on-other-side-of

יִשְׂרָאֵל עֹרֶף לִפְנֵי אֹיְבָיו׃ וְיִשְׁמְעוּ הַכְּנַעֲנִי
the-Canaanite now-they-will-hear (9) being-enemies-of-him before back Israel

וְכֹל יֹשְׁבֵי הָאָרֶץ וְנָסַבּוּ עָלֵינוּ
around-us and-they-will-surround the-country ones-living-of and-all-of

וְהִכְרִיתוּ אֶת־שְׁמֵנוּ מִן־הָאָרֶץ וּמַה־תַּעֲשֶׂה
will-you-do then-what? the-earth from name-of-us *** and-they-will-wipe-out

לְשִׁמְךָ הַגָּדוֹל׃ וַיֹּאמֶר יְהוָה אֶל־יְהוֹשֻׁעַ קֻם לָךְ
for-you stand-up! Joshua to Yahweh and-he-said (10) the-great for-name-of-you

לָמָּה זֶּה אַתָּה נֹפֵל עַל־פָּנֶיךָ׃ חָטָא יִשְׂרָאֵל וְגַם
and-also Israel he-sinned (11) faces-of-you on being-down you this why?

Joshua, they said, "Not all the
people will have to go up
against Ai. Send two or three
thousand men to take it and
do not weary all the people, for
only a few men are there." [4]So
about three thousand men
went up; but they were routed
by the men of Ai, [5]who killed
about thirty-six of them. They
chased the Israelites from the
city gate as far as the stone
quarries[q] and struck them
down on the slopes. At this
the hearts of the people melted
and became like water.

[6]Then Joshua tore his clothes
and fell facedown to the
ground before the ark of the
LORD, remaining there till evening. The elders of Israel did
the same, and sprinkled dust
on their heads. [7]And Joshua
said, "Ah, Sovereign LORD,
why did you ever bring this
people across the Jordan to deliver us into the hands of the
Amorites to destroy us? If only
we had been content to stay
on the other side of the Jordan!
[8]O Lord, what can I say, now
that Israel has been routed by
its enemies? [9]The Canaanites
and the other people of the
country will hear about this
and they will surround us and
wipe out our name from the
earth. What then will you do
for your own great name?"

[10]The LORD said to Joshua,
"Stand up! What are you doing down on your face? [11]Israel

q5 Or *as far as Shebarim*

עָבְרוּ אֶת־ בְּרִיתִי אֲשֶׁר צִוִּיתִי אוֹתָם וְגַם לָקְחוּ
they-took and-also them I-commanded which covenant-of-me *** they-violated

מִן־ הַחֵרֶם וְגַם גָּנְבוּ וְגַם כִּחֲשׁוּ וְגַם
and-also they-lied and-also they-stole and-also the-devoted-thing from

שָׂמוּ בִכְלֵיהֶם׃ (12) וְלֹא יָכְלוּ בְּנֵי יִשְׂרָאֵל לָקוּם
to-stand Israel sons-of they-can so-not (12) with-possessions-of-them they-put

לִפְנֵי אֹיְבֵיהֶם עֹרֶף יִפְנוּ לִפְנֵי אֹיְבֵיהֶם
being-enemies-of-them before they-turn back being-enemies-of-them against

כִּי הָיוּ לְחֵרֶם לֹא אוֹסִיף לִהְיוֹת עִמָּכֶם אִם־ לֹא
not if with-you to-be I-will-continue not for-destruction they-are for

תַשְׁמִידוּ הַחֵרֶם מִקִּרְבְּכֶם׃ (13) קֻם קַדֵּשׁ אֶת־
*** consecrate! go! (13) from-among-you the-devoted-thing you-destroy

הָעָם וְאָמַרְתָּ הִתְקַדְּשׁוּ לְמָחָר כִּי כֹה אָמַר
he-says this for for-tomorrow consecrate-yourselves! and-you-tell the-people

יְהוָה אֱלֹהֵי יִשְׂרָאֵל חֵרֶם בְּקִרְבְּךָ יִשְׂרָאֵל לֹא תוּכַל לָקוּם
to-stand you-can not Israel in-among-you devoted-thing Israel God-of Yahweh

לִפְנֵי אֹיְבֶיךָ עַד־ הֲסִירְכֶם הַחֵרֶם
the-devoted-thing to-remove-you until being-enemies-of-you against

מִקִּרְבְּכֶם׃ (14) וְנִקְרַבְתֶּם בַּבֹּקֶר לְשִׁבְטֵיכֶם
by-tribes-of-you in-the-morning and-you-present-yourselves (14) from-among-you

וְהָיָה הַשֵּׁבֶט אֲשֶׁר־ יִלְכְּדֶנּוּ יְהוָה יִקְרַב
he-shall-come-forward Yahweh he-takes-him that the-tribe and-he-shall-be

לַמִּשְׁפָּחוֹת וְהַמִּשְׁפָּחָה אֲשֶׁר־ יִלְכְּדֶנָּה יְהוָה תִּקְרַב
she-shall-come-forward Yahweh he-takes-her that and-the-clan by-the-clans

לַבָּתִּים וְהַבַּיִת אֲשֶׁר יִלְכְּדֶנּוּ יְהוָה יִקְרַב
he-shall-come-forward Yahweh he-takes-him that and-the-family by-the-families

לַגְּבָרִים׃ (15) וְהָיָה הַנִּלְכָּד בַּחֵרֶם
with-the-devoted-thing the-one-being-caught and-he-shall-be (15) by-the-men

יִשָּׂרֵף בָּאֵשׁ אֹתוֹ וְאֶת־ כָּל־ אֲשֶׁר־ לוֹ כִּי עָבַר
he-violated for to-him that all and him by-the-fire he-shall-be-destroyed

אֶת־ בְּרִית יְהוָה וְכִי־ עָשָׂה נְבָלָה בְּיִשְׂרָאֵל׃
in-Israel disgraceful-thing he-did and-for Yahweh covenant-of ***

(16) וַיַּשְׁכֵּם יְהוֹשֻׁעַ בַּבֹּקֶר וַיַּקְרֵב אֶת־יִשְׂרָאֵל
Israel *** and-he-had-come-forward in-the-morning Joshua and-he-rose (16)

לִשְׁבָטָיו וַיִּלָּכֵד שֵׁבֶט יְהוּדָה׃ (17) וַיַּקְרֵב
so-he-had-come-forward (17) Judah tribe-of and-he-was-taken by-tribes-of-him

אֶת־מִשְׁפַּחַת יְהוּדָה וַיִּלְכֹּד אֵת מִשְׁפַּחַת הַזַּרְחִי וַיַּקְרֵב
so-he-had-come-forward the-Zerahite clan-of *** and-he-took Judah clan-of ***

has sinned; they have violated
my covenant, which I com-
manded them to keep. They
have taken some of the devoted things; they have stolen,
they have lied, they have put
them with their own possessions. 12That is why the Israelites cannot stand against their
enemies; they turn their backs
and run because they have
been made liable to destruction. I will not be with you
anymore unless you destroy
whatever among you is devoted to destruction.

13"Go, consecrate the people.
Tell them, 'Consecrate yourselves in preparation for tomorrow; for this is what the
LORD, the God of Israel, says:
That which is devoted is
among you, O Israel. You cannot stand against your enemies until you remove it.

14" 'In the morning, present
yourselves tribe by tribe. The
tribe that the LORD takes shall
come forward clan by clan; the
clan that the LORD takes shall
come forward family by
family; and the family that the
LORD takes shall come forward
man by man. 15He who is
caught with the devoted
things shall be destroyed by
fire, along with all that belongs to him. He has violated
the covenant of the LORD and
has done a disgraceful thing in
Israel!' "

16Early the next morning
Joshua had Israel come forward by tribes, and Judah was
taken. 17The clans of Judah
came forward, and he took the
Zerahites. He had the clan of
the Zerahites come forward by

אֶת־ מִשְׁפַּחַת הַזַּרְחִי לַגְּבָרִים וַיִּלָּכֵד זַבְדִּי׃
Zabdi and-he-was-taken by-the-families the-Zerahite clan-of ***

וַיַּקְרֵב אֶת־ בֵּיתוֹ לַגְּבָרִים וַיִּלָּכֵד
and-he-was-taken by-the-men family-of-him *** so-he-had-come-forward (18)

עָכָן בֶּן־ כַּרְמִי בֶן־ זַבְדִּי בֶּן־ זֶרַח לְמַטֵּה יְהוּדָה׃
Judah of-tribe-of Zerah son-of Zabdi son-of Carmi son-of Achan

וַיֹּאמֶר יְהוֹשֻׁעַ אֶל־ עָכָן בְּנִי שִׂים־ נָא כָבוֹד לַיהוָה
to-Yahweh glory now! give! son-of-me Achan to Joshua then-he-said (19)

אֱלֹהֵי יִשְׂרָאֵל וְתֶן־ לוֹ תוֹדָה וְהַגֶּד־ נָא לִי מֶה עָשִׂיתָ אַל־
not you-did what to-me now! and-tell! praise to-him and-give! Israel God-of

תְּכַחֵד מִמֶּנִּי׃ וַיַּעַן עָכָן אֶת־ יְהוֹשֻׁעַ וַיֹּאמַר אָמְנָה אָנֹכִי
I true and-he-said Joshua *** Achan and-he-replied (20) from-me you-hide

חָטָאתִי לַיהוָה אֱלֹהֵי יִשְׂרָאֵל וְכָזֹאת וְכָזֹאת עָשִׂיתִי׃
I-did and-as-this and-as-this Israel God-of against-Yahweh I-sinned

וָאֶרְאֶה° בַשָּׁלָל אַדֶּרֶת שִׁנְעָר אַחַת טוֹבָה וּמָאתַיִם
and-two-hundreds beautiful one Shinar robe-of in-the-plunder when-I-saw (21)

שְׁקָלִים כֶּסֶף וּלְשׁוֹן זָהָב אֶחָד חֲמִשִּׁים שְׁקָלִים מִשְׁקָלוֹ
weight-of-him shekels fifty one gold and-wedge-of silver shekels

וָאֶחְמְדֵם וָאֶקָּחֵם וְהִנָּם טְמוּנִים
ones-being-hidden and-see-they! and-I-took-them then-I-coveted-them

בָּאָרֶץ בְּתוֹךְ הָאָהֳלִי וְהַכֶּסֶף תַּחְתֶּיהָ׃
under-her and-the-silver the-tent-of-me inside-of in-the-ground

וַיִּשְׁלַח יְהוֹשֻׁעַ מַלְאָכִים וַיָּרֻצוּ הָאֹהֱלָה וְהִנֵּה
and-see! to-the-tent and-they-ran messengers Joshua so-he-sent (22)

טְמוּנָה בְּאָהֳלוֹ וְהַכֶּסֶף תַּחְתֶּיהָ׃ וַיִּקָּחוּם
and-they-took-them (23) under-her and-the-silver in-tent-of-him being-hidden

מִתּוֹךְ הָאֹהֶל וַיְבִאוּם אֶל־ יְהוֹשֻׁעַ וְאֶל כָּל־ בְּנֵי
sons-of all-of and-to Joshua to and-they-brought-them the-tent from-inside-of

יִשְׂרָאֵל וַיַּצִּקֻם לִפְנֵי יְהוָה׃ וַיִּקַּח יְהוֹשֻׁעַ אֶת־
*** Joshua then-he-took (24) Yahweh before and-they-spread-out-them Israel

עָכָן בֶּן־ זֶרַח וְאֶת־ הַכֶּסֶף וְאֶת־הָאַדֶּרֶת וְאֶת־ לְשׁוֹן הַזָּהָב וְאֶת־
and the-gold wedge-of and the-robe and the-silver and Zerah son-of Achan

בָּנָיו וְאֶת־ בְּנֹתָיו וְאֶת־ שׁוֹרוֹ וְאֶת־ חֲמֹרוֹ וְאֶת־
and donkey-of-him and cattle-of-him and daughters-of-him and sons-of-him

צֹאנוֹ וְאֶת־ אָהֳלוֹ וְאֶת־כָּל־אֲשֶׁר־ לוֹ וְכָל־ יִשְׂרָאֵל עִמּוֹ
with-him Israel and-all-of to-him that all and tent-of-him and sheep-of-him

וַיַּעֲלוּ אֹתָם עֵמֶק עָכוֹר׃ וַיֹּאמֶר יְהוֹשֻׁעַ מֶה
why? Joshua and-he-said (25) Achor Valley-of them and-they-took

families, and Zimri was taken.
18 Joshua had his family come
forward man by man, and
Achan son of Carmi, the son
of Zimri, the son of Zerah, of
the tribe of Judah, was taken.
19 Then Joshua said to Achan,
"My son, give glory to the
LORD,[r] the God of Israel, and
give him the praise.[s] Tell me
what you have done; do not
hide it from me."
20 Achan replied, "It is true! I
have sinned against the LORD,
the God of Israel. This is what
I have done: 21 When I saw in
the plunder a beautiful robe
from Babylonia,[t] two hundred
shekels[u] of silver and a wedge
of gold weighing fifty
shekels,[v] I coveted them and
took them. They are hidden in
the ground inside my tent,
with the silver underneath."
22 So Joshua sent messengers,
and they ran to the tent, and
there it was, hidden in his
tent, with the silver underneath. 23 They took the things
from the tent, brought them to
Joshua and all the Israelites
and spread them out before
the LORD.
24 Then Joshua, together with
all Israel, took Achan son of
Zerah, the silver, the robe, the
gold wedge, his sons and
daughters, his cattle, donkeys
and sheep, his tent and all that
he had, to the Valley of Achor.
25 Joshua said, "Why have you

[r]19 A solemn charge to tell the truth
[s]19 Or *and confess to him*
[t]21 Hebrew *Shinar*
[u]21 That is, about 5 pounds (about 2.3 kilograms)
[v]21 That is, about 1 1/4 pounds (about 0.6 kilogram)

°*21* ק וארא

עֲכַרְתָּנוּ יַעְכָּרְךָ יְהוָה בַּיּוֹם
on-the-day Yahweh he-will-bring-disaster-on-you you-brought-disaster-on-us

הַזֶּה וַיִּרְגְּמוּ אֹתוֹ כָל־ יִשְׂרָאֵל אֶבֶן וַיִּשְׂרְפוּ אֹתָם
them and-they-burned stone Israel all-of him then-they-stoned the-this

בָּאֵשׁ וַיִּסְקְלוּ אֹתָם בָּאֲבָנִים׃ (26) וַיָּקִימוּ
and-they-heaped-up (26) with-the-stones them after-they-stoned in-the-fire

עָלָיו גַּל־ אֲבָנִים גָּדוֹל עַד הַיּוֹם הַזֶּה וַיָּשָׁב יְהוָה
Yahweh then-he-turned the-this the-day to large rocks pile-of over-him

מֵחֲרוֹן אַפּוֹ עַל־ כֵּן קָרָא שֵׁם הַמָּקוֹם הַהוּא
the-that the-place name-of he-calls this for anger-of-him from-fierceness-of

עֵמֶק עָכוֹר עַד הַיּוֹם הַזֶּה׃ (8:1) וַיֹּאמֶר יְהוָה אֶל־יְהוֹשֻׁעַ אַל־
not Joshua to Yahweh and-he-said (8:1) the-this the-day to Achor Valley-of

תִּירָא וְאַל־ תֵּחָת קַח עִמְּךָ אֵת כָּל־ עַם
people-of all-of *** with-you take! you-be-discouraged and-not you-be-afraid

הַמִּלְחָמָה וְקוּם עֲלֵה הָעָי רְאֵה נָתַתִּי בְיָדְךָ אֶת־
*** into-hand-of-you I-delivered see! the-Ai attack! and-go-up! the-army

מֶלֶךְ הָעַי וְאֶת־ עַמּוֹ וְאֶת־ עִירוֹ וְאֶת־ אַרְצוֹ׃
land-of-him and city-of-him and people-of-him and the-Ai king-of

(2) וְעָשִׂיתָ לָעַי וּלְמַלְכָּהּ כַּאֲשֶׁר עָשִׂיתָ לִירִיחוֹ
to-Jericho you-did just-as and-to-king-of-her to-the-Ai and-you-shall-do (2)

וּלְמַלְכָּהּ רַק־ שְׁלָלָהּ וּבְהֶמְתָּהּ תָּבֹזּוּ
you-may-carry-off and-stock-of-her plunder-of-her except and-to-king-of-her

לָכֶם שִׂים־ לְךָ אֹרֵב לָעִיר מֵאַחֲרֶיהָ׃
at-behind-her for-the-city being-ambush for-you set! for-you

(3) וַיָּקָם יְהוֹשֻׁעַ וְכָל־ עַם הַמִּלְחָמָה לַעֲלוֹת הָעָי
the-Ai to-attack the-army people-of and-all-of Joshua so-he-moved-out (3)

וַיִּבְחַר יְהוֹשֻׁעַ שְׁלֹשִׁים אֶלֶף אִישׁ גִּבּוֹרֵי הַחַיִל וַיִּשְׁלָחֵם
and-he-sent-out-them the-fight men-of man thousand thirty Joshua and-he-chose

לָיְלָה׃ (4) וַיְצַו אֹתָם לֵאמֹר רְאוּ אַתֶּם אֹרְבִים לָעִיר
against-the-city ones-ambushing you see! to-say them and-he-ordered (4) night

מֵאַחֲרֵי הָעִיר אַל־ תַּרְחִיקוּ מִן־ הָעִיר מְאֹד וִהְיִיתֶם כֻּלְּכֶם
all-of-you and-you-be very the-city from you-go-far not the-city at-behind

נְכֹנִים׃ (5) וַאֲנִי וְכָל־ הָעָם אֲשֶׁר אִתִּי נִקְרַב
we-will-advance with-me who the-people and-all-of now-I (5) ones-being-alert

אֶל־ הָעִיר וְהָיָה כִּי־ יֵצְאוּ לִקְרָאתֵנוּ כַּאֲשֶׁר
just-as to-attack-us they-come-out when and-he-will-be the-city on

בָּרִאשֹׁנָה וְנַסְנוּ לִפְנֵיהֶם׃ (6) וְיָצְאוּ אַחֲרֵינוּ
after-us and-they-will-pursue (6) before-them then-we-will-flee at-the-first

brought this disaster on us?
The LORD will bring disaster
on you today."
Then all Israel stoned him,
and after they had stoned the
rest, they burned them. [26]Over
Achan they heaped up a large
pile of rocks, which remains to
this day. Then the LORD
turned from his fierce anger.
Therefore that place has been
called the Valley of Achor[w]
ever since.

Ai Destroyed

8 Then the LORD said to
Joshua, "Do not be afraid;
do not be discouraged. Take
the whole army with you, and
go up and attack Ai. For I have
delivered into your hands the
king of Ai, his people, his city
and his land. [2]You shall do to
Ai and its king as you did to
Jericho and its king, except
that you may carry off their
plunder and livestock for
yourselves. Set an ambush behind the city."
[3]So Joshua and the whole
army moved out to attack Ai.
He chose thirty thousand of
his best fighting men and sent
them out at night [4]with these
orders: "Listen carefully. You
are to set an ambush behind
the city. Don't go very far from
it. All of you be on the alert. [5]I
and all those with me will advance on the city, and when
the men come out against us,
as they did before, we will flee
from them. [6]They will pursue

[w]26 *Achor* means *disaster*.

*25 Most mss have *qamets* under the *kaph* (כָּ—).

עַד הַתִּיקֵנוּ אוֹתָם מִן־ הָעִיר כִּי יֹאמְרוּ נָסִים
ones-running-away they-will-say for the-city from them to-lure-us until

לְפָנֵינוּ כַּאֲשֶׁר בָּרִאשֹׁנָה וְנַסְנוּ לִפְנֵיהֶם׃ וְאַתֶּם תָּקֻמוּ
you-rise then-you (7) before-them when-we-flee at-the-first just-as before-us

מֵהָאוֹרֵב וְהוֹרַשְׁתֶּם אֶת־ הָעִיר וּנְתָנָהּ יְהוָה
Yahweh and-he-will-give-her the-city *** and-you-take from-the-being-ambush

אֱלֹהֵיכֶם בְּיֶדְכֶם׃ וְהָיָה כְּתָפְשְׂכֶם אֶת־ הָעִיר
the-city *** when-to-take-you and-he-will-be (8) into-hand-of-you God-of-you

תַּצִּיתוּ אֶת־ הָעִיר בָּאֵשׁ כִּדְבַר יְהוָה תַּעֲשׂוּ רְאוּ
see! you-do Yahweh as-command-of with-the-fire the-city *** then-you-burn

צִוִּיתִי אֶתְכֶם׃ וַיִּשְׁלָחֵם יְהוֹשֻׁעַ וַיֵּלְכוּ אֶל־ הַמַּאְרָב
the-ambush-place to and-they-went Joshua then-he-sent-them (9) you I-ordered

וַיֵּשְׁבוּ בֵּין בֵּית־ אֵל וּבֵין הָעַי מִיָּם לָעָי
of-the-Ai to-west the-Ai and-between El Beth between and-they-waited

וַיָּלֶן יְהוֹשֻׁעַ בַּלַּיְלָה הַהוּא בְּתוֹךְ הָעָם׃
the-people in-among the-that on-the-night Joshua but-he-spent-night

וַיַּשְׁכֵּם יְהוֹשֻׁעַ בַּבֹּקֶר וַיִּפְקֹד אֶת־ הָעָם
the-people *** and-he-mustered in-the-morning Joshua and-he-rose (10)

וַיַּעַל הוּא וְזִקְנֵי יִשְׂרָאֵל לִפְנֵי הָעָם הָעָי׃
the-Ai the-people before Israel and-leaders-of he and-he-marched

וְכָל־ הָעָם הַמִּלְחָמָה אֲשֶׁר אִתּוֹ עָלוּ
they-marched-up with-him that the-force the-people and-entire-of (11)

וַיִּגְּשׁוּ וַיָּבֹאוּ נֶגֶד הָעִיר וַיַּחֲנוּ
and-they-camped the-city in-front-of and-they-arrived and-they-approached

מִצְּפוֹן לָעַי וְהַגַּי בֵּינָו° וּבֵין־ הָעָי׃
the-Ai and-between between-him and-the-valley of-the-Ai to-north

וַיִּקַּח כַּחֲמֵשֶׁת אֲלָפִים אִישׁ וַיָּשֶׂם אוֹתָם אֹרֵב
being-ambush them and-he-set man thousands about-five-of and-he-took (12)

בֵּין בֵּית־ אֵל וּבֵין הָעַי מִיָּם לָעִיר׃ וַיָּשִׂימוּ
and-they-positioned (13) of-the-city to-west the-Ai and-between El Beth between

הָעָם אֶת־ כָּל־ הַמַּחֲנֶה אֲשֶׁר מִצְּפוֹן לָעִיר וְאֶת־ עֲקֵבוֹ
ambush-of-him and of-the-city to-north that the-camp all-of *** the-people

מִיָּם לָעִיר וַיֵּלֶךְ יְהוֹשֻׁעַ בַּלַּיְלָה הַהוּא בְּתוֹךְ הָעֵמֶק׃
the-valley into the-that on-the-night Joshua and-he-went of-the-city to-west

וַיְהִי כִּרְאוֹת מֶלֶךְ־ הָעַי וַיְמַהֲרוּ וַיַּשְׁכִּימוּ
and-they-got-up then-they-hurried the-Ai king-of when-to-see and-he-was (14)

וַיֵּצְאוּ אַנְשֵׁי־ הָעִיר לִקְרַאת־ יִשְׂרָאֵל לַמִּלְחָמָה הוּא וְכָל־
and-all-of he in-the-battle Israel to-meet the-city men-of and-they-went-out

°11 ק ביניו

us until we have lured them
away from the city, for they
will say, 'They are running
away from us as they did before.' So when we flee from
them, [7]you are to rise up from
ambush and take the city. The
LORD your God will give it into
your hand. [8]When you have
taken the city, set it on fire. Do
what the LORD has com-
manded. See to it; you have
my orders."
[9]Then Joshua sent them off,
and they went to the place of
ambush and lay in wait between Bethel and Ai, to the
west of Ai—but Joshua spent
that night with the people.
[10]Early the next morning
Joshua mustered his men, and
he and the leaders of Israel
marched before them to Ai.
[11]The entire force that was
with him marched up and approached the city and arrived
in front of it. They set up camp
north of Ai, with the valley between them and the city.
[12]Joshua had taken about five
thousand men and set them in
ambush between Bethel and
Ai, to the west of the city.
[13]They had the soldiers take up
their positions—all those in
the camp to the north of the
city and the ambush to the
west of it. That night Joshua
went into the valley.
[14]When the king of Ai saw
this, he and all the men of the
city hurried out early in the

עִמּוֹ לַמּוֹעֵד לִפְנֵי הָעֲרָבָה וְהוּא לֹא יָדַע כִּי־
that he-knew not but-he the-Arabah overlooking at-the-place people-of-him

אֹרֵב לוֹ מֵאַחֲרֵי הָעִיר׃ וַיִּנָּגְעוּ
and-they-let-selves-be-driven (15) the-city at-behind against-him being-ambush

יְהוֹשֻׁעַ וְכָל־ יִשְׂרָאֵל לִפְנֵיהֶם וַיָּנֻסוּ דֶּרֶךְ הַמִּדְבָּר׃
the-desert direction-of and-they-fled before-them Israel and-all-of Joshua

וַיִּזָּעֲקוּ כָּל־ הָעָם אֲשֶׁר בָּעִיר° לִרְדֹּף אַחֲרֵיהֶם
after-them to-pursue *in-the-city who the-man all-of and-they-were-called (16)

וַיִּרְדְּפוּ אַחֲרֵי יְהוֹשֻׁעַ וַיִּנָּתְקוּ מִן־ הָעִיר׃ וְלֹא־
and-not (17) the-city from and-they-were-lured Joshua after and-they-pursued

נִשְׁאַר אִישׁ בָּעַי וּבֵית אֵל אֲשֶׁר לֹא־ יָצְאוּ אַחֲרֵי יִשְׂרָאֵל
Israel after they-went not who El or-Beth in-the-Ai man he-remained

וַיַּעַזְבוּ אֶת־ הָעִיר פְּתוּחָה וַיִּרְדְּפוּ אַחֲרֵי יִשְׂרָאֵל׃
Israel after and-they-pursued being-open the-city *** and-they-left

וַיֹּאמֶר יְהוָה אֶל־ יְהוֹשֻׁעַ נְטֵה בַּכִּידוֹן אֲשֶׁר־
that with-the-javelin hold-out! Joshua to Yahweh then-he-said (18)

בְּיָדְךָ אֶל־ הָעַי כִּי בְיָדְךָ אֶתְּנֶנָּה
I-will-deliver-her into-hand-of-you for the-Ai toward in-hand-of-you

וַיֵּט יְהוֹשֻׁעַ בַּכִּידוֹן אֲשֶׁר־ בְּיָדוֹ אֶל־ הָעִיר׃
the-city toward in-hand-of-him that with-the-javelin Joshua so-he-held-out

וְהָאוֹרֵב קָם מְהֵרָה מִמְּקוֹמוֹ וַיָּרוּצוּ
and-they-rushed from-position-of-him quickly he-rose and-the-being-ambush (19)

כִּנְטוֹת יָדוֹ וַיָּבֹאוּ הָעִיר וַיִּלְכְּדוּהָ
and-they-captured-her the-city and-they-entered hand-of-him when-to-hold-out

וַיְמַהֲרוּ וַיַּצִּיתוּ אֶת־ הָעִיר בָּאֵשׁ׃
with-the-fire the-city *** and-they-burned and-they-were-quick

וַיִּפְנוּ אַנְשֵׁי הָעַי אַחֲרֵיהֶם וַיִּרְאוּ וְהִנֵּה
and-see! and-they-looked back-of-them the-Ai men-of and-they-turned (20)

עָלָה עֲשַׁן הָעִיר הַשָּׁמַיְמָה וְלֹא־ הָיָה בָהֶם יָדַיִם
ways for-them he-was but-not against-the-skies the-city smoke-of he-rose

לָנוּס הֵנָּה וָהֵנָּה וְהָעָם הַנָּס הַמִּדְבָּר
the-desert the-one-fleeing for-the-people or-there here to-escape

נֶהְפַּךְ אֶל־ הָרוֹדֵף׃ וִיהוֹשֻׁעַ וְכָל־ יִשְׂרָאֵל
Israel and-all-of when-Joshua (21) the-one-pursuing against he-turned-back

רָאוּ כִּי־ לָכַד הָאֹרֵב אֶת־ הָעִיר וְכִי עָלָה
he-went-up and-that the-city *** the-being-ambush he-took that they-saw

עֲשַׁן הָעִיר וַיָּשֻׁבוּ וַיַּכּוּ אֶת־ אַנְשֵׁי הָעָי׃
the-Ai men-of *** and-they-attacked then-they-turned the-city smoke-of

morning to meet Israel in battle at a certain place overlooking the Arabah. But he did not know that an ambush had been set against him behind
the city. [15]Joshua and all Israel let themselves be driven back before them, and they fled
toward the desert. [16]All the men of Ai were called to pursue them, and they pursued Joshua and were lured away
from the city. [17]Not a man remained in Ai or Bethel who did not go after Israel. They left the city open and went in pursuit of Israel.
[18]Then the LORD said to Joshua, "Hold out toward Ai the javelin that is in your hand, for into your hand I will deliver the city." So Joshua held out his javelin toward Ai.
[19]As soon as he did this, the men in the ambush rose quickly from their position and rushed forward. They entered the city and captured it and quickly set it on fire.
[20]The men of Ai looked back and saw the smoke of the city rising against the sky, but they had no chance to escape in any direction, for the Israelites who had been fleeing toward the desert had turned back against their pursuers.
[21]For when Joshua and all Israel saw that the ambush had taken the city and that smoke was going up from the city, they turned around and attacked the men of Ai. [22]The

*16 Western mss read *in-the-city* (בָּעִיר) with no *Qere* form; eastern mss have the *Qere in-the-Ai* (בָּעַי).

°16 ק בעי

וְאֵלֶּה יָצְאוּ מִן־ הָעִיר לִקְרָאתָם וַיִּהְיוּ
so-they-were to-attack-them the-city from they-came-out and-these (22)

לְיִשְׂרָאֵל בַּתָּוֶךְ אֵלֶּה מִזֶּה וְאֵלֶּה מִזֶּה
on-other-side and-these on-one-side these in-the-middle by-Israel

וַיַּכּוּ אוֹתָם עַד־בִּלְתִּי הִשְׁאִיר־לוֹ שָׂרִיד וּפָלִיט׃ וְאֶת־
but (23) or-fugitive survivor to-him he-left not until them and-they-cut-down

מֶלֶךְ הָעַי תָּפְשׂוּ חָי וַיַּקְרִבוּ אֹתוֹ אֶל־יְהוֹשֻׁעַ׃ וַיְהִי
and-he-was (24) Joshua to him and-they-brought alive they-took the-Ai king-of

כְּכַלּוֹת יִשְׂרָאֵל לַהֲרֹג אֶת־ כָּל־ יֹשְׁבֵי הָעַי בַּשָּׂדֶה
in-the-field the-Ai one-living-of all-of *** to-kill Israel when-to-finish

בַּמִּדְבָּר אֲשֶׁר רְדָפוּם בּוֹ וַיִּפְּלוּ כֻלָּם
all-of-them when-they-fell into-him they-chased-them where in-the-desert

לְפִי־ חֶרֶב עַד־ תֻּמָּם וַיָּשֻׁבוּ כָל־ יִשְׂרָאֵל הָעַי
the-Ai Israel all-of then-they-returned to-finish-them when sword by-edge-of

וַיַּכּוּ אֹתָהּ לְפִי־ חָרֶב׃ וַיְהִי כָל־ הַנֹּפְלִים
the-ones-falling all-of and-he-was (25) sword with-edge-of her and-they-killed

בַּיּוֹם הַהוּא מֵאִישׁ וְעַד־ אִשָּׁה שְׁנֵים עָשָׂר אֶלֶף כֹּל אַנְשֵׁי
people-of all-of thousand ten two woman even-to from-man the-that on-the-day

הָעָי׃ וִיהוֹשֻׁעַ לֹא־ הֵשִׁיב יָדוֹ אֲשֶׁר נָטָה
he-held-out that hand-of-him he-drew-back not for-Joshua (26) the-Ai

בַּכִּידוֹן עַד אֲשֶׁר הֶחֱרִים אֵת כָּל־ יֹשְׁבֵי הָעָי׃
the-Ai ones-living-of all-of *** he-destroyed when until with-the-javelin

רַק הַבְּהֵמָה וּשְׁלַל הָעִיר הַהִיא בָּזְזוּ לָהֶם
for-them they-carried-off the-this the-city and-plunder-of the-stock but (27)

יִשְׂרָאֵל כִּדְבַר יְהוָה אֲשֶׁר צִוָּה אֶת־ יְהוֹשֻׁעַ׃ וַיִּשְׂרֹף
so-he-burned (28) Joshua *** he-gave that Yahweh as-instruction-of Israel

יְהוֹשֻׁעַ אֶת־הָעָי וַיְשִׂימֶהָ תֵּל־ עוֹלָם שְׁמָמָה עַד הַיּוֹם
the-day to desolate-place permanent heap and-he-made-her the-Ai *** Joshua

הַזֶּה׃ וְאֶת־ מֶלֶךְ הָעַי תָּלָה עַל־ הָעֵץ עַד־ עֵת
time-of until the-tree on he-hung the-Ai king-of and (29) the-this

הָעֶרֶב וּכְבוֹא הַשֶּׁמֶשׁ צִוָּה יְהוֹשֻׁעַ וַיֹּרִידוּ אֶת־
*** and-they-took Joshua he-ordered the-sun and-when-to-set the-evening

נִבְלָתוֹ מִן־ הָעֵץ וַיַּשְׁלִיכוּ אוֹתָהּ אֶל־ פֶּתַח שַׁעַר הָעִיר
the-city gate-of entrance-of at her and-they-threw the-tree from body-of-him

וַיָּקִימוּ עָלָיו גַּל־ אֲבָנִים גָּדוֹל עַד הַיּוֹם הַזֶּה׃ אָז
then (30) the-this the-day to large rocks pile-of over-him and-they-raised

יִבְנֶה יְהוֹשֻׁעַ מִזְבֵּחַ לַיהוָה אֱלֹהֵי יִשְׂרָאֵל בְּהַר עֵיבָל׃ כַּאֲשֶׁר
just-as (31) Ebal on-Mount-of Israel God-of to-Yahweh altar Joshua he-built

men of the ambush also came
out of the city against them, so
that they were caught in the
middle, with Israelites on both
sides. Israel cut them down,
leaving them neither survivors nor fugitives. 23But they
took the king of Ai alive and
brought him to Joshua.
24When Israel had finished
killing all the men of Ai in the
fields and in the desert where
they had chased them, and
when every one of them had
been put to the sword, all the
Israelites returned to Ai and
killed those who were in it.
25Twelve thousand men and
women fell that day—all the
people of Ai. 26For Joshua did
not draw back the hand that
held out his javelin until he
had destroyed[x] all who lived
in Ai. 27But Israel did carry off
for themselves the livestock
and plunder of this city, as the
LORD had instructed Joshua.
28So Joshua burned Ai and
made it a permanent heap of
ruins, a desolate place to this
day. 29He hung the king of Ai
on a tree and left him there
until evening. At sunset,
Joshua ordered them to take
his body from the tree and
throw it down at the entrance
of the city gate. And they
raised a large pile of rocks over
it, which remains to this day.

The Covenant Renewed at Mount Ebal

30Then Joshua built on
Mount Ebal an altar to the
LORD, the God of Israel, 31as

[x]26 The Hebrew term refers to the irrevocable giving over of things or persons to the LORD, often by totally destroying them.

צִוָּה מֹשֶׁה עֶבֶד־ יְהוָה אֶת־ בְּנֵי יִשְׂרָאֵל כַּכָּתוּב
as-the-being-written Israel sons-of *** Yahweh servant-of Moses he-commanded

בְּסֵפֶר תּוֹרַת מֹשֶׁה מִזְבַּח אֲבָנִים שְׁלֵמוֹת אֲשֶׁר לֹא־ הֵנִיף עֲלֵיהֶן
on-them he-used not that uncut-ones stones altar-of Moses Law-of in-Book-of

בַּרְזֶל וַיַּעֲלוּ עָלָיו עֹלוֹת לַיהוָה וַיִּזְבְּחוּ
and-they-sacrificed to-Yahweh burnt-offerings on-him and-they-offered iron-tool

שְׁלָמִים׃ וַיִּכְתָּב־ שָׁם עַל־ הָאֲבָנִים אֵת מִשְׁנֵה תּוֹרַת
law-of copy-of *** the-stones on there and-he-wrote (32) fellowship-offerings

מֹשֶׁה אֲשֶׁר כָּתַב לִפְנֵי בְּנֵי יִשְׂרָאֵל׃ וְכָל־ יִשְׂרָאֵל
Israel and-all-of (33) Israel sons-of in-presences-of he-wrote which Moses

וּזְקֵנָיו וְשֹׁטְרִים ׀ וְשֹׁפְטָיו עֹמְדִים
ones-standing and-ones-judging-him and-being-officials and-elders-of-him

מִזֶּה ׀ וּמִזֶּה ׀ לָאָרוֹן נֶגֶד הַכֹּהֲנִים הַלְוִיִּם
the-Levites the-priests facing of-the-ark and-on-other-side on-one-side

נֹשְׂאֵי ׀ אֲרוֹן בְּרִית־ יְהוָה כַּגֵּר כָּאֶזְרָח
as-the-citizen so-the-alien Yahweh covenant-of ark-of ones-carrying-of

חֶצְיוֹ אֶל־ מוּל הַר־ גְּרִזִים וְהַחֶצְיוֹ אֶל־ מוּל
front-of in and-the-half-of-him Gerizim Mount-of front-of in half-of-him

הַר־ עֵיבָל כַּאֲשֶׁר צִוָּה מֹשֶׁה עֶבֶד־ יְהוָה לְבָרֵךְ אֶת־
*** to-bless Yahweh servant-of Moses he-commanded just-as Ebal Mount-of

הָעָם יִשְׂרָאֵל בָּרִאשֹׁנָה׃ וְאַחֲרֵי־ כֵן קָרָא אֶת־ כָּל־
all-of *** he-read this and-after (34) at-the-formerly Israel the-people

דִּבְרֵי הַתּוֹרָה הַבְּרָכָה וְהַקְּלָלָה כְּכָל־ הַכָּתוּב
the-being-written as-all-of and-the-curse the-blessing the-law words-of

בְּסֵפֶר הַתּוֹרָה׃ לֹא־ הָיָה דָבָר מִכֹּל אֲשֶׁר־ צִוָּה מֹשֶׁה אֲשֶׁר
that Moses he-commanded that of-all word he-was not (35) the-Law In-Book-of

לֹא־ קָרָא יְהוֹשֻׁעַ נֶגֶד כָּל־ קְהַל יִשְׂרָאֵל וְהַנָּשִׁים
even-the-women Israel assembly-of whole-of before Joshua he-read not

וְהַטַּף וְהַגֵּר הַהֹלֵךְ בְּקִרְבָּם׃ וַיְהִי
and-he-was (9:1) in-among-them the-one-living and-the-alien and-the-child

כִשְׁמֹעַ כָל־ הַמְּלָכִים אֲשֶׁר בְּעֵבֶר הַיַּרְדֵּן בָּהָר
in-the-hill-country the-Jordan on-west-of who the-kings all-of when-to-hear

וּבַשְּׁפֵלָה וּבְכֹל חוֹף הַיָּם הַגָּדוֹל אֶל־ מוּל
edge-of to the-Great the-Sea coast-of and-along-entire-of and-in-the-foothill

הַלְּבָנוֹן הַחִתִּי וְהָאֱמֹרִי הַכְּנַעֲנִי הַפְּרִזִּי הַחִוִּי
the-Hivite the-Perizzite the-Canaanite and-the-Amorite the-Hittite the-Lebanon

וְהַיְבוּסִי׃ וַיִּתְקַבְּצוּ יַחְדָּו לְהִלָּחֵם עִם־ יְהוֹשֻׁעַ
Joshua against to-make-war together then-they-gathered (2) and-the-Jebusite

Moses the servant of the LORD
had commanded the Israelites.
He built it according to what is
written in the Book of the Law
of Moses—an altar of uncut
stones, on which no iron tool
had been used. On it they
offered to the LORD burnt
offerings and sacrificed fellowship offerings.[y] 32There in
the presence of the Israelites,
Joshua copied on stones the
law of Moses, which he had
written. 33All Israel, aliens and
citizens alike, with their elders, officials and judges, were
standing on both sides of the
ark of the covenant of the
LORD, facing those who carried it—the priests, who were
Levites. Half of the people
stood in front of Mount Gerizim and half of them in front
of Mount Ebal, as Moses the
servant of the LORD had formerly commanded when he
gave instructions to bless the
people of Israel.
34Afterward, Joshua read all
the words of the law—the
blessings and the curses—just
as it is written in the Book of
the Law. 35There was not a
word of all that Moses had
commanded that Joshua did
not read to the whole assembly of Israel, including the
women and children, and the
aliens who lived among them.

The Gibeonite Deception

9 Now when all the kings
west of the Jordan heard
about these things—those in
the hill country, in the western foothills, and along the entire coast of the Great Sea[z] as
far as Lebanon (the kings of
the Hittites, Amorites, Canaanites, Perizzites, Hivites
and Jebusites)— 2they came together to make war against

[y]31 Traditionally *peace offerings*
[z]1 That is, the Mediterranean

*33 Most mss have *dagesh* in the *zayin* (זִּים־).

וְעִם־ יִשְׂרָאֵל פֶּה אֶחָד׃ וְיֹשְׁבֵי גִבְעוֹן שָׁמְעוּ אֵת
*** they-heard Gibeon but-ones-living-of (3) one force Israel and-against

אֲשֶׁר עָשָׂה יְהוֹשֻׁעַ לִירִיחוֹ וְלָעָי׃ וַיַּעֲשׂוּ גַם־
indeed and-they-resorted (4) and-to-the-Ai to-Jericho Joshua he-did what

הֵמָּה בְעָרְמָה וַיֵּלְכוּ וַיִּצְטַיָּרוּ* וַיִּקְחוּ שַׂקִּים
sacks and-they-loaded *and-they-acted-as-delegation and-they-went to-ruse they

בָּלִים לַחֲמוֹרֵיהֶם וְנֹאדוֹת יַיִן בָּלִים וּמְבֻקָּעִים
and-ones-being-cracked old-ones wine and-skins-of on-donkeys-of-them ones-worn

וּמְצֹרָרִים׃ וּנְעָלוֹת בָּלוֹת וּמְטֻלָּאוֹת
and-ones-being-patched ones-worn and-sandals (5) and-ones-being-mended

בְּרַגְלֵיהֶם וּשְׂלָמוֹת בָּלוֹת עֲלֵיהֶם וְכֹל לֶחֶם
bread-of and-all-of on-them old-ones and-clothes on-feet-of-them

צֵידָם יָבֵשׁ הָיָה נִקֻּדִים׃ וַיֵּלְכוּ
then-they-went (6) ones-being-moldy he-was he-was-dry food-supply-of-them

אֶל־יְהוֹשֻׁעַ אֶל־הַמַּחֲנֶה הַגִּלְגָּל וַיֹּאמְרוּ אֵלָיו וְאֶל־ אִישׁ יִשְׂרָאֵל
Israel man-of and-to to-him and-they-said the-Gilgal the-camp in Joshua to

מֵאֶרֶץ רְחוֹקָה בָּאנוּ וְעַתָּה כִּרְתוּ־ לָנוּ בְרִית׃ °וַיֹּאמְרוּ
and-he-said (7) treaty with-us make! and-now we-came distant from-country

אִישׁ־ יִשְׂרָאֵל אֶל־ הַחִוִּי אוּלַי בְּקִרְבִּי אַתָּה יוֹשֵׁב וְאֵיךְ
then-how? living you at-near-me perhaps the-Hivite to Israel man-of

°אֶכְרָות־ לְךָ בְּרִית׃ וַיֹּאמְרוּ אֶל־ יְהוֹשֻׁעַ עֲבָדֶיךָ
servants-of-you Joshua to and-they-said (8) treaty with-you can-I-make

אֲנָחְנוּ וַיֹּאמֶר אֲלֵהֶם יְהוֹשֻׁעַ מִי אַתֶּם וּמֵאַיִן תָּבֹאוּ׃
you-come and-from-where? you who? Joshua to-them but-he-asked we

וַיֹּאמְרוּ אֵלָיו מֵאֶרֶץ רְחוֹקָה מְאֹד בָּאוּ
they-came very distant from-country to-him and-they-answered (9)

עֲבָדֶיךָ לְשֵׁם יְהוָה אֱלֹהֶיךָ כִּי־ שָׁמַעְנוּ שָׁמְעוֹ
report-of-him we-heard for God-of-you Yahweh because-of-fame-of servants-of-you

וְאֵת כָּל־אֲשֶׁר עָשָׂה בְּמִצְרָיִם׃ וְאֵת׀ כָּל־אֲשֶׁר עָשָׂה לִשְׁנֵי מַלְכֵי
kings-of to-two-of he-did that all and (10) in-Egypt he-did that all and

הָאֱמֹרִי אֲשֶׁר בְּעֵבֶר הַיַּרְדֵּן לְסִיחוֹן מֶלֶךְ חֶשְׁבּוֹן וּלְעוֹג
and-to-Og Heshbon king-of to-Sihon the-Jordan on-east-of who the-Amorite

מֶלֶךְ־ הַבָּשָׁן אֲשֶׁר בְּעַשְׁתָּרוֹת׃ וַיֹּאמְרוּ אֵלֵינוּ זְקֵינֵינוּ
elders-of-us to-us and-they-said (11) in-Ashtaroth who the-Bashan king-of

וְכָל־ יֹשְׁבֵי אַרְצֵנוּ לֵאמֹר קְחוּ בְיֶדְכֶם צֵידָה
provision in-hand-of-you take! to-say land-of-us ones-living-of and-all-of

לַדֶּרֶךְ וּלְכוּ לִקְרָאתָם וַאֲמַרְתֶּם אֲלֵיהֶם עַבְדֵיכֶם
servants-of-you to-them and-you-say to-meet-them and-go! for-the-journey

Joshua and Israel.
[3]However, when the people
of Gibeon heard what Joshua
had done to Jericho and Ai,
[4]they resorted to a ruse: They
went as a delegation whose
donkeys were loaded[a] with
worn-out sacks and old wineskins, cracked and mended.
[5]The men put worn and
patched sandals on their feet
and wore old clothes. All the
bread of their food supply was
dry and moldy. [6]Then they
went to Joshua in the camp at
Gilgal and said to him and the
men of Israel, "We have come
from a distant country; make a
treaty with us."
[7]The men of Israel said to the
Hivites, "But perhaps you live
near us. How then can we
make a treaty with you?"
[8]"We are your servants,"
they said to Joshua.
But Joshua asked, "Who are
you and where do you come
from?"
[9]They answered: "Your servants have come from a very
distant country because of the
fame of the LORD your God.
For we have heard reports of
him: all that he did in Egypt,
[10]and all that he did to the two
kings of the Amorites east of
the Jordan—Sihon king of
Heshbon, and Og king of Bashan, who reigned in Ash-
taroth. [11]And our elders and all
those living in our country
said to us, 'Take provisions for
your journey; go and meet
them and say to them, "We are

[a]4 Most Hebrew manuscripts; some Hebrew manuscripts, Vulgate and Syriac (see also Septuagint) *They prepared provisions and loaded their donkeys*

*4 Some mss and versions read *daleth* for *resh* (ויצטידו) as in verse 12, *and-they-prepared-provision.*

°7a ק ויאמר

°7b ק אכרת

אֲנַחְנוּ וְעַתָּה כִּרְתוּ־ לָנוּ בְרִית: זֶה׀ לַחְמֵנוּ חָם הִצְטַיַּדְנוּ אֹתוֹ
him we-packed warm bread-of-us this (12) treaty with-us make! so-now we

מִבָּתֵּינוּ בְּיוֹם צֵאתֵנוּ לָלֶכֶת אֲלֵיכֶם וְעַתָּה הִנֵּה יָבֵשׁ
he-is-dry see! but-now to-you to-come to-leave-us on-day at-homes-of-us

וְהָיָה נִקֻּדִים: וְאֵלֶּה נֹאדוֹת הַיַּיִן אֲשֶׁר מִלֵּאנוּ
we-filled that the-wine skins-of and-these (13) ones-being-moldy and-he-is

חֲדָשִׁים וְהִנֵּה הִתְבַּקָּעוּ וְאֵלֶּה שַׂלְמוֹתֵינוּ וּנְעָלֵינוּ
and-sandals-of-us clothes-of-us and-these they-are-cracked but-see! new-ones

בָּלוּ מֵרֹב הַדֶּרֶךְ מְאֹד: וַיִּקְחוּ הָאֲנָשִׁים
the-men so-they-sampled (14) very the-journey by-length-of they-are-worn-out

מִצֵּידָם וְאֶת־ פִּי יְהוָה לֹא שָׁאָלוּ: וַיַּעַשׂ
then-he-made (15) they-inquired not Yahweh word-of but from-provision-of-them

לָהֶם יְהוֹשֻׁעַ שָׁלוֹם וַיִּכְרֹת לָהֶם בְּרִית לְחַיּוֹתָם
to-let-live-them treaty with-them and-he-made peace Joshua with-them

וַיִּשָּׁבְעוּ לָהֶם נְשִׂיאֵי הָעֵדָה: וַיְהִי
and-he-was (16) the-assembly leaders-of with-them and-they-ratified-by-oath

מִקְצֵה שְׁלֹשֶׁת יָמִים אַחֲרֵי אֲשֶׁר־ כָּרְתוּ לָהֶם בְּרִית וַיִּשְׁמְעוּ
then-they-heard treaty with-them they-made when after days three-of at-end-of

כִּי־ קְרֹבִים הֵם אֵלָיו וּבְקִרְבּוֹ הֵם יֹשְׁבִים:
ones-living they and-at-near-to-him to-him they neighbors that

וַיִּסְעוּ בְנֵי־ יִשְׂרָאֵל וַיָּבֹאוּ אֶל־ עָרֵיהֶם בַּיּוֹם
on-the-day cities-of-them to and-they-came Israel sons-of so-they-set-out (17)

הַשְּׁלִישִׁי וְעָרֵיהֶם גִּבְעוֹן וְהַכְּפִירָה וּבְאֵרוֹת וְקִרְיַת
and-Kiriath and-Beeroth and-the-Kephirah Gibeon now-cities-of-them the-third

יְעָרִים: וְלֹא הִכּוּם בְּנֵי יִשְׂרָאֵל כִּי־ נִשְׁבְּעוּ
they-swore-oath for Israel sons-of they-attacked-them but-not (18) Jearim

לָהֶם נְשִׂיאֵי הָעֵדָה בַּיהוָה אֱלֹהֵי יִשְׂרָאֵל וַיִּלֹּנוּ
and-they-grumbled Israel God-of by-Yahweh the-assembly leaders-of to-them

כָל־ הָעֵדָה עַל־ הַנְּשִׂיאִים: וַיֹּאמְרוּ כָל־
all-of but-they-answered (19) the-leaders against the-assembly whole-of

הַנְּשִׂיאִים אֶל־ כָּל־ הָעֵדָה אֲנַחְנוּ נִשְׁבַּעְנוּ לָהֶם בַּיהוָה
by-Yahweh to-them we-gave-oath we the-assembly whole-of to the-leaders

אֱלֹהֵי יִשְׂרָאֵל וְעַתָּה לֹא נוּכַל לִנְגֹּעַ בָּהֶם: זֹאת נַעֲשֶׂה
we-will-do this (20) on-them to-touch we-can not and-now Israel God-of

לָהֶם וְהַחֲיֵה אוֹתָם וְלֹא־ יִהְיֶה עָלֵינוּ קֶצֶף עַל־הַשְּׁבוּעָה
the-oath for wrath on-us he-will-fall so-not them even-to-let-live to-them

אֲשֶׁר־ נִשְׁבַּעְנוּ לָהֶם: וַיֹּאמְרוּ אֲלֵיהֶם הַנְּשִׂיאִים יִחְיוּ
let-them-live the-leaders to-them and-they-said (21) to-them we-swore that

your servants; make a treaty
with us." ' [12]This bread of ours
was warm when we packed it
at home on the day we left to
come to you. But now see how
dry and moldy it is. [13]And
these wineskins that we filled
were new, but see how
cracked they are. And our
clothes and sandals are worn
out by the very long journey."
[14]The men of Israel sampled
their provisions but did not
inquire of the LORD. [15]Then
Joshua made a treaty of peace
with them to let them live, and
the leaders of the assembly
ratified it by oath.
[16]Three days after they made
the treaty with the Gibeonites,
the Israelites heard that they
were neighbors, living near
them. [17]So the Israelites set out
and on the third day came to
their cities: Gibeon, Kephirah,
Beeroth and Kiriath Jearim.
[18]But the Israelites did not attack them, because the leaders
of the assembly had sworn an
oath to them by the LORD, the
God of Israel.
The whole assembly grum-
bled against the leaders, [19]but
all the leaders answered, "We
have given them our oath by
the LORD, the God of Israel,
and we cannot touch them
now. [20]This is what we will do
to them: We will let them live,
so that wrath will not fall on
us for breaking the oath we
swore to them." [21]They continued, "Let them live, but let

וַיִּהְיוּ חֹטְבֵי עֵצִים וְשֹׁאֲבֵי־ מַיִם לְכָל־
for-all-of waters and-ones-carrying-of woods ones-cutting-of but-let-them-be

הָעֵדָה כַּאֲשֶׁר דִּבְּרוּ לָהֶם הַנְּשִׂיאִים׃ וַיִּקְרָא
then-he-summoned (22) the-leaders to-them they-promised just-as the-community

לָהֶם יְהוֹשֻׁעַ וַיְדַבֵּר אֲלֵיהֶם לֵאמֹר לָמָּה רִמִּיתֶם אֹתָנוּ לֵאמֹר
to-say us you-deceived why? to-say to-them and-he-said Joshua to-them

רְחוֹקִים אֲנַחְנוּ מִכֶּם מְאֹד וְאַתֶּם בְּקִרְבֵּנוּ יֹשְׁבִים׃ וְעַתָּה
and-now (23) ones-living at-near-us while-you very from-you we ones-distant

אֲרוּרִים אַתֶּם וְלֹא־ יִכָּרֵת מִכֶּם עֶבֶד וְחֹטְבֵי
and-ones-cutting-of servant from-you he-will-cease and-not you ones-being-cursed

עֵצִים וְשֹׁאֲבֵי־ מַיִם לְבֵית אֱלֹהָי׃ וַיַּעֲנוּ
and-they-replied (24) God-of-me for-house-of waters and-ones-carrying-of woods

אֶת־ יְהוֹשֻׁעַ וַיֹּאמְרוּ כִּי הֻגֵּד הֻגַּד לַעֲבָדֶיךָ
to-servants-of-you he-was-told to-be-told clearly and-they-said Joshua ***

אֵת אֲשֶׁר צִוָּה יְהוָה אֱלֹהֶיךָ אֶת־ מֹשֶׁה עַבְדּוֹ לָתֵת
to-give servant-of-him Moses *** God-of-you Yahweh he-commanded how ***

לָכֶם אֶת־ כָּל־ הָאָרֶץ וּלְהַשְׁמִיד אֶת־ כָּל־ יֹשְׁבֵי
ones-inhabiting-of all-of *** and-to-wipe-out the-land whole-of *** to-you

הָאָרֶץ מִפְּנֵיכֶם וַנִּירָא מְאֹד לְנַפְשֹׁתֵינוּ מִפְּנֵיכֶם
because-of-you for-lives-of-us greatly so-we-feared from-before-you the-land

וַנַּעֲשֵׂה אֶת־ הַדָּבָר הַזֶּה׃ וְעַתָּה הִנְנוּ בְיָדֶךָ
in-hand-of-you see-we! and-now (25) the-this the-thing *** so-we-did

כַּטּוֹב וְכַיָּשָׁר בְּעֵינֶיךָ לַעֲשׂוֹת לָנוּ עֲשֵׂה׃ וַיַּעַשׂ
so-he-did (26) do! to-us to-do in-eyes-of-you and-as-the-right as-the-good

לָהֶם כֵּן וַיַּצֵּל אוֹתָם מִיַּד בְּנֵי־ יִשְׂרָאֵל וְלֹא
and-not Israel sons-of from-hand-of them and-he-saved this to-them

הֲרָגוּם׃ וַיִּתְּנֵם יְהוֹשֻׁעַ בַּיּוֹם הַהוּא
the-that on-the-day Joshua and-he-made-them (27) they-killed-them

חֹטְבֵי עֵצִים וְשֹׁאֲבֵי מַיִם לָעֵדָה
for-the-community waters and-ones-carrying-of woods ones-cutting-of

וּלְמִזְבַּח יְהוָה עַד־ הַיּוֹם הַזֶּה אֶל־ הַמָּקוֹם אֲשֶׁר יִבְחָר׃
he-would-choose that the-place at the-this the-day to Yahweh and-for-altar-of

וַיְהִי כִשְׁמֹעַ אֲדֹנִי־ צֶדֶק מֶלֶךְ יְרוּשָׁלַם כִּי־ לָכַד
he-took that Jerusalem king-of Zedek Adoni when-to-hear now-he-was (10:1)

יְהוֹשֻׁעַ אֶת־ הָעַי וַיַּחֲרִימָהּ כַּאֲשֶׁר עָשָׂה לִירִיחוֹ
to-Jericho he-did just-as and-he-destroyed-her the-Ai *** Joshua

וּלְמַלְכָּהּ כֵּן־ עָשָׂה לָעַי וּלְמַלְכָּהּ וְכִי
and-that and-to-king-of-her to-the-Ai he-did same and-to-king-of-her

them be woodcutters and water carriers for the entire community." So the leaders' promise to them was kept.

[22]Then Joshua summoned the Gibeonites and said, "Why did you deceive us by saying, 'We live a long way from you,' while actually you live near us? [23]You are now under a curse: You will never cease to serve as woodcutters and water carriers for the house of my God."

[24]They answered Joshua, "Your servants were clearly told how the LORD your God had commanded his servant Moses to give you the whole land and to wipe out all its inhabitants from before you. So we feared for our lives because of you, and that is why we did this. [25]We are now in your hands. Do to us whatever seems good and right to you."

[26]So Joshua saved them from the Israelites, and they did not kill them. [27]That day he made the Gibeonites woodcutters and water carriers for the community and for the altar of the LORD at the place the LORD would choose. And that is what they are to this day.

The Sun Stands Still

10 Now Adoni-Zedek king of Jerusalem heard that Joshua had taken Ai and totally destroyed[b] it, doing to Ai and its king as he had done to Jericho and its king, and that the people of

[b]1 The Hebrew term refers to the irrevocable giving over of things or persons to the LORD, often by totally destroying them; also in verses 28, 35, 37, 39 and 40.

הִשְׁלִימוּ יֹשְׁבֵי גִבְעוֹן אֶת־יִשְׂרָאֵל וַיִּהְיוּ
and-they-lived Israel with Gibeon ones-living-of they-made-peace-treaty

בְּקִרְבָּם׃ וַיִּירְאוּ מְאֹד כִּי עִיר גְּדוֹלָה גִּבְעוֹן
Gibeon important city for very then-they-were-alarmed (2) at-near-them

כְּאַחַת עָרֵי הַמַּמְלָכָה וְכִי הִיא גְדוֹלָה מִן־הָעַי וְכָל־
and-all-of the-Ai than larger she and-indeed the-royal cities-of like-one-of

אֲנָשֶׁיהָ גִּבֹּרִים׃ וַיִּשְׁלַח אֲדֹנִי־צֶדֶק מֶלֶךְ יְרוּשָׁלַם
Jerusalem king-of Zedek Adoni so-he-appealed (3) good-fighters men-of-her

אֶל־הוֹהָם מֶלֶךְ־חֶבְרוֹן וְאֶל־פִּרְאָם מֶלֶךְ־יַרְמוּת וְאֶל־יָפִיעַ מֶלֶךְ־
king-of Japhia and-to Jarmuth king-of Piram and-to Hebron king-of Hoham to

לָכִישׁ וְאֶל־דְּבִיר מֶלֶךְ־עֶגְלוֹן לֵאמֹר׃ עֲלוּ־אֵלַי וְעִזְרֻנִי
and-help-me! to-me come-up! (4) to-say Eglon king-of Debir and-to Lachish

וְנַכֶּה אֶת־גִּבְעוֹן כִּי־הִשְׁלִימָה אֶת־יְהוֹשֻׁעַ וְאֶת־בְּנֵי
sons-of and-with Joshua with she-made-peace for Gibeon *** and-we-will-attack

יִשְׂרָאֵל׃ וַיֵּאָסְפוּ וַיַּעֲלוּ חֲמֵשֶׁת׀ מַלְכֵי הָאֱמֹרִי
the-Amorite kings-of five-of and-they-moved-up then-they-joined (5) Israel

מֶלֶךְ יְרוּשָׁלַם מֶלֶךְ־חֶבְרוֹן מֶלֶךְ־יַרְמוּת מֶלֶךְ־לָכִישׁ מֶלֶךְ־
king-of Lachish king-of Jarmuth king-of Hebron king-of Jerusalem king-of

עֶגְלוֹן הֵם וְכָל־מַחֲנֵיהֶם וַיַּחֲנוּ עַל־גִּבְעוֹן
Gibeon against and-they-positioned troops-of-them and-all-of they Eglon

וַיִּלָּחֲמוּ עָלֶיהָ׃ וַיִּשְׁלְחוּ אַנְשֵׁי גִבְעוֹן אֶל־יְהוֹשֻׁעַ
Joshua to Gibeon men-of then-they-sent (6) against-her and-they-attacked

אֶל־הַמַּחֲנֶה הַגִּלְגָּלָה לֵאמֹר אַל־תֶּרֶף יָדֶיךָ
hands-of-you you-abandon not to-say at-the-Gilgal the-camp in

מֵעֲבָדֶיךָ עֲלֵה אֵלֵינוּ מְהֵרָה וְהוֹשִׁיעָה לָּנוּ וְעָזְרֵנוּ
and-help-us! to-us and-save! quickly to-us come-up! from-servants-of-you

כִּי נִקְבְּצוּ אֵלֵינוּ כָּל־מַלְכֵי הָאֱמֹרִי יֹשְׁבֵי
ones-living-of the-Amorite kings-of all-of against-us they-joined for

הָהָר׃ וַיַּעַל יְהוֹשֻׁעַ מִן־הַגִּלְגָּל הוּא וְכָל־
and-entire-of he the-Gilgal from Joshua so-he-marched-up (7) the-hill-country

עַם הַמִּלְחָמָה עִמּוֹ וְכֹל גִּבּוֹרֵי הֶחָיִל׃ וַיֹּאמֶר
and-he-said (8) the-fight men-of and-all-of with-him the-army people-of

יְהוָה אֶל־יְהוֹשֻׁעַ אַל־תִּירָא מֵהֶם כִּי בְיָדְךָ נְתַתִּים
I-gave-them into-hand-of-you for of-them you-be-afraid not Joshua to Yahweh

לֹא־יַעֲמֹד אִישׁ מֵהֶם בְּפָנֶיךָ׃ וַיָּבֹא אֲלֵיהֶם יְהוֹשֻׁעַ
Joshua against-them and-he-came (9) against-you of-them one he-can-stand not

פִּתְאֹם כָּל־הַלַּיְלָה עָלָה מִן־הַגִּלְגָּל׃ וַיְהֻמֵּם
and-he-confused-them (10) the-Gilgal from he-marched the-night all-of surprise

Gibeon had made a treaty of
peace with Israel and were living near them. 2He and his
people were very much
alarmed at this, because Gibeon was an important city, like
one of the royal cities; it was
larger than Ai, and all its men
were good fighters. 3So Adoni-
Zedek king of Jerusalem ap-
pealed to Hoham king of Hebron, Piram king of Jarmuth,
Japhia king of Lachish and
Debir king of Eglon. 4"Come
up and help me attack Gibeon," he said, "because it has
made peace with Joshua and
the Israelites."
5Then the five kings of the
Amorites—the kings of Jerusalem, Hebron, Jarmuth, La-
chish and Eglon—joined
forces. They moved up with all
their troops and took up positions against Gibeon and attacked it.
6The Gibeonites then sent
word to Joshua in the camp at
Gilgal: "Do not abandon your
servants. Come up to us quickly and save us! Help us, because all the Amorite kings
from the hill country have
joined forces against us."
7So Joshua marched up from
Gilgal with his entire army,
including all the best fighting
men. 8The LORD said to Joshua,
"Do not be afraid of them; I
have given them into your
hand. Not one of them will be
able to withstand you."
9After an all-night march
from Gilgal, Joshua took them
by surprise. 10The LORD threw

יְהוָה לִפְנֵי יִשְׂרָאֵל וַיַּכֵּם מַכָּה־ גְדוֹלָה בְּגִבְעוֹן
at-Gibeon great victory and-he-defeated-them Israel before Yahweh

וַיִּרְדְּפֵם דֶּרֶךְ מַעֲלֵה בֵית־ חוֹרֹן וַיַּכֵּם עַד־
to and-he-cut-down-them Horon Beth going-up-of road-of and-he-pursued-them

עֲזֵקָה וְעַד־ מַקֵּדָה׃ וַיְהִי בְּנֻסָם ׀ מִפְּנֵי יִשְׂרָאֵל
Israel from-before as-to-flee-them and-he-was (11) Makkedah and-to Azekah

הֵם בְּמוֹרַד בֵּית־ חוֹרֹן וַיהוָה הִשְׁלִיךְ עֲלֵיהֶם אֲבָנִים
hailstones on-them he-hurled then-Yahweh Horon Beth on-road-down-of they

גְּדֹלוֹת מִן־ הַשָּׁמַיִם עַד־ עֲזֵקָה וַיָּמֻתוּ רַבִּים אֲשֶׁר־ מֵתוּ
they-died who ones-more and-they-died Azekah to the-skies from large-ones

בְּאַבְנֵי הַבָּרָד מֵאֲשֶׁר הָרְגוּ בְּנֵי יִשְׂרָאֵל בֶּחָרֶב׃
by-the-sword Israel sons-of they-killed than-whom the-hail from-stones-of

אָז יְדַבֵּר יְהוֹשֻׁעַ לַיהוָה בְּיוֹם תֵּת יְהוָה אֶת־ הָאֱמֹרִי
the-Amorite *** Yahweh to-give on-day to-Yahweh Joshua he-said then (12)

לִפְנֵי בְּנֵי יִשְׂרָאֵל וַיֹּאמֶר ׀ לְעֵינֵי יִשְׂרָאֵל שֶׁמֶשׁ בְּגִבְעוֹן
over-Gibeon sun Israel before-eyes-of and-he-said Israel sons-of over-to

דּוֹם וְיָרֵחַ בְּעֵמֶק אַיָּלוֹן׃ וַיִּדֹּם הַשֶּׁמֶשׁ
the-sun so-he-stood-still (13) Aijalon over-Valley-of and-moon stand-still!

וְיָרֵחַ עָמָד עַד־ יִקֹּם גּוֹי אֹיְבָיו הֲלֹא־
not? being-enemies-of-him nation he-avenged-self till he-stopped and-moon

הִיא כְתוּבָה עַל־ סֵפֶר הַיָּשָׁר וַיַּעֲמֹד הַשֶּׁמֶשׁ בַּחֲצִי
in-middle-of the-sun and-he-stopped the-Jashar Book-of in being-written this

הַשָּׁמַיִם וְלֹא־ אָץ לָבוֹא כְּיוֹם תָּמִים׃ וְלֹא הָיָה
he-was and-never (14) full about-day to-go-down he-hurried and-not the-skies

כַּיּוֹם הַהוּא לְפָנָיו וְאַחֲרָיו לִשְׁמֹעַ יְהוָה בְּקוֹל
to-voice-of Yahweh to-listen or-since-him before-him the-that like-the-day

אִישׁ כִּי יְהוָה נִלְחָם לְיִשְׂרָאֵל׃ וַיָּשָׁב יְהוֹשֻׁעַ
Joshua then-he-returned (15) for-Israel one-fighting Yahweh surely man

וְכָל־ יִשְׂרָאֵל עִמּוֹ אֶל־ הַמַּחֲנֶה הַגִּלְגָּלָה׃ וַיָּנֻסוּ
now-they-fled (16) at-the-Gilgal the-camp to with-him Israel and-all-of

חֲמֵשֶׁת הַמְּלָכִים הָאֵלֶּה וַיֵּחָבְאוּ בַמְּעָרָה בְּמַקֵּדָה׃
at-the-Makkedah in-the-cave and-they-hid the-these the-kings five-of

וַיֻּגַּד לִיהוֹשֻׁעַ לֵאמֹר נִמְצְאוּ חֲמֵשֶׁת הַמְּלָכִים
the-kings five-of they-were-found to-say to-Joshua when-he-was-told (17)

נֶחְבְּאִים בַּמְּעָרָה בְּמַקֵּדָה׃ וַיֹּאמֶר יְהוֹשֻׁעַ גֹּלּוּ אֲבָנִים
rocks roll! Joshua and-he-said (18) at-the-Makkedah in-the-cave ones-hiding

גְּדֹלוֹת אֶל־ פִּי הַמְּעָרָה וְהַפְקִידוּ עָלֶיהָ אֲנָשִׁים לְשָׁמְרָם׃
to-guard-them men by-her and-post! the-cave mouth-of up-to large-ones

them into confusion before Israel, who defeated them in a great victory at Gibeon. Israel pursued them along the road going up to Beth Horon and cut them down all the way to Azekah and Makkedah. [11]As they fled before Israel on the road down from Beth Horon to Azekah, the LORD hurled large hailstones down on them from the sky, and more of them died from the hailstones than were killed by the swords of the Israelites.

[12]On the day the LORD gave the Amorites over to Israel, Joshua said to the LORD in the presence of Israel:

"O sun, stand still over
Gibeon,
O moon, over the Valley
of Aijalon."
[13]So the sun stood still,
and the moon stopped,
till the nation avenged
itself on[c] its enemies,

as it is written in the Book of Jashar.

The sun stopped in the middle of the sky and delayed going down about a full day. [14]There has never been a day like it before or since, a day when the LORD listened to a man. Surely the LORD was fighting for Israel!

[15]Then Joshua returned with all Israel to the camp at Gilgal.

Five Amorite Kings Killed

[16]Now the five kings had fled and hidden in the cave at Makkedah. [17]When Joshua was told that the five kings had been found hiding in the cave at Makkedah, [18]he said, "Roll large rocks up to the mouth of the cave, and post some men there to guard it.

[c]13 Or *nation triumphed over*

וְאַתֶּם אַל־ תַּעֲמֹדוּ רִדְפוּ אַחֲרֵי אֹיְבֵיכֶם וְזִנַּבְתֶּם
and-you-attack being-enemies-of-you after pursue! you-stop not but-you (19)

אוֹתָם אַל־ תִּתְּנוּם לָבוֹא אֶל־ עָרֵיהֶם כִּי נְתָנָם יְהוָה
Yahweh he-gave-them for cities-of-them to to-reach you-let-them not them

אֱלֹהֵיכֶם בְּיֶדְכֶם׃ וַיְהִי כְּכַלּוֹת יְהוֹשֻׁעַ וּבְנֵי
and-sons-of Joshua that-to-complete so-he-was (20) into-hand-of-you God-of-you

יִשְׂרָאֵל לְהַכּוֹתָם מַכָּה גְדוֹלָה־ מְאֹד עַד־ תֻּמָּם
to-finish-them almost very great destruction to-destroy-them Israel

וְהַשְּׂרִידִים שָׂרְדוּ מֵהֶם וַיָּבֹאוּ אֶל־ עָרֵי
cities-of to and-they-reached of-them they-were-left but-the-ones-left

הַמִּבְצָר׃ וַיָּשֻׁבוּ כָל־ הָעָם אֶל־ הַמַּחֲנֶה אֶל־
to the-camp to the-army whole-of then-they-returned (21) the-fortified

יְהוֹשֻׁעַ מַקֵּדָה בְּשָׁלוֹם לֹא־ חָרַץ לִבְנֵי יִשְׂרָאֵל לְאִישׁ
against-man Israel against-sons-of he-uttered no-one in-safety Makkedah Joshua

אֶת־ לְשֹׁנוֹ׃ וַיֹּאמֶר יְהוֹשֻׁעַ פִּתְחוּ אֶת־ פִּי הַמְּעָרָה
the-cave mouth-of *** open! Joshua then-he-said (22) word-of-him ***

וְהוֹצִיאוּ אֵלַי אֶת־ חֲמֵשֶׁת הַמְּלָכִים הָאֵלֶּה מִן־ הַמְּעָרָה׃
the-cave from the-those the-kings five-of *** to-me and-bring-out!

וַיַּעֲשׂוּ כֵן וַיֹּצִיאוּ אֵלָיו אֶת־ חֲמֵשֶׁת הַמְּלָכִים
the-kings five-of *** to-him and-they-brought-out this so-they-did (23)

הָאֵלֶּה מִן־ הַמְּעָרָה אֵת ׀ מֶלֶךְ יְרוּשָׁלַם אֶת־ מֶלֶךְ חֶבְרוֹן אֶת־ מֶלֶךְ
king-of *** Hebron king-of *** Jerusalem king-of *** the-cave from the-those

יַרְמוּת אֶת־מֶלֶךְ לָכִישׁ אֶת־ מֶלֶךְ עֶגְלוֹן׃ וַיְהִי כְּהוֹצִיאָם
when-to-bring-them and-he-was (24) Eglon king-of *** Lachish king-of *** Jarmuth

אֶת־הַמְּלָכִים הָאֵלֶּה אֶל־יְהוֹשֻׁעַ וַיִּקְרָא יְהוֹשֻׁעַ אֶל־ כָּל־ אִישׁ
man-of every-of to Joshua then-he-summoned Joshua to the-these the-kings ***

יִשְׂרָאֵל וַיֹּאמֶר אֶל־ קְצִינֵי אַנְשֵׁי הַמִּלְחָמָה הֶהָלְכוּא אִתּוֹ
with-him who-they-came the-army men-of commanders-of to and-he-said Israel

קִרְבוּ שִׂימוּ אֶת־ רַגְלֵיכֶם עַל־ צַוְּארֵי הַמְּלָכִים הָאֵלֶּה וַיִּקְרְבוּ
so-they-came the-these the-kings necks-of on feet-of-you *** put! come!

וַיָּשִׂימוּ אֶת־ רַגְלֵיהֶם עַל־ צַוְּארֵיהֶם׃ וַיֹּאמֶר אֲלֵיהֶם
to-them and-he-said (25) necks-of-them on feet-of-them *** and-they-placed

יְהוֹשֻׁעַ אַל־ תִּירְאוּ וְאַל־ תֵּחָתּוּ חִזְקוּ וְאִמְצוּ
and-be-courageous! be-strong! you-be-discouraged and-not you-fear not Joshua

כִּי כָכָה יַעֲשֶׂה יְהוָה לְכָל־ אֹיְבֵיכֶם אֲשֶׁר אַתֶּם
you whom being-enemies-of-you to-all-of Yahweh he-will-do this for

נִלְחָמִים אוֹתָם׃ וַיַּכֵּם יְהוֹשֻׁעַ אַחֲרֵי־ כֵן
this after Joshua then-he-struck-them (26) them ones-fighting

19But don't stop! Pursue your
enemies, attack them from the
rear and don't let them reach
their cities, for the LORD your
God has given them into your
hand."
20So Joshua and the Israelites
destroyed them completely—
almost to a man—but the few
who were left reached their
fortified cities. 21The whole
army then returned safely to
Joshua in the camp at Makkedah, and no one uttered a
word against the Israelites.
22Joshua said, "Open the
mouth of the cave and bring
those five kings out to me."
23So they brought the five
kings out of the cave—the
kings of Jerusalem, Hebron,
Jarmuth, Lachish and Eglon.
24When they had brought
these kings to Joshua, he summoned all the men of Israel
and said to the army com-
manders who had come with
him, "Come here and put your
feet on the necks of these
kings." So they came forward
and placed their feet on their
necks.
25Joshua said to them, "Do
not be afraid; do not be discouraged. Be strong and courageous. This is what the LORD
will do to all the enemies you
are going to fight." 26Then
Joshua struck and killed the

וַיְמִיתֵם וַיִּתְלֵם עַל חֲמִשָּׁה עֵצִים וַיִּהְיוּ תְּלוּיִם
ones-hanging and-they-were trees five on and-he-hung-them and-he-killed-them

עַל־ הָעֵצִים עַד־ הָעָרֶב׃ וַיְהִי לְעֵת בּוֹא הַשֶּׁמֶשׁ
the-sun to-set at-time and-he-was (27) the-evening until the-trees on

צִוָּה יְהוֹשֻׁעַ וַיֹּרִידוּם מֵעַל הָעֵצִים וַיַּשְׁלִכֻם
and-they-threw-them the-trees from-on and-they-took-down-them Joshua he-ordered

אֶל־ הַמְּעָרָה אֲשֶׁר נֶחְבְּאוּ־ שָׁם וַיָּשִׂמוּ אֲבָנִים גְּדֹלוֹת עַל־
at large-ones rocks and-they-placed there they-hid where the-cave into

פִּי הַמְּעָרָה עַד־ עֶצֶם הַיּוֹם הַזֶּה׃ וְאֶת־ מַקֵּדָה לָכַד
he-took Makkedah and (28) the-this the-day very-of to the-cave mouth-of

יְהוֹשֻׁעַ בַּיּוֹם הַהוּא וַיַּכֶּהָ לְפִי־ חֶרֶב וְאֶת־ מַלְכָּהּ
king-of-her and sword to-edge-of and-he-put-her the-that on-the-day Joshua

הֶחֱרִם אוֹתָם וְאֶת־ כָּל־ הַנֶּפֶשׁ אֲשֶׁר־ בָּהּ לֹא הִשְׁאִיר שָׂרִיד
survivor he-left not in-her who the-person every-of and them he-destroyed

וַיַּעַשׂ לְמֶלֶךְ מַקֵּדָה כַּאֲשֶׁר עָשָׂה לְמֶלֶךְ יְרִיחוֹ׃
Jericho to-king-of he-did just-as Makkedah to-king-of and-he-did

וַיַּעֲבֹר יְהוֹשֻׁעַ וְכָל־ יִשְׂרָאֵל עִמּוֹ מִמַּקֵּדָה
from-Makkedah with-him Israel and-all-of Joshua then-he-moved-on (29)

לִבְנָה וַיִּלָּחֶם עִם־ לִבְנָה׃ וַיִּתֵּן יְהוָה גַּם־אוֹתָהּ
her also Yahweh and-he-gave (30) Libnah against and-he-attacked Libnah

בְּיַד יִשְׂרָאֵל וְאֶת־ מַלְכָּהּ וַיַּכֶּהָ לְפִי־ חֶרֶב וְאֶת־
and sword to-edge-of and-he-put-her king-of-her and Israel into-hand-of

כָּל־ הַנֶּפֶשׁ אֲשֶׁר־ בָּהּ לֹא־ הִשְׁאִיר בָּהּ שָׂרִיד וַיַּעַשׂ
and-he-did survivor in-her he-left not in-her who the-person every-of

לְמַלְכָּהּ כַּאֲשֶׁר עָשָׂה לְמֶלֶךְ יְרִיחוֹ׃ וַיַּעֲבֹר
then-he-moved-on (31) Jericho to-king-of he-did just-as to-king-of-her

יְהוֹשֻׁעַ וְכָל־ יִשְׂרָאֵל עִמּוֹ מִלִּבְנָה לָכִישָׁה וַיִּחַן
and-he-positioned to-Lachish from-Libnah with-him Israel and-all-of Joshua

עָלֶיהָ וַיִּלָּחֶם בָּהּ׃ וַיִּתֵּן יְהוָה אֶת־ לָכִישׁ
Lachish *** Yahweh and-he-gave (32) against-her and-he-attacked against-her

בְּיַד יִשְׂרָאֵל וַיִּלְכְּדָהּ בַּיּוֹם הַשֵּׁנִי וַיַּכֶּהָ
and-he-put-her the-second on-the-day and-he-took-her Israel into-hand-of

לְפִי־ חֶרֶב וְאֶת־ כָּל־ הַנֶּפֶשׁ אֲשֶׁר־ בָּהּ כְּכֹל אֲשֶׁר־ עָשָׂה
he-did that as-all in-her who the-person every-of and sword to-edge-of

לְלִבְנָה׃ אָז עָלָה הֹרָם מֶלֶךְ גֶּזֶר לַעְזֹר אֶת־לָכִישׁ
Lachish *** to-help Gezer king-of Horam he-came-up meanwhile (33) to-Libnah

וַיַּכֵּהוּ יְהוֹשֻׁעַ וְאֶת־ עַמּוֹ עַד־ בִּלְתִּי הִשְׁאִיר־ לוֹ שָׂרִיד׃
survivor to-him he-left not until army-of-him and Joshua but-he-defeated-him

kings and hung them on five
trees, and they were left hanging on the trees until evening.
27 At sunset Joshua gave the
order and they took them
down from the trees and
threw them into the cave
where they had been hiding.
At the mouth of the cave they
placed large rocks, which are
there to this day.
28 That day Joshua took Makkedah. He put the city and its
king to the sword and totally
destroyed everyone in it. He
left no survivors. And he did
to the king of Makkedah as he
had done to the king of Jericho.

Southern Cities Conquered

29 Then Joshua and all Israel
with him moved on from
Makkedah to Libnah and attacked it. 30 The LORD also gave
that city and its king into Israel's hand. The city and everyone in it Joshua put to the
sword. He left no survivors
there. And he did to its king as
he had done to the king of Jericho.
31 Then Joshua and all Israel
with him moved on from Libnah to Lachish; he took up positions against it and attacked
it. 32 The LORD handed Lachish
over to Israel, and Joshua took
it on the second day. The city
and everyone in it he put to
the sword, just as he had done
to Libnah. 33 Meanwhile,
Horam king of Gezer had
come up to help Lachish, but
Joshua defeated him and his
army—until no survivors were
left.

וַיַּעֲבֹר יְהוֹשֻׁעַ וְכָל־ יִשְׂרָאֵל עִמּוֹ מִלָּכִישׁ

from-Lachish with-him Israel and-all-of Joshua then-he-moved-on (34)

עֶגְלֹנָה וַיַּחֲנוּ עָלֶיהָ וַיִּלָּחֲמוּ עָלֶיהָ׃

against-her and-they-attacked against-her and-they-positioned to-Eglon

וַיִּלְכְּדוּהָ בַּיּוֹם הַהוּא וַיַּכּוּהָ לְפִי־

to-edge-of and-they-put-her the-same on-the-day and-they-captured-her (35)

חֶרֶב וְאֵת כָּל־ הַנֶּפֶשׁ אֲשֶׁר־ בָּהּ בַּיּוֹם הַהוּא הֶחֱרִים

he-destroyed the-same on-the-day in-her who the-person every-of and sword

כְּכֹל אֲשֶׁר־ עָשָׂה לְלָכִישׁ׃ וַיַּעַל יְהוֹשֻׁעַ וְכָל־ יִשְׂרָאֵל

Israel and-all-of Joshua then-he-went-up (36) to-Lachish he-did that as-all

עִמּוֹ מֵעֶגְלוֹנָה חֶבְרוֹנָה וַיִּלָּחֲמוּ עָלֶיהָ׃

against-her and-they-attacked to-Hebron from-Eglon with-him

וַיִּלְכְּדוּהָ וַיַּכּוּהָ־ לְפִי־ חֶרֶב וְאֶת־ מַלְכָּהּ וְאֶת־

and king-of-her and sword to-edge-of and-they-put-her and-they-took-her (37)

כָּל־ עָרֶיהָ וְאֶת־ כָּל־ הַנֶּפֶשׁ אֲשֶׁר־ בָּהּ לֹא־ הִשְׁאִיר

he-left not in-her who the-person every-of and villages-of-her all-of

שָׂרִיד כְּכֹל אֲשֶׁר־ עָשָׂה לְעֶגְלוֹן וַיַּחֲרֵם אוֹתָהּ וְאֶת־ כָּל־

every-of and her and-he-destroyed to-Eglon he-did that as-all survivor

הַנֶּפֶשׁ אֲשֶׁר־ בָּהּ׃ וַיָּשָׁב יְהוֹשֻׁעַ וְכָל־ יִשְׂרָאֵל עִמּוֹ

with-him Israel and-all-of Joshua then-he-turned (38) in-her who the-person

דְּבִרָה וַיִּלָּחֶם עָלֶיהָ׃ וַיִּלְכְּדָהּ וְאֶת־ מַלְכָּהּ

king-of-her and and-he-took-her (39) against-her and-he-attacked to-Debir

וְאֶת־ כָּל־ עָרֶיהָ וַיַּכּוּם לְפִי־ חֶרֶב וַיַּחֲרִימוּ

and-they-destroyed sword to-edge-of and-they-put-them villages-of-her all-of and

אֶת־ כָּל־ נֶפֶשׁ אֲשֶׁר־ בָּהּ לֹא הִשְׁאִיר שָׂרִיד כַּאֲשֶׁר עָשָׂה לְחֶבְרוֹן

to-Hebron he-did just-as survivor he-left not in-her who person every-of ***

כֵּן־ עָשָׂה לִדְבִרָה וּלְמַלְכָּהּ וְכַאֲשֶׁר עָשָׂה לְלִבְנָה

to-Libnah he-did and-just-as and-to-king-of-her to-Debir he-did so

וּלְמַלְכָּהּ׃ וַיַּכֶּה יְהוֹשֻׁעַ אֶת־ כָּל־ הָאָרֶץ

the-region whole-of *** Joshua so-he-subdued (40) and-to-king-of-her

הָהָר וְהַנֶּגֶב וְהַשְּׁפֵלָה וְהָאֲשֵׁדוֹת וְאֵת כָּל־

all-of and and-the-slopes and-the-foothill and-the-Negev the-hill-country

מַלְכֵיהֶם לֹא הִשְׁאִיר שָׂרִיד וְאֵת כָּל־ הַנְּשָׁמָה הֶחֱרִים

he-destroyed the-breather every-of and survivor he-left not kings-of-them

כַּאֲשֶׁר צִוָּה יְהוָה אֱלֹהֵי יִשְׂרָאֵל׃ וַיַּכֵּם יְהוֹשֻׁעַ

Joshua and-he-subdued-them (41) Israel God-of Yahweh he-commanded just-as

מִקָּדֵשׁ בַּרְנֵעַ וְעַד־ עַזָּה וְאֵת כָּל־ אֶרֶץ גֹּשֶׁן וְעַד־ גִּבְעוֹן׃

Gibeon even-to Goshen region-of whole-of and Gaza even-to Barnea from-Kadesh

[34]Then Joshua and all Israel
with him moved on from Lachish to Eglon; they took up
positions against it and attacked it. [35]They captured it
that same day and put it to the
sword and totally destroyed
everyone in it, just as they had
done to Lachish.
[36]Then Joshua and all Israel
with him went up from Eglon
to Hebron and attacked it.
[37]They took the city and put it
to the sword, together with its
king, its villages and everyone
in it. They left no survivors.
Just as at Eglon, they totally
destroyed it and everyone in
it.
[38]Then Joshua and all Israel
with him turned around and
attacked Debir. [39]They took
the city, its king and its villages, and put them to the
sword. Everyone in it they totally destroyed. They left no
survivors. They did to Debir
and its king as they had done
to Libnah and its king and to
Hebron.
[40]So Joshua subdued the
whole region, including the
hill country, the Negev, the
western foothills and the
mountain slopes, together
with all their kings. He left no
survivors. He totally destroyed
all who breathed, just as the
LORD, the God of Israel, had
commanded. [41]Joshua subdued them from Kadesh Barnea to Gaza and from the
whole region of Goshen to

וְאֵת כָּל־ הַמְּלָכִים הָאֵלֶּה וְאֶת־ אַרְצָם לָכַד יְהוֹשֻׁעַ
Joshua he-conquered land-of-them and the-these the-kings all-of and (42)

פַּעַם אֶחָת כִּי יְהוָה אֱלֹהֵי יִשְׂרָאֵל נִלְחָם לְיִשְׂרָאֵל׃
for-Israel one-fighting Israel God-of Yahweh for one campaign

וַיָּשָׁב יְהוֹשֻׁעַ וְכָל־ יִשְׂרָאֵל עִמּוֹ אֶל־ הַמַּחֲנֶה
the-camp to with-him Israel and-all-of Joshua then-he-returned (43)

הַגִּלְגָּלָה׃ וַיְהִי כִּשְׁמֹעַ יָבִין מֶלֶךְ־ חָצוֹר וַיִּשְׁלַח
then-he-sent Hazor king-of Jabin when-to-hear and-he-was (11:1) at-the-Gilgal

אֶל־יוֹבָב מֶלֶךְ מָדוֹן וְאֶל־ מֶלֶךְ שִׁמְרוֹן וְאֶל־ מֶלֶךְ אַכְשָׁף׃
Acshaph king-of and-to Shimron king-of and-to Madon king-of Jobab to

וְאֶל־ הַמְּלָכִים אֲשֶׁר מִצְּפוֹן בָּהָר וּבָעֲרָבָה נֶגֶב
south-of and-in-the-Arabah in-the-mountain in-north-of who the-kings and-to (2)

כִּנְרוֹת וּבַשְּׁפֵלָה וּבְנָפוֹת דּוֹר מִיָּם׃ הַכְּנַעֲנִי
the-Canaanite (3) on-west Dor and-in-Naphoth and-in-the-foothill Kinnereth

מִמִּזְרָח וּמִיָּם וְהָאֱמֹרִי וְהַחִתִּי וְהַפְּרִזִּי
and-the-Perizzite and-the-Hittite and-the-Amorite and-in-west in-east

וְהַיְבוּסִי בָּהָר וְהַחִוִּי תַּחַת חֶרְמוֹן בְּאֶרֶץ
in-region-of Hermon below and-the-Hivite in-the-hill-country and-the-Jebusite

הַמִּצְפָּה׃ וַיֵּצְאוּ הֵם וְכָל־ מַחֲנֵיהֶם עִמָּם
with-them troops-of-them and-all-of they and-they-came-out (4) the-Mizpah

עַם־ רָב כַּחוֹל אֲשֶׁר עַל־ שְׂפַת־ הַיָּם לָרֹב וְסוּס
and-horse by-number the-sea shore-of on that as-the-sand numerous army

וָרֶכֶב רַב־ מְאֹד׃ וַיִּוָּעֲדוּ כֹּל הַמְּלָכִים הָאֵלֶּה
the-these the-kings all-of and-they-joined (5) large number and-chariot

וַיָּבֹאוּ וַיַּחֲנוּ יַחְדָּו אֶל־ מֵי מֵרוֹם לְהִלָּחֵם עִם־
against to-fight Merom Waters-of at together and-they-camped and-they-came

יִשְׂרָאֵל׃ וַיֹּאמֶר יְהוָה אֶל־יְהוֹשֻׁעַ אַל־ תִּירָא מִפְּנֵיהֶם כִּי־
for from-before-them you-fear not Joshua to Yahweh and-he-said (6) Israel

מָחָר כָּעֵת הַזֹּאת אָנֹכִי נֹתֵן אֶת־ כֻּלָּם חֲלָלִים לִפְנֵי
over-to ones-slain all-of-them *** handing I the-this by-the-time tomorrow

יִשְׂרָאֵל אֶת־ סוּסֵיהֶם תְּעַקֵּר וְאֶת־ מַרְכְּבֹתֵיהֶם תִּשְׂרֹף
you-burn chariots-of-them and you-hamstring horses-of-them *** Israel

בָּאֵשׁ׃ וַיָּבֹא יְהוֹשֻׁעַ וְכָל־ עַם הַמִּלְחָמָה עִמּוֹ
with-him the-battle army-of and-whole-of Joshua so-he-came (7) with-the-fire

עֲלֵיהֶם עַל־ מֵי מֵרוֹם פִּתְאֹם וַיִּפְּלוּ בָּהֶם׃
against-them and-they-attacked suddenly Merom Waters-of at against-them

וַיִּתְּנֵם יְהוָה בְּיַד־ יִשְׂרָאֵל וַיַּכּוּם
and-they-defeated-them Israel into-hand-of Yahweh and-he-gave-them (8)

Gibeon. 42All these kings and
their lands Joshua conquered
in one campaign, because the
LORD, the God of Israel, fought
for Israel.
43Then Joshua returned with
all Israel to the camp at Gilgal.

Northern Kings Defeated

11 When Jabin king of
Hazor heard of this, he
sent word to Jobab king of Madon, to the kings of Shimron
and Acshaph, 2and to the
northern kings who were in
the mountains, in the Arabah
south of Kinnereth, in the
western foothills and in Naphoth Dor[d] on the west; 3to the
Canaanites in the east and
west; to the Amorites, Hittites,
Perizzites and Jebusites in the
hill country; and to the Hivites
below Hermon in the region
of Mizpah. 4They came out
with all their troops and a
large number of horses and
chariots—a huge army, as numerous as the sand on the seashore. 5All these kings joined
forces and made camp to-
gether at the Waters of Merom, to fight against Israel.
6The LORD said to Joshua,
"Do not be afraid of them, because by this time tomorrow I
will hand all of them over to
Israel, slain. You are to ham-
string their horses and burn
their chariots."
7So Joshua and his whole
army came against them suddenly at the Waters of Merom
and attacked them, 8and the
LORD gave them into the hand
of Israel. They defeated them

[d] 2 Or *in the heights of Dor*

וַֽיִּרְדְּפוּם עַד־צִידוֹן רַבָּה וְעַד מִשְׂרְפוֹת מַיִם וְעַד־ בִּקְעַת
Valley-of and-to Maim Misrephoth and-to Greater Sidon to and-they-pursued-them

מִצְפֶּה מִזְרָחָה וַיַּכֻּם עַד־ בִּלְתִּי הִשְׁאִיר־ לָהֶם שָׂרִיד׃
survivor to-them he-left not until and-they-defeated-them on-east Mizpah

וַיַּעַשׂ לָהֶם יְהוֹשֻׁעַ כַּאֲשֶׁר אָמַר־ לוֹ יְהוָה אֶת־
*** Yahweh to-him he-directed just-as Joshua to-them and-he-did (9)

סוּסֵיהֶם עִקֵּר וְאֶת־ מַרְכְּבֹתֵיהֶם שָׂרַף בָּאֵשׁ׃
with-the-fire he-burned chariots-of-them and he-hamstrung horses-of-them

וַיָּשָׁב יְהוֹשֻׁעַ בָּעֵת הַהִיא וַיִּלְכֹּד אֶת־ חָצוֹר
Hazor *** and-he-captured the-that at-the-time Joshua and-he-turned-back (10)

וְאֶת־ מַלְכָּהּ הִכָּה בֶחָרֶב כִּֽי־ חָצוֹר לְפָנִים הִיא רֹאשׁ כָּל־
all-of head-of she formerly Hazor for to-the-sword he-put king-of-her and

הַמַּמְלָכוֹת הָאֵלֶּה׃ וַיַּכּוּ אֶת־ כָּל־ הַנֶּפֶשׁ אֲשֶׁר־ בָּהּ
in-her who the-person every-of *** and-they-put (11) the-these the-kingdoms

לְפִי־ חֶרֶב הַחֲרֵם לֹא נוֹתַר כָּל־ נְשָׁמָה וְאֶת־ חָצוֹר
Hazor and breather any-of he-was-spared not to-destroy sword to-edge-of

שָׂרַף בָּאֵשׁ׃ וְאֶת־ כָּל־ עָרֵי הַמְּלָכִים־ הָאֵלֶּה וְאֶת־
and the-these the-royalties cities-of all-of and (12) with-the-fire he-burned

כָּל־ מַלְכֵיהֶם לָכַד יְהוֹשֻׁעַ וַיַּכֵּם לְפִי־ חֶרֶב
sword to-edge-of and-he-put-them Joshua he-took kings-of-them all-of

הֶחֱרִים אוֹתָם כַּאֲשֶׁר צִוָּה מֹשֶׁה עֶבֶד יְהוָה׃ רַק
yet (13) Yahweh servant-of Moses he-commanded just-as them he-destroyed

כָּל־ הֶעָרִים הָעֹמְדוֹת עַל־ תִּלָּם לֹא שְׂרָפָם
he-burned-them not mound-of-them on the-ones-being-built the-cities any-of

יִשְׂרָאֵל זוּלָתִי אֶת־ חָצוֹר לְבַדָּהּ שָׂרַף יְהוֹשֻׁעַ׃ וְכֹל
and-all-of (14) Joshua he-burned by-self-of-her Hazor *** except Israel

שְׁלַל הֶעָרִים הָאֵלֶּה וְהַבְּהֵמָה בָּזְזוּ לָהֶם
for-them they-carried-off and-the-livestock the-these the-cities plunder-of

בְּנֵי יִשְׂרָאֵל רַק אֶת־ כָּל־ הָאָדָם הִכּוּ לְפִי־ חֶרֶב עַד־
until sword to-edge-of they-put the-person every-of *** but Israel sons-of

הִשְׁמִדָם אוֹתָם לֹא הִשְׁאִירוּ כָּל־ נְשָׁמָה׃ כַּאֲשֶׁר
just-as (15) breather any-of they-spared not them he-destroyed-them

צִוָּה יְהוָה אֶת־ מֹשֶׁה עַבְדּוֹ כֵּן־ צִוָּה מֹשֶׁה אֶת־
*** Moses he-commanded so servant-of-him Moses *** Yahweh he-commanded

יְהוֹשֻׁעַ וְכֵן עָשָׂה יְהוֹשֻׁעַ לֹא־ הֵסִיר דָּבָר מִכֹּל אֲשֶׁר־
that of-all anything he-left-undone not Joshua he-did and-so Joshua

צִוָּה יְהוָה אֶת־ מֹשֶׁה׃ וַיִּקַּח יְהוֹשֻׁעַ אֶת־ כָּל־ הָאָרֶץ
the-land entire-of *** Joshua so-he-took (16) Moses *** Yahweh he-commanded

and pursued them all the way to Greater Sidon, to Misrephoth Maim, and to the Valley of Mizpah on the east, until no survivors were left. [9]Joshua did to them as the LORD had directed: He hamstrung their horses and burned their chariots.

[10]At that time Joshua turned back and captured Hazor and put its king to the sword. (Hazor had been the head of all these kingdoms.) [11]Everyone in it they put to the sword. They totally destroyed[e] them, not sparing anything that breathed, and he burned up Hazor itself.

[12]Joshua took all these royal cities and their kings and put them to the sword. He totally destroyed them, as Moses the servant of the LORD had commanded. [13]Yet Israel did not burn any of the cities built on their mounds—except Hazor, which Joshua burned. [14]The Israelites carried off for themselves all the plunder and livestock of these cities, but all the people they put to the sword until they completely destroyed them, not sparing anyone that breathed. [15]As the LORD commanded his servant Moses, so Moses commanded Joshua, and Joshua did it; he left nothing undone of all that the LORD commanded Moses.

[16]So Joshua took this entire

[e]11 The Hebrew term refers to the irrevocable giving over of things or persons to the LORD, often by totally destroying them; also in verses 12, 20 and 21.

הַזֹּאת הָהָר וְאֶת־ כָּל־ הַנֶּגֶב וְאֵת כָּל־ אֶרֶץ
region-of whole-of and the-Negev all-of and the-hill-country the-this

הַגֹּשֶׁן וְאֶת־ הַשְּׁפֵלָה וְאֶת־ הָעֲרָבָה וְאֶת־ הַר יִשְׂרָאֵל
Israel mountain-of and the-Arabah and the-foothill and the-Goshen

וּשְׁפֵלָתֹה׃ מִן־ הָהָר הֶחָלָק הָעוֹלֶה שֵׂעִיר
Seir the-one-rising the-Halak the-Mount from (17) and-foothill-of-her

וְעַד־ בַּעַל־ גָּד בְּבִקְעַת הַלְּבָנוֹן תַּחַת הַר־ חֶרְמוֹן וְאֵת כָּל־
all-of and Hermon Mount-of below the-Lebanon in-Valley-of Gad Baal even-to

מַלְכֵיהֶם לָכַד וַיַּכֵּם וַיְמִיתֵם׃ יָמִים
days (18) and-he-killed-them and-he-struck-them he-captured kings-of-her

רַבִּים עָשָׂה יְהוֹשֻׁעַ אֶת־ כָּל־ הַמְּלָכִים הָאֵלֶּה מִלְחָמָה׃ לֹא־ הָיְתָה
she-was not (19) war the-these the-kings all-of *** Joshua he-waged many

עִיר אֲשֶׁר הִשְׁלִימָה אֶל־ בְּנֵי יִשְׂרָאֵל בִּלְתִּי הַחִוִּי יֹשְׁבֵי
ones-living-of the-Hivite except Israel sons-of with she-made-treaty that city

גִבְעוֹן אֶת־ הַכֹּל לָקְחוּ בַמִּלְחָמָה׃ כִּי מֵאֵת יְהוָה ׀ הָיְתָה
she-was Yahweh from for (20) in-the-battle they-took the-all *** Gibeon

לְחַזֵּק אֶת־ לִבָּם לִקְרַאת הַמִּלְחָמָה אֶת־ יִשְׂרָאֵל לְמַעַן
so-that Israel *** the-war to-wage heart-of-them *** to-harden

הַחֲרִימָם לְבִלְתִּי הֱיוֹת־ לָהֶם תְּחִנָּה כִּי לְמַעַן הַשְׁמִידָם
to-exterminate-them so-that indeed mercy to-them to-be not to-destroy-them

כַּאֲשֶׁר צִוָּה יְהוָה אֶת־ מֹשֶׁה׃ וַיָּבֹא יְהוֹשֻׁעַ בָּעֵת
at-the-time Joshua then-he-went (21) Moses *** Yahweh he-commanded just-as

הַהִיא וַיַּכְרֵת אֶת־ הָעֲנָקִים מִן־ הָהָר מִן־ חֶבְרוֹן
Hebron from the-hill-country from the-Anakite *** and-he-destroyed the-that

מִן־ דְּבִר מִן־ עֲנָב וּמִכֹּל הַר יְהוּדָה וּמִכֹּל
and-from-all-of Judah hill-country-of and-from-all-of Anab from Debir from

הַר יִשְׂרָאֵל עִם־ עָרֵיהֶם הֶחֱרִימָם יְהוֹשֻׁעַ׃ לֹא־
not (22) Joshua he-destroyed-them cities-of-them with Israel hill-country-of

נוֹתַר עֲנָקִים בְּאֶרֶץ בְּנֵי יִשְׂרָאֵל רַק בְּעַזָּה בְּגַת
in-Gath in-Gaza only Israel sons-of in-territory-of Anakites he-was-left

וּבְאַשְׁדּוֹד נִשְׁאָרוּ׃ וַיִּקַּח יְהוֹשֻׁעַ אֶת־ כָּל־ הָאָרֶץ
the-land entire-of *** Joshua so-he-took (23) they-survived and-in-Ashdod

כְּכֹל אֲשֶׁר דִּבֶּר יְהוָה אֶל־ מֹשֶׁה וַיִּתְּנָהּ יְהוֹשֻׁעַ לְנַחֲלָה
as-inheritance Joshua and-he-gave-her Moses to Yahweh he-directed that as-all

לְיִשְׂרָאֵל כְּמַחְלְקֹתָם לְשִׁבְטֵיהֶם וְהָאָרֶץ שָׁקְטָה
she-had-rest then-the-land as-tribes-of-them as-divisions-of-them to-Israel

מִמִּלְחָמָה׃ וְאֵלֶּה ׀ מַלְכֵי הָאָרֶץ אֲשֶׁר הִכּוּ בְנֵי־
sons-of they-defeated whom the-land kings-of now-these (12:1) from-war

land: the hill country, all the Negev, the whole region of Goshen, the western foothills, the Arabah and the mountains of Israel with their foothills,
[17]from Mount Halak, which rises toward Seir, to Baal Gad in the Valley of Lebanon below Mount Hermon. He captured all their kings and struck them down, putting them to death.
[18]Joshua waged war against all these kings for a long time.
[19]Except for the Hivites living in Gibeon, not one city made a treaty of peace with the Israelites, who took them all in battle.
[20]For it was the LORD himself who hardened their hearts to wage war against Israel, so that he might destroy them totally, exterminating them without mercy, as the LORD had commanded Moses.

[21]At that time Joshua went and destroyed the Anakites from the hill country: from Hebron, Debir and Anab, from all the hill country of Judah, and from all the hill country of Israel. Joshua totally destroyed them and their towns.
[22]No Anakites were left in Israelite territory; only in Gaza, Gath and Ashdod did any survive.
[23]So Joshua took the entire land, just as the LORD had directed Moses, and he gave it as an inheritance to Israel according to their tribal divisions.

Then the land had rest from war.

List of Defeated Kings

12 These are the kings of the land whom the Israelites had defeated and

יִשְׂרָאֵל וַיִּרְשׁוּ אֶת־ אַרְצָם בְּעֵבֶר הַיַּרְדֵּן
the-Jordan on-side-of territory-of-them *** and-they-took-over Israel

מִזְרְחָה הַשֶּׁמֶשׁ מִנַּחַל אַרְנוֹן עַד־ הַר חֶרְמוֹן וְכָל־
and-all-of Hermon Mount-of to Arnon from-Gorge-of the-sun toward-rise-of

הָעֲרָבָה מִזְרָחָה׃ סִיחוֹן מֶלֶךְ הָאֱמֹרִי הַיּוֹשֵׁב בְּחֶשְׁבּוֹן
in-Heshbon the-one-reigning the-Amorite king-of Sihon (2) on-east the-Arabah

מֹשֵׁל מֵעֲרוֹעֵר אֲשֶׁר עַל־ שְׂפַת־ נַחַל אַרְנוֹן וְתוֹךְ הַנַּחַל
the-gorge and-middle-of Arnon Gorge-of rim-of on that from-Aroer ruling

וַחֲצִי הַגִּלְעָד וְעַד יַבֹּק הַנַּחַל גְּבוּל בְּנֵי עַמּוֹן׃
Ammon sons-of border-of the-River Jabbok even-to the-Gilead and-half-of

וְהָעֲרָבָה עַד־ יָם כִּנְרוֹת מִזְרָחָה וְעַד יָם הָעֲרָבָה
the-Arabah Sea-of and-to on-east Kinnereth Sea-of to and-the-Arabah (3)

יָם־ הַמֶּלַח מִזְרָחָה דֶּרֶךְ בֵּית הַיְשִׁמוֹת וּמִתֵּימָן תַּחַת
below and-on-south the-Jeshimoth Beth toward on-east the-Salt Sea-of

אַשְׁדּוֹת הַפִּסְגָּה׃ וּגְבוּל עוֹג מֶלֶךְ הַבָּשָׁן מִיֶּתֶר
from-last-of the-Bashan king-of Og and-territory-of (4) the-Pisgah slopes-of

הָרְפָאִים הַיּוֹשֵׁב בְּעַשְׁתָּרוֹת וּבְאֶדְרֶעִי׃ וּמֹשֵׁל
and-ruling (5) and-in-Edrei in-Ashtaroth the-one-reigning the-Rephaites

בְּהַר חֶרְמוֹן וּבְסַלְכָה וּבְכָל־ הַבָּשָׁן עַד־ גְּבוּל
border-of to the-Bashan and-over-all-of and-over-Salecah Hermon over-Mount-of

הַגְּשׁוּרִי וְהַמַּעֲכָתִי וַחֲצִי הַגִּלְעָד גְּבוּל סִיחוֹן
Sihon border-of the-Gilead and-half-of and-the-Maacathite the-Geshurite

מֶלֶךְ־ חֶשְׁבּוֹן׃ מֹשֶׁה עֶבֶד־ יְהוָה וּבְנֵי יִשְׂרָאֵל
Israel and-sons-of Yahweh servant-of Moses (6) Heshbon king-of

הִכּוּם וַיִּתְּנָהּ מֹשֶׁה עֶבֶד־ יְהוָה יְרֻשָּׁה
possession Yahweh servant-of Moses and-he-gave-her they-conquered-them

לָרְאוּבֵנִי וְלַגָּדִי וְלַחֲצִי שֵׁבֶט הַמְנַשֶּׁה׃
the-Manasseh tribe-of and-to-half-of and-to-the-Gadite to-the-Reubenite

וְאֵלֶּה מַלְכֵי הָאָרֶץ אֲשֶׁר הִכָּה יְהוֹשֻׁעַ וּבְנֵי יִשְׂרָאֵל
Israel and-sons-of Joshua he-conquered that the-land kings-of and-these (7)

בְּעֵבֶר הַיַּרְדֵּן יָמָּה מִבַּעַל גָּד בְּבִקְעַת הַלְּבָנוֹן וְעַד־
even-to the-Lebanon in-Valley-of Gad from-Baal to-west the-Jordan on-side-of

הָהָר הֶחָלָק הָעֹלֶה שֵׂעִירָה וַיִּתְּנָהּ יְהוֹשֻׁעַ
Joshua and-he-gave-her toward-Seir the-one-rising the-Halak the-Mount

לְשִׁבְטֵי יִשְׂרָאֵל יְרֻשָּׁה כְּמַחְלְקֹתָם׃ בָּהָר
in-the-hill-country (8) by-divisions-of-them possession Israel to-tribes-of

וּבַשְּׁפֵלָה וּבָעֲרָבָה וּבָאֲשֵׁדוֹת וּבַמִּדְבָּר
and-in-the-desert and-in-the-slopes and-in-the-Arabah and-in-the-foothill

whose territory they took over
east of the Jordan, from the
Arnon Gorge to Mount Her-
mon, including all the eastern
side of the Arabah:

2Sihon king of the Amorites,
who reigned in Heshbon.
He ruled from Aroer on the
rim of the Arnon Gorge—
from the middle of the
gorge—to the Jabbok River,
which is the border of the
Ammonites. This included
half of Gilead. 3He also
ruled over the eastern Arabah from the Sea of Kin-
nereth[f] to the Sea of the
Arabah (the Salt Sea[g]), to
Beth Jeshimoth, and then
southward below the slopes
of Pisgah.

4And the territory of Og king
of Bashan,
one of the last of the Rephaites, who reigned in
Ashtaroth and Edrei. 5He
ruled over Mount Hermon,
Salecah, all of Bashan to the
border of the people of Geshur and Maacah, and half
of Gilead to the border of
Sihon king of Heshbon.

6Moses, the servant of the
LORD, and the Israelites conquered them. And Moses the
servant of the LORD gave their
land to the Reubenites, the
Gadites and the half-tribe of
Manasseh to be their possession.
7These are the kings of the
land that Joshua and the Israelites conquered on the west
side of the Jordan, from Baal
Gad in the Valley of Lebanon
to Mount Halak, which rises
toward Seir (their lands
Joshua gave as an inheritance
to the tribes of Israel according
to their tribal divisions— 8the
hill country, the western foothills, the Arabah, the mountain slopes, the desert and the

f3 That is, Galilee
g3 That is, the Dead Sea

*6 Most mss have no *qibbuts* under the *resh* (לָרְאוּבֵנִי).

וּבַנֶּגֶב הַחִתִּי הָאֱמֹרִי וְהַכְּנַעֲנִי הַפְּרִזִּי
the-Perizzite and-the-Canaanite the-Amorite the-Hittite and-in-the-Negev

הַחִוִּי וְהַיְבוּסִי׃ מֶלֶךְ יְרִיחוֹ אֶחָד מֶלֶךְ הָעַי אֲשֶׁר־
that the-Ai king-of one Jericho king-of (9) and-the-Jebusite the-Hivite

מִצַּד בֵּית־אֵל אֶחָד׃ מֶלֶךְ יְרוּשָׁלַםִ אֶחָד מֶלֶךְ חֶבְרוֹן אֶחָד׃
one Hebron king-of one Jerusalem king-of (10) one El Beth at-near

מֶלֶךְ יַרְמוּת אֶחָד מֶלֶךְ לָכִישׁ אֶחָד׃ מֶלֶךְ עֶגְלוֹן אֶחָד מֶלֶךְ
king-of one Eglon king-of (12) one Lachish king-of one Jarmuth king-of (11)

גֶּזֶר אֶחָד׃ מֶלֶךְ דְּבִר אֶחָד מֶלֶךְ גֶּדֶר אֶחָד׃ מֶלֶךְ חָרְמָה אֶחָד
one Hormah king-of (14) one Geder king-of one Debir king-of (13) one Gezer

מֶלֶךְ עֲרָד אֶחָד׃ מֶלֶךְ לִבְנָה אֶחָד מֶלֶךְ עֲדֻלָּם אֶחָד׃ מֶלֶךְ
king-of (16) one Adullam king-of one Libnah king-of (15) one Arad king-of

מַקֵּדָה אֶחָד מֶלֶךְ בֵּית־אֵל אֶחָד׃ מֶלֶךְ תַּפּוּחַ אֶחָד מֶלֶךְ חֵפֶר אֶחָד׃
one Hepher king-of one Tappuah king-of (17) one El Beth king-of one Makkedah

מֶלֶךְ אֲפֵק אֶחָד מֶלֶךְ לַשָּׁרוֹן אֶחָד׃ מֶלֶךְ מָדוֹן אֶחָד מֶלֶךְ
king-of one Madon king-of (19) one Lasharon king-of one Aphek king-of (18)

חָצוֹר אֶחָד׃ מֶלֶךְ שִׁמְרוֹן מְרֹאון אֶחָד מֶלֶךְ אַכְשָׁף אֶחָד׃ מֶלֶךְ
king-of (21) one Acshaph king-of one Meron Shimron king-of (20) one Hazor

תַּעְנַךְ אֶחָד מֶלֶךְ מְגִדּוֹ אֶחָד׃ מֶלֶךְ קֶדֶשׁ אֶחָד מֶלֶךְ־יָקְנְעָם
Jokneam king-of one Kedesh king-of (22) one Megiddo king-of one Taanach

לַכַּרְמֶל אֶחָד׃ מֶלֶךְ דּוֹר לְנָפַת דּוֹר אֶחָד מֶלֶךְ־גּוֹיִם לְגִלְגָּל
in-Gilgal Goyim king-of one Dor in-Naphoth Dor king-of (23) one in-the-Carmel

אֶחָד׃ מֶלֶךְ תִּרְצָה אֶחָד כָּל־מְלָכִים שְׁלֹשִׁים וְאֶחָד׃ וִיהוֹשֻׁעַ
when-Joshua (13:1) and-one thirty kings all-of one Tirzah king-of (24) one

זָקֵן בָּא בַּיָּמִים וַיֹּאמֶר יְהוָה אֵלָיו אַתָּה
you to-him Yahweh then-he-said in-the-days he-was-advanced he-was-old

זָקַנְתָּה בָּאתָ בַיָּמִים וְהָאָרֶץ נִשְׁאֲרָה הַרְבֵּה־
to-be-large she-remains and-the-land in-the-days you-are-advanced you-are-old

מְאֹד לְרִשְׁתָּהּ׃ זֹאת הָאָרֶץ הַנִּשְׁאָרֶת כָּל־ גְּלִילוֹת
regions-of all-of the-remaining the-land this (2) to-take-over-her very

הַפְּלִשְׁתִּים וְכָל־ הַגְּשׁוּרִי׃ מִן־ הַשִּׁיחוֹר אֲשֶׁר עַל־ פְּנֵי
east-of on that the-Shihor from (3) the-Geshurite and-all-of the-Philistines

מִצְרַיִם וְעַד גְּבוּל עֶקְרוֹן צָפוֹנָה לַכְּנַעֲנִי תֵּחָשֵׁב
she-was-counted as-the-Canaanite on-north Ekron territory-of and-to Egypt

חֲמֵשֶׁת סַרְנֵי פְלִשְׁתִּים הָעַזָּתִי וְהָאַשְׁדּוֹדִי הָאֶשְׁקְלוֹנִי
the-Ashkelonite and-the-Ashdodite the-Gazathite Philistines rulers-of five-of

הַגִּתִּי וְהָעֶקְרוֹנִי וְהָעַוִּים׃ מִתֵּימָן כָּל־ אֶרֶץ
land-of all-of from-south (4) and-the-Avvites and-the-Ekronite the-Gathite

Negev—the lands of the Hittites, Amorites, Canaanites, Perizzites, Hivites and Jebusites):

9 the king of Jericho one
the king of Ai (near Bethel) one
10 the king of Jerusalem one
the king of Hebron one
11 the king of Jarmuth one
the king of Lachish one
12 the king of Eglon one
the king of Gezer one
13 the king of Debir one
the king of Geder one
14 the king of Hormah one
the king of Arad one
15 the king of Libnah one
the king of Adullam one
16 the king of Makkedah one
the king of Bethel one
17 the king of Tappuah one
the king of Hepher one
18 the king of Aphek one
the king of Lasharon one
19 the king of Madon one
the king of Hazor one
20 the king of Shimron Meron one
the king of Acshaph one
21 the king of Taanach one
the king of Megiddo one
22 the king of Kedesh one
the king of Jokneam in Carmel one
23 the king of Dor (in Naphoth Dor[h]) one
the king of Goyim in Gilgal one
24 the king of Tirzah one
thirty-one kings in all.

Land Still to Be Taken

13 When Joshua was old and well advanced in years, the LORD said to him, "You are very old, and there are still very large areas of land to be taken over.

2 "This is the land that remains: all the regions of the Philistines and Geshurites:
3 from the Shihor River on the east of Egypt to the territory of Ekron on the north, all of it counted as Canaanite (the territory of the five Philistine rulers in Gaza, Ashdod, Ashkelon, Gath and Ekron—that of the Avvites);
4 from the south, all the land of the

h23 Or *in the heights of Dor*

הַכְּנַעֲנִי וּמְעָרָה אֲשֶׁר לַצִּידֹנִים עַד־אֲפֵקָה עַד
to to-Aphek as-far-as of-the-Sidonians that and-from-Arah the-Canaanite

גְּבוּל הָאֱמֹרִי׃ וְהָאָרֶץ הַגִּבְלִי וְכָל־הַלְּבָנוֹן
the-Lebanon and-all-of the-Gebalite and-the-area (5) the-Amorite region-of

מִזְרַח הַשֶּׁמֶשׁ מִבַּעַל גָּד תַּחַת הַר־חֶרְמוֹן עַד לְבוֹא חֲמָת׃ כָּל־
all-of (6) Hamath Lebo to Hermon Mount-of below Gad from-Baal the-sun rise-of

יֹשְׁבֵי הָהָר מִן־הַלְּבָנוֹן עַד־מִשְׂרְפֹת מַיִם
Maim Misrephoth to the-Lebanon from the-mountain-region ones-inhabiting-of

כָּל־צִידֹנִים אָנֹכִי אוֹרִישֵׁם מִפְּנֵי בְּנֵי יִשְׂרָאֵל רַק
only Israel sons-of from-before I-will-drive-out-them I Sidonians all-of

הַפִּלֶהָ לְיִשְׂרָאֵל בְּנַחֲלָה כַּאֲשֶׁר צִוִּיתִךָ׃ וְעַתָּה
and-now (7) I-instructed-you just-as for-inheritance to-Israel allocate-her!

חַלֵּק אֶת־הָאָרֶץ הַזֹּאת בְּנַחֲלָה לְתִשְׁעַת הַשְּׁבָטִים
the-tribes among-nine-of as-inheritance the-this the-land *** divide!

וַחֲצִי הַשֵּׁבֶט הַמְנַשֶּׁה׃ עִמּוֹ הָרְאוּבֵנִי וְהַגָּדִי
and-the-Gadite the-Reubenite with-him (8) the-Manasseh the-tribe and-half-of

לָקְחוּ נַחֲלָתָם אֲשֶׁר נָתַן לָהֶם מֹשֶׁה בְּעֵבֶר
on-side-of Moses to-them he-gave that inheritance-of-them they-received

הַיַּרְדֵּן מִזְרָחָה כַּאֲשֶׁר נָתַן לָהֶם מֹשֶׁה עֶבֶד יְהוָה׃
Yahweh servant-of Moses to-them he-assigned just-as to-east the-Jordan

מֵעֲרוֹעֵר אֲשֶׁר עַל־שְׂפַת־נַחַל אַרְנוֹן וְהָעִיר אֲשֶׁר בְּתוֹךְ־
in-middle-of that and-the-town Arnon Gorge-of rim-of on that from-Aroer (9)

הַנַּחַל וְכָל־הַמִּישֹׁר מֵידְבָא עַד־דִּיבוֹן׃ וְכֹל
and-all-of (10) Dibon as-far-as Medeba the-plateau and-whole-of the-gorge

עָרֵי סִיחוֹן מֶלֶךְ הָאֱמֹרִי אֲשֶׁר מָלַךְ בְּחֶשְׁבּוֹן עַד־גְּבוּל
border-of to in-Heshbon he-ruled who the-Amorite king-of Sihon towns-of

בְּנֵי עַמּוֹן׃ וְהַגִּלְעָד וּגְבוּל הַגְּשׁוּרִי
the-Geshurite and-territory-of and-the-Gilead (11) Ammon sons-of

וְהַמַּעֲכָתִי וְכֹל הַר חֶרְמוֹן וְכָל־הַבָּשָׁן עַד־
as-far-as the-Bashan and-all-of Hermon Mount-of and-all-of and-the-Maacathite

סַלְכָה׃ כָּל־מַמְלְכוּת עוֹג בַּבָּשָׁן אֲשֶׁר־מָלַךְ בְּעַשְׁתָּרוֹת
in-Ashtaroth he-reigned who in-the-Bashan Og kingdom-of whole-of (12) Salecah

וּבְאֶדְרֶעִי הוּא נִשְׁאַר מִיֶּתֶר הָרְפָאִים וַיַּכֵּם
and-he-defeated-them the-Rephaites among-last-of he-survived he and-in-Edrei

מֹשֶׁה וַיֹּרִשֵׁם׃ וְלֹא הוֹרִישׁוּ בְּנֵי יִשְׂרָאֵל אֶת־
*** Israel sons-of they-drove-out but-not (13) and-he-took-over-them Moses

הַגְּשׁוּרִי וְאֶת־הַמַּעֲכָתִי וַיֵּשֶׁב גְּשׁוּר וּמַעֲכָת בְּקֶרֶב
in-among and-Maacah Geshur so-he-lives the-Maacathite and the-Geshurite

Canaanites, from Arah of
the Sidonians as far as
Aphek, the region of the
Amorites, [5]the area of the
Gebalites[i]; and all Lebanon
to the east, from Baal Gad
below Mount Hermon to
Lebo[j] Hamath.

[6]"As for all the inhabitants
of the mountain regions from
Lebanon to Misrephoth
Maim, that is, all the Sidonians, I myself will drive them
out before the Israelites. Be
sure to allocate this land to Israel for an inheritance, as I
have instructed you, [7]and divide it as an inheritance
among the nine tribes and
half of the tribe of Manasseh."

Division of the Land East of the Jordan

[8]The other half of Manasseh,[k]
the Reubenites and the Gadites had received the inheritance that Moses had given
them east of the Jordan, as he,
the servant of the LORD, had
assigned it to them.

[9]It extended from Aroer on
the rim of the Arnon Gorge,
and from the town in the
middle of the gorge, and included the whole plateau of
Medeba as far as Dibon,
[10]and all the towns of Sihon
king of the Amorites, who
ruled in Heshbon, out to
the border of the Ammon-
ites. [11]It also included Gilead, the territory of the
people of Geshur and Maa-
cah, all of Mount Hermon
and all Bashan as far as
Salecah— [12]that is, the
whole kingdom of Og in
Bashan, who had reigned
in Ashtaroth and Edrei and
had survived as one of the
last of the Rephaites. Moses
had defeated them and tak-
en over their land. [13]But the
Israelites did not drive out
the people of Geshur and
Maacah, so they continue
to live among the Israelites

[i]5 That is, the area of Byblos
[j]5 Or *to the entrance to*
[k]8 Hebrew *With it* (that is, with the other half of Manasseh)

יִשְׂרָאֵל עַד הַיּוֹם הַזֶּה׃ רַק לְשֵׁבֶט הַלֵּוִי לֹא נָתַן
he-gave not the-Levite to-tribe-of but (14) the-this the-day to Israel

נַחֲלָה אִשֵּׁי יְהוָה אֱלֹהֵי יִשְׂרָאֵל הוּא נַחֲלָתוֹ
inheritance-of-him this Israel God-of Yahweh fire-offerings-of inheritance

כַּאֲשֶׁר דִּבֶּר־ לוֹ׃ וַיִּתֵּן מֹשֶׁה לְמַטֵּה בְנֵי־ רְאוּבֵן
Reuben sons-of to-tribe-of Moses and-he-gave (15) to-him he-promised just-as

לְמִשְׁפְּחֹתָם׃ וַיְהִי לָהֶם הַגְּבוּל מֵעֲרוֹעֵר אֲשֶׁר עַל־
on that from-Aroer the-territory to-them and-he-was (16) by-clans-of-them

שְׂפַת־ נַחַל אַרְנוֹן וְהָעִיר אֲשֶׁר בְּתוֹךְ־ הַנַּחַל וְכָל־
and-whole-of the-gorge in-middle-of that and-the-town Arnon Gorge-of rim-of

הַמִּישֹׁר עַל־ מֵידְבָא׃ חֶשְׁבּוֹן וְכָל־ עָרֶיהָ אֲשֶׁר
that towns-of-her and-all-of Heshbon (17) Medeba past the-plateau

בַּמִּישֹׁר דִּיבוֹן וּבָמוֹת בַּעַל וּבֵית בַּעַל מְעוֹן׃ וְיַהְצָה
and-Jahaz (18) Meon Baal and-Beth Baal and-Bamoth Dibon on-the-plateau

וּקְדֵמֹת וּמֵפָעַת׃ וְקִרְיָתַיִם וְשִׂבְמָה וְצֶרֶת
and-Zereth and-Sibmah and-Kiriathaim (19) and-Mephaath and-Kedemoth

הַשַּׁחַר בְּהַר הָעֵמֶק׃ וּבֵית פְּעוֹר וְאַשְׁדּוֹת הַפִּסְגָּה
the-Pisgah and-slopes-of Peor and-Beth (20) the-Valley on-hill-of the-Shahar

וּבֵית הַיְשִׁמוֹת׃ וְכֹל עָרֵי הַמִּישֹׁר וְכָל־
and-entire-of the-plateau towns-of and-all-of (21) the-Jeshimoth and-Beth

מַמְלְכוּת סִיחוֹן מֶלֶךְ הָאֱמֹרִי אֲשֶׁר מָלַךְ בְּחֶשְׁבּוֹן אֲשֶׁר הִכָּה
he-defeated whom at-Heshbon he-ruled who the-Amorite king-of Sihon realm-of

מֹשֶׁה אֹתוֹ ׀ וְאֶת־נְשִׂיאֵי מִדְיָן אֶת־אֱוִי וְאֶת־רֶקֶם וְאֶת־צוּר וְאֶת־חוּר וְאֶת־רֶבַע
Reba and Hur and Zur and Rekem and Evi *** Midian chiefs-of and him Moses

נְסִיכֵי סִיחוֹן יֹשְׁבֵי הָאָרֶץ׃ וְאֶת־ בִּלְעָם בֶּן־ בְּעוֹר
Beor son-of Balaam and (22) the-country ones-living-of Sihon princes-of

הַקּוֹסֵם הָרְגוּ בְנֵי־ יִשְׂרָאֵל בַּחֶרֶב אֶל־
beside to-the-sword Israel sons-of they-put the-one-practicing-divination

חַלְלֵיהֶם׃ וַיְהִי גְּבוּל בְּנֵי רְאוּבֵן הַיַּרְדֵּן
the-Jordan Reuben sons-of boundary-of and-he-was (23) ones-slain-of-them

וּגְבוּל זֹאת נַחֲלַת בְּנֵי־ רְאוּבֵן לְמִשְׁפְּחֹתָם הֶעָרִים
the-towns by-clans-of-them Reuben sons-of inheritance-of this and-bank

וְחַצְרֵיהֶן׃ וַיִּתֵּן מֹשֶׁה לְמַטֵּה־ גָד לִבְנֵי־ גָד
Gad to-sons-of Gad to-tribe-of Moses and-he-gave (24) and-villages-of-them

לְמִשְׁפְּחֹתָם׃ וַיְהִי לָהֶם הַגְּבוּל יַעְזֵר וְכָל־
and-all-of Jazer the-territory to-them and-he-was (25) by-clans-of-them

עָרֵי הַגִּלְעָד וַחֲצִי אֶרֶץ בְּנֵי עַמּוֹן עַד־ עֲרוֹעֵר
Aroer as-far-as Ammon sons-of country-of and-half-of the-Gilead towns-of

to this day.

14 But to the tribe of Levi he gave no inheritance, since the offerings made by fire to the LORD, the God of Israel, are their inheritance, as he promised them.

15 This is what Moses had given to the tribe of Reuben, clan by clan:

16 The territory from Aroer on the rim of the Arnon Gorge, and from the town in the middle of the gorge, and the whole plateau past Medeba 17 to Heshbon and all its towns on the plateau, including Dibon, Bamoth Baal, Beth Baal Meon, 18 Jahaz, Kedemoth, Mephaath, 19 Kiriathaim, Sibmah, Zereth Shahar on the hill in the valley, 20 Beth Peor, the slopes of Pisgah, and Beth Jeshimoth 21 —all the towns on the plateau and the entire realm of Sihon king of the Amorites, who ruled at Heshbon. Moses had defeated him and the Midianite chiefs, Evi, Rekem, Zur, Hur and Reba—princes allied with Sihon—who lived in that country. 22 In addition to those slain in battle, the Israelites had put to the sword Balaam son of Beor, who practiced divination. 23 The boundary of the Reubenites was the bank of the Jordan. These towns and their villages were the inheritance of the Reubenites, clan by clan.

24 This is what Moses had given to the tribe of Gad, clan by clan:

25 The territory of Jazer, all the towns of Gilead and half the Ammonite country

אֲשֶׁר עַל־ פְּנֵי רַבָּה׃ וּמֵחֶשְׁבּוֹן עַד־ רָמַת הַמִּצְפֶּה וּבְטֹנִים
and-Betonim the-Mizpah Ramath to and-from-Heshbon (26) Rabbah near at that

וּמִמַּחֲנַיִם עַד־ גְּבוּל לִדְבִר׃ וּבָעֵמֶק בֵּית הָרָם
Haram Beth and-in-the-valley (27) of-Debir territory to and-from-Mahanaim

וּבֵית נִמְרָה וְסֻכּוֹת וְצָפוֹן יֶתֶר מַמְלְכוּת סִיחוֹן מֶלֶךְ חֶשְׁבּוֹן
Heshbon king-of Sihon realm-of rest-of and-Zaphon and-Succoth Nimrah and-Beth

הַיַּרְדֵּן וּגְבֻל עַד־ קְצֵה יָם־ כִּנֶּרֶת עֵבֶר הַיַּרְדֵּן
the-Jordan side-of Kinnereth Sea-of end-of to and-territory the-Jordan

מִזְרָחָה׃ זֹאת נַחֲלַת בְּנֵי־ גָד לְמִשְׁפְּחֹתָם הֶעָרִים
the-towns by-clans-of-them Gad sons-of inheritance-of this (28) on-east

וְחַצְרֵיהֶם׃ וַיִּתֵּן מֹשֶׁה לַחֲצִי שֵׁבֶט מְנַשֶּׁה
Manasseh tribe-of to-half-of Moses and-he-gave (29) and-villages-of-them

וַיְהִי לַחֲצִי מַטֵּה בְנֵי־ מְנַשֶּׁה לְמִשְׁפְּחוֹתָם׃
by-clans-of-them Manasseh descendants-of family-of to-half-of and-he-was

וַיְהִי גְּבוּלָם מִמַּחֲנַיִם כָּל־ הַבָּשָׁן כָּל־
entire-of the-Bashan all-of from-Mahanaim territory-of-them and-he-was (30)

מַמְלְכוּת ׀ עוֹג מֶלֶךְ־ הַבָּשָׁן וְכָל־ חַוֹּת יָאִיר אֲשֶׁר
that Jair settlements-of and-all-of the-Bashan king-of Og realm-of

בַּבָּשָׁן שִׁשִּׁים עִיר׃ וַחֲצִי הַגִּלְעָד וְעַשְׁתָּרוֹת וְאֶדְרֶעִי
and-Edrei and-Ashtaroth the-Gilead and-half-of (31) town sixty in-the-Bashan

עָרֵי מַמְלְכוּת עוֹג בַּבָּשָׁן לִבְנֵי מָכִיר בֶּן־ מְנַשֶּׁה
Manasseh son-of Makir for-sons-of in-the-Bashan Og royalty-of cities-of

לַחֲצִי בְנֵי־ מָכִיר לְמִשְׁפְּחוֹתָם׃ אֵלֶּה אֲשֶׁר־ נִחַל
he-gave-inheritance that these (32) by-clans-of-them Makir sons-of for-half-of

מֹשֶׁה בְּעַרְבוֹת מוֹאָב מֵעֵבֶר לְיַרְדֵּן יְרִיחוֹ מִזְרָחָה׃
to-east Jericho of-Jordan-of on-across Moab in-plains-of Moses

וּלְשֵׁבֶט הַלֵּוִי לֹא־ נָתַן מֹשֶׁה נַחֲלָה יְהוָה אֱלֹהֵי
God-of Yahweh inheritance Moses he-gave not the-Levi but-to-tribe-of (33)

יִשְׂרָאֵל הוּא נַחֲלָתָם כַּאֲשֶׁר דִּבֶּר לָהֶם׃ וְאֵלֶּה
now-these (14:1) to-them he-promised just-as inheritance-of-them he Israel

אֲשֶׁר־ נָחֲלוּ בְנֵי־ יִשְׂרָאֵל בְּאֶרֶץ כְּנָעַן אֲשֶׁר נִחֲלוּ
they-allotted which Canaan in-land-of Israel sons-of they-inherited that

אוֹתָם אֶלְעָזָר הַכֹּהֵן וִיהוֹשֻׁעַ בִּן־ נוּן וְרָאשֵׁי אֲבוֹת
fathers-of and-heads-of Nun son-of and-Joshua the-priest Eleazar them

הַמַּטּוֹת לִבְנֵי יִשְׂרָאֵל׃ בְּגוֹרַל נַחֲלָתָם כַּאֲשֶׁר
just-as inheritance-of-them by-lot (2) Israel of-sons-of the-tribes

צִוָּה יְהוָה בְּיַד־ מֹשֶׁה לְתִשְׁעַת הַמַּטּוֹת וַחֲצִי
and-half-of the-tribes to-nine-of Moses by-hand-of Yahweh he-commanded

as far as Aroer, near Rabbah; [26]and from Heshbon to
Ramath Mizpah and Beto-
nim, and from Mahanaim
to the territory of Debir;
[27]and in the valley, Beth
Haram, Beth Nimrah, Suc-
coth and Zaphon with the
rest of the realm of Sihon
king of Heshbon (the east
side of the Jordan, the territory up to the end of the Sea
of Kinnereth[l]). [28]These
towns and their villages
were the inheritance of the
Gadites, clan by clan.

[29]This is what Moses had giv-
en to the half-tribe of Manasseh, that is, to half the family
of the descendants of Manasseh, clan by clan:

[30]The territory extending
from Mahanaim and in-
cluding all of Bashan, the
entire realm of Og king of
Bashan—all the settlements
of Jair in Bashan, sixty
towns, [31]half of Gilead, and
Ashtaroth and Edrei (the
royal cities of Og in Ba-
shan). This was for the descendants of Makir son of
Manasseh—for half of the
sons of Makir, clan by clan.

[32]This is the inheritance
Moses had given when he was
in the plains of Moab across
the Jordan east of Jericho. [33]But
to the tribe of Levi, Moses had
given no inheritance; the
LORD, the God of Israel, is their
inheritance, as he promised
them.

Division of the Land West of the Jordan

14 Now these are the
areas the Israelites re-
ceived as an inheritance in the
land of Canaan, which Eleazar
the priest, Joshua son of Nun
and the heads of the tribal
clans of Israel allotted to them.
[2]Their inheritances were assigned by lot to the nine-and-
a-half tribes, as the LORD had
commanded through Moses.

[l]27 That is, Galilee

הַמַּטֶּה׃ כִּֽי־ נָתַ֨ן מֹשֶׁ֜ה נַחֲלַ֨ת שְׁנֵ֤י הַמַּטּוֹת֙

the-tribes two-of inheritance-of Moses he-granted for (3) the-tribe

וַחֲצִ֣י הַמַּטֶּ֔ה מֵעֵ֖בֶר לַיַּרְדֵּ֑ן וְלַ֨לְוִיִּ֔ם לֹא־ נָתַ֥ן

he-granted not but-to-the-Levites of-the-Jordan on-east the-tribe and-half-of

נַחֲלָ֖ה בְּתוֹכָֽם׃ כִּֽי־ הָי֧וּ בְנֵֽי־ יוֹסֵ֛ף שְׁנֵ֥י מַטּ֖וֹת

tribes two-of Joseph sons-of they-became for (4) in-among-them inheritance

מְנַשֶּׁ֣ה וְאֶפְרָ֑יִם וְלֹֽא־ נָתְנוּ֩ חֵ֨לֶק לַלְוִיִּ֜ם בָּאָ֗רֶץ כִּ֤י

but in-the-land to-the-Levites share they-gave and-not and-Ephraim Manasseh

אִם־ עָרִים֙ לָשֶׁ֔בֶת וּמִ֨גְרְשֵׁיהֶ֔ם לְמִקְנֵיהֶ֖ם וּלְקִנְיָנָֽם׃

and-for-herd-of-them for-flocks-of-them and-pastures-of-them to-live towns only

כַּאֲשֶׁ֨ר צִוָּ֤ה יְהוָה֙ אֶת־ מֹשֶׁ֔ה כֵּ֥ן עָשׂ֖וּ בְּנֵ֣י יִשְׂרָאֵ֑ל

Israel sons-of they-did so Moses * Yahweh he-commanded just-as (5)**

וַֽיַּחְלְק֖וּ אֶת־ הָאָֽרֶץ׃ וַיִּגְּשׁ֨וּ בְנֵֽי־ יְהוּדָ֤ה אֶל־יְהוֹשֻׁ֙עַ֙

Joshua to Judah men-of now-they-approached (6) the-land * and-they-divided**

בַּגִּלְגָּ֔ל וַיֹּ֣אמֶר אֵלָ֔יו כָּלֵ֥ב בֶּן־ יְפֻנֶּ֖ה הַקְּנִזִּ֑י אַתָּ֣ה

you the-Kenizzite Jephunneh son-of Caleb to-him and-he-said at-the-Gilgal

יָדַ֡עְתָּ אֶֽת־ הַדָּבָר֩ אֲשֶׁר־ דִּבֶּ֨ר יְהוָ֜ה אֶל־מֹשֶׁ֣ה אִישׁ־הָאֱלֹהִ֗ים עַ֧ל

about the-God man-of Moses to Yahweh he-said that the-thing * you-know**

אֹדוֹתַ֛י וְעַ֥ל אֹדוֹתֶ֖יךָ בְּקָדֵ֥שׁ בַּרְנֵֽעַ׃ בֶּן־אַרְבָּעִ֨ים

forty son-of (7) Barnea at-Kadesh because-of-you and-about because-of-me

שָׁנָ֜ה אָנֹכִ֗י בִּ֠שְׁלֹחַ מֹשֶׁ֨ה עֶבֶד־ יְהוָ֥ה אֹתִ֛י מִקָּדֵ֥שׁ בַּרְנֵ֖עַ לְרַגֵּ֣ל

to-explore Barnea from-Kadesh me Yahweh servant-of Moses when-to-send I year

אֶת־ הָאָ֑רֶץ וָאָשֵׁ֤ב אֹתוֹ֙ דָּבָ֔ר כַּאֲשֶׁ֖ר עִם־ לְבָבִֽי׃

heart-of-me in just-as report him and-I-brought-back the-land ***

וְאַחַ֗י אֲשֶׁ֤ר עָלוּ֙ עִמִּ֔י הִמְסִ֖יו אֶת־ לֵ֣ב

heart-of * they-made-melt with-me they-went-up who but-brothers-of-me (8)**

הָעָ֑ם וְאָנֹכִ֣י מִלֵּ֔אתִי אַחֲרֵ֖י יְהוָ֥ה אֱלֹהָֽי׃ וַיִּשָּׁבַ֣ע

so-he-swore (9) God-of-me Yahweh after I-was-wholehearted but-I the-people

מֹשֶׁ֗ה בַּיּ֣וֹם הַהוּא֮ לֵאמֹר֒ אִם־ לֹ֗א הָאָ֙רֶץ֙ אֲשֶׁ֨ר דָּרְכָ֤ה

she-walked that the-land indeed now to-say the-that on-the-day Moses

רַגְלְךָ֙ בָּ֔הּ לְךָ֨ תִהְיֶ֧ה לְֽנַחֲלָ֛ה וּלְבָנֶ֖יךָ

and-to-children-of-you as-inheritance she-will-be to-you on-her foot-of-you

עַד־עוֹלָ֑ם כִּ֚י מִלֵּ֔אתָ אַחֲרֵ֖י יְהוָ֥ה אֱלֹהָֽי׃ וְעַתָּ֗ה הִנֵּה֩

see! and-now (10) God-of-me Yahweh after you-were-wholehearted for ever for

הֶחֱיָ֨ה יְהוָ֣ה ׀ אוֹתִי֮ כַּאֲשֶׁ֣ר דִּבֵּר֒ זֶה֩ אַרְבָּעִ֨ים וְחָמֵ֜שׁ שָׁנָ֗ה

year and-five forty this he-promised just-as me Yahweh he-kept-alive

מֵ֠אָז דִּבֶּ֨ר יְהוָ֜ה אֶת־ הַדָּבָ֤ר הַזֶּה֙ אֶל־מֹשֶׁ֔ה אֲשֶׁר־ הָלַ֥ךְ

he-moved while Moses to the-this the-thing * Yahweh he-said since-when**

[3]Moses had granted the two-
and-a-half tribes their inheritance east of the Jordan but
had not granted the Levites an
inheritance among the rest,
[4]for the sons of Joseph had
become two tribes—Manasseh
and Ephraim. The Levites received no share of the land but
only towns to live in, with
pasturelands for their flocks
and herds. [5]So the Israelites divided the land, just as the
LORD had commanded Moses.

Hebron Given to Caleb

[6]Now the men of Judah approached Joshua at Gilgal, and
Caleb son of Jephunneh the
Kenizzite said to him, "You
know what the LORD said to
Moses the man of God at Kadesh Barnea about you and
me. [7]I was forty years old
when Moses the servant of the
LORD sent me from Kadesh
Barnea to explore the land.
And I brought him back a report according to my convic-
tions, [8]but my brothers who
went up with me made the
hearts of the people melt with
fear. I, however, followed the
LORD my God wholeheartedly.
[9]So on that day Moses swore to
me, 'The land on which your
feet have walked will be your
inheritance and that of your
children forever, because you
have followed the LORD my
God wholeheartedly.'[m]
[10]"Now then, just as the
LORD promised, he has kept
me alive for forty-five years
since the time he said this to
Moses, while Israel moved

[m]9 Deut. 1:36

ישראל במדבר ועתה הנה אנכי היום בן־ חמש ושמונים שנה׃
year and-eighty five son-of the-day I see! so-now in-the-desert Israel

עודני היום חזק כאשר ביום שלח אותי משה ככחי
as-vigor-of-me Moses me to-send on-day just-as strong the-day still-I (11)

אז וככחי עתה למלחמה ולצאת ולבוא׃ ועתה
so-now (12) and-to-go even-to-go-out to-the-battle now so-vigor-of-me then

תנה־ לי את־ ההר הזה אשר־ דבר יהוה ביום
on-the-day Yahweh he-promised that the-this the-hill-country *** to-me give!

ההוא כי אתה־ שמעת ביום ההוא כי־ ענקים שם וערים
and-cities there Anakites that the-that on-the-day you-heard you for the-that

גדלות בצרות אולי יהוה אותי והורשתים
then-I-will-drive-out-them with-me Yahweh but fortified-ones large-ones

כאשר דבר יהוה׃ ויברכהו יהושע ויתן את־
*** and-he-gave Joshua then-he-blessed-him (13) Yahweh he-said just-as

חברון לכלב בן־ יפנה לנחלה׃ על־ כן היתה־
she-belonged this for (14) as-inheritance Jephunneh son-of to-Caleb Hebron

חברון לכלב בן־ יפנה הקנזי לנחלה עד היום
the-day to as-inheritance the-Kenizzite Jephunneh son-of to-Caleb Hebron

הזה יען אשר מלא אחרי יהוה אלהי ישראל׃
Israel God-of Yahweh after he-was-wholehearted that because the-this

ושם חברון לפנים קרית ארבע האדם הגדול
the-greatest the-man Arba Kiriath before Hebron now-name-of (15)

בענקים הוא והארץ שקטה ממלחמה׃ ויהי
and-he-was (15:1) from-war she-had-rest then-the-land he among-the-Anakites

הגורל למטה בני יהודה למשפחתם אל־ גבול
territory-of to by-clans-of-them Judah sons-of for-tribe-of the-allotment

אדום מדבר־ צן נגבה מקצה תימן׃ ויהי להם
to-them and-he-was (2) south in-extreme-of in-south Zin Desert-of Edom

גבול נגב מקצה ים המלח מן־ הלשן הפנה
the-one-facing the-bay from the-Salt Sea-of from-end-of south boundary-of

נגבה׃ ויצא אל־ מנגב למעלה עקרבים ועבר
and-he-continued Scorpions of-Pass-of on-south at and-he-crossed (3) to-south

צנה ועלה מנגב לקדש ברנע ועבר חצרון
Hezron then-he-ran-past Barnea of-Kadesh to-south and-he-went to-Zin

ועלה אדרה ונסב הקרקעה׃ ועבר
then-he-passed-along (4) to-the-Karka then-he-curved to-Addar then-he-went-up

עצמונה ויצא נחל מצרים והיה תצאות הגבול
the-boundary ends-of and-they-were Egypt Wadi-of and-he-joined to-Azmon

°4 ק והיו

about in the desert. So here I am today, eighty-five years old! [11]I am still as strong today as the day Moses sent me out; I'm just as vigorous to go out to battle now as I was then. [12]Now give me this hill country that the LORD promised me that day. You yourself heard then that the Anakites were there and their cities were large and fortified, but, the LORD helping me, I will drive them out just as he said."

[13]Then Joshua blessed Caleb son of Jephunneh and gave him Hebron as his inheritance. [14]So Hebron has belonged to Caleb son of Jephunneh the Kenizzite ever since, because he followed the LORD, the God of Israel, wholeheartedly. [15](Hebron used to be called Kiriath Arba after Arba, who was the greatest man among the Anakites.)

Then the land had rest from war.

Allotment for Judah

15 The allotment for the tribe of Judah, clan by clan, extended down to the territory of Edom, to the Desert of Zin in the extreme south.

[2]Their southern boundary started from the bay at the southern end of the Salt Sea,[n] [3]crossed south of Scorpion[o] Pass, continued on to Zin and went over to the south of Kadesh Barnea. Then it ran past Hezron up to Addar and curved around to Karka. [4]It then passed along to Azmon and joined the Wadi of Egypt,

[n]2 That is, the Dead Sea; also in verse 5
[o]3 Hebrew *Akrabbim*

יָמָּה זֶה־ יִהְיֶה לָכֶם גְּבוּל נֶגֶב׃ וּגְבוּל קֵדְמָה
to-east and-boundary-of (5) southern boundary-of for-you he-is this at-sea

יָם הַמֶּלַח עַד־ קְצֵה הַיַּרְדֵּן וּגְבוּל לִפְאַת
on-side-of and-boundary the-Jordan mouth-of as-far-as the-Salt Sea-of

צָפוֹנָה מִלְּשׁוֹן הַיָּם מִקְצֵה הַיַּרְדֵּן׃ וְעָלָה
and-he-went-up (6) the-Jordan at-mouth-of the-sea from-bay-of to-north

הַגְּבוּל בֵּית חָגְלָה וְעָבַר מִצְּפוֹן לְבֵית הָעֲרָבָה
the-Arabah of-Beth to-north and-he-continued Hoglah Beth the-boundary

וְעָלָה הַגְּבוּל אֶבֶן בֹּהַן בֶּן־ רְאוּבֵן׃ וְעָלָה
then-he-went-up (7) Reuben son-of Bohan Stone-of the-boundary and-he-went

הַגְּבוּל ׀ דְּבִרָה מֵעֵמֶק עָכוֹר וְצָפוֹנָה פֹּנֶה אֶל־ הַגִּלְגָּל
the-Gilgal to turning and-at-north Achor from-Valley-of to-Debir the-boundary

אֲשֶׁר־ נֹכַח לְמַעֲלֵה אֲדֻמִּים אֲשֶׁר מִנֶּגֶב לַנָּחַל וְעָבַר
and-he-continued of-the-gorge at-south that Adummim to-Pass-of facing which

הַגְּבוּל אֶל־ מֵי־ עֵין שֶׁמֶשׁ וְהָיוּ תֹצְאֹתָיו אֶל־עֵין רֹגֵל׃
Rogel En at ends-of-him and-they-were Shemesh En Waters-of to the-boundary

וְעָלָה הַגְּבוּל גֵּי בֶן־ הִנֹּם אֶל־ כֶּתֶף
slope-of along Hinnom Ben Valley-of the-boundary then-he-ran-up (8)

הַיְבוּסִי מִנֶּגֶב הִיא יְרוּשָׁלִָם וְעָלָה הַגְּבוּל אֶל־ רֹאשׁ
top-of to the-boundary and-he-climbed Jerusalem that on-south the-Jebusite

הָהָר אֲשֶׁר עַל־ פְּנֵי גֵי־ הִנֹּם יָמָּה אֲשֶׁר בִּקְצֵה עֵמֶק־
Valley-of at-end-of that on-west Hinnom Valley-of front-of at that the-hill

רְפָאִים צָפֹנָה׃ וְתָאַר הַגְּבוּל מֵרֹאשׁ הָהָר אֶל־
toward the-hill from-top-of the-boundary then-he-headed (9) at-north Rephaim

מַעְיַן מֵי נֶפְתּוֹחַ וְיָצָא אֶל־ עָרֵי הַר־ עֶפְרוֹן
Ephron Mount-of towns-of to and-he-came Nephtoah Waters-of spring-of

וְתָאַר הַגְּבוּל בַּעֲלָה הִיא קִרְיַת יְעָרִים׃ וְנָסַב
then-he-curved (10) Jearim Kiriath that Baalah the-boundary and-he-went

הַגְּבוּל מִבַּעֲלָה יָמָּה אֶל־ הַר שֵׂעִיר וְעָבַר אֶל־ כֶּתֶף
slope-of along and-he-ran Seir Mount-of to to-west from-Baalah the-boundary

הַר־ יְעָרִים מִצָּפוֹנָה הִיא כְסָלוֹן וְיָרַד בֵּית־ שֶׁמֶשׁ
Shemesh Beth and-he-continued-down Kesalon that on-north Jearim Mount-of

וְעָבַר תִּמְנָה׃ וְיָצָא הַגְּבוּל אֶל־ כֶּתֶף עֶקְרוֹן
Ekron slope-of to the-boundary and-he-went (11) Timnah and-he-crossed

צָפוֹנָה וְתָאַר הַגְּבוּל שִׁכְּרוֹנָה וְעָבַר הַר־
Mount-of and-he-passed-along to-Shikkeron the-boundary and-he-turned on-north

הַבַּעֲלָה וְיָצָא יַבְנְאֵל וְהָיוּ תֹּצְאוֹת הַגְּבוּל יָמָּה׃
at-sea the-boundary ends-of and-they-were Jabneel and-he-reached the-Baalah

ending at the sea. This is
their[p] southern boundary.
5 The eastern boundary is
the Salt Sea as far as the
mouth of the Jordan.
The northern boundary
started from the bay of the
sea at the mouth of the Jordan, 6 went up to Beth Hoglah and continued north of
Beth Arabah to the Stone of
Bohan son of Reuben. 7 The
boundary then went up to
Debir from the Valley of
Achor and turned north to
Gilgal, which faces the Pass
of Adummim south of the
gorge. It continued along to
the Waters of En Shemesh
and came out at En Rogel.
8 Then it ran up the Valley
of Ben Hinnom along the
southern slope of the Jebusite city (that is, Jerusalem).
From there it climbed to the
top of the hill west of the
Hinnom Valley at the
northern end of the Valley
of Rephaim. 9 From the hill-
top the boundary headed
toward the spring of the
Waters of Nephtoah, came
out at the towns of Mount
Ephron and went down
toward Baalah (that is,
Kiriath Jearim). 10 Then it
curved westward from Baa-
lah to Mount Seir, ran
along the northern slope of
Mount Jearim (that is,
Kesalon), continued down
to Beth Shemesh and
crossed to Timnah. 11 It
went to the northern slope
of Ekron, turned toward
Shikkeron, passed along to
Mount Baalah and reached
Jabneel. The boundary
ended at the sea.

p4 Hebrew *your*

וּגְב֣וּל יָ֔ם הַיָּ֥מָּה הַגָּד֖וֹל וּגְב֑וּל זֶ֣ה גְב֔וּל
boundary-of this and-coast the-Great to-the-Sea west and-boundary-of (12)

בְּנֵֽי־יְהוּדָ֛ה סָבִ֖יב לְמִשְׁפְּחֹתָֽם׃ וּלְכָלֵ֣ב בֶּן־יְפֻנֶּ֗ה
Jephunneh son-of and-to-Caleb (13) by-clans-of-them around Judah people-of

נָ֤תַן חֵ֙לֶק֙ בְּת֣וֹךְ בְּנֵֽי־יְהוּדָ֔ה אֶל־פִּ֥י יְהוָ֖ה לִיהוֹשֻׁ֑עַ
to-Joshua Yahweh command-of at Judah sons-of in-midst-of portion he-gave

אֶת־קִרְיַ֥ת אַרְבַּ֛ע אֲבִ֥י הָעֲנָ֖ק הִ֥יא חֶבְרֽוֹן׃ וַיֹּ֤רֶשׁ
and-he-drove-out (14) Hebron that the-Anak forefather-of Arba Kiriath ***

מִשָּׁם֙ כָּלֵ֔ב אֶת־שְׁלוֹשָׁ֖ה בְּנֵ֣י הָעֲנָ֑ק אֶת־שֵׁשַׁ֤י וְאֶת־אֲחִימַן֙ וְאֶת־
and Ahiman and Sheshai *** the-Anak sons-of three *** Caleb from-there

תַּלְמַ֔י יְלִידֵ֖י הָעֲנָֽק׃ וַיַּ֣עַל מִשָּׁ֔ם אֶל־
against from-there and-he-marched (15) the-Anak descendants-of Talmai

יֹשְׁבֵ֖י דְּבִ֑ר וְשֵׁם־דְּבִ֥ר לְפָנִ֖ים קִרְיַת־סֵֽפֶר׃ וַיֹּ֖אמֶר
and-he-said (16) Sepher Kiriath formerly Debir now-name-of Debir ones-living-of

כָּלֵ֑ב אֲשֶׁר־יַכֶּ֧ה אֶת־קִרְיַת־סֵ֛פֶר וּלְכָדָ֖הּ
and-he-captures-her Sepher Kiriath *** he-attacks whoever Caleb

וְנָתַ֥תִּי ל֛וֹ אֶת־עַכְסָ֥ה בִתִּ֖י לְאִשָּֽׁה׃ וַֽיִּלְכְּדָ֔הּ
and-he-took-her (17) as-wife daughter-of-me Acsah *** to-him then-I-will-give

עָתְנִיאֵ֥ל בֶּן־קְנַ֖ז אֲחִ֣י כָלֵ֑ב וַיִּתֶּן־ל֛וֹ אֶת־עַכְסָ֥ה
Acsah *** to-him so-he-gave Caleb brother-of Kenaz son-of Othniel

בִתּ֖וֹ לְאִשָּֽׁה׃ וַיְהִ֣י בְּבוֹאָ֗הּ וַתְּסִיתֵ֙הוּ֙
then-she-urged-him when-to-come-her and-he-was (18) as-wife daughter-of-him

לִשְׁא֤וֹל מֵֽאֵת־אָבִ֙יהָ֙ שָׂדֶ֔ה וַתִּצְנַ֖ח מֵעַ֣ל הַחֲמ֑וֹר
the-donkey from-on when-she-got-off field father-of-her from to-ask

וַיֹּאמֶר־לָ֥הּ כָּלֵ֖ב מַה־לָּֽךְ׃ וַתֹּ֜אמֶר תְּנָה־לִּ֣י
for-me do! and-she-replied (19) for-you what? Caleb to-her then-he-asked

בְרָכָ֗ה כִּ֣י אֶ֤רֶץ הַנֶּ֙גֶב֙ נְתַתָּ֔נִי וְנָתַתָּ֥ה לִ֖י גֻּלֹּ֣ת
springs-of to-me also-you-give you-gave-me the-Negev land-of since favor

מָ֑יִם וַיִּתֶּן־לָ֗הּ אֵ֚ת גֻּלֹּ֣ת עִלִּיּ֔וֹת וְאֵ֖ת גֻּלֹּ֥ת תַּחְתִּיּֽוֹת׃
lower-ones springs-of and upper-ones springs-of *** to-her so-he-gave waters

זֹ֗את נַחֲלַ֛ת מַטֵּ֥ה בְנֵֽי־יְהוּדָ֖ה לְמִשְׁפְּחֹתָֽם׃
by-clans-of-them Judah sons-of tribe-of inheritance-of this (20)

וַיִּֽהְי֣וּ הֶעָרִ֗ים מִקְצֵה֙ לְמַטֵּ֣ה בְנֵֽי־יְהוּדָ֔ה אֶל־
toward Judah sons-of of-tribe-of at-end the-towns and-they-were (21)

גְּב֥וּל אֱד֖וֹם בַּנֶּ֑גְבָּה קַבְצְאֵ֥ל וְעֵ֖דֶר וְיָגֽוּר׃ וְקִינָ֥ה
and-Kinah (22) and-Jagur and-Eder Kabzeel in-the-Negev Edom boundary-of

וְדִימוֹנָ֖ה וְעַדְעָדָֽה׃ וְקֶ֥דֶשׁ וְחָצ֖וֹר וְיִתְנָֽן׃ זִ֥יף
Ziph (24) and-Ithnan and-Hazor and-Kedesh (23) and-Adadah and-Dimonah

[12]The western boundary
is the coastline of the Great
Sea.[q]
These are the boundaries
around the people of Judah by
their clans.

[13]In accordance with the
LORD's command to him,
Joshua gave to Caleb son of Je-
phunneh a portion in Judah—
Kiriath Arba, that is, Hebron.
(Arba was the forefather of
Anak.) [14]From Hebron Caleb
drove out the three Anakites—
Sheshai, Ahiman and Tal-
mai—descendants of Anak.
[15]From there he marched
against the people living in
Debir (formerly called Kiriath
Sepher). [16]And Caleb said, "I
will give my daughter Acsah
in marriage to the man who
attacks and captures Kiriath
Sepher." [17]Othniel son of
Kenaz, Caleb's brother, took
it; so Caleb gave his daughter
Acsah to him in marriage.
[18]One day when she came to
Othniel, she urged him[r] to ask
her father for a field.
When she got off the don-
key, Caleb asked her, "What
can I do for you?"
[19]She replied, "Do me a
special favor. Since you have
given me land in the Negev,
give me also springs of water."
So Caleb gave her the upper
and lower springs.

[20]This is the inheritance of
the tribe of Judah, clan by
clan:

[21]The southernmost towns of
the tribe of Judah in the Negev
toward the boundary of Edom
were:
Kabzeel, Eder, Jagur,
[22]Kinah, Dimonah, Ada-
dah, [23]Kedesh, Hazor, Ith-
nan, [24]Ziph, Telem,

[q]12 That is, the Mediterranean; also in verse 47
[r]18 Hebrew and some Septuagint manuscripts; other Septuagint manuscripts (see also note at Judges 1:14) *Othniel, he urged her*

וְטֶלֶם וּבְעָלוֹת׃ וְחָצוֹר ׀ חֲדַתָּה וּקְרִיּוֹת חֶצְרוֹן הִיא חָצוֹר׃
Hazor that Hezron and-Kerioth Hadattah and-Hazor (25) and-Bealoth and-Telem

אֲמָם וּשְׁמַע וּמוֹלָדָה׃ וַחֲצַר גַּדָּה וְחֶשְׁמוֹן וּבֵית
and-Beth and-Heshmon Gaddah and-Hazar (27) and-Moladah and-Shema Amam (26)

פָּלֶט׃ וַחֲצַר שׁוּעָל וּבְאֵר שֶׁבַע וּבִזְיוֹתְיָה׃ בַּעֲלָה וְעִיִּים
and-Iim Baalah (29) and-Biziothiah Sheba and-Beer Shual and-Hazar (28) Pelet

וָעֶצֶם׃ וְאֶלְתּוֹלַד וּכְסִיל וְחָרְמָה׃ וְצִקְלַג וּמַדְמַנָּה
and-Madmannah and-Ziklag (31) and-Hormah and-Kesil and-Eltolad (30) and-Ezem

וְסַנְסַנָּה׃ וּלְבָאוֹת וְשִׁלְחִים וְעַיִן וְרִמּוֹן כָּל־
total-of and-Rimmon and-Ain and-Shilhim and-Lebaoth (32) and-Sansannah

עָרִים עֶשְׂרִים וָתֵשַׁע וְחַצְרֵיהֶן׃ בַּשְּׁפֵלָה אֶשְׁתָּאוֹל
Eshtaol in-the-foothill (33) and-villages-of-them and-nine twenty towns

וְצָרְעָה וְאַשְׁנָה׃ וְזָנוֹחַ וְעֵין גַּנִּים תַּפּוּחַ וְהָעֵינָם׃
and-the-Enam Tappuah Gannim and-En and-Zanoah (34) and-Ashnah and-Zorah

יַרְמוּת וַעֲדֻלָּם שׂוֹכֹה וַעֲזֵקָה׃ וְשַׁעֲרַיִם וַעֲדִיתַיִם
and-Adithaim and-Shaaraim (36) and-Azekah Socoh and-Adullam Jarmuth (35)

וְהַגְּדֵרָה וּגְדֵרֹתָיִם עָרִים אַרְבַּע־עֶשְׂרֵה וְחַצְרֵיהֶן׃ צְנָן
Zenan (37) and-villages-of-them ten four towns or-Gederothaim and-the-Gederah

וַחֲדָשָׁה וּמִגְדַּל־גָּד׃ וְדִלְעָן וְהַמִּצְפֶּה וְיָקְתְאֵל׃
and-Joktheel and-the-Mizpah and-Dilean (38) Gad and-Migdal and-Hadashah

לָכִישׁ וּבָצְקַת וְעֶגְלוֹן׃ וְכַבּוֹן וְלַחְמָס וְכִתְלִישׁ׃
and-Kitlish and-Lahmas and-Cabbon (40) and-Eglon and-Bozkath Lachish (39)

וּגְדֵרוֹת בֵּית־דָּגוֹן וְנַעֲמָה וּמַקֵּדָה עָרִים שֵׁשׁ־עֶשְׂרֵה
ten six towns and-Makkedah and-Naamah Dagon Beth and-Gederoth (41)

וְחַצְרֵיהֶן׃ לִבְנָה וָעֶתֶר וְעָשָׁן׃ וְיִפְתָּח
and-Iphtah (43) and-Ashan and-Ether Libnah (42) and-villages-of-them

וְאַשְׁנָה וּנְצִיב׃ וּקְעִילָה וְאַכְזִיב וּמָרֵאשָׁה עָרִים תֵּשַׁע
nine towns and-Mareshah and-Aczib and-Keilah (44) and-Nezib and-Ashnah

וְחַצְרֵיהֶן׃ עֶקְרוֹן וּבְנֹתֶיהָ וַחֲצֵרֶיהָ׃
and-villages-of-her and-settlements-of-her Ekron (45) and-villages-of-them

מֵעֶקְרוֹן וָיָמָּה כֹּל אֲשֶׁר־עַל־יַד אַשְׁדּוֹד וְחַצְרֵיהֶן׃
and-villages-of-them Ashdod vicinity-of in that all and-to-west from-Ekron (46)

אַשְׁדּוֹד בְּנוֹתֶיהָ וַחֲצֵרֶיהָ עַזָּה בְּנוֹתֶיהָ
settlements-of-her Gaza and-villages-of-her settlements-of-her Ashdod (47)

וַחֲצֵרֶיהָ עַד־נַחַל מִצְרָיִם וְהַיָּם הַגָּבוֹל וּגְבוּל׃
and-coast the-Great and-the-Sea Egypt Wadi-of as-far-as and-villages-of-her

וּבָהָר שָׁמִיר וְיַתִּיר וְשׂוֹכֹה׃ וְדַנָּה
and-Dannah (49) and-Socoh and-Jattir Shamir and-in-the-hill-country (48)

Bealoth, [25]Hazor Hadattah,
Kerioth Hezron (that is,
Hazor), [26]Amam, Shema,
Moladah, [27]Hazar Gaddah,
Heshmon, Beth Pelet, [28]Ha-
zar Shual, Beersheba, Bizio-
thiah, [29]Baalah, Iim, Ezem,
[30]Eltolad, Kesil, Hormah,
[31]Ziklag, Madmannah, San-
sannah, [32]Lebaoth, Shil-
him, Ain and Rimmon—a
total of twenty-nine towns
and their villages.

[33]In the western foothills:
Eshtaol, Zorah, Ashnah,
[34]Zanoah, En Gannim, Tappuah, Enam, [35]Jarmuth,
Adullam, Socoh, Azekah,
[36]Shaaraim, Adithaim and
Gederah (or Gedero-
thaim)[s]—fourteen towns
and their villages.
[37]Zenan, Hadashah, Mig-
dal Gad, [38]Dilean, Mizpah,
Joktheel, [39]Lachish, Bozkath, Eglon, [40]Cabbon, Lah-
mas, Kitlish, [41]Gederoth,
Beth Dagon, Naamah and
Makkedah—sixteen towns
and their villages.
[42]Libnah, Ether, Ashan,
[43]Iphtah, Ashnah, Nezib,
[44]Keilah, Aczib and Mare-
shah—nine towns and
their villages.
[45]Ekron, with its sur-
rounding settlements and
villages; [46]west of Ekron, all
that were in the vicinity of
Ashdod, together with
their villages; [47]Ashdod, its
surrounding settlements
and villages; and Gaza, its
settlements and villages, as
far as the Wadi of Egypt
and the coastline of the
Great Sea.

[48]In the hill country:
Shamir, Jattir, Socoh,

[s]36 Or *Gederah and Gederothaim*

°47 ק הגדול

וְקִרְיַת־ סַנָּה הִיא דְבִר׃ וַעֲנָב וְאֶשְׁתְּמֹה וְעָנִים׃
and-Anim and-Eshtemoh and-Anab (50) Debir that Sannah and-Kiriath

וְגֹשֶׁן וְחֹלֹן וְגִלֹה עָרִים אַחַת־עֶשְׂרֵה וְחַצְרֵיהֶן׃
and-villages-of-them ten one towns and-Giloh and-Holon and-Goshen (51)

אֲרַב וְרוּמָה* וְאֶשְׁעָן׃ וְיָנִים† וּבֵית־ תַּפּוּחַ וַאֲפֵקָה׃
and-Aphekah Tappuah and-Beth and-Janim (53) and-Eshan and-Dumah Arab (52)

וְחֻמְטָה וְקִרְיַת אַרְבַּע הִיא חֶבְרוֹן וְצִיעֹר עָרִים תֵּשַׁע
nine towns and-Zior Hebron that Arba and-Kiriath and-Humtah (54)

וְחַצְרֵיהֶן׃ מָעוֹן | כַּרְמֶל וָזִיף וְיוּטָּה׃ וְיִזְרְעֶאל
and-Jezreel (56) and-Juttah and-Ziph Carmel Maon (55) and-villages-of-them

וְיָקְדְעָם וְזָנוֹחַ׃ הַקַּיִן גִּבְעָה וְתִמְנָה עָרִים עֶשֶׂר
ten towns and-Timnah Gibeah the-Kain (57) and-Zanoah and-Jokdeam

וְחַצְרֵיהֶן׃ חַלְחוּל בֵּית־ צוּר וּגְדוֹר׃ וּמַעֲרָת
and-Maarath (59) and-Gedor Zur Beth Halhul (58) and-villages-of-them

וּבֵית־ עֲנוֹת וְאֶלְתְּקֹן עָרִים שֵׁשׁ וְחַצְרֵיהֶן׃ קִרְיַת־ בַּעַל
Baal Kiriath (60) and-villages-of-them six towns and-Eltekon Anoth and-Beth

הִיא קִרְיַת יְעָרִים וְהָרַבָּה עָרִים שְׁתָּיִם וְחַצְרֵיהֶן׃
and-villages-of-them two towns and-the-Rabbah Jearim Kiriath that

בַּמִּדְבָּר בֵּית הָעֲרָבָה מִדִּין וּסְכָכָה׃ וְהַנִּבְשָׁן
and-the-Nibshan (62) and-Secacah Middin the-Arabah Beth in-the-desert (61)

וְעִיר־ הַמֶּלַח וְעֵין גֶּדִי עָרִים שֵׁשׁ וְחַצְרֵיהֶן׃ וְאֶת־
but (63) and-villages-of-them six towns Gedi and-En the-Salt and-City-of

הַיְבוּסִי יוֹשְׁבֵי יְרוּשָׁלִַם לֹא־ יוּכְלוּ בְנֵי־ יְהוּדָה
Judah people-of they-could not Jerusalem ones-living-of the-Jebusite

לְהוֹרִישָׁם וַיֵּשֶׁב הַיְבוּסִי אֶת־ בְּנֵי יְהוּדָה בִּירוּשָׁלִָם
in-Jerusalem Judah people-of with the-Jebusite so-he-lives to-dislodge-them

עַד הַיּוֹם הַזֶּה׃ וַיֵּצֵא הַגּוֹרָל לִבְנֵי יוֹסֵף
Joseph for-sons-of the-allotment and-he-began (16:1) the-this the-day to

מִיַּרְדֵּן יְרִיחוֹ לְמֵי יְרִיחוֹ מִזְרָחָה הַמִּדְבָּר עֹלֶה
going-up the-desert to-east Jericho by-waters-of Jericho at-Jordan-of

מִירִיחוֹ בָּהָר בֵּית־ אֵל׃ וְיָצָא מִבֵּית־ אֵל לוּזָה
to-Luz El from-Beth and-he-went (2) El Beth into-the-hill-country from-Jericho

וְעָבַר אֶל־ גְּבוּל הָאַרְכִּי עֲטָרוֹת׃ וְיָרַד־
and-he-descended (3) Ataroth the-Arkite territory-of to and-he-crossed-over

יָמָּה אֶל־ גְּבוּל הַיַּפְלֵטִי עַד גְּבוּל בֵּית־ חוֹרֹן תַּחְתּוֹן
Lower Horon Beth region-of as-far-as the-Japhletite territory-of to to-west

וְעַד־ גָּזֶר וְהָיוּ תֹצְאֹתָו יָמָּה׃ וַיִּנְחֲלוּ בְנֵי־
sons-of and-they-inherited (4) at-sea ends-of-him and-they-were Gezer and-to

49 Dannah, Kiriath Sannah
(that is, Debir), 50 Anab,
Eshtemoh, Anim, 51 Go-
shen, Holon and Giloh—
eleven towns and their villages.
52 Arab, Dumah, Eshan,
53 Janim, Beth Tappuah,
Aphekah, 54 Humtah,
Kiriath Arba (that is, Hebron) and Zior—nine
towns and their villages.
55 Maon, Carmel, Ziph,
Juttah, 56 Jezreel, Jokdeam,
Zanoah, 57 Kain, Gibeah
and Timnah—ten towns
and their villages.
58 Halhul, Beth Zur, Ge-
dor, 59 Maarath, Beth Anoth
and Eltekon—six towns
and their villages.
60 Kiriath Baal (that is,
Kiriath Jearim) and Rab-
bah—two towns and their
villages.

61 In the desert:
Beth Arabah, Middin,
Secacah, 62 Nibshan, the
City of Salt and En Gedi—
six towns and their vil-
lages.
63 Judah could not dislodge
the Jebusites, who were living
in Jerusalem; to this day the
Jebusites live there with the
people of Judah.

Allotment for Ephraim and Manasseh

16 The allotment for Jo-
seph began at the
Jordan of Jericho,[t] east of
the waters of Jericho, and
went up from there
through the desert into the
hill country of Bethel. 2 It
went on from Bethel (that
is, Luz),[u] crossed over to the
territory of the Arkites in
Ataroth, 3 descended westward to the territory of the
Japhletites as far as the region of Lower Beth Horon
and on to Gezer, ending at
the sea.

t1 *Jordan of Jericho* was possibly an ancient name for the Jordan River.
u2 Septuagint; Hebrew *Bethel to Luz*

*52 Most mss read *and-Dumah* (ודומה); L reads *and-Rumah.*

†53 Most mss have *hireq* under the *nun* and have no *dagesh* in the *yod* (־ִים). The *Kethib* form thus reads *and-Janim*, and the *Qere* reads *and-Janum.*

°53 ק וינום
°63 ק יכלו
°3 ק תצאתיו

יוֹסֵף מְנַשֶּׁה וְאֶפְרָיִם׃ וַיְהִי גְּבוּל בְּנֵי־ אֶפְרַיִם
Ephraim sons-of territory-of and-he-was (5) and-Ephraim Manasseh Joseph

לְמִשְׁפְּחֹתָם וַיְהִי גְּבוּל נַחֲלָתָם מִזְרָחָה עַטְרוֹת
Ataroth in-east inheritance-of-them boundary-of and-he-was by-clans-of-them

אַדָּר עַד־ בֵּית חוֹרֹן עֶלְיוֹן׃ וְיָצָא הַגְּבוּל הַיָּמָּה
to-the-sea the-boundary and-he-continued (6) Upper Horon Beth to Addar

הַמִּכְמְתָת מִצָּפוֹן וְנָסַב הַגְּבוּל מִזְרָחָה תַּאֲנַת שִׁלֹה
Shiloh Taanath to-east the-boundary and-he-curved on-north the-Micmethath

וְעָבַר אוֹתוֹ מִמִּזְרַח יָנוֹחָה׃ וְיָרַד מִיָּנוֹחָה
from-Janoah then-he-went-down (7) to-Janoah on-east him and-he-passed

עֲטָרוֹת וְנַעֲרָתָה וּפָגַע בִּירִיחוֹ וְיָצָא הַיַּרְדֵּן׃
the-Jordan and-he-came-out on-Jericho and-he-touched and-to-Naarah Ataroth

מִתַּפּוּחַ יֵלֵךְ הַגְּבוּל יָמָּה נַחַל קָנָה וְהָיוּ
and-they-were Kanah Ravine-of to-west the-border he-went from-Tappuah (8)

תֹצְאֹתָיו הַיָּמָּה זֹאת נַחֲלַת מַטֵּה בְנֵי־ אֶפְרַיִם
Ephraim sons-of tribe-of inheritance-of this at-the-sea ends-of-him

לְמִשְׁפְּחֹתָם׃ וְהֶעָרִים הַמִּבְדָּלוֹת לִבְנֵי אֶפְרַיִם
Ephraim for-sons-of the-ones-set-aside and-the-towns (9) by-clans-of-them

בְּתוֹךְ נַחֲלַת בְּנֵי־ מְנַשֶּׁה כָּל־ הֶעָרִים וְחַצְרֵיהֶן׃
and-villages-of-them the-towns all-of Manasseh sons-of inheritance-of within

וְלֹא הוֹרִישׁוּ אֶת־ הַכְּנַעֲנִי הַיּוֹשֵׁב בְּגָזֶר
in-Gezer the-one-living the-Canaanite *** they-dislodged but-not (10)

וַיֵּשֶׁב הַכְּנַעֲנִי בְּקֶרֶב אֶפְרַיִם עַד־ הַיּוֹם הַזֶּה וַיְהִי
but-he-is the-this the-day to Ephraim in-among the-Canaanite so-he-lives

לְמַס־ עֹבֵד׃ וַיְהִי הַגּוֹרָל לְמַטֵּה מְנַשֶּׁה
Manasseh for-tribe-of the-allotment and-he-was (17:1) working at-forced-labor

כִּי־הוּא בְּכוֹר יוֹסֵף לְמָכִיר בְּכוֹר מְנַשֶּׁה אֲבִי
ancestor-of Manasseh firstborn-of for-Makir Joseph firstborn-of he as

הַגִּלְעָד כִּי הוּא הָיָה אִישׁ מִלְחָמָה וַיְהִי־ לוֹ הַגִּלְעָד
the-Gilead to-him and-he-was war man-of he-was he for the-Gilead

וְהַבָּשָׁן׃ וַיְהִי לִבְנֵי מְנַשֶּׁה הַנּוֹתָרִים
the-ones-remaining Manasseh for-people-of so-he-was (2) and-the-Bashan

לְמִשְׁפְּחֹתָם לִבְנֵי אֲבִיעֶזֶר וְלִבְנֵי־ חֵלֶק
Helek and-for-people-of Abiezer for-people-of by-clans-of-them

וְלִבְנֵי אַשְׂרִיאֵל וְלִבְנֵי־ שֶׁכֶם וְלִבְנֵי־ חֵפֶר
Hepher and-for-people-of Shechem and-for-people-of Asriel and-for-people-of

וְלִבְנֵי שְׁמִידָע אֵלֶּה בְּנֵי מְנַשֶּׁה בֶּן־ יוֹסֵף הַזְּכָרִים
the-males Joseph son-of Manasseh descendants-of these Shemida and-for-people-of

4 So Manasseh and Ephraim,
the descendants of Joseph, received their inheritance.

5 This was the territory of
Ephraim, clan by clan:

The boundary of their in-
heritance went from
Ataroth Addar in the east to
Upper Beth Horon 6 and
continued to the sea. From
Micmethath on the north it
curved eastward to Taanath
Shiloh, passing by it to Janoah on the east. 7 Then it
went down from Janoah to
Ataroth and Naarah,
touched Jericho and came
out at the Jordan. 8 From
Tappuah the border went
west to the Kanah Ravine
and ended at the sea. This
was the inheritance of the
tribe of the Ephraimites,
clan by clan. 9 It also included all the towns and
their villages that were set
aside for the Ephraimites
within the inheritance of
the Manassites.

10 They did not dislodge the
Canaanites living in Gezer; to
this day the Canaanites live
among the people of Ephraim
but are required to do forced
labor.

17 This was the allotment
for the tribe of Manas-
seh as Joseph's firstborn, that
is, for Makir, Manasseh's
firstborn. Makir was the
ancestor of the Gileadites,
who had received Gilead and
Bashan because the Makirites
were great soldiers. 2 So this allotment was for the rest of the
people of Manasseh—the clans
of Abiezer, Helek, Asriel, Shechem, Hepher and Shemida.
These are the other male descendants of Manasseh son of

לְמִשְׁפְּחֹתָם׃ וְלִצְלָפְחָד בֶּן־ חֵפֶר בֶּן־ גִּלְעָד בֶּן־
son-of Gilead son-of Hepher son-of now-to-Zelophehad (3) by-clans-of-them

מָכִיר בֶּן־ מְנַשֶּׁה לֹא־ הָיוּ לוֹ בָּנִים כִּי אִם־ בָּנוֹת וְאֵלֶּה
and-these daughters only but sons to-him they-were not Manasseh son-of Makir

שְׁמוֹת בְּנֹתָיו מַחְלָה וְנֹעָה חָגְלָה מִלְכָּה וְתִרְצָה׃
and-Tirzah Milcah Hoglah and-Noah Mahlah daughters-of-him names-of

וַתִּקְרַבְנָה לִפְנֵי אֶלְעָזָר הַכֹּהֵן וְלִפְנֵי ׀ יְהוֹשֻׁעַ בִּן־ נוּן
Nun son-of Joshua and-before the-priest Eleazar before and-they-went (4)

וְלִפְנֵי הַנְּשִׂיאִים לֵאמֹר יְהוָה צִוָּה אֶת־ מֹשֶׁה לָתֶת־ לָנוּ
to-us to-give Moses *** he-commanded Yahweh to-say the-leaders and-before

נַחֲלָה בְּתוֹךְ אַחֵינוּ וַיִּתֵּן לָהֶם אֶל־ פִּי יְהוָה
Yahweh command-of at to-them so-he-gave brothers-of-us in-among inheritance

נַחֲלָה בְּתוֹךְ אֲחֵי אֲבִיהֶן׃ וַיִּפְּלוּ
and-they-consisted (5) father-of-them brothers-of along-with inheritance

חַבְלֵי־ מְנַשֶּׁה עֲשָׂרָה לְבַד מֵאֶרֶץ הַגִּלְעָד וְהַבָּשָׁן
and-the-Bashan the-Gilead of-land-of besides ten Manasseh tracts-of-land-of

אֲשֶׁר מֵעֵבֶר לַיַּרְדֵּן׃ כִּי בְּנוֹת מְנַשֶּׁה נָחֲלוּ
they-received Manasseh daughters-of for (6) of-the-Jordan on-east that

נַחֲלָה בְּתוֹךְ בָּנָיו וְאֶרֶץ הַגִּלְעָד הָיְתָה
she-belonged the-Gilead and-land-of sons-of-him in-among inheritance

לִבְנֵי־ מְנַשֶּׁה הַנּוֹתָרִים׃ וַיְהִי גְבוּל־ מְנַשֶּׁה
Manasseh territory-of and-he-was (7) the-ones-remaining Manasseh to-sons-of

מֵאָשֵׁר הַמִּכְמְתָת אֲשֶׁר עַל־ פְּנֵי שְׁכֶם וְהָלַךְ הַגְּבוּל
the-boundary and-he-ran Shechem east-of to that the-Micmethath from-Asher

אֶל־ הַיָּמִין אֶל־ יֹשְׁבֵי עֵין תַּפּוּחַ׃ לִמְנַשֶּׁה הָיְתָה אֶרֶץ
land-of she-was for-Manasseh (8) Tappuah En ones-living-of to the-south to

תַּפּוּחַ וְתַפּוּחַ אֶל־ גְּבוּל מְנַשֶּׁה לִבְנֵי אֶפְרָיִם׃
Ephraim for-sons-of Manasseh boundary-of on but-Tappuah Tappuah

וְיָרַד הַגְּבוּל נַחַל קָנָה נֶגְבָּה לַנַּחַל
of-the-ravine to-south Kanah Ravine-of the-boundary then-he-continued (9)

עָרִים הָאֵלֶּה לְאֶפְרַיִם בְּתוֹךְ עָרֵי מְנַשֶּׁה וּגְבוּל
but-boundary-of Manasseh towns-of in-among to-Ephraim the-these towns

מְנַשֶּׁה מִצְּפוֹן לַנַּחַל וַיְהִי תֹצְאֹתָיו הַיָּמָּה׃
at-the-sea ends-of-him and-he-was of-the-ravine on-north Manasseh

נֶגְבָּה לְאֶפְרַיִם וְצָפוֹנָה לִמְנַשֶּׁה וַיְהִי הַיָּם
the-sea and-he-reached for-Manasseh and-on-north for-Ephraim on-south (10)

גְּבוּלוֹ וּבְאָשֵׁר יִפְגְּעוּן מִצָּפוֹן וּבְיִשָּׂשכָר מִמִּזְרָח׃
on-east and-on-Issachar on-north they-bordered and-on-Asher territory-of-him

Joseph by their clans.
3Now Zelophehad son of Hepher, the son of Gilead, the son of Makir, the son of Manasseh, had no sons but only daughters, whose names were Mahlah, Noah, Hoglah, Milcah and Tirzah.
4They went to Eleazar the priest, Joshua son of Nun, and the leaders and said, "The LORD commanded Moses to give us an inheritance among our brothers." So Joshua gave them an inheritance along with the brothers of their father, according to the LORD's command.
5Manasseh's share consisted of ten tracts of land besides Gilead and Bashan east of the Jordan,
6because the daughters of the tribe of Manasseh received an inheritance among the sons. The land of Gilead belonged to the rest of the descendants of Manasseh.

7The territory of Manasseh extended from Asher to Micmethath east of Shechem. The boundary ran southward from there to include the people living at En Tappuah.
8(Manasseh had the land of Tappuah, but Tappuah itself, on the boundary of Manasseh, belonged to the Ephraimites.)
9Then the boundary continued south to the Kanah Ravine. There were towns belonging to Ephraim lying among the towns of Manasseh, but the boundary of Manasseh was the northern side of the ravine and ended at the sea.
10On the south the land belonged to Ephraim, on the north to Manasseh. The territory of Manasseh reached the sea and bordered Asher on the north and Issachar on the east.

וַיְהִי לִמְנַשֶּׁה בְּיִשָּׂשכָר וּבְאָשֵׁר בֵּית־ שְׁאָן
Shan Beth and-within-Asher within-Issachar for-Manasseh and-he-was (11)

וּבְנוֹתֶיהָ וְיִבְלְעָם וּבְנוֹתֶיהָ וְאֶת־ יֹשְׁבֵי
ones-living-of and and-settlements-of-her and-Ibleam and-settlements-of-her

דֹאר וּבְנוֹתֶיהָ וְיֹשְׁבֵי עֵין־ דֹּר וּבְנֹתֶיהָ
and-settlements-of-her Dor En and-ones-living-of and-settlements-of-her Dor

וְיֹשְׁבֵי תַעְנַךְ וּבְנֹתֶיהָ וְיֹשְׁבֵי מְגִדּוֹ
Megiddo and-ones-living-of and-settlements-of-her Taanach and-ones-living-of

וּבְנוֹתֶיהָ שְׁלֹשֶׁת הַנָּפֶת׃ וְלֹא יָכְלוּ בְּנֵי
sons-of they-could yet-not (12) the-Naphoth third-of and-settlements-of-her

מְנַשֶּׁה לְהוֹרִישׁ אֶת־ הֶעָרִים הָאֵלֶּה וַיּוֹאֶל
for-he-was-determined the-these the-towns *** to-occupy Manasseh

הַכְּנַעֲנִי לָשֶׁבֶת בָּאָרֶץ הַזֹּאת׃ וַיְהִי כִּי
when and-he-was (13) the-that in-the-region to-live the-Canaanite

חָזְקוּ בְּנֵי יִשְׂרָאֵל וַיִּתְּנוּ אֶת־ הַכְּנַעֲנִי
the-Canaanite *** and-they-subjected Israel sons-of they-grew-stronger

לָמַס וְהוֹרֵשׁ לֹא הוֹרִישׁוֹ׃ וַיְדַבְּרוּ
and-they-said (14) he-drove-out-him not but-to-drive-out to-forced-labor

בְּנֵי יוֹסֵף אֶת־יְהוֹשֻׁעַ לֵאמֹר מַדּוּעַ נָתַתָּה לִּי נַחֲלָה גּוֹרָל
allotment inheritance to-me you-gave why? to-say Joshua *** Joseph people-of

אֶחָד וְחֶבֶל אֶחָד וַאֲנִי עַם־ רָב עַד אֲשֶׁר־ עַד־ כֹּה בֵּרְכַנִי
he-blessed-me so until now until numerous people yet-I one and-portion one

יְהוָה׃ וַיֹּאמֶר אֲלֵיהֶם יְהוֹשֻׁעַ אִם־ עַם־ רַב אַתָּה עֲלֵה
go-up! you numerous people if Joshua to-them and-he-answered (15) Yahweh

לְךָ הַיַּעְרָה וּבֵרֵאתָ לְךָ שָׁם בְּאֶרֶץ הַפְּרִזִּי
the-Perizzite in-land-of there for-you and-you-clear into-the-forest for-you

וְהָרְפָאִים כִּי־ אָץ לְךָ הַר־ אֶפְרָיִם׃
Ephraim hill-country-of for-you being-small if and-the-Rephaites

וַיֹּאמְרוּ בְּנֵי יוֹסֵף לֹא־ יִמָּצֵא לָנוּ הָהָר
the-hill-country for-us he-is-enough not Joseph people-of and-they-replied (16)

וְרֶכֶב בַּרְזֶל בְּכָל־ הַכְּנַעֲנִי הַיֹּשֵׁב בְּאֶרֶץ־
in-region-of the-one-living the-Canaanite among-all-of iron and-chariot-of

הָעֵמֶק לַאֲשֶׁר בְּבֵית־ שְׁאָן וּבְנוֹתֶיהָ וְלַאֲשֶׁר בְּעֵמֶק
in-Valley-of and-to-whom and-settlements-of-her Shan in-Beth to-whom the-plain

יִזְרְעֶאל׃ וַיֹּאמֶר יְהוֹשֻׁעַ אֶל־ בֵּית יוֹסֵף לְאֶפְרַיִם וְלִמְנַשֶּׁה
and-to-Manasseh to-Ephraim Joseph house-of to Joshua but-he-said (17) Jezreel

לֵאמֹר עַם־ רַב אַתָּה וְכֹחַ גָּדוֹל לְךָ לֹא־ יִהְיֶה לְךָ
for-you he-will-be not to-you great and-power you numerous people to-say

11 Within Issachar and
Asher, Manasseh also had
Beth Shan, Ibleam and the
people of Dor, Endor, Taanach and Megiddo, to-
gether with their surrounding settlements (the third
in the list is Naphoth[v]).
12 Yet the Manassites were not
able to occupy these towns, for
the Canaanites were determined to live in that region.
13 However, when the Israelites grew stronger, they sub-
jected the Canaanites to forced
labor but did not drive them
out completely.
14 The people of Joseph said
to Joshua, "Why have you giv-
en us only one allotment and
one portion for an inheritance? We are a numerous
people and the LORD has
blessed us abundantly."
15 "If you are so numerous,"
Joshua answered, "and if the
hill country of Ephraim is too
small for you, go up into the
forest and clear land for yourselves there in the land of the
Perizzites and Rephaites."
16 The people of Joseph replied, "The hill country is not
enough for us, and all the Canaanites who live in the plain
have iron chariots, both those
in Beth Shan and its settlements and those in the Valley
of Jezreel."
17 But Joshua said to the
house of Joseph—to Ephraim
and Manasseh—"You are nu-
merous and very powerful.

[v] 11 That is, Naphoth Dor

גּוֹרָל אֶחָד׃ כִּי הַר יִהְיֶה־לָּךְ כִּי־יַעַר הוּא
that forest but for-you he-will-be hill-country but (18) one allotment

וּבֵרֵאתוֹ וְהָיָה לְךָ תֹּצְאֹתָיו כִּי־תוֹרִישׁ
you-drive-out indeed limits-of-him for-you and-he-will-be so-you-clear-him

אֶת־הַכְּנַעֲנִי כִּי רֶכֶב בַּרְזֶל לוֹ כִּי חָזָק הוּא׃
he strong though to-him iron chariot-of though the-Canaanite ***

וַיִּקָּהֲלוּ כָּל־עֲדַת בְּנֵי־יִשְׂרָאֵל שִׁלֹה
Shiloh Israel sons-of assembly-of whole-of and-they-gathered (18:1)

וַיַּשְׁכִּינוּ שָׁם אֶת־אֹהֶל מוֹעֵד וְהָאָרֶץ נִכְבְּשָׁה
she-was-controlled and-the-country Meeting Tent-of *** there and-they-set-up

לִפְנֵיהֶם׃ וַיִּוָּתְרוּ בִּבְנֵי יִשְׂרָאֵל אֲשֶׁר לֹא־חָלְקוּ
they-received not who Israel among-sons-of but-they-remained (2) before-them

אֶת־נַחֲלָתָם שִׁבְעָה שְׁבָטִים׃ וַיֹּאמֶר יְהוֹשֻׁעַ אֶל־בְּנֵי יִשְׂרָאֵל
Israel sons-of to Joshua so-he-said (3) tribes seven inheritance-of-them ***

עַד־אָנָה אַתֶּם מִתְרַפִּים לָבוֹא לָרֶשֶׁת אֶת־הָאָרֶץ אֲשֶׁר נָתַן
he-gave that the-land *** to-possess to-begin ones-waiting you how? long

לָכֶם יְהוָה אֱלֹהֵי אֲבוֹתֵיכֶם׃ הָבוּ לָכֶם שְׁלֹשָׁה אֲנָשִׁים
men three for-you appoint! (4) fathers-of-you God-of Yahweh to-you

לַשָּׁבֶט וְאֶשְׁלָחֵם וְיָקֻמוּ וְיִתְהַלְּכוּ
and-they-will-make-survey and-they-will-go and-I-will-send-them from-the-tribe

בָאָרֶץ וְיִכְתְּבוּ אוֹתָהּ לְפִי נַחֲלָתָם
inheritance-of-them by-portion-of about-her and-they-will-write of-the-land

וְיָבֹאוּ אֵלָי׃ וְהִתְחַלְּקוּ אֹתָהּ לְשִׁבְעָה חֲלָקִים יְהוּדָה
Judah parts into-seven her and-divide! (5) to-me then-they-will-return

יַעֲמֹד עַל־גְּבוּלוֹ מִנֶּגֶב וּבֵית יוֹסֵף
Joseph and-house-of on-south territory-of-him in he-will-remain

יַעַמְדוּ עַל־גְּבוּלָם מִצָּפוֹן׃ וְאַתֶּם תִּכְתְּבוּ
you-write-description and-you (6) on-north territory-of-them in they-will-remain

אֶת־הָאָרֶץ שִׁבְעָה חֲלָקִים וַהֲבֵאתֶם אֵלַי הֵנָּה וְיָרִיתִי לָכֶם
for-you and-I-will-cast here to-me then-you-bring parts seven the-land ***

גּוֹרָל פֹּה לִפְנֵי יְהוָה אֱלֹהֵינוּ׃ כִּי אֵין־חֵלֶק לַלְוִיִּם
for-the-Levites portion not but (7) God-of-us Yahweh in-presences-of here lot

בְּקִרְבְּכֶם כִּי־כְהֻנַּת יְהוָה נַחֲלָתוֹ וְגָד
and-Gad inheritance-of-him Yahweh priestly-service-of for in-among-you

וּרְאוּבֵן וַחֲצִי שֵׁבֶט הַמְנַשֶּׁה לָקְחוּ נַחֲלָתָם
inheritance-of-them they-received the-Manasseh tribe-of and-half-of and-Reuben

מֵעֵבֶר לַיַּרְדֵּן מִזְרָחָה אֲשֶׁר נָתַן לָהֶם מֹשֶׁה עֶבֶד יְהוָה׃
Yahweh servant-of Moses to-them he-gave that on-east of-the-Jordan on-side

You will have not only one allotment 18but the forested hill
country as well. Clear it, and
its farthest limits will be
yours; though the Canaanites
have iron chariots and though
they are strong, you can drive
them out."

Division of the Rest of the Land

18 The whole assembly of
the Israelites gathered
at Shiloh and set up the Tent
of Meeting there. The country
was brought under their control, 2but there were still seven
Israelite tribes who had not
yet received their inheritance.
3So Joshua said to the Israelites: "How long will you wait
before you begin to take
possession of the land that the
LORD, the God of your fathers,
has given you? 4Appoint three
men from each tribe. I will
send them out to make a survey of the land and to write a
description of it, according to
the inheritance of each. Then
they will return to me. 5You
are to divide the land into sev-
en parts. Judah is to remain in
its territory on the south and
the house of Joseph in its territory on the north. 6After you
have written descriptions of
the seven parts of the land,
bring them here to me and I
will cast lots for you in the
presence of the LORD our God.
7The Levites, however, do not
get a portion among you, because the priestly service of
the LORD is their inheritance.
And Gad, Reuben and the
half-tribe of Manasseh have
already received their inheritance on the east side of the
Jordan. Moses the servant of
the LORD gave it to them."

וַיָּקֻמוּ הָאֲנָשִׁים וַיֵּלֵכוּ וַיְצַו יְהוֹשֻׁעַ אֶת־

*** Joshua and-he-instructed and-they-went the-men and-they-started (8)

הַהֹלְכִים לִכְתֹּב אֶת־הָאָרֶץ לֵאמֹר לְכוּ וְהִתְהַלְּכוּ בָאָרֶץ

of-the-land and-make-survey! go! to-say the-land *** to-map the-ones-going

וְכִתְבוּ אוֹתָהּ וְשׁוּבוּ אֵלַי וּפֹה אַשְׁלִיךְ לָכֶם גּוֹרָל

lot for-you I-will-cast and-here to-me then-return! about-her and-write!

לִפְנֵי יְהוָה בְּשִׁלֹה׃ וַיֵּלְכוּ הָאֲנָשִׁים וַיַּעַבְרוּ

and-they-went the-men so-they-left (9) at-Shiloh Yahweh in-presences-of

בָאָרֶץ וַיִּכְתְּבוּהָ לֶעָרִים לְשִׁבְעָה חֲלָקִים עַל־

on parts in-seven by-the-towns and-they-described-her through-the-land

סֵפֶר וַיָּבֹאוּ אֶל־יְהוֹשֻׁעַ אֶל־הַמַּחֲנֶה שִׁלֹה׃ וַיַּשְׁלֵךְ

then-he-cast (10) Shiloh the-camp in Joshua to and-they-returned scroll

לָהֶם יְהוֹשֻׁעַ גּוֹרָל בְּשִׁלֹה לִפְנֵי יְהוָה וַיְחַלֶּק־

and-he-distributed Yahweh in-presences-of in-Shiloh lot Joshua for-them

שָׁם יְהוֹשֻׁעַ אֶת־הָאָרֶץ לִבְנֵי יִשְׂרָאֵל כְּמַחְלְקֹתָם׃

according-to-tribes-of-them Israel to-sons-of the-land *** Joshua there

וַיַּעַל גּוֹרַל מַטֵּה בְנֵי־בִנְיָמִן לְמִשְׁפְּחֹתָם וַיֵּצֵא

and-he-lay by-clans-of-them Benjamin sons-of tribe-of lot and-he-came-up (11)

גְּבוּל גּוֹרָלָם בֵּין בְּנֵי יְהוּדָה וּבֵין בְּנֵי

sons-of and-between Judah sons-of between allotment-of-them territory-of

יוֹסֵף׃ וַיְהִי לָהֶם הַגְּבוּל לִפְאַת צָפוֹנָה מִן־

at on-north on-side-of the-boundary for-them and-he-began (12) Joseph

הַיַּרְדֵּן וְעָלָה הַגְּבוּל אֶל־כֶּתֶף יְרִיחוֹ מִצָּפוֹן

on-north Jericho slope-of by the-boundary and-he-passed the-Jordan

וְעָלָה בָהָר יָמָּה וְהָיָה° תֹּצְאֹתָיו

ends-of-him and-they-came-out to-west into-the-hill-country and-he-headed

מִדְבַּרָה בֵּית אָוֶן׃ וְעָבַר מִשָּׁם הַגְּבוּל לוּזָה אֶל־

to to-Luz the-boundary from-there and-he-crossed (13) Aven Beth at-desert-of

כֶּתֶף לוּזָה נֶגְבָּה הִיא בֵּית־אֵל וְיָרַד הַגְּבוּל עַטְרוֹת

Ataroth the-boundary and-he-went-down El Beth that to-south to-Luz slope

אַדָּר עַל־הָהָר אֲשֶׁר מִנֶּגֶב לְבֵית־חֹרוֹן תַּחְתּוֹן׃ וְתָאַר

and-he-turned (14) Lower Horon of-Beth on-south that the-hill on Addar

הַגְּבוּל וְנָסַב לִפְאַת־יָם נֶגְבָּה מִן־הָהָר אֲשֶׁר

that the-hill from to-south west along-side-of and-he-turned the-boundary

עַל־פְּנֵי בֵית־חֹרוֹן נֶגְבָּה וְהָיָה° תֹּצְאֹתָיו אֶל־קִרְיַת־

Kiriath at ends-of-him and-they-came-out on-south Horon Beth face-of to

בַּעַל הִיא קִרְיַת יְעָרִים עִיר בְּנֵי יְהוּדָה זֹאת פְּאַת־יָם׃

west side-of this Judah people-of town-of Jearim Kiriath that Baal

[8]As the men started on their way to map out the land, Joshua instructed them, "Go and make a survey of the land and write a description of it. Then return to me, and I will cast lots for you here at Shiloh in the presence of the LORD." [9]So the men left and went through the land. They wrote its description on a scroll, town by town, in seven parts, and returned to Joshua in the camp at Shiloh. [10]Joshua then cast lots for them in Shiloh in the presence of the LORD, and there he distributed the land to the Israelites according to their tribal divisions.

Allotment for Benjamin

[11]The lot came up for the tribe of Benjamin, clan by clan. Their allotted territory lay between the tribes of Judah and Joseph:

[12]On the north side their boundary began at the Jordan, passed the northern slope of Jericho and headed west into the hill country, coming out at the desert of Beth Aven. [13]From there it crossed to the south slope of Luz (that is, Bethel) and went down to Ataroth Addar on the hill south of Lower Beth Horon.

[14]From the hill facing Beth Horon on the south the boundary turned south along the western side and came out at Kiriath Baal (that is, Kiriath Jearim), a town of the people of Judah. This was the western side.

°12 ק והיו
°14 ק והיו

וּפְאַת־ נֶ֫גְבָּה מִקְצֵה קִרְיַת יְעָרִים וְיָצָא הַגְּבוּל
the-boundary and-he-began Jearim Kiriath outskirt-of at-south and-side-of (15)

יָ֫מָּה וְיָצָא אֶל־ מַעְיַן מֵי נֶפְתּוֹחַ׃ וְיָרַד
and-he-went-down (16) Nephtoah waters-of spring-of at and-he-came-out on-west

הַגְּבוּל אֶל־קְצֵה הָהָר אֲשֶׁר עַל־ פְּנֵי גֵּי בֶן־ הִנֹּם אֲשֶׁר
that Hinnom Ben Valley-of face-of at that the-hill foot-of to the-boundary

בְּעֵמֶק רְפָאִים צָפֹנָה וְיָרַד גֵּי הִנֹּם אֶל־
along Hinnom Valley-of and-he-continued-down to-north Rephaim by-Valley-of

כֶּתֶף הַיְבוּסִי נֶגְבָּה וְיָרַד עֵין רֹגֵל׃ וְתָאַר
then-he-curved (17) Rogel En and-he-went on-south the-Jebusite slope-of

מִצָּפוֹן וְיָצָא עֵין שֶׁמֶשׁ וְיָצָא אֶל־גְּלִילוֹת אֲשֶׁר־ נֹכַח
facing which Geliloth to and-he-continued Shemesh En and-he-went to-north

מַעֲלֵה אֲדֻמִּים וְיָרַד אֶבֶן בֹּהַן בֶּן־ רְאוּבֵן׃ וְעָבַר
and-he-went (18) Reuben son-of Bohan Stone-of and-he-ran-down Adummim Pass-of

אֶל־ כֶּתֶף מוּל־ הָעֲרָבָה צָפוֹנָה וְיָרַד הָעֲרָבָתָה׃
into-the-Arabah and-he-continued on-north the-Arabah facing-of slope-of to

וְעָבַר הַגְּבוּל אֶל־ כֶּתֶף בֵּית־ חָגְלָה צָפוֹנָה°
on-north Hoglah Beth slope-of to the-boundary then-he-went (19)

°וְהָיָה ׀ °תֹּצְאוֹתָיו הַגְּבוּל אֶל־לְשׁוֹן יָם־ הַמֶּלַח צָפוֹנָה אֶל־
at on-north the-Salt Sea-of bay-of at the-boundary ends-of and-they-came-out

קְצֵה הַיַּרְדֵּן נֶגְבָּה זֶה גְּבוּל נֶגֶב׃ וְהַיַּרְדֵּן
and-the-Jordan (20) south boundary-of this in-south the-Jordan mouth-of

יִגְבֹּל־ אֹתוֹ לִפְאַת־ קֵדְמָה זֹאת נַחֲלַת בְּנֵי
sons-of inheritance-of this on-east on-side-of him he-formed-boundary

בִנְיָמִן לִגְבוּלֹתֶיהָ סָבִיב לְמִשְׁפְּחֹתָם׃ וְהָיוּ
and-they-were (21) for-clans-of-them around by-boundaries-of-her Benjamin

הֶעָרִים לְמַטֵּה בְּנֵי בִנְיָמִן לְמִשְׁפְּחוֹתֵיהֶם יְרִיחוֹ וּבֵית־
and-Beth Jericho by-clans-of-them Benjamin sons-of to-tribe-of the-cities

חָגְלָה וְעֵמֶק קְצִיץ׃ וּבֵית הָעֲרָבָה וּצְמָרַיִם וּבֵית־אֵל׃
El and-Beth and-Zemaraim the-Arabah and-Beth (22) Keziz and-Emek Hoglah

וְהָעַוִּים וְהַפָּרָה וְעָפְרָה׃ וּכְפַר °הָעַמֹּנָי*
the-Ammoni and-Kephar (24) and-Ophrah and-the-Parah and-the-Avvim (23)

וְהָעָפְנִי וָגָבַע עָרִים שְׁתֵּים־עֶשְׂרֵה וְחַצְרֵיהֶן׃ גִּבְעוֹן
Gibeon (25) and-villages-of-them ten two towns and-Geba and-the-Ophni

וְהָרָמָה וּבְאֵרוֹת׃ וְהַמִּצְפֶּה וְהַכְּפִירָה
and-the-Kephirah and-the-Mizpah (26) and-the-Beeroth and-the-Ramah

וְהַמֹּצָה׃ וְרֶקֶם וְיִרְפְּאֵל וְתַרְאֲלָה׃ וְצֵלַע הָאֶלֶף
Haeleph and-Zelah (28) and-Taralah and-Irpeel and-Rekem (27) and-the-Mozah

[15]The southern side began at the outskirts of
Kiriath Jearim on the west,
and the boundary came out
at the spring of the Waters
of Nephtoah. [16]The boundary went down to the foot
of the hill facing the Valley
of Ben Hinnom, north of
the Valley of Rephaim. It
continued down the Hinnom Valley along the
southern slope of the Jebusite city and so to En Rogel.
[17]It then curved north, went
to En Shemesh, continued
to Geliloth, which faces the
Pass of Adummim, and ran
down to the Stone of Bohan
son of Reuben. [18]It continued to the northern
slope of Beth Arabah[w] and
on down into the Arabah.
[19]It then went to the northern slope of Beth Hoglah
and came out at the northern bay of the Salt Sea,[x] at
the mouth of the Jordan in
the south. This was the
southern boundary.

[20]The Jordan formed the
boundary on the eastern
side.

These were the boundaries that marked out the inheritance of the clans of Benjamin on all sides.

[21]The tribe of Benjamin, clan
by clan, had the following cities:

Jericho, Beth Hoglah,
Emek Keziz, [22]Beth Arabah,
Zemaraim, Bethel, [23]Avvim, Parah, Ophrah, [24]Kephar Ammoni, Ophni and
Geba—twelve towns and
their villages.

[25]Gibeon, Ramah,
Beeroth, [26]Mizpah, Kephirah, Mozah, [27]Rekem,
Irpeel, Taralah, [28]Zelah, Haeleph, the Jebusite city (that

[w]18 Septuagint; Hebrew *slope facing the Arabah*

[x]19 That is, the Dead Sea

*24 The *Qere* reads *the-Ammonah;* the NIV has translated according to the Septuagint, reading *hireq* under the *nun* instead of *qamets* (ׇ).

°19a ק והיו

°19b ק תצאות

°24 ק העמנה

וְהַיְבוּסִי הִיא יְרוּשָׁלִַם גִּבְעַת קִרְיַת עָרִים אַרְבַּע־עֶשְׂרֵה
ten four towns Kiriath Gibeah Jerusalem that and-the-Jebusite

וְחַצְרֵיהֶן זֹאת נַחֲלַת בְּנֵי־ בִנְיָמִן לְמִשְׁפְּחֹתָם׃
for-clans-of-them Benjamin sons-of inheritance-of this and-villages-of-them

וַיֵּצֵא הַגּוֹרָל הַשֵּׁנִי לְשִׁמְעוֹן לְמַטֵּה בְנֵי־
sons-of for-tribe-of for-Simeon the-second the-lot and-he-came-out (19:1)

שִׁמְעוֹן לְמִשְׁפְּחוֹתָם וַיְהִי נַחֲלָתָם בְּתוֹךְ נַחֲלַת
territory-of within inheritance-of-them and-he-lay by-clans-of-them Simeon

בְּנֵי־ יְהוּדָה׃ וַיְהִי לָהֶם בְּנַחֲלָתָם בְּאֵר־ שֶׁבַע
Sheba Beer in-inheritance-of-them for-them and-he-was (2) Judah sons-of

וְשֶׁבַע וּמוֹלָדָה׃ וַחֲצַר שׁוּעָל וּבָלָה וָעָצֶם׃ וְאֶלְתּוֹלַד
and-Eltolad (4) and-Ezem and-Balah Shual and-Hazar (3) and-Moladah or-Sheba

וּבְתוּל וְחָרְמָה׃ וְצִקְלַג וּבֵית־ הַמַּרְכָּבוֹת וַחֲצַר סוּסָה׃
Susah and-Hazar the-Marcaboth and-Beth and-Ziklag (5) and-Hormah and-Bethul

וּבֵית לְבָאוֹת וְשָׁרוּחֶן עָרִים שְׁלֹשׁ־ עֶשְׂרֵה וְחַצְרֵיהֶן׃
and-villages-of-them ten three-of towns and-Sharuhen Lebaoth and-Beth (6)

עַיִן ׀ רִמּוֹן וָעֶתֶר וְעָשָׁן עָרִים אַרְבַּע וְחַצְרֵיהֶן׃
and-villages-of-them four towns and-Ashan and-Ether Rimmon Ain (7)

וְכָל־ הַחֲצֵרִים אֲשֶׁר סְבִיבוֹת הֶעָרִים הָאֵלֶּה עַד־
as-far-as the-these the-towns ones-around that the-villages and-all-of (8)

בַּעֲלַת בְּאֵר רָאמַת נֶגֶב זֹאת נַחֲלַת מַטֵּה בְנֵי־ שִׁמְעוֹן
Simeon sons-of tribe-of inheritance-of this Negev Ramah-of Beer Baalath

לְמִשְׁפְּחֹתָם׃ מֵחֶבֶל בְּנֵי יְהוּדָה נַחֲלַת בְּנֵי
sons-of inheritance-of Judah sons-of from-share-of (9) by-clans-of-them

שִׁמְעוֹן כִּי־ הָיָה חֵלֶק בְּנֵי־ יְהוּדָה רַב מֵהֶם וַיִּנְחֲלוּ
so-they-inherited for-them too-much Judah sons-of portion-of he-was for Simeon

בְנֵי־ שִׁמְעוֹן בְּתוֹךְ נַחֲלָתָם׃ וַיַּעַל הַגּוֹרָל
the-lot and-he-came-up (10) territory-of-them within Simeon sons-of

הַשְּׁלִישִׁי לִבְנֵי זְבוּלֻן לְמִשְׁפְּחֹתָם וַיְהִי גְּבוּל
boundary-of and-he-went by-clans-of-them Zebulun for-sons-of the-third

נַחֲלָתָם עַד־ שָׂרִיד׃ וְעָלָה גְבוּלָם ׀
boundary-of-them and-he-went (11) Sarid as-far-as inheritance-of-them

לַיָּמָּה וּמַרְעֲלָה וּפָגַע בְּדַבָּשֶׁת וּפָגַע
and-he-extended on-Dabbesheth and-he-touched and-to-Maralah to-the-west

אֶל־ הַנַּחַל אֲשֶׁר עַל־ פְּנֵי יָקְנְעָם׃ וְשָׁב מִשָּׂרִיד
from-Sarid and-he-turned (12) Jokneam areas-of near that the-ravine to

קֵדְמָה מִזְרַח הַשֶּׁמֶשׁ עַל־ גְּבוּל כִּסְלֹת תָּבֹר וְיָצָא אֶל־
to and-he-went-on Tabor Kisloth territory-of to the-sun rise-of to-east

is, Jerusalem), Gibeah and Kiriath—fourteen towns and their villages.
This was the inheritance of Benjamin for its clans.

Allotment for Simeon

19 The second lot came out for the tribe of Simeon, clan by clan. Their inheritance lay within the territory of Judah.
2 It included:
Beersheba (or Sheba),[y] Moladah,
3 Hazar Shual, Balah, Ezem,
4 Eltolad, Bethul, Hormah,
5 Ziklag, Beth Marcaboth, Hazar Susah,
6 Beth Lebaoth and Sharuhen—thirteen towns and their villages;
7 Ain, Rimmon, Ether and Ashan—four towns and their villages—
8 and all the villages around these towns as far as Baalath Beer (Ramah in the Negev).
This was the inheritance of the tribe of the Simeonites, clan by clan.
9 The inheritance of the Simeonites was taken from the share of Judah, because Judah's portion was more than they needed. So the Simeonites received their inheritance within the territory of Judah.

Allotment for Zebulun

10 The third lot came up for Zebulun, clan by clan:
The boundary of their inheritance went as far as Sarid.
11 Going west it ran to Maralah, touched Dabbesheth, and extended to the ravine near Jokneam.
12 It turned east from Sarid toward the sunrise to the territory of Kisloth Tabor and went on to Daberath

y2 Or *Beersheba, Sheba;* 1 Chronicles 4:28 does not have *Sheba.*

הַדָּבְרַת וְעָלָה יָפִיעַ׃ וּמִשָּׁם עָבַר קֵדְמָה
to-east he-continued then-from-there (13) Japhia and-he-went-up the-Daberath

מִזְרָחָה גִּתָּה חֵפֶר עִתָּה קָצִין וְיָצָא רִמּוֹן הַמְּתֹאָר
the-one-turning Rimmon and-he-came-out Kazin to-Eth Hepher to-Gath to-east

הַנֵּעָה׃ וְנָסַב אֹתוֹ הַגְּבוּל מִצְּפוֹן חַנָּתֹן
Hannathon on-north-of the-boundary him then-he-went-around (14) the-Neah

וְהָיוּ תֹּצְאֹתָיו גֵּי יִפְתַּח־אֵל׃ וְקַטָּת וְנַהֲלָל
and-Nahalal and-Kattath (15) El Iphtah Valley-of ends-of-him and-they-were

וְשִׁמְרוֹן וְיִדְאֲלָה וּבֵית לָחֶם עָרִים שְׁתֵּים־עֶשְׂרֵה וְחַצְרֵיהֶן׃
and-villages-of-them ten two towns Lehem and-Beth and-Idalah and-Shimron

זֹאת נַחֲלַת בְּנֵי־ זְבוּלֻן לְמִשְׁפְּחוֹתָם הֶעָרִים הָאֵלֶּה
the-these the-towns clans-of-them Zebulun sons-of inheritance-of this (16)

וְחַצְרֵיהֶן׃ לְיִשָּׂשכָר יָצָא הַגּוֹרָל הָרְבִיעִי
the-fourth the-lot he-came-out for-Issachar (17) and-villages-of-them

לִבְנֵי יִשָּׂשכָר לְמִשְׁפְּחוֹתָם׃ וַיְהִי גְּבוּלָם
territory-of-them and-he-was (18) by-clans-of-them Issachar for-sons-of

יִזְרְעֶאלָה וְהַכְּסוּלֹת וְשׁוּנֵם׃ וַחֲפָרַיִם וְשִׁיאֹן
and-Shion and-Hapharaim (19) and-Shunem and-the-Kesulloth to-Jezreel

וַאֲנָחֲרַת׃ וְהָרַבִּית וְקִשְׁיוֹן וָאֶבֶץ׃ וְרֶמֶת
and-Remeth (21) and-Ebez and-Kishion and-the-Rabbith (20) and-Anaharath

וְעֵין־ גַּנִּים וְעֵין חַדָּה וּבֵית פַּצֵּץ׃ וּפָגַע הַגְּבוּל
the-boundary and-he-touched (22) Pazzez and-Beth Haddah and-En Gannim and-En

בְּתָבוֹר וְשַׁחֲצוּמָה וּבֵית שֶׁמֶשׁ וְהָיוּ תֹּצְאוֹת
ends-of and-they-were Shemesh and-Beth and-Shahazumah on-Tabor

גְּבוּלָם הַיַּרְדֵּן עָרִים שֵׁשׁ־ עֶשְׂרֵה וְחַצְרֵיהֶן׃ זֹאת
this (23) and-villages-of-them ten six towns the-Jordan boundary-of-them

נַחֲלַת מַטֵּה בְּנֵי־ יִשָּׂשכָר לְמִשְׁפְּחֹתָם הֶעָרִים
the-towns by-clans-of-them Issachar sons-of tribe-of inheritance-of

וְחַצְרֵיהֶן׃ וַיֵּצֵא הַגּוֹרָל הַחֲמִישִׁי לְמַטֵּה
for-tribe-of the-fifth the-lot and-he-came-out (24) and-villages-of-them

בְנֵי־ אָשֵׁר לְמִשְׁפְּחוֹתָם׃ וַיְהִי גְּבוּלָם חֶלְקַת
Helkath territory-of-them and-he-was (25) by-clans-of-them Asher sons-of

וַחֲלִי וָבֶטֶן וְאַכְשָׁף׃ וְאַלַּמֶּלֶךְ וְעַמְעָד וּמִשְׁאָל
and-Mishal and-Amad and-Allammelech (26) and-Acshaph and-Beten and-Hali

וּפָגַע בְּכַרְמֶל הַיָּמָּה וּבְשִׁיחוֹר לִבְנָת׃ וְשָׁב
and-he-turned (27) Libnath and-on-Shihor on-the-west on-Carmel and-he-touched

מִזְרַח הַשֶּׁמֶשׁ בֵּית דָּגֹן וּפָגַע בִּזְבֻלוּן וּבְגֵי יִפְתַּח־
Iphtah and-on-Valley-of on-Zebulun and-he-touched Dagon Beth the-sun rise-of

and up to Japhia. 13Then it
continued eastward to Gath
Hepher and Eth Kazin; it
came out at Rimmon and
turned toward Neah.
14There the boundary went
around on the north to
Hannathon and ended at
the Valley of Iphtah El. 15In-
cluded were Kattath, Na-
halal, Shimron, Idalah and
Bethlehem. There were
twelve towns and their villages.
16These towns and their villages were the inheritance of
Zebulun, clan by clan.

Allotment for Issachar

17The fourth lot came out for
Issachar, clan by clan. 18Their
territory included:
Jezreel, Kesulloth, Shu-
nem, 19Hapharaim, Shion,
Anaharath, 20Rabbith,
Kishion, Ebez, 21Remeth,
En Gannim, En Haddah
and Beth Pazzez. 22The
boundary touched Tabor,
Shahazumah and Beth She-
mesh, and ended at the Jordan. There were sixteen
towns and their villages.
23These towns and their villages were the inheritance of
the tribe of Issachar, clan by
clan.

Allotment for Asher

24The fifth lot came out for the
tribe of Asher, clan by clan.
25Their territory included:
Helkath, Hali, Beten, Ac-
shaph, 26Allammelech,
Amad and Mishal. On the
west the boundary touched
Carmel and Shihor Lib-
nath. 27It then turned east
toward Beth Dagon,
touched Zebulun and the
Valley of Iphtah El, and

*22 Most mss have no *hireq* under the *tsade* and point the *vav* as *shureq* (צוּ—); thus, the *Ketbib* reads *and-Shahazumah* and the *Qere* reads *and-Shahazimah*.

°22 ק ושחצימה

אֶל צָפוֹנָה בֵּית הָעֵמֶק וּנְעִיאֵל וְיָצָא אֶל־ כָּבוּל מִשְּׂמֹאל׃
on-left Cabul by and-he-passed and-Neiel the-Emek Beth on-north El

וְעֶבְרֹן וּרְחֹב וְחַמּוֹן וְקָנָה עַד צִידוֹן רַבָּה׃
Greater Sidon as-far-as and-Kanah and-Hammon and-Rehob and-Ebron (28)

וְשָׁב הַגְּבוּל הָרָמָה וְעַד־ עִיר מִבְצַר־ צֹר
Tyre fortified city-of and-to the-Ramah the-boundary then-he-turned (29)

וְשָׁב הַגְּבוּל חֹסָה וַיִּהְיוּ תֹּצְאֹתָיו הַיָּמָּה
at-the-sea ends-of-him and-they-came-out Hosah the-boundary and-he-turned

מֵחֶבֶל אַכְזִיבָה׃ וְעֻמָה וַאֲפֵק וּרְחֹב עָרִים עֶשְׂרִים
twenty towns and-Rehob and-Aphek and-Ummah (30) at-Aczib in-region-of

וּשְׁתַּיִם וְחַצְרֵיהֶן׃ זֹאת נַחֲלַת מַטֵּה בְנֵי־ אָשֵׁר
Asher sons-of tribe-of inheritance-of this (31) and-villages-of-them and-two

לְמִשְׁפְּחֹתָם הֶעָרִים הָאֵלֶּה וְחַצְרֵיהֶן׃ לִבְנֵי
for-sons-of (32) and-villages-of-them the-these the-towns by-clans-of-them

נַפְתָּלִי יָצָא הַגּוֹרָל הַשִּׁשִּׁי לִבְנֵי נַפְתָּלִי לְמִשְׁפְּחֹתָם׃
by-clans-of-them Naphtali for-sons-of the-sixth the-lot he-came-out Naphtali

וַיְהִי גְבוּלָם מֵחֵלֶף מֵאֵלוֹן בְּצַעֲנַנִּים
in-Zaanannim from-large-tree from-Heleph boundary-of-them and-he-went (33)

וַאֲדָמִי הַנֶּקֶב וְיַבְנְאֵל עַד־ לַקּוּם וַיְהִי תֹּצְאֹתָיו הַיַּרְדֵּן׃
the-Jordan ends-of-him and-he-was Lakkum to and-Jabneel the-Nekeb and-Adami

וְשָׁב הַגְּבוּל יָמָּה אַזְנוֹת תָּבוֹר וְיָצָא מִשָּׁם
from-there and-he-came-out Tabor Aznoth to-west the-boundary and-he-ran (34)

חוּקֹקָה וּפָגַע בִּזְבֻלוּן מִנֶּגֶב וּבְאָשֵׁר פָּגַע מִיָּם
on-west he-touched and-on-Asher on-south on-Zebulun and-he-touched at-Hukkok

וּבִיהוּדָה הַיַּרְדֵּן מִזְרַח הַשָּׁמֶשׁ׃ וְעָרֵי מִבְצָר
fortified and-cities-of (35) the-sun rise-of the-Jordan and-on-Judah

הַצִּדִּים צֵר וְחַמַּת רַקַּת וְכִנָּרֶת׃ וַאֲדָמָה וְהָרָמָה
and-the-Ramah and-Adamah (36) and-Kinnereth Rakkath and-Hamath Zer the-Ziddim

וְחָצוֹר׃ וְקֶדֶשׁ וְאֶדְרֶעִי וְעֵין חָצוֹר׃ וְיִרְאוֹן וּמִגְדַּל־
and-Migdal and-Iron (38) Hazor and-En and-Edrei and-Kedesh (37) and-Hazor

אֵל חֳרֵם וּבֵית־עֲנָת וּבֵית שָׁמֶשׁ עָרִים תְּשַׁע־עֶשְׂרֵה וְחַצְרֵיהֶן׃
and-villages-of-them ten nine-of towns Shemesh and-Beth Anath and-Beth Horem El

זֹאת נַחֲלַת מַטֵּה בְנֵי־ נַפְתָּלִי לְמִשְׁפְּחֹתָם הֶעָרִים
the-towns by-clans-of-them Naphtali sons-of tribe-of inheritance-of this (39)

וְחַצְרֵיהֶן׃ לְמַטֵּה בְנֵי־ דָן לְמִשְׁפְּחֹתָם
by-clans-of-them Dan sons-of for-tribe-of (40) and-villages-of-them

יָצָא הַגּוֹרָל הַשְּׁבִיעִי׃ וַיְהִי גְּבוּל
territory-of and-he-was (41) the-seventh the-lot he-came-out

went north to Beth Emek
and Neiel, passing Cabul
on the left.
28 It went to Ab-
don,[z] Rehob, Hammon and
Kanah, as far as Greater Sidon.
29 The boundary then
turned back toward Ramah
and went to the fortified
city of Tyre, turned toward
Hosah and came out at the
sea in the region of Aczib,
30 Ummah, Aphek and
Rehob. There were twenty-
two towns and their vil-
lages.
31 These towns and their villages were the inheritance of
the tribe of Asher, clan by
clan.

Allotment for Naphtali

32 The sixth lot came out for
Naphtali, clan by clan:
33 Their boundary went
from Heleph and the large
tree in Zaanannim, passing
Adami Nekeb and Jabneel
to Lakkum and ending at
the Jordan.
34 The boundary
ran west through Aznoth
Tabor and came out at Huk-
kok. It touched Zebulun on
the south, Asher on the
west and the Jordan[a] on the
east.
35 The fortified cities
were Ziddim, Zer, Ham-
math, Rakkath, Kinnereth,
36 Adamah, Ramah, Hazor,
37 Kedesh, Edrei, En Hazor,
38 Iron, Migdal El, Horem,
Beth Anath and Beth She-
mesh. There were nineteen
towns and their villages.
39 These towns and their villages were the inheritance of
the tribe of Naphtali, clan by
clan.

Allotment for Dan

40 The seventh lot came out for
the tribe of Dan, clan by clan.
41 The territory of their inheritance included:

[z] 28 Some Hebrew manuscripts (see also Joshua 21:30); most Hebrew manuscripts *Ebron*

[a] 34 Septuagint; Hebrew *west, and Judah, the Jordan,*

*30 Most mss have *dagesh* in the *mem* (מ׳־).

°29 ק והיו

וְשַׁעֲלַבִּין שָׁמֶשׁ׃ וְעִיר וְאֶשְׁתָּאוֹל צָרְעָה נַחֲלָתָם
and-Shaalabbin (42) Shemesh and-Ir and-Eshtaol Zorah inheritance-of-them

וְאֶלְתְּקֵה וְעֶקְרוֹן׃ וְתִמְנָתָה וְאֵילוֹן וְיִתְלָה׃ וְאַיָּלוֹן
and-Eltekeh (44) and-Ekron and-at-Timnah and-Elon (43) and-Ithlah and-Aijalon

רִמּוֹן׃ וְגַת־ בְרַק וּבְנֵי־ וִיהֻד וּבַעֲלָת׃ וְגִבְּתוֹן
Rimmon and-Gath Berak and-Bene and-Jehud (45) and-Baalath and-Gibbethon

יָפוֹ׃ מוּל הַגְּבוּל עִם־ וְהָרַקּוֹן הַיַּרְקוֹן וּמֵי
Joppa facing the-area with and-the-Rakkon the-Jarkon and-Me (46)

וַיַּעֲלוּ מֵהֶם דָן בְּנֵי־ גְבוּל־ וַיֵּצֵא
so-they-went-up from-them Dan sons-of territory-of but-he-went-out (47)

וַיַּכּוּ ׀ אוֹתָהּ וַיִּלְכְּדוּ לֶשֶׁם עִם־ וַיִּלָּחֲמוּ דָן בְנֵי־
and-they-put her and-they-took Leshem against and-they-attacked Dan sons-of

בָהּ וַיֵּשְׁבוּ אוֹתָהּ וַיִּרְשׁוּ חֶרֶב לְפִי־ אוֹתָהּ
in-her and-they-settled her and-they-occupied sword to-edge-of her

זֹאת אֲבִיהֶם׃ דָּן כְּשֵׁם דָּן לְלֶשֶׁם וַיִּקְרְאוּ
this (48) forefather-of-them Dan after-name-of Dan to-Leshem and-they-named

הָאֵלֶּה הֶעָרִים לְמִשְׁפְּחֹתָם דָן בְנֵי־ מַטֵּה נַחֲלַת
the-these the-towns by-clans-of-them Dan sons-of tribe-of inheritance-of

הָאָרֶץ אֶת־ לִנְחֹל־ וַיְכַלּוּ וְחַצְרֵיהֶן׃
the-land *** to-divide when-they-finished (49) and-villages-of-them

לִיהוֹשֻׁעַ נַחֲלָה יִשְׂרָאֵל בְנֵי־ וַיִּתְּנוּ לִגְבוּלֹתֶיהָ
to-Joshua inheritance Israel sons-of then-they-gave into-portions-of-her

אֶת־ לוֹ נָתְנוּ יְהוָה פִּי עַל־ בְּתוֹכָם׃ נוּן בִּן־
*** to-him they-gave Yahweh command-of at (50) in-among-them Nun son-of

אֶפְרָיִם בְּהַר סֶרַח תִּמְנַת־ אֶת־ שָׁאָל אֲשֶׁר הָעִיר
Ephraim in-hill-country-of Serah Timnath *** he-asked-for which the-town

הַנְּחָלֹת אֵלֶּה בָּהּ׃ וַיֵּשֶׁב הָעִיר אֶת־ וַיִּבְנֶה
the-territories these (51) in-her and-he-settled the-town *** and-he-built-up

וְרָאשֵׁי נוּן בִּן־ וִיהוֹשֻׁעַ ׀ הַכֹּהֵן אֶלְעָזָר נִחֲלוּ אֲשֶׁר
and-heads-of Nun son-of and-Joshua the-priest Eleazar they-assigned that

לִפְנֵי בְּשִׁלֹה ׀ בְּגוֹרָל ׀ יִשְׂרָאֵל בְּנֵי־ לְמַטּוֹת הָאָבוֹת
in-presences-of at-Shiloh by-lot Israel sons-of of-tribes-of the-fathers

אֶת־ מֵחַלֵּק וַיְכַלּוּ מוֹעֵד אֹהֶל פֶּתַח יְהוָה
*** from-to-divide so-they-finished Meeting Tent-of entrance-of Yahweh

אֶל־ דַּבֵּר לֵאמֹר׃ יְהוֹשֻׁעַ אֶל־ יְהוָה וַיְדַבֵּר הָאָרֶץ׃
to tell! (2) to-say Joshua to Yahweh then-he-spoke (20:1) the-land

אֲשֶׁר־ הַמִּקְלָט עָרֵי אֶת־ לָכֶם תְּנוּ לֵאמֹר יִשְׂרָאֵל בְּנֵי
as the-refuge cities-of *** for-you designate! to-say Israel sons-of

Zorah, Eshtaol, Ir She-
mesh, 42Shaalabbin, Aija-
lon, Ithlah, 43Elon, Timnah,
Ekron, 44Eltekeh, Gibbe-
thon, Baalath, 45Jehud, Bene
Berak, Gath Rimmon, 46Me
Jarkon and Rakkon, with
the area facing Joppa.
47(But the Danites had
difficulty taking possession of
their territory, so they went up
and attacked Leshem, took it,
put it to the sword and occupied it. They settled in Leshem and named it Dan after
their forefather.)
48These towns and their villages were the inheritance of
the tribe of Dan, clan by clan.

Allotment for Joshua

49When they had finished
dividing the land into its allotted portions, the Israelites
gave Joshua son of Nun an inheritance among them, 50as
the LORD had commanded.
They gave him the town he
asked for—Timnath Serah[b] in
the hill country of Ephraim.
And he built up the town and
settled there.
51These are the territories
that Eleazar the priest, Joshua
son of Nun and the heads of
the tribal clans of Israel assigned by lot at Shiloh in the
presence of the LORD at the entrance to the Tent of Meeting.
And so they finished dividing
the land.

Cities of Refuge

20 Then the LORD said to
Joshua: 2"Tell the Isra-
elites to designate the cities of

[b]50 Also known as *Timnath Heres* (see Judges 2:9)

דִּבַּרְתִּי אֲלֵיכֶם בְּיַד־ מֹשֶׁה׃ לָנוּס שָׁמָּה רוֹצֵחַ
one-killing to-there to-flee (3) Moses by-hand-of to-you I-instructed

מַכֵּה־ נֶפֶשׁ בִּשְׁגָגָה בִּבְלִי־ דָעַת וְהָיוּ לָכֶם
for-you so-they-may-be intention without by-accident person one-killing-of

לְמִקְלָט מִגֹּאֵל הַדָּם׃ וְנָס אֶל־ אַחַת ׀
one-of to when-he-flees (4) the-blood from-one-avenging-of for-protection

מֵהֶעָרִים הָאֵלֶּה וְעָמַד פֶּתַח שַׁעַר הָעִיר
the-city gate-of entrance-of then-he-must-stand the-these from-the-cities

וְדִבֶּר בְּאָזְנֵי זִקְנֵי הָעִיר־ הַהִיא אֶת־ דְּבָרָיו
cases-of-him *** the-that the-city elders-of in-ears-of and-he-must-state

וְאָסְפוּ אֹתוֹ הָעִירָה אֲלֵיהֶם וְנָתְנוּ־ לוֹ
to-him and-they-must-give to-them into-the-city him then-they-must-admit

מָקוֹם וְיָשַׁב עִמָּם׃ וְכִי יִרְדֹּף גֹּאֵל
one-avenging-of he-pursues and-if (5) with-them so-he-can-live place

הַדָּם אַחֲרָיו וְלֹא־ יַסְגִּרוּ אֶת־ הָרֹצֵחַ
the-one-killing *** they-must-surrender then-not after-him the-blood

בְּיָדוֹ כִּי בִבְלִי־ דַעַת הִכָּה אֶת־ רֵעֵהוּ וְלֹא־
and-not neighbor-of-him *** he-killed intention without for into-hand-of-him

שֹׂנֵא הוּא לוֹ מִתְּמוֹל שִׁלְשׁוֹם׃ וְיָשַׁב ׀
and-he-must-stay (6) before on-yesterday against-him he having-malice

בָּעִיר הַהִיא עַד־ עָמְדוֹ לִפְנֵי הָעֵדָה לַמִּשְׁפָּט
for-the-trial the-assembly before to-stand-him until the-that in-the-city

עַד־ מוֹת הַכֹּהֵן הַגָּדוֹל אֲשֶׁר יִהְיֶה בַּיָּמִים הָהֵם אָז ׀
then the-those in-the-days he-is who the-high the-priest death-of until

יָשׁוּב הָרוֹצֵחַ וּבָא אֶל־ עִירוֹ וְאֶל־
and-to town-of-him to and-he-may-go the-one-killing he-may-go-back

בֵּיתוֹ אֶל־ הָעִיר אֲשֶׁר־ נָס מִשָּׁם׃ וַיַּקְדִּשׁוּ אֶת־
*** so-they-set-apart (7) from-there he-fled which the-town in home-of-him

קֶדֶשׁ בַּגָּלִיל בְּהַר נַפְתָּלִי וְאֶת־ שְׁכֶם בְּהַר
in-hill-country-of Shechem and Naphtali in-hill-country-of in-the-Galilee Kedesh

אֶפְרַיִם וְאֶת־קִרְיַת אַרְבַּע הִיא חֶבְרוֹן בְּהַר יְהוּדָה׃ וּמֵעֵבֶר
and-on-side (8) Judah in-hill-country-of Hebron that Arba Kiriath and Ephraim

לְיַרְדֵּן יְרִיחוֹ מִזְרָחָה נָתְנוּ אֶת־ בֶּצֶר בַּמִּדְבָּר
in-the-desert Bezer *** they-designated on-east Jericho of-Jordan-of

בַּמִּישֹׁר מִמַּטֵּה רְאוּבֵן וְאֶת־ רָאמֹת בַּגִּלְעָד מִמַּטֵּה־ גָד
Gad in-tribe-of in-the-Gilead Ramoth and Reuben in-tribe-of on-the-plateau

וְאֶת־ גָּלוֹן בַּבָּשָׁן מִמַּטֵּה מְנַשֶּׁה׃ אֵלֶּה הָיוּ עָרֵי
cities-of they-were these (9) Manasseh in-tribe-of in-the-Bashan Golan and

°8 ק גולן

refuge, as I instructed you
through Moses, [3]so that anyone who kills a person accidentally and unintentionally
may flee there and find protec-
tion from the avenger of
blood.
[4]"When he flees to one of
these cities, he is to stand in
the entrance of the city gate
and state his case before the
elders of that city. Then they
are to admit him into their city
and give him a place to live
with them. [5]If the avenger of
blood pursues him, they must
not surrender the one accused,
because he killed his neighbor
unintentionally and without
malice aforethought. [6]He is to
stay in that city until he has
stood trial before the assembly
and until the death of the high
priest who is serving at that
time. Then he may go back to
his own home in the town
from which he fled."
[7]So they set apart Kedesh in
Galilee in the hill country of
Naphtali, Shechem in the hill
country of Ephraim, and
Kiriath Arba (that is, Hebron)
in the hill country of Judah.
[8]On the east side of the Jordan
of Jericho[c] they designated Bezer in the desert on the plateau
in the tribe of Reuben,
Ramoth in Gilead in the tribe
of Gad, and Golan in Bashan
in the tribe of Manasseh. [9]Any

[c]8 *Jordan of Jericho* was possibly an ancient name for the Jordan River.

הַמּוּעָדָה לְכֹל ׀ בְּנֵי יִשְׂרָאֵל וְלַגֵּר הַגָּר
the-one-living or-for-the-alien Israel sons-of for-any-of the-designated

בְּתוֹכָם לָנוּס שָׁמָּה כָּל־ מַכֵּה־ נֶפֶשׁ בִּשְׁגָגָה
by-accident person one-killing-of any-of to-there to-flee in-among-them

וְלֹא יָמוּת בְּיַד גֹּאֵל הַדָּם עַד־
prior the-blood one-avenging-of by-hand-of he-would-be-killed so-not

עָמְדוֹ לִפְנֵי הָעֵדָה׃ וַיִּגְּשׁוּ רָאשֵׁי
heads-of now-they-approached (21:1) the-assembly before to-stand-him

אֲבוֹת הַלְוִיִּם אֶל־אֶלְעָזָר הַכֹּהֵן וְאֶל־ יְהוֹשֻׁעַ בִּן־ נוּן וְאֶל־
and-to Nun son-of Joshua and-to the-priest Eleazar to the-Levites fathers-of

רָאשֵׁי אֲבוֹת הַמַּטּוֹת לִבְנֵי יִשְׂרָאֵל׃ וַיְדַבְּרוּ אֲלֵיהֶם
to-them and-they-spoke (2) Israel of-sons-of the-tribes fathers-of heads-of

בְּשִׁלֹה בְּאֶרֶץ כְּנַעַן לֵאמֹר יְהוָה צִוָּה בְיַד־ מֹשֶׁה
Moses by-hand-of he-commanded Yahweh to-say Canaan in-land-of at-Shiloh

לָתֶת־ לָנוּ עָרִים לָשָׁבֶת וּמִגְרְשֵׁיהֶן לִבְהֶמְתֵּנוּ׃
for-livestock-of-us and-pasturelands-of-them to-live towns to-us to-give

וַיִּתְּנוּ בְנֵי־ יִשְׂרָאֵל לַלְוִיִּם מִנַּחֲלָתָם אֶל־
at from-inheritance-of-them to-the-Levites Israel sons-of so-they-gave (3)

פִּי יְהוָה אֶת־ הֶעָרִים הָאֵלֶּה וְאֶת־ מִגְרְשֵׁיהֶן׃
pasturelands-of-them and the-these the-towns *** Yahweh command-of

וַיֵּצֵא הַגּוֹרָל לְמִשְׁפְּחֹת הַקְּהָתִי וַיְהִי לִבְנֵי
for-sons-of and-he-was the-Kohathite for-clans-of the-lot and-he-came-out (4)

אַהֲרֹן הַכֹּהֵן מִן־ הַלְוִיִּם מִמַּטֵּה יְהוּדָה וּמִמַּטֵּה
and-from-tribe-of Judah from-tribe-of the-Levites from the-priest Aaron

הַשִּׁמְעֹנִי וּמִמַּטֵּה בִנְיָמִן בַּגּוֹרָל עָרִים שְׁלֹשׁ עֶשְׂרֵה׃
ten three-of towns by-the-lot Benjamin and-from-tribe-of the-Simeonite

וְלִבְנֵי קְהָת הַנּוֹתָרִים מִמִּשְׁפְּחֹת מַטֵּה־ אֶפְרַיִם
Ephraim tribe-of from-clans-of the-ones-remaining Kohath and-for-sons-of (5)

וּמִמַּטֵּה־ דָן וּמֵחֲצִי מַטֵּה מְנַשֶּׁה בַּגּוֹרָל עָרִים
towns by-the-lot Manasseh tribe-of and-from-half-of Dan and-from-tribe-of

עָשֶׂר׃ וְלִבְנֵי גֵרְשׁוֹן מִמִּשְׁפְּחוֹת מַטֵּה־ יִשָּׂשכָר
Issachar tribe-of from-clans-of Gershon and-for-sons-of (6) ten

וּמִמַּטֵּה־ אָשֵׁר וּמִמַּטֵּה נַפְתָּלִי וּמֵחֲצִי מַטֵּה
tribe-of and-from-half-of Naphtali and-from-tribe-of Asher and-from-tribe-of

מְנַשֶּׁה בַבָּשָׁן בַּגּוֹרָל עָרִים שְׁלֹשׁ עֶשְׂרֵה׃ לִבְנֵי מְרָרִי
Merari for-sons-of (7) ten three-of towns by-the-lot in-the-Bashan Manasseh

לְמִשְׁפְּחֹתָם מִמַּטֵּה רְאוּבֵן וּמִמַּטֵּה־ גָד וּמִמַּטֵּה
and-from-tribe-of Gad and-from-tribe-of Reuben from-tribe-of by-clans-of-them

of the Israelites or any alien living among them who killed someone accidentally could flee to these designated cities and not be killed by the avenger of blood prior to standing trial before the assembly.

Towns for the Levites

21 Now the family heads of the Levites approached Eleazar the priest, Joshua son of Nun, and the heads of the other tribal families of Israel [2]at Shiloh in Canaan and said to them, "The LORD commanded through Moses that you give us towns to live in, with pasturelands for our livestock." [3]So, as the LORD had commanded, the Israelites gave the Levites the following towns and pasturelands out of their own inheritance:

[4]The first lot came out for the Kohathites, clan by clan. The Levites who were descendants of Aaron the priest were allotted thirteen towns from the tribes of Judah, Simeon and Benjamin. [5]The rest of Kohath's descendants were allotted ten towns from the clans of the tribes of Ephraim, Dan and half of Manasseh.

[6]The descendants of Gershon were allotted thirteen towns from the clans of the tribes of Issachar, Asher, Naphtali and the half-tribe of Manasseh in Bashan.

[7]The descendants of Merari, clan by clan, received twelve towns from the tribes of Reuben, Gad and Zebulun.

זְבוּלֻן עָרִים שְׁתֵּים עֶשְׂרֵה׃ וַיִּתְּנוּ בְנֵי־ יִשְׂרָאֵל לַלְוִיִּם אֶת־

*** to-the-Levites Israel sons-of so-they-gave (8) ten two towns Zebulun

הֶעָרִים הָאֵלֶּה וְאֶת־ מִגְרְשֵׁיהֶן כַּאֲשֶׁר צִוָּה יְהוָה

Yahweh he-commanded just-as pasturelands-of-them and the-these the-towns

בְּיַד־ מֹשֶׁה בַּגּוֹרָל׃ וַיִּתְּנוּ מִמַּטֵּה בְּנֵי יְהוּדָה

Judah sons-of from-tribe-of and-they-allotted (9) by-the-lot Moses by-hand-of

וּמִמַּטֵּה בְּנֵי שִׁמְעוֹן אֵת הֶעָרִים הָאֵלֶּה אֲשֶׁר־ יִקְרָא

he-called which the-these the-towns *** Simeon sons-of and-from-tribe-of

אֶתְהֶן בְּשֵׁם׃ וַיְהִי לִבְנֵי אַהֲרֹן מִמִּשְׁפְּחוֹת הַקְּהָתִי

the-Kohathite from-clans-of Aaron to-sons-of and-he-was (10) by-name them

מִבְּנֵי לֵוִי כִּי לָהֶם הָיָה הַגּוֹרָל רִיאשֹׁנָה׃ וַיִּתְּנוּ לָהֶם אֶת־

*** to-them and-they-gave (11) first the-lot he-fell to-them for Levi from-sons-of

קִרְיַת אַרְבַּע אֲבִי הָעֲנוֹק הִיא חֶבְרוֹן בְּהַר יְהוּדָה

Judah in-hill-country-of Hebron that the-Anak forefather-of Arba Kiriath

וְאֶת־ מִגְרָשֶׁהָ סְבִיבֹתֶיהָ׃ וְאֶת־ שְׂדֵה הָעִיר

the-city field-of but (12) ones-surrounding-her pastureland-of-her and

וְאֶת־ חֲצֵרֶיהָ נָתְנוּ לְכָלֵב בֶּן־ יְפֻנֶּה בַּאֲחֻזָּתוֹ׃

as-possession-of-him Jephunneh son-of to-Caleb they-gave villages-of-her and

וְלִבְנֵי ׀ אַהֲרֹן הַכֹּהֵן נָתְנוּ אֶת־ עִיר מִקְלַט

refuge-of city-of *** they-gave the-priest Aaron so-to-sons-of (13)

הָרֹצֵחַ אֶת־ חֶבְרוֹן וְאֶת־ מִגְרָשֶׁהָ וְאֶת־לִבְנָה וְאֶת־ מִגְרָשֶׁהָ׃

pasture-of-her and Libnah and pasture-of-her and Hebron *** the-one-killing

וְאֶת־ יַתִּר וְאֶת־ מִגְרָשֶׁהָ וְאֶת־אֶשְׁתְּמֹעַ וְאֶת־ מִגְרָשֶׁהָ׃ וְאֶת־

and (15) pasture-of-her and Eshtemoa and pasture-of-her and Jattir and (14)

חֹלֹן וְאֶת־ מִגְרָשֶׁהָ וְאֶת־ דְּבִר וְאֶת־ מִגְרָשֶׁהָ׃ וְאֶת־ עַיִן וְאֶת־

and Ain and (16) pasture-of-her and Debir and pasture-of-her and Holon

מִגְרָשֶׁהָ וְאֶת־ יֻטָּה וְאֶת־ מִגְרָשֶׁהָ אֶת־ בֵּית שֶׁמֶשׁ וְאֶת־

and Shemesh Beth *** pasture-of-her and Juttah and pasture-of-her

מִגְרָשֶׁהָ עָרִים תֵּשַׁע מֵאֵת שְׁנֵי הַשְּׁבָטִים הָאֵלֶּה׃

the-these the-tribes two-of from nine towns pasture-of-her

וּמִמַּטֵּה בִנְיָמִן אֶת־ גִּבְעוֹן וְאֶת־ מִגְרָשֶׁהָ אֶת־ גֶּבַע וְאֶת־

and Geba *** pasture-of-her and Gibeon *** Benjamin and-from-tribe-of (17)

מִגְרָשֶׁהָ׃ אֶת־ עֲנָתוֹת וְאֶת־ מִגְרָשֶׁהָ וְאֶת־ עַלְמוֹן וְאֶת־

and Almon and pasture-of-her and Anathoth *** (18) pasture-of-her

מִגְרָשֶׁהָ עָרִים אַרְבַּע׃ כָּל־ עָרֵי בְנֵי־ אַהֲרֹן הַכֹּהֲנִים

the-priests Aaron sons-of towns-of all-of (19) four towns pasture-of-her

שְׁלֹשׁ־ עֶשְׂרֵה עָרִים וּמִגְרְשֵׁיהֶן׃ וּלְמִשְׁפְּחוֹת בְּנֵי־ קְהָת

Kohath sons-of and-to-clans-of (20) and-pastures-of-them towns ten three-of

8 So the Israelites allotted to
the Levites these towns and
their pasturelands, as the LORD
had commanded through
Moses.

9 From the tribes of Judah and
Simeon they allotted the following towns by name
10 (these towns were assigned
to the descendants of Aaron
who were from the Kohathite
clans of the Levites, because
the first lot fell to them):
11 They gave them Kiriath
Arba (that is, Hebron),
with its surrounding pas-
tureland, in the hill country
of Judah. (Arba was the
forefather of Anak.) 12 But
the fields and villages
around the city they had
given to Caleb son of Je-
phunneh as his possession.
13 So to the descendants of
Aaron the priest they gave
Hebron (a city of refuge for
one accused of murder),
Libnah, 14 Jattir, Eshtemoa,
15 Holon, Debir, 16 Ain, Juttah and Beth Shemesh, to-
gether with their pasturelands—nine towns from
these two tribes.
17 And from the tribe of
Benjamin they gave them
Gibeon, Geba, 18 Anathoth
and Almon, together with
their pasturelands—four
towns.
19 All the towns for the priests,
the descendants of Aaron,
were thirteen, together with
their pasturelands.

20 The rest of the Kohathite

הַלְוִיִּם הַנּוֹתָרִים מִבְּנֵי קְהָת וַיְהִי עָרֵי
towns-of and-he-was Kohath from-sons-of the-ones-remaining the-Levites

גּוֹרָלָם מִמַּטֵּה אֶפְרָיִם׃ וַיִּתְּנוּ לָהֶם אֶת־
*** to-them and-they-gave (21) Ephraim from-tribe-of allotment-of-them

עִיר מִקְלַט הָרֹצֵחַ אֶת־שְׁכֶם וְאֶת־מִגְרָשֶׁהָ
pasture-of-her and Shechem *** the-one-killing refuge-of city-of

בְּהַר אֶפְרָיִם וְאֶת־גֶּזֶר וְאֶת־מִגְרָשֶׁהָ׃ וְאֶת־קִבְצַיִם
Kibzaim and (22) pasture-of-her and Gezer and Ephraim in-hill-country-of

וְאֶת־מִגְרָשֶׁהָ וְאֶת־בֵּית חוֹרֹן וְאֶת־מִגְרָשֶׁהָ עָרִים אַרְבַּע׃
four towns pasture-of-her and Horon Beth and pasture-of-her and

וּמִמַּטֵּה־דָן אֶת־אֶלְתְּקֵא וְאֶת־מִגְרָשֶׁהָ אֶת־גִּבְּתוֹן
Gibbethon *** pasture-of-her and Eltekeh *** Dan and-from-tribe-of (23)

וְאֶת־מִגְרָשֶׁהָ׃ אֶת־אַיָּלוֹן וְאֶת־מִגְרָשֶׁהָ אֶת־גַּת־רִמּוֹן וְאֶת־
and Rimmon Gath *** pasture-of-her and Aijalon *** (24) pasture-of-her and

מִגְרָשֶׁהָ עָרִים אַרְבַּע׃ וּמִמַּחֲצִית מַטֵּה מְנַשֶּׁה אֶת־תַּעְנַךְ
Taanach *** Manasseh tribe-of and-from-half-of (25) four towns pasture-of-her

וְאֶת־מִגְרָשֶׁהָ וְאֶת־גַּת־רִמּוֹן וְאֶת־מִגְרָשֶׁהָ עָרִים שְׁתָּיִם׃ כָּל־
all-of (26) two towns pasture-of-her and Rimmon Gath and pasture-of-her and

עָרִים עֶשֶׂר וּמִגְרְשֵׁיהֶן לְמִשְׁפְּחוֹת בְּנֵי־קְהָת הַנּוֹתָרִים׃
the-ones-remaining Kohath sons-of to-clans-of and-pasturelands-of-them ten towns

וְלִבְנֵי גֵרְשׁוֹן מִמִּשְׁפְּחֹת הַלְוִיִּם מֵחֲצִי מַטֵּה
tribe-of from-half-of the-Levites from-clans-of Gershon and-to-sons-of (27)

מְנַשֶּׁה אֶת־עִיר מִקְלַט הָרֹצֵחַ אֶת־גֹּלָן בַּבָּשָׁן וְאֶת־
and in-the-Bashan Golan *** the-one-killing refuge-of city-of *** Manasseh

מִגְרָשֶׁהָ וְאֶת־בְּעֶשְׁתְּרָה וְאֶת־מִגְרָשֶׁהָ עָרִים שְׁתָּיִם׃
two towns pasture-of-her and Be-Eshtarah and pasture-of-her

וּמִמַּטֵּה יִשָּׂשכָר אֶת־קִשְׁיוֹן וְאֶת־מִגְרָשֶׁהָ אֶת־דָּבְרַת
Daberath *** pasture-of-her and Kishion *** Issachar and-from-tribe-of (28)

וְאֶת־מִגְרָשֶׁהָ׃ אֶת־יַרְמוּת וְאֶת־מִגְרָשֶׁהָ אֶת־עֵין גַּנִּים וְאֶת־
and Gannim En *** pasture-of-her and Jarmuth *** (29) pasture-of-her and

מִגְרָשֶׁהָ עָרִים אַרְבַּע׃ וּמִמַּטֵּה אָשֵׁר אֶת־מִשְׁאָל וְאֶת־
and Mishal *** Asher and-from-tribe-of (30) four towns pasture-of-her

מִגְרָשֶׁהָ אֶת־עַבְדּוֹן וְאֶת־מִגְרָשֶׁהָ׃ אֶת־חֶלְקָת וְאֶת־מִגְרָשֶׁהָ
pasture-of-her and Helkath *** (31) pasture-of-her and Abdon *** pasture-of-her

וְאֶת־רְחֹב וְאֶת־מִגְרָשֶׁהָ עָרִים אַרְבַּע׃ וּמִמַּטֵּה נַפְתָּלִי אֶת־
*** Naphtali and-from-tribe-of (32) four towns pasture-of-her and Rehob and

עִיר | מִקְלַט הָרֹצֵחַ אֶת־קֶדֶשׁ בַּגָּלִיל וְאֶת־מִגְרָשֶׁהָ
pasture-of-her and in-the-Galilee Kedesh *** the-one-killing refuge-of city-of

clans of the Levites were allotted towns from the tribe of Ephraim:

[21]In the hill country of Ephraim they were given Shechem (a city of refuge for one accused of murder) and Gezer,
[22]Kibzaim and Beth Horon, together with their pasturelands—four towns.

[23]Also from the tribe of Dan they received Eltekeh, Gibbethon,
[24]Aijalon and Gath Rimmon, together with their pasturelands—four towns.

[25]From half the tribe of Manasseh they received Taanach and Gath Rimmon, together with their pasturelands—two towns.

[26]All these ten towns and their pasturelands were given to the rest of the Kohathite clans.

[27]The Levite clans of the Gershonites were given:

from the half-tribe of Manasseh,

Golan in Bashan (a city of refuge for one accused of murder) and Be Eshtarah, together with their pasturelands—two towns;

[28]from the tribe of Issachar,

Kishion, Daberath,
[29]Jarmuth and En Gannim, together with their pasturelands—four towns;

[30]from the tribe of Asher,

Mishal, Abdon,
[31]Helkath and Rehob, together with their pasturelands—four towns;

[32]from the tribe of Naphtali,

Kedesh in Galilee (a city of refuge for one accused of

°27 ק גולן

וְאֶת־חַמֹּת דֹּאר וְאֶת־מִגְרָשֶׁהָ וְאֶת־קַרְתָּן וְאֶת־מִגְרָשֶׁהָ עָרִים שָׁלֹשׁ׃
three towns pasture-of-her and Kartan and pasture-of-her and Dor Hammoth and

כָּל־עָרֵי הַגֵּרְשֻׁנִּי לְמִשְׁפְּחֹתָם שְׁלֹשׁ־עֶשְׂרֵה עִיר
town ten three-of by-clans-of-them the-Gershonite towns-of all-of (33)

וּמִגְרְשֵׁיהֶן׃ וּלְמִשְׁפְּחוֹת בְּנֵי־מְרָרִי הַלְוִיִּם
the-Levites Merari sons-of and-to-clans-of (34) and-pasturelands-of-them

הַנּוֹתָרִים מֵאֵת מַטֵּה זְבוּלֻן אֶת־יָקְנְעָם וְאֶת־מִגְרָשֶׁהָ אֶת־
*** pasture-of-her and Jokneam *** Zebulun tribe-of from the-ones-remaining

קַרְתָּה וְאֶת־מִגְרָשֶׁהָ׃ אֶת־דִּמְנָה וְאֶת־מִגְרָשֶׁהָ אֶת־נַהֲלָל וְאֶת־
and Nahalal *** pasture-of-her and Dimnah *** (35) pasture-of-her and Kartah

מִגְרָשֶׁהָ עָרִים אַרְבַּע׃ וּמִמַּטֵּה רְאוּבֵן אֶת־בֶּצֶר וְאֶת־
and Bezer *** Reuben and-from-tribe-of *(36) four towns pasture-of-her

מִגְרָשֶׁהָ וְאֶת־יַהְצָה וְאֶת־מִגְרָשֶׁהָ׃ אֶת־קְדֵמוֹת וְאֶת־
and Kedemoth *** (37) pasture-of-her and Jahaz and pasture-of-her

מִגְרָשֶׁהָ וְאֶת־מֵיפַעַת וְאֶת־מִגְרָשֶׁהָ עָרִים אַרְבַּע׃
four towns pasture-of-her and Mephaath and pasture-of-her

וּמִמַּטֵּה־גָד אֶת־עִיר מִקְלַט הָרֹצֵחַ אֶת־רָמֹת
Ramoth *** the-one-killing refuge-of city-of *** Gad and-from-tribe-of (38)

בַּגִּלְעָד וְאֶת־מִגְרָשֶׁהָ וְאֶת־מַחֲנַיִם וְאֶת־מִגְרָשֶׁהָ׃ אֶת־
*** (39) pasture-of-her and Mahanaim and pasture-of-her and in-the-Gilead

חֶשְׁבּוֹן וְאֶת־מִגְרָשֶׁהָ אֶת־יַעְזֵר וְאֶת־מִגְרָשֶׁהָ כָּל־עָרִים אַרְבַּע׃
four towns all-of pasture-of-her and Jazer *** pasture-of-her and Heshbon

כָּל־הֶעָרִים לִבְנֵי מְרָרִי לְמִשְׁפְּחֹתָם הַנּוֹתָרִים
the-ones-remaining by-clans-of-them Merari to-sons-of the-towns all-of (40)

מִמִּשְׁפְּחוֹת הַלְוִיִּם וַיְהִי גּוֹרָלָם עָרִים שְׁתֵּים עֶשְׂרֵה׃
ten two towns allotment-of-them and-he-was the-Levites from-clans-of

כֹּל עָרֵי הַלְוִיִּם בְּתוֹךְ אֲחֻזַּת בְּנֵי־יִשְׂרָאֵל עָרִים
towns Israel sons-of territory-of in-among the-Levites towns-of all-of (41)

אַרְבָּעִים וּשְׁמֹנֶה וּמִגְרְשֵׁיהֶן׃ תִּהְיֶינָה הֶעָרִים הָאֵלֶּה
the-these the-towns they-had (42) and-pasturelands-of-them and-eight forty

עִיר עִיר וּמִגְרָשֶׁיהָ סְבִיבֹתֶיהָ כֵּן לְכָל־
for-all-of true ones-surrounding-her also-pasturelands-of-her city city

הֶעָרִים הָאֵלֶּה׃ וַיִּתֵּן יְהוָה לְיִשְׂרָאֵל אֶת־כָּל־הָאָרֶץ
the-land all-of *** to-Israel Yahweh so-he-gave (43) the-these the-towns

אֲשֶׁר נִשְׁבַּע לָתֵת לַאֲבוֹתָם וַיִּרָשׁוּהָ וַיֵּשְׁבוּ
and-they-settled and-they-possessed-her to-fathers-of-them to-give he-swore that

בָהּ׃ וַיָּנַח יְהוָה לָהֶם מִסָּבִיב כְּכֹל אֲשֶׁר־נִשְׁבַּע
he-swore that as-all on-every-side to-them Yahweh and-he-gave-rest (44) in-her

murder), Hammoth Dor and Kartan, together with their pasturelands—three towns.
[33]All the towns of the Gershonite clans were thirteen, together with their pasturelands.

[34]The Merarite clans (the rest of the Levites) were given:
from the tribe of Zebulun, Jokneam, Kartah, [35]Dimnah and Nahalal, together with their pasturelands—four towns;
[36]from the tribe of Reuben, Bezer, Jahaz, [37]Kedemoth and Mephaath, together with their pasturelands—four towns;
[38]from the tribe of Gad, Ramoth in Gilead (a city of refuge for one accused of murder), Mahanaim, [39]Heshbon and Jazer, together with their pasturelands—four towns in all.
[40]All the towns allotted to the Merarite clans, who were the rest of the Levites, were twelve.
[41]The towns of the Levites in the territory held by the Israelites were forty-eight in all, together with their pasturelands. [42]Each of these towns had pasturelands surrounding it; this was true for all these towns.

[43]So the LORD gave Israel all the land he had sworn to give

***36** Most mss and versions include verses 36 and 37, although L does not; thus BHS reproduces them from the majority MT in a reduced type. See the introduction, page xiii.

לַאֲבוֹתָ֑ם וְלֹא־ עָ֨מַד אִ֤ישׁ בִּפְנֵיהֶם֙ מִכָּל־
of-any-of against-faces-of-them man he-withstood and-not to-fathers-of-them

אֹֽיְבֵיהֶ֔ם אֵ֚ת כָּל־ אֹֽיְבֵיהֶ֔ם נָתַ֥ן יְהוָ֖ה
Yahweh he-gave being-enemies-of-them all-of *** being-enemies-of-them

בְּיָדָֽם׃ לֹֽא־ נָפַ֣ל דָּבָ֗ר מִכֹּל֙ הַדָּבָ֣ר הַטּ֔וֹב
the-good the-promise from-any-of promise he-failed not (45) into-hand-of-them

אֲשֶׁר־ דִּבֶּ֥ר יְהוָ֖ה אֶל־ בֵּ֣ית יִשְׂרָאֵ֑ל הַכֹּ֖ל בָּֽא׃
he-fulfilled the-every-one Israel house-of to Yahweh he-promised that

אָ֚ז יִקְרָ֣א יְהוֹשֻׁ֔עַ לָרֻֽאוּבֵנִ֖י וְלַגָּדִ֑י
and-to-the-Gadite to-the-Reubenite Joshua he-summoned then (22:1)

וְלַחֲצִ֖י מַטֵּ֥ה מְנַשֶּֽׁה׃ וַיֹּ֣אמֶר אֲלֵיהֶ֔ם אַתֶּ֣ם שְׁמַרְתֶּ֔ם אֵ֚ת כָּל־
all *** you-did you to-them and-he-said (2) Manasseh tribe-of and-to-half-of

אֲשֶׁ֣ר צִוָּ֣ה אֶתְכֶ֔ם מֹשֶׁ֖ה עֶ֣בֶד יְהוָ֑ה וַתִּשְׁמְע֣וּ בְקוֹלִ֔י
to-voice-of-me and-you-obeyed Yahweh servant-of Moses you he-commanded that

לְכֹ֥ל אֲשֶׁר־ צִוִּ֖יתִי אֶתְכֶֽם׃ לֹֽא־ עֲזַבְתֶּ֣ם אֶת־ אֲחֵיכֶ֗ם
brothers-of-you *** you-deserted not (3) you I-commanded that in-everything

זֶ֚ה יָמִ֣ים רַבִּ֔ים עַ֖ד הַיּ֣וֹם הַזֶּ֑ה וּשְׁמַרְתֶּ֕ם אֶת־ מִשְׁמֶ֕רֶת מִצְוַ֖ת
given-of mission-of *** but-you-carried-out the-this the-day to many days this

יְהוָ֥ה אֱלֹהֵיכֶֽם׃ וְעַתָּ֗ה הֵנִ֨יחַ יְהוָ֤ה אֱלֹהֵיכֶם֙ לַאֲחֵיכֶ֔ם
to-brothers-of-you God-of-you Yahweh he-gave-rest and-now (4) God-of-you Yahweh

כַּאֲשֶׁ֖ר דִּבֶּ֣ר לָהֶ֑ם וְעַתָּ֡ה פְּנוּ֩ וּלְכ֨וּ לָכֶ֜ם לְאָהֳלֵיכֶ֗ם
to-homes-of-you for-you and-go! return! and-now to-them he-promised just-as

אֶל־אֶ֙רֶץ֙ אֲחֻזַּתְכֶ֔ם אֲשֶׁ֣ר ׀ נָתַ֣ן לָכֶ֗ם מֹשֶׁה֙ עֶ֣בֶד יְהוָ֔ה
Yahweh servant-of Moses to-you he-gave that possession-of-you land-of to

בְּעֵ֖בֶר הַיַּרְדֵּֽן׃ רַ֣ק ׀ שִׁמְר֣וּ מְאֹד֮ לַעֲשׂ֣וֹת אֶת־ הַמִּצְוָ֣ה
the-command *** to-keep very be-careful! but (5) the-Jordan on-other-side-of

וְאֶת־הַתּוֹרָה֒ אֲשֶׁ֨ר צִוָּ֣ה אֶתְכֶם֮ מֹשֶׁ֣ה עֶֽבֶד־ יְהוָה֒ לְאַהֲבָ֞ה אֶת־יְהוָ֤ה
Yahweh *** to-love Yahweh servant-of Moses you he-gave that the-law and

אֱלֹהֵיכֶם֙ וְלָלֶ֣כֶת בְּכָל־ דְּרָכָ֔יו וְלִשְׁמֹ֥ר מִצְוֺתָ֖יו
commands-of-him and-to-obey ways-of-him in-all-of and-to-walk God-of-you

וּלְדָבְקָה־ ב֑וֹ וּלְעָבְד֕וֹ בְּכָל־ לְבַבְכֶ֖ם
heart-of-you with-all-of and-to-serve-him to-him and-to-hold-fast

וּבְכָל־ נַפְשְׁכֶֽם׃ וַֽיְבָרְכֵ֖ם יְהוֹשֻׁ֑עַ וַֽיְשַׁלְּחֵ֔ם
and-he-sent-them Joshua then-he-blessed-them (6) soul-of-you and-with-all-of

וַיֵּלְכ֖וּ אֶל־ אָהֳלֵיהֶֽם׃ וְלַחֲצִ֣י ׀ שֵׁ֣בֶט הַֽמְנַשֶּׁ֗ה
the-Manasseh tribe-of and-to-half-of (7) homes-of-them to and-they-went

נָתַ֣ן מֹשֶׁה֮ בַּבָּשָׁן֒ וּלְחֶצְי֗וֹ נָתַ֤ן יְהוֹשֻׁ֙עַ֙ עִם־
with Joshua he-gave and-to-half-of-him in-the-Bashan Moses he-gave

their forefathers, and they
took possession of it and settled there. 44The LORD gave
them rest on every side, just as
he had sworn to their forefathers. Not one of their enemies withstood them; the
LORD handed all their enemies
over to them. 45Not one of all
the LORD's good promises to
the house of Israel failed;
every one was fulfilled.

Eastern Tribes Return Home

22 Then Joshua sum-
moned the Reubenites,
the Gadites and the half-tribe
of Manasseh 2and said to
them, "You have done all that
Moses the servant of the LORD
commanded, and you have
obeyed me in everything I
commanded. 3For a long time
now—to this very day—you
have not deserted your brothers but have carried out the
mission the LORD your God
gave you. 4Now that the LORD
your God has given your
brothers rest as he promised,
return to your homes in the
land that Moses the servant of
the LORD gave you on the other
side of the Jordan. 5But be very
careful to keep the command-
ment and the law that Moses
the servant of the LORD gave
you: to love the LORD your
God, to walk in all his ways, to
obey his commands, to hold
fast to him and to serve him
with all your heart and all your
soul."

6Then Joshua blessed them
and sent them away, and they
went to their homes. 7(To the
half-tribe of Manasseh Moses
had given land in Bashan, and
to the other half of the tribe

אֲחֵיהֶם מֵעֵבֶר הַיַּרְדֵּן יָמָּה וְגַם כִּי שִׁלְּחָם
he-sent-them when and-also on-west the-Jordan on-side-of brothers-of-them

יְהוֹשֻׁעַ אֶל־ אָהֳלֵיהֶם וַיְבָרְכֵם׃ וַיֹּאמֶר אֲלֵיהֶם לֵאמֹר
to-say to-them and-he-said (8) then-he-blessed-them homes-of-them to Joshua

בִּנְכָסִים רַבִּים שׁוּבוּ אֶל־ אָהֳלֵיכֶם וּבְמִקְנֶה רַב־ מְאֹד
very large and-with-herd homes-of-you to return! great-ones with-wealths

בְּכֶסֶף וּבְזָהָב וּבִנְחֹשֶׁת וּבְבַרְזֶל וּבִשְׂלָמוֹת
and-with-clothes and-with-iron and-with-bronze and-with-gold with-silver

הַרְבֵּה מְאֹד חִלְקוּ שְׁלַל־ אֹיְבֵיכֶם עִם־ אֲחֵיכֶם׃
brothers-of-you with being-enemies-of-you plunder-of divide! very to-be-great

וַיָּשֻׁבוּ וַיֵּלְכוּ בְּנֵי־ רְאוּבֵן וּבְנֵי־ גָד וַחֲצִי ׀
and-half-of Gad and-sons-of Reuben sons-of and-they-left so-they-returned (9)

שֵׁבֶט הַמְנַשֶּׁה מֵאֵת בְּנֵי יִשְׂרָאֵל מִשִּׁלֹה אֲשֶׁר בְּאֶרֶץ־ כְּנָעַן
Canaan in-land-of that at-Shiloh Israel sons-of from the-Manasseh tribe-of

לָלֶכֶת אֶל־אֶרֶץ הַגִּלְעָד אֶל־ אֶרֶץ אֲחֻזָּתָם אֲשֶׁר נֹאחֲזוּ־
they-acquired which possession-of-them land-of to the-Gilead land-of to to-go

בָהּ עַל־ פִּי יְהוָה בְּיַד־ מֹשֶׁה׃ וַיָּבֹאוּ אֶל־ גְּלִילוֹת
Geliloth-of to when-they-came (10) Moses by-hand-of Yahweh command-of by to-her

הַיַּרְדֵּן אֲשֶׁר בְּאֶרֶץ כְּנָעַן וַיִּבְנוּ בְנֵי־ רְאוּבֵן וּבְנֵי־
and-sons-of Reuben sons-of then-they-built Canaan in-land-of that the-Jordan

גָד וַחֲצִי שֵׁבֶט הַמְנַשֶּׁה שָׁם מִזְבֵּחַ עַל־ הַיַּרְדֵּן מִזְבֵּחַ
altar the-Jordan by altar there the-Manasseh tribe-of and-half-of Gad

גָּדוֹל לְמַרְאֶה׃ וַיִּשְׁמְעוּ בְנֵי־ יִשְׂרָאֵל לֵאמֹר הִנֵּה
see! to-say Israel sons-of when-they-heard (11) in-appearance imposing

בָנוּ בְּנֵי־ רְאוּבֵן וּבְנֵי־ גָד וַחֲצִי שֵׁבֶט הַמְנַשֶּׁה
the-Manasseh tribe-of and-half-of Gad and-sons-of Reuben sons-of they-built

אֶת־ הַמִּזְבֵּחַ אֶל־ מוּל אֶרֶץ כְּנַעַן אֶל־ גְּלִילוֹת הַיַּרְדֵּן אֶל־
on the-Jordan Geliloth-of at Canaan land-of border-of on the-altar ***

עֵבֶר בְּנֵי יִשְׂרָאֵל׃ וַיִּשְׁמְעוּ בְּנֵי יִשְׂרָאֵל וַיִּקָּהֲלוּ
then-they-gathered Israel sons-of when-they-heard (12) Israel sons-of side-of

כָּל־ עֲדַת בְּנֵי־ יִשְׂרָאֵל שִׁלֹה לַעֲלוֹת עֲלֵיהֶם לַצָּבָא׃
to-the-war against-them to-go Shiloh Israel sons-of assembly-of whole-of

וַיִּשְׁלְחוּ בְנֵי־ יִשְׂרָאֵל אֶל־בְּנֵי־ רְאוּבֵן וְאֶל־ בְּנֵי־ גָד וְאֶל־
and-to Gad sons-of and-to Reuben sons-of to Israel sons-of so-they-sent (13)

חֲצִי שֵׁבֶט־ מְנַשֶּׁה אֶל־ אֶרֶץ הַגִּלְעָד אֶת־ פִּינְחָס בֶּן־ אֶלְעָזָר
Eleazar son-of Phinehas *** the-Gilead land-of to Manasseh tribe-of half-of

הַכֹּהֵן׃ וַעֲשָׂרָה נְשִׂאִים עִמּוֹ נָשִׂיא אֶחָד נָשִׂיא אֶחָד לְבֵית
for-house-of one chief one chief with-him chief-men and-ten (14) the-priest

Joshua gave land on the west
side of the Jordan with their
brothers.) When Joshua sent
them home, he blessed them,
[8]saying, "Return to your
homes with your great
wealth—with large herds of
livestock, with silver, gold,
bronze and iron, and a great
quantity of clothing—and divide with your brothers the
plunder from your enemies."
[9]So the Reubenites, the Gadites and the half-tribe of
Manasseh left the Israelites at
Shiloh in Canaan to return to
Gilead, their own land, which
they had acquired in accordance with the command of the
LORD through Moses.
[10]When they came to Geliloth near the Jordan in the
land of Canaan, the Reubenites, the Gadites and the half-
tribe of Manasseh built an imposing altar there by the Jordan. [11]And when the Israelites
heard that they had built the
altar on the border of Canaan
at Geliloth near the Jordan on
the Israelite side, [12]the whole
assembly of Israel gathered at
Shiloh to go to war against
them.
[13]So the Israelites sent
Phinehas son of Eleazar, the
priest, to the land of Gilead—
to Reuben, Gad and the half-
tribe of Manasseh. [14]With him
they sent ten of the chief men,
one for each of the tribes of

°7 ק בעבר

אָב לְכֹל מַטּוֹת יִשְׂרָאֵל וְאִישׁ רָאשׁ בֵּית־ אֲבוֹתָם
fathers-of-them house-of head-of also-each Israel tribes-of for-each-of father

הֵמָּה לְאַלְפֵי יִשְׂרָאֵל׃ וַיָּבֹאוּ אֶל־ בְּנֵי־ רְאוּבֵן וְאֶל־
and-to Reuben sons-of to when-they-went (15) Israel among-clans-of they

בְּנֵי־ גָד וְאֶל־ חֲצִי שֵׁבֶט־ מְנַשֶּׁה אֶל־ אֶרֶץ הַגִּלְעָד
the-Gilead land-of to Manasseh tribe-of half-of and-to Gad sons-of

וַיְדַבְּרוּ אִתָּם לֵאמֹר׃ כֹּה אָמְרוּ כֹּל ׀ עֲדַת יְהוָה
Yahweh assembly-of whole-of they-say this (16) to-say to-them then-they-said

מָה־ הַמַּעַל הַזֶּה אֲשֶׁר מְעַלְתֶּם בֵּאלֹהֵי יִשְׂרָאֵל
Israel with-God-of-you you-broke-faith that the-this the-breech-of-faith what?

לָשׁוּב הַיּוֹם מֵאַחֲרֵי יְהוָה בִּבְנוֹתְכֶם לָכֶם מִזְבֵּחַ
altar for-you by-to-build-you Yahweh from-after the-day to-turn-away

לִמְרָדְכֶם הַיּוֹם בַּיהוָה׃ הַמְעַט־ לָנוּ אֶת־ עֲוֹן
sin-of *** for-us not-enough? (17) against-Yahweh the-day in-to-rebel-you

פְּעוֹר אֲשֶׁר לֹא־ הִטַּהַרְנוּ מִמֶּנּוּ עַד הַיּוֹם הַזֶּה וַיְהִי
though-he-fell the-this the-day to from-him to-be-cleansed-us not that Peor

הַנֶּגֶף בַּעֲדַת יְהוָה׃ וְאַתֶּם תָּשֻׁבוּ הַיּוֹם
the-day you-turn-away and-you (18) Yahweh on-community-of the-plague

מֵאַחֲרֵי יְהוָה וְהָיָה אַתֶּם תִּמְרְדוּ הַיּוֹם בַּיהוָה
against-Yahweh the-day you-rebel you and-he-will-be Yahweh from-after

וּמָחָר אֶל־ כָּל־ עֲדַת יִשְׂרָאֵל יִקְצֹף׃ וְאַךְ
and-now (19) he-will-be-angry Israel community-of whole-of with and-tomorrow

אִם־טְמֵאָה אֶרֶץ אֲחֻזַּתְכֶם עִבְרוּ לָכֶם אֶל־ אֶרֶץ אֲחֻזַּת
possession-of land-of to for-you come-over! possession-of-you land-of defiled if

יְהוָה אֲשֶׁר שָׁכַן־ שָׁם מִשְׁכַּן יְהוָה וְהֵאָחֲזוּ בְּתוֹכֵנוּ
in-among-us and-share! Yahweh tabernacle-of there he-stands where Yahweh

וּבַיהוָה אַל־ תִּמְרֹדוּ וְאֹתָנוּ אֶל־* תִּמְרֹדוּ בִּבְנֹתְכֶם
by-to-build-you you-rebel not or-against-us you-rebel not but-against-Yahweh

לָכֶם מִזְבֵּחַ מִבַּלְעֲדֵי מִזְבַּח יְהוָה אֱלֹהֵינוּ׃ הֲלוֹא ׀ עָכָן בֶּן־
son-of Achan not? (20) God-of-us Yahweh altar-of other-than altar for-you

זֶרַח מָעַל מַעַל בַּחֵרֶם וְעַל־ כָּל־
whole-of and-upon with-devoted-thing unfaithfulness he-acted-unfaithfully Zerah

עֲדַת יִשְׂרָאֵל הָיָה קָצֶף וְהוּא אִישׁ אֶחָד לֹא גָוַע בַּעֲוֹנוֹ׃
for-sin-of-him he-died not only man and-he wrath he-came Israel community-of

וַיַּעֲנוּ בְּנֵי־ רְאוּבֵן וּבְנֵי־ גָד וַחֲצִי שֵׁבֶט
tribe-of and-half-of Gad and-sons-of Reuben sons-of and-they-replied (21)

הַמְנַשֶּׁה וַיְדַבְּרוּ אֶת־ רָאשֵׁי אַלְפֵי יִשְׂרָאֵל׃ אֵל ׀ אֱלֹהִים ׀
God Mighty-One (22) Israel clans-of heads-of *** and-they-said the-Manasseh

Israel, each the head of a
family division among the Israelite clans.
15When they went to Gil-
ead—to Reuben, Gad and the
half-tribe of Manasseh—they
said to them: 16"The whole assembly of the LORD says: 'How
could you break faith with the
God of Israel like this? How
could you turn away from the
LORD and build yourselves an
altar in rebellion against him
now? 17Was not the sin of Peor
enough for us? Up to this very
day we have not cleansed ourselves from that sin, even
though a plague fell on the
community of the LORD! 18And
are you now turning away
from the LORD?
" 'If you rebel against the
LORD today, tomorrow he will
be angry with the whole community of Israel. 19If the land
you possess is defiled, come
over to the LORD's land, where
the LORD's tabernacle stands,
and share the land with us.
But do not rebel against the
LORD or against us by building
an altar for yourselves, other
than the altar of the LORD our
God. 20When Achan son of
Zerah acted unfaithfully re-
garding the devoted things,[d]
did not wrath come upon the
whole community of Israel?
He was not the only one who
died for his sin.' "
21Then Reuben, Gad and the
half-tribe of Manasseh replied
to the heads of the clans of Israel: 22"The Mighty One, God,

[d]20 The Hebrew term refers to the irrevocable giving over of things or persons to the LORD, often by totally destroying them.

*19 Most mss have *pathah* under the *aleph* (אַל).

יְהוָה אֵל ׀ אֱלֹהִים ׀ יְהוָה הוּא יֹדֵעַ וְיִשְׂרָאֵל הוּא יֵדָע אִם־
if let-him-know he and-Israel knowing he Yahweh God Mighty-One Yahweh

בְּמֶרֶד וְאִם־ בְּמַעַל בַּיהוָה אַל־ תּוֹשִׁיעֵנוּ הַיּוֹם הַזֶּה׃
the-this the-day you-spare-us not to-Yahweh in-disobedience or-if in-rebellion

(23) לִבְנוֹת לָנוּ מִזְבֵּחַ לָשׁוּב מֵאַחֲרֵי יְהוָה וְאִם־לְהַעֲלוֹת
to-offer or-if Yahweh from-after to-turn-away altar for-us to-build (23)

עָלָיו עוֹלָה וּמִנְחָה וְאִם־ לַעֲשׂוֹת עָלָיו
on-him to-sacrifice or-if and-grain-offering burnt-offering on-him

זִבְחֵי שְׁלָמִים יְהוָה הוּא יְבַקֵּשׁ׃ (24) וְאִם־
but-indeed (24) may-he-call-account himself Yahweh fellowships offerings-of

לֹא מִדְּאָגָה מִדָּבָר עָשִׂינוּ אֶת־ זֹאת לֵאמֹר מָחָר יֹאמְרוּ
they-might-say some-day to-say this *** we-did for-reason for-fear no

בְנֵיכֶם לְבָנֵינוּ לֵאמֹר מַה־ לָּכֶם וְלַיהוָה
and-with-Yahweh with-you what? to-say to-descendants-of-us descendants-of-you

אֱלֹהֵי יִשְׂרָאֵל׃ (25) וּגְבוּל נָתַן־ יְהוָה בֵּינֵנוּ וּבֵינֵיכֶם
and-between-you between-us Yahweh he-made now-boundary (25) Israel God-of

בְּנֵי־ רְאוּבֵן וּבְנֵי־ גָד אֶת־ הַיַּרְדֵּן אֵין־ לָכֶם חֵלֶק בַּיהוָה
in-Yahweh share for-you not the-Jordan *** Gad and-sons-of Reuben sons-of

וְהִשְׁבִּיתוּ בְנֵיכֶם אֶת־ בָּנֵינוּ לְבִלְתִּי יְרֹא
to-fear not descendants-of-us *** descendants-of-you so-they-might-make-stop

אֶת־ יְהוָה׃ (26) וַנֹּאמֶר נַעֲשֶׂה־ נָּא לָנוּ לִבְנוֹת אֶת־הַמִּזְבֵּחַ
the-altar *** to-build for-us now! let-us-get-ready so-we-said (26) Yahweh ***

לֹא לְעוֹלָה וְלֹא לְזָבַח׃ (27) כִּי עֵד הוּא
he witness on-contrary (27) for-sacrifice and-not for-burnt-offering not

בֵּינֵינוּ וּבֵינֵיכֶם וּבֵין דֹּרוֹתֵינוּ אַחֲרֵינוּ לַעֲבֹד
to-worship after-us generations-of-us and-between and-between-you between-us

אֶת־ עֲבֹדַת יְהוָה לְפָנָיו בְּעֹלוֹתֵינוּ
*** worship-of Yahweh before-him with-burnt-offerings-of-us

וּבִזְבָחֵינוּ וּבִשְׁלָמֵינוּ וְלֹא־
then-not and-with-fellowship-offerings-of-us and-with-sacrifices-of-us

יֹאמְרוּ בְנֵיכֶם מָחָר לְבָנֵינוּ אֵין־ לָכֶם
for-you not to-descendants-of-us future descendants-of-you they-will-say

חֵלֶק בַּיהוָה׃ (28) וַנֹּאמֶר וְהָיָה כִּי־ יֹאמְרוּ אֵלֵינוּ וְאֶל־
or-to to-us they-say if now-he-will-be and-we-said (28) in-Yahweh share

דֹּרֹתֵינוּ מָחָר וְאָמַרְנוּ רְאוּ אֶת־ תַּבְנִית מִזְבַּח
altar-of replica-of *** look! then-we-will-answer future descendants-of-us

יְהוָה אֲשֶׁר־ עָשׂוּ אֲבוֹתֵינוּ לֹא לְעוֹלָה וְלֹא
and-not for-burnt-offering not fathers-of-us they-built which Yahweh

the LORD! The Mighty One,
God, the LORD! He knows! And
let Israel know! If this has
been in rebellion or disobedi-
ence to the LORD, do not spare
us this day. 23If we have built
our own altar to turn away
from the LORD and to offer
burnt offerings and grain
offerings, or to sacrifice fellowship offerings[c] on it, may
the LORD himself call us to account.

24"No! We did it for fear that
some day your descendants
might say to ours, 'What do
you have to do with the LORD,
the God of Israel? 25The LORD
has made the Jordan a boundary between us and you—you
Reubenites and Gadites! You
have no share in the LORD.' So
your descendants might cause
ours to stop fearing the LORD.

26"That is why we said, 'Let
us get ready and build an altar—but not for burnt
offerings or sacrifices.' 27On
the contrary, it is to be a witness between us and you and
the generations that follow,
that we will worship the LORD
at his sanctuary with our
burnt offerings, sacrifices and
fellowship offerings. Then in
the future your descendants
will not be able to say to ours,
'You have no share in the
LORD.'

28"And we said, 'If they ever
say this to us, or to our descendants, we will answer:
Look at the replica of the
LORD's altar, which our fathers
built, not for burnt offerings

[c]23 Traditionally *peace offerings;* also in verse 27

לְזֶבַח כִּי־ עֵד הוּא בֵּינֵינוּ וּבֵינֵיכֶם׃ חָלִילָה
far-be-it! (29) and-between-you between-us he witness but for-sacrifice

לָּנוּ מִמֶּנּוּ לִמְרֹד בַּיהוָה וְלָשׁוּב הַיּוֹם מֵאַחֲרֵי
from-after the-day and-to-turn-away against-Yahweh to-rebel from-him from-us

יְהוָה לִבְנוֹת מִזְבֵּחַ לְעֹלָה לְמִנְחָה וּלְזָבַח
and-for-sacrifice for-grain-offering for-burnt-offering altar to-build Yahweh

מִלְּבַד מִזְבַּח יְהוָה אֱלֹהֵינוּ אֲשֶׁר לִפְנֵי מִשְׁכָּנוֹ׃
tabernacle-of-him before that God-of-us Yahweh altar-of other-than

וַיִּשְׁמַע פִּינְחָס הַכֹּהֵן וּנְשִׂיאֵי הָעֵדָה
the-community and-leaders-of the-priest Phinehas when-he-heard (30)

וְרָאשֵׁי אַלְפֵי יִשְׂרָאֵל אֲשֶׁר אִתּוֹ אֶת־ הַדְּבָרִים אֲשֶׁר דִּבְּרוּ
they-said that the-things *** with-him who Israel clans-of even-heads-of

בְּנֵי־ רְאוּבֵן וּבְנֵי־ גָד וּבְנֵי מְנַשֶּׁה וַיִּיטַב
then-he-was-pleasant Manasseh and-sons-of Gad and-sons-of Reuben sons-of

בְּעֵינֵיהֶם׃ וַיֹּאמֶר פִּינְחָס בֶּן־ אֶלְעָזָר הַכֹּהֵן אֶל־
to the-priest Eleazar son-of Phinehas and-he-said (31) in-eyes-of-them

בְּנֵי־ רְאוּבֵן וְאֶל־ בְּנֵי־ גָד וְאֶל־ בְּנֵי מְנַשֶּׁה הַיּוֹם ׀ יָדַעְנוּ
we-know the-day Manasseh sons-of and-to Gad sons-of and-to Reuben sons-of

כִּי־ בְתוֹכֵנוּ יְהוָה אֲשֶׁר לֹא־ מְעַלְתֶּם בַּיהוָה
toward-Yahweh you-acted-unfaithfully not because Yahweh in-among-us that

הַמַּעַל הַזֶּה אָז הִצַּלְתֶּם אֶת־ בְּנֵי יִשְׂרָאֵל מִיַּד
from-hand-of Israel sons-of *** you-rescued now the-this the-unfaithfulness

יְהוָה׃ וַיָּשָׁב פִּינְחָס בֶּן־ אֶלְעָזָר הַכֹּהֵן ׀ וְהַנְּשִׂיאִים
and-the-leaders the-priest Eleazar son-of Phinehas then-he-returned (32) Yahweh

מֵאֵת בְּנֵי־ רְאוּבֵן וּמֵאֵת בְּנֵי־ גָד מֵאֶרֶץ הַגִּלְעָד אֶל־ אֶרֶץ
land-of to the-Gilead in-land-of Gad sons-of and-from Reuben sons-of from

כְּנַעַן אֶל־ בְּנֵי יִשְׂרָאֵל וַיָּשִׁבוּ אוֹתָם דָּבָר׃ וַיִּיטַב
and-he-was-good (33) report them and-they-brought Israel sons-of to Canaan

הַדָּבָר בְּעֵינֵי בְּנֵי יִשְׂרָאֵל וַיְבָרְכוּ אֱלֹהִים בְּנֵי יִשְׂרָאֵל
Israel sons-of God and-they-praised Israel sons-of in-eyes-of the-report

וְלֹא אָמְרוּ לַעֲלוֹת עֲלֵיהֶם לַצָּבָא לְשַׁחֵת אֶת־ הָאָרֶץ
the-country *** to-devastate to-the-war against-them to-go they-talked and-not

אֲשֶׁר בְּנֵי־ רְאוּבֵן וּבְנֵי־ גָד יֹשְׁבִים בָּהּ׃ וַיִּקְרְאוּ
and-they-named (34) in-her ones-living Gad and-sons-of Reuben sons-of where

בְּנֵי־ רְאוּבֵן וּבְנֵי־ גָד לַמִּזְבֵּחַ כִּי עֵד הוּא בֵּינֹתֵינוּ כִּי
that between-us he witness that to-the-altar Gad and-sons-of Reuben sons-of

יְהוָה הָאֱלֹהִים׃ וַיְהִי מִיָּמִים רַבִּים אַחֲרֵי אֲשֶׁר־ הֵנִיחַ
he-gave-rest when after many after-days and-he-was (23:1) the-God Yahweh

and sacrifices, but as a witness
between us and you.'
[29]"Far be it from us to rebel
against the LORD and turn
away from him today by
building an altar for burnt
offerings, grain offerings and
sacrifices, other than the altar
of the LORD our God that
stands before his tabernacle."
[30]When Phinehas the priest
and the leaders of the community—the heads of the
clans of the Israelites—heard
what Reuben, Gad and
Manasseh had to say, they
were pleased. [31]And Phinehas
son of Eleazar, the priest, said
to Reuben, Gad and Manas-
seh, "Today we know that the
LORD is with us, because you
have not acted unfaithfully
toward the LORD in this matter. Now you have rescued the
Israelites from the LORD's
hand."
[32]Then Phinehas son of Eleazar, the priest, and the leaders
returned to Canaan from their
meeting with the Reubenites
and Gadites in Gilead and reported to the Israelites. [33]They
were glad to hear the report
and praised God. And they
talked no more about going to
war against them to devastate
the country where the Reubenites and the Gadites lived.
[34]And the Reubenites and
the Gadites gave the altar this
name: A WITNESS BETWEEN US
THAT THE LORD IS GOD.

Joshua's Farewell to the Leaders

23 After a long time had
passed and the LORD
had given Israel rest from all

יְהוָה לְיִשְׂרָאֵל מִכָּל־ אֹיְבֵיהֶם מִסָּבִיב וִיהוֹשֻׁעַ

then-Joshua from-around being-enemies-of-them from-all-of to-Israel Yahweh

זָקֵן בָּא בַּיָּמִים׃ וַיִּקְרָא יְהוֹשֻׁעַ לְכָל־

to-all-of Joshua and-he-summoned (2) in-the-days he-was-advanced he-was-old

יִשְׂרָאֵל לִזְקֵנָיו וּלְרָאשָׁיו וּלְשֹׁפְטָיו

and-to-ones-judging-him and-to-leaders-of-him to-elders-of-him Israel

וּלְשֹׁטְרָיו וַיֹּאמֶר אֲלֵהֶם אֲנִי זָקַנְתִּי בָּאתִי

I-am-advanced I-am-old I to-them and-he-said and-to-being-officials-of-him

בַּיָּמִים׃ וְאַתֶּם רְאִיתֶם אֵת כָּל־ אֲשֶׁר עָשָׂה יְהוָה אֱלֹהֵיכֶם

God-of-you Yahweh he-did that everything *** you-saw and-you (3) in-the-days

לְכָל־ הַגּוֹיִם הָאֵלֶּה מִפְּנֵיכֶם כִּי יְהוָה אֱלֹהֵיכֶם

God-of-you Yahweh indeed for-sakes-of-you the-these the-nations to-all-of

הוּא הַנִּלְחָם לָכֶם׃ רְאוּ הִפַּלְתִּי לָכֶם אֶת־ הַגּוֹיִם

the-nations *** for-you I-allotted remember! (4) for-you the-one-fighting he

הַנִּשְׁאָרִים הָאֵלֶּה בְּנַחֲלָה לְשִׁבְטֵיכֶם מִן־ הַיַּרְדֵּן

the-Jordan between for-tribes-of-you as-inheritance the-these the-ones-remaining

וְכָל־ הַגּוֹיִם אֲשֶׁר הִכְרַתִּי וְהַיָּם הַגָּדוֹל מְבוֹא הַשָּׁמֶשׁ׃

the-sun set-of the-Great and-the-Sea I-conquered that the-nations even-all-of

וַיהוָה אֱלֹהֵיכֶם הוּא יֶהְדֳּפֵם מִפְּנֵיכֶם

from-before-you he-will-drive-out-them he God-of-you now-Yahweh (5)

וְהוֹרִישׁ אֹתָם מִלִּפְנֵיכֶם וִירִשְׁתֶּם אֶת־ אַרְצָם

land-of-them *** and-you-will-possess from-before-you them and-he-will-push-out

כַּאֲשֶׁר דִּבֶּר יְהוָה אֱלֹהֵיכֶם לָכֶם׃ וַחֲזַקְתֶּם מְאֹד

very but-you-be-strong (6) to-you God-of-you Yahweh he-promised just-as

לִשְׁמֹר וְלַעֲשׂוֹת אֶת כָּל־ הַכָּתוּב בְּסֵפֶר תּוֹרַת

Law-of in-Book-of the-being-written all-of *** and-to-obey to-be-careful

מֹשֶׁה לְבִלְתִּי סוּר־ מִמֶּנּוּ יָמִין וּשְׂמֹאול׃ לְבִלְתִּי־ בוֹא בַּגּוֹיִם

with-the-nations to-associate not (7) or-left right from-him to-turn not Moses

הָאֵלֶּה הַנִּשְׁאָרִים הָאֵלֶּה אִתְּכֶם וּבְשֵׁם אֱלֹהֵיהֶם

gods-of-them and-with-name-of among-you the-these the-ones-remaining the-these

לֹא־ תַזְכִּירוּ וְלֹא תַשְׁבִּיעוּ וְלֹא תַעַבְדוּם וְלֹא תִשְׁתַּחֲווּ

you-bow-down and-not you-serve-them and-not you-swear and-not you-invoke not

לָהֶם׃ כִּי אִם־ בַּיהוָה אֱלֹהֵיכֶם תִּדְבָּקוּ כַּאֲשֶׁר עֲשִׂיתֶם

you-did just-as you-hold-fast God-of-you to-Yahweh only but (8) to-them

עַד הַיּוֹם הַזֶּה׃ וַיּוֹרֶשׁ יְהוָה מִפְּנֵיכֶם גּוֹיִם

nations from-before-you Yahweh now-he-drove-out (9) the-this the-day until

גְּדֹלִים וַעֲצוּמִים וְאַתֶּם לֹא־ עָמַד אִישׁ בִּפְנֵיכֶם עַד

to against-you anyone he-withstood not and-you and-powerful-ones great-ones

their enemies around them,
Joshua, by then old and well
advanced in years, 2summoned all Israel—their elders,
leaders, judges and
officials—and said to them: "I
am old and well advanced in
years. 3You yourselves have
seen everything the LORD your
God has done to all these nations for your sake; it was the
LORD your God who fought for
you. 4Remember how I have
allotted as an inheritance for
your tribes all the land of the
nations that remain—the nations I conquered—between
the Jordan and the Great Sea[f]
in the west. 5The LORD your
God himself will drive them
out of your way. He will push
them out before you, and you
will take possession of their
land, as the LORD your God
promised you.
6"Be very strong; be careful
to obey all that is written in
the Book of the Law of Moses,
without turning aside to the
right or to the left. 7Do not associate with these nations that
remain among you; do not invoke the names of their gods
or swear by them. You must
not serve them or bow down
to them. 8But you are to hold
fast to the LORD your God, as
you have until now.
9"The LORD has driven out
before you great and powerful
nations; to this day no one has
been able to withstand you.

[f]4 That is, the Mediterranean

הַיּוֹם הַזֶּה׃ אִישׁ־אֶחָד מִכֶּם יִרְדָּף־ אָלֶף כִּי יְהוָה אֱלֹהֵיכֶם
God-of-you Yahweh for thousand he-routs from-you one man (10) the-this the-day

הוּא הַנִּלְחָם לָכֶם כַּאֲשֶׁר דִּבֶּר לָכֶם׃ וְנִשְׁמַרְתֶּם
so-you-be-careful (11) to-you he-promised just-as for-you the-one-fighting he

מְאֹד לְנַפְשֹׁתֵיכֶם לְאַהֲבָה אֶת־ יְהוָה אֱלֹהֵיכֶם׃ כִּי אִם־ שׁוֹב
to-turn if but (12) God-of-you Yahweh *** to-love with-selves-of-you very

תָּשׁוּבוּ וּדְבַקְתֶּם בְּיֶתֶר הַגּוֹיִם הָאֵלֶּה
the-these the-nations with-survivor-of and-you-ally-yourselves you-turn-away

הַנִּשְׁאָרִים הָאֵלֶּה אִתְּכֶם וְהִתְחַתַּנְתֶּם בָּהֶם
with-them and-you-intermarry among-you the-these the-ones-remaining

וּבָאתֶם בָּהֶם וְהֵם בָּכֶם׃ יָדוֹעַ תֵּדְעוּ
you-be-sure to-be-sure (13) with-you and-they with-them and-you-associate

כִּי לֹא יוֹסִיף יְהוָה אֱלֹהֵיכֶם לְהוֹרִישׁ אֶת־ הַגּוֹיִם
the-nations *** to-drive-out God-of-you Yahweh he-will-continue not that

הָאֵלֶּה מִלִּפְנֵיכֶם וְהָיוּ לָכֶם לְפַח וּלְמוֹקֵשׁ
and-as-trap as-snare for-you and-they-will-become from-before-you the-these

וּלְשֹׁטֵט בְּצִדֵּיכֶם וְלִצְנִנִים בְּעֵינֵיכֶם עַד־ אֲבָדְכֶם
you-perish until in-eyes-of-you and-as-thorns on-backs-of-you and-as-whip

מֵעַל הָאֲדָמָה הַטּוֹבָה הַזֹּאת אֲשֶׁר נָתַן לָכֶם יְהוָה אֱלֹהֵיכֶם׃
God-of-you Yahweh to-you he-gave which the-this the-good the-land from-on

וְהִנֵּה אָנֹכִי הוֹלֵךְ הַיּוֹם בְּדֶרֶךְ כָּל־ הָאָרֶץ וִידַעְתֶּם
and-you-know the-earth all-of on-way-of the-day going I now-see! (14)

בְּכָל־ לְבַבְכֶם וּבְכָל־ נַפְשְׁכֶם כִּי לֹא־ נָפַל
he-failed not that soul-of-you and-with-all-of heart-of-you with-all-of

דָּבָר אֶחָד מִכֹּל הַדְּבָרִים הַטּוֹבִים אֲשֶׁר דִּבֶּר יְהוָה
Yahweh he-gave that the-good-ones the-promises of-all-of one promise

אֱלֹהֵיכֶם עֲלֵיכֶם הַכֹּל בָּאוּ לָכֶם לֹא־ נָפַל מִמֶּנּוּ
of-him he-failed not for-you they-were-fulfilled the-all to-you God-of-you

דָּבָר אֶחָד׃ וְהָיָה כַּאֲשֶׁר־ בָּא עֲלֵיכֶם כָּל־
every-of for-you he-came-true just-as but-he-will-be (15) one promise

הַדָּבָר הַטּוֹב אֲשֶׁר דִּבֶּר יְהוָה אֱלֹהֵיכֶם אֲלֵיכֶם כֵּן יָבִיא
he-will-bring so to-you God-of-you Yahweh he-gave that the-good the-promise

יְהוָה עֲלֵיכֶם אֵת כָּל־ הַדָּבָר הָרָע עַד־ הַשְׁמִידוֹ אוֹתְכֶם
you to-destroy-him until the-evil the-thing every-of *** on-you Yahweh

מֵעַל הָאֲדָמָה הַטּוֹבָה הַזֹּאת אֲשֶׁר נָתַן לָכֶם יְהוָה אֱלֹהֵיכֶם׃
God-of-you Yahweh to-you he-gave that the-this the-good the-land from-on

בְּעָבְרְכֶם אֶת־ בְּרִית יְהוָה אֱלֹהֵיכֶם אֲשֶׁר צִוָּה
he-commanded which God-of-you Yahweh covenant-of *** if-to-violate-you (16)

10One of you routs a thousand,
because the LORD your God
fights for you, just as he promised. 11So be very careful to
love the LORD your God.
12"But if you turn away and
ally yourselves with the survivors of these nations that remain among you and if you
intermarry with them and associate with them, 13then you
may be sure that the LORD
your God will no longer drive
out these nations before you.
Instead, they will become
snares and traps for you,
whips on your backs and
thorns in your eyes, until you
perish from this good land,
which the LORD your God has
given you.
14"Now I am about to go the
way of all the earth. You know
with all your heart and soul
that not one of all the good
promises the LORD your God
gave you has failed. Every
promise has been fulfilled; not
one has failed. 15But just as
every good promise of the
LORD your God has come true,
so the LORD will bring on you
all the evil he has threatened,
until he has destroyed you
from this good land he has
given you. 16If you violate the
covenant of the LORD your
God, which he commanded

אֶתְכֶם֮ וַהֲלַכְתֶּ֗ם וַעֲבַדְתֶּם֙ אֱלֹהִ֣ים אֲחֵרִ֔ים וְהִשְׁתַּחֲוִיתֶ֖ם לָהֶ֑ם

to-them and-you-bow-down other-ones gods and-you-serve and-you-go you

וְחָרָ֤ה אַף־ יְהוָה֙ בָּכֶ֔ם וַאֲבַדְתֶּ֣ם מְהֵרָ֔ה

quickly and-you-will-perish against-you Yahweh anger-of then-he-will-burn

מֵעַל֙ הָאָ֣רֶץ הַטּוֹבָ֔ה אֲשֶׁ֖ר נָתַ֥ן לָכֶֽם׃ וַיֶּאֱסֹ֧ף*

then-he-assembled (24:1) to-you he-gave that the-good the-land from-on

יְהוֹשֻׁ֛עַ אֶֽת־ כָּל־ שִׁבְטֵ֥י יִשְׂרָאֵ֖ל שְׁכֶ֑מָה וַיִּקְרָא֩ לְזִקְנֵ֨י

to-elders-of and-he-summoned at-Shechem Israel tribes-of all-of *** Joshua

יִשְׂרָאֵ֜ל וּלְרָאשָׁ֗יו וּלְשֹֽׁפְטָיו֙ וּלְשֹׁ֣טְרָ֔יו

and-to-being-officials-of-him and-to-ones-judging-him and-to-leaders-of-him Israel

וַיִּֽתְיַצְּב֖וּ לִפְנֵ֥י הָאֱלֹהִֽים׃ וַיֹּ֨אמֶר יְהוֹשֻׁ֜עַ אֶל־ כָּל־

all-of to Joshua and-he-said (2) the-God before and-they-presented-themselves

הָעָ֗ם כֹּֽה־ אָמַ֣ר יְהוָה֮ אֱלֹהֵ֣י יִשְׂרָאֵל֒ בְּעֵ֣בֶר הַנָּהָ֗ר יָשְׁב֤וּ

they-lived the-River at-beyond Israel God-of Yahweh he-says this the-people

אֲבֽוֹתֵיכֶם֙ מֵֽעוֹלָ֔ם תֶּ֛רַח אֲבִ֥י אַבְרָהָ֖ם וַאֲבִ֣י נָח֑וֹר

Nahor and-father-of Abraham father-of Terah at-long-ago fathers-of-you

וַיַּעַבְד֖וּ אֱלֹהִ֥ים אֲחֵרִֽים׃ וָ֠אֶקַּח אֶת־ אֲבִיכֶ֤ם אֶת־

*** father-of-you *** but-I-took (3) other-ones gods and-they-worshiped

אַבְרָהָם֙ מֵעֵ֣בֶר הַנָּהָ֔ר וָאוֹלֵ֥ךְ אוֹת֖וֹ בְּכָל־ אֶ֣רֶץ כְּנָ֑עַן

Canaan land-of through-all-of him and-I-led the-River from-beyond Abraham

וָאַרְבֶּ֙ אֶת־ זַרְע֔וֹ וָאֶתֶּן־ ל֖וֹ אֶת־ יִצְחָֽק׃

Isaac *** to-him and-I-gave descendant-of-him *** and-I-made-many

וָאֶתֵּ֣ן לְיִצְחָ֔ק אֶֽת־יַעֲקֹ֖ב וְאֶת־עֵשָׂ֑ו וָאֶתֵּ֨ן לְעֵשָׂ֜ו אֶת־ הַ֤ר

mountain-of *** to-Esau and-I-gave Esau and Jacob *** to-Isaac and-I-gave (4)

שֵׂעִיר֙ לָרֶ֣שֶׁת אוֹת֔וֹ וְיַעֲקֹ֥ב וּבָנָ֖יו יָרְד֥וּ מִצְרָֽיִם׃

Egypt they-went-down and-sons-of-him but-Jacob him to-possess Seir

וָאֶשְׁלַ֞ח אֶת־ מֹשֶׁ֤ה וְאֶת־ אַהֲרֹן֙ וָאֶגֹּ֣ף אֶת־מִצְרַ֔יִם כַּאֲשֶׁ֥ר עָשִׂ֖יתִי

I-did by-what Egypt *** then-I-afflicted Aaron and Moses *** then-I-sent (5)

בְּקִרְבּ֑וֹ וְאַחַ֖ר הוֹצֵ֥אתִי אֶתְכֶֽם׃ וָאוֹצִ֤יא אֶת־

*** when-I-brought-out (6) you I-brought-out and-afterward in-among-him

אֲבֽוֹתֵיכֶם֙ מִמִּצְרַ֔יִם וַתָּבֹ֖אוּ הַיָּ֑מָּה וַיִּרְדְּפ֨וּ

and-they-pursued to-the-sea then-you-came from-Egypt fathers-of-you

מִצְרַ֜יִם אַחֲרֵ֧י אֲבוֹתֵיכֶ֛ם בְּרֶ֥כֶב וּבְפָרָשִׁ֖ים יַם־ סֽוּף׃

Reed Sea-of and-with-horsemen with-chariot fathers-of-you after Egyptians

וַיִּצְעֲק֣וּ אֶל־ יְהוָ֗ה וַיָּ֨שֶׂם מַאֲפֵ֜ל בֵּינֵיכֶ֣ם ׀ וּבֵ֣ין

and-between between-you darkness and-he-put Yahweh to but-they-cried-out (7)

הַמִּצְרִ֗ים וַיָּבֵ֨א עָלָ֤יו אֶת־ הַיָּם֙ וַיְכַסֵּ֔הוּ

and-he-covered-him the-sea *** over-him and-he-brought the-Egyptians

you, and go and serve other
gods and bow down to them,
the LORD's anger will burn
against you, and you will
quickly perish from the good
land he has given you."

The Covenant Renewed at Shechem

24 Then Joshua assembled
all the tribes of Israel at
Shechem. He summoned the
elders, leaders, judges and
officials of Israel, and they
presented themselves before
God.
2Joshua said to all the people,
"This is what the LORD, the
God of Israel, says: 'Long ago
your forefathers, including
Terah the father of Abraham
and Nahor, lived beyond the
River[g] and worshiped other
gods. 3But I took your father
Abraham from the land
beyond the River and led him
throughout Canaan and gave
him many descendants. I gave
him Isaac, 4and to Isaac I gave
Jacob and Esau. I assigned the
hill country of Seir to Esau, but
Jacob and his sons went down
to Egypt.
5" 'Then I sent Moses and
Aaron, and I afflicted the
Egyptians by what I did there,
and I brought you out. 6When
I brought your fathers out
of Egypt, you came to the sea,
and the Egyptians pursued
them with chariots and horsemen[h] as far as the Red Sea.[i]
7But they cried to the LORD for
help, and he put darkness between you and the Egyptians;
he brought the sea over them
and covered them. You saw

[g]2 That is, the Euphrates; also in verses 3, 14 and 15
[h]6 Or *charioteers*
[i]6 Hebrew *Yam Suph*; that is, Sea of Reeds

*1 Most mss have **hateph segol** under the *aleph* (וַיֶּאֱ).

°3 ק וארבה

וַתִּרְאֶינָה עֵינֵיכֶם אֵת אֲשֶׁר־עָשִׂיתִי בְּמִצְרַיִם וַתֵּשְׁבוּ
then-you-lived to-Egyptians I-did what *** eyes-of-you and-they-saw

בַּמִּדְבָּר יָמִים רַבִּים׃ וָאָבִאָה אֶתְכֶם אֶל־אֶרֶץ הָאֱמֹרִי
the-Amorite land-of to you and-I-brought (8) many days in-the-desert

הַיּוֹשֵׁב בְּעֵבֶר הַיַּרְדֵּן וַיִּלָּחֲמוּ אִתְּכֶם וָאֶתֵּן
but-I-gave against-you and-they-fought the-Jordan on-east-of the-one-living

אוֹתָם בְּיֶדְכֶם וַתִּירְשׁוּ אֶת־אַרְצָם וָאַשְׁמִידֵם
and-I-destroyed-them land-of-them *** and-you-possessed into-hand-of-you them

מִפְּנֵיכֶם׃ וַיָּקָם בָּלָק בֶּן־צִפּוֹר מֶלֶךְ מוֹאָב
Moab king-of Zippor son-of Balak when-he-prepared (9) from-before-you

וַיִּלָּחֶם בְּיִשְׂרָאֵל וַיִּשְׁלַח וַיִּקְרָא לְבִלְעָם בֶּן־
son-of for-Balaam and-he-summoned then-he-sent against-Israel and-he-fought

בְּעוֹר לְקַלֵּל אֶתְכֶם׃ וְלֹא אָבִיתִי לִשְׁמֹעַ לְבִלְעָם וַיְבָרֶךְ
so-he-blessed to-Balaam to-listen I-would but-not (10) you to-curse Beor

בָּרוֹךְ אֶתְכֶם וָאַצִּל אֶתְכֶם מִיָּדוֹ׃ וַתַּעַבְרוּ אֶת־
*** then-you-crossed (11) from-hand-of-him you and-I-delivered you to-bless

הַיַּרְדֵּן וַתָּבֹאוּ אֶל־יְרִיחוֹ וַיִּלָּחֲמוּ בָכֶם בַּעֲלֵי־
citizens-of against-you and-they-fought Jericho to and-you-came the-Jordan

יְרִיחוֹ הָאֱמֹרִי וְהַפְּרִזִּי וְהַכְּנַעֲנִי וְהַחִתִּי
and-the-Hittite and-the-Canaanite and-the-Perizzite the-Amorite Jericho

וְהַגִּרְגָּשִׁי הַחִוִּי וְהַיְבוּסִי וָאֶתֵּן אוֹתָם בְּיֶדְכֶם׃
into-hand-of-you them but-I-gave and-the-Jebusite the-Hivite and-the-Girgashite

וָאֶשְׁלַח לִפְנֵיכֶם אֶת־הַצִּרְעָה וַתְּגָרֶשׁ אוֹתָם
them and-she-drove-out the-hornet *** ahead-of-you and-I-sent (12)

מִפְּנֵיכֶם שְׁנֵי מַלְכֵי הָאֱמֹרִי לֹא בְחַרְבְּךָ וְלֹא
and-not with-sword-of-you not the-Amorite kings-of two-of from-before-you

בְקַשְׁתֶּךָ׃ וָאֶתֵּן לָכֶם אֶרֶץ׀ אֲשֶׁר לֹא־יָגַעְתָּ בָּהּ
on-her you-toiled not which land to-you so-I-gave (13) with-bow-of-you

וְעָרִים אֲשֶׁר לֹא־בְנִיתֶם וַתֵּשְׁבוּ בָּהֶם כְּרָמִים וְזֵיתִים
and-olive-groves vineyards in-them and-you-live you-built not which and-cities

אֲשֶׁר לֹא־נְטַעְתֶּם אַתֶּם אֹכְלִים׃ וְעַתָּה יְראוּ אֶת־יְהוָה וְעִבְדוּ
and-serve! Yahweh *** fear! and-now (14) ones-eating you you-planted not that

אֹתוֹ בְּתָמִים וּבֶאֱמֶת וְהָסִירוּ אֶת־אֱלֹהִים אֲשֶׁר
that gods *** and-throw-away! and-in-faithfulness in-wholeness him

עָבְדוּ אֲבוֹתֵיכֶם בְּעֵבֶר הַנָּהָר וּבְמִצְרַיִם וְעִבְדוּ
and-serve! and-in-Egypt the-River at-beyond fathers-of-you they-worshiped

אֶת־יְהוָה׃ וְאִם רַע בְּעֵינֵיכֶם לַעֲבֹד אֶת־יְהוָה בַּחֲרוּ
choose! Yahweh *** to-serve in-eyes-of-you undesirable but-if (15) Yahweh ***

with your own eyes what I did
to the Egyptians. Then you
lived in the desert for a long
time.
[8]" 'I brought you to the land
of the Amorites who lived east
of the Jordan. They fought
against you, but I gave them
into your hands. I destroyed
them from before you, and
you took possession of their
land. [9]When Balak son of Zippor, the king of Moab, prepared to fight against Israel, he
sent for Balaam son of Beor to
put a curse on you. [10]But I
would not listen to Balaam, so
he blessed you again and
again, and I delivered you out
of his hand.
[11]" 'Then you crossed the
Jordan and came to Jericho.
The citizens of Jericho fought
against you, as did also the
Amorites, Perizzites, Canaanites, Hittites, Girgashites, Hivites and Jebusites, but I gave
them into your hands. [12]I sent
the hornet ahead of you,
which drove them out before
you—also the two Amorite
kings. You did not do it with
your own sword and bow. [13]So
I gave you a land on which
you did not toil and cities you
did not build; and you live in
them and eat from vineyards
and olive groves that you did
not plant.'
[14]"Now fear the LORD and
serve him with all faithfulness. Throw away the gods
your forefathers worshiped
beyond the River and in
Egypt, and serve the LORD.
[15]But if serving the LORD seems
undesirable to you, then

8° ק ואביא

לָכֶם הַיּוֹם אֶת־ מִי תַעֲבֹדוּן אִם אֶת־אֱלֹהִים אֲשֶׁר־ עָבְדוּ
they-served that gods *** whether you-will-serve whom *** the-day for-you

אֲבוֹתֵיכֶם אֲשֶׁר °בְּעֵבֶר הַנָּהָר וְאִם אֶת־ אֱלֹהֵי הָאֱמֹרִי
the-Amorite gods-of *** or-whether the-River at-beyond when fathers-of-you

אֲשֶׁר אַתֶּם יֹשְׁבִים בְּאַרְצָם וְאָנֹכִי וּבֵיתִי נַעֲבֹד
we-will-serve and-household-of-me but-I in-land-of-them ones-living you whom

אֶת־ יְהוָה׃ וַיַּעַן הָעָם וַיֹּאמֶר חָלִילָה לָּנוּ
from-us far-be-it! and-he-said the-people then-he-answered (16) Yahweh ***

מֵעֲזֹב אֶת־ יְהוָה לַעֲבֹד אֱלֹהִים אֲחֵרִים׃ כִּי יְהוָה
Yahweh for (17) other-ones gods to-serve Yahweh *** from-to-forsake

אֱלֹהֵינוּ הוּא הַמַּעֲלֶה אֹתָנוּ וְאֶת־ אֲבוֹתֵינוּ מֵאֶרֶץ מִצְרַיִם
Egypt from-land-of fathers-of-us and us the-one-bringing-up he God-of-us

מִבֵּית עֲבָדִים וַאֲשֶׁר עָשָׂה לְעֵינֵינוּ אֶת־ הָאֹתוֹת
the-signs *** before-eyes-of-us he-performed and-who slaveries from-house-of

הַגְּדֹלוֹת הָאֵלֶּה וַיִּשְׁמְרֵנוּ בְּכָל־ הַדֶּרֶךְ אֲשֶׁר
that the-journey on-entire-of and-he-protected-us the-those the-great-ones

הָלַכְנוּ בָהּ וּבְכֹל הָעַמִּים אֲשֶׁר עָבַרְנוּ
we-traveled which the-nations and-among-all-of on-her we-traveled

בְּקִרְבָּם׃ וַיְגָרֶשׁ יְהוָה אֶת־ כָּל־ הָעַמִּים
the-nations all-of *** Yahweh and-he-drove-out (18) through-midst-of-them

וְאֶת־ הָאֱמֹרִי יֹשֵׁב הָאָרֶץ מִפָּנֵינוּ גַּם־ אֲנַחְנוּ נַעֲבֹד אֶת־
*** we-will-serve we also from-before-us the-land living-of the-Amorite and

יְהוָה כִּי־ הוּא אֱלֹהֵינוּ׃ וַיֹּאמֶר יְהוֹשֻׁעַ אֶל־ הָעָם לֹא
not the-people to Joshua then-he-said (19) God-of-us he for Yahweh

תוּכְלוּ לַעֲבֹד אֶת־ יְהוָה כִּי־אֱלֹהִים קְדֹשִׁים הוּא אֵל־קַנּוֹא הוּא לֹא־
not he jealous God he holy-ones God for Yahweh *** to-serve you-are-able

יִשָּׂא לְפִשְׁעֲכֶם וּלְחַטֹּאותֵיכֶם׃ כִּי תַעַזְבוּ
you-forsake if (20) and-to-sins-of-you to-rebellion-of-you he-will-forgive

אֶת־ יְהוָה וַעֲבַדְתֶּם אֱלֹהֵי נֵכָר וְשָׁב
then-he-will-turn foreign gods-of and-you-serve Yahweh ***

וְהֵרַע לָכֶם וְכִלָּה אֶתְכֶם אַחֲרֵי אֲשֶׁר־
when after you and-he-will-make-end on-you and-he-will-bring-disaster

הֵיטִיב לָכֶם׃ וַיֹּאמֶר הָעָם אֶל־יְהוֹשֻׁעַ לֹא כִּי אֶת־ יְהוָה
Yahweh *** but no Joshua to the-people but-he-said (21) to-you he-was-good

נַעֲבֹד׃ וַיֹּאמֶר יְהוֹשֻׁעַ אֶל־ הָעָם עֵדִים אַתֶּם
you witnesses the-people to Joshua then-he-said (22) we-will-serve

בָּכֶם כִּי־ אַתֶּם בְּחַרְתֶּם לָכֶם אֶת־ יְהוָה לַעֲבֹד אוֹתוֹ וַיֹּאמְרוּ
and-they-said him to-serve Yahweh *** for-you you-chose you that against-you

choose for yourselves this day whom you will serve, whether the gods your forefathers served beyond the River, or the gods of the Amorites, in whose land you are living. But as for me and my household, we will serve the LORD."

[16]Then the people answered, "Far be it from us to forsake the LORD to serve other gods! [17]It was the LORD our God himself who brought us and our forefathers up out of Egypt, from that land of slavery, and performed those great signs before our eyes. He protected us on our entire journey and among all the nations through which we traveled. [18]And the LORD drove out before us all the nations, including the Amorites, who lived in the land. We too will serve the LORD, because he is our God."

[19]Joshua said to the people, "You are not able to serve the LORD. He is a holy God; he is a jealous God. He will not forgive your rebellion and your sins. [20]If you forsake the LORD and serve foreign gods, he will turn and bring disaster on you and make an end of you, after he has been good to you."

[21]But the people said to Joshua, "No! We will serve the LORD."

[22]Then Joshua said, "You are witnesses against yourselves that you have chosen to serve the LORD."

°15 ק מעבר

עֵדִים׃ (23) וְעַתָּה הָסִירוּ אֶת־אֱלֹהֵי הַנֵּכָר אֲשֶׁר בְּקִרְבְּכֶם
in-among-you that the-foreign gods-of *** throw-away! then-now (23) witnesses

וְהַטּוּ אֶת־לְבַבְכֶם אֶל־יְהוָה אֱלֹהֵי יִשְׂרָאֵל׃ (24) וַיֹּאמְרוּ
and-they-said (24) Israel God-of Yahweh to heart-of-you *** and-yield!

הָעָם אֶל־יְהוֹשֻׁעַ אֶת־יְהוָה אֱלֹהֵינוּ נַעֲבֹד וּבְקוֹלוֹ
and-to-voice-of-him we-will-serve God-of-us Yahweh *** Joshua to the-people

נִשְׁמָע׃ (25) וַיִּכְרֹת יְהוֹשֻׁעַ בְּרִית לָעָם בַּיּוֹם
on-the-day for-the-people covenant Joshua and-he-made (25) we-will-obey

הַהוּא וַיָּשֶׂם לוֹ חֹק וּמִשְׁפָּט בִּשְׁכֶם׃ (26) וַיִּכְתֹּב
and-he-recorded (26) at-Shechem and-law decree for-him and-he-drew-up the-that

יְהוֹשֻׁעַ אֶת־הַדְּבָרִים הָאֵלֶּה בְּסֵפֶר תּוֹרַת אֱלֹהִים וַיִּקַּח אֶבֶן
stone then-he-took God Law-of in-Book-of the-these the-things *** Joshua

גְּדוֹלָה וַיְקִימֶהָ שָּׁם תַּחַת הָאַלָּה אֲשֶׁר בְּמִקְדַּשׁ יְהוָה׃
Yahweh near-holy-place-of that the-oak under there and-he-set-up-her large

(27) וַיֹּאמֶר יְהוֹשֻׁעַ אֶל־כָּל־הָעָם הִנֵּה הָאֶבֶן הַזֹּאת
the-this the-stone see! the-people all-of to Joshua and-he-said (27)

תִּהְיֶה־בָּנוּ לְעֵדָה כִּי־הִיא שָׁמְעָה אֵת כָּל־אִמְרֵי
words-of all-of *** she-heard she for as-witness against-us she-will-be

יְהוָה אֲשֶׁר דִּבֶּר עִמָּנוּ וְהָיְתָה בָכֶם לְעֵדָה פֶּן־
if as-witness against-you and-she-will-be to-us he-said that Yahweh

תְּכַחֲשׁוּן בֵּאלֹהֵיכֶם׃ (28) וַיְשַׁלַּח יְהוֹשֻׁעַ אֶת־הָעָם
the-people *** Joshua then-he-sent-away (28) to-God-of-you you-are-untrue

אִישׁ לְנַחֲלָתוֹ׃ (29) וַיְהִי אַחֲרֵי הַדְּבָרִים הָאֵלֶּה
the-these the-things after and-he-was (29) to-inheritance-of-him each

וַיָּמָת יְהוֹשֻׁעַ בִּן־נוּן עֶבֶד יְהוָה בֶּן־מֵאָה וָעֶשֶׂר
and-ten hundred son-of Yahweh servant-of Nun son-of Joshua that-he-died

שָׁנִים׃ (30) וַיִּקְבְּרוּ אֹתוֹ בִּגְבוּל נַחֲלָתוֹ בְּתִמְנַת־
at-Timnath inheritance-of-him in-land-of him and-they-buried (30) years

סֶרַח אֲשֶׁר בְּהַר־אֶפְרָיִם מִצְּפוֹן לְהַר־גָּעַשׁ׃
Gaash of-Mount-of to-north Ephraim in-hill-country-of that Serah

(31) וַיַּעֲבֹד יִשְׂרָאֵל אֶת־יְהוָה כֹּל יְמֵי יְהוֹשֻׁעַ וְכֹל ׀
and-all-of Joshua days-of all-of Yahweh *** Israel and-he-served (31)

יְמֵי הַזְּקֵנִים אֲשֶׁר הֶאֱרִיכוּ יָמִים אַחֲרֵי יְהוֹשֻׁעַ וַאֲשֶׁר
and-who Joshua after days they-outlived who the-elders days-of

יָדְעוּ אֵת כָּל־מַעֲשֵׂה יְהוָה אֲשֶׁר עָשָׂה לְיִשְׂרָאֵל׃ (32) וְאֶת־
and (32) for-Israel he-did that Yahweh work-of all-of *** they-experienced

עַצְמוֹת יוֹסֵף אֲשֶׁר־הֶעֱלוּ בְנֵי־יִשְׂרָאֵל ׀ מִמִּצְרַיִם קָבְרוּ
they-buried from-Egypt Israel sons-of they-brought-up which Joseph bones-of

"Yes, we are witnesses,"
they replied.
23"Now then," said Joshua,
"throw away the foreign gods
that are among you and yield
your hearts to the LORD, the
God of Israel."
24And the people said to
Joshua, "We will serve the
LORD our God and obey him."
25On that day Joshua made a
covenant for the people, and
there at Shechem he drew up
for them decrees and laws.
26And Joshua recorded these
things in the Book of the Law
of God. Then he took a large
stone and set it up there under
the oak near the holy place of
the LORD.
27"See!" he said to all the
people. "This stone will be a
witness against us. It has
heard all the words the LORD
has said to us. It will be a witness against you if you are un-
true to your God."

Buried in the Promised Land

28Then Joshua sent the
people away, each to his own
inheritance.
29After these things, Joshua
son of Nun, the servant of the
LORD, died at the age of a hundred and ten. 30And they buried him in the land of his inheritance, at Timnath Serah[j]
in the hill country of Ephraim,
north of Mount Gaash.
31Israel served the LORD
throughout the lifetime of
Joshua and of the elders who
outlived him and who had
experienced everything the
LORD had done for Israel.
32And Joseph's bones, which
the Israelites had brought up
from Egypt, were buried at

j30 Also known as *Timnath Heres* (see Judges 2:9)

חֲמוֹר	בְּנֵי־	מֵאֵת	יַעֲקֹב	קָנָה	אֲשֶׁר	הַשָּׂדֶה	בְּחֶלְקַת	בִשְׁכֶם
Hamor	sons-of	from	Jacob	he-bought	that	the-land	in-tract-of	at-Shechem

יוֹסֵף	לִבְנֵי־	וַיִּהְיוּ	קְשִׂיטָה	בְּמֵאָה	שְׁכֶם	אֲבִי־
Joseph	for-sons-of	and-they-became	kesitah	for-hundred	Shechem	father-of

אֹתוֹ	וַיִּקְבְּרוּ	מֵת	אַהֲרֹן	בֶּן־	וְאֶלְעָזָר		לְנַחֲלָה׃
him	and-they-buried	he-died	Aaron	son-of	and-Eleazar	(33)	as-inheritance

לוֹ	נִתַּן־	אֲשֶׁר	בְּנוֹ	פִּינְחָס	בְּגִבְעַת
to-him	he-was-allotted	which	son-of-him	Phinehas	at-Gibeah-of

אֶפְרָיִם׃	בְּהַר
Ephraim	in-hill-country-of

Shechem in the tract of land that Jacob bought for a hundred pieces of silver[k] from the sons of Hamor, the father of Shechem. This became the inheritance of Joseph's descendants.

33 And Eleazar son of Aaron died and was buried at Gibeah, which had been allotted to his son Phinehas in the hill country of Ephraim.

k32 Hebrew *hundred kesitahs;* a kesitah was a unit of money of unknown weight and value.

וַיְהִי אַחֲרֵי מוֹת יְהוֹשֻׁעַ וַיִּשְׁאֲלוּ בְּנֵי יִשְׂרָאֵל
Israel sons-of then-they-asked Joshua death-of after and-he-was (1:1)

בַּיהוָה לֵאמֹר מִי יַעֲלֶה־ לָּנוּ אֶל־ הַכְּנַעֲנִי בַתְּחִלָּה
as-the-first the-Canaanite against for-us will-he-go-up who? to-say of-Yahweh

לְהִלָּחֶם בּוֹ׃ וַיֹּאמֶר יְהוָה יְהוּדָה יַעֲלֶה הִנֵּה נָתַתִּי
I-gave see! he-must-go Judah Yahweh and-he-answered (2) against-him to-fight

אֶת־ הָאָרֶץ בְּיָדוֹ׃ וַיֹּאמֶר יְהוּדָה לְשִׁמְעוֹן אָחִיו
brother-of-him to-Simeon Judah then-he-said (3) into-hand-of-him the-land ***

עֲלֵה אִתִּי בְגוֹרָלִי וְנִלָּחֲמָה בַּכְּנַעֲנִי
against-the-Canaanite and-we-will-fight into-territory-of-me with-me come-up!

וְהָלַכְתִּי גַם־ אֲנִי אִתְּךָ בְּגוֹרָלֶךָ וַיֵּלֶךְ אִתּוֹ
with-him so-he-went into-territory-of-you with-you I also then-I-will-go

שִׁמְעוֹן׃ וַיַּעַל יְהוּדָה וַיִּתֵּן יְהוָה אֶת־ הַכְּנַעֲנִי
the-Canaanite *** Yahweh then-he-gave Judah when-he-attached (4) Simeon

וְהַפְּרִזִּי בְּיָדָם וַיַּכּוּם בְּבֶזֶק עֲשֶׂרֶת
ten at-Bezek and-they-struck-down-them into-hand-of-them and-the-Perizzite

אֲלָפִים אִישׁ׃ וַיִּמְצְאוּ אֶת־ אֲדֹנִי בֶזֶק בְּבֶזֶק וַיִּלָּחֲמוּ
and-they-fought at-Bezek Bezek Adoni *** and-they-found (5) man thousands

בּוֹ וַיַּכּוּ אֶת־ הַכְּנַעֲנִי וְאֶת־ הַפְּרִזִּי׃
the-Perizzite and the-Canaanite *** and-they-routed against-him

וַיָּנָס אֲדֹנִי בֶזֶק וַיִּרְדְּפוּ אַחֲרָיו וַיֹּאחֲזוּ אֹתוֹ
him and-they-caught after-him but-they-chased Bezek Adoni and-he-fled (6)

וַיְקַצְּצוּ אֶת־ בְּהֹנוֹת* יָדָיו וְרַגְלָיו׃
and-feet-of-him hands-of-him *thumbs/big-toes-of *** and-they-cut-off

וַיֹּאמֶר אֲדֹנִי־ בֶזֶק שִׁבְעִים ׀ מְלָכִים בְּהֹנוֹת* יְדֵיהֶם
hands-of-them *thumbs/big-toes-of kings seventy Bezek Adoni then-he-said (7)

וְרַגְלֵיהֶם מְקֻצָּצִים הָיוּ מְלַקְּטִים תַּחַת
under ones-picking-up-scraps they-are ones-being-cut-off and-feet-of-them

שֻׁלְחָנִי כַּאֲשֶׁר עָשִׂיתִי כֵּן שִׁלַּם־ לִי אֱלֹהִים וַיְבִיאֻהוּ
and-they-brought-him God to-me he-paid-back same I-did just-as table-of-me

יְרוּשָׁלִַם וַיָּמָת שָׁם׃ וַיִּלָּחֲמוּ בְנֵי־ יְהוּדָה
Judah men-of and-they-attacked (8) there and-he-died Jerusalem

בִּירוּשָׁלִַם וַיִּלְכְּדוּ אוֹתָהּ וַיַּכּוּהָ לְפִי־ חָרֶב וְאֶת־
and sword to-edge-of and-they-put-her her and-they-took against-Jerusalem

הָעִיר שִׁלְּחוּ בָאֵשׁ׃ וְאַחַר יָרְדוּ בְּנֵי יְהוּדָה
Judah men-of they-went-down then-after (9) on-fire they-set the-city

לְהִלָּחֵם בַּכְּנַעֲנִי יוֹשֵׁב הָהָר וְהַנֶּגֶב
and-the-Negev the-hill-country living-of against-the-Canaanite to-fight

Israel Fights the Remaining Canaanites

1 After the death of Joshua, the Israelites asked the
LORD, "Who will be the first to
go up and fight for us against
the Canaanites?"
2The LORD answered, "Judah
is to go; I have given the land
into their hands."
3Then the men of Judah said
to the Simeonites their brothers, "Come up with us into the
territory allotted to us, to fight
against the Canaanites. We in
turn will go with you into
yours." So the Simeonites
went with them.
4When Judah attacked, the
LORD gave the Canaanites and
Perizzites into their hands and
they struck down ten thousand men at Bezek.
5It was
there that they found Adoni-Bezek and fought against him,
putting to rout the Canaanites
and Perizzites.
6Adoni-Bezek
fled, but they chased him and
caught him, and cut off his
thumbs and big toes.
7Then Adoni-Bezek said,
"Seventy kings with their
thumbs and big toes cut off
have picked up scraps under
my table. Now God has paid
me back for what I did to
them." They brought him to
Jerusalem, and he died there.
8The men of Judah attacked
Jerusalem also and took it.
They put the city to the sword
and set it on fire.
9After that, the men of Judah
went down to fight against the
Canaanites living in the hill
country, the Negev and the

*6,7 This Hebrew word means both *thumb* and *big toe* as it is in construct to both *hands* and *feet*.

וְהַשְּׁפֵלָה׃ וַיֵּלֶךְ יְהוּדָה אֶל־ הַכְּנַעֲנִי
the-Canaanite against Judah so-he-advanced (10) and-the-foothill

הַיּוֹשֵׁב בְּחֶבְרוֹן וְשֵׁם־ חֶבְרוֹן לְפָנִים קִרְיַת אַרְבַּע
Arba Kiriath formerly Hebron now-name-of in-Hebron the-one-living

וַיַּכּוּ אֶת־ שֵׁשַׁי וְאֶת־ אֲחִימַן וְאֶת־ תַּלְמָי׃ וַיֵּלֶךְ
and-he-advanced (11) Talmai and Ahiman and Sheshai *** and-they-defeated

מִשָּׁם אֶל־ יוֹשְׁבֵי דְּבִיר וְשֵׁם־ דְּבִיר לְפָנִים קִרְיַת־
Kiriath formerly Debir now-name-of Debir ones-living-of against from-there

סֵפֶר׃ וַיֹּאמֶר כָּלֵב אֲשֶׁר־ יַכֶּה אֶת־ קִרְיַת־ סֵפֶר
Sepher Kiriath *** he-attacks whoever Caleb and-he-said (12) Sepher

וּלְכָדָהּ וְנָתַתִּי לוֹ אֶת־ עַכְסָה בִתִּי לְאִשָּׁה׃
as-wife daughter-of-me Acsah *** to-him then-I-will-give and-he-captures-her

וַיִּלְכְּדָהּ עָתְנִיאֵל בֶּן־ קְנַז אֲחִי כָלֵב הַקָּטֹן
the-younger Caleb brother-of Kenaz son-of Othniel and-he-took-her (13)

מִמֶּנּוּ וַיִּתֶּן־ לוֹ אֶת־ עַכְסָה בִתּוֹ לְאִשָּׁה׃ וַיְהִי
and-he-was (14) as-wife daughter-of-him Acsah *** to-him so-he-gave than-him

בְּבוֹאָהּ וַתְּסִיתֵהוּ לִשְׁאוֹל מֵאֵת־ אָבִיהָ הַשָּׂדֶה
the-field father-of-her from to-ask then-she-urged-him when-to-come-her

וַתִּצְנַח מֵעַל הַחֲמוֹר וַיֹּאמֶר־ לָהּ כָּלֵב מַה־ לָּךְ׃
for-you what? Caleb to-her then-he-asked the-donkey from-on when-she-got-off

וַתֹּאמֶר לוֹ הָבָה־ לִּי בְרָכָה כִּי אֶרֶץ הַנֶּגֶב
the-Negev land-of since favor for-me do! to-him and-she-replied (15)

נְתַתָּנִי וְנָתַתָּה לִי גֻּלֹּת מָיִם וַיִּתֶּן־ לָהּ כָּלֵב
Caleb to-her then-he-gave waters springs-of to-me then-you-give you-gave-me

אֵת גֻּלֹּת עִלִּית וְאֵת גֻּלֹּת תַּחְתִּית׃ וּבְנֵי קֵינִי
Kenite and-descendants-of (16) lower springs-of and upper springs-of ***

חֹתֵן מֹשֶׁה עָלוּ מֵעִיר הַתְּמָרִים אֶת־ בְּנֵי יְהוּדָה
Judah men-of with the-Palms from-City-of they-went-up Moses father-in-law-of

מִדְבַּר יְהוּדָה אֲשֶׁר בְּנֶגֶב עֲרָד וַיֵּלֶךְ וַיֵּשֶׁב אֶת־
among and-he-lived and-he-went Arad in-Negev-of that Judah Desert-of

הָעָם׃ וַיֵּלֶךְ יְהוּדָה אֶת־ שִׁמְעוֹן אָחִיו וַיַּכּוּ
and-they-attacked brother-of-him Simeon with Judah then-he-went (17) the-people

אֶת־ הַכְּנַעֲנִי יוֹשֵׁב צְפַת וַיַּחֲרִימוּ אוֹתָהּ וַיִּקְרָא אֶת־
*** and-he-called her and-they-destoyed Zephath living-of the-Canaanite ***

שֵׁם־ הָעִיר חָרְמָה׃ וַיִּלְכֹּד יְהוּדָה אֶת־עַזָּה וְאֶת־ גְּבוּלָהּ
territory-of-her and Gaza *** Judah and-he-took (18) Hormah the-city name-of

וְאֶת־ אַשְׁקְלוֹן וְאֶת־ גְּבוּלָהּ וְאֶת־ עֶקְרוֹן וְאֶת־ גְּבוּלָהּ׃
territory-of-her and Ekron and territory-of-her and Ashkelon and

western foothills. 10They advanced against the Canaanites
living in Hebron (formerly
called Kiriath Arba) and defeated Sheshai, Ahiman and
Talmai.
11From there they advanced
against the people living in
Debir (formerly called Kiriath
Sepher). 12And Caleb said, "I
will give my daughter Acsah
in marriage to the man who
attacks and captures Kiriath
Sepher." 13Othniel son of
Kenaz, Caleb's younger brother, took it; so Caleb gave his
daughter Acsah to him in marriage. 14One day when she
came to Othniel, she urged
him[a] to ask her father for a
field. When she got off her
donkey, Caleb asked her,
"What can I do for you?"
15She replied, "Do me a
special favor. Since you have
given me land in the Negev,
give me also springs of water."
Then Caleb gave her the upper
and lower springs.
16The descendants of Moses'
father-in-law, the Kenite,
went up from the City of
Palms[b] with the men of Judah
to live among the people of the
Desert of Judah in the Negev
near Arad.
17Then the men of Judah
went with the Simeonites
their brothers and attacked the
Canaanites living in Zephath,
and they totally destroyed[c] the
city. Therefore it was called
Hormah.[d] 18The men of Judah
also took[e] Gaza, Ashkelon and
Ekron—each city with its territory.

[a]14 Hebrew; Septuagint and Vulgate *Othniel, he urged her*
[b]16 That is, Jericho
[c]17 The Hebrew term refers to the irrevocable giving over of things or persons to the LORD, often by totally destroying them.
[d]17 *Hormah* means *destruction.*
[e]18 Hebrew; Septuagint *Judah did not take*

וַיְהִ֤י יְהוָה֙ אֶת־ יְהוּדָ֔ה וַיֹּ֖רֶשׁ אֶת־ הָהָ֑ר כִּ֣י
but the-hill-country *** and-he-possessed Judah with Yahweh and-he-was (19)

לֹ֤א לְהוֹרִישׁ֙ אֶת־ יֹשְׁבֵ֣י הָעֵ֔מֶק כִּי־ רֶ֥כֶב בַּרְזֶ֖ל לָהֶֽם׃
to-them iron chariot-of for the-plain ones-living-of *** to-drive-out not

וַיִּתְּנ֤וּ לְכָלֵב֙ אֶת־חֶבְר֔וֹן כַּאֲשֶׁ֖ר דִּבֶּ֣ר מֹשֶׁ֑ה וַיּ֣וֹרֶשׁ
and-he-drove Moses he-promised just-as Hebron *** to-Caleb and-they-gave (20)

מִשָּׁ֔ם אֶת־ שְׁלֹשָׁ֖ה בְּנֵ֥י הָעֲנָֽק׃ וְאֶת־ הַיְבוּסִי֙ יֹשֵׁ֣ב
living-of the-Jebusite but (21) the-Anak sons-of three *** from-there

יְרוּשָׁלִַ֔ם לֹ֥א הוֹרִ֖ישׁוּ בְּנֵ֣י בִנְיָמִ֑ן וַיֵּ֨שֶׁב הַיְבוּסִ֜י אֶת־
with the-Jebusite and-he-lives Benjamin sons-of they-dislodged not Jerusalem

בְּנֵ֤י בִנְיָמִן֙ בִּיר֣וּשָׁלִַ֔ם עַ֖ד הַיּ֥וֹם הַזֶּֽה׃ וַיַּעֲל֛וּ
now-they-attacked (22) the-this the-day to in-Jerusalem Benjamin sons-of

בֵית־ יוֹסֵ֛ף גַּם־ הֵ֖ם בֵּֽית־ אֵ֑ל וַיהוָ֖ה עִמָּֽם׃
with-them and-Yahweh El Beth they indeed Joseph house-of

וַיָּתִ֥ירוּ בֵית־ יוֹסֵ֖ף בְּבֵֽית־ אֵ֑ל וְשֵֽׁם־ הָעִ֥יר
the-city now-name-of El to-Beth Joseph house-of and-they-sent-spies (23)

לְפָנִ֖ים לֽוּז׃ וַיִּרְאוּ֙ הַשֹּׁ֣מְרִ֔ים אִ֖ישׁ יוֹצֵ֣א מִן־ הָעִ֑יר
the-city from coming-out man the-ones-spying and-they-saw (24) Luz formerly

וַיֹּ֣אמְרוּ ל֗וֹ הַרְאֵ֤נוּ נָא֙ אֶת־ מְב֣וֹא הָעִ֔יר וְעָשִׂ֥ינוּ
and-we-will-treat the-city entrance-of *** now! show-us! to-him and-they-said

עִמְּךָ֖ חָֽסֶד׃ וַיַּרְאֵם֙ אֶת־ מְב֣וֹא הָעִ֔יר וַיַּכּ֥וּ
and-they-put the-city entrance-of *** so-he-showed-them (25) well with-you

אֶת־ הָעִ֖יר לְפִי־ חָ֑רֶב וְאֶת־ הָאִ֥ישׁ וְאֶת־ כָּל־ מִשְׁפַּחְתּ֖וֹ
family-of-him whole-of and the-man but sword to-edge-of the-city ***

שִׁלֵּֽחוּ׃ וַיֵּ֣לֶךְ הָאִ֔ישׁ אֶ֖רֶץ הַחִתִּ֑ים וַיִּ֣בֶן עִ֔יר
city and-he-built the-Hittites land-of the-man then-he-went (26) they-spared

וַיִּקְרָ֤א שְׁמָהּ֙ ל֔וּז ה֣וּא שְׁמָ֔הּ עַ֖ד הַיּ֥וֹם הַזֶּֽה׃
the-this the-day to name-of-her which Luz name-of-her and-he-called

וְלֹא־ הוֹרִ֣ישׁ מְנַשֶּׁ֗ה אֶת־ בֵּית־ שְׁאָ֣ן וְאֶת־ בְּנוֹתֶ֘יהָ֮ וְאֶת־
or settlements-of-her and Shan Beth *** Manasseh he-drove-out but-not (27)

תַּעְנַ֣ךְ וְאֶת־ בְּנֹתֶ֒יהָ֒ וְאֶת־ יוֹשְׁבֵ֨י ד֜וֹר וְאֶת־ בְּנוֹתֶ֗יהָ
settlements-of-her and Dor ones-living-of or settlements-of-her and Taanach

וְאֶת־ יוֹשְׁבֵ֤י יִבְלְעָם֙ וְאֶת־ בְּנֹתֶ֔יהָ וְאֶת־ יוֹשְׁבֵ֥י מְגִדּ֖וֹ
Meggido ones-living-of or settlements-of-her and Ibleam ones-living-of or

וְאֶת־ בְּנוֹתֶ֑יהָ וַיּ֙וֹאֶל֙ הַֽכְּנַעֲנִ֔י לָשֶׁ֖בֶת בָּאָ֥רֶץ
in-the-land to-live the-Canaanite for-he-was-determined settlements-of-her and

הַזֹּֽאת׃ וַֽיְהִי֙ כִּֽי־ חָזַ֣ק יִשְׂרָאֵ֔ל וַיָּ֥שֶׂם אֶת־
*** then-he-pressed Israel he-became-strong when and-he-was (28) the-that

[19]The LORD was with the
men of Judah. They took
possession of the hill country,
but they were unable to drive
the people from the plains, because they had iron chariots.
[20]As Moses had promised, Hebron was given to Caleb, who
drove from it the three sons of
Anak. [21]The Benjamites, however, failed to dislodge the Jebusites, who were living in
Jerusalem; to this day the Jebusites live there with the Benjamites.
[22]Now the house of Joseph
attacked Bethel, and the LORD
was with them. [23]When they
sent men to spy out Bethel
(formerly called Luz), [24]the
spies saw a man coming out of
the city and they said to him,
"Show us how to get into the
city and we will see that you
are treated well." [25]So he
showed them, and they put
the city to the sword but
spared the man and his whole
family. [26]He then went to the
land of the Hittites, where he
built a city and called it Luz,
which is its name to this day.
[27]But Manasseh did not
drive out the people of Beth
Shan or Taanach or Dor or
Ibleam or Megiddo and their
surrounding settlements, for
the Canaanites were determined to live in that land.
[28]When Israel became strong,
they pressed the Canaanites

°27 ק יֹשְׁבֵי

הַכְּנַעֲנִי לָמַס וְהוֹרֵישׁ לֹא הוֹרִישׁוֹ׃
he-drove-out-him not but-to-drive-out into-forced-labor the-Canaanite

וְאֶפְרַיִם לֹא הוֹרִישׁ אֶת־ הַכְּנַעֲנִי הַיּוֹשֵׁב בְּגָזֶר
in-Gezer the-one-living the-Canaanite *** he-drove-out not and-Ephraim (29)

וַיֵּשֶׁב הַכְּנַעֲנִי בְּקִרְבּוֹ בְּגָזֶר׃ זְבוּלֻן לֹא
not Zebulun (30) in-Gezer in-among-him the-Canaanite but-he-lives

הוֹרִישׁ אֶת־ יוֹשְׁבֵי קִטְרוֹן וְאֶת־ יוֹשְׁבֵי נַהֲלֹל וַיֵּשֶׁב
but-he-remained Nahalol ones-living-of or Kitron ones-living-of *** he-drove-out

הַכְּנַעֲנִי בְּקִרְבּוֹ וַיִּהְיוּ לָמַס׃ אָשֵׁר לֹא
not Asher (31) at-forced-labor but-they-became in-among-him the-Canaanite

הוֹרִישׁ אֶת־ יֹשְׁבֵי עַכּוֹ וְאֶת־ יוֹשְׁבֵי צִידוֹן וְאֶת־אַחְלָב וְאֶת־
or Ahlab or Sidon ones-living-of or Acco ones-living-of *** he-drove-out

אַכְזִיב וְאֶת־ חֶלְבָּה וְאֶת־אֲפִיק וְאֶת־רְחֹב׃ וַיֵּשֶׁב הָאָשֵׁרִי בְּקֶרֶב
in-among the-Asherite so-he-lived (32) Rehob or Aphek or Helbah or Aczib

הַכְּנַעֲנִי יֹשְׁבֵי הָאָרֶץ כִּי לֹא הוֹרִישׁוֹ׃
he-drove-out-him not for the-land ones-inhabiting-of the-Canaanite

נַפְתָּלִי לֹא־ הוֹרִישׁ אֶת־ יֹשְׁבֵי בֵית־ שֶׁמֶשׁ וְאֶת־ יֹשְׁבֵי
ones-living-of or Shemesh Beth ones-living-of *** he-drove-out not Naphtali (33)

בֵית־ עֲנָת וַיֵּשֶׁב בְּקֶרֶב הַכְּנַעֲנִי יֹשְׁבֵי הָאָרֶץ
the-land ones-inhabiting-of the-Canaanite in-among but-he-lived Anath Beth

וְיֹשְׁבֵי בֵית־ שֶׁמֶשׁ וּבֵית עֲנָת הָיוּ לָהֶם
for-them they-became Anath and-Beth Shemesh Beth and-ones-living-of

לָמַס׃ וַיִּלְחֲצוּ הָאֱמֹרִי אֶת־ בְּנֵי־ דָן
Dan sons-of *** the-Amorite and-they-confined (34) at-forced-labor

הָהָרָה כִּי־ לֹא נְתָנוֹ לָרֶדֶת לָעֵמֶק׃
into-the-plain to-come-down he-allowed-him not and to-the-hill-country

וַיּוֹאֶל הָאֱמֹרִי לָשֶׁבֶת בְּהַר־ חֶרֶס
Heres in-Mount-of to-hold-out the-Amorite and-he-was-determined (35)

בְּאַיָּלוֹן וּבְשַׁעַלְבִים וַתִּכְבַּד יַד בֵּית־ יוֹסֵף
Joseph house-of power-of when-she-increased and-in-Shaalbim in-Aijalon

וַיִּהְיוּ לָמַס׃ וּגְבוּל הָאֱמֹרִי מִמַּעֲלֵה
from-Pass-of the-Amorite now-boundary-of (36) at-forced-labor then-they-became

עַקְרַבִּים מֵהַסֶּלַע וָמָעְלָה׃ וַיַּעַל מַלְאַךְ־ יְהוָה מִן־
from Yahweh angel-of and-he-went-up (2:1) and-beyond to-the-Sela Scorpions

הַגִּלְגָּל אֶל־ הַבֹּכִים וַיֹּאמֶר אַעֲלֶה אֶתְכֶם מִמִּצְרַיִם וָאָבִיא
and-I-led from-Egypt you I-brought-up and-he-said the-Bokim to the-Gilgal

אֶתְכֶם אֶל־הָאָרֶץ אֲשֶׁר נִשְׁבַּעְתִּי לַאֲבֹתֵיכֶם וָאֹמַר לֹא־ אָפֵר
I-will-break not and-I-said to-fathers-of-you I-swore that the-land into you

into forced labor but never
drove them out completely.
[29]Nor did Ephraim drive out
the Canaanites living in Gezer, but the Canaanites continued to live there among
them. [30]Neither did Zebulun
drive out the Canaanites living in Kitron or Nahalol, who
remained among them; but
they did subject them to
forced labor. [31]Nor did Asher
drive out those living in Acco
or Sidon or Ahlab or Aczib or
Helbah or Aphek or Rehob,
[32]and because of this the
people of Asher lived among
the Canaanite inhabitants of
the land. [33]Neither did Naphtali drive out those living in
Beth Shemesh or Beth Anath;
but the Naphtalites too lived
among the Canaanite inhabitants of the land, and those living in Beth Shemesh and Beth
Anath became forced laborers
for them. [34]The Amorites
confined the Danites to the
hill country, not allowing
them to come down into the
plain. [35]And the Amorites
were determined also to hold
out in Mount Heres, Aijalon
and Shaalbim, but when the
power of the house of Joseph
increased, they too were
pressed into forced labor.
[36]The boundary of the Amorites was from Scorpion[f] Pass
to Sela and beyond.

The Angel of the LORD at Bokim

2 The angel of the LORD
went up from Gilgal to
Bokim and said, "I brought
you up out of Egypt and led
you into the land that I swore
to give to your forefathers. I
said, 'I will never break my

[f]36 Hebrew *Akrabbim*

בְּרִיתִ֛י אִתְּכֶ֖ם לְעוֹלָֽם׃ וְאַתֶּ֗ם לֹֽא־ תִכְרְת֤וּ בְרִית֙
covenant you-shall-make not and-you (2) for-ever with-you covenant-of-me

לְיוֹשְׁבֵי֙ הָאָ֣רֶץ הַזֹּ֔את מִזְבְּחוֹתֵיהֶ֖ם תִּתֹּצ֑וּן
you-shall-break-down altars-of-them the-this the-land with-ones-living-of

וְלֹֽא־ שְׁמַעְתֶּ֥ם בְּקֹלִ֖י מַה־ זֹּ֥את עֲשִׂיתֶֽם׃ וְגַ֣ם אָמַ֔רְתִּי לֹֽא־
not I-tell so-now (3) you-did this why? to-voice-of-me you-obeyed yet-not

אֲגָרֵ֥שׁ אוֹתָ֖ם מִפְּנֵיכֶ֑ם וְהָי֤וּ לָכֶם֙ לְצִדִּ֔ים
in-sides to-you and-they-will-be from-before-you them I-will-drive-out

וֵאלֹ֣הֵיהֶ֔ם יִהְי֥וּ לָכֶ֖ם לְמוֹקֵֽשׁ׃ וַיְהִ֗י כְּדַבֵּ֞ר
when-to-speak and-he-was (4) as-snare to-you they-will-be and-gods-of-them

מַלְאַ֤ךְ יְהוָה֙ אֶת־ הַדְּבָרִ֣ים הָאֵ֔לֶּה אֶל־ כָּל־ בְּנֵ֖י יִשְׂרָאֵ֑ל
Israel sons-of all-of to the-these the-things *** Yahweh angel-of

וַיִּשְׂא֥וּ הָעָ֛ם אֶת־ קוֹלָ֖ם וַיִּבְכּֽוּ׃ וַיִּקְרְא֛וּ
and-they-called (5) and-they-wept voice-of-them *** the-people then-they-lifted

שֵֽׁם־ הַמָּק֥וֹם הַה֖וּא בֹּכִ֑ים וַיִּזְבְּחוּ־ שָׁ֖ם לַיהוָֽה׃
to-Yahweh there and-they-sacrificed Bokim the-that the-place name-of

וַיְשַׁלַּ֥ח יְהוֹשֻׁ֖עַ אֶת־ הָעָ֑ם וַיֵּלְכ֤וּ בְנֵֽי־ יִשְׂרָאֵל֙ אִ֣ישׁ
each Israel sons-of and-they-went the-people *** Joshua then-he-dismissed (6)

לְנַחֲלָת֖וֹ לָרֶ֥שֶׁת אֶת־ הָאָֽרֶץ׃ וַיַּעַבְד֤וּ הָעָם֙
the-people and-they-served (7) the-land *** to-possess to-inheritance-of-him

אֶת־ יְהוָ֔ה כֹּ֖ל יְמֵ֣י יְהוֹשֻׁ֑עַ וְכֹ֣ל ׀ יְמֵ֣י הַזְּקֵנִ֗ים אֲשֶׁ֨ר
who the-elders days-of and-all-of Joshua days-of all-of Yahweh ***

הֶאֱרִ֤יכוּ יָמִים֙ אַחֲרֵ֣י יְהוֹשׁ֔וּעַ אֲשֶׁ֣ר רָא֗וּ אֵ֚ת כָּל־ מַעֲשֵׂ֤ה יְהוָה֙
Yahweh thing-of every-of *** they-saw who Joshua after days they-outlived

הַגָּד֔וֹל אֲשֶׁ֥ר עָשָׂ֖ה לְיִשְׂרָאֵֽל׃ וַיָּ֛מָת יְהוֹשֻׁ֥עַ בִּן־ נ֖וּן עֶ֣בֶד
servant-of Nun son-of Joshua and-he-died (8) for-Israel he-did that the-great

יְהוָ֑ה בֶּן־ מֵאָ֥ה וָעֶ֖שֶׂר שָׁנִֽים׃ וַיִּקְבְּר֤וּ אוֹתוֹ֙ בִּגְב֣וּל
in-land-of him and-they-buried (9) years and-ten hundred son-of Yahweh

נַחֲלָת֔וֹ בְּתִמְנַת־ חֶ֖רֶס בְּהַ֣ר אֶפְרָ֑יִם מִצְּפ֖וֹן
to-north Ephraim in-hill-country-of Heres at-Timnath inheritance-of-him

לְהַר־ גָּֽעַשׁ׃ וְגַם֙ כָּל־ הַדּ֣וֹר הַה֔וּא
the-that the-generation whole-of and-also (10) Gaash of-Mount-of

נֶאֶסְפ֖וּ אֶל־ אֲבוֹתָ֑יו וַיָּקָם֩ דּ֨וֹר אַחֵ֜ר
another generation then-he-grew-up fathers-of-him to they-were-gathered

אַחֲרֵיהֶ֗ם אֲשֶׁ֤ר לֹא־ יָֽדְעוּ֙ אֶת־ יְהוָ֔ה וְגַם֙ אֶת־הַֽמַּעֲשֶׂ֔ה אֲשֶׁ֥ר עָשָׂ֖ה
he-did that the-deed *** nor-either Yahweh *** they-knew not who after-them

לְיִשְׂרָאֵֽל׃ וַיַּעֲשׂ֧וּ בְנֵֽי־ יִשְׂרָאֵ֛ל אֶת־ הָרַ֖ע בְּעֵינֵ֣י יְהוָ֑ה
Yahweh in-eyes-of the-evil *** Israel sons-of then-they-did (11) for-Israel

covenant with you, [2]and you shall not make a covenant with the people of this land, but you shall break down their altars.' Yet you have disobeyed me. Why have you done this? [3]Now therefore I tell you that I will not drive them out before you; they will be ⌊thorns⌋ in your sides and their gods will be a snare to you."

[4]When the angel of the LORD had spoken these things to all the Israelites, the people wept aloud, [5]and they called that place Bokim.[g] There they offered sacrifices to the LORD.

Disobedience and Defeat

[6]After Joshua had dismissed the Israelites, they went to take possession of the land, each to his own inheritance. [7]The people served the LORD throughout the lifetime of Joshua and of the elders who outlived him and who had seen all the great things the LORD had done for Israel.

[8]Joshua son of Nun, the servant of the LORD, died at the age of a hundred and ten. [9]And they buried him in the land of his inheritance, at Timnath Heres[h] in the hill country of Ephraim, north of Mount Gaash.

[10]After that whole generation had been gathered to their fathers, another generation grew up, who knew neither the LORD nor what he had done for Israel. [11]Then the Israelites did evil in the eyes of

g5 *Bokim* means *weepers*.
h9 Also known as *Timnath Serah* (see Joshua 19:50 and 24:30)

וַיַּעַבְדוּ אֶת־ הַבְּעָלִים׃ וַיַּעַזְבוּ אֶת־ יְהוָה ׀ אֱלֹהֵי
God-of Yahweh *** and-they-forsook (12) the-Baals *** and-they-served

אֲבוֹתָם הַמּוֹצִיא אוֹתָם מֵאֶרֶץ מִצְרַיִם וַיֵּלְכוּ
and-they-followed Egypt from-land-of them the-one-bringing fathers-of-them

אַחֲרֵי ׀ אֱלֹהִים אֲחֵרִים מֵאֱלֹהֵי הָעַמִּים אֲשֶׁר סְבִיבוֹתֵיהֶם
ones-around-them who the-peoples from-gods-of other-ones gods after

וַיִּשְׁתַּחֲווּ לָהֶם וַיַּכְעִסוּ אֶת־ יְהוָה׃ וַיַּעַזְבוּ
for-they-forsook (13) Yahweh *** and-they-angered to-them and-they-worshiped

אֶת־ יְהוָה וַיַּעַבְדוּ לַבַּעַל וְלָעַשְׁתָּרוֹת׃ וַיִּחַר־
and-he-burned (14) and-to-the-Ashtoreths to-the-Baal and-they-served Yahweh ***

אַף יְהוָה בְּיִשְׂרָאֵל וַיִּתְּנֵם בְּיַד־ שֹׁסִים
ones-raiding into-hand-of and-he-gave-them against-Israel Yahweh anger-of

וַיָּשֹׁסּוּ אוֹתָם וַיִּמְכְּרֵם בְּיַד אוֹיְבֵיהֶם
being-enemies-of-them into-hand-of and-he-sold-them them and-they-plundered

מִסָּבִיב וְלֹא־ יָכְלוּ עוֹד לַעֲמֹד לִפְנֵי אוֹיְבֵיהֶם׃
being-enemies-of-them against to-resist longer they-were-able and-not at-around

בְּכֹל ׀ אֲשֶׁר יָצְאוּ יַד־ יְהוָה הָיְתָה־ בָּם
against-them she-was Yahweh hand-of they-went-out when in-every (15)

לְרָעָה כַּאֲשֶׁר דִּבֶּר יְהוָה וְכַאֲשֶׁר נִשְׁבַּע יְהוָה לָהֶם
to-them Yahweh he-swore and-just-as Yahweh he-said just-as for-defeat

וַיֵּצֶר לָהֶם מְאֹד׃ וַיָּקֶם יְהוָה שֹׁפְטִים
ones-judging Yahweh then-he-raised-up (16) greatly to-them and-he-distressed

וַיּוֹשִׁיעוּם מִיַּד שֹׁסֵיהֶם׃ וְגַם אֶל־
to and-yet (17) ones-raiding-them from-hand-of and-they-saved-them

שֹׁפְטֵיהֶם לֹא שָׁמֵעוּ כִּי זָנוּ אַחֲרֵי אֱלֹהִים אֲחֵרִים
other-ones gods to they-prostituted but they-listened not ones-judging-them

וַיִּשְׁתַּחֲווּ לָהֶם סָרוּ מַהֵר מִן־ הַדֶּרֶךְ אֲשֶׁר
which the-way from to-be-quick they-turned to-them and-they-worshiped

הָלְכוּ אֲבוֹתָם לִשְׁמֹעַ מִצְוֺת־ יְהוָה לֹא־ עָשׂוּ כֵן׃
this they-did not Yahweh commands-of to-obey fathers-of-them they-walked

וְכִי־ הֵקִים יְהוָה ׀ לָהֶם שֹׁפְטִים וְהָיָה יְהוָה
Yahweh then-he-was ones-judging for-them Yahweh he-raised-up and-when (18)

עִם־ הַשֹּׁפֵט וְהוֹשִׁיעָם מִיַּד אֹיְבֵיהֶם
being-enemies-of-them from-hand-of and-he-saved-them the-one-judging with

כֹּל יְמֵי הַשּׁוֹפֵט כִּי־ יִנָּחֵם יְהוָה מִנַּאֲקָתָם
on-groan-of-them Yahweh he-had-compassion for the-one-judging days-of all-of

מִפְּנֵי לֹחֲצֵיהֶם וְדֹחֲקֵיהֶם׃ וְהָיָה ׀
but-he-was (19) and-ones-afflicting-them ones-oppressing-them from-under

the LORD and served the Baals.
[12]They forsook the LORD, the
God of their fathers, who had
brought them out of Egypt.
They followed and worshiped
various gods of the peoples
around them. They provoked
the LORD to anger [13]because
they forsook him and served
Baal and the Ashtoreths. [14]In
his anger against Israel the
LORD handed them over to
raiders who plundered them.
He sold them to their enemies
all around, whom they were
no longer able to resist.
[15]Whenever Israel went out to
fight, the hand of the LORD
was against them to defeat
them, just as he had sworn to
them. They were in great distress.
[16]Then the LORD raised up
judges,[i] who saved them out
of the hands of these raiders.
[17]Yet they would not listen to
their judges but prostituted
themselves to other gods and
worshiped them. Unlike their
fathers, they quickly turned
from the way in which their
fathers had walked, the way of
obedience to the LORD's commands. [18]Whenever the LORD
raised up a judge for them, he
was with the judge and saved
them out of the hands of their
enemies as long as the judge
lived; for the LORD had compassion on them as they
groaned under those who oppressed and afflicted them.

[i]16 Or *leaders;* similarly in verses 17-19

בְּמוֹת הַשּׁוֹפֵט יָשֻׁבוּ וְהִשְׁחִיתוּ
and-they-were-corrupt they-returned the-one-judging when-to-die

מֵאֲבוֹתָם לָלֶכֶת אַחֲרֵי אֱלֹהִים אֲחֵרִים לְעָבְדָם
to-serve-them other-ones gods after to-follow more-than-fathers-of-them

וּלְהִשְׁתַּחֲוֺת לָהֶם לֹא הִפִּילוּ מִמַּעַלְלֵיהֶם
from-practices-of-them they-gave-up not to-them and-to-worship

וּמִדַּרְכָּם הַקָּשָׁה׃ (20) וַיִּחַר־ אַף יְהוָה בְּיִשְׂרָאֵל
with-Israel Yahweh anger-of and-he-burned (20) the-stubborn and-from-way-them

וַיֹּאמֶר יַעַן אֲשֶׁר עָבְרוּ הַגּוֹי הַזֶּה אֶת־ בְּרִיתִי
covenant-of-me *** the-this the-nation they-violated that because and-he-said

אֲשֶׁר צִוִּיתִי אֶת־ אֲבוֹתָם וְלֹא שָׁמְעוּ לְקוֹלִי׃
to-voice-of-me they-listened and-not fathers-of-them for I-laid-down that

(21) גַּם־ אֲנִי לֹא אוֹסִיף לְהוֹרִישׁ אִישׁ מִפְּנֵיהֶם מִן־
from from-before-them any to-drive-out I-will-continue not I indeed (21)

הַגּוֹיִם אֲשֶׁר־ עָזַב יְהוֹשֻׁעַ וַיָּמֹת׃ (22) לְמַעַן נַסּוֹת בָּם
with-them to-test so-that (22) when-he-died Joshua he-left that the-nations

אֶת־יִשְׂרָאֵל הֲשֹׁמְרִים הֵם אֶת־ דֶּרֶךְ יְהוָה לָלֶכֶת בָּם
in-them to-walk Yahweh way-of *** they whether-ones-keeping Israel ***

כַּאֲשֶׁר שָׁמְרוּ אֲבוֹתָם אִם־לֹא׃ (23) וַיַּנַּח יְהוָה אֶת־
*** Yahweh and-he-let-remain (23) not or fathers-of-them they-did just-as

הַגּוֹיִם הָאֵלֶּה לְבִלְתִּי הוֹרִישָׁם מַהֵר וְלֹא נְתָנָם
he-gave-them and-not to-be-quick to-drive-out-them not the-those the-nations

בְּיַד־ יְהוֹשֻׁעַ׃ (3:1) וְאֵלֶּה הַגּוֹיִם אֲשֶׁר הִנִּיחַ יְהוָה לְנַסּוֹת
to-test Yahweh he-left that the-nations and-these (3:1) Joshua into-hand-of

בָּם אֶת־ יִשְׂרָאֵל אֵת כָּל־אֲשֶׁר לֹא־ יָדְעוּ אֵת כָּל־ מִלְחֲמוֹת
wars-of any-of *** they-experienced not who all *** Israel *** with-them

כְּנָעַן׃ (2) רַק לְמַעַן דַּעַת דֹּרוֹת בְּנֵי־ יִשְׂרָאֵל
Israel sons-of generations-of to-experience so-that only (2) Canaan

לְלַמְּדָם מִלְחָמָה רַק אֲשֶׁר־ לְפָנִים לֹא יְדָעוּם׃
they-experienced-them not previously who only warfare to-teach-them

(3) חֲמֵשֶׁת ׀ סַרְנֵי פְלִשְׁתִּים וְכָל־ הַכְּנַעֲנִי וְהַצִּידֹנִי
and-the-Sidonian the-Canaanite and-all-of Philistines rulers-of five-of (3)

וְהַחִוִּי יֹשֵׁב הַר הַלְּבָנוֹן מֵהַר בַּעַל חֶרְמוֹן
Hermon Baal from-Mount-of the-Lebanon mountain-of living-of and-the-Hivite

עַד לְבוֹא חֲמָת׃ (4) וַיִּהְיוּ לְנַסּוֹת בָּם אֶת־יִשְׂרָאֵל לָדַעַת
to-see Israel *** with-them to-test and-they-were (4) Hamath Lebo to

הֲיִשְׁמְעוּ אֶת־ מִצְוֺת יְהוָה אֲשֶׁר־ צִוָּה אֶת־ אֲבוֹתָם
fathers-of-them *** he-gave which Yahweh commands-of *** whether-they-would-obey

19But when the judge died, the
people returned to ways even
more corrupt than those of
their fathers, following other
gods and serving and wor-
shiping them. They refused to
give up their evil practices and
stubborn ways.
20Therefore the LORD was
very angry with Israel and
said, "Because this nation has
violated the covenant that I
laid down for their forefathers
and has not listened to me, 21I
will no longer drive out before
them any of the nations
Joshua left when he died. 22I
will use them to test Israel and
see whether they will keep the
way of the LORD and walk in it
as their forefathers did." 23The
LORD had allowed those nations to remain; he did not
drive them out at once by giving them into the hands of
Joshua.

3 These are the nations the
LORD left to test all those
Israelites who had not experienced any of the wars in Canaan 2(he did this only to
teach warfare to the descendants of the Israelites who had
not had previous battle experi-
ence): 3the five rulers of the
Philistines, all the Canaanites,
the Sidonians, and the Hivites
living in the Lebanon mountains from Mount Baal Hermon to Lebo[i] Hamath. 4They
were left to test the Israelites to
see whether they would obey
the LORD's commands, which
he had given their forefathers

[i]3 *Or to the entrance to*

בְּיַד־ מֹשֶׁה׃ וּבְנֵי יִשְׂרָאֵל יָשְׁבוּ בְּקֶרֶב הַכְּנַעֲנִי
the-Canaanite in-among they-lived Israel and-sons-of (5) Moses by-hand-of

הַחִתִּי וְהָאֱמֹרִי וְהַפְּרִזִּי וְהַחִוִּי וְהַיְבוּסִי׃
and-the-Jebusite and-the-Hivite and-the-Perizzite and-the-Amorite the-Hittite

וַיִּקְחוּ אֶת־ בְּנוֹתֵיהֶם לָהֶם לְנָשִׁים וְאֶת־ בְּנוֹתֵיהֶם
daughters-of-them and as-wives for-them daughters-of-them *** and-they-took (6)

נָתְנוּ לִבְנֵיהֶם וַיַּעַבְדוּ אֶת־ אֱלֹהֵיהֶם׃ וַיַּעֲשׂוּ
and-they-did (7) gods-of-them *** and-they-served to-sons-of-them they-gave

בְנֵי־ יִשְׂרָאֵל אֶת־ הָרַע בְּעֵינֵי יְהוָה וַיִּשְׁכְּחוּ אֶת־ יְהוָה
Yahweh *** and-they-forgot Yahweh in-eyes-of the-evil *** Israel sons-of

אֱלֹהֵיהֶם וַיַּעַבְדוּ אֶת־הַבְּעָלִים וְאֶת־הָאֲשֵׁרוֹת׃ וַיִּחַר־
and-he-burned (8) the-Asherahs and the-Baals *** and-they-served God-of-them

אַף יְהוָה בְּיִשְׂרָאֵל וַיִּמְכְּרֵם בְּיַד כּוּשַׁן רִשְׁעָתַיִם
Rishathaim Cushan into-hand-of so-he-sold-them against-Israel Yahweh anger-of

מֶלֶךְ אֲרַם נַהֲרָיִם וַיַּעַבְדוּ בְנֵי־ יִשְׂרָאֵל אֶת־ כּוּשַׁן רִשְׁעָתַיִם
Rishathaim Cushan *** Israel sons-of and-they-served Naharaim Aram king-of

שְׁמֹנֶה שָׁנִים׃ וַיִּזְעֲקוּ בְנֵי־ יִשְׂרָאֵל אֶל־ יְהוָה וַיָּקֶם
so-he-raised-up Yahweh to Israel sons-of but-they-cried (9) years eight

יְהוָה מוֹשִׁיעַ לִבְנֵי יִשְׂרָאֵל וַיּוֹשִׁיעֵם אֵת עָתְנִיאֵל בֶּן־
son-of Othniel *** and-he-saved-them Israel for-sons-of one-delivering Yahweh

קְנַז אֲחִי כָלֵב הַקָּטֹן מִמֶּנּוּ׃ וַתְּהִי עָלָיו רוּחַ־
Spirit-of upon-him and-she-came (10) than-him the-younger Caleb brother-of Kenaz

יְהוָה וַיִּשְׁפֹּט אֶת־ יִשְׂרָאֵל וַיֵּצֵא לַמִּלְחָמָה וַיִּתֵּן יְהוָה
Yahweh and-he-gave to-the-war and-he-went Israel *** and-he-judged Yahweh

בְּיָדוֹ אֶת־ כּוּשַׁן רִשְׁעָתַיִם מֶלֶךְ אֲרָם וַתָּעָז
and-she-overpowered Aram king-of Rishathaim Cushan *** into-hand-of-him

יָדוֹ עַל כּוּשַׁן רִשְׁעָתָיִם׃ וַתִּשְׁקֹט הָאָרֶץ אַרְבָּעִים
forty the-land so-she-had-peace (11) Rishathaim Cushan over hand-of-him

שָׁנָה וַיָּמָת עָתְנִיאֵל בֶּן־ קְנַז׃ וַיֹּסִפוּ בְּנֵי יִשְׂרָאֵל
Israel sons-of and-they-did-again (12) Kenaz son-of Othniel and-he-died year

לַעֲשׂוֹת הָרַע בְּעֵינֵי יְהוָה וַיְחַזֵּק יְהוָה אֶת־ עֶגְלוֹן מֶלֶךְ־
king-of Eglon *** Yahweh and-he-gave-power Yahweh in-eyes-of the-evil to-do

מוֹאָב עַל־יִשְׂרָאֵל עַל כִּי־ עָשׂוּ אֶת־ הָרַע בְּעֵינֵי יְהוָה׃
Yahweh in-eyes-of the-evil *** they-did that because Israel over Moab

וַיֶּאֱסֹף אֵלָיו אֶת־ בְּנֵי עַמּוֹן וַעֲמָלֵק וַיֵּלֶךְ
and-he-came and-Amalek Ammon sons-of *** with-him and-he-joined (13)

וַיַּךְ אֶת־ יִשְׂרָאֵל וַיִּירְשׁוּ אֶת־ עִיר הַתְּמָרִים׃
the-Palms City-of *** and-they-possessed Israel *** and-he-attacked

through Moses.
5 The Israelites lived among
the Canaanites, Hittites, Amorites, Perizzites, Hivites and
Jebusites. 6 They took their
daughters in marriage and
gave their own daughters to
their sons, and served their
gods.

Othniel

7 The Israelites did evil in the
eyes of the LORD; they forgot
the LORD their God and served
the Baals and the Asherahs.
8 The anger of the LORD burned
against Israel so that he sold
them into the hands of Cushan-Rishathaim king of
Aram Naharaim,[k] to whom
the Israelites were subject for
eight years. 9 But when they
cried out to the LORD, he raised
up for them a deliverer, Othniel son of Kenaz, Caleb's
younger brother, who saved
them. 10 The Spirit of the LORD
came upon him, so that he
became Israel's judge[l] and
went to war. The LORD gave
Cushan-Rishathaim king of
Aram into the hands of Othniel, who overpowered him.
11 So the land had peace for
forty years, until Othniel son
of Kenaz died.

Ehud

12 Once again the Israelites
did evil in the eyes of the
LORD, and because they did
this evil the LORD gave Eglon
king of Moab power over Israel. 13 Getting the Ammonites
and Amalekites to join him,
Eglon came and attacked Israel, and they took possession of

[k] 8 That is, Northwest Mesopotamia
[l] 10 Or *leader*

וַיַּעַבְדוּ בְנֵי־ יִשְׂרָאֵל אֶת־עֶגְלוֹן מֶלֶךְ־מוֹאָב שְׁמוֹנֶה עֶשְׂרֵה שָׁנָה׃
year ten eight Moab king-of Eglon *** Israel sons-of and-they-served (14)

וַיִּזְעֲקוּ בְנֵי־ יִשְׂרָאֵל אֶל־ יְהוָה וַיָּקֶם יְהוָה לָהֶם
to-them Yahweh and-he-gave Yahweh to Israel sons-of and-they-cried (15)

מוֹשִׁיעַ אֶת־ אֵהוּד בֶּן־ גֵּרָא בֶּן־הַיְמִינִי אִישׁ אִטֵּר יַד־
hand-of bound-of man the-Benjamite Gera son-of Ehud *** one-delivering

יְמִינוֹ וַיִּשְׁלְחוּ בְנֵי־ יִשְׂרָאֵל בְּיָדוֹ מִנְחָה לְעֶגְלוֹן
to-Eglon tribute in-hand-of-him Israel sons-of and-they-sent right-of-him

מֶלֶךְ מוֹאָב׃ וַיַּעַשׂ לוֹ אֵהוּד חֶרֶב וְלָהּ שְׁנֵי פֵיוֹת
edges two-of and-on-her sword Ehud for-him now-he-made (16) Moab king-of

גֹּמֶד אָרְכָּהּ וַיַּחְגֹּר אוֹתָהּ מִתַּחַת לְמַדָּיו עַל
to to-clothes-of-him at-under her and-he-strapped length-of-her cubit

יֶרֶךְ יְמִינוֹ׃ וַיַּקְרֵב אֶת־ הַמִּנְחָה לְעֶגְלוֹן מֶלֶךְ
king-of to-Eglon the-tribute *** and-he-presented (17) right-of-him thigh-of

מוֹאָב וְעֶגְלוֹן אִישׁ בָּרִיא מְאֹד׃ וַיְהִי כַּאֲשֶׁר כִּלָּה לְהַקְרִיב אֶת־
*** to-present he-finished just-as and-he-was (18) very fat man now-Eglon Moab

הַמִּנְחָה וַיְשַׁלַּח אֶת־ הָעָם נֹשְׂאֵי הַמִּנְחָה׃
the-tribute ones-carrying-of the-people *** then-he-sent-away the-tribute

וְהוּא שָׁב מִן־הַפְּסִילִים אֲשֶׁר אֶת־ הַגִּלְגָּל וַיֹּאמֶר
and-he-said the-Gilgal near that the-idols at he-turned-back but-he (19)

דְּבַר־ סֵתֶר לִי אֵלֶיךָ הַמֶּלֶךְ וַיֹּאמֶר הָס וַיֵּצְאוּ
and-they-left quiet! and-he-said the-king for-you to-me secret message-of

מֵעָלָיו כָּל־ הָעֹמְדִים עָלָיו׃ וְאֵהוּד | בָּא
he-approached then-Ehud (20) to-him the-ones-attending all-of from-with-him

אֵלָיו וְהוּא־ יֹשֵׁב בַּעֲלִיַּת הַמְּקֵרָה אֲשֶׁר־ לוֹ
to-him that the-summer-palace in-upper-room-of sitting while-he to-him

לְבַדּוֹ וַיֹּאמֶר אֵהוּד דְּבַר־ אֱלֹהִים לִי אֵלֶיךָ וַיָּקָם מֵעַל
from-on and-he-rose for-you to-me God message-of Ehud and-he-said by-himself

הַכִּסֵּא׃ וַיִּשְׁלַח אֵהוּד אֶת־ יַד שְׂמֹאלוֹ וַיִּקַּח אֶת־
and-he-drew left-of-him hand-of *** Ehud and-he-reached (21) the-seat

הַחֶרֶב מֵעַל יֶרֶךְ יְמִינוֹ וַיִּתְקָעֶהָ בְּבִטְנוֹ׃
into-belly-of-him and-he-plunged-her right-of-him thigh-of from-on the-sword

וַיָּבֹא גַם־ הַנִּצָּב אַחַר הַלַּהַב וַיִּסְגֹּר הַחֵלֶב בְּעַד
over the-fat and-he-closed the-blade after the-handle even and-he-sank-in (22)

הַלַּהַב כִּי לֹא שָׁלַף הַחֶרֶב מִבִּטְנוֹ וַיֵּצֵא
and-he-came-out from-belly-of-him the-sword he-pulled-out not for the-blade

הַפַּרְשְׁדֹנָה׃ וַיֵּצֵא אֵהוּד הַמִּסְדְּרוֹנָה וַיִּסְגֹּר דַּלְתוֹת
doors-of and-he-shut to-the-porch Ehud then-he-went-out (23) of-the-back

the City of Palms.[m] 14The Israelites were subject to Eglon king of Moab for eighteen years.

15Again the Israelites cried out to the LORD, and he gave them a deliverer—Ehud, a left-handed man, the son of Gera the Benjamite. The Israelites sent him with tribute to Eglon king of Moab. 16Now Ehud had made a double-edged sword about a foot and a half[n] long, which he strapped to his right thigh under his clothing. 17He presented the tribute to Eglon king of Moab, who was a very fat man. 18After Ehud had presented the tribute, he sent on their way the men who had carried it. 19At the idols[o] near Gilgal he himself turned back and said, "I have a secret message for you, O king."

The king said, "Quiet!" And all his attendants left him.

20Ehud then approached him while he was sitting alone in the upper room of his summer palace[p] and said, "I have a message from God for you." As the king rose from his seat, 21Ehud reached with his left hand, drew the sword from his right thigh and plunged it into the king's belly. 22Even the handle sank in after the blade, which came out his back. Ehud did not pull the sword out, and the fat closed in over it. 23Then Ehud went out to the porch[q]; he shut the

[m] *13* That is, Jericho
[n] *16* Hebrew *a cubit* (about 0.5 meter)
[o] *19* Or *the stone quarries*; also in verse 26
[p] *20* The meaning of the Hebrew for this phrase is uncertain.
[q] *23* The meaning of the Hebrew for this word is uncertain.

הָעֲלִיָּה* בַּעֲדוֹ וְנָעָל: (24) וְהוּא יָצָא וַעֲבָדָיו
and-servants-of-him he-went now-he (24) and-he-locked behind-him the-upper-room

בָּאוּ וַיִּרְאוּ וְהִנֵּה דַּלְתוֹת הָעֲלִיָּה נְעֻלוֹת
ones-being-locked the-upper-room doors-of and-see! and-they-looked they-came

וַיֹּאמְרוּ אַךְ מֵסִיךְ הוּא אֶת־ רַגְלָיו בַּחֲדַר הַמְּקֵרָה:
the-house in-inner-room-of feet-of-him *** he covering indeed and-they-said

(25) וַיָּחִילוּ עַד־ בּוֹשׁ וְהִנֵּה אֵינֶנּוּ פֹתֵחַ דַּלְתוֹת
doors-of opening not-he but-see! to-be-embarrassed until and-they-waited (25)

הָעֲלִיָּה וַיִּקְחוּ אֶת־ הַמַּפְתֵּחַ וַיִּפְתָּחוּ וְהִנֵּה אֲדֹנֵיהֶם
lords-of-them and-see! and-they-unlocked the-key *** so-they-took the-upper-room

נֹפֵל אַרְצָה מֵת: (26) וְאֵהוּד נִמְלַט עַד הִתְמַהְמְהָם
to-wait-them while he-got-away and-Ehud (26) being-dead on-floor one-falling

וְהוּא עָבַר אֶת־ הַפְּסִילִים וַיִּמָּלֵט הַשְּׂעִירָתָה: (27) וַיְהִי
and-he-was (27) to-the-Seirah and-he-escaped the-idols *** he-passed-by and-he

בְּבוֹאוֹ וַיִּתְקַע בַּשּׁוֹפָר בְּהַר אֶפְרָיִם
Ephraim in-hill-country-of on-the-trumpet then-he-blew when-to-arrive-him

וַיֵּרְדוּ עִמּוֹ בְנֵי־ יִשְׂרָאֵל מִן־ הָהָר וְהוּא לִפְנֵיהֶם:
before-them and-he the-hill from Israel sons-of with-him and-they-went-down

(28) וַיֹּאמֶר אֲלֵהֶם רִדְפוּ אַחֲרַי כִּי־ נָתַן יְהוָה אֶת־
*** Yahweh he-gave for after-me follow! to-them and-he-ordered (28)

אֹיְבֵיכֶם אֶת־ מוֹאָב בְּיֶדְכֶם וַיֵּרְדוּ אַחֲרָיו
after-him so-they-followed into-hand-of-you Moab *** being-enemies-of-you

וַיִּלְכְּדוּ אֶת־ מַעְבְּרוֹת הַיַּרְדֵּן לְמוֹאָב וְלֹא־ נָתְנוּ
they-allowed and-not to-Moab the-Jordan fords-of *** and-they-possessed

אִישׁ לַעֲבֹר: (29) וַיַּכּוּ אֶת־ מוֹאָב בָּעֵת הַהִיא
the-that at-the-time Moab *** and-he-struck-down (29) to-cross-over anyone

כַּעֲשֶׂרֶת אֲלָפִים אִישׁ כָּל־ שָׁמֵן וְכָל־ אִישׁ חָיִל וְלֹא
and-not strong man-of and-all-of vigorous all-of man thousands about-ten-of

נִמְלַט אִישׁ: (30) וַתִּכָּנַע מוֹאָב בַּיּוֹם הַהוּא תַּחַת
under the-that on-the-day Moab and-she-was-made-subject (30) man he-escaped

יַד יִשְׂרָאֵל וַתִּשְׁקֹט הָאָרֶץ שְׁמוֹנִים שָׁנָה: (31) וְאַחֲרָיו
and-after-him (31) year eighty the-land and-she-had-peace Israel hand-of

הָיָה שַׁמְגַּר בֶּן־ עֲנָת וַיַּךְ אֶת־ פְּלִשְׁתִּים שֵׁשׁ־ מֵאוֹת
hundreds six Philistines *** and-he-struck-down Anath son-of Shamgar he-came

אִישׁ בְּמַלְמַד הַבָּקָר וַיֹּשַׁע גַּם־ הוּא אֶת־ יִשְׂרָאֵל: (4:1) וַיֹּסִפוּ
and-they-repeated (4:1) Israel *** he also and-he-saved the-ox with-goad-of man

בְּנֵי יִשְׂרָאֵל לַעֲשׂוֹת הָרַע בְּעֵינֵי יְהוָה וְאֵהוּד מֵת:
he-died now-Ehud Yahweh in-eyes-of the-evil to-do Israel sons-of

doors of the upper room behind him and locked them.

[24]After he had gone, the servants came and found the doors of the upper room locked. They said, "He must be relieving himself in the inner room of the house." [25]They waited to the point of embarrassment, but when he did not open the doors of the room, they took a key and unlocked them. There they saw their lord fallen to the floor, dead.

[26]While they waited, Ehud got away. He passed by the idols and escaped to Seirah. [27]When he arrived there, he blew a trumpet in the hill country of Ephraim, and the Israelites went down with him from the hills, with him leading them.

[28]"Follow me," he ordered, "for the LORD has given Moab, your enemy, into your hands." So they followed him down and, taking possession of the fords of the Jordan that led to Moab, they allowed no one to cross over. [29]At that time they struck down about ten thousand Moabites, all vigorous and strong; not a man escaped. [30]That day Moab was made subject to Israel, and the land had peace for eighty years.

Shamgar

[31]After Ehud came Shamgar son of Anath, who struck down six hundred Philistines with an oxgoad. He too saved Israel.

Deborah

4 After Ehud died, the Israelites once again did evil in the eyes of the LORD. [2]So the

***23 Most mss have *hateph pathah* under the *ayin* (הָעֲ).**

וַיִּמְכְּרֵם יְהוָה בְּיַד יָבִין מֶלֶךְ־כְּנַעַן אֲשֶׁר מָלַךְ
he-reigned who Canaan king-of Jabin into-hand-of Yahweh so-he-sold-them (2)

בְּחָצוֹר וְשַׂר־צְבָאוֹ סִיסְרָא וְהוּא יוֹשֵׁב בַּחֲרֹשֶׁת
in-Harosheth living and-he Sisera army-of-him and-commander-of in-Hazor

הַגּוֹיִם׃ וַיִּצְעֲקוּ בְנֵי־יִשְׂרָאֵל אֶל־יְהוָה כִּי תְּשַׁע מֵאוֹת
hundreds nine-of for Yahweh to Israei sons-of and-they-cried (3) Haggoyim

רֶכֶב־בַּרְזֶל לוֹ וְהוּא לָחַץ אֶת־בְּנֵי יִשְׂרָאֵל בְּחָזְקָה
with-cruelty Israel sons-of *** he-oppressed and-he to-him iron chariot-of

עֶשְׂרִים שָׁנָה׃ וּדְבוֹרָה אִשָּׁה נְבִיאָה אֵשֶׁת לַפִּידוֹת הִיא שֹׁפְטָה
leading she Lappidoth wife-of prophetess woman now-Deborah (4) year twenty

אֶת־יִשְׂרָאֵל בָּעֵת הַהִיא׃ וְהִיא יוֹשֶׁבֶת תַּחַת־תֹּמֶר
Palm-of under holding-court and-she (5) the-that at-the-time Israel ***

דְּבוֹרָה בֵּין הָרָמָה וּבֵין בֵּית־אֵל בְּהַר אֶפְרָיִם
Ephraim in-hill-country-of El Beth and-between the-Ramah between Deborah

וַיַּעֲלוּ אֵלֶיהָ בְּנֵי יִשְׂרָאֵל לַמִּשְׁפָּט׃ וַתִּשְׁלַח
and-she-sent (6) for-the-decision Israel sons-of to-her and-they-came

וַתִּקְרָא לְבָרָק בֶּן־אֲבִינֹעַם מִקֶּדֶשׁ נַפְתָּלִי וַתֹּאמֶר
and-she-said Naphtali from-Kedesh-of Abinoam son-of for-Barak and-she-called

אֵלָיו הֲלֹא צִוָּה ׀ יְהוָה אֱלֹהֵי־יִשְׂרָאֵל לֵךְ וּמָשַׁכְתָּ בְּהַר
to-Mount-of and-you-lead-way go! Israel God-of Yahweh he-commands not? to-him

תָּבוֹר וְלָקַחְתָּ עִמְּךָ עֲשֶׂרֶת אֲלָפִים אִישׁ מִבְּנֵי נַפְתָּלִי
Naphtali from-sons-of man thousands ten-of with-you and-you-take Tabor

וּמִבְּנֵי זְבֻלוּן׃ וּמָשַׁכְתִּי אֵלֶיךָ אֶל־נַחַל קִישׁוֹן אֶת־
*** Kishon River-of to to-you and-I-will-lure (7) Zebulun and-from-sons-of

סִיסְרָא שַׂר־צְבָא יָבִין וְאֶת־רִכְבּוֹ וְאֶת־הֲמוֹנוֹ
troop-of-him and-with chariot-of-him with Jabin army-of commander-of Sisera

וּנְתַתִּיהוּ בְּיָדֶךָ׃ וַיֹּאמֶר אֵלֶיהָ בָּרָק אִם־תֵּלְכִי
you-go if Barak to-her and-he-said (8) into-hand-of-you and-I-will-give-him

עִמִּי וְהָלָכְתִּי וְאִם־לֹא תֵלְכִי עִמִּי לֹא אֵלֵךְ׃ וַתֹּאמֶר
and-she-said (9) I-will-go not with-me you-go not but-if then-I-will-go with-me

הָלֹךְ אֵלֵךְ עִמָּךְ אֶפֶס כִּי לֹא תִהְיֶה תִּפְאַרְתְּךָ עַל־
because-of honor-of-you she-will-be not indeed but with-you I-will-go to-go

הַדֶּרֶךְ אֲשֶׁר אַתָּה הוֹלֵךְ כִּי בְיַד־אִשָּׁה יִמְכֹּר יְהוָה אֶת־
*** Yahweh he-will-give woman into-hand-of rather going you that the-way

סִיסְרָא וַתָּקָם דְּבוֹרָה וַתֵּלֶךְ עִם־בָּרָק קֶדְשָׁה׃
to-Kedesh Barak with and-she-went Deborah so-she-got-up Sisera

וַיַּזְעֵק בָּרָק אֶת־זְבוּלֻן וְאֶת־נַפְתָּלִי קֶדְשָׁה וַיַּעַל
and-he-followed at-Kedesh Naphtali and Zebulun *** Barak and-he-summoned (10)

LORD sold them into the hands
of Jabin, a king of Canaan,
who reigned in Hazor. The
commander of his army was
Sisera, who lived in
Harosheth Haggoyim. 3 Be-
cause he had nine hundred
iron chariots and had cruelly
oppressed the Israelites for
twenty years, they cried to the
LORD for help.

4 Deborah, a prophetess, the
wife of Lappidoth, was leading[r] Israel at that time. 5 She
held court under the Palm of
Deborah between Ramah and
Bethel in the hill country of
Ephraim, and the Israelites
came to her to have their dis-
putes decided. 6 She sent for
Barak son of Abinoam from
Kedesh in Naphtali and said
to him, "The LORD, the God of
Israel, commands you: 'Go,
take with you ten thousand
men of Naphtali and Zebulun
and lead the way to Mount Tabor. 7 I will lure Sisera, the
commander of Jabin's army,
with his chariots and his
troops to the Kishon River
and give him into your
hands.' "

8 Barak said to her, "If you go
with me, I will go; but if you
don't go with me, I won't go."
9 "Very well," Deborah said,
"I will go with you. But because of the way you are going
about this,[s] the honor will not
be yours, for the LORD will
hand Sisera over to a woman."
So Deborah went with Barak
to Kedesh, 10 where he summoned Zebulun and Naphtali.

[r]4 Traditionally *judging*
[s]9 Or *But on the expedition you are undertaking*

בְּרַגְלָיו עֲשֶׂרֶת אַלְפֵי אִישׁ וַתַּעַל עִמּוֹ דְּבוֹרָה׃
Deborah with-him and-she-went man thousands-of ten-of on-feet-of-him

(11) וְחֶבֶר הַקֵּינִי נִפְרָד מִקַּיִן מִבְּנֵי חֹבָב חֹתֵן
father-in-law-of Hobab from-sons-of from-Ken leaving the-Kenite now-Heber (11)

מֹשֶׁה וַיֵּט אָהֳלוֹ עַד־אֵלוֹן בְּצַעֲנַיִם° אֲשֶׁר אֶת־קֶדֶשׁ׃
Kedesh near that in-Zaanannim great-tree by tent-of-him and-he-pitched Moses

(12) וַיַּגִּדוּ לְסִיסְרָא כִּי עָלָה בָּרָק בֶּן־אֲבִינֹעַם הַר־
Mount-of Abinoam son-of Barak he-went-up that to-Sisera when-they-told (12)

תָּבוֹר׃ (13) וַיַּזְעֵק סִיסְרָא אֶת־כָּל־רִכְבּוֹ תְּשַׁע מֵאוֹת
hundreds nine-of chariot-of-him all-of *** Sisera then-he-gathered (13) Tabor

רֶכֶב בַּרְזֶל וְאֶת־כָּל־הָעָם אֲשֶׁר אִתּוֹ מֵחֲרֹשֶׁת הַגּוֹיִם
Haggoyim from-Harosheth with-him who the-people all-of and iron chariot-of

אֶל־נַחַל קִישׁוֹן׃ (14) וַתֹּאמֶר דְּבֹרָה אֶל־בָּרָק קוּם כִּי זֶה הַיּוֹם
the-day this for go! Barak to Deborah then-she-said (14) Kishon River-of to

אֲשֶׁר נָתַן יְהוָה אֶת־סִיסְרָא בְּיָדֶךָ הֲלֹא יְהוָה יָצָא
he-went Yahweh not? into-hand-of-you Sisera *** Yahweh he-gave that

לְפָנֶיךָ וַיֵּרֶד בָּרָק מֵהַר תָּבוֹר וַעֲשֶׂרֶת אֲלָפִים
thousands and-ten-of Tabor from-Mount-of Barak so-he-went-down ahead-of-you

אִישׁ אַחֲרָיו׃ (15) וַיָּהָם יְהוָה אֶת־סִיסְרָא וְאֶת־כָּל־הָרֶכֶב
the-chariot all-of and Sisera *** Yahweh and-he-routed (15) after-him man

וְאֶת־כָּל־הַמַּחֲנֶה לְפִי־חֶרֶב לִפְנֵי בָרָק וַיֵּרֶד סִיסְרָא
Sisera and-he-abandoned Barak before sword by-edge-of the-army all-of and

מֵעַל הַמֶּרְכָּבָה וַיָּנָס בְּרַגְלָיו׃ (16) וּבָרָק רָדַף
he-pursued but-Barak (16) on-feet-of-him and-he-fled the-chariot from-on

אַחֲרֵי הָרֶכֶב וְאַחֲרֵי הַמַּחֲנֶה עַד חֲרֹשֶׁת הַגּוֹיִם וַיִּפֹּל
and-he-fell Haggoyim Harosheth as-far-as the-army and-after the-chariot after

כָּל־מַחֲנֵה סִיסְרָא לְפִי־חֶרֶב לֹא נִשְׁאַר עַד־אֶחָד׃
one even he-was-left not sword by-edge-of Sisera troop-of all-of

(17) וְסִיסְרָא נָס בְּרַגְלָיו אֶל־אֹהֶל יָעֵל אֵשֶׁת חֶבֶר
Heber wife-of Jael tent-of to on-feet-of-him he-fled but-Sisera (17)

הַקֵּינִי כִּי שָׁלוֹם בֵּין יָבִין מֶלֶךְ־חָצוֹר וּבֵין
and-between Hazor king-of Jabin between friendly-relation for the-Kenite

בֵּית חֶבֶר הַקֵּינִי׃ (18) וַתֵּצֵא יָעֵל לִקְרַאת סִיסְרָא
Sisera to-meet Jael and-she-went-out (18) the-Kenite Heber clan-of

וַתֹּאמֶר אֵלָיו סוּרָה אֲדֹנִי סוּרָה אֵלַי אַל־תִּירָא
you-be-afraid not with-me come-in! lord-of-me come! to-him and-she-said

וַיָּסַר אֵלֶיהָ הָאֹהֱלָה וַתְּכַסֵּהוּ בַּשְּׂמִיכָה׃
with-the-covering and-she-covered-him into-the-tent with-her so-he-entered

Ten thousand men followed
him, and Deborah also went
with him.
[11]Now Heber the Kenite had
left the other Kenites, the descendants of Hobab, Moses'
brother-in-law,[f] and pitched
his tent by the great tree in
Zaanannim near Kedesh.
[12]When they told Sisera that
Barak son of Abinoam had
gone up to Mount Tabor, [13]Sis-
era gathered together his nine
hundred iron chariots and all
the men with him, from
Harosheth Haggoyim to the
Kishon River.
[14]Then Deborah said to
Barak, "Go! This is the day the
LORD has given Sisera into
your hands. Has not the LORD
gone ahead of you?" So Barak
went down Mount Tabor, followed by ten thousand men.
[15]At Barak's advance, the LORD
routed Sisera and all his chariots and army by the sword,
and Sisera abandoned his
chariot and fled on foot. [16]But
Barak pursued the chariots
and army as far as Harosheth
Haggoyim. All the troops of
Sisera fell by the sword; not a
man was left.
[17]Sisera, however, fled on
foot to the tent of Jael, the wife
of Heber the Kenite, because
there were friendly relations
between Jabin king of Hazor
and the clan of Heber the Kenite.
[18]Jael went out to meet Sisera
and said to him, "Come, my
lord, come right in. Don't be
afraid." So he entered her tent,
and she put a covering over
him.

[f]11 *Or father-in-law*

°*11* ק בצעננים

וַיֹּאמֶר אֵלֶיהָ הַשְׁקִינִי־נָא מְעַט־מַיִם כִּי צָמֵאתִי
I-am-thirsty for waters little-of now! give-me! to-her and-he-said (19)

וַתִּפְתַּח אֶת־נֹאוד* הֶחָלָב וַתַּשְׁקֵהוּ וַתְּכַסֵּהוּ׃
and-she-covered-him and-she-gave-drink-him the-milk skin-of *** and-she-opened

וַיֹּאמֶר אֵלֶיהָ עֲמֹד פֶּתַח הָאֹהֶל וְהָיָה אִם־אִישׁ
someone if and-he-will-be the-tent doorway-of stand! to-her and-he-told (20)

יָבוֹא וּשְׁאֵלֵךְ וְאָמַר הֲיֵשׁ־פֹּה אִישׁ וְאָמַרְתְּ
then-you-say anyone here is-there? and-he-says and-he-asks-you he-comes-by

אָיִן׃ וַתִּקַּח יָעֵל אֵשֶׁת־חֶבֶר אֶת־יְתַד הָאֹהֶל וַתָּשֶׂם
and-she-took the-tent peg-of *** Heber wife-of Jael but-she-picked-up (21) no

אֶת־הַמַּקֶּבֶת בְּיָדָהּ וַתָּבוֹא אֵלָיו בַּלָּאט† וַתִּתְקַע
and-she-drove in-the-quiet to-him and-she-went in-hand-of-her the-hammer ***

אֶת־הַיָּתֵד בְּרַקָּתוֹ וַתִּצְנַח בָּאָרֶץ וְהוּא־
while-he in-the-ground and-she-stuck through-temple-of-him the-peg ***

נִרְדָּם וַיָּעַף וַיָּמֹת׃ וְהִנֵּה בָרָק רֹדֵף אֶת־
*** pursuing Barak and-see! (22) and-he-died for-he-was-exhausted sleeping

סִיסְרָא וַתֵּצֵא יָעֵל לִקְרָאתוֹ וַתֹּאמֶר לוֹ לֵךְ
come! to-him and-she-said to-meet-him Jael and-she-went-out Sisera

וְאַרְאֶךָּ אֶת־הָאִישׁ אֲשֶׁר־אַתָּה מְבַקֵּשׁ וַיָּבֹא אֵלֶיהָ
with-her so-he-went-in looking-for you whom the-man *** and-I-will-show-you

וְהִנֵּה סִיסְרָא נֹפֵל מֵת וְהַיָּתֵד בְּרַקָּתוֹ׃
through-temple-of-him and-the-tent-peg being-dead lying Sisera and-see!

וַיַּכְנַע אֱלֹהִים בַּיּוֹם הַהוּא אֵת יָבִין מֶלֶךְ־כְּנָעַן לִפְנֵי
before Canaan king-of Jabin *** the-that on-the-day God so-he-subdued (23)

בְּנֵי יִשְׂרָאֵל׃ וַתֵּלֶךְ יַד בְּנֵי־יִשְׂרָאֵל הָלוֹךְ וְקָשָׁה
also-strong to-grow Israel sons-of hand-of and-she-grew (24) Israel sons-of

עַל יָבִין מֶלֶךְ־כְּנָעַן עַד אֲשֶׁר הִכְרִיתוּ אֵת יָבִין מֶלֶךְ־
king-of Jabin *** they-destroyed when until Canaan king-of Jabin against

כְּנָעַן׃ וַתָּשַׁר דְּבוֹרָה וּבָרָק בֶּן־אֲבִינֹעַם בַּיּוֹם
on-the-day Abinoam son-of and-Barak Deborah and-she-sang (5:1) Canaan

הַהוּא לֵאמֹר׃ בִּפְרֹעַ פְּרָעוֹת בְּיִשְׂרָאֵל בְּהִתְנַדֵּב
when-to-offer-themselves in-Israel princes when-to-take-lead (2) to-say the-that

עָם בָּרְכוּ יְהוָה׃ שִׁמְעוּ מְלָכִים הַאֲזִינוּ רֹזְנִים אָנֹכִי לַיהוָה אָנֹכִי
I to-Yahweh I rulers listen! kings hear! (3) Yahweh praise! people

אָשִׁירָה אֲזַמֵּר לַיהוָה אֱלֹהֵי יִשְׂרָאֵל׃ יְהוָה
Yahweh (4) Israel God-of to-Yahweh I-will-make-music I-will-sing

בְּצֵאתְךָ מִשֵּׂעִיר בְּצַעְדְּךָ מִשְּׂדֵה אֱדוֹם אֶרֶץ
earth Edom from-land-of when-to-march-you from-Seir when-to-go-out-you

19"I'm thirsty," he said.
"Please give me some water."
She opened a skin of milk,
gave him a drink, and covered
him up.
20"Stand in the doorway of
the tent," he told her. "If
someone comes by and asks
you, 'Is anyone here?' say
'No.' "
21But Jael, Heber's wife,
picked up a tent peg and a
hammer and went quietly to
him while he lay fast asleep,
exhausted. She drove the peg
through his temple into the
ground, and he died.
22Barak came by in pursuit of
Sisera, and Jael went out to
meet him. "Come," she said,
"I will show you the man
you're looking for." So he
went in with her, and there
lay Sisera with the tent peg
through his temple—dead.
23On that day God subdued
Jabin, the Canaanite king, before the Israelites. 24And the
hand of the Israelites grew
stronger and stronger against
Jabin, the Canaanite king, until they destroyed him.

The Song of Deborah

5 On that day Deborah and
Barak son of Abinoam
sang this song:

2"When the princes in Israel
take the lead,
when the people
willingly offer
themselves—
praise the LORD!

3"Hear this, you kings!
Listen, you rulers!
I will sing to the LORD, I
will sing;
I will make music to the
LORD, the God of
Israel.

4"O LORD, when you went
out from Seir,
when you marched from
the land of Edom,
the earth shook, the
heavens poured,
the clouds poured down
water.

***19 Many mss omit the *vav* or have (נאד) as a *Qere* form.**

†21 Many mss omit the *aleph* or have (בַּלָּט) as a *Qere* form.

רָֽעָשָׁה גַּם־ שָׁמַיִם נָטָפוּ גַּם־ עָבִים נָטְפוּ מָֽיִם׃
waters they-poured-down clouds also they-poured heavens also she-shook

הָרִים נָזְלוּ מִפְּנֵי יְהוָה זֶה סִינַי מִפְּנֵי יְהוָה
Yahweh at-before Sinai One-of Yahweh at-before they-quaked mountains (5)

אֱלֹהֵי יִשְׂרָאֵל׃ בִּימֵי שַׁמְגַּר בֶּן־ עֲנָת בִּימֵי יָעֵל
Jael in-days-of Anath son-of Shamgar in-days-of (6) Israel God-of

חָדְלוּ אֳרָחוֹת וְהֹלְכֵי נְתִיבוֹת יֵלְכוּ אֳרָחוֹת
roads they-took paths and-ones-travelling-of roads they-were-abandoned

עֲקַלְקַלּוֹת׃ חָדְלוּ פְרָזוֹן בְּיִשְׂרָאֵל חָדֵלּוּ עַד
until they-ceased in-Israel village-life they-ceased (7) winding-ones

שַׁקַּמְתִּי דְּבוֹרָה שַׁקַּמְתִּי אֵם בְּיִשְׂרָאֵל׃ יִבְחַר אֱלֹהִים חֲדָשִׁים אָז
then new-ones gods they-chose (8) in-Israel mother I-arose Deborah I-arose

לָחֶם שְׁעָרִים מָגֵן אִם־ יֵרָאֶה וָרֹמַח בְּאַרְבָּעִים אֶלֶף
thousand among-forty or-spear he-was-seen not shield city-gates war-of

בְּיִשְׂרָאֵל׃ לִבִּי לְחוֹקְקֵי יִשְׂרָאֵל הַמִּתְנַדְּבִים
the-ones-volunteering Israel with-ones-ruling-of heart-of-me (9) in-Israel

בָּעָם בָּרְכוּ יְהוָה׃ רֹכְבֵי אֲתֹנוֹת צְחֹרוֹת
white-ones donkeys ones-riding-of (10) Yahweh praise! among-the-people

יֹשְׁבֵי עַל־ מִדִּין וְהֹלְכֵי עַל־ דֶּרֶךְ שִׂיחוּ׃
consider! road on and-ones-walking-of saddle-blanket on ones-sitting-of

מִקּוֹל מְחַצְצִים בֵּין מַשְׁאַבִּים שָׁם יְתַנּוּ
they-recite there watering-places at ones-singing to-voice-of (11)

צִדְקוֹת יְהוָה צִדְקֹת פִּרְזֹנוֹ בְּיִשְׂרָאֵל אָז
then in-Israel warrior-of-him righteous-acts-of Yahweh righteous-acts-of

יָרְדוּ לַשְּׁעָרִים עַם־ יְהוָה׃ עוּרִי עוּרִי
wake-up! wake-up! (12) Yahweh people-of to-the-city-gates they-went-down

דְּבוֹרָה עוּרִי עוּרִי דַּבְּרִי־ שִׁיר קוּם בָּרָק וּֽשְׁבֵה
and-capture! Barak arise! song break-out! wake-up! wake-up! Deborah

שֶׁבְיְךָ בֶּן־ אֲבִינֹעַם׃ אָז יְרַד שָׂרִיד לְאַדִּירִים
to-nobles one-left he-came-down then (13) Abinoam son-of captive-of-you

עַם יְהוָה יְרַד־ לִי בַּגִּבּוֹרִים׃ מִנִּי אֶפְרַיִם
Ephraim from (14) with-the-mighty-ones to-me he-came Yahweh people-of

שָׁרְשָׁם בַּעֲמָלֵק אַחֲרֶיךָ בִנְיָמִין בַּעֲמָמֶיךָ מִנִּי מָכִיר
Makir from with-people-of-you Benjamin following-you in-Amelek root-of-them

יָרְדוּ מְחֹקְקִים וּמִזְּבוּלֻן מֹשְׁכִים בְּשֵׁבֶט
of-staff-of ones-bearing and-from-Zebulun ones-commanding they-came-down

סֹפֵר׃ וְשָׂרַי בְּיִשָּׂשכָר עִם־ דְּבֹרָה וְיִשָּׂשכָר
and-Issachar Deborah with in-Issachar and-princes-of-me (15) one-commanding

5The mountains quaked before the LORD, the One of Sinai,
before the LORD, the God of Israel.

6"In the days of Shamgar son of Anath,
in the days of Jael, the roads were abandoned;
travelers took to winding paths.
7Village life[u] in Israel ceased,
ceased until I,[v] Deborah, arose,
arose a mother in Israel.
8When they chose new gods,
war came to the city gates,
and not a shield or spear was seen
among forty thousand in Israel.
9My heart is with Israel's princes,
with the willing volunteers among the people.
Praise the LORD!

10"You who ride on white donkeys,
sitting on your saddle blankets,
and you who walk along the road,
consider 11the voice of the singers[w] at the watering places.
They recite the righteous acts of the LORD,
the righteous acts of his warriors[x] in Israel.
Then the people of the LORD
went down to the city gates.

12"Wake up, wake up, Deborah!
Wake up, wake up, break out in song!
Arise, O Barak!
Take captive your captives, O son of Abinoam.

13"Then the men who were left
came down to the nobles;
the people of the LORD
came to me with the mighty.
14Some came from Ephraim, whose roots were in Amalek;
Benjamin was with the people who followed you.
From Makir captains came down,
from Zebulun those who bear a commander's staff.

[u]7 Or *Warriors* [v]7 Or *you*
[w]11 Or *archers;* the meaning of the Hebrew for this word is uncertain. [x]11 Or *villagers*

כֵּן בָּרָק בָּעֵמֶק שֻׁלַּח בְּרַגְלָיו בִּפְלַגּוֹת רְאוּבֵן
Reuben in-districts-of on-feet-of-him he-rushed into-the-valley Barak same

גְּדֹלִים חִקְקֵי־לֵב׃ (16) לָמָּה יָשַׁבְתָּ בֵּין הַמִּשְׁפְּתַיִם לִשְׁמֹעַ
to-hear the-campfires among you-stayed why? (16) heart searchings-of many

שְׁרִקוֹת עֲדָרִים לִפְלַגּוֹת רְאוּבֵן גְּדוֹלִים חִקְרֵי־לֵב׃
heart searchings-of many Reuben in-districts-of flocks whistlings-of

(17) גִּלְעָד בְּעֵבֶר הַיַּרְדֵּן שָׁכֵן וְדָן לָמָּה יָגוּר אֳנִיּוֹת
ships he-lingered why? and-Dan he-stayed the-Jordan at-beyond Gilead (17)

אָשֵׁר יָשַׁב לְחוֹף יַמִּים וְעַל מִפְרָצָיו יִשְׁכּוֹן׃
he-stayed coves-of-him and-in seas on-coast-of he-remained Asher

(18) זְבֻלוּן עַם חֵרֵף נַפְשׁוֹ לָמוּת וְנַפְתָּלִי עַל מְרוֹמֵי
heights-of on and-Naphtali to-die life-of-him he-risked people Zebulun (18)

שָׂדֶה׃ (19) בָּאוּ מְלָכִים נִלְחָמוּ אָז נִלְחֲמוּ מַלְכֵי כְנַעַן
Canaan kings-of they-fought then they-fought kings they-came (19) field

בְּתַעְנַךְ עַל־מֵי מְגִדּוֹ בֶּצַע כֶּסֶף לֹא לָקָחוּ׃
they-carried-off not silver plunder Megiddo waters-of by at-Taanach

(20) מִן־שָׁמַיִם נִלְחָמוּ הַכּוֹכָבִים מִמְּסִלּוֹתָם נִלְחֲמוּ עִם־
against they-fought from-courses-them the-stars they-fought heavens from (20)

סִיסְרָא׃ (21) נַחַל קִישׁוֹן גְּרָפָם נַחַל קְדוּמִים נַחַל
River-of old-ages river-of he-swept-away-them Kishon River-of (21) Sisera

קִישׁוֹן תִּדְרְכִי נַפְשִׁי עֹז׃ (22) אָז הָלְמוּ עִקְּבֵי־
hoofs-of they-thundered then (22) strong soul-of-me you-march-on Kishon

סוּס מִדַּהֲרוֹת דַּהֲרוֹת אַבִּירָיו׃ (23) אוֹרוּ מֵרוֹז
Meroz curse! (23) mighty-ones-of-him gallopings-of from-gallopings-of horse

אָמַר מַלְאַךְ יְהוָה אֹרוּ אָרוֹר יֹשְׁבֶיהָ כִּי לֹא־בָאוּ
they-came not for ones-populating-her to-curse curse! Yahweh angel-of he-said

לְעֶזְרַת יְהוָה לְעֶזְרַת יְהוָה בַּגִּבּוֹרִים׃ (24) תְּבֹרַךְ
you-are-blessed (24) against-mighty-ones Yahweh to-help-of Yahweh to-help-of

מִנָּשִׁים יָעֵל אֵשֶׁת חֶבֶר הַקֵּינִי מִנָּשִׁים בָּאֹהֶל
in-the-tent most-of-women the-Kenite Heber wife-of Jael most-of-women

תְּבֹרָךְ׃ (25) מַיִם שָׁאַל חָלָב נָתָנָה בְּסֵפֶל אַדִּירִים
nobles in-bowl-of she-gave milk he-asked waters (25) you-are-blessed

הִקְרִיבָה חֶמְאָה׃ (26) יָדָהּ לַיָּתֵד תִּשְׁלַחְנָה
they-reached for-the-tent-peg hand-of-her (26) curdled-milk she-brought

וִימִינָהּ לְהַלְמוּת עֲמֵלִים וְהָלְמָה סִיסְרָא מָחֲקָה
she-crushed Sisera and-she-struck workmen for-hammer-of and-right-of-her

רֹאשׁוֹ וּמָחֲצָה וְחָלְפָה רַקָּתוֹ׃ (27) בֵּין
at (27) temple-of-him and-she-pierced and-she-shattered head-of-him

15 The princes of Issachar were with Deborah;
yes, Issachar was with Barak,
rushing after him into the valley.
In the districts of Reuben there was much searching of heart.
16 Why did you stay among the campfires
to hear the whistling for the flocks?
In the districts of Reuben there was much searching of heart.
17 Gilead stayed beyond the Jordan.
And Dan, why did he linger by the ships?
Asher remained on the seacoast
and stayed in his coves.
18 The people of Zebulun risked their very lives;
so did Naphtali on the heights of the field.

19 "Kings came, they fought;
the kings of Canaan fought
at Taanach by the waters of Megiddo,
but they carried off no silver, no plunder.
20 From the heavens the stars fought,
from their courses they fought against Sisera.
21 The river Kishon swept them away,
the age-old river, the river Kishon.
March on, my soul; be strong!
22 Then thundered the horses' hoofs—
galloping, galloping go his mighty steeds.
23 'Curse Meroz,' said the angel of the LORD.
'Curse its people bitterly,
because they did not come to help the LORD,
to help the LORD against the mighty.'

24 "Most blessed of women be Jael,
the wife of Heber the Kenite,
most blessed of tent-dwelling women.
25 He asked for water, and she gave him milk;
in a bowl fit for nobles she brought him curdled milk.
26 Her hand reached for the tent peg,
her right hand for the workman's hammer.
She struck Sisera, she crushed his head,
she shattered and pierced his temple.

רַגְלֶיהָ כָּרַע נָפַל שָׁכָב בֵּין רַגְלֶיהָ כָּרַע נָפָל בַּאֲשֶׁר
at-where he-fell he-sank feet-of-her at he-lay he-fell he-sank feet-of-her

כָּרַע שָׁם נָפַל שָׁדוּד׃ (28) בְּעַד הַחַלּוֹן נִשְׁקְפָה
she-peered the-window through (28) being-dead he-fell there he-sank

וַתְּיַבֵּב אֵם סִיסְרָא בְּעַד הָאֶשְׁנָב מַדּוּעַ בֹּשֵׁשׁ
taking-long why? the-lattice behind Sisera mother-of and-she-cried-out

רִכְבּוֹ לָבוֹא מַדּוּעַ אֶחֱרוּ פַּעֲמֵי מַרְכְּבוֹתָיו׃
chariots-of-him clatters-of they-delay why? to-come chariot-of-him

(29) חַכְמוֹת שָׂרוֹתֶיהָ תַּעֲנֶינָּה אַף־ הִיא תָּשִׁיב
she-repeats she indeed they-answer-her ladies-of-her wisest-ones-of (29)

אֲמָרֶיהָ לָהּ׃ (30) הֲלֹא יִמְצְאוּ יְחַלְּקוּ שָׁלָל רַחַם רַחֲמָתַיִם
two-girls girl spoil they-divide they-find not? (30) to-her words-of-her

לְרֹאשׁ גֶּבֶר שְׁלַל צְבָעִים לְסִיסְרָא שְׁלַל
plunder-of for-Sisera colorful-garments plunder-of man for-each-of

צְבָעִים רִקְמָה צֶבַע רִקְמָתַיִם לְצַוְּארֵי
for-necks-of ones-embroidered garment-of embroidered colorful-garments

שָׁלָל׃ (31) כֵּן יֹאבְדוּ כָל־ אוֹיְבֶיךָ יְהוָה
Yahweh being-enemies-of-you all-of may-they-perish so (31) plunder

וְאֹהֲבָיו כְּצֵאת הַשֶּׁמֶשׁ בִּגְבֻרָתוֹ וַתִּשְׁקֹט
then-she-had-peace in-strength-of-him the-sun like-to-rise but-ones-loving-him

הָאָרֶץ אַרְבָּעִים שָׁנָה׃ (6:1) וַיַּעֲשׂוּ בְנֵי־ יִשְׂרָאֵל הָרַע בְּעֵינֵי
in-eyes-of the-evil Israel sons-of and-they-did (6:1) year forty the-land

יְהוָה וַיִּתְּנֵם יְהוָה בְּיַד־ מִדְיָן שֶׁבַע שָׁנִים׃
years seven Midian into-hand-of Yahweh and-he-gave-them Yahweh

(2) וַתָּעָז יַד־ מִדְיָן עַל־ יִשְׂרָאֵל מִפְּנֵי מִדְיָן
Midian because-of Israel over Midian hand-of and-she-was-oppressive (2)

עָשׂוּ* לָהֶם ׀ בְּנֵי יִשְׂרָאֵל אֶת־ הַמִּנְהָרוֹת אֲשֶׁר בֶּהָרִים
in-the-mountains that the-shelters *** Israel sons-of for-them they-prepared

וְאֶת־הַמְּעָרוֹת וְאֶת־ הַמְּצָדוֹת׃ (3) וְהָיָה אִם־ זָרַע יִשְׂרָאֵל
Israel he-planted when and-he-was (3) the-strongholds and the-caves and

וְעָלָה מִדְיָן וַעֲמָלֵק וּבְנֵי־ קֶדֶם וְעָלוּ
and-they-invaded east and-people-of and-Amalek Midian then-he-invaded

עָלָיו׃ (4) וַיַּחֲנוּ עֲלֵיהֶם וַיַּשְׁחִיתוּ אֶת־ יְבוּל
crop-of *** and-they-ruined against-them and-they-camped (4) against-him

הָאָרֶץ עַד־ בּוֹאֲךָ עַזָּה וְלֹא־ יַשְׁאִירוּ מִחְיָה בְּיִשְׂרָאֵל
for-Israel from-living-thing they-spared and-not Gaza to-go-you as the-land

וְשֶׂה וָשׁוֹר וַחֲמוֹר׃ (5) כִּי הֵם וּמִקְנֵיהֶם יַעֲלוּ
they-came-up and-stock-of-them they for (5) nor-donkey nor-cattle neither-sheep

---

27 At her feet he sank,
he fell; there he lay.
At her feet he sank, he fell;
where he sank, there he
fell—dead.

28 "Through the window
peered Sisera's mother;
behind the lattice she
cried out,
'Why is his chariot so long
in coming?
Why is the clatter of his
chariots delayed?'
29 The wisest of her ladies
answer her;
indeed, she keeps saying
to herself,
30 'Are they not finding and
dividing the spoils:
a girl or two for each
man,
colorful garments as
plunder for Sisera,
colorful garments
embroidered,
highly embroidered
garments for my
neck—
all this as plunder?'

31 "So may all your enemies
perish, O LORD!
But may they who love
you be like the sun
when it rises in its
strength."

Then the land had peace forty years.

Gideon

6 Again the Israelites did
evil in the eyes of the
LORD, and for seven years he
gave them into the hands of
the Midianites. 2 Because the
power of Midian was so op-
pressive, the Israelites prepared shelters for themselves
in mountain clefts, caves and
strongholds. 3 Whenever the
Israelites planted their crops,
the Midianites, Amalekites
and other eastern peoples invaded the country. 4 They
camped on the land and
ruined the crops all the way to
Gaza and did not spare a living thing for Israel, neither
sheep nor cattle nor donkeys.
5 They came up with their livestock and their tents like

*2 Most mss have *maqqeph* binding this word to the following (עשׂו־).

וְאָהֳלֵיהֶם יָבֹאוּ כְדֵי־ אַרְבֶּה לָרֹב וְלָהֶם
and-to-them in-number locust like-swarm-of and-they-came and-tents-of-them

וְלִגְמַלֵּיהֶם אֵין מִסְפָּר וַיָּבֹאוּ בָאָרֶץ לְשַׁחֲתָהּ׃
to-ravish-her on-the-land and-they-invaded number not and-to-camels-of-them

וַיִּדַּל יִשְׂרָאֵל מְאֹד מִפְּנֵי מִדְיָן וַיִּזְעֲקוּ
so-they-cried Midian because-of very Israel and-he-was-impoverished (6)

בְנֵי־ יִשְׂרָאֵל אֶל־ יְהוָה׃ וַיְהִי כִּי־ זָעֲקוּ בְנֵי־יִשְׂרָאֵל אֶל־
to Israel sons-of they-cried when and-he-was (7) Yahweh to Israel sons-of

יְהוָה עַל אֹדוֹת מִדְיָן׃ וַיִּשְׁלַח יְהוָה אִישׁ נָבִיא אֶל־ בְּנֵי
sons-of to prophet man Yahweh then-he-sent (8) Midian reasons-of for Yahweh

יִשְׂרָאֵל וַיֹּאמֶר לָהֶם כֹּה־ אָמַר יְהוָה ׀ אֱלֹהֵי יִשְׂרָאֵל אָנֹכִי הֶעֱלֵיתִי
I-brought-up I Israel God-of Yahweh he-says this to-them and-he-said Israel

אֶתְכֶם מִמִּצְרַיִם וָאֹצִיא אֶתְכֶם מִבֵּית עֲבָדִים׃ וָאַצִּל
and-I-snatched (9) slaveries from-house-of you and-I-brought from-Egypt you

אֶתְכֶם מִיַּד מִצְרַיִם וּמִיַּד כָּל־ לֹחֲצֵיכֶם וָאֲגָרֵשׁ
and-I-drove ones-oppressing-you all-of and-from-hand-of Egypt from-hand-of you

אוֹתָם מִפְּנֵיכֶם וָאֶתְּנָה לָכֶם אֶת־ אַרְצָם׃ וָאֹמְרָה
and-I-said (10) land-of-them *** to-you and-I-gave from-before-you them

לָכֶם אֲנִי יְהוָה אֱלֹהֵיכֶם לֹא תִירְאוּ אֶת־ אֱלֹהֵי הָאֱמֹרִי אֲשֶׁר
who the-Amorite gods-of *** you-worship not God-of-you Yahweh I to-you

אַתֶּם יוֹשְׁבִים בְּאַרְצָם וְלֹא שְׁמַעְתֶּם בְּקוֹלִי׃
to-voice-of-me you-listened but-not in-land-of-them ones-living you

וַיָּבֹא מַלְאַךְ יְהוָה וַיֵּשֶׁב תַּחַת הָאֵלָה אֲשֶׁר בְּעָפְרָה
in-Ophrah that the-oak under and-he-sat Yahweh angel-of and-he-came (11)

אֲשֶׁר לְיוֹאָשׁ אֲבִי הָעֶזְרִי וְגִדְעוֹן בְּנוֹ חֹבֵט חִטִּים
wheats threshing son-of-him and-Gideon the-Abiezrite to-Joash that

בַּגַּת לְהָנִיס מִפְּנֵי מִדְיָן׃ וַיֵּרָא אֵלָיו
to-him when-he-appeared (12) Midian from-before to-keep in-the-winepress

מַלְאַךְ יְהוָה וַיֹּאמֶר אֵלָיו יְהוָה עִמְּךָ גִּבּוֹר הֶחָיִל׃
the-mighty warrior-of with-you Yahweh to-him then-he-said Yahweh angel-of

וַיֹּאמֶר אֵלָיו גִּדְעוֹן בִּי אֲדֹנִי וְיֵשׁ יְהוָה עִמָּנוּ
with-us Yahweh if-he-is sir-of-me but Gideon to-him and-he-replied (13)

וְלָמָּה מְצָאַתְנוּ כָּל־ זֹאת וְאַיֵּה כָל־ נִפְלְאֹתָיו
being-wonders-of-him all-of and-where? this all-of she-happened-to-us then-why?

אֲשֶׁר סִפְּרוּ־ לָנוּ אֲבוֹתֵינוּ לֵאמֹר הֲלֹא מִמִּצְרַיִם הֶעֱלָנוּ
he-brought-us from-Egypt not? to-say fathers-of-us to-us they-told that

יְהוָה וְעַתָּה נְטָשָׁנוּ יְהוָה וַיִּתְּנֵנוּ בְּכַף־ מִדְיָן׃
Midian into-hand-of and-he-put-us Yahweh he-abandoned-us but-now Yahweh

swarms of locusts. It was impossible to count the men and
their camels; they invaded the
land to ravage it. [6]Midian so
impoverished the Israelites
that they cried out to the LORD
for help.
[7]When the Israelites cried to
the LORD because of Midian,
[8]he sent them a prophet, who
said, "This is what the LORD,
the God of Israel, says: I
brought you up out of Egypt,
out of the land of slavery. [9]I
snatched you from the power
of Egypt and from the hand of
all your oppressors. I drove
them from before you and
gave you their land. [10]I said to
you, 'I am the LORD your God;
do not worship the gods of the
Amorites, in whose land you
live.' But you have not listened
to me."
[11]The angel of the LORD came
and sat down under the oak in
Ophrah that belonged to Joash
the Abiezrite, where his son
Gideon was threshing wheat
in a winepress to keep it from
the Midianites. [12]When the
angel of the LORD appeared to
Gideon, he said, "The LORD is
with you, mighty warrior."
[13]"But sir," Gideon replied,
"if the LORD is with us, why
has all this happened to us?
Where are all his wonders that
our fathers told us about when
they said, 'Did not the LORD
bring us up out of Egypt?' But
now the LORD has abandoned
us and put us into the hand of
Midian."

°5 ק ובאו

וַיִּפֶן אֵלָיו יְהוָה וַיֹּאמֶר לֵךְ בְּכֹחֲךָ זֶה
this in-strength-of-you go! and-he-said Yahweh to-him and-he-turned (14)

וְהוֹשַׁעְתָּ אֶת־יִשְׂרָאֵל מִכַּף מִדְיָן הֲלֹא שְׁלַחְתִּיךָ׃ וַיֹּאמֶר
and-he-asked (15) I-send-you not? Midian from-hand-of Israel *** and-you-save

אֵלָיו בִּי אֲדֹנָי בַּמָּה אוֹשִׁיעַ אֶת־יִשְׂרָאֵל הִנֵּה אַלְפִּי הַדַּל
the-weakest clan-of-me see! Israel *** I-save by-the-how? Lord but to-him

בִּמְנַשֶּׁה וְאָנֹכִי הַצָּעִיר בְּבֵית אָבִי׃ וַיֹּאמֶר
and-he-answered (16) father-of-me in-house-of the-least and-I in-Manasseh

אֵלָיו יְהוָה כִּי אֶהְיֶה עִמָּךְ וְהִכִּיתָ אֶת־מִדְיָן
Midian *** and-you-will-strike-down with-you I-will-be indeed Yahweh to-him

כְּאִישׁ אֶחָד׃ וַיֹּאמֶר אֵלָיו אִם־נָא מָצָאתִי חֵן בְּעֵינֶיךָ
in-eyes-of-you favor I-found now! if to-him and-he-replied (17) one as-man

וְעָשִׂיתָ לִּי אוֹת שָׁאַתָּה מְדַבֵּר עִמִּי׃ אַל־נָא תָמֻשׁ
you-go-away now! not (18) to-me talking that-you sign to-me then-you-give

מִזֶּה עַד־בֹּאִי אֵלֶיךָ וְהֹצֵאתִי אֶת־מִנְחָתִי וְהִנַּחְתִּי
and-I-set offering-of-me *** and-I-bring to-you to-come-back-me until from-here

לְפָנֶיךָ וַיֹּאמַר אָנֹכִי אֵשֵׁב עַד שׁוּבֶךָ׃ וְגִדְעוֹן
and-Gideon (19) to-return-you until I-will-wait I and-he-said before-you

בָּא וַיַּעַשׂ גְּדִי־עִזִּים וְאֵיפַת־קֶמַח
flour and-ephah-of goats young-one-of and-he-prepared he-went-in

מַצּוֹת הַבָּשָׂר שָׂם בַּסַּל וְהַמָּרָק שָׂם
he-put and-the-broth in-the-basket he-put the-meat breads-without-yeast

בַּפָּרוּר וַיּוֹצֵא אֵלָיו אֶל־תַּחַת הָאֵלָה וַיַּגַּשׁ׃
and-he-offered the-oak under at to-him and-he-brought-out in-the-pot

וַיֹּאמֶר אֵלָיו מַלְאַךְ הָאֱלֹהִים קַח אֶת־הַבָּשָׂר וְאֶת־
and the-meat *** take! the-God angel-of to-him and-he-said (20)

הַמַּצּוֹת וְהַנַּח אֶל־הַסֶּלַע הַלָּז וְאֶת־הַמָּרָק שְׁפוֹךְ
pour-out! the-broth and the-this the-rock on and-place! the-unleavened-breads

וַיַּעַשׂ כֵּן׃ וַיִּשְׁלַח מַלְאַךְ יְהוָה אֶת־קְצֵה הַמִּשְׁעֶנֶת
the-staff tip-of *** Yahweh angel-of and-he-reached-out (21) so and-he-did

אֲשֶׁר בְּיָדוֹ וַיִּגַּע בַּבָּשָׂר וּבַמַּצּוֹת
and-on-the-unleavened-breads on-the-meat and-he-touched in-hand-of-him that

וַתַּעַל הָאֵשׁ מִן־הַצּוּר וַתֹּאכַל אֶת־הַבָּשָׂר וְאֶת־
and the-meat *** and-she-consumed the-rock from the-fire and-she-flared

הַמַּצּוֹת וּמַלְאַךְ יְהוָה הָלַךְ מֵעֵינָיו׃
from-eyes-of-him he-went-away Yahweh and-angel-of the-unleavened-breads

וַיַּרְא גִּדְעוֹן כִּי־מַלְאַךְ יְהוָה הוּא וַיֹּאמֶר גִּדְעוֹן
Gideon then-he-exclaimed he Yahweh angel-of that Gideon when-he-realized (22)

14The LORD turned to him
and said, "Go in the strength
you have and save Israel out of
Midian's hand. Am I not
sending you?"
15"But Lord,[y]" Gideon asked,
"how can I save Israel? My
clan is the weakest in Manasseh, and I am the least in my
family."
16The LORD answered, "I will
be with you, and you will
strike down the Midianites as
if they were but one man."
17Gideon replied, "If now I
have found favor in your eyes,
give me a sign that it is really
you talking to me.
18Please do
not go away until I come back
and bring my offering and set
it before you."
And the LORD said, "I will
wait until you return."
19Gideon went in, prepared
a young goat, and from an
ephah[z] of flour he made bread
without yeast. Putting the
meat in a basket and its broth
in a pot, he brought them out
and offered them to him under
the oak.
20The angel of God said to
him, "Take the meat and the
unleavened bread, place them
on this rock, and pour out the
broth." And Gideon did so.
21With the tip of the staff that
was in his hand, the angel of
the LORD touched the meat
and the unleavened bread.
Fire flared from the rock, consuming the meat and the
bread. And the angel of the
LORD disappeared.
22When
Gideon realized that it was the
angel of the LORD, he exclaimed, "Ah, Sovereign LORD!

y15 Or *sir*
z19 That is, probably about 1/2 bushel (about 22 liters)

אֲהָהּ אֲדֹנָי יְהוִה כִּי־ עַל־ כֵּן רָאִיתִי מַלְאַךְ יְהוָה פָּנִים אֶל־פָּנִים׃
faces to faces Yahweh angel-of I-saw that because for Yahweh Lord ah!

וַיֹּאמֶר לוֹ יְהוָה שָׁלוֹם לְךָ אַל־ תִּירָא לֹא תָּמוּת׃
you-will-die not you-be-afraid not to-you peace Yahweh to-him but-he-said (23)

וַיִּבֶן שָׁם גִּדְעוֹן מִזְבֵּחַ לַיהוָה וַיִּקְרָא־ לוֹ יְהוָה
Yahweh to-him and-he-called to-Yahweh altar Gideon there so-he-built (24)

שָׁלוֹם עַד הַיּוֹם הַזֶּה עוֹדֶנּוּ בְּעָפְרַת אֲבִי הָעֶזְרִי׃ וַיְהִי
and-he-was (25) the-Abiezite in-Ophrah-of still-he the-this the-day to Peace

בַּלַּיְלָה הַהוּא וַיֹּאמֶר לוֹ יְהוָה קַח אֶת־ פַּר־ הַשּׁוֹר
the-herd bull-of *** take! Yahweh to-him that-he-said the-that in-the-night

אֲשֶׁר לְאָבִיךָ וּפַר הַשֵּׁנִי שֶׁבַע שָׁנִים וְהָרַסְתָּ
and-you-tear-down years seven the-second even-bull-of to-father-of-you that

אֶת־ מִזְבַּח הַבַּעַל אֲשֶׁר לְאָבִיךָ וְאֶת־ הָאֲשֵׁרָה אֲשֶׁר־
that the-Asherah-pole and to-father-of-you that the-Baal altar-of ***

עָלָיו תִּכְרֹת׃ וּבָנִיתָ מִזְבֵּחַ לַיהוָה אֱלֹהֶיךָ עַל
on God-of-you to-Yahweh altar then-you-build (26) you-cut-down beside-him

רֹאשׁ הַמָּעוֹז הַזֶּה בַּמַּעֲרָכָה וְלָקַחְתָּ אֶת־ הַפָּר הַשֵּׁנִי
the-second the-bull *** then-you-take by-the-layer the-this the-bluff top-of

וְהַעֲלִיתָ עוֹלָה בַּעֲצֵי הָאֲשֵׁרָה אֲשֶׁר תִּכְרֹת׃
you-cut-down that the-Asherah-pole with-woods-of burnt-offering and-you-offer

וַיִּקַּח גִּדְעוֹן עֲשָׂרָה אֲנָשִׁים מֵעֲבָדָיו וַיַּעַשׂ כַּאֲשֶׁר
just-as and-he-did from-servants-of-him men ten Gideon so-he-took (27)

דִּבֶּר אֵלָיו יְהוָה וַיְהִי כַּאֲשֶׁר יָרֵא אֶת־ בֵּית
house-of *** he-was-afraid because but-he-was Yahweh to-him he-told

אָבִיו וְאֶת־ אַנְשֵׁי הָעִיר מֵעֲשׂוֹת יוֹמָם וַיַּעַשׂ לָיְלָה׃
night so-he-did by-day from-to-do the-town men-of and father-of-him

וַיַּשְׁכִּימוּ אַנְשֵׁי הָעִיר בַּבֹּקֶר וְהִנֵּה נֻתַּץ
he-was-demolished then-see! in-the-morning the-town men-of when-they-got-up (28)

מִזְבַּח הַבַּעַל וְהָאֲשֵׁרָה אֲשֶׁר־ עָלָיו כֹּרָתָה וְאֵת
and being-cut-down beside-him that and-the-Asherah-pole the-Baal altar-of

הַפָּר הַשֵּׁנִי הֹעֲלָה עַל־ הַמִּזְבֵּחַ הַבָּנוּי׃
the-one-being-built the-altar on he-was-sacrificed the-second the-bull

וַיֹּאמְרוּ אִישׁ אֶל־ רֵעֵהוּ מִי עָשָׂה הַדָּבָר הַזֶּה
the-this the-thing he-did who? other-of-him to each and-they-asked (29)

וַיִּדְרְשׁוּ וַיְבַקְשׁוּ וַיֹּאמְרוּ גִּדְעוֹן בֶּן־ יוֹאָשׁ
Joash son-of Gideon then-they-said and-they-searched when-they-investigated

עָשָׂה הַדָּבָר הַזֶּה׃ וַיֹּאמְרוּ אַנְשֵׁי הָעִיר אֶל־ יוֹאָשׁ
Joash to the-town men-of and-they-demanded (30) the-this the-thing he-did

I have seen the angel of the
LORD face to face!"
23But the LORD said to him,
"Peace! Do not be afraid. You
are not going to die."
24So Gideon built an altar to
the LORD there and called it
"The LORD is Peace." To this
day it stands in Ophrah of the
Abiezrites.
25That same night the LORD
said to him, "Take the second
bull from your father's herd,
the one seven years old.[a] Tear
down your father's altar to
Baal and cut down the
Asherah pole[b] beside it.
26Then build a proper kind of[c]
altar to the LORD your God on
the top of this bluff. Using the
wood of the Asherah pole that
you cut down, offer the second[d] bull as a burnt offering."
27So Gideon took ten of his
servants and did as the LORD
told him. But because he was
afraid of his family and the
men of the town, he did it at
night rather than in the day-
time.
28In the morning when the
men of the town got up, there
was Baal's altar, demolished,
with the Asherah pole beside
it cut down and the second
bull sacrificed on the newly
built altar!
29They asked each other,
"Who did this?"
When they carefully investi-
gated, they were told, "Gideon
son of Joash did it."
30The men of the town de-
manded of Joash, "Bring out

[a]25 Or *Take a full-grown, mature bull from your father's herd*
[b]25 That is, a symbol of the goddess Asherah; here and elsewhere in Judges
[c]26 Or *build with layers of stone an*
[d]26 Or *full-grown;* also in verse 28

*24 Most mss have *patbah* under the *resh* (תַ־).

הוֹצֵא אֶת־ בִּנְךָ וְיָמֹת כִּי נָתַץ אֶת־ מִזְבַּח
altar-of *** he-broke-down because for-he-must-die son-of-you *** bring-out!

הַבַּעַל וְכִי כָרַת הָאֲשֵׁרָה אֲשֶׁר־ עָלָיו׃
beside-him that the-Asherah-pole he-cut-down and-because the-Baal

וַיֹּאמֶר יוֹאָשׁ לְכֹל אֲשֶׁר־ עָמְדוּ עָלָיו הַאַתֶּם ׀ תְּרִיבוּן
will-you-plead you? around-him they-stood who to-all Joash but-he-replied (31)

לַבַּעַל אִם־אַתֶּם תּוֹשִׁיעוּן אוֹתוֹ אֲשֶׁר יָרִיב לוֹ יוּמַת
he-will-die for-him he-fights whoever him will-you-save you or for-the-Baal

עַד־ הַבֹּקֶר אִם־אֱלֹהִים הוּא יָרֶב לוֹ כִּי נָתַץ אֶת־
*** he-breaks-down when for-him he-can-defend he god if the-morning by

מִזְבְּחוֹ׃ וַיִּקְרָא־ לוֹ בַיּוֹם־ הַהוּא יְרֻבַּעַל לֵאמֹר
to-say Jerub-Baal the-that on-the-day to-him so-he-called (32) altar-of-him

יָרֶב בּוֹ הַבַּעַל כִּי נָתַץ אֶת־ מִזְבְּחוֹ׃
altar-of-him *** he-broke-down for the-Baal with-him let-him-contend

וְכָל־ מִדְיָן וַעֲמָלֵק וּבְנֵי־ קֶדֶם נֶאֶסְפוּ יַחְדָּו
together they-joined east and-peoples-of and-Amalek Midian now-all-of (33)

וַיַּעַבְרוּ וַיַּחֲנוּ בְּעֵמֶק יִזְרְעֶאל׃ וְרוּחַ
then-Spirit-of (34) Jezreel in-Valley-of and-they-camped and-they-crossed

יְהוָה לָבְשָׁה אֶת־ גִּדְעוֹן וַיִּתְקַע בַּשּׁוֹפָר וַיִּזָּעֵק
and-he-summoned on-the-trumpet and-he-blew Gideon *** she-came-upon Yahweh

אֲבִיעֶזֶר אַחֲרָיו׃ וּמַלְאָכִים שָׁלַח בְּכָל־ מְנַשֶּׁה
Manasseh through-all-of he-sent and-messengers (35) after-him Abiezer

וַיִּזָּעֵק גַּם־ הוּא אַחֲרָיו וּמַלְאָכִים שָׁלַח בְּאָשֵׁר
into-Asher he-sent and-messengers after-him he also and-he-called

וּבִזְבֻלוּן וּבְנַפְתָּלִי וַיַּעֲלוּ לִקְרָאתָם׃ וַיֹּאמֶר
and-he-said (36) to-meet-them so-they-went-up and-into-Naphtali and-into-Zebulun

גִּדְעוֹן אֶל־הָאֱלֹהִים אִם־ יֶשְׁךָ מוֹשִׁיעַ בְּיָדִי אֶת־ יִשְׂרָאֵל כַּאֲשֶׁר
just-as Israel *** by-hand-of-me one-saving it-is-you if the-God to Gideon

דִּבַּרְתָּ׃ הִנֵּה אָנֹכִי מַצִּיג אֶת־ גִּזַּת הַצֶּמֶר בַּגֹּרֶן
on-the-threshing-floor the-wool fleece-of *** placing I look! (37) you-promised

אִם טַל יִהְיֶה עַל־ הַגִּזָּה לְבַדָּהּ וְעַל־ כָּל־ הָאָרֶץ חֹרֶב
dryness the-ground all-of and-on by-herself the-fleece on he-is dew if

וְיָדַעְתִּי כִּי־ תוֹשִׁיעַ בְּיָדִי אֶת־ יִשְׂרָאֵל כַּאֲשֶׁר
you-said just-as Israel *** by-hand-of-me you-will-save that then-I-will-know

וַיְהִי־ כֵן וַיַּשְׁכֵּם מִמָּחֳרָת וַיָּזַר אֶת־
*** then-he-squeezed on-next-day when-he-rose so and-he-happened (38)

הַגִּזָּה וַיִּמֶץ טַל מִן־ הַגִּזָּה מְלוֹא הַסֵּפֶל מָיִם׃
waters the-bowl fullness-of the-fleece from dew and-he-wrung-out the-fleece

your son. He must die, because he has broken down
Baal's altar and cut down the
Asherah pole beside it."
31But Joash replied to the
hostile crowd around him,
"Are you going to plead Baal's
cause? Are you trying to save
him? Whoever fights for him
shall be put to death by morning! If Baal really is a god, he
can defend himself when
someone breaks down his altar." 32So that day they called
Gideon "Jerub-Baal,[c]" saying,
"Let Baal contend with him,"
because he broke down Baal's
altar.
33Now all the Midianites,
Amalekites and other eastern
peoples joined forces and
crossed over the Jordan and
camped in the Valley of Jezreel. 34Then the Spirit of the
LORD came upon Gideon, and
he blew a trumpet, summon-
ing the Abiezrites to follow
him. 35He sent messengers
throughout Manasseh, calling
them to arms, and also into
Asher, Zebulun and Naphtali,
so that they too went up to
meet them.
36Gideon said to God, "If you
will save Israel by my hand as
you have promised—look, 37I
will place a wool fleece on the
threshing floor. If there is dew
only on the fleece and all the
ground is dry, then I will
know that you will save Israel
by my hand, as you said."
38And that is what happened.
Gideon rose early the next
day; he squeezed the fleece
and wrung out the dew—a
bowlful of water.

[c]32 *Jerub-Baal* means *let Baal contend.*

וַיֹּאמֶר גִּדְעוֹן אֶל־הָאֱלֹהִים אַל־ יִחַר אַפְּךָ בִּי

against-me anger-of-you let-him-burn not the-God to Gideon then-he-said (39)

וַאֲדַבְּרָה אַךְ הַפָּעַם אֲנַסֶּה נָּא־ רַק־ הַפַּעַם

the-once only now! let-me-test the-once again but-let-me-request

בַּגִּזָּה יְהִי־ נָא חֹרֶב אֶל־ הַגִּזָּה לְבַדָּהּ וְעַל־ כָּל־

all-of and-on by-herself the-fleece on dryness now! may-he-be with-the-fleece

הָאָרֶץ יִהְיֶה־ טָּל׃ וַיַּעַשׂ אֱלֹהִים כֵּן בַּלַּיְלָה הַהוּא

the-that on-the-night so God and-he-did (40) dew may-he-be the-ground

וַיְהִי־ חֹרֶב אֶל־ הַגִּזָּה לְבַדָּהּ וְעַל־ כָּל־ הָאָרֶץ הָיָה

he-was the-ground all-of and-on by-herself the-fleece on dryness and-he-was

טָל׃ וַיַּשְׁכֵּם יְרֻבַּעַל הוּא גִדְעוֹן וְכָל־ הָעָם אֲשֶׁר

who the-people and-all-of Gideon that Jerub-Baal and-he-rose (7:1) dew

אִתּוֹ וַיַּחֲנוּ עַל־ עֵין חֲרֹד וּמַחֲנֵה מִדְיָן הָיָה־ לוֹ

by-him he-was Midian now-camp-of Harod spring-of at and-they-camped with-him

מִצָּפוֹן מִגִּבְעַת הַמּוֹרֶה בָּעֵמֶק׃ וַיֹּאמֶר יְהוָה אֶל־

to Yahweh and-he-said (2) in-the-valley the-Moreh near-hill-of to-north

גִּדְעוֹן רַב הָעָם אֲשֶׁר אִתָּךְ מִתִּתִּי אֶת־ מִדְיָן

Midian *** for-to-deliver-me with-you who the-people too-many Gideon

בְּיָדָם פֶּן־ יִתְפָּאֵר עָלַי יִשְׂרָאֵל לֵאמֹר יָדִי

hand-of-me to-say Israel against-me he-may-boast so-not into-hand-of-them

הוֹשִׁיעָה לִּי׃ וְעַתָּה קְרָא נָא בְּאָזְנֵי הָעָם לֵאמֹר מִי־

whoever to-say the-people in-ears-of now! announce! so-now (3) to-me she-saved

יָרֵא וְחָרֵד יָשֹׁב וְיִצְפֹּר מֵהַר

from-Mount-of and-he-may-leave he-may-turn-back and-trembling fearful

הַגִּלְעָד וַיָּשָׁב מִן־ הָעָם עֶשְׂרִים וּשְׁנַיִם אֶלֶף וַעֲשֶׂרֶת

and-ten-of thousand and-two twenty the-people from so-he-left the-Gilead

אֲלָפִים נִשְׁאָרוּ׃ וַיֹּאמֶר יְהוָה אֶל־ גִּדְעוֹן עוֹד הָעָם

the-people still Gideon to Yahweh but-he-said (4) they-remained thousands

רָב הוֹרֵד אוֹתָם אֶל־ הַמַּיִם וְאֶצְרְפֶנּוּ לְךָ שָׁם

there for-you and-I-will-sift-him the-waters to them take-down! too-many

וְהָיָה אֲשֶׁר אֹמַר אֵלֶיךָ זֶה ׀ יֵלֵךְ אִתָּךְ הוּא יֵלֵךְ

he-shall-go he with-you he-shall-go this to-you I-say whom and-he-will-be

אִתָּךְ וְכֹל אֲשֶׁר־ אֹמַר אֵלֶיךָ זֶה לֹא־ יֵלֵךְ עִמָּךְ הוּא לֹא

not he with-you he-shall-go not this to-you I-say whom but-all with-you

יֵלֵךְ׃ וַיּוֹרֶד אֶת־ הָעָם אֶל־ הַמָּיִם וַיֹּאמֶר

and-he-told the-waters to the-people *** so-he-took-down (5) he-shall-go

יְהוָה אֶל־גִּדְעוֹן כֹּל אֲשֶׁר־ יָלֹק בִּלְשׁוֹנוֹ מִן־ הַמַּיִם כַּאֲשֶׁר

just-as the-waters from with-tongue-of-him he-laps who all Gideon to Yahweh

39 Then Gideon said to God, "Do not be angry with me. Let me make just one more request. Allow me one more test with the fleece. This time make the fleece dry and the ground covered with dew."
40 That night God did so. Only the fleece was dry; all the ground was covered with dew.

Gideon Defeats the Midianites

7 Early in the morning, Jerub-Baal (that is, Gideon) and all his men camped at the spring of Harod. The camp of Midian was north of them in the valley near the hill of Moreh.
2 The LORD said to Gideon, "You have too many men for me to deliver Midian into their hands. In order that Israel may not boast against me that her own strength has saved her,
3 announce now to the people, 'Anyone who trembles with fear may turn back and leave Mount Gilead.'" So twenty-two thousand men left, while ten thousand remained.
4 But the LORD said to Gideon, "There are still too many men. Take them down to the water, and I will sift them for you there. If I say, 'This one shall go with you,' he shall go; but if I say, 'This one shall not go with you,' he shall not go."
5 So Gideon took the men down to the water. There the LORD told him, "Separate those who lap the water with

יָלֹק הַכֶּלֶב תַּצִּיג אוֹתוֹ לְבָד וְכֹל אֲשֶׁר־יִכְרַע עַל־בִּרְכָּיו
knees-of-him on he-kneels who and-all by-self him you-separate the-dog he-laps

לִשְׁתּוֹת׃ וַיְהִי מִסְפַּר הַֽמְלַקְקִים בְּיָדָם אֶל־
to with-hand-of-them the-ones-lapping number-of and-he-was (6) to-drink

פִּיהֶם שְׁלֹשׁ מֵאוֹת אִישׁ וְכֹל יֶתֶר הָעָם כָּרְעוּ
they-kneeled the-people rest-of and-all-of man hundreds three-of mouth-of-them

עַל־בִּרְכֵיהֶם לִשְׁתּוֹת מָיִם׃ וַיֹּאמֶר יְהוָה אֶל־גִּדְעוֹן
Gideon to Yahweh then-he-said (7) waters to-drink knees-of-them on

בִּשְׁלֹשׁ מֵאוֹת הָאִישׁ הַֽמְלַקְקִים אוֹשִׁיעַ אֶתְכֶם וְנָתַתִּי
and-I-will-give you I-will-save the-ones-lapping the-man hundreds with-three-of

אֶת־מִדְיָן בְּיָדֶךָ וְכָל־הָעָם יֵלְכוּ אִישׁ לִמְקֹמוֹ׃
to-place-of-him each let-them-go the-people and-all-of into-hand-you Midian ***

וַיִּקְחוּ אֶת־צֵדָה הָעָם בְּיָדָם וְאֵת
and in-hand-of-them the-people provision *** so-they-took-over (8)

שׁוֹפְרֹתֵיהֶם וְאֵת כָּל־אִישׁ יִשְׂרָאֵל שִׁלַּח אִישׁ לְאֹהָלָיו
to-tents-of-him each he-sent Israel man-of rest-of and trumpets-of-them

וּבִשְׁלֹשׁ־מֵאוֹת הָאִישׁ הֶחֱזִיק וּמַחֲנֵה מִדְיָן הָיָה לוֹ
by-him he-was Midian now-camp-of he-kept the-man hundreds but-to-three-of

מִתַּחַת בָּעֵמֶק׃ וַיְהִי בַּלַּיְלָה הַהוּא וַיֹּאמֶר
then-he-said the-that in-the-night and-he-was (9) in-the-valley at-below

אֵלָיו יְהוָה קוּם רֵד בַּמַּחֲנֶה כִּי נְתַתִּיו בְּיָדֶךָ׃
into-hand-of-you I-gave-him for against-the-camp go-down! get-up! Yahweh to-him

וְאִם־יָרֵא אַתָּה לָרֶדֶת רֵד אַתָּה וּפֻרָה נַעַרְךָ אֶל־
to servant-of-you and-Purah you go-down! to-attack you afraid but-if (10)

הַמַּחֲנֶה׃ וְשָׁמַעְתָּ מַה־יְדַבֵּרוּ וְאַחַר תֶּחֱזַקְנָה
they-will-be-encouraged and-after they-say what and-you-listen (11) the-camp

יָדֶיךָ וְיָרַדְתָּ בַּמַּחֲנֶה וַיֵּרֶד הוּא
he so-he-went-down against-the-camp and-you-will-attack hands-of-you

וּפֻרָה נַעֲרוֹ אֶל־קְצֵה הַחֲמֻשִׁים אֲשֶׁר בַּמַּחֲנֶה׃
around-the-camp who the-ones-being-posted end-of to servant-of-him and-Purah

וּמִדְיָן וַעֲמָלֵק וְכָל־בְּנֵי־קֶדֶם נֹפְלִים
ones-being-settled east peoples-of and-all-of and-Amalek now-Midian (12)

בָּעֵמֶק כָּאַרְבֶּה לָרֹב וְלִגְמַלֵּיהֶם אֵין מִסְפָּר
count not and-to-camels-of-them in-number as-the-locust in-the-valley

כַּחוֹל שֶׁעַל־שְׂפַת הַיָּם לָרֹב׃ וַיָּבֹא גִדְעוֹן
Gideon and-he-arrived (13) in-number the-sea shore-of that-on as-the-sand

וְהִנֵּה־אִישׁ מְסַפֵּר לְרֵעֵהוּ חֲלוֹם וַיֹּאמֶר הִנֵּה חֲלוֹם חָלַמְתִּי
I-dreamed dream see! and-he-said dream to-friend-of-him telling man and-see!

their tongues like a dog from
those who kneel down to
drink." 6Three hundred men
lapped with their hands to
their mouths. All the rest got
down on their knees to drink.
7The LORD said to Gideon,
"With the three hundred men
that lapped I will save you and
give the Midianites into your
hands. Let all the other men
go, each to his own place." 8So
Gideon sent the rest of the Israelites to their tents but kept
the three hundred, who took
over the provisions and trumpets of the others.

Now the camp of Midian lay
below him in the valley. 9During that night the LORD said to
Gideon, "Get up, go down
against the camp, because I
am going to give it into your
hands. 10If you are afraid to attack, go down to the camp
with your servant Purah 11and
listen to what they are saying.
Afterward, you will be encouraged to attack the camp."
So he and Purah his servant
went down to the outposts of
the camp. 12The Midianites,
the Amalekites and all the other eastern peoples had settled
in the valley, thick as locusts.
Their camels could no more be
counted than the sand on the
seashore.
13Gideon arrived just as a
man was telling a friend his
dream. "I had a dream," he

וְהִנֵּה צְלוֹל לֶחֶם שְׂעֹרִים מִתְהַפֵּךְ בְּמַחֲנֵה מִדְיָן וַיָּבֹא
and-he-came Midian into-camp-of tumbling barleys bread-of round-loaf and-see!

עַד־הָאֹהֶל וַיַּכֵּהוּ וַיִּפֹּל וַיַּהַפְכֵהוּ לְמַעְלָה
to-on-top and-he-overturned-him so-he-fell and-he-struck-him the-tent to

וְנָפַל הָאֹהֶל׃ וַיַּעַן רֵעֵהוּ וַיֹּאמֶר אֵין
not and-he-said friend-of-him and-he-responded (14) the-tent and-he-collapsed

זֹאת בִּלְתִּי אִם־חֶרֶב גִּדְעוֹן בֶּן־יוֹאָשׁ אִישׁ יִשְׂרָאֵל נָתַן הָאֱלֹהִים
the-God he-gave Israel man-of Joash son-of Gideon sword-of but nothing this

בְּיָדוֹ אֶת־מִדְיָן וְאֶת־כָּל־הַמַּחֲנֶה׃ וַיְהִי כִשְׁמֹעַ
when-to-hear and-he-was (15) the-camp whole-of and Midian *** into-hand-of-him

גִדְעוֹן אֶת־מִסְפַּר הַחֲלוֹם וְאֶת־שִׁבְרוֹ וַיִּשְׁתָּחוּ
then-he-worshiped interpretation-of-him and the-dream account-of *** Gideon

וַיָּשָׁב אֶל־מַחֲנֵה יִשְׂרָאֵל וַיֹּאמֶר קוּמוּ כִּי־נָתַן
he-gave for get-up! and-he-called-out Israel camp-of to and-he-returned

יְהוָה בְּיֶדְכֶם אֶת־מַחֲנֵה מִדְיָן׃ וַיַּחַץ אֶת־שְׁלֹשׁ־
three-of *** and-he-divided (16) Midian camp-of *** into-hand-of-you Yahweh

מֵאוֹת הָאִישׁ שְׁלֹשָׁה רָאשִׁים וַיִּתֵּן שׁוֹפָרוֹת בְּיַד־כֻּלָּם
all-of-them in-hand-of trumpets and-he-placed companies three the-man hundreds

וְכַדִּים רֵקִים וְלַפִּדִים בְּתוֹךְ הַכַּדִּים׃ וַיֹּאמֶר אֲלֵיהֶם
to-them and-he-told (17) the-jars inside-of and-torches empty-ones and-jars

מִמֶּנִּי תִרְאוּ וְכֵן תַּעֲשׂוּ וְהִנֵּה אָנֹכִי בָא בִּקְצֵה הַמַּחֲנֶה
the-camp to-edge-of going I now-see! you-do and-same you-watch to-me

וְהָיָה כַאֲשֶׁר־אֶעֱשֶׂה כֵּן תַּעֲשׂוּן׃ וְתָקַעְתִּי בַּשּׁוֹפָר אָנֹכִי
I on-the-trumpet when-I-blow (18) you-do same I-do just-as and-he-will-be

וְכָל־אֲשֶׁר אִתִּי וּתְקַעְתֶּם גַּם־אַתֶּם בַּשּׁוֹפָרוֹת סְבִיבוֹת כָּל־
all-of ones-around you also on-the-trumpets then-you-blow with-me who and-all

הַמַּחֲנֶה וַאֲמַרְתֶּם לַיהוָה וּלְגִדְעוֹן׃ וַיָּבֹא גִדְעוֹן
Gideon and-he-reached (19) and-for-Gideon for-Yahweh and-you-shout the-camp

וּמֵאָה־אִישׁ אֲשֶׁר־אִתּוֹ בִּקְצֵה הַמַּחֲנֶה רֹאשׁ הָאַשְׁמֹרֶת
the-watch beginning-of the-camp to-edge-of with-him who man and-hundred

הַתִּיכוֹנָה אַךְ הָקֵם הֵקִימוּ אֶת־הַשֹּׁמְרִים וַיִּתְקְעוּ
and-they-blew the-ones-guarding *** they-changed to-change after the-middle

בַּשּׁוֹפָרוֹת וְנָפוֹץ הַכַּדִּים אֲשֶׁר בְּיָדָם׃ וַיִּתְקְעוּ
and-they-blew (20) in-hand-of-them that the-jars and-to-break on-the-trumpets

שְׁלֹשֶׁת הָרָאשִׁים בַּשּׁוֹפָרוֹת וַיִּשְׁבְּרוּ הַכַּדִּים
the-jars and-they-smashed on-the-trumpets the-companies three-of

וַיַּחֲזִיקוּ בְיַד־שְׂמֹאולָם בַּלַּפִּדִים וּבְיַד־
and-in-hand-of on-the-torches left-of-them in-hand-of and-they-grasped

°13 ק צליל

was saying. "A round loaf of barley bread came tumbling into the Midianite camp. It struck the tent with such force that the tent overturned and collapsed."
14His friend responded, "This can be nothing other than the sword of Gideon son of Joash, the Israelite. God has given the Midianites and the whole camp into his hands."
15When Gideon heard the dream and its interpretation, he worshiped God. He returned to the camp of Israel and called out, "Get up! The LORD has given the Midianite camp into your hands."
16Dividing the three hundred men into three companies, he placed trumpets and empty jars in the hands of all of them, with torches inside.
17"Watch me," he told them. "Follow my lead. When I get to the edge of the camp, do exactly as I do.
18When I and all who are with me blow our trumpets, then from all around the camp blow yours and shout, 'For the LORD and for Gideon.'"
19Gideon and the hundred men with him reached the edge of the camp at the beginning of the middle watch, just after they had changed the guard. They blew their trumpets and broke the jars that were in their hands.
20The three companies blew the trumpets and smashed the jars. Grasping the torches in their left hands and holding in

יְמִינָם הַשּׁוֹפָרוֹת לִתְקוֹעַ וַֽיִּקְרְאוּ חֶרֶב לַיהוָה
right-of-them the-trumpets to-blow and-they-shouted sword for-Yahweh

וּלְגִדְעוֹן׃ וַיַּעַמְדוּ אִישׁ תַּחְתָּיו סָבִיב לַמַּחֲנֶה
and-for-Gideon (21) and-they-held each position-of-him around to-the-camp

וַיָּרָץ כָּל־ הַמַּחֲנֶה וַיָּרִיעוּ וַיָּנִיסוּ׃ וַיִּתְקְעוּ
and-he-ran all-of the-camp and-they-cried-out and-they-fled (22) when-they-sounded

שְׁלֹשׁ־ מֵאוֹת הַשּׁוֹפָרוֹת וַיָּשֶׂם יְהוָה אֵת חֶרֶב אִישׁ
three-of hundreds the-trumpets then-he-caused Yahweh *** sword-of each

בְּרֵעֵהוּ וּבְכָל־ הַמַּחֲנֶה וַיָּנָס הַמַּחֲנֶה עַד־
against-other-of-him even-through-all-of the-camp and-he-fled the-army to

בֵּית הַשִּׁטָּה צְרֵרָתָה עַד שְׂפַת־ אָבֵל מְחוֹלָה עַל־ טַבָּת׃
Beth the-Shittah toward-Zererah as-far-as border-of Abel Meholah near Tabbath

וַיִּצָּעֵק אִישׁ־ יִשְׂרָאֵל מִנַּפְתָּלִי וּמִן־ אָשֵׁר
(23) and-he-was-called-out man-of Israel from-Naphtali and-from Asher

וּמִן־ כָּל־ מְנַשֶּׁה וַֽיִּרְדְּפוּ אַחֲרֵי מִדְיָן׃ וּמַלְאָכִים
and-from all-of Manasseh and-they-pursued after Midian (24) and-messengers

שָׁלַח גִּדְעוֹן בְּכָל־ הַר אֶפְרַיִם לֵאמֹר רְדוּ
he-sent Gideon through-all-of hill-country-of Ephraim to-say come-down!

לִקְרַאת מִדְיָן וְלִכְדוּ לָהֶם אֶת־ הַמַּיִם עַד בֵּית
to-encounter Midian and-sieze! ahead-of-them *** the-waters as-far-as Beth

בָּרָה וְאֶת־ הַיַּרְדֵּן וַיִּצָּעֵק כָּל־ אִישׁ אֶפְרַיִם וַיִּלְכְּדוּ
Barah even the-Jordan so-he-was-called-out all-of man-of Ephraim and-they-took

אֶת־ הַמַּיִם עַד בֵּית בָּרָה וְאֶת־ הַיַּרְדֵּן׃ וַיִּלְכְּדוּ
*** the-waters as-far-as Beth Barah even the-Jordan (25) and-they-captured

שְׁנֵי־ שָׂרֵי מִדְיָן אֶת־ עֹרֵב וְאֶת־ זְאֵב וַיַּהַרְגוּ אֶת־ עוֹרֵב
two-of leaders-of Midian *** Oreb and Zeeb and-they-killed *** Oreb

בְּצוּר־ עוֹרֵב וְאֶת־ זְאֵב הָרְגוּ בְיֶקֶב־ זְאֵב וַֽיִּרְדְּפוּ
at-rock-of Oreb and Zeeb they-killed at-winepress-of Zeeb and-they-pursued

אֶל־ מִדְיָן וְרֹאשׁ־ עֹרֵב וּזְאֵב הֵבִיאוּ אֶל־ גִּדְעוֹן מֵעֵבֶר
after Midian and-head-of Oreb and-Zeeb they-brought to Gideon by-side

לַיַּרְדֵּן׃ וַיֹּאמְרוּ אֵלָיו אִישׁ אֶפְרַיִם מָה־ הַדָּבָר
of-the-Jordan (8:1) now-they-asked to-him man-of Ephraim what? the-thing

הַזֶּה עָשִׂיתָ לָּנוּ לְבִלְתִּי קְרֹאות לָנוּ כִּי הָלַכְתָּ לְהִלָּחֵם
the-this you-treated to-us not to-call to-us when you-went to-fight

בְּמִדְיָן וַיְרִיבוּן אִתּוֹ בְּחָזְקָה׃ וַיֹּאמֶר
against-Midian and-they-criticized at-him with-sharpness (2) but-he-answered

אֲלֵיהֶם מֶה־ עָשִׂיתִי עַתָּה כָּכֶם הֲלוֹא טוֹב עֹלְלוֹת
to-them what? I-accomplished now compared-to-you not? better gleanings-of

their right hands the trumpets
they were to blow, they shouted, "A sword for the LORD and
for Gideon!" 21While each man
held his position around the
camp, all the Midianites ran,
crying out as they fled.
22When the three hundred
trumpets sounded, the LORD
caused the men throughout
the camp to turn on each other
with their swords. The army
fled to Beth Shittah toward
Zererah as far as the border of
Abel Meholah near Tabbath.
23Israelites from Naphtali,
Asher and all Manasseh were
called out, and they pursued
the Midianites. 24Gideon sent
messengers throughout the
hill country of Ephraim, saying, "Come down against the
Midianites and seize the waters of the Jordan ahead of
them as far as Beth Barah."
So all the men of Ephraim
were called out and they took
the waters of the Jordan as far
as Beth Barah. 25They also captured two of the Midianite
leaders, Oreb and Zeeb. They
killed Oreb at the rock of Oreb,
and Zeeb at the winepress of
Zeeb. They pursued the
Midianites and brought the
heads of Oreb and Zeeb to
Gideon, who was by the Jordan.

Zebah and Zalmunna

8 Now the Ephraimites
asked Gideon, "Why have
you treated us like this? Why
didn't you call us when you
went to fight Midian?" And
they criticized him sharply.
2But he answered them,
"What have I accomplished
compared to you? Aren't the
gleanings of Ephraim's grapes

°21 ק וינוסו

אֶפְרַיִם מִבְצִיר אֲבִיעֶזֶר׃ בְּיֶדְכֶם נָתַן אֱלֹהִים
God he-gave into-hand-of-you (3) Abiezer than-grape-harvest-of Ephraim

אֶת־ שָׂרֵי מִדְיָן אֶת־ עֹרֵב וְאֶת־ זְאֵב וּמַה־ יָּכֹלְתִּי עֲשׂוֹת
to-do was-I-able and-what? Zeeb and Oreb *** Midian leaders-of ***

כָּכֶם אָז רָפְתָה רוּחָם מֵעָלָיו
from-against-him resentment-of-them she-subsided then compared-to-you

בְּדַבְּרוֹ הַדָּבָר הַזֶּה׃ וַיָּבֹא גִדְעוֹן הַיַּרְדֵּנָה
to-the-Jordan Gideon and-he-came (4) the-this the-thing when-to-say-him

עֹבֵר הוּא וּשְׁלֹשׁ־ מֵאוֹת הָאִישׁ אֲשֶׁר אִתּוֹ עֲיֵפִים
ones-exhausted with-him who the-man hundreds and-three-of he crossing

וְרֹדְפִים׃ וַיֹּאמֶר לְאַנְשֵׁי סֻכּוֹת תְּנוּ־ נָא כִּכְּרוֹת לֶחֶם
bread cakes-of now! give! Succoth to-men-of and-he-said (5) yet-ones-pursuing

לָעָם אֲשֶׁר בְּרַגְלָי כִּי־ עֲיֵפִים הֵם וְאָנֹכִי רֹדֵף אַחֲרֵי
after pursuing and-I they ones-worn-out for at-feet-of-me who to-the-troop

זֶבַח וְצַלְמֻנָּע מַלְכֵי מִדְיָן׃ וַיֹּאמֶר שָׂרֵי סֻכּוֹת
Succoth officials-of but-he-said (6) Midian kings-of and-Zalmunna Zebah

הֲכַף זֶבַח וְצַלְמֻנָּע עַתָּה בְּיָדֶךָ כִּי־ נִתֵּן
we-should-give that in-hand-of-you already and-Zalmunna Zebah hand-of?

לִצְבָאֲךָ לָחֶם׃ וַיֹּאמֶר גִּדְעוֹן לָכֵן בְּתֵת יְהוָה
Yahweh when-to-give for-that Gideon then-he-replied (7) bread to-troop-of-you

אֶת־ זֶבַח וְאֶת־ צַלְמֻנָּע בְּיָדִי וְדַשְׁתִּי אֶת־ בְּשַׂרְכֶם
flesh-of-you *** then-I-will-tear into-hand-of-me Zalmunna and Zebah ***

אֶת־ קוֹצֵי הַמִּדְבָּר וְאֶת־ הַבַּרְקֳנִים׃ וַיַּעַל מִשָּׁם
from-there and-he-went-up (8) the-briers and-with the-desert thorns-of with

פְּנוּאֵל וַיְדַבֵּר אֲלֵיהֶם כָּזֹאת וַיַּעֲנוּ אוֹתוֹ אַנְשֵׁי פְנוּאֵל
Penuel men-of him but-they-answered as-that of-them and-he-requested Penuel

כַּאֲשֶׁר עָנוּ אַנְשֵׁי סֻכּוֹת׃ וַיֹּאמֶר גַּם־ לְאַנְשֵׁי פְנוּאֵל
Penuel to-men-of also so-he-said (9) Succoth men-of they-answered just-as

לֵאמֹר בְּשׁוּבִי בְשָׁלוֹם אֶתֹּץ אֶת־ הַמִּגְדָּל הַזֶּה׃
the-this the-tower *** I-will-tear-down in-triumph when-to-return-me to-say

וְזֶבַח וְצַלְמֻנָּע בַּקַּרְקֹר וּמַחֲנֵיהֶם עִמָּם
with-them and-forces-of-them in-the-Karkor and-Zalmunna now-Zebah (10)

כַּחֲמֵשֶׁת עָשָׂר אֶלֶף כֹּל הַנּוֹתָרִים מִכֹּל מַחֲנֵה
army-of from-all-of the-ones-being-left all-of thousand ten about-five-of

בְנֵי־ קֶדֶם וְהַנֹּפְלִים מֵאָה וְעֶשְׂרִים אֶלֶף אִישׁ
man thousand and-twenty hundred and-the-ones-having-fallen east peoples-of

שֹׁלֵף חָרֶב׃ וַיַּעַל גִּדְעוֹן דֶּרֶךְ הַשְּׁכוּנֵי
the-ones-dwelling-of way-of Gideon and-he-went-up (11) sword bearing-of

better than the full grape harvest of Abiezer? 3God gave
Oreb and Zeeb, the Midianite
leaders, into your hands. What
was I able to do compared to
you?" At this, their resent-
ment against him subsided.
4Gideon and his three hundred men, exhausted yet keeping up the pursuit, came to the
Jordan and crossed it. 5He said
to the men of Succoth, "Give
my troops some bread; they
are worn out, and I am still
pursuing Zebah and Zalmunna, the kings of Midian."
6But the officials of Succoth
said, "Do you already have the
hands of Zebah and Zalmunna in your possession? Why
should we give bread to your
troops?"
7Then Gideon replied, "Just
for that, when the LORD has
given Zebah and Zalmunna
into my hand, I will tear your
flesh with desert thorns and
briers."
8From there he went up to
Peniel[f] and made the same request of them, but they answered as the men of Succoth
had. 9So he said to the men of
Peniel, "When I return in triumph, I will tear down this
tower."
10Now Zebah and Zalmunna
were in Karkor with a force of
about fifteen thousand men,
all that were left of the armies
of the eastern peoples; a hundred and twenty thousand
swordsmen had fallen. 11Gide-
on went up by the route of the

[f] 8 Hebrew *Penuel*, a variant of *Peniel;* also in verses 9 and 17

בָּאֳהָלִים מִקֶּדֶם לְנֹבַח וְיָגְבֳּהָה* וַיַּךְ אֶת־ הַמַּחֲנֶה
the-army *** and-he-fell-upon and-Jogbehah of-Nobah to-east in-tents

וְהַמַּחֲנֶה הָיָה בֶטַח׃ וַיָּנוּסוּ† זֶבַח וְצַלְמֻנָּע
and-Zalmunna Zebah and-they-fled (12) unsuspecting he-was and-the-army

וַיִּרְדֹּף אַחֲרֵיהֶם וַיִּלְכֹּד אֶת־ שְׁנֵי ׀ מַלְכֵי מִדְיָן אֶת־
*** Midian kings-of two-of *** and-he-captured after-them but-he-pursued

זֶבַח וְאֶת־ צַלְמֻנָּע וְכָל־ הַמַּחֲנֶה הֶחֱרִיד׃ וַיָּשָׁב
then-he-returned (13) he-routed the-army and-entire-of Zalmunna and Zebah

גִּדְעוֹן בֶּן־ יוֹאָשׁ מִן־ הַמִּלְחָמָה מִלְמַעֲלֵה הֶחָרֶס׃ וַיִּלְכָּד־
and-he-caught (14) the-Heres by-Pass-of the-battle from Joash son-of Gideon

נַעַר מֵאַנְשֵׁי סֻכּוֹת וַיִּשְׁאָלֵהוּ וַיִּכְתֹּב אֵלָיו אֶת־
*** for-him and-he-wrote and-he-questioned-him Succoth from-men-of young-man

שָׂרֵי סֻכּוֹת וְאֶת־ זְקֵנֶיהָ שִׁבְעִים וְשִׁבְעָה אִישׁ׃ וַיָּבֹא
then-he-came (15) man and-seven seventy elders-of-her even Succoth officials-of

אֶל־אַנְשֵׁי סֻכּוֹת וַיֹּאמֶר הִנֵּה זֶבַח וְצַלְמֻנָּע אֲשֶׁר חֵרַפְתֶּם אוֹתִי
me you-taunted whom and-Zalmunna Zebah here! and-he-said Succoth men-of to

לֵאמֹר הֲכַף זֶבַח וְצַלְמֻנָּע עַתָּה בְּיָדֶךָ כִּי נִתֵּן
we-should-give that in-hand-of-you already and-Zalmunna Zebah hand-of? to-say

לַאֲנָשֶׁיךָ הַיְּעֵפִים לָחֶם׃ וַיִּקַּח אֶת־ זִקְנֵי הָעִיר
the-town elders-of *** and-he-took (16) bread the-exhausted-ones to-men-of-you

וְאֶת־ קוֹצֵי הַמִּדְבָּר וְאֶת־ הַבַּרְקֳנִים וַיֹּדַע בָּהֶם אֵת
*** with-them and-he-taught-lesson the-briers and the-desert thorns-of and

אַנְשֵׁי סֻכּוֹת׃ וְאֶת־ מִגְדַּל פְּנוּאֵל נָתָץ וַיַּהֲרֹג אֶת־
*** and-he-killed he-pulled-down Penuel tower-of also (17) Succoth men-of

אַנְשֵׁי הָעִיר׃ וַיֹּאמֶר אֶל־זֶבַח וְאֶל־ צַלְמֻנָּע אֵיפֹה
what-kind? Zalmunna and-to Zebah to then-he-asked (18) the-town men-of

הָאֲנָשִׁים אֲשֶׁר הֲרַגְתֶּם בְּתָבוֹר וַיֹּאמְרוּ כָּמוֹךָ כְמוֹהֶם אֶחָד
each so-they like-you and-they-answered at-Tabor you-killed whom the-men

כְּתֹאַר בְּנֵי הַמֶּלֶךְ׃ וַיֹּאמַר אַחַי בְּנֵי־
sons-of brothers-of-me and-he-replied (19) the-king sons-of like-bearing-of

אִמִּי הֵם חַי־ יְהוָה לוּ הַחֲיִתֶם אוֹתָם לֹא הָרַגְתִּי אֶתְכֶם׃
you I-would-kill not them you-spared if Yahweh life-of they mother-of-me

וַיֹּאמֶר לְיֶתֶר בְּכוֹרוֹ קוּם הֲרֹג אוֹתָם וְלֹא־ שָׁלַף
he-drew but-not them kill! rise! oldest-son-of-him to-Jether and-he-said (20)

הַנַּעַר חַרְבּוֹ כִּי יָרֵא כִּי עוֹדֶנּוּ נָעַר׃ וַיֹּאמֶר זֶבַח
Zebah and-he-said (21) boy only-he for he-was-afraid for sword-of-him the-boy

וְצַלְמֻנָּע קוּם אַתָּה וּפְגַע־ בָּנוּ כִּי כָאִישׁ גְּבוּרָתוֹ
strength-of-him as-the-man for against-us and-strike! you come! and-Zalmunna

nomads east of Nobah and Jogbehah and fell upon the unsuspecting army. [12]Zebah and Zalmunna, the two kings of Midian, fled, but he pursued them and captured them, routing their entire army.

[13]Gideon son of Joash then returned from the battle by the Pass of Heres. [14]He caught a young man of Succoth and questioned him, and the young man wrote down for him the names of the seventy-seven officials of Succoth, the elders of the town. [15]Then Gideon came and said to the men of Succoth, "Here are Zebah and Zalmunna, about whom you taunted me by saying, 'Do you already have the hands of Zebah and Zalmunna in your possession? Why should we give bread to your exhausted men?' " [16]He took the elders of the town and taught the men of Succoth a lesson by punishing them with desert thorns and briers. [17]He also pulled down the tower of Peniel and killed the men of the town.

[18]Then he asked Zebah and Zalmunna, "What kind of men did you kill at Tabor?"

"Men like you," they answered, "each one with the bearing of a prince."

[19]Gideon replied, "Those were my brothers, the sons of my own mother. As surely as the LORD lives, if you had spared their lives, I would not kill you." [20]Turning to Jether, his oldest son, he said, "Kill them!" But Jether did not draw his sword, because he was only a boy and was afraid.

[21]Zebah and Zalmunna said, "Come, do it yourself. 'As is the man, so is his strength.' "

**11* Most mss have no *dagesh* in and have simple *sheva* under the *beth* (בְ–).

†*12* Most mss have *qibbuts* instead of *shureq* (וינֻסו).

וַיָּקָם גִּדְעוֹן וַיַּהֲרֹג אֶת־ זֶבַח וְאֶת־ צַלְמֻנָּע וַיִּקַּח
and-he-took Zalmunna and Zebah *** and-he-killed Gideon so-he-stepped-forward

אֶת־ הַשַּׂהֲרֹנִים אֲשֶׁר בְּצַוְּארֵי גְמַלֵּיהֶם׃ וַיֹּאמְרוּ אִישׁ־
man-of and-they-said (22) camels-of-them on-necks-of that the-ornaments ***

יִשְׂרָאֵל אֶל־גִּדְעוֹן מְשָׁל־ בָּנוּ גַּם־ אַתָּה גַּם־ בִּנְךָ גַּם בֶּן־
son-of also son-of-you also you indeed over-us rule! Gideon to Israel

בִּנֶךָ כִּי הוֹשַׁעְתָּנוּ מִיַּד מִדְיָן׃ וַיֹּאמֶר אֲלֵהֶם
to-them but-he-told (23) Midian from-hand-of you-saved-us for son-of-you

גִּדְעוֹן לֹא־ אֶמְשֹׁל אֲנִי בָּכֶם וְלֹא־ יִמְשֹׁל בְּנִי בָּכֶם
over-you son-of-me he-will-rule and-not over-you I I-will-rule not Gideon

יְהוָה יִמְשֹׁל בָּכֶם׃ וַיֹּאמֶר אֲלֵהֶם גִּדְעוֹן אֶשְׁאֲלָה
I-will-request Gideon to-them and-he-said (24) over-you he-will-rule Yahweh

מִכֶּם שְׁאֵלָה וּתְנוּ־ לִי אִישׁ נֶזֶם שְׁלָלוֹ כִּי־
for plunder-of-him earring-of each to-me that-give! request from-you

נִזְמֵי זָהָב לָהֶם כִּי יִשְׁמְעֵאלִים הֵם׃ וַיֹּאמְרוּ נָתוֹן
to-give and-they-answered (25) they Ishmaelites for to-them gold earrings-of

נִתֵּן וַיִּפְרְשׂוּ אֶת־ הַשִּׂמְלָה וַיַּשְׁלִיכוּ שָׁמָּה
onto-there and-they-threw the-garment *** so-they-spread-out we-will-give

אִישׁ נֶזֶם שְׁלָלוֹ׃ וַיְהִי מִשְׁקַל נִזְמֵי הַזָּהָב
the-gold earrings-of weight-of and-he-was (26) plunder-of-him earring-of each

אֲשֶׁר שָׁאָל אֶלֶף וּשְׁבַע־ מֵאוֹת זָהָב לְבַד מִן־ הַשַּׂהֲרֹנִים
the-ornaments from apart gold hundreds and-seven-of thousand he-asked-for that

וְהַנְּטִפוֹת וּבִגְדֵי הָאַרְגָּמָן שֶׁעַל מַלְכֵי מִדְיָן וּלְבַד
and-apart Midian kings-of that-on the-purple and-garments-of and-the-pendants

מִן־ הָעֲנָקוֹת אֲשֶׁר בְּצַוְּארֵי גְמַלֵּיהֶם׃ וַיַּעַשׂ אוֹתוֹ גִדְעוֹן
Gideon him and-he-made (27) camels-of-them on-necks-of that the-chains from

לְאֵפוֹד וַיַּצֵּג אוֹתוֹ בְעִירוֹ בְּעָפְרָה וַיִּזְנוּ
and-they-prostituted in-Ophrah in-town-of-him him and-he-placed into-ephod

כָל־ יִשְׂרָאֵל אַחֲרָיו שָׁם וַיְהִי לְגִדְעוֹן וּלְבֵיתוֹ
and-to-family-of-him to-Gideon and-he-became there after-him Israel all-of

לְמוֹקֵשׁ׃ וַיִּכָּנַע מִדְיָן לִפְנֵי בְּנֵי יִשְׂרָאֵל וְלֹא
and-not Israel sons-of before Midian thus-he-was-subdued (28) as-snare

יָסְפוּ לָשֵׂאת רֹאשָׁם וַתִּשְׁקֹט הָאָרֶץ אַרְבָּעִים שָׁנָה
year forty the-land and-she-had-peace head-of-them to-raise they-repeated

בִּימֵי גִדְעוֹן׃ וַיֵּלֶךְ יְרֻבַּעַל בֶּן־ יוֹאָשׁ וַיֵּשֶׁב
and-he-lived Joash son-of Jerub-Baal and-he-went-back (29) Gideon in-days-of

בְּבֵיתוֹ׃ וּלְגִדְעוֹן הָיוּ שִׁבְעִים בָּנִים יֹצְאֵי
ones-coming-out-of sons seventy they-were and-to-Gideon (30) in-home-of-him

So Gideon stepped forward and killed them, and took the ornaments off their camels' necks.

Gideon's Ephod

22The Israelites said to Gideon, "Rule over us—you, your son and your grandson—because you have saved us out of the hand of Midian."

23But Gideon told them, "I will not rule over you, nor will my son rule over you. The LORD will rule over you."
24And he said, "I do have one request, that each of you give me an earring from your share of the plunder." (It was the custom of the Ishmaelites to wear gold earrings.)

25They answered, "We'll be glad to give them." So they spread out a garment, and each man threw a ring from his plunder onto it.
26The weight of the gold rings he asked for came to seventeen hundred shekels,[g] not counting the ornaments, the pendants and the purple garments worn by the kings of Midian or the chains that were on their camels' necks.
27Gideon made the gold into an ephod, which he placed in Ophrah, his town. All Israel prostituted themselves by worshiping it there, and it became a snare to Gideon and his family.

Gideon's Death

28Thus Midian was subdued before the Israelites and did not raise its head again. During Gideon's lifetime, the land enjoyed peace forty years.

29Jerub-Baal son of Joash went back home to live.
30He had seventy sons of his own,

g26 That is, about 43 pounds (about 19.5 kilograms)

יְרֵכוֹ כִּי־ נָשִׁים רַבּוֹת הָיוּ לוֹ׃ וּפִֽילַגְשׁוֹ אֲשֶׁר
who and-concubine-of-him (31) to-him they-were many wives for body-of-him

בִּשְׁכֶם יָֽלְדָה־ לּוֹ גַם־ הִיא בֵּן וַיָּשֶׂם אֶת־ שְׁמוֹ אֲבִימֶלֶךְ׃
Abimelech name-of-him *** and-he-gave son she also to-him she-bore in-Shechem

וַיָּמָת גִּדְעוֹן בֶּן־ יוֹאָשׁ בְּשֵׂיבָה טוֹבָה וַיִּקָּבֵר
and-he-was-buried good at-old-age Joash son-of Gideon and-he-died (32)

בְּקֶבֶר יוֹאָשׁ אָבִיו בְּעָפְרָה אֲבִי הָעֶזְרִי׃ וַיְהִי
and-he-was (33) the-Abiezrite in-Ophrah father-of-him Joash in-tomb-of

כַּאֲשֶׁר מֵת גִּדְעוֹן וַיָּשׁוּבוּ בְּנֵי יִשְׂרָאֵל וַיִּזְנוּ
and-they-prostituted Israel sons-of then-they-turned Gideon he-died just-as

אַחֲרֵי הַבְּעָלִים וַיָּשִׂימוּ לָהֶם בַּעַל בְּרִית לֵאלֹהִים׃ וְלֹא
and-not (34) as-god Berith Baal for-them and-they-set-up the-Baals to

זָכְרוּ בְּנֵי יִשְׂרָאֵל אֶת־ יְהוָה אֱלֹהֵיהֶם הַמַּצִּיל אוֹתָם
them the-one-rescuing God-of-them Yahweh *** Israel sons-of they-remembered

מִיַּד כָּל־ אֹיְבֵיהֶם מִסָּבִיב׃ וְלֹא־
and-not (35) on-every-side being-enemies-of-them all-of from-hand-of

עָשׂוּ חֶסֶד עִם־ בֵּית יְרֻבַּעַל גִּדְעוֹן כְּכָל־ הַטּוֹבָה
the-good for-all-of Gideon Jerub-Baal family-of to gratitude they-showed

אֲשֶׁר עָשָׂה עִם־ יִשְׂרָאֵל׃ וַיֵּלֶךְ אֲבִימֶלֶךְ בֶּן־ יְרֻבַּעַל
Jerub-Baal son-of Abimelech and-he-went (9:1) Israel for he-did that

שְׁכֶמָה אֶל־ אֲחֵי אִמּוֹ וַיְדַבֵּר אֲלֵיהֶם וְאֶל־ כָּל־
all-of and-to to-them and-he-spoke mother-of-him brothers-of to to-Shechem

מִשְׁפַּחַת בֵּית־ אֲבִי אִמּוֹ לֵאמֹר׃ דַּבְּרוּ־ נָא בְּאָזְנֵי
in-ears-of now! ask! (2) to-say mother-of-him father-of house-of clan-of

כָל־ בַּעֲלֵי שְׁכֶם מַה־ טּוֹב לָכֶם הֲמְשֹׁל בָּכֶם שִׁבְעִים
seventy over-you to-rule? for-you better which? Shechem citizens-of all-of

אִישׁ כֹּל בְּנֵי יְרֻבַּעַל אִם־ מְשֹׁל בָּכֶם אִישׁ אֶחָד וּזְכַרְתֶּם
and-you-remember one man over-you to-rule or Jerub-Baal sons-of all-of man

כִּי־ עַצְמֵכֶם* וּבְשַׂרְכֶם אָנִי׃ וַיְדַבְּרוּ אֲחֵי־
brothers-of and-they-spoke (3) I and-flesh-of-you bone-of-you that

אִמּוֹ עָלָיו בְּאָזְנֵי כָּל־ בַּעֲלֵי שְׁכֶם אֵת כָּל־
all-of *** Shechem citizens-of all-of in-ears-of for-him mother-of-him

הַדְּבָרִים הָאֵלֶּה וַיֵּט לִבָּם אַחֲרֵי אֲבִימֶלֶךְ כִּי
for Abimelech after heart-of-them and-he-inclined the-these the-things

אָמְרוּ אָחִינוּ הוּא׃ וַיִּתְּנוּ־ לוֹ שִׁבְעִים כֶּסֶף
silver seventy to-him and-they-gave (4) he brother-of-us they-said

מִבֵּית בַּעַל בְּרִית וַיִּשְׂכֹּר בָּהֶם אֲבִימֶלֶךְ אֲנָשִׁים רֵיקִים
reckless-ones men Abimelech with-them and-he-hired Berith Baal from-temple-of

for he had many wives. [31]His
concubine, who lived in Shechem, also bore him a son,
whom he named Abimelech.
[32]Gideon son of Joash died at a
good old age and was buried
in the tomb of his father Joash
in Ophrah of the Abiezrites.
[33]No sooner had Gideon
died than the Israelites again
prostituted themselves to the
Baals. They set up Baal-Berith
as their god and [34]did not
remember the LORD their God,
who had rescued them from
the hands of all their enemies
on every side. [35]They also
failed to show gratitude to the
family of Jerub-Baal (that is,
Gideon) for all the good things
he had done for them.

Abimelech

9 Abimelech son of Jerub-
Baal went to his mother's
brothers in Shechem and said
to them and to all his mother's
clan, [2]"Ask all the citizens of
Shechem, 'Which is better for
you: to have all seventy of
Jerub-Baal's sons rule over
you, or just one man?'
Remember, I am your flesh
and blood."
[3]When the brothers repeated
all this to the citizens of Shechem, they were inclined to
follow Abimelech, for they
said, "He is our brother."
[4]They gave him seventy silver
shekels[h] from the temple of
Baal-Berith, and Abimelech
used them to hire reckless adventurers, who became his

[h]4 That is, about 1 3/4 pounds (about 0.8 kilogram)

*2 Most mss have *sheva* under the first *mem* (־מְ׳).

וּפֹחֲזִים וַיֵּלְכוּ אַחֲרָיו׃ וַיָּבֹא בֵית־
home-of and-he-went (5) after-him and-they-followed and-ones-adventuring

אָבִיו עָפְרָתָה וַיַּהֲרֹג אֶת־ אֶחָיו בְנֵי־ יְרֻבַּעַל
Jerub-Baal sons-of brothers-of-him *** and-he-murdered in-Ophrah father-of-him

שִׁבְעִים אִישׁ עַל־אֶבֶן אֶחָת וַיִּוָּתֵר יוֹתָם בֶּן־ יְרֻבַּעַל הַקָּטֹן
the-young Jerub-Baal son-of Jotham but-he-escaped one stone on man seventy

כִּי נֶחְבָּא׃ וַיֵּאָסְפוּ כָּל־ בַּעֲלֵי שְׁכֶם וְכָל־ בֵּית
Beth and-all-of Shechem citizens-of all-of then-they-gathered (6) he-hid for

מִלּוֹא וַיֵּלְכוּ וַיַּמְלִיכוּ אֶת־ אֲבִימֶלֶךְ לְמֶלֶךְ עִם־ אֵלוֹן
great-tree beside as-king Abimelech *** and-they-crowned and-they-went Millo

מֻצָּב אֲשֶׁר בִּשְׁכֶם׃ וַיַּגִּדוּ לְיוֹתָם וַיֵּלֶךְ
then-he-climbed to-Jotham when-they-told (7) in-Shechem that *standing

וַיַּעֲמֹד בְּרֹאשׁ הַר־ גְּרִזִים וַיִּשָּׂא קוֹלוֹ
voice-of-him and-he-raised Gerizim Mount-of on-top-of and-he-stood

וַיִּקְרָא וַיֹּאמֶר לָהֶם שִׁמְעוּ אֵלַי בַּעֲלֵי שְׁכֶם
Shechem citizens-of to-me listen! to-them and-he-said and-he-shouted

וְיִשְׁמַע אֲלֵיכֶם אֱלֹהִים׃ הָלוֹךְ הָלְכוּ הָעֵצִים לִמְשֹׁחַ
to-anoint the-trees they-went-out to-go-out (8) God to-you so-he-may-listen

עֲלֵיהֶם מֶלֶךְ וַיֹּאמְרוּ לַזַּיִת מָלְוֹכָה עָלֵינוּ׃ וַיֹּאמֶר
but-he-said (9) over-us be-king! to-the-olive-tree and-they-said king for-them

לָהֶם הַזַּיִת הֶחֳדַלְתִּי אֶת־ דִּשְׁנִי אֲשֶׁר־ בִּי יְכַבְּדוּ
they-honor by-me which oil-of-me *** should-I-give-up? the-olive-tree to-them

אֱלֹהִים וַאֲנָשִׁים וְהָלַכְתִּי לָנוּעַ עַל־ הָעֵצִים׃ וַיֹּאמְרוּ הָעֵצִים
the-trees then-they-said (10) the-trees over to-wave and-I-go and-men gods

לַתְּאֵנָה לְכִי־ אַתְּ מָלְכִי עָלֵינוּ׃ וַתֹּאמֶר לָהֶם
to-them but-she-replied (11) over-us be-king! you come! to-the-fig-tree

הַתְּאֵנָה הֶחֳדַלְתִּי אֶת־ מָתְקִי וְאֶת־ תְּנוּבָתִי הַטּוֹבָה
the-good fruit-of-me and sweetness-of-me *** should-I-give-up! the-fig-tree

וְהָלַכְתִּי לָנוּעַ עַל־ הָעֵצִים׃ וַיֹּאמְרוּ הָעֵצִים לַגָּפֶן
to-the-vine the-trees then-they-said (12) the-trees over to-wave and-I-go

לְכִי־אַתְּ מָלְוֹכִי עָלֵינוּ׃ וַתֹּאמֶר לָהֶם הַגֶּפֶן הֶחֳדַלְתִּי
should-I-give-up? the-vine to-them but-she-said (13) over-us be-king! you come!

אֶת־ תִּירוֹשִׁי הַמְשַׂמֵּחַ אֱלֹהִים וַאֲנָשִׁים וְהָלַכְתִּי לָנוּעַ עַל־ הָעֵצִים׃
the-trees over to-wave and-I-go and-men gods the-one-cheering wine-of-me ***

וַיֹּאמְרוּ כָל־ הָעֵצִים אֶל־ הָאָטָד לֵךְ אַתָּה מְלָךְ־
be-king! you come! the-thornbush to the-trees all-of then-they-said (14)

עָלֵינוּ׃ וַיֹּאמֶר הָאָטָד אֶל־ הָעֵצִים אִם בֶּאֱמֶת אַתֶּם
you in-reality if the-trees to the-thornbush and-he-said (15) over-us

followers. 5He went to his father's home in Ophrah and on
one stone murdered his seventy brothers, the sons of
Jerub-Baal. But Jotham, the
youngest son of Jerub-Baal, escaped by hiding. 6Then all the
citizens of Shechem and Beth
Millo gathered beside the
great tree at the pillar in Shechem to crown Abimelech
king.
7When Jotham was told
about this, he climbed up on
the top of Mount Gerizim and
shouted to them, "Listen to
me, citizens of Shechem, so
that God may listen to you.
8One day the trees went out to
anoint a king for themselves.
They said to the olive tree, 'Be
our king.'
9"But the olive tree an-
swered, 'Should I give up my
oil, by which both gods and
men are honored, to go waving over the trees?'
10"Next, the trees said to the
fig tree, 'Come and be our
king.'
11"But the fig tree replied,
'Should I give up my fruit, so
good and sweet, to go waving
over the trees?'
12"Then the trees said to the
vine, 'Come and be our king.'
13"But the vine answered,
'Should I give up my wine,
which cheers both gods and
men, to go waving over the
trees?'
14"Finally all the trees said to
the thornbush, 'Come and be
our king.'
15"The thornbush said to the
trees, 'If you really want to

*6 On the basis of the Septuagint, the NIV adds the definite article and repoints this word as הַמַּצָּב, *the-pillar.*

°8 ק מלכה

°12 ק מלכי

משחים אתי למלך עליכם באו חסו בצלי ואם־
but-if in-shade-of-me take-refuge! come! over-you as-king me ones-anointing

אין תצא אש מן־ האטד ותאכל את־ ארזי
cedars-of *** and-let-her-consume the-thornbush from fire let-her-come-out not

הלבנון: ועתה אם־ באמת ובתמים עשיתם
you-acted and-in-good-faith in-honor if and-now (16) the-Lebanon

ותמליכו את־ אבימלך ואם־ טובה עשיתם עם־ ירבעל ועם־
and-to Jerub-Baal to you-were fair and-if Abimelech *** when-you-made-king

ביתו ואם־ כגמול ידיו עשיתם לו: אשר־
for (17) to-him you-did hands-of-him as-deserving-of and-if family-of-him

נלחם אבי עליכם וישלך את־ נפשו מנגד
in-front life-of-him *** and-he-risked for-you father-of-me he-fought

ויצל אתכם מיד מדין: ואתם קמתם על־
against you-revolted but-you (18) Midian from-hand-of you when-he-rescued

בית אבי היום ותהרגו את־ בניו שבעים איש
man seventy sons-of-him *** and-you-murdered the-day father-of-me family-of

על־ אבן אחת ותמליכו את־ אבימלך בן־ אמתו
slave-girl-of-him son-of Abimelech *** and-you-made-king single stone on

על־ בעלי שכם כי אחיכם הוא: ואם־ באמת
in-honor then-if (19) he brother-of-you because Shechem citizens-of over

ובתמים עשיתם עם־ ירבעל ועם־ ביתו
family-of-him and-toward Jerub-Baal toward you-acted and-in-good-faith

היום הזה שמחו באבימלך וישמח גם־ הוא בכם:
in-you he also and-may-he-have-joy in-Abimelech have-joy! the-this the-day

ואם־ אין תצא אש מאבימלך ותאכל את־
*** and-let-her-consume from-Abimelech fire let-her-come-out not but-if (20)

בעלי שכם ואת־ בית מלוא ותצא אש מבעלי
from-citizens-of fire and-let-her-come-out Millo Beth and Shechem citizens-of

שכם ומבית מלוא ותאכל את־ אבימלך: וינס
then-he-fled (21) Abimelech *** and-let-her-consume Millo and-from-Beth Shechem

יותם ויברח וילך בארה וישב שם מפני
because-of there and-he-lived to-Beer and-he-went and-he-escaped Jotham

אבימלך אחיו: וישר אבימלך על־ ישראל שלש
three Israel over Abimelech and-he-governed (22) brother-of-him Abimelech

שנים: וישלח אלהים רוח רעה בין אבימלך ובין
and-between Abimelech between evil spirit God and-he-sent (23) years

בעלי שכם ויבגדו בעלי־ שכם
Shechem citizens-of and-they-acted-treacherously Shechem citizens-of

anoint me king over you, come and take refuge in my shade; but if not, then let fire come out of the thornbush and consume the cedars of Lebanon!'

[16]"Now if you have acted honorably and in good faith when you made Abimelech king, and if you have been fair to Jerub-Baal and his family, and if you have treated him as he deserves— [17]and to think that my father fought for you, risked his life to rescue you from the hand of Midian [18](but today you have revolted against my father's family, murdered his seventy sons on a single stone, and made Abimelech, the son of his slave girl, king over the citizens of Shechem because he is your brother)— [19]if then you have acted honorably and in good faith toward Jerub-Baal and his family today, may Abimelech be your joy, and may you be his, too! [20]But if you have not, let fire come out from Abimelech and consume you, citizens of Shechem and Beth Millo, and let fire come out from you, citizens of Shechem and Beth Millo, and consume Abimelech!"

[21]Then Jotham fled, escaping to Beer, and he lived there because he was afraid of his brother Abimelech.

[22]After Abimelech had governed Israel three years, [23]God sent an evil spirit between Abimelech and the citizens of Shechem, who acted treacherously against Abimelech.

בַּאֲבִימֶלֶךְ׃ לָבוֹא חֲמַס שִׁבְעִים בְּנֵי־ יְרֻבַּעַל
Jerub-Baal sons-of seventy crime-of to-bring (24) against-Abimelech

וְדָמָם לָשׂוּם עַל־ אֲבִימֶלֶךְ אֲחִיהֶם אֲשֶׁר הָרַג אוֹתָם
them he-murdered who brother-of-them Abimelech on to-avenge and-blood-of-them

וְעַל בַּעֲלֵי שְׁכֶם אֲשֶׁר־ חִזְּקוּ אֶת־ יָדָיו לַהֲרֹג אֶת־
*** to-murder hands-of-him *** they-helped who Shechem citizens-of and-on

אֶחָיו׃ וַיָּשִׂימוּ לוֹ בַּעֲלֵי שְׁכֶם
Shechem citizens-of against-him and-they-set (25) brothers-of-him

מְאָרְבִים עַל רָאשֵׁי הֶהָרִים וַיִּגְזְלוּ אֵת כָּל־ אֲשֶׁר־ יַעֲבֹר
he-passed who everyone *** and-they-robbed the-hills tops-of on ones-ambushing

עֲלֵיהֶם בַּדָּרֶךְ וַיֻּגַּד לַאֲבִימֶלֶךְ׃ וַיָּבֹא גַּעַל
Gaal now-he-came (26) to-Abimelech and-he-was-reported on-the-road by-them

בֶּן־ עֶבֶד וְאֶחָיו וַיַּעַבְרוּ בִּשְׁכֶם וַיִּבְטְחוּ־
and-they-confided into-Shechem and-they-moved and-brothers-of-him Ebed son-of

בוֹ בַּעֲלֵי שְׁכֶם׃ וַיֵּצְאוּ הַשָּׂדֶה וַיִּבְצְרוּ
and-they-gathered the-field and-they-went-out (27) Shechem citizens-of in-him

אֶת־ כַּרְמֵיהֶם וַיִּדְרְכוּ וַיַּעֲשׂוּ הִלּוּלִים וַיָּבֹאוּ
and-they-entered festivals and-they-held and-they-trod grapes-of-them ***

בֵּית אֱלֹהֵיהֶם וַיֹּאכְלוּ וַיִּשְׁתּוּ וַיְקַלְלוּ אֶת־
*** and-they-cursed and-they-drank and-they-ate god-of-them temple-of

אֲבִימֶלֶךְ׃ וַיֹּאמֶר ׀ גַּעַל בֶּן־ עֶבֶד מִי־ אֲבִימֶלֶךְ וּמִי־ שְׁכֶם
Shechem and-who? Abimelech who? Ebed son-of Gaal then-he-said (28) Abimelech

כִּי נַעַבְדֶנּוּ הֲלֹא בֶן־ יְרֻבַּעַל וּזְבֻל פְּקִידוֹ
deputy-of-him and-Zebul Jerub-Baal son-of not? we-should-serve-him that

עִבְדוּ אֶת־ אַנְשֵׁי חֲמוֹר אֲבִי שְׁכֶם וּמַדּוּעַ נַעַבְדֶנּוּ אֲנָחְנוּ׃
we should-we-serve-him now-why? Shechem father-of Hamor men-of *** serve!

וּמִי יִתֵּן אֶת־ הָעָם הַזֶּה בְּיָדִי
under-command-of-me the-this the-people *** he-could-put now-who? (29)

וְאָסִירָה אֶת־ אֲבִימֶלֶךְ וַיֹּאמֶר לַאֲבִימֶלֶךְ רַבֶּה
gather! to-Abimelech and-I-would-say Abimelech *** then-I-would-get-rid

צְבָאֲךָ וָצֵאָה׃ וַיִּשְׁמַע זְבֻל שַׂר־ הָעִיר אֶת־
*** the-city governor-of Zebul when-he-heard (30) and-come-out! army-of-you

דִּבְרֵי גַּעַל בֶּן־ עָבֶד וַיִּחַר אַפּוֹ׃ וַיִּשְׁלַח
and-he-sent (31) anger-of-him then-he-burned Ebed son-of Gaal words-of

מַלְאָכִים אֶל־ אֲבִימֶלֶךְ בְּתָרְמָה לֵאמֹר הִנֵּה גַעַל בֶּן־ עֶבֶד
Ebed son-of Gaal see! to-say under-cover Abimelech to messengers

וְאֶחָיו בָּאִים שְׁכֶמָה וְהִנָּם צָרִים אֶת־
*** ones-stirring-up and-see-they! to-Shechem ones-coming and-brothers-of-him

[24]God did this in order that the
crime against Jerub-Baal's seventy sons, the shedding of
their blood, might be avenged
on their brother Abimelech
and on the citizens of Shechem, who had helped him
murder his brothers. [25]In op-
position to him these citizens
of Shechem set men on the
hilltops to ambush and rob
everyone who passed by, and
this was reported to Abimelech.

[26]Now Gaal son of Ebed
moved with his brothers into
Shechem, and its citizens put
their confidence in him. [27]Af-
ter they had gone out into the
fields and gathered the grapes
and trodden them, they held a
festival in the temple of their
god. While they were eating
and drinking, they cursed
Abimelech. [28]Then Gaal son of
Ebed said, "Who is Abime-
lech, and who is Shechem,
that we should be subject to
him? Isn't he Jerub-Baal's son,
and isn't Zebul his deputy?
Serve the men of Hamor, Shechem's father! Why should we
serve Abimelech? [29]If only this
people were under my com-
mand! Then I would get rid of
him. I would say to Abimelech, 'Call out your whole
army!' "[i]

[30]When Zebul the governor
of the city heard what Gaal
son of Ebed said, he was very
angry. [31]Under cover he sent
messengers to Abimelech,
saying, "Gaal son of Ebed and
his brothers have come to Shechem and are stirring up the

[i]29 Septuagint; Hebrew *him." Then he said to Abimelech, "Call out your whole army!"*

הָעִיר עָלֶיךָ׃ וְעַתָּה קוּם לַיְלָה אַתָּה וְהָעָם אֲשֶׁר־אִתָּךְ
with-you who and-the-people you night come! and-now (32) against-you the-city

וֶאֱרֹב בַּשָּׂדֶה׃ וְהָיָה בַבֹּקֶר כִּזְרֹחַ
as-to-rise in-the-morning and-he-will-be (33) in-the-field and-lie-in-wait!

הַשֶּׁמֶשׁ תַּשְׁכִּים וּפָשַׁטְתָּ עַל־הָעִיר וְהִנֵּה־הוּא וְהָעָם
and-the-people he and-see! the-city against and-you-advance you-get-up the-sun

אֲשֶׁר־אִתּוֹ יֹצְאִים אֵלֶיךָ וְעָשִׂיתָ לּוֹ כַּאֲשֶׁר תִּמְצָא
she-finds just-as to-him then-you-do against-you ones-coming-out with-him who

יָדֶךָ׃ וַיָּקָם אֲבִימֶלֶךְ וְכָל־הָעָם אֲשֶׁר־עִמּוֹ
with-him that the-troop and-all-of Abimelech so-he-set-out (34) hand-of-you

לַיְלָה וַיֶּאֶרְבוּ עַל־שְׁכֶם אַרְבָּעָה רָאשִׁים׃ וַיֵּצֵא גַּעַל
Gaal now-he-went-out (35) companies four Shechem near and-they-hid night

בֶּן־עֶבֶד וַיַּעֲמֹד פֶּתַח שַׁעַר הָעִיר וַיָּקָם
and-he-came-out the-city gate-of entrace-of and-he-stood Ebed son-of

אֲבִימֶלֶךְ וְהָעָם אֲשֶׁר־אִתּוֹ מִן־הַמַּאְרָב׃ וַיַּרְא־
when-he-saw (36) the-hiding-place from with-him who and-the-troop Abimelech

גַעַל אֶת־הָעָם וַיֹּאמֶר אֶל־זְבֻל הִנֵּה־עָם יוֹרֵד
coming-down people look! Zebul to then-he-said the-people *** Gaal

מֵרָאשֵׁי הֶהָרִים וַיֹּאמֶר אֵלָיו זְבֻל אֵת צֵל
shadow-of *** Zebul to-him and-he-replied the-mountains from-tops-of

הֶהָרִים אַתָּה רֹאֶה כַּאֲנָשִׁים*׃ וַיֹּסֶף עוֹד גַּעַל לְדַבֵּר
to-speak Gaal again but-he-repeated (37) as-men seeing you the-mountains

וַיֹּאמֶר הִנֵּה־עָם יוֹרְדִים מֵעִם טַבּוּר הָאָרֶץ
the-land center-of from-in ones-coming-down people look! and-he-said

וְרֹאשׁ־אֶחָד בָּא מִדֶּרֶךְ אֵלוֹן מְעוֹנְנִים׃ וַיֹּאמֶר
then-he-said (38) ones-soothsaying oak-of from-direction-of coming one and-company

אֵלָיו זְבֻל אַיֵּה אֵפוֹא פִיךָ אֲשֶׁר תֹּאמַר מִי אֲבִימֶלֶךְ כִּי
that Abimelech who? you-said when talk-of-you now where? Zebul to-him

נַעַבְדֶנּוּ הֲלֹא זֶה הָעָם אֲשֶׁר מָאַסְתָּה בּוֹ צֵא־
go! against-him you-ridiculed whom the-people this not? we-should-serve-him

נָא עַתָּה וְהִלָּחֶם בּוֹ׃ וַיֵּצֵא גַעַל לִפְנֵי בַּעֲלֵי
citizens-of before Gaal so-he-went-out (39) against-him and-fight! now now!

שְׁכֶם וַיִּלָּחֶם בַּאֲבִימֶלֶךְ׃ וַיִּרְדְּפֵהוּ אֲבִימֶלֶךְ
Abimelech and-he-chased-him (40) against-Abimelech and-he-fought Shechem

וַיָּנָס מִפָּנָיו וַיִּפְּלוּ חֲלָלִים רַבִּים עַד־פֶּתַח
entrance-of to many ones-wounded and-they-fell from-before-him and-he-fled

הַשָּׁעַר׃ וַיֵּשֶׁב אֲבִימֶלֶךְ בָּארוּמָה וַיְגָרֶשׁ זְבֻל אֶת־גַּעַל
Gaal *** Zebul and-he-drove in-Arumah Abimelech and-he-stayed (41) the-gate

city against you. [32]Now then,
during the night you and your
men should come and lie in
wait in the fields. [33]In the
morning at sunrise, advance
against the city. When Gaal
and his men come out against
you, do whatever your hand
finds to do."
[34]So Abimelech and all his
troops set out by night and
took up concealed positions
near Shechem in four companies. [35]Now Gaal son of Ebed
had gone out and was standing at the entrance to the city
gate just as Abimelech and his
soldiers came out from their
hiding place.
[36]When Gaal saw them, he
said to Zebul, "Look, people
are coming down from the
tops of the mountains!"
Zebul replied, "You mistake
the shadows of the mountains
for men."
[37]But Gaal spoke up again:
"Look, people are coming
down from the center of the
land, and a company is coming from the direction of the
soothsayers' tree."
[38]Then Zebul said to him,
"Where is your big talk now,
you who said, 'Who is Abimelech that we should be subject
to him?' Aren't these the men
you ridiculed? Go out and
fight them!"
[39]So Gaal led out[j] the citizens of Shechem and fought
Abimelech. [40]Abimelech
chased him, and many fell
wounded in the flight—all the
way to the entrance to the
gate. [41]Abimelech stayed in
Arumah, and Zebul drove

j39 Or *Gaal went out in the sight of*

*36 Most mss have *pathah* under the *kaph* (’כַּ).

וְאֶת־ אֶחָיו מִשֶּׁבֶת בִּשְׁכֶם׃ וַיְהִי מִמָּחֳרָת
on-next-day and-he-was (42) in-Shechem from-to-live brothers-of-him and

וַיֵּצֵא הָעָם הַשָּׂדֶה וַיַּגִּדוּ לַאֲבִימֶלֶךְ׃
to-Abimelech and-they-reported the-field the-people that-he-went-out

וַיִּקַּח אֶת־ הָעָם וַיֶּחֱצֵם לִשְׁלֹשָׁה רָאשִׁים
companies into-three and-he-divided-them the-people *** so-he-took (43)

וַיֶּאֱרֹב בַּשָּׂדֶה וַיַּרְא וְהִנֵּה הָעָם יֹצֵא מִן־
from coming the-people and-see! and-he-saw in-the-field and-he-set-ambush

הָעִיר וַיָּקָם עֲלֵיהֶם וַיַּכֵּם׃ וַאֲבִימֶלֶךְ
and-Abimelech (44) and-he-attacked-them against-them then-he-rose the-city

וְהָרָאשִׁים אֲשֶׁר עִמּוֹ פָּשְׁטוּ וַיַּעַמְדוּ
and-they-took-position they-rushed-forward with-him who and-the-companies

פֶּתַח שַׁעַר הָעִיר וּשְׁנֵי הָרָאשִׁים פָּשְׁטוּ עַל־ כָּל־
all upon they-rushed the-companies then-two-of the-city gate-of entrance-of

אֲשֶׁר בַּשָּׂדֶה וַיַּכּוּם׃ וַאֲבִימֶלֶךְ נִלְחָם
he-attacked and-Abimelech (45) and-they-struck-down-them in-the-field who

בָּעִיר כֹּל הַיּוֹם הַהוּא וַיִּלְכֹּד אֶת־ הָעִיר וְאֶת־
and the-city *** and-he-captured the-that the-day all-of against-the-city

הָעָם אֲשֶׁר־ בָּהּ הָרָג וַיִּתֹּץ אֶת־ הָעִיר
the-city *** then-he-destroyed he-killed in-her who the-people

וַיִּזְרָעֶהָ מֶלַח׃ וַיִּשְׁמְעוּ כָּל־ בַּעֲלֵי
citizens-of all-of when-they-heard (46) salt and-he-scattered-over-her

מִגְדַּל־ שְׁכֶם וַיָּבֹאוּ אֶל־ צְרִיחַ בֵּית אֵל בְּרִית׃
Berith El temple-of stronghold-of into then-they-went Shechem tower-of

וַיֻּגַּד לַאֲבִימֶלֶךְ כִּי הִתְקַבְּצוּ כָּל־ בַּעֲלֵי
citizens-of all-of they-assembled that to-Abimelech when-he-was-told (47)

מִגְדַּל־ שְׁכֶם׃ וַיַּעַל אֲבִימֶלֶךְ הַר־ צַלְמוֹן הוּא וְכָל־
and-all-of he Zalmon Mount-of Abimelech then-he-went-up (48) Shechem tower-of

הָעָם אֲשֶׁר־ אִתּוֹ וַיִּקַּח אֲבִימֶלֶךְ אֶת־הַקַּרְדֻּמּוֹת בְּיָדוֹ
in-hand-of-him the-axes *** Abimelech and-he-took with-him who the-people

וַיִּכְרֹת שׂוֹכַת עֵצִים וַיִּשָּׂאֶהָ וַיָּשֶׂם עַל־ שִׁכְמוֹ
shoulder-of-him on and-he-put and-he-lifted-her trees branch-of and-he-cut-off

וַיֹּאמֶר אֶל־ הָעָם אֲשֶׁר־ עִמּוֹ מָה רְאִיתֶם עָשִׂיתִי מַהֲרוּ
be-quick! I-did you-saw what with-him who the-people to and-he-ordered

עֲשׂוּ כָמוֹנִי׃ וַיִּכְרְתוּ גַם־ כָּל־ הָעָם אִישׁ שׂוֹכֹה
branch-of-him each the-people all-of also so-they-cut (49) like-me do!

וַיֵּלְכוּ אַחֲרֵי אֲבִימֶלֶךְ וַיָּשִׂימוּ עַל־ הַצְּרִיחַ
the-stronghold against and-they-piled Abimelech after and-they-followed

Gaal and his brothers out of
Shechem.
42The next day the people of
Shechem went out to the
fields, and this was reported to
Abimelech. 43So he took his
men, divided them into three
companies and set an ambush
in the fields. When he saw the
people coming out of the city,
he rose to attack them.
44Abimelech and the companies with him rushed forward
to a position at the entrance to
the city gate. Then two companies rushed upon those in the
fields and struck them down.
45All that day Abimelech
pressed his attack against the
city until he had captured it
and killed its people. Then he
destroyed the city and scattered salt over it.
46On hearing this, the citizens in the tower of Shechem
went into the stronghold of
the temple of El-Berith.
47When Abimelech heard that
they had assembled there, 48he
and all his men went up
Mount Zalmon. He took an ax
and cut off some branches,
which he lifted to his shoulders. He ordered the men with
him, "Quick! Do what you
have seen me do!" 49So all the
men cut branches and fol-
lowed Abimelech. They piled
them against the stronghold

וַיַּצִּיתוּ עֲלֵיהֶם אֶת־ הַצְּרִיחַ בָּאֵשׁ וַיָּמֻתוּ
and-they-died with-the-fire the-stronghold *** over-them and-they-set-fire

גַּם כָּל־ אַנְשֵׁי מִגְדַּל־ שְׁכֶם כְּאֶלֶף אִישׁ וְאִשָּׁה׃
and-woman man about-thousand Shechem tower-of people-of all-of also

וַיֵּלֶךְ אֲבִימֶלֶךְ אֶל־ תֵּבֵץ וַיִּחַן בְּתֵבֵץ
against-Thebez and-he-besieged Thebez to Abimelech and-he-went (50)

וַיִּלְכְּדָהּ׃ וּמִגְדַּל־ עֹז הָיָה בְתוֹךְ־ הָעִיר
the-city inside-of he-was strong now-tower-of (51) and-he-captured-her

וַיָּנֻסוּ שָׁמָּה כָּל־ הָאֲנָשִׁים וְהַנָּשִׁים וְכֹל בַּעֲלֵי
people-of and-all-of and-the-women the-men all-of to-there and-they-fled

הָעִיר וַיִּסְגְּרוּ בַּעֲדָם וַיַּעֲלוּ עַל־ גַּג הַמִּגְדָּל׃
the-tower roof-of on and-they-climbed-up after-them and-they-locked the-city

וַיָּבֹא אֲבִימֶלֶךְ עַד־ הַמִּגְדָּל וַיִּלָּחֶם בּוֹ
against-him and-he-stormed the-tower to Abimelech and-he-went (52)

וַיִּגַּשׁ עַד־ פֶּתַח הַמִּגְדָּל לְשָׂרְפוֹ בָאֵשׁ׃
with-the-fire to-burn-him the-tower entrance-of to and-he-approached

וַתַּשְׁלֵךְ אִשָּׁה אַחַת פֶּלַח רֶכֶב עַל־ רֹאשׁ אֲבִימֶלֶךְ
Abimelech head-of on upper millstone one woman but-she-dropped (53)

וַתָּרִץ אֶת־ גֻּלְגָּלְתּוֹ׃ וַיִּקְרָא מְהֵרָה אֶל־ הַנַּעַר ׀
the-servant to hurriedly and-he-called (54) skull-of-him *** and-she-cracked

נֹשֵׂא כֵלָיו וַיֹּאמֶר לוֹ שְׁלֹף חַרְבְּךָ וּמוֹתְתֵנִי
and-kill-me! sword-of-you draw! to-him and-he-said armors-of-him bearing

פֶּן־ יֹאמְרוּ לִי אִשָּׁה הֲרָגָתְהוּ וַיִּדְקְרֵהוּ
so-he-ran-through-him she-killed-him woman about-me they-can-say so-not

נַעֲרוֹ וַיָּמֹת׃ וַיִּרְאוּ אִישׁ־ יִשְׂרָאֵל כִּי מֵת
he-was-dead that Israel man-of when-they-saw (55) and-he-died servant-of-him

אֲבִימֶלֶךְ וַיֵּלְכוּ אִישׁ לִמְקֹמוֹ׃ וַיָּשֶׁב אֱלֹהִים אֶת
*** God so-he-repaid (56) to-home-of-him each then-they-went Abimelech

רָעַת אֲבִימֶלֶךְ אֲשֶׁר עָשָׂה לְאָבִיו לַהֲרֹג אֶת־שִׁבְעִים
seventy *** to-murder to-father-of-him he-did that Abimelech wickedness-of

אֶחָיו׃ וְאֵת כָּל־ רָעַת אַנְשֵׁי שְׁכֶם הֵשִׁיב
he-brought Shechem men-of wickedness-of all-of and (57) brothers-of-him

אֱלֹהִים בְּרֹאשָׁם וַתָּבֹא אֲלֵיהֶם קִלְלַת יוֹתָם בֶּן־ יְרֻבָּעַל׃
Jerub-Baal son-of Jotham curse-of on-them and-she-came on-head-of-them God

וַיָּקָם אַחֲרֵי אֲבִימֶלֶךְ לְהוֹשִׁיעַ אֶת־ יִשְׂרָאֵל תּוֹלָע בֶּן־ פּוּאָה
Puah son-of Tola Israel *** to-save Abimelech after and-he-rose (10:1)

בֶּן־ דּוֹדוֹ אִישׁ יִשָּׂשכָר וְהוּא־ יֹשֵׁב בְּשָׁמִיר בְּהַר אֶפְרָיִם׃
Ephraim in-hill-country-of in-Shamir living and-he Issachar man-of Dodo son-of

and set it on fire over the
people inside. So all the people
in the tower of Shechem,
about a thousand men and
women, also died.
50 Next Abimelech went to
Thebez and besieged it and
captured it. 51 Inside the city,
however, was a strong tower,
to which all the men and
women—all the people of the
city—fled. They locked themselves in and climbed up on
the tower roof. 52 Abimelech
went to the tower and stormed
it. But as he approached the
entrance to the tower to set it
on fire, 53 a woman dropped an
upper millstone on his head
and cracked his skull.
54 Hurriedly he called to his
armor-bearer, "Draw your
sword and kill me, so that they
can't say, 'A woman killed
him.' " So his servant ran him
through, and he died. 55 When
the Israelites saw that Abimelech was dead, they went
home.
56 Thus God repaid the
wickedness that Abimelech
had done to his father by mur-
dering his seventy brothers.
57 God also made the men of
Shechem pay for all their
wickedness. The curse of Jotham son of Jerub-Baal came
on them.

Tola

10 After the time of
Abimelech a man of Is-
sachar, Tola son of Puah, the
son of Dodo, rose to save Israel. He lived in Shamir, in the
hill country of Ephraim. 2 He

וַיִּשְׁפֹּט אֶת־יִשְׂרָאֵל עֶשְׂרִים וְשָׁלֹשׁ שָׁנָה וַיָּמָת וַיִּקָּבֵר

and-he-was-buried then-he-died year and-three twenty Israel *** and-he-led (2)

בְּשָׁמִיר׃ וַיָּקָם אַחֲרָיו יָאִיר הַגִּלְעָדִי וַיִּשְׁפֹּט אֶת־יִשְׂרָאֵל

Israel *** and-he-led the-Gileadite Jair after-him and-he-rose (3) in-Shamir

עֶשְׂרִים וּשְׁתַּיִם שָׁנָה׃ וַיְהִי־ לוֹ שְׁלֹשִׁים בָּנִים רֹכְבִים עַל־שְׁלֹשִׁים

thirty on ones-riding sons thirty to-him and-he-was (4) year and-two twenty

עֲיָרִים וּשְׁלֹשִׁים עֲיָרִים* לָהֶם לָהֶם יִקְרְאוּ ׀ חַוֺּת יָאִיר עַד

to Jair Havvoth they-called to-them to-them *donkeys and-thirty donkeys

הַיּוֹם הַזֶּה אֲשֶׁר בְּאֶרֶץ הַגִּלְעָד׃ וַיָּמָת יָאִיר

Jair when-he-died (5) the-Gilead in-land-of that the-this the-day

וַיִּקָּבֵר בְּקָמוֹן׃ וַיֹּסִפוּ ׀ בְּנֵי יִשְׂרָאֵל לַעֲשׂוֹת

to-do Israel sons-of and-they-continued (6) in-Kamon then-he-was-buried

הָרַע בְּעֵינֵי יְהוָה וַיַּעַבְדוּ אֶת־ הַבְּעָלִים וְאֶת־ הָעַשְׁתָּרוֹת

the-Ashtoreths and the-Baals *** and-they-served Yahweh in-eyes-of the-evil

וְאֶת־אֱלֹהֵי אֲרָם וְאֶת־ אֱלֹהֵי צִידוֹן וְאֵת ׀ אֱלֹהֵי מוֹאָב וְאֵת אֱלֹהֵי בְנֵי־

sons-of gods-of and Moab gods-of and Sidon gods-of and Aram gods-of and

עַמּוֹן וְאֵת אֱלֹהֵי פְלִשְׁתִּים וַיַּעַזְבוּ אֶת־ יְהוָה וְלֹא

and-not Yahweh *** and-they-forsook Philistines gods-of and Ammon

עֲבָדוּהוּ׃ וַיִּחַר־ אַף יְהוָה בְּיִשְׂרָאֵל

against-Israel Yahweh anger-of and-he-burned (7) they-served-him

וַיִּמְכְּרֵם בְּיַד־ פְּלִשְׁתִּים וּבְיַד בְּנֵי עַמּוֹן׃

Ammon sons-of and-into-hand-of Philistines into-hand-of and-he-sold-them

וַיִּרְעֲצוּ וַיְרֹצְצוּ אֶת־ בְּנֵי יִשְׂרָאֵל בַּשָּׁנָה הַהִיא

the-that in-the-year Israel sons-of *** and-they-crushed and-they-shattered (8)

שְׁמֹנֶה עֶשְׂרֵה שָׁנָה אֶת־כָּל־ בְּנֵי יִשְׂרָאֵל אֲשֶׁר בְּעֵבֶר הַיַּרְדֵּן

the-Jordan on-east-side-of who Israel sons-of all-of *** year ten eight

בְּאֶרֶץ הָאֱמֹרִי אֲשֶׁר בַּגִּלְעָד׃ וַיַּעַבְרוּ בְנֵי־

sons-of and-they-crossed (9) in-the-Gilead that the-Amorite in-land-of

עַמּוֹן אֶת־ הַיַּרְדֵּן לְהִלָּחֵם גַּם־ בִּיהוּדָה וּבְבִנְיָמִין

and-against-Benjamin against-Judah also to-fight the-Jordan *** Ammon

וּבְבֵית אֶפְרָיִם וַתֵּצֶר לְיִשְׂרָאֵל מְאֹד׃

greatly to-Israel and-she-was-distressing Ephraim and-against-house-of

וַיִּזְעֲקוּ בְּנֵי יִשְׂרָאֵל אֶל־יְהוָה לֵאמֹר חָטָאנוּ לָךְ

against-you we-sinned to-say Yahweh to Israel sons-of then-they-cried-out (10)

וְכִי עָזַבְנוּ אֶת־ אֱלֹהֵינוּ וַנַּעֲבֹד אֶת־הַבְּעָלִים׃ וַיֹּאמֶר

and-he-said (11) the-Baals *** and-we-served God-of-us *** we-forsook and-indeed

יְהוָה אֶל־ בְּנֵי יִשְׂרָאֵל הֲלֹא מִמִּצְרַיִם וּמִן־ הָאֱמֹרִי וּמִן־

and-when the-Amorite and-when when-Egypt not? Israel sons-of to Yahweh

led[k] Israel twenty-three years; then he died, and was buried in Shamir.

Jair

[3]He was followed by Jair of Gilead, who led Israel twenty-two years. [4]He had thirty sons, who rode thirty donkeys. They controlled thirty towns in Gilead, which to this day are called Havvoth Jair.[l] [5]When Jair died, he was buried in Kamon.

Jephthah

[6]Again the Israelites did evil in the eyes of the LORD. They served the Baals and the Ashtoreths, and the gods of Aram, the gods of Sidon, the gods of Moab, the gods of the Ammonites and the gods of the Philistines. And because the Israelites forsook the LORD and no longer served him, [7]he became angry with them. He sold them into the hands of the Philistines and the Ammonites, [8]who that year shattered and crushed them. For eighteen years they oppressed all the Israelites on the east side of the Jordan in Gilead, the land of the Amorites. [9]The Ammonites also crossed the Jordan to fight against Judah, Benjamin and the house of Ephraim; and Israel was in great distress. [10]Then the Israelites cried out to the LORD, "We have sinned against you, forsaking our God and serving the Baals."

[11]The LORD replied, "When the Egyptians, the Amorites,

k2 Traditionally *judged;* also in verse 3

l4 Or *called the settlements of Jair*

4 This word should probably be repointed with the ancient versions as עָרִים , *towns.

בְּנֵי עַמּוֹן וּמִן־ פְּלִשְׁתִּים׃ וְצִידוֹנִים וַעֲמָלֵק וּמָעוֹן
and-Maon and-Amalek and-Sidonians (12) Philistines and-when Ammon sons-of

לָחֲצוּ אֶתְכֶם וַתִּצְעֲקוּ אֵלַי וָאוֹשִׁיעָה אֶתְכֶם מִיָּדָם׃
from-hand-of-them you then-I-saved to-me and-you-cried you they-oppressed

וְאַתֶּם עֲזַבְתֶּם אוֹתִי וַתַּעַבְדוּ אֱלֹהִים אֲחֵרִים לָכֵן לֹא־
not so other-ones gods and-you-served me you-forsook but-you (13)

אוֹסִיף לְהוֹשִׁיעַ אֶתְכֶם׃ לְכוּ וְזַעֲקוּ אֶל־הָאֱלֹהִים אֲשֶׁר בְּחַרְתֶּם
you-chose whom the-gods to and-cry-out! go! (14) you to-save I-will-continue

בָּם הֵמָּה יוֹשִׁיעוּ לָכֶם בְּעֵת צָרַתְכֶם׃ וַיֹּאמְרוּ
but-they-said (15) trouble-of-you in-time-of to-you let-them-save they to-them

בְנֵי־ יִשְׂרָאֵל אֶל־ יְהוָה חָטָאנוּ עֲשֵׂה־אַתָּה לָנוּ כְּכָל־ הַטּוֹב
the-good as-all-of to-us you do! we-sinned Yahweh to Israel sons-of

בְּעֵינֶיךָ אַךְ הַצִּילֵנוּ נָא הַיּוֹם הַזֶּה׃ וַיָּסִירוּ
then-they-got-rid (16) the-this the-day now! rescue-us! but in-eyes-of-you

אֶת־ אֱלֹהֵי הַנֵּכָר מִקִּרְבָּם וַיַּעַבְדוּ אֶת־ יְהוָה
Yahweh *** and-they-served from-among-them the-foreign gods-of ***

וַתִּקְצַר נַפְשׁוֹ בַּעֲמַל יִשְׂרָאֵל׃ וַיִּצָּעֲקוּ
and-they-gathered (17) Israel with-misery-of soul-of-him and-she-could-not-bear

בְּנֵי עַמּוֹן וַיַּחֲנוּ בַּגִּלְעָד וַיֵּאָסְפוּ בְּנֵי
sons-of and-they-assembled in-the-Gilead and-they-camped Ammon sons-of

יִשְׂרָאֵל וַיַּחֲנוּ בַּמִּצְפָּה׃ וַיֹּאמְרוּ הָעָם שָׂרֵי
leaders-of the-people and-they-said (18) at-the-Mizpah and-they-camped Israel

גִלְעָד אִישׁ אֶל־ רֵעֵהוּ מִי הָאִישׁ אֲשֶׁר יָחֵל לְהִלָּחֵם
to-attack he-launches who the-man whoever other-of-him to each Gilead

בִּבְנֵי עַמּוֹן יִהְיֶה לְרֹאשׁ לְכֹל יֹשְׁבֵי גִלְעָד׃
Gilead ones-living-of of-all-of as-head he-will-be Ammon against-sons-of

וְיִפְתָּח הַגִּלְעָדִי הָיָה גִּבּוֹר חַיִל וְהוּא בֶּן־ אִשָּׁה
woman son-of and-he mighty warrior-of he-was the-Gileadite now-Jephthah (11:1)

זוֹנָה וַיּוֹלֶד גִּלְעָד אֶת־ יִפְתָּח׃ וַתֵּלֶד אֵשֶׁת־
wife-of and-she-bore (2) Jephthah *** Gilead and-he-fathered being-prostitute

גִּלְעָד לוֹ בָּנִים וַיִּגְדְּלוּ בְנֵי־ הָאִשָּׁה וַיְגָרְשׁוּ
then-they-drove-away the-woman sons-of when-they-grew-up sons to-him Gilead

אֶת־ יִפְתָּח וַיֹּאמְרוּ לוֹ לֹא־ תִנְחַל בְּבֵית־
in-family-of you-will-inherit not to-him and-they-said Jephthah ***

אָבִינוּ כִּי בֶן־ אִשָּׁה אַחֶרֶת אָתָּה׃ וַיִּבְרַח יִפְתָּח מִפְּנֵי
from-before Jephthah so-he-fled (3) you another woman son-of for father-of-us

אֶחָיו וַיֵּשֶׁב בְּאֶרֶץ טוֹב וַיִּתְלַקְּטוּ אֶל־
around and-they-gathered Tob in-land-of and-he-settled brothers-of-him

the Ammonites, the Philistines, 12the Sidonians, the
Amalekites and the Maonites[m]
oppressed you and you cried
to me for help, did I not save
you from their hands? 13But
you have forsaken me and
served other gods, so I will no
longer save you. 14Go and cry
out to the gods you have chosen. Let them save you when
you are in trouble!"

15But the Israelites said to the
LORD, "We have sinned. Do
with us whatever you think
best, but please rescue us
now." 16Then they got rid of
the foreign gods among them
and served the LORD. And he
could bear Israel's misery no
longer.

17When the Ammonites
were called to arms and
camped in Gilead, the Israelites assembled and camped at
Mizpah. 18The leaders of the
people of Gilead said to each
other, "Whoever will launch
the attack against the Ammonites will be the head of all
those living in Gilead."

11 Jephthah the Gileadite
was a mighty warrior.
His father was Gilead; his
mother was a prostitute. 2Gil-
ead's wife also bore him sons,
and when they were grown
up, they drove Jephthah away.
"You are not going to get any
inheritance in our family,"
they said, "because you are
the son of another woman."
3So Jephthah fled from his
brothers and settled in the
land of Tob, where a group of
adventurers gathered around

[m]12 Hebrew; some Septuagint manuscripts *Midianites*

יִפְתָּח אֲנָשִׁים רֵיקִים וַיֵּצְאוּ עִמּוֹ׃ וַיְהִי מִיָּמִים

after-days and-he-was (4) after-him and-they-followed adventurers men Jephthah

וַיִּלָּחֲמוּ בְנֵי־עַמּוֹן עִם־יִשְׂרָאֵל׃ וַיְהִי כַּאֲשֶׁר־נִלְחֲמוּ

they-made-war just-as and-he-was (5) Israel on Ammon sons-of then-they-made-war

בְנֵי־עַמּוֹן עִם־יִשְׂרָאֵל וַיֵּלְכוּ זִקְנֵי גִלְעָד לָקַחַת אֶת־יִפְתָּח

Jephthah *** to-get Gilead elders-of then-they-went Israel on Ammon sons-of

מֵאֶרֶץ טוֹב׃ וַיֹּאמְרוּ לְיִפְתָּח לְכָה וְהָיִיתָה לָּנוּ

to-us and-you-be come! to-Jephthah and-they-said (6) Tob from-land-of

לְקָצִין וְנִלָּחֲמָה בִּבְנֵי עַמּוֹן׃ וַיֹּאמֶר יִפְתָּח

Jephthah and-he-said (7) Ammon against-sons-of so-we-can-fight as-commander

לְזִקְנֵי גִלְעָד הֲלֹא אַתֶּם שְׂנֵאתֶם אוֹתִי וַתְּגָרְשׁוּנִי מִבֵּית

from-house-of and-you-drove-me me you-hated you not? Gilead to-elders-of

אָבִי וּמַדּוּעַ בָּאתֶם אֵלַי עַתָּה כַּאֲשֶׁר צַר לָכֶם׃

to-you trouble just-when now to-me you-come so-why? father-of-me

וַיֹּאמְרוּ זִקְנֵי גִלְעָד אֶל־יִפְתָּח לָכֵן עַתָּה שַׁבְנוּ

we-turn now nevertheless Jephthah to Gilead elders-of and-they-said (8)

אֵלֶיךָ וְהָלַכְתָּ עִמָּנוּ וְנִלְחַמְתָּ בִּבְנֵי עַמּוֹן וְהָיִיתָ

and-you-will-be Ammon against-sons-of and-you-fight with-us so-you-come to-you

לָּנוּ לְרֹאשׁ לְכֹל יֹשְׁבֵי גִלְעָד׃ וַיֹּאמֶר יִפְתָּח אֶל־

to Jephthah and-he-said (9) Gilead ones-living-of over-all-of as-head to-us

זִקְנֵי גִלְעָד אִם־מְשִׁיבִים אַתֶּם אוֹתִי לְהִלָּחֵם בִּבְנֵי

against-sons-of to-fight me you ones-taking-back suppose Gilead elders-of

עַמּוֹן וְנָתַן יְהוָה אוֹתָם לְפָנָי אָנֹכִי אֶהְיֶה לָכֶם לְרֹאשׁ׃

as-head to-you will-I-be I to-me them Yahweh and-he-gives Ammon

וַיֹּאמְרוּ זִקְנֵי־גִלְעָד אֶל־יִפְתָּח יְהוָה יִהְיֶה שֹׁמֵעַ

witnessing he-is Yahweh Jephthah to Gilead elders-of and-they-replied (10)

בֵּינוֹתֵינוּ אִם־לֹא כִדְבָרְךָ כֵּן נַעֲשֶׂה׃ וַיֵּלֶךְ יִפְתָּח

Jephthah so-he-went (11) we-will-do so as-word-of-you not if against-us

עִם־זִקְנֵי גִלְעָד וַיָּשִׂימוּ הָעָם אוֹתוֹ עֲלֵיהֶם לְרֹאשׁ

as-head over-them him the-people and-they-made Gilead elders-of with

וּלְקָצִין וַיְדַבֵּר יִפְתָּח אֶת־כָּל־דְּבָרָיו לִפְנֵי

before words-of-him all-of *** Jephthah and-he-repeated and-as-commander

יְהוָה בַּמִּצְפָּה׃ וַיִּשְׁלַח יִפְתָּח מַלְאָכִים אֶל־מֶלֶךְ בְּנֵי־

sons-of king-of to messengers Jephthah then-he-sent (12) in-the-Mizpah Yahweh

עַמּוֹן לֵאמֹר מַה־לִּי וָלָךְ כִּי־בָאתָ אֵלַי לְהִלָּחֵם

to-attack to-me you-came that and-to-you to-me what? to-say Ammon

בְּאַרְצִי׃ וַיֹּאמֶר מֶלֶךְ בְּנֵי־עַמּוֹן אֶל־

to Ammon sons-of king-of and-he-answered (13) against-country-of-me

him and followed him.

4Some time later, when the Ammonites made war on Israel, 5the elders of Gilead went to get Jephthah from the land of Tob. 6"Come," they said, "be our commander, so we can fight the Ammonites."

7Jephthah said to them, "Didn't you hate me and drive me from my father's house? Why do you come to me now, when you're in trouble?"

8The elders of Gilead said to him, "Nevertheless, we are turning to you now; come with us to fight the Ammonites, and you will be our head over all who live in Gilead."

9Jephthah answered, "Suppose you take me back to fight the Ammonites and the LORD gives them to me—will I really be your head?"

10The elders of Gilead replied, "The LORD is our witness; we will certainly do as you say." 11So Jephthah went with the elders of Gilead, and the people made him head and commander over them. And he repeated all his words before the LORD in Mizpah.

12Then Jephthah sent messengers to the Ammonite king with the question: "What do you have against us that you have attacked our country?"

13The king of the Ammonites answered Jephthah's messengers, "When Israel came

מַלְאֲכֵי יִפְתָּח כִּֽי־ לָקַח יִשְׂרָאֵל אֶת־ אַרְצִי בַּעֲלוֹתוֹ
when-to-come-him land-of-me *** Israel he-took because Jephthah messengers-of

מִמִּצְרַיִם מֵאַרְנוֹן וְעַד־ הַיַּבֹּק וְעַד־ הַיַּרְדֵּן וְעַתָּה
and-now the-Jordan even-to the-Jabbok even-to from-Arnon from-Egypt

הָשִׁיבָה אֶתְהֶן בְּשָׁלוֹם׃ וַיּוֹסֶף עוֹד יִפְתָּח וַיִּשְׁלַח
and-he-sent Jephthah again and-he-repeated (14) in-peace them give-back!

מַלְאָכִים אֶל־ מֶלֶךְ בְּנֵי עַמּוֹן׃ וַיֹּאמֶר לוֹ כֹּה אָמַר
he-says this to-him and-he-said (15) Ammon sons-of king-of to messengers

יִפְתָּח לֹא־ לָקַח יִשְׂרָאֵל אֶת־אֶרֶץ מוֹאָב וְאֶת־ אֶרֶץ בְּנֵי עַמּוֹן׃
Ammon sons-of land-of or Moab land-of *** Israel he-took not Jephthah

כִּי בַּעֲלוֹתָם מִמִּצְרָיִם וַיֵּלֶךְ יִשְׂרָאֵל בַּמִּדְבָּר
through-the-desert Israel then-he-went from-Egypt when-to-come-up-them but (16)

עַד־ יַם־ סוּף וַיָּבֹא קָדֵשָׁה׃ וַיִּשְׁלַח יִשְׂרָאֵל מַלְאָכִים ׀
messengers Israel then-he-sent (17) to-Kadesh and-he-went-on Reed Sea-of to

אֶל־ מֶלֶךְ אֱדוֹם ׀ לֵאמֹר אֶעְבְּרָה־ נָּא בְאַרְצֶךָ וְלֹא
but-not through-country-of-you now! let-me-go to-say Edom king-of to

שָׁמַע מֶלֶךְ אֱדוֹם וְגַם אֶל־ מֶלֶךְ מוֹאָב שָׁלַח וְלֹא אָבָה
he-allowed but-not he-sent Moab king-of to and-also Edom king-of he-listened

וַיֵּשֶׁב יִשְׂרָאֵל בְּקָדֵשׁ׃ וַיֵּלֶךְ בַּמִּדְבָּר
through-the-desert so-he-travelled (18) at-Kadesh Israel so-he-stayed

וַיָּסָב אֶת־ אֶרֶץ אֱדוֹם וְאֶת־ אֶרֶץ מוֹאָב וַיָּבֹא מִמִּזְרַח־
along-rise-of and-he-passed Moab land-of and Edom land-of *** and-he-skirted

שֶׁמֶשׁ לְאֶרֶץ מוֹאָב וַֽיַּחֲנוּן בְּעֵבֶר אַרְנוֹן וְלֹא־
but-not Arnon on-other-side-of and-they-camped Moab of-country-of sun

בָאוּ בִּגְבוּל מוֹאָב כִּי אַרְנוֹן גְּבוּל מוֹאָב׃ וַיִּשְׁלַח
then-he-sent (19) Moab border-of Arnon for Moab into-territory-of they-entered

יִשְׂרָאֵל מַלְאָכִים אֶל־סִיחוֹן מֶלֶךְ־ הָאֱמֹרִי מֶלֶךְ חֶשְׁבּוֹן וַיֹּאמֶר
and-he-said Heshbon king-of the-Amorite king-of Sihon to messengers Israel

לוֹ יִשְׂרָאֵל נַעְבְּרָה־ נָּא בְאַרְצְךָ עַד־ מְקוֹמִי׃
place-of-me to through-country-of-you now! let-us-pass Israel to-him

וְלֹא־ הֶאֱמִין סִיחוֹן אֶת־ יִשְׂרָאֵל עֲבֹר בִּגְבֻלוֹ
through-territory-of-him to-pass Israel *** Sihon he-trusted but-not (20)

וַיֶּאֱסֹף סִיחוֹן אֶת־ כָּל־ עַמּוֹ וַיַּחֲנוּ בְּיָהְצָה
at-Jahaz and-they-camped people-of-him all-of *** Sihon and-he-mustered

וַיִּלָּחֶם עִם־ יִשְׂרָאֵל׃ וַיִּתֵּן יְהוָה אֱלֹהֵי־ יִשְׂרָאֵל אֶת־סִיחוֹן
Sihon *** Israeh God-of Yahweh then-he-gave (21) Israel with and-he-fought

וְאֶת־ כָּל־ עַמּוֹ בְּיַד יִשְׂרָאֵל וַיַּכּוּם
and-they-defeated-them Israel into-hand-of people-of-him all-of and

up out of Egypt, they took away my land from the Arnon to the Jabbok, all the way to the Jordan. Now give it back peaceably."

[14]Jephthah sent back messengers to the Ammonite king, [15]saying:

"This is what Jephthah says: Israel did not take the land of Moab or the land of the Ammonites. [16]But when they came up out of Egypt, Israel went through the desert to the Red Sea[n] and on to Kadesh. [17]Then Israel sent messengers to the king of Edom, saying, 'Give us permission to go through your country,' but the king of Edom would not listen. They sent also to the king of Moab, and he refused. So Israel stayed at Kadesh.

[18]"Next they traveled through the desert, skirted the lands of Edom and Moab, passed along the eastern side of the country of Moab, and camped on the other side of the Arnon. They did not enter the territory of Moab, for the Arnon was its border.

[19]"Then Israel sent messengers to Sihon king of the Amorites, who ruled in Heshbon, and said to him, 'Let us pass through your country to our own place.' [20]Sihon, however, did not trust Israel[o] to pass through his territory. He mustered all his men and encamped at Jahaz and fought with Israel.

[21]"Then the LORD, the God of Israel, gave Sihon and all his men into Israel's hands, and they defeated

[n]16 Hebrew *Yam Suph;* that is, Sea of Reeds
[o]20 Or *however, would not make an agreement for Israel*

וַיִּירַשׁ יִשְׂרָאֵל אֵת כָּל־אֶרֶץ הָאֱמֹרִי יוֹשֵׁב הָאָרֶץ
the-country living-of the-Amorite land-of all-of *** Israel and-he-took-over

הַהִיא׃ וַיִּירְשׁוּ אֵת כָּל־גְּבוּל הָאֱמֹרִי מֵאַרְנוֹן
from-Arnon the-Amorite territory-of all-of *** and-they-captured (22) the-that

וְעַד־הַיַּבֹּק וּמִן־הַמִּדְבָּר וְעַד־הַיַּרְדֵּן׃ וְעַתָּה
and-now (23) the-Jordan even-to the-desert and-from the-Jabbok even-to

יְהוָה ׀ אֱלֹהֵי יִשְׂרָאֵל הוֹרִישׁ אֶת־הָאֱמֹרִי מִפְּנֵי עַמּוֹ
people-of-him from-before the-Amorite *** he-drove-out Israel God-of Yahweh

יִשְׂרָאֵל וְאַתָּה תִּירָשֶׁנּוּ׃ הֲלֹא אֵת אֲשֶׁר יוֹרִישְׁךָ כְּמוֹשׁ
Chemosh he-gives-you what *** not? (24) will-you-take-over-him so-you Israel

אֱלֹהֶיךָ אוֹתוֹ תִירָשׁ וְאֵת כָּל־אֲשֶׁר הוֹרִישׁ יְהוָה אֱלֹהֵינוּ
God-of-us Yahweh he-gave that all likewise you-will-take him god-of-you

מִפָּנֵינוּ אוֹתוֹ נִירָשׁ׃ וְעַתָּה הֲטוֹב טוֹב אַתָּה
you to-be-better to-be-better? and-indeed (25) we-will-possess him to-us

מִבָּלָק בֶּן־צִפּוֹר מֶלֶךְ מוֹאָב הֲרוֹב רָב עִם־יִשְׂרָאֵל
Israel with he-quarrelled to-quarrel? Moab king-of Zippor son-of than-Balak

אִם־נִלְחֹם נִלְחַם בָּם׃ בְּשֶׁבֶת יִשְׂרָאֵל בְּחֶשְׁבּוֹן
in-Heshbon Israel while-to-occupy (26) with-them he-fought to-fight or

וּבִבְנוֹתֶיהָ וּבְעַרְעוֹר וּבִבְנוֹתֶיהָ וּבְכָל־
and-in-all-of and-in-settlements-of-her and-in-Aroer and-in-settlements-of-her

הֶעָרִים אֲשֶׁר עַל־יְדֵי אַרְנוֹן שְׁלֹשׁ מֵאוֹת שָׁנָה וּמַדּוּעַ לֹא־
not then-why? year hundreds three-of Arnon banks-of along that the-towns

הִצַּלְתֶּם בָּעֵת הַהִיא׃ וְאָנֹכִי לֹא־חָטָאתִי לָךְ
against-you I-wronged not now-I (27) the-that during-the-time you-retook

וְאַתָּה עֹשֶׂה אִתִּי רָעָה לְהִלָּחֶם בִּי יִשְׁפֹּט יְהוָה
Yahweh let-him-decide against-me to-wage-war wrong to-me doing but-you

הַשֹּׁפֵט הַיּוֹם בֵּין בְּנֵי יִשְׂרָאֵל וּבֵין בְּנֵי עַמּוֹן׃
Ammon sons-of and-between Israel sons-of between the-day the-One-Judging

וְלֹא שָׁמַע מֶלֶךְ בְּנֵי עַמּוֹן אֶל־דִּבְרֵי יִפְתָּח אֲשֶׁר
that Jephthah messages-of to Ammon sons-of king-of he-attended but-not (28)

שָׁלַח אֵלָיו׃ וַתְּהִי עַל־יִפְתָּח רוּחַ יְהוָה וַיַּעֲבֹר
and-he-crossed Yahweh Spirit-of Jephthah upon then-she-came (29) to-him he-sent

אֶת־הַגִּלְעָד וְאֶת־מְנַשֶּׁה וַיַּעֲבֹר אֶת־מִצְפֵּה גִלְעָד
Gilead Mizpah-of *** and-he-passed-through Manasseh and the-Gilead ***

וּמִמִּצְפֵּה גִלְעָד עָבַר בְּנֵי עַמּוֹן׃ וַיִּדַּר
and-he-vowed (30) Ammon sons-of he-advanced Gilead and-from-Mizpah-of

יִפְתָּח נֶדֶר לַיהוָה וַיֹּאמַר אִם־נָתוֹן תִּתֵּן אֶת־בְּנֵי עַמּוֹן
Ammon sons-of *** you-give to-give if and-he-said to-Yahweh vow Jephthah

them. Israel took over all
the land of the Amorites
who lived in that country,
22capturing all of it from the
Arnon to the Jabbok and
from the desert to the Jordan.
23"Now since the LORD,
the God of Israel, has
driven the Amorites out before his people Israel, what
right have you to take it
over? 24Will you not take
what your god Chemosh
gives you? Likewise, whatever the LORD our God has
given us, we will possess.
25Are you better than Balak
son of Zippor, king of
Moab? Did he ever quarrel
with Israel or fight with
them? 26For three hundred
years Israel occupied Heshbon, Aroer, the surround-
ing settlements and all the
towns along the Arnon.
Why didn't you retake
them during that time? 27I
have not wronged you, but
you are doing me wrong by
waging war against me. Let
the LORD, the Judge, decide
the dispute this day be-
tween the Israelites and the
Ammonites."

28The king of Ammon, how-
ever, paid no attention to the
message Jephthah sent him.
29Then the Spirit of the LORD
came upon Jephthah. He
crossed Gilead and Manasseh,
passed through Mizpah of Gilead, and from there he advanced against the Ammon-
ites. 30And Jephthah made a
vow to the LORD: "If you give
the Ammonites into my

בְּיָדִֽי׃ (31) וְהָיָה הַיּוֹצֵא אֲשֶׁר יֵצֵא

he-comes-out that the-one-coming-out then-he-will-be (31) into-hand-of-me

מִדַּלְתֵי בֵיתִי לִקְרָאתִי בְּשׁוּבִי בְשָׁלוֹם מִבְּנֵי

from-sons-of in-triumph when-to-return-me to-meet-me house-of-me from-doors-of

עַמּוֹן וְהָיָה לַיהוָה וְהַעֲלִיתִהוּ עוֹלָה׃

burnt-offering and-I-will-sacrifice-him for-Yahweh then-he-will-be Ammon

(32) וַיַּעֲבֹר יִפְתָּח אֶל־ בְּנֵי עַמּוֹן לְהִלָּחֶם בָּם

against-them to-fight Ammon sons-of to Jephthah then-he-went-over (32)

וַיִּתְּנֵם יְהוָה בְּיָדוֹ׃ (33) וַיַּכֵּם מֵעֲרוֹעֵר

from-Aroer and-he-devastated-them (33) into-hand-of-him Yahweh and-he-gave-them

וְעַד־ בּוֹאֲךָ מִנִּית עֶשְׂרִים עִיר וְעַד אָבֵל כְּרָמִים מַכָּה

devastation Keramim Abel and-as-far-as town twenty Minnith to-go-you even-to

גְּדוֹלָה מְאֹד וַיִּכָּנְעוּ בְּנֵי עַמּוֹן מִפְּנֵי בְּנֵי יִשְׂרָאֵל׃

Israel sons-of from-before Ammon sons-of thus-they-were-subdued very great

(34) וַיָּבֹא יִפְתָּח הַמִּצְפָּה אֶל־ בֵּיתוֹ וְהִנֵּה

then-see! home-of-him to the-Mizpah Jephthah when-he-returned (34)

בִתּוֹ יֹצֵאת לִקְרָאתוֹ בְּתֻפִּים* וּבִמְחֹלוֹת

and-with-dances with-tambourines to-meet-him coming-out daughter-of-him

וְרַק הִיא יְחִידָה אֵין־ לוֹ מִמֶּנּוּ† בֵּן אוֹ־ בָת׃ (35) וַיְהִי

and-he-was (35) daughter or son from-him to-him not along she and-only

כִרְאוֹתוֹ אוֹתָהּ וַיִּקְרַע אֶת־ בְּגָדָיו וַיֹּאמֶר אֲהָהּ

oh! and-he-cried clothes-of-him *** then-he-tore her when-see-him

בִּתִּי הַכְרֵעַ הִכְרַעְתִּנִי וְאַתְּ הָיִיתְ††

you-are and-you you-made-wretched-me to-make-wretched daughter-of-me

בְּעֹכְרָי וְאָנֹכִי פָּצִיתִי־ פִי אֶל־ יְהוָה וְלֹא אוּכַל

I-can and-not Yahweh to mouth-of-me I-opened for-I being-miseries-of-me

לָשׁוּב׃ (36) וַתֹּאמֶר אֵלָיו אָבִי פָּצִיתָה אֶת־ פִּיךָ

mouth-of-you *** you-opened father-of-me to-him and-she-said (36) to-break

אֶל־יְהוָה עֲשֵׂה לִי כַּאֲשֶׁר יָצָא מִפִּיךָ אַחֲרֵי אֲשֶׁר עָשָׂה

he-gave that now from-mouth-of-you he-came-out just-as to-me do! Yahweh to

לְךָ יְהוָה נְקָמוֹת מֵאֹיְבֶיךָ מִבְּנֵי עַמּוֹן׃

Ammon on-sons-of on-being-enemies-of-you vengeances Yahweh to-you

(37) וַתֹּאמֶר אֶל־ אָבִיהָ יֵעָשֶׂה לִּי הַדָּבָר הַזֶּה

the-this the-request to-me let-him-be-granted father-of-her to and-she-said (37)

הַרְפֵּה מִמֶּנִּי שְׁנַיִם חֳדָשִׁים וְאֵלְכָה וְיָרַדְתִּי עַל־ הֶהָרִים

the-hills on and-I-will-wander and-I-will-roam months two from-me let-alone!

וְאֶבְכֶּה עַל־ בְּתוּלַי אָנֹכִי וְרֵעְיֹתָי°׃ (38) וַיֹּאמֶר

and-he-said (38) and-friends-of-me I virginities-of-me over and-I-will-weep

hands, [31]whatever comes out
of the door of my house to
meet me when I return in triumph from the Ammonites
will be the LORD's, and I will
sacrifice it as a burnt offering."
[32]Then Jephthah went over
to fight the Ammonites, and
the LORD gave them into his
hands. [33]He devastated twenty
towns from Aroer to the
vicinity of Minnith, as far as
Abel Keramim. Thus Israel
subdued Ammon.
[34]When Jephthah returned
to his home in Mizpah, who
should come out to meet him
but his daughter, dancing to
the sound of tambourines! She
was an only child. Except for
her he had neither son nor
daughter. [35]When he saw her,
he tore his clothes and cried,
"Oh! My daughter! You have
made me miserable and
wretched, because I have
made a vow to the LORD that I
cannot break."
[36]"My father," she replied,
"you have given your word to
the LORD. Do to me just as you
promised, now that the LORD
has avenged you of your enemies, the Ammonites. [37]But
grant me this one request,"
she said. "Give me two
months to roam the hills and
weep with my friends, be-
cause I will never marry."

*34 Most mss have *dagesh* in the *beth* (בּ).

†34 The NIV, with the ancient versions, replaces the masculine suffix with the feminine (מִמֶּנָּה), *except-her*.

††35 Most mss have no *sheva* under the *tav* (ת).

°37 ק ורעותי

לְכִי וַיִּשְׁלַח אוֹתָהּ שְׁנֵי חֳדָשִׁים וַתֵּלֶךְ הִיא וְרֵעוֹתֶיהָ
and-girl-friends-of-her she and-she-went months two-of her and-he-let-go go!

וַתֵּבְךְּ עַל־ בְּתוּלֶיהָ עַל־ הֶהָרִים׃ וַיְהִי מִקֵּץ ׀
at-end-of and-he-was (39) the-hills into virginities-of-her over and-she-wept

שְׁנַיִם חֳדָשִׁים וַתָּשָׁב אֶל־ אָבִיהָ וַיַּעַשׂ לָהּ אֶת־
*** to-her and-he-did father-of-her to then-she-returned months two

נִדְרוֹ אֲשֶׁר נָדָר וְהִיא לֹא־ יָדְעָה אִישׁ וַתְּהִי־ חֹק
custom and-she-became man she-knew not and-she he-vowed that vow-of-him

בְּיִשְׂרָאֵל׃ מִיָּמִים ׀ יָמִימָה תֵּלַכְנָה בְּנוֹת יִשְׂרָאֵל
Israel young-women-of they-go-out at-days from-days (40) in-Israel

לְתַנּוֹת לְבַת־ יִפְתָּח הַגִּלְעָדִי אַרְבַּעַת יָמִים בַּשָּׁנָה׃
in-the-year days four-of the-Gileadite Jephthah for-daughter-of to-commemorate

וַיִּצָּעֵק אִישׁ אֶפְרַיִם וַיַּעֲבֹר צָפוֹנָה
to-Zaphon and-he-crossed-over Ephraim man-of and-he-was-called-out (12:1)

וַיֹּאמְרוּ לְיִפְתָּח מַדּוּעַ ׀ עָבַרְתָּ ׀ לְהִלָּחֵם בִּבְנֵי־ עַמּוֹן
Ammon against-sons-of to-fight you-went why? to-Jephthah and-they-said

וְלָנוּ לֹא קָרָאתָ לָלֶכֶת עִמָּךְ בֵּיתְךָ נִשְׂרֹף
we-will-burn-down house-of-you with-you to-go you-called not and-to-us

עָלֶיךָ בָּאֵשׁ׃ וַיֹּאמֶר יִפְתָּח אֲלֵיהֶם אִישׁ רִיב
struggle man-of to-them Jephthah and-he-answered (2) with-the-fire over-you

הָיִיתִי אֲנִי וְעַמִּי וּבְנֵי־ עַמּוֹן מְאֹד וָאֶזְעַק אֶתְכֶם
to-you and-I-called great Ammon with-sons-of and-people-of-me I I-was

וְלֹא־ הוֹשַׁעְתֶּם אוֹתִי מִיָּדָם׃ וָאֶרְאֶה כִּי־ אֵינְךָ מוֹשִׁיעַ
helping not-you that when-I-saw (3) from-hand-of-them me you-saved but-not

וָאָשִׂימָה נַפְשִׁי בְכַפִּי וָאֶעְבְּרָה אֶל־ בְּנֵי עַמּוֹן
Ammon sons-of to and-I-crossed-over in-hand-of-me life-of-me then-I-took

וַיִּתְּנֵם יְהוָה בְּיָדִי וְלָמָּה עֲלִיתֶם אֵלַי הַיּוֹם
the-day to-me you-came-up now-why? into-hand-of-me Yahweh and-he-gave-them

הַזֶּה לְהִלָּחֶם בִּי׃ וַיִּקְבֹּץ יִפְתָּח אֶת־ כָּל־ אַנְשֵׁי
men-of all-of *** Jephthah then-he-called (4) against-me to-fight the-this

גִלְעָד וַיִּלָּחֶם אֶת־ אֶפְרָיִם וַיַּכּוּ אַנְשֵׁי גִלְעָד אֶת־
*** Gilead men-of and-they-struck-down Ephraim *** and-he-fought Gilead

אֶפְרַיִם כִּי אָמְרוּ פְּלִיטֵי אֶפְרַיִם אַתֶּם גִּלְעָד בְּתוֹךְ אֶפְרַיִם
Ephraim in-among Gilead you Ephraim renegades-of they-said because Ephraim

בְּתוֹךְ מְנַשֶּׁה׃ וַיִּלְכֹּד גִּלְעָד אֶת־ מַעְבְּרוֹת הַיַּרְדֵּן
the-Jordan fords-of *** Gilead and-he-captured (5) Manasseh in-among

לְאֶפְרָיִם וְהָיָה כִּי יֹאמְרוּ פְּלִיטֵי אֶפְרַיִם אֶעֱבֹרָה
let-me-cross-over Ephraim survivors-of they-said when and-he-was to-Ephraim

[38]"You may go," he said.
And he let her go for two
months. She and the girls
went into the hills and wept
because she would never marry. [39]After the two months, she
returned to her father and he
did to her as he had vowed.
And she was a virgin.
From this comes the Israelite
custom [40]that each year the
young women of Israel go out
for four days to commemorate
the daughter of Jephthah the
Gileadite.

Jephthah and Ephraim

12 The men of Ephraim
called out their forces,
crossed over to Zaphon and
said to Jephthah, "Why did
you go to fight the Ammonites
without calling us to go with
you? We're going to burn
down your house over your
head."
[2]Jephthah answered, "I and
my people were engaged in a
great struggle with the Ammonites, and although I
called, you didn't save me out
of their hands. [3]When I saw
that you wouldn't help, I took
my life in my hands and
crossed over to fight the Ammonites, and the LORD gave
me the victory over them.
Now why have you come up
today to fight me?"
[4]Jephthah then called together the men of Gilead and
fought against Ephraim. The
Gileadites struck them down
because the Ephraimites had
said, "You Gileadites are rene-
gades from Ephraim and
Manasseh." [5]The Gileadites
captured the fords of the Jordan leading to Ephraim, and
whenever a survivor of
Ephraim said, "Let me cross

וַיֹּאמְרוּ לוֹ אַנְשֵׁי־גִלְעָד הַאֶפְרָתִי אַתָּה וַיֹּאמֶר ׀ לֹא׃
no and-he-replied you Ephramite? Gilead men-of to-him then-they-asked

וַיֹּאמְרוּ לוֹ אֱמָר־נָא שִׁבֹּלֶת וַיֹּאמֶר סִבֹּלֶת וְלֹא
for-not sibboleth and-he-said shibboleth now! say! to-him then-they-said (6)

יָכִין לְדַבֵּר כֵּן וַיֹּאחֲזוּ אוֹתוֹ וַיִּשְׁחָטוּהוּ אֶל־
at and-they-killed-him him then-they-seized correctly to-pronounce he-could

מַעְבְּרוֹת הַיַּרְדֵּן וַיִּפֹּל בָּעֵת הַהִיא מֵאֶפְרַיִם אַרְבָּעִים
forty from-Ephraim the-that at-the-time and-he-fell the-Jordan fords-of

וּשְׁנַיִם אָלֶף׃ וַיִּשְׁפֹּט יִפְתָּח אֶת־יִשְׂרָאֵל שֵׁשׁ שָׁנִים וַיָּמָת
then-he-died years six Israel *** Jephthah and-he-led (7) thousand and-two

יִפְתָּח הַגִּלְעָדִי וַיִּקָּבֵר בְּעָרֵי גִלְעָד׃ וַיִּשְׁפֹּט
and-he-led (8) Gilead in-towns-of and-he-was-buried the-Gileadite Jephthah

אַחֲרָיו אֶת־יִשְׂרָאֵל אִבְצָן מִבֵּית לָחֶם׃ וַיְהִי־לוֹ שְׁלֹשִׁים בָּנִים
sons thirty to-him and-he-was (9) Lehem of-Beth Ibzan Israel *** after-him

וּשְׁלֹשִׁים בָּנוֹת שִׁלַּח הַחוּצָה וּשְׁלֹשִׁים בָּנוֹת
young-women and-thirty to-the-outside he-gave-away daughters and-thirty

הֵבִיא לְבָנָיו מִן־הַחוּץ וַיִּשְׁפֹּט אֶת־יִשְׂרָאֵל שֶׁבַע
seven Israel *** and-he-led the-outside from for-sons-of-him he-brought-in

שָׁנִים׃ וַיָּמָת אִבְצָן וַיִּקָּבֵר בְּבֵית לָחֶם׃ וַיִּשְׁפֹּט
and-he-led (11) Lehem in-Beth and-he-was-buried Ibzan then-he-died (10) years

אַחֲרָיו אֶת־יִשְׂרָאֵל אֵילוֹן הַזְּבוּלֹנִי וַיִּשְׁפֹּט אֶת־יִשְׂרָאֵל עֶשֶׂר שָׁנִים׃
years ten Israel *** and-he-led the-Zebulunite Elon Israel *** after-him

וַיָּמָת אֵלוֹן* הַזְּבוּלֹנִי וַיִּקָּבֵר בְּאַיָּלוֹן בְּאֶרֶץ
in-land-of in-Aijalon and-he-was-buried the-Zebulunite Elon then-he-died (12)

זְבוּלֻן׃ וַיִּשְׁפֹּט אַחֲרָיו אֶת־יִשְׂרָאֵל עַבְדּוֹן בֶּן־הִלֵּל
Hillel son-of Abdon Israel *** after-him and-he-led (13) Zebulun

הַפִּרְעָתוֹנִי׃ וַיְהִי־לוֹ אַרְבָּעִים בָּנִים וּשְׁלֹשִׁים בְּנֵי בָנִים
sons sons-of and-thirty sons forty to-him and-he-was (14) the-Pirathonite

רֹכְבִים עַל־שִׁבְעִים עֲיָרִם וַיִּשְׁפֹּט אֶת־יִשְׂרָאֵל שְׁמֹנֶה שָׁנִים׃
years eight Israel *** and-he-led donkeys seventy on ones-riding

וַיָּמָת עַבְדּוֹן בֶּן־הִלֵּל הַפִּרְעָתוֹנִי וַיִּקָּבֵר
and-he-was-buried the-Pirathonite Hillel son-of Abdon then-he-died (15)

בְּפִרְעָתוֹן בְּאֶרֶץ אֶפְרַיִם בְּהַר הָעֲמָלֵקִי׃
the-Amalekite in-hill-country-of Ephraim in-land-of at-Pirathon

וַיֹּסִפוּ בְּנֵי יִשְׂרָאֵל לַעֲשׂוֹת הָרַע בְּעֵינֵי יְהוָה
Yahweh in-eyes-of the-evil to-do Israel sons-of and-they-repeated (13:1)

וַיִּתְּנֵם יְהוָה בְּיַד־פְּלִשְׁתִּים אַרְבָּעִים שָׁנָה׃ וַיְהִי
and-he-was (2) year forty Philistines into-hand-of Yahweh so-he-delivered-them

over," the men of Gilead asked him, "Are you an Ephraimite?" If he replied, "No,"
6they said, "All right, say 'Shibboleth.'" If he said, "Sibboleth," because he could not pronounce the word correctly, they seized him and killed him at the fords of the Jordan. Forty-two thousand Ephraimites were killed at that time.
7Jephthah led[P] Israel six years. Then Jephthah the Gileadite died, and was buried in a town in Gilead.

Ibzan, Elon and Abdon

8After him, Ibzan of Bethlehem led Israel.
9He had thirty sons and thirty daughters. He gave his daughters away in marriage to those outside his clan, and for his sons he brought in thirty young women as wives from outside his clan. Ibzan led Israel seven years.
10Then Ibzan died, and was buried in Bethlehem.
11After him, Elon the Zebulunite led Israel ten years.
12Then Elon died, and was buried in Aijalon in the land of Zebulun.
13After him, Abdon son of Hillel, from Pirathon, led Israel.
14He had forty sons and thirty grandsons, who rode on seventy donkeys. He led Israel eight years.
15Then Abdon son of Hillel died, and was buried at Pirathon in Ephraim, in the hill country of the Amalekites.

The Birth of Samson

13 Again the Israelites did evil in the eyes of the LORD, so the LORD delivered them into the hands of the Philistines for forty years.

P7 Traditionally *judged;* also in verses 8-14

*12 Most mss have *yod* after the *aleph* (אילון), as in verse 11.

אִישׁ אֶחָד מִצָּרְעָה מִמִּשְׁפַּחַת הַדָּנִי וּשְׁמוֹ מָנוֹחַ
Manoah and-name-of-him the-Danite from-clan-of of-Zorah certain man

וְאִשְׁתּוֹ עֲקָרָה וְלֹא יָלָדָה׃ וַיֵּרָא מַלְאַךְ־
angel-of and-he-appeared (3) she-bore-child and-not sterile and-wife-of-him

יְהוָה אֶל־הָאִשָּׁה וַיֹּאמֶר אֵלֶיהָ הִנֵּה־נָא אַתְּ־עֲקָרָה וְלֹא
and-not sterile you now! see! to-her and-he-said the-woman to Yahweh

יָלַדְתְּ וְהָרִית וְיָלַדְתְּ בֵּן׃ וְעַתָּה
and-now (4) son and-you-will-bear but-you-will-conceive you-bore-child

הִשָּׁמְרִי נָא וְאַל־תִּשְׁתִּי יַיִן וְשֵׁכָר וְאַל־תֹּאכְלִי
you-eat and-not or-fermented-drink wine you-drink that-not now! see!

כָּל־טָמֵא׃ כִּי הִנָּךְ הָרָה וְיֹלַדְתְּ בֵּן
son and-you-will-bear conceiving see-you! because (5) unclean-thing any-of

וּמוֹרָה לֹא־יַעֲלֶה עַל־רֹאשׁוֹ כִּי־נְזִיר אֱלֹהִים יִהְיֶה הַנַּעַר
the-boy he-will-be God Nazirite-of for head-of-him on he-may-go not and-razor

מִן־הַבֶּטֶן וְהוּא יָחֵל לְהוֹשִׁיעַ אֶת־יִשְׂרָאֵל מִיַּד
from-hand-of Israel *** to-deliver he-will-begin and-he the-womb from

פְּלִשְׁתִּים׃ וַתָּבֹא הָאִשָּׁה וַתֹּאמֶר לְאִישָׁהּ לֵאמֹר
to-say to-husband-of-her and-she-told the-woman then-she-went (6) Philistines

אִישׁ הָאֱלֹהִים בָּא אֵלַי וּמַרְאֵהוּ כְּמַרְאֵה מַלְאַךְ
angel-of like-appearance-of and-appearance-of-him to-me he-came the-God man-of

הָאֱלֹהִים נוֹרָא מְאֹד וְלֹא שְׁאִלְתִּיהוּ אֵי־מִזֶּה הוּא וְאֶת־
and he from-there where? I-asked-him and-not very being-awesome the-God

שְׁמוֹ לֹא־הִגִּיד לִי׃ וַיֹּאמֶר לִי הִנָּךְ הָרָה
conceiving see-you! to-me but-he-said (7) to-me he-told not name-of-him

וְיֹלַדְתְּ בֵּן וְעַתָּה אַל־תִּשְׁתִּי יַיִן וְשֵׁכָר וְאַל־
and-not or-fermented-drink wine you-drink not now-then son and-you-will-bear

תֹּאכְלִי כָּל־טֻמְאָה כִּי־נְזִיר אֱלֹהִים יִהְיֶה הַנַּעַר מִן־
from the-boy he-will-be God Nazirite-of for unclean-thing any-of you-eat

הַבֶּטֶן עַד יוֹם מוֹתוֹ׃ וַיֶּעְתַּר מָנוֹחַ אֶל־יְהוָה
Yahweh to Manoah then-he-prayed (8) death-of-him day-of until the-womb

וַיֹּאמַר בִּי אֲדוֹנָי אִישׁ הָאֱלֹהִים אֲשֶׁר שָׁלַחְתָּ יָבוֹא־נָא עוֹד
again now! let-him-come you-sent whom the-God man-of Lord O! and-he-said

אֵלֵינוּ וְיוֹרֵנוּ מַה־נַּעֲשֶׂה לַנַּעַר הַיּוּלָּד׃
the-one-being-born with-the-boy we-must-do what so-he-may-teach-us to-us

וַיִּשְׁמַע הָאֱלֹהִים בְּקוֹל מָנוֹחַ וַיָּבֹא מַלְאַךְ הָאֱלֹהִים
the-God angel-of and-he-came Manoah to-voice-of the-God and-he-heard (9)

עוֹד אֶל־הָאִשָּׁה וְהִיא יוֹשֶׁבֶת בַּשָּׂדֶה וּמָנוֹחַ אִישָׁהּ אֵין
not husband-of-her but-Manoah in-the-field being and-she the-woman to again

2 A certain man of Zorah,
named Manoah, from the clan
of the Danites, had a wife who
was sterile and remained
childless. 3 The angel of the
LORD appeared to her and said,
"You are sterile and childless,
but you are going to conceive
and have a son. 4 Now see to it
that you drink no wine or other fermented drink and that
you do not eat anything unclean, 5 because you will conceive and give birth to a son.
No razor may be used on his
head, because the boy is to be
a Nazirite, set apart to God
from birth, and he will begin
the deliverance of Israel from
the hands of the Philistines."

6 Then the woman went to
her husband and told him, "A
man of God came to me. He
looked like an angel of God,
very awesome. I didn't ask
him where he came from, and
he didn't tell me his name.
7 But he said to me, 'You will
conceive and give birth to a
son. Now then, drink no wine
or other fermented drink and
do not eat anything unclean,
because the boy will be a Nazirite of God from birth until the
day of his death.' "

8 Then Manoah prayed to the
LORD: "O Lord, I beg you, let
the man of God you sent to us
come again to teach us how to
bring up the boy who is to be
born."

9 God heard Manoah, and the
angel of God came again to the
woman while she was out in
the field; but her husband Manoah was not with her. 10 The

עִמָּהּ׃ וַתְּמַהֵר הָאִשָּׁה וַתָּרָץ וַתַּגֵּד
and-she-told and-she-ran the-woman and-she-hurried (10) with-her

לְאִישָׁהּ וַתֹּאמֶר אֵלָיו הִנֵּה נִרְאָה אֵלַי הָאִישׁ אֲשֶׁר־
who the-man to-me he-appeared see! to-him and-she-said to-husband-of-her

בָּא בַיּוֹם אֵלָי׃ וַיָּקָם וַיֵּלֶךְ מָנוֹחַ אַחֲרֵי
after Manoah and-he-followed and-he-got-up (11) to-me on-the-day he-came

אִשְׁתּוֹ וַיָּבֹא אֶל־הָאִישׁ וַיֹּאמֶר לוֹ הַאַתָּה הָאִישׁ אֲשֶׁר־
who the-man you? to-him then-he-said the-man to when-he-came wife-of-him

דִּבַּרְתָּ אֶל־הָאִשָּׁה וַיֹּאמֶר אָנִי׃ וַיֹּאמֶר מָנוֹחַ עַתָּה
when Manoah so-he-asked (12) I and-he-said the-wife to you-talked

יָבֹא דְבָרֶיךָ מַה־יִּהְיֶה מִשְׁפַּט־הַנַּעַר וּמַעֲשֵׂהוּ׃
and-work-of-him the-boy rule-of he-will-be what? words-of-you he-fulfills

וַיֹּאמֶר מַלְאַךְ יְהוָה אֶל־מָנוֹחַ מִכֹּל אֲשֶׁר־אָמַרְתִּי אֶל־
to I-told that from-all Manoah to Yahweh angel-of and-he-answered (13)

הָאִשָּׁה תִּשָּׁמֵר׃ מִכֹּל אֲשֶׁר־יֵצֵא מִגֶּפֶן הַיַּיִן
the-grape from-vine-of he-comes that from-anything (14) she-must-do the-wife

לֹא תֹאכַל וְיַיִן וְשֵׁכָר אַל־תֵּשְׁתְּ וְכָל־
and-any-of she-must-drink not or-fermented-drink and-wine she-must-eat not

טֻמְאָה אַל־תֹּאכַל כֹּל אֲשֶׁר־צִוִּיתִיהָ תִּשְׁמֹר׃
she-must-do I-commanded-her that everything she-must-eat not unclean-thing

וַיֹּאמֶר מָנוֹחַ אֶל־מַלְאַךְ יְהוָה נַעְצְרָה־נָּא אוֹתָךְ
you now! let-us-detain Yahweh angel-of to Manoah then-he-said (15)

וְנַעֲשֶׂה לְפָנֶיךָ גְּדִי עִזִּים׃ וַיֹּאמֶר מַלְאַךְ
angel-of and-he-replied (16) goats young-goat-of for-you so-we-may-prepare

יְהוָה אֶל־מָנוֹחַ אִם־תַּעְצְרֵנִי לֹא־אֹכַל בְּלַחְמֶךָ וְאִם־
but-if from-food-of-you I-will-eat not you-detain-me though Manoah to Yahweh

תַּעֲשֶׂה עֹלָה לַיהוָה תַּעֲלֶנָּה כִּי לֹא־יָדַע מָנוֹחַ
Manoah he-realized not now you-offer-her to-Yahweh burnt-offering you-prepare

כִּי־מַלְאַךְ יְהוָה הוּא׃ וַיֹּאמֶר מָנוֹחַ אֶל־מַלְאַךְ יְהוָה
Yahweh angel-of of Manoah then-he-inquired (17) he Yahweh angel-of that

מִי שְׁמֶךָ כִּי־יָבֹא °דְבָרְיךָ וְכִבַּדְנוּךָ׃
then-we-may-honor-you word-of-you he-comes-true when name-of-you what?

וַיֹּאמֶר לוֹ מַלְאַךְ יְהוָה לָמָּה זֶּה תִּשְׁאַל לִשְׁמִי
about-name-of-me you-ask this why? Yahweh angel-of to-him and-he-replied (18)

וְהוּא־פֶלְאִי*׃ וַיִּקַּח מָנוֹחַ אֶת־גְּדִי הָעִזִּים וְאֶת־
and the-goats young-goat-of *** Manoah then-he-took (19) wonderful now-he

הַמִּנְחָה וַיַּעַל עַל־הַצּוּר לַיהוָה וּמַפְלִא
and-amazing-thing to-Yahweh the-rock on and-he-sacrificed the-grain-offering

woman hurried to tell her husband, "He's here! The man
who appeared to me the other
day!"
11Manoah got up and fol-
lowed his wife. When he came
to the man, he said, "Are you
the one who talked to my
wife?"
"I am," he said.
12So Manoah asked him,
"When your words are
fulfilled, what is to be the rule
for the boy's life and work?"
13The angel of the LORD answered, "Your wife must do all
that I have told her. 14She must
not eat anything that comes
from the grapevine, nor drink
any wine or other fermented
drink nor eat anything unclean. She must do everything
I have commanded her."
15Manoah said to the angel
of the LORD, "We would like
you to stay until we prepare a
young goat for you."
16The angel of the LORD replied, "Even though you de-
tain me, I will not eat any of
your food. But if you prepare a
burnt offering, offer it to the
LORD." (Manoah did not realize that it was the angel of the
LORD.)
17Then Manoah inquired of
the angel of the LORD, "What
is your name, so that we may
honor you when your word
comes true?"
18He replied, "Why do you
ask my name? It is beyond
understanding.[q]" 19Then Manoah took a young goat, together with the grain offering,
and sacrificed it on a rock to

[q] 18 Or *is wonderful*

*18 Most mss point the textual form פֶּלְאִי and offer a *Qere* form פֶּלִי(א).

°17 ק דברך

לַעֲשׂוֹת וּמָנוֹחַ וְאִשְׁתּוֹ רֹאִים׃ וַיְהִי בַעֲלוֹת

as-to-blaze-up and-he-was (20) ones-watching and-wife-of-him and-Manoah to-do

הַלַּהַב מֵעַל הַמִּזְבֵּחַ הַשָּׁמַיְמָה וַיַּעַל מַלְאַךְ־

angel-of then-he-ascended toward-the-heavens the-altar from-on the-flame

יְהוָה בְּלַהַב הַמִּזְבֵּחַ וּמָנוֹחַ וְאִשְׁתּוֹ רֹאִים

ones-seeing and-wife-of-him and-Manoah the-altar in-flame-of Yahweh

וַיִּפְּלוּ עַל־ פְּנֵיהֶם אָרְצָה׃ וְלֹא־ יָסַף עוֹד

again he-repeated when-not (21) to-ground faces-of-them on then-they-fell

מַלְאַךְ יְהוָה לְהֵרָאֹה אֶל־ מָנוֹחַ וְאֶל־ אִשְׁתּוֹ אָז יָדַע

he-realized then wife-of-him and-to Manoah to to-show-himself Yahweh angel-of

מָנוֹחַ כִּי־ מַלְאַךְ יְהוָה הוּא׃ וַיֹּאמֶר מָנוֹחַ אֶל־ אִשְׁתּוֹ מוֹת

to-die wife-of-him to Manoah and-he-said (22) he Yahweh angel-of that Manoah

נָמוּת כִּי אֱלֹהִים רָאִינוּ׃ וַתֹּאמֶר לוֹ אִשְׁתּוֹ לוּ

if wife-of-him to-him but-she-answered (23) we-saw God for we-will-die

חָפֵץ יְהוָה לַהֲמִיתֵנוּ לֹא־ לָקַח מִיָּדֵנוּ עֹלָה

burnt-offering from-hand-of-us he-would-accept not to-kill-us Yahweh he-meant

וּמִנְחָה וְלֹא הֶרְאָנוּ אֶת־ כָּל־ אֵלֶּה וְכָעֵת

or-at-the-time these all-of *** he-would-show-us and-not and-grain-offering

לֹא הִשְׁמִיעָנוּ כָּזֹאת׃ וַתֵּלֶד הָאִשָּׁה בֵּן וַתִּקְרָא

and-she-called son the-woman and-she-bore (24) as-this he-would-tell-us not

אֶת־ שְׁמוֹ שִׁמְשׁוֹן וַיִּגְדַּל הַנַּעַר וַיְבָרְכֵהוּ יְהוָה׃

Yahweh and-he-blessed-him the-boy and-he-grew Samson name-of-him ***

וַתָּחֶל רוּחַ יְהוָה לְפַעֲמוֹ בְּמַחֲנֵה־ דָן בֵּין צָרְעָה

Zorah between Dan in-Mahaneh to-stir-him Yahweh Spirit-of and-she-began (25)

וּבֵין אֶשְׁתָּאֹל׃ וַיֵּרֶד שִׁמְשׁוֹן תִּמְנָתָה וַיַּרְא

and-he-saw to-Timnah Samson and-he-went-down (14:1) Eshtaol and-between

אִשָּׁה בְּתִמְנָתָה מִבְּנוֹת פְּלִשְׁתִּים׃ וַיַּעַל

when-he-returned (2) Philistines from-young-women-of in-Timnah woman

וַיַּגֵּד לְאָבִיו וּלְאִמּוֹ וַיֹּאמֶר אִשָּׁה רָאִיתִי

I-saw woman and-he-said and-to-mother-of-him to-father-of-him then-he-told

בְתִמְנָתָה מִבְּנוֹת פְּלִשְׁתִּים וְעַתָּה קְחוּ־אוֹתָהּ לִי לְאִשָּׁה׃

as-wife for-me her get! and-now Philistines from-young-women-of in-Timnah

וַיֹּאמֶר לוֹ אָבִיו וְאִמּוֹ הַאֵין בִּבְנוֹת

among-women-of not? and-mother-of-him father-of-him to-him and-he-said (3)

אַחֶיךָ וּבְכָל־ עַמִּי אִשָּׁה כִּי־ אַתָּה הוֹלֵךְ לָקַחַת אִשָּׁה

wife to-get going you that woman people-of-me or-among-all-of relatives-of-you

מִפְּלִשְׁתִּים הָעֲרֵלִים וַיֹּאמֶר שִׁמְשׁוֹן אֶל־ אָבִיו

father-of-him to Samson but-he-said the-uncircumcised-ones from-Philistines

---

the LORD. And the LORD did an amazing thing while Manoah and his wife watched: [20]As the flame blazed up from the altar toward heaven, the angel of the LORD ascended in the flame. Seeing this, Manoah and his wife fell with their faces to the ground. [21]When the angel of the LORD did not show himself again to Manoah and his wife, Manoah realized that it was the angel of the LORD.

[22]"We are doomed to die!" he said to his wife. "We have seen God!"

[23]But his wife answered, "If the LORD had meant to kill us, he would not have accepted a burnt offering and grain offering from our hands, nor shown us all these things or now told us this."

[24]The woman gave birth to a boy and named him Samson. He grew and the LORD blessed him, [25]and the Spirit of the LORD began to stir him while he was in Mahaneh Dan, between Zorah and Eshtaol.

Samson's Marriage

14 Samson went down to Timnah and saw there a young Philistine woman. [2]When he returned, he said to his father and mother, "I have seen a Philistine woman in Timnah; now get her for me as my wife."

[3]His father and mother replied, "Isn't there an acceptable woman among your relatives or among all our people? Must you go to the uncircumcised Philistines to get a wife?"

But Samson said to his father, "Get her for me. She's the

אותה קח־ לי כי־ היא ישרה בעיני׃ ואביו

now-father-of-him (4) in-eyes-of-me she-is-right she for for-me get! her

ואמו לא ידעו כי מיהוה היא כי־ תאנה הוא־

he occasion for this from-Yahweh that they-knew not and-mother-of-him

מבקש מפלשתים ובעת ההיא פלשתים משלים

ones-ruling Philistines the-that for-at-the-time from-Philistines seeking

בישראל׃ וירד שמשון ואביו ואמו

and-mother-of-him and-father-of-him Samson and-he-went-down (5) over-Israel

תמנתה ויבאו עד־ כרמי תמנתה והנה כפיר

young-lion-of and-see! Timnah vineyards-of to and-they-approached to-Timnah

אריות שאג לקראתו׃ ותצלח עליו רוח יהוה

Yahweh Spirit-of upon-him then-she-came (6) to-attack-him roaring lions

וישסעהו כשסע הגדי ומאומה אין בידו

in-hand-of-him not but-anything the-young-goat as-to-tear and-he-tore-apart-him

ולא הגיד לאביו ולאמו את אשר עשה׃

he-did what *** or-to-mother-of-him to-father-of-him he-told but-not

וירד וידבר לאשה ותישר בעיני

in-eyes-of and-she-was-right with-the-woman and-he-talked then-he-went-down (7)

שמשון׃ וישב מימים לקחתה ויסר

then-he-turned-aside to-marry-her after-days when-he-went-back (8) Samson

לראות את מפלת האריה והנה עדת דבורים בגוית האריה

the-lion in-body-of bees swarm-of and-see! the-lion carcass-of *** to-look

ודבש׃ וירדהו אל־ כפיו וילך הלוך

to-walk and-he-went hands-of-him with and-he-scooped-out-him (9) and-honey

ואכל וילך אל־ אביו ואל־ אמו ויתן

then-he-gave mother-of-him and-to father-of-him to when-he-came and-to-eat

להם ויאכלו ולא־ הגיד להם כי מגוית האריה

the-lion from-carcass-of that to-them he-told but-not and-they-ate to-them

רדה הדבש׃ וירד אביהו אל־ האשה ויעש

and-he-made the-woman to father-of-him now-he-went-down (10) the-honey he-took

שם שמשון משתה כי כן יעשו הבחורים׃ ויהי

and-he-was (11) the-bridegrooms they-did customary as feast Samson there

כראותם אותו ויקחו שלשים מרעים ויהיו אתו׃

with-him and-they-were companions thirty then-they-gave him when-to-see-them

ויאמר להם שמשון אחודה־ נא לכם חידה אם־ הגד

to-tell if riddle to-you now! let-me-tell Samson to-them and-he-said (12)

תגידו אותה לי שבעת ימי המשתה ומצאתם

and-you-find-answer the-feast days-of seven-of to-me her you-tell

right one for me." [4](His parents did not know that this
was from the LORD, who was
seeking an occasion to confront the Philistines; for at that
time they were ruling over Israel.) [5]Samson went down to
Timnah together with his father and mother. As they approached the vineyards of
Timnah, suddenly a young
lion came roaring toward him.
[6]The Spirit of the LORD came
upon him in power so that he
tore the lion apart with his
bare hands as he might have
torn a young goat. But he told
neither his father nor his
mother what he had done.
[7]Then he went down and
talked with the woman, and
he liked her.

[8]Some time later, when he
went back to marry her, he
turned aside to look at the
lion's carcass. In it was a
swarm of bees and some
honey, [9]which he scooped out
with his hands and ate as he
went along. When he rejoined
his parents, he gave them
some, and they too ate it. But
he did not tell them that he
had taken the honey from the
lion's carcass.

[10]Now his father went down
to see the woman. And Samson made a feast there, as was
customary for bridegrooms.
[11]When he appeared, he was
given thirty companions.

[12]"Let me tell you a riddle,"
Samson said to them. "If you
can give me the answer within the seven days of the feast,

וְנָתַתִּי לָכֶם שְׁלֹשִׁים סְדִינִים וּשְׁלֹשִׁים חֲלִפֹת בְּגָדִים׃
clothes sets-of and-thirty linen-garments thirty to-you then-I-will-give

וְאִם־ לֹא תוּכְלוּ לְהַגִּיד לִי וּנְתַתֶּם אַתֶּם לִי שְׁלֹשִׁים
thirty to-me you then-you-must-give to-me to-answer you-can not but-if (13)

סְדִינִים וּשְׁלֹשִׁים חֲלִיפוֹת בְּגָדִים וַיֹּאמְרוּ לוֹ חוּדָה
tell! to-him and-they-said clothes sets-of and-thirty linen-garments

חִידָתְךָ וְנִשְׁמָעֶנָּה׃ וַיֹּאמֶר לָהֶם מֵהָאֹכֵל
from-the-one-eating to-them and-he-replied (14) and-let-us-hear-her riddle-of-you

יָצָא מַאֲכָל וּמֵעַז יָצָא מָתוֹק וְלֹא יָכְלוּ
they-could and-not sweet-thing he-came and-from-strong edible-thing he-came

לְהַגִּיד הַחִידָה שְׁלֹשֶׁת יָמִים׃ וַיְהִי ׀ בַּיּוֹם הַשְּׁבִיעִי*
*the-seventh on-the-day and-he-was (15) days three-of the-riddle to-answer

וַיֹּאמְרוּ לְאֵשֶׁת־ שִׁמְשׁוֹן פַּתִּי אֶת־ אִישֵׁךְ וְיַגֶּד־ לָנוּ
for-us so-he-explains husband-of-you *** coax! Samson to-wife-of then-they-said

אֶת־הַחִידָה פֶּן־ נִשְׂרֹף אוֹתָךְ וְאֶת־ בֵּית אָבִיךְ בָּאֵשׁ
with-the-fire father-of-you household-of and you we-will-burn or the-riddle ***

הַלְיָרְשֵׁנוּ קְרָאתֶם לָנוּ הֲלֹא׃ וַתֵּבְךְּ אֵשֶׁת שִׁמְשׁוֹן
Samson wife-of then-she-sobbed (16) or-not to-us you-invited to-rob-us?

עָלָיו וַתֹּאמֶר רַק־ שְׂנֵאתַנִי וְלֹא אֲהַבְתָּנִי הַחִידָה
the-riddle you-love-me and-not you-hate-me indeed and-she-said on-him

חַדְתָּ לִבְנֵי עַמִּי וְלִי לֹא הִגַּדְתָּה וַיֹּאמֶר
and-he-replied you-told-answer not but-to-me people-of-me to-men-of you-gave

לָהּ הִנֵּה לְאָבִי וּלְאִמִּי לֹא הִגַּדְתִּי וְלָךְ
so-to-you I-explained not and-to-mother-of-me to-father-of-me see! to-her

אַגִּיד׃ וַתֵּבְךְּ עָלָיו שִׁבְעַת הַיָּמִים אֲשֶׁר־ הָיָה
he-was that the-days seven-of on-him and-she-cried (17) should-I-explain

לָהֶם הַמִּשְׁתֶּה וַיְהִי ׀ בַּיּוֹם הַשְּׁבִיעִי וַיַּגֶּד־ לָהּ כִּי
for to-her then-he-told the-seventh on-the-day so-he-was the-feast to-them

הֱצִיקַתְהוּ וַתַּגֵּד הַחִידָה לִבְנֵי עַמָּהּ׃
people-of-her to-men-of the-riddle then-she-explained she-pressed-him

וַיֹּאמְרוּ לוֹ אַנְשֵׁי הָעִיר בַּיּוֹם הַשְּׁבִיעִי בְּטֶרֶם
at-before the-seventh on-the-day the-town men-of to-him and-they-said (18)

יָבֹא הַחַרְסָה מַה־ מָּתוֹק מִדְּבַשׁ וּמֶה עַז מֵאֲרִי
than-lion stronger and-what? than-honey sweeter what? the-sun he-set

וַיֹּאמֶר לָהֶם לוּלֵא חֲרַשְׁתֶּם בְּעֶגְלָתִי לֹא מְצָאתֶם
you-would-solve not with-heifer-of-me you-plowed if-not to-them and-he-said

חִידָתִי׃ וַתִּצְלַח עָלָיו רוּחַ יְהוָה וַיֵּרֶד
and-he-went-down Yahweh Spirit-of upon-him then-she-came (19) riddle-of-me

I will give you thirty linen garments and thirty sets of
clothes. 13 If you can't tell me
the answer, you must give me thirty linen garments and thirty sets of clothes."
"Tell us your riddle," they said. "Let's hear it."
14 He replied,

"Out of the eater,
something to eat;
out of the strong,
something sweet."

For three days they could not give the answer.
15 On the fourth[r] day, they
said to Samson's wife, "Coax your husband into explaining the riddle for us, or we will burn you and your father's household to death. Did you invite us here to rob us?"
16 Then Samson's wife threw
herself on him, sobbing, "You hate me! You don't really love me. You've given my people a riddle, but you haven't told me the answer."
"I haven't even explained it to my father or mother," he replied, "so why should I explain it to you?" 17 She cried
the whole seven days of the feast. So on the seventh day he finally told her, because she continued to press him. She in turn explained the riddle to her people.
18 Before sunset on the sev-
enth day the men of the town said to him,

"What is sweeter than honey?
What is stronger than a lion?"

Samson said to them,

"If you had not plowed with my heifer,
you would not have solved my riddle."

19 Then the Spirit of the LORD
came upon him in power. He went down to Ashkelon,

[r]15 Some Septuagint manuscripts and Syriac; Hebrew *seventh*

*15 The NIV, with some ancient versions, reads *resh* instead of *shin* הָרְבִיעִי, *the-fourth*.

אַשְׁקְלוֹן וַיַּךְ מֵהֶם ׀ שְׁלֹשִׁים אִישׁ וַיִּקַּח אֶת־
*** and-he-stripped man thirty from-them and-he-struck-down Ashkelon

חֲלִיצוֹתָם וַיִּתֵּן הַחֲלִיפוֹת לְמַגִּידֵי הַחִידָה
the-riddle to-ones-answering-of the-clothes and-he-gave belongings-of-them

וַיִּחַר אַפּוֹ וַיַּעַל בֵּית אָבִיהוּ׃
father-of-him house-of and-he-went-up anger-of-him and-he-burned

וַתְּהִי אֵשֶׁת שִׁמְשׁוֹן לְמֵרֵעֵהוּ אֲשֶׁר רֵעָה לוֹ׃
to-him he-attended who to-friend-of-him Samson wife-of and-she-became (20)

וַיְהִי מִיָּמִים בִּימֵי קְצִיר־ חִטִּים וַיִּפְקֹד
then-he-visited wheats harvest-of in-days-of after-days and-he-was (15:1)

שִׁמְשׁוֹן אֶת־ אִשְׁתּוֹ בִּגְדִי עִזִּים וַיֹּאמֶר אָבֹאָה אֶל־
into I-will-go and-he-said goats with-young-goat-of wife-of-him *** Samson

אִשְׁתִּי הֶחָדְרָה וְלֹא־ נְתָנוֹ אָבִיהָ לָבוֹא׃
to-go-in father-of-her he-let-him but-not into-the-room wife-of-me

וַיֹּאמֶר אָבִיהָ אָמֹר אָמַרְתִּי כִּי־ שָׂנֹא שְׂנֵאתָהּ
you-hated-her to-hate that I-say to-say father-of-her and-he-said (2)

וָאֶתְּנֶנָּה לְמֵרֵעֶךָ הֲלֹא אֲחֹתָהּ הַקְּטַנָּה טוֹבָה
attractive the-young sister-of-her not? to-friend-of-you so-I-gave-her

מִמֶּנָּה תְּהִי־ נָא לְךָ תַּחְתֶּיהָ׃ וַיֹּאמֶר לָהֶם
to-them and-he-said (3) instead-of-her for-you now! let-her-be more-than-her

שִׁמְשׁוֹן נִקֵּיתִי הַפַּעַם מִפְּלִשְׁתִּים כִּי־ עֹשֶׂה אֲנִי עִמָּם רָעָה׃
harm to-them I doing now from-Philistines the-time I-am-innocent Samson

וַיֵּלֶךְ שִׁמְשׁוֹן וַיִּלְכֹּד שְׁלֹשׁ־ מֵאוֹת שׁוּעָלִים וַיִּקַּח
and-he-got foxes hundreds three-of and-he-caught Samson so-he-went-out (4)

לַפִּדִים וַיֶּפֶן זָנָב אֶל־ זָנָב וַיָּשֶׂם לַפִּיד אֶחָד בֵּין־ שְׁנֵי
pair-of between one torch then-he-fastened tail to tail and-he-tied torches

הַזְּנָבוֹת בַּתָּוֶךְ׃ וַיַּבְעֶר־ אֵשׁ בַּלַּפִּידִים וַיְשַׁלַּח
and-he-let-loose on-the-torches fire and-he-lit (5) in-the-middle the-tails

בְּקָמוֹת פְּלִשְׁתִּים וַיַּבְעֵר מִגָּדִישׁ וְעַד־
even-to from-shock and-he-burned-up Philistines in-standing-grain-of

קָמָה וְעַד־ כֶּרֶם זָיִת׃ וַיֹּאמְרוּ פְלִשְׁתִּים מִי
who? Philistines when-they-asked (6) olive-grove vineyard even-to standing-grain

עָשָׂה זֹאת וַיֹּאמְרוּ שִׁמְשׁוֹן חֲתַן הַתִּמְנִי כִּי לָקַח
he-took because the-Timnite son-in-law-of Samson then-they-said this he-did

אֶת־ אִשְׁתּוֹ וַיִּתְּנָהּ לְמֵרֵעֵהוּ וַיַּעֲלוּ פְלִשְׁתִּים
Philistines so-they-went-up to-friend-of-him and-he-gave-her wife-of-him ***

וַיִּשְׂרְפוּ אוֹתָהּ וְאֶת־ אָבִיהָ בָּאֵשׁ׃ וַיֹּאמֶר לָהֶם
to-them and-he-said (7) with-the-fire father-of-her and her and-they-burned

struck down thirty of their
men, stripped them of their
belongings and gave their
clothes to those who had explained the riddle. Burning
with anger, he went up to his
father's house. [20]And Samson's wife was given to the
friend who had attended him
at his wedding.

Samson's Vengeance on the Philistines

15 Later on, at the time of
wheat harvest, Samson
took a young goat and went to
visit his wife. He said, "I'm
going to my wife's room." But
her father would not let him
go in.
[2]"I was so sure you
thoroughly hated her," he
said, "that I gave her to your
friend. Isn't her younger sister
more attractive? Take her instead."
[3]Samson said to them, "This
time I have a right to get even
with the Philistines; I will
really harm them." [4]So he
went out and caught three
hundred foxes and tied them
tail to tail in pairs. He then
fastened a torch to every pair
of tails, [5]lit the torches and let
the foxes loose in the standing
grain of the Philistines. He
burned up the shocks and
standing grain, together with
the vineyards and olive
groves.
[6]When the Philistines asked,
"Who did this?" they were
told, "Samson, the Timnite's
son-in-law, because his wife
was given to his friend."
So the Philistines went up
and burned her and her father
to death. [7]Samson said to

שִׁמְשׁוֹן אִם־ תַּעֲשׂוּן כָּזֹאת כִּי אִם־ נִקַּמְתִּי בָּכֶם
on-you I-will-get-revenge indeed then like-this you-acted since Samson

וְאַחַר אֶחְדָּל׃ וַיַּךְ אוֹתָם שׁוֹק עַל־ יָרֵךְ מַכָּה גְדוֹלָה
great slaughter thigh on leg them and-he-attacked (8) I-will-stop and-after

וַיֵּרֶד וַיֵּשֶׁב בִּסְעִיף סֶלַע עֵיטָם׃ וַיַּעֲלוּ
and-they-went-up (9) Etam rock-of in-cave-of and-he-stayed then-he-went-down

פְלִשְׁתִּים וַיַּחֲנוּ בִּיהוּדָה וַיִּנָּטְשׁוּ בַּלֶּחִי׃
near-the-Lehi and-they-spread-out in-Judah and-they-camped Philistines

וַיֹּאמְרוּ אִישׁ יְהוּדָה לָמָה עֲלִיתֶם עָלֵינוּ וַיֹּאמְרוּ
and-they-answered against-us you-came-up why? Judah man-of and-they-asked (10)

לֶאֱסוֹר אֶת־ שִׁמְשׁוֹן עָלִינוּ לַעֲשׂוֹת לוֹ כַּאֲשֶׁר עָשָׂה לָנוּ׃
to-us he-did just-as to-him to-do we-came Samson *** to-take-prisoner

וַיֵּרְדוּ שְׁלֹשֶׁת אֲלָפִים אִישׁ מִיהוּדָה אֶל־ סְעִיף סֶלַע
rock-of cave-of to from-Judah man thousands three-of then-they-went-down (11)

עֵיטָם וַיֹּאמְרוּ לְשִׁמְשׁוֹן הֲלֹא יָדַעְתָּ כִּי־ מֹשְׁלִים בָּנוּ
over-us ones-ruling that you-realize not? to-Samon and-they-said Etam

פְּלִשְׁתִּים וּמַה־ זֹּאת עָשִׂיתָ לָּנוּ וַיֹּאמֶר לָהֶם כַּאֲשֶׁר
just-as to-them and-he-answered to-us you-did this now-what? Philistines

עָשׂוּ לִי כֵּן עָשִׂיתִי לָהֶם׃ וַיֹּאמְרוּ לוֹ לֶאֱסָרְךָ
to-tie-up-you to-him and-they-said (12) to-them I-did same to-me they-did

יָרַדְנוּ לְתִתְּךָ בְּיַד־ פְּלִשְׁתִּים וַיֹּאמֶר לָהֶם שִׁמְשׁוֹן
Samson to-them and-he-said Philistines into-hand-of to-give-you we-came

הִשָּׁבְעוּ לִי פֶּן־ תִּפְגְּעוּן בִּי אַתֶּם׃ וַיֹּאמְרוּ
and-they-answered (13) yourselves to-me you-will-kill not to-me swear!

לוֹ לֵאמֹר לֹא כִּי־ אָסֹר נֶאֱסָרְךָ וּנְתַנּוּךָ
and-we-will-give-you we-will-tie-up-you to-tie-up only agreed to-say to-him

בְיָדָם וְהָמֵת לֹא נְמִיתֶךָ וַיַּאַסְרֻהוּ בִּשְׁנַיִם
with-two so-they-bound-him we-will-kill-you not but-to-kill into-hand-of-them

עֲבֹתִים חֲדָשִׁים וַיַּעֲלוּהוּ מִן־ הַסָּלַע׃ הוּא־ בָא עַד־
to he-approached he (14) the-rock from and-they-led-him new-ones ropes

לֶחִי וּפְלִשְׁתִּים הֵרִיעוּ לִקְרָאתוֹ וַתִּצְלַח עָלָיו
upon-him and-she-came to-come-to-him they-shouted and-Philistines Lehi

רוּחַ יְהוָה וַתִּהְיֶינָה הָעֲבֹתִים אֲשֶׁר עַל־ זְרוֹעוֹתָיו כַּפִּשְׁתִּים
like-the-flax arms-of-him on that the-ropes and-they-became Yahweh Spirit-of

אֲשֶׁר בָּעֲרוּ בָאֵשׁ וַיִּמַּסּוּ אֱסוּרָיו מֵעַל
from-on ones-binding-him and-they-dropped with-fire they-burned that

יָדָיו׃ וַיִּמְצָא לְחִי־ חֲמוֹר טְרִיָּה וַיִּשְׁלַח
and-he-reached fresh donkey jawbone-of and-he-found (15) hands-of-him

them, "Since you've acted like
this, I won't stop until I get my
revenge on you." [8]He attacked
them viciously and slaughtered many of them. Then he
went down and stayed in a
cave in the rock of Etam.
[9]The Philistines went up and
camped in Judah, spreading
out near Lehi. [10]The men of
Judah asked, "Why have you
come to fight us?"
"We have come to take Samson prisoner," they answered,
"to do to him as he did to us."
[11]Then three thousand men
from Judah went down to the
cave in the rock of Etam and
said to Samson, "Don't you
realize that the Philistines are
rulers over us? What have you
done to us?"
He answered, "I merely did
to them what they did to me."
[12]They said to him, "We've
come to tie you up and hand
you over to the Philistines."
Samson said, "Swear to me
that you won't kill me yourselves."
[13]"Agreed," they answered.
"We will only tie you up and
hand you over to them. We
will not kill you." So they
bound him with two new
ropes and led him up from the
rock. [14]As he approached Lehi,
the Philistines came toward
him shouting. The Spirit of
the LORD came upon him in
power. The ropes on his arms
became like charred flax, and
the bindings dropped from his
hands. [15]Finding a fresh jawbone of a donkey, he grabbed

יָדוֹ וַיִּקָּחֶהָ וַיַּךְ־ בָּהּ אֶלֶף אִישׁ׃
man thousand with-her and-he-struck-down and-he-grabbed-her hand-of-him

וַיֹּאמֶר שִׁמְשׁוֹן בִּלְחִי הַחֲמוֹר חֲמוֹר חֲמֹרָתָיִם
two-heaps heap the-donkey with-jawbone-of Samson then-he-said (16)

בִּלְחִי הַחֲמוֹר הִכֵּיתִי אֶלֶף אִישׁ׃ וַיְהִי
and-he-was (17) man thousand I-killed the-donkey with-jawbone-of

כְּכַלֹּתוֹ לְדַבֵּר וַיַּשְׁלֵךְ הַלְּחִי מִיָּדוֹ
from-hand-of-him the-jawbone then-he-threw-away to-speak when-to-finish-him

וַיִּקְרָא לַמָּקוֹם הַהוּא רָמַת לֶחִי׃ וַיִּצְמָא מְאֹד
very and-he-was-thirsty (18) Lehi Ramath the-that to-the-place and-he-called

וַיִּקְרָא אֶל־ יְהוָה וַיֹּאמַר אַתָּה נָתַתָּ בְיַד־ עַבְדְּךָ
servant-of-you into-hand-of you-gave you and-he-said Yahweh to and-he-cried

אֶת־ הַתְּשׁוּעָה הַגְּדֹלָה הַזֹּאת וְעַתָּה אָמוּת בַּצָּמָא
of-the-thirst must-I-die and-now the-this the-great the-victory ***

וְנָפַלְתִּי בְּיַד הָעֲרֵלִים׃ וַיִּבְקַע אֱלֹהִים
God then-he-opened (19) the-uncircumcised-ones into-hand-of and-must-I-fall

אֶת־ הַמַּכְתֵּשׁ אֲשֶׁר־ בַּלֶּחִי וַיֵּצְאוּ מִמֶּנּוּ מַיִם
waters from-him and-they-came-out in-the-Lehi that the-hollow-place ***

וַיֵּשְׁתְּ וַתָּשָׁב רוּחוֹ וַיֶּחִי עַל־ כֵּן ׀
this for and-he-revived strength-of-him then-she-returned when-he-drank

קָרָא שְׁמָהּ עֵין הַקּוֹרֵא אֲשֶׁר בַּלֶּחִי עַד הַיּוֹם הַזֶּה׃
the-this the-day to in-the-Lehi that Hakkore En name-of-her he-called

וַיִּשְׁפֹּט אֶת־ יִשְׂרָאֵל בִּימֵי פְלִשְׁתִּים עֶשְׂרִים שָׁנָה׃ וַיֵּלֶךְ
and-he-went (16:1) year twenty Philistines in-days-of Israel *** and-he-led (20)

שִׁמְשׁוֹן עַזָּתָה וַיַּרְא־ שָׁם אִשָּׁה זוֹנָה וַיָּבֹא אֵלֶיהָ׃
into-her and-he-went being-prostitute woman there and-he-saw to-Gaza Samson

לָעַזָּתִים ׀ לֵאמֹר בָּא שִׁמְשׁוֹן הֵנָּה וַיָּסֹבּוּ
so-they-surrounded to-here Samson he-came to-say to-the-Gazathites (2)

וַיֶּאֶרְבוּ־ לוֹ כָל־ הַלַּיְלָה בְּשַׁעַר הָעִיר
the-city at-gate-of the-night all-of for-him and-they-lay-in-wait

וַיִּתְחָרְשׁוּ כָל־ הַלַּיְלָה לֵאמֹר עַד־ אוֹר הַבֹּקֶר
the-morning dawn-of at to-say the-night all-of and-they-were-still

וַהֲרַגְנֻהוּ׃ וַיִּשְׁכַּב שִׁמְשׁוֹן עַד־ חֲצִי הַלַּיְלָה
the-night middle-of until Samson but-he-lay (3) then-we-will-kill-him

וַיָּקָם ׀ בַּחֲצִי הַלַּיְלָה וַיֶּאֱחֹז בְּדַלְתוֹת שַׁעַר־
gate-of of-doors-of and-he-took-hold the-night in-middle-of then-he-got-up

הָעִיר וּבִשְׁתֵּי הַמְּזוּזוֹת וַיִּסָּעֵם עִם־ הַבְּרִיחַ
the-bar with and-he-tore-loose-them the-posts and-of-two-of the-city

it and struck down a thousand men.

16Then Samson said,

"With a donkey's jawbone
I have made donkeys of them.[s]
With a donkey's jawbone
I have killed a thousand men."

17When he finished speaking, he threw away the jawbone; and the place was called Ramath Lehi.[t]

18Because he was very
thirsty, he cried out to the
LORD, "You have given your
servant this great victory.
Must I now die of thirst and
fall into the hands of the uncircumcised?" 19Then God
opened up the hollow place in
Lehi, and water came out of it.
When Samson drank, his
strength returned and he
revived. So the spring was
called En Hakkore,[u] and it is
still there in Lehi.
20Samson led[v] Israel for
twenty years in the days of the
Philistines.

Samson and Delilah

16 One day Samson went
to Gaza, where he saw
a prostitute. He went in to
spend the night with her. 2The
people of Gaza were told,
"Samson is here!" So they surrounded the place and lay in
wait for him all night at the
city gate. They made no move
during the night, saying, "At
dawn we'll kill him."
3But Samson lay there only
until the middle of the night.
Then he got up and took hold
of the doors of the city gate,
together with the two posts,
and tore them loose, bar and

[s]16 Or *made a heap or two;* the Hebrew for *donkey* sounds like the Hebrew for *heap.*
[t]17 *Ramath Lehi* means *jawbone hill.*
[u]19 *En Hakkore* means *caller's spring.*
[v]20 Traditionally *judged*

*2 Most mss have *pathah* under the *resh* (וַהֲרַגְ).

וַיָּשֶׂם עַל־ כְּתֵפָיו וַיַּעֲלֵם אֶל־ רֹאשׁ הָהָר אֲשֶׁר
that the-hill top-of to and-he-carried-them shoulders-of-him to and-he-lifted

עַל־ פְּנֵי חֶבְרוֹן׃ וַיְהִי אַחֲרֵי־ כֵן וַיֶּאֱהַב אִשָּׁה
woman then-he-fell-in-love this after and-he-was (4) Hebron faces-of to

בְּנַחַל שֹׂרֵק וּשְׁמָהּ דְּלִילָה׃ וַיַּעֲלוּ אֵלֶיהָ סַרְנֵי
rulers-of to-her and-they-went (5) Delilah and-name-of-her Sorek in-Valley-of

פְלִשְׁתִּים וַיֹּאמְרוּ לָהּ פַּתִּי אוֹתוֹ וּרְאִי בַּמֶּה כֹּחוֹ
strength-of-him in-the-what and-see! him lure! to-her and-they-said Philistines

גָדוֹל וּבַמֶּה נוּכַל לוֹ וַאֲסַרְנֻהוּ
so-we-may-tie-up-him over-him we-can-overpower and-with-the-what great

לְעַנֹּתוֹ וַאֲנַחְנוּ נִתַּן־ לָךְ אִישׁ אֶלֶף וּמֵאָה כָּסֶף׃
silver and-hundred thousand each to-you we-will-give and-we to-subdue-him

וַתֹּאמֶר דְּלִילָה אֶל־שִׁמְשׁוֹן הַגִּידָה־נָּא לִי בַּמֶּה כֹּחֲךָ
strength-of-you in-the-what to-me now! tell! Samson to Delilah so-she-said (6)

גָדוֹל וּבַמֶּה תֵאָסֵר לְעַנּוֹתֶךָ׃ וַיֹּאמֶר
and-he-answered (7) to-subdue-you you-can-be-tied-up and-with-the-what great

אֵלֶיהָ שִׁמְשׁוֹן אִם־ יַאַסְרֻנִי בְּשִׁבְעָה יְתָרִים לַחִים אֲשֶׁר לֹא־
not that fresh-ones thongs with-seven they-tie-me if Samson to-her

חֹרָבוּ וְחָלִיתִי וְהָיִיתִי כְּאַחַד הָאָדָם׃
the-man as-any-of and-I-will-be then-I-will-become-weak they-were-dried

וַיַּעֲלוּ־ לָהּ סַרְנֵי פְלִשְׁתִּים שִׁבְעָה יְתָרִים לַחִים
fresh-ones thongs seven Philistines rulers-of to-her then-they-brought (8)

אֲשֶׁר לֹא־ חֹרָבוּ וַתַּאַסְרֵהוּ בָּהֶם׃ וְהָאֹרֵב
and-the-one-hiding (9) with-them and-she-tied-him they-were-dried not that

יֹשֵׁב לָהּ בַּחֶדֶר וַתֹּאמֶר אֵלָיו פְּלִשְׁתִּים עָלֶיךָ
upon-you Philistines to-him then-she-called in-the-room with-her staying

שִׁמְשׁוֹן וַיְנַתֵּק אֶת־ הַיְתָרִים כַּאֲשֶׁר יִנָּתֵק פְּתִיל־ הַנְּעֹרֶת
the-string piece-of he-snaps just-as the-thongs *** but-he-snapped Samson

בַּהֲרִיחוֹ אֵשׁ וְלֹא נוֹדַע כֹּחוֹ׃
strength-of-him he-was-discovered so-not flame when-to-come-close-him

וַתֹּאמֶר דְּלִילָה אֶל־שִׁמְשׁוֹן הִנֵּה הֵתַלְתָּ בִּי וַתְּדַבֵּר
and-you-told of-me you-made-fool see! Samson to Delilah then-she-said (10)

אֵלַי כְּזָבִים עַתָּה הַגִּידָה־נָּא לִי בַּמֶּה תֵּאָסֵר׃ וַיֹּאמֶר
and-he-said (11) you-can-be-tied with-the-what to-me now! tell! now lies to-me

אֵלֶיהָ אִם־ אָסוֹר יַאַסְרוּנִי בַּעֲבֹתִים חֲדָשִׁים אֲשֶׁר לֹא־ נַעֲשָׂה
he-was-done not that new-ones with-ropes they-tie-me to-tie if to-her

בָהֶם מְלָאכָה וְחָלִיתִי וְהָיִיתִי כְּאַחַד הָאָדָם׃
the-man as-any-of and-I-will-be then-I-will-become-weak work with-them

all. He lifted them to his shoulders and carried them to the top of the hill that faces Hebron.
4Some time later, he fell in love with a woman in the Valley of Sorek whose name was
Delilah. 5The rulers of the Philistines went to her and said, "See if you can lure him into showing you the secret of his great strength and how we can overpower him so we may tie him up and subdue him. Each one of us will give you eleven hundred shekels[w] of silver."
6So Delilah said to Samson, "Tell me the secret of your great strength and how you can be tied up and subdued."
7Samson answered her, "If anyone ties me with seven fresh thongs[x] that have not been dried, I'll become as weak as any other man."
8Then the rulers of the Philistines brought her seven fresh thongs that had not been dried, and she tied him with
them. 9With men hidden in the room, she called to him, "Samson, the Philistines are upon you!" But he snapped the thongs as easily as a piece of string snaps when it comes close to a flame. So the secret of his strength was not discovered.
10Then Delilah said to Samson, "You have made a fool of me; you lied to me. Come now, tell me how you can be tied."
11He said, "If anyone ties me securely with new ropes that have never been used, I'll become as weak as any other man."

w5 That is, about 28 pounds (about 13 kilograms)
x7 Or *bowstrings;* also in verses 8 and 9

וַתִּקַּח דְּלִילָה עֲבֹתִים חֲדָשִׁים וַתַּאַסְרֵהוּ בָהֶם
with-them and-she-tied-him new-ones ropes Delilah so-she-took (12)

וַתֹּאמֶר אֵלָיו פְּלִשְׁתִּים עָלֶיךָ שִׁמְשׁוֹן וְהָאֹרֵב יֹשֵׁב
staying and-the-one-hiding Samson upon-you Philistines to-him and-she-called

בֶּחָדֶר וַיְנַתְּקֵם מֵעַל זְרֹעֹתָיו כַּחוּט׃
as-the-thread arms-of-him from-on but-he-snapped-them in-the-room

וַתֹּאמֶר דְּלִילָה אֶל־ שִׁמְשׁוֹן עַד־ הֵנָּה הֵתַלְתָּ בִּי
of-me you-made-fool to-now until Samson to Delilah then-she-said (13)

וַתְּדַבֵּר אֵלַי כְּזָבִים הַגִּידָה לִּי בַּמֶּה תֵּאָסֵר וַיֹּאמֶר
and-he-said you-can-be-tied with-the-what to-me tell! lies to-me and-you-told

אֵלֶיהָ אִם־ תַּאַרְגִי אֶת־ שֶׁבַע מַחְלְפוֹת רֹאשִׁי עִם־ הַמַּסָּכֶת׃
the-fabric into head-of-me braids-of seven *** you-weave if to-her

*[וְתָקַעַתְּ בַּיָּתֵד וְחָלִיתִי וְהָיִיתִי כְּאַחַד הָאָדָם
the-man as-any-of and-I-will-be then-I-will-become-weak with-pin and-you-tighten]*

וַתְּיַשְּׁנֵהוּ וַתַּאֲרֹג אֶת־ שֶׁבַע מַחְלְפוֹת רֹאשׁוֹ עִם־ הַמַּסָּכֶת]*
*[the-fabric into head-of-him braids-of seven *** and-she-wove so-she-put-to-sleep-him

וַתִּתְקַע בַּיָּתֵד וַתֹּאמֶר אֵלָיו פְּלִשְׁתִּים עָלֶיךָ
upon-you Philistines to-him and-she-called with-the-pin and-she-tightened (14)

שִׁמְשׁוֹן וַיִּיקַץ מִשְּׁנָתוֹ וַיִּסַּע אֶת־ הַיְתַד הָאֶרֶג
the-loom the-pin *** and-he-pulled-up from-sleep-of-him and-he-awoke Samson

וְאֶת־ הַמַּסָּכֶת׃ וַתֹּאמֶר אֵלָיו אֵיךְ תֹּאמַר אֲהַבְתִּיךְ
I-love-you can-you-say how? to-him then-she-said (15) the-fabric with

וְלִבְּךָ אֵין אִתִּי זֶה שָׁלֹשׁ פְּעָמִים הֵתַלְתָּ בִּי וְלֹא־
and-not of-me you-made-fool times three this with-me not when-heart-of-you

הִגַּדְתָּ לִּי בַּמֶּה כֹּחֲךָ גָדוֹל׃ וַיְהִי כִּי־
that and-he-was (16) great strength-of-you in-the-what to-me you-told

הֵצִיקָה לּוֹ בִדְבָרֶיהָ כָּל־ הַיָּמִים וַתְּאַלְצֵהוּ
and-she-prodded-him the-days all-of with-words-of-her to-him she-nagged

וַתִּקְצַר נַפְשׁוֹ לָמוּת׃ וַיַּגֶּד־ לָהּ אֶת־ כָּל־
all-of *** to-her so-he-told (17) to-die life-of-him so-she-was-tired

לִבּוֹ וַיֹּאמֶר לָהּ מוֹרָה לֹא־ עָלָה עַל־ רֹאשִׁי כִּי־
for head-of-me on he-went not razor to-her and-he-said heart-of-him

נְזִיר אֱלֹהִים אֲנִי מִבֶּטֶן אִמִּי אִם־ גֻּלַּחְתִּי וְסָר
then-he-would-leave I-was-shaved if mother-of-me from-womb-of I God Nazirite-of

מִמֶּנִּי כֹחִי וְחָלִיתִי וְהָיִיתִי כְּכָל־
as-any-of and-I-would-be and-I-would-become-weak strength-of-me from-me

הָאָדָם׃ וַתֵּרֶא דְלִילָה כִּי־ הִגִּיד לָהּ אֶת־ כָּל־ לִבּוֹ
heart-of-him all-of *** to-her he-told that Delilah when-she-saw (18) the-man

12So Delilah took new ropes
and tied him with them. Then,
with men hidden in the room,
she called to him, "Samson,
the Philistines are upon you!"
But he snapped the ropes off
his arms as if they were
threads.
13Delilah then said to Samson, "Until now, you have
been making a fool of me and
lying to me. Tell me how you
can be tied."
He replied, "If you weave
the seven braids of my head
into the fabric ⌊on the loom⌋
and tighten it with the pin, I'll
become as weak as any other
man." So while he was sleeping, Delilah took the seven
braids of his head, wove them
into the fabric 14and[y] tight-
ened it with the pin.
Again she called to him,
"Samson, the Philistines are
upon you!" He awoke from his
sleep and pulled up the pin
and the loom, with the fabric.
15Then she said to him,
"How can you say, 'I love
you,' when you won't confide
in me? This is the third time
you have made a fool of me
and haven't told me the secret
of your great strength." 16With
such nagging she prodded
him day after day until he was
tired to death.
17So he told her everything.
"No razor has ever been used
on my head," he said, "because I have been a Nazirite
set apart to God since birth. If
my head were shaved, my
strength would leave me, and
I would become as weak as
any other man."
18When Delilah saw that he
had told her everything, she

[y]*13,14* Some Septuagint manuscripts; Hebrew *"⌊I can⌋ if you weave the seven braids of my head into the fabric ⌊on the loom⌋." 14So she*

**13* The Hebrew text in brackets is conjectured on the basis of the Septuagint mss the NIV translates. See the introduction, page xiii.

וַתִּשְׁלַח וַתִּקְרָא לְסַרְנֵי פְלִשְׁתִּים לֵאמֹר עֲלוּ
come-back! to-say Philistines to-rulers-of and-she-called then-she-sent

הַפַּעַם כִּֽי־ הִגִּיד לָה° אֶת־ כָּל־ לִבּוֹ וְעָלוּ אֵלֶיהָ
to-her so-they-returned heart-of-him all-of *** to-me he-told for the-once

סַרְנֵי פְלִשְׁתִּים וַיַּעֲלוּ הַכֶּסֶף בְּיָדָם׃
in-hand-of-them the-silver and-they-brought Philistines rulers-of

וַתְּיַשְּׁנֵהוּ עַל־ בִּרְכֶּיהָ וַתִּקְרָא לָאִישׁ
to-the-man and-she-called knees-of-her on and-she-put-to-sleep-him (19)

וַתְּגַלַּח אֶת־ שֶׁבַע מַחְלְפוֹת רֹאשׁוֹ וַתָּחֶל לְעַנּוֹתוֹ
to-subdue-him and-she-began head-of-him braids-of seven *** and-she-shaved

וַיָּסַר כֹּחוֹ מֵעָלָיו׃ וַתֹּאמֶר פְּלִשְׁתִּים
Philistines then-she-called (20) from-on-him strength-of-him and-he-left

עָלֶיךָ שִׁמְשׁוֹן וַיִּקַץ מִשְּׁנָתוֹ וַיֹּאמֶר אֵצֵא
I-will-go-out and-he-thought from-sleep-of-him and-he-awoke Samson upon-you

כְּפַעַם בְּפַעַם וְאִנָּעֵר וְהוּא לֹא יָדַע כִּי יְהוָה
Yahweh that he-knew not but-he and-I-will-shake-myself-free in-time as-time

סָר מֵעָלָיו׃ וַיֹּאחֲזוּהוּ פְלִשְׁתִּים וַיְנַקְּרוּ
and-they-gouged-out Philistines then-they-seized-him (21) from-on-him he-left

אֶת־ עֵינָיו וַיּוֹרִידוּ אוֹתוֹ עַזָּתָה וַיַּאַסְרוּהוּ
and-they-bound-him to-Gaza him and-they-took-down eyes-of-him ***

בַּנְחֻשְׁתַּיִם וַיְהִי טוֹחֵן בְּבֵית הָאֲסִירִים°׃
the-prisons in-house-of one-grinding and-he-was with-the-bronze-shackles

וַיָּחֶל שְׂעַר־ רֹאשׁוֹ לְצַמֵּחַ כַּאֲשֶׁר גֻּלָּח׃
he-was-shaved just-as to-grow head-of-him hair-of but-he-began (22)

וְסַרְנֵי פְלִשְׁתִּים נֶאֶסְפוּ לִזְבֹּחַ זֶבַח־ גָּדוֹל
great sacrifice to-offer they-assembled Philistines now-rulers-of (23)

לְדָגוֹן אֱלֹהֵיהֶם וּלְשִׂמְחָה וַיֹּאמְרוּ נָתַן אֱלֹהֵינוּ
god-of-us he-delivered and-they-said and-for-celebration god-of-them to-Dagon

בְּיָדֵנוּ אֵת שִׁמְשׁוֹן אוֹיְבֵנוּ׃ וַיִּרְאוּ אֹתוֹ
him when-they-saw (24) being-enemies-of-us Samson *** into-hand-of-us

הָעָם וַיְהַלְלוּ אֶת־ אֱלֹהֵיהֶם כִּי אָמְרוּ נָתַן
he-delivered they-said for god-of-them *** then-they-praised the-people

אֱלֹהֵינוּ בְּיָדֵנוּ אֶת־ אוֹיְבֵנוּ וְאֵת מַחֲרִיב
one-laying-waste and being-enemy-of-us *** into-hand-of-us god-of-us

אַרְצֵנוּ וַאֲשֶׁר הִרְבָּה אֶת־ חֲלָלֵינוּ׃ וַיְהִי כִּי°*
when and-he-was (25) ones-slain-of-us *** he-multiplied and-who land-of-us

טוֹב לִבָּם וַיֹּאמְרוּ קִרְאוּ לְשִׁמְשׁוֹן
to-Samson call-out! and-they-shouted spirit-of-them to-be-high

sent word to the rulers of the
Philistines, "Come back once
more; he has told me everything." So the rulers of the
Philistines returned with the
silver in their hands. 19Having
put him to sleep on her lap,
she called a man to shave off
the seven braids of his hair,
and so began to subdue him.[z]
And his strength left him.
20Then she called, "Samson,
the Philistines are upon you!"
He awoke from his sleep
and thought, "I'll go out as before and shake myself free."
But he did not know that the
LORD had left him.
21Then the Philistines seized
him, gouged out his eyes and
took him down to Gaza. Binding him with bronze shackles,
they set him to grinding in the
prison. 22But the hair on his
head began to grow again after it had been shaved.

The Death of Samson

23Now the rulers of the Philistines assembled to offer a
great sacrifice to Dagon their
god and to celebrate, saying,
"Our god has delivered Samson, our enemy, into our
hands."
24When the people saw him,
they praised their god, saying,

"Our god has delivered our enemy
into our hands,
the one who laid waste our land
and multiplied our slain."

25While they were in high
spirits, they shouted, "Bring
out Samson to entertain us."

z19 Hebrew; some Septuagint manuscripts *and he began to weaken*

*25 Most mss have *hirek* under the *kaph* and *maqqeph* after the *yodh* (כִּי־טוֹב). L here supplies the pointing for the *Qere*.

°18 ק לי
°21 ק האסורים
°25 ק כטוב

וִישַׂחֶק־ לָנוּ וַיִּקְרְאוּ לְשִׁמְשׁוֹן מִבֵּית
from-house-of to-Samson so-they-called-out for-us so-he-may-entertain

הָאֲסִירִים וַיְצַחֵק לִפְנֵיהֶם וַיַּעֲמִידוּ אוֹתוֹ בֵּין הָעַמּוּדִים׃
the-pillars among him and-they-stood before-them and-he-performed the-prisons

וַיֹּאמֶר שִׁמְשׁוֹן אֶל־ הַנַּעַר הַמַּחֲזִיק בְּיָדוֹ הַנִּיחָה
put! on-hand-of-him the-one-holding the-servant to Samson and-he-said (26)

אוֹתִי וְהֵימִשֵׁנִי אֶת־ הָעַמֻּדִים אֲשֶׁר הַבַּיִת נָכוֹן עֲלֵיהֶם
by-them he-is-supported the-temple that the-pillars *** and-make-feel-me! me

וְאֶשָּׁעֵן עֲלֵיהֶם׃ וְהַבַּיִת מָלֵא הָאֲנָשִׁים
the-men he-was-crowded now-the-temple (27) against-them so-I-may-lean

וְהַנָּשִׁים וְשָׁמָּה כֹּל סַרְנֵי פְלִשְׁתִּים וְעַל־ הַגָּג
the-roof and-on Philistines rulers-of all-of and-at-there and-the-women

כִּשְׁלֹשֶׁת אֲלָפִים אִישׁ וְאִשָּׁה הָרֹאִים בִּשְׂחוֹק
at-performance-of the-ones-watching and-woman man thousands about-three-of

שִׁמְשׁוֹן׃ וַיִּקְרָא שִׁמְשׁוֹן אֶל־ יְהוָה וַיֹּאמַר אֲדֹנָי יֱהֹוִה
Yahweh Lord and-he-said Yahweh to Samson then-he-prayed (28) Samson

זָכְרֵנִי נָא וְחַזְּקֵנִי נָא אַךְ הַפַּעַם הַזֶּה הָאֱלֹהִים
the-God the-this the-once just now! and-strengthen-me! now! remember-me!

וְאִנָּקְמָה נְקַם־ אַחַת מִשְּׁתֵי עֵינַי מִפְּלִשְׁתִּים׃
on-Philistines eyes-of-me for-two-of one vengeance-of and-let-me-get-revenge

וַיִּלְפֹּת שִׁמְשׁוֹן אֶת־ שְׁנֵי ׀ עַמּוּדֵי הַתָּוֶךְ אֲשֶׁר הַבַּיִת
the-temple which the-center pillars-of two-of *** Samson then-he-reached (29)

נָכוֹן עֲלֵיהֶם וַיִּסָּמֵךְ עֲלֵיהֶם אֶחָד בִּימִינוֹ
on-right-of-him one against-them and-he-braced-himself on-them he-stood

וְאֶחָד בִּשְׂמֹאלוֹ׃ וַיֹּאמֶר שִׁמְשׁוֹן תָּמוֹת נַפְשִׁי עִם־
with life-of-me let-her-die Samson and-he-said (30) on-left-of-him and-one

פְּלִשְׁתִּים וַיֵּט בְּכֹחַ וַיִּפֹּל הַבַּיִת עַל־
on the-temple and-he-came-down with-might then-he-pushed Philistines

הַסְּרָנִים וְעַל־ כָּל־ הָעָם אֲשֶׁר־ בּוֹ וַיִּהְיוּ הַמֵּתִים
the-dead-ones and-they-were in-him who the-people all-of and-on the-rulers

אֲשֶׁר הֵמִית בְּמוֹתוֹ רַבִּים מֵאֲשֶׁר הֵמִית בְּחַיָּיו׃
in-lives-of-him he-killed more-than many in-death-of-him he-killed whom

וַיֵּרְדוּ אֶחָיו וְכָל־ בֵּית אָבִיהוּ
father-of-him family-of and-whole-of brothers-of-him then-they-went-down (31)

וַיִּשְׂאוּ אֹתוֹ וַיַּעֲלוּ ׀ וַיִּקְבְּרוּ אוֹתוֹ בֵּין צָרְעָה
Zorah between him and-they-buried and-they-brought-back him and-they-got

וּבֵין אֶשְׁתָּאֹל בְּקֶבֶר מָנוֹחַ אָבִיו וְהוּא שָׁפַט אֶת־יִשְׂרָאֵל
Israel *** he-led now-he father-of-him Manoah in-tomb-of Eshtaol and-between

So they called Samson out of
the prison, and he performed
for them.
When they stood him
among the pillars, [26]Samson
said to the servant who held
his hand, "Put me where I can
feel the pillars that support the
temple, so that I may lean
against them." [27]Now the temple was crowded with men
and women; all the rulers of
the Philistines were there, and
on the roof were about three
thousand men and women
watching Samson perform.
[28]Then Samson prayed to the
LORD, "O Sovereign LORD,
remember me. O God, please
strengthen me just once more,
and let me with one blow get
revenge on the Philistines for
my two eyes." [29]Then Samson
reached toward the two cen-
tral pillars on which the temple stood. Bracing himself
against them, his right hand
on the one and his left hand
on the other, [30]Samson said,
"Let me die with the Philistines!" Then he pushed with
all his might, and down came
the temple on the rulers and all
the people in it. Thus he killed
many more when he died
than while he lived.
[31]Then his brothers and his
father's whole family went
down to get him. They
brought him back and buried
him between Zorah and Eshtaol in the tomb of Manoah
his father. He had led[a] Israel

[a]31 Traditionally *judged*

°25 ק׳ האסורים
°26 ק׳ והמשני

עֶשְׂרִים שָׁנָה׃ וַיְהִי־ אִישׁ מֵהַר־ אֶפְרָיִם וּשְׁמוֹ
and-name-of-him Ephraim from-hill-country-of man now-he-was (17:1) year twenty

מִיכָיְהוּ׃ וַיֹּאמֶר לְאִמּוֹ אֶלֶף וּמֵאָה הַכֶּסֶף
the-silver and-hundred thousand to-mother-of-him and-he-said (2) Micah

אֲשֶׁר לֻקַּח־ לָךְ וְאַתְּי אָלִית וְגַם אָמַרְתְּ
you-spoke and-also you-uttered-curse and-you from-you he-was-taken that

בְּאָזְנַי הִנֵּה־ הַכֶּסֶף אִתִּי אֲנִי לְקַחְתִּיו וַתֹּאמֶר אִמּוֹ
mother-of-him then-she-said I-took-him I with-me the-silver see! in-ears-of-me

בָּרוּךְ בְּנִי לַיהוָה׃ וַיָּשֶׁב אֶת־ אֶלֶף־
thousand *** when-he-returned (3) by-Yahweh son-of-me being-blessed

וּמֵאָה הַכֶּסֶף לְאִמּוֹ וַתֹּאמֶר אִמּוֹ
mother-of-him then-she-said to-mother-of-him the-silver and-hundred

הַקְדֵּשׁ הִקְדַּשְׁתִּי אֶת־ הַכֶּסֶף לַיהוָה מִיָּדִי
from-hand-of-me to-Yahweh the-silver *** I-consecrate to-consecrate

לִבְנִי לַעֲשׂוֹת פֶּסֶל וּמַסֵּכָה וְעַתָּה אֲשִׁיבֶנּוּ
I-will-give-back-him and-now and-cast-idol carved-image to-make for-son-of-me

לָךְ׃ וַיָּשֶׁב אֶת־ הַכֶּסֶף לְאִמּוֹ וַתִּקַּח
and-she-took to-mother-of-him the-silver *** so-he-returned (4) to-you

אִמּוֹ מָאתַיִם כֶּסֶף וַתִּתְּנֵהוּ לַצּוֹרֵף
to-the-one-being-silversmith and-she-gave-him silver two-hundreds mother-of-him

וַיַּעֲשֵׂהוּ פֶּסֶל וּמַסֵּכָה וַיְהִי בְּבֵית מִיכָיְהוּ׃ וְהָאִישׁ
now-the-man (5) Micah in-house-of and-he-was and-idol image and-he-made-him

מִיכָה לוֹ בֵּית אֱלֹהִים וַיַּעַשׂ אֵפוֹד וּתְרָפִים וַיְמַלֵּא אֶת־
*** and-he-installed and-idols ephod and-he-made gods shrine-of to-him Micah

יַד אַחַד מִבָּנָיו וַיְהִי־ לוֹ לְכֹהֵן׃ בַּיָּמִים
in-the-days (6) as-priest for-him and-he-was from-sons-of-him one hand-of

הָהֵם אֵין מֶלֶךְ בְּיִשְׂרָאֵל אִישׁ הַיָּשָׁר בְּעֵינָיו יַעֲשֶׂה׃
he-did in-eyes-of-him the-thing-fit everyone in-Israel king not the-those

וַיְהִי־ נַעַר מִבֵּית לֶחֶם יְהוּדָה מִמִּשְׁפַּחַת יְהוּדָה וְהוּא
and-he Judah from-clan-of Judah Lehem-of from-Beth young-man and-he-was (7)

לֵוִי וְהוּא גָר־ שָׁם׃ וַיֵּלֶךְ הָאִישׁ מֵהָעִיר מִבֵּית
from-Beth from-the-town the-man and-he-left (8) there he-lived but-he Levite

לֶחֶם יְהוּדָה לָגוּר בַּאֲשֶׁר יִמְצָא וַיָּבֹא הַר־
hill-country-of and-he-came he-would-find in-where to-stay Judah Lehem-of

אֶפְרַיִם עַד־ בֵּית מִיכָה לַעֲשׂוֹת דַּרְכּוֹ׃ וַיֹּאמֶר־ לוֹ
to-him and-he-asked (9) way-of-him to-carry-on Micah house-of to Ephraim

מִיכָה מֵאַיִן תָּבוֹא וַיֹּאמֶר אֵלָיו לֵוִי אָנֹכִי מִבֵּית לֶחֶם
Lehem-of from-Beth I Levite to-him and-he-said you-come from-where? Micah

°2 ק ואת

twenty years.

Micah's Idols

17 Now a man named
Micah from the hill
country of Ephraim 2said to
his mother, "The eleven hundred shekels[b] of silver that
were taken from you and
about which I heard you utter
a curse—I have that silver with
me; I took it."
Then his mother said, "The
LORD bless you, my son!"
3When he returned the elev-
en hundred shekels of silver to
his mother, she said, "I solemnly consecrate my silver to
the LORD for my son to make a
carved image and a cast idol. I
will give it back to you."
4So he returned the silver to
his mother, and she took two
hundred shekels[c] of silver and
gave them to a silversmith,
who made them into the image and the idol. And they
were put in Micah's house.
5Now this man Micah had a
shrine, and he made an ephod
and some idols and installed
one of his sons as his priest.
6In those days Israel had no
king; everyone did as he saw
fit.
7A young Levite from Bethlehem in Judah, who had been
living within the clan of
Judah, 8left that town in search
of some other place to stay. On
his way[d] he came to Micah's
house in the hill country of
Ephraim.
9Micah asked him, "Where
are you from?"
"I'm a Levite from Beth-
lehem in Judah," he said,

[b]2 That is, about 28 pounds (about 13 kilograms)
[c]4 That is, about 5 pounds (about 2.3 kilograms)
[d]8 Or *To carry on his profession*

יְהוּדָה וְאָנֹכִי הֹלֵךְ לָגוּר בַּאֲשֶׁר אֶמְצָא׃ וַיֹּאמֶר לוֹ מִיכָה
Micah to-him then-he-said (10) I-find at-where to-stay going and-I Judah

שְׁבָה עִמָּדִי וֶהְיֵה־ לִי לְאָב וּלְכֹהֵן וְאָנֹכִי אֶתֶּן־
I-will-give and-I and-as-priest as-father for-me and-be! with-me live!

לְךָ עֲשֶׂרֶת כֶּסֶף לַיָּמִים וְעֵרֶךְ בְּגָדִים וּמִחְיָתֶךָ
and-food-of-you clothes and-set-of for-the-days silver ten-of to-you

וַיֵּלֶךְ הַלֵּוִי׃ וַיּוֹאֶל הַלֵּוִי לָשֶׁבֶת אֶת־ הָאִישׁ
the-man with to-live the-Levite so-he-agreed (11) the-Levite and-he-came

וַיְהִי הַנַּעַר לוֹ כְּאַחַד מִבָּנָיו׃ וַיְמַלֵּא
then-he-installed (12) of-sons-of-him like-one to-him the-young-man and-he-was

מִיכָה אֶת־ יַד הַלֵּוִי וַיְהִי־ לוֹ הַנַּעַר לְכֹהֵן
as-priest the-young-man for-him and-he-became the-Levite hand-of *** Micah

וַיְהִי בְּבֵית מִיכָה׃ וַיֹּאמֶר מִיכָה עַתָּה יָדַעְתִּי כִּי־
that I-know now Micah and-he-said (13) Micah in-house-of and-he-lived

יֵיטִיב יְהוָה לִי כִּי הָיָה־ לִי הַלֵּוִי לְכֹהֵן׃
as-priest the-Levite for-me he-became since to-me Yahweh he-will-be-good

בַּיָּמִים הָהֵם אֵין מֶלֶךְ בְּיִשְׂרָאֵל וּבַיָּמִים הָהֵם
the-those and-in-the-days in-Israel king not the-those in-the-days (18:1)

שֵׁבֶט הַדָּנִי מְבַקֶּשׁ־ לוֹ נַחֲלָה לָשֶׁבֶת כִּי לֹא־ נָפְלָה
she-came not because to-settle place for-him seeking the-Danite tribe-of

לּוֹ עַד־ הַיּוֹם הַהוּא בְּתוֹךְ־ שִׁבְטֵי יִשְׂרָאֵל בְּנַחֲלָה׃
for-inheritance Israel tribes-of in-among the-that the-day to for-him

וַיִּשְׁלְחוּ בְנֵי־ דָן ׀ מִמִּשְׁפַּחְתָּם חֲמִשָּׁה אֲנָשִׁים מִקְצוֹתָם
from-all-of-them men five from-clan-of-them Dan sons-of so-they-sent (2)

אֲנָשִׁים בְּנֵי־ חַיִל מִצָּרְעָה וּמֵאֶשְׁתָּאֹל לְרַגֵּל אֶת־ הָאָרֶץ
the-land *** to-spy-out and-from-Eshtaol from-Zorah war men-of men

וּלְחָקְרָהּ וַיֹּאמְרוּ אֲלֵהֶם לְכוּ חִקְרוּ אֶת־ הָאָרֶץ
the-land *** explore! go! to-them and-they-told and-to-explore-her

וַיָּבֹאוּ הַר־ אֶפְרַיִם עַד־ בֵּית מִיכָה וַיָּלִינוּ
and-they-spent-night Micah house-of to Ephraim hill-country-of and-they-entered

שָׁם׃ הֵמָּה עִם־ בֵּית מִיכָה וְהֵמָּה הִכִּירוּ אֶת־ קוֹל
voice-of *** they-recognized and-they Micah house-of near they (3) there

הַנַּעַר הַלֵּוִי וַיָּסוּרוּ שָׁם וַיֹּאמְרוּ לוֹ מִי־
who? to-him and-they-asked there so-they-turned-in the-Levite the-young-man

הֱבִיאֲךָ הֲלֹם וּמָה־ אַתָּה עֹשֶׂה בָּזֶה וּמַה־ לְּךָ פֹה׃
here to-you and-why? in-this doing you and-what? here he-brought-you

וַיֹּאמֶר אֲלֵהֶם כָּזֹה וְכָזֶה עָשָׂה לִי מִיכָה
Micah for-me he-did and-as-that as-this to-them and-he-told (4)

"and I'm looking for a place to stay."
[10]Then Micah said to him, "Live with me and be my father and priest, and I'll give you ten shekels[e] of silver a year, your clothes and your
food." [11]So the Levite agreed to live with him, and the young man was to him like one of his
sons. [12]Then Micah installed the Levite, and the young man became his priest and lived in
his house. [13]And Micah said, "Now I know that the LORD will be good to me, since this Levite has become my priest."

Danites Settle in Laish

18 In those days Israel had no king.

And in those days the tribe of the Danites was seeking a place of their own where they might settle, because they had not yet come into an inheritance among the tribes of Israel. [2]So the Danites sent five warriors from Zorah and Eshtaol to spy out the land and explore it. These men represented all their clans. They told them, "Go, explore the land."

The men entered the hill country of Ephraim and came to the house of Micah, where
they spent the night. [3]When they were near Micah's house, they recognized the voice of the young Levite; so they turned in there and asked him, "Who brought you here? What are you doing in this place? Why are you here?"
[4]He told them what Micah had done for him, and said,

[e]10 That is, about 4 ounces (about 110 grams)

וַיִּשְׂכְּרֵנִי וָאֱהִי־ לוֹ לְכֹהֵן׃ וַיֹּאמְרוּ לוֹ שְׁאַל־
inquire! to-him then-they-said (5) as-priest for-him and-I-am and-he-hired-me

נָא בֵאלֹהִים וְנֵדְעָה הֲתַצְלִיחַ דַּרְכֵּנוּ אֲשֶׁר אֲנַחְנוּ
we that journey-of-us whether-she-will-succeed so-we-may-learn of-God now!

הֹלְכִים עָלֶיהָ׃ וַיֹּאמֶר לָהֶם הַכֹּהֵן לְכוּ לְשָׁלוֹם נֹכַח
approved-of in-peace go! the-priest to-them and-he-answered (6) on-her ones-going

יְהוָה דַּרְכְּכֶם אֲשֶׁר תֵּלְכוּ־ בָהּ׃ וַיֵּלְכוּ חֲמֵשֶׁת הָאֲנָשִׁים
the-men five-of so-they-left (7) on-her you-go that journey-of-you Yahweh

וַיָּבֹאוּ לָיְשָׁה וַיִּרְאוּ אֶת־ הָעָם אֲשֶׁר־ בְּקִרְבָּהּ
in-midst-of-her who the-people *** and-they-saw to-Laish and-they-came

יוֹשֶׁבֶת־ לָבֶטַח כְּמִשְׁפַּט צִדֹנִים שֹׁקֵט ׀ וּבֹטֵחַ
and-being-secure unsuspecting Sidonians like-custom-of in-safety living

וְאֵין־ מַכְלִים דָּבָר בָּאָרֶץ יוֹרֵשׁ עֶצֶר וּרְחֹקִים
and-ones-distant prosperity possessing in-the-land thing lacking since-not

הֵמָּה מִצִּדֹנִים וְדָבָר אֵין־ לָהֶם עִם־ אָדָם׃ וַיָּבֹאוּ
and-they-returned (8) anyone with to-them not and-relationship from-Sidonians they

אֶל־ אֲחֵיהֶם צָרְעָה וְאֶשְׁתָּאֹל וַיֹּאמְרוּ לָהֶם אֲחֵיהֶם
brothers-of-them to-them and-they-asked and-Eshtaol Zorah brothers-of-them to

מָה אַתֶּם׃ וַיֹּאמְרוּ קוּמָה וְנַעֲלֶה עֲלֵיהֶם כִּי רָאִינוּ
we-saw for against-them and-let-us-attack come! and-they-answered (9) you how?

אֶת־ הָאָרֶץ וְהִנֵּה טוֹבָה מְאֹד וְאַתֶּם מַחְשִׁים אַל־ תֵּעָצְלוּ
you-hesitate not ones-doing-nothing but-you very good and-see! the-land ***

לָלֶכֶת לָבֹא לָרֶשֶׁת אֶת־ הָאָרֶץ׃ כְּבֹאֲכֶם תָּבֹאוּ ׀
you-will-come when-to-arrive-you (10) the-land *** to-take-over to-enter to-go

אֶל־ עַם בֹּטֵחַ וְהָאָרֶץ רַחֲבַת יָדַיִם כִּי־ נְתָנָהּ
he-put-her that measures spacious-of and-the-land unsuspecting people to

אֱלֹהִים בְּיֶדְכֶם מְקוֹם אֲשֶׁר אֵין־ שָׁם מַחְסוֹר כָּל־ דָּבָר אֲשֶׁר בָּאָרֶץ׃
in-the-land that thing any-of lack there not that place into-hand-of-you God

וַיִּסְעוּ מִשָּׁם מִמִּשְׁפַּחַת הַדָּנִי מִצָּרְעָה
from-Zorah the-Danite from-clan-of from-there then-they-set-out (11)

וּמֵאֶשְׁתָּאֹל שֵׁשׁ־ מֵאוֹת אִישׁ חָגוּר כְּלֵי מִלְחָמָה׃
battle things-of being-armed man hundreds six and-from-Eshtaol

וַיַּעֲלוּ וַיַּחֲנוּ בְּקִרְיַת יְעָרִים בִּיהוּדָה עַל־ כֵּן
this for in-Judah Jearim near-Kiriath and-they-camped and-they-went (12)

קָרְאוּ לַמָּקוֹם הַהוּא מַחֲנֵה־ דָן עַד הַיּוֹם הַזֶּה הִנֵּה
see! the-this the-day to Dan Mahaneh the-that to-the-place they-called

אַחֲרֵי קִרְיַת יְעָרִים׃ וַיַּעַבְרוּ מִשָּׁם הַר־ אֶפְרָיִם
Ephraim hill-country-of from-there and-they-went (13) Jearim Kiriath west-of

"He has hired me and I am his priest."

5Then they said to him, "Please inquire of God to learn whether our journey will be successful."

6The priest answered them, "Go in peace. Your journey has the LORD's approval."

7So the five men left and came to Laish, where they saw that the people were living in safety, like the Sidonians, unsuspecting and secure. And since their land lacked nothing, they were prosperous.[f] Also, they lived a long way from the Sidonians and had no relationship with anyone else.[g]

8When they returned to Zorah and Eshtaol, their brothers asked them, "How did you find things?"

9They answered, "Come on, let's attack them! We have seen that the land is very good. Aren't you going to do something? Don't hesitate to go there and take it over.
10When you get there, you will find an unsuspecting people and a spacious land that God has put into your hands, a land that lacks nothing whatever."

11Then six hundred men from the clan of the Danites, armed for battle, set out from Zorah and Eshtaol. 12On their way they set up camp near Kiriath Jearim in Judah. This is why the place west of Kiriath Jearim is called Mahaneh Dan[h] to this day. 13From there they went on to the hill country of Ephraim and came

[f]7 The meaning of the Hebrew for this clause is uncertain.
[g]7 Hebrew; some Septuagint manuscripts *with the Arameans*
[h]12 *Mahaneh Dan* means *Dan's camp.*

וַיָּבֹאוּ עַד־ בֵּית מִיכָה׃ וַיַּעֲנוּ חֲמֵשֶׁת הָאֲנָשִׁים
the-men five-of then-they-said (14) Micah house-of to and-they-came

הַהֹלְכִים לְרַגֵּל אֶת־ הָאָרֶץ לַיִשׁ וַיֹּאמְרוּ אֶל־ אֲחֵיהֶם
brothers-of-them to and-they-said Laish the-land *** to-spy-out the-ones-going

הֲיְדַעְתֶּם כִּי יֵשׁ בַּבָּתִּים הָאֵלֶּה אֵפוֹד וּתְרָפִים
and-idols ephod the-these in-the-houses there-is that you-know?

וּפֶסֶל וּמַסֵּכָה וְעַתָּה דְּעוּ מַה־ תַּעֲשׂוּ׃
you-must-do what you-know and-now and-cast-idol and-carved-image

וַיָּסוּרוּ שָׁמָּה וַיָּבֹאוּ אֶל־ בֵּית־ הַנַּעַר
the-young-man house-of to and-they-went to-there so-they-turned-in (15)

הַלֵּוִי בֵּית מִיכָה וַיִּשְׁאֲלוּ־ לוֹ לְשָׁלוֹם׃ וְשֵׁשׁ־
and-six (16) for-peace to-him and-they-greeted Micah place-of the-Levite

מֵאוֹת אִישׁ חֲגוּרִים כְּלֵי מִלְחַמְתָּם נִצָּבִים
ones-standing battle-of-them things-of ones-being-armed man hundreds

פֶּתַח הַשָּׁעַר אֲשֶׁר מִבְּנֵי־ דָן׃ וַיַּעֲלוּ חֲמֵשֶׁת הָאֲנָשִׁים
the-men five-of and-they-went (17) Dan from-sons-of who the-gate entrance-of

הַהֹלְכִים לְרַגֵּל אֶת־ הָאָרֶץ בָּאוּ שָׁמָּה לָקְחוּ
they-took into-there they-entered the-land *** to-spy-out the-ones-going

אֶת־ הַפֶּסֶל וְאֶת־ הָאֵפוֹד וְאֶת־ הַתְּרָפִים וְאֶת־ הַמַּסֵּכָה
the-cast-idol and the-household-gods and the-ephod and the-carved-image ***

וְהַכֹּהֵן נִצָּב פֶּתַח הַשַּׁעַר וְשֵׁשׁ־ מֵאוֹת הָאִישׁ
the-man hundreds and-six the-gate entrance-of standing and-the-priest

הֶחָגוּר כְּלֵי הַמִּלְחָמָה׃ וְאֵלֶּה בָּאוּ בֵּית
house-of they-entered when-these (18) the-battle things-of the-one-being-armed

מִיכָה וַיִּקְחוּ אֶת־ פֶּסֶל הָאֵפוֹד וְאֶת־ הַתְּרָפִים
the-household-gods and the-ephod carved-image *** then-they-took Micah

וְאֶת־ הַמַּסֵּכָה וַיֹּאמֶר אֲלֵיהֶם הַכֹּהֵן מָה אַתֶּם עֹשִׂים׃
ones-doing you what? the-priest to-them and-he-said the-cast-idol and

וַיֹּאמְרוּ לוֹ הַחֲרֵשׁ שִׂים־ יָדְךָ עַל־ פִּיךָ
mouth-of-you over hand-of-you put! be-quiet! to-him and-they-answered (19)

וְלֵךְ עִמָּנוּ וֶהְיֵה־ לָנוּ לְאָב וּלְכֹהֵן הֲטוֹב ׀ הֱיוֹתְךָ
to-be-you better? and-as-priest as-father for-us and-be! with-us and-come!

כֹהֵן לְבֵית אִישׁ אֶחָד אוֹ הֱיוֹתְךָ כֹהֵן לְשֵׁבֶט וּלְמִשְׁפָּחָה
and-for-clan for-tribe priest to-be-you or one man for-household-of priest

בְּיִשְׂרָאֵל׃ וַיִּיטַב לֵב הַכֹּהֵן וַיִּקַּח אֶת־ הָאֵפוֹד
the-ephod *** and-he-took the-priest heart-of then-he-was-glad (20) in-Israel

וְאֶת־ הַתְּרָפִים הַפָּסֶל וַיָּבֹא בְּקֶרֶב הָעָם׃ וַיִּפְנוּ
the-people in-among and-he-went the-carved-image and the-household-gods and

to Micah's house.
[14]Then the five men who
had spied out the land of Laish
said to their brothers, "Do you
know that one of these houses
has an ephod, other
household gods, a carved image and a cast idol? Now you
know what to do." [15]So they
turned in there and went to
the house of the young Levite
at Micah's place and greeted
him. [16]The six hundred Danites, armed for battle, stood at
the entrance to the gate. [17]The
five men who had spied out
the land went inside and took
the carved image, the ephod,
the other household gods and
the cast idol while the priest
and the six hundred armed
men stood at the entrance to
the gate.
[18]When these men went into
Micah's house and took the
carved image, the ephod, the
other household gods and the
cast idol, the priest said to
them, "What are you doing?"
[19]They answered him, "Be
quiet! Don't say a word. Come
with us, and be our father and
priest. Isn't it better that you
serve a tribe and clan in Israel
as priest rather than just one
man's household?" [20]Then the
priest was glad. He took the
ephod, the other household
gods and the carved image
and went along with the

וַיִּפְנוּ וַיֵּלֵכוּ וַיָּשִׂימוּ אֶת־ הַטַּף וְאֶת־
and the-little-child *** and-they-put and-they-left and-they-turned (21)

הַמִּקְנֶה וְאֶת־ הַכְּבוּדָּה לִפְנֵיהֶם׃ הֵמָּה הִרְחִיקוּ
they-went-distance they (22) in-front-of-them the-possession and the-livestock

מִבֵּית מִיכָה וְהָאֲנָשִׁים אֲשֶׁר בַּבָּתִּים אֲשֶׁר עִם־ בֵּית מִיכָה
Micah house-of near that in-the-houses who and-the-men Micah from-house-of

נִזְעֲקוּ וַיַּדְבִּיקוּ אֶת־ בְּנֵי־ דָן׃ וַיִּקְרְאוּ
and-they-shouted (23) Dan sons-of *** and-they-overtook they-were-called-together

אֶל־ בְּנֵי־ דָן וַיַּסֵּבּוּ פְּנֵיהֶם וַיֹּאמְרוּ לְמִיכָה מַה־
what? to-Micah and-they-said faces-of-them and-they-turned Dan sons-of after

לְּךָ כִּי נִזְעָקְתָּ׃ וַיֹּאמֶר אֶת־ אֱלֹהַי אֲשֶׁר־ עָשִׂיתִי
I-made that gods-of-me *** and-he-replied (24) you-called-out that to-you

לְקַחְתֶּם וְאֶת־ הַכֹּהֵן וַתֵּלְכוּ וּמַה־ לִּי עוֹד וּמַה־ זֶּה
this now-how? else to-me so-what? and-you-went-away the-priest and you-took

תֹּאמְרוּ אֵלַי מַה־ לָּךְ׃ וַיֹּאמְרוּ אֵלָיו בְּנֵי־ דָן אַל־
not Dan sons-of to-him and-they-answered (25) to-you what? of-me you-ask

תַּשְׁמַע קוֹלְךָ עִמָּנוּ פֶּן־ יִפְגְּעוּ בָכֶם אֲנָשִׁים
men against-you they-will-attack or with-us voice-of-you you-make-heard

מָרֵי נֶפֶשׁ וְאָסַפְתָּה נַפְשְׁךָ וְנֶפֶשׁ בֵּיתֶךָ׃
family-of-you and-life-of life-of-you and-you-will-lose temper ones-hot-of

וַיֵּלְכוּ בְנֵי־ דָן לְדַרְכָּם וַיַּרְא מִיכָה כִּי־
that Micah and-he-saw on-way-of-them Dan sons-of so-they-went (26)

חֲזָקִים הֵמָּה מִמֶּנּוּ וַיִּפֶן וַיָּשָׁב אֶל־ בֵּיתוֹ׃
home-of-him to and-he-went-back so-he-turned than-him they stronger-ones

וְהֵמָּה לָקְחוּ אֵת אֲשֶׁר־ עָשָׂה מִיכָה וְאֶת־ הַכֹּהֵן אֲשֶׁר הָיָה־
he-was who the-priest and Micah he-made what *** they-took then-they (27)

לוֹ וַיָּבֹאוּ עַל־ לַיִשׁ עַל־ עַם שֹׁקֵט וּבֹטֵחַ
and-unsuspecting being-peaceful people against Laish to and-they-went for-him

וַיַּכּוּ אוֹתָם לְפִי־ חָרֶב וְאֶת־ הָעִיר שָׂרְפוּ בָאֵשׁ׃
with-fire they-burned the-city and sword with-edge-of them and-they-attacked

וְאֵין מַצִּיל כִּי רְחוֹקָה־ הִיא מִצִּידוֹן וְדָבָר אֵין־
not and-relationship from-Sidon she long-way for one-rescuing and-not (28)

לָהֶם עִם־ אָדָם וְהִיא בְּעֵמֶק אֲשֶׁר לְבֵית־ רְחוֹב וַיִּבְנוּ
and-they-rebuilt Rehob near-Beth that in-the-valley now-she anyone with to-them

אֶת־ הָעִיר וַיֵּשְׁבוּ בָהּ׃ וַיִּקְרְאוּ שֵׁם־ הָעִיר
the-city name-of and-they-called (29) in-her and-they-settled the-city ***

דָּן בְּשֵׁם דָּן אֲבִיהֶם אֲשֶׁר יוּלַּד לְיִשְׂרָאֵל וְאוּלָם
even-though to-Israel he-was-born who forefather-of-them Dan after-name-of Dan

people. 21 Putting their little
children, their livestock and
their possessions in front of
them, they turned away and
left.
22 When they had gone some
distance from Micah's house,
the men who lived near Micah
were called together and overtook the Danites. 23 As they
shouted after them, the Danites turned and said to Micah,
"What's the matter with you
that you called out your men
to fight?"
24 He replied, "You took the
gods I made, and my priest,
and went away. What else do
I have? How can you ask,
'What's the matter with
you?' "
25 The Danites answered,
"Don't argue with us, or some
hot-tempered men will attack
you, and you and your family
will lose your lives." 26 So the
Danites went their way, and
Micah, seeing that they were
too strong for him, turned
around and went back home.
27 Then they took what
Micah had made, and his
priest, and went on to Laish,
against a peaceful and unsuspecting people. They attacked
them with the sword and
burned down their city.
28 There was no one to rescue
them because they lived a long
way from Sidon and had no
relationship with anyone else.
The city was in a valley near
Beth Rehob.
The Danites rebuilt the city
and settled there. 29 They
named it Dan after their
forefather Dan, who was born

לַיִשׁ שֵׁם־ הָעִיר לָרִאשֹׁנָה׃ וַיָּקִימוּ לָהֶם בְּנֵי־
sons-of for-them and-they-set-up (30) before the-city name-of Laish

דָן אֶת־ הַפָּסֶל וִיהוֹנָתָן בֶּן־ גֵּרְשֹׁם בֶּן־ מְנַשֶּׁה הוּא וּבָנָיו
and-sons-of-him he *Moses son-of Gershom son-of and-Jonathan the-idol *** Dan

הָיוּ כֹהֲנִים לְשֵׁבֶט הַדָּנִי עַד־ יוֹם גְּלוֹת הָאָרֶץ׃
the-land to-be-captured day to the-Danite for-tribe-of priests they-were

וַיָּשִׂימוּ לָהֶם אֶת־ פֶּסֶל מִיכָה אֲשֶׁר עָשָׂה כָּל־ יְמֵי
days-of all-of he-made that Micah idol-of *** for-them and-they-set-up (31)

הֱיוֹת בֵּית־ הָאֱלֹהִים בְּשִׁלֹה׃ וַיְהִי בַּיָּמִים הָהֵם
the-those in-the-days and-he-was (19:1) in-Shiloh the-God house-of to-be

וּמֶלֶךְ אֵין בְּיִשְׂרָאֵל וַיְהִי ׀ אִישׁ לֵוִי גָּר בְּיַרְכְּתֵי
in-remote-areas-of living Levite man now-he-was in-Israel he-was-not that-king

הַר־ אֶפְרַיִם וַיִּקַּח־ לוֹ אִשָּׁה פִילֶגֶשׁ מִבֵּית
from-Beth concubine woman for-him and-he-took Ephraim hill-country-of

לֶחֶם יְהוּדָה׃ וַתִּזְנֶה עָלָיו פִּילַגְשׁוֹ וַתֵּלֶךְ
and-she-left concubine-of-him to-him but-she-was-unfaithful (2) Judah Lehem-of

מֵאִתּוֹ אֶל־ בֵּית אָבִיהָ אֶל־ בֵּית לֶחֶם יְהוּדָה וַתְּהִי־
and-she-was Judah Lehem-of Beth to father-of-her house-of to from-with-him

שָׁם יָמִים אַרְבָּעָה חֳדָשִׁים׃ וַיָּקָם אִישָׁהּ וַיֵּלֶךְ אַחֲרֶיהָ
after-her and-he-went husband-of-her then-he-rose (3) months four days there

לְדַבֵּר עַל־ לִבָּהּ לַהֲשִׁיבוֹ° וְנַעֲרוֹ עִמּוֹ וְצֶמֶד
and-two-of with-him and-servant-of-him to-return-her heart-of-her to to-speak

חֲמֹרִים וַתְּבִיאֵהוּ בֵּית אָבִיהָ וַיִּרְאֵהוּ אֲבִי
father-of when-he-saw-him father-of-her house-of and-she-took-him donkeys

הַנַּעֲרָה וַיִּשְׂמַח לִקְרָאתוֹ׃ וַיֶּחֱזַק־† בּוֹ
upon-him and-he-prevailed (4) to-welcome-him then-he-was-glad the-girl

חֹתְנוֹ אֲבִי הַנַּעֲרָה וַיֵּשֶׁב אִתּוֹ שְׁלֹשֶׁת
three-of with-him so-he-remained the-girl father-of father-in-law-of-him

יָמִים וַיֹּאכְלוּ וַיִּשְׁתּוּ וַיָּלִינוּ שָׁם׃ וַיְהִי
and-he-was (5) there and-they-slept and-they-drank and-they-ate days

בַּיּוֹם הָרְבִיעִי וַיַּשְׁכִּימוּ בַבֹּקֶר וַיָּקָם לָלֶכֶת
to-leave and-he-prepared in-the-morning that-they-got-up the-fourth on-the-day

וַיֹּאמֶר אֲבִי הַנַּעֲרָה אֶל־ חֲתָנוֹ סְעָד לִבְּךָ
heart-of-you refresh! son-in-law-of-him to the-girl father-of but-he-said

פַּת־ לֶחֶם וְאַחַר תֵּלֵכוּ׃ וַיֵּשְׁבוּ וַיֹּאכְלוּ שְׁנֵיהֶם
two-of-them and-they-ate so-they-sat (6) you-can-go and-then food piece-of

יַחְדָּו וַיִּשְׁתּוּ וַיֹּאמֶר אֲבִי הַנַּעֲרָה אֶל־ הָאִישׁ הוֹאֶל־
be-pleased! the-man to the-girl father-of then-he-said and-they-drank together

to Israel—though the city used to be called Laish. [30]There the Danites set up for themselves the idols, and Jonathan son of Gershom, the son of Moses,[i] and his sons were priests for the tribe of Dan until the time of the captivity of the land. [31]They continued to use the idols Micah had made, all the time the house of God was in Shiloh.

A Levite and His Concubine

19 In those days Israel had no king.

Now a Levite who lived in a remote area in the hill country of Ephraim took a concubine from Bethlehem in Judah. [2]But she was unfaithful to him. She left him and went back to her father's house in Bethlehem, Judah. After she had been there four months, [3]her husband went to her to persuade her to return. He had with him his servant and two donkeys. She took him into her father's house, and when her father saw him, he gladly welcomed him. [4]His father-in-law, the girl's father, prevailed upon him to stay; so he remained with him three days, eating and drinking, and sleeping there.

[5]On the fourth day they got up early and he prepared to leave, but the girl's father said to his son-in-law, "Refresh yourself with something to eat; then you can go." [6]So the two of them sat down to eat and drink together. Afterward the girl's father said, "Please

[i]30 An ancient scribal tradition, some Septuagint manuscripts and Vulgate; Masoretic Text *Manasseh*

*30 The "suspended nun" appears to have been an ancient scribal insertion to alter the name *Moses* to *Manasseh* (see Ginsburg, pp. 335ff).

†4 Most mss point this verb as a *Hiphil* (וַיַּחְזֵק) rather than a *Qal*.

°3 ק להשיבה

נָא וְלִין וְיִטַב לִבֶּךָ׃ וַיָּקָם הָאִישׁ

the-man when-he-got-up (7) heart-of-you and-let-him-enjoy and-stay! now!

לָלֶכֶת וַיִּפְצַר־ בּוֹ חֹתְנוֹ וַיֵּשֶׁב

so-he-stayed father-in-law-of-him over-him then-he-persuaded to-go

וַיָּלֶן שָׁם׃ וַיַּשְׁכֵּם בַּבֹּקֶר בַּיּוֹם הַחֲמִישִׁי

the-fifth of-the-day on-the-morning when-he-rose (8) there and-he-spent-night

לָלֶכֶת וַיֹּאמֶר ׀ אֲבִי הַנַּעֲרָה סְעָד־ נָא לְבָבְךָ וְהִתְמַהְמְהוּ

and-wait! heart-of-you now! refresh! the-girl father-of then-he-said to-go

עַד־ נְטוֹת הַיּוֹם וַיֹּאכְלוּ שְׁנֵיהֶם׃ וַיָּקָם

when-he-got-up (9) two-of-them so-they-ate the-day to-stretch-out till

הָאִישׁ לָלֶכֶת הוּא וּפִילַגְשׁוֹ וְנַעֲרוֹ וַיֹּאמֶר לוֹ

to-him then-he-said and-servant-of-him and-concubine-of-him he to-go the-man

חֹתְנוֹ אֲבִי הַנַּעֲרָה הִנֵּה נָא רָפָה הַיּוֹם

the-day he-is-gone now! see! the-girl father-of father-in-law-of-him

לַעֲרֹב לִינוּ־ נָא הִנֵּה חֲנוֹת הַיּוֹם לִין פֹּה

here stay! the-day to-be-over see! now! spend-night! to-be-evening

וְיִיטַב לְבָבֶךָ וְהִשְׁכַּמְתֶּם מָחָר לְדַרְכְּכֶם

on-way-of-you tomorrow then-you-get-up heart-of-you and-let-him-enjoy

וְהָלַכְתָּ לְאֹהָלֶךָ׃ וְלֹא־ אָבָה הָאִישׁ לָלוּן

to-stay the-man he-was-willing but-not (10) to-tent-of-you and-you-can-go

וַיָּקָם וַיֵּלֶךְ וַיָּבֹא עַד־ נֹכַח יְבוּס הִיא יְרוּשָׁלָםִ

Jerusalem that Jebus direction-of toward and-he-went and-he-left so-he-got-up

וְעִמּוֹ צֶמֶד חֲמוֹרִים חֲבוּשִׁים וּפִילַגְשׁוֹ עִמּוֹ׃

with-him and-concubine-of-him ones-being-saddled donkeys two-of and-with-him

הֵם עִם־ יְבוּס וְהַיּוֹם רַד מְאֹד וַיֹּאמֶר הַנַּעַר

the-servant and-he-said almost he-was-gone and-the-day Jebus near they (11)

אֶל־ אֲדֹנָיו לְכָה־ נָּא וְנָסוּרָה אֶל־ עִיר־ הַיְבוּסִי

the-Jebusite city-of into and-let-us-go now! come! masters-of-him to

הַזֹּאת וְנָלִין בָּהּ׃ וַיֹּאמֶר אֵלָיו אֲדֹנָיו

masters-of-him to-him and-he-replied (12) in-her and-let-us-spend-night the-this

לֹא נָסוּר אֶל־ עִיר נָכְרִי אֲשֶׁר לֹא־ מִבְּנֵי יִשְׂרָאֵל הֵנָּה

they Israel from-sons-of not who alien city into we-will-go not

וְעָבַרְנוּ עַד־ גִּבְעָה׃ וַיֹּאמֶר לְנַעֲרוֹ לְךָ

come! to-servant-of-him and-he-said (13) Gibeah to so-we-will-go-on

וְנִקְרְבָה בְּאַחַד הַמְּקֹמוֹת וְלַנּוּ בַגִּבְעָה

in-the-Gibeah and-let-us-spend-night the-places to-one-of and-let-us-reach

אוֹ בָרָמָה׃ וַיַּעַבְרוּ וַיֵּלֵכוּ וַתָּבֹא לָהֶם

before-them and-she-set and-they-walked ʼ so-they-went (14) in-the-Ramah or

°13 ק לכה

stay tonight and enjoy yourself."
7And when the man got up to go, his father-in-law persuaded him, so he stayed there that night.
8On the morning of the fifth day, when he rose to go, the girl's father said, "Refresh yourself. Wait till afternoon!" So the two of them ate together.
9Then when the man, with his concubine and his servant, got up to leave, his father-in-law, the girl's father, said, "Now look, it's almost evening. Spend the night here; the day is nearly over. Stay and enjoy yourself. Early tomorrow morning you can get up and be on your way home."
10But, unwilling to stay another night, the man left and went toward Jebus (that is, Jerusalem), with his two saddled donkeys and his concubine.
11When they were near Jebus and the day was almost gone, the servant said to his master, "Come, let's stop at this city of the Jebusites and spend the night."
12His master replied, "No. We won't go into an alien city, whose people are not Israelites. We will go on to Gibeah."
13He added, "Come, let's try to reach Gibeah or Ramah and spend the night in one of those places."
14So they went

הַשֶּׁמֶשׁ אֵצֶל הַגִּבְעָה אֲשֶׁר לְבִנְיָמִן׃ וַיָּסֻרוּ שָׁם לָבוֹא

to-go there so-they-stopped (15) in-Benjamin that the-Gibeah near the-sun

לָלוּן בַּגִּבְעָה וַיָּבֹא וַיֵּשֶׁב בִּרְחוֹב הָעִיר

the-city in-square-of and-he-sat and-he-went in-the-Gibeah to-spend-night

וְאֵין אִישׁ מְאַסֵּף־אוֹתָם הַבַּיְתָה לָלוּן׃ וְהִנֵּה ׀ אִישׁ זָקֵן

old man then-see! (16) to-spend-night into-the-home them taking man but-no

בָּא מִן־ מַעֲשֵׂהוּ מִן־ הַשָּׂדֶה בָּעֶרֶב וְהָאִישׁ

now-the-man in-the-evening the-field from work-of-him from coming-in

מֵהַר אֶפְרַיִם וְהוּא־ גָר בַּגִּבְעָה וְאַנְשֵׁי הַמָּקוֹם

the-place now-men-of in-the-Gibeah he-lived and-he Ephraim from-hill-country-of

בְּנֵי יְמִינִי׃ וַיִּשָּׂא עֵינָיו וַיַּרְא אֶת־ הָאִישׁ

the-man *** and-he-saw eyes-of-him when-he-lifted (17) Benjamites

הָאֹרֵחַ בִּרְחֹב הָעִיר וַיֹּאמֶר הָאִישׁ הַזָּקֵן אָנָה תֵלֵךְ

you-go where? the-old the-man then-he-asked the-city in-square-of the-traveling

וּמֵאַיִן תָּבוֹא׃ וַיֹּאמֶר אֵלָיו עֹבְרִים אֲנַחְנוּ מִבֵּית־

from-Beth we ones-going to-him and-he-answered (18) you-come and-from-where?

לֶחֶם יְהוּדָה עַד־ יַרְכְּתֵי הַר־ אֶפְרַיִם מִשָּׁם אָנֹכִי

I from-there Ephraim hill-country-of remote-areas-of to Judah Lehem-of

וָאֵלֵךְ עַד־ בֵּית לֶחֶם יְהוּדָה וְאֶת־ בֵּית יְהוָה אֲנִי הֹלֵךְ וְאֵין

but-no going I Yahweh house-of and Judah Lehem-of Beth to and-I-went

אִישׁ מְאַסֵּף אוֹתִי הַבָּיְתָה׃ וְגַם־ תֶּבֶן גַּם־ מִסְפּוֹא יֵשׁ

there-is fodder also straw now-both (19) into-the-house me taking man

לַחֲמוֹרֵינוּ וְגַם לֶחֶם וָיַיִן יֶשׁ־ לִי וְלַאֲמָתֶךָ

and-for-maid-of-you for-me there-is and-wine bread and-also for-donkeys-of-us

וְלַנַּעַר עִם־ עֲבָדֶיךָ אֵין מַחְסוֹר כָּל־ דָּבָר׃

thing any-of need there-is-no servants-of-you with and-for-the-young-man

וַיֹּאמֶר הָאִישׁ הַזָּקֵן שָׁלוֹם לָךְ רַק כָּל־ מַחְסוֹרְךָ

need-of-you all-of only to-you welcome the-old the-man and-he-said (20)

עָלָי רַק בָּרְחוֹב אַל־ תָּלַן׃ וַיְבִיאֵהוּ

so-he-took-him (21) you-spend-night not in-the-square only with-me

לְבֵיתוֹ וַיָּבָול לַחֲמוֹרִים וַיִּרְחֲצוּ רַגְלֵיהֶם

feet-of-them and-they-washed for-donkeys and-he-fed into-house-of-him

וַיֹּאכְלוּ וַיִּשְׁתּוּ׃ הֵמָּה מֵיטִיבִים אֶת־ לִבָּם

heart-of-them *** ones-making-enjoy they (22) and-they-drank and-they-ate

וְהִנֵּה אַנְשֵׁי הָעִיר אַנְשֵׁי בְנֵי־ בְלִיַּעַל נָסַבּוּ אֶת־ הַבַּיִת

the-house *** they-surrounded wickedness sons-of men-of the-city men-of then-see!

מִתְדַּפְּקִים עַל־ הַדָּלֶת וַיֹּאמְרוּ אֶל־ הָאִישׁ בַּעַל הַבַּיִת

the-house owner-of the-man to and-they-shouted the-door on ones-pounding

°21 ק ויבל

on, and the sun set as they
neared Gibeah in Benjamin.
[15]There they stopped to spend
the night. They went and sat
in the city square, but no one
took them into his home for
the night.
[16]That evening an old man
from the hill country of
Ephraim, who was living in
Gibeah (the men of the place
were Benjamites), came in
from his work in the fields.
[17]When he looked and saw the
traveler in the city square, the
old man asked, "Where are
you going? Where did you
come from?"
[18]He answered, "We are on
our way from Bethlehem in
Judah to a remote area in the
hill country of Ephraim where
I live. I have been to Bethlehem in Judah and now I am
going to the house of the LORD.
No one has taken me into his
house. [19]We have both straw
and fodder for our donkeys
and bread and wine for ourselves your servants—me,
your maidservant, and the
young man with us. We don't
need anything."
[20]"You are welcome at my
house," the old man said. "Let
me supply whatever you need.
Only don't spend the night in
the square." [21]So he took him
into his house and fed his
donkeys. After they had
washed their feet, they had
something to eat and drink.
[22]While they were enjoying
themselves, some of the
wicked men of the city surrounded the house. Pounding
on the door, they shouted to
the old man who owned the

הַזָּקֵן לֵאמֹר הוֹצֵא אֶת־ הָאִישׁ אֲשֶׁר־ בָּא אֶל־ בֵּיתְךָ
house-of-you to he-came who the-man *** bring-out! to-say the-old

וְנֵדָעֶנּוּ׃ וַיֵּצֵא אֲלֵיהֶם הָאִישׁ בַּעַל
owner-of the-man to-them and-he-went-out (23) so-we-can-have-sex-with-him

הַבַּיִת וַיֹּאמֶר אֲלֵהֶם אַל־ אַחַי אַל־ תָּרֵעוּ נָא אַחֲרֵי
since now! you-be-vile not friends-of-me no to-them and-he-said the-house

אֲשֶׁר־ בָּא הָאִישׁ הַזֶּה אֶל־* בֵּיתִי אַל־ תַּעֲשׂוּ אֶת־ הַנְּבָלָה
the-disgrace *** you-do not house-of-me into the-this the-man he-came that

הַזֹּאת׃ הִנֵּה בִתִּי הַבְּתוּלָה וּפִילַגְשֵׁהוּ
and-concubine-of-him the-virgin daughter-of-me look! (24) the-this

אוֹצִיאָה־ נָּא אוֹתָם וְעַנּוּ אוֹתָם וַעֲשׂוּ לָהֶם הַטּוֹב
the-good to-them and-do! them and-use! them now! I-will-bring-out

בְּעֵינֵיכֶם וְלָאִישׁ הַזֶּה לֹא תַעֲשׂוּ דְּבַר הַנְּבָלָה
the-disgrace thing-of you-do not the-this but-to-the-man in-eyes-of-you

הַזֹּאת׃ וְלֹא־ אָבוּ הָאֲנָשִׁים לִשְׁמֹעַ לוֹ וַיַּחֲזֵק הָאִישׁ
the-man so-he-took to-him to-listen the-men they-wanted but-not (25) the-this

בְּפִילַגְשׁוֹ וַיֹּצֵא אֲלֵיהֶם הַחוּץ וַיֵּדְעוּ אוֹתָהּ
her and-they-raped the-outside to-them and-he-sent to-concubine-of-him

וַיִּתְעַלְּלוּ־ בָהּ כָּל־ הַלַּיְלָה עַד־ הַבֹּקֶר וַיְשַׁלְּחוּהָ
and-they-let-go-her the-morning to the-night all-of against-her and-they-abused

בַּעֲלוֹת° הַשָּׁחַר׃ וַתָּבֹא הָאִשָּׁה לִפְנוֹת הַבֹּקֶר
the-day to-break the-woman and-she-went-back (26) the-dawn when-to-come

וַתִּפֹּל פֶּתַח בֵּית־ הָאִישׁ אֲשֶׁר־ אֲדוֹנֶיהָ שָּׁם עַד־
until there masters-of-her where the-man house-of door-of and-she-fell

הָאוֹר׃ וַיָּקָם אֲדֹנֶיהָ בַּבֹּקֶר וַיִּפְתַּח
then-he-opened in-the-morning masters-of-her when-he-got-up (27) the-daylight

דַּלְתוֹת הַבַּיִת וַיֵּצֵא לָלֶכֶת לְדַרְכּוֹ וְהִנֵּה
and-see! on-way-of-him to-continue and-he-stepped-out the-house doors-of

הָאִשָּׁה פִילַגְשׁוֹ נֹפֶלֶת פֶּתַח הַבַּיִת וְיָדֶיהָ
and-hands-of-her the-house doorway-of having-fallen concubine-of-him the-woman

עַל־ הַסַּף׃ וַיֹּאמֶר אֵלֶיהָ קוּמִי וְנֵלֵכָה וְאֵין
but-not and-let-us-go get-up! to-her and-he-said (28) the-threshold on

עֹנֶה וַיִּקָּחֶהָ עַל־ הַחֲמוֹר וַיָּקָם הָאִישׁ וַיֵּלַךְ
and-he-went the-man and-he-set-out the-donkey on then-he-put-her answering

לִמְקֹמוֹ׃ וַיָּבֹא אֶל־ בֵּיתוֹ וַיִּקַּח אֶת־ הַמַּאֲכֶלֶת
the-knife *** then-he-took home-of-him to when-he-reached (29) to-home-of-him

וַיַּחֲזֵק בְּפִילַגְשׁוֹ וַיְנַתְּחֶהָ לַעֲצָמֶיהָ לִשְׁנֵים
into-two by-limbs-of-her and-he-cut-up-her onto-concubine-of-him and-he-held

house, "Bring out the man
who came to your house so we
can have sex with him."
23 The owner of the house
went outside and said to them,
"No, my friends, don't be so
vile. Since this man is my
guest, don't do this disgraceful
thing. 24 Look, here is my virgin daughter, and his concubine. I will bring them out to
you now, and you can use
them and do to them whatever
you wish. But to this man,
don't do such a disgraceful
thing."
25 But the men would not listen to him. So the man took
his concubine and sent her
outside to them, and they
raped her and abused her
throughout the night, and at
dawn they let her go. 26 At daybreak the woman went back to
the house where her master
was staying, fell down at the
door and lay there until daylight.
27 When her master got up in
the morning and opened the
door of the house and stepped
out to continue on his way,
there lay his concubine, fallen
in the doorway of the house,
with her hands on the threshold. 28 He said to her, "Get up;
let's go." But there was no answer. Then the man put her on
his donkey and set out for
home.
29 When he reached home, he
took a knife and cut up his
concubine, limb by limb, into

*23 Most mss have *segol* under the *aleph* (אֶל).

°25 ק כעלות

עָשָׂר נְתָחִים וַיְשַׁלְּחֶהָ בְּכֹל גְּבוּל יִשְׂרָאֵל׃ וְהָיָה
and-he-was (30) Israel area-of into-every-of and-he-sent-her parts ten

כָל־ הָרֹאֶה וְאָמַר לֹא־ נִהְיְתָה וְלֹא־ נִרְאֲתָה
she-was-seen and-not she-was not then-he-said the-one-seeing every-of

כָּזֹאת לְמִיּוֹם עֲלוֹת בְּנֵי־ יִשְׂרָאֵל מֵאֶרֶץ מִצְרַיִם עַד
to Egypt from-land-of Israel sons-of to-come-up on-since-day such-as-this

הַיּוֹם הַזֶּה שִׂימוּ־ לָכֶם עָלֶיהָ עֻצוּ וְדַבֵּרוּ׃
and-tell! consider! about-her for-you think! the-this the-day

וַיֵּצְאוּ כָּל־ בְּנֵי יִשְׂרָאֵל וַתִּקָּהֵל הָעֵדָה
the-assembly and-she-assembled Israel sons-of all-of then-they-came-out (20:1)

כְּאִישׁ אֶחָד לְמִדָּן וְעַד־ בְּאֵר שֶׁבַע וְאֶרֶץ הַגִּלְעָד אֶל־
before the-Gilead and-land-of Sheba Beer even-to at-from-Dan one as-man

יְהוָה הַמִּצְפָּה׃ וַיִּתְיַצְּבוּ פִּנּוֹת כָּל־ הָעָם כֹּל
all-of the-people all-of leaders-of and-they-took-places (2) the-Mizpah Yahweh

שִׁבְטֵי יִשְׂרָאֵל בִּקְהַל עַם הָאֱלֹהִים אַרְבַּע מֵאוֹת אֶלֶף
thousand hundreds four the-God people-of in-assembly-of Israel tribes-of

אִישׁ רַגְלִי שֹׁלֵף חָרֶב׃ וַיִּשְׁמְעוּ בְּנֵי בִנְיָמִן כִּי־
that Benjamin sons-of and-they-heard (3) sword being-armed soldier man

עָלוּ בְנֵי־ יִשְׂרָאֵל הַמִּצְפָּה וַיֹּאמְרוּ בְּנֵי יִשְׂרָאֵל דַּבְּרוּ
tell! Israel sons-of then-they-said the-Mizpah Israel sons-of they-went-up

אֵיכָה נִהְיְתָה הָרָעָה הַזֹּאת׃ וַיַּעַן הָאִישׁ הַלֵּוִי
the-Levite the-man so-he-said (4) the-this the-awful-thing she-happened how?

אִישׁ הָאִשָּׁה הַנִּרְצָחָה וַיֹּאמַר הַגִּבְעָתָה אֲשֶׁר
that to-the-Gibeah and-he-said the-being-murdered the-woman husband-of

לְבִנְיָמִן בָּאתִי אֲנִי וּפִילַגְשִׁי לָלוּן׃ וַיָּקֻמוּ
and-they-came (5) to-spend-night and-concubine-of-me I I-came in-Benjamin

עָלַי בַּעֲלֵי הַגִּבְעָה וַיָּסֹבּוּ עָלַי אֶת־ הַבַּיִת
the-house *** against-me and-they-surrounded the-Gibeah men-of after-me

לַיְלָה אוֹתִי דִּמּוּ לַהֲרֹג וְאֶת־ פִּילַגְשִׁי עִנּוּ וַתָּמֹת׃
and-she-died they-raped concubine-of-me and to-kill they-intended me night

וָאֹחֵז בְּפִילַגְשִׁי וָאֲנַתְּחֶהָ וָאֲשַׁלְּחֶהָ בְּכָל־
to-each-of and-I-sent-her and-I-cut-up-her to-concubine-of-me so-I-took (6)

שְׂדֵה נַחֲלַת יִשְׂרָאֵל כִּי עָשׂוּ זִמָּה וּנְבָלָה
and-disgrace lewd-act they-committed for Israel inheritance-of region-of

בְּיִשְׂרָאֵל׃ הִנֵּה כֻלְּכֶם בְּנֵי יִשְׂרָאֵל הָבוּ לָכֶם דָּבָר וְעֵצָה
and-verdict word for-you give! Israel sons-of all-of-you now! (7) in-Israel

הֲלֹם׃ וַיָּקָם כָּל־ הָעָם כְּאִישׁ אֶחָד לֵאמֹר לֹא נֵלֵךְ אִישׁ
man he-will-go not to-say one as-man the-people all-of and-he-rose (8) here

twelve parts and sent them
into all the areas of Israel.
30 Everyone who saw it said,
"Such a thing has never been
seen or done, not since the day
the Israelites came up out of
Egypt. Think about it! Consider it! Tell us what to do!"

Israelites Fight the Benjamites

20 Then all the Israelites
from Dan to Beersheba
and from the land of Gilead
came out as one man and assembled before the LORD in
Mizpah. 2 The leaders of all the
people of the tribes of Israel
took their places in the assembly of the people of God, four
hundred thousand soldiers
armed with swords. 3 (The
Benjamites heard that the Israelites had gone up to Mizpah.) Then the Israelites said,
"Tell us how this awful thing
happened."
4 So the Levite, the husband
of the murdered woman, said,
"I and my concubine came to
Gibeah in Benjamin to spend
the night. 5 During the night
the men of Gibeah came after
me and surrounded the house,
intending to kill me. They
raped my concubine, and she
died. 6 I took my concubine,
cut her into pieces and sent
one piece to each region of Israel's inheritance, because
they committed this lewd and
disgraceful act in Israel. 7 Now,
all you Israelites, speak up and
give your verdict."
8 All the people rose as one
man, saying, "None of us will

לְאָהֳלוֹ וְלֹא נָסוּר אִישׁ לְבֵיתוֹ׃ וְעַתָּה זֶה
this but-now (9) to-house-of-him man he-will-return and-not to-home-of-him

הַדָּבָר אֲשֶׁר נַעֲשֶׂה לַגִּבְעָה עָלֶיהָ בְּגוֹרָל׃ וְלָקַחְנוּ
now-we-will-take (10) by-lot against-her to-the-Gibeah we-will-do that the-thing

עֲשָׂרָה אֲנָשִׁים לַמֵּאָה לְכֹל ׀ שִׁבְטֵי יִשְׂרָאֵל וּמֵאָה
and-hundred Israel tribes-of from-all-of from-the-hundred men ten

לָאֶלֶף וְאֶלֶף לָרְבָבָה לָקַחַת צֵדָה
provision to-get from-the-ten-thousand and-thousand from-the-thousand

לָעָם לַעֲשׂוֹת לְבוֹאָם לְגֶבַע בִּנְיָמִן כְּכָל־ הַנְּבָלָה
the-vileness as-all-of Benjamin to-Gibeah-of to-arrive-them to-give for-the-army

אֲשֶׁר עָשָׂה בְּיִשְׂרָאֵל׃ וַיֵּאָסֵף כָּל־ אִישׁ יִשְׂרָאֵל אֶל־
against Israel man-of every-of so-he-got-together (11) in-Israel he-did that

הָעִיר כְּאִישׁ אֶחָד חֲבֵרִים׃ וַיִּשְׁלְחוּ שִׁבְטֵי יִשְׂרָאֵל אֲנָשִׁים
men Israel tribes-of and-they-sent (12) ones-united one as-man the-city

בְּכָל־ שִׁבְטֵי בִנְיָמִן לֵאמֹר מָה הָרָעָה הַזֹּאת אֲשֶׁר
that the-this the-awful-crime what? to-say Benjamin tribes-of through-all-of

נִהְיְתָה בָּכֶם׃ וְעַתָּה תְּנוּ אֶת־ הָאֲנָשִׁים בְּנֵי־
sons-of the-men *** surrender! and-now (13) among-you she-was-committed

בְלִיַּעַל אֲשֶׁר בַּגִּבְעָה וּנְמִיתֵם וּנְבַעֲרָה רָעָה מִיִּשְׂרָאֵל
from-Israel evil and-we-may-purge so-we-may-kill-them of-the-Gibeah who wickedness

וְלֹא אָבוּ * בִּנְיָמִן לִשְׁמֹעַ בְּקוֹל אֲחֵיהֶם
fellows-of-them to-voice-of to-listen Benjamin *sons-of they-wanted but-not

בְּנֵי־ יִשְׂרָאֵל׃ וַיֵּאָסְפוּ בְנֵי־ בִנְיָמִן מִן־ הֶעָרִים
the-towns from Benjamin sons-of and-they-came-together (14) Israel sons-of

הַגִּבְעָתָה לָצֵאת לַמִּלְחָמָה עִם־ בְּנֵי יִשְׂרָאֵל׃
Israel sons-of against to-the-fight to-go-out at-the-Gibeah

וַיִּתְפָּקְדוּ בְּנֵי בִנְיָמִן בַּיּוֹם הַהוּא מֵהֶעָרִים
from-the-towns the-that on-the-day Benjamin sons-of and-they-mobilized (15)

עֶשְׂרִים וְשִׁשָּׁה אֶלֶף אִישׁ שֹׁלֵף חָרֶב לְבַד מִיֹּשְׁבֵי
from-ones-living-of aside sword carrying man thousand and-six twenty

הַגִּבְעָה הִתְפָּקְדוּ שְׁבַע מֵאוֹת אִישׁ בָּחוּר׃ מִכֹּל ׀
among-all-of (16) being-chosen man hundreds seven-of they-mobilized the-Gibeah

הָעָם הַזֶּה שְׁבַע מֵאוֹת אִישׁ בָּחוּר אִטֵּר יַד־
hand-of bound-of being-chosen man hundreds seven-of the-this the-people

יְמִינוֹ כָּל־ זֶה קֹלֵעַ בָּאֶבֶן אֶל־ הַשַּׂעֲרָה וְלֹא
and-not the-hair at with-the-stone slinging this each-of right-of-him

יַחֲטִא׃ וְאִישׁ יִשְׂרָאֵל הִתְפָּקְדוּ לְבַד מִבִּנְיָמִן אַרְבַּע
four from-Benjamin apart they-mustered Israel and-man-of (17) he-would-miss

go home. No, not one of us
will return to his house. 9But
now this is what we'll do to
Gibeah: We'll go up against it
as the lot directs. 10We'll take
ten men out of every hundred
from all the tribes of Israel,
and a hundred from a thousand, and a thousand from ten
thousand, to get provisions for
the army. Then, when the
army arrives at Gibeah in Benjamin, it can give them what
they deserve for all this vileness done in Israel." 11So all
the men of Israel got together
and united as one man against
the city.

12The tribes of Israel sent
men throughout the tribe of
Benjamin, saying, "What
about this awful crime that
was committed among you?
13Now surrender those wicked
men of Gibeah so that we may
put them to death and purge
the evil from Israel."

But the Benjamites would
not listen to their fellow Israelites. 14From their towns they
came together at Gibeah to
fight against the Israelites. 15At
once the Benjamites mobilized twenty-six thousand
swordsmen from their towns,
in addition to seven hundred
chosen men from those living
in Gibeah. 16Among all these
soldiers there were seven hundred chosen men who were
left-handed, each of whom
could sling a stone at a hair
and not miss.

17Israel, apart from Benjamin, mustered four hundred

**13* Most mss have the *Qere* בְּנֵי without a *Kethib* form.

מֵאוֹת אֶלֶף אִישׁ שֹׁלֵף חָרֶב כָּל־ זֶה אִישׁ מִלְחָמָה׃
fight man-of this every-of sword carrying man thousand hundreds

וַיָּקֻמוּ וַיַּעֲלוּ בֵית־ אֵל וַיִּשְׁאֲלוּ בֵאלֹהִים
of-God and-they-inquired El Beth and-they-went-up and-they-rose (18)

וַיֹּאמְרוּ בְּנֵי יִשְׂרָאֵל מִי יַעֲלֶה־ לָּנוּ בַתְּחִלָּה לַמִּלְחָמָה
to-the-fight as-the-first of-us he-shall-go who? Israel sons-of and-they-said

עִם־ בְּנֵי בִנְיָמִן וַיֹּאמֶר יְהוָה יְהוּדָה בַתְּחִלָּה׃
as-the-first Judah Yahweh and-he-replied Benjamin sons-of against

וַיָּקוּמוּ בְנֵי־ יִשְׂרָאֵל בַּבֹּקֶר וַיַּחֲנוּ עַל־
near and-they-pitched-camp in-the-morning Israel sons-of and-they-got-up (19)

הַגִּבְעָה׃ וַיֵּצֵא אִישׁ יִשְׂרָאֵל לַמִּלְחָמָה עִם־ בִּנְיָמִן
Benjamin against to-the-fight Israel man-of and-he-went-out (20) the-Gibeah

וַיַּעַרְכוּ אִתָּם אִישׁ־ יִשְׂרָאֵל מִלְחָמָה אֶל־ הַגִּבְעָה׃
the-Gibeah at battle Israel man-of against-them and-they-took-positions

וַיֵּצְאוּ בְנֵי־ בִנְיָמִן מִן־ הַגִּבְעָה וַיַּשְׁחִיתוּ
and-they-cut-down the-Gibeah from Benjamin sons-of and-they-came-out (21)

בְיִשְׂרָאֵל בַּיּוֹם הַהוּא שְׁנַיִם וְעֶשְׂרִים אֶלֶף אִישׁ אָרְצָה׃
on-battlefield man thousand and-twenty two the-that on-the-day from-Israel

וַיִּתְחַזֵּק הָעָם אִישׁ יִשְׂרָאֵל וַיֹּסִפוּ
and-they-repeated Israel man-of the-people but-he-encouraged (22)

לַעֲרֹךְ מִלְחָמָה בַּמָּקוֹם אֲשֶׁר־ עָרְכוּ שָׁם בַּיּוֹם
on-the-day there they-stationed where in-the-place battle to-take-position

הָרִאשׁוֹן׃ וַיַּעֲלוּ בְנֵי־ יִשְׂרָאֵל וַיִּבְכּוּ לִפְנֵי־ יְהוָה
Yahweh before and-they-wept Israel sons-of and-they-went-up (23) the-first

עַד־ הָעֶרֶב וַיִּשְׁאֲלוּ בַיהוָה לֵאמֹר הַאוֹסִיף לָגֶשֶׁת
to-go-up shall-I-repeat? to-say of-Yahweh and-they-inquired the-evening until

לַמִּלְחָמָה עִם־ בְּנֵי בִּנְיָמִן אָחִי וַיֹּאמֶר יְהוָה
Yahweh and-he-answered brother-of-me Benjamin sons-of against to-the-battle

עֲלוּ אֵלָיו׃ וַיִּקְרְבוּ בְנֵי־ יִשְׂרָאֵל אֶל־ בְּנֵי בִנְיָמִן
Benjamin sons-of to Israel sons-of then-they-drew-near (24) against-him go-up!

בַּיּוֹם הַשֵּׁנִי׃ וַיֵּצֵא בִנְיָמִן | לִקְרָאתָם | מִן־
from to-oppose-them Benjamin when-he-came-out (25) the-second on-the-day

הַגִּבְעָה בַּיּוֹם הַשֵּׁנִי וַיַּשְׁחִיתוּ בִבְנֵי יִשְׂרָאֵל
Israel from-sons-of then-they-cut-down the-second on-the-day the-Gibeah

עוֹד שְׁמֹנַת עָשָׂר אֶלֶף אִישׁ אָרְצָה כָּל־ אֵלֶּה שֹׁלְפֵי
ones-bearing-of these all-of on-battlefield man thousand ten eight-of another

חָרֶב׃ וַיַּעֲלוּ כָל־ בְּנֵי יִשְׂרָאֵל וְכָל־ הָעָם
the-people and-all-of Israel sons-of all-of then-they-went-up (26) sword

thousand swordsmen, all of
them fighting men.
18The Israelites went up to
Bethel[j] and inquired of God.
They said, "Who of us shall go
first to fight against the Benjamites?"
The LORD replied, "Judah
shall go first."
19The next morning the Israelites got up and pitched camp
near Gibeah. 20The men of Israel went out to fight the Benjamites and took up battle positions against them at Gibeah. 21The Benjamites came out
of Gibeah and cut down
twenty-two thousand Israelites on the battlefield that day.
22But the men of Israel encouraged one another and
again took up their positions
where they had stationed
themselves the first day. 23The
Israelites went up and wept
before the LORD until evening,
and they inquired of the LORD.
They said, "Shall we go up
again to battle against the
Benjamites, our brothers?"
The LORD answered, "Go up
against them."
24Then the Israelites drew
near to Benjamin the second
day. 25This time, when the
Benjamites came out from
Gibeah to oppose them, they
cut down another eighteen
thousand Israelites, all of them
armed with swords.
26Then the Israelites, all the
people, went up to Bethel, and

j18 Or *to the house of God*; also in verse 26

וַיָּבֹאוּ בֵית־ אֵל וַיִּבְכּוּ וַיֵּשְׁבוּ שָׁם לִפְנֵי יְהוָה
Yahweh before there and-they-sat and-they-wept El Beth and-they-came

וַיָּצוּמוּ בַיּוֹם־ הַהוּא עַד־ הָעָרֶב וַיַּעֲלוּ
and-they-presented the-evening until the-that on-the-day and-they-fasted

עֹלוֹת וּשְׁלָמִים לִפְנֵי יְהוָה׃ וַיִּשְׁאֲלוּ
and-they-inquired (27) Yahweh before and-fellowship-offerings burnt-offerings

בְנֵי־ יִשְׂרָאֵל בַּיהוָה וְשָׁם אֲרוֹן בְּרִית הָאֱלֹהִים בַּיָּמִים
in-the-days the-God covenant-of ark-of now-there of-Yahweh Israel sons-of

הָהֵם׃ וּפִינְחָס בֶּן־ אֶלְעָזָר בֶּן־ אַהֲרֹן עֹמֵד ׀
ministering Aaron son-of Eleazar son-of and-Phinehas (28) the-those

לְפָנָיו בַּיָּמִים הָהֵם לֵאמֹר הַאוֹסִף עוֹד לָצֵאת
to-go-up again shall-I-repeat? to-ask the-those in-the-days before-him

לַמִּלְחָמָה עִם־ בְּנֵי־ בִנְיָמִן אָחִי אִם־ אֶחְדָּל
shall-I-not-go or brother-of-me Benjamin sons-of with to-the-battle

וַיֹּאמֶר יְהוָה עֲלוּ כִּי מָחָר אֶתְּנֶנּוּ בְיָדֶךָ׃
into-hand-of-you I-will-give-him tomorrow for go! Yahweh and-he-responded

וַיָּשֶׂם יִשְׂרָאֵל אֹרְבִים אֶל־ הַגִּבְעָה סָבִיב׃
around the-Gibeah against ones-ambushing Israel then-he-set (29)

וַיַּעֲלוּ בְנֵי־ יִשְׂרָאֵל אֶל־ בְּנֵי בִנְיָמִן בַּיּוֹם
on-the-day Benjamin sons-of against Israel sons-of and-they-went-up (30)

הַשְּׁלִישִׁי וַיַּעַרְכוּ אֶל־ הַגִּבְעָה כְּפַעַם בְּפָעַם׃
on-time as-time the-Gibeah against and-they-took-positions the-third

וַיֵּצְאוּ בְנֵי־ בִנְיָמִן לִקְרַאת הָעָם הָנְתְּקוּ
they-were-drawn-away the-people to-meet Benjamin sons-of and-they-came-out (31)

מִן־ הָעִיר וַיָּחֵלּוּ לְהַכּוֹת מֵהָעָם חֲלָלִים כְּפַעַם ׀
as-time casualties on-the-people to-inflict and-they-began the-city from

בְּפַעַם בַּמְסִלּוֹת אֲשֶׁר אַחַת עֹלָה בֵית־ אֵל וְאַחַת גִּבְעָתָה
to-Gibeah and-one-of El Beth leading one-of that on-the-roads on-time

בַּשָּׂדֶה כִּשְׁלֹשִׁים אִישׁ בְּיִשְׂרָאֵל׃ וַיֹּאמְרוּ בְּנֵי בִנְיָמִן
Benjamin sons-of and-they-said (32) from-Israel man about-thirty in-the-field

נִגָּפִים הֵם לְפָנֵינוּ כְּבָרִאשֹׁנָה וּבְנֵי יִשְׂרָאֵל
Israel and-sons-of as-at-the-first before-us they ones-being-defeated

אָמְרוּ נָנוּסָה וּנְתַקְּנֻהוּ מִן־ הָעִיר אֶל־הַמְסִלּוֹת׃
the-roads to the-city from and-let-us-draw-away-him let-us-retreat they-said

וְכֹל ׀ אִישׁ יִשְׂרָאֵל קָמוּ מִמְּקוֹמוֹ וַיַּעַרְכוּ
and-they-positioned from-place-of-him they-moved Israel man-of and-every-of (33)

בְּבַעַל תָּמָר וְאֹרֵב יִשְׂרָאֵל מֵגִיחַ מִמְּקֹמוֹ
from-place-of-him charging Israel and-one-ambushing-of Tamar at-Baal

there they sat weeping before
the LORD. They fasted that day
until evening and presented
burnt offerings and fellowship
offerings[k] to the LORD. 27And
the Israelites inquired of the
LORD. (In those days the ark of
the covenant of God was
there, 28with Phinehas son of
Eleazar, the son of Aaron,
ministering before it.) They
asked, "Shall we go up again
to battle with Benjamin our
brother, or not?"

The LORD responded, "Go,
for tomorrow I will give them
into your hands."

29Then Israel set an ambush
around Gibeah. 30They went
up against the Benjamites on
the third day and took up positions against Gibeah as they
had done before. 31The Benjamites came out to meet them
and were drawn away from
the city. They began to inflict
casualties on the Israelites as
before, so that about thirty
men fell in the open field and
on the roads—the one leading
to Bethel and the other to Gibeah.

32While the Benjamites were
saying, "We are defeating
them as before," the Israelites
were saying, "Let's retreat and
draw them away from the city
to the roads."

33All the men of Israel
moved from their places and
took up positions at Baal Tamar, and the Israelite ambush
charged out of its place on the

k26 Traditionally *peace offerings*

מִמַּעֲרֵה־ גָבַע׃ וַיָּבֹאוּ מִנֶּגֶד לַגִּבְעָה עֲשֶׂרֶת
ten-of of-the-Gibeah against-front and-they-went (34) Gibeah *from-plain-of

אֲלָפִים אִישׁ בָּחוּר מִכָּל־ יִשְׂרָאֵל וְהַמִּלְחָמָה כָּבֵדָה
she-was-heavy and-the-fight Israel from-all-of being-chosen man thousands

וְהֵם לֹא יָדְעוּ כִּי־ נֹגַעַת עֲלֵיהֶם הָרָעָה׃
the-disaster to-them being-near that they-realized not and-they

וַיִּגֹּף יְהוָה ׀ אֶת־ בִּנְיָמִן לִפְנֵי יִשְׂרָאֵל וַיַּשְׁחִיתוּ
and-they-struck-down Israel before Benjamin *** Yahweh and-he-defeated (35)

בְנֵי יִשְׂרָאֵל בְּבִנְיָמִן בַּיּוֹם הַהוּא עֶשְׂרִים וַחֲמִשָּׁה אֶלֶף
thousand and-five twenty the-that on-the-day from-Benjamin Israel sons-of

וּמֵאָה אִישׁ כָּל־ אֵלֶּה שֹׁלֵף חָרֶב׃ וַיִּרְאוּ בְנֵי־ בִנְיָמִן
Benjamin sons-of then-they-saw (36) sword bearing these all-of man and-hundred

כִּי נִגָּפוּ וַיִּתְּנוּ אִישׁ־ יִשְׂרָאֵל מָקוֹם לְבִנְיָמִן כִּי
for before-Benjamin way Israel man-of now-they-gave they-were-beaten that

בָטְחוּ אֶל־ הָאֹרֵב אֲשֶׁר† שָׂמוּ אֶל־ הַגִּבְעָה׃
the-Gibeah near they-set that the-one-ambushing on they-relied

וְהָאֹרֵב הֵחִישׁוּ וַיִּפְשְׁטוּ אֶל־ הַגִּבְעָה
the-Gibeah into and-they-dashed they-moved-suddenly and-the-one-ambushing (37)

וַיִּמְשֹׁךְ הָאֹרֵב וַיַּךְ אֶת־ כָּל־ הָעִיר
the-city whole-of *** and-he-put the-one-ambushing and-he-spread-out

לְפִי־ חָרֶב׃ וְהַמּוֹעֵד הָיָה לְאִישׁ יִשְׂרָאֵל עִם־
with Israel for-man-of he-was and-the-arrangement (38) sword to-edge-of

הָאֹרֵב הֶרֶב לְהַעֲלוֹתָם מַשְׂאַת הֶעָשָׁן מִן־
from the-smoke cloud-of to-send-up-them make-great! the-one-ambushing

הָעִיר׃ וַיַּהֲפֹךְ אִישׁ־ יִשְׂרָאֵל בַּמִּלְחָמָה וּבִנְיָמִן
now-Benjamin in-the-battle Israel man-of then-he-would-turn (39) the-city

הֵחֵל לְהַכּוֹת חֲלָלִים בְּאִישׁ־ יִשְׂרָאֵל כִּשְׁלֹשִׁים אִישׁ כִּי אָמְרוּ
they-said and man about-thirty Israel on-man-of casualties to-inflict he-began

אַךְ נִגּוֹף נִגָּף הוּא לְפָנֵינוּ כַּמִּלְחָמָה הָרִאשֹׁנָה׃
the-first as-the-battle before-us he being-defeated to-be-defeated indeed

וְהַמַּשְׂאֵת הֵחֵלָּה לַעֲלוֹת מִן־ הָעִיר עַמּוּד עָשָׁן
smoke column-of the-city from to-rise she-began but-the-cloud (40)

וַיִּפֶן בִּנְיָמִן אַחֲרָיו וְהִנֵּה עָלָה כְלִיל־ הָעִיר
the-city whole-of he-went-up and-see! behind-him Benjamin and-he-turned

הַשָּׁמָיְמָה׃ וְאִישׁ יִשְׂרָאֵל הָפַךְ וַיִּבָּהֵל אִישׁ
man-of and-he-was-terrified he-turned Israel then-men-of (41) into-the-skies

בִּנְיָמִן כִּי רָאָה כִּי־ נָגְעָה עָלָיו הָרָעָה׃ וַיִּפְנוּ
so-they-fled (42) the-disaster upon-him she-came that he-realized for Benjamin

west[l] of Gibeah. [34]Then ten
thousand of Israel's finest men
made a frontal attack on Gibeah. The fighting was so heavy
that the Benjamites did not
realize how near disaster was.
[35]The LORD defeated Benjamin
before Israel, and on that day
the Israelites struck down 25,-
100 Benjamites, all armed
with swords. [36]Then the Benjamites saw that they were
beaten.

Now the men of Israel had
given way before Benjamin,
because they relied on the ambush they had set near Gibeah. [37]The men who had been
in ambush made a sudden
dash into Gibeah, spread out
and put the whole city to the
sword. [38]The men of Israel had
arranged with the ambush
that they should send up a
great cloud of smoke from the
city, [39]and then the men of Israel would turn in the battle.

The Benjamites had begun
to inflict casualties on the men
of Israel (about thirty), and
they said, "We are defeating
them as in the first battle."
[40]But when the column of
smoke began to rise from the
city, the Benjamites turned
and saw the smoke of the
whole city going up into the
sky. [41]Then the men of Israel
turned on them, and the men
of Benjamin were terrified, because they realized that disaster had come upon them. [42]So

[l]33 Some Septuagint manuscripts and Vulgate; the meaning of the Hebrew for this word is uncertain.

*33 The NIV, with the versions listed above in footnote *l*, reads *beth* for *be* (רַב־–), *on-west-of*.

†36 Most mss include the accent *mereka* (אֲשֶׁר).

לִפְנֵי אִישׁ יִשְׂרָאֵל אֶל־ דֶּרֶךְ הַמִּדְבָּר וְהַמִּלְחָמָה הִדְבִּיקָתְהוּ

she-pursued-him but-the-battle the-desert direction-of in Israel man-of before

וַאֲשֶׁר מֵהֶעָרִים מַשְׁחִיתִים אוֹתוֹ בְּתוֹכוֹ׃ כִּתְּרוּ

they-surrounded (43) among-him him ones-cutting-down from-the-towns and-whoever

אֶת־ בִּנְיָמִן הִרְדִיפֻהוּ מְנוּחָה הִדְרִיכֻהוּ עַד נֹכַח הַגִּבְעָה

the-Gibeah vicinity-of in they-overran-him *easily they-chased-him Benjamin ***

מִמִּזְרַח־ שָׁמֶשׁ׃ וַיִּפְּלוּ מִבִּנְיָמִן שְׁמֹנָה־ עָשָׂר אֶלֶף אִישׁ

man thousand ten eight from-Benjamin and-they-fell (44) sun toward-rise-of

אֶת־ כָּל־ אֵלֶּה אַנְשֵׁי־ חָיִל׃ וַיִּפְנוּ וַיָּנֻסוּ הַמִּדְבָּרָה

to-the-desert and-they-fled and-they-turned (45) valor men-of these all-of ***

אֶל־ סֶלַע הָרִמּוֹן וַיְעֹלְלֻהוּ בַּמְסִלּוֹת חֲמֵשֶׁת אֲלָפִים

thousands five-of along-the-roads and-they-cut-down-him the-Rimmon Rock-of to

אִישׁ וַיַּדְבִּיקוּ אַחֲרָיו עַד־ גִּדְעֹם וַיַּכּוּ מִמֶּנּוּ

from-him and-they-struck-down Gidom as-far-as after-him and-they-pressed man

אַלְפַּיִם אִישׁ׃ וַיְהִי כָל־ הַנֹּפְלִים מִבִּנְיָמִן

from-Benjamin the-ones-falling all-of and-he-was (46) man two-thousands

עֶשְׂרִים וַחֲמִשָּׁה אֶלֶף אִישׁ שֹׁלֵף חֶרֶב בַּיּוֹם הַהוּא אֶת־ כָּל־

all-of *** the-that on-the-day sword bearing man thousand and-five twenty

אֵלֶּה אַנְשֵׁי־ חָיִל׃ וַיִּפְנוּ וַיָּנֻסוּ הַמִּדְבָּרָה אֶל־

to into-the-desert and-they-fled but-they-turned (47) valor men-of these

סֶלַע הָרִמּוֹן שֵׁשׁ מֵאוֹת אִישׁ וַיֵּשְׁבוּ בְּסֶלַע רִמּוֹן אַרְבָּעָה

four Rimmon at-Rock-of and-they-stayed man hundreds six the-Rimmon Rock-of

חֳדָשִׁים׃ וְאִישׁ יִשְׂרָאֵל שָׁבוּ אֶל־ בְּנֵי בִנְיָמִן

Benjamin sons-of to they-went-back Israel and-man-of (48) months

וַיַּכּוּם לְפִי־ חֶרֶב מֵעִיר מְתֹם עַד־ בְּהֵמָה עַד

even animal including everything from-town sword to-edge-of and-they-put-them

כָּל־ הַנִּמְצָא גַּם כָּל־ הֶעָרִים הַנִּמְצָאוֹת

the-ones-being-found the-towns all-of also the-one-being-found every-of

שִׁלְּחוּ בָאֵשׁ׃ וְאִישׁ יִשְׂרָאֵל נִשְׁבַּע בַּמִּצְפָּה

at-the-Mizpah he-took-oath Israel and-man-of (21:1) with-fire they-burned

לֵאמֹר אִישׁ מִמֶּנּוּ לֹא־ יִתֵּן בִּתּוֹ לְבִנְיָמִן לְאִשָּׁה׃

as-wife to-Benjamin daughter-of-him he-will-give not of-us one to-say

וַיָּבֹא הָעָם בֵּית־ אֵל וַיֵּשְׁבוּ שָׁם עַד־ הָעֶרֶב

the-evening until there and-they-sat El Beth the-people and-he-went (2)

לִפְנֵי הָאֱלֹהִים וַיִּשְׂאוּ קוֹלָם וַיִּבְכּוּ בְּכִי גָדוֹל׃

great weeping and-they-wept voice-of-them and-they-raised the-God before

וַיֹּאמְרוּ לָמָה יְהוָה אֱלֹהֵי יִשְׂרָאֵל הָיְתָה זֹּאת בְיִשְׂרָאֵל

to-Israel this she-happened Israel God-of Yahweh why? and-they-cried (3)

they fled before the Israelites
in the direction of the desert,
but they could not escape the
battle. And the men of Israel
who came out of the towns cut
them down there. 43They surrounded the Benjamites,
chased them and easily[m] over-
ran them in the vicinity of
Gibeah on the east. 44Eighteen
thousand Benjamites fell, all of
them valiant fighters. 45As
they turned and fled toward
the desert to the rock of Rimmon, the Israelites cut down
five thousand men along the
roads. They kept pressing after
the Benjamites as far as Gidom
and struck down two thou-
sand more.
46On that day twenty-five
thousand Benjamite swordsmen fell, all of them valiant
fighters. 47But six hundred
men turned and fled into the
desert to the rock of Rimmon,
where they stayed four
months. 48The men of Israel
went back to Benjamin and
put all the towns to the sword,
including the animals and
everything else they found.
All the towns they came across
they set on fire.

Wives for the Benjamites

21 The men of Israel had
taken an oath at Miz-
pah: "Not one of us will give
his daughter in marriage to a
Benjamite."
2The people went to Bethel,[n]
where they sat before God until evening, raising their
voices and weeping bitterly.
3"O LORD, the God of Israel,"
they cried, "why has this happened to Israel? Why should

[m]43 The meaning of the Hebrew for this word is uncertain.
[n]2 Or *to the house of God*

*43 Perhaps a place name, *from-Nubah* or *-Nobah*, as in the Septuagint, Codex B.

לְהִפָּקֵד הַיּוֹם מִיִּשְׂרָאֵל שֵׁבֶט אֶחָד׃ וַיְהִי מִמָּחֳרָת
on-next-day and-he-was (4) one tribe from-Israel the-day to-be-missing

וַיַּשְׁכִּימוּ הָעָם וַיִּבְנוּ־ שָׁם מִזְבֵּחַ וַיַּעֲלוּ
and-they-presented altar there and-they-built the-people that-they-got-up

עֹלוֹת וּשְׁלָמִים׃ וַיֹּאמְרוּ בְּנֵי יִשְׂרָאֵל
Israel sons-of then-they-asked (5) and-fellowship-offerings burnt-offerings

מִי אֲשֶׁר לֹא־ עָלָה בַקָּהָל מִכָּל־ שִׁבְטֵי יִשְׂרָאֵל אֶל־
before Israel tribes-of from-all-of to-the-assembly he-came-up not that who?

יְהוָה כִּי הַשְּׁבוּעָה הַגְּדוֹלָה הָיְתָה לַאֲשֶׁר לֹא־ עָלָה אֶל־
before he-came-up not that-whoever she-was the-solemn the-oath for Yahweh

יְהוָה הַמִּצְפָּה לֵאמֹר מוֹת יוּמָת׃ וַיִּנָּחֲמוּ בְּנֵי
sons-of now-they-grieved (6) he-must-die to-die to-say the-Mizpah Yahweh

יִשְׂרָאֵל אֶל־ בִּנְיָמִן אָחִיו וַיֹּאמְרוּ נִגְדַּע הַיּוֹם שֵׁבֶט
tribe the-day he-is-cut-off and-they-said brother-of-him Benjamin for Israel

אֶחָד מִיִּשְׂרָאֵל׃ מַה־ נַּעֲשֶׂה לָהֶם לַנּוֹתָרִים
for-the-ones-being-left for-them can-we-provide how? (7) from-Israel one

לְנָשִׁים וַאֲנַחְנוּ נִשְׁבַּעְנוּ בַיהוָה לְבִלְתִּי תֵּת־ לָהֶם
to-them to-give not by-Yahweh we-took-oath since-we as-wives

מִבְּנוֹתֵינוּ לְנָשִׁים׃ וַיֹּאמְרוּ מִי אֶחָד מִשִּׁבְטֵי
of-tribes-of one which? then-they-asked (8) as-wives from-daughters-of-us

יִשְׂרָאֵל אֲשֶׁר לֹא־ עָלָה אֶל־ יְהוָה הַמִּצְפָּה וְהִנֵּה לֹא בָא־
he-came not and-see! the-Mizpah Yahweh before he-came-up not that Israel

אִישׁ אֶל־ הַמַּחֲנֶה מִיָּבֵישׁ גִּלְעָד אֶל־ הַקָּהָל׃ וַיִּתְפָּקֵד
for-they-counted (9) the-assembly for Gilead from-Jabesh the-camp to man

הָעָם וְהִנֵּה אֵין־ שָׁם אִישׁ מִיּוֹשְׁבֵי יָבֵשׁ גִּלְעָד׃
Gilead Jabesh from-ones-living-of person there not and-see! the-people

וַיִּשְׁלְחוּ־ שָׁם הָעֵדָה שְׁנֵים־עָשָׂר אֶלֶף אִישׁ מִבְּנֵי הֶחָיִל
the-fight from-men-of man thousand ten two the-assembly there so-they-sent (10)

וַיְצַוּוּ אוֹתָם לֵאמֹר לְכוּ וְהִכִּיתֶם אֶת־ יוֹשְׁבֵי יָבֵשׁ
Jabesh ones-living-of *** and-you-put go! to-say them and-they-instructed

גִּלְעָד לְפִי־ חֶרֶב וְהַנָּשִׁים וְהַטָּף׃ וְזֶה הַדָּבָר
the-thing and-this (11) and-the-child and-the-women sword to-edge-of Gilead

אֲשֶׁר תַּעֲשׂוּ כָּל־ זָכָר וְכָל־ אִשָּׁה יֹדַעַת מִשְׁכַּב־ זָכָר
male relation-of experiencing woman and-every-of male every-of you-do that

תַּחֲרִימוּ׃ וַיִּמְצְאוּ מִיּוֹשְׁבֵי ׀ יָבֵישׁ גִּלְעָד אַרְבַּע מֵאוֹת
hundreds four Gilead Jabesh among-ones-living-of and-they-found (12) you-kill

נַעֲרָה בְתוּלָה אֲשֶׁר לֹא־ יָדְעָה אִישׁ לְמִשְׁכַּב זָכָר
male for-relation-of man she-experienced not who virgin young-woman

one tribe be missing from Israel today?"
4 Early the next day the
people built an altar and
presented burnt offerings and
fellowship offerings.[o]
5 Then the Israelites asked,
"Who from all the tribes of Israel has failed to assemble before the LORD?" For they had
taken a solemn oath that anyone who failed to assemble before the LORD at Mizpah
should certainly be put to
death.
6 Now the Israelites grieved
for their brothers, the Benjamites. "Today one tribe is cut
off from Israel," they said.
7 "How can we provide wives
for those who are left, since we
have taken an oath by the
LORD not to give them any of
our daughters in marriage?"
8 Then they asked, "Which one
of the tribes of Israel failed to
assemble before the LORD at
Mizpah?" They discovered
that no one from Jabesh Gilead had come to the camp for
the assembly. 9 For when they
counted the people, they
found that none of the people
of Jabesh Gilead were there.
10 So the assembly sent
twelve thousand fighting men
with instructions to go to Jabesh Gilead and put to the
sword those living there, including the women and children. 11 "This is what you are
to do," they said. "Kill every
male and every woman who is
not a virgin." 12 They found
among the people living in Jabesh Gilead four hundred
young women who had never
slept with a man, and they

[o]4 Traditionally *peace offerings*

וַיָּבִיאוּ אוֹתָם אֶל־ הַמַּחֲנֶה שִׁלֹה אֲשֶׁר בְּאֶרֶץ כְּנָעַן׃
Canaan in-land-of that Shiloh the-camp to them and-they-took

וַיִּשְׁלְחוּ כָּל־ הָעֵדָה וַיְדַבְּרוּ אֶל־ בְּנֵי בִנְיָמִן
Benjamin sons-of to and-they-spoke the-assembly whole-of then-they-sent (13)

אֲשֶׁר בְּסֶלַע רִמּוֹן וַיִּקְרְאוּ לָהֶם שָׁלוֹם׃ וַיָּשָׁב
so-he-returned (14) peace to-them and-they-offered Rimmon at-Rock-of who

בִּנְיָמִן בָּעֵת הַהִיא וַיִּתְּנוּ לָהֶם הַנָּשִׁים אֲשֶׁר
whom the-women to-them and-they-gave the-that at-the-time Benjamin

חִיּוּ מִנְּשֵׁי יָבֵשׁ גִּלְעָד וְלֹא־ מָצְאוּ לָהֶם כֵּן׃
enough for-them they-found but-not Gilead Jabesh from-women-of they-spared

וְהָעָם נִחָם לְבִנְיָמִן כִּי־ עָשָׂה יְהוָה פֶּרֶץ
gap Yahweh he-made because for-Benjamin he-grieved and-the-people (15)

בְּשִׁבְטֵי יִשְׂרָאֵל׃ וַיֹּאמְרוּ זִקְנֵי הָעֵדָה מַה־
how? the-assembly elders-of and-they-said (16) Israel in-tribes-of

נַּעֲשֶׂה לַנּוֹתָרִים לְנָשִׁים כִּי־ נִשְׁמְדָה
she-is-destroyed since as-wives for-the-ones-being-left shall-we-provide

מִבִּנְיָמִן אִשָּׁה׃ וַיֹּאמְרוּ יְרֻשַּׁת פְּלֵיטָה לְבִנְיָמִן וְלֹא־
so-not for-Benjmain survivor heir-of and-they-said (17) woman from-Benjamin

יִמָּחֶה שֵׁבֶט מִיִּשְׂרָאֵל׃ וַאֲנַחְנוּ לֹא נוּכַל לָתֵת־
to-give we-can not and-we (18) from-Israel tribe he-will-be-wiped-out

לָהֶם נָשִׁים מִבְּנוֹתֵינוּ כִּי־ נִשְׁבְּעוּ בְנֵי־ יִשְׂרָאֵל
Israel sons-of they-took-oath since from-daughters-of-us wives to-them

לֵאמֹר אָרוּר נֹתֵן אִשָּׁה לְבִנְיָמִן׃ וַיֹּאמְרוּ הִנֵּה
look! but-they-said (19) to-Benjamin wife one-giving being-cursed to-say

חַג־ יְהוָה בְּשִׁלוֹ מִיָּמִים ׀ יָמִימָה אֲשֶׁר מִצְּפוֹנָה לְבֵית־אֵל
El of-Beth to-north that on-days from-days in-Shiloh Yahweh festival-of

מִזְרְחָה הַשֶּׁמֶשׁ לִמְסִלָּה הָעֹלָה מִבֵּית־ אֵל שְׁכֶמָה וּמִנֶּגֶב
and-to-south to-Shechem El from-Beth the-one-going of-road the-sun rise-of

לִלְבוֹנָה׃ וַיְצַוּ אֶת־ בְּנֵי בִנְיָמִן לֵאמֹר לְכוּ
go! to-say Benjamin sons-of *** so-they-instructed (20) of-Lebonah

וַאֲרַבְתֶּם בַּכְּרָמִים׃ וּרְאִיתֶם וְהִנֵּה אִם־ יֵצְאוּ
they-come-out when and-see! and-you-watch (21) in-the-vineyards and-you-hide

בְנוֹת־ שִׁילוֹ לָחוּל בַּמְּחֹלוֹת וִיצָאתֶם מִן־ הַכְּרָמִים
the-vineyards from then-you-rush-out in-the-dances to-join Shiloh girls-of

וַחֲטַפְתֶּם לָכֶם אִישׁ אִשְׁתּוֹ מִבְּנוֹת שִׁילוֹ וַהֲלַכְתֶּם
and-you-go Shiloh from-girls-of wife-of-him each for-you and-you-seize

אֶרֶץ בִּנְיָמִן׃ וְהָיָה כִּי־ יָבֹאוּ אֲבוֹתָם אוֹ
or fathers-of-them they-come when and-he-will-be (22) Benjamin land-of

took them to the camp at Shiloh in Canaan.
13 Then the assembly sent an
offer of peace to the Benjamites at the rock of Rimmon.
14 So the Benjamites returned
at that time and were given
the women of Jabesh Gilead
who had been spared. But
there were not enough for all
of them.
15 The people grieved for
Benjamin, because the LORD
had made a gap in the tribes of
Israel. 16 And the elders of the
assembly said, "With the
women of Benjamin de-
stroyed, how shall we provide
wives for the men who are
left? 17 The Benjamite survivors
must have heirs," they said,
"so that a tribe of Israel will
not be wiped out. 18 We can't
give them our daughters as
wives, since we Israelites have
taken this oath: 'Cursed be
anyone who gives a wife to a
Benjamite.' 19 But look, there is
the annual festival of the LORD
in Shiloh, to the north of Bethel, and east of the road that
goes from Bethel to Shechem,
and to the south of Lebonah."
20 So they instructed the Benjamites, saying, "Go and hide
in the vineyards 21 and watch.
When the girls of Shiloh come
out to join in the dancing,
then rush from the vineyards
and each of you seize a wife
from the girls of Shiloh and go
to the land of Benjamin.
22 When their fathers or brothers complain to us, we will say

°20 ק ויצוו

אֲחֵיהֶם לָרוֹב | אֵלֵינוּ וְאָמַרְנוּ אֲלֵיהֶם חָנּוּנוּ
do-kindness-to-us! to-them then-we-will-say to-us to-complain brothers-of-them

אוֹתָם כִּי לֹא לָקַחְנוּ אִישׁ אִשְׁתּוֹ בַּמִּלְחָמָה כִּי לֹא אַתֶּם
you not since during-the-war wife-of-him man we-got not because them

נְתַתֶּם לָהֶם כָּעֵת תֶּאְשָׁמוּ׃ (23) וַיַּעֲשׂוּ־
so-they-did (23) you-would-have-been-guilty at-the-time to-them you-gave

כֵן בְּנֵי בִנְיָמִן וַיִּשְׂאוּ נָשִׁים לְמִסְפָּרָם מִן־
from by-number-of-them girls and-they-carried-off Benjamin sons-of that

הַמְחֹלְלוֹת אֲשֶׁר גָּזָלוּ וַיֵּלְכוּ וַיָּשׁוּבוּ אֶל־
to and-they-returned then-they-went they-caught whom the-ones-dancing

נַחֲלָתָם וַיִּבְנוּ אֶת־ הֶעָרִים וַיֵּשְׁבוּ בָּהֶם׃
in-them and-they-settled the-towns *** and-they-rebuilt inheritance-of-them

(24) וַיִּתְהַלְּכוּ מִשָּׁם בְּנֵי־ יִשְׂרָאֵל בָּעֵת הַהִיא אִישׁ
each the-that at-the-time Israel sons-of from-there and-they-left (24)

לְשִׁבְטוֹ וּלְמִשְׁפַּחְתּוֹ וַיֵּצְאוּ מִשָּׁם אִישׁ
each from-there and-they-went and-to-clan-of-him to-tribe-of-him

לְנַחֲלָתוֹ׃ (25) בַּיָּמִים הָהֵם אֵין מֶלֶךְ בְּיִשְׂרָאֵל
in-Israel king there-was-no the-those in-the-days (25) to-inheritance-of-him

אִישׁ הַיָּשָׁר בְּעֵינָיו יַעֲשֶׂה׃
he-did in-eyes-of-him the-thing-fit everyone

to them, 'Do us a kindness by
helping them, because we did
not get wives for them during
the war, and you are innocent,
since you did not give your
daughters to them.' "
23So that is what the Benjamites did. While the girls were
dancing, each man caught one
and carried her off to be his
wife. Then they returned to
their inheritance and rebuilt
the towns and settled in them.
24At that time the Israelites
left that place and went home
to their tribes and clans, each
to his own inheritance.
25In those days Israel had no
king; everyone did as he saw
fit.

°22 ק לריב

וַיְהִי בִּימֵי שְׁפֹט הַשֹּׁפְטִים וַיְהִי רָעָב
famine that-he-was the-ones-judging to-judge in-days-of and-he-was (1:1)

בָּאָרֶץ וַיֵּלֶךְ אִישׁ מִבֵּית לֶחֶם יְהוּדָה לָגוּר בִּשְׂדֵי
in-regions-of to-live Judah Lehem-of from-Beth man and-he-went in-the-land

מוֹאָב הוּא וְאִשְׁתּוֹ וּשְׁנֵי בָנָיו׃ וְשֵׁם הָאִישׁ
the-man now-name-of (2) sons-of-him and-two-of and-wife-of-him he Moab

אֱלִימֶלֶךְ וְשֵׁם אִשְׁתּוֹ נָעֳמִי וְשֵׁם שְׁנֵי־בָנָיו ׀
sons-of-him two-of and-name-of Naomi wife-of-him and-name-of Elimelech

מַחְלוֹן וְכִלְיוֹן אֶפְרָתִים מִבֵּית לֶחֶם יְהוּדָה וַיָּבֹאוּ
and-they-went Judah Lehem-of from-Beth Ephrathites and-Kilion Mahlon

שְׂדֵי־מוֹאָב וַיִּהְיוּ־שָׁם׃ וַיָּמָת אֱלִימֶלֶךְ אִישׁ
husband-of Elimelech now-he-died (3) there and-they-lived Moab regions-of

נָעֳמִי וַתִּשָּׁאֵר הִיא וּשְׁנֵי בָנֶיהָ׃ וַיִּשְׂאוּ
and-they-married (4) sons-of-her and-two-of she and-she-was-left Naomi

לָהֶם נָשִׁים מֹאֲבִיּוֹת שֵׁם הָאַחַת עָרְפָּה וְשֵׁם הַשֵּׁנִית רוּת
Ruth the-other and-name-of Orpah the-one name-of Moabites women for-them

וַיֵּשְׁבוּ שָׁם כְּעֶשֶׂר שָׁנִים׃ וַיָּמוּתוּ גַם־שְׁנֵיהֶם
both-of-them also and-they-died (5) years about-ten there and-they-lived

מַחְלוֹן וְכִלְיוֹן וַתִּשָּׁאֵר הָאִשָּׁה מִשְּׁנֵי יְלָדֶיהָ
sons-of-her without-two-of the-woman and-she-was-left and-Kilion Mahlon

וּמֵאִישָׁהּ׃ וַתָּקָם הִיא וְכַלֹּתֶיהָ
and-daughters-in-law-of-her she and-she-prepared (6) and-without-husband-of-her

וַתָּשָׁב מִשְּׂדֵי מוֹאָב כִּי שָׁמְעָה בִּשְׂדֵה מוֹאָב כִּי־
that Moab in-region-of she-heard when Moab from-regions-of and-she-returned

פָקַד יְהוָה אֶת־עַמּוֹ לָתֵת לָהֶם לָחֶם׃ וַתֵּצֵא
and-she-left (7) food for-them to-provide people-of-him *** Yahweh he-aided

מִן־הַמָּקוֹם אֲשֶׁר הָיְתָה־שָׁמָּה וּשְׁתֵּי כַלֹּתֶיהָ
daughters-in-law-of-her and-two-of at-there she-lived where the-place from

עִמָּהּ וַתֵּלַכְנָה בַדֶּרֶךְ לָשׁוּב אֶל־אֶרֶץ יְהוּדָה׃
Judah land-of to to-go-back on-the-road and-they-set-out with-her

וַתֹּאמֶר נָעֳמִי לִשְׁתֵּי כַלֹּתֶיהָ לֵכְנָה שֹּׁבְנָה אִשָּׁה
each go-back! go! daughters-in-law-of-her to-two-of Naomi then-she-said (8)

לְבֵית אִמָּהּ יַעֲשֶׂה יְהוָה עִמָּכֶם חֶסֶד כַּאֲשֶׁר
just-as kindness to-you Yahweh may-he-show mother-of-her to-home-of

עֲשִׂיתֶם עִם־הַמֵּתִים וְעִמָּדִי׃ יִתֵּן יְהוָה לָכֶם
to-you Yahweh may-he-grant (9) and-to-me the-dead-ones to you-showed

וּמְצֶאןָ מְנוּחָה אִשָּׁה בֵּית אִישָׁהּ וַתִּשַּׁק לָהֶן
on-them then-she-kissed husband-of-her home-of each rest and-find!

Naomi and Ruth

1 In the days when the
judges ruled,[a] there was a
famine in the land, and a man
from Bethlehem in Judah, together with his wife and two
sons, went to live for a while
in the country of Moab. [2]The
man's name was Elimelech,
his wife's name Naomi, and
the names of his two sons
were Mahlon and Kilion.
They were Ephrathites from
Bethlehem, Judah. And they
went to Moab and lived there.
[3]Now Elimelech, Naomi's
husband, died, and she was
left with her two sons. [4]They
married Moabite women, one
named Orpah and the other
Ruth. After they had lived
there about ten years, [5]both
Mahlon and Kilion also died,
and Naomi was left without
her two sons and her hus-
band.
[6]When she heard in Moab
that the LORD had come to the
aid of his people by providing
food for them, Naomi and her
daughters-in-law prepared to
return home from there. [7]With
her two daughters-in-law she
left the place where she had
been living and set out on the
road that would take them
back to the land of Judah.
[8]Then Naomi said to her two
daughters-in-law, "Go back,
each of you, to your mother's
home. May the LORD show
kindness to you, as you have
shown to your dead and to me.
[9]May the LORD grant that each
of you will find rest in the
home of another husband."
Then she kissed them and

[a]1 Traditionally *judged*

°8 ק יעש

וַתִּשֶּׂאנָה קוֹלָן וַתִּבְכֶּינָה׃ (10) וַתֹּאמַרְנָה־ לָּהּ כִּי־
indeed to-her and-they-said (10) and-they-wept voice-of-them and-they-raised

אִתָּךְ נָשׁוּב לְעַמֵּךְ׃ (11) וַתֹּאמֶר נָעֳמִי שֹׁבְנָה
return! Naomi but-she-said (11) to-people-of-you we-will-go-back with-you

בְנֹתַי לָמָּה תֵלַכְנָה עִמִּי הַעוֹד־ לִי בָנִים
sons to-me any-more? with-me would-you-come why? daughters-of-me

בְּמֵעַי וְהָיוּ לָכֶם לַאֲנָשִׁים׃ (12) שֹׁבְנָה
return! (12) as-husbands for-you that-they-could-become in-insides-of-me

בְנֹתַי לֵכְןָ כִּי זָקַנְתִּי מִהְיוֹת לְאִישׁ כִּי אָמַרְתִּי
I-thought if to-husband than-to-be I-am-too-old for go! daughters-of-me

יֶשׁ־ לִי תִקְוָה גַּם הָיִיתִי הַלַּיְלָה לְאִישׁ וְגַם יָלַדְתִּי בָנִים׃
sons I-bore and-then to-husband the-night I-was if hope for-me there-was

(13) הֲלָהֵן ׀ תְּשַׂבֵּרְנָה עַד אֲשֶׁר יִגְדָּלוּ הֲלָהֵן תֵּעָגֵנָה
would-you-remain for-them? they-grew-up when until would-you-wait for-them? (13)

לְבִלְתִּי הֱיוֹת לְאִישׁ אַל בְּנֹתַי כִּי־ מַר־ לִי מְאֹד מִכֶּם
than-you more for-me bitter for daughters-of-me no to-husband to-become not

כִּי־ יָצְאָה בִי יַד־ יְהוָה׃ (14) וַתִּשֶּׂנָה קוֹלָן
voice-of-them and-they-raised (14) Yahweh hand-of against-me she-went-out for

וַתִּבְכֶּינָה עוֹד וַתִּשַּׁק עָרְפָּה לַחֲמוֹתָהּ וְרוּת
but-Ruth on-mother-in-law-of-her Orpah then-she-kissed again and-they-wept

דָּבְקָה בָּהּ׃ (15) וַתֹּאמֶר הִנֵּה שָׁבָה יְבִמְתֵּךְ
sister-in-law-of-you she-goes-back look! and-she-said (15) to-her she-clung

אֶל־ עַמָּהּ וְאֶל־ אֱלֹהֶיהָ שׁוּבִי אַחֲרֵי יְבִמְתֵּךְ׃
sister-in-law-of-you with go-back! gods-of-her and-to people-of-her to

(16) וַתֹּאמֶר רוּת אַל־ תִּפְגְּעִי־ בִי לְעָזְבֵךְ לָשׁוּב
to-turn-back to-leave-you to-me you-urge not Ruth but-she-replied (16)

מֵאַחֲרָיִךְ כִּי אֶל־ אֲשֶׁר תֵּלְכִי אֵלֵךְ וּבַאֲשֶׁר תָּלִינִי אָלִין
I-will-stay you-stay and-at-where I-will-go you-go where to for from-after-you

עַמֵּךְ עַמִּי וֵאלֹהַיִךְ אֱלֹהָי׃ (17) בַּאֲשֶׁר תָּמוּתִי
you-die at-where (17) God-of-me and-God-of-you people-of-me people-of-you

אָמוּת וְשָׁם אֶקָּבֵר כֹּה יַעֲשֶׂה יְהוָה לִי וְכֹה
and-so with-me Yahweh may-he-deal so I-will-be-buried and-there I-will-die

יֹסִיף כִּי הַמָּוֶת יַפְרִיד בֵּינִי וּבֵינֵךְ׃
and-between-you between-me he-separates the-death unless may-he-be-severe

(18) וַתֵּרֶא כִּי־ מִתְאַמֶּצֶת הִיא לָלֶכֶת אִתָּהּ
with-her to-go she being-determined that when-she-realized (18)

וַתֶּחְדַּל לְדַבֵּר אֵלֶיהָ׃ (19) וַתֵּלַכְנָה שְׁתֵּיהֶם עַד־
until two-of-them so-they-went-on (19) to-her to-urge then-she-stopped

they wept aloud [10]and said to
her, "We will go back with
you to your people."
[11]But Naomi said, "Return
home, my daughters. Why
would you come with me? Am
I going to have any more sons,
who could become your hus-
bands? [12]Return home, my
daughters; I am too old to have
another husband. Even if I
thought there was still hope
for me—even if I had a husband tonight and then gave
birth to sons— [13]would you
wait until they grew up?
Would you remain unmarried
for them? No, my daughters. It
is more bitter for me than for
you, because the LORD's hand
has gone out against me!"
[14]At this they wept again.
Then Orpah kissed her
mother-in-law good-by, but
Ruth clung to her.
[15]"Look," said Naomi, "your
sister-in-law is going back to
her people and her gods. Go
back with her."
[16]But Ruth replied, "Don't
urge me to leave you or to turn
back from you. Where you go
I will go, and where you stay I
will stay. Your people will be
my people and your God my
God. [17]Where you die I will
die, and there I will be buried.
May the LORD deal with me, be
it ever so severely, if anything
but death separates you and
me." [18]When Naomi realized
that Ruth was determined to
go with her, she stopped urging her.
[19]So the two women went on

בָּאָנָה בֵּית לָחֶם וַיְהִי כְּבֹאָנָה בֵּית לֶחֶם
Lehem Beth when-to-arrive-them and-he-was Lehem Beth to-come-them

וַתֵּהֹם כָּל־ הָעִיר עֲלֵיהֶן וַתֹּאמַרְנָה
and-they-exclaimed because-of-them the-town whole-of then-she-was-stirred

הֲזֹאת נָעֳמִי׃ וַתֹּאמֶר אֲלֵיהֶן אַל־תִּקְרֶאנָה לִי נָעֳמִי קְרֶאןָ לִי
to-me call! Naomi to-me you-call not to-them and-she-told (20) Naomi this?

מָרָא כִּי־ הֵמַר שַׁדַּי לִי מְאֹד׃ אֲנִי מְלֵאָה הָלַכְתִּי
I-went-away full I (21) very for-me Almighty he-made-bitter because Mara

וְרֵיקָם הֱשִׁיבַנִי יְהוָה לָמָּה תִקְרֶאנָה לִי נָעֳמִי וַיהוָה
now-Yahweh Naomi to-me you-call why? Yahweh he-brought-back-me but-empty

עָנָה בִי וְשַׁדַּי הֵרַע לִי׃
upon-me he-brought-misfortune and-Almighty to-me he-afflicted

וַתָּשָׁב נָעֳמִי וְרוּת הַמּוֹאֲבִיָּה כַלָּתָהּ
daughter-in-law-of-her the-Moabitess and-Ruth Naomi so-she-returned (22)

עִמָּהּ הַשָּׁבָה מִשְּׂדֵי מוֹאָב וְהֵמָּה בָּאוּ בֵּית
Beth they-arrived and-they Moab from-regions-of who-she-returned with-her

לֶחֶם בִּתְחִלַּת קְצִיר שְׂעֹרִים׃ וּלְנָעֳמִי מִידַּע
relative now-to-Naomi (2:1) barleys harvest-of at-beginning-of Lehem

לְאִישָׁהּ אִישׁ גִּבּוֹר חַיִל מִמִּשְׁפַּחַת אֱלִימֶלֶךְ וּשְׁמוֹ
and-name-of-him Elimelech from-clan-of standing great-of man of-husband-of-her

בֹּעַז׃ וַתֹּאמֶר רוּת הַמּוֹאֲבִיָּה אֶל־ נָעֳמִי אֵלְכָה־ נָּא הַשָּׂדֶה
the-field now! let-me-go Naomi to the-Moabitess Ruth and-she-said (2) Boaz

וַאֲלַקֳטָה בַשִּׁבֳּלִים אַחַר אֲשֶׁר אֶמְצָא־ חֵן בְּעֵינָיו
in-eyes-of-him favor I-find whom behind among-the-grains and-let-me-pick-up

וַתֹּאמֶר לָהּ לְכִי בִתִּי׃ וַתֵּלֶךְ וַתָּבוֹא
and-she-went so-she-left (3) daughter-of-me go! to-her and-she-said

וַתְּלַקֵּט בַּשָּׂדֶה אַחֲרֵי הַקֹּצְרִים וַיִּקֶר
and-he-happened the-ones-harvesting behind in-the-field and-she-gleaned

מִקְרֶהָ חֶלְקַת הַשָּׂדֶה לְבֹעַז אֲשֶׁר מִמִּשְׁפַּחַת אֱלִימֶלֶךְ׃
Elimelech from-clan-of who to-Boaz the-field section-of happening-of-her

וְהִנֵּה־ בֹעַז בָּא מִבֵּית לֶחֶם וַיֹּאמֶר
and-he-greeted Lehem from-Beth arriving Boaz then-see! (4)

לַקּוֹצְרִים יְהוָה עִמָּכֶם וַיֹּאמְרוּ לוֹ יְבָרֶכְךָ
may-he-bless-you to-him and-they-called with-you Yahweh to-the-ones-harvesting

יְהוָה׃ וַיֹּאמֶר בֹּעַז לְנַעֲרוֹ הַנִּצָּב עַל־
over the-one-being-foreman to-servant-of-him Boaz and-he-asked (5) Yahweh

הַקּוֹצְרִים לְמִי הַנַּעֲרָה הַזֹּאת׃ וַיַּעַן הַנַּעַר
the-servant and-he-replied (6) the-that the-woman to-whom? the-ones-harvesting

1° ק מודע

until they came to Bethlehem.
When they arrived in Bethlehem, the whole town was
stirred because of them, and
the women exclaimed, "Can
this be Naomi?"
20"Don't call me Naomi,[b]"
she told them. "Call me Mara,[c]
because the Almighty[d] has
made my life very bitter. 21I
went away full, but the LORD
has brought me back empty.
Why call me Naomi? The LORD
has afflicted[e] me; the Almighty has brought misfor-
tune upon me."
22So Naomi returned from
Moab accompanied by Ruth
the Moabitess, her daughter-
in-law, arriving in Bethlehem
as the barley harvest was beginning.

Ruth Meets Boaz

2 Now Naomi had a relative
on her husband's side,
from the clan of Elimelech, a
man of standing, whose name
was Boaz.
2And Ruth the Moabitess
said to Naomi, "Let me go to
the fields and pick up the left-
over grain behind anyone in
whose eyes I find favor."
Naomi said to her, "Go
ahead, my daughter." 3So she
went out and began to glean
in the fields behind the harvesters. As it turned out, she
found herself working in a
field belonging to Boaz, who
was from the clan of Elimelech.
4Just then Boaz arrived from
Bethlehem and greeted the
harvesters, "The LORD be with
you!"
"The LORD bless you!" they
called back.
5Boaz asked the foreman of
his harvesters, "Whose young
woman is that?"
6The foreman replied, "She

[b]20 *Naomi* means *pleasant;* also in verse 21.
[c]20 *Mara* means *bitter.*
[d]20 Hebrew *Shaddai;* also in verse 21
[e]21 Or *has testified against*

הַנִּצָּב עַל־ הַקּוֹצְרִים וַיֹּאמַר נַעֲרָה
young-woman and-he-said the-ones-harvesting over the-one-being-foreman

מוֹאֲבִיָּה הִיא הַשָּׁבָה עִם־ נָעֳמִי מִשְּׂדֵה מוֹאָב׃ וַתֹּאמֶר
and-she-said (7) Moab from-region-of Naomi with who-she-came-back she Moabitess

אֲלַקֳטָה־ נָּא וְאָסַפְתִּי בָעֳמָרִים אַחֲרֵי הַקּוֹצְרִים
the-ones-harvesting behind among-the-sheaves and-let-me-gather now! let-me-glean

וַתָּבוֹא וַתַּעֲמוֹד מֵאָז הַבֹּקֶר וְעַד־ עַתָּה זֶה שִׁבְתָּהּ
to-rest-her except now even-till the-morning from-then and-she-worked so-she-went

הַבַּיִת מְעָט׃ וַיֹּאמֶר בֹּעַז אֶל־ רוּת הֲלוֹא שָׁמַעַתְּ בִּתִּי אַל־
not daughter-of-me you-heard not? Ruth to Boaz so-he-said (8) short the-shelter

תֵּלְכִי לִלְקֹט בְּשָׂדֶה אַחֵר וְגַם לֹא תַעֲבוּרִי מִזֶּה וְכֹה
but-here from-here you-go-away not and-also another in-field to-glean you-go

תִדְבָּקִין עִם־ נַעֲרֹתָי׃ עֵינַיִךְ בַּשָּׂדֶה אֲשֶׁר־
where in-the-field eyes-of-you (9) servant-girls-of-me with you-stay

יִקְצֹרוּן וְהָלַכְתְּ אַחֲרֵיהֶן הֲלוֹא צִוִּיתִי אֶת־הַנְּעָרִים לְבִלְתִּי
not the-men *** I-told not? after-them and-you-follow they-harvest

נָגְעֵךְ וְצָמִת וְהָלַכְתְּ אֶל־ הַכֵּלִים וְשָׁתִית
and-you-get-drink the-jars to then-you-go when-you-are-thirsty to-touch-you

מֵאֲשֶׁר יִשְׁאֲבוּן הַנְּעָרִים׃ וַתִּפֹּל עַל־ פָּנֶיהָ וַתִּשְׁתַּחוּ
and-she-bowed faces-of-her to and-she-fell (10) the-men they-filled from-what

אַרְצָה וַתֹּאמֶר אֵלָיו מַדּוּעַ מָצָאתִי חֵן בְּעֵינֶיךָ
in-eyes-of-you favor I-found why? to-him and-she-exclaimed to-ground

לְהַכִּירֵנִי וְאָנֹכִי נָכְרִיָּה׃ וַיַּעַן בֹּעַז וַיֹּאמֶר לָהּ
to-her and-he-said Boaz and-he-replied (11) foreigner yet-I to-notice-me

הֻגֵּד הֻגַּד לִי כֹּל אֲשֶׁר־ עָשִׂית אֶת־ חֲמוֹתֵךְ אַחֲרֵי
since mother-in-law-of-you for you-did that all to-me he-was-told to-be-told

מוֹת אִישֵׁךְ וַתַּעַזְבִי אָבִיךְ וְאִמֵּךְ
and-mother-of-you father-of-you that-you-left husband-of-you death-of

וְאֶרֶץ מוֹלַדְתֵּךְ וַתֵּלְכִי אֶל־ עַם אֲשֶׁר לֹא־ יָדַעַתְּ תְּמוֹל
yesterday you-knew not who people to and-you-came home-of-you and-land-of

שִׁלְשׁוֹם׃ יְשַׁלֵּם יְהוָה פָּעֳלֵךְ וּתְהִי מַשְׂכֻּרְתֵּךְ
reward-of-you and-may-she-be deed-of-you Yahweh may-he-repay (12) before

שְׁלֵמָה מֵעִם יְהוָה אֱלֹהֵי יִשְׂרָאֵל אֲשֶׁר־ בָּאת לַחֲסוֹת תַּחַת־
under to-take-refuge you-came whom Israel God-of Yahweh from-with rich

כְּנָפָיו׃ וַתֹּאמֶר אֶמְצָא־ חֵן בְּעֵינֶיךָ אֲדֹנִי
lord-of-me in-eyes-of-you favor may-I-find and-she-said (13) wings-of-him

כִּי נִחַמְתָּנִי וְכִי דִבַּרְתָּ עַל־ לֵב שִׁפְחָתֶךָ וְאָנֹכִי
though-I servant-of-you heart-of to you-spoke and-for you-comforted-me for

is the Moabitess who came
back from Moab with Naomi.
7She said, 'Please let me glean
and gather among the sheaves
behind the harvesters.' She
went into the field and has
worked steadily from morning
till now, except for a short rest
in the shelter."
8So Boaz said to Ruth, "My
daughter, listen to me. Don't
go and glean in another field
and don't go away from here.
Stay here with my servant
girls. 9Watch the field where
the men are harvesting, and
follow along after the girls. I
have told the men not to touch
you. And whenever you are
thirsty, go and get a drink
from the water jars the men
have filled."
10At this, she bowed down
with her face to the ground.
She exclaimed, "Why have I
found such favor in your eyes
that you notice me—a foreigner?"
11Boaz replied, "I've been
told all about what you have
done for your mother-in-law
since the death of your husband—how
you left your father
and mother and your
homeland and came to live
with a people you did not
know before. 12May the LORD
repay you for what you have
done. May you be richly rewarded
by the LORD, the God
of Israel, under whose wings
you have come to take refuge."
13"May I continue to find favor
in your eyes, my lord," she
said. "You have given me
comfort and have spoken
kindly to your servant—

לֹא אֶהְיֶה כְּאַחַת שִׁפְחֹתֶיךָ׃ וַיֹּאמֶר לָה בֹעַז
Boaz to-her and-he-said (14) servant-girls-of-you as-one-of I-am not

לְעֵת הָאֹכֶל גֹּשִׁי הֲלֹם וְאָכַלְתְּ מִן־ הַלֶּחֶם וְטָבַלְתְּ
and-you-dip the-bread from and-you-eat here come! the-meal at-time-of

פִּתֵּךְ בַּחֹמֶץ וַתֵּשֶׁב מִצַּד הַקֹּצְרִים
the-ones-harvesting at-side-of when-she-sat in-the-wine-vinegar piece-of-you

וַיִּצְבָּט־ לָהּ קָלִי וַתֹּאכַל וַתִּשְׂבַּע
and-she-was-filled and-she-ate roasted-grain to-her and-he-offered

וַתֹּתַר׃ וַתָּקָם לְלַקֵּט וַיְצַו בֹּעַז אֶת־
*** Boaz then-he-ordered to-glean as-she-got-up (15) and-she-had-left-over

נְעָרָיו לֵאמֹר גַּם בֵּין הָעֳמָרִים תְּלַקֵּט וְלֹא
then-not she-gathers the-sheaves among even-if to-say men-of-him

תַכְלִימוּהָ׃ וְגַם שֹׁל־ תָּשֹׁלּוּ לָהּ מִן־
from for-her you-pull-out to-pull-out but-rather (16) you-embarrass-her

הַצְּבָתִים וַעֲזַבְתֶּם וְלִקְּטָה וְלֹא תִגְעֲרוּ־ בָהּ׃
to-her you-rebuke and-not so-she-can-pick-up and-you-leave the-bundles

וַתְּלַקֵּט בַּשָּׂדֶה עַד־ הָעָרֶב וַתַּחְבֹּט אֵת
*** then-she-threshed the-evening until in-the-field so-she-gleaned (17)

אֲשֶׁר־ לִקֵּטָה וַיְהִי כְּאֵיפָה שְׂעֹרִים׃ וַתִּשָּׂא
and-she-carried (18) barleys about-ephah and-he-was she-gathered what

וַתָּבוֹא הָעִיר וַתֵּרֶא חֲמוֹתָהּ אֵת אֲשֶׁר־ לִקֵּטָה
she-gathered what *** mother-in-law-of-her and-she-saw the-town and-she-took

וַתּוֹצֵא וַתִּתֶּן־ לָהּ אֵת אֲשֶׁר־ הוֹתִרָה
she-had-left-over what *** to-her and-she-gave and-she-brought-out

מִשָּׂבְעָהּ׃ וַתֹּאמֶר לָהּ חֲמוֹתָהּ אֵיפֹה
where? mother-in-law-of-her to-her and-she-asked (19) from-to-be-filled-her

לִקַּטְתְּ הַיּוֹם וְאָנָה עָשִׂית יְהִי מַכִּירֵךְ
one-noticing-you may-he-be you-worked and-at-where? the-day you-gleaned

בָּרוּךְ וַתַּגֵּד לַחֲמוֹתָהּ אֵת אֲשֶׁר־ עָשְׂתָה
she-worked whom *** to-mother-in-law-of-her then-she-told being-blessed

עִמּוֹ וַתֹּאמֶר שֵׁם הָאִישׁ אֲשֶׁר עָשִׂיתִי עִמּוֹ הַיּוֹם בֹּעַז׃
Boaz the-day with-him I-worked whom the-man name-of and-she-said with-him

וַתֹּאמֶר נָעֳמִי לְכַלָּתָהּ בָּרוּךְ הוּא לַיהוָה
by-Yahweh he being-blessed to-daughter-in-law-of-her Naomi and-she-said (20)

אֲשֶׁר לֹא־ עָזַב חַסְדּוֹ אֶת־ הַחַיִּים וְאֶת־ הַמֵּתִים
the-dead-ones and-with the-living-ones with kindness-of-him he-stopped not who

וַתֹּאמֶר לָהּ נָעֳמִי קָרוֹב לָנוּ הָאִישׁ מִגֹּאֲלֵנוּ הוּא׃
he of-one-redeeming-us the-man to-us close Naomi to-her then-she-said

though I do not have the standing of one of your servant girls."
14 At mealtime Boaz said to her, "Come over here. Have some bread and dip it in the wine vinegar."

When she sat down with the harvesters, he offered her some roasted grain. She ate all she wanted and had some left over.
15 As she got up to glean, Boaz gave orders to his men, "Even if she gathers among the sheaves, don't embarrass her.
16 Rather, pull out some stalks for her from the bundles and leave them for her to pick up, and don't rebuke her."
17 So Ruth gleaned in the field until evening. Then she threshed the barley she had gathered, and it amounted to about an ephah.[f]
18 She carried it back to town, and her mother-in-law saw how much she had gathered. Ruth also brought out and gave her what she had left over after she had eaten enough.
19 Her mother-in-law asked her, "Where did you glean today? Where did you work? Blessed be the man who took notice of you!"

Then Ruth told her mother-in-law about the one at whose place she had been working. "The name of the man I worked with today is Boaz," she said.
20 "The LORD bless him!" Naomi said to her daughter-in-law. "The LORD has not stopped showing his kindness to the living and the dead." She added, "That man is our close relative; he is one of our kinsman-redeemers."

[f] 17 That is, probably about 1/2 bushel (about 22 liters)

וַתֹּאמֶר רוּת הַמּוֹאֲבִיָּה גַּם ׀ כִּי־ אָמַר אֵלַי עִם־ הַנְּעָרִים
the-workers with to-me he-said even also the-Moabitess Ruth then-she-said (21)

אֲשֶׁר־ לִי תִּדְבָּקִין עַד אִם־ כִּלּוּ אֵת כָּל־ הַקָּצִיר אֲשֶׁר־ לִי׃
to-me that the-harvest all-of *** they-finish when until you-stay to-me who

וַתֹּאמֶר נָעֳמִי אֶל־ רוּת כַּלָּתָהּ טוֹב בִּתִּי
daughter-of-me good daughter-in-law-of-her Ruth to Naomi and-she-said (22)

כִּי תֵצְאִי עִם־ נַעֲרוֹתָיו וְלֹא יִפְגְּעוּ־ בָךְ בְּשָׂדֶה אַחֵר׃
another in-field to-you they-will-harm for-not girls-of-him with you-go that

וַתִּדְבַּק בְּנַעֲרוֹת בֹּעַז לְלַקֵּט עַד־ כְּלוֹת
to-be-finished until to-glean Boaz to-servant-girls-of so-she-stayed-close (23)

קְצִיר־ הַשְּׂעֹרִים וּקְצִיר הַחִטִּים וַתֵּשֶׁב אֶת־
with and-she-lived the-wheats and-harvest-of the-barleys harvest-of

חֲמוֹתָהּ׃ וַתֹּאמֶר לָהּ נָעֳמִי חֲמוֹתָהּ
mother-in-law-of-her Naomi to-her now-she-said (3:1) mother-in-law-of-her

בִּתִּי הֲלֹא אֲבַקֶּשׁ־ לָךְ מָנוֹחַ אֲשֶׁר יִיטַב־ לָךְ׃
for-you he-will-be-good where rest for-you I-should-seek not? daughter-of-me

וְעַתָּה הֲלֹא בֹעַז מֹדַעְתָּנוּ אֲשֶׁר הָיִית אֶת־ נַעֲרוֹתָיו
servant-girls-of-him with you-are whom kinsman-of-us Boaz not? and-now (2)

הִנֵּה־ הוּא זֹרֶה אֶת־ גֹּרֶן הַשְּׂעֹרִים הַלָּיְלָה׃ וְרָחַצְתְּ ׀
so-you-wash (3) the-night the-barleys threshing-floor-of *** winnowing he see!

וָסַכְתְּ וְשַׂמְתְּ שִׂמְלֹתַיִךְ עָלַיִךְ וְיָרַדְתִּי
then-you-go-down on-you clothes-of-you and-you-put-on and-you-perfume

הַגֹּרֶן אַל־ תִּוָּדְעִי לָאִישׁ עַד כַּלֹּתוֹ
to-finish-him until to-the-man you-make-yourself-known not the-threshing-floor

לֶאֱכֹל וְלִשְׁתּוֹת׃ וִיהִי בְשָׁכְבוֹ וְיָדַעַתְּ
then-you-note when-to-lie-down-him and-he-will-be (4) and-to-drink to-eat

אֶת־ הַמָּקוֹם אֲשֶׁר יִשְׁכַּב־ שָׁם וּבָאת וְגִלִּית מַרְגְּלֹתָיו
feet-of-him and-you-uncover then-you-go there he-lies where the-place ***

וְשָׁכָבְתִּי וְהוּא יַגִּיד לָךְ אֵת אֲשֶׁר תַּעֲשִׂין׃
you-must-do what *** to-you he-will-tell then-he and-you-lie-down

וַתֹּאמֶר אֵלֶיהָ כֹּל אֲשֶׁר־ תֹּאמְרִי * אֶעֱשֶׂה׃ וַתֵּרֶד
so-she-went-down (6) I-will-do *to-me you-say that all to-her and-she-answered (5)

הַגֹּרֶן וַתַּעַשׂ כְּכֹל אֲשֶׁר־ צִוַּתָּה חֲמוֹתָהּ׃
mother-in-law-of-her she-said that as-all and-she-did the-threshing-floor

וַיֹּאכַל בֹּעַז וַיֵּשְׁתְּ וַיִּיטַב לִבּוֹ וַיָּבֹא
then-he-went spirit-of-him and-he-was-good and-he-drank Boaz when-he-ate (7)

לִשְׁכַּב בִּקְצֵה הָעֲרֵמָה וַתָּבֹא בַלָּט
quietly and-she-approached the-grain-pile at-far-end-of to-lie-down

21 Then Ruth the Moabitess said, "He even said to me, 'Stay with my workers until they finish harvesting all my grain.'"

22 Naomi said to Ruth her daughter-in-law, "It will be good for you, my daughter, to go with his girls, because in someone else's field you might be harmed."

23 So Ruth stayed close to the servant girls of Boaz to glean until the barley and wheat harvests were finished. And she lived with her mother-in-law.

Ruth and Boaz at the Threshing Floor

3 One day Naomi her mother-in-law said to her, "My daughter, should I not try to find a home[g] for you, where you will be well provided for? 2 Is not Boaz, with whose servant girls you have been, a kinsman of ours? Tonight he will be winnowing barley on the threshing floor. 3 Wash and perfume yourself, and put on your best clothes. Then go down to the threshing floor, but don't let him know you are there until he has finished eating and drinking. 4 When he lies down, note the place where he is lying. Then go and uncover his feet and lie down. He will tell you what to do."

5 "I will do whatever you say," Ruth answered. 6 So she went down to the threshing floor and did everything her mother-in-law told her to do.

7 When Boaz had finished eating and drinking and was in good spirits, he went over to lie down at the far end of the grain pile. Ruth approached quietly, uncovered

g1 Hebrew *find rest* (see Ruth 1:9)

*5 Most mss include the *Qere* אֵלַי *to-me*, with no *Ketbib* form.

°3a ק שמלתיך
°3b ק וירדת
°4 ק ושכבת

וַתְּגַל מַרְגְּלֹתָיו וַתִּשְׁכָּב׃ וַיְהִי בַּחֲצִי
in-middle-of and-he-was (8) and-she-lay-down feet-of-him and-she-uncovered

הַלַּיְלָה וַיֶּחֱרַד הָאִישׁ וַיִּלָּפֵת וְהִנֵּה אִשָּׁה שֹׁכֶבֶת
lying woman and-see! and-he-turned the-man that-he-was-startled the-night

מַרְגְּלֹתָיו׃ וַיֹּאמֶר מִי־ אָתְּ* וַתֹּאמֶר אָנֹכִי רוּת אֲמָתֶךָ
servant-of-you Ruth I and-she-said you who? and-he-asked (9) feet-of-him

וּפָרַשְׂתָּ כְנָפֶךָ עַל־ אֲמָתְךָ כִּי גֹאֵל
one-redeeming since servant-of-you over garment-corner-of-you now-you-spread

אָתָּה׃ וַיֹּאמֶר בְּרוּכָה אַתְּ לַיהוָה בִּתִּי
daughter-of-me by-Yahweh you being-blessed and-he-replied (10) you

הֵיטַבְתְּ חַסְדֵּךְ הָאַחֲרוֹן מִן־ הָרִאשׁוֹן לְבִלְתִּי־לֶכֶת
to-run not the-earlier greater-than the-latter kindness-of-you you-showed

אַחֲרֵי הַבַּחוּרִים אִם־ דַּל וְאִם־ עָשִׁיר׃ וְעַתָּה בִּתִּי
daughter-of-me and-now (11) rich or-whether poor whether the-young-men after

אַל־ תִּירְאִי כֹּל אֲשֶׁר־ תֹּאמְרִי אֶעֱשֶׂה־ לָּךְ כִּי יוֹדֵעַ כָּל־
whole-of knowing for for-you I-will-do you-ask that all you-be-afraid not

שַׁעַר עַמִּי כִּי אֵשֶׁת חַיִל אָתְּ׃ וְעַתָּה כִּי אָמְנָם
true although and-now (12) you noble woman-of that people-of-me gate-of

כִּי אִם† גֹאֵל אָנֹכִי וְגַם יֵשׁ גֹּאֵל קָרוֹב מִמֶּנִּי׃
than-I nearer one-redeeming there-is and-also I one-redeeming †indeed that

לִינִי הַלַּיְלָה וְהָיָה בַבֹּקֶר אִם־ יִגְאָלֵךְ טוֹב
good he-redeems-you if in-the-morning and-he-will-be the-night stay! (13)

יִגְאָל וְאִם־ לֹא יַחְפֹּץ לְגָאֳלֵךְ וּגְאַלְתִּיךְ
then-I-will-redeem-you to-redeem-you he-is-willing not but-if let-him-redeem

אָנֹכִי חַי־ יְהוָה שִׁכְבִי עַד־ הַבֹּקֶר׃ וַתִּשְׁכַּב מַרְגְּלֹתָו° עַד־
until feet-of-him so-she-lay (14) the-morning until lie! Yahweh life-of I

הַבֹּקֶר וַתָּקָם בְּטֶרוֹם° יַכִּיר אִישׁ אֶת־ רֵעֵהוּ
neighbor-of-him *** man he-could-recognize at-before but-she-got-up the-morning

וַיֹּאמֶר אַל־ יִוָּדַע כִּי־ בָאָה הָאִשָּׁה הַגֹּרֶן׃
the-threshing-floor the-woman she-came that he-must-be-known not and-he-said

וַיֹּאמֶר הָבִי הַמִּטְפַּחַת אֲשֶׁר־עָלַיִךְ וְאֶחֳזִי־ בָהּ וַתֹּאחֶז
when-she-held onto-her and-hold! on-you that the-shawl bring! and-he-said (15)

בָּהּ וַיָּמָד שֵׁשׁ־ שְׂעֹרִים וַיָּשֶׁת עָלֶיהָ וַיָּבֹא
then-he-went-back on-her and-he-put barleys six-of then-he-poured onto-her

הָעִיר׃ וַתָּבוֹא אֶל־ חֲמוֹתָהּ וַתֹּאמֶר מִי־ אַתְּ
you who? then-she-asked mother-in-law-of-her to when-she-came (16) the-town

בִּתִּי וַתַּגֶּד־ לָהּ אֵת כָּל־ אֲשֶׁר עָשָׂה־ לָהּ הָאִישׁ׃
the-man for-her he-did that all *** to-her then-she-told daughter-of-me

his feet and lay down. 8In the
middle of the night something
startled the man, and he
turned and discovered a
woman lying at his feet.
9"Who are you?" he asked.
"I am your servant Ruth,"
she said. "Spread the corner of
your garment over me, since
you are a kinsman-redeemer."
10"The LORD bless you, my
daughter," he replied. "This
kindness is greater than that
which you showed earlier:
You have not run after the
younger men, whether rich or
poor. 11And now, my daughter, don't be afraid. I will do
for you all you ask. All my fellow townsmen know that you
are a woman of noble char-
acter. 12Although it is true that
I am near of kin, there is a
kinsman-redeemer nearer
than I. 13Stay here for the
night, and in the morning if
he wants to redeem, good; let
him redeem. But if he is not
willing, I vow that, as surely as
the LORD lives, I will do it. Lie
here until morning."
14So she lay at his feet until
morning, but got up before
anyone could be recognized;
and he said, "Don't let it be
known that a woman came to
the threshing floor."
15He also said, "Bring me the
shawl you are wearing and
hold it out." When she did so,
he poured into it six measures
of barley and put it on her.
Then he[h] went back to town.
16When Ruth came to her
mother-in-law, Naomi asked,
"How did it go, my daugh-
ter?"
Then she told her every-
thing Boaz had done for her

[h]15 Most Hebrew manuscripts; many Hebrew manuscripts, Vulgate and Syriac *she*

*9 Most mss have *sheva* under the *tav* (אָתְּ).

†12 Most mss have no vowel or *Qere* reading, indicating the Masoretes felt the word to be unnecessary and not to be read.

°14a ק מרגלתיו

°14b ק בטרם

וַתֹּאמֶר שֵׁשׁ־ הַשְּׂעֹרִים הָאֵלֶּה נָתַן לִי כִּי אָמַר
he-said for to-me he-gave the-these the-barleys six-of and-she-said (17)

* אַל־ תָּבוֹאִי רֵיקָם אֶל־ חֲמוֹתֵךְ׃ וַתֹּאמֶר
then-she-said (18) mother-in-law-of-you to empty-handed you-go-back not *to-me

שְׁבִי בִתִּי עַד אֲשֶׁר תֵּדְעִין אֵיךְ יִפֹּל דָּבָר כִּי
for matter he-happens what you-find-out when until daughter-of-me wait!

לֹא יִשְׁקֹט הָאִישׁ כִּי־ אִם־ כִּלָּה הַדָּבָר הַיּוֹם׃
the-day the-matter he-settles when until the-man he-will-rest not

וּבֹעַז עָלָה הַשַּׁעַר וַיֵּשֶׁב שָׁם וְהִנֵּה הַגֹּאֵל
the-one-redeeming and-see! there and-he-sat the-gate he-went-up now-Boaz (4:1)

עֹבֵר אֲשֶׁר דִּבֶּר־ בֹּעַז וַיֹּאמֶר סוּרָה שְׁבָה־ פֹּה
here sit-down! come-over! and-he-said Boaz he-mentioned whom coming-along

פְּלֹנִי אַלְמֹנִי וַיָּסַר וַיֵּשֵׁב׃ וַיִּקַּח עֲשָׂרָה אֲנָשִׁים
men ten and-he-took (2) and-he-sat-down so-he-went-over †friend-of-me

מִזִּקְנֵי הָעִיר וַיֹּאמֶר שְׁבוּ־ פֹה וַיֵּשֵׁבוּ׃ וַיֹּאמֶר
then-he-said (3) and-they-sat here sit! and-he-said the-town from-elders-of

לַגֹּאֵל חֶלְקַת הַשָּׂדֶה אֲשֶׁר לְאָחִינוּ לֶאֱלִימֶלֶךְ
to-Elimelech to-brother-of-us that the-land piece-of to-the-one-redeeming

מָכְרָה נָעֳמִי הַשָּׁבָה מִשְּׂדֵה מוֹאָב׃ וַאֲנִי אָמַרְתִּי
I-thought now-I (4) Moab from-region-of who-she-came-back Naomi she-sells

אֶגְלֶה אָזְנְךָ לֵאמֹר קְנֵה נֶגֶד הַיֹּשְׁבִים וְנֶגֶד
and-before the-ones-sitting before buy! to-suggest ear-of-you I-should-inform

זִקְנֵי עַמִּי אִם־ תִּגְאַל גְּאָל וְאִם־ לֹא יִגְאַל
he-will-redeem not but-if redeem! you-will-redeem if people-of-me elders-of

הַגִּידָה לִּי וְאֵדְעָ° כִּי אֵין זוּלָתְךָ לִגְאוֹל וְאָנֹכִי אַחֲרֶיךָ
after-you and-I to-redeem except-you no-one for so-I-will-know to-me tell!

וַיֹּאמֶר אָנֹכִי אֶגְאָל׃ וַיֹּאמֶר בֹּעַז בְּיוֹם־ קְנוֹתְךָ הַשָּׂדֶה
the-land to-buy-you on-day Boaz then-he-said (5) I-will-redeem I and-he-said

מִיַּד נָעֳמִי וּמֵאֵת רוּת הַמּוֹאֲבִיָּה אֵשֶׁת־ הַמֵּת
the-dead-man widow-of the-Moabitess Ruth and-from Naomi from-hand-of

קָנִיתִי° לְהָקִים שֵׁם־ הַמֵּת עַל־ נַחֲלָתוֹ׃
property-of-him with the-dead-man name-of to-maintain you-acquire

וַיֹּאמֶר הַגֹּאֵל לֹא אוּכַל לִגְאָול°־ לִי פֶּן־
because for-me to-redeem I-can not the-one-redeeming then-he-said (6)

אַשְׁחִית אֶת־ נַחֲלָתִי גְּאַל־ לְךָ אַתָּה אֶת־ גְּאֻלָּתִי
redemption-of-me *** you for-you redeem! estate-of-me *** I-might-endanger

כִּי לֹא־ אוּכַל לִגְאֹל׃ וְזֹאת לְפָנִים בְּיִשְׂרָאֵל עַל־
for in-Israel in-earlier-times now-this (7) to-redeem I-can not for

[17]and added, "He gave me these six measures of barley, saying, 'Don't go back to your mother-in-law empty-handed.' "

[18]Then Naomi said, "Wait, my daughter, until you find out what happens. For the man will not rest until the matter is settled today."

Boaz Marries Ruth

4 Meanwhile Boaz went up to the town gate and sat there. When the kinsman-redeemer he had mentioned came along, Boaz said, "Come over here, my friend, and sit down." So he went over and sat down.

[2]Boaz took ten of the elders of the town and said, "Sit here," and they did so. [3]Then he said to the kinsman-redeemer, "Naomi, who has come back from Moab, is selling the piece of land that belonged to our brother Elimelech. [4]I thought I should bring the matter to your attention and suggest that you buy it in the presence of these seated here and in the presence of the elders of my people. If you will redeem it, do so. But if you[i] will not, tell me, so I will know. For no one has the right to do it except you, and I am next in line."

"I will redeem it," he said.

[5]Then Boaz said, "On the day you buy the land from Naomi and from Ruth the Moabitess, you acquire[j] the dead man's widow, in order to maintain the name of the dead with his property."

[6]At this, the kinsman-redeemer said, "Then I cannot redeem it because I might endanger my own estate. You redeem it yourself. I cannot do it."

[i]4 Many Hebrew manuscripts, Septuagint, Vulgate and Syriac; most Hebrew manuscripts *he*

[j]5 Hebrew; Vulgate and Syriac *Naomi, you acquire Ruth the Moabitess,*

*17 Most mss include the Qere אֵלַי, *to-me,* with no *Ketib* form.

†1 The meaning of this phrase is uncertain, perhaps used in place of a proper name, as the English idiom "so-and-so."

°4 ק ואדעה

°5 ק קניתה

°6 ק לגאל

הַגְּאוּלָּה וְעַל־ הַתְּמוּרָה לְקַיֵּם כָּל־ דָּבָר שָׁלַף

he-took-off matter any-of to-finalize the-transfer and-for the-redemption

אִישׁ נַעֲלוֹ וְנָתַן לְרֵעֵהוּ וְזֹאת הַתְּעוּדָה

the-legalizing-method now-this to-other-of-him and-he-gave sandal-of-him man

בְּיִשְׂרָאֵל׃ וַיֹּאמֶר הַגֹּאֵל לְבֹעַז קְנֵה־ לָךְ וַיִּשְׁלֹף

and-he-removed for-you buy! to-Boaz the-one-redeeming so-he-said (8) in-Israel

נַעֲלוֹ׃ וַיֹּאמֶר בֹּעַז לַזְּקֵנִים וְכָל־ הָעָם

the-people and-all-of to-the-elders Boaz then-he-announced (9) sandal-of-him

עֵדִים אַתֶּם הַיּוֹם כִּי קָנִיתִי אֶת־ כָּל־ אֲשֶׁר לֶאֱלִימֶלֶךְ וְאֵת כָּל־ אֲשֶׁר

that all and to-Elimelech that all *** I-bought that the-day you witnesses

לְכִלְיוֹן וּמַחְלוֹן מִיַּד נָעֳמִי׃ וְגַם אֶת־ רוּת הַמֹּאֲבִיָּה

the-Moabitess Ruth *** and-also (10) Naomi from-hand-of and-Mahlon to-Kilion

אֵשֶׁת מַחְלוֹן קָנִיתִי לִי לְאִשָּׁה לְהָקִים שֵׁם־ הַמֵּת עַל־

with the-dead name-of to-maintain as-wife for-me I-acquired Mahlon widow-of

נַחֲלָתוֹ וְלֹא־ יִכָּרֵת שֵׁם־ הַמֵּת מֵעִם

from-among the-dead name-of he-will-disappear so-not property-of-him

אֶחָיו וּמִשַּׁעַר מְקוֹמוֹ עֵדִים אַתֶּם הַיּוֹם׃

the-day you witnesses town-of-him or-from-gate-of brothers-of-him

וַיֹּאמְרוּ כָּל־ הָעָם אֲשֶׁר־ בַּשַּׁעַר וְהַזְּקֵנִים עֵדִים

witnesses and-the-elders at-the-gate who the-people all-of then-they-said (11)

יִתֵּן יְהוָה אֶת־ הָאִשָּׁה הַבָּאָה אֶל־ בֵּיתֶךָ כְּרָחֵל ׀

like-Rachel home-of-you into the-one-coming the-woman *** Yahweh may-he-make

וּכְלֵאָה אֲשֶׁר בָּנוּ שְׁתֵּיהֶם אֶת־ בֵּית יִשְׂרָאֵל וַעֲשֵׂה־

and-have! Israel house-of *** two-of-them they-built-up who and-like-Leah

חַיִל בְּאֶפְרָתָה וּקְרָא־ שֵׁם בְּבֵית לָחֶם׃ וִיהִי

and-may-he-be (12) Lehem in-Beth name and-call! in-Ephratah standing

בֵיתְךָ כְּבֵית פֶּרֶץ אֲשֶׁר־ יָלְדָה תָמָר לִיהוּדָה מִן־

through to-Judah Tamar she-bore whom Perez like-family-of family-of-you

הַזֶּרַע אֲשֶׁר יִתֵּן יְהוָה לְךָ מִן־ הַנַּעֲרָה הַזֹּאת׃

the-this the-young-woman by to-you Yahweh he-gives that the-offspring

וַיִּקַּח בֹּעַז אֶת־ רוּת וַתְּהִי־ לוֹ לְאִשָּׁה וַיָּבֹא

and-he-went for-wife to-him and-she-became Ruth *** Boaz so-he-took (13)

אֵלֶיהָ וַיִּתֵּן יְהוָה לָהּ הֵרָיוֹן וַתֵּלֶד בֵּן׃

son and-she-bore conception to-her Yahweh and-he-gave into-her

וַתֹּאמַרְנָה הַנָּשִׁים אֶל־ נָעֳמִי בָּרוּךְ יְהוָה אֲשֶׁר לֹא

not who Yahweh being-praised Naomi to the-women and-they-said (14)

הִשְׁבִּית לָךְ גֹּאֵל הַיּוֹם וְיִקָּרֵא שְׁמוֹ

name-of-him now-may-he-be-called the-day one-redeeming for-you he-let-cease

7(Now in earlier times in Israel, for the redemption and
transfer of property to become
final, one party took off his
sandal and gave it to the other.
This was the method of legal-
izing transactions in Israel.)
8So the kinsman-redeemer
said to Boaz, "Buy it yourself."
And he removed his sandal.
9Then Boaz announced to
the elders and all the people,
"Today you are witnesses that
I have bought from Naomi all
the property of Elimelech, Kilion and Mahlon. 10I have also
acquired Ruth the Moabitess,
Mahlon's widow, as my wife,
in order to maintain the name
of the dead with his property,
so that his name will not
disappear from among his
family or from the town
records. Today you are witnesses!"
11Then the elders and all
those at the gate said, "We are
witnesses. May the LORD make
the woman who is coming
into your home like Rachel
and Leah, who together built
up the house of Israel. May
you have standing in
Ephratah and be famous in
Bethlehem. 12Through the
offspring the LORD gives you
by this young woman, may
your family be like that of
Perez, whom Tamar bore to
Judah."

The Genealogy of David

13So Boaz took Ruth and she
became his wife. And the
LORD enabled her to conceive,
and she gave birth to a son.
14The women said to Naomi:
"Praise be to the LORD, who
this day has not left you without a kinsman-redeemer. May
he become famous throughout

בְּיִשְׂרָאֵל׃ (15) וְהָיָה לָךְ לְמֵשִׁיב נֶפֶשׁ
life as-one-renewing for-you and-he-will-be (15) throughout-Israel

וּלְכַלְכֵּל אֶת־ שֵׂיבָתֵךְ כִּי כַלָּתֵךְ אֲשֶׁר־ אֲהֵבַתֶךְ
she-loves-you who daughter-in-law-of-you for old-age-of-you *** and-to-sustain

יְלָדַתּוּ אֲשֶׁר־ הִיא טוֹבָה לָךְ מִשִּׁבְעָה בָּנִים׃ (16) וַתִּקַּח
then-she-took (16) sons than-seven to-you better she who she-bore-him

נָעֳמִי אֶת־ הַיֶּלֶד וַתְּשִׁתֵהוּ בְחֵיקָהּ וַתְּהִי־ לוֹ
for-him and-she-was in-lap-of-her and-she-laid-him the-child *** Naomi

לְאֹמֶנֶת׃ (17) וַתִּקְרֶאנָה לוֹ הַשְּׁכֵנוֹת שֵׁם לֵאמֹר
to-say name the-women-living to-him and-they-called (17) as-one-caring

יֻלַּד־ בֵּן לְנָעֳמִי וַתִּקְרֶאנָה שְׁמוֹ עוֹבֵד הוּא אֲבִי־
father-of he Obed name-of-him and-they-called to-Naomi son he-was-born

יִשַׁי אֲבִי דָוִד׃ (18) וְאֵלֶּה תּוֹלְדוֹת פָּרֶץ פֶּרֶץ הוֹלִיד
he-fathered Perez Perez family-lines-of so-these (18) David father-of Jesse

אֶת־ חֶצְרוֹן׃ (19) וְחֶצְרוֹן הוֹלִיד אֶת־ רָם וְרָם הוֹלִיד אֶת־
*** he-fathered and-Ram Ram *** he-fathered and-Hezron (19) Hezron ***

עַמִּינָדָב׃ (20) וְעַמִּינָדָב הוֹלִיד אֶת־ נַחְשׁוֹן וְנַחְשׁוֹן הוֹלִיד
he-fathered and-Nahshon Nahshon *** he-fathered and-Amminadab (20) Amminadab

אֶת־ שַׂלְמָה׃ (21) וְשַׂלְמוֹן הוֹלִיד אֶת־ בֹּעַז וּבֹעַז הוֹלִיד אֶת־
*** he-fathered and-Boaz Boaz *** he-fathered and-Salmon (21) Salma ***

עוֹבֵד׃ (22) וְעֹבֵד הוֹלִיד אֶת־ יִשָׁי וְיִשַׁי הוֹלִיד אֶת־ דָּוִד׃
David *** he-fathered and-Jesse Jesse *** he-fathered and-Obed (22) Obed

Israel! 15He will renew your
life and sustain you in your
old age. For your daughter-in-
law, who loves you and who is
better to you than seven sons,
has given him birth."
16Then Naomi took the
child, laid him in her lap and
cared for him. 17The women
living there said, "Naomi has
a son." And they named him
Obed. He was the father of
Jesse, the father of David.
18This, then, is the family
line of Perez:

Perez was the father of Hezron,
19Hezron the father of Ram
Ram the father of Amminadab,
20Amminadab the father of Nahshon,
Nahshon the father of Salmon,[k]
21Salmon the father of Boaz,
Boaz the father of Obed,
22Obed the father of Jesse,
and Jesse the father of David.

[k] 20 A few Hebrew manuscripts, some Septuagint manuscripts and Vulgate (see also verse 21 and Septuagint of 1 Chron. 2:11); most Hebrew manuscripts *Salma*

וַיְהִי אִישׁ אֶחָד מִן־ הָרָמָתַיִם צוֹפִים מֵהַר
from-hill-country-of Zuphites the-Ramathaim from certain man now-he-was (1:1)

אֶפְרָיִם וּשְׁמוֹ אֶלְקָנָה בֶּן־ יְרֹחָם בֶּן־ אֱלִיהוּא בֶּן־ תֹּחוּ
Tohu son-of Elihu son-of Jeroham son-of Elkanah and-name-of-him Ephraim

בֶּן־ צוּף אֶפְרָתִי׃ וְלוֹ שְׁתֵּי נָשִׁים שֵׁם אַחַת חַנָּה
Hannah one name-of wives two-of now-to-him (2) Ephramite Zuph son-of

וְשֵׁם הַשֵּׁנִית פְּנִנָּה וַיְהִי לִפְנִנָּה יְלָדִים וּלְחַנָּה
but-to-Hannah children to-Peninnah and-he-was Peninnah the-other and-name-of

אֵין יְלָדִים׃ וְעָלָה הָאִישׁ הַהוּא מֵעִירוֹ מִיָּמִים ׀
from-days from-town-of-him the-this the-man and-he-went-up (3) children no

יָמִימָה לְהִשְׁתַּחֲוֺת וְלִזְבֹּחַ לַיהוָה צְבָאוֹת בְּשִׁלֹה וְשָׁם
and-there at-Shiloh Hosts to-Yahweh-of and-to-sacrifice to-worship at-days

שְׁנֵי בְנֵי־ עֵלִי חָפְנִי וּפִנְחָס כֹּהֲנִים לַיהוָה׃ וַיְהִי
when-he-came (4) of-Yahweh priests and-Phinehas Hophni Eli sons-of two-of

הַיּוֹם וַיִּזְבַּח אֶלְקָנָה וְנָתַן לִפְנִנָּה אִשְׁתּוֹ
wife-of-him to-Peninnah then-he-gave Elkanah and-he-sacrificed the-day

וּלְכָל־ בָּנֶיהָ וּבְנוֹתֶיהָ מָנוֹת׃ וּלְחַנָּה
but-to-Hannah (5) portions and-daughters-of-her sons-of-her and-to-all-of

יִתֵּן מָנָה אַחַת אַפָּיִם כִּי אֶת־ חַנָּה אָהֵב וַיהוָה סָגַר
he-closed and-Yahweh he-loved Hannah *** because double one portion he-gave

רַחְמָהּ׃ וְכִעֲסַתָּה צָרָתָהּ גַּם־ כַּעַס בַּעֲבוּר
in-order provocation indeed rival-of-her and-she-provoked-her (6) womb-of-her

הַרְּעִמָהּ כִּי־ סָגַר יְהוָה בְּעַד רַחְמָהּ׃ וְכֵן
and-this (7) womb-of-her completely Yahweh he-closed because to-irritate-her

יַעֲשֶׂה שָׁנָה בְשָׁנָה מִדֵּי עֲלֹתָהּ בְּבֵית יְהוָה כֵּן
then Yahweh to-house-of to-go-up-her whenever after-year year he-went-on

תַּכְעִסֶנָּה וַתִּבְכֶּה וְלֹא תֹאכַל׃ וַיֹּאמֶר לָהּ אֶלְקָנָה
Elkanah to-her and-he-said (8) she-ate and-not so-she-wept she-provoked-her

אִישָׁהּ חַנָּה לָמֶה תִבְכִּי וְלָמֶה לֹא תֹאכְלִי וְלָמֶה יֵרַע
he-is-sad and-why? you-eat not and-why? you-weep why? Hannah husband-of-her

לְבָבֵךְ הֲלוֹא אָנֹכִי טוֹב לָךְ מֵעֲשָׂרָה בָּנִים׃ וַתָּקָם חַנָּה
Hannah now-she-stood-up (9) sons than-ten to-you better I not? heart-of-you

אַחֲרֵי אָכְלָה בְשִׁלֹה וְאַחֲרֵי שָׁתֹה וְעֵלִי הַכֹּהֵן יֹשֵׁב עַל־
on sitting the-priest now-Eli to-drink and-after in-Shiloh to-eat-her after

הַכִּסֵּא עַל־ מְזוּזַת הֵיכַל יְהוָה׃ וְהִיא מָרַת נָפֶשׁ
soul bitter-of and-she (10) Yahweh temple-of doorpost-of by the-chair

וַתִּתְפַּלֵּל עַל־ יְהוָה וּבָכֹה תִבְכֶּה׃ וַתִּדֹּר נֶדֶר
vow and-she-vowed (11) she-wept and-to-weep Yahweh to and-she-prayed

The Birth of Samuel

1 There was a certain man
from Ramathaim, a Zuph-
ite[a] from the hill country of
Ephraim, whose name was Elkanah son of Jeroham, the son
of Elihu, the son of Tohu, the
son of Zuph, an Ephraimite.
2 He had two wives; one was
called Hannah and the other
Peninnah. Peninnah had children, but Hannah had none.
3 Year after year this man
went up from his town to worship and sacrifice to the LORD
Almighty at Shiloh, where
Hophni and Phinehas, the
two sons of Eli, were priests of
the LORD. 4 Whenever the day
came for Elkanah to sacrifice,
he would give portions of the
meat to his wife Peninnah and
to all her sons and daughters.
5 But to Hannah he gave a double portion because he loved
her, and the LORD had closed
her womb. 6 And because the
LORD had closed her womb,
her rival kept provoking her in
order to irritate her. 7 This
went on year after year.
Whenever Hannah went up to
the house of the LORD, her rival provoked her till she wept
and would not eat. 8 Elkanah
her husband would say to her,
"Hannah, why are you weeping? Why don't you eat? Why
are you downhearted? Don't I
mean more to you than ten
sons?"
9 Once when they had
finished eating and drinking
in Shiloh, Hannah stood up.
Now Eli the priest was sitting
on a chair by the doorpost of
the LORD's temple.[b] 10 In bitterness of soul Hannah wept
much and prayed to the LORD.
11 And she made a vow, saying,

[a]1 Or *from Ramathaim Zuphim*
[b]9 That is, tabernacle

וַתֹּאמַר יְהוָה צְבָאוֹת אִם־ רָאֹה תִרְאֶה ׀ בָּעֳנִי

upon-misery-of you-will-look to-look if Hosts Yahweh-of and-she-said

אֲמָתֶךָ וּזְכַרְתַּנִי וְלֹא־ תִשְׁכַּח אֶת־

*** you-will-forget and-not and-you-will-remember-me servant-of-you

אֲמָתֶךָ וְנָתַתָּה לַאֲמָתְךָ זֶרַע אֲנָשִׁים

men offspring-of to-servant-of-you but-you-will-give servant-of-you

וּנְתַתִּיו לַיהוָה כָּל־ יְמֵי חַיָּיו וּמוֹרָה לֹא־

not and-razor lives-of-him days-of all-of to-Yahweh then-I-will-give-him

יַעֲלֶה עַל־ רֹאשׁוֹ׃ וְהָיָה כִּי הִרְבְּתָה לְהִתְפַּלֵּל לִפְנֵי

to to-pray she-kept-on as and-he-was (12) head-of-him on he-will-use

יְהוָה וְעֵלִי שֹׁמֵר אֶת־ פִּיהָ׃ וְחַנָּה הִיא מְדַבֶּרֶת עַל־

in praying she now-Hannah (13) mouth-of-her *** observing then-Eli Yahweh

לִבָּהּ רַק שְׂפָתֶיהָ נָּעוֹת וְקוֹלָהּ לֹא יִשָּׁמֵעַ

he-was-heard not but-voice-of-her ones-moving lips-of-her only heart-of-her

וַיַּחְשְׁבֶהָ עֵלִי לְשִׁכֹּרָה׃ וַיֹּאמֶר אֵלֶיהָ עֵלִי עַד־ מָתַי

when? until Eli to-her and-he-said (14) to-be-drunk Eli and-he-thought-her

תִּשְׁתַּכָּרִין הָסִירִי אֶת־ יֵינֵךְ מֵעָלָיִךְ׃ וַתַּעַן

and-she-replied (15) from-with-you wine-of-you *** get-rid! will-you-be-drunk

חַנָּה וַתֹּאמֶר לֹא אֲדֹנִי אִשָּׁה קְשַׁת־ רוּחַ אָנֹכִי וְיַיִן

and-wine I spirit troubled-of woman lord-of-me not-so and-she-said Hannah

וְשֵׁכָר לֹא שָׁתִיתִי וָאֶשְׁפֹּךְ אֶת־ נַפְשִׁי לִפְנֵי יְהוָה׃ אַל־

not (16) Yahweh to soul-of-me *** but-I-poured-out I-drank not or-beer

תִּתֵּן אֶת־ אֲמָתְךָ לִפְנֵי בַּת־ בְּלִיָּעַל כִּי־ מֵרֹב

in-greatness-of for wickedness daughter-of for servant-of-you *** you-take

שִׂיחִי וְכַעְסִי דִּבַּרְתִּי עַד־ הֵנָּה׃ וַיַּעַן עֵלִי

Eli and-he-answered (17) at-here at I-prayed and-grief-of-me anguish-of-me

וַיֹּאמֶר לְכִי לְשָׁלוֹם וֵאלֹהֵי יִשְׂרָאֵל יִתֵּן אֶת־ שֵׁלָתֵךְ

request-of-you *** may-he-grant Israel and-God-of in-peace go! and-he-said

אֲשֶׁר שָׁאַלְתְּ מֵעִמּוֹ׃ וַתֹּאמֶר תִּמְצָא שִׁפְחָתְךָ

servant-of-you may-she-find and-she-said (18) from-with-him you-asked that

חֵן בְּעֵינֶיךָ וַתֵּלֶךְ הָאִשָּׁה לְדַרְכָּהּ וַתֹּאכַל

and-she-ate on-way-of-her the-woman then-she-went in-eyes-of-you favor

וּפָנֶיהָ לֹא־ הָיוּ־ לָהּ עוֹד׃ וַיַּשְׁכִּמוּ

and-they-arose (19) longer to-her they-were not and-faces-of-her

בַבֹּקֶר וַיִּשְׁתַּחֲווּ לִפְנֵי יְהוָה וַיָּשֻׁבוּ

then-they-returned Yahweh before and-they-worshiped in-the-morning

וַיָּבֹאוּ אֶל־ בֵּיתָם הָרָמָתָה וַיֵּדַע אֶלְקָנָה אֶת־

*** Elkanah and-he-lay-with at-the-Ramah home-of-them to and-they-went-back

"O Lord Almighty, if you will
only look upon your servant's
misery and remember me, and
not forget your servant but
give her a son, then I will give
him to the Lord for all the days
of his life, and no razor will
ever be used on his head."
12As she kept on praying to
the Lord, Eli observed her
mouth. 13Hannah was praying
in her heart, and her lips were
moving but her voice was not
heard. Eli thought she was
drunk 14and said to her, "How
long will you keep on getting
drunk? Get rid of your wine."
15"Not so, my lord," Hannah
replied, "I am a woman who is
deeply troubled. I have not
been drinking wine or beer; I
was pouring out my soul to the
Lord. 16Do not take your servant for a wicked woman; I
have been praying here out of
my great anguish and grief."
17Eli answered, "Go in
peace, and may the God of Israel grant you what you have
asked of him."
18She said, "May your servant find favor in your eyes."
Then she went her way and
ate something, and her face
was no longer downcast.
19Early the next morning
they arose and worshiped before the Lord and then went
back to their home at Ramah.
Elkanah lay with Hannah his

חַנָּה אִשְׁתּוֹ וַיִּזְכְּרֶהָ יְהוָה׃ וַיְהִי לִתְקֻפוֹת
in-courses-of so-he-was (20) Yahweh and-he-remembered-her wife-of-him Hannah

הַיָּמִים וַתַּהַר חַנָּה וַתֵּלֶד בֵּן וַתִּקְרָא אֶת־
*** and-she-called son and-she-bore Hannah then-she-conceived the-days

שְׁמוֹ שְׁמוּאֵל כִּי מֵיְהוָה שְׁאִלְתִּיו׃ וַיַּעַל
when-he-went-up (21) I-asked-for-him from-Yahweh because Samuel name-of-him

הָאִישׁ אֶלְקָנָה וְכָל־ בֵּיתוֹ לִזְבֹּחַ לַיהוָה אֶת־ זֶבַח
sacrifice-of *** to-Yahweh to-offer family-of-him and-all-of Elkanah the-man

הַיָּמִים וְאֶת־ נִדְרוֹ׃ וְחַנָּה לֹא עָלָתָה כִּי־ אָמְרָה
she-said for she-went not but-Hannah (22) vow-of-him and the-days

לְאִישָׁהּ עַד יִגָּמֵל הַנַּעַר וַהֲבִאֹתִיו
then-I-will-take-him the-boy he-is-weaned after to-husband-of-her

וְנִרְאָה אֶת־ פְּנֵי יְהוָה וְיָשַׁב שָׁם עַד־ עוֹלָם׃
always for there and-he-will-live Yahweh before *** and-he-will-be-presented

וַיֹּאמֶר לָהּ אֶלְקָנָה אִישָׁהּ עֲשִׂי הַטּוֹב בְּעֵינַיִךְ
in-eyes-of-you the-good do! husband-of-her Elkanah to-her and-he-told (23)

שְׁבִי עַד־ גָּמְלֵךְ אֹתוֹ אַךְ יָקֵם יְהוָה אֶת־ דְּבָרוֹ
word-of-him *** Yahweh may-he-make-good only him to-wean-you until stay!

וַתֵּשֶׁב הָאִשָּׁה וַתֵּינֶק אֶת־ בְּנָהּ עַד־ גָמְלָהּ אֹתוֹ׃
him to-wean-her until son-of-her *** and-she-nursed the-woman so-she-stayed

וַתַּעֲלֵהוּ עִמָּהּ כַּאֲשֶׁר גְּמָלַתּוּ *בְּפָרִים שְׁלֹשָׁה*
three with-bulls she-weaned-him just-as with-her and-she-took-him (24)

וְאֵיפָה אַחַת קֶמַח וְנֵבֶל יַיִן וַתְּבִאֵהוּ בֵית־ יְהוָה
Yahweh house-of and-she-brought-him wine and-skin-of flour one and-ephah

שִׁלוֹ וְהַנַּעַר נָעַר׃ וַיִּשְׁחֲטוּ אֶת־ הַפָּר
the-bull *** when-they-slaughtered (25) young now-the-boy Shiloh

וַיָּבִיאוּ אֶת־ הַנַּעַר אֶל־ עֵלִי׃ וַתֹּאמֶר בִּי אֲדֹנִי חֵי
life-of lord-of-me oh! and-she-said (26) Eli to the-boy *** then-they-brought

נַפְשְׁךָ אֲדֹנִי אֲנִי הָאִשָּׁה הַנִּצֶּבֶת עִמְּכָה בָּזֶה
at-here beside-you the-one-standing the-woman I lord-of-me soul-of-you

לְהִתְפַּלֵּל אֶל־ יְהוָה׃ אֶל־ הַנַּעַר הַזֶּה הִתְפַּלָּלְתִּי וַיִּתֵּן יְהוָה
Yahweh and-he-granted I-prayed the-this the-child for (27) Yahweh to to-pray

לִי אֶת־ שְׁאֵלָתִי אֲשֶׁר שָׁאַלְתִּי מֵעִמּוֹ׃ וְגַם אָנֹכִי הִשְׁאִלְתִּהוּ
I-give-him I so-now (28) from-with-him I-asked that request-of-me *** to-me

לַיהוָה כָּל־ הַיָּמִים אֲשֶׁר הָיָה הוּא שָׁאוּל לַיהוָה
to-Yahweh being-given he he-lives that the-days all-of to-Yahweh

וַיִּשְׁתַּחוּ שָׁם לַיהוָה׃ וַתִּתְפַּלֵּל חַנָּה וַתֹּאמַר
and-she-said Hannah then-she-prayed (2:1) to-Yahweh there and-he-worshiped

wife, and the LORD remem-
bered her. [20]So in the course of
time Hannah conceived and
gave birth to a son. She named
him Samuel,[e] saying, "Because I asked the LORD for
him."

Hannah Dedicates Samuel

[21]When the man Elkanah
went up with all his family to
offer the annual sacrifice to the
LORD and to fulfill his vow,
[22]Hannah did not go. She said
to her husband, "After the boy
is weaned, I will take him and
present him before the LORD,
and he will live there always."
[23]"Do what seems best to
you," Elkanah her husband
told her. "Stay here until you
have weaned him; only may
the LORD make good his[f]
word." So the woman stayed
at home and nursed her son
until she had weaned him.
[24]After he was weaned, she
took the boy with her, young
as he was, along with a three-
year-old bull,[g] an ephah[h] of
flour and a skin of wine, and
brought him to the house of
the LORD at Shiloh. [25]When
they had slaughtered the bull,
they brought the boy to Eli,
[26]and she said to him, "As
surely as you live, my lord, I
am the woman who stood
here beside you praying to the
LORD. [27]I prayed for this child,
and the LORD has granted me
what I asked of him. [28]So now
I give him to the LORD. For his
whole life he will be given
over to the LORD." And he
worshiped the LORD there.

Hannah's Prayer

2 Then Hannah prayed and
said:

[e]20 *Samuel* sounds like the Hebrew for *heard of God.*
[f]23 Masoretic Text; Dead Sea Scrolls, Septuagint and Syriac *your*
[g]24 Dead Sea Scrolls, Septuagint and Syriac; Masoretic Text *with three bulls*
[h]24 That is, probably about 1/2 bushel (about 22 liters)

*24 The Dead Sea Scrolls read
בקר משלש ולחם
and-bread being-three-years-old bull as do the ancient versions listed above in footnote *g*, (cf. verse 25).

עָלַץ לִבִּי בַּיהוָה רָמָה קַרְנִי בַּיהוָה
in-Yahweh horn-of-me she-is-lifted-high in-Yahweh heart-of-me he-rejoices

רָחַב פִּי עַל־ אוֹיְבַי כִּי שָׂמַחְתִּי
I-delight for being-enemies-of-me over mouth-of-me he-boasts

בִּישׁוּעָתֶךָ׃ (2) אֵין־ קָדוֹשׁ כַּיהוָה כִּי
indeed like-Yahweh holy there-is-no-one (2) in-deliverance-of-you

אֵין בִּלְתֶּךָ וְאֵין צוּר כֵּאלֹהֵינוּ׃ (3) אַל־
not (3) like-God-of-us Rock and-there-is-no besides-you there-is-no-one

תַּרְבּוּ תְדַבְּרוּ גְּבֹהָה גְבֹהָה יֵצֵא עָתָק מִפִּיכֶם
from-mouth-of-you arrogance he-comes proudly proudly you-talk you-keep-on

כִּי אֵל דֵּעוֹת יְהוָה וְלֹא נִתְכְּנוּ עֲלִלוֹת׃ (4) קֶשֶׁת
bow-of (4) deeds they-are-weighed and-by-him Yahweh knowings God-of for

גִּבֹּרִים חַתִּים וְנִכְשָׁלִים אָזְרוּ חָיִל׃
strength they-are-armed but-ones-stumbling ones-broken warriors

(5) שְׂבֵעִים בַּלֶּחֶם נִשְׂכָּרוּ וּרְעֵבִים חָדֵלּוּ
they-stop but-hungry-ones they-hire-themselves-out for-the-food full-ones (5)

עַד־ עֲקָרָה יָלְדָה שִׁבְעָה וְרַבַּת בָּנִים אֻמְלָלָה׃ (6) יְהוָה
Yahweh (6) pining-away sons but-many-of seven she-bore barren even

מֵמִית וּמְחַיֶּה מוֹרִיד שְׁאוֹל וַיָּעַל׃
and-he-raises-up Sheol bringing-down and-making-alive bringing-death

(7) יְהוָה מוֹרִישׁ וּמַעֲשִׁיר מַשְׁפִּיל אַף־ מְרוֹמֵם׃
exalting and humbling and-sending-wealth sending-poverty Yahweh (7)

(8) מֵקִים מֵעָפָר דָּל מֵאַשְׁפֹּת יָרִים אֶבְיוֹן לְהוֹשִׁיב עִם־
with to-seat needy he-lifts from-ash-heaps poor from-dust raising (8)

נְדִיבִים וְכִסֵּא כָבוֹד יַנְחִלֵם כִּי לַיהוָה מְצֻקֵי
foundations-of to-Yahweh for he-has-inherit-them honor and-throne-of princes

אֶרֶץ וַיָּשֶׁת עֲלֵיהֶם תֵּבֵל׃ (9) רַגְלֵי חֲסִידָו יִשְׁמֹר
he-will-guard saints-of-him feet-of (9) world upon-them and-he-set earth

וּרְשָׁעִים בַּחֹשֶׁךְ יִדָּמּוּ כִּי־ לֹא בְכֹחַ
by-strength not for they-will-be-silenced in-the-darkness but-wicked-ones

יִגְבַּר־ אִישׁ׃ (10) יְהוָה יֵחַתּוּ מְרִיבָו עָלָו
against-him ones-opposing-him he-shatters Yahweh (10) one he-prevails

בַּשָּׁמַיִם יַרְעֵם יְהוָה יָדִין אַפְסֵי־ אָרֶץ וְיִתֶּן־
he-will-give earth ends-of he-will-judge Yahweh he-thunders from-the-heavens

עֹז לְמַלְכּוֹ וְיָרֵם קֶרֶן מְשִׁיחוֹ׃
anointed-of-him horn-of he-will-exalt to-king-of-him strength

(11) וַיֵּלֶךְ אֶלְקָנָה הָרָמָתָה עַל־ בֵּיתוֹ וְהַנַּעַר הָיָה
he-was but-the-boy home-of-him to to-the-Ramah Elkanah then-he-went (11)

"My heart rejoices in the LORD;
in the LORD my horn[i] is lifted high.
My mouth boasts over my enemies,
for I delight in your deliverance.
2 "There is no one holy[j] like the LORD;
there is no one besides you;
there is no Rock like our God.
3 "Do not keep talking so proudly
or let your mouth speak such arrogance,
for the LORD is a God who knows,
and by him deeds are weighed.
4 "The bows of the warriors are broken,
but those who stumbled are armed with strength.
5 Those who were full hire themselves out for food,
but those who were hungry hunger no more.
She who was barren has borne seven children,
but she who has had many sons pines away.
6 "The LORD brings death and makes alive;
he brings down to the grave[k] and raises up.
7 The LORD sends poverty and wealth;
he humbles and he exalts.
8 He raises the poor from the dust
and lifts the needy from the ash heap;
he seats them with princes
and has them inherit a throne of honor.
"For the foundations of the earth are the LORD's;
upon them he has set the world.
9 He will guard the feet of his saints,
but the wicked will be silenced in darkness.
"It is not by strength that one prevails;
10 those who oppose the LORD will be shattered.
He will thunder against them from heaven;

[i] 1 *Horn* here symbolizes strength; also in verse 10.
[j] 2 Or *no Holy One*
[k] 6 Hebrew *Sheol*

°3 ק ולו , °9 ק חסידיו
°10a ק מריביו , °10b ק עליו

מְשָׁרֵת אֶת־ יְהוָה אֶת־ פְּנֵי עֵלִי הַכֹּהֵן׃ וּבְנֵי עֵלִי
Eli now-sons-of (12) the-priest Eli faces-of before Yahweh before ministering

בְּנֵי בְלִיָּעַל לֹא יָדְעוּ אֶת־ יְהוָה׃ וּמִשְׁפַּט הַכֹּהֲנִים
the-priests now-practice-of (13) Yahweh *** they-regarded not wickedness sons-of

אֶת־ הָעָם כָּל־ אִישׁ זֹבֵחַ זֶבַח וּבָא נַעַר
servant-of then-he-came sacrifice offering one any-of the-people with

הַכֹּהֵן כְּבַשֵּׁל הַבָּשָׂר וְהַמַּזְלֵג שְׁלֹשׁ־ הַשִּׁנַּיִם
the-prongs three-of and-the-fork the-meat while-to-boil the-priest

בְּיָדוֹ׃ וְהִכָּה בַכִּיּוֹר אוֹ בַדּוּד אוֹ
or into-the-kettle or into-the-pan and-he-plunged (14) in-hand-of-him

בַקַּלַּחַת אוֹ בַפָּרוּר כֹּל אֲשֶׁר יַעֲלֶה הַמַּזְלֵג יִקַּח
he-took the-fork he-brought-up that all into-the-pot or into-the-caldron

הַכֹּהֵן בּוֹ כָּכָה יַעֲשׂוּ לְכָל־ יִשְׂרָאֵל הַבָּאִים שָׁם
there the-ones-coming Israel to-all-of they-treated so for-him the-priest

בְּשִׁלֹה׃ גַּם בְּטֶרֶם יַקְטִרוּן אֶת־ הַחֵלֶב וּבָא ׀ נַעַר
servant-of then-he-came the-fat *** they-burned even-before but (15) to-Shiloh

הַכֹּהֵן וְאָמַר לָאִישׁ הַזֹּבֵחַ תְּנָה בָשָׂר לִצְלוֹת
to-roast meat give! the-one-sacrificing to-the-man and-he-said the-priest

לַכֹּהֵן וְלֹא־ יִקַּח מִמְּךָ בָּשָׂר מְבֻשָּׁל כִּי אִם־ חָי׃
raw only but being-boiled meat from-you he-will-accept for-not to-the-priest

וַיֹּאמֶר אֵלָיו הָאִישׁ קַטֵּר יַקְטִירוּן כַּיּוֹם הַחֵלֶב
the-fat as-the-day let-them-burn to-burn the-man to-him if-he-said (16)

וְקַח־ לְךָ כַּאֲשֶׁר תְּאַוֶּה נַפְשֶׁךָ וְאָמַר ׀ לוֹ° כִּי
but no then-he-answered self-of-you she-wants just-as for-you then-take!

עַתָּה תִתֵּן וְאִם־ לֹא לָקַחְתִּי בְחָזְקָה׃ וַתְּהִי חַטַּאת
sin-of and-she-was (17) by-force I-will-take not and-if you-hand-over now

הַנְּעָרִים גְּדוֹלָה מְאֹד אֶת־ פְּנֵי יְהוָה כִּי נִאֲצוּ
they-treated-with-contempt for Yahweh faces-of before very great the-young-men

הָאֲנָשִׁים אֵת מִנְחַת יְהוָה׃ וּשְׁמוּאֵל מְשָׁרֵת אֶת־ פְּנֵי
faces-of before ministering but-Samuel (18) Yahweh offering-of *** the-men

יְהוָה נַעַר חָגוּר אֵפוֹד בָּד׃ וּמְעִיל קָטֹן תַּעֲשֶׂה־ לּוֹ
for-him she-made little and-robe (19) linen ephod wearing boy Yahweh

אִמּוֹ וְהַעַלְתָה לוֹ מִיָּמִים ׀ יָמִימָה בַּעֲלוֹתָהּ אֶת־
with when-to-go-up-her at-days on-days to-him and-she-took mother-of-him

אִישָׁהּ לִזְבֹּחַ אֶת־ זֶבַח הַיָּמִים׃ וּבֵרַךְ עֵלִי
Eli and-he-blessed (20) the-days sacrifice-of *** to-offer husband-of-her

אֶת־ אֶלְקָנָה וְאֶת־ אִשְׁתּוֹ וְאָמַר יָשֵׂם יְהוָה לְךָ זֶרַע מִן־
by child to-you Yahweh may-he-give and-he-said wife-of-him and Elkanah ***

the LORD will judge the
ends of the earth.

"He will give strength to
his king
and exalt the horn of his
anointed."

11Then Elkanah went home
to Ramah, but the boy minis-
tered before the LORD under
Eli the priest.

Eli's Wicked Sons

12Eli's sons were wicked
men; they had no regard for
the LORD. 13Now it was the
practice of the priests with the
people that whenever anyone
offered a sacrifice and while
the meat was being boiled, the
servant of the priest would
come with a three-pronged
fork in his hand. 14He would
plunge it into the pan or kettle
or caldron or pot, and the
priest would take for himself
whatever the fork brought up.
This is how they treated all the
Israelites who came to Shiloh.
15But even before the fat was
burned, the servant of the
priest would come and say to
the man who was sacrificing,
"Give the priest some meat to
roast; he won't accept boiled
meat from you, but only raw."
16If the man said to him,
"Let the fat be burned up first,
and then take whatever you
want," the servant would then
answer, "No, hand it over
now; if you don't, I'll take it by
force."
17This sin of the young men
was very great in the LORD's
sight, for they[l] were treating
the LORD's offering with contempt.
18But Samuel was ministering before the LORD—a boy
wearing a linen ephod. 19Each
year his mother made him a
little robe and took it to him
when she went up with her
husband to offer the annual
sacrifice. 20Eli would bless Elkanah and his wife, saying,
"May the LORD give you children by this woman to take

[l]17 Or *men*

°16 ק לא

הָאִשָּׁה הַזֹּאת תַּחַת הַשְּׁאֵלָה אֲשֶׁר שָׁאַל לַיהוָה
of-Yahweh he-asked that the-request in-place-of the-this the-woman

וְהָלְכוּ לִמְקֹמוֹ׃ כִּי־ פָקַד יְהוָה אֶת־ חַנָּה
Hannah to Yahweh he-was-gracious and (21) to-home-of-him then-they-went

וַתַּהַר וַתֵּלֶד שְׁלֹשָׁה־ בָנִים וּשְׁתֵּי בָנוֹת וַיִּגְדַּל
and-he-grew-up daughters and-two-of sons three and-she-bore and-she-conceived

הַנַּעַר שְׁמוּאֵל עִם־ יְהוָה׃ וְעֵלִי זָקֵן מְאֹד וְשָׁמַע אֵת כָּל־
all *** and-he-heard very he-was-old now-Eli (22) Yahweh with Samuel the-boy

אֲשֶׁר יַעֲשׂוּן בָּנָיו לְכָל־ יִשְׂרָאֵל וְאֵת אֲשֶׁר־ יִשְׁכְּבוּן אֶת־ הַנָּשִׁים
the-women with they-slept how and Israel to-all-of sons-of-him they-did that

הַצֹּבְאוֹת פֶּתַח אֹהֶל מוֹעֵד׃ וַיֹּאמֶר לָהֶם לָמָּה
why? to-them so-he-said (23) Meeting Tent-of entrance-of the-ones-serving

תַעֲשׂוּן כַּדְּבָרִים הָאֵלֶּה אֲשֶׁר אָנֹכִי שֹׁמֵעַ אֶת־ דִּבְרֵיכֶם רָעִים
wicked-ones deeds-of-you *** hearing I that the-these as-the-things you-do

מֵאֵת כָּל־ הָעָם אֵלֶּה׃ אַל בָּנָי כִּי לוֹא־טוֹבָה הַשְּׁמֻעָה אֲשֶׁר
that the-report good not for sons-of-me no (24) these the-people all-of from

אָנֹכִי שֹׁמֵעַ מַעֲבִרִים עַם־ יְהוָה׃ אִם־ יֶחֱטָא אִישׁ לְאִישׁ
against-man man he-sins if (25) Yahweh people-of ones-spreading hearing I

וּפִלְלוֹ אֱלֹהִים וְאִם לַיהוָה יֶחֱטָא־ אִישׁ מִי
who? man he-sins against-Yahweh but-if God then-he-may-mediate-for-him

יִתְפַּלֶּל־ לוֹ וְלֹא יִשְׁמְעוּ לְקוֹל אֲבִיהֶם
father-of-them to-rebuke-of they-listened but-not for-him he-will-intercede

כִּי־ חָפֵץ יְהוָה לַהֲמִיתָם׃ וְהַנַּעַר שְׁמוּאֵל הֹלֵךְ
growing Samuel and-the-boy (26) to-kill-them Yahweh he-willed for

וְגָדֵל וָטוֹב גַּם עִם־ יְהוָה וְגַם עִם־ אֲנָשִׁים׃ וַיָּבֹא
now-he-came (27) men with and-also Yahweh with both and-favor both-stature

אִישׁ־אֱלֹהִים אֶל־עֵלִי וַיֹּאמֶר אֵלָיו כֹּה אָמַר יְהוָה הֲנִגְלֹה
to-reveal-myself? Yahweh he-says this to-him and-he-said Eli to God man-of

נִגְלֵיתִי אֶל־ בֵּית אָבִיךָ בִּהְיוֹתָם בְּמִצְרַיִם
in-Egypt when-to-be-them father-of-you house-of to I-revealed-myself

לְבֵית פַּרְעֹה׃ וּבָחֹר אֹתוֹ מִכָּל־ שִׁבְטֵי יִשְׂרָאֵל
Israel tribes-of from-all-of him and-to-choose (28) Pharaoh under-house-of

לִי לְכֹהֵן לַעֲלוֹת עַל־ מִזְבְּחִי לְהַקְטִיר קְטֹרֶת לָשֵׂאת אֵפוֹד
ephod to-wear incense to-burn altar-of-me to to-go-up as-priest for-me

לְפָנָי וָאֶתְּנָה לְבֵית אָבִיךָ אֶת־ כָּל־
all-of *** father-of-you to-house-of and-I-gave in-presences-of-me

אִשֵּׁי בְּנֵי יִשְׂרָאֵל׃ לָמָּה תִבְעֲטוּ בְּזִבְחִי
at-sacrifice-of-me you-scorn why? (29) Israel sons-of fire-offerings-of

the place of the one she prayed
for and gave to the LORD."
Then they would go home.
[21]And the LORD was gracious
to Hannah; she conceived and
gave birth to three sons and
two daughters. Meanwhile,
the boy Samuel grew up in the
presence of the LORD.
[22]Now Eli, who was very old,
heard about everything his
sons were doing to all Israel
and how they slept with the
women who served at the entrance to the Tent of Meeting.
[23]So he said to them, "Why do
you do such things? I hear
from all the people about these
wicked deeds of yours. [24]No,
my sons; it is not a good report
that I hear spreading among
the LORD's people. [25]If a man
sins against another man,
God[m] may mediate for him;
but if a man sins against the
LORD, who will intercede for
him?" His sons, however, did
not listen to their father's
rebuke, for it was the LORD's
will to put them to death.
[26]And the boy Samuel continued to grow in stature and
in favor with the LORD and
with men.

Prophecy Against the House of Eli

[27]Now a man of God came to
Eli and said to him, "This is
what the LORD says: 'Did I not
clearly reveal myself to your
father's house when they were
in Egypt under Pharaoh? [28]I
chose your father out of all the
tribes of Israel to be my priest,
to go up to my altar, to burn
incense, and to wear an ephod
in my presence. I also gave
your father's house all the
offerings made with fire by
the Israelites. [29]Why do you[n]
scorn my sacrifice and

[m]25 Or *the judges*
[n]29 The Hebrew is plural.

וּבְמִנְחָתִי אֲשֶׁר צִוִּיתִי מָעוֹן וַתְּכַבֵּד אֶת־ בָּנֶיךָ
sons-of-you *** and-you-honor dwelling I-prescribed that and-at-offering-of-me

מִמֶּנִּי לְהַבְרִיאֲכֶם מֵרֵאשִׁית כָּל־ מִנְחַת יִשְׂרָאֵל
Israel offering-of every-of on-choice-part-of to-make-fat-you more-than-me

לְעַמִּי׃ (30) לָכֵן נְאֻם־ יְהוָה אֱלֹהֵי יִשְׂרָאֵל אָמוֹר
to-promise Israel God-of Yahweh declaration-of therefore (30) of-people-of-me

אָמַרְתִּי בֵּיתְךָ וּבֵית אָבִיךָ יִתְהַלְּכוּ
they-would-minister father-of-you and-house-of house-of-you I-promised

לְפָנַי עַד־ עוֹלָם וְעַתָּה נְאֻם־ יְהוָה חָלִילָה לִּי כִּי־
for from-me far-be-it! Yahweh declaration-of but-now forever for before-me

מְכַבְּדַי אֲכַבֵּד וּבֹזַי יֵקָלּוּ׃
they-will-be-disdained but-ones-despising-me I-will-honor ones-honoring-me

(31) הִנֵּה יָמִים בָּאִים וְגָדַעְתִּי אֶת־ זְרֹעֲךָ וְאֶת־
and strength-of-you *** when-I-will-cut-short ones-coming days see! (31)

זְרֹעַ בֵּית אָבִיךָ מִהְיוֹת זָקֵן בְּבֵיתֶךָ׃
in-family-of-you old-man not-to-be father-of-you house-of strength-of

(32) וְהִבַּטְתָּ צַר מָעוֹן בְּכֹל אֲשֶׁר־ יֵיטִיב
he-will-do-good that though-all dwelling distress-of and-you-will-see (32)

אֶת־ יִשְׂרָאֵל וְלֹא־ יִהְיֶה זָקֵן בְּבֵיתְךָ כָּל־ הַיָּמִים׃
the-days all-of in-family-of-you old-man he-will-be yet-not Israel ***

(33) וְאִישׁ לֹא־ אַכְרִית לְךָ מֵעִם מִזְבְּחִי לְכַלּוֹת אֶת־
*** to-blind altar-of-me from-at of-you I-cut-off not and-everyone (33)

עֵינֶיךָ וְלַאֲדִיב אֶת־ נַפְשֶׁךָ וְכָל־ מַרְבִּית
many-descendant-of and-all-of heart-of-you *** and-to-grieve eyes-of-you

בֵּיתְךָ יָמוּתוּ אֲנָשִׁים׃ (34) וְזֶה־ לְּךָ הָאוֹת אֲשֶׁר יָבֹא
he-happens that the-sign to-you and-this (34) men they-will-die family of-you

אֶל־ שְׁנֵי בָנֶיךָ אֶל־ חָפְנִי וּפִינְחָס בְּיוֹם אֶחָד יָמוּתוּ
they-will-die same on-day and-Phinehas Hophni to sons-of-you two-of to

שְׁנֵיהֶם׃ (35) וַהֲקִימֹתִי לִי כֹּהֵן נֶאֱמָן כַּאֲשֶׁר
as-what being-faithful priest for-me and-I-will-raise-up (35) both-of-them

בִּלְבָבִי וּבְנַפְשִׁי יַעֲשֶׂה וּבָנִיתִי לוֹ
for-him and-I-will-establish he-will-do and-in-mind-of-me in-heart-of-me

בַּיִת נֶאֱמָן וְהִתְהַלֵּךְ לִפְנֵי־ מְשִׁיחִי כָּל־ הַיָּמִים׃
the-days all-of anointed-of-me before and-he-will-minister being-firm house

(36) וְהָיָה כָּל־ הַנּוֹתָר בְּבֵיתְךָ יָבוֹא
he-will-come in-family-of-you the-one-being-left every-of then-he-will-be (36)

לְהִשְׁתַּחֲוֺת לוֹ לַאֲגוֹרַת כֶּסֶף וְכִכַּר־ לֶחֶם וְאָמַר
and-he-will-plead bread and-crust-of silver for-piece-of before-him to-bow

offering that I prescribed for
my dwelling? Why do you
honor your sons more than
me by fattening yourselves on
the choice parts of every
offering made by my people
Israel?'

[30]"Therefore the LORD, the
God of Israel, declares: 'I
promised that your house and
your father's house would
minister before me forever.'
But now the LORD declares:
'Far be it from me! Those who
honor me I will honor, but
those who despise me will be
disdained. [31]The time is coming when I will cut short your
strength and the strength of
your father's house, so that
there will not be an old man in
your family line [32]and you will
see distress in my dwelling.
Although good will be done to
Israel, in your family line
there will never be an old
man. [33]Every one of you that I
do not cut off from my altar
will be spared only to blind
your eyes with tears and to
grieve your heart, and all your
descendants will die in the
prime of life.

[34]" 'And what happens to
your two sons, Hophni and
Phinehas, will be a sign to
you—they will both die on the
same day. [35]I will raise up for
myself a faithful priest, who
will do according to what is in
my heart and mind. I will
firmly establish his house, and
he will minister before my
anointed one always. [36]Then
everyone left in your family
line will come and bow down
before him for a piece of silver
and a crust of bread and plead,

*35 Most mss have *hireq* under the *he* (וְהִתְ׳).

סְפָחֵנִי נָא אֶל־ אַחַת הַכְּהֻנּוֹת לֶאֱכֹל פַּת־ לָחֶם׃
food bit-of to-eat the-priestly-offices one-of to now! appoint-me!

וְהַנַּעַר שְׁמוּאֵל מְשָׁרֵת אֶת־ יְהוָה לִפְנֵי עֵלִי וּדְבַר־
and-word-of Eli under Yahweh before ministering Samuel now-the-boy (3:1)

יְהוָה הָיָה יָקָר בַּיָּמִים הָהֵם אֵין חָזוֹן נִפְרָץ׃
being-many vision there-was-not the-those in-the-days rare he-was Yahweh

וַיְהִי בַּיּוֹם הַהוּא וְעֵלִי שֹׁכֵב בִּמְקֹמוֹ
in-place-of-him lying-down that-Eli the-that on-the-day and-he-was (2)

וְעֵינָו הֵחֵלּוּ כֵהוֹת לֹא יוּכַל לִרְאוֹת׃ וְנֵר
and-lamp-of (3) to-see he-could not weak-ones they-became now-eyes-of-him

אֱלֹהִים טֶרֶם יִכְבֶּה וּשְׁמוּאֵל שֹׁכֵב בְּהֵיכַל יְהוָה אֲשֶׁר־
where Yahweh in-temple-of lying-down and-Samuel he-went-out not-yet God

שָׁם אֲרוֹן אֱלֹהִים׃ וַיִּקְרָא יְהוָה אֶל־שְׁמוּאֵל וַיֹּאמֶר הִנֵּנִי׃
here-I! and-he-answered Samuel to Yahweh then-he-called (4) God ark-of there

וַיָּרָץ אֶל־ עֵלִי וַיֹּאמֶר הִנְנִי כִּי־ קָרָאתָ לִּי וַיֹּאמֶר
but-he-said to-me you-called for here-I! and-he-said Eli to and-he-ran (5)

לֹא־קָרָאתִי שׁוּב שְׁכָב וַיֵּלֶךְ וַיִּשְׁכָּב׃ וַיֹּסֶף
and-he-repeated (6) and-he-lay-down so-he-went lie-down! go-back! I-called not

יְהוָה קְרֹא עוֹד שְׁמוּאֵל וַיָּקָם שְׁמוּאֵל וַיֵּלֶךְ אֶל־עֵלִי
Eli to and-he-went Samuel and-he-got-up Samuel again to-call Yahweh

וַיֹּאמֶר הִנְנִי כִּי קָרָאתָ לִי וַיֹּאמֶר לֹא־ קָרָאתִי בְנִי
son-of-me I-called not but-he-said to-me you-called for here-I! and-he-said

שׁוּב שְׁכָב׃ וּשְׁמוּאֵל טֶרֶם יָדַע אֶת־ יְהוָה וְטֶרֶם
and-not-yet Yahweh *** he-knew not-yet now-Samuel (7) lie-down! go-back!

יִגָּלֶה אֵלָיו דְּבַר־ יְהוָה׃ וַיֹּסֶף יְהוָה קְרֹא־
to-call Yahweh and-he-repeated (8) Yahweh word-of to-him he-was-revealed

שְׁמוּאֵל בַּשְּׁלִשִׁית וַיָּקָם וַיֵּלֶךְ אֶל־ עֵלִי וַיֹּאמֶר הִנְנִי
here-I! and-he-said Eli to and-he-went and-he-got-up on-the-third Samuel

כִּי קָרָאתָ לִי וַיָּבֶן עֵלִי כִּי יְהוָה קֹרֵא לַנָּעַר׃
to-the-boy calling Yahweh that Eli then-he-realized to-me you-called for

וַיֹּאמֶר עֵלִי לִשְׁמוּאֵל לֵךְ שְׁכָב וְהָיָה אִם־ יִקְרָא אֵלֶיךָ
to-you he-calls if and-he-will-be lie-down! go! to-Samuel Eli so-he-told (9)

וְאָמַרְתָּ דַּבֵּר יְהוָה כִּי שֹׁמֵעַ עַבְדֶּךָ וַיֵּלֶךְ שְׁמוּאֵל
Samuel so-he-went servant-of-you listening for Yahweh speak! they-you-say

וַיִּשְׁכַּב בִּמְקוֹמוֹ׃ וַיָּבֹא יְהוָה וַיִּתְיַצַּב
and-he-stood Yahweh and-he-came (10) in-place-of-him and-he-lay-down

וַיִּקְרָא כְפַעַם־ בְּפַעַם שְׁמוּאֵל | שְׁמוּאֵל וַיֹּאמֶר שְׁמוּאֵל דַּבֵּר כִּי
for speak! Samuel then-he-said Samuel Samuel at-time as-time and-he-called

"Appoint me to some priestly
office so I can have food to
eat.' "

The LORD Calls Samuel

3 The boy Samuel minis-
tered before the LORD un-
der Eli. In those days the word
of the LORD was rare; there
were not many visions.
2One night Eli, whose eyes
were becoming so weak that
he could barely see, was lying
down in his usual place. 3The
lamp of God had not yet gone
out, and Samuel was lying
down in the temple° of the
LORD, where the ark of God
was. 4Then the LORD called
Samuel.
Samuel answered, "Here I
am." 5And he ran to Eli and
said, "Here I am; you called
me."
But Eli said, "I did not call;
go back and lie down." So he
went and lay down.
6Again the LORD called,
"Samuel!" And Samuel got up
and went to Eli and said,
"Here I am; you called me."
"My son," Eli said, "I did
not call; go back and lie
down."
7Now Samuel did not yet
know the LORD: The word of
the LORD had not yet been revealed to him.
8The LORD called Samuel a
third time, and Samuel got up
and went to Eli and said,
"Here I am; you called me."
Then Eli realized that the
LORD was calling the boy. 9So
Eli told Samuel, "Go and lie
down, and if he calls you, say,
'Speak, LORD, for your servant
is listening.' " So Samuel went
and lay down in his place.
10The LORD came and stood
there, calling as at the other
times, "Samuel! Samuel!"
Then Samuel said, "Speak,

°3 That is, tabernacle

°2 ק ועיניו

שֹׁמֵעַ עַבְדֶּךָ׃ וַיֹּאמֶר יְהוָה אֶל־שְׁמוּאֵל הִנֵּה אָנֹכִי עֹשֶׂה
doing I see! Samuel to Yahweh and-he-said (11) servant-of-you listening

דָבָר בְּיִשְׂרָאֵל אֲשֶׁר כָּל־ שֹׁמְעוֹ תְּצִלֶּינָה שְׁתֵּי
both-of they-will-tingle one-hearing-him every-of that in-Israel something

אָזְנָיו׃ בַּיּוֹם הַהוּא אָקִים אֶל־ עֵלִי אֵת כָּל־
all *** Eli against I-will-carry-out the-that on-the-day (12) ears-of-him

אֲשֶׁר דִּבַּרְתִּי אֶל־ בֵּיתוֹ הָחֵל וְכַלֵּה׃ וְהִגַּדְתִּי
for-I-told (13) and-to-end to-begin family-of-him against I-spoke that

לוֹ כִּי־ שֹׁפֵט אֲנִי אֶת־ בֵּיתוֹ עַד־ עוֹלָם בַּעֲוֺן אֲשֶׁר־ יָדַע
he-knew that for-sin forever for family-of-him *** I judging that to-him

כִּי־ מְקַלְלִים לָהֶם בָּנָיו וְלֹא כִהָה
he-restrained and-not sons-of-him to-them ones-bringing-contempt for

בָּם׃ וְלָכֵן נִשְׁבַּעְתִּי לְבֵית עֵלִי אִם־ יִתְכַּפֵּר
he-will-be-atoned not Eli to-house-of I-swore so-therefore (14) against-them

עֲוֺן בֵּית־ עֵלִי בְּזֶבַח וּבְמִנְחָה עַד־ עוֹלָם׃ וַיִּשְׁכַּב
and-he-lay (15) forever for or-by-offering by-sacrifice Eli house-of guilt-of

שְׁמוּאֵל עַד־ הַבֹּקֶר וַיִּפְתַּח אֶת־ דַּלְתוֹת בֵּית־ יְהוָה
Yahweh house-of doors-of *** then-he-opened the-morning until Samuel

וּשְׁמוּאֵל יָרֵא מֵהַגִּיד אֶת־ הַמַּרְאָה אֶל־עֵלִי׃ וַיִּקְרָא
but-he-called (16) Eli to the-vision *** from-to-tell he-was-afraid now-Samuel

עֵלִי אֶת־ שְׁמוּאֵל וַיֹּאמֶר שְׁמוּאֵל בְּנִי וַיֹּאמֶר הִנֵּנִי׃
here-I! and-he-answered son-of-me Samuel and-he-said Samuel *** Eli

וַיֹּאמֶר מָה הַדָּבָר אֲשֶׁר דִּבֶּר אֵלֶיךָ אַל־ נָא תְכַחֵד
you-hide now! not to-you he-said that the-message what? and-he-asked (17)

מִמֶּנִּי כֹּה יַעֲשֶׂה־ לְּךָ אֱלֹהִים וְכֹה יוֹסִיף אִם־ תְּכַחֵד
you-hide if may-he-be-severe and-so God with-you may-he-deal so from-me

מִמֶּנִּי דָּבָר מִכָּל־ הַדָּבָר אֲשֶׁר־ דִּבֶּר אֵלֶיךָ׃ וַיַּגֶּד־
so-he-told (18) to-you he-told that the-message from-any-of anything from-me

לוֹ שְׁמוּאֵל אֶת־ כָּל־ הַדְּבָרִים וְלֹא כִחֵד מִמֶּנּוּ וַיֹּאמַר
and-he-said from-him he-hid and-not the-things all-of *** Samuel to-him

יְהוָה הוּא הַטּוֹב בְּעֵינָו יַעֲשֶׂה׃ וַיִּגְדַּל שְׁמוּאֵל
Samuel and-he-grew (19) let-him-do in-eyes-of-him the-good he Yahweh

וַיהוָה הָיָה עִמּוֹ וְלֹא־ הִפִּיל מִכָּל־ דְּבָרָיו
words-of-him from-any-of he-let-fall and-not with-him he-was and-Yahweh

אָרְצָה׃ וַיֵּדַע כָּל־ יִשְׂרָאֵל מִדָּן וְעַד־ בְּאֵר שָׁבַע
Sheba Beer even-to from-Dan Israel all-of and-he-recognized (20) to-ground

כִּי נֶאֱמָן שְׁמוּאֵל לְנָבִיא לַיהוָה׃ וַיֹּסֶף יְהוָה
Yahweh and-he-continued (21) of-Yahweh as-prophet Samuel being-attested that

for your servant is listening."
[11]And the LORD said to Samuel: "See, I am about to do
something in Israel that will
make the ears of everyone
who hears of it tingle. [12]At that
time I will carry out against Eli
everything I spoke against his
family—from beginning to
end. [13]For I told him that I
would judge his family forever
because of the sin he knew
about; his sons made themselves contemptible,[p] and he
failed to restrain them.
[14]Therefore, I swore to the
house of Eli, 'The guilt of Eli's
house will never be atoned for
by sacrifice or offering.' "
[15]Samuel lay down until
morning and then opened the
doors of the house of the LORD.
He was afraid to tell Eli the vision, [16]but Eli called him and
said, "Samuel, my son."
Samuel answered, "Here I
am."
[17]"What was it he said to
you?" Eli asked. "Do not hide
it from me. May God deal with
you, be it ever so severely, if
you hide from me anything he
told you." [18]So Samuel told
him everything, hiding nothing from him. Then Eli said,
"He is the LORD; let him do
what is good in his eyes."
[19]The LORD was with Samuel
as he grew up, and he let none
of his words fall to the ground.
[20]And all Israel from Dan to
Beersheba recognized that
Samuel was attested as a
prophet of the LORD. [21]The
LORD continued to appear at

[p]13 Masoretic Text; an ancient Hebrew scribal tradition and Septuagint *sons blasphemed God*

°*18* ק בעיניו

לְהֵרָאֹה בְּשִׁלֹה כִּֽי־ נִגְלָה יְהוָה אֶל־ שְׁמוּאֵל בְּשִׁלוֹ
at-Shiloh Samuel to Yahweh he-revealed-himself for at-Shiloh to-appear

בִּדְבַר יְהוָֽה׃ וַיְהִי דְבַר־ שְׁמוּאֵל לְכָל־ יִשְׂרָאֵל
Israel to-all-of Samuel word-of and-he-came (4:1) Yahweh through-word-of

וַיֵּצֵא יִשְׂרָאֵל[q] לִקְרַאת פְּלִשְׁתִּים לַמִּלְחָמָה וַיַּחֲנוּ עַל־
at and-they-camped in-the-fight Philistines to-meet Israel now-he-went-out

הָאֶבֶן הָעֵזֶר וּפְלִשְׁתִּים חָנוּ בַאֲפֵֽק׃ וַיַּעַרְכוּ
and-they-deployed (2) at-Aphek they-camped and-Philistines the-Ezer the-Eben

פְלִשְׁתִּים לִקְרַאת יִשְׂרָאֵל וַתִּטֹּשׁ הַמִּלְחָמָה וַיִּנָּגֶף
and-he-was-defeated the-battle and-she-spread Israel to-meet Philistines

יִשְׂרָאֵל לִפְנֵי פְלִשְׁתִּים וַיַּכּוּ בַמַּעֲרָכָה בַּשָּׂדֶה
in-the-field on-the-battleground and-they-killed Philistines before Israel

כְּאַרְבַּעַת אֲלָפִים אִֽישׁ׃ וַיָּבֹא הָעָם אֶל־הַֽמַּחֲנֶה
the-camp to the-people when-he-returned (3) man thousands about-four-of

וַיֹּאמְרוּ זִקְנֵי יִשְׂרָאֵל לָמָּה נְגָפָנוּ יְהוָה הַיּוֹם לִפְנֵי
before the-day Yahweh he-defeated-us why? Israel elders-of then-they-asked

פְלִשְׁתִּים נִקְחָה אֵלֵינוּ מִשִּׁלֹה אֶת־ אֲרוֹן בְּרִית יְהוָה
Yahweh covenant-of ark-of *** from-Shiloh to-us let-us-bring Philistines

וְיָבֹא בְקִרְבֵּנוּ וְיֹשִׁעֵנוּ מִכַּף אֹיְבֵֽינוּ׃
being-enemies-of-us from-hand-of and-he-may-save-us in-among-us so-he-may-go

וַיִּשְׁלַח הָעָם שִׁלֹה וַיִּשְׂאוּ מִשָּׁם אֵת אֲרוֹן
ark-of *** from-there and-they-brought Shiloh the-people so-he-sent (4)

בְּרִית־ יְהוָה צְבָאוֹת יֹשֵׁב הַכְּרֻבִים וְשָׁם שְׁנֵי
two-of and-there the-cherubim being-enthroned-of Hosts Yahweh-of covenant-of

בְנֵֽי־ עֵלִי עִם־ אֲרוֹן בְּרִית הָאֱלֹהִים חָפְנִי וּפִינְחָֽס׃ וַיְהִי
and-he-was (5) and-Phinehas Hophni the-God covenant-of ark-of with Eli sons-of

כְּבוֹא אֲרוֹן בְּרִית־ יְהוָה אֶל־ הַמַּחֲנֶה וַיָּרִעוּ כָל־
all-of and-they-shouted the-camp into Yahweh covenant-of ark-of when-to-come

יִשְׂרָאֵל תְּרוּעָה גְדוֹלָה וַתֵּהֹם הָאָֽרֶץ׃ וַיִּשְׁמְעוּ פְלִשְׁתִּים
Philistines when-they-heard (6) the-ground so-she-shook great shout Israel

אֶת־ קוֹל הַתְּרוּעָה וַיֹּאמְרוּ מֶה קוֹל הַתְּרוּעָה הַגְּדוֹלָה
the-great the-shout sound-of what? then-they-asked the-uproar sound-of ***

הַזֹּאת בְּמַחֲנֵה הָעִבְרִים וַיֵּדְעוּ כִּי אֲרוֹן יְהוָה בָּא
he-came Yahweh ark-of that when-they-learned the-Hebrews in-camp-of the-this

אֶל־ הַמַּחֲנֶֽה׃ וַיִּרְאוּ הַפְּלִשְׁתִּים כִּי אָמְרוּ בָּא
he-came they-said for the-Philistines then-they-were-afraid (7) the-camp into

אֱלֹהִים אֶל־הַמַּחֲנֶה וַיֹּאמְרוּ אוֹי לָנוּ כִּי לֹא הָיְתָה כָּזֹאת
like-this she-happened not for to-us woe! and-they-said the-camp into god

Shiloh, and there he revealed
himself to Samuel through his
word.

4 And Samuel's word came
to all Israel.

The Philistines Capture the Ark

Now the Israelites went out
to fight against the Philistines.
The Israelites camped at Ebenezer, and the Philistines at
Aphek. 2The Philistines deployed their forces to meet Israel, and as the battle spread,
Israel was defeated by the
Philistines, who killed about
four thousand of them on the
battlefield. 3When the soldiers
returned to camp, the elders of
Israel asked, "Why did the
LORD bring defeat upon us today before the Philistines? Let
us bring the ark of the LORD's
covenant from Shiloh, so that
it[q] may go with us and save us
from the hand of our ene-
mies."
4So the people sent men to
Shiloh, and they brought back
the ark of the covenant of the
LORD Almighty, who is en-
throned between the cherubim. And Eli's two sons,
Hophni and Phinehas, were
there with the ark of the covenant of God.
5When the ark of the LORD's
covenant came into the camp,
all Israel raised such a great
shout that the ground shook.
6Hearing the uproar, the Philistines asked, "What's all this
shouting in the Hebrew
camp?"
When they learned that the
ark of the LORD had come into
the camp, 7the Philistines
were afraid. "A god has come
into the camp," they said.
"We're in trouble! Nothing
like this has happened before.

[q]3 Or *he*

אֶתְמוֹל שִׁלְשֹׁם׃ אוֹי לָנוּ מִי יַצִּילֵנוּ מִיַּד הָאֱלֹהִים
the-gods from-hand-of he-will-deliver-us who? to-us woe! (8) before yesterday

הָאַדִּירִים הָאֵלֶּה אֵלֶּה הֵם הָאֱלֹהִים הַמַּכִּים אֶת־ מִצְרַיִם
Egyptians *** the-ones-striking the-gods they these the-these the-mighty-ones

בְּכָל־ מַכָּה בַּמִּדְבָּר׃ הִתְחַזְּקוּ וִהְיוּ לַאֲנָשִׁים פְּלִשְׁתִּים
Philistines like-men and-be! be-strong! (9) in-the-desert plague with-every-of

פֶּן תַּעַבְדוּ לָעִבְרִים כַּאֲשֶׁר עָבְדוּ לָכֶם
to-you they-are-subject just-as to-the-Hebrews you-will-be-subject or

וִהְיִיתֶם לַאֲנָשִׁים וְנִלְחַמְתֶּם׃ וַיִּלָּחֲמוּ פְלִשְׁתִּים
Philistines so-they-fought (10) and-you-fight like-men so-you-be

וַיִּנָּגֶף יִשְׂרָאֵל וַיָּנֻסוּ אִישׁ לְאֹהָלָיו וַתְּהִי
and-she-was to-tents-of-him each and-they-fled Israel and-he-was-defeated

הַמַּכָּה גְּדוֹלָה מְאֹד וַיִּפֹּל מִיִּשְׂרָאֵל שְׁלֹשִׁים אֶלֶף רַגְלִי׃
foot-soldier thousand thirty from-Israel and-he-fell very great the-slaughter

וַאֲרוֹן אֱלֹהִים נִלְקָח וּשְׁנֵי בְנֵי־ עֵלִי מֵתוּ חָפְנִי
Hophni they-died Eli sons-of and-two-of he-was-captured God and-ark-of (11)

וּפִינְחָס׃ וַיָּרָץ אִישׁ־ בִּנְיָמִן מֵהַמַּעֲרָכָה וַיָּבֹא
and-he-went from-the-battle-line Benjamin man-of and-he-ran (12) and-Phinehas

שִׁלֹה בַּיּוֹם הַהוּא וּמַדָּיו קְרֻעִים וַאֲדָמָה עַל־
on and-dust ones-being-torn and-clothes-of-him the-that on-the-day Shiloh

רֹאשׁוֹ׃ וַיָּבוֹא וְהִנֵּה עֵלִי יֹשֵׁב עַל־ הַכִּסֵּא יַךְ
side-of the-chair on sitting Eli then-see! when-he-arrived (13) head-of-him

דֶּרֶךְ מְצַפֶּה כִּי־ הָיָה לִבּוֹ חָרֵד עַל אֲרוֹן הָאֱלֹהִים וְהָאִישׁ
when-the-man the-God ark-of for afraid heart-of-him he-was for watching road

בָּא לְהַגִּיד בָּעִיר וַתִּזְעַק כָּל־ הָעִיר׃
the-town whole-of then-she-cried in-the-town to-tell he-entered

וַיִּשְׁמַע עֵלִי אֶת־ קוֹל הַצְּעָקָה וַיֹּאמֶר מֶה קוֹל
sound-of what? and-he-asked the-outcry sound-of *** Eli and-he-heard (14)

הֶהָמוֹן הַזֶּה וְהָאִישׁ מִהַר וַיָּבֹא וַיַּגֵּד לְעֵלִי׃
to-Eli and-he-told and-he-went he-hurried and-the-man the-this the-uproar

וְעֵלִי בֶּן־ תִּשְׁעִים וּשְׁמֹנֶה שָׁנָה וְעֵינָיו קָמָה וְלֹא
so-not being-set and-eyes-of-him year and-eight ninety son-of now-Eli (15)

יָכוֹל לִרְאוֹת׃ וַיֹּאמֶר הָאִישׁ אֶל־ עֵלִי אָנֹכִי הַבָּא מִן־
from the-one-coming I Eli to the-man and-he-told (16) to-see he-could

הַמַּעֲרָכָה וַאֲנִי מִן־ הַמַּעֲרָכָה נַסְתִּי הַיּוֹם וַיֹּאמֶר מֶה־
what? and-he-asked the-day I-fled the-battle-line from and-I the-battle-line

הָיָה הַדָּבָר בְּנִי׃ וַיַּעַן הַמְבַשֵּׂר
the-one-bringing-news and-he-replied (17) son-of-me the-thing he-happened

8Woe to us! Who will deliver us
from the hand of these mighty
gods? They are the gods who
struck the Egyptians with all
kinds of plagues in the desert.
9Be strong, Philistines! Be
men, or you will be subject to
the Hebrews, as they have
been to you. Be men, and
fight!"
10So the Philistines fought,
and the Israelites were defeated
and every man fled to
his tent. The slaughter was
very great; Israel lost thirty
thousand foot soldiers. 11The
ark of God was captured, and
Eli's two sons, Hophni and
Phinehas, died.

Death of Eli

12That same day a Benjamite
ran from the battle line and
went to Shiloh, his clothes
torn and dust on his head.
13When he arrived, there was
Eli sitting on his chair by the
side of the road, watching, because
his heart feared for the
ark of God. When the man entered
the town and told what
had happened, the whole
town sent up a cry.
14Eli heard the outcry and
asked, "What is the meaning
of this uproar?"
The man hurried over to Eli,
15who was ninety-eight years
old and whose eyes were set so
that he could not see. 16He told
Eli, "I have just come from the
battle line; I fled from it this
very day."
Eli asked, "What happened,
my son?"
17The man who brought the

°13 ק יד

וַיֹּאמֶר נָס יִשְׂרָאֵל לִפְנֵי פְלִשְׁתִּים וְגַם מַגֵּפָה גְדוֹלָה הָיְתָה
she-was heavy loss and-also Philistines before Israel he-fled and-he-said

בָעָם וְגַם־ שְׁנֵי בָנֶיךָ מֵתוּ חָפְנִי וּפִינְחָס
and-Phinehas Hophni they-died sons-of-you two-of and-also among-the-people

וַאֲרוֹן הָאֱלֹהִים נִלְקָחָה׃ וַיְהִי כְּהַזְכִּירוֹ | אֶת־
*** when-to-mention-him and-he-was (18) she-was-captured the-God and-ark-of

אֲרוֹן הָאֱלֹהִים וַיִּפֹּל מֵעַל־ הַכִּסֵּא אֲחֹרַנִּית בְּעַד | יַד הַשַּׁעַר
the-gate side-of by backward the-chair from-on and-he-fell the-God ark-of

וַתִּשָּׁבֵר מַפְרַקְתּוֹ וַיָּמֹת כִּי־ זָקֵן הָאִישׁ וְכָבֵד
and-heavy the-man he-was-old for and-he-died neck-of-him and-she-was-broken

וְהוּא שָׁפַט אֶת־ יִשְׂרָאֵל אַרְבָּעִים שָׁנָה׃ וְכַלָּתוֹ אֵשֶׁת־
wife-of now-daughter-in-law-of-him (19) year forty Israel *** he-led and-he

פִּינְחָס הָרָה לָלַת וַתִּשְׁמַע אֶת־ הַשְּׁמֻעָה אֶל־ הִלָּקַח
to-be-captured that the-news *** when-she-heard to-deliver pregnant Phinehas

אֲרוֹן הָאֱלֹהִים וּמֵת חָמִיהָ וְאִישָׁהּ
and-husband-of-her father-in-law-of-her and-he-died the-God ark-of

וַתִּכְרַע וַתֵּלֶד כִּי־ נֶהֶפְכוּ עָלֶיהָ
over-her they-overcame but and-she-gave-birth then-she-went-into-labor

צִרֶיהָ׃ וּכְעֵת מוּתָהּ וַתְּדַבֵּרְנָה
then-they-said to-die-her and-at-time-of (20) labor-pains-of-her

הַנִּצָּבוֹת עָלֶיהָ אַל־ תִּירְאִי כִּי בֵן יָלָדְתְּ וְלֹא
but-not you-bore son for you-despair not to-her the-ones-attending

עָנְתָה וְלֹא־ שָׁתָה לִבָּהּ׃ וַתִּקְרָא לַנַּעַר
to-the-boy and-she-named (21) heart-of-her she-attended and-not she-responded

אִי־כָבוֹד לֵאמֹר גָּלָה כָבוֹד מִיִּשְׂרָאֵל אֶל־ הִלָּקַח אֲרוֹן
ark-of to-be-captured because from-Israel glory he-departed to-say Ichabod

הָאֱלֹהִים וְאֶל־ חָמִיהָ וְאִישָׁהּ׃
and-husband-of-her father-in-law-of-her and-because-of the-God

וַתֹּאמֶר גָּלָה כָבוֹד מִיִּשְׂרָאֵל כִּי נִלְקַח אֲרוֹן
ark-of he-was-captured for from-Israel glory he-departed and-she-said (22)

הָאֱלֹהִים׃ וּפְלִשְׁתִּים לָקְחוּ אֵת אֲרוֹן הָאֱלֹהִים וַיְבִאֻהוּ
and-they-took-him the-God ark-of *** they-captured now-Philistines (5:1) the-God

מֵאֶבֶן הָעֵזֶר אַשְׁדּוֹדָה׃ וַיִּקְחוּ פְלִשְׁתִּים אֶת־ אֲרוֹן
ark-of *** Philistines then-they-carried (2) to-Ashdod the-Ezer from-Eben

הָאֱלֹהִים וַיָּבִיאוּ אֹתוֹ בֵּית דָּגוֹן וַיַּצִּיגוּ אֹתוֹ אֵצֶל דָּגוֹן׃
Dagon beside him and-they-set Dagon temple-of him and-they-took the-God

וַיַּשְׁכִּמוּ אַשְׁדּוֹדִים מִמָּחֳרָת וְהִנֵּה דָגוֹן נֹפֵל
having-fallen Dagon then-see! on-next-day Ashdodites when-they-rose (3)

news replied, "Israel fled before the Philistines, and the army has suffered heavy losses. Also your two sons, Hophni and Phinehas, are dead, and the ark of God has been captured."

[18]When he mentioned the ark of God, Eli fell backward off his chair by the side of the gate. His neck was broken and he died, for he was an old man and heavy. He had led[r] Israel forty years.

[19]His daughter-in-law, the wife of Phinehas, was pregnant and near the time of delivery. When she heard the news that the ark of God had been captured and that her father-in-law and her husband were dead, she went into labor and gave birth, but was overcome by her labor pains. [20]As she was dying, the women attending her said, "Don't despair; you have given birth to a son." But she did not respond or pay any attention.

[21]She named the boy Ichabod,[s] saying, "The glory has departed from Israel"—because of the capture of the ark of God and the deaths of her father-in-law and her husband. [22]She said, "The glory has departed from Israel, for the ark of God has been captured."

The Ark in Ashdod and Ekron

5 After the Philistines had captured the ark of God, they took it from Ebenezer to Ashdod. [2]Then they carried the ark into Dagon's temple and set it beside Dagon. [3]When the people of Ashdod rose early the next day, there was Dagon, fallen on his face

[r]18 Traditionally *judged*
[s]21 *Ichabod* means *no glory.*

לְפָנָיו אַרְצָה לִפְנֵי אֲרוֹן יְהוָה וַיִּקְחוּ אֶת־ דָּגוֹן
Dagon *** and-they-took Yahweh ark-of before on-ground on-faces-of-him

וַיָּשִׁבוּ אֹתוֹ לִמְקוֹמוֹ׃ וַיַּשְׁכִּמוּ בַבֹּקֶר
in-the-morning but-they-rose (4) in-place-of-him him and-they-put-back

מִמָּחֳרָת וְהִנֵּה דָגוֹן נֹפֵל לְפָנָיו אַרְצָה לִפְנֵי
before on-ground on-faces-of-him having-fallen Dagon and-see! on-next-day

אֲרוֹן יְהוָה וְרֹאשׁ דָּגוֹן וּשְׁתֵּי׀ כַּפּוֹת יָדָיו
hands-of-him palms-of and-two-of Dagon and-head-of Yahweh ark-of

כְּרֻתוֹת אֶל־ הַמִּפְתָּן רַק דָּגוֹן נִשְׁאַר עָלָיו׃ עַל־
for (5) on-him he-remained Dagon only the-threshold on ones-being-broken-off

כֵּן לֹא־ יִדְרְכוּ כֹהֲנֵי דָגוֹן וְכָל־ הַבָּאִים בֵּית־
temple-of the-ones-entering or-any-of Dagon priests-of they-step not this

דָּגוֹן עַל־ מִפְתַּן דָּגוֹן בְּאַשְׁדּוֹד עַד הַיּוֹם הַזֶּה׃ וַתִּכְבַּד
and-she-was-heavy (6) the-this the-day to at-Ashdod Dagon threshold-of on Dagon

יַד־ יְהוָה אֶל־ הָאַשְׁדּוֹדִים וַיְשִׁמֵּם וַיַּךְ
and-he-afflicted and-he-brought-desolation the-Ashdodites upon Yahweh hand-of

אֹתָם בַּעְפֹלִים° אֶת־אַשְׁדּוֹד וְאֶת־ גְּבוּלֶיהָ׃ וַיִּרְאוּ אַנְשֵׁי־
men-of when-they-saw (7) vicinities-of-her and Ashdod *** *with-the-tumors them

אַשְׁדּוֹד כִּי־ כֵן וְאָמְרוּ לֹא־ יֵשֵׁב אֲרוֹן אֱלֹהֵי יִשְׂרָאֵל עִמָּנוּ
with-us Israel god-of ark-of he-must-stay not then-they-said so that Ashdod

כִּי־ קָשְׁתָה יָדוֹ עָלֵינוּ וְעַל דָּגוֹן אֱלֹהֵינוּ׃ וַיִּשְׁלְחוּ
so-they-sent (8) god-of-us Dagon and-upon upon-us hand-of-him she-is-heavy for

וַיַּאַסְפוּ אֶת־ כָּל־ סַרְנֵי פְלִשְׁתִּים אֲלֵיהֶם וַיֹּאמְרוּ
and-they-asked to-them Philistines rulers-of all-of *** and-they-called-together

מַה־ נַּעֲשֶׂה לַאֲרוֹן אֱלֹהֵי יִשְׂרָאֵל וַיֹּאמְרוּ גַּת
Gath and-they-answered Israel god-of with-ark-of shall-we-do what?

יִסֹּב אֲרוֹן אֱלֹהֵי יִשְׂרָאֵל וַיַּסֵּבּוּ אֶת־ אֲרוֹן אֱלֹהֵי יִשְׂרָאֵל׃
Israel God-of ark-of *** so-they-moved Israel god-of ark-of let-him-move

וַיְהִי אַחֲרֵי׀ הֵסַבּוּ אֹתוֹ וַתְּהִי יַד־ יְהוָה׀
Yahweh hand-of then-she-was him they-moved after but-he-was (9)

בָּעִיר מְהוּמָה גְּדוֹלָה מְאֹד וַיַּךְ אֶת־ אַנְשֵׁי הָעִיר
the-city people-of *** and-he-afflicted very great panic against-the-city

מִקָּטֹן וְעַד־ גָּדוֹל וַיִּשָּׂתְרוּ לָהֶם עְפָלִים°׃ וַיְשַׁלְּחוּ
so-they-sent (10) *tumors on-them so-they-broke-out old even-to from-young

אֶת־ אֲרוֹן הָאֱלֹהִים עֶקְרוֹן וַיְהִי כְּבוֹא אֲרוֹן הָאֱלֹהִים עֶקְרוֹן
Ekron the-God ark-of as-to-enter and-he-was Ekron the-God ark-of ***

וַיִּזְעֲקוּ הָעֶקְרֹנִים לֵאמֹר הֵסַבּוּ אֵלַי אֶת־ אֲרוֹן אֱלֹהֵי
god-of ark-of *** to-me they-brought to-say the-Ekronites then-they-cried

on the ground before the ark of the LORD! They took Dagon and put him back in his place.
4But the following morning when they rose, there was Dagon, fallen on his face on the ground before the ark of the LORD! His head and hands had been broken off and were lying on the threshold; only his body remained.
5That is why to this day neither the priests of Dagon nor any others who enter Dagon's temple at Ashdod step on the threshold.

6The LORD's hand was heavy upon the people of Ashdod and its vicinity; he brought devastation upon them and afflicted them with tumors.[t]
7When the men of Ashdod saw what was happening, they said, "The ark of the god of Israel must not stay here with us, because his hand is heavy upon us and upon Dagon our god."
8So they called together all the rulers of the Philistines and asked them, "What shall we do with the ark of the god of Israel?"

They answered, "Have the ark of the god of Israel moved to Gath." So they moved the ark of the God of Israel.

9But after they had moved it, the LORD's hand was against that city, throwing it into a great panic. He afflicted the people of the city, both young and old, with an outbreak of tumors.[u]
10So they sent the ark of God to Ekron.

As the ark of God was entering Ekron, the people of Ekron cried out, "They have brought the ark of the god of Israel

t6 Hebrew; Septuagint and Vulgate *tumors. And rats appeared in their land, and death and destruction were throughout the city*
u9 Or *with tumors in the groin* (see Septuagint)

*6, 9 The *Qere* is a less graphic synonym of the *Kethib*, see footnote *u* above.

°6 ק בטחרים
°9 ק טחרים

יִשְׂרָאֵל לַהֲמִיתֵנִי וְאֶת־ עַמִּי׃ וַיִּשְׁלְחוּ וַיַּאַסְפוּ

and-they-called-together so-they-sent (11) people-of-me and to-kill-me Israel

אֶת־ כָּל־ סַרְנֵי פְלִשְׁתִּים וַיֹּאמְרוּ שַׁלְּחוּ אֶת־ אֲרוֹן אֱלֹהֵי

god-of ark-of *** send-away! and-they-said Philistines rulers-of all-of ***

יִשְׂרָאֵל וְיָשֹׁב לִמְקֹמוֹ וְלֹא־ יָמִית אֹתִי וְאֶת־

and me he-will-kill so-not to-place-of-him and-let-him-go-back Israel

עַמִּי כִּי־ הָיְתָה מְהוּמַת־ מָוֶת בְּכָל־ הָעִיר כָּבְדָה

she-was-heavy the-city in-all-of death panic-of she-was for people-of-me

מְאֹד יַד הָאֱלֹהִים שָׁם׃ וְהָאֲנָשִׁים אֲשֶׁר לֹא־ מֵתוּ

they-died not who and-the-people (12) there the-God hand-of very

הֻכּוּ בַּעְפָלִים° וַתַּעַל שַׁוְעַת הָעִיר

the-city outcry-of and-she-went-up *with-the-tumors they-were-afflicted

הַשָּׁמָיִם׃ וַיְהִי אֲרוֹן־ יְהוָה בִּשְׂדֵה פְלִשְׁתִּים שִׁבְעָה

seven Philistines in-territory-of Yahweh ark-of when-he-was (6:1) the-heavens

חֳדָשִׁים׃ וַיִּקְרְאוּ פְלִשְׁתִּים לַכֹּהֲנִים וְלַקֹּסְמִים

and-for-the-ones-divining for-the-priests Philistines then-he-called (2) months

לֵאמֹר מַה־ נַּעֲשֶׂה לַאֲרוֹן יְהוָה הוֹדִעֻנוּ בַּמֶּה

by-the-how tell-us! Yahweh with-ark-of shall-we-do what? to-say

נְשַׁלְּחֶנּוּ לִמְקוֹמוֹ׃ וַיֹּאמְרוּ אִם־ מְשַׁלְּחִים

ones-returning if and-they-answered (3) to-place-of-him we-should-send-him

אֶת־ אֲרוֹן אֱלֹהֵי יִשְׂרָאֵל אַל־ תְּשַׁלְּחוּ אֹתוֹ רֵיקָם כִּי־ הָשֵׁב תָּשִׁיבוּ

you-send to-send but empty him you-send-away not Israel god-of ark-of ***

לוֹ אָשָׁם אָז תֵּרָפְאוּ וְנוֹדַע לָכֶם

to-you and-he-will-be-made-known you-will-be-healed then guilt-offering to-him

לָמָּה לֹא־ תָסוּר יָדוֹ מִכֶּם׃ וַיֹּאמְרוּ מָה

what? and-they-asked (4) from-you hand-of-him she-was-lifted not why

הָאָשָׁם אֲשֶׁר נָשִׁיב לוֹ וַיֹּאמְרוּ מִסְפַּר

by-number-of and-they-replied to-him we-should-send that the-guilt-offering

סַרְנֵי פְלִשְׁתִּים חֲמִשָּׁה עָפְלֵי° זָהָב וַחֲמִשָּׁה עַכְבְּרֵי זָהָב כִּי־ מַגֵּפָה

plague for gold rats-of and-five gold *tumors-of five Philistines rulers-of

אַחַת לְכֻלָּם וּלְסַרְנֵיכֶם׃ וַעֲשִׂיתֶם צַלְמֵי

models-of so-you-make (5) and-to-rulers-of-you to-all-of-them same

עָפְלֵיכֶם° וְצַלְמֵי עַכְבְּרֵיכֶם הַמַּשְׁחִיתִם אֶת־ הָאָרֶץ

the-country *** the-ones-destroying rats-of-you and-models-of *tumors-of-you

וּנְתַתֶּם לֵאלֹהֵי יִשְׂרָאֵל כָּבוֹד אוּלַי יָקֵל אֶת־ יָדוֹ

hand-of-him *** he-will-lift perhaps honor Israel to-god-of and-you-give

מֵעֲלֵיכֶם וּמֵעַל אֱלֹהֵיכֶם וּמֵעַל אַרְצְכֶם׃ וְלָמָּה

now-why? (6) land-of-you and-from-on gods-of-you and-from-on from-on-you

around to us to kill us and our
people." [11]So they called together all the rulers of the Philistines and said, "Send the ark
of the god of Israel away; let it
go back to its own place, or it[v]
will kill us and our people."
For death had filled the city
with panic; God's hand was
very heavy upon it. [12]Those
who did not die were afflicted
with tumors, and the outcry of
the city went up to heaven.

The Ark Returned to Israel

6 When the ark of the LORD
had been in Philistine territory seven months, [2]the Philistines called for the priests
and the diviners and said,
"What shall we do with the
ark of the LORD? Tell us how
we should send it back to its
place."

[3]They answered, "If you return the ark of the god of Israel, do not send it away empty,
but by all means send a guilt
offering to him. Then you will
be healed, and you will know
why his hand has not been
lifted from you."

[4]The Philistines asked,
"What guilt offering should
we send to him?"

They replied, "Five gold tumors and five gold rats, according to the number of the
Philistine rulers, because the
same plague has struck both
you and your rulers. [5]Make
models of the tumors and of
the rats that are destroying the
country, and pay honor to Israel's god. Perhaps he will lift
his hand from you and your
gods and your land. [6]Why do

[v]11 Or *he*

*12, 4, 5 The *Qere* is a less graphic synonym of the *Kethib*.

°12 ק בטחרים
°4 ק טחרי
°5 ק טחריכם

תְכַבְּדוּ אֶת־ לְבַבְכֶם כַּאֲשֶׁר כִּבְּדוּ מִצְרַיִם וּפַרְעֹה אֶת־
*** and-Pharoah Egyptians they-hardened just-as heart-of-you *** you-harden

לִבָּם הֲלוֹא כַּאֲשֶׁר הִתְעַלֵּל בָּהֶם וַיְשַׁלְּחוּם
then-they-sent-them against-them he-treated-harshly as-when not? heart-of-them

וַיֵּלֵכוּ׃ וְעַתָּה קְחוּ וַעֲשׂוּ עֲגָלָה חֲדָשָׁה אֶחָת
one new cart and-make-ready! get! now-then (7) so-they-could-go-away

וּשְׁתֵּי פָרוֹת עָלוֹת אֲשֶׁר לֹא־ עָלָה עֲלֵיהֶם עֹל וַאֲסַרְתֶּם
and-you-hitch yoke on-them he-went not that ones-having-calved cows and-two-of

אֶת־ הַפָּרוֹת בָּעֲגָלָה וַהֲשֵׁבֹתֶם בְּנֵיהֶם מֵאַחֲרֵיהֶם
from-after-them calves-of-them but-you-take-away to-the-cart the-cows ***

הַבָּיְתָה׃ וּלְקַחְתֶּם אֶת־ אֲרוֹן יְהוָה וּנְתַתֶּם אֹתוֹ אֶל־ הָעֲגָלָה
the-cart on him and-you-put Yahweh ark-of *** and-you-take (8) in-the-pen

וְאֵת כְּלֵי הַזָּהָב אֲשֶׁר הֲשֵׁבֹתֶם לוֹ אָשָׁם תָּשִׂימוּ
you-put guilt-offering to-him you-send-back that the-gold objects-of and

בָאַרְגַּז מִצִּדּוֹ וְשִׁלַּחְתֶּם אֹתוֹ וְהָלָךְ׃ וּרְאִיתֶם
but-you-watch (9) and-he-will-go him and-you-send at-side-of-him in-the-chest

אִם־ דֶּרֶךְ גְּבוּלוֹ יַעֲלֶה בֵּית שֶׁמֶשׁ הוּא עָשָׂה לָנוּ אֶת־
*** on-us he-brought he Shemesh Beth he-goes-up territory-of-him way-of if

הָרָעָה הַגְּדוֹלָה הַזֹּאת וְאִם־ לֹא וְיָדַעְנוּ כִּי לֹא
not that then-we-will-know not but-if the-this the-great the-disaster

יָדוֹ נָגְעָה בָּנוּ מִקְרֶה הוּא הָיָה לָנוּ׃ וַיַּעֲשׂוּ
so-they-did (10) to-us he-happened he chance against-us she-struck hand-of-him

הָאֲנָשִׁים כֵּן וַיִּקְחוּ שְׁתֵּי פָרוֹת עָלוֹת וַיַּאַסְרוּם
and-they-hitched-them ones-having-calved cows two-of and-they-took this the-men

בָּעֲגָלָה וְאֶת־ בְּנֵיהֶם כָּלוּ בַבָּיִת׃ וַיָּשִׂמוּ
and-they-placed (11) in-the-pen they-penned-up calves-of-them and to-the-cart

אֶת־ אֲרוֹן יְהוָה אֶל־ הָעֲגָלָה וְאֵת הָאַרְגַּז וְאֵת עַכְבְּרֵי הַזָּהָב וְאֵת
and the-gold rats-of and the-chest and the-cart on Yahweh ark-of ***

צַלְמֵי טְחֹרֵיהֶם׃ וַיִּשַּׁרְנָה* הַפָּרוֹת בַּדֶּרֶךְ
up-the-road the-cows and-they-went-straight (12) tumors-of-them models-of

עַל־ דֶּרֶךְ בֵּית שֶׁמֶשׁ בִּמְסִלָּה אַחַת הָלְכוּ הָלֹךְ וְגָעוֹ וְלֹא־
and-not and-to-low to-go they-went one on-path Shemesh Beth road-of on

סָרוּ יָמִין וּשְׂמֹאול וְסַרְנֵי פְלִשְׁתִּים הֹלְכִים אַחֲרֵיהֶם
after-them ones-following Philistines and-rulers-of or-left right they-turned

עַד־ גְּבוּל בֵּית שָׁמֶשׁ׃ וּבֵית שֶׁמֶשׁ קֹצְרִים
ones-harvesting Shemesh now-Beth (13) Shemesh Beth border-of as-far-as

קְצִיר־ חִטִּים בָּעֵמֶק וַיִּשְׂאוּ אֶת־ עֵינֵיהֶם וַיִּרְאוּ
and-they-saw eyes-of-them *** when-they-lifted in-the-valley wheats harvest-of

you harden your hearts as the
Egyptians and Pharaoh did?
When he[w] treated them harshly, did they not send the Israelites out so they could go on
their way?
7"Now then, get a new cart
ready, with two cows that
have calved and have never
been yoked. Hitch the cows to
the cart, but take their calves
away and pen them up. 8Take
the ark of the LORD and put it
on the cart, and in a chest beside it put the gold objects you
are sending back to him as a
guilt offering. Send it on its
way, 9but keep watching it. If
it goes up to its own territory,
toward Beth Shemesh, then
the LORD has brought this
great disaster on us. But if it
does not, then we will know
that it was not his hand that
struck us and that it happened
to us by chance."
10So they did this. They took
two such cows and hitched
them to the cart and penned
up their calves. 11They placed
the ark of the LORD on the cart
and along with it the chest
containing the gold rats and
the models of the tumors.
12Then the cows went straight
up toward Beth Shemesh,
keeping on the road and lowing all the way; they did not
turn to the right or to the left.
The rulers of the Philistines
followed them as far as the
border of Beth Shemesh.
13Now the people of Beth
Shemesh were harvesting
their wheat in the valley, and
when they looked up and saw

[w]6 That is, God

*12 Most mss have *dagesh* in the *yod* (וַיִּ).

אֶת־הָאָרוֹן וַיִּשְׂמְחוּ לִרְאוֹת׃ וְהָעֲגָלָה בָּאָה אֶל־שְׂדֵה
field-of to she-came and-the-cart (14) to-see then-they-rejoiced the-ark ***

יְהוֹשֻׁעַ בֵּית־הַשִּׁמְשִׁי וַתַּעֲמֹד שָׁם וְשָׁם אֶבֶן גְּדוֹלָה
large stone now-there there and-she-stopped the-Shemeshite Beth Joshua

וַיְבַקְּעוּ אֶת־עֲצֵי הָעֲגָלָה וְאֶת־הַפָּרוֹת הֶעֱלוּ
they-sacrificed the-cows and the-cart woods-of *** and-they-chopped-up

עֹלָה לַיהוָה׃ וְהַלְוִיִּם הוֹרִידוּ ׀ אֶת־אֲרוֹן
ark-of *** they-took-down and-the-Levites (15) to-Yahweh burnt-offering

יְהוָה וְאֶת־הָאַרְגַּז אֲשֶׁר־אִתּוֹ אֲשֶׁר־בּוֹ כְלֵי־זָהָב וַיָּשִׂמוּ
and-they-placed gold objects-of in-him that with-him that the-chest and Yahweh

אֶל־הָאֶבֶן הַגְּדוֹלָה וְאַנְשֵׁי בֵית־שֶׁמֶשׁ הֶעֱלוּ עֹלוֹת
burnt-offerings they-offered Shemesh Beth people-of the-large the-rock on

וַיִּזְבְּחוּ זְבָחִים בַּיּוֹם הַהוּא לַיהוָה׃ וַחֲמִשָּׁה
now-five (16) to-Yahweh the-that on-the-day sacrifices and-they-sacrificed

סַרְנֵי־פְלִשְׁתִּים רָאוּ וַיָּשֻׁבוּ עֶקְרוֹן בַּיּוֹם הַהוּא׃
the-that on-the-day Ekron then-they-returned they-saw Philistines rulers-of

וְאֵלֶּה טְחֹרֵי הַזָּהָב אֲשֶׁר הֵשִׁיבוּ פְלִשְׁתִּים אָשָׁם
guilt-offering Philistines they-sent that the-gold tumors-of now-these (17)

לַיהוָה לְאַשְׁדּוֹד אֶחָד לְעַזָּה אֶחָד לְאַשְׁקְלוֹן אֶחָד לְגַת אֶחָד
one for-Gath one for-Ashkelon one for-Gaza one for-Ashdod to-Yahweh

לְעֶקְרוֹן אֶחָד׃ וְעַכְבְּרֵי הַזָּהָב מִסְפַּר כָּל־עָרֵי
towns-of all-of by-number-of the-gold and-rats-of (18) one for-Ekron

פְלִשְׁתִּים לַחֲמֵשֶׁת הַסְּרָנִים מֵעִיר מִבְצָר וְעַד כֹּפֶר
village-of even-to fortified from-city-of the-rulers to-five-of Philistines

הַפְּרָזִי וְעַד* ׀ אָבֵל† הַגְּדוֹלָה אֲשֶׁר הִנִּיחוּ עָלֶיהָ אֵת
*** by-her they-set where the-Greater †Abel *even-to the-country-dweller

אֲרוֹן יְהוָה עַד הַיּוֹם הַזֶּה בִּשְׂדֵה יְהוֹשֻׁעַ בֵּית־הַשִּׁמְשִׁי׃
the-Shemeshite Beth Joshua in-field-of the-this the-day to Yahweh ark-of

וַיַּךְ בְּאַנְשֵׁי בֵית־שֶׁמֶשׁ כִּי רָאוּ בַּאֲרוֹן
into-ark-of they-looked because Shemesh Beth from-men-of but-he-struck-down (19)

יְהוָה וַיַּךְ בָּעָם שִׁבְעִים אִישׁ חֲמִשִּׁים אֶלֶף אִישׁ
man thousand fifty man seventy from-the-people and-he-struck-down Yahweh

וַיִּתְאַבְּלוּ הָעָם כִּי־הִכָּה יְהוָה בָּעָם מַכָּה
blow against-the-people Yahweh he-struck because the-people and-they-mourned

גְּדוֹלָה†† וַיֹּאמְרוּ אַנְשֵׁי בֵית־שֶׁמֶשׁ מִי יוּכַל לַעֲמֹד
to-stand he-can who? Shemesh Beth men-of and-they-asked (20) heavy

לִפְנֵי יְהוָה הָאֱלֹהִים הַקָּדוֹשׁ הַזֶּה וְאֶל־מִי יַעֲלֶה
he-will-go-up whom? and-to the-this the-holy the-God Yahweh in-presences-of

the ark, they rejoiced at the
sight. [14]The cart came to the
field of Joshua of Beth Shemesh, and there it stopped beside a large rock. The people
chopped up the wood of the
cart and sacrificed the cows as
a burnt offering to the LORD.
[15]The Levites took down the
ark of the LORD, together with
the chest containing the gold
objects, and placed them on
the large rock. On that day the
people of Beth Shemesh
offered burnt offerings and
made sacrifices to the LORD.
[16]The five rulers of the Philistines saw all this and then returned that same day to Ekron.
[17]These are the gold tumors
the Philistines sent as a guilt
offering to the LORD—one each
for Ashdod, Gaza, Ashkelon,
Gath and Ekron. [18]And the
number of the gold rats was
according to the number of
Philistine towns belonging to
the five rulers—the fortified
towns with their country villages. The large rock, on
which[x] they set the ark of the
LORD, is a witness to this day
in the field of Joshua of Beth
Shemesh.
[19]But God struck down some
of the men of Beth Shemesh,
putting seventy[y] of them to
death because they had looked
into the ark of the LORD. The
people mourned because of
the heavy blow the LORD had
dealt them, [20]and the men of
Beth Shemesh asked, "Who
can stand in the presence of
the LORD, this holy God? To
whom will the ark go up from

[x]*18* A few Hebrew manuscripts and Septuagint; most Hebrew manuscripts *villages as far as Greater Abel, where*
[y]*19* A few Hebrew manuscripts; most Hebrew manuscripts and Septuagint *50,070*

***18a The NIV repoints the *ayin* with *tsere* and adds *qamets he* ending to read וְעֵדָה, *and-witness* (cf. Joshua 24:27).**

***18b The NIV, based on the versions listed above in footnote *x*, translates אבן, *rock*.**

††19 Most mss end the verse with *soph pasuq* (:).

מֵעָלֵֽינוּ׃ וַֽיִּשְׁלְחוּ֙ מַלְאָכִ֔ים אֶל־ יוֹשְׁבֵ֥י קִרְיַת־ יְעָרִ֖ים
Jearim Kiriath ones-living-of to messengers then-they-sent (21) from-with-us

לֵאמֹ֔ר הֵשִׁ֤בוּ פְלִשְׁתִּים֙ אֶת־ אֲר֣וֹן יְהוָ֑ה רְד֕וּ הַעֲל֥וּ אֹת֖וֹ
him take-up! come-down! Yahweh ark-of *** Philistines they-returned to-say

אֲלֵיכֶֽם׃ וַיָּבֹ֜אוּ אַנְשֵׁ֣י ׀ קִרְיַ֣ת יְעָרִ֗ים וַיַּעֲלוּ֙ אֶת־ אֲר֣וֹן
ark-of *** and-they-took-up Jearim Kiriath men-of so-they-came (7:1) to-you

יְהוָ֔ה וַיָּבִ֣אוּ אֹת֔וֹ אֶל־ בֵּ֥ית אֲבִינָדָ֖ב בַּגִּבְעָ֑ה וְאֶת־ אֶלְעָזָ֤ר
Eleazar and on-the-hill Abinadab house-of to him and-they-took Yahweh

בְּנוֹ֙ קִדְּשׁ֔וּ לִשְׁמֹ֖ר אֶת־ אֲר֥וֹן יְהוָֽה׃ וַיְהִ֞י מִיּ֗וֹם
from-day and-he-was (2) Yahweh ark-of *** to-guard they-consecrated son-of-him

שֶׁ֤בֶת הָֽאָרוֹן֙ בְּקִרְיַ֣ת יְעָרִ֔ים וַיִּרְבּוּ֙ הַיָּמִ֔ים וַיִּהְי֖וּ
and-they-were the-days and-they-were-many Jearim at-Kiriath the-ark to-remain

עֶשְׂרִ֣ים שָׁנָ֑ה וַיִּנָּה֛וּ כָּל־ בֵּ֥ית יִשְׂרָאֵ֖ל אַחֲרֵ֥י יְהוָֽה׃
Yahweh after Israel house-of all-of then-they-mourned year twenty

וַיֹּ֣אמֶר שְׁמוּאֵ֗ל אֶל־ כָּל־ בֵּ֣ית יִשְׂרָאֵל֮ לֵאמֹר֒ אִם־ בְּכָל־
with-all-of if to-say Israel house-of whole-of to Samuel and-he-said (3)

לְבַבְכֶ֗ם אַתֶּם֙ שָׁבִ֣ים אֶל־ יְהוָ֔ה הָסִ֜ירוּ אֶת־ אֱלֹהֵ֧י הַנֵּכָ֛ר
the-foreign gods-of *** be-rid! Yahweh to ones-returning you heart-of-you

מִתּוֹכְכֶ֖ם וְהָעַשְׁתָּר֑וֹת וְהָכִ֨ינוּ לְבַבְכֶ֤ם אֶל־ יְהוָה֙
Yahweh to heart-of-you and-commit! and-the-Ashtoreths from-among-you

וְעִבְדֻ֣הוּ לְבַדּ֔וֹ וְיַצֵּ֥ל אֶתְכֶ֖ם מִיַּ֥ד פְּלִשְׁתִּֽים׃
Philistines from-hand-of you and-he-will-deliver only-him and-serve-him!

וַיָּסִ֙ירוּ֙ בְּנֵ֣י יִשְׂרָאֵ֔ל אֶת־ הַבְּעָלִ֖ים וְאֶת־ הָעַשְׁתָּרֹ֑ת
the-Ashtoreths and the-Baals *** Israel sons-of so-they-put-away (4)

וַיַּעַבְד֥וּ אֶת־ יְהוָ֖ה לְבַדּֽוֹ׃ וַיֹּ֣אמֶר שְׁמוּאֵ֔ל קִבְצ֥וּ אֶת־
*** assemble! Samuel then-he-said (5) only-him Yahweh *** and-they-served

כָּל־ יִשְׂרָאֵ֖ל הַמִּצְפָּ֑תָה וְאֶתְפַּלֵּ֥ל בַּעַדְכֶ֖ם אֶל־ יְהוָֽה׃
Yahweh with for-you and-I-will-intercede at-the-Mizpah Israel all-of

וַיִּקָּבְצ֣וּ הַמִּצְפָּ֗תָה וַיִּֽשְׁאֲבוּ־ מַ֜יִם וַֽיִּשְׁפְּכ֣וּ ׀
and-they-poured-out waters then-they-drew at-the-Mizpah when-they-assembled (6)

לִפְנֵ֣י יְהוָ֗ה וַיָּצ֙וּמוּ֙ בַּיּ֣וֹם הַה֔וּא וַיֹּ֣אמְרוּ שָׁ֔ם
there and-they-confessed the-that on-the-day and-they-fasted Yahweh before

חָטָ֖אנוּ לַיהוָ֑ה וַיִּשְׁפֹּ֧ט שְׁמוּאֵ֛ל אֶת־ בְּנֵ֥י יִשְׂרָאֵ֖ל בַּמִּצְפָּֽה׃
at-the-Mizpah Israel sons-of *** Samuel and-he-led against-Yahweh we-sinned

וַיִּשְׁמְע֣וּ פְלִשְׁתִּ֗ים כִּֽי־ הִתְקַבְּצ֣וּ בְנֵֽי־ יִשְׂרָאֵל֙
Israel sons-of they-assembled that Philistines when-they-heard (7)

הַמִּצְפָּ֔תָה וַיַּעֲל֥וּ סַרְנֵֽי־ פְלִשְׁתִּ֖ים אֶל־ יִשְׂרָאֵ֑ל
Israel against Philistines rulers-of then-they-came-up at-the-Mizpah

here?"
[21]Then they sent messengers
to the people of Kiriath Jearim,
saying, "The Philistines have
returned the ark of the LORD.
Come down and take it up to
7 your place." [1]So the men
of Kiriath Jearim came
and took up the ark of the
LORD. They took it to Abinadab's house on the hill and
consecrated Eleazar his son to
guard the ark of the LORD.

The Philistines Subdued at Mizpah

[2]It was a long time, twenty
years in all, that the ark remained at Kiriath Jearim, and
all the people of Israel
mourned and sought after the
LORD. [3]And Samuel said to the
whole house of Israel, "If you
are returning to the LORD with
all your hearts, then rid yourselves of the foreign gods and
the Ashtoreths and commit
yourselves to the LORD and
serve him only, and he will
deliver you out of the hand of
the Philistines." [4]So the Israelites put away their Baals and
Ashtoreths, and served the
LORD only.
[5]Then Samuel said, "Assemble all Israel at Mizpah and I
will intercede with the LORD
for you." [6]When they had assembled at Mizpah, they drew
water and poured it out before
the LORD. On that day they
fasted and there they con-
fessed, "We have sinned
against the LORD." And Samuel was leader[z] of Israel at
Mizpah.
[7]When the Philistines heard
that Israel had assembled at
Mizpah, the rulers of the Philistines came up to attack them.

[z]6 Traditionally *judge*

וַיִּשְׁמְעוּ בְּנֵֽי יִשְׂרָאֵל וַיִּרְאוּ מִפְּנֵי פְּלִשְׁתִּֽים׃
Philistines because-of then-they-were-afraid Israel sons-of when-they-heard

וַיֹּאמְרוּ בְנֵֽי־יִשְׂרָאֵל אֶל־שְׁמוּאֵל אַל־תַּחֲרֵשׁ מִמֶּנּוּ מִזְּעֹק
from-to-cry for-us you-stop not Samuel to Israel sons-of and-they-said (8)

אֶל־יְהוָה אֱלֹהֵינוּ וְיֹשִׁעֵנוּ מִיַּד פְּלִשְׁתִּֽים׃
Philistines from-hand-of so-he-may-rescue-us God-of-us Yahweh to

וַיִּקַּח שְׁמוּאֵל טְלֵה חָלָב אֶחָד °וַיַּעֲלֶהָ עוֹלָה
burnt-offering and-he-offered-him one suckling lamb-of Samuel then-he-took (9)

כָּלִיל לַיהוָה וַיִּזְעַק שְׁמוּאֵל אֶל־יְהוָה בְּעַד יִשְׂרָאֵל
Israel on-behalf-of Yahweh to Samuel and-he-cried-out to-Yahweh whole

וַיַּעֲנֵהוּ יְהוָה׃ וַיְהִי שְׁמוּאֵל מַעֲלֶה
sacrificing Samuel while-he-was (10) Yahweh and-he-answered-him

הָעוֹלָה וּפְלִשְׁתִּים נִגְּשׁוּ לַמִּלְחָמָה בְּיִשְׂרָאֵל
with-Israel to-the-battle they-drew-near then-Philistines the-burnt-offering

וַיַּרְעֵם יְהוָה ׀ בְּקוֹל־גָּדוֹל בַּיּוֹם הַהוּא עַל־
against the-that on-the-day loud with-thunder Yahweh but-he-thundered

פְּלִשְׁתִּים וַיְהֻמֵּם וַיִּנָּגְפוּ לִפְנֵי יִשְׂרָאֵל׃
Israel before so-they-were-routed and-he-made-panic-them Philistines

וַיֵּצְאוּ אַנְשֵׁי יִשְׂרָאֵל מִן־הַמִּצְפָּה וַיִּרְדְּפוּ אֶת־
*** and-they-pursued the-Mizpah from Israel men-of and-they-rushed-out (11)

פְּלִשְׁתִּים וַיַּכּוּם עַד־מִתַּחַת לְבֵית כָּר׃ וַיִּקַּח
then-he-took (12) Car to-Beth at-below to and-they-slaughtered-them Philistines

שְׁמוּאֵל אֶבֶן אַחַת וַיָּשֶׂם בֵּין־הַמִּצְפָּה וּבֵין הַשֵּׁן
the-Shen and-between the-Mizpah between and-he-set-up one stone Samuel

וַיִּקְרָא אֶת־שְׁמָהּ אֶבֶן הָעָזֶר וַיֹּאמַר עַד־הֵנָּה
at-here to and-he-said the-Ezer Eben name-of-her *** and-he-called

עֲזָרָנוּ יְהוָה׃ וַיִּכָּנְעוּ הַפְּלִשְׁתִּים וְלֹא־
and-not the-Philistines so-they-were-subdued (13) Yahweh he-helped-us

יָסְפוּ עוֹד לָבוֹא בִּגְבוּל יִשְׂרָאֵל וַתְּהִי יַד־
hand-of and-she-was Israel into-territory-of to-invade again they-repeated

יְהוָה בַּפְּלִשְׁתִּים כֹּל יְמֵי שְׁמוּאֵל׃ וַתָּשֹׁבְנָה
and-they-were-restored (14) Samuel days-of all-of against-the-Philistines Yahweh

הֶעָרִים אֲשֶׁר לָקְחוּ־פְלִשְׁתִּים מֵאֵת יִשְׂרָאֵל ׀ לְיִשְׂרָאֵל מֵעֶקְרוֹן
from-Ekron to-Israel Israel from Philistines they-captured that the-towns

וְעַד־גַּת וְאֶת־גְּבוּלָן הִצִּיל יִשְׂרָאֵל מִיַּד פְּלִשְׁתִּים
Philistines from-hand-of Israel he-delivered territory-of-them and Gath even-to

וַיְהִי שָׁלוֹם בֵּין יִשְׂרָאֵל וּבֵין הָאֱמֹרִי׃ וַיִּשְׁפֹּט
and-he-judged (15) the-Amorite and-between Israel between peace and-he-was

And when the Israelites heard
of it, they were afraid because
of the Philistines. 8They said
to Samuel, "Do not stop crying
out to the LORD our God for us,
that he may rescue us from the
hand of the Philistines."
9Then Samuel took a suckling
lamb and offered it up as a
whole burnt offering to the
LORD. He cried out to the LORD
on Israel's behalf, and the
LORD answered him.
10While Samuel was sac-
rificing the burnt offering, the
Philistines drew near to en-
gage Israel in battle. But that
day the LORD thundered with
loud thunder against the Philistines and threw them into
such a panic that they were
routed before the Israelites.
11The men of Israel rushed out
of Mizpah and pursued the
Philistines, slaughtering them
along the way to a point below
Beth Car.
12Then Samuel took a stone
and set it up between Mizpah
and Shen. He named it Ebenezer,[a] saying, "Thus far has the
LORD helped us." 13So the Philistines were subdued and did
not invade Israelite territory
again.
Throughout Samuel's life-
time, the hand of the LORD was
against the Philistines. 14The
towns from Ekron to Gath that
the Philistines had captured
from Israel were restored to
her, and Israel delivered the
neighboring territory from the
power of the Philistines. And
there was peace between Israel and the Amorites.
15Samuel continued as judge

[a]12 *Ebenezer* means *stone of help.*

°9 ק ויעלהו

שְׁמוּאֵל אֶת־יִשְׂרָאֵל כֹּל יְמֵי חַיָּיו׃ וְהָלַךְ מִדֵּי
as-needs-of and-he-went (16) lives-of-him days-of all-of Israel *** Samuel

שָׁנָה בְּשָׁנָה וְסָבַב בֵּית־אֵל וְהַגִּלְגָּל וְהַמִּצְפָּה
and-the-Mizpah and-the-Gilgal El Beth and-he-went-on-circuit by-year year

וְשָׁפַט אֶת־יִשְׂרָאֵל אֵת כָּל־הַמְּקוֹמוֹת הָאֵלֶּה׃ וּתְשֻׁבָתוֹ
but-return-of-him (17) the-those the-places all-of *** Israel *** and-he-judged

הָרָמָתָה כִּי־שָׁם בֵּיתוֹ וְשָׁם שָׁפָט אֶת־יִשְׂרָאֵל וַיִּבֶן־
and-he-built Israel *** he-judged and-there home-of-him there for to-the-Ramah

שָׁם מִזְבֵּחַ לַיהוָה׃ וַיְהִי כַּאֲשֶׁר זָקֵן שְׁמוּאֵל
Samuel he-grew-old as-when and-he-was (8:1) to-Yahweh altar there

וַיָּשֶׂם אֶת־ בָּנָיו שֹׁפְטִים לְיִשְׂרָאֵל׃ וַיְהִי
now-he-was (2) for-Israel ones-judging sons-of-him *** then-he-appointed

שֶׁם־ בְּנוֹ הַבְּכוֹר יוֹאֵל וְשֵׁם מִשְׁנֵהוּ אֲבִיָּה
Abijah second-of-him and-name-of Joel the-firstborn son-of-him name-of

שֹׁפְטִים בִּבְאֵר שָׁבַע׃ וְלֹא־ הָלְכוּ בָנָיו °בִּדְרָכָו
in-ways-of-him sons-of-him they-walked but-not (3) Sheba at-Beer ones-judging

וַיִּטּוּ אַחֲרֵי הַבָּצַע וַיִּקְחוּ־ שֹׁחַד
bribe and-they-accepted the-dishonest-gain after and-they-turned-aside

וַיַּטּוּ מִשְׁפָּט׃ וַיִּתְקַבְּצוּ כֹּל זִקְנֵי יִשְׂרָאֵל
Israel elders-of all-of so-they-gathered (4) justice and-they-perverted

וַיָּבֹאוּ אֶל־שְׁמוּאֵל הָרָמָתָה׃ וַיֹּאמְרוּ אֵלָיו הִנֵּה אַתָּה
you see! to-him and-they-said (5) at-the-Ramah Samuel to and-they-came

זָקַנְתָּ וּבָנֶיךָ לֹא הָלְכוּ בִּדְרָכֶיךָ עַתָּה שִׂימָה־ לָּנוּ
for-us appoint! now in-ways-of-you they-walk not and-sons-of-you you-are-old

מֶלֶךְ לְשָׁפְטֵנוּ כְּכָל־ הַגּוֹיִם׃ וַיֵּרַע הַדָּבָר
the-thing but-he-was-displeasing (6) the-nations as-all-of to-lead-us king

בְּעֵינֵי שְׁמוּאֵל כַּאֲשֶׁר אָמְרוּ תְּנָה־ לָּנוּ מֶלֶךְ לְשָׁפְטֵנוּ וַיִּתְפַּלֵּל
so-he-prayed to-lead-us king to-us give! they-said as-when Samuel in-eyes-of

שְׁמוּאֵל אֶל־ יְהוָה׃ וַיֹּאמֶר יְהוָה אֶל־שְׁמוּאֵל שְׁמַע בְּקוֹל
to-voice-of listen! Samuel to Yahweh and-he-told (7) Yahweh to Samuel

הָעָם לְכֹל אֲשֶׁר־ יֹאמְרוּ אֵלֶיךָ כִּי לֹא אֹתְךָ מָאָסוּ כִּי־אֹתִי
me but they-rejected you not for to-you they-say that to-all the-people

מָאֲסוּ מִמְּלֹךְ עֲלֵיהֶם׃ כְּכָל־ הַמַּעֲשִׂים אֲשֶׁר־ עָשׂוּ
they-did that the-deeds as-all-of (8) over-them from-to-be-king they-rejected

מִיּוֹם הַעֲלֹתִי אֹתָם מִמִּצְרַיִם וְעַד־ הַיּוֹם הַזֶּה
the-this the-day even-to from-Egypt them to-bring-up-me from-day

וַיַּעַזְבֻנִי וַיַּעַבְדוּ אֱלֹהִים אֲחֵרִים כֵּן הֵמָּה עֹשִׂים גַּם־
also ones-doing they so other-ones gods and-they-served then-they-forsook-me

over Israel all the days of his
life. [16]From year to year he
went on a circuit from Bethel
to Gilgal to Mizpah, judging
Israel in all those places. [17]But
he always went back to
Ramah, where his home was,
and there he also judged Israel. And he built an altar there
to the LORD.

Israel Asks for a King

8 When Samuel grew old,
he appointed his sons as
judges for Israel. [2]The name of
his firstborn was Joel and the
name of his second was Abijah, and they served at Beersheba. [3]But his sons did not
walk in his ways. They turned
aside after dishonest gain and
accepted bribes and perverted
justice.

[4]So all the elders of Israel
gathered together and came to
Samuel at Ramah. [5]They said
to him, "You are old, and your
sons do not walk in your
ways; now appoint a king to
lead[c] us, such as all the other
nations have."

[6]But when they said, "Give
us a king to lead us," this displeased Samuel; so he prayed
to the LORD. [7]And the LORD
told him: "Listen to all that the
people are saying to you; it is
not you they have rejected as
their king, but me. [8]As they
have done from the day I
brought them up out of Egypt
until this day, forsaking me
and serving other gods, so

[c]5 Traditionally *judge;* also in verses 6 and 20

°3 ק בדרכיו

לָךְ׃ (9) וְעַתָּה שְׁמַע בְּקוֹלָם אַךְ כִּי־ הָעֵד תָּעִיד
you-warn to-warn indeed but to-voice-of-them listen! and-now (9) to-you

בָּהֶם וְהִגַּדְתָּ לָהֶם מִשְׁפַּט הַמֶּלֶךְ אֲשֶׁר יִמְלֹךְ
he-will-reign who the-king leadership-of to-them and-you-make-known to-them

עֲלֵיהֶם׃ (10) וַיֹּאמֶר שְׁמוּאֵל אֵת כָּל־ דִּבְרֵי יְהוָה אֶל־ הָעָם
the-people to Yahweh words-of all-of *** Samuel so-he-told (10) over-them

הַשֹּׁאֲלִים מֵאִתּוֹ מֶלֶךְ׃ (11) וַיֹּאמֶר זֶה יִהְיֶה מִשְׁפַּט
leadership-of he-will-be this and-he-said (11) king from-him the-ones-asking

הַמֶּלֶךְ אֲשֶׁר יִמְלֹךְ עֲלֵיכֶם אֶת־ בְּנֵיכֶם יִקָּח
he-will-take sons-of-you *** over-you he-will-reign who the-king

וְשָׂם לוֹ בְּמֶרְכַּבְתּוֹ וּבְפָרָשָׁיו
and-with-horses-of-him with-chariot-of-him for-him and-he-will-place

וְרָצוּ לִפְנֵי מֶרְכַּבְתּוֹ׃ (12) וְלָשׂוּם לוֹ
for-him and-to-assign (12) chariot-of-him in-front-of and-they-will-run

שָׂרֵי אֲלָפִים וְשָׂרֵי חֲמִשִּׁים וְלַחֲרֹשׁ חֲרִישׁוֹ
ground-of-him and-to-plow fifties and-commanders-of thousands commanders-of

וְלִקְצֹר קְצִירוֹ וְלַעֲשׂוֹת כְּלֵי־ מִלְחַמְתּוֹ וּכְלֵי
and-equipments-of war-of-him weapons-of and-to-make harvest-of-him and-to-reap

רִכְבּוֹ׃ (13) וְאֶת־ בְּנוֹתֵיכֶם יִקָּח לְרַקָּחוֹת
as-perfumers he-will-take daughters-of-you and (13) chariot-of-him

וּלְטַבָּחוֹת וּלְאֹפוֹת׃ (14) וְאֶת־ שְׂדוֹתֵיכֶם וְאֶת־ כַּרְמֵיכֶם
vineyards-of-you and fields-of-you and (14) and-as-ones-baking and-as-cooks

וְזֵיתֵיכֶם הַטּוֹבִים יִקָּח וְנָתַן
and-he-will-give he-will-take the-best-ones and-olive-groves-of-you

לַעֲבָדָיו׃ (15) וְזַרְעֵיכֶם וְכַרְמֵיכֶם יַעְשֹׂר
he-will-take-tenth and-vintages-of-you and-grains-of-you (15) to-attendants-of-him

וְנָתַן לְסָרִיסָיו וְלַעֲבָדָיו׃ (16) וְאֶת־
and (16) and-to-servants-of-him to-officials-of-him and-he-will-give

עַבְדֵיכֶם וְאֶת־ שִׁפְחוֹתֵיכֶם וְאֶת־ בַּחוּרֵיכֶם הַטּוֹבִים
the-best-ones young-men-of-you and maidservants-of-you and menservants-of-you

וְאֶת־ חֲמוֹרֵיכֶם יִקָּח וְעָשָׂה לִמְלַאכְתּוֹ׃
for-kingdom-of-him and-he-will-use he-will-take donkeys-of-you and

(17) צֹאנְכֶם יַעְשֹׂר וְאַתֶּם תִּהְיוּ־ לוֹ לַעֲבָדִים׃
as-slaves for-him you-will-become and-you he-will-take-tenth flock-of-you (17)

(18) וּזְעַקְתֶּם בַּיּוֹם הַהוּא מִלִּפְנֵי מַלְכְּכֶם אֲשֶׁר
whom king-of-you because-of the-that on-the-day and-you-will-cry-out (18)

בְּחַרְתֶּם לָכֶם וְלֹא־ יַעֲנֶה יְהוָה אֶתְכֶם בַּיּוֹם הַהוּא׃
the-that on-the-day you Yahweh he-will-answer but-not for-you you-chose

they are doing to you. [9]Now
listen to them; but warn them
solemnly and let them know
what the king who will reign
over them will do."
[10]Samuel told all the words
of the LORD to the people who
were asking him for a king.
[11]He said, "This is what the
king who will reign over you
will do: He will take your sons
and make them serve with his
chariots and horses, and they
will run in front of his chariots. [12]Some he will assign to be
commanders of thousands
and commanders of fifties,
and others to plow his ground
and reap his harvest, and still
others to make weapons of
war and equipment for his
chariots. [13]He will take your
daughters to be perfumers and
cooks and bakers. [14]He will
take the best of your fields and
vineyards and olive groves
and give them to his attendants. [15]He will take a tenth of
your grain and of your vintage
and give it to his officials and
attendants. [16]Your men-
servants and maidservants
and the best of your cattle[d]
and donkeys he will take for
his own use. [17]He will take a
tenth of your flocks, and you
yourselves will become his
slaves. [18]When that day comes,
you will cry out for relief from
the king you have chosen, and
the LORD will not answer you
in that day."

[d]16 Septuagint; Hebrew *young men*

וַיְמָאֲנוּ הָעָם לִשְׁמֹעַ בְּקוֹל שְׁמוּאֵל וַיֹּאמְרוּ

and-they-said Samuel to-voice-of to-listen the-people but-they-refused (19)

לֹּא כִּי אִם־ מֶלֶךְ יִהְיֶה עָלֵינוּ׃ וְהָיִינוּ גַם־ אֲנַחְנוּ כְּכָל־

like-all-of we also then-we-will-be (20) over-us he-must-be king indeed but no

הַגּוֹיִם וּשְׁפָטָנוּ מַלְכֵּנוּ וְיָצָא לְפָנֵינוּ

before-us and-he-will-go-out king-of-us and-he-will-lead-us the-nations

וְנִלְחַם אֶת־ מִלְחֲמֹתֵנוּ׃ וַיִּשְׁמַע שְׁמוּאֵל אֵת כָּל־

all-of *** Samuel when-he-heard (21) battles-of-us *** and-he-will-fight

דִּבְרֵי הָעָם וַיְדַבְּרֵם בְּאָזְנֵי יְהוָה׃ וַיֹּאמֶר

and-he-said (22) Yahweh in-ears-of then-he-repeated-them the-people words-of

יְהוָה אֶל־ שְׁמוּאֵל שְׁמַע בְּקוֹלָם וְהִמְלַכְתָּ לָהֶם מֶלֶךְ

king to-them and-you-give-king to-voice-of-them listen! Samuel to Yahweh

וַיֹּאמֶר שְׁמוּאֵל אֶל־ אַנְשֵׁי יִשְׂרָאֵל לְכוּ אִישׁ לְעִירוֹ׃

to-town-of-him everyone go-back! Israel men-of to Samuel then-he-said

וַיְהִי־ אִישׁ מִבִּן־° יָמִין וּשְׁמוֹ קִישׁ בֶּן־ אֲבִיאֵל בֶּן־

son-of Abiel son-of Kish and-name-of-him Jamin from-Ben man now-he-was (9:1)

צְרוֹר בֶּן־ בְּכוֹרַת בֶּן־ אֲפִיחַ בֶּן־ אִישׁ יְמִינִי גִּבּוֹר חָיִל׃

standing man-of *Jamite man-of son-of Aphiah son-of Becorath son-of Zeror

וְלוֹ־ הָיָה בֵן וּשְׁמוֹ שָׁאוּל בָּחוּר וָטוֹב

and-impressive young-man Saul and-name-of-him son he-was and-to-him (2)

וְאֵין אִישׁ מִבְּנֵי יִשְׂרָאֵל טוֹב מִמֶּנּוּ מִשִּׁכְמוֹ וָמַעְלָה

and-above from-shoulder-of-him than-him better Israel from-sons-of man and-not

גָּבֹהַּ מִכָּל־ הָעָם׃ וַתֹּאבַדְנָה הָאֲתֹנוֹת לְקִישׁ

of-Kish the-donkeys now-they-were-lost (3) the-people than-any-of taller

אֲבִי שָׁאוּל וַיֹּאמֶר קִישׁ אֶל־שָׁאוּל בְּנוֹ קַח־ נָא אִתְּךָ אֶת־

*** with-you now! take! son-of-him Saul to Kish and-he-said Saul father-of

אַחַד מֵהַנְּעָרִים וְקוּם לֵךְ בַּקֵּשׁ אֶת־ הָאֲתֹנֹת׃ וַיַּעֲבֹר

so-he-passed (4) the-donkeys *** look-for! go! and-rise! from-the-servants one

בְּהַר־ אֶפְרַיִם וַיַּעֲבֹר בְּאֶרֶץ־ שָׁלִשָׁה וְלֹא

but-not Shalisha through-area-of and-he-passed Ephraim through-hill-country-of

מָצָאוּ וַיַּעַבְרוּ בְאֶרֶץ־ שַׁעֲלִים וָאַיִן וַיַּעֲבֹר

so-he-passed but-there-was-not Shaalim into-district-of so-they-went they-found

בְּאֶרֶץ־ יְמִינִי וְלֹא מָצָאוּ׃ הֵמָּה בָּאוּ

they-reached they (5) they-found but-not *Jamite through-territory-of

בְּאֶרֶץ צוּף וְשָׁאוּל אָמַר לְנַעֲרוֹ אֲשֶׁר־ עִמּוֹ לְכָה

come! with-him who to-servant-of-him he-said and-Saul Zuph to-district-of

וְנָשׁוּבָה פֶּן־ יֶחְדַּל אָבִי מִן־ הָאֲתֹנוֹת

the-donkeys about father-of-me he-will-stop-thinking or and-let-us-go-back

[19]But the people refused to
listen to Samuel. "No!" they
said. "We want a king over us.
[20]Then we will be like all the
other nations, with a king to
lead us and to go out before us
and fight our battles."
[21]When Samuel heard all
that the people said, he repeated it before the LORD.
[22]The LORD answered, "Listen
to them and give them a
king."
Then Samuel said to the
men of Israel, "Everyone go
back to his town."

Samuel Anoints Saul

9 There was a Benjamite, a
man of standing, whose
name was Kish son of Abiel,
the son of Zeror, the son of
Becorath, the son of Aphiah of
Benjamin. [2]He had a son
named Saul, an impressive
young man without equal
among the Israelites—a head
taller than any of the others.
[3]Now the donkeys belonging to Saul's father Kish were
lost, and Kish said to his son
Saul, "Take one of the servants
with you and go and look for
the donkeys." [4]So he passed
through the hill country of
Ephraim and through the area
around Shalisha, but they did
not find them. They went on
into the district of Shaalim,
but the donkeys were not
there. Then he passed through
the territory of Benjamin, but
they did not find them.
[5]When they reached the district of Zuph, Saul said to the
servant who was with him,
"Come, let's go back, or my father will stop thinking about

*1,4 Or *Benjamite.*

°1 ק מבנימין

וְדָאַג לָנוּ׃ וַיֹּאמֶר לוֹ הִנֵּה־נָא אִישׁ־אֱלֹהִים
God man-of now! look! to-him but-he-replied (6) about-us and-he-will-worry

בָּעִיר הַזֹּאת וְהָאִישׁ נִכְבָּד כֹּל אֲשֶׁר־יְדַבֵּר בּוֹא
to-come-true he-says that all being-respected and-the-man the-this in-the-town

יָבוֹא עַתָּה נֵלֲכָה שָּׁם אוּלַי יַגִּיד לָנוּ אֶת־דַּרְכֵּנוּ
way-of-us *** to-us he-will-tell perhaps there let-us-go now he-comes-true

אֲשֶׁר־הָלַכְנוּ עָלֶיהָ׃ וַיֹּאמֶר שָׁאוּל לְנַעֲרוֹ וְהִנֵּה
now-see! to-servant-of-him Saul and-he-said (7) on-her you-should-go that

נֵלֵךְ וּמַה־נָּבִיא לָאִישׁ כִּי הַלֶּחֶם אָזַל מִכֵּלֵינוּ
from-sacks-of-us he-is-gone the-food for to-the-man can-we-give then-what? we-go

וּתְשׁוּרָה אֵין־לְהָבִיא לְאִישׁ הָאֱלֹהִים מָה אִתָּנוּ׃ וַיֹּסֶף
and-he-repeated (8) to-us what? the-God to-man-of to-take not and-gift

הַנַּעַר לַעֲנוֹת אֶת־שָׁאוּל וַיֹּאמֶר הִנֵּה נִמְצָא בְיָדִי
in-hand-of-me being-found look! and-he-said Saul *** to-answer the-servant

רֶבַע שֶׁקֶל כָּסֶף וְנָתַתִּי לְאִישׁ הָאֱלֹהִים וְהִגִּיד
so-he-will-tell the-God to-man-of now-I-will-give silver shekel-of quarter-of

לָנוּ אֶת־דַּרְכֵּנוּ׃ לְפָנִים ׀ בְּיִשְׂרָאֵל כֹּה־אָמַר הָאִישׁ בְּלֶכְתּוֹ
when-to-go-him the-man he-said this in-Israel formerly (9) way-of-us *** to-us

לִדְרוֹשׁ אֱלֹהִים לְכוּ וְנֵלְכָה עַד־הָרֹאֶה כִּי לַנָּבִיא הַיּוֹם
the-day to-the-prophet for the-seer to and-we-will-go come! God to-inquire

יִקָּרֵא לְפָנִים הָרֹאֶה׃ וַיֹּאמֶר שָׁאוּל לְנַעֲרוֹ
to-servant-of-him Saul and-he-said (10) the-seer formerly he-was-called

טוֹב דְּבָרְךָ לְכָה ׀ נֵלֵכָה וַיֵּלְכוּ אֶל־הָעִיר אֲשֶׁר־שָׁם
there were the-town for so-they-set-out let-us-go come! word-of-you good

אִישׁ הָאֱלֹהִים׃ הֵמָּה עֹלִים בְּמַעֲלֵה הָעִיר וְהֵמָּה מָצְאוּ
they-met and-they the-town on-hill-of ones-going-up they (11) the-God man-of

נְעָרוֹת יֹצְאוֹת לִשְׁאֹב מָיִם וַיֹּאמְרוּ לָהֶן הֲיֵשׁ בָּזֶה
at-here is-he? to-them and-they-asked waters to-draw ones-coming-out girls

הָרֹאֶה׃ וַתַּעֲנֶינָה אוֹתָם וַתֹּאמַרְנָה יֵּשׁ הִנֵּה לְפָנֶיךָ
ahead-of-you see! he-is and-they-said them and-they-answered (12) the-seer

מַהֵר ׀ עַתָּה כִּי הַיּוֹם בָּא לָעִיר כִּי זֶבַח הַיּוֹם
the-day sacrifice for to-the-town he-came the-day for now hurry!

לָעָם בַּבָּמָה׃ כְּבֹאֲכֶם הָעִיר כֵּן
so the-town as-to-enter-you (13) at-the-high-place for-the-people

תִּמְצְאוּן אֹתוֹ בְּטֶרֶם יַעֲלֶה הַבָּמָתָה לֶאֱכֹל כִּי לֹא־
not for to-eat to-the-high-place he-goes-up at-before him you-will-find

יֹאכַל הָעָם עַד־בֹּאוֹ כִּי־הוּא יְבָרֵךְ הַזֶּבַח
the-sacrifice he-must-bless he for to-come-him until the-people he-will-eat

the donkeys and start worrying about us."
6 But the servant replied, "Look, in this town there is a man of God; he is highly respected, and everything he says comes true. Let's go there now. Perhaps he will tell us what way to take."
7 Saul said to his servant, "If we go, what can we give the man? The food in our sacks is gone. We have no gift to take to the man of God. What do we have?"
8 The servant answered him again. "Look," he said, "I have a quarter of a shekel[e] of silver. I will give it to the man of God so that he will tell us what way to take."
9 (Formerly in Israel, if a man went to inquire of God, he would say, "Come, let us go to the seer," because the prophet of today used to be called a seer.)
10 "Good," Saul said to his servant. "Come, let's go." So they set out for the town where the man of God was.
11 As they were going up the hill to the town, they met some girls coming out to draw water, and they asked them, "Is the seer here?"
12 "He is," they answered. "He's ahead of you. Hurry now; he has just come to our town today, for the people have a sacrifice at the high place.
13 As soon as you enter the town, you will find him before he goes up to the high place to eat. The people will not begin eating until he comes, because he must bless

[e] 8 That is, about 1/10 ounce (about 3 grams)

אַחֲרֵי־כֵ֖ן יֹאכְל֣וּ הַקְּרֻאִ֑ים וְעַתָּ֣ה עֲל֔וּ כִּֽי־אֹת֥וֹ

him for go-up! so-now the-ones-being-invited they-will-eat that after

כְהַיּ֖וֹם תִּמְצְא֥וּן אֹתֽוֹ׃ וַֽיַּעֲל֖וּ הָעִ֑יר הֵ֗מָּה בָּאִים֙

ones-coming they the-town so-they-went-up (14) him you-will-find about-the-day

בְּת֣וֹךְ הָעִ֔יר וְהִנֵּ֧ה שְׁמוּאֵ֛ל יֹצֵ֥א לִקְרָאתָ֖ם לַעֲל֥וֹת

to-go-up to-meet-them coming-out Samuel and-see! the-town into-midst-of

הַבָּמָֽה׃ וַֽיהוָ֔ה גָּלָ֖ה אֶת־אֹ֣זֶן שְׁמוּאֵ֑ל י֣וֹם אֶחָ֔ד לִפְנֵ֥י

before one day Samuel ear-of *** he-revealed now-Yahweh (15) the-high-place

ב֣וֹא־שָׁא֔וּל לֵאמֹֽר׃ כָּעֵ֣ת ׀ מָחָ֗ר אֶשְׁלַ֨ח אֵלֶ֜יךָ אִ֗ישׁ

man to-you I-will-send tomorrow about-the-time (16) to-say Saul to-come

מֵאֶ֙רֶץ֙ בִּנְיָמִ֔ן וּמְשַׁחְתּ֥וֹ לְנָגִ֖יד עַל־עַמִּ֣י יִשְׂרָאֵ֑ל

Israel people-of-me over as-leader and-you-anoint-him Benjamin from-land-of

וְהוֹשִׁ֥יעַ אֶת־עַמִּ֖י מִיַּ֣ד פְּלִשְׁתִּ֑ים כִּ֤י רָאִ֙יתִי֙

I-looked indeed Philistines from-hand-of people-of-me *** and-he-will-deliver

אֶת־עַמִּ֔י כִּ֛י בָּ֥אָה צַעֲקָת֖וֹ אֵלָֽי׃ וּשְׁמוּאֵ֖ל רָאָ֣ה אֶת־

*** he-saw when-Samuel (17) to-me cry-of-him she-reached for people-of-me ***

שָׁא֑וּל וַֽיהוָ֣ה עָנָ֔הוּ הִנֵּ֤ה הָאִישׁ֙ אֲשֶׁ֣ר אָמַ֣רְתִּי אֵלֶ֔יךָ זֶ֖ה

this-one to-you I-spoke whom the-man see! he-told-to-him then-Yahweh Saul

יַעְצֹ֥ר בְּעַמִּֽי׃ וַיִּגַּ֥שׁ שָׁא֛וּל אֶת־שְׁמוּאֵ֖ל

Samuel *** Saul and-he-approached (18) over-people-of-me he-will-govern

בְּת֣וֹךְ הַשָּׁ֑עַר וַיֹּ֙אמֶר֙ הַגִּֽידָה־נָּ֣א לִ֔י אֵי־זֶ֖ה בֵּ֥ית

house-of this where? to-me now! tell! and-he-asked the-gateway inside-of

הָרֹאֶֽה׃ וַיַּ֨עַן שְׁמוּאֵ֜ל אֶת־שָׁא֗וּל וַיֹּ֙אמֶר֙ אָנֹכִ֣י הָרֹאֶ֔ה עֲלֵ֤ה

go-up! the-seer I and-he-said Saul *** Samuel and-he-replied (19) the-seer

לְפָנַי֙ הַבָּמָ֔ה וַאֲכַלְתֶּ֥ם עִמִּ֖י הַיּ֑וֹם וְשִׁלַּחְתִּ֣יךָ

and-I-will-let-go-you the-day with-me for-you-must-eat the-high-place ahead-of-me

בַבֹּ֔קֶר וְכֹ֛ל אֲשֶׁ֥ר בִּֽלְבָבְךָ֖ אַגִּ֥יד לָֽךְ׃

to-you I-will-tell in-heart-of-you that and-all in-the-morning

וְלָאֲתֹנ֞וֹת הָאֹבְד֣וֹת לְךָ֗ הַיּוֹם֙ שְׁלֹ֣שֶׁת

three-of the-day from-you the-ones-being-lost as-for-the-donkeys (20)

הַיָּמִ֔ים אַל־תָּ֧שֶׂם אֶֽת־לִבְּךָ֛ לָהֶ֖ם כִּ֣י נִמְצָ֑אוּ

they-were-found for about-them heart-of-you *** you-upset not the-days

וּלְמִי֙ כָּל־חֶמְדַּ֣ת יִשְׂרָאֵ֔ל הֲל֣וֹא לְךָ֔ וּלְכֹ֖ל בֵּ֥ית

family-of and-to-all-of to-you not? Israel desire-of all-of and-to-whom?

אָבִֽיךָ׃ וַיַּ֨עַן שָׁא֜וּל וַיֹּ֗אמֶר הֲל֨וֹא בֶן־יְמִינִ֜י אָנֹ֗כִי

I Benjamite not? and-he-said Saul and-he-answered (21) father-of-you

מִקְּטַנֵּי֙ שִׁבְטֵ֣י יִשְׂרָאֵ֔ל וּמִשְׁפַּחְתִּי֙ הַצְּעִרָ֔ה מִכָּל־

from-all-of the-least and-clan-of-me Israel tribes-of from-smallest-ones-of

the sacrifice; afterward, those
who are invited will eat. Go up
now; you should find him
about this time."
14 They went up to the town,
and as they were entering it,
there was Samuel, coming
toward them on his way up to
the high place.
15 Now the day before Saul
came, the LORD had revealed
this to Samuel: 16 "About this
time tomorrow I will send you
a man from the land of Benjamin. Anoint him leader over
my people Israel; he will deliver my people from the hand
of the Philistines. I have
looked upon my people, for
their cry has reached me."
17 When Samuel caught sight
of Saul, the LORD said to him,
"This is the man I spoke to
you about; he will govern my
people."
18 Saul approached Samuel in
the gateway and asked,
"Would you please tell me
where the seer's house is?"
19 "I am the seer," Samuel replied. "Go up ahead of me to
the high place, for today you
are to eat with me, and in the
morning I will let you go and
will tell you all that is in your
heart. 20 As for the donkeys you
lost three days ago, do not
worry about them; they have
been found. And to whom is
all the desire of Israel turned,
if not to you and all your father's family?"
21 Saul answered, "But am I
not a Benjamite, from the
smallest tribe of Israel, and is
not my clan the least of all the

מִשְׁפְּחוֹת שִׁבְטֵי בִנְיָמִן וְלָמָּה דִּבַּרְתָּ אֵלַי כַּדָּבָר הַזֶּה׃
the-this as-the-thing to-me you-say now-why? Benjamin tribes-of clans-of

וַיִּקַּח שְׁמוּאֵל אֶת־שָׁאוּל וְאֶת־נַעֲרוֹ וַיְבִיאֵם
and-he-brought-them servant-of-him and Saul *** Samuel then-he-took (22)

לִשְׁכָּתָה וַיִּתֵּן לָהֶם מָקוֹם בְּרֹאשׁ הַקְּרוּאִים וְהֵמָּה
now-they the-ones-being-invited at-head-of seat to-them and-he-gave into-hall

כִּשְׁלֹשִׁים אִישׁ׃ וַיֹּאמֶר שְׁמוּאֵל לַטַּבָּח תְּנָה אֶת־הַמָּנָה
the-piece *** bring! to-the-cook Samuel and-he-said (23) person about-thirty

אֲשֶׁר נָתַתִּי לָךְ אֲשֶׁר אָמַרְתִּי אֵלֶיךָ שִׂים אֹתָהּ עִמָּךְ׃ וַיָּרֶם
so-he-took (24) with-you her set-aside! to-you I-told that to-you I-gave that

הַטַּבָּח אֶת־הַשּׁוֹק וְהֶעָלֶיהָ וַיָּשֶׂם ׀ לִפְנֵי שָׁאוּל וַיֹּאמֶר הִנֵּה
see! and-he-said Saul before and-he-set and-what-on-her the-leg *** the-cook

הַנִּשְׁאָר שִׂים־לְפָנֶיךָ אֱכֹל כִּי לַמּוֹעֵד שָׁמוּר־
being-kept for-the-occasion for eat! before-you to-set the-one-being-kept

לְךָ לֵאמֹר הָעָם ׀ קָרָאתִי וַיֹּאכַל שָׁאוּל עִם־שְׁמוּאֵל בַּיּוֹם
on-the-day Samuel with Saul and-he-dined I-invited the-people to-say for-you

הַהוּא׃ וַיֵּרְדוּ מֵהַבָּמָה הָעִיר וַיְדַבֵּר
then-he-talked the-city from-the-high-place after-they-came-down (25) the-that

עִם־שָׁאוּל עַל־הַגָּג׃ וַיַּשְׁכִּמוּ וַיְהִי כַּעֲלוֹת הַשַּׁחַר
the-daybreak about-to-come and-he-was and-they-rose (26) the-roof on Saul with

וַיִּקְרָא שְׁמוּאֵל אֶל־שָׁאוּל הַגָּג לֵאמֹר קוּמָה וַאֲשַׁלְּחֶךָּ
and-I-will-send-you get-ready! to-say on-the-roof Saul to Samuel and-he-called

וַיָּקָם שָׁאוּל וַיֵּצְאוּ שְׁנֵיהֶם הוּא וּשְׁמוּאֵל
and-Samuel he two-of-them then-they-went-out Saul when-he-got-ready

הַחוּצָה׃ הֵמָּה יוֹרְדִים בִּקְצֵה הָעִיר וּשְׁמוּאֵל
and-Samuel the-town to-edge-of ones-going-down they (27) to-the-outside

אָמַר אֶל־שָׁאוּל אֱמֹר לַנַּעַר וְיַעֲבֹר לְפָנֵינוּ וַיַּעֲבֹר
and-he-went-on ahead-of-us so-he-goes to-the-servant tell! Saul to he-said

וְאַתָּה עֲמֹד כַּיּוֹם וְאַשְׁמִיעֲךָ אֶת־דְּבַר אֱלֹהִים׃ וַיִּקַּח
then-he-took (10:1) God message-of *** so-I-may-tell-you as-the-day stay! but-you

שְׁמוּאֵל אֶת־פַּךְ הַשֶּׁמֶן וַיִּצֹק עַל־רֹאשׁוֹ וַיִּשָּׁקֵהוּ
and-he-kissed-him head-of-him on and-he-poured the-oil flask-of *** Samuel

וַיֹּאמֶר הֲלוֹא כִּי־מְשָׁחֲךָ יְהוָה עַל־נַחֲלָתוֹ לְנָגִיד׃
as-leader inheritance-of-him over Yahweh he-anointed-you indeed not? and-he-said

בְּלֶכְתְּךָ הַיּוֹם מֵעִמָּדִי וּמָצָאתָ שְׁנֵי אֲנָשִׁים
men two-of then-you-will-meet from-with-me the-day when-to-leave-you (2)

עִם־קְבֻרַת רָחֵל בִּגְבוּל בִּנְיָמִן בְּצֶלְצַח וְאָמְרוּ אֵלֶיךָ
to-you and-they-will-say at-Zelzah Benjamin on-border-of Rachel tomb-of near

ק הגגה 26°

clans of the tribe of Benjamin? Why do you say such a thing to me?"

[22]Then Samuel brought Saul and his servant into the hall and seated them at the head of those who were invited—about thirty in number. [23]Samuel said to the cook, "Bring the piece of meat I gave you, the one I told you to lay aside."

[24]So the cook took up the leg with what was on it and set it in front of Saul. Samuel said, "Here is what has been kept for you. Eat, because it was set aside for you for this occasion, from the time I said, 'I have invited guests.'" And Saul dined with Samuel that day.

[25]After they came down from the high place to the town, Samuel talked with Saul on the roof of his house. [26]They rose about daybreak and Samuel called to Saul on the roof, "Get ready, and I will send you on your way." When Saul got ready, he and Samuel went outside together. [27]As they were going down to the edge of the town, Samuel said to Saul, "Tell the servant to go on ahead of us"—and the servant did so—"but you stay here awhile, so that I may give you a message from God."

10 Then Samuel took a flask of oil and poured it on Saul's head and kissed him, saying, "Has not the LORD anointed you leader over his inheritance?[f] [2]When you leave me today, you will meet two men near Rachel's tomb, at Zelzah on the border of Benjamin. They will say to you,

[f]1 Hebrew; Septuagint and Vulgate *over his people Israel? You will reign over the LORD's people and save them from the power of their enemies round about. And this will be a sign to you that the LORD has anointed you leader over his inheritance:*

נִמְצְאוּ הָאֲתֹנוֹת אֲשֶׁר הָלַכְתָּ לְבַקֵּשׁ וְהִנֵּה נָטַשׁ
he-stopped and-see! to-look-for you-set-out that the-donkeys they-were-found

אָבִיךָ אֶת־ דִּבְרֵי הָאֲתֹנוֹת וְדָאַג לָכֶם לֵאמֹר מָה
what? to-say about-you and-he-worries the-donkeys thoughts-of *** father-of-you

אֶעֱשֶׂה לִבְנִי׃ (3) וְחָלַפְתָּ מִשָּׁם וָהָלְאָה
and-onward from-there then-you-will-go (3) about-son-of-me shall-I-do

וּבָאתָ עַד־ אֵלוֹן תָּבוֹר וּמְצָאוּךָ שָּׁם שְׁלֹשָׁה
three there and-they-will-meet-you Tabor great-tree-of to and-you-will-come

אֲנָשִׁים עֹלִים אֶל־הָאֱלֹהִים בֵּית־אֵל אֶחָד נֹשֵׂא ׀ שְׁלֹשָׁה גְדָיִים
young-goats three carrying one El Beth the-God to ones-going-up men

וְאֶחָד נֹשֵׂא שְׁלֹשֶׁת כִּכְּרוֹת לֶחֶם וְאֶחָד נֹשֵׂא נֵבֶל־
skin-of carrying and-another bread loaves-of three-of carrying and-another

יָיִן׃ (4) וְשָׁאֲלוּ לְךָ לְשָׁלוֹם וְנָתְנוּ לְךָ
to-you and-they-will-give for-peace to-you and-they-will-greet (4) wine

שְׁתֵּי־ לֶחֶם וְלָקַחְתָּ מִיָּדָם׃ (5) אַחַר כֵּן תָּבוֹא
you-will-go that after (5) from-hand-of-them and-you-will-accept bread two-of

גִּבְעַת הָאֱלֹהִים אֲשֶׁר־ שָׁם נְצִבֵי פְלִשְׁתִּים וִיהִי
and-he-will-be Philistines ones-being-posted-of there where the-God Gibeah-of

כְבֹאֲךָ שָׁם הָעִיר וּפָגַעְתָּ חֶבֶל נְבִיאִים
prophets procession-of then-you-will-meet the-town there as-to-approach-you

יֹרְדִים מֵהַבָּמָה וְלִפְנֵיהֶם נֵבֶל וְתֹף
and-tambourine lyre and-before-them from-the-high-place ones-coming-down

וְחָלִיל וְכִנּוֹר וְהֵמָּה מִתְנַבְּאִים׃ (6) וְצָלְחָה עָלֶיךָ
upon-you and-she-will-come (6) ones-prophesying and-they and-harp and-flute

רוּחַ יְהוָה וְהִתְנַבִּיתָ עִמָּם וְנֶהְפַּכְתָּ
and-you-will-be-changed with-them and-you-will-prophesy Yahweh Spirit-of

לְאִישׁ אַחֵר׃ (7) וְהָיָה כִּי תָבֹאינָה הָאֹתוֹת
the-signs they-are-fulfilled once and-he-will-be (7) different into-person

הָאֵלֶּה לָךְ עֲשֵׂה לְךָ אֲשֶׁר תִּמְצָא יָדֶךָ כִּי הָאֱלֹהִים
the-God for hand-of-you she-finds whatever for-you do! for-you the-these

עִמָּךְ׃ (8) וְיָרַדְתָּ לְפָנַי הַגִּלְגָּל וְהִנֵּה אָנֹכִי יֹרֵד
coming-down I and-see! the-Gilgal ahead-of-me now-you-go-down (8) with-you

אֵלֶיךָ לְהַעֲלוֹת עֹלוֹת לִזְבֹּחַ זִבְחֵי שְׁלָמִים שִׁבְעַת
seven-of fellowships offerings-of to-sacrifice burnt-offerings to-offer to-you

יָמִים תּוֹחֵל עַד־ בּוֹאִי אֵלֶיךָ וְהוֹדַעְתִּי לְךָ אֵת אֲשֶׁר
what *** to-you and-I-tell to-you to-come-me until you-must-wait days

תַּעֲשֶׂה׃ (9) וְהָיָה כְּהַפְנֹתוֹ שִׁכְמוֹ לָלֶכֶת מֵעִם
from-with to-leave shoulder-of-him as-to-turn-him and-he-was (9) you-must-do

'The donkeys you set out to
look for have been found. And
now your father has stopped
thinking about them and is
worried about you. He is asking, "What shall I do about my
son?" '
3"Then you will go on from
there until you reach the great
tree of Tabor. Three men going
up to God at Bethel will meet
you there. One will be carrying three young goats, another
three loaves of bread, and another a skin of wine. 4They
will greet you and offer you
two loaves of bread, which
you will accept from them.
5"After that you will go to
Gibeah of God, where there is
a Philistine outpost. As you
approach the town, you will
meet a procession of prophets
coming down from the high
place with lyres, tambourines,
flutes and harps being played
before them, and they will be
prophesying. 6The Spirit of the
LORD will come upon you in
power, and you will prophesy
with them; and you will be
changed into a different person. 7Once these signs are
fulfilled, do whatever your
hand finds to do, for God is
with you.
8"Go down ahead of me to
Gilgal. I will surely come
down to you to sacrifice burnt
offerings and fellowship
offerings,[8] but you must wait
seven days until I come to you
and tell you what you are to
do."

Saul Made King

9As Saul turned to leave

8 8 Traditionally *peace offerings*

°7 ק תבאנה

שְׁמוּאֵל וַיַּהֲפָךְ־ לוֹ אֱלֹהִים לֵב אַחֵר וַיָּבֹאוּ
and-they-were-fulfilled different heart God for-him then-he-changed Samuel

כָּל־ הָאֹתוֹת הָאֵלֶּה בַּיּוֹם הַהוּא׃ וַיָּבֹאוּ שָׁם
there when-they-arrived (10) the-that on-the-day the-these the-signs all-of

הַגִּבְעָתָה וְהִנֵּה חֶבֶל־ נְבִאִים לִקְרָאתוֹ וַתִּצְלַח
and-she-came to-meet-him prophets procession-of then-see! at-the-Gibeah

עָלָיו רוּחַ אֱלֹהִים וַיִּתְנַבֵּא בְּתוֹכָם׃ וַיְהִי
and-he-was (11) in-among-them and-he-prophesied God Spirit-of upon-him

כָּל־ יוֹדְעוֹ מֵאִתְּמוֹל שִׁלְשׁוֹם וַיִּרְאוּ וְהִנֵּה עִם־
with and-see! when-they-saw before from-yesterday one-knowing-him every-of

נְבִאִים נִבָּא וַיֹּאמֶר הָעָם אִישׁ אֶל־ רֵעֵהוּ מַה־
what? other-of-him to each the-people then-they-asked prophesying prophets

זֶּה הָיָה לְבֶן־ קִישׁ הֲגַם שָׁאוּל בַּנְּבִיאִים׃ וַיַּעַן
and-he-replied (12) among-the-prophets Saul also? Kish to-son-of he-happened this

אִישׁ מִשָּׁם וַיֹּאמֶר וּמִי אֲבִיהֶם עַל־ כֵּן הָיְתָה
she-became this for father-of-them and-who? and-he-said from-there man

לְמָשָׁל הֲגַם שָׁאוּל בַּנְּבִאִים׃ וַיְכַל מֵהִתְנַבּוֹת
from-to-prophesy after-he-stopped (13) among-the-prophets Saul also? as-saying

וַיָּבֹא הַבָּמָה׃ וַיֹּאמֶר דּוֹד שָׁאוּל אֵלָיו וְאֶל־
and-to to-him Saul uncle-of now-he-asked (14) the-high-place then-he-went

נַעֲרוֹ אָן הֲלַכְתֶּם וַיֹּאמֶר לְבַקֵּשׁ אֶת־ הָאֲתֹנוֹת
the-donkeys *** to-look-for and-he-said you-were where? servant-of-him

וַנִּרְאֶה כִּי־ אַיִן וַנָּבוֹא אֶל־שְׁמוּאֵל׃ וַיֹּאמֶר
and-he-said (15) Samuel to then-we-went there-was-not that when-we-saw

דּוֹד שָׁאוּל הַגִּידָה־נָּא לִי מָה־ אָמַר לָכֶם שְׁמוּאֵל׃ וַיֹּאמֶר
and-he-replied (16) Samuel to-you he-said what to-me now! tell! Saul uncle-of

שָׁאוּל אֶל־ דּוֹדוֹ הַגֵּד הִגִּיד לָנוּ כִּי נִמְצְאוּ
they-were-found that to-us he-assured to-assure uncle-of-him to Saul

הָאֲתֹנוֹת וְאֶת־ דְּבַר הַמְּלוּכָה לֹא־ הִגִּיד לוֹ אֲשֶׁר אָמַר
he-said what to-him he-told not the-kingship matter-of but the-donkeys

שְׁמוּאֵל׃ וַיַּצְעֵק שְׁמוּאֵל אֶת־ הָעָם אֶל־ יְהוָה הַמִּצְפָּה׃
the-Mizpah Yahweh to the-people *** Samuel and-he-summoned (17) Samuel

וַיֹּאמֶר ׀ אֶל־ בְּנֵי יִשְׂרָאֵל כֹּה־ אָמַר יְהוָה אֱלֹהֵי יִשְׂרָאֵל אָנֹכִי
I Israel God-of Yahweh he-says this Israel sons-of to and-he-said (18)

הֶעֱלֵיתִי אֶת־ יִשְׂרָאֵל מִמִּצְרָיִם וָאַצִּיל אֶתְכֶם מִיַּד מִצְרַיִם
Egypt from-hand-of you and-I-delivered from-Egypt Israel *** I-brought-up

וּמִיַּד כָּל־ הַמַּמְלָכוֹת הַלֹּחֲצִים אֶתְכֶם׃ וְאַתֶּם
but-you (19) you the-ones-oppressing the-kingdoms all-of and-from-hand-of

Samuel, God changed Saul's
heart, and all these signs were
fulfilled that day. 10 When they
arrived at Gibeah, a pro-
cession of prophets met him;
the Spirit of God came upon
him in power, and he joined
in their prophesying. 11 When
all those who had formerly
known him saw him prophe-
sying with the prophets, they
asked each other, "What is
this that has happened to the
son of Kish? Is Saul also
among the prophets?"
12 A man who lived there answered, "And who is their father?" So it became a saying:
"Is Saul also among the prophets?" 13 After Saul stopped
prophesying, he went to the
high place.
14 Now Saul's uncle asked
him and his servant, "Where
have you been?"
"Looking for the donkeys,"
he said. "But when we saw
they were not to be found, we
went to Samuel."
15 Saul's uncle said, "Tell me
what Samuel said to you."
16 Saul replied, "He assured
us that the donkeys had been
found." But he did not tell his
uncle what Samuel had said
about the kingship.
17 Samuel summoned the
people of Israel to the LORD at
Mizpah 18 and said to them,
"This is what the LORD, the
God of Israel, says: 'I brought
Israel up out of Egypt, and I
delivered you from the power
of Egypt and all the kingdoms
that oppressed you.' 19 But you

הַיּוֹם מְאַסְתֶּם אֶת־ אֱלֹהֵיכֶם אֲשֶׁר־ הוּא מוֹשִׁיעַ לָכֶם מִכָּל־
from-all-of to-you saving he who God-of-you *** you-rejected the-day

רָעוֹתֵיכֶם וְצָרֹתֵיכֶם וַתֹּאמְרוּ לֹו כִּי־ מֶלֶךְ
king indeed to-him and-you-said and-distresses-of-you calamities-of-you

תָּשִׂים עָלֵינוּ וְעַתָּה הִתְיַצְּבוּ לִפְנֵי יְהוָה לְשִׁבְטֵיכֶם
by-tribes-of-you Yahweh before you-present-yourselves so-now over-us you-set

וּלְאַלְפֵיכֶם׃ וַיַּקְרֵב שְׁמוּאֵל אֵת כָּל־ שִׁבְטֵי
tribes-of all-of *** Samuel when-he-brought-near (20) and-by-clans-of-you

יִשְׂרָאֵל וַיִּלָּכֵד שֵׁבֶט בִּנְיָמִן׃ וַיַּקְרֵב אֶת־
*** then-he-brought-forward (21) Benjamin tribe-of then-he-was-chosen Israel

שֵׁבֶט בִּנְיָמִן לְמִשְׁפְּחֹתָו וַתִּלָּכֵד מִשְׁפַּחַת הַמַּטְרִי
the-Matri clan-of and-she-was-chosen by-clans-of-him Benjamin tribe-of

וַיִּלָּכֵד שָׁאוּל בֶּן־ קִישׁ וַיְבַקְשֻׁהוּ וְלֹא
and-not but-they-looked-for-him Kish son-of Saul then-he-was-chosen

נִמְצָא׃ וַיִּשְׁאֲלוּ־ עוֹד בַּיהוָה הֲבָא עוֹד הֲלֹם
here yet has-he-come? of-Yahweh further so-they-inquired (22) he-was-found

אִישׁ וַיֹּאמֶר יְהוָה הִנֵּה־ הוּא נֶחְבָּא אֶל־ הַכֵּלִים׃
the-baggages among he-hid-himself he see! Yahweh and-he-said man

וַיָּרֻצוּ וַיִּקָּחֻהוּ מִשָּׁם וַיִּתְיַצֵּב בְּתוֹךְ
in-among and-he-stood from-there and-they-brought-out-him and-they-ran (23)

הָעָם וַיִּגְבַּהּ מִכָּל־ הָעָם מִשִּׁכְמוֹ
from-shoulder-of-him the-people than-all-of and-he-was-taller the-people

וָמָעְלָה׃ וַיֹּאמֶר שְׁמוּאֵל אֶל־ כָּל־ הָעָם הַרְאִיתֶם אֲשֶׁר
whom you-see? the-people all-of to Samuel and-he-said (24) and-upward

בָּחַר־ בּוֹ יְהוָה כִּי אֵין כָּמֹהוּ בְּכָל־ הָעָם
the-people among-all-of like-him there-is-not indeed Yahweh to-him he-chose

וַיָּרִעוּ כָל־ הָעָם וַיֹּאמְרוּ יְחִי הַמֶּלֶךְ׃
the-king may-he-live and-they-said the-people all-of then-they-shouted

וַיְדַבֵּר שְׁמוּאֵל אֶל־ הָעָם אֵת מִשְׁפַּט הַמְּלֻכָה
the-kingship regulation-of *** the-people to Samuel then-he-explained (25)

וַיִּכְתֹּב בַּסֵּפֶר וַיַּנַּח לִפְנֵי יְהוָה וַיְשַׁלַּח
then-he-dismissed Yahweh before and-he-deposited on-the-scroll and-he-wrote

שְׁמוּאֵל אֶת־כָּל־ הָעָם אִישׁ לְבֵיתוֹ׃ וְגַם־ שָׁאוּל הָלַךְ
he-went Saul and-also (26) to-home-of-him each the-people all-of *** Samuel

לְבֵיתוֹ גִּבְעָתָה וַיֵּלְכוּ עִמּוֹ הַחַיִל אֲשֶׁר־
whom the-valiant-man with-him and-they-went in-Gibeah to-home-of-him

נָגַע אֱלֹהִים בְּלִבָּם׃ וּבְנֵי בְלִיַּעַל אָמְרוּ מַה־
how? they-said trouble but-sons-of (27) on-heart-of-them God he-touched

have now rejected your God,
who saves you out of all your
calamities and distresses. And
you have said, 'No, set a king
over us.' So now present yourselves before the LORD by your
tribes and clans."
20 When Samuel brought all
the tribes of Israel near, the
tribe of Benjamin was chosen.
21 Then he brought forward the
tribe of Benjamin, clan by
clan, and Matri's clan was
chosen. Finally Saul son of
Kish was chosen. But when
they looked for him, he was
not to be found. 22 So they inquired further of the LORD,
"Has the man come here yet?"
And the LORD said, "Yes, he
has hidden himself among the
baggage."
23 They ran and brought him
out, and as he stood among
the people he was a head taller
than any of the others. 24 Samuel said to all the people, "Do
you see the man the LORD has
chosen? There is no one like
him among all the people."
Then the people shouted,
"Long live the king!"
25 Samuel explained to the
people the regulations of the
kingship. He wrote them
down on a scroll and deposit-
ed it before the LORD. Then
Samuel dismissed the people,
each to his own home.
26 Saul also went to his home
in Gibeah, accompanied by
valiant men whose hearts God
had touched. 27 But some troublemakers said, "How can this

°21 ק למשפחתיו

יֹשִׁעֵ֫נוּ זֶ֔ה וַיִּבְזֻ֕הוּ וְלֹֽא־ הֵבִ֥יאוּ ל֖וֹ מִנְחָ֑ה
gift to-him they-brought and-not and-they-despised-him this can-he-save-us

וַיְהִ֖י כְּמַחֲרִֽישׁ׃ וַיַּ֗עַל נָחָשׁ֙ הָֽעַמּוֹנִ֔י
the-Ammonite Nahash and-he-went-up (11:1) as-one-being-silent but-he-was

וַיִּ֖חַן עַל־ יָבֵ֣שׁ גִּלְעָ֑ד וַיֹּ֨אמְר֜וּ כָּל־ אַנְשֵׁ֤י יָבֵישׁ֙ אֶל־
to Jabesh men-of all-of and-they-said Gilead Jabesh against and-he-besieged

נָחָ֔שׁ כְּרָת־ לָ֥נוּ בְרִ֖ית וְנַעַבְדֶֽךָּ׃ וַיֹּ֣אמֶר אֲלֵיהֶ֗ם
to-them but-he-replied (2) and-we-will-serve-you treaty with-us make! Nahash

נָחָשׁ֙ הָֽעַמּוֹנִ֔י בְּזֹאת֙ אֶכְרֹ֣ת לָכֶ֔ם בִּנְק֥וֹר לָכֶ֖ם
of-you that-to-gouge-out with-you I-will-make-treaty on-this the-Ammonite Nahash

כָּל־ עֵ֣ין יָמִ֑ין וְשַׂמְתִּ֥יהָ חֶרְפָּ֖ה עַל־ כָּל־ יִשְׂרָאֵֽל׃ וַיֹּ֣אמְרוּ
and-they-said (3) Israel all-of on disgrace so-I-bring-her right eye every-of

אֵלָ֜יו זִקְנֵ֣י יָבֵ֗ישׁ הֶ֤רֶף לָ֙נוּ֙ שִׁבְעַ֣ת יָמִ֔ים וְנִשְׁלְחָה֙ מַלְאָכִ֔ים
messengers so-we-can-send days seven-of to-us give! Jabesh elders-of to-him

בְּכֹ֖ל גְּב֣וּל יִשְׂרָאֵ֑ל וְאִם־ אֵ֥ין מוֹשִׁ֛יעַ אֹתָ֖נוּ
us rescuing no-one and-if Israel territory-of through-all-of

וְיָצָ֥אנוּ אֵלֶֽיךָ׃ וַיָּבֹ֤אוּ הַמַּלְאָכִים֙ גִּבְעַ֣ת שָׁא֔וּל
Saul Gibeah-of the-messengers when-they-came (4) to-you then-we-will-surrender

וַֽיְדַבְּר֥וּ הַדְּבָרִ֖ים בְּאָזְנֵ֣י הָעָ֑ם וַיִּשְׂא֧וּ כָל־
all-of then-they-raised the-people in-ears-of the-terms and-they-reported

הָעָ֛ם אֶת־ קוֹלָ֖ם וַיִּבְכּֽוּ׃ וְהִנֵּ֣ה שָׁא֗וּל בָּ֚א
returning Saul then-see! (5) and-they-wept voice-of-them *** the-people

אַחֲרֵ֤י הַבָּקָר֙ מִן־ הַשָּׂדֶ֔ה וַיֹּ֣אמֶר שָׁא֔וּל מַה־ לָּעָ֖ם כִּ֣י
that with-the-people what? Saul and-he-asked the-field from the-ox behind

יִבְכּ֑וּ וַיְסַפְּרוּ־ ל֔וֹ אֶת־ דִּבְרֵ֖י אַנְשֵׁ֥י יָבֵֽישׁ׃
Jabesh men-of words-of *** to-him then-they-repeated they-weep

וַתִּצְלַ֤ח רֽוּחַ־ אֱלֹהִים֙ עַל־ שָׁא֔וּל בְּשָׁמְע֖וֹ אֶת־הַדְּבָרִ֣ים
the-words *** when-to-hear-him Saul upon God Spirit-of and-she-came (6)

הָאֵ֑לֶּה וַיִּ֥חַר אַפּ֖וֹ מְאֹֽד׃ וַיִּקַּח֩ צֶ֨מֶד בָּקָ֜ר
ox pair-of and-he-took (7) greatly anger-of-him and-he-burned the-these

וַֽיְנַתְּחֵ֗הוּ וַיְשַׁלַּ֞ח בְּכָל־ גְּב֣וּל יִשְׂרָאֵל֮ בְּיַ֣ד
by-hand-of Israel area-of to-every-of and-he-sent and-he-cut-up-him

הַמַּלְאָכִ֣ים ׀ לֵאמֹ֡ר אֲשֶׁר֩ אֵינֶ֨נּוּ יֹצֵ֜א אַחֲרֵ֤י שָׁאוּל֙ וְאַחַ֣ר שְׁמוּאֵ֔ל כֹּ֥ה
this Samuel and-after Saul after following not-he who to-say the-messengers

יֵעָשֶׂ֖ה לִבְקָר֑וֹ וַיִּפֹּ֤ל פַּֽחַד־ יְהוָה֙ עַל־ הָעָ֔ם
the-people on Yahweh terror-of then-he-fell to-ox-of-him he-will-be-done

וַיֵּצְא֖וּ כְּאִ֥ישׁ אֶחָֽד׃ וַֽיִּפְקְדֵ֖ם בְּבָ֑זֶק
at-Bezek when-he-mustered-them (8) one as-man and-they-turned-out

fellow save us?" They despised him and brought him no gifts. But Saul kept silent.

Saul Rescues the City of Jabesh

11 Nahash the Ammonite went up and besieged Jabesh Gilead. And all the men of Jabesh said to him, "Make a treaty with us, and we will be subject to you."
2But Nahash the Ammonite replied, "I will make a treaty with you only on the condition that I gouge out the right eye of every one of you and so bring disgrace on all Israel."
3The elders of Jabesh said to him, "Give us seven days so we can send messengers throughout Israel; if no one comes to rescue us, we will surrender to you."
4When the messengers came to Gibeah of Saul and reported these terms to the people, they all wept aloud. 5Just then Saul
was returning from the fields, behind his oxen, and he asked, "What is wrong with the people? Why are they weeping?" Then they repeated to him what the men of Jabesh had said.
6When Saul heard their words, the Spirit of God came upon him in power, and he burned with anger. 7He took a
pair of oxen, cut them into pieces, and sent the pieces by messengers throughout Israel, proclaiming, "This is what will be done to the oxen of anyone who does not follow Saul and Samuel." Then the terror of the LORD fell on the people, and they turned out as one man. 8When Saul mustered them at Bezek, the men

°6 ק כשמעו

וַיִּהְיוּ בְנֵי־ יִשְׂרָאֵל שְׁלֹשׁ מֵאוֹת אֶלֶף וְאִישׁ יְהוּדָה
Judah and-man-of thousand hundreds three-of Israel sons-of then-they-were

שְׁלֹשִׁים אָלֶף׃ וַיֹּאמְרוּ לַמַּלְאָכִים הַבָּאִים כֹּה
this the-ones-coming to-the-messengers and-they-told (9) thousand thirty

תֹאמְרוּן לְאִישׁ יָבֵישׁ גִּלְעָד מָחָר תִּהְיֶה־ לָכֶם תְּשׁוּעָה
deliverance to-you she-will-come tomorrow Gilead Jabesh to-man-of you-say

בְּחֹם הַשָּׁמֶשׁ וַיָּבֹאוּ הַמַּלְאָכִים וַיַּגִּידוּ
and-they-reported the-messengers then-they-went the-sun when-to-be-hot

לְאַנְשֵׁי יָבֵישׁ וַיִּשְׂמָחוּ׃ וַיֹּאמְרוּ אַנְשֵׁי יָבֵישׁ
Jabesh men-of and-they-said (10) then-they-were-elated Jabesh to-men-of

מָחָר נֵצֵא אֲלֵיכֶם וַעֲשִׂיתֶם לָּנוּ כְּכָל־ הַטּוֹב
the-good as-all-of to-us and-you-can-do to-you we-will-surrender tomorrow

בְּעֵינֵיכֶם׃ וַיְהִי מִמָּחֳרָת וַיָּשֶׂם שָׁאוּל אֶת־
*** Saul that-he-separated on-next-day and-he-was (11) in-eyes-of-you

הָעָם שְׁלֹשָׁה רָאשִׁים וַיָּבֹאוּ בְתוֹךְ־ הַמַּחֲנֶה בְּאַשְׁמֹרֶת
in-watch-of the-camp into-midst-of and-they-broke divisions three the-people

הַבֹּקֶר וַיַּכּוּ אֶת־ עַמּוֹן עַד־ חֹם הַיּוֹם וַיְהִי
and-he-was the-day heat-of until Ammon *** and-they-slaughtered the-morning

הַנִּשְׁאָרִים וַיָּפֻצוּ וְלֹא נִשְׁאֲרוּ־ בָם שְׁנָיִם
two of-them they-were-left so-not that-they-were-scattered the-ones-surviving

יָחַד׃ וַיֹּאמֶר הָעָם אֶל־ שְׁמוּאֵל מִי הָאֹמֵר שָׁאוּל
Saul the-one-asking who? Samuel to the-people then-he-said (12) together

יִמְלֹךְ עָלֵינוּ תְּנוּ הָאֲנָשִׁים וּנְמִיתֵם׃ וַיֹּאמֶר
but-he-said (13) and-we-will-kill-them the-men bring! over-us shall-he-reign

שָׁאוּל לֹא־ יוּמַת אִישׁ בַּיּוֹם הַזֶּה כִּי הַיּוֹם עָשָׂה־
bringing the-day for the-this on-the-day man he-shall-be-killed not Saul

יְהוָה תְּשׁוּעָה בְּיִשְׂרָאֵל׃ וַיֹּאמֶר שְׁמוּאֵל אֶל־ הָעָם לְכוּ
come! the-people to Samuel then-he-said (14) to-Israel rescue Yahweh

וְנֵלְכָה הַגִּלְגָּל וּנְחַדֵּשׁ שָׁם הַמְּלוּכָה׃
the-kingship there and-we-will-reaffirm the-Gilgal and-let-us-go

וַיֵּלְכוּ כָל־ הָעָם הַגִּלְגָּל וַיַּמְלִכוּ
and-they-confirmed-as-king the-Gilgal the-people all-of so-they-went (15)

שָׁם אֶת־ שָׁאוּל לִפְנֵי יְהוָה בַּגִּלְגָּל וַיִּזְבְּחוּ־ שָׁם
there and-they-sacrificed at-the-Gilgal Yahweh in-presences-of Saul *** there

זְבָחִים שְׁלָמִים לִפְנֵי יְהוָה וַיִּשְׂמַח שָׁם שָׁאוּל וְכָל־
and-all-of Saul there and-he-celebrated Yahweh before fellowship-ones offerings

אַנְשֵׁי יִשְׂרָאֵל עַד־ מְאֹד׃ וַיֹּאמֶר שְׁמוּאֵל אֶל־ כָּל־ יִשְׂרָאֵל הִנֵּה
see! Israel all-of to Samuel and-he-said (12:1) greatly to Israel men-of

°9 ק כחם

of Israel numbered three hundred thousand and the men of
Judah thirty thousand.
9They told the messengers
who had come, "Say to the
men of Jabesh Gilead, 'By the
time the sun is hot tomorrow,
you will be delivered.' " When
the messengers went and reported this to the men of Jabesh, they were elated. 10They
said to the Ammonites, "Tomorrow we will surrender to
you, and you can do to us
whatever seems good to you."
11The next day Saul sepa-
rated his men into three divisions; during the last watch of
the night they broke into the
camp of the Ammonites and
slaughtered them until the
heat of the day. Those who
survived were scattered, so
that no two of them were left
together.

Saul Confirmed as King

12The people then said to
Samuel, "Who was it that
asked, 'Shall Saul reign over
us?' Bring these men to us and
we will put them to death."
13But Saul said, "No one
shall be put to death today, for
this day the LORD has rescued
Israel."
14Then Samuel said to the
people, "Come, let us go to Gilgal and there reaffirm the
kingship." 15So all the people
went to Gilgal and confirmed
Saul as king in the presence of
the LORD. There they sacrificed
fellowship offerings[h] before
the LORD, and Saul and all the
Israelites held a great celebra-
tion.

Samuel's Farewell Speech

12 Samuel said to all Israel, "I have listened to

[h]15 Traditionally *peace offerings*

שָׁמַעְתִּי בְקֹלְכֶם לְכֹל אֲשֶׁר־אֲמַרְתֶּם לִי וָאַמְלִיךְ עֲלֵיכֶם
over-you and-I-set-king to-me you-said that to-all to-voice-of-you I-listened

מֶלֶךְ׃ וְעַתָּה הִנֵּה הַמֶּלֶךְ ׀ מִתְהַלֵּךְ לִפְנֵיכֶם וַאֲנִי זָקַנְתִּי וָשַׂבְתִּי
and-I-am-gray I-am-old and-I before-you going the-king see! and-now (2) king

וּבָנַי הִנָּם אִתְּכֶם וַאֲנִי הִתְהַלַּכְתִּי לִפְנֵיכֶם מִנְּעֻרַי
from-youths-of-me before-you I-went and-I with-you here-they! and-sons-of-me

עַד־הַיּוֹם הַזֶּה׃ הִנְנִי עֲנוּ בִי נֶגֶד יְהוָה
Yahweh before against-me testify! here-I! (3) the-this the-day until

וְנֶגֶד מְשִׁיחוֹ אֶת־שׁוֹר ׀ מִי לָקַחְתִּי וַחֲמוֹר מִי לָקַחְתִּי וְאֶת־
and I-took whose? and-donkey I-took whose? ox *** anointed-of-him and-before

מִי עָשַׁקְתִּי אֶת־מִי רַצּוֹתִי וּמִיַּד־מִי לָקַחְתִּי
I-accepted whom? and-from-hand-of I-oppressed whom? *** I-cheated whom?

כֹפֶר וְאַעְלִים עֵינַי בּוֹ וְאָשִׁיב לָכֶם׃
to-you and-I-will-make-right against-him eyes-of-me so-I-shut bribe

וַיֹּאמְרוּ לֹא עֲשַׁקְתָּנוּ וְלֹא רַצּוֹתָנוּ וְלֹא־
and-not you-oppressed-us and-not you-cheated-us not and-they-replied (4)

לָקַחְתָּ מִיַּד־אִישׁ מְאוּמָה׃ וַיֹּאמֶר אֲלֵיהֶם עֵד יְהוָה
Yahweh witness to-them and-he-said (5) anything anyone from-hand-of you-took

בָּכֶם וְעֵד מְשִׁיחוֹ הַיּוֹם הַזֶּה כִּי לֹא מְצָאתֶם
you-found not that the-this the-day anointed-of-him and-witness against-you

בְּיָדִי מְאוּמָה וַיֹּאמֶר עֵד׃ וַיֹּאמֶר שְׁמוּאֵל אֶל־
to Samuel then-he-said (6) witness and-they-said anything in-hand-of-me

הָעָם יְהוָה אֲשֶׁר עָשָׂה אֶת־מֹשֶׁה וְאֶת־אַהֲרֹן וַאֲשֶׁר הֶעֱלָה
he-brought-out and-who Aaron and Moses *** he-appointed who Yahweh the-people

אֶת־אֲבֹתֵיכֶם מֵאֶרֶץ מִצְרָיִם׃ וְעַתָּה הִתְיַצְּבוּ וְאִשָּׁפְטָה
for-I-will-give-evidence stand! then-now (7) Egypt from-land-of fathers-of-you ***

אִתְּכֶם לִפְנֵי יְהוָה אֵת כָּל־צִדְקוֹת יְהוָה אֲשֶׁר־עָשָׂה
he-performed that Yahweh righteous-acts-of all-of *** Yahweh before to-you

אִתְּכֶם וְאֶת־אֲבוֹתֵיכֶם׃ כַּאֲשֶׁר־בָּא יַעֲקֹב מִצְרָיִם
Egypt Jacob he-entered after-when (8) fathers-of-you and-for for-you

וַיִּזְעֲקוּ אֲבוֹתֵיכֶם אֶל־יְהוָה וַיִּשְׁלַח יְהוָה אֶת־מֹשֶׁה וְאֶת־
and Moses *** Yahweh and-he-sent Yahweh to fathers-of-you then-they-cried

אַהֲרֹן וַיּוֹצִיאוּ אֶת־אֲבֹתֵיכֶם מִמִּצְרַיִם וַיֹּשִׁבוּם
and-they-settled-them from-Egypt fathers-of-you *** and-they-brought Aaron

בַּמָּקוֹם הַזֶּה׃ וַיִּשְׁכְּחוּ אֶת־יְהוָה אֱלֹהֵיהֶם וַיִּמְכֹּר
so-he-sold God-of-them Yahweh *** but-they-forgot (9) the-this in-the-place

אֹתָם בְּיַד סִיסְרָא שַׂר־צְבָא חָצוֹר וּבְיַד־פְּלִשְׁתִּים
Philistines and-into-hand-of Hazor army-of commander-of Sisera into-hand-of them

everything you said to me and
have set a king over you. [2]Now
you have a king as your leader.
As for me, I am old and gray,
and my sons are here with
you. I have been your leader
from my youth until this day.
[3]Here I stand. Testify against
me in the presence of the LORD
and his anointed. Whose ox
have I taken? Whose donkey
have I taken? Whom have I
cheated? Whom have I oppressed?
From whose hand
have I accepted a bribe to
make me shut my eyes? If I
have done any of these, I will
make it right."

[4]"You have not cheated or
oppressed us," they replied.
"You have not taken anything
from anyone's hand."

[5]Samuel said to them, "The
LORD is witness against you,
and also his anointed is witness
this day, that you have
not found anything in my
hand."

"He is witness," they said.

[6]Then Samuel said to the
people, "It is the LORD who appointed
Moses and Aaron and
brought your forefathers up
out of Egypt. [7]Now then, stand
here, because I am going to
confront you with evidence
before the LORD as to all the
righteous acts performed by
the LORD for you and your fathers.

[8]"After Jacob entered Egypt,
they cried to the LORD for help,
and the LORD sent Moses and
Aaron, who brought your
forefathers out of Egypt and
settled them in this place.

[9]"But they forgot the LORD
their God; so he sold them into
the hand of Sisera, the commander
of the army of Hazor,

וּבְיַד מֶלֶךְ מוֹאָב וַיִּלָּחֲמוּ בָּם׃ וַיִּזְעֲקוּ
and-they-cried (10) against-them and-they-fought Moab king-of and-into-hand-of

אֶל־יְהוָה וַיֹּאמְרֻ° חָטָאנוּ כִּי עָזַבְנוּ אֶת־יְהוָה וַנַּעֲבֹד
and-we-served Yahweh *** we-forsook for we-sinned and-they-said Yahweh to

אֶת־הַבְּעָלִים וְאֶת־הָעַשְׁתָּרוֹת וְעַתָּה הַצִּילֵנוּ מִיַּד
from-hand-of deliver-us! but-now the-Ashtoreths and the-Baals ***

אֹיְבֵינוּ וְנַעַבְדֶךָּ׃ וַיִּשְׁלַח יְהוָה אֶת־
*** Yahweh then-he-sent (11) and-we-will-serve-you being-enemies-of-us

יְרֻבַּעַל וְאֶת־בְּדָן וְאֶת־יִפְתָּח וְאֶת־שְׁמוּאֵל וַיַּצֵּל אֶתְכֶם מִיַּד
from-hand-of you and-he-delivered Samuel and Jephthah and Bedan and Jerub Baal

אֹיְבֵיכֶם מִסָּבִיב וַתֵּשְׁבוּ בֶּטַח׃ וַתִּרְאוּ
when-you-saw (12) securely so-you-lived on-every-side being-enemies-of-you

כִּי־נָחָשׁ מֶלֶךְ בְּנֵי־עַמּוֹן בָּא עֲלֵיכֶם וַתֹּאמְרוּ לִי
to-me then-you-said against-you moving Ammon sons-of king-of Nahash that

לֹא כִּי־מֶלֶךְ יִמְלֹךְ עָלֵינוּ וַיהוָה אֱלֹהֵיכֶם מַלְכְּכֶם׃
king-of-you God-of-you though-Yahweh over-us let-him-rule king indeed no

וְעַתָּה הִנֵּה הַמֶּלֶךְ אֲשֶׁר בְּחַרְתֶּם אֲשֶׁר שְׁאֶלְתֶּם וְהִנֵּה נָתַן
he-set and-see! you-asked-for whom you-chose whom the-king here! so-now (13)

יְהוָה עֲלֵיכֶם מֶלֶךְ׃ אִם־תִּירְאוּ אֶת־יְהוָה וַעֲבַדְתֶּם אֹתוֹ
him and-you-serve Yahweh *** you-fear if (14) king over-you Yahweh

וּשְׁמַעְתֶּם בְּקֹלוֹ וְלֹא תַמְרוּ אֶת־פִּי יְהוָה
Yahweh command-of against you-rebel and-not to-voice-of-him and-you-obey

וִהְיִתֶם גַּם־אַתֶּם וְגַם־הַמֶּלֶךְ אֲשֶׁר מָלַךְ עֲלֵיכֶם אַחַר יְהוָה
Yahweh after over-you he-reigns who the-king and-also you both and-you-are

אֱלֹהֵיכֶם׃ וְאִם־לֹא תִשְׁמְעוּ בְּקוֹל יְהוָה וּמְרִיתֶם אֶת־
against and-you-rebel Yahweh to-voice-of you-obey not but-if (15) God-of-you

פִּי יְהוָה וְהָיְתָה יַד־יְהוָה בָּכֶם
against-you Yahweh hand-of then-she-will-be Yahweh command-of

וּבַאֲבֹתֵיכֶם׃ גַּם־עַתָּה הִתְיַצְּבוּ וּרְאוּ אֶת־הַדָּבָר
the-thing *** and-see! stand-still! now then (16) as-against-fathers-of-you

הַגָּדוֹל הַזֶּה אֲשֶׁר יְהוָה עֹשֶׂה לְעֵינֵיכֶם׃ הֲלוֹא קְצִיר־
harvest-of not? (17) before-eyes-of-you doing Yahweh that the-this the-great

חִטִּים הַיּוֹם אֶקְרָא אֶל־יְהוָה וְיִתֵּן קֹלוֹת וּמָטָר
and-rain thunders so-he-sends Yahweh upon I-will-call the-day wheats

וּדְעוּ וּרְאוּ כִּי־רָעַתְכֶם רַבָּה אֲשֶׁר עֲשִׂיתֶם בְּעֵינֵי יְהוָה
Yahweh in-eyes-of you-did that great evil-of-you that and-see! and-realize!

לִשְׁאוֹל לָכֶם מֶלֶךְ׃ וַיִּקְרָא שְׁמוּאֵל אֶל־יְהוָה וַיִּתֵּן יְהוָה
Yahweh and-he-sent Yahweh upon Samuel then-he-called (18) king for-you to-ask

°10 ק ויאמרו

and into the hands of the Philistines and the king of Moab,
who fought against them.
10They cried out to the LORD
and said, 'We have sinned; we
have forsaken the LORD and
served the Baals and the Ashtoreths. But now deliver us
from the hands of our enemies, and we will serve you.'
11Then the LORD sent Jerub-
Baal,[i] Barak,[j] Jephthah and
Samuel,[k] and he delivered you
from the hands of your enemies on every side, so that you
lived securely.
12"But when you saw that
Nahash king of the Ammon-
ites was moving against you,
you said to me, 'No, we want
a king to rule over us'—even
though the LORD your God was
your king. 13Now here is the
king you have chosen, the one
you asked for; see, the LORD
has set a king over you. 14If
you fear the LORD and serve
and obey him and do not rebel
against his commands, and if
both you and the king who
reigns over you follow the
LORD your God—good! 15But if
you do not obey the LORD, and
if you rebel against his commands, his hand will be
against you, as it was against
your fathers.
16"Now then, stand still and
see this great thing the LORD is
about to do before your eyes!
17Is it not wheat harvest now?
I will call upon the LORD to
send thunder and rain. And
you will realize what an evil
thing you did in the eyes of
the LORD when you asked for a
king."
18Then Samuel called upon
the LORD, and that same day
the LORD sent thunder and

[i]11 Also called *Gideon*
[j]11 Some Septuagint manuscripts and Syriac; Hebrew *Bedan*
[k]11 Hebrew; some Septuagint manuscripts and Syriac *Samson*

קֹלֹת וּמָטָר בַּיּוֹם הַהוּא וַיִּירָא כָל־ הָעָם
the-people all-of so-he-stood-in-awe the-that on-the-day and-rain thunders

מְאֹד אֶת־ יְהוָה וְאֶת־ שְׁמוּאֵל׃ וַיֹּאמְרוּ כָל־ הָעָם אֶל־שְׁמוּאֵל
Samuel to the-people all-of and-they-said (19) Samuel and Yahweh *** greatly

הִתְפַּלֵּל בְּעַד־ עֲבָדֶיךָ אֶל־ יְהוָה אֱלֹהֶיךָ וְאַל־ נָמוּת כִּי־
for we-will-die so-not God-of-you Yahweh to servants-of-you for pray!

יָסַפְנוּ עַל־ כָּל־ חַטֹּאתֵינוּ רָעָה לִשְׁאֹל לָנוּ מֶלֶךְ׃ וַיֹּאמֶר
and-he-replied (20) king for-us to-ask evil sins-of-us all-of to we-added

שְׁמוּאֵל אֶל־ הָעָם אַל־ תִּירָאוּ אַתֶּם עֲשִׂיתֶם אֵת כָּל־ הָרָעָה
the-evil all-of *** you-did you you-be-afraid not the-people to Samuel

הַזֹּאת אַךְ אַל־ תָּסוּרוּ מֵאַחֲרֵי יְהוָה וַעֲבַדְתֶּם אֶת־ יְהוָה
Yahweh *** but-you-serve Yahweh from-after you-turn not yet the-this

בְּכָל־ לְבַבְכֶם׃ וְלֹא תָּסוּרוּ כִּי ׀ אַחֲרֵי הַתֹּהוּ
the-useless-idol after indeed you-turn and-not (21) heart-of-you with-all-of

אֲשֶׁר לֹא־ יוֹעִילוּ וְלֹא יַצִּילוּ כִּי־ תֹהוּ הֵמָּה׃ כִּי לֹא־
not for (22) they useless for they-rescue and-not they-do-good not that

יִטֹּשׁ יְהוָה אֶת־ עַמּוֹ בַּעֲבוּר שְׁמוֹ הַגָּדוֹל
the-great name-of-him for-sake-of people-of-him *** Yahweh he-will-reject

כִּי הוֹאִיל יְהוָה לַעֲשׂוֹת אֶתְכֶם לוֹ לְעָם׃ גַּם אָנֹכִי חָלִילָה
far-be-it! I now (23) as-people for-him you to-make Yahweh he-was-pleased for

לִּי מֵחֲטֹא לַיהוָה מֵחֲדֹל לְהִתְפַּלֵּל בַּעַדְכֶם וְהוֹרֵיתִי
and-I-will-teach for-you to-pray by-to-fail against-Yahweh from-to-sin from-me

אֶתְכֶם בְּדֶרֶךְ הַטּוֹבָה וְהַיְשָׁרָה׃ אַךְ ׀ יְראוּ אֶת־ יְהוָה וַעֲבַדְתֶּם
and-you-serve Yahweh *** fear! but (24) and-the-right the-good on-way-of you

אֹתוֹ בֶּאֱמֶת בְּכָל־ לְבַבְכֶם כִּי רְאוּ אֵת אֲשֶׁר־ הִגְדִּל
he-did-great-thing how *** consider! indeed heart-of-you with-all-of in-faith him

עִמָּכֶם׃ וְאִם־ הָרֵעַ תָּרֵעוּ גַּם־ אַתֶּם גַּם־ מַלְכְּכֶם
king-of-you and you both you-do-evil to-do-evil yet-if (25) for-you

תִּסָּפוּ׃ בֶּן־ שָׁנָה שָׁאוּל בְּמָלְכוֹ וּשְׁתֵּי
and-two-of when-to-become-king-him Saul year son-of (13:1) you-will-be-swept-away

שָׁנִים מָלַךְ עַל־ יִשְׂרָאֵל׃ וַיִּבְחַר־ לוֹ שָׁאוּל שְׁלֹשֶׁת
three-of Saul for-him and-he-chose (2) Israel over he-reigned years

אֲלָפִים מִיִּשְׂרָאֵל וַיִּהְיוּ עִם־ שָׁאוּל אַלְפַּיִם בְּמִכְמָשׂ
at-Micmash two-thousands Saul with and-they-were from-Israel thousands

וּבְהַר בֵּית־ אֵל וְאֶלֶף הָיוּ עִם־ יוֹנָתָן
Jonathan with they-were and-thousand El Beth and-in-hill-country-of

בְּגִבְעַת בִּנְיָמִין וְיֶתֶר הָעָם שִׁלַּח אִישׁ לְאֹהָלָיו׃
to-homes-of-him each he-sent-back the-people and-rest-of Benjamin at-Gibeah-of

rain. So all the people stood in awe of the LORD and of Samuel.

[19]The people all said to Samuel, "Pray to the LORD your God for your servants so that we will not die, for we have added to all our other sins the evil of asking for a king."

[20]"Do not be afraid," Samuel replied. "You have done all this evil; yet do not turn away from the LORD, but serve the LORD with all your heart. [21]Do not turn away after useless idols. They can do you no good, nor can they rescue you, because they are useless. [22]For the sake of his great name the LORD will not reject his people, because the LORD was pleased to make you his own. [23]As for me, far be it from me that I should sin against the LORD by failing to pray for you. And I will teach you the way that is good and right. [24]But be sure to fear the LORD and serve him faithfully with all your heart; consider what great things he has done for you. [25]Yet if you persist in doing evil, both you and your king will be swept away."

Samuel Rebukes Saul

13 Saul was ⌊thirty⌋[l] years old when he became king, and he reigned over Israel ⌊forty-⌋[m] two years.

[2]Saul[n] chose three thousand men from Israel; two thousand were with him at Micmash and in the hill country of Bethel, and a thousand were with Jonathan at Gibeah of Benjamin. The rest of the men he sent back to their homes.

[l]1 A few late manuscripts of the Septuagint; Hebrew does not have *thirty*.
[m]1 See the round number in Acts 13:21; Hebrew does not have *forty-*.
[n]1,2 Or *and when he had reigned over Israel two years,* [2]*he*

וַיַּךְ יוֹנָתָן אֵת נְצִיב פְּלִשְׁתִּים אֲשֶׁר בְּגֶבַע
at-Geba that Philistines outpost-of *** Jonathan and-he-attacked (3)

וַיִּשְׁמְעוּ פְּלִשְׁתִּים וְשָׁאוּל תָּקַע בַּשּׁוֹפָר בְּכָל־
through-all-of on-the-trumpet he-blew then-Saul Philistines and-they-heard

הָאָרֶץ לֵאמֹר יִשְׁמְעוּ הָעִבְרִים׃ וְכָל־ יִשְׂרָאֵל שָׁמְעוּ
they-heard Israel so-all-of (4) the-Hebrews let-them-hear to-say the-land

לֵאמֹר הִכָּה שָׁאוּל אֶת־ נְצִיב פְּלִשְׁתִּים וְגַם־ נִבְאַשׁ*
he-became-stench and-now Philistines outpost-of *** Saul he-attacked to-say

יִשְׂרָאֵל בַּפְּלִשְׁתִּים וַיִּצָּעֲקוּ הָעָם אַחֲרֵי שָׁאוּל
Saul after the-people and-they-were-summoned to-the-Philistines Israel

הַגִּלְגָּל׃ וּפְלִשְׁתִּים נֶאֶסְפוּ ׀ לְהִלָּחֵם עִם־ יִשְׂרָאֵל שְׁלֹשִׁים
thirty Israel against to-fight they-assembled and-Philistines (5) the-Gilgal

אֶלֶף רֶכֶב וְשֵׁשֶׁת אֲלָפִים פָּרָשִׁים וְעָם כַּחוֹל אֲשֶׁר
that as-the-sand and-soldier charioteers thousands and-six-of chariot thousand

עַל־ שְׂפַת־ הַיָּם לָרֹב וַיַּעֲלוּ וַיַּחֲנוּ בְמִכְמָשׂ
at-Micmash and-they-camped and-they-went-up in-number the-sea shore-of on

קִדְמַת בֵּית אָוֶן׃ וְאִישׁ יִשְׂרָאֵל רָאוּ כִּי צַר־
he-was-critical that they-saw Israel when-man-of (6) Aven Beth east-of

לוֹ כִּי נִגַּשׂ הָעָם וַיִּתְחַבְּאוּ הָעָם בַּמְּעָרוֹת
in-the-caves the-army then-they-hid the-army he-was-hard-pressed for to-him

וּבַחֲוָחִים וּבַסְּלָעִים וּבַצְּרִחִים וּבַבֹּרוֹת׃
and-in-the-cisterns and-in-the-pits and-among-the-rocks and-in-the-thickets

וְעִבְרִים עָבְרוּ אֶת־ הַיַּרְדֵּן אֶרֶץ גָּד וְגִלְעָד וְשָׁאוּל
and-Saul and-Gilead Gad land-of the-Jordan *** they-crossed and-Hebrews (7)

עוֹדֶנּוּ בַגִּלְגָּל וְכָל־ הָעָם חָרְדוּ אַחֲרָיו׃
with-him they-quaked-with-fear the-troop and-all-of at-the-Gilgal still-he

וַיִּיחֶל° ׀ שִׁבְעַת יָמִים לַמּוֹעֵד אֲשֶׁר שְׁמוּאֵל וְלֹא־ בָא
he-came but-not Samuel that as-the-set-time days seven-of and-he-waited (8)

שְׁמוּאֵל הַגִּלְגָּל וַיָּפֶץ הָעָם מֵעָלָיו׃ וַיֹּאמֶר
so-he-said (9) from-with-him the-people and-he-scattered the-Gilgal Samuel

שָׁאוּל הַגִּשׁוּ אֵלַי הָעֹלָה וְהַשְּׁלָמִים וַיַּעַל
and-he-offered and-the-fellowship-offerings the-burnt-offering to-me bring! Saul

הָעֹלָה׃ וַיְהִי כְּכַלֹּתוֹ לְהַעֲלוֹת הָעֹלָה
the-burnt-offering to-offer as-to-finish-him and-he-was (10) the-burnt-offering

וְהִנֵּה שְׁמוּאֵל בָּא וַיֵּצֵא שָׁאוּל לִקְרָאתוֹ לְבָרְכוֹ׃
to-greet-him to-meet-him Saul and-he-went-out arriving Samuel then-see!

וַיֹּאמֶר שְׁמוּאֵל מֶה עָשִׂיתָ וַיֹּאמֶר שָׁאוּל כִּי־ רָאִיתִי כִּי־
that I-saw when Saul and-he-replied you-did what? Samuel and-he-asked (11)

3Jonathan attacked the Philistine outpost at Geba, and the
Philistines heard about it.
Then Saul had the trumpet
blown throughout the land
and said, "Let the Hebrews
hear!" 4So all Israel heard the
news: "Saul has attacked the
Philistine outpost, and now
Israel has become a stench to
the Philistines." And the
people were summoned to
join Saul at Gilgal.
5The Philistines assembled
to fight Israel, with three thousand[o] chariots, six thousand
charioteers, and soldiers as
numerous as the sand on the
seashore. They went up and
camped at Micmash, east of
Beth Aven. 6When the men of
Israel saw that their situation
was critical and that their
army was hard pressed, they
hid in caves and thickets,
among the rocks, and in pits
and cisterns. 7Some Hebrews
even crossed the Jordan to the
land of Gad and Gilead.
Saul remained at Gilgal, and
all the troops with him were
quaking with fear. 8He waited
seven days, the time set by
Samuel; but Samuel did not
come to Gilgal, and Saul's men
began to scatter. 9So he said,
"Bring me the burnt offering
and the fellowship
offerings.[p]" And Saul offered
up the burnt offering. 10Just as
he finished making the
offering, Samuel arrived, and
Saul went out to greet him.
11"What have you done?"
asked Samuel.
Saul replied, "When I saw

[o]5 Some Septuagint manuscripts and Syriac; Hebrew *thirty thousand*
[p]9 Traditionally *peace offerings*

*4 Most mss have the accent *mereka* under the *aleph* (אַשׁ֥–).

°8 ק ויוחל

נָפַץ הָעָם מֵעָלַי וְאַתָּה לֹא־בָאתָ לְמוֹעֵד
at-set-time-of you-came not and-you from-with-me the-people he-scattered

הַיָּמִים וּפְלִשְׁתִּים נֶאֱסָפִים מִכְמָשׂ׃ וָאֹמַר עַתָּה
now and-I-thought (12) Micmash ones-assembling and-Philistines the-days

יֵרְדוּ פְלִשְׁתִּים אֵלַי הַגִּלְגָּל וּפְנֵי יְהוָה
Yahweh and-faces-of the-Gilgal against-me Philistines they-will-come-down

לֹא חִלִּיתִי וָאֶתְאַפַּק וָאַעֲלֶה הָעֹלָה׃
the-burnt-offering and-I-offered so-I-felt-compelled I-sought not

וַיֹּאמֶר שְׁמוּאֵל אֶל־שָׁאוּל נִסְכָּלְתָּ לֹא שָׁמַרְתָּ אֶת־מִצְוַת
command-of *** you-kept not you-were-foolish Saul to Samuel and-he-said (13)

יְהוָה אֱלֹהֶיךָ אֲשֶׁר צִוָּךְ כִּי עַתָּה הֵכִין יְהוָה אֶת־
*** Yahweh he-would-establish now or he-gave-you that God-of-you Yahweh

מַמְלַכְתְּךָ אֶל־יִשְׂרָאֵל עַד־עוֹלָם׃ וְעַתָּה מַמְלַכְתְּךָ לֹא־
not kingdom-of-you but-now (14) all-time for Israel over kingdom-of-you

תָקוּם בִּקֵּשׁ יְהוָה לוֹ אִישׁ כִּלְבָבוֹ
after-heart-of-him man for-him Yahweh he-sought she-will-endure

וַיְצַוֵּהוּ יְהוָה לְנָגִיד עַל־עַמּוֹ כִּי לֹא שָׁמַרְתָּ
you-kept not for people-of-him over as-leader Yahweh and-he-appointed-him

אֵת אֲשֶׁר־צִוְּךָ יְהוָה׃ וַיָּקָם שְׁמוּאֵל וַיַּעַל
and-he-went-up Samuel then-he-left (15) Yahweh he-commanded-you what ***

מִן־הַגִּלְגָּל גִּבְעַת בִּנְיָמִן וַיִּפְקֹד שָׁאוּל אֶת־הָעָם
the-people *** Saul and-he-counted Benjamin Gibeah-of the-Gilgal from

הַנִּמְצְאִים עִמּוֹ כְּשֵׁשׁ מֵאוֹת אִישׁ׃ וְשָׁאוּל
now-Saul (16) man hundreds about-six with-him the-ones-being-found

וְיוֹנָתָן בְּנוֹ וְהָעָם הַנִּמְצָא עִמָּם
with-them the-ones-being-found and-the-people son-of-him and-Jonathan

יֹשְׁבִים בְּגֶבַע בִּנְיָמִן וּפְלִשְׁתִּים חָנוּ בְמִכְמָשׂ׃
at-Micmash they-camped and-Philistines Benjamin in-Geba-of ones-staying

וַיֵּצֵא הַמַּשְׁחִית מִמַּחֲנֵה פְלִשְׁתִּים שְׁלֹשָׁה
three Philistines from-camp-of the-one-raiding and-he-went-out (17)

רָאשִׁים הָרֹאשׁ אֶחָד יִפְנֶה אֶל־דֶּרֶךְ עָפְרָה אֶל־אֶרֶץ
vicinity-of in Ophrah way-of toward he-turned one the-detachment detachments

שׁוּעָל׃ וְהָרֹאשׁ אֶחָד יִפְנֶה דֶּרֶךְ בֵּית חֹרוֹן
Horon Beth way-of he-turned another and-the-detachment (18) Shual

וְהָרֹאשׁ אֶחָד יִפְנֶה דֶּרֶךְ הַגְּבוּל הַנִּשְׁקָף
the-overlooking the-borderland way-of he-turned another and-the-detachment

עַל־גֵּי הַצְּבֹעִים הַמִּדְבָּרָה׃ וְחָרָשׁ לֹא יִמָּצֵא
he-was-found not and-blacksmith (19) to-the-desert the-Zeboim Valley-of over

that the men were scattering,
and that you did not come at
the set time, and that the Philistines were assembling at
Micmash, [12]I thought, 'Now
the Philistines will come
down against me at Gilgal,
and I have not sought the
LORD's favor.' So I felt com-
pelled to offer the burnt
offering."

[13]"You acted foolishly,"
Samuel said. "You have not
kept the command the LORD
your God gave you; if you had,
he would have established
your kingdom over Israel for
all time. [14]But now your kingdom will not endure; the LORD
has sought out a man after his
own heart and appointed him
leader of his people, because
you have not kept the LORD's
command."

[15]Then Samuel left Gilgal[s]
and went up to Gibeah of Benjamin, and Saul counted the
men who were with him.
They numbered about six
hundred.

Israel Without Weapons

[16]Saul and his son Jonathan
and the men with them were
staying in Geba of Benjamin,
while the Philistines camped
at Micmash. [17]Raiding parties
went out from the Philistine
camp in three detachments.
One turned toward Ophrah in
the vicinity of Shual, [18]another
toward Beth Horon, and the
third toward the borderland
overlooking the Valley of Ze-
boim facing the desert.

[19]Not a blacksmith could be

[s]15 Hebrew; Septuagint *Gilgal and went his way; the rest of the people went after Saul to meet the army, and they went out of Gilgal*

בְּכֹל אֶרֶץ יִשְׂרָאֵל כִּי־ אָמְרֻ° פְלִשְׁתִּים פֶּן יַעֲשׂוּ
they-will-make otherwise Philistines they-said for Israel land-of in-whole-of

הָעִבְרִים חֶרֶב אוֹ חֲנִית׃ (20) וַיֵּרְדוּ כָל־ יִשְׂרָאֵל
Israel all-of so-they-went-down (20) spear or sword the-Hebrews

הַפְּלִשְׁתִּים לִלְטוֹשׁ אִישׁ אֶת־ מַחֲרַשְׁתּוֹ וְאֶת־ אֵתוֹ וְאֶת־
and mattock-of-him and plowshare-of-him *** each to-sharpen the-Philistines

קַרְדֻּמּוֹ וְאֵת מַחֲרֵשָׁתוֹ׃ (21) וְהָיְתָה הַפְּצִירָה פִים*
*pim the-sharpening and-she-was (21) plowshare-of-him and ax-of-him

לַמַּחֲרֵשֹׁת וְלָאֵתִים וְלִשְׁלֹשׁ קִלְּשׁוֹן וּלְהַקַּרְדֻּמִּים
and-for-the-axes fork and-for-third and-for-the-mattocks for-the-plowshares

וּלְהַצִּיב הַדָּרְבָן׃ (22) וְהָיָה בְּיוֹם מִלְחֶמֶת וְלֹא נִמְצָא
he-was-found that-not battle on-day-of so-he-was (22) the-goad and-to-repoint

חֶרֶב וַחֲנִית בְּיַד כָּל־ הָעָם אֲשֶׁר אֶת־ שָׁאוּל וְאֶת־ יוֹנָתָן
Jonathan and-with Saul with who the-soldier any-of in-hand-of or-spear sword

וַתִּמָּצֵא לְשָׁאוּל וּלְיוֹנָתָן בְּנוֹ׃ (23) וַיֵּצֵא
now-he-went-out (23) son-of-him and-with-Jonathan with-Saul but-she-was-found

מַצַּב פְּלִשְׁתִּים אֶל־ מַעֲבַר מִכְמָשׂ׃ (14:1) וַיְהִי הַיּוֹם
the-day and-he-was (14:1) Micmash pass-of to Philistines detachment-of

וַיֹּאמֶר יוֹנָתָן בֶּן־ שָׁאוּל אֶל־ הַנַּעַר נֹשֵׂא כֵלָיו
armors-of-him bearing the-young-man to Saul son-of Jonathan that-he-said

לְכָה וְנַעְבְּרָה אֶל־ מַצַּב פְּלִשְׁתִּים אֲשֶׁר מֵעֵבֶר
on-other-side that Philistines outpost-of to and-let-us-go-over come!

הַלָּז וּלְאָבִיו לֹא הִגִּיד׃ (2) וְשָׁאוּל יוֹשֵׁב בִּקְצֵה
at-outskirt-of staying now-Saul (2) he-told not but-to-father-of-him the-this

הַגִּבְעָה תַּחַת הָרִמּוֹן אֲשֶׁר בְּמִגְרוֹן וְהָעָם אֲשֶׁר
who and-the-people in-Migron that the-pomegranate-tree under the-Gibeah

עִמּוֹ כְּשֵׁשׁ מֵאוֹת אִישׁ׃ (3) וַאֲחִיָּה בֶן־ אֲחִטוּב אֲחִי
brother-of Ahitub son-of and-Ahijah (3) man hundreds about-six-of with-him

אִיכָבוֹד ׀ בֶּן־ פִּינְחָס בֶּן־ עֵלִי כֹּהֵן ׀ יְהוָה בְּשִׁלוֹ נֹשֵׂא אֵפוֹד
ephod wearing in-Shiloh Yahweh priest-of Eli son-of Phinehas son-of Ichabod

וְהָעָם לֹא יָדַע כִּי הָלַךְ יוֹנָתָן׃ (4) וּבֵין
now-between (4) Jonathan he-left that he-was-aware not now-the-people

הַמַּעְבְּרוֹת אֲשֶׁר בִּקֵּשׁ יוֹנָתָן לַעֲבֹר עַל־ מַצַּב פְּלִשְׁתִּים
Philistines outpost-of to to-cross Jonathan he-intended that the-passes

שֵׁן־ הַסֶּלַע מֵהָעֵבֶר מִזֶּה וְשֵׁן־ הַסֶּלַע מֵהָעֵבֶר
on-the-pass the-rock and-cliff-of on-one-side on-the-pass the-rock cliff-of

מִזֶּה וְשֵׁם הָאֶחָד בּוֹצֵץ וְשֵׁם הָאֶחָד סֶנֶּה׃
Seneh the-other and-name-of Bozez the-one and-name-of on-other-side

found in the whole land of Israel, because the Philistines had said, "Otherwise the Hebrews will make swords or spears!"
20 So all Israel went down to the Philistines to have their plowshares, mattocks, axes and sickles[t] sharpened.
21 The price was two thirds of a shekel[u] for sharpening plowshares and mattocks, and a third of a shekel[v] for sharpening forks and axes and for repointing goads.
22 So on the day of the battle not a soldier with Saul and Jonathan had a sword or spear in his hand; only Saul and his son Jonathan had them.

Jonathan Attacks the Philistines

14 23 Now a detachment of Philistines had gone out to the pass at Micmash.
1 One day Jonathan son of Saul said to the young man bearing his armor, "Come, let's go over to the Philistine outpost on the other side." But he did not tell his father.
2 Saul was staying on the outskirts of Gibeah under a pomegranate tree in Migron. With him were about six hundred men,
3 among whom was Ahijah, who was wearing an ephod. He was a son of Ichabod's brother Ahitub son of Phinehas, the son of Eli, the LORD's priest in Shiloh. No one was aware that Jonathan had left.
4 On each side of the pass that Jonathan intended to cross to reach the Philistine outpost was a cliff; one was called Bozez, and the other

[t]20 Septuagint; Hebrew *plowshares*
[u]21 Hebrew *pim,* that is, about 1/4 ounce (about 8 grams)
[v]21 That is, about 1/8 ounce (about 4 grams)

***21 This word occurs only here in the Hebrew Scriptures. Its weight is given in footnote *u*.**

°19 ק אמרו

(5) הַשֵּׁן הָאֶחָד מָצוּק מִצָּפוֹן מוּל מִכְמָשׂ וְהָאֶחָד מִנֶּגֶב
to-south and-the-other Micmash toward to-north pillar the-one the-cliff (5)

מוּל גָּבַע׃ (6) וַיֹּאמֶר יְהוֹנָתָן אֶל־הַנַּעַר ׀ נֹשֵׂא כֵלָיו
armors-of-him bearing the-young-man to Jonathan and-he-said (6) Geba toward

לְכָה וְנַעְבְּרָה אֶל־מַצַּב הָעֲרֵלִים הָאֵלֶּה
the-those the-uncircumcised-ones outpost-of to and-let-us-go-over come!

אוּלַי יַעֲשֶׂה יְהוָה לָנוּ כִּי אֵין לַיהוָה מַעְצוֹר לְהוֹשִׁיעַ
to-save hindrance to-Yahweh nothing for for-us Yahweh he-will-act perhaps

בְּרַב אוֹ בִמְעָט׃ (7) וַיֹּאמֶר לוֹ נֹשֵׂא כֵלָיו עֲשֵׂה כָּל־
all do! armors-of-him one-bearing to-him and-he-said (7) by-few or by-many

אֲשֶׁר בִּלְבָבֶךָ נְטֵה לָךְ הִנְנִי עִמְּךָ כִּלְבָבֶךָ׃
after-heart-of-you with-you see-I! for-you go-ahead! in-mind-of-you that

(8) וַיֹּאמֶר יְהוֹנָתָן הִנֵּה אֲנַחְנוּ עֹבְרִים אֶל־הָאֲנָשִׁים וְנִגְלִינוּ
and-we-will-show the-men toward ones-crossing we see! Jonathan and-he-said (8)

אֲלֵיהֶם׃ (9) אִם־כֹּה יֹאמְרוּ אֵלֵינוּ דֹּמּוּ עַד־הַגִּיעֵנוּ אֲלֵיכֶם וְעָמַדְנוּ
then-we-stay to-you to-come-us until wait! to-us they-say this if (9) to-them

תַחְתֵּינוּ וְלֹא נַעֲלֶה אֲלֵיהֶם׃ (10) וְאִם־כֹּה יֹאמְרוּ עֲלוּ
come-up! they-say this but-if (10) to-them we-will-go-up and-not place-of-us

עָלֵינוּ וְעָלִינוּ כִּי־נְתָנָם יְהוָה בְּיָדֵנוּ וְזֶה־
and-this into-hand-of-us Yahweh he-gave-them for then-we-will-climb-up to-us

לָּנוּ הָאוֹת׃ (11) וַיִּגָּלוּ שְׁנֵיהֶם אֶל־מַצַּב
outpost-of to both-of-them so-they-showed-themselves (11) the-sign to-us

פְּלִשְׁתִּים וַיֹּאמְרוּ פְלִשְׁתִּים הִנֵּה עִבְרִים יֹצְאִים מִן־
from ones-crawling-out Hebrews look! Philistines and-they-said Philistines

הַחֹרִים אֲשֶׁר הִתְחַבְּאוּ־שָׁם׃ (12) וַיַּעֲנוּ אַנְשֵׁי הַמַּצָּבָה אֶת־
*** the-outpost men-of and-they-shouted (12) there they-hid that the-holes

יוֹנָתָן ׀ וְאֶת־נֹשֵׂא כֵלָיו וַיֹּאמְרוּ עֲלוּ אֵלֵינוּ
to-us come-up! and-they-said armors-of-him one-bearing and Jonathan

וְנוֹדִיעָה אֶתְכֶם דָּבָר וַיֹּאמֶר יוֹנָתָן אֶל־נֹשֵׂא כֵלָיו
armors-of-him one-bearing to Jonathan so-he-said lesson you and-we-will-teach

עֲלֵה אַחֲרַי כִּי־נְתָנָם יְהוָה בְּיַד יִשְׂרָאֵל׃
Israel into-hand-of Yahweh he-gave-them for after-me climb-up!

(13) וַיַּעַל יוֹנָתָן עַל־יָדָיו וְעַל־רַגְלָיו
feet-of-him and-on hands-of-him on Jonathan and-he-climbed-up (13)

וְנֹשֵׂא כֵלָיו אַחֲרָיו וַיִּפְּלוּ לִפְנֵי יוֹנָתָן
Jonathan before and-they-fell after-him armors-of-him and-one-bearing

וְנֹשֵׂא כֵלָיו מְמוֹתֵת אַחֲרָיו׃ (14) וַתְּהִי הַמַּכָּה
the-attack and-she-was (14) behind-him killing armors-of-him and-one-bearing

Seneh. 5One cliff stood to the
north toward Micmash, the
other to the south toward
Geba.
6Jonathan said to his young
armor-bearer, "Come, let's go
over to the outpost of those
uncircumcised fellows. Perhaps the LORD will act in our
behalf. Nothing can hinder
the LORD from saving,
whether by many or by few."
7"Do all that you have in
mind," his armor-bearer said.
"Go ahead; I am with you
heart and soul."
8Jonathan said, "Come,
then; we will cross over
toward the men and let them
see us. 9If they say to us, 'Wait
there until we come to you,'
we will stay where we are and
not go up to them. 10But if they
say, 'Come up to us,' we will
climb up, because that will be
our sign that the LORD has giv-
en them into our hands."
11So both of them showed
themselves to the Philistine
outpost. "Look!" said the Philistines. "The Hebrews are
crawling out of the holes they
were hiding in." 12The men of
the outpost shouted to Jonathan and his armor-bearer,
"Come up to us and we'll
teach you a lesson."
So Jonathan said to his armor-bearer, "Climb up after
me; the LORD has given them
into the hand of Israel."
13Jonathan climbed up, using his hands and feet, with
his armor-bearer right behind
him. The Philistines fell before
Jonathan, and his armor-bearer followed and killed behind

הָרִאשֹׁנָה אֲשֶׁר הִכָּה יוֹנָתָן וְנֹשֵׂא כֵלָיו כְּעֶשְׂרִים
about-twenty armors-of-him and-one-bearing Jonathan he-killed that the-first

אִישׁ כְּבַחֲצִי מַעֲנָה צֶמֶד שָׂדֶה׃ וַתְּהִי חֲרָדָה
panic then-she-struck (15) field yoke work-area in-about-half-of man

בַמַּחֲנֶה בַשָּׂדֶה וּבְכָל־ הָעָם הַמַּצָּב וְהַמַּשְׁחִית
and-the-raiding the-outpost the-army and-in-whole-of in-the-field in-the-camp

חָרְדוּ גַּם־ הֵמָּה וַתִּרְגַּז הָאָרֶץ וַתְּהִי לְחֶרְדַּת אֱלֹהִים׃
God as-panic-of and-she-was the-ground and-she-shook they also they-panicked

וַיִּרְאוּ הַצֹּפִים לְשָׁאוּל בְּגִבְעַת בִּנְיָמִן וְהִנֵּה
and-see! Benjamin at-Gibeah-of of-Saul the-ones-looking-out and-they-saw (16)

הֶהָמוֹן נָמוֹג וַיֵּלֶךְ וַהֲלֹם׃ וַיֹּאמֶר שָׁאוּל
Saul then-he-said (17) indeed-everywhere and-he-went melting-away the-army

לָעָם אֲשֶׁר אִתּוֹ פִּקְדוּ־ נָא וּרְאוּ מִי הָלַךְ
he-left who and-see! now! muster-forces! with-him who to-the-people

מֵעִמָּנוּ וַיִּפְקְדוּ וְהִנֵּה אֵין יוֹנָתָן
Jonathan there-was-not then-see! when-they-mustered from-with-us

וְנֹשֵׂא כֵלָיו׃ וַיֹּאמֶר שָׁאוּל לַאֲחִיָּה הַגִּישָׁה אֲרוֹן
ark-of bring! to-Ahijah Saul and-he-said (18) armors-of-him and-one-bearing

הָאֱלֹהִים כִּי־ הָיָה אֲרוֹן הָאֱלֹהִים בַּיּוֹם הַהוּא וּבְנֵי יִשְׂרָאֵל׃
Israel with-sons-of the-that on-the-day the-God ark-of he-was for the-God

וַיְהִי עַד דִּבֶּר שָׁאוּל אֶל־ הַכֹּהֵן וְהֶהָמוֹן אֲשֶׁר
that that-the-tumult the-priest to Saul he-talked while and-he-was (19)

בְּמַחֲנֵה פְלִשְׁתִּים וַיֵּלֶךְ הָלוֹךְ וָרָב וַיֹּאמֶר שָׁאוּל אֶל־
to Saul so-he-said even-more to-go and-he-increased Philistines in-camp-of

הַכֹּהֵן אֱסֹף יָדֶךָ׃ וַיִּזָּעֵק שָׁאוּל וְכָל־
and-all-of Saul then-he-assembled (20) hand-of-you withdraw! the-priest

הָעָם אֲשֶׁר אִתּוֹ וַיָּבֹאוּ עַד־הַמִּלְחָמָה וְהִנֵּה הָיְתָה חֶרֶב
sword-of she-was and-see! the-battle to and-they-went with-him who the-people

אִישׁ בְּרֵעֵהוּ מְהוּמָה גְּדוֹלָה מְאֹד׃ וְהָעִבְרִים הָיוּ
they-were and-the-Hebrews (21) very great confusion against-fellow-of-him man

לַפְּלִשְׁתִּים כְּאֶתְמוֹל שִׁלְשׁוֹם אֲשֶׁר עָלוּ עִמָּם
with-them they-went-up who before as-yesterday with-the-Philistines

בַּמַּחֲנֶה סָבִיב וְגַם־ הֵמָּה לִהְיוֹת עִם־יִשְׂרָאֵל אֲשֶׁר עִם־שָׁאוּל וְיוֹנָתָן׃
and-Jonathan Saul with who Israel with to-be they and-also around to-the-camp

וְכֹל אִישׁ יִשְׂרָאֵל הַמִּתְחַבְּאִים בְּהַר־ אֶפְרַיִם
Ephraim in-hill-country-of the-ones-hiding Israel man-of when-all-of (22)

שָׁמְעוּ כִּי־ נָסוּ פְּלִשְׁתִּים וַיַּדְבְּקוּ גַּם־ הֵמָּה אַחֲרֵיהֶם
after-them they also then-they-joined Philistines they-ran that they-heard

him. 14In that first attack Jonathan and his armor-bearer
killed some twenty men in an
area of about half an acre.[w]

Israel Routs the Philistines

15Then panic struck the
whole army—those in the
camp and field, and those in
the outposts and raiding parties—and the ground shook. It
was a panic sent by God.[x]
16Saul's lookouts at Gibeah
of Benjamin saw the army
melting away in all directions.
17Then Saul said to the men
who were with him, "Muster
the forces and see who has left
us." When they did, it was
Jonathan and his armor-bearer who were not there.
18Saul said to Ahijah, "Bring
the ark of God." (At that time
it was with the Israelites.)[y]
19While Saul was talking to the
priest, the tumult in the Philistine camp increased more and
more. So Saul said to the
priest, "Withdraw your
hand."
20Then Saul and all his men
assembled and went to the
battle. They found the Philistines in total confusion, striking each other with their
swords. 21Those Hebrews who
had previously been with the
Philistines and had gone up
with them to their camp went
over to the Israelites who were
with Saul and Jonathan.
22When all the Israelites who
had hidden in the hill country
of Ephraim heard that the
Philistines were on the run,
they joined the battle in hot

[w]14 Hebrew *half a yoke*; a "yoke" was the land plowed by a yoke of oxen in one day.
[x]15 Or *a terrible panic*
[y]18 Hebrew; some Septuagint manuscripts *"Bring the ephod." (At that time he wore the ephod before the Israelites.)*

בַּמִּלְחָמָה׃ וַיּוֹשַׁע יְהוָה בַּיּוֹם הַהוּא אֶת־יִשְׂרָאֵל
Israel *** the-that on-the-day Yahweh so-he-rescued (23) in-the-battle

וְהַמִּלְחָמָה עָבְרָה אֶת־בֵּית אָוֶן׃ וְאִישׁ־יִשְׂרָאֵל
Israel now-man-of (24) Aven Beth *** she-moved-on and-the-battle

נִגַּשׂ בַּיּוֹם הַהוּא וַיֹּאֶל שָׁאוּל אֶת־הָעָם
the-people *** Saul for-he-bound-oath the-that on-the-day he-was-distressed

לֵאמֹר אָרוּר הָאִישׁ אֲשֶׁר־יֹאכַל לֶחֶם עַד־הָעֶרֶב וְנִקַּמְתִּי
and-I-am-avenged the-evening before food he-eats who the-man being-cursed to-say

מֵאֹיְבַי *וְלֹא טָעַם* כָּל־הָעָם לָחֶם׃ וְכָל־
and-all-of (25) food the-troop any-of he-tasted so-not on-being-enemies-of-me

הָאָרֶץ בָּאוּ בַיָּעַר וַיְהִי דְבַשׁ עַל־פְּנֵי הַשָּׂדֶה׃
the-ground surface-of on honey and-he-was into-the-wood they-entered the-land

וַיָּבֹא הָעָם אֶל־הַיַּעַר וְהִנֵּה הֵלֶךְ דְּבָשׁ וְאֵין־
yet-not honey oozing-of then-see! the-wood into the-army when-he-went (26)

מַשִּׂיג יָדוֹ אֶל־פִּיו כִּי־יָרֵא הָעָם אֶת־הַשְּׁבֻעָה׃
the-oath *** the-people he-feared for mouth-of-him to hand-of-him one-putting

וְיוֹנָתָן לֹא־שָׁמַע בְּהַשְׁבִּיעַ אָבִיו אֶת־הָעָם
the-people *** father-of-him that-to-bind-oath he-heard not but-Jonathan (27)

וַיִּשְׁלַח אֶת־קְצֵה הַמַּטֶּה אֲשֶׁר בְּיָדוֹ וַיִּטְבֹּל אוֹתָהּ
her and-he-dipped in-hand-of-him that the-staff end-of *** so-he-reached

בְּיַעְרַת הַדְּבָשׁ וַיָּשֶׁב יָדוֹ אֶל־פִּיו
mouth-of-him to hand-of-him then-he-raised the-honey into-honeycomb-of

°וַתָּרֹאנָה עֵינָיו׃ וַיַּעַן אִישׁ מֵהָעָם
from-the-soldier man then-he-told (28) eyes-of-him and-they-brightened

וַיֹּאמֶר הַשְׁבֵּעַ הִשְׁבִּיעַ אָבִיךָ אֶת־הָעָם לֵאמֹר
to-say the-army *** father-of-you he-bound-oath to-bind-oath and-he-said

אָרוּר הָאִישׁ אֲשֶׁר־יֹאכַל לֶחֶם הַיּוֹם וַיָּעַף הָעָם׃
the-people so-he-is-faint the-day food he-eats who the-man being-cursed

וַיֹּאמֶר יוֹנָתָן עָכַר אָבִי אֶת־הָאָרֶץ רְאוּ־
see! the-country for father-of-me he-made-trouble Jonathan and-he-said (29)

נָא כִּי־אֹרוּ עֵינַי כִּי טָעַמְתִּי מְעַט דְּבַשׁ הַזֶּה׃
the-this honey little-of I-tasted when eyes-of-me they-brightened how now!

אַף כִּי לוּא אָכֹל אָכַל הַיּוֹם הָעָם מִשְּׁלַל
from-plunder-of the-people the-day he-ate to-eat if how-much indeed (30)

אֹיְבָיו אֲשֶׁר מָצָא כִּי עַתָּה לֹא־רָבְתָה מַכָּה
slaughter she-would-be-greater not now for they-took that being-enemies-of-him

בַּפְּלִשְׁתִּים׃ וַיַּכּוּ בַּיּוֹם הַהוּא
the-that on-the-day and-they-struck-down (31) of-the-Philistines

pursuit. [23]So the LORD rescued Israel that day, and the battle moved on beyond Beth Aven.

Jonathan Eats Honey

[24]Now the men of Israel were in distress that day, because Saul had bound the people under an oath, saying, "Cursed be any man who eats food before evening comes, before I have avenged myself on my enemies!" So none of the troops tasted food.

[25]The entire army[a] entered the woods, and there was honey on the ground. [26]When they went into the woods, they saw the honey oozing out, yet no one put his hand to his mouth, because they feared the oath. [27]But Jonathan had not heard that his father had bound the people with the oath, so he reached out the end of the staff that was in his hand and dipped it into the honeycomb. He raised his hand to his mouth, and his eyes brightened.[b] [28]Then one of the soldiers told him, "Your father bound the army under a strict oath, saying, 'Cursed be any man who eats food today!' That is why the men are faint."

[29]Jonathan said, "My father has made trouble for the country. See how my eyes brightened[c] when I tasted a little of this honey. [30]How much better it would have been if the men had eaten today some of the plunder they took from their enemies. Would not the slaughter of the Philistines have been even greater?"

[a]25 Or *Now all the people of the land*
[b]27 Or *his strength was renewed*
[c]29 Or *my strength was renewed*

*24 Most mss bind these two words with *maqqeph* (ולא־טעם).

°27 ק ותארנה

בַּפְּלִשְׁתִּים מִמִּכְמָשׂ אַיָּלֹנָה וַיָּעַף הָעָם מְאֹד׃
very the-people and-he-was-exhausted to-Aijalon from-Micmash of-the-Philistines

(32) וַיַּעַשׂ הָעָם אֶל־ שָׁלָל וַיִּקְחוּ צֹאן וּבָקָר
and-cattle sheep and-they-took the-plunder on the-people and-he-pounced (32)

וּבְנֵי בָקָר וַיִּשְׁחֲטוּ־ אָרְצָה וַיֹּאכַל הָעָם עַל־
with the-people and-he-ate on-ground and-they-butchered cattle and-calves-of

הַדָּם׃ (33) וַיַּגִּדוּ לְשָׁאוּל לֵאמֹר הִנֵּה הָעָם חֹטְאִים
ones-sinning the-people look! to-say to-Saul and-he-told (33) the-blood

לַיהוָה לֶאֱכֹל עַל־ הַדָּם וַיֹּאמֶר בְּגַדְתֶּם גֹּלּוּ־
roll! you-broke-faith and-he-said the-blood with to-eat against-Yahweh

אֵלַי הַיּוֹם אֶבֶן גְּדוֹלָה׃ (34) וַיֹּאמֶר שָׁאוּל פֻּצוּ בָעָם
among-the-people go-out! Saul then-he-said (34) large stone the-day to-me

וַאֲמַרְתֶּם לָהֶם הַגִּישׁוּ אֵלַי אִישׁ שׁוֹרוֹ וְאִישׁ שֵׂיֵהוּ
sheep-of-him and-each cattle-of-him each to-me bring! to-them and-you-tell

וּשְׁחַטְתֶּם בָּזֶה וַאֲכַלְתֶּם וְלֹא־ תֶחֶטְאוּ לַיהוָה לֶאֱכֹל
to-eat against-Yahweh you-sin and-not and-you-eat at-here and-you-slaughter

אֶל־ הַדָּם וַיַּגִּשׁוּ כָל־ הָעָם אִישׁ שׁוֹרוֹ בְיָדוֹ
in-hand-of-him ox-of-him each the-people all-of so-they-brought the-blood with

הַלַּיְלָה וַיִּשְׁחֲטוּ־ שָׁם׃ (35) וַיִּבֶן שָׁאוּל מִזְבֵּחַ לַיהוָה
to-Yahweh altar Saul and-he-built (35) there and-they-slaughtered the-night

אֹתוֹ הֵחֵל לִבְנוֹת מִזְבֵּחַ לַיהוָה׃ (36) וַיֹּאמֶר שָׁאוּל נֵרְדָה
let-us-go-down Saul and-he-said (36) to-Yahweh altar to-build he-was-first him

אַחֲרֵי פְלִשְׁתִּים ׀ לַיְלָה וְנָבֹזָה בָהֶם ׀ עַד־ אוֹר הַבֹּקֶר
the-morning dawn-of till from-them and-let-us-plunder night Philistines after

וְלֹא־ נַשְׁאֵר בָּהֶם אִישׁ וַיֹּאמְרוּ כָּל־ הַטּוֹב
the-good all-of and-they-replied one of-them let-us-leave and-not

בְּעֵינֶיךָ עֲשֵׂה וַיֹּאמֶר הַכֹּהֵן נִקְרְבָה הֲלֹם אֶל־הָאֱלֹהִים׃
the-God of here let-us-inquire the-priest but-he-said do! in-eyes-of-you

(37) וַיִּשְׁאַל שָׁאוּל בֵּאלֹהִים הַאֵרֵד אַחֲרֵי פְלִשְׁתִּים
Philistines after shall-I-go-down? of-God Saul so-he-asked (37)

הֲתִתְּנֵם בְּיַד יִשְׂרָאֵל וְלֹא עָנָהוּ בַּיּוֹם
on-the-day he-answered-him but-not Israel into-hand-of will-you-give-them?

הַהוּא׃ (38) וַיֹּאמֶר שָׁאוּל גֹּשׁוּ הֲלֹם כֹּל פִּנּוֹת הָעָם
the-army leaders-of all-of here come! Saul so-he-said (38) the-that

וּדְעוּ וּרְאוּ בַּמָּה הָיְתָה הַחַטָּאת הַזֹּאת הַיּוֹם׃
the-day the-this the-sin she-was-committed as-the-what and-see! and-know!

(39) כִּי חַי־ יְהוָה הַמּוֹשִׁיעַ אֶת־יִשְׂרָאֵל כִּי אִם־ יֶשְׁנוֹ
it-is-him if even Israel *** the-one-rescuing Yahweh life-of for (39)

31That day, after the Israelites had struck down the Philistines from Micmash to Aijalon, they were exhausted.
32They pounced on the plunder and, taking sheep, cattle
and calves, they butchered
them on the ground and ate
them, together with the blood.
33Then someone said to Saul,
"Look, the men are sinning
against the LORD by eating
meat that has blood in it."
"You have broken faith," he
said. "Roll a large stone over
here at once." 34Then he said,
"Go out among the men and
tell them, 'Each of you bring
me your cattle and sheep, and
slaughter them here and eat
them. Do not sin against the
LORD by eating meat with
blood still in it.' "
So everyone brought his ox
that night and slaughtered it
there. 35Then Saul built an altar to the LORD; it was the first
time he had done this.
36Saul said, "Let us go down
after the Philistines by night
and plunder them till dawn,
and let us not leave one of
them alive."
"Do whatever seems best to
you," they replied.
But the priest said, "Let us
inquire of God here."
37So Saul asked God, "Shall I
go down after the Philistines?
Will you give them into Israel's hand?" But God did not
answer him that day.
38Saul therefore said, "Come
here, all you who are leaders of
the army, and let us find out
what sin has been committed
today. 39As surely as the LORD
who rescues Israel lives, even

[d]41 Hebrew; Septuagint *"Why have you not answered your servant today? If the fault is in me or my son Jonathan, respond with Urim, but if the men of Israel are at fault, respond with Thummim."*

°32a ק ויעט
°32b ק השלל

בְּיוֹנָתָן בְּנִי כִּי מוֹת יָמוּת וְאֵין עֹנֵהוּ
answering-him but-not he-must-die to-die indeed son-of-me with-Jonathan

מִכָּל־ הָעָם׃ (40) וַיֹּאמֶר אֶל־ כָּל־ יִשְׂרָאֵל אַתֶּם תִּהְיוּ
you-stand you Israel all-of to then-he-said (40) the-people from-any-of

לְעֵבֶר אֶחָד וַאֲנִי וְיוֹנָתָן בְּנִי נִהְיֶה לְעֵבֶר
at-over-here we-will-stand son-of-me and-Jonathan and-I one at-over-there

אֶחָד וַיֹּאמְרוּ הָעָם אֶל־ שָׁאוּל הַטּוֹב בְּעֵינֶיךָ עֲשֵׂה׃
do! in-eyes-of-you the-good Saul to the-people and-they-replied one

(41) וַיֹּאמֶר שָׁאוּל אֶל־ יְהוָה אֱלֹהֵי יִשְׂרָאֵל הָבָה תָמִים
right-answer give! Israel God-of Yahweh to Saul then-he-prayed (41)

וַיִּלָּכֵד יוֹנָתָן וְשָׁאוּל וְהָעָם יָצָאוּ׃
they-went-away and-the-people and-Saul Jonathan and-he-was-taken

(42) וַיֹּאמֶר שָׁאוּל הַפִּילוּ בֵּינִי וּבֵין יוֹנָתָן בְּנִי
son-of-me Jonathan and-between between-me cast-lot! Saul and-he-said (42)

וַיִּלָּכֵד יוֹנָתָן׃ (43) וַיֹּאמֶר שָׁאוּל אֶל־ יוֹנָתָן הַגִּידָה לִּי מֶה
what to-me tell! Jonathan to Saul then-he-said (43) Jonathan and-he-was-taken

עָשִׂיתָה וַיַּגֶּד־ לוֹ יוֹנָתָן וַיֹּאמֶר טָעֹם טָעַמְתִּי בִּקְצֵה
with-end-of I-tasted to-taste and-he-said Jonathan to-him and-he-told you-did

הַמַּטֶּה אֲשֶׁר־ בְּיָדִי מְעַט דְּבַשׁ הִנְנִי אָמוּת׃ (44) וַיֹּאמֶר
and-he-said (44) must-I-die now-I! honey little-of in-hand-of-me that the-staff

שָׁאוּל כֹּה־ יַעֲשֶׂה אֱלֹהִים וְכֹה יוֹסִף כִּי־ מוֹת תָּמוּת יוֹנָתָן׃
Jonathan you-die to-die if-not may-he-be-severe and-so God may-he-deal so Saul

(45) וַיֹּאמֶר הָעָם אֶל־ שָׁאוּל הֲיוֹנָתָן ׀ יָמוּת אֲשֶׁר עָשָׂה
he-brought who should-he-die Jonathan? Saul to the-people but-he-said (45)

הַיְשׁוּעָה הַגְּדוֹלָה הַזֹּאת בְּיִשְׂרָאֵל חָלִילָה חַי־ יְהוָה אִם־
not Yahweh life-of never! in-Israel the-this the-great the-deliverance

יִפֹּל מִשַּׂעֲרַת רֹאשׁוֹ אַרְצָה כִּי־ עִם־ אֱלֹהִים עָשָׂה
he-did God with for to-ground head-of-him from-hair-of he-shall-fall

הַיּוֹם הַזֶּה וַיִּפְדּוּ הָעָם אֶת־ יוֹנָתָן וְלֹא־ מֵת׃
he-died and-not Jonathan *** the-people so-they-rescued the-this the-day

(46) וַיַּעַל שָׁאוּל מֵאַחֲרֵי פְּלִשְׁתִּים וּפְלִשְׁתִּים הָלְכוּ
they-withdrew and-Philistines Philistines from-after Saul then-he-stopped (46)

לִמְקוֹמָם׃ (47) וְשָׁאוּל לָכַד הַמְּלוּכָה עַל־ יִשְׂרָאֵל וַיִּלָּחֶם
and-he-fought Israel over the-rule he-assumed and-Saul (47) to-land-of-them

סָבִיב ׀ בְּכָל־ אֹיְבָיו בְּמוֹאָב ׀ וּבִבְנֵי־
and-against-sons-of against-Moab being-enemies-of-him against-all-of every-side

עַמּוֹן וּבֶאֱדוֹם וּבְמַלְכֵי צוֹבָה וּבַפְּלִשְׁתִּים
and-against-the-Philistines Zobah and-against-kings-of and-against-Edom Ammon

---

if it lies with my son Jonathan,
he must die." But not one of
the men said a word.
40Saul then said to all the Israelites, "You stand over
there; I and Jonathan my son
will stand over here."
"Do what seems best to
you," the men replied.
41Then Saul prayed to the
LORD, the God of Israel, "Give
me the right answer."[d] And
Jonathan and Saul were taken
by lot, and the men were
cleared. 42Saul said, "Cast the
lot between me and Jonathan
my son." And Jonathan was
taken.
43Then Saul said to Jona-
than, "Tell me what you have
done."
So Jonathan told him, "I
merely tasted a little honey
with the end of my staff. And
now must I die?"
44Saul said, "May God deal
with me, be it ever so severely,
if you do not die, Jonathan."
45But the men said to Saul,
"Should Jonathan die—he
who has brought about this
great deliverance in Israel?
Never! As surely as the LORD
lives, not a hair of his head
will fall to the ground, for he
did this today with God's
help." So the men rescued
Jonathan, and he was not put
to death.
46Then Saul stopped pursuing the Philistines, and they
withdrew to their own land.
47After Saul had assumed
rule over Israel, he fought
against their enemies on
every side: Moab, the Am-
monites, Edom, the kings of
Zobah, and the Philistines.

וּבְכֹל אֲשֶׁר־ יִפְנֶה יַרְשִׁיעַ׃ וַיַּעַשׂ

and-he-fought (48) he-inflicted-punishment he-turned where and-at-every

חַיִל וַיַּךְ אֶת־ עֲמָלֵק וַיַּצֵּל אֶת־ יִשְׂרָאֵל מִיַּד

from-hand-of Israel *** and-he-delivered Amalek *** and-he-defeated valiantly

שֹׁסֵהוּ׃ וַיִּהְיוּ בְּנֵי שָׁאוּל יוֹנָתָן וְיִשְׁוִי

and-Ishvi Jonathan Saul sons-of now-they-were (49) one-plundering-him

וּמַלְכִּי־ שׁוּעַ וְשֵׁם שְׁתֵּי בְנֹתָיו שֵׁם הַבְּכִירָה

the-older-daughter name-of daughters-of-him two-of and-name-of Shua and-Malki

מֵרַב וְשֵׁם הַקְּטַנָּה מִיכַל׃ וְשֵׁם אֵשֶׁת שָׁאוּל אֲחִינֹעַם

Ahinoam Saul wife-of and-name-of (50) Michal the-younger and-name-of Merab

בַּת־ אֲחִימָעַץ וְשֵׁם שַׂר־ צְבָאוֹ אֲבִינֵר בֶּן־נֵר

Ner son-of Abner army-of-him commander-of and-name-of Ahimaaz daughter-of

דּוֹד שָׁאוּל׃ וְקִישׁ אֲבִי־ שָׁאוּל וְנֵר אֲבִי־ אַבְנֵר בֶּן־

son-of Abner father-of and-Ner Saul father-of and-Kish (51) Saul uncle-of

אֲבִיאֵל׃ וַתְּהִי הַמִּלְחָמָה חֲזָקָה עַל־ פְּלִשְׁתִּים כֹּל יְמֵי שָׁאוּל

Saul days-of all-of Philistines with bitter the-war and-she-was (52) Abiel

וְרָאָה שָׁאוּל כָּל־ אִישׁ גִּבּוֹר וְכָל־ בֶּן־ חַיִל וַיַּאַסְפֵהוּ

then-he-added-him bravery son-of or-any-of mighty man any-of Saul when-he-saw

אֵלָיו׃ וַיֹּאמֶר שְׁמוּאֵל אֶל־שָׁאוּל אֹתִי שָׁלַח יְהוָה לִמְשָׁחֲךָ

to-anoint-you Yahweh he-sent me Saul to Samuel and-he-said (15:1) to-him

לְמֶלֶךְ עַל־ עַמּוֹ עַל־ יִשְׂרָאֵל וְעַתָּה שְׁמַע לְקוֹל דִּבְרֵי

words-of to-message-of listen! so-now Israel over people-of-him over as-king

יְהוָה׃ כֹּה אָמַר יְהוָה צְבָאוֹת פָּקַדְתִּי אֵת אֲשֶׁר־עָשָׂה עֲמָלֵק

Amalek he-did what *** I-will-punish Hosts Yahweh-of he-says this (2) Yahweh

לְיִשְׂרָאֵל אֲשֶׁר־ שָׂם לוֹ בַּדֶּרֶךְ בַּעֲלֹתוֹ מִמִּצְרָיִם׃

from-Egypt as-to-come-up-them on-the-way to-him he-waylaid when to-Israel

עַתָּה לֵךְ וְהִכִּיתָה אֶת־ עֲמָלֵק וְהַחֲרַמְתֶּם אֶת־כָּל־אֲשֶׁר־ לוֹ

to-him that all *** and-you-destroy Amalek *** and-you-attack go! now (3)

וְלֹא תַחְמֹל עָלָיו וְהֵמַתָּה מֵאִישׁ עַד־ אִשָּׁה מֵעֹלֵל

from-child woman to from-man but-you-kill from-them you-spare and-not

וְעַד־ יוֹנֵק מִשּׁוֹר וְעַד־ שֶׂה מִגָּמָל וְעַד־ חֲמוֹר׃

donkey even-to from-camel sheep even-to from-cattle one-nursing even-to

וַיְשַׁמַּע שָׁאוּל אֶת־ הָעָם וַיִּפְקְדֵם בַּטְּלָאִים

at-the-Telaim and-he-mustered-them the-people *** Saul so-he-summoned (4)

מָאתַיִם אֶלֶף רַגְלִי וַעֲשֶׂרֶת אֲלָפִים אֶת־ אִישׁ יְהוּדָה׃

Judah man-of *** thousands and-ten-of foot-soldier thousand two-hundreds

וַיָּבֹא שָׁאוּל עַד־ עִיר עֲמָלֵק וַיָּרֶב בַּנָּחַל׃

in-the-ravine and-he-set-ambush Amalek city-of to Saul and-he-went (5)

Wherever he turned, he inflicted punishment on them.[e] [48]He fought valiantly and defeated the Amalekites, delivering Israel from the hands of those who had plundered them.

Saul's Family

[49]Saul's sons were Jonathan, Ishvi[f] and Malki-Shua. The name of his older daughter was Merab, and that of the younger was Michal. [50]His wife's name was Ahinoam daughter of Ahimaaz. The name of the commander of Saul's army was Abner son of Ner, and Ner was Saul's uncle. [51]Saul's father Kish and Abner's father Ner were sons of Abiel.

[52]All the days of Saul there was bitter war with the Philistines, and whenever Saul saw a mighty or brave man, he took him into his service.

The LORD Rejects Saul as King

15 Samuel said to Saul, "I am the one the LORD sent to anoint you king over his people Israel; so listen now to the message from the LORD. [2]This is what the LORD Almighty says: 'I will punish the Amalekites for what they did to Israel when they waylaid them as they came up from Egypt. [3]Now go, attack the Amalekites and totally destroy[g] everything that belongs to them. Do not spare them; put to death men and women, children and infants, cattle and sheep, camels and donkeys.' "

[4]So Saul summoned the men and mustered them at Telaim—two hundred thousand foot soldiers and ten thousand men from Judah. [5]Saul went to the city of Amalek and set an ambush in the ravine. [6]Then

[e]47 Hebrew; Septuagint *he was victorious*
[f]49 Also known as *Ish-Bosheth* and *Esh-Baal*

וַיֹּאמֶר שָׁאוּל אֶל־הַקֵּינִי לְכוּ סֻּרוּ רְדוּ מִתּוֹךְ עֲמָלֵקִי
Amalekite from-among go-away! leave! go! the-Kenite to Saul then-he-said (6)

פֶּן־אֹסִפְךָ עִמּוֹ וְאַתָּה עָשִׂיתָה חֶסֶד עִם־כָּל־בְּנֵי
sons-of all-of to kindness you-showed for-you with-him I-destroy-you so-not

יִשְׂרָאֵל בַּעֲלוֹתָם מִמִּצְרָיִם וַיָּסַר קֵינִי מִתּוֹךְ
from-among Kenite so-he-moved-away from-Egypt when-to-come-up-them Israel

עֲמָלֵק׃ וַיַּךְ שָׁאוּל אֶת־עֲמָלֵק מֵחֲוִילָה בּוֹאֲךָ שׁוּר אֲשֶׁר
that Shur to-go-you from-Havilah Amalek *** Saul then-he-attacked (7) Amalek

עַל־פְּנֵי מִצְרָיִם׃ וַיִּתְפֹּשׂ אֶת־אֲגַג מֶלֶךְ־עֲמָלֵק חָי וְאֶת־כָּל־
all-of and alive Amalek king-of Agag *** and-he-took (8) Egypt east-of to

הָעָם הֶחֱרִים לְפִי־חָרֶב׃ וַיַּחְמֹל שָׁאוּל וְהָעָם
and-the-army Saul but-he-spared (9) sword with-edge-of he-destroyed the-people

עַל־אֲגָג וְעַל־מֵיטַב הַצֹּאן וְהַבָּקָר וְהַמִּשְׁנִים וְעַל־
and-to and-the-fat-calves and-the-cattle the-sheep best-of and-to Agag to

הַכָּרִים וְעַל־כָּל־הַטּוֹב וְלֹא אָבוּ הַחֲרִימָם
to-destroy-them they-were-willing and-not the-good all-of and-to the-lambs

וְכָל־הַמְּלָאכָה נְמִבְזָה* וְנָמֵס אֹתָהּ הֶחֱרִימוּ׃
they-destroyed her and-being-weak *being-despised the-thing but-every-of

וַיְהִי דְּבַר־יְהוָה אֶל־שְׁמוּאֵל לֵאמֹר׃ נִחַמְתִּי כִּי־
that I-am-grieved (11) to-say Samuel to Yahweh word-of then-he-came (10)

הִמְלַכְתִּי אֶת־שָׁאוּל לְמֶלֶךְ כִּי־שָׁב מֵאַחֲרַי וְאֶת־דְּבָרַי
instructions-of-me and from-after-me he-turned for as-king Saul *** I-made-king

לֹא הֵקִים וַיִּחַר לִשְׁמוּאֵל וַיִּזְעַק אֶל־יְהוָה כָּל־
all-of Yahweh to and-he-cried-out to-Samuel and-he-troubled he-carried-out not

הַלָּיְלָה׃ וַיַּשְׁכֵּם שְׁמוּאֵל לִקְרַאת שָׁאוּל בַּבֹּקֶר וַיֻּגַּד
but-he-was-told in-the-morning Saul to-meet Samuel and-he-got-up (12) the-night

לִשְׁמוּאֵל לֵאמֹר בָּא־שָׁאוּל הַכַּרְמֶלָה וְהִנֵּה מַצִּיב לוֹ
to-him setting-up and-see! to-the-Carmel Saul he-went to-say to-Samuel

יָד וַיִּסֹּב וַיַּעֲבֹר וַיֵּרֶד הַגִּלְגָּל׃
the-Gilgal and-he-went-down and-he-left and-he-turned monument

וַיָּבֹא שְׁמוּאֵל אֶל־שָׁאוּל וַיֹּאמֶר לוֹ שָׁאוּל בָּרוּךְ
being-blessed Saul to-him then-he-said Saul to Samuel when-he-reached (13)

אַתָּה לַיהוָה הֲקִימֹתִי אֶת־דְּבַר יְהוָה׃ וַיֹּאמֶר שְׁמוּאֵל
Samuel but-he-said (14) Yahweh instruction-of *** I-carried-out by-Yahweh you

וּמֶה קוֹל־הַצֹּאן הַזֶּה בְּאָזְנָי וְקוֹל
and-lowing-of in-ears-of-me the-this the-sheep bleating-of then-what?

הַבָּקָר אֲשֶׁר אָנֹכִי שֹׁמֵעַ׃ וַיֹּאמֶר שָׁאוּל מֵעֲמָלֵקִי
from-Amalekite Saul and-he-answered (15) hearing I that the-cattle

he said to the Kenites, "Go
away, leave the Amalekites so
that I do not destroy you along
with them; for you showed
kindness to all the Israelites
when they came up out of
Egypt." So the Kenites moved
away from the Amalekites.
7Then Saul attacked the
Amalekites all the way from
Havilah to Shur, to the east of
Egypt. 8He took Agag king of
the Amalekites alive, and all
his people he totally destroyed
with the sword. 9But Saul and
the army spared Agag and the
best of the sheep and cattle,
the fat calves[h] and lambs—
everything that was good.
These they were unwilling to
destroy completely, but everything that was despised and
weak they totally destroyed.
10Then the word of the LORD
came to Samuel: 11"I am
grieved that I have made Saul
king, because he has turned
away from me and has not
carried out my instructions."
Samuel was troubled, and he
cried out to the LORD all that
night.
12Early in the morning Samuel got up and went to meet
Saul, but he was told, "Saul
has gone to Carmel. There he
has set up a monument in his
own honor and has turned
and gone on down to Gilgal."
13When Samuel reached
him, Saul said, "The LORD
bless you! I have carried out
the LORD's instructions."
14But Samuel said, "What
then is this bleating of sheep
in my ears? What is this lowing of cattle that I hear?"
15Saul answered, "The soldiers brought them from the

g3 The Hebrew term refers to the irrevocable giving over of things or persons to the LORD, often by totally destroying them; also in verses 8, 9, 15, 18, 20 and 21.
h9 Or *the grown bulls;* the meaning of the Hebrew for this phrase is uncertain.

***9 Without the *mem*, this word would read as a normal Niphal participle. Most lexicons suggest this letter resulted from a scribal error.**

הֱבִיאוּם אֲשֶׁר חָמַל הָעָם עַל־מֵיטַב הַצֹּאן
the-sheep best-of from the-soldier he-spared which they-brought-them

וְהַבָּקָר לְמַעַן זְבֹחַ לַיהוָה אֱלֹהֶיךָ וְאֶת־הַיּוֹתֵר
the-remaining but God-of-you to-Yahweh to-sacrifice in-order-to and-the-cattle

הֶחֱרַמְנוּ׃ וַיֹּאמֶר שְׁמוּאֵל אֶל־שָׁאוּל הֶרֶף וְאַגִּידָה לְּךָ
to-you and-let-me-tell stop! Saul to Samuel and-he-said (16) we-destroyed

אֵת אֲשֶׁר דִּבֶּר יְהוָה אֵלַי הַלָּיְלָה וַיֹּאמְרוּ לוֹ דַּבֵּר׃
tell! to-him and-he-replied the-night to-me Yahweh he-said what ***

וַיֹּאמֶר שְׁמוּאֵל הֲלוֹא אִם־קָטֹן אַתָּה בְּעֵינֶיךָ רֹאשׁ
head-of in-eyes-of-you you small although not? Samuel and-he-said (17)

שִׁבְטֵי יִשְׂרָאֵל אָתָּה וַיִּמְשָׁחֲךָ יְהוָה לְמֶלֶךְ עַל־יִשְׂרָאֵל׃
Israel over as-king Yahweh and-he-anointed-you you Israel tribes-of

וַיִּשְׁלָחֲךָ יְהוָה בְּדָרֶךְ וַיֹּאמֶר לֵךְ וְהַחֲרַמְתָּה אֶת־
*** and-you-destroy go! and-he-said on-mission Yahweh and-he-sent-you (18)

הַחַטָּאִים אֶת־עֲמָלֵק וְנִלְחַמְתָּ בוֹ עַד כַּלּוֹתָם
to-wipe-out-them until on-him and-you-make-war Amalek *** the-wicked-ones

אֹתָם׃ וְלָמָּה לֹא־שָׁמַעְתָּ בְּקוֹל יְהוָה וַתַּעַט אֶל־
on and-you-pounced Yahweh to-voice-of you-obeyed not so-why? (19) them

הַשָּׁלָל וַתַּעַשׂ הָרַע בְּעֵינֵי יְהוָה׃ וַיֹּאמֶר שָׁאוּל אֶל־
to Saul and-he-said (20) Yahweh in-eyes-of the-evil and-you-did the-plunder

שְׁמוּאֵל אֲשֶׁר שָׁמַעְתִּי בְּקוֹל יְהוָה וָאֵלֵךְ בַּדֶּרֶךְ אֲשֶׁר־
that on-the-mission and-I-went Yahweh to-voice-of I-obeyed that Samuel

שְׁלָחַנִי יְהוָה וָאָבִיא אֶת־אֲגַג מֶלֶךְ עֲמָלֵק וְאֶת־עֲמָלֵק
Amalek and Amalek king-of Agag *** and-I-brought-back Yahweh he-assigned-me

הֶחֱרַמְתִּי׃ וַיִּקַּח הָעָם מֵהַשָּׁלָל צֹאן וּבָקָר
and cattle sheep from-the-plunder the-soldier and-he-took (21) I-destroyed

רֵאשִׁית הַחֵרֶם לִזְבֹּחַ לַיהוָה אֱלֹהֶיךָ בַּגִּלְגָּל׃
at-the-Gilgal God-of-you to-Yahweh to-sacrifice the-devoted-thing best-of

וַיֹּאמֶר שְׁמוּאֵל הַחֵפֶץ לַיהוָה בְּעֹלוֹת וּזְבָחִים
and-sacrifices in-burnt-offerings to-Yahweh delight? Samuel but-he-replied (22)

כִּשְׁמֹעַ בְּקוֹל יְהוָה הִנֵּה שְׁמֹעַ מִזֶּבַח טוֹב לְהַקְשִׁיב
to-heed better than-sacrifice to-obey see! Yahweh to-voice-of as-to-obey

מֵחֵלֶב אֵילִים׃ כִּי חַטַּאת־קֶסֶם מֶרִי וְאָוֶן וּתְרָפִים
and-idolatries and-evil rebellion divination sin-of for (23) rams than-fat-of

הַפְצַר יַעַן מָאַסְתָּ אֶת־דְּבַר יְהוָה וַיִּמְאָסְךָ
so-he-rejected-you Yahweh word-of *** you-rejected because to-be-arrogant

מִמֶּלֶךְ׃ וַיֹּאמֶר שָׁאוּל אֶל־שְׁמוּאֵל חָטָאתִי כִּי־עָבַרְתִּי אֶת־
*** I-violated indeed I-sinned Samuel to Saul then-he-said (24) as-king

°16 ק ויאמר

Amalekites; they spared the
best of the sheep and cattle to
sacrifice to the LORD your God,
but we totally destroyed the
rest."
[16]"Stop!" Samuel said to
Saul. "Let me tell you what the
LORD said to me last night."
"Tell me," Saul replied.
[17]Samuel said, "Although
you were once small in your
own eyes, did you not become
the head of the tribes of Israel?
The LORD anointed you king
over Israel. [18]And he sent you
on a mission, saying, 'Go and
completely destroy those
wicked people, the Amalekites; make war on them until
you have wiped them out.'
[19]Why did you not obey the
LORD? Why did you pounce on
the plunder and do evil in the
eyes of the LORD?"
[20]"But I did obey the LORD,"
Saul said. "I went on the mission the LORD assigned me. I
completely destroyed the
Amalekites and brought back
Agag their king. [21]The soldiers
took sheep and cattle from the
plunder, the best of what was
devoted to God, in order to
sacrifice them to the LORD your
God at Gilgal."
[22]But Samuel replied:

"Does the LORD delight in
burnt offerings and
sacrifices
as much as in obeying
the voice of the LORD?
To obey is better than
sacrifice,
and to heed is better
than the fat of rams.
[23]For rebellion is like the sin
of divination,
and arrogance like the
evil of idolatry.
Because you have rejected
the word of the LORD,
he has rejected you as
king."

[24]Then Saul said to Samuel,
"I have sinned. I violated the

פִּי־ יְהוָה וְאֶת־ דְּבָרֶיךָ כִּי יָרֵאתִי אֶת־ הָעָם
the-people *** I-was-afraid for instructions-of-you and Yahweh command-of

וָאֶשְׁמַע בְּקוֹלָם׃ (25) וְעַתָּה שָׂא נָא אֶת־ חַטָּאתִי
sin-of-me *** now! forgive! and-now (25) to-voice-of-them so-I-gave-in

וְשׁוּב עִמִּי וְאֶשְׁתַּחֲוֶה לַיהוָה׃ (26) וַיֹּאמֶר שְׁמוּאֵל
Samuel but-he-said (26) to-Yahweh so-I-may-worship with-me and-come-back!

אֶל־שָׁאוּל לֹא אָשׁוּב עִמָּךְ כִּי מָאַסְתָּה אֶת־ דְּבַר יְהוָה
Yahweh word-of *** you-rejected for with-you I-will-go-back not Saul to

וַיִּמְאָסְךָ יְהוָה מִהְיוֹת מֶלֶךְ עַל־ יִשְׂרָאֵל׃ (27) וַיִּסֹּב
as-he-turned (27) Israel over king from-to-be Yahweh and-he-rejected-you

שְׁמוּאֵל לָלֶכֶת וַיַּחֲזֵק בִּכְנַף־ מְעִילוֹ וַיִּקָּרַע׃
and-he-tore robe-of-him of-edge-of then-he-caught-hold to-leave Samuel

(28) וַיֹּאמֶר אֵלָיו שְׁמוּאֵל קָרַע יְהוָה אֶת־ מַמְלְכוּת יִשְׂרָאֵל
Israel kingdom-of *** Yahweh he-tore Samuel to-him and-he-said (28)

מֵעָלֶיךָ הַיּוֹם וּנְתָנָהּ לְרֵעֲךָ הַטּוֹב מִמֶּךָּ׃
than-you the-better to-neighbor-of-you and-he-gave-her the-day from-with-you

(29) וְגַם נֵצַח יִשְׂרָאֵל לֹא יְשַׁקֵּר וְלֹא יִנָּחֵם כִּי לֹא
not for he-changes-mind and-not he-lies not Israel Glory-of and-also (29)

אָדָם הוּא לְהִנָּחֵם׃ (30) וַיֹּאמֶר חָטָאתִי עַתָּה כַּבְּדֵנִי נָא נֶגֶד
before now! honor-me! but I-sinned and-he-replied (30) to-change-mind he man

זִקְנֵי־ עַמִּי וְנֶגֶד יִשְׂרָאֵל וְשׁוּב עִמִּי וְהִשְׁתַּחֲוֵיתִי
so-I-may-worship with-me and-come-back! Israel and-before people-of-me elders-of

לַיהוָה אֱלֹהֶיךָ׃ (31) וַיָּשָׁב שְׁמוּאֵל אַחֲרֵי שָׁאוּל וַיִּשְׁתַּחוּ
and-he-worshipped Saul with Samuel so-he-went-back (31) God-of-you to-Yahweh

שָׁאוּל לַיהוָה׃ (32) וַיֹּאמֶר שְׁמוּאֵל הַגִּישׁוּ אֵלַי אֶת־ אֲגַג מֶלֶךְ עֲמָלֵק
Amalek king-of Agag *** to-me bring! Samuel then-he-said (32) to-Yahweh Saul

וַיֵּלֶךְ אֵלָיו אֲגַג מַעֲדַנֹּת וַיֹּאמֶר אֲגַג אָכֵן סָר
he-is-past surely Agag and-he-thought confidently Agag to-him and-he-came

מַר־ הַמָּוֶת׃ (33) וַיֹּאמֶר שְׁמוּאֵל כַּאֲשֶׁר שִׁכְּלָה
she-made-childless just-as Samuel but-he-said (33) the-death bitterness-of

נָשִׁים חַרְבֶּךָ כֵּן־ תִּשְׁכַּל מִנָּשִׁים אִמֶּךָ
mother-of-you among-women she-will-be-childless so sword-of-you women

וַיְשַׁסֵּף שְׁמוּאֵל אֶת־ אֲגָג לִפְנֵי יְהוָה בַּגִּלְגָּל׃ (34) וַיֵּלֶךְ
then-he-left (34) at-the-Gilgal Yahweh before Agag *** Samuel and-he-killed

שְׁמוּאֵל הָרָמָתָה וְשָׁאוּל עָלָה אֶל־ בֵּיתוֹ גִּבְעַת שָׁאוּל׃
Saul Gibeah-of home-of-him to he-went-up but-Saul for-the-Ramah Samuel

(35) וְלֹא־ יָסַף שְׁמוּאֵל לִרְאוֹת אֶת־שָׁאוּל עַד־ יוֹם מוֹתוֹ
death-of-him day-of until Saul *** to-see Samuel he-went-again and-not (35)

LORD's command and your instructions. I was afraid of the people and so I gave in to them.
25 Now I beg you, forgive my sin and come back with me, so that I may worship the LORD."
26 But Samuel said to him, "I will not go back with you. You have rejected the word of the LORD, and the LORD has rejected you as king over Israel!"
27 As Samuel turned to leave, Saul caught hold of the edge of his robe, and it tore.
28 Samuel said to him, "The LORD has torn the kingdom of Israel from you today and has given it to one of your neighbors—to one better than you.
29 He who is the Glory of Israel does not lie or change his mind; for he is not a man, that he should change his mind."
30 Saul replied, "I have sinned. But please honor me before the elders of my people and before Israel; come back with me, so that I may worship the LORD your God."
31 So Samuel went back with Saul, and Saul worshiped the LORD.
32 Then Samuel said, "Bring me Agag king of the Amalekites."

Agag came to him confidently,[i] thinking, "Surely the bitterness of death is past."
33 But Samuel said,

"As your sword has made
women childless,
so will your mother be
childless among
women."

And Samuel put Agag to death before the LORD at Gilgal.
34 Then Samuel left for Ramah, but Saul went up to his home in Gibeah of Saul.
35 Until the day Samuel died, he did not go to see Saul again,

[i]32 Or *him trembling, yet*

כִּֽי־ הִתְאַבֵּל שְׁמוּאֵל אֶל־שָׁאוּל וַיהוָה נִחָם כִּֽי־ הִמְלִיךְ
he-made-king that he-was-grieved and-Yahweh Saul for Samuel he-mourned though

אֶת־שָׁאוּל עַל־יִשְׂרָאֵל׃ וַיֹּאמֶר יְהוָה אֶל־שְׁמוּאֵל עַד־ מָתַי אַתָּה
you when? until Samuel to Yahweh and-he-said (16:1) Israel over Saul ***

מִתְאַבֵּל אֶל־ שָׁאוּל וַאֲנִי מְאַסְתִּיו מִמְּלֹךְ עַל־יִשְׂרָאֵל מַלֵּא קַרְנְךָ
horn-of-you fill! Israel over as-king I-rejected-him since-I Saul for mourning

שֶׁמֶן וְלֵךְ אֶשְׁלָחֲךָ אֶל־ יִשַׁי בֵּית־הַלַּחְמִי כִּֽי־ רָאִיתִי בְּבָנָיו
of-sons-of-him I-chose for the-Bethlehemite Jesse to I-send-you and-go! oil

לִי מֶֽלֶךְ׃ וַיֹּאמֶר שְׁמוּאֵל אֵיךְ אֵלֵךְ וְשָׁמַע שָׁאוּל
Saul for-he-will-hear can-I-go how? Samuel but-he-said (2) king for-me

וַהֲרָגָנִי וַיֹּאמֶר יְהוָה עֶגְלַת בָּקָר תִּקַּח בְּיָדֶךָ
in-hand-of-you you-take herd heifer-of Yahweh and-he-said and-he-will-kill-me

וְאָמַרְתָּ לִזְבֹּחַ לַיהוָה בָּאתִי׃ וְקָרָאתָ לְיִשַׁי
to-Jesse and-you-invite (3) I-came to-Yahweh to-sacrifice and-you-say

בַּזָּבַח וְאָנֹכִי אוֹדִיעֲךָ אֵת אֲשֶׁר־ תַּעֲשֶׂה וּמָשַׁחְתָּ
and-you-anoint you-must-do what *** I-will-show-you and-I to-the-sacrifice

לִי אֵת אֲשֶׁר־ אֹמַר אֵלֶיךָ׃ וַיַּעַשׂ שְׁמוּאֵל אֵת אֲשֶׁר דִּבֶּר
he-said what *** Samuel and-he-did (4) to-you I-indicate whom *** for-me

יְהוָה וַיָּבֹא בֵּית לָחֶם וַיֶּחֶרְדוּ זִקְנֵי הָעִיר
the-town elders-of then-they-trembled Lehem Beth when-he-arrived Yahweh

לִקְרָאתוֹ וַיֹּאמֶר שָׁלֹם בּוֹאֶךָ׃ וַיֹּאמֶר ׀ שָׁלוֹם
peacefully and-he-replied (5) to-come-you peacefully and-they-asked to-meet-him

לִזְבֹּחַ לַיהוָה בָּאתִי הִתְקַדְּשׁוּ וּבָאתֶם אִתִּי
with-me and-you-come consecrate-yourselves! I-came to-Yahweh to-sacrifice

בַּזָּבַח וַיְקַדֵּשׁ אֶת־ יִשַׁי וְאֶת־ בָּנָיו וַיִּקְרָא
and-he-invited sons-of-him and Jesse *** then-he-consecrated to-the-sacrifice

לָהֶם לַזָּבַח׃ וַיְהִי בְּבוֹאָם וַיַּרְא אֶת־
*** then-he-saw when-to-arrive-them and-he-was (6) to-the-sacrifice to-them

אֱלִיאָב וַיֹּאמֶר אַךְ נֶגֶד יְהוָה מְשִׁיחוֹ׃ וַיֹּאמֶר
but-he-said (7) anointed-of-him Yahweh before surely and-he-thought Eliab

יְהוָה אֶל־שְׁמוּאֵל אַל־ תַּבֵּט אֶל־ מַרְאֵהוּ וְאֶל־ גְּבֹהַּ
height-of or-to appearance-of-him to you-consider not Samuel to Yahweh

קוֹמָתוֹ כִּי מְאַסְתִּיהוּ כִּי ׀ לֹא אֲשֶׁר יִרְאֶה הָאָדָם כִּי הָאָדָם
the-man for the-man he-looks-at what not for I-rejected-him for height-of-him

יִרְאֶה לַעֵינַיִם וַיהוָה יִרְאֶה לַלֵּבָב׃ וַיִּקְרָא
then-he-called (8) at-the-heart he-looks but-Yahweh at-the-eyes he-looks

יִשַׁי אֶל־אֲבִינָדָב וַיַּעֲבִרֵהוּ לִפְנֵי שְׁמוּאֵל וַיֹּאמֶר גַּם־
also but-he-said Samuel in-front-of and-he-had-pass-him Abinadab to Jesse

though Samuel mourned for
him. And the LORD was
grieved that he had made Saul
king over Israel.

Samuel Anoints David

16 The LORD said to Sam-
uel, "How long will
you mourn for Saul, since I
have rejected him as king over
Israel? Fill your horn with oil
and be on your way; I am
sending you to Jesse of Bethlehem. I have chosen one of
his sons to be king."
[2]But Samuel said, "How can
I go? Saul will hear about it
and kill me."
The LORD said, "Take a heifer with you and say, 'I have
come to sacrifice to the LORD.'
[3]Invite Jesse to the sacrifice,
and I will show you what to
do. You are to anoint for me
the one I indicate."
[4]Samuel did what the LORD
said. When he arrived at Bethlehem, the elders of the town
trembled when they met him.
They asked, "Do you come in
peace?"
[5]Samuel replied, "Yes, in
peace; I have come to sacrifice
to the LORD. Consecrate yourselves and come to the sacrifice with me." Then he consecrated Jesse and his sons
and invited them to the sacrifice.
[6]When they arrived, Samuel
saw Eliab and thought, "Surely the LORD's anointed stands
here before the LORD."
[7]But the LORD said to Samuel,
"Do not consider his appearance or his height, for I have
rejected him. The LORD does
not look at the things man
looks at. Man looks at the out-
ward appearance, but the
LORD looks at the heart."
[8]Then Jesse called Abinadab
and had him pass in front of
Samuel. But Samuel said, "The

בָּזֶה לֹא־ בָחַר יְהוָה׃ וַיַּעֲבֵר יִשַׁי שַׁמָּה וַיֹּאמֶר
but-he-said Shammah Jesse then-he-had-pass (9) Yahweh he-chose not to-this

גַּם־ בָּזֶה לֹא־ בָחַר יְהוָה׃ וַיַּעֲבֵר יִשַׁי שִׁבְעַת
seven-of Jesse and-he-had-pass (10) Yahweh he-chose not to-this also

בָּנָיו לִפְנֵי שְׁמוּאֵל וַיֹּאמֶר שְׁמוּאֵל אֶל־יִשַׁי לֹא־ בָחַר יְהוָה
Yahweh he-chose not Jesse to Samuel but-he-said Samuel before sons-of-him

בָּאֵלֶּה׃ וַיֹּאמֶר שְׁמוּאֵל אֶל־יִשַׁי הֲתַמּוּ הַנְּעָרִים וַיֹּאמֶר
and-he-said the-sons are-they-all? Jesse to Samuel so-he-asked (11) to-these

עוֹד שָׁאַר הַקָּטָן וְהִנֵּה רֹעֶה בַּצֹּאן וַיֹּאמֶר שְׁמוּאֵל
Samuel and-he-said to-the-sheep tending but-see! the-young he-remains still

אֶל־יִשַׁי שִׁלְחָה וְקָחֶנּוּ כִּי לֹא־ נָסֹב עַד־ בֹּאוֹ פֹה׃
here to-arrive-him until we-will-gather not for and-get-him! send! Jesse to

וַיִּשְׁלַח וַיְבִיאֵהוּ וְהוּא אַדְמוֹנִי עִם־ יְפֵה עֵינַיִם
eyes fineness-of with ruddy now-he and-he-had-brought-him so-he-sent (12)

וְטוֹב רֹאִי וַיֹּאמֶר יְהוָה קוּם מְשָׁחֵהוּ כִּי־ זֶה הוּא׃
he this for anoint-him! rise! Yahweh then-he-said feature and-handsome-of

וַיִּקַּח שְׁמוּאֵל אֶת־ קֶרֶן הַשֶּׁמֶן וַיִּמְשַׁח אֹתוֹ בְּקֶרֶב
in-presence-of him and-he-anointed the-oil horn-of *** Samuel so-he-took (13)

אֶחָיו וַתִּצְלַח רוּחַ־ יְהוָה אֶל־ דָּוִד מֵהַיּוֹם הַהוּא
the-that from-the-day David upon Yahweh Spirit-of and-she-came brothers-of-him

וָמָעְלָה וַיָּקָם שְׁמוּאֵל וַיֵּלֶךְ הָרָמָתָה׃ וְרוּחַ
now-Spirit-of (14) to-the-Ramah and-he-went Samuel then-he-rose and-onward

יְהוָה סָרָה מֵעִם שָׁאוּל וּבִעֲתַתּוּ רוּחַ־ רָעָה מֵאֵת
from evil spirit and-she-tormented-him Saul from-with she-departed Yahweh

יְהוָה׃ וַיֹּאמְרוּ עַבְדֵי־ שָׁאוּל אֵלָיו הִנֵּה־ נָא רוּחַ־אֱלֹהִים
God spirit-of now! see! to-him Saul attendants-of and-they-said (15) Yahweh

רָעָה מְבַעִתֶּךָ׃ יֹאמַר־ נָא אֲדֹנֵנוּ עֲבָדֶיךָ
servants-of-you lord-of-us now! let-him-command (16) tormenting-you evil

לְפָנֶיךָ יְבַקְשׁוּ אִישׁ יֹדֵעַ מְנַגֵּן בַּכִּנּוֹר וְהָיָה
and-he-will-be on-the-harp playing knowing someone let-them-seek before-you

בִּהְיוֹת עָלֶיךָ רוּחַ־ אֱלֹהִים רָעָה וְנִגֵּן בְּיָדוֹ
with-hand-of-him then-he-will-play evil God spirit-of upon-you when-to-come

וְטוֹב לָךְ׃ וַיֹּאמֶר שָׁאוּל אֶל־ עֲבָדָיו רְאוּ־ נָא
now! find! attendants-of-him to Saul so-he-said (17) for-you and-better

לִי אִישׁ מֵיטִיב לְנַגֵּן וַהֲבִיאוֹתֶם אֵלָי׃ וַיַּעַן
and-he-answered (18) to-me and-you-bring to-play doing-well someone for-me

אֶחָד מֵהַנְּעָרִים וַיֹּאמֶר הִנֵּה רָאִיתִי בֵּן לְיִשַׁי בֵּית הַלַּחְמִי
the-Bethlehemite of-Jesse son I-saw see! and-he-said of-the-servants one

LORD has not chosen this one
either." [9]Jesse then had Shammah pass by, but Samuel said,
"Nor has the LORD chosen this
one." [10]Jesse had seven of his
sons pass before Samuel, but
Samuel said to him, "The LORD
has not chosen these." [11]So he
asked Jesse, "Are these all the
sons you have?"

"There is still the youngest,"
Jesse answered, "but he is
tending the sheep."

Samuel said, "Send for him;
we will not sit down[j] until he
arrives."

[12]So he sent and had him
brought in. He was ruddy,
with a fine appearance and
handsome features.

Then the LORD said, "Rise
and anoint him; he is the
one."

[13]So Samuel took the horn of
oil and anointed him in the
presence of his brothers, and
from that day on the Spirit of
the LORD came upon David in
power. Samuel then went to
Ramah.

David in Saul's Service

[14]Now the Spirit of the LORD
had departed from Saul, and
an evil[k] spirit from the LORD
tormented him.

[15]Saul's attendants said to
him, "See, an evil spirit from
God is tormenting you. [16]Let
our lord command his ser-
vants here to search for someone who can play the harp. He
will play when the evil spirit
from God comes upon you,
and you will feel better."

[17]So Saul said to his attendants, "Find someone who
plays well and bring him to
me."

[18]One of the servants answered, "I have seen a son of
Jesse of Bethlehem who

[j]11 Some Septuagint manuscripts; Hebrew *not gather around*
[k]14 Or *injurious;* also in verses 15, 16 and 23

יֹדֵעַ נַגֵּן וְגִבּוֹר חַיִל וְאִישׁ מִלְחָמָה וּנְבוֹן דָּבָר
speech and-being-wise-of war and-man-of valor and-brave-of to-play knowing

וְאִישׁ תֹּאַר וַיהוָה עִמּוֹ׃ וַיִּשְׁלַח שָׁאוּל מַלְאָכִים
messengers Saul then-he-sent (19) with-him and-Yahweh fine-looking and-man

אֶל־יִשָׁי וַיֹּאמֶר שִׁלְחָה אֵלַי אֶת־דָּוִד בִּנְךָ אֲשֶׁר בַּצֹּאן׃
with-the-sheep who son-of-you David *** to-me send! and-he-said Jesse to

וַיִּקַּח יִשַׁי חֲמוֹר לֶחֶם וְנֹאד יַיִן וּגְדִי
and-young-goat-of wine and-skin-of bread donkey-of Jesse so-he-took (20)

עִזִּים אֶחָד וַיִּשְׁלַח בְּיַד־דָּוִד בְּנוֹ אֶל־שָׁאוּל׃ וַיָּבֹא
and-he-came (21) Saul to son-of-him David in-hand-of and-he-sent one goats

דָוִד אֶל־שָׁאוּל וַיַּעֲמֹד לְפָנָיו וַיֶּאֱהָבֵהוּ מְאֹד
very-much and-he-liked-him before-him and-he-served Saul to David

וַיְהִי־לוֹ נֹשֵׂא כֵלִים׃ וַיִּשְׁלַח שָׁאוּל אֶל־יִשַׁי
Jesse to Saul then-he-sent (22) armors one-bearing for-him and-he-became

לֵאמֹר יַעֲמָד־נָא דָוִד לְפָנַי כִּי־מָצָא חֵן בְּעֵינָי׃
in-eyes-of-me favor he-found for before-me David now! let-him-serve to-say

וְהָיָה בִּהְיוֹת רוּחַ־אֱלֹהִים אֶל־שָׁאוּל וְלָקַח דָּוִד אֶת־
*** David then-he-took Saul to God spirit-of when-to-come and-he-was (23)

הַכִּנּוֹר וְנִגֵּן בְּיָדוֹ וְרָוַח לְשָׁאוּל וְטוֹב
and-better to-Saul and-he-was-relief with-hand-of-him and-he-played the-harp

לוֹ וְסָרָה מֵעָלָיו רוּחַ הָרָעָה׃ וַיַּאַסְפוּ
now-they-gathered (17:1) the-evil spirit-of from-upon-him and-she-left for-him

פְלִשְׁתִּים אֶת־מַחֲנֵיהֶם לַמִּלְחָמָה וַיֵּאָסְפוּ שֹׂכֹה אֲשֶׁר
that Socoh and-they-assembled for-the-war forces-of-them *** Philistines

לִיהוּדָה וַיַּחֲנוּ בֵּין־שׂוֹכֹה וּבֵין־עֲזֵקָה בְּאֶפֶס דַּמִּים׃
Dammim at-Ephes Azekah and-between Socoh between and-they-camped in-Judah

וְשָׁאוּל וְאִישׁ־יִשְׂרָאֵל נֶאֶסְפוּ וַיַּחֲנוּ בְּעֵמֶק
in-Valley-of and-they-camped they-assembled Israel and-man-of and-Saul (2)

הָאֵלָה וַיַּעַרְכוּ מִלְחָמָה לִקְרַאת פְּלִשְׁתִּים׃ וּפְלִשְׁתִּים
and-Philistines (3) Philistines to-meet battle-line and-they-drew-up the-Elah

עֹמְדִים אֶל־הָהָר מִזֶּה וְיִשְׂרָאֵל עֹמְדִים אֶל־הָהָר
the-hill on ones-occupying and-Israel on-this-side the-hill on ones-occupying

מִזֶּה וְהַגַּיְא בֵּינֵיהֶם׃ וַיֵּצֵא אִישׁ־
man-of now-he-came-out (4) between-them and-the-valley on-other-side

הַבֵּנַיִם מִמַּחֲנוֹת פְּלִשְׁתִּים גָּלְיָת שְׁמוֹ מִגַּת
from-Gath name-of-him Goliath Philistines from-camps-of the-spaces-between

גָּבְהוֹ שֵׁשׁ אַמּוֹת וָזָרֶת׃ וְכוֹבַע נְחֹשֶׁת עַל־רֹאשׁוֹ
head-of-him on bronze and-helmet-of (5) and-span cubits six height-of-him

knows how to play the harp. He is a brave man and a warrior. He speaks well and is a fine-looking man. And the LORD is with him."
19Then Saul sent messengers to Jesse and said, "Send me your son David, who is with the sheep."
20So Jesse took a donkey loaded with bread, a skin of wine and a young goat and sent them with his son David to Saul.
21David came to Saul and entered his service. Saul liked him very much, and David became one of his armor-bearers.
22Then Saul sent word to Jesse, saying, "Allow David to remain in my service, for I am pleased with him."
23Whenever the spirit from God came upon Saul, David would take his harp and play. Then relief would come to Saul; he would feel better, and the evil spirit would leave him.

David and Goliath

17 Now the Philistines gathered their forces for war and assembled at Socoh in Judah. They pitched camp at Ephes Dammim, between Socoh and Azekah.
2Saul and the Israelites assembled and camped in the Valley of Elah and drew up their battle line to meet the Philistines.
3The Philistines occupied one hill and the Israelites another, with the valley between them.
4A champion named Goliath, who was from Gath, came out of the Philistine camp. He was over nine feet[l] tall.
5He had a bronze helmet

[l]4 Hebrew *was six cubits and a span* (about 3 meters)

וְשִׁרְי֥וֹן קַשְׂקַשִּׂ֖ים ה֣וּא לָב֑וּשׁ וּמִשְׁקַל֙ הַשִּׁרְי֔וֹן חֲמֵשֶׁת־ אֲלָפִ֥ים
thousands five-of the-coat and-weight-of wearing he scale-armors and-coat-of

שְׁקָלִ֖ים נְחֹֽשֶׁת׃ וּמִצְחַ֣ת נְחֹ֔שֶׁת עַל־ רַגְלָ֑יו וְכִיד֥וֹן נְחֹ֖שֶׁת
bronze and-javelin-of legs-of-him on bronze and-greave-of (6) bronze shekels

בֵּ֥ין כְּתֵפָֽיו׃ וְחֵ֣ץ חֲנִית֗וֹ כִּמְנוֹר֙ אֹֽרְגִ֔ים
ones-weaving like-rod-of spear-of-him and-shaft-of (7) shoulders-of-him between

וְלַהֶ֣בֶת חֲנִית֔וֹ שֵׁשׁ־ מֵא֥וֹת שְׁקָלִ֖ים בַּרְזֶ֑ל וְנֹשֵׂ֥א הַצִּנָּ֖ה
the-shield and-one-bearing iron shekels hundreds six spear-of-him and-point-of

הֹלֵ֥ךְ לְפָנָֽיו׃ וַֽיַּעֲמֹ֗ד וַיִּקְרָא֙ אֶל־מַעַרְכֹ֣ת יִשְׂרָאֵ֔ל
Israel ranks-of to and-he-shouted and-he-stood (8) ahead-of-him going

וַיֹּ֣אמֶר לָהֶ֔ם לָ֥מָּה תֵצְא֖וּ לַעֲרֹ֣ךְ מִלְחָמָ֑ה הֲל֧וֹא אָנֹכִ֣י הַפְּלִשְׁתִּ֗י
the-Philistine I not? battle to-line-up you-come-out why? to-them and-he-said

וְאַתֶּם֙ עֲבָדִ֣ים לְשָׁא֔וּל בְּרוּ־ לָכֶ֥ם אִ֖ישׁ וְיֵרֵ֥ד אֵלָֽי׃
to-me and-have-him-come-down man for-you choose! of-Saul servants and-you

אִם־ יוּכַ֞ל לְהִלָּחֵ֤ם אִתִּי֙ וְהִכָּ֔נִי וְהָיִ֥ינוּ לָכֶ֖ם
to-you then-we-will-become and-he-kills-me with-me to-fight he-is-able if (9)

לַעֲבָדִ֑ים וְאִם־ אֲנִ֤י אֽוּכַל־ לוֹ֙ וְהִכִּיתִ֔יו וִהְיִ֤יתֶם
then-you-will-become and-I-kill-him over-him I-overcome I but-if as-subjects

לָ֙נוּ֙ לַעֲבָדִ֔ים וַעֲבַדְתֶּ֖ם אֹתָֽנוּ׃ וַיֹּ֙אמֶר֙ הַפְּלִשְׁתִּ֔י אֲנִ֗י
I the-Philistine then-he-said (10) us and-you-will-serve as-subjects to-us

חֵרַ֛פְתִּי אֶת־ מַעַרְכ֥וֹת יִשְׂרָאֵ֖ל הַיּ֣וֹם הַזֶּ֑ה תְּנוּ־ לִ֣י אִ֔ישׁ וְנִֽלָּחֲמָ֖ה
and-let-us-fight man to-me! give! the-this the-day Israel ranks-of *** I-defy

יָֽחַד׃ וַיִּשְׁמַ֤ע שָׁאוּל֙ וְכָל־ יִשְׂרָאֵ֔ל אֶת־ דִּבְרֵ֥י
words-of *** Israel and-all-of Saul when-he-heard (11) each-other

הַפְּלִשְׁתִּ֖י הָאֵ֑לֶּה וַיֵּחַ֥תּוּ וַיִּרְא֖וּ מְאֹֽד׃
very and-they-were-terrified then-they-were-dismayed the-these the-Philistine

וְדָוִ֡ד בֶּן־ אִישׁ֩ אֶפְרָתִ֨י הַזֶּ֜ה מִבֵּ֧ית לֶ֣חֶם יְהוּדָ֗ה
Judah Lehem-of from-Beth the-this Ephrathite man son-of now-David (12)

וּשְׁמ֣וֹ יִשַׁ֔י וְל֖וֹ שְׁמֹנָ֣ה בָנִ֑ים וְהָאִישׁ֙ בִּימֵ֣י שָׁא֔וּל
Saul in-days-of and-the-man sons eight and-to-him Jesse and-name-of-him

זָקֵ֖ן בָּ֥א בַאֲנָשִֽׁים׃ וַיֵּלְכ֞וּ שְׁלֹ֤שֶׁת בְּנֵֽי־
sons-of three-of and-they-followed (13) among-men he-was-advanced he-was-old

יִשַׁי֙ הַגְּדֹלִ֔ים הָלְכ֥וּ אַחֲרֵֽי־ שָׁא֖וּל לַמִּלְחָמָ֑ה וְשֵׁ֣ם ׀ שְׁלֹ֣שֶׁת
three-of and-name-of to-the-war Saul after they-went the-old-ones Jesse

בָּנָ֗יו אֲשֶׁ֤ר הָֽלְכוּ֙ בַּמִּלְחָמָ֔ה אֱלִיאָ֣ב הַבְּכ֔וֹר וּמִשְׁנֵ֙הוּ֙
and-second-of-him the-firstborn Eliab to-the-war they-went who sons-of-him

אֲבִֽינָדָ֔ב וְהַשְּׁלִשִׁ֖י שַׁמָּֽה׃ וְדָוִ֖ד ה֣וּא הַקָּטָ֑ן וּשְׁלֹשָׁה֙
and-three the-youngest he now-David (14) Shammah and-the-third Abinadab

on his head and wore a coat of
scale armor of bronze weighing five thousand shekels[m]; 6on
his legs he wore bronze
greaves, and a bronze javelin
was slung on his back. 7His
spear shaft was like a weaver's
rod, and its iron point
weighed six hundred shekels.[o]
His shield bearer went ahead
of him.
8Goliath stood and shouted
to the ranks of Israel, "Why do
you come out and line up for
battle? Am I not a Philistine,
and are you not the servants of
Saul? Choose a man and have
him come down to me. 9If he is
able to fight and kill me, we
will become your subjects; but
if I overcome him and kill
him, you will become our subjects and serve us." 10Then the
Philistine said, "This day I
defy the ranks of Israel! Give
me a man and let us fight each
other." 11On hearing the Philistine's words, Saul and all the
Israelites were dismayed and
terrified.
12Now David was the son of
an Ephrathite named Jesse,
who was from Bethlehem in
Judah. Jesse had eight sons,
and in Saul's time he was old
and well advanced in years.
13Jesse's three oldest sons had
followed Saul to the war: The
firstborn was Eliab; the second, Abinadab; and the third,
Shammah. 14David was the

[m]5 That is, about 125 pounds (about 57 kilograms)
[o]7 That is, about 15 pounds (about 7 kilograms)
[p]17 That is, probably about 1/2 bushel (about 22 liters)

°7 ק ועץ

הַגְּדֹלִים הָלְכוּ אַחֲרֵי שָׁאוּל׃ וְדָוִד הֹלֵךְ וָשָׁב
and-returning going but-David (15) Saul after they-followed the-old-ones

מֵעַל שָׁאוּל לִרְעוֹת אֶת־ צֹאן אָבִיו בֵּית־ לָחֶם׃
Lehem Beth father-of-him sheep-of *** to-tend Saul from-with

וַיִּגַּשׁ הַפְּלִשְׁתִּי הַשְׁכֵּם וְהַעֲרֵב
and-to-be-evening to-be-morning the-Philistine and-he-came-forward (16)

וַיִּתְיַצֵּב אַרְבָּעִים יוֹם׃ וַיֹּאמֶר יִשַׁי לְדָוִד בְּנוֹ קַח־
take! son-of-him to-David Jesse now-he-said (17) day forty and-he-took-stand

נָא לְאַחֶיךָ אֵיפַת הַקָּלִיא הַזֶּה וַעֲשָׂרָה לֶחֶם
bread and-ten the-this the-roasted-grain ephah-of to-brothers-of-you now!

הַזֶּה וְהָרֵץ הַמַּחֲנֶה לְאַחֶיךָ׃ וְאֵת עֲשֶׂרֶת חֲרִצֵי
pieces-of ten and (18) to-brothers-of-you the-camp and-hurry! the-this

הֶחָלָב הָאֵלֶּה תָּבִיא לְשַׂר־ הָאָלֶף וְאֶת־ אַחֶיךָ
brothers-of-you and the-unit to-commander-of you-take the-these the-cheese

תִּפְקֹד לְשָׁלוֹם וְאֶת־ עֲרֻבָּתָם תִּקָּח׃ וְשָׁאוּל
now-Saul (19) you-bring-back assurance-of-them and about-welfare you-see

וְהֵמָּה וְכָל־ אִישׁ יִשְׂרָאֵל בְּעֵמֶק הָאֵלָה נִלְחָמִים עִם־
against ones-fighting the-Elah in-Valley-of Israel man-of and-all-of and-they

פְלִשְׁתִּים׃ וַיַּשְׁכֵּם דָּוִד בַּבֹּקֶר וַיִּטֹּשׁ אֶת־ הַצֹּאן
the-flock *** and-he-left in-the-morning David so-he-rose (20) Philistines

עַל־ שֹׁמֵר וַיִּשָּׂא וַיֵּלֶךְ כַּאֲשֶׁר צִוָּהוּ
he-directed-him just-as and-he-set-out and-he-loaded-up one-shepherding with

יִשָׁי וַיָּבֹא הַמַּעְגָּלָה וְהַחַיִל הַיֹּצֵא אֶל־ הַמַּעֲרָכָה
the-position to the-one-going-out and-the-army the-camp and-he-reached Jesse

וְהֵרֵעוּ בַּמִּלְחָמָה׃ וַתַּעֲרֹךְ יִשְׂרָאֵל וּפְלִשְׁתִּים
and-Philistines Israel and-he-drew-up (21) for-the-battle and-they-shouted

מַעֲרָכָה לִקְרַאת מַעֲרָכָה׃ וַיִּטֹּשׁ דָּוִד אֶת־ הַכֵּלִים מֵעָלָיו עַל־
with from-with-him the-things *** David and-he-left (22) line to-face line

יַד שׁוֹמֵר הַכֵּלִים וַיָּרָץ הַמַּעֲרָכָה וַיָּבֹא
and-he-came the-battle-line and-he-ran the-supplies one-keeping hand-of

וַיִּשְׁאַל לְאֶחָיו לְשָׁלוֹם׃ וְהוּא ׀ מְדַבֵּר עִמָּם
with-them talking and-he (23) for-peace to-brothers-of-him and-he-greeted

וְהִנֵּה אִישׁ הַבֵּנַיִם עוֹלֶה גָּלְיָת הַפְּלִשְׁתִּי
the-Philistine Goliath stepping-out the-spaces-between man-of and-see!

שְׁמוֹ מִגַּת מִמַּעַרְוֹת פְּלִשְׁתִּים וַיְדַבֵּר כַּדְּבָרִים
as-the-words and-he-shouted Philistines from-lines-of from-Gath name-of-him

הָאֵלֶּה וַיִּשְׁמַע דָּוִד׃ וְכֹל אִישׁ יִשְׂרָאֵל בִּרְאוֹתָם
when-to-see-them Israel man-of and-every-of (24) David and-he-heard the-these

youngest. The three oldest followed Saul, 15but David went
back and forth from Saul to
tend his father's sheep at
Bethlehem.
16For forty days the Philistine came forward every
morning and evening and
took his stand.
17Now Jesse said to his son
David, "Take this ephah[p] of
roasted grain and these ten
loaves of bread for your brothers and hurry to their camp.
18Take along these ten cheeses
to the commander of their
unit.[q] See how your brothers
are and bring back some as-
surance[r] from them. 19They
are with Saul and all the men
of Israel in the Valley of Elah,
fighting against the Philistines."
20Early in the morning David left the flock with a shepherd, loaded up and set out, as
Jesse had directed. He reached
the camp as the army was going out to its battle positions,
shouting the war cry. 21Israel
and the Philistines were drawing up their lines facing each
other. 22David left his things
with the keeper of supplies,
ran to the battle lines and
greeted his brothers. 23As he
was talking with them,
Goliath, the Philistine champion from Gath, stepped out
from his lines and shouted his
usual defiance, and David
heard it. 24When the Israelites

q18 Hebrew *thousand*
r18 Or *some token;* or *some pledge of spoils*

°23 ק ממערכות

אֶת־ הָאִישׁ וַיָּנֻסוּ מִפָּנָיו וַיִּירְאוּ מְאֹד׃
greatly and-they-feared from-before-him then-they-ran the-man ***

וַיֹּאמֶר ׀ אִישׁ יִשְׂרָאֵל הַרְּאִיתֶם הָאִישׁ הָעֹלֶה הַזֶּה
the-this the-one-coming-out the-man you-see? Israel man-of now-he-said (25)

כִּי לְחָרֵף אֶת־ יִשְׂרָאֵל עֹלֶה וְהָיָה הָאִישׁ אֲשֶׁר־ יַכֶּנּוּ
he-kills-him who the-man and-he-will-be coming-out Israel *** to-defy that

יַעְשְׁרֶנּוּ הַמֶּלֶךְ ׀ עֹשֶׁר גָּדוֹל וְאֶת־ בִּתּוֹ יִתֶּן־ לוֹ
to-him he-will-give daughter-of-him and great wealth the-king he-will-give-him

וְאֵת בֵּית אָבִיו יַעֲשֶׂה חָפְשִׁי בְּיִשְׂרָאֵל׃ וַיֹּאמֶר
and-he-asked (26) in-Israel tax-exempt he-will-make father-of-him family-of and

דָּוִד אֶל־ הָאֲנָשִׁים הָעֹמְדִים עִמּוֹ לֵאמֹר מַה־ יֵּעָשֶׂה
he-will-be-done what? to-say near-him the-ones-standing the-men to David

לָאִישׁ אֲשֶׁר יַכֶּה אֶת־ הַפְּלִשְׁתִּי הַלָּז וְהֵסִיר חֶרְפָּה
disgrace and-he-removes the-this the-Philistine *** he-kills who for-the-man

מֵעַל יִשְׂרָאֵל כִּי מִי הַפְּלִשְׁתִּי הֶעָרֵל הַזֶּה כִּי
that the-this the-uncircumcised the-Philistine who for Israel from-on

חֵרֵף מַעַרְכוֹת אֱלֹהִים חַיִּים׃ וַיֹּאמֶר לוֹ הָעָם
the-people to-him and-he-told (27) ones-living God armies-of he-defies

כַּדָּבָר הַזֶּה לֵאמֹר כֹּה יֵעָשֶׂה לָאִישׁ אֲשֶׁר יַכֶּנּוּ׃
he-kills-him who for-the-man he-will-be-done this to-say the-this as-the-saying

וַיִּשְׁמַע אֱלִיאָב אָחִיו הַגָּדוֹל בְּדַבְּרוֹ אֶל־הָאֲנָשִׁים
the-men to when-to-speak-him the-old brother-of-him Eliab when-he-heard (28)

וַיִּחַר־ אַף אֱלִיאָב בְּדָוִד וַיֹּאמֶר ׀ לָמָּה־ זֶּה יָרַדְתָּ
you-came-down this why? and-he-asked at-David Eliab anger-of then-he-burned

וְעַל־ מִי נָטַשְׁתָּ מְעַט הַצֹּאן הָהֵנָּה בַּמִּדְבָּר אֲנִי יָדַעְתִּי
I-know I in-the-desert the-those the-sheep few-of you-left whom? and-with

אֶת־ זְדֹנְךָ וְאֵת רֹעַ לְבָבֶךָ כִּי לְמַעַן רְאוֹת
to-watch in-order-to only heart-of-you wickedness-of and conceit-of-you ***

הַמִּלְחָמָה יָרָדְתָּ׃ וַיֹּאמֶר דָּוִד מֶה עָשִׂיתִי עָתָּה הֲלוֹא דָּבָר
word not? now I-did what? David and-he-said (29) you-came-down the-battle

הוּא׃ וַיִּסֹּב מֵאֶצְלוֹ אֶל־ מוּל אַחֵר וַיֹּאמֶר
and-he-asked another face-of to from-with-him then-he-turned (30) he

כַּדָּבָר הַזֶּה וַיְשִׁבֻהוּ הָעָם דָּבָר כַּדָּבָר
as-the-answer answer the-people and-they-answered-him the-same as-the-matter

הָרִאשׁוֹן׃ וַיִּשָּׁמְעוּ הַדְּבָרִים אֲשֶׁר דִּבֶּר דָּוִד
David he-said that the-words and-they-were-overheard (31) the-previous

וַיַּגִּדוּ לִפְנֵי־ שָׁאוּל וַיִּקָּחֵהוּ׃ וַיֹּאמֶר דָּוִד
David and-he-said (32) and-he-sent-for-him Saul to-before and-they-reported

saw the man, they all ran from
him in great fear.
[25]Now the Israelites had
been saying, "Do you see how
this man keeps coming out?
He comes out to defy Israel.
The king will give great
wealth to the man who kills
him. He will also give him his
daughter in marriage and will
exempt his father's family
from taxes in Israel."
[26]David asked the men
standing near him, "What will
be done for the man who kills
this Philistine and removes
this disgrace from Israel? Who
is this uncircumcised Philistine that he should defy the armies of the living God?"
[27]They repeated to him what
they had been saying and told
him, "This is what will be
done for the man who kills
him."
[28]When Eliab, David's oldest
brother, heard him speaking
with the men, he burned with
anger at him and asked, "Why
have you come down here?
And with whom did you leave
those few sheep in the desert?
I know how conceited you are
and how wicked your heart is;
you came down only to watch
the battle."
[29]"Now what have I done?"
said David. "Can't I even
speak?" [30]He then turned
away to someone else and
brought up the same matter,
and the men answered him as
before. [31]What David said was
overheard and reported to
Saul, and Saul sent for him.
[32]David said to Saul, "Let no

*31 Most mss have *hireq* under the *yod* (יִ).

אֶל־שָׁאוּל אַל־יִפֹּל לֵב־אָדָם עָלָיו עַבְדְּךָ
servant-of-you on-account-of-him anyone heart-of let-him-lose not Saul to

יֵלֵךְ וְנִלְחַם עִם־הַפְּלִשְׁתִּי הַזֶּה׃ וַיֹּאמֶר
and-he-replied (33) the-this the-Philistine with and-he-will-fight he-will-go

שָׁאוּל אֶל־דָּוִד לֹא תוּכַל לָלֶכֶת אֶל־הַפְּלִשְׁתִּי הַזֶּה
the-this the-Philistine against to-go-out you-are-able not David to Saul

לְהִלָּחֵם עִמּוֹ כִּי־נַעַר אַתָּה וְהוּא אִישׁ מִלְחָמָה מִנְּעֻרָיו׃
from-youths-of-him fighting man-of and-he you boy for with-him to-fight

וַיֹּאמֶר דָּוִד אֶל־שָׁאוּל רֹעֶה הָיָה עַבְדְּךָ
servant-of-you he-is one-keeping Saul to David but-he-said (34)

לְאָבִיו בַּצֹּאן וּבָא הָאֲרִי וְאֶת־הַדּוֹב
the-bear or the-lion when-he-came over-the-sheep for-father-of-him

וְנָשָׂא שֶׂה מֵהָעֵדֶר׃ וְיָצָאתִי אַחֲרָיו
after-him then-I-went (35) from-the-flock sheep and-he-carried-off

וְהִכִּתִיו וְהִצַּלְתִּי מִפִּיו וַיָּקָם עָלָי
on-me when-he-turned from-mouth-of-him and-I-rescued and-I-struck-him

וְהֶחֱזַקְתִּי בִּזְקָנוֹ וְהִכִּתִיו וַהֲמִיתִּיו׃ גַּם אֶת־
*** both (36) and-I-killed-him and-I-struck-him by-hair-of-him then-I-seized

הָאֲרִי גַּם־הַדּוֹב הִכָּה עַבְדֶּךָ וְהָיָה הַפְּלִשְׁתִּי
the-Philistine and-he-will-be servant-of-you he-killed the-bear and the-lion

הֶעָרֵל הַזֶּה כְּאַחַד מֵהֶם כִּי חֵרֵף מַעַרְכֹת אֱלֹהִים
God armies-of he-defied for of-them like-one the-this the-uncircumcised

חַיִּים׃ וַיֹּאמֶר דָּוִד יְהוָה אֲשֶׁר הִצִּלַנִי מִיַּד
from-paw-of he-delivered-me who Yahweh David and-he-said (37) ones-living

הָאֲרִי וּמִיַּד הַדֹּב הוּא יַצִּילֵנִי מִיַּד
from-hand-of he-will-deliver-me he the-bear and-from-paw-of the-lion

הַפְּלִשְׁתִּי הַזֶּה וַיֹּאמֶר שָׁאוּל אֶל־דָּוִד לֵךְ וַיהוָה יִהְיֶה
may-he-be and-Yahweh go! David to Saul and-he-said the-this the-Philistine

עִמָּךְ׃ וַיַּלְבֵּשׁ שָׁאוּל אֶת־דָּוִד מַדָּיו וְנָתַן
and-he-put tunics-of-him David *** Saul then-he-dressed (38) with-you

קוֹבַע נְחֹשֶׁת עַל־רֹאשׁוֹ וַיַּלְבֵּשׁ אֹתוֹ שִׁרְיוֹן׃
coat-of-armor him and-he-dressed head-of-him on bronze helmet-of

וַיַּחְגֹּר דָּוִד אֶת־חַרְבּוֹ מֵעַל לְמַדָּיו
to-tunics-of-him on-over sword-of-him *** David and-he-fastened (39)

וַיֹּאֶל לָלֶכֶת כִּי לֹא־נִסָּה וַיֹּאמֶר דָּוִד אֶל־שָׁאוּל לֹא אוּכַל
I-can not Saul to David and-he-said he-tested not for to-walk and-he-tried

לָלֶכֶת בָּאֵלֶּה כִּי לֹא נִסִּיתִי וַיְסִרֵם דָּוִד מֵעָלָיו׃
from-on-him David so-he-took-off-them I-tested not for in-the-these to-go

one lose heart on account of
this Philistine; your servant
will go and fight him."
33 Saul replied, "You are not
able to go out against this Philistine and fight him; you are
only a boy, and he has been a
fighting man from his youth."
34 But David said to Saul,
"Your servant has been keeping his father's sheep. When a
lion or a bear came and carried
off a sheep from the flock, 35 I
went after it, struck it and rescued the sheep from its mouth.
When it turned on me, I seized
it by its hair, struck it and
killed it. 36 Your servant has
killed both the lion and the
bear; this uncircumcised Philistine will be like one of them,
because he has defied the armies of the living God. 37 The
LORD who delivered me from
the paw of the lion and the
paw of the bear will deliver me
from the hand of this Philistine."
Saul said to David, "Go, and
the LORD be with you."
38 Then Saul dressed David
in his own tunic. He put a coat
of armor on him and a bronze
helmet on his head. 39 David
fastened on his sword over the
tunic and tried walking
around, because he was not
used to them.
"I cannot go in these," he
said to Saul, "because I am not
used to them." So he took

וַיִּקַּח מַקְלוֹ בְּיָדוֹ וַיִּבְחַר־ לוֹ חֲמִשָּׁה
five for-him and-he-chose in-hand-of-him staff-of-him then-he-took (40)

חַלֻּקֵי־ אֲבָנִים׀ מִן־ הַנַּחַל וַיָּשֶׂם אֹתָם בִּכְלִי הָרֹעִים
ones-herding in-bag-of them and-he-put the-stream from stones smooth-ones-of

אֲשֶׁר־ לוֹ וּבַיַּלְקוּט וְקַלְעוֹ בְיָדוֹ וַיִּגַּשׁ
and-he-approached in-hand-of-him and-sling-of-him even-in-the-pouch to-him that

אֶל־ הַפְּלִשְׁתִּי׃ וַיֵּלֶךְ הַפְּלִשְׁתִּי הֹלֵךְ וְקָרֵב אֶל־ דָּוִד
David to and-closer coming the-Philistine and-he-came (41) the-Philistine to

וְהָאִישׁ נֹשֵׂא הַצִּנָּה לְפָנָיו׃ וַיַּבֵּט
and-he-looked-over (42) in-front-of-him the-shield bearing and-the-man

הַפְּלִשְׁתִּי וַיִּרְאֶה אֶת־ דָּוִד וַיִּבְזֵהוּ כִּי־ הָיָה נַעַר
boy he-was for and-he-despised-him David *** and-he-saw the-Philistine

וְאַדְמֹנִי עִם־ יְפֵה מַרְאֶה׃ וַיֹּאמֶר הַפְּלִשְׁתִּי אֶל־ דָּוִד
David to the-Philistine and-he-said (43) feature handsome-of with and-ruddy

הֲכֶלֶב אָנֹכִי כִּי־אַתָּה בָא־ אֵלַי בַּמַּקְלוֹת וַיְקַלֵּל הַפְּלִשְׁתִּי
the-Philistine and-he-cursed with-the-sticks at-me coming you that I dog?

אֶת־ דָּוִד בֵּאלֹהָיו׃ וַיֹּאמֶר הַפְּלִשְׁתִּי אֶל־ דָּוִד לְכָה
come! David to the-Philistine and-he-said (44) by-gods-of-him David ***

אֵלַי וְאֶתְּנָה אֶת־ בְּשָׂרְךָ לְעוֹף הַשָּׁמַיִם וּלְבֶהֱמַת
and-to-beast-of the-airs to-bird-of flesh-of-you *** and-I-will-give to-me

הַשָּׂדֶה׃ וַיֹּאמֶר דָּוִד אֶל־ הַפְּלִשְׁתִּי אַתָּה בָּא אֵלַי
against-me coming you the-Philistine to David and-he-said (45) the-field

בְּחֶרֶב וּבַחֲנִית וּבְכִידוֹן וְאָנֹכִי בָא־ אֵלֶיךָ בְּשֵׁם
in-name-of against-you coming but-I and-with-javelin and-with-spear with-sword

יְהוָה צְבָאוֹת אֱלֹהֵי מַעַרְכוֹת יִשְׂרָאֵל אֲשֶׁר חֵרַפְתָּ׃ הַיּוֹם
the-day (46) you-defied whom Israel armies-of God-of Hosts Yahweh-of

הַזֶּה יְסַגֶּרְךָ יְהוָה בְּיָדִי וְהִכִּיתִךָ
and-I-will-strike-down-you to-hand-of-me Yahweh he-will-hand-over-you the-this

וַהֲסִרֹתִי אֶת־ רֹאשְׁךָ מֵעָלֶיךָ וְנָתַתִּי פֶּגֶר
carcass-of and-I-will-give from-on-you head-of-you *** and-I-will-cut-off

מַחֲנֵה פְלִשְׁתִּים הַיּוֹם הַזֶּה לְעוֹף הַשָּׁמַיִם וּלְחַיַּת
and-to-beast-of the-airs to-bird-of the-this the-day Philistines army-of

הָאָרֶץ וְיֵדְעוּ כָּל־ הָאָרֶץ כִּי יֵשׁ אֱלֹהִים לְיִשְׂרָאֵל׃
in-Israel God there-is that the-world whole-of and-they-will-know the-earth

וְיֵדְעוּ כָּל־ הַקָּהָל הַזֶּה כִּי־ לֹא בְּחֶרֶב
by-sword not that the-this the-gathering all-of and-they-will-know (47)

וּבַחֲנִית יְהוֹשִׁיעַ יְהוָה כִּי לַיהוָה הַמִּלְחָמָה וְנָתַן אֶתְכֶם
you and-he-will-give the-battle to-Yahweh for Yahweh he-saves or-by-spear

them off. 40 Then he took his
staff in his hand, chose five
smooth stones from the
stream, put them in the pouch
of his shepherd's bag and,
with his sling in his hand, approached the Philistine.
41 Meanwhile, the Philistine,
with his shield bearer in front
of him, kept coming closer to
David. 42 He looked David over
and saw that he was only a
boy, ruddy and handsome,
and he despised him. 43 He said
to David, "Am I a dog, that
you come at me with sticks?"
And the Philistine cursed David by his gods. 44 "Come
here," he said, "and I'll give
your flesh to the birds of the
air and the beasts of the field!"
45 David said to the Philistine, "You come against me
with sword and spear and
javelin, but I come against you
in the name of the LORD Almighty, the God of the armies
of Israel, whom you have
defied. 46 This day the LORD
will hand you over to me, and
I'll strike you down and cut off
your head. Today I will give
the carcasses of the Philistine
army to the birds of the air
and the beasts of the earth,
and the whole world will
know that there is a God in
Israel. 47 All those gathered
here will know that it is not by
sword or spear that the LORD
saves; for the battle is the
LORD's, and he will give all of

בְּיָדֵנוּ׃ וְהָיָה כִּי־ קָם הַפְּלִשְׁתִּי וַיֵּלֶךְ
and-he-moved the-Philistine he-rose as and-he-was (48) into-hand-of-us

וַיִּקְרַב לִקְרַאת דָּוִד וַיְמַהֵר דָּוִד וַיָּרָץ
and-he-ran David then-he-was-quick David to-attack and-he-came-closer

הַמַּעֲרָכָה לִקְרַאת הַפְּלִשְׁתִּי׃ וַיִּשְׁלַח דָּוִד אֶת־
*** David and-he-reached (49) the-Philistine to-meet the-battle-line

יָדוֹ אֶל־ הַכְּלִי וַיִּקַּח מִשָּׁם אֶבֶן וַיְקַלַּע
and-he-slung stone from-there and-he-took the-bag into hand-of-him

וַיַּךְ אֶת־ הַפְּלִשְׁתִּי אֶל־ מִצְחוֹ וַתִּטְבַּע הָאֶבֶן
the-stone and-she-sank forehead-of-him on the-Philistine *** and-he-struck

בְּמִצְחוֹ וַיִּפֹּל עַל־ פָּנָיו אָרְצָה׃ וַיֶּחֱזַק
so-he-triumphed (50) on-ground faces-of-him on and-he-fell into-forehead-of-him

דָּוִד מִן־ הַפְּלִשְׁתִּי בַּקֶּלַע וּבָאֶבֶן וַיַּךְ
and-he-struck-down and-with-the-stone with-the-sling the-Philistine over David

אֶת־ הַפְּלִשְׁתִּי וַיְמִיתֵהוּ וְחֶרֶב אֵין בְּיַד־ דָּוִד׃
David in-hand-of not and-sword and-he-killed-him the-Philistine ***

וַיָּרָץ דָּוִד וַיַּעֲמֹד אֶל־ הַפְּלִשְׁתִּי וַיִּקַּח אֶת־
*** and-he-took-hold the-Philistine over and-he-stood David and-he-ran (51)

חַרְבּוֹ וַיִּשְׁלְפָהּ מִתַּעְרָהּ וַיְמֹתְתֵהוּ
and-he-killed-him from-scabbard-of-her and-he-drew-her sword-of-him

וַיִּכְרָת־ בָּהּ אֶת־ רֹאשׁוֹ וַיִּרְאוּ הַפְּלִשְׁתִּים כִּי־
that the-Philistines when-they-saw head-of-him *** with-her and-he-cut-off

מֵת גִּבּוֹרָם וַיָּנֻסוּ׃ וַיָּקֻמוּ אַנְשֵׁי
men-of then-they-surged-forward (52) then-they-ran hero-of-them he-was-dead

יִשְׂרָאֵל וִיהוּדָה וַיָּרִעוּ וַיִּרְדְּפוּ אֶת־ הַפְּלִשְׁתִּים עַד־
to the-Philistines *** and-they-pursued and-they-shouted and-Judah Israel

בּוֹאֲךָ גַיְא וְעַד שַׁעֲרֵי עֶקְרוֹן וַיִּפְּלוּ חַלְלֵי
ones-dead-of and-they-were-strewn Ekron gates-of and-to valley to-enter-you

פְלִשְׁתִּים בְּדֶרֶךְ שַׁעֲרַיִם וְעַד־ גַּת וְעַד־ עֶקְרוֹן*
*Ekron and-to Gath even-to Shaaraim along-road-of Philistines

וַיָּשֻׁבוּ בְּנֵי יִשְׂרָאֵל מִדְּלֹק אַחֲרֵי פְלִשְׁתִּים
Philistines after from-to-chase Israel sons-of when-they-returned (53)

וַיָּשֹׁסּוּ אֶת־ מַחֲנֵיהֶם׃ וַיִּקַּח דָּוִד אֶת־ רֹאשׁ
head-of *** David and-he-took (54) camps-of-them *** then-they-plundered

הַפְּלִשְׁתִּי וַיְבִאֵהוּ יְרוּשָׁלִָם וְאֶת־ כֵּלָיו שָׂם
he-put weapons-of-him and Jerusalem and-he-brought-him the-Philistine

בְּאָהֳלוֹ׃ וְכִרְאוֹת שָׁאוּל אֶת־ דָּוִד יֹצֵא לִקְרַאת
to-meet going-out David *** Saul and-as-to-watch (55) in-tent-of-him

you into our hands."
48As the Philistine moved
closer to attack him, David ran
quickly toward the battle line
to meet him. 49Reaching into
his bag and taking out a stone,
he slung it and struck the Philistine on the forehead. The
stone sank into his forehead,
and he fell facedown on the
ground.
50So David triumphed over
the Philistine with a sling and
a stone; without a sword in his
hand he struck down the Philistine and killed him.
51David ran and stood over
him. He took hold of the Philistine's sword and drew it
from the scabbard. After he
killed him, he cut off his head
with the sword.
When the Philistines saw
that their hero was dead, they
turned and ran. 52Then the
men of Israel and Judah
surged forward with a shout
and pursued the Philistines to
the entrance of Gath[s] and to
the gates of Ekron. Their dead
were strewn along the Shaaraim road to Gath and Ekron.
53When the Israelites returned
from chasing the Philistines,
they plundered their camp.
54David took the Philistine's
head and brought it to Jerusalem, and he put the Philistine's weapons in his own
tent.
55As Saul watched David going out to meet the Philistine,

s52 Some Septuagint manuscripts; Hebrew *a valley*

*52 Most mss end verse 52 with *sopb pasuq* (:).

הַפְּלִשְׁתִּי אָמַר אֶל־אַבְנֵר שַׂר הַצָּבָא בֶּן־מִי־זֶה

that whom? son-of the-army commander-of Abner to he-said the-Philistine

הַנַּעַר אַבְנֵר וַיֹּאמֶר אַבְנֵר חֵי־נַפְשְׁךָ הַמֶּלֶךְ אִם־

not the-king soul-of-you life-of Abner and-he-replied Abner the-young-man

יָדָעְתִּי׃ וַיֹּאמֶר הַמֶּלֶךְ שְׁאַל אַתָּה בֶּן־מִי־זֶה הָעָלֶם׃

the-young-man this whom? son-of you find-out! the-king and-he-said (56) I-know

וּכְשׁוּב דָּוִד מֵהַכּוֹת אֶת־הַפְּלִשְׁתִּי וַיִּקַּח אֹתוֹ

him then-he-took the-Philistine *** from-to-kill David and-as-to-return (57)

אַבְנֵר וַיְבִאֵהוּ לִפְנֵי שָׁאוּל וְרֹאשׁ הַפְּלִשְׁתִּי בְּיָדוֹ׃

in-hand-of-him the-Philistine and-head-of Saul before and-he-brought-him Abner

וַיֹּאמֶר אֵלָיו שָׁאוּל בֶּן־מִי אַתָּה הַנַּעַר וַיֹּאמֶר

and-he-said the-young-man you whom? son-of Saul to-him and-he-asked (58)

דָּוִד בֶּן־עַבְדְּךָ יִשַׁי בֵּית הַלַּחְמִי׃ וַיְהִי

and-he-was (18:1) the-Bethlehemite Jesse servant-of-you son-of David

כְּכַלֹּתוֹ לְדַבֵּר אֶל־שָׁאוּל וְנֶפֶשׁ יְהוֹנָתָן נִקְשְׁרָה

she-became-one Jonathan then-spirit-of Saul with to-talk after-to-finish-him

בְּנֶפֶשׁ דָּוִד וַיֶּאֱהָבוֹ° יְהוֹנָתָן כְּנַפְשׁוֹ׃

as-self-of-him Jonathan and-he-loved-him David with-spirit-of

וַיִּקָּחֵהוּ שָׁאוּל בַּיּוֹם הַהוּא וְלֹא נְתָנוֹ לָשׁוּב

to-return he-let-him and-not the-that from-the-day Saul and-he-kept-him (2)

בֵּית אָבִיו׃ וַיִּכְרֹת יְהוֹנָתָן וְדָוִד בְּרִית

covenant with-David Jonathan and-he-made (3) father-of-him house-of

בְּאַהֲבָתוֹ אֹתוֹ כְּנַפְשׁוֹ׃ וַיִּתְפַּשֵּׁט יְהוֹנָתָן אֶת־

*** Jonathan and-he-took-off (4) as-self-of-him him because-to-love-him

הַמְּעִיל אֲשֶׁר עָלָיו וַיִּתְּנֵהוּ לְדָוִד וּמַדָּיו וְעַד־

and-even and-tunics-of-him to-David and-he-gave-him on-him that the-robe

חַרְבּוֹ וְעַד־קַשְׁתּוֹ וְעַד־חֲגֹרוֹ׃ וַיֵּצֵא

when-he-went-out (5) belt-of-him and-even bow-of-him and-even sword-of-him

דָוִד בְּכֹל° אֲשֶׁר יִשְׁלָחֶנּוּ שָׁאוּל יַשְׂכִּיל וַיְשִׂמֵהוּ

and-he-set-him he-did-successfully Saul he-sent-him that in-anything David

שָׁאוּל עַל אַנְשֵׁי הַמִּלְחָמָה וַיִּיטַב בְּעֵינֵי כָל־הָעָם

the-people all-of in-eyes-of and-he-was-pleasing the-army men-of over Saul

וְגַם בְּעֵינֵי עַבְדֵי שָׁאוּל׃ וַיְהִי בְּבוֹאָם

when-to-return-them and-he-was (6) Saul officers-of in-eyes-of and-also

בְּשׁוּב דָּוִד מֵהַכּוֹת אֶת־הַפְּלִשְׁתִּי וַתֵּצֶאנָה

then-they-came-out the-Philistine *** from-to-kill David after-to-come-back

הַנָּשִׁים מִכָּל־עָרֵי יִשְׂרָאֵל לָשׁוּר וְהַמְּחֹלוֹת לִקְרַאת שָׁאוּל

Saul to-meet and-the-dances to-sing Israel towns-of from-all-of the-women

°1 ק ויאהבהו

°6 ק לשיר

he said to Abner, commander of the army, "Abner, whose son is that young man?"

Abner replied, "As surely as you live, O king, I don't know."

[56]The king said, "Find out whose son this young man is."

[57]As soon as David returned from killing the Philistine, Abner took him and brought him before Saul, with David still holding the Philistine's head.

[58]"Whose son are you, young man?" Saul asked him.

David said, "I am the son of your servant Jesse of Bethlehem."

Saul's Jealousy of David

18 After David had finished talking with Saul, Jonathan became one in spirit with David, and he loved him as himself. [2]From that day Saul kept David with him and did not let him return to his father's house. [3]And Jonathan made a covenant with David because he loved him as himself. [4]Jonathan took off the robe he was wearing and gave it to David, along with his tunic, and even his sword, his bow and his belt.

[5]Whatever Saul sent him to do, David did it so successfully[t] that Saul gave him a high rank in the army. This pleased all the people, and Saul's officers as well.

[6]When the men were returning home after David had killed the Philistine, the women came out from all the towns of Israel to meet King

[t]5 Or *wisely*

הַמֶּ֫לֶךְ בְּתֻפִּים בְּשִׂמְחָה וּבְשָׁלִשִׁים׃ (7) וַֽתַּעֲנֶינָה
and-they-sang (7) and-with-lutes with-joyful-song with-tambourines the-king

הַנָּשִׁים הַֽמְשַׂחֲקוֹת וַתֹּאמַ֫רְןָ הִכָּה שָׁאוּל בַּאֲלָפָו
to-thousands-of-him Saul he-has-slain and-they-said the-ones-dancing the-women

וְדָוִד בְּרִבְבֹתָיו׃ (8) וַיִּחַר לְשָׁאוּל מְאֹד
very to-Saul and-he-was-angry (8) to-tens-of-thousands-of-him and-David

וַיֵּרַע בְּעֵינָיו הַדָּבָר הַזֶּה וַיֹּאמֶר
and-he-thought the-this the-refrain in-eyes-of-him and-he-was-galling

נָתְנוּ לְדָוִד רְבָבוֹת וְלִי נָתְנוּ הָאֲלָפִים
the-thousands they-credited but-to-me tens-of-thousands to-David they-credited

וְעוֹד לוֹ אַךְ הַמְּלוּכָה׃ (9) וַיְהִי שָׁאוּל עָוֺן אֶת־
*** jealously-eyeing Saul and-he-was (9) the-kingdom but to-him and-more

דָּוִד מֵהַיּוֹם הַהוּא וָהָלְאָה׃ (10) וַיְהִי מִמָּחֳרָת וַתִּצְלַח
then-she-came on-next-day and-he-was (10) and-on the-that from-the-day David

רוּחַ אֱלֹהִים ׀ רָעָה ׀ אֶל־שָׁאוּל וַיִּתְנַבֵּא בְתוֹךְ־ הַבַּיִת וְדָוִד
and-David the-house inside-of and-he-prophesied Saul upon evil God spirit-of

מְנַגֵּן בְּיָדוֹ כְּיוֹם ׀ בְּיוֹם וְהַחֲנִית בְּיַד־ שָׁאוּל׃
Saul in-hand-of and-the-spear on-day as-day with-hand-of-him playing

(11) וַיָּטֶל שָׁאוּל אֶת־ הַחֲנִית וַיֹּאמֶר אַכֶּה בְדָוִד
through-David I-will-pin and-he-said the-spear *** Saul and-he-hurled (11)

וּבַקִּיר וַיִּסֹּב דָּוִד מִפָּנָיו פַּעֲמָיִם׃ (12) וַיִּרָא
and-he-feared (12) twice from-before-him David but-he-eluded and-to-the-wall

שָׁאוּל מִלִּפְנֵי דָוִד כִּי־ הָיָה יְהוָה עִמּוֹ וּמֵעִם שָׁאוּל סָר׃
he-left Saul but-from-with with-him Yahweh he-was for David because-of Saul

(13) וַיְסִרֵהוּ שָׁאוּל מֵעִמּוֹ וַיְשִׂמֵהוּ לוֹ שַׂר־
commander-of for-him and-he-made-him from-with-him Saul so-he-sent-him (13)

אֶלֶף וַיֵּצֵא וַיָּבֹא לִפְנֵי הָעָם׃ (14) וַיְהִי דָוִד
David and-he-was (14) the-troop before and-he-led so-he-went-out thousand

לְכָל־ דְּרָכָו מַשְׂכִּיל וַיהוָה עִמּוֹ׃ (15) וַיַּרְא שָׁאוּל
Saul when-he-saw (15) with-him for-Yahweh succeeding ways-of-him in-all-of

אֲשֶׁר־הוּא מַשְׂכִּיל מְאֹד וַיָּגָר מִפָּנָיו׃ (16) וְכָל־
but-all-of (16) because-of-him then-he-was-afraid greatly succeeding he that

יִשְׂרָאֵל וִיהוּדָה אֹהֵב אֶת־ דָּוִד כִּי־ הוּא יוֹצֵא וָבָא לִפְנֵיהֶם׃
before-them and-leading going-out he for David *** loving and-Judah Israel

(17) וַיֹּאמֶר שָׁאוּל אֶל־ דָּוִד הִנֵּה בִתִּי הַגְּדוֹלָה מֵרַב אֹתָהּ
her Merab the-old daughter-of-me see! David to Saul and-he-said (17)

אֶתֶּן־ לְךָ לְאִשָּׁה אַךְ הֱיֵה־ לִּי לְבֶן־ חַיִל וְהִלָּחֵם
and-fight! bravery as-man-of to-me be! only as-wife to-you I-will-give

Saul with singing and dancing, with joyful songs and with tambourines and lutes. [7]As they danced, they sang:

"Saul has slain his
thousands,
and David his tens of
thousands."

[8]Saul was very angry; this refrain galled him. "They have credited David with tens of thousands," he thought, "but me with only thousands. What more can he get but the kingdom?" [9]And from that time on Saul kept a jealous eye on David.

[10]The next day an evil[u] spirit from God came forcefully upon Saul. He was prophesying in his house, while David was playing the harp, as he usually did. Saul had a spear in his hand [11]and he hurled it, saying to himself, "I'll pin David to the wall." But David eluded him twice.

[12]Saul was afraid of David, because the LORD was with David but had left Saul. [13]So he sent David away from him and gave him command over a thousand men, and David led the troops in their campaigns. [14]In everything he did he had great success,[v] because the LORD was with him. [15]When Saul saw how successful[w] he was, he was afraid of him. [16]But all Israel and Judah loved David, because he led them in their campaigns.

[17]Saul said to David, "Here is my older daughter Merab. I will give her to you in marriage; only serve me bravely

[u]10 Or *injurious* [v]14 Or *he was very wise*
[w]15 Or *wise*

°7 ק באלפיו
°9 ק עוין
°14 ק דרכיו

מִלְחֲמוֹת יְהוָה וְשָׁאוּל אָמַר אַל־ תְּהִי יָדִי בּוֹ
against-him hand-of-me she-will-be not he-said for-Saul Yahweh battles-of

וּתְהִי־ בוֹ יַד־ פְּלִשְׁתִּים׃ וַיֹּאמֶר דָּוִד אֶל־
to David but-he-said (18) Philistines hand-of against-him but-let-her-be

שָׁאוּל מִי אָנֹכִי וּמִי חַיַּי מִשְׁפַּחַת אָבִי בְּיִשְׂרָאֵל כִּי־
that in-Israel father-of-me clan-of families-of-me and-what? I who? Saul

אֶהְיֶה חָתָן לַמֶּלֶךְ׃ וַיְהִי בְּעֵת תֵּת אֶת־ מֵרַב
Merab *** to-give at-time-of so-he-was (19) of-the-king son-in-law I-become

בַּת־ שָׁאוּל לְדָוִד וְהִיא נִתְּנָה לְעַדְרִיאֵל הַמְּחֹלָתִי
the-Meholathite to-Adriel she-was-given then-she to-David Saul daughter-of

לְאִשָּׁה׃ וַתֶּאֱהַב מִיכַל בַּת־ שָׁאוּל אֶת־דָּוִד וַיַּגִּדוּ
when-they-told David *** Saul daughter-of Michal now-she-loved (20) as-wife

לְשָׁאוּל וַיִּשַׁר הַדָּבָר בְּעֵינָיו׃ וַיֹּאמֶר
and-he-thought (21) in-eyes-of-him the-thing then-he-was-pleasing to-Saul

שָׁאוּל אֶתְּנֶנָּה לּוֹ וּתְהִי־ לוֹ לְמוֹקֵשׁ וּתְהִי־
so-she-may-be as-snare to-him so-she-may-be to-him I-will-give-her Saul

בוֹ יַד־ פְּלִשְׁתִּים וַיֹּאמֶר שָׁאוּל אֶל־ דָּוִד בִּשְׁתַּיִם
for-second-time David to Saul so-he-said Philistines hand-of against-him

תִּתְחַתֵּן בִּי הַיּוֹם׃ וַיְצַו שָׁאוּל אֶת־
*** Saul then-he-ordered (22) the-day of-me you-may-become-son-in-law

עֲבָדָו דַּבְּרוּ אֶל־ דָּוִד בַּלָּט לֵאמֹר הִנֵּה חָפֵץ
he-is-pleased see! to-say in-the-private David to speak! attendants-of-him

בְּךָ הַמֶּלֶךְ וְכָל־ עֲבָדָיו אֲהֵבוּךָ וְעַתָּה
so-now they-like-you attendants-of-him and-all-of the-king with-you

הִתְחַתֵּן בַּמֶּלֶךְ׃ וַיְדַבְּרוּ עַבְדֵי שָׁאוּל
Saul attendants-of so-they-spoke (23) of-the-king become-son-in-law!

בְּאָזְנֵי דָוִד אֶת־ הַדְּבָרִים הָאֵלֶּה וַיֹּאמֶר דָּוִד הֲנִקַלָּה
being-small? David but-he-said the-these the-words *** David in-ears-of

בְעֵינֵיכֶם הִתְחַתֵּן בַּמֶּלֶךְ וְאָנֹכִי אִישׁ־ רָשׁ
being-poor man now-I of-the-king to-become-son-in-law in-eyes-of-you

וְנִקְלֶה׃ וַיַּגִּדוּ עַבְדֵי שָׁאוּל לוֹ לֵאמֹר
to-say to-him Saul servants-of when-they-told (24) and-being-little-known

כַּדְּבָרִים הָאֵלֶּה, דִּבֶּר דָּוִד׃ וַיֹּאמֶר שָׁאוּל כֹּה־ תֹאמְרוּ
you-say this Saul and-he-replied (25) David he-says the-these as-the-words

לְדָוִד אֵין־ חֵפֶץ לַמֶּלֶךְ בְּמֹהַר כִּי בְּמֵאָה
for-hundred other-than for-bride-price to-the-king desire not to-David

עָרְלוֹת פְּלִשְׁתִּים לְהִנָּקֵם בְּאֹיְבֵי הַמֶּלֶךְ וְשָׁאוּל
now-Saul the-king on-being-enemies-of to-take-revenge Philistines foreskins-of

and fight the battles of the LORD." For Saul said to himself, "I will not raise a hand against him. Let the Philistines do that!"

[18]But David said to Saul, "Who am I, and what is my family or my father's clan in Israel, that I should become the king's son-in-law?" [19]So[x] when the time came for Merab, Saul's daughter, to be given to David, she was given in marriage to Adriel of Meholah.

[20]Now Saul's daughter Michal was in love with David, and when they told Saul about it, he was pleased. [21]"I will give her to him," he thought, "so that she may be a snare to him and so that the hand of the Philistines may be against him." So Saul said to David, "Now you have a second opportunity to become my son-in-law."

[22]Then Saul ordered his attendants: "Speak to David privately and say, 'Look, the king is pleased with you, and his attendants all like you; now become his son-in-law.' "

[23]They repeated these words to David. But David said, "Do you think it is a small matter to become the king's son-in-law? I'm only a poor man and little known."

[24]When Saul's servants told him what David had said, [25]Saul replied, "Say to David, 'The king wants no other price for the bride than a hundred Philistine foreskins, to take revenge on his enemies.' "

x19 Or *However,*

°22 ק עבדיו

חָשַׁב לְהַפִּיל אֶת־ דָּוִד בְּיַד־ פְּלִשְׁתִּים׃ וַיַּגִּדוּ
when-they-told (26) Philistines by-hand-of David *** to-have-fall he-planned

עֲבָדָיו לְדָוִד אֶת־ הַדְּבָרִים הָאֵלֶּה וַיִּשַׁר
then-he-was-pleasing the-these the-things *** to-David attendants-of-him

הַדָּבָר בְּעֵינֵי דָוִד לְהִתְחַתֵּן בַּמֶּלֶךְ וְלֹא
and-not of-the-king to-become-son-in-law David in-eyes-of the-thing

מָלְאוּ הַיָּמִים׃ וַיָּקָם דָּוִד וַיֵּלֶךְ ׀ הוּא וַאֲנָשָׁיו
and-men-of-him he and-he-went-out David and-he-rose (27) the-days they-elapsed

וַיַּךְ בַּפְּלִשְׁתִּים מָאתַיִם אִישׁ וַיָּבֵא דָוִד אֶת־
*** David and-he-brought man two-hundreds of-the-Philistines and-he-killed

עָרְלֹתֵיהֶם וַיְמַלְאוּם לַמֶּלֶךְ לְהִתְחַתֵּן
to-be-son-in-law to-the-king and-they-gave-fullness-of-them foreskins-of-them

בַּמֶּלֶךְ וַיִּתֶּן־ לוֹ שָׁאוּל אֶת־ מִיכַל בִּתּוֹ לְאִשָּׁה׃
as-wife daughter-of-him Michal *** Saul to-him then-he-gave of-the-king

וַיַּרְא שָׁאוּל וַיֵּדַע כִּי יְהוָה עִם־ דָּוִד וּמִיכַל
and-Michal David with Yahweh that and-he-knew Saul when-he-realized (28)

בַּת־ שָׁאוּל אֲהֵבַתְהוּ׃ וַיֹּאסֶף שָׁאוּל לֵרֹא מִפְּנֵי
because-of to-fear Saul then-he-increased (29) she-loved-him Saul daughter-of

דָוִד עוֹד וַיְהִי שָׁאוּל אֹיֵב אֶת־ דָּוִד כָּל־ הַיָּמִים׃
the-days all-of David *** being-enemy Saul and-he-remained more David

וַיֵּצְאוּ שָׂרֵי פְלִשְׁתִּים וַיְהִי ׀ מִדֵּי
as-often-of and-he-was Philistines commanders-of and-they-went-out (30)

צֵאתָם שָׂכַל דָּוִד מִכֹּל עַבְדֵי שָׁאוּל
Saul officers-of over-all-of David he-succeeded to-go-out-them

וַיִּיקַר שְׁמוֹ מְאֹד׃ וַיְדַבֵּר שָׁאוּל אֶל־ יוֹנָתָן
Jonathan to Saul and-he-told (19:1) well name-of-him and-he-became-known

בְּנוֹ וְאֶל־ כָּל־ עֲבָדָיו לְהָמִית אֶת־ דָּוִד וִיהוֹנָתָן
but-Jonathan David *** to-kill attendants-of-him all-of and-to son-of-him

בֶּן־ שָׁאוּל חָפֵץ בְּדָוִד מְאֹד׃ וַיַּגֵּד יְהוֹנָתָן לְדָוִד
to-David Jonathan and-he-warned (2) very of-David he-was-fond Saul son-of

לֵאמֹר מְבַקֵּשׁ שָׁאוּל אָבִי לַהֲמִיתֶךָ וְעַתָּה הִשָּׁמֶר־ נָא
now! be-on-guard! so-now to-kill-you father-of-me Saul looking to-say

בַבֹּקֶר וְיָשַׁבְתָּ בַסֵּתֶר וְנַחְבֵּאתָ׃ וַאֲנִי אֵצֵא
I-will-go-out and-I (3) and-you-stay into-the-hiding and-you-go in-the-morning

וְעָמַדְתִּי לְיַד־ אָבִי בַּשָּׂדֶה אֲשֶׁר אַתָּה שָׁם וַאֲנִי
and-I there you where in-the-field father-of-me by-hand-of and-I-will-stand

אֲדַבֵּר בְּךָ אֶל־ אָבִי וְרָאִיתִי מָה וְהִגַּדְתִּי
and-I-will-tell what and-I-will-find-out father-of-me to about-you I-will-speak

Saul's plan was to have David fall by the hands of the Philistines.

26When the attendants told David these things, he was pleased to become the king's son-in-law. So before the allotted time elapsed, 27David and his men went out and killed two hundred Philistines. He brought their foreskins and presented the full number to the king so that he might become the king's son-in-law. Then Saul gave him his daughter Michal in marriage.

28When Saul realized that the LORD was with David and that his daughter Michal loved David, 29Saul became still more afraid of him, and he remained his enemy the rest of his days.

30The Philistine commanders continued to go out to battle, and as often as they did, David met with more success[y] than the rest of Saul's officers, and his name became well known.

Saul Tries to Kill David

19 Saul told his son Jonathan and all the attendants to kill David. But Jonathan was very fond of David 2and warned him, "My father Saul is looking for a chance to kill you. Be on your guard tomorrow morning; go into hiding and stay there. 3I will go out and stand with my father in the field where you are. I'll speak to him about you and will tell you what I find out."

[y]30 Or *David acted more wisely*

וַיְדַבֵּר יְהוֹנָתָן בְּדָוִד טוֹב אֶל־שָׁאוּל אָבִיו :לָךְ
father-of-him Saul to well of-David Jonathan and-he-spoke (4) to-you

וַיֹּאמֶר אֵלָיו אַל־ יֶחֱטָא הַמֶּלֶךְ בְּעַבְדּוֹ בְדָוִד
to-David to-servant-of-him the-king let-him-do-wrong not to-him and-he-said

כִּי לוֹא חָטָא לָךְ וְכִי מַעֲשָׂיו טוֹב־ לְךָ מְאֹד׃
greatly to-you beneficial deeds-of-him and-for to-you he-wronged not for

וַיָּשֶׂם אֶת־ נַפְשׁוֹ בְכַפּוֹ וַיַּךְ אֶת־
*** when-he-killed in-hand-of-him life-of-him *** and-he-took (5)

הַפְּלִשְׁתִּי וַיַּעַשׂ יְהוָה תְּשׁוּעָה גְדוֹלָה לְכָל־ יִשְׂרָאֵל רָאִיתָ
you-saw Israel for-all-of great victory Yahweh and-he-won the-Philistine

וַתִּשְׂמָח וְלָמָּה תֶחֱטָא בְּדָם נָקִי לְהָמִית
to-kill innocent to-blood you-would-do-wrong then-why? and-you-were-glad

אֶת־ דָּוִד חִנָּם׃ וַיִּשְׁמַע שָׁאוּל בְּקוֹל יְהוֹנָתָן
Jonathan to-voice-of Saul and-he-listened (6) without-reason David ***

וַיִּשָּׁבַע שָׁאוּל חַי־ יְהוָה אִם־ יוּמָת׃ וַיִּקְרָא
so-he-called (7) he-will-be-killed not Yahweh life-of Saul and-he-took-oath

יְהוֹנָתָן לְדָוִד וַיַּגֶּד־ לוֹ יְהוֹנָתָן אֵת כָּל־ הַדְּבָרִים
the-conversations all-of *** Jonathan to-him and-he-told to-David Jonathan

הָאֵלֶּה וַיָּבֵא יְהוֹנָתָן אֶת־ דָּוִד אֶל־שָׁאוּל וַיְהִי לְפָנָיו
before-him and-he-was Saul to David *** Jonathan and-he-brought the-these

כְּאֶתְמוֹל שִׁלְשׁוֹם׃ וַתּוֹסֶף הַמִּלְחָמָה לִהְיוֹת וַיֵּצֵא
and-he-went-out to-break-out the-war and-she-repeated (8) before as-yesterday

דָוִד וַיִּלָּחֶם בַּפְּלִשְׁתִּים וַיַּךְ בָּהֶם מַכָּה
force against-them and-he-struck with-the-Philistines and-he-fought David

גְדוֹלָה וַיָּנֻסוּ מִפָּנָיו׃ וַתְּהִי רוּחַ יְהוָה רָעָה
evil Yahweh spirit-of but-she-came (9) from-before-him and-they-fled great

אֶל־ שָׁאוּל וְהוּא בְּבֵיתוֹ יוֹשֵׁב וַחֲנִיתוֹ בְּיָדוֹ
in-hand-of-him and-spear-of-him sitting in-house-of-him as-he Saul upon

וְדָוִד מְנַגֵּן בְּיָד׃ וַיְבַקֵּשׁ שָׁאוּל לְהַכּוֹת בַּחֲנִית
with-spear to-pin Saul and-he-tried (10) with-hand playing and-David

בְּדָוִד וּבַקִּיר וַיִּפְטַר מִפְּנֵי שָׁאוּל וַיַּךְ
and-he-drove Saul from-before but-he-eluded and-to-the-wall through-David

אֶת־ הַחֲנִית בַּקִּיר וְדָוִד נָס וַיִּמָּלֵט בַּלַּיְלָה
in-the-night and-he-escaped he-fled and-David into-the-wall the-spear ***

הוּא׃ וַיִּשְׁלַח שָׁאוּל מַלְאָכִים אֶל־ בֵּית דָּוִד לְשָׁמְרוֹ
to-watch-him David house-of to men Saul and-he-sent (11) the-that

וְלַהֲמִיתוֹ בַּבֹּקֶר וַתַּגֵּד לְדָוִד מִיכַל אִשְׁתּוֹ
wife-of-him Michal to-David but-she-warned in-the-morning and-to-kill-him

4 Jonathan spoke well of David to Saul his father and said
to him, "Let not the king do
wrong to his servant David;
he has not wronged you, and
what he has done has
benefited you greatly. 5 He took
his life in his hands when he
killed the Philistine. The LORD
won a great victory for all Israel, and you saw it and were
glad. Why then would you do
wrong to an innocent man
like David by killing him for
no reason?"
6 Saul listened to Jonathan
and took this oath: "As surely
as the LORD lives, David will
not be put to death."
7 So Jonathan called David
and told him the whole con-
versation. He brought him to
Saul, and David was with Saul
as before.
8 Once more war broke out,
and David went out and
fought the Philistines. He
struck them with such force
that they fled before him.
9 But an evil[z] spirit from the
LORD came upon Saul as he
was sitting in his house with
his spear in his hand. While
David was playing the harp,
10 Saul tried to pin him to the
wall with his spear, but David
eluded him as Saul drove the
spear into the wall. That night
David made good his escape.
11 Saul sent men to David's
house to watch it and to kill
him in the morning. But Michal, David's wife, warned

[z]9 Or *injurious*

לֵאמֹר אִם־ אֵינְךָ מְמַלֵּט אֶת־ נַפְשְׁךָ הַלַּיְלָה מָחָר אַתָּה מוּמָת׃
being-killed you tomorrow the-night life-of-you for running not-you if to-say

וַתֹּרֶד מִיכַל אֶת־ דָּוִד בְּעַד הַחַלּוֹן וַיֵּלֶךְ
and-he-went the-window through David *** Michal so-she-let-down (12)

וַיִּבְרַח וַיִּמָּלֵט׃ וַתִּקַּח מִיכַל אֶת־ הַתְּרָפִים
the-idols *** Michal then-she-took (13) and-he-escaped and-he-fled

וַתָּשֶׂם אֶל־ הַמִּטָּה וְאֵת כְּבִיר הָעִזִּים שָׂמָה מְרַאֲשֹׁתָיו
at-heads-of-him she-put the-goat-hairs material-of and the-bed on and-she-laid

וַתְּכַס בַּבָּגֶד׃ וַיִּשְׁלַח שָׁאוּל מַלְאָכִים לָקַחַת אֶת־
*** to-capture men Saul when-he-sent (14) with-the-garment and-she-covered

דָּוִד וַתֹּאמֶר חֹלֶה הוּא׃ וַיִּשְׁלַח שָׁאוּל אֶת־הַמַּלְאָכִים
the-men *** Saul but-he-sent-back (15) he being-ill then-she-said David

לִרְאוֹת אֶת־ דָּוִד לֵאמֹר הַעֲלוּ אֹתוֹ בַמִּטָּה אֵלַי לַהֲמִתוֹ׃
to-kill-him to-me in-the-bed him bring-up! to-say David *** to-see

וַיָּבֹאוּ הַמַּלְאָכִים וְהִנֵּה הַתְּרָפִים אֶל־הַמִּטָּה וּכְבִיר
and-material-of the-bed in the-idols then-see! the-men when-they-entered (16)

הָעִזִּים מְרַאֲשֹׁתָיו׃ וַיֹּאמֶר שָׁאוּל אֶל־מִיכַל לָמָּה כָּכָה
like-this why? Michal to Saul and-he-said (17) at-heads-of-him the-goat-hairs

רִמִּיתִנִי וַתְּשַׁלְּחִי אֶת־ אֹיְבִי וַיִּמָּלֵט
so-he-escaped being-enemy-of-me *** and-you-sent-away you-deceived-me

וַתֹּאמֶר מִיכַל אֶל־שָׁאוּל הוּא־ אָמַר אֵלַי שַׁלְּחֵנִי לָמָה
why? let-get-away-me! to-me he-said he Saul to Michal and-she-told

אֲמִיתֵךְ׃ וְדָוִד בָּרַח וַיִּמָּלֵט וַיָּבֹא אֶל־
to then-he-went and-he-escaped he-fled when-David (18) should-I-kill-you

שְׁמוּאֵל הָרָמָתָה וַיַּגֶּד־ לוֹ אֵת כָּל־ אֲשֶׁר עָשָׂה־ לוֹ שָׁאוּל
Saul to-him he-did that all *** to-him and-he-told at-the-Ramah Samuel

וַיֵּלֶךְ הוּא וּשְׁמוּאֵל וַיֵּשְׁבוּ בְּנָוֹית׃ וַיֻּגַּד
and-he-was-told (19) in-Naioth and-they-stayed and-Samuel he then-he-went

לְשָׁאוּל לֵאמֹר הִנֵּה דָוִד בְּנָוֹית בָּרָמָה׃ וַיִּשְׁלַח שָׁאוּל מַלְאָכִים
men Saul so-he-sent (20) at-the-Ramah in-Naioth David see! to-say to-Saul

לָקַחַת אֶת־ דָּוִד וַיַּרְא אֶת־ לַהֲקַת הַנְּבִיאִים נִבְּאִים
ones-prophesying the-prophets group-of *** but-they-saw David *** to-capture

וּשְׁמוּאֵל עֹמֵד נִצָּב עֲלֵיהֶם וַתְּהִי עַל־ מַלְאֲכֵי שָׁאוּל
Saul men-of upon and-she-came over-them leading standing and-Samuel

רוּחַ אֱלֹהִים וַיִּתְנַבְּאוּ גַּם־ הֵמָּה׃ וַיַּגִּדוּ לְשָׁאוּל
to-Saul and-they-told (21) they also and-they-prophesied God Spirit-of

וַיִּשְׁלַח מַלְאָכִים אֲחֵרִים וַיִּתְנַבְּאוּ גַּם־ הֵמָּה וַיֹּסֶף שָׁאוּל
Saul and-he-repeated they also and-they-prophesied more-ones men and-he-sent

him, "If you don't run for your life tonight, tomorrow you'll be killed." [12]So Michal let David down through a window, and he fled and escaped. [13]Then Michal took an idol[a] and laid it on the bed, covering it with a garment and putting some goats' hair at the head.

[14]When Saul sent the men to capture David, Michal said, "He is ill."

[15]Then Saul sent the men back to see David and told them, "Bring him up to me in his bed so that I may kill him." [16]But when the men entered, there was the idol in the bed, and at the head was some goats' hair.

[17]Saul said to Michal, "Why did you deceive me like this and send my enemy away so that he escaped?"

Michal told him, "He said to me, 'Let me get away. Why should I kill you?' "

[18]When David had fled and made his escape, he went to Samuel at Ramah and told him all that Saul had done to him. Then he and Samuel went to Naioth and stayed there. [19]Word came to Saul: "David is in Naioth at Ramah"; [20]so he sent men to capture him. But when they saw a group of prophets prophesying, with Samuel standing there as their leader, the Spirit of God came upon Saul's men and they also prophesied. [21]Saul was told about it, and he sent more men, and they prophesied too.

[a]13 Hebrew *teraphim;* also in verse 16

°18 ק בניות
°19 ק בניות

וַיִּשְׁלַח מַלְאָכִים שְׁלִשִׁים וַיִּתְנַבְּאוּ גַּם־ הֵמָּה׃ וַיֵּלֶךְ
then-he-left (22) they also and-they-prophesied third-ones men and-he-sent

גַּם־ הוּא הָרָמָתָה וַיָּבֹא עַד־ בּוֹר הַגָּדוֹל אֲשֶׁר בַּשֶּׂכוּ
at-the-Secu that the-great cistern-of to and-he-went for-the-Ramah he also

וַיִּשְׁאַל וַיֹּאמֶר אֵיפֹה שְׁמוּאֵל וְדָוִד וַיֹּאמֶר הִנֵּה בְּנָוֺית
in-Naioth see! and-he-said and-David Samuel where? and-he-said and-he-asked

בָּרָמָה׃ וַיֵּלֶךְ שָׁם אֶל־ נָוֺית בָּרָמָה וַתְּהִי
but-she-came at-the-Ramah Naioth to there so-he-went (23) at-the-Ramah

עָלָיו גַּם־ הוּא רוּחַ אֱלֹהִים וַיֵּלֶךְ הָלוֹךְ וַיִּתְנַבֵּא עַד־
until and-he-prophesied to-walk and-he-walked God Spirit-of he also upon-him

בֹּאוֹ בְּנָוֺית בָּרָמָה׃ וַיִּפְשַׁט גַּם־ הוּא
he also and-he-stripped-off (24) at-the-Ramah to-Naioth to-come-him

בְּגָדָיו וַיִּתְנַבֵּא גַם־ הוּא לִפְנֵי שְׁמוּאֵל וַיִּפֹּל עָרֹם
naked and-he-lay Samuel in-presences-of he also and-he-prophesied robes-of-him

כָּל־ הַיּוֹם הַהוּא וְכָל־ הַלָּיְלָה עַל־ כֵּן יֹאמְרוּ הֲגַם שָׁאוּל
Saul also? they-say this for the-night and-all-of the-that the-day all-of

בַּנְּבִיאִם׃ וַיִּבְרַח דָּוִד מִנָּוֺת בָּרָמָה
at-the-Ramah from-Naioth David then-he-fled (20:1) among-the-prophets

וַיָּבֹא וַיֹּאמֶר ׀ לִפְנֵי יְהוֹנָתָן מֶה עָשִׂיתִי מֶה־ עֲוֹנִי וּמֶה־
and-how? crime-of-me what? I-did what? Jonathan to and-he-asked and-he-went

חַטָּאתִי לִפְנֵי אָבִיךָ כִּי מְבַקֵּשׁ אֶת־ נַפְשִׁי׃ וַיֹּאמֶר
and-he-replied (2) life-of-me *** seeking that father-of-you to I-did-wrong

לוֹ חָלִילָה לֹא תָמוּת הִנֵּה לוֹ־ עָשָׂה אָבִי דָּבָר גָּדוֹל
great anything father-of-me he-does not look! you-will-die not never! to-him

אוֹ דָּבָר קָטֹן וְלֹא יִגְלֶה אֶת־ אָזְנִי וּמַדּוּעַ יַסְתִּיר
would-he-hide now-why? ear-of-me *** he-confides that-not small anything or

אָבִי מִמֶּנִּי אֶת־ הַדָּבָר הַזֶּה אֵין זֹאת׃ וַיִּשָּׁבַע
but-he-took-oath (3) so not the-this the-thing *** from-me father-of-me

עוֹד דָּוִד וַיֹּאמֶר יָדֹעַ יָדַע אָבִיךָ כִּי־ מָצָאתִי חֵן
favor I-found that father-of-you he-knows to-know and-he-said David again

בְּעֵינֶיךָ וַיֹּאמֶר אַל־ יֵדַע־ זֹאת יְהוֹנָתָן פֶּן־ יֵעָצֵב
he-will-be-grieved or Jonathan this he-must-know not and-he-said in-eyes-of-you

וְאוּלָם חַי־ יְהוָה וְחֵי נַפְשֶׁךָ כִּי כְפֶשַׂע בֵּינִי
between-me only-step indeed self-of-you and-life-of Yahweh life-of and-yet

וּבֵין הַמָּוֶת׃ וַיֹּאמֶר יְהוֹנָתָן אֶל־ דָּוִד מַה־ תֹּאמַר
she-asks whatever David to Jonathan and-he-said (4) the-death and-between

נַפְשְׁךָ וְאֶעֱשֶׂה־ לָּךְ׃ וַיֹּאמֶר דָּוִד אֶל־ יְהוֹנָתָן הִנֵּה־
look! Jonathan to David so-he-said (5) for-you then-I-will-do self-of-you

Saul sent men a third time, and they also prophesied. 22Finally, he himself left for Ramah and went to the great cistern at Secu. And he asked, "Where are Samuel and David?"

"Over in Naioth at Ramah," they said.

23So Saul went to Naioth at Ramah. But the Spirit of God came even upon him, and he walked along prophesying until he came to Naioth. 24He stripped off his robes and also prophesied in Samuel's presence. He lay that way all that day and night. This is why people say, "Is Saul also among the prophets?"

David and Jonathan

20 Then David fled from Naioth at Ramah and went to Jonathan and asked, "What have I done? What is my crime? How have I wronged your father, that he is trying to take my life?"

2"Never!" Jonathan replied. "You are not going to die! Look, my father doesn't do anything, great or small, without confiding in me. Why would he hide this from me? It's not so!"

3But David took an oath and said, "Your father knows very well that I have found favor in your eyes, and he has said to himself, 'Jonathan must not know this or he will be grieved.' Yet as surely as the LORD lives and as you live, there is only a step between me and death."

4Jonathan said to David, "Whatever you want me to do, I'll do for you."

°22 ק בניות
°23a ק ניות
°23b ק בניות
°1 ק מניות
°2a ק לא
°2b ק יעשה

חֹדֶשׁ מָחָר וְאָנֹכִי יָשֹׁב־ אֵשֵׁב עִם־ הַמֶּלֶךְ לֶאֱכוֹל

to-dine the-king with I-should-sit to-sit and-I tomorrow New-Moon-festival

וְשִׁלַּחְתַּנִי וְנִסְתַּרְתִּי בַשָּׂדֶה עַד הָעֶרֶב הַשְּׁלִשִׁית׃

the-third the-evening until in-the-field and-I-will-hide but-you-let-go-me

אִם־ פָּקֹד יִפְקְדֵנִי אָבִיךָ וְאָמַרְתָּ נִשְׁאֹל נִשְׁאַל

he-asked to-ask then-you-tell father-of-you he-misses-me to-miss if (6)

מִמֶּנִּי דָוִד לָרוּץ בֵּית־ לֶחֶם עִירוֹ כִּי זֶבַח הַיָּמִים

the-days sacrifice-of for town-of-him Lehem Beth to-hurry David from-me

שָׁם לְכָל־ הַמִּשְׁפָּחָה׃ אִם־ כֹּה יֹאמַר טוֹב שָׁלוֹם

safe very-well he-says this if (7) the-clan for-whole-of there

לְעַבְדֶּךָ וְאִם־ חָרֹה יֶחֱרֶה לוֹ דַּע כִּי־

that be-sure! to-him he-is-angry to-be-angry but-if for-servant-of-you

כָלְתָה הָרָעָה מֵעִמּוֹ׃ וְעָשִׂיתָ חֶסֶד עַל־

to kindness then-you-show (8) from-with-him the-harm she-is-determined

עַבְדֶּךָ כִּי בִּבְרִית יְהוָה הֵבֵאתָ אֶת־ עַבְדְּךָ

servant-of-you *** you-brought Yahweh into-covenant-of for servant-of-you

עִמָּךְ וְאִם־ יֶשׁ־ בִּי עָוֺן הֲמִיתֵנִי אַתָּה וְעַד־ אָבִיךָ לָמָּה־

why? father-of-you for-to you kill-me! guilt in-me there-is but-if with-you

זֶּה תְבִיאֵנִי׃ וַיֹּאמֶר יְהוֹנָתָן חָלִילָה לָּךְ כִּי ׀ אִם־ יָדֹעַ

to-know if for to-you never! Jonathan and-he-said (9) you-hand-over-me this

אֵדַע כִּי־ כָלְתָה הָרָעָה מֵעִם אָבִי לָבוֹא

to-go father-of-me from-with the-harm she-was-determined that I-knew

עָלֶיךָ וְלֹא אֹתָהּ אַגִּיד לָךְ׃ וַיֹּאמֶר דָּוִד אֶל־

to David and-he-asked (10) to-you I-would-tell her then-not against-you

יְהוֹנָתָן מִי יַגִּיד לִי אוֹ מַה־ יַּעַנְךָ אָבִיךָ

father-of-you he-answers-you something if to-me he-will-tell who? Jonathan

קָשָׁה׃ וַיֹּאמֶר יְהוֹנָתָן אֶל־ דָּוִד לְכָה וְנֵצֵא הַשָּׂדֶה

the-field and-let-us-go-out come! David to Jonathan then-he-said (11) harsh

וַיֵּצְאוּ שְׁנֵיהֶם הַשָּׂדֶה׃ וַיֹּאמֶר יְהוֹנָתָן אֶל־ דָּוִד

David to Jonathan then-he-said (12) the-field two-of-them so-they-went

יְהוָה אֱלֹהֵי יִשְׂרָאֵל כִּי־ אֶחְקֹר אֶת־ אָבִי כָּעֵת ׀

by-the-time father-of-me *** I-will-sound-out surely Israel God-of Yahweh

מָחָר הַשְּׁלִשִׁית וְהִנֵּה־ טוֹב אֶל־ דָּוִד וְלֹא־ אָז אֶשְׁלַח

I-will-send then then-not David to favorable and-if the-third tomorrow

אֵלֶיךָ וְגָלִיתִי אֶת־ אָזְנֶךָ׃ כֹּה־ יַעֲשֶׂה יְהוָה

Yahweh may-he-deal so (13) ear-of-you *** and-I-will-let-know to-you

לִיהוֹנָתָן וְכֹה יֹסִיף כִּי־ יֵיטִב אֶל־ אָבִי אֶת־

*** father-of-me to he-pleases if may-he-be-severe and-so with-Jonathan

5So David said, "Look, tomorrow is the New Moon festival, and I am supposed to
dine with the king; but let me
go and hide in the field until
the evening of the day after tomorrow. 6If your father misses
me at all, tell him, 'David earnestly asked my permission to
hurry to Bethlehem, his home
town, because an annual sacrifice is being made there for
his whole clan.' 7If he says,
'Very well,' then your servant
is safe. But if he loses his temper, you can be sure that he is
determined to harm me. 8As
for you, show kindness to
your servant, for you have
brought him into a covenant
with you before the LORD. If I
am guilty, then kill me yourself! Why hand me over to
your father?"

9"Never!" Jonathan said. "If
I had the least inkling that my
father was determined to
harm you, wouldn't I tell
you?"

10David asked, "Who will tell
me if your father answers you
harshly?"

11"Come," Jonathan said,
"let's go out into the field." So
they went there together.

12Then Jonathan said to David: "By the LORD, the God of
Israel, I will surely sound out
my father by this time the day
after tomorrow! If he is favorably disposed toward you, will
I not send you word and let
you know? 13But if my father is
inclined to harm you, may the
LORD deal with me, be it ever

הָרָעָה עָלֶיךָ וְגָלִיתִי אֶת־ אָזְנֶךָ וְשִׁלַּחְתִּיךָ וְהָלַכְתָּ
and-you-go and-I-send-you ear-of-you *** and-I-let-know to-you the-harm

לְשָׁלוֹם וִיהִי יְהוָה עִמָּךְ כַּאֲשֶׁר הָיָה עִם־ אָבִי׃
father-of-me with he-was just-as with-you Yahweh and-may-he-be in-safety

וְלֹא אִם־עוֹדֶנִּי חָי וְלֹא־ תַעֲשֶׂה עִמָּדִי חֶסֶד יְהוָה
Yahweh kindness-of to-me will-you-show then-not alive still-I if and-not (14)

וְלֹא אָמוּת׃ וְלֹא־ תַכְרִת אֶת־ חַסְדְּךָ מֵעִם
from-with kindness-of-you *** you-cut-off and-not (15) I-die so-not

בֵּיתִי עַד־ עוֹלָם וְלֹא בְּהַכְרִת יְהוָה אֶת־ אֹיְבֵי
being-enemies-of *** Yahweh when-to-cut-off even-not ever for family-of-me

דָוִד אִישׁ מֵעַל פְּנֵי הָאֲדָמָה׃ וַיִּכְרֹת יְהוֹנָתָן עִם־
with Jonathan so-he-made-covenant (16) the-earth faces-of from-on each David

בֵּית דָּוִד וּבִקֵּשׁ יְהוָה מִיַּד אֹיְבֵי
being-enemies-of from-hand-of Yahweh and-may-he-call-account David house-of

דָוִד׃ וַיּוֹסֶף יְהוֹנָתָן לְהַשְׁבִּיעַ אֶת־ דָּוִד בְּאַהֲבָתוֹ
from-love-of-him David *** to-make-swear Jonathan and-he-repeated (17) David

אֹתוֹ כִּי־אַהֲבַת נַפְשׁוֹ אֲהֵבוֹ׃ וַיֹּאמֶר־ לוֹ יְהוֹנָתָן
Jonathan to-him then-he-said (18) he-loved-him self-of-him love-of for for-him

מָחָר חֹדֶשׁ וְנִפְקַדְתָּ כִּי יִפָּקֵד
he-will-be-empty for and-you-will-be-missed New-Moon-festival tomorrow

מוֹשָׁבֶךָ׃ וְשִׁלַּשְׁתָּ תֵּרֵד מְאֹד וּבָאתָ אֶל־
to and-you-go quickly you-go-down and-you-act-on-third-day (19) seat-of-you

הַמָּקוֹם אֲשֶׁר־ נִסְתַּרְתָּ שָּׁם בְּיוֹם הַמַּעֲשֶׂה וְיָשַׁבְתָּ אֵצֶל הָאֶבֶן
the-stone by and-you-wait the-deed on-day-of there you-hid where the-place

הָאָזֶל׃ וַאֲנִי שְׁלֹשֶׁת הַחִצִּים צִדָּה אוֹרֶה לְשַׁלַּח־
to-shoot I-will-shoot side-of-her the-arrows three-of and-I (20) the-Ezel

לִי לְמַטָּרָה׃ וְהִנֵּה אֶשְׁלַח אֶת־ הַנַּעַר לֵךְ מְצָא אֶת־
*** find! go! the-boy *** I-will-send then-see! (21) at-target for-me

הַחִצִּים אִם־ אָמֹר אֹמַר לַנַּעַר הִנֵּה הַחִצִּים ׀ מִמְּךָ וָהֵנָּה
and-beside by-you the-arrows look! to-the-boy I-say to-say if the-arrows

קָחֶנּוּ ׀ וָבֹאָה כִּי־ שָׁלוֹם לְךָ וְאֵין דָּבָר חַי־ יְהוָה׃
Yahweh life-of danger and-no for-you safe for then-come! bring-him!

וְאִם־ כֹּה אֹמַר לָעֶלֶם הִנֵּה הַחִצִּים מִמְּךָ וָהָלְאָה לֵךְ
go! and-beyond from-you the-arrows look! to-the-boy I-say this but-if (22)

כִּי שִׁלַּחֲךָ יְהוָה׃ וְהַדָּבָר אֲשֶׁר דִּבַּרְנוּ אֲנִי וָאָתָּה
and-you I we-discussed that and-the-matter (23) Yahweh he-sent-away-you for

הִנֵּה יְהוָה בֵּינִי וּבֵינְךָ עַד־ עוֹלָם׃ וַיִּסָּתֵר דָּוִד
David so-he-hid (24) forever to and-between-you between-me Yahweh see!

so severely, if I do not let you
know and send you away
safely. May the LORD be with
you as he has been with my
father. [14]But show me unfailing kindness like that of the
LORD as long as I live, so that I
may not be killed, [15]and do not
ever cut off your kindness
from my family—not even
when the LORD has cut off
every one of David's enemies
from the face of the earth."
[16]So Jonathan made a covenant with the house of David, saying, "May the LORD
call David's enemies to account." [17]And Jonathan had
David reaffirm his oath out of
love for him, because he loved
him as he loved himself.
[18]Then Jonathan said to David: "Tomorrow is the New
Moon festival. You will be
missed, because your seat will
be empty. [19]The day after tomorrow, toward evening, go
to the place where you hid
when this trouble began, and
wait by the stone Ezel. [20]I will
shoot three arrows to the side
of it, as though I were shooting at a target. [21]Then I will
send a boy and say, 'Go, find
the arrows.' If I say to him,
'Look, the arrows are on this
side of you; bring them here,'
then come, because, as surely
as the LORD lives, you are safe;
there is no danger. [22]But if I
say to the boy, 'Look, the arrows are beyond you,' then
you must go, because the LORD
has sent you away. [23]And
about the matter you and I discussed—remember, the LORD
is witness between you and
me forever."
[24]So David hid in the field,

בשדה ויהי החדש וישב המלך על־
at the-king then-he-sat-down the-New-Moon-festival when-he-came in-the-field

הלחם לאכול: וישב המלך על־ מושבו כפעם בפעם אל־
at at-time as-time place-of-him in the-king and-he-sat (25) to-eat the-meal

מושב הקיר ויקם יהונתן וישב אבנר מצד שאול
Saul at-side-of Abner and-he-sat Jonathan and-he-arose the-wall place-of

ויפקד מקום דוד: ולא־ דבר שאול מאומה ביום
on-the-day anything Saul he-said and-not (26) David place-of but-he-was-empty

ההוא כי אמר מקרה הוא בלתי טהור הוא כי־ לא טהור:
clean not surely he clean not he happening he-thought for the-that

ויהי ממחרת החדש השני ויפקד
then-he-was-empty the-second the-month on-next-day-of but-he-was (27)

מקום דוד ויאמר שאול אל־יהונתן בנו מדוע לא־ בא
he-came not why? son-of-him Jonathan to Saul then-he-said David place-of

בן־ ישי גם־ תמול גם־ היום אל־ הלחם: ויען
and-he-answered (28) the-meal to the-day or yesterday either Jesse son-of

יהונתן את־ שאול נשאל נשאל דוד מעמדי עד־ בית לחם:
Lehem Beth to from-with-me David he-asked to-ask Saul *** Jonathan

ויאמר שלחני נא כי זבח משפחה לנו בעיר
in-the-town of-us family sacrifice-of for now! let-go-me! and-he-said (29)

והוא צוה־ לי אחי ועתה אם־מצאתי חן בעיניך
in-eyes-of-you favor I-found if so-now brother-of-me to-me he-ordered and-he

אמלטה נא ואראה את־ אחי על־ כן לא־ בא
he-came not this for brothers-of-me *** and-let-me-see now! let-me-get-away

אל־ שלחן המלך: ויחר־ אף שאול ביהונתן
against-Jonathan Saul anger-of and-he-flared-up (30) the king table-of to

ויאמר לו בן־ נעות המרדות הלוא ידעתי
I-know not? the-rebellion woman-being-perverse-of son-of to-him and-he-said

כי־ בחר אתה לבן־ ישי לבשתך ולבשת ערות
nakedness-of and-to-shame-of to-shame-of-you Jesse with-son-of you siding that

אמך: כי כל־ הימים אשר בן־ ישי חי על־האדמה
the-earth on alive Jesse son-of that the-days all-of for (31) mother-of-you

לא תכון אתה ומלכותך ועתה שלח וקח
and-bring! send! and-now or-kingdom-of-you you you-will-be-established not

אתו אלי כי בן־ מות הוא: ויען יהונתן את־שאול
Saul *** Jonathan and-he-asked (32) he death son-of for to-me him

אביו ויאמר אליו למה יומת מה עשה:
he-did what? should-he-die why? to-him and-he-said father-of-him

and when the New Moon festival came, the king sat down
to eat. [25]He sat in his customary place by the wall. Jonathan
sat opposite him,[b] and Abner
sat next to Saul, but David's
place was empty. [26]Saul said
nothing that day, for he
thought, "Something must
have happened to David to
make him ceremonially un-
clean—surely he is unclean."
[27]But the next day, the second
day of the month, David's
place was empty again. Then
Saul said to his son Jonathan,
"Why hasn't the son of Jesse
come to the meal, either yesterday or today?"
[28]Jonathan answered, "David earnestly asked me for permission to go to Bethlehem.
[29]He said, 'Let me go, because
our family is observing a sacrifice in the town and my
brother has ordered me to be
there. If I have found favor in
your eyes, let me get away to
see my brothers.' That is why
he has not come to the king's
table."
[30]Saul's anger flared up at
Jonathan and he said to him,
"You son of a perverse and re-
bellious woman! Don't I know
that you have sided with the
son of Jesse to your own
shame and to the shame of the
mother who bore you? [31]As
long as the son of Jesse lives
on this earth, neither you nor
your kingdom will be established. Now send and bring
him to me, for he must die!"
[32]"Why should he be put to
death? What has he done?"
Jonathan asked his father.

[b]25 Septuagint; Hebrew *Jonathan arose*

°24 ק אל

וַיָּטֶל שָׁאוּל אֶת־ הַחֲנִית עָלָיו לְהַכֹּתוֹ וַיֵּדַע
then-he-knew to-kill-him at-him the-spear *** Saul but-he-hurled (33)

יְהוֹנָתָן כִּי־ כָלָה הִיא מֵעִם אָבִיו לְהָמִית אֶת־ דָּוִד׃
David *** to-kill father-of-him from-with this he-intended that Jonathan

וַיָּקָם יְהוֹנָתָן מֵעִם הַשֻּׁלְחָן בָּחֳרִי־ אָף וְלֹא־
and-not anger in-fierceness-of the-table from-at Jonathan so-he-got-up (34)

אָכַל בְּיוֹם־ הַחֹדֶשׁ הַשֵּׁנִי לֶחֶם כִּי נֶעְצַב אֶל־ דָּוִד כִּי
for David for he-was-grieved for food the-second the-month on-day-of he-ate

הִכְלִמוֹ אָבִיו׃ וַיְהִי בַבֹּקֶר וַיֵּצֵא
then-he-went-out in-the-morning and-he-was (35) father-of-him he-shamed-him

יְהוֹנָתָן הַשָּׂדֶה לְמוֹעֵד דָּוִד וְנַעַר קָטֹן עִמּוֹ׃ וַיֹּאמֶר
and-he-said (36) with-him small and-boy David for-meeting-of the-field Jonathan

לְנַעֲרוֹ רֻץ מְצָא נָא אֶת־ הַחִצִּים אֲשֶׁר אָנֹכִי מוֹרֶה הַנַּעַר רָץ
he-ran the-boy shooting I that the-arrows *** now! find! run! to-boy-of-him

וְהוּא־ יָרָה הַחֵצִי לְהַעֲבִרוֹ׃ וַיָּבֹא הַנַּעַר עַד־
to the-boy when-he-came (37) to-go-beyond-him the-arrow he-shot and-he

מְקוֹם הַחֵצִי אֲשֶׁר יָרָה יְהוֹנָתָן וַיִּקְרָא יְהוֹנָתָן אַחֲרֵי
after Jonathan then-he-called Jonathan he-shot where the-arrow place-of

הַנַּעַר וַיֹּאמֶר הֲלוֹא הַחֵצִי מִמְּךָ וָהָלְאָה׃ וַיִּקְרָא
then-he-shouted (38) and-beyond from-you the-arrow not? and-he-said the-boy

יְהוֹנָתָן אַחֲרֵי הַנַּעַר מְהֵרָה חוּשָׁה אַל־ תַּעֲמֹד וַיְלַקֵּט נַעַר
boy-of and-he-picked-up you-stop not go-quickly! hurry the-boy after Jonathan

יְהוֹנָתָן אֶת־ הַחִצִּי° וַיָּבֹא אֶל־ אֲדֹנָיו׃ וְהַנַּעַר
now-the-boy (39) masters-of-him to and-he-returned the-arrows *** Jonathan

לֹא־ יָדַע מְאוּמָה אַךְ יְהוֹנָתָן וְדָוִד יָדְעוּ אֶת־ הַדָּבָר׃
the-matter *** they-knew and-David Jonathan only anything he-knew not

וַיִּתֵּן יְהוֹנָתָן אֶת־ כֵּלָיו אֶל־ הַנַּעַר אֲשֶׁר־ לוֹ
with-him who the-boy to weapons-of-him *** Jonathan then-he-gave (40)

וַיֹּאמֶר לוֹ לֵךְ הָבֵיא הָעִיר׃ הַנַּעַר בָּא וְדָוִד
then-David he-went the-boy (41) the-town carry-back! go! to-him and-he-said

קָם מֵאֵצֶל הַנֶּגֶב וַיִּפֹּל לְאַפָּיו אַרְצָה
to-ground on-faces-of-him and-he-fell the-south from-side-of he-got-up

וַיִּשְׁתַּחוּ שָׁלֹשׁ פְּעָמִים וַיִּשְּׁקוּ ׀ אִישׁ אֶת־ רֵעֵהוּ וַיִּבְכּוּ
and-they-wept other-of-him *** each then-they-kissed times three and-he-bowed

אִישׁ אֶת־ רֵעֵהוּ עַד־ דָּוִד הִגְדִּיל׃ וַיֹּאמֶר יְהוֹנָתָן
Jonathan and-he-said (42) he-did-more David but other-of-him with each

לְדָוִד לֵךְ לְשָׁלוֹם אֲשֶׁר נִשְׁבַּעְנוּ שְׁנֵינוּ אֲנַחְנוּ בְּשֵׁם יְהוָה לֵאמֹר
to-say Yahweh in-name-of we both-of-us we-swore for in-peace go! to-David

[33]But Saul hurled his spear at him to kill him. Then Jonathan knew that his father intended to kill David.

[34]Jonathan got up from the table in fierce anger; on that second day of the month he did not eat, because he was grieved at his father's shameful treatment of David.

[35]In the morning Jonathan went out to the field for his meeting with David. He had a small boy with him, [36]and he said to the boy, "Run and find the arrows I shoot." As the boy ran, he shot an arrow beyond him. [37]When the boy came to the place where Jonathan's arrow had fallen, Jonathan called out after him, "Isn't the arrow beyond you?" [38]Then he shouted, "Hurry! Go quickly! Don't stop!" The boy picked up the arrow and returned to his master. [39](The boy knew nothing of all this; only Jonathan and David knew.) [40]Then Jonathan gave his weapons to the boy and said, "Go, carry them back to town."

[41]After the boy had gone, David got up from the south side of the stone[c] and bowed down before Jonathan three times, with his face to the ground. Then they kissed each other and wept together—but David wept the most.

[42]Jonathan said to David, "Go in peace, for we have sworn friendship with each other in the name of the LORD,

[c]41 Septuagint; Hebrew does not have *of the stone*.

°38 ק החצים

יְהֹוָה יִהְיֶה ׀ בֵּינִי וּבֵינֶךָ וּבֵין זַרְעִי
descendant-of-me and-between and-between-you between-me he-is Yahweh

וּבֵין זַרְעֲךָ עַד־ עוֹלָם׃ וַיָּקָם וַיֵּלַךְ
and-he-left then-he-got-up *(21:1) forever to descendant-of-you and-between

וִיהוֹנָתָן בָּא הָעִיר׃ וַיָּבֹא דָוִד נֹבֶה אֶל־אֲחִימֶלֶךְ
Ahimelech to to-Nob David and-he-went (2) the-town he-went-back and-Jonathan

הַכֹּהֵן וַיֶּחֱרַד אֲחִימֶלֶךְ לִקְרַאת דָּוִד וַיֹּאמֶר לוֹ מַדּוּעַ
why? to-him and-he-said David to-meet Ahimelech and-he-trembled the-priest

אַתָּה לְבַדֶּךָ וְאִישׁ אֵין אִתָּךְ׃ וַיֹּאמֶר דָּוִד
David and-he-answered (3) with-you not and-man by-self-of-you you

לַאֲחִימֶלֶךְ הַכֹּהֵן הַמֶּלֶךְ צִוַּנִי דָבָר וַיֹּאמֶר אֵלַי אִישׁ
man to-me and-he-said matter he-charged-me the-king the-priest to-Ahimelech

אַל־ יֵדַע מְאוּמָה אֶת־ הַדָּבָר אֲשֶׁר־ אָנֹכִי שֹׁלֵחֲךָ וַאֲשֶׁר
and-that sending-you I that the-mission *** anything he-must-know not

צִוִּיתִךָ וְאֶת־הַנְּעָרִים יוֹדַעְתִּי אֶל־מְקוֹם פְּלֹנִי אַלְמוֹנִי׃ וְעַתָּה מַה־
what? then-now (4) some certain place at I-told the-men and I-instruct-you

יֵשׁ תַּחַת־ יָדְךָ חֲמִשָּׁה־ לֶחֶם תְּנָה בְיָדִי אוֹ
or into-hand-of-me give! bread five hand-of-you under there-is

הַנִּמְצָא׃ וַיַּעַן הַכֹּהֵן אֶת־ דָּוִד וַיֹּאמֶר
and-he-said David *** the-priest but-he-answered (5) the-thing-being-found

אֵין־לֶחֶם חֹל אֶל־ תַּחַת יָדִי כִּי־ אִם־ לֶחֶם קֹדֶשׁ יֵשׁ
there-is consecrated bread however but hand-of-me under at ordinary bread not

אִם־ נִשְׁמְרוּ הַנְּעָרִים אַךְ מֵאִשָּׁה׃ וַיַּעַן דָּוִד אֶת־
*** David and-he-replied (6) from-woman only the-men they-kept-themselves if

הַכֹּהֵן וַיֹּאמֶר לוֹ כִּי אִם־ אִשָּׁה עֲצֻרָה־ לָנוּ
from-us being-kept woman indeed that to-him and-he-said the-priest

כִּתְמוֹל שִׁלְשֹׁם בְּצֵאתִי וַיִּהְיוּ כְלֵי־ הַנְּעָרִים קֹדֶשׁ
holy the-men things-of and-they-are when-to-set-out-me before as-yesterday

וְהוּא דֶּרֶךְ חֹל וְאַף כִּי הַיּוֹם יִקְדַּשׁ בַּכֶּלִי׃
concerning-the-thing he-is-holy the-day more so-also not-holy mission when-he

וַיִּתֶּן־ לוֹ הַכֹּהֵן קֹדֶשׁ כִּי לֹא־ הָיָה שָׁם לֶחֶם
bread there he-was not since consecrated the-priest to-him so-he-gave (7)

כִּי־ אִם־ לֶחֶם הַפָּנִים הַמּוּסָרִים מִלִּפְנֵי יְהֹוָה
Yahweh from-before the-ones-being-removed the-Presences bread-of only except

לָשׂוּם לֶחֶם חֹם בְּיוֹם הִלָּקְחוֹ׃ וְשָׁם אִישׁ
man now-there (8) to-be-taken-him on-day hot bread to-be-replaced

מֵעַבְדֵי שָׁאוּל בַּיּוֹם הַהוּא נֶעְצָר לִפְנֵי יְהֹוָה
Yahweh before being-detained the-that on-the-day Saul from-servants-of

saying, 'The LORD is witness
between you and me, and between your descendants and
my descendants forever.' "
Then David left, and Jonathan
went back to the town.

David at Nob

21 David went to Nob, to
Ahimelech the priest.
Ahimelech trembled when he
met him, and asked, "Why are
you alone? Why is no one
with you?"
2David answered Ahimelech
the priest, "The king charged
me with a certain matter and
said to me, 'No one is to know
anything about your mission
and your instructions.' As for
my men, I have told them to
meet me at a certain place.
3Now then, what do you have
on hand? Give me five loaves
of bread, or whatever you can
find."
4But the priest answered David, "I don't have any ordinary bread on hand; however,
there is some consecrated
bread here—provided the men
have kept themselves from
women."
5David replied, "Indeed
women have been kept from
us, as usual whenever[d] I set
out. The men's things[e] are
holy even on missions that are
not holy. How much more so
today!" 6So the priest gave him
the consecrated bread, since
there was no bread there except the bread of the Presence
that had been removed from
before the LORD and replaced
by hot bread on the day it was
taken away.
7Now one of Saul's servants
was there that day, detained

[d]5 *Or from us in the past few days since*
[e]5 *Or bodies*

*1 The Hebrew enumeration of chapter 21 begins in the middle of verse 42 of chapter 20 in the English; thus there is a one-verse discrepancy throughout chapter 21.

וּשְׁמוֹ דֹּאֵג הָאֲדֹמִי אַבִּיר הָרֹעִים אֲשֶׁר לְשָׁאוּל׃

to-Saul who the-ones-shepherding head-of the-Edomite Doeg and-name-of-him

וַיֹּאמֶר דָּוִד לַאֲחִימֶלֶךְ וְאִין יֶשׁ־ פֹּה תַחַת־ יָדְךָ

hand-of-you under here there-is now-not to-Ahimelech David and-he-asked (9)

חֲנִית אוֹ־ חָרֶב כִּי גַם־ חַרְבִּי וְגַם־ כֵּלַי לֹא־ לָקַחְתִּי

I-brought not weapons-of-me or-even sword-of-me either for sword or spear

בְיָדִי כִּי־ הָיָה דְבַר־ הַמֶּלֶךְ נָחוּץ׃ וַיֹּאמֶר

and-he-replied (10) being-urgent the-king business-of he-was for in-hand-of-me

הַכֹּהֵן חֶרֶב גָּלְיָת הַפְּלִשְׁתִּי אֲשֶׁר־ הִכִּיתָ בְּעֵמֶק

in-Valley-of you-killed whom the-Philistine Goliath sword-of the-priest

הָאֵלָה הִנֵּה־ הִיא לוּטָה בַשִּׂמְלָה אַחֲרֵי הָאֵפוֹד אִם־ אֹתָהּ

her if the-ephod behind in-the-cloth being-wrapped she see! the-Elah

תִּקַּח־ לְךָ קָח כִּי אֵין אַחֶרֶת זוּלָתָהּ בָּזֶה וַיֹּאמֶר

and-he-said at-here except-her other not for take! for-you you-would-take

דָּוִד אֵין כָּמוֹהָ תְּנֶנָּה לִּי׃ וַיָּקָם דָּוִד וַיִּבְרַח

and-he-fled David then-he-rose (11) to-me give-her! like-her not David

בַּיּוֹם־ הַהוּא מִפְּנֵי שָׁאוּל וַיָּבֹא אֶל־ אָכִישׁ מֶלֶךְ גַּת׃

Gath king-of Achish to and-he-went Saul from-before the-that on-the-day

וַיֹּאמְרוּ עַבְדֵי אָכִישׁ אֵלָיו הֲלוֹא־ זֶה דָוִד מֶלֶךְ

king-of David this not? to-him Achish servants-of but-they-said (12)

הָאָרֶץ הֲלוֹא לָזֶה יַעֲנוּ בַמְּחֹלוֹת לֵאמֹר הִכָּה שָׁאוּל

Saul he-killed to-say in-the-dances they-sing about-this not? the-land

°בַּאֲלָפָו וְדָוִד °בְּרִבְבֹתָו׃ וַיָּשֶׂם

and-he-took (13) to-ten-of-thousands-of-him and-David to-thousands-of-him

דָּוִד אֶת־ הַדְּבָרִים הָאֵלֶּה בִּלְבָבוֹ וַיִּרָא מְאֹד

very-much and-he-was-afraid to-heart-of-him the-these the-words *** David

מִפְּנֵי אָכִישׁ מֶלֶךְ־ גַּת׃ וַיְשַׁנּוֹ אֶת־ טַעְמוֹ

insanity-of-him *** and-he-feigned-him (14) Gath king-of Achish from-before

בְּעֵינֵיהֶם וַיִּתְהֹלֵל בְּיָדָם °וַיְתָו

and-he-marked in-hand-of-them and-he-acted-like-madman before-eyes-of-them

עַל־ דַּלְתוֹת הַשַּׁעַר וַיּוֹרֶד רִירוֹ אֶל־ זְקָנוֹ׃

beard-of-him into saliva-of-him and-he-let-run-down the-gate doors-of on

וַיֹּאמֶר אָכִישׁ אֶל־ עֲבָדָיו הִנֵּה תִרְאוּ אִישׁ מִשְׁתַּגֵּעַ

being-insane man you-see look! servants-of-him to Achish and-he-said (15)

לָמָּה תָּבִיאוּ אֹתוֹ אֵלָי׃ חֲסַר מְשֻׁגָּעִים אָנִי כִּי־ הֲבֵאתֶם

you-bring that I ones-being-mad short-of (16) to-me him you-bring why?

אֶת־ זֶה לְהִשְׁתַּגֵּעַ עָלָי הֲזֶה יָבוֹא אֶל־ בֵּיתִי׃

house-of-me into must-he-come this? in-front-of-me to-act-madly this ***

before the LORD; he was Doeg
the Edomite, Saul's head shepherd.
[8]David asked Ahimelech,
"Don't you have a spear or a
sword here? I haven't brought
my sword or any other weapon, because the king's
business was urgent."
[9]The priest replied, "The
sword of Goliath the Philistine, whom you killed in the
Valley of Elah, is here; it is
wrapped in a cloth behind the
ephod. If you want it, take it;
there is no sword here but that
one."
David said, "There is none
like it; give it to me."

David at Gath

[10]That day David fled from
Saul and went to Achish king
of Gath. [11]But the servants of
Achish said to him, "Isn't this
David, the king of the land?
Isn't he the one they sing
about in their dances:

"'Saul has slain his
thousands,
and David his tens of
thousands'?"

[12]David took these words to
heart and was very much
afraid of Achish king of Gath.
[13]So he feigned insanity in
their presence; and while he
was in their hands he acted
like a madman, making marks
on the doors of the gate and
letting saliva run down his
beard.
[14]Achish said to his servants,
"Look at the man! He is in-
sane! Why bring him to me?
[15]Am I so short of madmen
that you have to bring this fellow here to carry on like this
in front of me? Must this man
come into my house?"

*See the note on page 220.

°12a ק באלפיו

°12b ק ברבבתיו

°14 ק ויתיו

וַיֵּלֶךְ דָּוִד מִשָּׁם וַיִּמָּלֵט אֶל־ מְעָרַת עֲדֻלָּם
Adullam cave-of to and-he-escaped from-there David and-he-left (22:1)

וַיִּשְׁמְעוּ אֶחָיו וְכָל־ בֵּית אָבִיו
father-of-him household-of and-all-of brothers-of-him when-they-heard

וַיֵּרְדוּ אֵלָיו שָׁמָּה׃ וַיִּתְקַבְּצוּ אֵלָיו כָּל־
every-of around-him and-they-gathered (2) at-there to-him then-they-went-down

אִישׁ מָצוֹק וְכָל־ אִישׁ אֲשֶׁר־ לוֹ נֹשֶׁא וְכָל־
and-every-of one-being-creditor to-him that man and-every-of distressed man

אִישׁ מַר־ נֶפֶשׁ וַיְהִי עֲלֵיהֶם לְשָׂר וַיִּהְיוּ
and-they-were as-leader to-them and-he-became spirit discontent-of man

עִמּוֹ כְּאַרְבַּע מֵאוֹת אִישׁ׃ וַיֵּלֶךְ דָּוִד מִשָּׁם מִצְפֵּה
Mizpah-of from-there David and-he-went (3) man hundreds about-four with-him

מוֹאָב וַיֹּאמֶר | אֶל־ מֶלֶךְ מוֹאָב יֵצֵא־ נָא אָבִי
father-of-me now! let-him-stay Moab king-of to and-he-said Moab

וְאִמִּי אִתְּכֶם עַד אֲשֶׁר אֵדַע מַה־ יַּעֲשֶׂה־ לִּי אֱלֹהִים׃
God for-me he-will-do what I-learn when until with-you and-mother-of-me

וַיַּנְחֵם אֶת־ פְּנֵי מֶלֶךְ מוֹאָב וַיֵּשְׁבוּ עִמּוֹ
with-him and-they-stayed Moab king-of presences-of in so-he-left-them (4)

כָּל־ יְמֵי הֱיוֹת־ דָּוִד בַּמְּצוּדָה׃ וַיֹּאמֶר גָּד הַנָּבִיא
the-prophet Gad but-he-said (5) in-the-stronghold David to-be days-of all-of

אֶל־ דָּוִד לֹא תֵשֵׁב בַּמְּצוּדָה לֵךְ וּבָאתָ־ לְּךָ אֶרֶץ
land-of for-you and-you-enter go! in-the-stronghold you-stay not David to

יְהוּדָה וַיֵּלֶךְ דָּוִד וַיָּבֹא יַעַר חָרֶת׃ וַיִּשְׁמַע שָׁאוּל
Saul now-he-heard (6) Hereth forest-of and-he-went David so-he-left Judah

כִּי נוֹדַע דָּוִד וַאֲנָשִׁים אֲשֶׁר אִתּוֹ וְשָׁאוּל יוֹשֵׁב
sitting and-Saul with-him who and-men David he-was-discovered that

בַּגִּבְעָה תַּחַת־ הָאֶשֶׁל* בָּרָמָה וַחֲנִיתוֹ בְיָדוֹ
in-hand-of-him and-spear-of-him on-the-hill the-tamarisk under in-the-Gibeah

וְכָל־ עֲבָדָיו נִצָּבִים עָלָיו׃ וַיֹּאמֶר שָׁאוּל
Saul and-he-said (7) around-him ones-standing officials-of-him and-all-of

לַעֲבָדָיו הַנִּצָּבִים עָלָיו שִׁמְעוּ־ נָא בְּנֵי יְמִינִי
†Jamite sons-of† now! listen! around-him the-ones-standing to-officials-of-him

גַּם־ לְכֻלְּכֶם יִתֵּן בֶּן־ יִשַׁי שָׂדוֹת וּכְרָמִים
and-vineyards fields Jesse son-of will-he-give to-all-of-you indeed

לְכֻלְּכֶם יָשִׂים שָׂרֵי אֲלָפִים וְשָׂרֵי מֵאוֹת׃
hundreds and-commanders-of thousands commanders-of will-he-make to-all-of-you

כִּי קְשַׁרְתֶּם כֻּלְּכֶם עָלַי וְאֵין־ גֹּלֶה אֶת־
*** he-tells and-no-one against-me all-of-you you-conspired indeed (8)

David at Adullam and Mizpah

22 David left Gath and escaped to the cave of
Adullam. When his brothers
and his father's household
heard about it, they went
down to him there. [2]All those
who were in distress or in
debt or discontented gathered
around him, and he became
their leader. About four hundred men were with him.
[3]From there David went to
Mizpah in Moab and said to
the king of Moab, "Would you
let my father and mother come
and stay with you until I learn
what God will do for me?" [4]So
he left them with the king of
Moab, and they stayed with
him as long as David was in
the stronghold.
[5]But the prophet Gad said to
David, "Do not stay in the
stronghold. Go into the land of
Judah." So David left and
went to the forest of Hereth.

Saul Kills the Priests of Nob

[6]Now Saul heard that David
and his men had been discovered. And Saul, spear in hand,
was seated under the tamarisk
tree on the hill at Gibeah, with
all his officials standing
around him. [7]Saul said to
them, "Listen, men of Benjamin! Will the son of Jesse give
all of you fields and vineyards? Will he make all of you
commanders of thousands
and commanders of hun-
dreds? [8]Is that why you have
all conspired against me? No
one tells me when my son

*6 Most mss have *tsere* under the *aleph* (הָאֵ֫).

†7 That is, *Benjamites.*

אָזְנִי בִּכְרָת־ בְּנִי עִם־ בֶּן־ יִשַׁי וְאֵין־
and-no-one Jesse son-of with son-of-me when-to-make-covenant ear-of-me

חֹלֶה מִכֶּם עָלַי וְגֹלֶה אֶת־ אָזְנִי כִּי הֵקִים
he-incited that ear-of-me *** or-telling about-me from-you being-concerned

בְּנִי אֶת־ עַבְדִּי עָלַי לְאֹרֵב כַּיּוֹם הַזֶּה׃
the-this as-the-day to-lie-in-wait against-me servant-of-me *** son-of-me

וַיַּעַן דֹּאֵג הָאֲדֹמִי וְהוּא נִצָּב עַל־ עַבְדֵי־ שָׁאוּל
Saul officials-of with standing now-he the-Edomite Doeg but-he-said (9)

וַיֹּאמַר רָאִיתִי אֶת־ בֶּן־ יִשַׁי בָּא נֹבֶה אֶל־ אֲחִימֶלֶךְ בֶּן־אֲחִטוּב׃
Ahitub son-of Ahimelech to to-Nob coming Jesse son-of *** I-saw and-he-said

וַיִּשְׁאַל־ לוֹ בַּיהוָה וְצֵידָה נָתַן לוֹ וְאֵת
and to-him he-gave and-provision of-Yahweh for-him and-he-inquired (10)

חֶרֶב גָּלְיָת הַפְּלִשְׁתִּי נָתַן לוֹ׃ וַיִּשְׁלַח הַמֶּלֶךְ
the-king then-he-sent (11) to-him he-gave the-Philistine Goliath sword-of

לִקְרֹא אֶת־ אֲחִימֶלֶךְ בֶּן־ אֲחִיטוּב הַכֹּהֵן וְאֵת כָּל־ בֵּית
family-of whole-of and the-priest Ahitub son-of Ahimelech *** to-call

אָבִיו הַכֹּהֲנִים אֲשֶׁר בְּנֹב וַיָּבֹאוּ כֻלָּם אֶל־ הַמֶּלֶךְ׃
the-king to all-of-them and-they-came at-Nob who the-priests father-of-him

וַיֹּאמֶר שָׁאוּל שְׁמַע־ נָא בֶּן־ אֲחִיטוּב וַיֹּאמֶר הִנְנִי
here-I and-he-answered Ahitub son-of now! listen! Saul and-he-said (12)

אֲדֹנִי׃ וַיֹּאמֶר אֵלָו שָׁאוּל לָמָּה קְשַׁרְתֶּם עָלַי אַתָּה
you against-me you-conspired why? Saul to-him and-he-said (13) lord-of-me

וּבֶן־ יִשָׁי בְּתִתְּךָ לוֹ לֶחֶם וְחֶרֶב וְשָׁאוֹל
and-to-inquire and-sword bread to-him when-to-give-you Jesse and-son-of

לוֹ בֵּאלֹהִים לָקוּם אֵלַי לְאֹרֵב כַּיּוֹם הַזֶּה׃
the-this as-the-day to-lie-in-wait against-me to-rebel of-God for-him

וַיַּעַן אֲחִימֶלֶךְ אֶת־ הַמֶּלֶךְ וַיֹּאמַר וּמִי בְכָל־
of-all-of and-who? and-he-said the-king *** Ahimelech and-he-answered (14)

עֲבָדֶיךָ כְּדָוִד נֶאֱמָן וַחֲתַן הַמֶּלֶךְ וְסָר
and-captain the-king even-son-in-law-of being-loyal as-David servants-of-you

אֶל־ מִשְׁמַעְתֶּךָ וְנִכְבָּד בְּבֵיתֶךָ׃ הַיּוֹם
the-day (15) in-household-of-you and-being-respected bodyguard-of-you of

הַחִלֹּתִי לִשְׁאָול־ לוֹ בֵאלֹהִים חָלִילָה לִּי אַל־ יָשֵׂם הַמֶּלֶךְ
the-king let-him-bring not for-me no! of-God for-him to-inquire was-I-first

בְּעַבְדּוֹ דָבָר בְּכָל־ בֵּית אָבִי כִּי
for father-of-me family-of against-any-of accusation against-servant-of-him

לֹא־ יָדַע עַבְדְּךָ בְּכָל־ זֹאת דָּבָר קָטֹן אוֹ גָדוֹל׃
great or small affair this about-any-of servant-of-you he-knows not

makes a covenant with the
son of Jesse. None of you is
concerned about me or tells
me that my son has incited my
servant to lie in wait for me, as
he does today."
[9]But Doeg the Edomite, who
was standing with Saul's
officials, said, "I saw the son
of Jesse come to Ahimelech
son of Ahitub at Nob.
[10]Ahimelech inquired of the
LORD for him; he also gave him
provisions and the sword of
Goliath the Philistine."
[11]Then the king sent for the
priest Ahimelech son of Ahitub and his father's whole
family, who were the priests at
Nob, and they all came to the
king. [12]Saul said, "Listen now,
son of Ahitub."
"Yes, my lord," he an-
swered.
[13]Saul said to him, "Why
have you conspired against
me, you and the son of Jesse,
giving him bread and a sword
and inquiring of God for him,
so that he has rebelled against
me and lies in wait for me, as
he does today?"
[14]Ahimelech answered the
king, "Who of all your servants is as loyal as David, the
king's son-in-law, captain of
your bodyguard and highly
respected in your household?
[15]Was that day the first time I
inquired of God for him? Of
course not! Let not the king accuse your servant or any of his
father's family, for your servant knows nothing at all
about this whole affair."

°13 ק אליו
°15 ק לשאל

וַיֹּאמֶר הַמֶּלֶךְ מוֹת תָּמוּת אֲחִימֶלֶךְ אַתָּה וְכָל־
and-whole-of you Ahimelech you-will-die to-die the-king but-he-said (16)

בֵּית אָבִיךָ׃ וַיֹּאמֶר הַמֶּלֶךְ לָרָצִים
to-the-ones-guarding the-king then-he-ordered (17) father-of-you family-of

הַנִּצָּבִים עָלָיו סֹבּוּ וְהָמִיתוּ ׀ כֹּהֲנֵי יְהוָה כִּי גַם־
also for Yahweh priests-of and-kill! turn! by-him the-ones-standing

יָדָם עִם־ דָּוִד וְכִי יָדְעוּ כִּי־ בֹרֵחַ הוּא וְלֹא גָלוּ
they-told yet-not he fleeing that they-knew and-for David with hand-of-them

אֶת־ אָזְנִו וְלֹא־ אָבוּ עַבְדֵי הַמֶּלֶךְ לִשְׁלֹחַ אֶת־
*** to-raise the-king officials-of they-were-willing but-not ear-of-me ***

יָדָם לִפְגֹעַ בְּכֹהֲנֵי יְהוָה׃ וַיֹּאמֶר
then-he-ordered (18) Yahweh against-priests-of to-strike hand-of-them

הַמֶּלֶךְ לְדוֹיֵג סֹב אַתָּה וּפְגַע בַּכֹּהֲנִים וַיִּסֹּב דּוֹיֵג
Doeg so-he-turned against-the-priests and-strike! you turn! to-Doeg the-king

הָאֲדֹמִי וַיִּפְגַּע־ הוּא בַּכֹּהֲנִים וַיָּמֶת ׀ בַּיּוֹם
on-the-day and-he-killed against-the-priests he and-he-struck the-Edomite

הַהוּא שְׁמֹנִים וַחֲמִשָּׁה אִישׁ נֹשֵׂא אֵפוֹד בָּד׃ וְאֵת נֹב עִיר־
town-of Nob also (19) linen ephod wearing man and-five eighty the-that

הַכֹּהֲנִים הִכָּה לְפִי־ חֶרֶב מֵאִישׁ וְעַד־ אִשָּׁה מֵעוֹלֵל
from-child woman even-to from-man sword to-edge-of he-put the-priests

וְעַד־ יוֹנֵק וְשׁוֹר וַחֲמוֹר וָשֶׂה לְפִי־ חָרֶב׃
sword to-edge-of and-sheep and-donkey and-cattle one-nursing even-to

וַיִּמָּלֵט בֵּן־ אֶחָד לַאֲחִימֶלֶךְ בֶּן־ אֲחִטוּב וּשְׁמוֹ
and-name-of-him Ahitub son-of of-Ahimelech one son but-he-escaped (20)

אֶבְיָתָר וַיִּבְרַח אַחֲרֵי דָוִד׃ וַיַּגֵּד אֶבְיָתָר לְדָוִד כִּי
that to-David Abiathar and-he-told (21) David after and-he-fled Abiathar

הָרַג שָׁאוּל אֵת כֹּהֲנֵי יְהוָה׃ וַיֹּאמֶר דָּוִד לְאֶבְיָתָר
to-Abiathar David then-he-said (22) Yahweh priests-of *** Saul he-killed

יָדַעְתִּי בַּיּוֹם הַהוּא כִּי־ שָׁם דּוֹיֵג הָאֲדֹמִי כִּי־ הַגֵּד
to-tell that the-Edomite Doeg there when the-that on-the-day I-knew

יַגִּיד לְשָׁאוּל אָנֹכִי סַבֹּתִי בְּכָל־ נֶפֶשׁ בֵּית
family-of life-of for-every-of I-am-responsible I to-Saul he-would-tell

אָבִיךָ׃ שְׁבָה אִתִּי אַל־ תִּירָא כִּי אֲשֶׁר־ יְבַקֵּשׁ אֶת־
*** he-seeks who for you-be-afraid not with-me stay! (23) father-of-you

נַפְשִׁי יְבַקֵּשׁ אֶת־ נַפְשֶׁךָ כִּי־ מִשְׁמֶרֶת אַתָּה עִמָּדִי׃
with-me you safe indeed life-of-you *** he-seeks life-of-me

וַיַּגִּדוּ לְדָוִד לֵאמֹר הִנֵּה פְלִשְׁתִּים נִלְחָמִים
ones-fighting Philistines look! to-say to-David when-they-told (23:1)

16But the king said, "You
will surely die, Ahimelech,
you and your father's whole
family."
17Then the king ordered the
guards at his side: "Turn and
kill the priests of the LORD, because they too have sided with
David. They knew he was fleeing, yet they did not tell me."
But the king's officials were
not willing to raise a hand to
strike the priests of the LORD.
18The king then ordered
Doeg, "You turn and strike
down the priests." So Doeg
the Edomite turned and struck
them down. That day he killed
eighty-five men who wore the
linen ephod. 19He also put to
the sword Nob, the town of
the priests, with its men and
women, its children and infants, and its cattle, donkeys
and sheep.
20But Abiathar, a son of
Ahimelech son of Ahitub, escaped and fled to join David.
21He told David that Saul had
killed the priests of the LORD.
22Then David said to Abiathar:
"That day, when Doeg the
Edomite was there, I knew he
would be sure to tell Saul. I am
responsible for the death of
your father's whole family.
23Stay with me; don't be
afraid; the man who is seeking
your life is seeking mine also.
You will be safe with me."

David Saves Keilah

23 When David was told,
"Look, the Philistines

°17 ק אזני
°18a ק לדואג
°18b ק דואג
°22 ק דואג

בִּקְעִילָה וְהֵמָּה שֹׁסִים אֶת־ הַגֳּרָנוֹת׃
the-threshing-floors *** ones-looting and-they against-Keilah

וַיִּשְׁאַל דָּוִד בַּיהוָה לֵאמֹר הַאֵלֵךְ וְהִכֵּיתִי
and-shall-I-attack shall-I-go? to-say of-Yahweh David and-he-inquired (2)

בַּפְּלִשְׁתִּים הָאֵלֶּה וַיֹּאמֶר יְהוָה אֶל־ דָּוִד לֵךְ
go! David to Yahweh and-he-answered the-these against-the-Philistines

וְהִכִּיתָ בַפְּלִשְׁתִּים וְהוֹשַׁעְתָּ אֶת־קְעִילָה׃ וַיֹּאמְרוּ
but-they-said (3) Keilah *** and-you-save against-the-Philistines and-you-attack

אַנְשֵׁי דָוִד אֵלָיו הִנֵּה אֲנַחְנוּ פֹה בִּיהוּדָה יְרֵאִים וְאַף כִּי־
if and-more ones-being-afraid in-Judah here we see! to-him David men-of

נֵלֵךְ קְעִלָה אֶל־ מַעַרְכוֹת פְּלִשְׁתִּים׃ וַיּוֹסֶף עוֹד דָּוִד
David again and-he-repeated (4) Philistines forces-of against Keilah we-go

לִשְׁאֹל בַּיהוָה וַיַּעֲנֵהוּ יְהוָה וַיֹּאמֶר קוּם רֵד
go-down! rise! and-he-said Yahweh and-he-answered-him of-Yahweh to-inquire

קְעִילָה כִּי־ אֲנִי נֹתֵן אֶת־ פְּלִשְׁתִּים בְּיָדֶךָ׃ וַיֵּלֶךְ דָּוִד
David so-he-went (5) into-hand-of-you Philistines *** giving I for Keilah

וַאֲנָשָׁו קְעִילָה וַיִּלָּחֶם בַּפְּלִשְׁתִּים וַיִּנְהַג
and-he-carried-off against-the-Philistines and-he-fought Keilah and-men-of-him

אֶת־ מִקְנֵיהֶם וַיַּךְ בָּהֶם מַכָּה גְדוֹלָה וַיֹּשַׁע
and-he-saved heavy loss on-them and-he-inflicted livestocks-of-them ***

דָּוִד אֵת יֹשְׁבֵי קְעִילָה׃ וַיְהִי בִּבְרֹחַ אֶבְיָתָר בֶּן־
son-of Abiathar when-to-flee now-he-was (6) Keilah ones-living-of *** David

אֲחִימֶלֶךְ אֶל־ דָּוִד קְעִילָה אֵפוֹד יָרַד בְּיָדוֹ׃
in-hand-of-him he-brought-down ephod Keilah David to Ahimelech

וַיֻּגַּד לְשָׁאוּל כִּי־ בָא דָוִד קְעִילָה וַיֹּאמֶר שָׁאוּל
Saul and-he-said Keilah David he-went that to-Saul and-he-was-told (7)

נִכַּר אֹתוֹ אֱלֹהִים בְּיָדִי כִּי נִסְגַּר לָבוֹא בְּעִיר
into-town to-enter he-imprisoned-himself for into-hand-of-me God him he-gave

דְּלָתַיִם וּבְרִיחַ׃ וַיְשַׁמַּע שָׁאוּל אֶת־ כָּל־ הָעָם לַמִּלְחָמָה
for-the-battle the-force all-of *** Saul and-he-called-up (8) and-bar gates

לָרֶדֶת קְעִילָה לָצוּר אֶל־ דָּוִד וְאֶל־ אֲנָשָׁיו׃
men-of-him and-against David against to-besiege Keilah to-go-down

וַיֵּדַע דָּוִד כִּי עָלָיו שָׁאוּל מַחֲרִישׁ הָרָעָה וַיֹּאמֶר
then-he-said the-harm plotting Saul against-him that David when-he-learned (9)

אֶל־אֶבְיָתָר הַכֹּהֵן הַגִּישָׁה הָאֵפוֹד׃ וַיֹּאמֶר דָּוִד יְהוָה אֱלֹהֵי
God-of Yahweh David and-he-said (10) the-ephod bring! the-priest Abiathar to

יִשְׂרָאֵל שָׁמֹעַ שָׁמַע עַבְדְּךָ כִּי־ מְבַקֵּשׁ שָׁאוּל לָבוֹא אֶל־קְעִילָה
Keilah to to-come Saul planning that servant-of-you he-heard to-hear Israel

are fighting against Keilah
and are looting the threshing
floors," 2 he inquired of the
LORD, saying, "Shall I go and
attack these Philistines?"
The LORD answered him,
"Go, attack the Philistines and
save Keilah."
3 But David's men said to
him, "Here in Judah we are
afraid. How much more, then,
if we go to Keilah against the
Philistine forces!"
4 Once again David inquired
of the LORD, and the LORD answered him, "Go down to Keilah, for I am going to give the
Philistines into your hand."
5 So David and his men went
to Keilah, fought the Philistines and carried off their livestock. He inflicted heavy
losses on the Philistines and
saved the people of Keilah.
6 (Now Abiathar son of Ahimelech had brought the ephod
down with him when he fled
to David at Keilah.)

Saul Pursues David

7 Saul was told that David
had gone to Keilah, and he
said, "God has handed him
over to me, for David has im-
prisoned himself by entering
a town with gates and bars."
8 And Saul called up all his
forces for battle, to go down to
Keilah to besiege David and
his men.
9 When David learned that
Saul was plotting against him,
he said to Abiathar the priest,
"Bring the ephod." 10 David
said, "O LORD, God of Israel,
your servant has heard
definitely that Saul plans to
come to Keilah and destroy

°5 ק ואנשיו

לְשַׁחֵת לָעִיר בַּעֲבוּרִי׃ הֲיַסְגִּרֻנִי בַעֲלֵי

citizens-of will-they-surrender-me? (11) on-account-of-me to-the-city to-destroy

קְעִילָה בְיָדוֹ הֲיֵרֵד שָׁאוּל כַּאֲשֶׁר שָׁמַע עַבְדֶּךָ

servant-of-you he-heard just-as Saul will-he-come-down? into-hand-of-him Keilah

יְהוָה אֱלֹהֵי יִשְׂרָאֵל הַגֶּד־ נָא לְעַבְדֶּךָ וַיֹּאמֶר יְהוָה

Yahweh and-he-said to-servant-of-you now! tell! Israel God-of Yahweh

יֵרֵד׃ וַיֹּאמֶר דָּוִד הֲיַסְגִּרוּ בַּעֲלֵי

citizens-of will-they-surrender? David and-he-asked (12) he-will-come-down

קְעִילָה אֹתִי וְאֶת־ אֲנָשַׁי בְּיַד־ שָׁאוּל וַיֹּאמֶר יְהוָה יַסְגִּירוּ׃

they-will-surrender Yahweh and-he-said Saul into-hand-of men-of-me and me Keilah

וַיָּקָם דָּוִד וַאֲנָשָׁיו כְּשֵׁשׁ־ מֵאוֹת אִישׁ וַיֵּצְאוּ

and-they-left man hundreds about-six and-men-of-him David so-he-rose (13)

מִקְּעִלָה וַיִּתְהַלְּכוּ בַּאֲשֶׁר יִתְהַלָּכוּ וּלְשָׁאוּל הֻגַּד כִּי־

that he-was-told when-to-Saul they-moved to-where and-they-moved from-Keilah

נִמְלַט דָּוִד מִקְּעִילָה וַיֶּחְדַּל לָצֵאת׃ וַיֵּשֶׁב דָּוִד

David and-he-stayed (14) to-go then-he-did-not from-Keilah David he-escaped

בַּמִּדְבָּר בַּמְּצָדוֹת וַיֵּשֶׁב בָּהָר בְּמִדְבַּר־ זִיף

Ziph in-Desert-of in-the-hill and-he-stayed in-the-strongholds in-the-desert

וַיְבַקְשֵׁהוּ שָׁאוּל כָּל־ הַיָּמִים וְלֹא־ נְתָנוֹ אֱלֹהִים

God he-gave-him but-not the-days all-of Saul and-he-searched-for-him

בְּיָדוֹ׃ וַיַּרְא דָּוִד* כִּי־ יָצָא שָׁאוּל לְבַקֵּשׁ

to-take Saul he-came-out that David and-he-learned (15) into-hand-of-him

אֶת־ נַפְשׁוֹ וְדָוִד בְּמִדְבַּר־ זִיף בַּחֹרְשָׁה׃ וַיָּקָם

and-he-rose (16) at-the-Horesh Ziph in-Desert-of while-David life-of-him ***

יְהוֹנָתָן בֶּן־ שָׁאוּל וַיֵּלֶךְ אֶל־ דָּוִד חֹרְשָׁה וַיְחַזֵּק אֶת־

*** and-he-strengthened at-Horesh David to and-he-went Saul son-of Jonathan

יָדוֹ בֵּאלֹהִים׃ וַיֹּאמֶר אֵלָיו אַל־ תִּירָא כִּי לֹא

not for you-be-afraid not to-him and-he-said (17) in-God hand-of-him

תִמְצָאֲךָ יַד שָׁאוּל אָבִי וְאַתָּה תִּמְלֹךְ עַל־

over you-will-be-king and-you father-of-me Saul hand-of she-will-find-you

יִשְׂרָאֵל וְאָנֹכִי אֶהְיֶה־ לְּךָ לְמִשְׁנֶה וְגַם־ שָׁאוּל אָבִי יֹדֵעַ

knowing father-of-me Saul and-even as-second to-you I-will-be and-I Israel

כֵּן׃ וַיִּכְרְתוּ שְׁנֵיהֶם בְּרִית לִפְנֵי יְהוָה וַיֵּשֶׁב

and-he-remained Yahweh before covenant two-of-them and-they-made (18) this

דָּוִד בַּחֹרְשָׁה וִיהוֹנָתָן הָלַךְ לְבֵיתוֹ׃ וַיַּעֲלוּ

and-they-went-up (19) to-home-of-him he-went but-Jonathan at-the-Horesh David

זִפִים אֶל־ שָׁאוּל הַגִּבְעָתָה לֵאמֹר הֲלוֹא דָוִד מִסְתַּתֵּר עִמָּנוּ

among-us hiding David not? to-say at-the-Gibeah Saul to Ziphites

the town on account of me.
[11]Will the citizens of Keilah
surrender me to him? Will
Saul come down, as your servant has heard? O LORD, God
of Israel, tell your servant."
And the LORD said, "He
will."
[12]Again David asked, "Will
the citizens of Keilah surrender me and my men to Saul?"
And the LORD said, "They
will."
[13]So David and his men,
about six hundred in number,
left Keilah and kept moving
from place to place. When Saul
was told that David had escaped from Keilah, he did not
go there.
[14]David stayed in the desert
strongholds and in the hills of
the Desert of Ziph. Day after
day Saul searched for him, but
God did not give David into
his hands.
[15]While David was at Horesh in the Desert of Ziph, he
learned that Saul had come out
to take his life. [16]And Saul's
son Jonathan went to David at
Horesh and helped him find
strength in God. [17]"Don't be
afraid," he said. "My father
Saul will not lay a hand on
you. You will be king over Israel, and I will be second to
you. Even my father Saul
knows this." [18]The two of
them made a covenant before
the LORD. Then Jonathan went
home, but David remained at
Horesh.
[19]The Ziphites went up to
Saul at Gibeah and said, "Is
not David hiding among us in

***15 Most mss have dagesh in the first *daleth* ('דּ).**

בִּמְצָדוֹת בַּחֹרְשָׁה בְּגִבְעַת הַחֲכִילָה אֲשֶׁר מִימִין

to-south-of that the-Hakilah on-hill-of at-the-Horesh in-the-strongholds

הַיְשִׁימוֹן׃ וְעַתָּה לְכָל־ אַוַּת נַפְשְׁךָ הַמֶּלֶךְ

the-king self-of-you pleasure-of as-any-of and-now (20) the-Jeshimon

לָרֶדֶת רֵד וְלָנוּ הַסְגִּירוֹ בְּיַד הַמֶּלֶךְ׃

the-king into-hand-of to-turn-over-him and-to-us come-down! to-come-down

וַיֹּאמֶר שָׁאוּל בְּרוּכִים אַתֶּם לַיהוָה כִּי חֲמַלְתֶּם

you-are-concerned for by-Yahweh you ones-being-blessed Saul and-he-replied (21)

עָלָי׃ לְכוּ־ נָא הָכִינוּ עוֹד וּדְעוּ וּרְאוּ אֶת־ מְקוֹמוֹ

place-of-him *** and-see! and-find-out! further prepare! now! go! (22) for-me

אֲשֶׁר תִּהְיֶה רַגְלוֹ מִי רָאָהוּ שָׁם כִּי אָמַר אֵלַי

to-me he-said for there he-saw-him who foot-of-him she-goes where

עָרוֹם יַעְרִם הוּא׃ וּרְאוּ וּדְעוּ מִכֹּל

about-all-of and-find-out! and-see! (23) he he-is-crafty to-be-crafty

הַמַּחֲבֹאִים אֲשֶׁר יִתְחַבֵּא שָׁם וְשַׁבְתֶּם אֵלַי אֶל־

with to-me and-you-come-back there he-hides where the-hiding-places

נָכוֹן וְהָלַכְתִּי אִתְּכֶם וְהָיָה אִם־ יֶשְׁנוֹ

there-is-him if and-he-will-be with-you then-I-will-go being-definite

בָאָרֶץ וְחִפַּשְׂתִּי אֹתוֹ בְּכֹל אַלְפֵי יְהוּדָה׃

Judah clans-of among-all-of him then-I-will-track-down in-the-area

וַיָּקוּמוּ וַיֵּלְכוּ זִיפָה לִפְנֵי שָׁאוּל וְדָוִד

now-David Saul ahead-of to-Ziph and-they-went so-they-set-out (24)

וַאֲנָשָׁיו בְּמִדְבַּר מָעוֹן בָּעֲרָבָה אֶל יְמִין הַיְשִׁימוֹן׃

the-Jeshimon south-of to in-the-Arabah Maon in-Desert-of and-men-of-him

וַיֵּלֶךְ שָׁאוּל וַאֲנָשָׁיו לְבַקֵּשׁ וַיַּגִּדוּ לְדָוִד

to-David when-they-told to-search and-men-of-him Saul and-he-began (25)

וַיֵּרֶד הַסֶּלַע וַיֵּשֶׁב בְּמִדְבַּר מָעוֹן וַיִּשְׁמַע

when-he-heard Maon in-Desert-of and-he-stayed the-rock then-he-went-down

שָׁאוּל וַיִּרְדֹּף אַחֲרֵי־ דָוִד מִדְבַּר מָעוֹן׃ וַיֵּלֶךְ שָׁאוּל

Saul and-he-went (26) Maon into-Desert-of David after then-he-pursued Saul

מִצַּד הָהָר מִזֶּה וְדָוִד וַאֲנָשָׁיו מִצַּד

along-side-of and-men-of-him and-David on-one the-mountain along-side-of

הָהָר מִזֶּה וַיְהִי דָוִד נֶחְפָּז לָלֶכֶת מִפְּנֵי שָׁאוּל

Saul from-before to-go hurrying David and-he-was on-other the-mountain

וְשָׁאוּל וַאֲנָשָׁיו עֹטְרִים אֶל־ דָּוִד וְאֶל־ אֲנָשָׁיו

men-of-him and-on David on ones-closing-in and-men-of-him and-Saul

לְתָפְשָׂם׃ וּמַלְאָךְ בָּא אֶל־שָׁאוּל לֵאמֹר מַהֲרָה וְלֵכָה

and-come! be-quick! to-say Saul to he-came and-messenger (27) to-capture-them

the strongholds at Horesh, on
the hill of Hakilah, south of Jeshimon? [20]Now, O king, come
down whenever it pleases you
to do so, and we will be responsible for handing him
over to the king."
[21]Saul replied, "The LORD
bless you for your concern for
me. [22]Go and make further
preparation. Find out where
David usually goes and who
has seen him there. They tell
me he is very crafty. [23]Find out
about all the hiding places he
uses and come back to me
with definite information.[f]
Then I will go with you; if he
is in the area, I will track him
down among all the clans of
Judah."
[24]So they set out and went to
Ziph ahead of Saul. Now David and his men were in the
Desert of Maon, in the Arabah
south of Jeshimon. [25]Saul and
his men began the search, and
when David was told about it,
he went down to the rock and
stayed in the Desert of Maon.
When Saul heard this, he went
into the Desert of Maon in
pursuit of David.
[26]Saul was going along one
side of the mountain, and David and his men were on the
other side, hurrying to get
away from Saul. As Saul and
his forces were closing in on
David and his men to capture
them, [27]a messenger came to
Saul, saying, "Come quickly!

[f]23 Or *me at Nacon*

כי־ פשטו פלשתים על־ הארץ׃ וישב שאול
Saul then-he-broke-off (28) the-land over Philistines they-raid for

מרדף אחרי דוד וילך לקראת פלשתים על־ כן קראו
they-call this for Philistines to-meet and-he-went David after from-to-pursue

למקום ההוא סלע המחלקות׃ ויעל דוד משם
from-there David and-he-went-up *(24:1) Hammahlekoth Sela the-this to-the-place

וישב במצדות עין־ גדי׃ ויהי כאשר שב
he-returned just-as and-he-was (2) Gedi En in-strongholds-of and-he-lived

שאול מאחרי פלשתים ויגדו לו לאמר הנה דוד
David see! to-say to-him then-they-told Philistines from-after Saul

במדבר עין גדי׃ ויקח שאול שלשת אלפים איש בחור
being-chosen man thousands three-of Saul so-he-took (3) Gedi En in-Desert-of

מכל־ ישראל וילך לבקש את־ דוד ואנשיו
and-men-of-him David *** to-look-for and-he-set-out Israel from-all-of

על־ פני צורי היעלים׃ ויבא אל־ גדרות הצאן
the-sheep pens-of to and-he-came (4) the-Wild-Goats Crags-of faces-of near

על־ הדרך ושם מערה ויבא שאול להסך את־ רגליו
feet-of-him *** to-cover Saul and-he-went-in cave and-there the-way along

ודוד ואנשיו בירכתי המערה ישבים׃
ones-staying the-cave in-back-parts-of and-men-of-him and-David

ויאמרו אנשי דוד אליו הנה היום אשר־ אמר יהוה
Yahweh he-said that the-day see! to-him David men-of and-they-said (5)

אליך הנה אנכי נתן את־ איביך בידך ועשית
and-you-deal into-hand-of-you being-enemy-of-you *** giving I see! to-you

לו כאשר יטב בעיניך ויקם דוד ויכרת
and-he-cut David then-he-crept-up in-eyes-of-you he-is-good just-as with-him

את־ כנף־ המעיל אשר־לשאול בלט׃ ויהי אחרי־ כן
this after and-he-was (6) unnoticed to-Saul that the-robe corner-of ***

ויך לב־ דוד אתו על אשר כרת את־ כנף אשר
that corner *** he-cut-off when for him David conscience-of then-he-struck

לשאול׃ ויאמר לאנשיו חלילה לי מיהוה אם־
that by-Yahweh from-me far-be-it! to-men-of-him and-he-said (7) to-Saul

אעשה את־ הדבר הזה לאדני למשיח יהוה
Yahweh to-anointed-of to-master-of-me the-this the-thing *** I-should-do

לשלח ידי בו כי־ משיח יהוה הוא׃ וישסע
and-he-rebuked (8) he Yahweh anointed-of for against-him hand-of-me to-lift

דוד את־ אנשיו בדברים ולא נתנם לקום אל־
against to-attack he-allowed-them and-not with-the-words men-of-him *** David

The Philistines are raiding the
land." 28Then Saul broke off
his pursuit of David and went
to meet the Philistines. That is
why they call this place Sela
Hammahlekoth.[g] 29And David
went up from there and lived
in the strongholds of En Gedi.

David Spares Saul's Life

24 After Saul returned
from pursuing the Phil-
istines, he was told, "David is
in the Desert of En Gedi." 2So
Saul took three thousand chosen men from all Israel and set
out to look for David and his
men near the Crags of the
Wild Goats.
3He came to the sheep pens
along the way; a cave was
there, and Saul went in to re-
lieve himself. David and his
men were far back in the cave.
4The men said, "This is the
very day the LORD spoke of
when he said to you, 'I will
give your enemy into your
hands for you to deal with as
you wish.'" Then David crept
up unnoticed and cut off a corner of Saul's robe.
5Afterward, David was conscience-stricken for having
cut off a corner of his robe. 6He
said to his men, "The LORD
forbid that I should do such a
thing to my master, the LORD's
anointed, or lift my hand
against him; for he is the
anointed of the LORD." 7With
these words David rebuked
his men and did not allow

g28 *Sela Hammahlekoth* means *rock of parting.*

***1 The Hebrew enumeration of chapter 24 begins with verse 29 of chapter 23 in the English; thus there is a one-verse discrepancy throughout chapter 24.**

°5 ק איבך

שָׁאוּל וְשָׁאוּל קָם מֵהַמְּעָרָה וַיֵּלֶךְ בַּדָּרֶךְ׃ וַיָּקָם
then-he-rose (9) on-the-way and-he-went from-the-cave he-left and-Saul Saul

דָּוִד אַחֲרֵי־כֵן וַיֵּצֵא מִן־הַמְּעָרָה וַיִּקְרָא אַחֲרֵי־שָׁאוּל
Saul after and-he-called the-cave from and-he-went-out this after David

לֵאמֹר אֲדֹנִי הַמֶּלֶךְ וַיַּבֵּט שָׁאוּל אַחֲרָיו וַיִּקֹּד דָּוִד
David then-he-bowed behind-him Saul when-he-looked the-king lord-of-me to-say

אַפַּיִם אַרְצָה וַיִּשְׁתָּחוּ׃ וַיֹּאמֶר דָּוִד לְשָׁאוּל לָמָּה
why? to-Saul David and-he-said (10) and-he-prostrated-himself to-ground faces

תִשְׁמַע אֶת־דִּבְרֵי אָדָם לֵאמֹר הִנֵּה דָוִד מְבַקֵּשׁ רָעָתֶךָ׃ הִנֵּה
see! (11) harm-of-you seeking David see! to-say man words-of *** you-listen

הַיּוֹם הַזֶּה רָאוּ עֵינֶיךָ אֵת אֲשֶׁר־נְתָנְךָ יְהוָה הַיּוֹם
the-day Yahweh he-delivered-you how *** eyes-of-you they-saw the-this the-day

בְּיָדִי בַּמְּעָרָה וְאָמַר לַהֲרָגְךָ וַתָּחָס עָלֶיךָ
to-you †but-she-spared to-kill-you and-he-urged in-the-cave into-hand-of-me

וָאֹמַר לֹא־אֶשְׁלַח יָדִי בַּאדֹנִי כִּי־מְשִׁיחַ
anointed-of for against-master-of-me hand-of-me I-will-lift not and-I-said

יְהוָה הוּא׃ וְאָבִי רְאֵה גַּם רְאֵה אֶת־כְּנַף מְעִילְךָ
robe-of-you piece-of *** look-at! indeed look-at! now-father-of-me (12) he Yahweh

בְּיָדִי כִּי בְּכָרְתִי אֶת־כְּנַף מְעִילְךָ וְלֹא הֲרַגְתִּיךָ
I-killed-you but-not robe-of-you corner-of *** to-cut-off-me for in-hand-of-me

דַּע וּרְאֵה כִּי אֵין בְּיָדִי רָעָה וָפֶשַׁע
or-rebellion wrong in-hand-of-me not that and-recognize! understand!

וְלֹא־חָטָאתִי לָךְ וְאַתָּה צֹדֶה אֶת־נַפְשִׁי לְקַחְתָּהּ׃
to-take-her life-of-me *** hunting but-you against-you I-wronged and-not

יִשְׁפֹּט יְהוָה בֵּינִי וּבֵינֶךָ וּנְקָמַנִי
and-may-he-avenge-me and-between-you between-me Yahweh may-he-judge (13)

יְהוָה מִמֶּךָּ וְיָדִי לֹא תִהְיֶה־בָּךְ׃ כַּאֲשֶׁר
just-as (14) against-you she-will-be not but-hand-of-me from-you Yahweh

יֹאמַר מְשַׁל הַקַּדְמֹנִי מֵרְשָׁעִים יֵצֵא רֶשַׁע וְיָדִי
so-hand-of-me evil-deed he-comes from-evildoers the-old saying-of she-says

לֹא תִהְיֶה־בָּךְ׃ אַחֲרֵי מִי יָצָא מֶלֶךְ יִשְׂרָאֵל
Israel king-of he-came-out whom? against (15) against-you she-will-be not

אַחֲרֵי מִי אַתָּה רֹדֵף אַחֲרֵי כֶּלֶב מֵת אַחֲרֵי פַּרְעֹשׁ אֶחָד׃
one flea after being-dead dog after pursuing you whom? after

וְהָיָה יְהוָה לְדַיָּן וְשָׁפַט בֵּינִי וּבֵינֶךָ
and-between-you between-me and-may-he-decide as-judge Yahweh now-may-he-be (16)

וְיֵרֶא וְיָרֵב אֶת־רִיבִי וְיִשְׁפְּטֵנִי
and-may-he-vindicate-me cause-of-me *** and-may-he-uphold and-may-he-consider

them to attack Saul. And Saul
left the cave and went his way.
8 Then David went out of the
cave and called out to Saul,
"My lord the king!" When
Saul looked behind him, David bowed down and prostrated himself with his face to the
ground. 9 He said to Saul,
"Why do you listen when men
say, 'David is bent on harming you'? 10 This day you have
seen with your own eyes how
the LORD delivered you into
my hands in the cave. Some
urged me to kill you, but I
spared you; I said, 'I will not
lift my hand against my master, because he is the LORD's
anointed.' 11 See, my father,
look at this piece of your robe
in my hand! I cut off the corner
of your robe but did not kill
you. Now understand and
recognize that I am not guilty
of wrongdoing or rebellion. I
have not wronged you, but
you are hunting me down to
take my life. 12 May the LORD
judge between you and me.
And may the LORD avenge the
wrongs you have done to me,
but my hand will not touch
you. 13 As the old saying goes,
'From evildoers come evil
deeds,' so my hand will not
touch you.
14 "Against whom has the
king of Israel come out?
Whom are you pursuing? A
dead dog? A flea? 15 May the
LORD be our judge and decide
between us. May he consider
my cause and uphold it; may
he vindicate me by delivering

*See the note on page 228.

†*11* The major ancient versions read this as first person, *"but-I-spared"*.

°9 ק מהמערה

מִיָּדֶךָ׃ וַיְהִי ׀ כְּכַלּוֹת דָּוִד לְדַבֵּר אֶת־הַדְּבָרִים
the-words *** to-say David when-to-finish and-he-was (17) from-hand-of-you

הָאֵלֶּה אֶל־שָׁאוּל וַיֹּאמֶר שָׁאוּל הֲקֹלְךָ זֶה בְּנִי דָוִד
David son-of-me that voice-of-you? Saul and-he-asked Saul to the-these

וַיִּשָּׂא שָׁאוּל קֹלוֹ וַיֵּבְךְּ׃ וַיֹּאמֶר אֶל־דָּוִד
David to and-he-said (18) and-he-wept voice-of-him Saul and-he-raised

צַדִּיק אַתָּה מִמֶּנִּי כִּי אַתָּה גְּמַלְתַּנִי הַטּוֹבָה וַאֲנִי גְּמַלְתִּיךָ
I-treated-you but-I the-good you-treated-me you for more-than-I you righteous

הָרָעָה׃ וְאַתְּ הִגַּדְתָּ הַיּוֹם אֵת אֲשֶׁר־עָשִׂיתָה אִתִּי טוֹבָה אֵת אֲשֶׁר
that *** good to-me you-did that *** the-day you-told and-you (19) the-bad

סִגְּרַנִי יְהוָה בְּיָדְךָ וְלֹא הֲרַגְתָּנִי׃ וְכִי־
now-when (20) you-killed-me but-not into-hand-of-you Yahweh he-delivered-me

יִמְצָא אִישׁ אֶת־אֹיְבוֹ וְשִׁלְּחוֹ בְּדֶרֶךְ טוֹבָה
unharmed on-way then-does-he-let-go-him being-enemy-of-him *** man he-finds

וַיהוָה יְשַׁלֶּמְךָ טוֹבָה תַּחַת הַיּוֹם הַזֶּה אֲשֶׁר עָשִׂיתָה
you-treated how the-this the-day for well may-he-reward-you now-Yahweh

לִי׃ וְעַתָּה הִנֵּה יָדַעְתִּי כִּי מָלֹךְ תִּמְלוֹךְ
you-will-be-king to-be-king that I-know see! and-now (21) to-me

וְקָמָה בְּיָדְךָ מַמְלֶכֶת יִשְׂרָאֵל׃ וְעַתָּה
and-now (22) Israel kingdom-of in-hand-of-you and-she-will-be-established

הִשָּׁבְעָה לִּי בַּיהוָה אִם־תַּכְרִית אֶת־זַרְעִי אַחֲרָי
after-me descendant-of-me *** you-will-cut-off not by-Yahweh to-me swear!

וְאִם־תַּשְׁמִיד אֶת־שְׁמִי מִבֵּית אָבִי׃
father-of-me from-family-of name-of-me *** you-will-wipe-out and-not

וַיִּשָּׁבַע דָּוִד לְשָׁאוּל וַיֵּלֶךְ שָׁאוּל אֶל־בֵּיתוֹ
home-of-him to Saul and-he-returned to-Saul David so-he-gave-oath (23)

וְדָוִד וַאֲנָשָׁיו עָלוּ עַל־הַמְּצוּדָה׃ וַיָּמָת
now-he-died (25:1) the-stronghold to they-went-up and-men-of-him but-David

שְׁמוּאֵל וַיִּקָּבְצוּ כָל־יִשְׂרָאֵל וַיִּסְפְּדוּ־לוֹ
for-him and-they-mourned Israel all-of and-they-assembled Samuel

וַיִּקְבְּרֻהוּ בְּבֵיתוֹ בָּרָמָה וַיָּקָם דָּוִד
David then-he-rose in-the-Ramah at-home-of-him and-they-buried-him

וַיֵּרֶד אֶל־מִדְבַּר פָּארָן׃ וְאִישׁ בְּמָעוֹן וּמַעֲשֵׂהוּ
and-property-of-him in-Maon now-man (2) Paran Desert-of to and-he-moved-down

בַכַּרְמֶל וְהָאִישׁ גָּדוֹל מְאֹד וְלוֹ צֹאן שְׁלֹשֶׁת־אֲלָפִים
thousands three-of sheep and-to-him very wealthy and-the-man at-the-Carmel

וְאֶלֶף עִזִּים וַיְהִי בִּגְזֹז אֶת־צֹאנוֹ בַּכַּרְמֶל׃
in-the-Carmel sheep-of-him *** when-to-shear and-he-was goats and-thousand

me from your hand."
[16]When David finished saying this, Saul asked, "Is that
your voice, David my son?"
And he wept aloud. [17]"You are
more righteous than I," he
said. "You have treated me
well, but I have treated you
badly. [18]You have just now
told me of the good you did to
me; the LORD delivered me
into your hands, but you did
not kill me. [19]When a man
finds his enemy, does he let
him get away unharmed? May
the LORD reward you well for
the way you treated me today.
[20]I know that you will surely
be king and that the kingdom
of Israel will be established in
your hands. [21]Now swear to
me by the LORD that you will
not cut off my descendants or
wipe out my name from my
father's family."
[22]So David gave his oath to
Saul. Then Saul returned
home, but David and his men
went up to the stronghold.

David, Nabal and Abigail

25 Now Samuel died, and
all Israel assembled
and mourned for him; and
they buried him at his home
in Ramah.
Then David moved down
into the Desert of Maon.[h] [2]A
certain man in Maon, who
had property there at Carmel,
was very wealthy. He had a
thousand goats and three
thousand sheep, which he
was shearing in Carmel. [3]His

[h]1 Some Septuagint manuscripts; Hebrew *Paran*

*See the note on page 228.

°19 ק ואתה

וְשֵׁם הָאִישׁ נָבָל וְשֵׁם אִשְׁתּוֹ אֲבִגָיִל וְהָאִשָּׁה
and-the-woman Abigail wife-of-him and-name-of Nabal the-man and-name-of (3)

טוֹבַת־ שֶׂכֶל וִיפַת תֹּאַר וְהָאִישׁ קָשֶׁה וְרַע
and-mean-of surly but-the-husband form and-beautiful-of intelligence good-of

מַעֲלָלִים וְהוּא כָלִבּוֹ׃ וַיִּשְׁמַע דָּוִד בַּמִּדְבָּר כִּי־ גֹזֵז
shearing that in-the-desert David and-he-heard (4) Calebite and-he dealings

נָבָל אֶת־ צֹאנוֹ׃ וַיִּשְׁלַח דָּוִד עֲשָׂרָה נְעָרִים וַיֹּאמֶר דָּוִד
David and-he-said young-men ten David so-he-sent (5) sheep-of-him *** Nabal

לַנְּעָרִים עֲלוּ כַרְמֶלָה וּבָאתֶם אֶל־ נָבָל וּשְׁאֶלְתֶּם־ לוֹ
to-him and-you-greet Nabal to and-you-go to-Carmel go-up! to-the-men

בִשְׁמִי לְשָׁלוֹם׃ וַאֲמַרְתֶּם כֹּה לֶחָי וְאַתָּה שָׁלוֹם
health and-you to-life this and-you-say (6) for-peace in-name-of-me

וּבֵיתְךָ שָׁלוֹם וְכֹל אֲשֶׁר־ לְךָ שָׁלוֹם׃ וְעַתָּה שָׁמַעְתִּי
I-hear and-now (7) health to-you that and-all health and-household-of-you

כִּי גֹזְזִים לָךְ עַתָּה הָרֹעִים אֲשֶׁר־ לְךָ הָיוּ עִמָּנוּ
with-us they-were to-you who the-ones-herding when to-you ones-shearing that

לֹא הֶכְלַמְנוּם וְלֹא־ נִפְקַד לָהֶם מְאוּמָה כָּל־ יְמֵי
days-of all-of anything of-them he-was-missed and-not we-mistreated-them not

הֱיוֹתָם בַּכַּרְמֶל׃ שְׁאַל אֶת־ נְעָרֶיךָ וְיַגִּידוּ
and-they-will-tell servants-of-you *** ask! (8) at-the-Carmel to-be-them

לָךְ וְיִמְצְאוּ הַנְּעָרִים חֵן בְּעֵינֶיךָ כִּי־ עַל־ יוֹם
day on since in-eyes-of-you favor the-young-men now-may-they-find to-you

טוֹב בָּנוּ תְּנָה־ נָּא אֵת אֲשֶׁר תִּמְצָא יָדְךָ לַעֲבָדֶיךָ
to-servants-of-you hand-of-you she-finds what *** now! give! to-us festive

וּלְבִנְךָ לְדָוִד׃ וַיָּבֹאוּ נַעֲרֵי דָוִד וַיְדַבְּרוּ
then-they-spoke David men-of when-they-arrived (9) to-David and-to-son-of-you

אֶל־נָבָל כְּכָל־ הַדְּבָרִים הָאֵלֶּה בְּשֵׁם דָּוִד וַיָּנוּחוּ׃
and-they-waited David in-name-of the-these the-messages as-all-of Nabal to

וַיַּעַן נָבָל אֶת־ עַבְדֵי דָוִד וַיֹּאמֶר מִי דָוִד
David who? and-he-said David servants-of *** Nabal and-he-answered (10)

וּמִי בֶן־ יִשָׁי הַיּוֹם רַבּוּ עֲבָדִים הַמִּתְפָּרְצִים
the-ones-breaking-away servants they-are-many the-day Jesse son-of and-who?

אִישׁ מִפְּנֵי אֲדֹנָיו׃ וְלָקַחְתִּי אֶת־ לַחְמִי וְאֶת־
and bread-of-me *** now-should-I-take (11) masters-of-him from-before each

מֵימַי וְאֵת טִבְחָתִי אֲשֶׁר טָבַחְתִּי לְגֹזְזָי
for-ones-shearing-of-me I-slaughtered that meat-of-me and waters-of-me

וְנָתַתִּי לַאֲנָשִׁים אֲשֶׁר לֹא יָדַעְתִּי אֵי מִזֶּה הֵמָּה׃ וַיַּהַפְכוּ
so-they-turned (12) they from-there where I-know not whom to-men and-I-give

name was Nabal and his
wife's name was Abigail. She
was an intelligent and beautiful woman, but her husband, a
Calebite, was surly and mean
in his dealings.
[4]While David was in the
desert, he heard that Nabal
was shearing sheep. [5]So he
sent ten young men and said
to them, "Go up to Nabal at
Carmel and greet him in my
name. [6]Say to him: 'Long life
to you! Good health to you and
your household! And good
health to all that is yours!
[7]"'Now I hear that it is
sheep-shearing time. When
your shepherds were with us,
we did not mistreat them, and
the whole time they were at
Carmel nothing of theirs was
missing. [8]Ask your own servants and they will tell you.
Therefore be favorable toward
my young men, since we come
at a festive time. Please give
your servants and your son
David whatever you can find
for them.'"
[9]When David's men arrived,
they gave Nabal this message
in David's name. Then they
waited.
[10]Nabal answered David's
servants, "Who is this David?
Who is this son of Jesse? Many
servants are breaking away
from their masters these days.
[11]Why should I take my bread
and water, and the meat I
have slaughtered for my
shearers, and give it to men
coming from who knows
where?"

°3 ק כלבי

נַעֲרֵי־ דָוִד לְדַרְכָּם וַיָּשֻׁבוּ וַיָּבֹאוּ וַיַּגִּדוּ
then-they-told when-they-arrived and-they-went-back to-way-of-them David men-of

לוֹ כְּכֹל הַדְּבָרִים הָאֵלֶּה׃ וַיֹּאמֶר דָּוִד לַאֲנָשָׁיו
to-men-of-him David and-he-said (13) the-these the-words as-all-of to-him

חִגְרוּ ׀ אִישׁ אֶת־ חַרְבּוֹ וַיַּחְגְּרוּ אִישׁ אֶת־ חַרְבּוֹ
sword-of-him *** each so-they-put-on sword-of-him *** each put-on!

וַיַּחְגֹּר גַּם־ דָּוִד אֶת־ חַרְבּוֹ וַיַּעֲלוּ ׀ אַחֲרֵי דָוִד
David with and-they-went-up sword-of-him *** David also and-he-put-on

כְּאַרְבַּע מֵאוֹת אִישׁ וּמָאתַיִם יָשְׁבוּ עַל־ הַכֵּלִים׃
the-supplies with they-stayed and-two-hundreds man hundreds about-four

וְלַאֲבִיגַיִל אֵשֶׁת נָבָל הִגִּיד נַעַר־ אֶחָד מֵהַנְּעָרִים לֵאמֹר
to-say from-servants one servant he-told Nabal wife-of now-to-Abigail (14)

הִנֵּה שָׁלַח דָּוִד מַלְאָכִים ׀ מֵהַמִּדְבָּר לְבָרֵךְ אֶת־ אֲדֹנֵינוּ
masters-of-us *** to-greet from-the-desert messengers David he-sent see!

וַיָּעַט בָּהֶם׃ וְהָאֲנָשִׁים טֹבִים לָנוּ מְאֹד וְלֹא
and-not very to-us ones-good yet-the-men (15) at-them but-he-insulted

הָכְלַמְנוּ וְלֹא־ פָקַדְנוּ מְאוּמָה כָּל־ יְמֵי הִתְהַלַּכְנוּ
to-walk-us days-of all-of anything we-missed and-not they-mistreated-us

אִתָּם בִּהְיוֹתֵנוּ בַּשָּׂדֶה׃ חוֹמָה הָיוּ עָלֵינוּ גַּם־
both around-us they-were wall (16) in-the-field when-to-be-us near-them

לַיְלָה גַּם־ יוֹמָם כָּל־ יְמֵי הֱיוֹתֵנוּ עִמָּם רֹעִים הַצֹּאן׃
the-sheep ones-herding near-them to-be-us days-of all-of by-day and night

וְעַתָּה דְּעִי וּרְאִי מַה־ תַּעֲשִׂי כִּי־ כָלְתָה הָרָעָה
the-disaster she-hangs for you-can-do what and-see! think-over! and-now (17)

אֶל־ אֲדֹנֵינוּ וְעַל כָּל־ בֵּיתוֹ וְהוּא בֶּן־ בְּלִיַּעַל
wicked son-of now-he household-of-him whole-of and-over masters-of-us over

מִדַּבֵּר אֵלָיו׃ וַתְּמַהֵר אֲבוֹגַיִל וַתִּקַּח מָאתַיִם
two-hundreds and-she-took Abigail and-she-hurried (18) to-him from-to-talk

לֶחֶם וּשְׁנַיִם נִבְלֵי־ יַיִן וְחָמֵשׁ צֹאן עֲשׂוּוֹת וְחָמֵשׁ
and-five ones-being-dressed sheep and-five wine skins-of and-two bread

סְאִים קָלִי וּמֵאָה צִמֻּקִים וּמָאתַיִם דְּבֵלִים
pressed-figs and-two-hundreds raisin-cakes and-hundred roasted-grain seahs

וַתָּשֶׂם עַל־ הַחֲמֹרִים׃ וַתֹּאמֶר לִנְעָרֶיהָ עִבְרוּ
go-on! to-servants-of-her then-she-told (19) the-donkeys on and-she-loaded

לְפָנַי הִנְנִי אַחֲרֵיכֶם בָּאָה וּלְאִישָׁהּ נָבָל לֹא
not Nabal but-to-husband-of-her following after-you see-I! ahead-of-me

הִגִּידָה׃ וְהָיָה הִיא ׀ רֹכֶבֶת עַל־הַחֲמוֹר וְיֹרֶדֶת בְּסֵתֶר
into-ravine-of and-descending the-donkey on riding she and-he-was (20) she-told

°18a ק אביגיל
°18b ק עשויות

12 David's men turned
around and went back. When
they arrived, they reported
every word. 13 David said to his
men, "Put on your swords!" So
they put on their swords, and
David put on his. About four
hundred men went up with
David, while two hundred
stayed with the supplies.
14 One of the servants told
Nabal's wife Abigail: "David
sent messengers from the
desert to give our master his
greetings, but he hurled insults at them. 15 Yet these men
were very good to us. They did
not mistreat us, and the whole
time we were out in the fields
near them nothing was missing. 16 Night and day they were
a wall around us all the time
we were herding our sheep
near them. 17 Now think it over
and see what you can do, because disaster is hanging over
our master and his whole
household. He is such a
wicked man that no one can
talk to him."
18 Abigail lost no time. She
took two hundred loaves of
bread, two skins of wine, five
dressed sheep, five seahs[i] of
roasted grain, a hundred cakes
of raisins and two hundred
cakes of pressed figs, and loaded them on donkeys. 19 Then
she told her servants, "Go on
ahead; I'll follow you." But she
did not tell her husband Nabal.
20 As she came riding her

[i]18 That is, probably about a bushel (about 37 liters)

הָהָר וְהִנֵּה דָוִד וַאֲנָשָׁיו יֹרְדִים לִקְרָאתָהּ
to-encounter-her ones-descending and-men-of-him David and-see! the-mountain

וַתִּפְגֹּשׁ אֹתָם׃ וְדָוִד אָמַר אַךְ לַשֶּׁקֶר שָׁמַרְתִּי
I-watched for-the-uselessness indeed he-said and-David (21) them and-she-met

אֶת־כָּל־אֲשֶׁר לָזֶה בַּמִּדְבָּר וְלֹא־נִפְקַד מִכָּל־אֲשֶׁר־
that from-all he-was-missed so-not in-the-desert to-this-one that all ***

לוֹ מְאוּמָה וַיָּשֶׁב־לִי רָעָה תַּחַת טוֹבָה׃ כֹּה־יַעֲשֶׂה
may-he-deal so (22) good for evil to-me now-he-paid-back anything to-him

אֱלֹהִים לְאֹיְבֵי דָוִד וְכֹה יֹסִיף אִם־אַשְׁאִיר
I-leave-alive if may-he-be-severe and-so David with-being-enemies-of God

מִכָּל־אֲשֶׁר־לוֹ עַד־הַבֹּקֶר מַשְׁתִּין בְּקִיר׃ וַתֵּרֶא
when-she-saw (23) against-wall one-urinating the-morning by to-him that of-all

אֲבִיגַיִל אֶת־דָּוִד וַתְּמַהֵר וַתֵּרֶד מֵעַל הַחֲמוֹר
the-donkey from-on and-she-got-off then-she-was-quick David *** Abigail

וַתִּפֹּל לְאַפֵּי דָוִד עַל־פָּנֶיהָ וַתִּשְׁתַּחוּ אָרֶץ׃
ground and-she-bowed faces-of-her on David before-faces-of and-she-fell

וַתִּפֹּל עַל־רַגְלָיו וַתֹּאמֶר בִּי־אֲנִי אֲדֹנִי הֶעָוֹן
the-blame lord-of-me me upon-me and-she-said feet-of-him at and-she-fell (24)

וּתְדַבֶּר־נָא אֲמָתְךָ בְּאָזְנֶיךָ וּשְׁמַע אֵת דִּבְרֵי
words-of *** and-hear! into-ears-of-you servant-of-you now! and-let-her-speak

אֲמָתֶךָ׃ אַל־נָא יָשִׂים אֲדֹנִי אֶת־לִבּוֹ אֶל־
to heart-of-him *** lord-of-me may-he-attend now! not (25) servant-of-you

אִישׁ הַבְּלִיַּעַל הַזֶּה עַל־נָבָל כִּי כִשְׁמוֹ כֶּן־הוּא נָבָל
Fool he so like-name-of-him for Nabal to the-this the-wickedness man-of

שְׁמוֹ וּנְבָלָה עִמּוֹ וַאֲנִי אֲמָתְךָ לֹא רָאִיתִי אֶת־נַעֲרֵי
men-of *** I-saw not servant-of-you but-I with-him and-folly name-of-him

אֲדֹנִי אֲשֶׁר שָׁלָחְתָּ׃ וְעַתָּה אֲדֹנִי חַי־יְהוָה
Yahweh life-of master-of-me and-now (26) you-sent whom master-of-me

וְחֵי־נַפְשְׁךָ אֲשֶׁר מְנָעֲךָ יְהוָה מִבּוֹא בְדָמִים
to-bloodsheds from-to-come Yahweh he-kept-you since self-of-you and-life-of

וְהוֹשֵׁעַ יָדְךָ לָךְ וְעַתָּה יִהְיוּ כְנָבָל
like-Nabal may-they-be and-now for-you hand-of-you and-to-avenge

אֹיְבֶיךָ וְהַמְבַקְשִׁים אֶל־אֲדֹנִי רָעָה׃ וְעַתָּה
and-now (27) harm master-of-me to and-the-ones-intending being-enemies-of-you

הַבְּרָכָה הַזֹּאת אֲשֶׁר־הֵבִיא שִׁפְחָתְךָ לַאדֹנִי
to-master-of-me servant-of-you he-brought which the-this the-gift

וְנִתְּנָה לַנְּעָרִים הַמִּתְהַלְּכִים בְּרַגְלֵי אֲדֹנִי׃
master-of-me at-feet-of the-ones-following to-the-men and-let-her-be-given

donkey into a mountain ravine, there were David and his men descending toward her, and she met them.
21 David had just said, "It's been useless—all my watching over this fellow's property in the desert so that nothing of his was missing. He has paid me back evil for good.
22 May God deal with David,[j] be it ever so severely, if by morning I leave alive one male of all who belong to him!"

23 When Abigail saw David, she quickly got off her donkey and bowed down before David with her face to the ground.
24 She fell at his feet and said: "My lord, let the blame be on me alone. Please let your servant speak to you; hear what your servant has to say.
25 May my lord pay no attention to that wicked man Nabal. He is just like his name—his name is Fool, and folly goes with him. But as for me, your servant, I did not see the men my master sent.

26 "Now since the LORD has kept you, my master, from bloodshed and from avenging yourself with your own hands, as surely as the LORD lives and as you live, may your enemies and all who intend to harm my master be like Nabal.
27 And let this gift, which your servant has brought to my master, be given to the men

j22 Some Septuagint manuscripts; Hebrew *with David's enemies*

שָׂא נָא לְפֶשַׁע אֲמָתֶךָ כִּי עָשֹׂה־ יַעֲשֶׂה
he-will-make to-make for servant-of-you to-offense-of now! forgive! (28)

יְהוָה לַאדֹנִי בַּיִת נֶאֱמָן כִּי־ מִלְחֲמוֹת יְהוָה אֲדֹנִי
master-of-me Yahweh battles-of for lasting dynasty for-master-of-me Yahweh

נִלְחָם וְרָעָה לֹא־ תִמָּצֵא בְךָ מִיָּמֶיךָ׃
during-days-of-you in-you let-her-be-found not and-wrongdoing fighting

וַיָּקָם אָדָם לִרְדָפְךָ וּלְבַקֵּשׁ אֶת־ נַפְשֶׁךָ
life-of-you *** and-to-take to-pursue-you someone though-he-rises (29)

וְהָיְתָה נֶפֶשׁ אֲדֹנִי צְרוּרָה׀ בִּצְרוֹר הַחַיִּים
the-ones-alive in-bundle-of being-bound master-of-me life-of then-she-will-be

אֵת יְהוָה אֱלֹהֶיךָ וְאֵת נֶפֶשׁ אֹיְבֶיךָ יְקַלְּעֶנָּה
he-will-hurl-away-her being-enemies-of-you life-of but God-of-you Yahweh by

בְּתוֹךְ כַּף הַקָּלַע׃ וְהָיָה כִּי־ יַעֲשֶׂה יְהוָה
Yahweh he-does when and-he-will-be (30) the-sling pocket-of inside-of

לַאדֹנִי כְּכֹל אֲשֶׁר־ דִּבֶּר אֶת־ הַטּוֹבָה עָלֶיךָ
about-you the-good *** he-promised that as-all for-master-of-me

וְצִוְּךָ לְנָגִיד עַל־ יִשְׂרָאֵל׃ וְלֹא תִהְיֶה זֹאת׀
this she-will-be then-not (31) Israel over as-leader and-he-appoints-you

לְךָ לְפוּקָה וּלְמִכְשׁוֹל לֵב לַאדֹנִי וְלִשְׁפָּךְ־
that-to-shed of-master-of-me conscience or-for-stumbling-of for-staggering to-you

דָּם חִנָּם וּלְהוֹשִׁיעַ אֲדֹנִי לוֹ וְהֵיטִב
when-he-brings-success for-him master-of-me or-to-avenge needlessly blood

יְהוָה לַאדֹנִי וְזָכַרְתָּ אֶת־ אֲמָתֶךָ׃ וַיֹּאמֶר
and-he-said (32) servant-of-you *** then-you-remember to-master-of-me Yahweh

דָּוִד לַאֲבִיגַל בָּרוּךְ יְהוָה אֱלֹהֵי יִשְׂרָאֵל אֲשֶׁר שְׁלָחֵךְ הַיּוֹם
the-day he-sent-you who Israel God-of Yahweh being-praised to-Abigail David

הַזֶּה לִקְרָאתִי׃ וּבָרוּךְ טַעְמֵךְ וּבְרוּכָה
and-being-blessed judgment-of-you and-being-blessed (33) to-meet-me the-this

אָתְּ אֲשֶׁר כְּלִתִנִי הַיּוֹם הַזֶּה מִבּוֹא בְדָמִים וְהֹשֵׁעַ
and-to-avenge to-bloodsheds from-to-come the-this the-day you-kept-me for you

יָדִי לִי׃ וְאוּלָם חַי־ יְהוָה אֱלֹהֵי יִשְׂרָאֵל אֲשֶׁר
who Israel God-of Yahweh life-of for-otherwise (34) for-me hand-of-me

מְנָעַנִי מֵהָרַע אֹתָךְ כִּי׀ לוּלֵי מִהַרְתְּ וַתָּבֹאתי לִקְרָאתִי
to-meet-me and-you-came you-were-quick not if you from-to-harm he-kept-me

כִּי אִם־ נוֹתַר לְנָבָל עַד־ אוֹר הַבֹּקֶר מַשְׁתִּין
one-urinating the-morning light-of by to-Nabal he-would-be-left not indeed

בְּקִיר׃ וַיִּקַּח דָּוִד מִיָּדָהּ אֵת אֲשֶׁר־ הֵבִיאָה
she-brought what *** from-hand-of-her David then-he-accepted (35) against-wall

who follow you. [28]Please forgive your servant's offense, for
the LORD will certainly make a
lasting dynasty for my master,
because he fights the LORD's
battles. Let no wrongdoing be
found in you as long as you
live. [29]Even though someone
is pursuing you to take your
life, the life of my master will
be bound securely in the bun-
dle of the living by the LORD
your God. But the lives of your
enemies he will hurl away as
from the pocket of a sling.
[30]When the LORD has done for
my master every good thing
he promised concerning him
and has appointed him leader
over Israel, [31]my master will
not have on his conscience the
staggering burden of needless
bloodshed or of having
avenged himself. And when
the LORD has brought my master success, remember your
servant."

[32]David said to Abigail,
"Praise be to the LORD, the God
of Israel, who has sent you today to meet me. [33]May you be
blessed for your good judg-
ment and for keeping me from
bloodshed this day and from
avenging myself with my own
hands. [34]Otherwise, as surely
as the LORD, the God of Israel,
lives, who has kept me from
harming you, if you had not
come quickly to meet me, not
one male belonging to Nabal
would have been left alive by
daybreak."

[35]Then David accepted from
her hand what she had

°34 ק ותבאת

לוֹ וְלָהּ אָמַר עֲלִי לְשָׁלוֹם לְבֵיתֵךְ רְאִי שָׁמַעְתִּי
I-heard see! to-home-of-you in-peace go! he-said and-to-her to-him

בְּקוֹלֵךְ וָאֶשָּׂא פָּנָיִךְ׃ וַתָּבֹא אֲבִיגַיִל ׀
Abigail when-she-went (36) requests-of-you and-I-granted to-word-of-you

אֶל־נָבָל וְהִנֵּה־לוֹ מִשְׁתֶּה בְּבֵיתוֹ כְּמִשְׁתֵּה הַמֶּלֶךְ
the-king like-banquet-of in-house-of-him banquet to-him then-see! Nabal to

וְלֵב נָבָל טוֹב עָלָיו וְהוּא שִׁכֹּר עַד־מְאֹד וְלֹא־הִגִּידָה לּוֹ
to-him she-told so-not very-much to drunk and-he in-him good Nabal and-heart-of

דָּבָר קָטֹן וְגָדוֹל עַד־אוֹר הַבֹּקֶר׃ וַיְהִי בַבֹּקֶר
in-the-morning then-he-was (37) the-morning light-of until or-great small thing

בְּצֵאת הַיַּיִן מִנָּבָל וַתַּגֶּד־לוֹ אִשְׁתּוֹ אֶת־
*** wife-of-him to-him then-she-told from-Nabal the-wine when-to-leave

הַדְּבָרִים הָאֵלֶּה וַיָּמָת לִבּוֹ בְּקִרְבּוֹ וְהוּא הָיָה
he-became and-he in-midst-of-him heart-of-him and-he-failed the-these the-things

לְאָבֶן׃ וַיְהִי כַּעֲשֶׂרֶת הַיָּמִים וַיִּגֹּף יְהוָה אֶת־
*** Yahweh and-he-struck the-days about-ten-of and-he-was (38) like-stone

נָבָל וַיָּמֹת׃ וַיִּשְׁמַע דָּוִד כִּי מֵת נָבָל וַיֹּאמֶר
then-he-said Nabal he-died that David when-he-heard (39) and-he-died Nabal

בָּרוּךְ יְהוָה אֲשֶׁר רָב אֶת־רִיב חֶרְפָּתִי מִיַּד
against-hand-of contempt-of-me cause-of *** he-upheld who Yahweh being-praised

נָבָל וְאֶת־עַבְדּוֹ חָשַׂךְ מֵרָעָה וְאֵת רָעַת נָבָל
Nabal wrongdoing-of and from-wrongdoing he-kept servant-of-him and Nabal

הֵשִׁיב יְהוָה בְּרֹאשׁוֹ וַיִּשְׁלַח דָּוִד וַיְדַבֵּר בַּאֲבִיגַיִל
to-Abigail and-he-asked David then-he-sent on-head-of-him Yahweh he-brought

לְקַחְתָּהּ לוֹ לְאִשָּׁה׃ וַיָּבֹאוּ עַבְדֵי דָוִד אֶל־אֲבִיגַיִל
Abigail to David servants-of and-they-went (40) as-wife for-him to-take-her

הַכַּרְמֶלָה וַיְדַבְּרוּ אֵלֶיהָ לֵאמֹר דָּוִד שְׁלָחָנוּ אֵלַיִךְ לְקַחְתֵּךְ
to-take-you to-you he-sent-us David to-say to-her and-they-said at-the-Carmel

לוֹ לְאִשָּׁה׃ וַתָּקָם וַתִּשְׁתַּחוּ אַפַּיִם אָרְצָה וַתֹּאמֶר
and-she-said to-ground faces and-she-bowed and-she-rose (41) as-wife for-him

הִנֵּה אֲמָתְךָ לְשִׁפְחָה לִרְחֹץ רַגְלֵי עַבְדֵי אֲדֹנִי׃
master-of-me servants-of feet-of to-wash for-service maidservant-of-you see!

וַתְּמַהֵר וַתָּקָם אֲבִיגַיִל וַתִּרְכַּב עַל־הַחֲמוֹר
the-donkey on and-she-got-on Abigail and-she-rose and-she-was-quick (42)

וְחָמֵשׁ נַעֲרֹתֶיהָ הַהֹלְכוֹת לְרַגְלָהּ וַתֵּלֶךְ אַחֲרֵי
with and-she-went at-foot-of-her the-ones-attending maids-of-her and-five

מַלְאֲכֵי דָוִד וַתְּהִי־לוֹ לְאִשָּׁה׃ וְאֶת־אֲחִינֹעַם לָקַח
he-married Ahinoam and (43) as-wife to-him and-she-became David messengers-of

brought him and said, "Go home in peace. I have heard your words and granted your request."
36When Abigail went to Nabal, he was in the house holding a banquet like that of a king. He was in high spirits and very drunk. So she told him nothing until daybreak.
37Then in the morning, when Nabal was sober, his wife told him all these things, and his heart failed him and he became like a stone.
38About ten days later, the LORD struck Nabal and he died.
39When David heard that Nabal was dead, he said, "Praise be to the LORD, who has upheld my cause against Nabal for treating me with contempt. He has kept me from doing wrong and has brought Nabal's wrongdoing down on his own head."
Then David sent word to Abigail, asking her to become his wife.
40His servants went to Carmel and said to Abigail, "David has sent us to you to take you to become his wife."
41She bowed down with her face to the ground and said, "Here is your maidservant, ready to serve you and wash the feet of my master's servants."
42Abigail quickly got on a donkey and, attended by her five maids, went with David's messengers and became his wife.
43David had also married Ahinoam of Jezreel, and

דָּוִד מִיִּזְרְעֶאל וַתִּהְיֶיןָ גַּם־ שְׁתֵּיהֶן לוֹ לְנָשִׁים׃
as-wives for-him both-of-them also and-they-were of-Jezreel David

וְשָׁאוּל נָתַן אֶת־ מִיכַל בִּתּוֹ אֵשֶׁת דָּוִד לְפַלְטִי
to-Palti David wife-of daughter-of-him Michal *** he-gave but-Saul (44)

בֶן־ לַיִשׁ אֲשֶׁר מִגַּלִּים׃ וַיָּבֹאוּ הַזִּפִים אֶל־שָׁאוּל
Saul to the-Ziphites and-they-went (26:1) from-Gallim who Laish son-of

הַגִּבְעָתָה לֵאמֹר הֲלוֹא דָוִד מִסְתַּתֵּר בְּגִבְעַת הַחֲכִילָה עַל פְּנֵי
faces-of to the-Hakilah on-hill-of hiding David not? to-say at-the-Gibeah

הַיְשִׁימֹן׃ וַיָּקָם שָׁאוּל וַיֵּרֶד אֶל־ מִדְבַּר־ זִיף
Ziph Desert-of to and-he-went-down Saul so-he-rose (2) the-Jeshimon

וְאִתּוֹ שְׁלֹשֶׁת־ אֲלָפִים אִישׁ בְּחוּרֵי יִשְׂרָאֵל לְבַקֵּשׁ
to-search Israel ones-being-chosen-of man thousands three-of and-with-him

אֶת־ דָּוִד בְּמִדְבַּר־ זִיף׃ וַיִּחַן שָׁאוּל בְּגִבְעַת הַחֲכִילָה
the-Hakilah on-hill-of Saul and-he-camped (3) Ziph in-Desert-of David ***

אֲשֶׁר עַל־ פְּנֵי הַיְשִׁימֹן עַל־ הַדָּרֶךְ וְדָוִד יֹשֵׁב בַּמִּדְבָּר
in-the-desert staying but-David the-road beside the-Jeshimon faces-of to that

וַיַּרְא כִּי בָא שָׁאוּל אַחֲרָיו הַמִּדְבָּרָה׃ וַיִּשְׁלַח
then-he-sent (4) to-the-desert after-him Saul he-followed that when-he-saw

דָּוִד מְרַגְּלִים וַיֵּדַע כִּי־ בָא שָׁאוּל אֶל־ נָכוֹן׃
to-be-definite to Saul he-arrived that and-he-learned ones-scouting David

וַיָּקָם דָּוִד וַיָּבֹא אֶל־ הַמָּקוֹם אֲשֶׁר חָנָה־ שָׁם
there he-camped where the-place to and-he-went David then-he-set-out (5)

שָׁאוּל וַיַּרְא דָּוִד אֶת־ הַמָּקוֹם אֲשֶׁר שָׁכַב־ שָׁם שָׁאוּל וְאַבְנֵר
and-Abner Saul there he-laid-down where the-place *** David and-he-saw Saul

בֶּן־ נֵר שַׂר־ צְבָאוֹ וְשָׁאוּל שֹׁכֵב בַּמַּעְגָּל
inside-the-camp lying now-Saul army-of-him commander-of Ner son-of

וְהָעָם חֹנִים סְבִיבֹתָו׃ וַיַּעַן דָּוִד וַיֹּאמֶר ׀ אֶל־
to and-he-said David then-he-asked (6) around-him ones-camping and-the-army

אֲחִימֶלֶךְ הַחִתִּי וְאֶל־ אֲבִישַׁי בֶּן־ צְרוּיָה אֲחִי יוֹאָב לֵאמֹר
to-say Joab brother-of Zeruiah son-of Abishai and-to the-Hittite Ahimelech

מִי־ יֵרֵד אִתִּי אֶל־שָׁאוּל אֶל־הַמַּחֲנֶה וַיֹּאמֶר אֲבִישַׁי אֲנִי
I Abishai and-he-said the-camp into Saul to with-me will-he-go-down who?

אֵרֵד עִמָּךְ׃ וַיָּבֹא דָוִד וַאֲבִישַׁי ׀ אֶל־ הָעָם לַיְלָה
night the-army to and-Abishai David so-he-went (7) with-you I-will-go

וְהִנֵּה שָׁאוּל שֹׁכֵב יָשֵׁן בַּמַּעְגָּל וַחֲנִיתוֹ מְעוּכָה־
being-stuck and-spear-of-him inside-the-camp asleep lying Saul and-see!

בָאָרֶץ מְרַאֲשֹׁתָו וְאַבְנֵר וְהָעָם שֹׁכְבִים
ones-lying and-the-soldier and-Abner near-heads-of-him in-the-ground

ק סביבתיו °5
ק מראשתיו °7

they both were his wives. 44But Saul had given his daughter Michal, David's wife, to Paltiel[k] son of Laish, who was from Gallim.

David Again Spares Saul's Life

26 The Ziphites went to Saul at Gibeah and said, "Is not David hiding on the hill of Hakilah, which faces Jeshimon?"

2So Saul went down to the Desert of Ziph, with his three thousand chosen men of Israel, to search there for David. 3Saul made his camp beside the road on the hill of Hakilah facing Jeshimon, but David stayed in the desert. When he saw that Saul had followed him there, 4he sent out scouts and learned that Saul had definitely arrived.[l]

5Then David set out and went to the place where Saul had camped. He saw where Saul and Abner son of Ner, the commander of the army, had lain down. Saul was lying inside the camp, with the army encamped around him.

6David then asked Ahimelech the Hittite and Abishai son of Zeruiah, Joab's brother, "Who will go down into the camp with me to Saul?"

"I'll go with you," said Abishai.

7So David and Abishai went to the army by night, and there was Saul, lying asleep inside the camp with his spear stuck in the ground near his head. Abner and the soldiers were lying around him.

k44 Hebrew *Palti*, a variant of *Paltiel*
l4 Or *had come to Nacon*

סְבִיבֹתָו׃ וַיֹּאמֶר אֲבִישַׁי אֶל־דָּוִד סִגַּר אֱלֹהִים הַיּוֹם אֶת־
*** the-day God he-delivered David to Abishai and-he-said (8) around-him

אוֹיִבְךָ בְּיָדֶךָ וְעַתָּה אַכֶּנּוּ נָא בַחֲנִית
with-the-spear now! let-me-pin-him and-now into-hand-of-you being-enemy-of-you

וּבָאָרֶץ פַּעַם אַחַת וְלֹא אֶשְׁנֶה לוֹ׃ וַיֹּאמֶר
but-he-said (9) to-him I-will-do-twice and-not one thrust and-into-the-ground

דָּוִד אֶל־אֲבִישַׁי אַל־תַּשְׁחִיתֵהוּ כִּי מִי שָׁלַח יָדוֹ
hand-of-him he-can-lay who? for you-destroy-him not Abishai to David

בִּמְשִׁיחַ יְהוָה וְנִקָּה׃ וַיֹּאמֶר דָּוִד חַי־
life-of David and-he-said (10) and-he-be-guiltless Yahweh on-anointed-of

יְהוָה כִּי אִם־יְהוָה יִגָּפֶנּוּ* אוֹ־יוֹמוֹ יָבוֹא
he-will-come day-of-him either he-will-strike-him Yahweh indeed that Yahweh

וָמֵת אוֹ בַמִּלְחָמָה יֵרֵד וְנִסְפָּה׃
and-he-will-perish he-will-go into-the-battle or and-he-will-die

חָלִילָה לִּי מֵיהוָה מִשְּׁלֹחַ יָדִי בִּמְשִׁיחַ
on-anointed-of hand-of-me from-to-lay by-Yahweh from-me far-be-it! (11)

יְהוָה וְעַתָּה קַח־נָא אֶת־הַחֲנִית אֲשֶׁר מְרַאֲשֹׁתָו° וְאֶת־צַפַּחַת
jug-of and at-heads-of-him that the-spear *** now! get! and-now Yahweh

הַמַּיִם וְנֵלְכָה לָּנוּ׃ וַיִּקַּח דָּוִד אֶת־הַחֲנִית וְאֶת־
and the-spear *** David so-he-took (12) for-us and-let-us-go the-waters

צַפַּחַת הַמַּיִם מֵרַאֲשֹׁתֵי שָׁאוּל וַיֵּלְכוּ לָהֶם וְאֵין רֹאֶה
seeing and-no-one for-them and-they-left Saul near-head-of the-waters jug-of

וְאֵין יוֹדֵעַ וְאֵין מֵקִיץ כִּי כֻלָּם יְשֵׁנִים כִּי
for ones-sleeping all-of-them for waking and-no-one knowing and-no-one

תַּרְדֵּמַת יְהוָה נָפְלָה עֲלֵיהֶם׃ וַיַּעֲבֹר דָּוִד
David then-he-crossed-over (13) upon-them she-fell Yahweh deep-sleep-of

הָעֵבֶר וַיַּעֲמֹד עַל־רֹאשׁ־הָהָר מֵרָחֹק רַב הַמָּקוֹם
the-space wide at-distance the-hill top-of on and-he-stood the-other-side

בֵּינֵיהֶם׃ וַיִּקְרָא דָוִד אֶל־הָעָם וְאֶל־אַבְנֵר בֶּן־נֵר
Ner son-of Abner and-to the-army to David and-he-called (14) between-them

לֵאמֹר הֲלוֹא תַעֲנֶה אַבְנֵר וַיַּעַן אַבְנֵר וַיֹּאמֶר מִי אַתָּה
you who? and-he-said Abner and-he-replied Abner will-you-answer not? to-say

קָרָאתָ אֶל־הַמֶּלֶךְ׃ וַיֹּאמֶר דָּוִד אֶל־אַבְנֵר הֲלוֹא־אִישׁ אַתָּה וּמִי
and-who? you man not? Abner to David and-he-said (15) the-king to you-call

כָמוֹךָ בְּיִשְׂרָאֵל וְלָמָּה לֹא שָׁמַרְתָּ אֶל־אֲדֹנֶיךָ הַמֶּלֶךְ כִּי־
for the-king lords-of-you over you-guarded not and-why? in-Israel like-you

בָא אַחַד הָעָם לְהַשְׁחִית אֶת־הַמֶּלֶךְ אֲדֹנֶיךָ׃ לֹא־טוֹב
good not (16) lords-of-you the-king *** to-destroy the-people one-of he-came

8Abishai said to David, "Today God has delivered your
enemy into your hands. Now
let me pin him to the ground
with one thrust of my spear; I
won't strike him twice."
9But David said to Abishai,
"Don't destroy him! Who can
lay a hand on the LORD's
anointed and be guiltless? 10As
surely as the LORD lives," he
said, "the LORD himself will
strike him; either his time will
come and he will die, or he
will go into battle and perish.
11But the LORD forbid that I
should lay a hand on the
LORD's anointed. Now get the
spear and water jug that are
near his head, and let's go."
12So David took the spear
and water jug near Saul's
head, and they left. No one
saw or knew about it, nor did
anyone wake up. They were
all sleeping, because the LORD
had put them into a deep
sleep.
13Then David crossed over to
the other side and stood on top
of the hill some distance away;
there was a wide space between them. 14He called out to
the army and to Abner son of
Ner, "Aren't you going to answer me, Abner?"
Abner replied, "Who are
you who calls to the king?"
15David said, "You're a man,
aren't you? And who is like
you in Israel? Why didn't you
guard your lord the king?
Someone came to destroy your
lord the king. 16What you have

*10 Most mss have *hateph qamets* under the *gimel* (יְגָּ).

°7 ק סביבתיו

°11 ק מראשתיו

הַדָּבָר הַזֶּה אֲשֶׁר עָשִׂיתָ חַי־ יְהוָה כִּי בְנֵי־ מָוֶת אַתֶּם אֲשֶׁר
who you death sons-of indeed Yahweh life-of you-did that the-this the-thing

לֹא־ שְׁמַרְתֶּם עַל־ אֲדֹנֵיכֶם עַל־ מְשִׁיחַ יְהוָה וְעַתָּה ׀ רְאֵה
look! and-now Yahweh anointed-of over masters-of-you over you-guarded not

אֵי־ חֲנִית הַמֶּלֶךְ וְאֶת־ צַפַּחַת הַמַּיִם אֲשֶׁר מְרַאֲשֹׁתָו׃
near-heads-of-him that the-waters jug-of and the-king spear-of where?

וַיַּכֵּר שָׁאוּל אֶת־ קוֹל דָּוִד וַיֹּאמֶר הֲקוֹלְךָ זֶה
that voice-of-you? and-he-said David voice-of *** Saul and-he-recognized (17)

בְּנִי דָוִד וַיֹּאמֶר דָּוִד קוֹלִי אֲדֹנִי הַמֶּלֶךְ׃
the-king lord-of-me voice-of-me David and-he-replied David son-of-me

וַיֹּאמֶר לָמָּה זֶּה אֲדֹנִי רֹדֵף אַחֲרֵי עַבְדּוֹ כִּי
for servant-of-him after pursuing lord-of-me this why? and-he-said (18)

מֶה עָשִׂיתִי וּמַה־ בְּיָדִי רָעָה׃ וְעַתָּה יִשְׁמַע־ נָא
now! let-him-listen and-now (19) wrong in-hand-of-me and-what? I-did what?

אֲדֹנִי הַמֶּלֶךְ אֵת דִּבְרֵי עַבְדּוֹ אִם־ יְהוָה הֱסִיתְךָ
he-incited-you Yahweh if servant-of-him words-of *** the-king lord-of-me

בִי יָרַח מִנְחָה וְאִם ׀ בְּנֵי הָאָדָם אֲרוּרִים
ones-being-cursed the-man sons-of but-if offering may-he-accept against-me

הֵם לִפְנֵי יְהוָה כִּי־ גֵרְשׁוּנִי הַיּוֹם מֵהִסְתַּפֵּחַ בְּנַחֲלַת
in-inheritance-of from-to-share the-day they-drove-me for Yahweh before they

יְהוָה לֵאמֹר לֵךְ עֲבֹד אֱלֹהִים אֲחֵרִים׃ וְעַתָּה אַל־ יִפֹּל
let-him-fall not and-now (20) other-ones gods serve! go! to-say Yahweh

דָּמִי אַרְצָה מִנֶּגֶד פְּנֵי יְהוָה כִּי־ יָצָא מֶלֶךְ
king-of he-came-out indeed Yahweh presences-of from-near to-ground blood-of-me

יִשְׂרָאֵל לְבַקֵּשׁ אֶת־פַּרְעֹשׁ אֶחָד כַּאֲשֶׁר יִרְדֹּף הַקֹּרֵא בֶּהָרִים׃
in-the-mountains the-partridge he-hunts just-as one flea *** to-look-for Israel

וַיֹּאמֶר שָׁאוּל חָטָאתִי שׁוּב בְּנִי־ דָוִד כִּי לֹא־ אָרַע
I-will-harm not for David son-of-me come-back! I-sinned Saul then-he-said (21)

לְךָ עוֹד תַּחַת אֲשֶׁר יָקְרָה נַפְשִׁי בְּעֵינֶיךָ הַיּוֹם
the-day in-eyes-of-you life-of-me she-was-precious that because again to-you

הַזֶּה הִנֵּה הִסְכַּלְתִּי וָאֶשְׁגֶּה הַרְבֵּה מְאֹד׃ וַיַּעַן
and-he-answered (22) very to-be-great and-I-erred I-was-foolish see! the-this

דָּוִד וַיֹּאמֶר הִנֵּה הַחֲנִית הַמֶּלֶךְ וְיַעֲבֹר אֶחָד
one now-let-him-come-over the-king spear-of see! and-he-said David

מֵהַנְּעָרִים וְיִקָּחֶהָ׃ וַיהוָה יָשִׁיב לָאִישׁ
to-the-man he-rewards now-Yahweh (23) and-let-him-get-her of-the-young-men

אֶת־ צִדְקָתוֹ וְאֶת־ אֱמֻנָתוֹ אֲשֶׁר נְתָנְךָ יְהוָה ׀
Yahweh he-delivered-you for faithfulness-of-him and righteousness-of-him ***

done is not good. As surely as
the LORD lives, you and your
men deserve to die, because
you did not guard your master, the LORD's anointed. Look
around you. Where are the
king's spear and water jug that
were near his head?"
17 Saul recognized David's
voice and said, "Is that your
voice, David my son?"
David replied, "Yes it is, my
lord the king." 18 And he
added, "Why is my lord pursuing his servant? What have
I done, and what wrong am I
guilty of? 19 Now let my lord
the king listen to his servant's
words. If the LORD has incited
you against me, then may he
accept an offering. If, however, men have done it, may
they be cursed before the
LORD! They have now driven
me from my share in the
LORD's inheritance and have
said, 'Go, serve other gods.'
20 Now do not let my blood fall
to the ground far from the
presence of the LORD. The king
of Israel has come out to look
for a flea—as one hunts a par-
tridge in the mountains."
21 Then Saul said, "I have
sinned. Come back, David my
son. Because you considered
my life precious today, I will
not try to harm you again.
Surely I have acted like a fool
and have erred greatly."
22 "Here is the king's spear,"
David answered. "Let one of
your young men come over
and get it. 23 The LORD rewards
every man for his righteousness and faithfulness. The
LORD delivered you into my

°16 ק מראשתיו
°22 ק חנית

הַיּוֹם בְּיָד וְלֹא אָבִיתִי לִשְׁלֹחַ יָדִי בִּמְשִׁיחַ יְהוָה׃
Yahweh on-anointed-of hand-of-me to-lay I-would but-not into-hand the-day

(24) וְהִנֵּה כַּאֲשֶׁר גָּדְלָה נַפְשְׁךָ הַיּוֹם הַזֶּה
the-this the-day life-of-you she-was-valued surely-as and-see! (24)

בְּעֵינָי כֵּן תִּגְדַּל נַפְשִׁי בְּעֵינֵי יְהוָה
Yahweh in-eyes-of life-of-me may-she-be-valued so in-eyes-of-me

וְיַצִּלֵנִי מִכָּל־ צָרָה׃ (25) וַיֹּאמֶר שָׁאוּל אֶל־ דָּוִד
David to Saul then-he-said (25) trouble from-all-of and-may-he-deliver-me

בָּרוּךְ אַתָּה בְּנִי דָוִד גַּם עָשֹׂה תַעֲשֶׂה וְגַם
and-indeed you-will-do to-do indeed David son-of-me you being-blessed

יָכֹל תּוּכָל וַיֵּלֶךְ דָּוִד לְדַרְכּוֹ וְשָׁאוּל
and-Saul on-way-of-him David so-he-went you-will-triumph to-triumph

שָׁב לִמְקוֹמוֹ׃ (27:1) וַיֹּאמֶר דָּוִד אֶל־ לִבּוֹ עַתָּה
now heart-of-him in David but-he-thought (27:1) to-home-of-him he-returned

אֶסָּפֶה יוֹם־אֶחָד בְּיַד־ שָׁאוּל אֵין־ לִי טוֹב כִּי הִמָּלֵט
to-escape unless good to-me not Saul by-hand-of one day I-will-be-destroyed

אִמָּלֵט ׀ אֶל־ אֶרֶץ פְּלִשְׁתִּים וְנוֹאַשׁ מִמֶּנִּי שָׁאוּל
Saul from-me then-he-will-give-up Philistines land-of to I-escape

לְבַקְשֵׁנִי עוֹד בְּכָל־ גְּבוּל יִשְׂרָאֵל וְנִמְלַטְתִּי
and-I-will-slip-out Israel part-of in-any-of ever to-search-for-me

מִיָּדוֹ׃ (2) וַיָּקָם דָּוִד וַיַּעֲבֹר הוּא וְשֵׁשׁ־ מֵאוֹת אִישׁ
man hundreds and-six he and-he-went-over David so-he-left (2) of-hand-of-him

אֲשֶׁר עִמּוֹ אֶל־אָכִישׁ בֶּן־ מָעוֹךְ מֶלֶךְ גַּת׃ (3) וַיֵּשֶׁב דָּוִד
David and-he-settled (3) Gath king-of Maoch son-of Achish to with-him who

עִם־אָכִישׁ בְּגַת הוּא וַאֲנָשָׁיו אִישׁ וּבֵיתוֹ דָּוִד וּשְׁתֵּי
and-two-of David and-family-of-him man and-men-of-him he in-Gath Achish with

נָשָׁיו אֲחִינֹעַם הַיִּזְרְעֵאלִית וַאֲבִיגַיִל אֵשֶׁת־ נָבָל הַכַּרְמְלִית׃
the-Carmelite Nabal widow-of and-Abigail the-Jezreelite Ahinoam wives-of-him

(4) וַיֻּגַּד לְשָׁאוּל כִּי־ בָרַח דָּוִד גַּת וְלֹא־ יָוסֶף
he-continued then-not Gath David he-fled that to-Saul when-he-was-told (4)

עוֹד לְבַקְשׁוֹ׃ (5) וַיֹּאמֶר דָּוִד אֶל־ אָכִישׁ אִם־ נָא מָצָאתִי
I-found now! if Achish to David then-he-said (5) to-search-for-him longer

חֵן בְּעֵינֶיךָ יִתְּנוּ־ לִי מָקוֹם בְּאַחַת עָרֵי
towns-of in-one-of place to-me let-them-assign in-eyes-of-you favor

הַשָּׂדֶה וְאֵשְׁבָה שָּׁם וְלָמָּה יֵשֵׁב עַבְדְּךָ
servants-of-you should-he-live for-why? there that-I-may-live the-country

בְּעִיר הַמַּמְלָכָה עִמָּךְ׃ (6) וַיִּתֶּן־ לוֹ אָכִישׁ בַּיּוֹם
on-the-day Achish to-him so-he-gave (6) with-you the-royal in-city-of

hands today, but I would not
lay a hand on the LORD's
anointed. [24]As surely as I
valued your life today, so may
the LORD value my life and deliver me from all trouble."
[25]Then Saul said to David,
"May you be blessed, my son
David; you will do great
things and surely triumph."
So David went on his way,
and Saul returned home.

David Among the Philistines

27 But David thought to
himself, "One of these
days I will be destroyed by the
hand of Saul. The best thing I
can do is to escape to the land
of the Philistines. Then Saul
will give up searching for me
anywhere in Israel, and I will
slip out of his hand."
[2]So David and the six hundred men with him left and
went over to Achish son of
Maoch king of Gath. [3]David
and his men settled in Gath
with Achish. Each man had
his family with him, and David had his two wives: Ahinoam of Jezreel and Abigail of
Carmel, the widow of Nabal.
[4]When Saul was told that David had fled to Gath, he no
longer searched for him.
[5]Then David said to Achish,
"If I have found favor in your
eyes, let a place be assigned to
me in one of the country
towns, that I may live there.
Why should your servant live
in the royal city with you?"
[6]So on that day Achish gave

°4 ק יסף

הַהוּא אֶת־צִקְלָג לָכֵן הָיְתָה צִקְלַג לְמַלְכֵי יְהוּדָה עַד הַיּוֹם
the-day to Judah to-kings-of Ziklag she-belongs thus Ziklag *** the-that

הַזֶּה׃ וַיְהִי מִסְפַּר הַיָּמִים אֲשֶׁר־יָשַׁב דָּוִד בִּשְׂדֵה
in-territory-of David he-lived that the-days number-of and-he-was (7) the-this

פְלִשְׁתִּים יָמִים וְאַרְבָּעָה חֳדָשִׁים׃ וַיַּעַל דָּוִד וַאֲנָשָׁיו
and-men-of-him David now-he-went-up (8) months and-four days Philistines

וַיִּפְשְׁטוּ אֶל־הַגְּשׁוּרִי וְהַגִּרְזִי וְהָעֲמָלֵקִי כִּי הֵנָּה
they now and-the-Amalekite *and-the-Girzite the-Geshurite on and-they-raided

יֹשְׁבוֹת הָאָרֶץ אֲשֶׁר מֵעוֹלָם בּוֹאֲךָ שׁוּרָה וְעַד־אֶרֶץ
land-of and-to to-Shur to-go-you from-ancient that the-land ones-living-of

מִצְרָיִם׃ וְהִכָּה דָוִד אֶת־הָאָרֶץ וְלֹא יְחַיֶּה אִישׁ
man he-left-alive then-not the-area *** David when-he-attacked (9) Egypt

וְאִשָּׁה וְלָקַח צֹאן וּבָקָר וַחֲמֹרִים וּגְמַלִּים וּבְגָדִים
and-clothes and-camels and-donkeys and-cattle sheep but-he-took or-woman

וַיָּשָׁב וַיָּבֹא אֶל־אָכִישׁ׃ וַיֹּאמֶר אָכִישׁ אַל־†
†not Achish when-he-asked (10) Achish to and-he-went then-he-returned

פְּשַׁטְתֶּם הַיּוֹם וַיֹּאמֶר דָּוִד עַל־נֶגֶב יְהוּדָה וְעַל־
or-against Judah Negev-of against David and-he-said the-day you-raided

נֶגֶב הַיַּרְחְמְאֵלִי†† וְאֶל־נֶגֶב הַקֵּינִי׃ וְאִישׁ וְאִשָּׁה
or-woman and-man (11) the-Kenite Negev-of or-against the-Jerahmeelite Negev-of

לֹא־יְחַיֶּה דָוִד לְהָבִיא גַת לֵאמֹר פֶּן־יַגִּדוּ עָלֵינוּ לֵאמֹר
to-say on-us they-inform lest to-say Gath to-bring David he-left-alive not

כֹּה־עָשָׂה דָוִד וְכֹה מִשְׁפָּטוֹ כָּל־הַיָּמִים אֲשֶׁר יָשַׁב
he-lived that the-days all-of practice-of-him and-such David he-did this

בִּשְׂדֵה פְלִשְׁתִּים׃ וַיַּאֲמֵן אָכִישׁ בְּדָוִד לֵאמֹר
to-say in-David Achish and-he-trusted (12) Philistines in-territory-of

הַבְאֵשׁ הִבְאִישׁ בְּעַמּוֹ בְיִשְׂרָאֵל וְהָיָה
so-he-will-be to-Israel to-people-of-him he-became-odious to-become-odious

לִי לְעֶבֶד עוֹלָם׃ וַיְהִי בַּיָּמִים הָהֵם
the-those in-the-days and-he-was (28:1) forever as-servant to-me

וַיִּקְבְּצוּ פְלִשְׁתִּים אֶת־מַחֲנֵיהֶם לַצָּבָא לְהִלָּחֵם
to-fight for-the-army forces-of-them *** Philistines then-they-gathered

בְּיִשְׂרָאֵל וַיֹּאמֶר אָכִישׁ אֶל־דָּוִד יָדֹעַ תֵּדַע
you-must-understand to-understand David to Achish and-he-said against-Israel

כִּי אִתִּי תֵּצֵא בַמַּחֲנֶה אַתָּה וַאֲנָשֶׁיךָ׃ וַיֹּאמֶר
and-he-said (2) and-men-of-you you in-the-army you-will-accompany with-me that

דָּוִד אֶל־אָכִישׁ לָכֵן אַתָּה תֵדַע אֵת אֲשֶׁר־יַעֲשֶׂה עַבְדֶּךָ
servant-of-you he-can-do what *** you-will-see you then Achish to David

him Ziklag, and it has belonged to the kings of Judah
ever since. [7]David lived in
Philistine territory a year and
four months.
[8]Now David and his men
went up and raided the Geshurites, the Girzites and the
Amalekites. (From ancient
times these peoples had lived
in the land extending to Shur
and Egypt.) [9]Whenever David
attacked an area, he did not
leave a man or woman alive,
but took sheep and cattle, donkeys and camels, and clothes.
Then he returned to Achish.
[10]When Achish asked,
"Where did you go raiding today?" David would say,
"Against the Negev of Judah"
or "Against the Negev of
Jerahmeel" or "Against the
Negev of the Kenites." [11]He
did not leave a man or woman
alive to be brought to Gath, for
he thought, "They might inform on us and say, 'This is
what David did.'" And such
was his practice as long as he
lived in Philistine territory.
[12]Achish trusted David and
said to himself, "He has
become so odious to his
people, the Israelites, that he
will be my servant forever."

Saul and the Witch of Endor

28 In those days the Philistines gathered their
forces to fight against Israel.
Achish said to David, "You
must understand that you and
your men will accompany me
in the army."
[2]David said, "Then you will
see for yourself what your servant can do."

*8 The NIV here translates the *Ketbib* form; the *Qere* reads *and-the-Gizrite.*

†*10* Some mss and versions read אִי, *where?*

††*10* Most mss have *sheva* under the *yod* and *pathah* under the *resh* (הַיְרַ).

°8 ק והגזרי

וַיֹּאמֶר אָכִישׁ אֶל־ דָּוִד לָכֵן שֹׁמֵר לְרֹאשִׁי
of-head-of-me being-guard very-well David to Achish and-he-replied

אֲשִׂימְךָ כָּל־ הַיָּמִים׃ וּשְׁמוּאֵל מֵת וַיִּסְפְּדוּ־
and-they-mourned he-was-dead now-Samuel (3) the-days all-of I-will-make-you

לוֹ כָּל־ יִשְׂרָאֵל וַיִּקְבְּרֻהוּ בָרָמָה וּבְעִירוֹ
even-in-town-of-him in-the-Ramah and-they-buried-him Israel all-of for-him

וְשָׁאוּל הֵסִיר הָאֹבוֹת וְאֶת־ הַיִּדְּעֹנִים מֵהָאָרֶץ׃
from-the-land the-spiritists and the-mediums he-expelled and-Saul

וַיִּקָּבְצוּ פְלִשְׁתִּים וַיָּבֹאוּ וַיַּחֲנוּ בְשׁוּנֵם
at-Shunem and-they-camped and-they-came Philistines and-they-assembled (4)

וַיִּקְבֹּץ שָׁאוּל אֶת־ כָּל־ יִשְׂרָאֵל וַיַּחֲנוּ בַּגִּלְבֹּעַ׃
at-the-Gilboa and-they-camped Israel all-of *** Saul and-he-gathered

וַיַּרְא שָׁאוּל אֶת־ מַחֲנֵה פְלִשְׁתִּים וַיִּרָא וַיֶּחֱרַד
and-he-was-terrified then-he-feared Philistines army-of *** Saul when-he-saw (5)

לִבּוֹ מְאֹד׃ וַיִּשְׁאַל שָׁאוּל בַּיהוָה וְלֹא עָנָהוּ
he-answered-him but-not of-Yahweh Saul and-he-inquired (6) greatly heart-of-him

יְהוָה גַּם בַּחֲלֹמוֹת גַּם בָּאוּרִים גַּם בַּנְּבִיאִם׃ וַיֹּאמֶר
then-he-said (7) by-the-prophets or by-the-Urim or by-dreams either Yahweh

שָׁאוּל לַעֲבָדָיו בַּקְּשׁוּ־ לִי אֵשֶׁת בַּעֲלַת־ אוֹב וְאֵלְכָה
so-I-may-go medium mistress-of woman-of for-me find! to-attendants-of-him Saul

אֵלֶיהָ וְאֶדְרְשָׁה־ בָּהּ וַיֹּאמְרוּ עֲבָדָיו אֵלָיו הִנֵּה
see! to-him attendants-of-him and-they-said of-her and-I-may-inquire to-her

אֵשֶׁת בַּעֲלַת־ אוֹב בְּעֵין דּוֹר׃ וַיִּתְחַפֵּשׂ שָׁאוּל
Saul so-he-disguised-himself (8) Dor in-En medium mistress-of woman-of

וַיִּלְבַּשׁ בְּגָדִים אֲחֵרִים וַיֵּלֶךְ הוּא וּשְׁנֵי אֲנָשִׁים עִמּוֹ
with-him men and-two-of he and-he-went other-ones clothes and-he-put-on

וַיָּבֹאוּ אֶל־ הָאִשָּׁה לָיְלָה וַיֹּאמֶר °קָסֳומִי־ נָא לִי
for-me now! consult! and-he-said night the-woman to and-they-came

בָּאוֹב וְהַעֲלִי לִי אֵת אֲשֶׁר־ אֹמַר אֵלָיִךְ׃ וַתֹּאמֶר
but-she-said (9) to-you I-name whom *** for-me and-bring-up! with-the-spirit

הָאִשָּׁה אֵלָיו הִנֵּה אַתָּה יָדַעְתָּ אֵת אֲשֶׁר־ עָשָׂה שָׁאוּל אֲשֶׁר הִכְרִית אֶת־
*** he-cut-off that Saul he-did what *** you-know you see! to-him the-woman

הָאֹבוֹת וְאֶת־ הַיִּדְּעֹנִי מִן־ הָאָרֶץ וְלָמָה אַתָּה מִתְנַקֵּשׁ
setting-trap you now-why? the-land from the-spiritist and the-mediums

בְנַפְשִׁי לַהֲמִיתֵנִי׃ וַיִּשָּׁבַע לָהּ שָׁאוּל בַּיהוָה לֵאמֹר
to-say by-Yahweh Saul to-her and-he-swore (10) to-kill-me for-life-of-me

חַי־ יְהוָה אִם־ יִקְּרֵךְ עָוֺן בַּדָּבָר הַזֶּה׃
the-this for-the-thing punishment he-will-come-on-you not Yahweh life-of

Achish replied, "Very well, I
will make you my bodyguard
for life."
3 Now Samuel was dead, and
all Israel had mourned for him
and buried him in his own
town of Ramah. Saul had ex-
pelled the mediums and
spiritists from the land.
4 The Philistines assembled
and came and set up camp at
Shunem, while Saul gathered
all the Israelites and set up
camp at Gilboa. 5 When Saul
saw the Philistine army, he
was afraid; terror filled his
heart. 6 He inquired of the
LORD, but the LORD did not answer him by dreams or Urim
or prophets. 7 Saul then said to
his attendants, "Find me a
woman who is a medium, so I
may go and inquire of her."
"There is one in Endor,"
they said.
8 So Saul disguised himself,
putting on other clothes, and
at night he and two men went
to the woman. "Consult a
spirit for me," he said, "and
bring up for me the one I
name."
9 But the woman said to him,
"Surely you know what Saul
has done. He has cut off the
mediums and spiritists from
the land. Why have you set a
trap for my life to bring about
my death?"
10 Saul swore to her by the
LORD, "As surely as the LORD
lives, you will not be punished
for this."

m13 Or *see spirits*; or *see gods*

°8 קְ קסמי

וַתֹּאמֶר הָאִשָּׁה אֶת־ מִי אַעֲלֶה־ לָּךְ וַיֹּאמֶר
and-he-said for-you shall-I-bring-up whom? *** the-woman then-she-asked (11)

אֶת־ שְׁמוּאֵל הַעֲלִי־ לִי׃ וַתֵּרֶא הָאִשָּׁה אֶת־ שְׁמוּאֵל
Samuel *** the-woman when-she-saw (12) for-me bring-up! Samuel ***

וַתִּזְעַק בְּקוֹל גָּדוֹל וַתֹּאמֶר הָאִשָּׁה אֶל־שָׁאוּל לֵאמֹר לָמָּה
why? to-say Saul to the-woman and-she-said loud with-voice then-she-cried-out

רִמִּיתָנִי וְאַתָּה שָׁאוּל׃ וַיֹּאמֶר לָהּ הַמֶּלֶךְ אַל־ תִּירְאִי
you-fear not the-king to-her and-he-said (13) Saul for-you you-deceived-me

כִּי מָה רָאִית וַתֹּאמֶר הָאִשָּׁה אֶל־שָׁאוּל אֱלֹהִים רָאִיתִי עֹלִים
ones-coming-up I-see spirits Saul to the-woman and-she-said you-see what? now

מִן־ הָאָרֶץ׃ וַיֹּאמֶר לָהּ מַה־ תָּאֳרוֹ וַתֹּאמֶר אִישׁ
man and-she-said look-of-him what? to-her and-he-asked (14) the-ground from

זָקֵן עֹלֶה וְהוּא עֹטֶה מְעִיל וַיֵּדַע שָׁאוּל כִּי־ שְׁמוּאֵל הוּא
he Samuel that Saul then-he-knew robe wearing and-he coming-up old

וַיִּקֹּד אַפַּיִם אַרְצָה וַיִּשְׁתָּחוּ׃ וַיֹּאמֶר שְׁמוּאֵל
Samuel and-he-said (15) and-he-prostrated-himself to-ground faces and-he-bowed

אֶל־שָׁאוּל לָמָּה הִרְגַּזְתַּנִי לְהַעֲלוֹת אֹתִי וַיֹּאמֶר שָׁאוּל צַר־
he-distresses Saul and-he-said me to-bring-up you-disturbed-me why? Saul to

לִי מְאֹד וּפְלִשְׁתִּים׀ נִלְחָמִים בִּי וֵאלֹהִים סָר
he-turned-away and-God against-me ones-fighting and-Philistines greatly to-me

מֵעָלַי וְלֹא־ עָנָנִי עוֹד גַּם בְּיַד־ הַנְּבִיאִם גַּם־
or the-prophets by-hand-of either longer he-answers-me and-not from-with-me

בַּחֲלֹמוֹת וָאֶקְרָאֶה לְךָ לְהוֹדִיעֵנִי מָה אֶעֱשֶׂה׃ וַיֹּאמֶר
and-he-said (16) I-should-do what to-tell-me on-you so-I-called by-dreams

שְׁמוּאֵל וְלָמָּה תִּשְׁאָלֵנִי וַיהוָה סָר מֵעָלֶיךָ וַיְהִי
and-he-became from-with-you he-turned for-Yahweh you-consult-me so-why? Samuel

עָרֶךָ׃ וַיַּעַשׂ יְהוָה לוֹ כַּאֲשֶׁר דִּבֶּר בְּיָדִי
by-hand-of-me he-predicted just-as for-him Yahweh and-he-did (17) enemy-of-you

וַיִּקְרַע יְהוָה אֶת־ הַמַּמְלָכָה מִיָּדֶךָ וַיִּתְּנָהּ
and-he-gave-her from-hand-of-you the-kingdom *** Yahweh and-he-tore

לְרֵעֲךָ לְדָוִד׃ כַּאֲשֶׁר לֹא־ שָׁמַעְתָּ בְּקוֹל יְהוָה
Yahweh to-voice-of you-obeyed not because (18) to-David to-neighbor-of-you

וְלֹא־ עָשִׂיתָ חֲרוֹן־ אַפּוֹ בַּעֲמָלֵק עַל־ כֵּן
this for against-Amalek wrath-of-him fierceness-of you-carried-out and-not

הַדָּבָר הַזֶּה עָשָׂה־ לְךָ יְהוָה הַיּוֹם הַזֶּה׃ וְיִתֵּן
and-he-will-give (19) the-this the-day Yahweh to-you he-did the-this the-thing

יְהוָה גַּם אֶת־ יִשְׂרָאֵל עִמְּךָ בְּיַד־ פְּלִשְׁתִּים וּמָחָר אַתָּה
you and-tomorrow Philistines into-hand-of with-you Israel *** both Yahweh

11 Then the woman asked,
"Whom shall I bring up for
you?"
"Bring up Samuel," he said.
12 When the woman saw
Samuel, she cried out at the
top of her voice and said to
Saul, "Why have you deceived
me? You are Saul!"
13 The king said to her,
"Don't be afraid. What do you
see?"
The woman said, "I see a
spirit[m] coming up out of the
ground."
14 "What does he look like?"
he asked.
"An old man wearing a robe
is coming up," she said.
Then Saul knew it was Samuel, and he bowed down and
prostrated himself with his
face to the ground.
15 Samuel said to Saul, "Why
have you disturbed me by
bringing me up?"
"I am in great distress," Saul
said. "The Philistines are
fighting against me, and God
has turned away from me. He
no longer answers me, either
by prophets or by dreams. So I
have called on you to tell me
what to do."
16 Samuel said, "Why do you
consult me, now that the LORD
has turned away from you and
become your enemy? 17 The
LORD has done what he pre-
dicted through me. The LORD
has torn the kingdom out of
your hands and given it to one
of your neighbors—to David.
18 Because you did not obey the
LORD or carry out his fierce
wrath against the Amalekites,
the LORD has done this to you
today. 19 The LORD will hand
over both Israel and you to the
Philistines, and tomorrow you

וּבָנֶיךָ עִמִּי גַּם אֶת־ מַחֲנֵה יִשְׂרָאֵל יִתֵּן יְהוָה
Yahweh he-will-give Israel army-of *** also with-me and-sons-of-you

בְּיַד־ פְלִשְׁתִּים׃ וַיְמַהֵר שָׁאוּל וַיִּפֹּל מְלֹא־
full-of and-he-fell Saul and-he-was-quick (20) Philistines into-hand-of

קוֹמָתוֹ אַרְצָה וַיִּרָא מְאֹד מִדִּבְרֵי שְׁמוּאֵל גַּם־
also Samuel from-words-of greatly and-he-feared on-ground length-of-him

כֹּחַ לֹא־ הָיָה בוֹ כִּי לֹא אָכַל לֶחֶם כָּל־ הַיּוֹם וְכָל־
and-all-of the-day all-of food he-ate not for in-him he-was not strength

הַלָּיְלָה׃ וַתָּבוֹא הָאִשָּׁה אֶל־שָׁאוּל וַתֵּרֶא כִּי־ נִבְהַל
being-shaken that and-she-saw Saul to the-woman when-she-came (21) the-night

מְאֹד וַתֹּאמֶר אֵלָיו הִנֵּה שָׁמְעָה שִׁפְחָתְךָ בְּקוֹלֶךָ
to-voice-of-you servant-of-you she-obeyed see! to-him then-she-said greatly

וָאָשִׂים נַפְשִׁי בְּכַפִּי וָאֶשְׁמַע אֶת־ דְּבָרֶיךָ אֲשֶׁר דִּבַּרְתָּ
you-told that words-of-you *** and-I-did in-hand-of-me life-of-me and-I-took

אֵלָי׃ וְעַתָּה שְׁמַע־ נָא גַם־ אַתָּה בְּקוֹל שִׁפְחָתֶךָ
servant-of-you to-voice-of you also now! listen! and-now (22) to-me

וְאָשִׂמָה לְפָנֶיךָ פַּת־ לֶחֶם וֶאֱכוֹל וִיהִי בְךָ כֹּחַ
strength in-you so-he-will-be and-eat! food some-of before-you and-let-me-set

כִּי תֵלֵךְ בַּדָּרֶךְ׃ וַיְמָאֵן וַיֹּאמֶר לֹא אֹכַל
I-will-eat not and-he-said and-he-refused (23) on-the-way you-can-go so

וַיִּפְרְצוּ־ בוֹ עֲבָדָיו וְגַם־ הָאִשָּׁה וַיִּשְׁמַע
and-he-listened the-woman and-also men-of-him with-him but-they-urged

לְקֹלָם וַיָּקָם מֵהָאָרֶץ וַיֵּשֶׁב אֶל־ הַמִּטָּה׃
the-couch on and-he-sat from-the-ground and-he-got-up to-voice-of-them

וְלָאִשָּׁה עֵגֶל־ מַרְבֵּק בַּבַּיִת וַתְּמַהֵר
and-she-hurried at-the-house fattened calf-of now-to-the-woman (24)

וַתִּזְבָּחֵהוּ וַתִּקַּח־ קֶמַח וַתָּלָשׁ וַתֹּפֵהוּ
and-she-baked-him and-she-kneaded flour and-she-took and-she-butchered-him

מַצּוֹת׃ וַתַּגֵּשׁ לִפְנֵי־ שָׁאוּל וְלִפְנֵי עֲבָדָיו
men-of-him and-before Saul before then-she-set (25) breads-without-yeast

וַיֹּאכֵלוּ וַיָּקֻמוּ וַיֵּלְכוּ בַּלַּיְלָה הַהוּא׃
the-that on-the-night and-they-left then-they-got-up and-they-ate

וַיִּקְבְּצוּ פְלִשְׁתִּים אֶת־ כָּל־ מַחֲנֵיהֶם אֲפֵקָה
at-Aphek forces-of-them all-of *** Philistines and-they-gathered (29:1)

וְיִשְׂרָאֵל חֹנִים בַּעַיִן אֲשֶׁר בְּיִזְרְעֶאל׃ וְסַרְנֵי
and-rulers-of (2) in-Jezreel that by-the-spring ones-camping and-Israel

פְלִשְׁתִּים עֹבְרִים לְמֵאוֹת וְלַאֲלָפִים וְדָוִד
and-David and-with-thousands with-hundreds ones-marching Philistines

and your sons will be with me.
The LORD will also hand over
the army of Israel to the Philistines."
[20]Immediately Saul fell full
length on the ground, filled
with fear because of Samuel's
words. His strength was gone,
for he had eaten nothing all
that day and night.
[21]When the woman came to
Saul and saw that he was
greatly shaken, she said,
"Look, your maidservant has
obeyed you. I took my life in
my hands and did what you
told me to do. [22]Now please listen to your servant and let me
give you some food so you
may eat and have the strength
to go on your way."
[23]He refused and said, "I will
not eat."
But his men joined the
woman in urging him, and he
listened to them. He got up
from the ground and sat on
the couch.
[24]The woman had a fattened
calf at the house, which she
butchered at once. She took
some flour, kneaded it and
baked bread without yeast.
[25]Then she set it before Saul
and his men, and they ate.
That same night they got up
and left.

Achish Sends David Back to Ziklag

29 The Philistines gath-
ered all their forces at
Aphek, and Israel camped by
the spring in Jezreel. [2]As the
Philistine rulers marched with
their units of hundreds and
thousands, David and his men

וַאֲנָשָׁיו עֹבְרִים בָּאַחֲרֹנָה עִם־ אָכִישׁ׃ וַיֹּאמְרוּ
and-they-asked (3) Achish with at-the-rear ones-marching and-men-of-him

שָׂרֵי פְלִשְׁתִּים מָה הָעִבְרִים הָאֵלֶּה וַיֹּאמֶר אָכִישׁ
Achish and-he-replied the-these the-Hebrews what? Philistines commanders-of

אֶל־ שָׂרֵי פְלִשְׁתִּים הֲלוֹא־ זֶה דָוִד עֶבֶד ׀ שָׁאוּל מֶלֶךְ־ יִשְׂרָאֵל
Israel king-of Saul officer-of David this not? Philistines commanders-of to

אֲשֶׁר הָיָה אִתִּי זֶה יָמִים אוֹ־ זֶה שָׁנִים וְלֹא־ מָצָאתִי בוֹ מְאוּמָה
anything in-him I-found and-not years this or days this with-me he-was who

מִיּוֹם נָפְלוֹ עַד־ הַיּוֹם הַזֶּה׃ וַיִּקְצְפוּ עָלָיו
with-him but-they-were-angry (4) the-this the-day to to-leave-him from-day

שָׂרֵי פְלִשְׁתִּים וַיֹּאמְרוּ לוֹ שָׂרֵי פְלִשְׁתִּים
Philistines commanders-of to-him and-they-said Philistines commanders-of

הָשֵׁב אֶת־ הָאִישׁ וְיָשֹׁב אֶל־ מְקוֹמוֹ אֲשֶׁר הִפְקַדְתּוֹ
you-assigned-him that place-of-him to that-he-may-return the-man *** send-back!

שָׁם וְלֹא־ יֵרֵד עִמָּנוּ בַּמִּלְחָמָה וְלֹא־ יִהְיֶה־
he-will-be so-not into-the-battle with-us he-must-go-down for-not there

לָּנוּ לְשָׂטָן בַּמִּלְחָמָה וּבַמֶּה יִתְרַצֶּה
could-he-regain-favor for-by-the-what? in-the-battle as-adversary against-us

זֶה אֶל־ אֲדֹנָיו הֲלוֹא בְּרָאשֵׁי הָאֲנָשִׁים הָהֵם׃ הֲלוֹא־ זֶה
this not? (5) the-these the-men with-heads-of not? masters-of-him with this

דָוִד אֲשֶׁר יַעֲנוּ־ לוֹ בַּמְּחֹלוֹת לֵאמֹר הִכָּה שָׁאוּל
Saul he-has-slain to-say in-the-dances about-him they-sang whom David

בַּאֲלָפָיו וְדָוִד בְּרִבְבֹתָו׃ וַיִּקְרָא
so-he-called (6) to-tens-of-thousands-of-him and-David to-thousands-of-him

אָכִישׁ אֶל־ דָּוִד וַיֹּאמֶר אֵלָיו חַי־ יְהוָה כִּי־ יָשָׁר אַתָּה
you reliable indeed Yahweh life-of to-him and-he-said David to Achish

וְטוֹב בְּעֵינַי צֵאתְךָ וּבֹאֲךָ אִתִּי בַּמַּחֲנֶה
in-the-army with-me and-to-serve-you to-go-out-you in-eyes-of-me and-pleasing

כִּי לֹא־ מָצָאתִי בְךָ רָעָה מִיּוֹם בֹּאֲךָ אֵלַי עַד־ הַיּוֹם
the-day until to-me to-come-you from-day fault in-you I-found not for

הַזֶּה וּבְעֵינֵי הַסְּרָנִים לֹא־ טוֹב אָתָּה׃ וְעַתָּה שׁוּב
turn-back! so-now (7) you pleasing not the-rulers but-in-eyes-of the-this

וְלֵךְ בְּשָׁלוֹם וְלֹא־ תַעֲשֶׂה רָע בְּעֵינֵי סַרְנֵי פְלִשְׁתִּים׃
Philistines rulers-of in-eyes-of displeasing you-do and-not in-peace and-go!

וַיֹּאמֶר דָּוִד אֶל־ אָכִישׁ כִּי מֶה עָשִׂיתִי וּמַה־ מָּצָאתָ
you-found and-what? I-did what? but Achish to David and-he-asked (8)

בְעַבְדְּךָ מִיּוֹם אֲשֶׁר הָיִיתִי לְפָנֶיךָ עַד הַיּוֹם הַזֶּה
the-this the-day until before-you I-came that from-day against-servant-of-you

were marching at the rear with Achish. 3The commanders of the Philistines asked, "What about these Hebrews?"

Achish replied, "Is this not David, who was an officer of Saul king of Israel? He has already been with me for over a year, and from the day he left Saul until now, I have found no fault in him."

4But the Philistine commanders were angry with him and said, "Send the man back, that he may return to the place you assigned him. He must not go with us into battle, or he will turn against us during the fighting. How better could he regain his master's favor than by taking the heads of our own men? 5Isn't this the David they sang about in their dances:

" 'Saul has slain his
thousands,
and David his tens of
thousands'?"

6So Achish called David and said to him, "As surely as the LORD lives, you have been reliable, and I would be pleased to have you serve with me in the army. From the day you came to me until now, I have found no fault in you, but the rulers don't approve of you. 7Turn back and go in peace; do nothing to displease the Philistine rulers."

8"But what have I done?" asked David. "What have you found against your servant from the day I came to you until now? Why can't I go and

°5 ק ברבבתיו

כִּי לֹא אָבוֹא וְנִלְחַמְתִּי בְּאֹיְבֵי אֲדֹנִי הַמֶּלֶךְ׃

the-king lord-of-me against-being-enemies-of and-I-can-fight I-can-go not that

וַיַּעַן אָכִישׁ וַיֹּאמֶר אֶל־דָּוִד יָדַעְתִּי כִּי טוֹב אַתָּה

you pleasing that I-know David to and-he-said Achish and-he-answered (9)

בְּעֵינַי כְּמַלְאַךְ אֱלֹהִים אַךְ שָׂרֵי פְלִשְׁתִּים אָמְרוּ

they-said Philistines commanders-of nevertheless God as-angel-of in-eyes-of-me

לֹא־יַעֲלֶה עִמָּנוּ בַּמִּלְחָמָה׃ וְעַתָּה הַשְׁכֵּם בַּבֹּקֶר

in-the-morning get-up! and-now (10) into-the-battle with-us he-must-go-up not

וְעַבְדֵי אֲדֹנֶיךָ אֲשֶׁר־בָּאוּ אִתָּךְ וְהִשְׁכַּמְתֶּם

and-you-get-up with-you they-came who masters-of-you and-servants-of

בַּבֹּקֶר וְאוֹר לָכֶם וָלֵכוּ׃ וַיַּשְׁכֵּם דָּוִד

David so-he-got-up (11) then-leave! to-you when-to-be-light in-the-morning

הוּא וַאֲנָשָׁיו לָלֶכֶת בַּבֹּקֶר לָשׁוּב אֶל־אֶרֶץ פְּלִשְׁתִּים

Philistines land-of to to-go-back in-the-morning to-leave and-men-of-him he

וּפְלִשְׁתִּים עָלוּ יִזְרְעֶאל׃ וַיְהִי בְּבֹא דָוִד

David when-to-reach and-he-was (30:1) Jezreel they-went-up and-Philistines

וַאֲנָשָׁיו צִקְלַג בַּיּוֹם הַשְּׁלִישִׁי וַעֲמָלֵקִי פָשְׁטוּ אֶל־נֶגֶב

Negev in they-raided now-Amalekite the-third on-the-day Ziklag and-men-of-him

וְאֶל־צִקְלַג וַיַּכּוּ אֶת־צִקְלַג וַיִּשְׂרְפוּ אֹתָהּ בָּאֵשׁ׃

with-fire her and-they-burned Ziklag *** and-they-attacked Ziklag and-in

וַיִּשְׁבּוּ אֶת־הַנָּשִׁים אֲשֶׁר־בָּהּ מִקָּטֹן וְעַד־גָּדוֹל לֹא

not old even-to from-young in-her who the-women *** and-they-captured (2)

הֵמִיתוּ אִישׁ וַיִּנְהֲגוּ וַיֵּלְכוּ לְדַרְכָּם׃

on-way-of-them and-they-went but-they-carried-off any they-killed

וַיָּבֹא דָוִד וַאֲנָשָׁיו אֶל־הָעִיר וְהִנֵּה שְׂרוּפָה

being-destroyed then-see! the-town to and-men-of-him David when-he-came (3)

בָּאֵשׁ וּנְשֵׁיהֶם וּבְנֵיהֶם וּבְנֹתֵיהֶם

and-daughters-of-them and-sons-of-them and-wives-of-them by-fire

נִשְׁבּוּ׃ וַיִּשָּׂא דָוִד וְהָעָם אֲשֶׁר־אִתּוֹ אֶת־

*** with-him who and-the-people David so-he-raised (4) they-were-captured

קוֹלָם וַיִּבְכּוּ עַד אֲשֶׁר אֵין־בָּהֶם כֹּחַ לִבְכּוֹת׃

to-weep strength in-them not when until and-they-wept voice-of-them

וּשְׁתֵּי נְשֵׁי־דָוִד נִשְׁבּוּ אֲחִינֹעַם הַיִּזְרְעֵלִית

the-Jezreelite Ahinoam they-were-captured David wives-of and-two-of (5)

וַאֲבִיגַיִל אֵשֶׁת נָבָל הַכַּרְמְלִי׃ וַתֵּצֶר לְדָוִד

to-David and-she-distressed (6) the-Carmelite Nabal widow-of and-Abigail

מְאֹד כִּי־אָמְרוּ הָעָם לְסָקְלוֹ כִּי־מָרָה נֶפֶשׁ

spirit-of she-was-bitter for to-stone-him the-people they-talked for greatly

fight against the enemies of my lord the king?"

[9]Achish answered, "I know that you have been as pleasing in my eyes as an angel of God; nevertheless, the Philistine commanders have said, 'He must not go up with us into battle.' [10]Now get up early, along with your master's servants who have come with you, and leave in the morning as soon as it is light."

[11]So David and his men got up early in the morning to go back to the land of the Philistines, and the Philistines went up to Jezreel.

David Destroys the Amalekites

30 David and his men reached Ziklag on the third day. Now the Amalekites had raided the Negev and Ziklag. They had attacked Ziklag and burned it, [2]and had taken captive the women and all who were in it, both young and old. They killed none of them, but carried them off as they went on their way.

[3]When David and his men came to Ziklag, they found it destroyed by fire and their wives and sons and daughters taken captive. [4]So David and his men wept aloud until they had no strength left to weep. [5]David's two wives had been captured—Ahinoam of Jezreel and Abigail, the widow of Nabal of Carmel. [6]David was greatly distressed because the men were talking of stoning him; each one was bitter in

כָּל־ הָעָם אִישׁ עַל־ בָּנָו° וְעַל־ בְּנֹתָיו
daughters-of-him and-because-of sons-of-him because-of each the-people all-of

וַיִּתְחַזֵּק דָּוִד בַּיהוָה אֱלֹהָיו׃ וַיֹּאמֶר דָּוִד אֶל־
to David then-he-said (7) God-of-him in-Yahweh David but-he-found-strength

אֶבְיָתָר הַכֹּהֵן בֶּן־ אֲחִימֶלֶךְ הַגִּישָׁה־ נָּא לִי הָאֵפֹד וַיַּגֵּשׁ
so-he-brought the-ephod to-me now! bring! Ahimelech son-of the-priest Abiathar

אֶבְיָתָר אֶת־ הָאֵפֹד אֶל־ דָּוִד׃ וַיִּשְׁאַל דָּוִד בַּיהוָה לֵאמֹר
to-say of-Yahweh David and-he-inquired (8) David to the-ephod *** Abiathar

אֶרְדֹּף אַחֲרֵי הַגְּדוּד־ הַזֶּה הַאַשִּׂגֶנּוּ
will-I-overtake-him? the-this the-raiding-party after shall-I-pursue

וַיֹּאמֶר לוֹ רְדֹף כִּי־ הַשֵּׂג תַּשִּׂיג וְהַצֵּל
and-to-rescue you-will-overtake to-overtake for pursue! to-him and-he-answered

תַּצִּיל׃ וַיֵּלֶךְ דָּוִד הוּא וְשֵׁשׁ־ מֵאוֹת אִישׁ אֲשֶׁר אִתּוֹ
with-him who man hundreds and-six he David and-he-went (9) you-will-rescue

וַיָּבֹאוּ עַד־ נַחַל הַבְּשׂוֹר וְהַנּוֹתָרִים עָמָדוּ׃
they-stayed and-the-ones-remaining the-Besor Ravine-of to and-they-came

וַיִּרְדֹּף דָּוִד הוּא וְאַרְבַּע־ מֵאוֹת אִישׁ וַיַּעַמְדוּ מָאתַיִם
two-hundreds but-they-stayed man hundreds and-four he David and-he-pursued (10)

אִישׁ אֲשֶׁר פִּגְּרוּ מֵעֲבֹר אֶת־ נַחַל הַבְּשׂוֹר׃
the-Besor Ravine-of *** from-to-cross they-were-exhausted who man

וַיִּמְצְאוּ אִישׁ־ מִצְרִי בַּשָּׂדֶה וַיִּקְחוּ אֹתוֹ אֶל־ דָּוִד
David to him and-they-brought in-the-field Egyptian man and-they-found (11)

וַיִּתְּנוּ־ לוֹ לֶחֶם וַיֹּאכַל וַיַּשְׁקֻהוּ מָיִם׃
waters and-they-gave-to-drink-him and-he-ate food to-him and-they-gave

וַיִּתְּנוּ־ לוֹ פֶלַח דְּבֵלָה וּשְׁנֵי צִמֻּקִים
raisin-cakes and-two-of pressed-fig-cake part-of to-him and-they-gave (12)

וַיֹּאכַל וַתָּשָׁב רוּחוֹ אֵלָיו כִּי לֹא־ אָכַל לֶחֶם וְלֹא־
and-not food he-ate not for to-him spirit-of-him and-she-returned and-he-ate

שָׁתָה מַיִם שְׁלֹשָׁה יָמִים וּשְׁלֹשָׁה לֵילוֹת׃ וַיֹּאמֶר לוֹ דָוִד
David to-him and-he-asked (13) nights and-three days three waters he-drank

לְמִי־ אַתָּה וְאֵי מִזֶּה אָתָּה וַיֹּאמֶר נַעַר מִצְרִי אָנֹכִי עֶבֶד
slave I Egyptian man and-he-said you from-there and-where? you to-whom?

לְאִישׁ עֲמָלֵקִי וַיַּעַזְבֵנִי אֲדֹנִי כִּי חָלִיתִי הַיּוֹם
the-day I-became-ill for master-of-me and-he-abandoned-me Amalekite of-man

שְׁלֹשָׁה׃ אֲנַחְנוּ פָּשַׁטְנוּ נֶגֶב הַכְּרֵתִי וְעַל־ אֲשֶׁר לִיהוּדָה וְעַל־
and-in to-Judah what and-in the-Kerethite Negev-of we-raided we (14) three

נֶגֶב כָּלֵב וְאֶת־ צִקְלַג שָׂרַפְנוּ בָאֵשׁ׃ וַיֹּאמֶר אֵלָיו דָּוִד
David to-him and-he-asked (15) with-fire we-burned Ziklag and Caleb Negev-of

spirit because of his sons and
daughters. But David found
strength in the LORD his God.
7Then David said to Abia-
thar the priest, the son of
Ahimelech, "Bring me the
ephod." Abiathar brought it to
him, 8and David inquired of
the LORD, "Shall I pursue this
raiding party? Will I overtake
them?"
"Pursue them," he an-
swered. "You will certainly
overtake them and succeed in
the rescue."
9David and the six hundred
men with him came to the Besor Ravine, where some
stayed behind, 10for two hundred men were too exhausted
to cross the ravine. But David
and four hundred men con-
tinued the pursuit.
11They found an Egyptian in
a field and brought him to David. They gave him water to
drink and food to eat— 12part
of a cake of pressed figs and
two cakes of raisins. He ate
and was revived, for he had
not eaten any food or drunk
any water for three days and
three nights.
13David asked him, "To
whom do you belong, and
where do you come from?"
He said, "I am an Egyptian,
the slave of an Amalekite. My
master abandoned me when I
became ill three days ago. 14We
raided the Negev of the Kerethites and the territory belonging to Judah and the
Negev of Caleb. And we
burned Ziklag."
15David asked him, "Can

°6 ק בניו

הֲתוֹרִדֵנִי אֶל־ הַגְּדוּד הַזֶּה וַיֹּאמֶר הִשָּׁבְעָה לִּי
to-me swear! and-he-answered the-this the-raiding-party to can-you-lead-me?

בֵאלֹהִים אִם־ תְּמִיתֵנִי וְאִם־ תַּסְגִּרֵנִי בְּיַד־
to-hand-of you-will-turn-over-me and-not you-will-kill-me not before-God

אֲדֹנִי וְאוֹרִדְךָ אֶל־ הַגְּדוּד הַזֶּה׃
the-this the-raiding-party to and-I-will-take-you master-of-me

(16) וַיֹּרִדֵהוּ וְהִנֵּה נְטֻשִׁים עַל־ פְּנֵי כָל־
all-of surfaces-of over ones-being-scattered and-see! so-he-led-down-him (16)

הָאָרֶץ אֹכְלִים וְשֹׁתִים וְחֹגְגִים בְּכֹל
over-all-of and-ones-reveling and-ones-drinking ones-eating the-country

הַשָּׁלָל הַגָּדוֹל אֲשֶׁר לָקְחוּ מֵאֶרֶץ פְּלִשְׁתִּים וּמֵאֶרֶץ
and-from-land-of Philistines from-land-of they-took that the-great the-plunder

יְהוּדָה׃ (17) וַיַּכֵּם דָּוִד מֵהַנֶּשֶׁף וְעַד־ הָעֶרֶב
the-evening even-to from-the-dusk David and-he-fought-them (17) Judah

לְמָחֳרָתָם וְלֹא־ נִמְלַט מֵהֶם אִישׁ כִּי אִם־אַרְבַּע
four only except any from-them he-got-away and-not of-next-day-of-them

מֵאוֹת אִישׁ־ נַעַר אֲשֶׁר־ רָכְבוּ עַל־ הַגְּמַלִּים וַיָּנֻסוּ׃
and-they-fled the-camels on they-rode-off who young man hundreds

(18) וַיַּצֵּל דָּוִד אֵת כָּל־אֲשֶׁר לָקְחוּ עֲמָלֵק וְאֶת־ שְׁתֵּי
two-of including Amalek they-took that all *** David so-he-recovered (18)

נָשָׁיו הִצִּיל דָּוִד׃ (19) וְלֹא נֶעְדַּר־ לָהֶם מִן־
from from-them he-was-missing and-nothing (19) David he-recovered wives-of-him

הַקָּטֹן וְעַד־ הַגָּדוֹל וְעַד־ בָּנִים וּבָנוֹת וּמִשָּׁלָל וְעַד
even-to or-from-plunder and-girls boys and-to the-old even-to the-young

כָּל־ אֲשֶׁר לָקְחוּ לָהֶם הַכֹּל הֵשִׁיב דָּוִד׃
David he-brought-back the-whole for-them they-took that anything

(20) וַיִּקַּח דָּוִד אֶת־ כָּל־ הַצֹּאן וְהַבָּקָר נָהֲגוּ לִפְנֵי
ahead-of they-drove and-the-herd the-flock all-of *** David and-he-took (20)

הַמִּקְנֶה הַהוּא וַיֹּאמְרוּ זֶה שְׁלַל דָּוִד׃ (21) וַיָּבֹא
then-he-came (21) David plunder-of this and-they-said the-this the-stock

דָוִד אֶל־ מָאתַיִם הָאֲנָשִׁים אֲשֶׁר־ פִּגְּרוּ ׀ מִלֶּכֶת ׀ אַחֲרֵי
after from-to-follow they-were-exhausted who the-men two-hundreds to David

דָוִד וַיֹּשִׁבֻם בְּנַחַל הַבְּשׂוֹר וַיֵּצְאוּ לִקְרַאת
to-meet and-they-came-out the-Besor at-Ravine-of and-they-left-them David

דָּוִד וְלִקְרַאת הָעָם אֲשֶׁר־ אִתּוֹ וַיִּגַּשׁ דָּוִד אֶת־
*** David and-he-approached with-him who the-people and-to-meet David

הָעָם וַיִּשְׁאַל לָהֶם לְשָׁלוֹם׃ (22) וַיַּעַן כָּל־ אִישׁ־
man every-of but-he-said (22) for-peace to-them and-he-greeted the-people

you lead me down to this raiding party?"

He answered, "Swear to me before God that you will not kill me or hand me over to my master, and I will take you down to them."

[16]He led David down, and there they were, scattered over the countryside, eating, drinking and reveling because of the great amount of plunder they had taken from the land of the Philistines and from
Judah. [17]David fought them from dusk until the evening of the next day, and none of them got away, except four hundred young men who rode off on camels and fled. [18]David
recovered everything the Amalekites had taken, including his two wives. [19]Nothing
was missing: young or old, boy or girl, plunder or anything else they had taken. David brought everything back.
[20]He took all the flocks and herds, and his men drove them ahead of the other livestock, saying, "This is David's plunder."

[21]Then David came to the two hundred men who had been too exhausted to follow him and who were left behind at the Besor Ravine. They came out to meet David and the people with him. As David and his men approached, he greeted them. [22]But all the evil

רָע וּבְלִיַּעַל מֵהָאֲנָשִׁים אֲשֶׁר הָלְכוּ עִם־דָּוִד וַיֹּאמְרוּ
and-they-said David with they-followed who among-the-men and-troublemaker evil

יַעַן אֲשֶׁר לֹא־הָלְכוּ עִמִּי לֹא־נִתֵּן לָהֶם
with-them he-will-be-shared not with-me they-went not that because

מֵהַשָּׁלָל אֲשֶׁר הִצַּלְנוּ כִּי־אִם־אִישׁ אֶת־אִשְׁתּוֹ וְאֶת־
and wife-of-him *** each that except we-recovered that from-the-plunder

בָּנָיו וְיִנְהֲגוּ וְיֵלֵכוּ׃ וַיֹּאמֶר דָּוִד
David but-he-replied (23) and-they-may-go and-they-make-take children-of-him

לֹא־תַעֲשׂוּ כֵן אֶחָי אֵת אֲשֶׁר־נָתַן יְהוָה לָנוּ וַיִּשְׁמֹר
for-he-protected to-us Yahweh he-gave what with brothers-of-me that you-do not

אֹתָנוּ וַיִּתֵּן אֶת־הַגְּדוּד הַבָּא עָלֵינוּ בְּיָדֵנוּ׃
into-hand-of-us against-us the-one-coming the-force *** and-he-gave us

וּמִי יִשְׁמַע לָכֶם לַדָּבָר הַזֶּה כִּי כְּחֵלֶק
as-share-of for the-this to-the-word to-you he-will-listen now-who? (24)

הַיֹּרֵד בַּמִּלְחָמָה וּכְחֵלֶק הַיֹּשֵׁב עַל־הַכֵּלִים
the-supplies with the-one-staying so-as-share-of to-the-battle the-one-going-down

יַחְדָּו יַחֲלֹקוּ׃ וַיְהִי מֵהַיּוֹם הַהוּא וָמָעְלָה
and-onward the-that from-the-day and-he-was (25) they-will-share alike

וַיְשִׂמֶהָ לְחֹק וּלְמִשְׁפָּט לְיִשְׂרָאֵל עַד הַיּוֹם הַזֶּה׃
the-this the-day to for-Israel and-as-ordinace as-statute that-he-made-her

וַיָּבֹא דָוִד אֶל־צִקְלַג וַיְשַׁלַּח מֵהַשָּׁלָל לְזִקְנֵי
to-elders-of from-the-plunder then-he-sent Ziklag in David when-he-arrived (26)

יְהוּדָה לְרֵעֵהוּ לֵאמֹר הִנֵּה לָכֶם בְּרָכָה מִשְּׁלַל
from-plunder-of present for-you see! to-say to-friends-of-him Judah

אֹיְבֵי יְהוָה׃ לַאֲשֶׁר בְּבֵית־אֵל וְלַאֲשֶׁר בְּרָמוֹת־נֶגֶב
Negev in-Ramoth and-to-whom El in-Beth to-whom (27) Yahweh being-enemies-of

וְלַאֲשֶׁר בְּיַתִּר׃ וְלַאֲשֶׁר בַּעֲרֹעֵר וְלַאֲשֶׁר בְּשִׂפְמוֹת
in-Siphmoth and-to-whom in-Aroer and-to-whom (28) in-Jattir and-to-whom

וְלַאֲשֶׁר בְּאֶשְׁתְּמֹעַ׃ וְלַאֲשֶׁר בְּרָכָל וְלַאֲשֶׁר בְּעָרֵי
in-towns-of and-to-whom in-Racal and-to-whom (29) in-Eshtemoa and-to-whom

הַיְּרַחְמְאֵלִי וְלַאֲשֶׁר בְּעָרֵי הַקֵּינִי׃ וְלַאֲשֶׁר בְּחָרְמָה
in-Hormah and-to-whom (30) the-Kenite in-towns-of and-to-whom the-Jerahmeelite

וְלַאֲשֶׁר בְּבוֹר־עָשָׁן וְלַאֲשֶׁר בַּעֲתָךְ׃ וְלַאֲשֶׁר בְּחֶבְרוֹן
in-Hebron and-to-whom (31) in-Athach and-to-whom Ashan in-Bor and-to-whom

וּלְכָל־הַמְּקֹמוֹת אֲשֶׁר־הִתְהַלֶּךְ־שָׁם דָּוִד הוּא וַאֲנָשָׁיו׃
and-men-of-him he David there he-roamed where the-places and-to-all-of

וּפְלִשְׁתִּים נִלְחָמִים בְּיִשְׂרָאֵל וַיָּנֻסוּ אַנְשֵׁי יִשְׂרָאֵל
Israel men-of and-they-fled against-Israel ones-fighting now-Philistines (31:1)

men and troublemakers among David's followers said, "Because they did not go out with us, we will not share with them the plunder we recovered. However, each man may take his wife and children and go."
[23]David replied, "No, my brothers, you must not do that with what the LORD has given us. He has protected us and handed over to us the forces
that came against us. [24]Who
will listen to what you say? The share of the man who stayed with the supplies is to be the same as that of him who went down to the battle.
All will share alike." [25]David
made this a statute and ordinance for Israel from that day to this.
[26]When David arrived in Ziklag, he sent some of the plunder to the elders of Judah, who were his friends, saying, "Here is a present for you from the plunder of the LORD's enemies."
[27]He sent it to those who were in Bethel, Ramoth Negev
and Jattir; [28]to those in Aroer,
Siphmoth, Eshtemoa [29]and
Racal; to those in the towns of the Jerahmeelites and the Kenites; [30]to those in Hormah,
Bor Ashan, Athach [31]and He-
bron; and to those in all the other places where David and his men had roamed.

Saul Takes His Life

31 Now the Philistines fought against Israel; the Israelites fled before them,

מִפְּנֵי פְלִשְׁתִּים וַיִּפְּלוּ חֲלָלִים בְּהַר הַגִּלְבֹּעַ׃
the-Gilboa on-Mount-of ones-slain and-they-fell Philistines from-before

וַיַּדְבְּקוּ פְלִשְׁתִּים אֶת־ שָׁאוּל וְאֶת־ בָּנָיו וַיַּכּוּ
and-they-killed sons-of-him and Saul *** Philistines and-they-pressed-after (2)

פְלִשְׁתִּים אֶת־ יְהוֹנָתָן וְאֶת־ אֲבִינָדָב וְאֶת־ מַלְכִּי־ שׁוּעַ בְּנֵי שָׁאוּל׃
Saul sons-of Shua Malki and Abinadab and Jonathan *** Philistines

וַתִּכְבַּד הַמִּלְחָמָה אֶל־ שָׁאוּל וַיִּמְצָאֻהוּ
and-they-overtook-him Saul around the-fighting and-she-grew-fierce (3)

הַמּוֹרִים אֲנָשִׁים בַּקָּשֶׁת וַיָּחֶל מְאֹד
critically and-he-was-wounded with-the-bow men the-ones-shooting

מֵהַמּוֹרִים׃ וַיֹּאמֶר שָׁאוּל לְנֹשֵׂא כֵלָיו שְׁלֹף
draw! armors-of-him to-one-bearing Saul and-he-said (4) by-the-ones-shooting

חַרְבְּךָ ׀ וְדָקְרֵנִי בָהּ פֶּן־ יָבוֹאוּ
they-will-come or with-her and-run-through-me! sword-of-you

הָעֲרֵלִים הָאֵלֶּה וּדְקָרֻנִי וְהִתְעַלְּלוּ־
and-they-will-abuse and-they-will-run-through-me the-these the-uncircumcised-ones

בִי וְלֹא אָבָה נֹשֵׂא כֵלָיו כִּי יָרֵא מְאֹד
very he-was-terrified for armors-of-him one-bearing he-would but-not at-me

וַיִּקַּח שָׁאוּל אֶת־ הַחֶרֶב וַיִּפֹּל עָלֶיהָ׃ וַיַּרְא נֹשֵׂא־
one-bearing when-he-saw (5) on-her and-he-fell the-sword *** Saul so-he-took

כֵלָיו כִּי מֵת שָׁאוּל וַיִּפֹּל גַּם־ הוּא עַל־ חַרְבּוֹ
sword-of-him on he also then-he-fell Saul he-was-dead that armors-of-him

וַיָּמָת עִמּוֹ׃ וַיָּמָת שָׁאוּל וּשְׁלֹשֶׁת בָּנָיו
sons-of-him and-three-of Saul so-he-died (6) with-him and-he-died

וְנֹשֵׂא כֵלָיו גַּם כָּל־ אֲנָשָׁיו בַּיּוֹם הַהוּא
the-that on-the-day men-of-him all-of and armors-of-him and-one-bearing

יַחְדָּו׃ וַיִּרְאוּ אַנְשֵׁי־ יִשְׂרָאֵל אֲשֶׁר־ בְּעֵבֶר הָעֵמֶק וַאֲשֶׁר ׀
and-who the-valley at-along who Israel men-of when-they-saw (7) together

בְּעֵבֶר הַיַּרְדֵּן כִּי־ נָסוּ אַנְשֵׁי יִשְׂרָאֵל וְכִי־ מֵתוּ
they-were-dead and-that Israel men-of they-fled that the-Jordan at-across

שָׁאוּל וּבָנָיו וַיַּעַזְבוּ אֶת־ הֶעָרִים וַיָּנֻסוּ
and-they-fled the-towns *** then-they-abandoned and-sons-of-him Saul

וַיָּבֹאוּ פְלִשְׁתִּים וַיֵּשְׁבוּ בָּהֶן׃ וַיְהִי
and-he-was (8) in-them and-they-occupied Philistines and-they-came

מִמָּחֳרָת וַיָּבֹאוּ פְלִשְׁתִּים לְפַשֵּׁט אֶת־ הַחֲלָלִים
the-ones-dead *** to-strip Philistines when-they-came on-next-day

וַיִּמְצְאוּ אֶת־ שָׁאוּל וְאֶת־ שְׁלֹשֶׁת בָּנָיו נֹפְלִים
ones-having-fallen sons-of-him three-of and Saul *** then-they-found

and many fell slain on Mount Gilboa. [2]The Philistines pressed hard after Saul and his sons, and they killed his sons Jonathan, Abinadab and Malki-Shua. [3]The fighting grew fierce around Saul, and when the archers overtook him, they wounded him critically.

[4]Saul said to his armor-bearer, "Draw your sword and run me through, or these uncircumcised fellows will come and run me through and abuse me."

But his armor-bearer was terrified and would not do it; so Saul took his own sword and fell on it. [5]When the armor-bearer saw that Saul was dead, he too fell on his sword and died with him. [6]So Saul and three of his sons and his armor-bearer and all his men died together that same day.

[7]When the Israelites along the valley and those across the Jordan saw that the Israelite army had fled and that Saul and his sons had died, they abandoned their towns and fled. And the Philistines came and occupied them.

[8]The next day, when the Philistines came to strip the dead, they found Saul and his three sons fallen on Mount

בְּהַר הַגִּלְבֹּעַ׃ וַיִּכְרְתוּ אֶת־ רֹאשׁוֹ וַיַּפְשִׁטוּ
on-Mount-of the-Gilboa (9) and-they-cut-off *** head-of-him and-they-stripped

אֶת־ כֵּלָיו וַיְשַׁלְּחוּ בְאֶרֶץ־ פְּלִשְׁתִּים סָבִיב
*** armors-of-him and-they-sent through-land-of Philistines around

לְבַשֵּׂר בֵּית עֲצַבֵּיהֶם וְאֶת־ הָעָם׃ וַיָּשִׂמוּ אֶת־
to-proclaim temple-of idols-of-them and the-people (10) and-they-put ***

כֵּלָיו בֵּית עַשְׁתָּרוֹת וְאֶת־ גְּוִיָּתוֹ תָּקְעוּ בְּחוֹמַת
armors-of-him temple-of Ashtoreths and body-of-him they-fastened to-wall-of

בֵּית שָׁן׃ וַיִּשְׁמְעוּ אֵלָיו יֹשְׁבֵי יָבֵישׁ גִּלְעָד אֵת
Beth Shan (11) when-they-heard about-him ones-living-of Jabesh Gilead ***

אֲשֶׁר־ עָשׂוּ פְלִשְׁתִּים לְשָׁאוּל׃ וַיָּקוּמוּ כָּל־ אִישׁ חַיִל
what they-did Philistines to-Saul (12) then-they-rose every-of man-of valor

וַיֵּלְכוּ כָל־ הַלַּיְלָה וַיִּקְחוּ אֶת־ גְּוִיַּת שָׁאוּל וְאֵת
and-they-journeyed all-of the-night and-they-took-down *** body-of Saul and

גְּוִיֹּת בָּנָיו מֵחוֹמַת בֵּית שָׁן וַיָּבֹאוּ יָבֵשָׁה
bodies-of sons-of-him from-wall-of Beth Shan and-they-went to-Jabesh

וַיִּשְׂרְפוּ אֹתָם שָׁם׃ וַיִּקְחוּ אֶת־ עַצְמֹתֵיהֶם
and-they-burned them there (13) then-they-took *** bones-of-them

וַיִּקְבְּרוּ תַחַת־ הָאֶשֶׁל בְּיָבֵשָׁה וַיָּצֻמוּ שִׁבְעַת יָמִים׃
and-they-buried under the-tamarisk in-Jabesh and-they-fasted seven-of days

Gilboa. 9They cut off his head
and stripped off his armor,
and they sent messengers
throughout the land of the
Philistines to proclaim the
news in the temple of their
idols and among their people.
10They put his armor in the
temple of the Ashtoreths and
fastened his body to the wall
of Beth Shan.

11When the people of Jabesh
Gilead heard of what the Philistines had done to Saul, 12all
their valiant men journeyed
through the night to Beth
Shan. They took down the
bodies of Saul and his sons
from the wall of Beth Shan
and went to Jabesh, where
they burned them. 13Then they
took their bones and buried
them under a tamarisk tree at
Jabesh, and they fasted seven
days.

וַיְהִ֗י אַחֲרֵי֙ מ֣וֹת שָׁא֔וּל וְדָוִ֣ד שָׁ֔ב מֵהַכּ֖וֹת
from-to-defeat he-returned then-David Saul death-of after and-he-was (1:1)

אֶת־הָעֲמָלֵ֑ק וַיֵּ֧שֶׁב דָּוִ֛ד בְּצִקְלָ֖ג יָמִ֥ים שְׁנָֽיִם׃ וַיְהִ֣י ׀
and-he-was (2) two days in-Ziklag David and-he-stayed the-Amalek ***

בַּיּ֣וֹם הַשְּׁלִישִׁ֗י וְהִנֵּ֨ה אִ֜ישׁ בָּ֤א מִן־הַֽמַּחֲנֶה֙ מֵעִ֣ם שָׁא֔וּל
Saul from-with the-camp from arriving man then-see! the-third on-the-day

וּבְגָדָ֣יו קְרֻעִ֔ים וַאֲדָמָ֖ה עַל־רֹאשׁ֑וֹ וַיְהִי֙
and-he-was head-of-him on and-dust ones-being-torn and-clothes-of-him

בְּבֹא֣וֹ אֶל־דָּוִ֔ד וַיִּפֹּ֥ל אַ֖רְצָה וַיִּשְׁתָּֽחוּ׃
and-he-paid-honor to-ground then-he-fell David to when-to-come-him

וַיֹּ֤אמֶר לוֹ֙ דָּוִ֔ד אֵ֥י מִזֶּ֖ה תָּב֑וֹא וַיֹּ֣אמֶר
and-he-answered you-came from-there where? David to-him and-he-asked (3)

אֵלָ֔יו מִמַּחֲנֵ֥ה יִשְׂרָאֵ֖ל נִמְלָֽטְתִּי׃ וַיֹּ֧אמֶר אֵלָ֛יו דָּוִ֖ד מֶה־
what? David to-him and-he-asked (4) I-escaped Israel from-camp-of to-him

הָיָ֥ה הַדָּבָ֖ר הַגֶּד־נָ֣א לִ֑י וַיֹּ֡אמֶר אֲשֶׁר־נָ֨ס הָעָ֜ם
the-people he-fled that and-he-said to-me now! tell! the-thing he-happened

מִן־הַמִּלְחָמָ֗ה וְגַם־הַרְבֵּ֞ה נָפַ֤ל מִן־הָעָם֙ וַיָּמֻ֔תוּ
and-they-died the-people from he-fell to-be-many and-also the-battle from

וְגַ֗ם שָׁא֛וּל וִיהוֹנָתָ֥ן בְּנ֖וֹ מֵֽתוּ׃ וַיֹּ֣אמֶר דָּוִ֔ד אֶל־
to David then-he-said (5) they-died son-of-him and-Jonathan Saul and-also

הַנַּ֖עַר הַמַּגִּ֣יד ל֑וֹ אֵ֣יךְ יָדַ֔עְתָּ כִּי־מֵ֥ת שָׁא֖וּל
Saul he-died that you-know how? to-him the-one-reporting the-young-man

וִיהוֹנָתָ֥ן בְּנֽוֹ׃ וַיֹּ֜אמֶר הַנַּ֣עַר ׀ הַמַּגִּ֣יד
the-one-reporting the-young-man and-he-said (6) son-of-him and-Jonathan

ל֗וֹ נִקְרֹ֤א נִקְרֵ֙יתִי֙ בְּהַ֣ר הַגִּלְבֹּ֔עַ וְהִנֵּ֥ה שָׁא֖וּל נִשְׁעָ֣ן עַל־
on leaning Saul and-see! the-Gilboa on-Mount-of I-happened to-happen to-him

חֲנִית֑וֹ וְהִנֵּ֧ה הָרֶ֛כֶב וּבַעֲלֵ֥י הַפָּרָשִׁ֖ים הִדְבִּקֻֽהוּ׃
they-were-upon-him the-horsemen and-masters-of the-chariot and-see! spear-of-him

וַיִּ֥פֶן אַחֲרָ֖יו וַיִּרְאֵ֑נִי וַיִּקְרָ֣א אֵלַ֔י וָאֹמַ֖ר
and-I-said to-me then-he-called and-he-saw-me after-me when-he-turned (7)

הִנֵּֽנִי׃ וַיֹּ֥אמֶר לִ֖י מִי־אָ֑תָּה וָיֹּאמַ֣ר אֵלָ֔יו עֲמָלֵקִ֖י אָנֹֽכִי׃
I Amalekite to-him and-I-answered you who? to-me and-he-asked (8) here-I!

וַיֹּ֣אמֶר אֵלַ֗י עֲמָד־נָ֤א עָלַי֙ וּמֹ֣תְתֵ֔נִי כִּ֥י אֲחָזַ֖נִי
he-holds-me for and-kill-me! over-me now! stand! to-me then-he-said (9)

הַשָּׁבָ֑ץ כִּֽי־כָל־ע֥וֹד נַפְשִׁ֖י בִּֽי׃ וָאֶעֱמֹ֣ד עָלָ֗יו
over-him so-I-stood (10) in-me life-of-me still all-of but the-death-throe

וַאֲמֹ֣תְתֵ֔הוּ כִּ֣י יָדַ֔עְתִּי כִּ֛י לֹ֥א יִחְיֶ֖ה אַחֲרֵ֣י נִפְל֑וֹ
to-fall-him after he-could-survive not that I-knew for and-I-killed-him

°8 ק ואמר

David Hears of Saul's Death

1 After the death of Saul,
David returned from de-
feating the Amalekites and
stayed in Ziklag two days. 2On
the third day a man arrived
from Saul's camp, with his
clothes torn and with dust on
his head. When he came to
David, he fell to the ground to
pay him honor.
3"Where have you come
from?" David asked him.
He answered, "I have es-
caped from the Israelite
camp."
4"What happened?" David
asked. "Tell me."
He said, "The men fled from
the battle. Many of them fell
and died. And Saul and his
son Jonathan are dead."
5Then David said to the
young man who brought him
the report, "How do you know
that Saul and his son Jonathan
are dead?"
6"I happened to be on
Mount Gilboa," the young
man said, "and there was
Saul, leaning on his spear,
with the chariots and riders almost upon him. 7When he
turned around and saw me, he
called out to me, and I said,
'What can I do?'
8"He asked me, 'Who are
you?'
" 'An Amalekite,' I an-
swered.
9"Then he said to me, 'Stand
over me and kill me! I am in
the throes of death, but I'm
still alive.'
10"So I stood over him and
killed him, because I knew
that after he had fallen he
could not survive. And I took

וָאֶקַּח הַנֵּזֶר ׀ אֲשֶׁר עַל־ רֹאשׁוֹ וְאֶצְעָדָה אֲשֶׁר עַל־ זְרֹעוֹ
arm-of-him on that and-band head-of-him on that the-crown and-I-took

וָאֲבִאֵם אֶל־ אֲדֹנִי הֵנָּה׃ וַיַּחֲזֵק דָּוִד
David and-he-took-hold (11) to-here lord-of-me to and-I-brought-them

בִּבְגָדוֹ° וַיִּקְרָעֵם וְגַם כָּל־ הָאֲנָשִׁים אֲשֶׁר אִתּוֹ׃
with-him who the-men all-of and-also and-he-tore-them of-clothes-of-him

וַיִּסְפְּדוּ וַיִּבְכּוּ וַיָּצֻמוּ עַד־ הָעֶרֶב עַל־
for the-evening till and-they-fasted and-they-wept and-they-mourned (12)

שָׁאוּל וְעַל־ יְהוֹנָתָן בְּנוֹ וְעַל־ עַם יְהוָה וְעַל־ בֵּית
house-of and-for Yahweh army-of and-for son-of-him Jonathan and-for Saul

יִשְׂרָאֵל כִּי נָפְלוּ בֶּחָרֶב׃ וַיֹּאמֶר דָּוִד אֶל־ הַנַּעַר
the-young-man to David and-he-said (13) by-the-sword they-fell for Israel

הַמַּגִּיד לוֹ אֵי מִזֶּה אַתָּה וַיֹּאמֶר בֶּן־ אִישׁ
man son-of and-he-answered you from-there where? to-him the-one-reporting

גֵּר עֲמָלֵקִי אָנֹכִי׃ וַיֹּאמֶר אֵלָיו דָּוִד אֵיךְ לֹא יָרֵאתָ
you-were-afraid not why? David to-him and-he-asked (14) I Amalekite alien

לִשְׁלֹחַ יָדְךָ לְשַׁחֵת אֶת־ מְשִׁיחַ יְהוָה׃ וַיִּקְרָא
then-he-called (15) Yahweh anointed-of *** to-destroy hand-of-you to-lift

דָוִד לְאַחַד מֵהַנְּעָרִים וַיֹּאמֶר גַּשׁ פְּגַע־ בּוֹ
against-him strike-down! go! and-he-said of-the-men to-one David

וַיַּכֵּהוּ וַיָּמֹת׃ וַיֹּאמֶר אֵלָיו דָּוִד דָּמְיךָ° עַל־
on blood-of-you David to-him for-he-said (16) and-he-died so-he-struck-him

רֹאשֶׁךָ כִּי פִיךָ עָנָה בְךָ לֵאמֹר אָנֹכִי מֹתַתִּי
I-killed I to-say against-you he-testified mouth-of-you for head-of-you

אֶת־ מְשִׁיחַ יְהוָה׃ וַיְקֹנֵן דָּוִד אֶת־ הַקִּינָה הַזֹּאת
the-this the-lament *** David and-he-lamented (17) Yahweh anointed-of ***

עַל־ שָׁאוּל וְעַל־ יְהוֹנָתָן בְּנוֹ׃ וַיֹּאמֶר
and-he-ordered (18) son-of-him Jonathan and-concerning Saul concerning

לְלַמֵּד בְּנֵי־ יְהוּדָה קָשֶׁת הִנֵּה כְתוּבָה עַל־ סֵפֶר הַיָּשָׁר׃
the-Jashar Book-of in being-written see! bow-lament Judah men-of to-teach

הַצְּבִי יִשְׂרָאֵל עַל־ בָּמוֹתֶיךָ חָלָל אֵיךְ נָפְלוּ גִבּוֹרִים׃
mighty-ones they-fell how! slain heights-of-you on Israel the-glory (19)

אַל־ תַּגִּידוּ בְגַת אַל־ תְּבַשְּׂרוּ בְּחוּצֹת אַשְׁקְלוֹן פֶּן־
lest Ashkelon in-streets-of you-proclaim not in-Gath you-tell not (20)

תִּשְׂמַחְנָה בְּנוֹת פְּלִשְׁתִּים פֶּן־ תַּעֲלֹזְנָה בְּנוֹת
daughters-of they-rejoice lest Philistines daughters-of they-be-glad

הָעֲרֵלִים׃ הָרֵי בַגִּלְבֹּעַ אַל־ טַל וְאַל־ מָטָר עֲלֵיכֶם
on-you rain and-no dew no of-the-Gilboa mountains-of (21) uncircumcised-ones

the crown that was on his head and the band on his arm and have brought them here to my lord."

11 Then David and all the men with him took hold of their clothes and tore them.
12 They mourned and wept and fasted till evening for Saul and his son Jonathan, and for the army of the LORD and the house of Israel, because they had fallen by the sword.

13 David said to the young man who brought him the report, "Where are you from?"

"I am the son of an alien, an Amalekite," he answered.

14 David asked him, "Why were you not afraid to lift your hand to destroy the LORD's anointed?"

15 Then David called one of his men and said, "Go, strike him down!" So he struck him down, and he died.
16 For David had said to him, "Your blood be on your own head. Your own mouth testified against you when you said, 'I killed the LORD's anointed.'"

David's Lament for Saul and Jonathan

17 David took up this lament concerning Saul and his son Jonathan,
18 and ordered that the men of Judah be taught this lament of the bow (it is written in the Book of Jashar):

19 "Your glory, O Israel, lies
slain on your heights.
How the mighty have
fallen!

20 "Tell it not in Gath,
proclaim it not in the
streets of Ashkelon,
lest the daughters of the
Philistines be glad,
lest the daughters of the
uncircumcised rejoice.

21 "O mountains of Gilboa,
may you have neither
dew nor rain,

°*11* ק בבגדיו
°*16* ק דמך

וּשְׂדֵי תְרוּמֹת כִּי שָׁם נִגְעַל מָגֵן גִּבּוֹרִים
mighty-ones shield-of he-was-defiled there for offerings nor-fields-of

מָגֵן שָׁאוּל בְּלִי מָשִׁיחַ בַּשָּׁמֶן׃ מִדַּם חֲלָלִים
ones-slain from-blood-of (22) with-the-oil rubbed no-longer Saul shield-of

מֵחֵלֶב גִּבּוֹרִים קֶשֶׁת יְהוֹנָתָן לֹא נָשׂוֹג אָחוֹר וְחֶרֶב
and-sword-of back he-turned not Jonathan bow-of mighty-ones from-flesh-of

שָׁאוּל לֹא תָשׁוּב רֵיקָם׃ שָׁאוּל וִיהוֹנָתָן הַנֶּאֱהָבִים
the-ones-being-loved and-Jonathan Saul (23) unsatisfied she-returned not Saul

וְהַנְּעִימִם בְּחַיֵּיהֶם וּבְמוֹתָם לֹא נִפְרָדוּ
they-were-parted not and-in-death-of-them in-lives-of-them and-the-gracious-ones

מִנְּשָׁרִים קַלּוּ מֵאֲרָיוֹת גָּבֵרוּ׃
they-were-strong more-than-lions they-were-swift more-than-eagles

בְּנוֹת יִשְׂרָאֵל אֶל־שָׁאוּל בְּכֶינָה הַמַּלְבִּשְׁכֶם שָׁנִי עִם־
and scarlet the-one-clothing-you weep! Saul for Israel daughters-of (24)

עֲדָנִים הַמַּעֲלֶה עֲדִי זָהָב עַל לְבוּשְׁכֶן׃ אֵיךְ
how! (25) garment-of-you on gold ornament-of the-one-adorning fineries

נָפְלוּ גִבֹּרִים בְּתוֹךְ הַמִּלְחָמָה יְהוֹנָתָן עַל־בָּמוֹתֶיךָ חָלָל׃
slain heights-of-you on Jonathan the-battle in-midst-of mighty-ones they-fell

צַר־לִי עָלֶיךָ אָחִי יְהוֹנָתָן נָעַמְתָּ לִּי
to-me you-were-dear Jonathan brother-of-me for-you to-me he-grieves (26)

מְאֹד נִפְלְאַתָה אַהֲבָתְךָ לִי מֵאַהֲבַת נָשִׁים׃ אֵיךְ
how! (27) women more-than-love-of for-me love-of-you she-was-wonderful very

נָפְלוּ גִבּוֹרִים וַיֹּאבְדוּ כְּלֵי מִלְחָמָה׃ וַיְהִי
and-he-was (2:1) war weapons-of and-they-perished mighty-ones they-fell

אַחֲרֵי־כֵן וַיִּשְׁאַל דָּוִד בַּיהוָה לֵאמֹר הַאֶעֱלֶה בְּאַחַת
to-one-of shall-I-go-up? to-say of-Yahweh David then-he-inquired this after

עָרֵי יְהוּדָה וַיֹּאמֶר יְהוָה אֵלָיו עֲלֵה וַיֹּאמֶר דָּוִד אָנָה
to-where? David and-he-asked go-up! to-him Yahweh and-he-said Judah towns-of

אֶעֱלֶה וַיֹּאמֶר חֶבְרֹנָה׃ וַיַּעַל שָׁם דָּוִד וְגַם
and-also David there so-he-went-up (2) to-Hebron and-he-answered shall-I-go

שְׁתֵּי נָשָׁיו אֲחִינֹעַם הַיִּזְרְעֵלִית וַאֲבִיגַיִל אֵשֶׁת נָבָל
Nabal widow-of and-Abigail the-Jezreelite Ahinoam wives-of-him two-of

הַכַּרְמְלִי׃ וַאֲנָשָׁיו אֲשֶׁר־עִמּוֹ הֶעֱלָה דָוִד אִישׁ
each David he-took with-him who and-men-of-him (3) the-Carmelite

וּבֵיתוֹ וַיֵּשְׁבוּ בְּעָרֵי חֶבְרוֹן׃ וַיָּבֹאוּ
then-they-came (4) Hebron in-towns-of and-they-settled with-family-of-him

אַנְשֵׁי יְהוּדָה וַיִּמְשְׁחוּ־שָׁם אֶת־דָּוִד לְמֶלֶךְ עַל־בֵּית יְהוּדָה
Judah house-of over as-king David *** there and-they-anointed Judah men-of

nor fields that yield
offerings ⌊of grain⌋.
For there the shield of the
mighty was defiled,
the shield of Saul—no
longer rubbed with oil.
22 From the blood of the
slain,
from the flesh of the
mighty,
the bow of Jonathan did
not turn back,
the sword of Saul did not
return unsatisfied.

23 "Saul and Jonathan—
in life they were loved
and gracious,
and in death they were
not parted.
They were swifter than
eagles,
they were stronger than
lions.

24 "O daughters of Israel,
weep for Saul,
who clothed you in scarlet
and finery,
who adorned your
garments with
ornaments of gold.

25 "How the mighty have
fallen in battle!
Jonathan lies slain on
your heights.
26 I grieve for you, Jonathan
my brother;
you were very dear to
me.
Your love for me was
wonderful,
more wonderful than
that of women.

27 "How the mighty have
fallen!
The weapons of war
have perished!"

David Anointed King Over Judah

2 In the course of time, David inquired of the LORD. "Shall I go up to one of the towns of Judah?" he asked.
The LORD said, "Go up."
David asked, "Where shall I go?"
"To Hebron," the LORD answered.
2 So David went up there with his two wives, Ahinoam of Jezreel and Abigail, the widow of Nabal of Carmel.
3 David also took the men who were with him, each with his family, and they settled in Hebron and its towns.
4 Then the men of Judah came to Hebron and there they anointed David king over the house of Judah.

וַיַּגִּדוּ לְדָוִד לֵאמֹר אַנְשֵׁי יָבֵישׁ גִּלְעָד אֲשֶׁר קָבְרוּ אֶת־שָׁאוּל׃
Saul *** they-buried who Gilead Jabesh men-of to-say to-David when-they-told

וַיִּשְׁלַח דָּוִד מַלְאָכִים אֶל־ אַנְשֵׁי יָבֵישׁ גִּלְעָד וַיֹּאמֶר אֲלֵיהֶם
to-them and-he-said Gilead Jabesh men-of to messengers David then-he-sent (5)

בְּרֻכִים אַתֶּם לַיהוָה אֲשֶׁר עֲשִׂיתֶם הַחֶסֶד הַזֶּה עִם־
to the-this the-kindness you-showed who by-Yahweh you ones-being-blessed

אֲדֹנֵיכֶם עִם־שָׁאוּל וַתִּקְבְּרוּ אֹתוֹ׃ וְעַתָּה יַעַשׂ־ יְהוָה
Yahweh may-he-show and-now (6) him when-you-buried Saul to masters-of-you

עִמָּכֶם חֶסֶד וֶאֱמֶת וְגַם אָנֹכִי אֶעֱשֶׂה אִתְּכֶם הַטּוֹבָה
the-favor to-you I-will-show I and-also and-faithfulness kindness to-you

הַזֹּאת אֲשֶׁר עֲשִׂיתֶם הַדָּבָר הַזֶּה׃ וְעַתָּה׀ תֶּחֱזַקְנָה
may-they-be-strong then-now (7) the-this the-thing you-did for the-this

יְדֵיכֶם וִהְיוּ לִבְנֵי־ חַיִל כִּי־ מֵת אֲדֹנֵיכֶם שָׁאוּל וְגַם־
and-also Saul masters-of-you dead for bravery as-men-of and-be! hands-of-you

אֹתִי מָשְׁחוּ בֵית־ יְהוּדָה לְמֶלֶךְ עֲלֵיהֶם׃ וְאַבְנֵר בֶּן־ נֵר
Ner son-of now-Abner (8) over-them as-king Judah house-of they-anointed me

שַׂר־ צָבָא אֲשֶׁר לְשָׁאוּל לָקַח אֶת־ אִישׁ בֹּשֶׁת בֶּן־ שָׁאוּל
Saul son-of Bosheth Ish *** he-took to-Saul that army commander-of

וַיַּעֲבִרֵהוּ מַחֲנָיִם׃ וַיַּמְלִכֵהוּ אֶל־ הַגִּלְעָד
the-Gilead over and-he-made-king-him (9) Mahanaim and-he-brought-him

וְאֶל־ הָאֲשׁוּרִי וְאֶל־ יִזְרְעֶאל וְעַל־ אֶפְרַיִם וְעַל־ בִּנְיָמִן
Benjamin and-over Ephraim and-over Jezreel and-over the-Ashuri and-over

וְעַל־ יִשְׂרָאֵל כֻּלֹּה׃ בֶּן־ אַרְבָּעִים שָׁנָה אִישׁ־ בֹּשֶׁת בֶּן־ שָׁאוּל
Saul son-of Bosheth Ish year forty son-of (10) all-of-him Israel and-over

בְּמָלְכוֹ עַל־ יִשְׂרָאֵל וּשְׁתַּיִם שָׁנִים מָלָךְ אַךְ בֵּית
house-of however he-reigned years and-two Israel over when-to-become-king-him

יְהוּדָה הָיוּ אַחֲרֵי דָוִד׃ וַיְהִי מִסְפַּר הַיָּמִים אֲשֶׁר הָיָה
he-was that the-days length-of and-he-was (11) David after they-went Judah

דָוִד מֶלֶךְ בְּחֶבְרוֹן עַל־ בֵּית יְהוּדָה שֶׁבַע שָׁנִים וְשִׁשָּׁה חֳדָשִׁים׃
months and-six years seven Judah house-of over in-Hebron king David

וַיֵּצֵא אַבְנֵר בֶּן־ נֵר וְעַבְדֵי אִישׁ־ בֹּשֶׁת בֶּן־ שָׁאוּל מִמַּחֲנַיִם
Mahanaim Saul son-of Bosheth Ish and-men-of Ner son-of Abner and-he-left (12)

גִּבְעוֹנָה׃ וְיוֹאָב בֶּן־ צְרוּיָה וְעַבְדֵי דָוִד יָצְאוּ
they-went-out David and-men-of Zeruiah son-of and-Joab (13) to-Gibeon

וַיִּפְגְּשׁוּם עַל־ בְּרֵכַת גִּבְעוֹן יַחְדָּו וַיֵּשְׁבוּ אֵלֶּה עַל־הַבְּרֵכָה
the-pool at these and-they-sat together Gibeon pool-of at and-they-met-them

מִזֶּה וְאֵלֶּה עַל־ הַבְּרֵכָה מִזֶּה׃ וַיֹּאמֶר אַבְנֵר אֶל־
to Abner then-he-said (14) at-other-side the-pool at and-these at-one-side

When David was told that it was the men of Jabesh Gilead who had buried Saul, [5]he sent messengers to the men of Jabesh Gilead to say to them, "The LORD bless you for showing this kindness to Saul your master by burying him. [6]May the LORD now show you kindness and faithfulness, and I too will show you the same favor because you have done this. [7]Now then, be strong and brave, for Saul your master is dead, and the house of Judah has anointed me king over them."

War Between the Houses of David and Saul

[8]Meanwhile, Abner son of Ner, the commander of Saul's army, had taken Ish-Bosheth son of Saul and brought him over to Mahanaim. [9]He made him king over Gilead, Ashuri[a] and Jezreel, and also over Ephraim, Benjamin and all Israel.

[10]Ish-Bosheth son of Saul was forty years old when he became king over Israel, and he reigned two years. The house of Judah, however, followed David. [11]The length of time David was king in Hebron over the house of Judah was seven years and six months.

[12]Abner son of Ner, together with the men of Ish-Bosheth son of Saul, left Mahanaim and went to Gibeon. [13]Joab son of Zeruiah and David's men went out and met them at the pool of Gibeon. One group sat down on one side of the pool and one group on the other side.

[14]Then Abner said to Joab,

[a]9 Or *Asher*

יוֹאָב יָקוּמוּ נָא הַנְּעָרִים וִישַׂחֲקוּ לְפָנֵינוּ
before-us and-let-them-fight the-young-men now! let-them-get-up Joab

וַיֹּאמֶר יוֹאָב יָקֻמוּ׃ וַיָּקֻמוּ וַיַּעַבְרוּ בְמִסְפָּר
by-number and-they-went so-they-stood-up (15) let-them-get-up Joab and-he-said

שְׁנֵים עָשָׂר לְבִנְיָמִן וּלְאִישׁ בֹּשֶׁת בֶּן־שָׁאוּל וּשְׁנֵים עָשָׂר מֵעַבְדֵי
from-men-of ten and-two Saul son-of Bosheth and-for-Ish for-Benjamin ten two

דָוִד׃ וַיַּחֲזִקוּ אִישׁ ׀ בְּרֹאשׁ רֵעֵהוּ וְחַרְבּוֹ
and-dagger-of-him opponent-of-him by-head each then-they-grabbed (16) David

בְּצַד רֵעֵהוּ וַיִּפְּלוּ יַחְדָּו וַיִּקְרָא לַמָּקוֹם
to-the-place so-he-called together and-they-fell opponent-of-him in-side-of

הַהוּא חֶלְקַת הַצֻּרִים אֲשֶׁר בְּגִבְעוֹן׃ וַתְּהִי הַמִּלְחָמָה קָשָׁה
fierce the-battle and-she-was (17) in-Gibeon that Hazzurim Helkath the-that

עַד־מְאֹד בַּיּוֹם הַהוּא וַיִּנָּגֶף אַבְנֵר וְאַנְשֵׁי יִשְׂרָאֵל
Israel and-men-of Abner and-he-was-defeated the-that on-the-day very-much to

לִפְנֵי עַבְדֵי דָוִד׃ וַיִּהְיוּ־שָׁם שְׁלֹשָׁה בְּנֵי צְרוּיָה יוֹאָב
Joab Zeruiah sons-of three there and-they-were (18) David men-of before

וַאֲבִישַׁי וַעֲשָׂהאֵל וַעֲשָׂהאֵל קַל בְּרַגְלָיו כְּאַחַד הַצְּבָיִם
the-gazelles as-one-of in-feet-of-him fleet now-Asahel and-Asahel and-Abishai

אֲשֶׁר בַּשָּׂדֶה׃ וַיִּרְדֹּף עֲשָׂהאֵל אַחֲרֵי אַבְנֵר וְלֹא־נָטָה
he-turned and-not Abner after Asahel and-he-chased (19) in-the-wild that

לָלֶכֶת עַל־הַיָּמִין וְעַל־הַשְּׂמֹאול מֵאַחֲרֵי אַבְנֵר׃ וַיִּפֶן אַבְנֵר
Abner and-he-looked (20) Abner from-after the-left or-to the-right to to-go

אַחֲרָיו וַיֹּאמֶר הַאַתָּה זֶה עֲשָׂהאֵל וַיֹּאמֶר אָנֹכִי׃ וַיֹּאמֶר
then-he-said (21) I and-he-answered Asahel that you? and-he-asked behind-him

לוֹ אַבְנֵר נְטֵה לְךָ עַל־יְמִינְךָ אוֹ עַל־שְׂמֹאלֶךָ וֶאֱחֹז
and-take-on! left-of-you to or right-of-you to for-you turn! Abner to-him

לְךָ אֶחָד מֵהַנְּעָרִים וְקַח־לְךָ אֶת־חֲלִצָתוֹ וְלֹא־
but-not weapon-of-him *** for-you and-strip! of-the-young-men one for-you

אָבָה עֲשָׂהאֵל לָסוּר מֵאַחֲרָיו׃ וַיֹּסֶף עוֹד אַבְנֵר
Abner again and-he-repeated (22) from-after-him to-turn Asahel he-would

לֵאמֹר אֶל־עֲשָׂהאֵל סוּר לְךָ מֵאַחֲרָי לָמָּה אַכֶּכָּה
should-I-strike-you why? from-after-me for-you turn! Asahel to to-warn

אַרְצָה וְאֵיךְ אֶשָּׂא פָנַי אֶל־יוֹאָב אָחִיךָ׃
brother-of-you Joab to faces-of-me could-I-lift and-how? to-ground

וַיְמָאֵן לָסוּר וַיַּכֵּהוּ אַבְנֵר בְּאַחֲרֵי הַחֲנִית
the-spear with-butt-of Abner so-he-struck-him to-turn but-he-refused (23)

אֶל־הַחֹמֶשׁ וַתֵּצֵא הַחֲנִית מֵאַחֲרָיו וַיִּפָּל־
and-he-fell through-back-of-him the-spear and-she-came-out the-stomach into

"Let's have some of the young men get up and fight hand to hand in front of us."

"All right, let them do it," Joab said.

15So they stood up and were counted off—twelve men for Benjamin and Ish-Bosheth son of Saul, and twelve for David.
16Then each man grabbed his opponent by the head and thrust his dagger into his opponent's side, and they fell down together. So that place in Gibeon was called Helkath Hazzurim.[b]

17The battle that day was very fierce, and Abner and the men of Israel were defeated by David's men.

18The three sons of Zeruiah were there: Joab, Abishai and Asahel. Now Asahel was as fleet-footed as a wild gazelle.
19He chased Abner, turning neither to the right nor to the left as he pursued him.
20Abner looked behind him and asked, "Is that you, Asahel?"

"It is," he answered.

21Then Abner said to him, "Turn aside to the right or to the left; take on one of the young men and strip him of his weapons." But Asahel would not stop chasing him.
22Again Abner warned Asahel, "Stop chasing me! Why should I strike you down? How could I look your brother Joab in the face?"

23But Asahel refused to give up the pursuit; so Abner thrust the butt of his spear into Asahel's stomach, and the spear came out through his back. He fell there and died on

[b]16 *Helkath Hazzurim* means *field of daggers* or *field of hostilities.*

שָׁם וַיָּמָת תַּחְתָּו וַיְהִי כָּל־ הַבָּא אֶל־
to the-one-coming every-of and-he-was in-place-of-him and-he-died there

הַמָּקוֹם אֲשֶׁר־ נָפַל שָׁם עֲשָׂהאֵל וַיָּמֹת וַיַּעֲמֹדוּ׃
then-they-stopped and-he-died Asahel there he-fell where the-place

(24) וַיִּרְדְּפוּ יוֹאָב וַאֲבִישַׁי אַחֲרֵי אַבְנֵר וְהַשֶּׁמֶשׁ בָּאָה
she-set and-the-sun Abner after and-Abishai Joab but-they-pursued (24)

וְהֵמָּה בָּאוּ עַד־ גִּבְעַת אַמָּה אֲשֶׁר עַל־ פְּנֵי־ גִיחַ דֶּרֶךְ
way-of Giah faces-of near that Ammah hill-of to they-came and-they

מִדְבַּר גִּבְעוֹן׃ (25) וַיִּתְקַבְּצוּ בְנֵי־ בִנְיָמִן אַחֲרֵי אַבְנֵר
Abner behind Benjamin men-of then-they-rallied (25) Gibeon wasteland-of

וַיִּהְיוּ לַאֲגֻדָּה אֶחָת וַיַּעַמְדוּ עַל רֹאשׁ־גִּבְעָה אֶחָת׃ (26) וַיִּקְרָא
and-he-called (26) one hill top-of on and-they-stood one as-group and-they-were

אַבְנֵר אֶל־יוֹאָב וַיֹּאמֶר הֲלָנֶצַח תֹּאכַל חֶרֶב הֲלוֹא יָדַעְתָּה
you-realize not? sword must-she-devour for-ever? and-he-said Joab to Abner

כִּי־ מָרָה תִהְיֶה בָּאַחֲרוֹנָה וְעַד־ מָתַי לֹא־ תֹאמַר
you-will-order not when? and-until in-the-end she-will-be bitter that

לָעָם לָשׁוּב מֵאַחֲרֵי אֲחֵיהֶם׃ (27) וַיֹּאמֶר יוֹאָב
Joab and-he-answered (27) brothers-of-them from-after to-turn to-the-people

חַי הָאֱלֹהִים כִּי לוּלֵא דִּבַּרְתָּ כִּי אָז מֵהַבֹּקֶר
until-the-morning then indeed you-spoke not if the-God life-of

נַעֲלָה הָעָם אִישׁ מֵאַחֲרֵי אָחִיו׃ (28) וַיִּתְקַע
so-he-blew (28) brother-of-him from-after each the-people he-would-continue

יוֹאָב בַּשּׁוֹפָר וַיַּעַמְדוּ כָּל־ הָעָם וְלֹא־ יִרְדְּפוּ
they-pursued and-not the-people all-of and-they-halted on-the-trumpet Joab

עוֹד אַחֲרֵי יִשְׂרָאֵל וְלֹא־ יָסְפוּ עוֹד לְהִלָּחֵם׃ (29) וְאַבְנֵר
and-Abner (29) to-fight-them again they-repeated and-not Israel after longer

וַאֲנָשָׁיו הָלְכוּ בָּעֲרָבָה כֹּל הַלַּיְלָה הַהוּא
the-that the-night all-of through-the-Arabah they-marched and-men-of-him

וַיַּעַבְרוּ אֶת־ הַיַּרְדֵּן וַיֵּלְכוּ כָּל־ הַבִּתְרוֹן
the-Bithron whole-of and-they-continued the-Jordan *** and-they-crossed

וַיָּבֹאוּ מַחֲנָיִם׃ (30) וְיוֹאָב שָׁב מֵאַחֲרֵי אַבְנֵר
Abner from-after he-returned then-Joab (30) Mahanaim and-they-came

וַיִּקְבֹּץ אֶת־ כָּל־ הָעָם וַיִּפָּקְדוּ מֵעַבְדֵי דָוִד
David from-men-of and-they-were-missing the-people all-of *** and-he-assembled

תִּשְׁעָה־ עָשָׂר אִישׁ וַעֲשָׂהאֵל׃ (31) וְעַבְדֵי דָוִד הִכּוּ מִבִּנְיָמִן
from-Benjamin they-killed David but-men-of (31) and-Asahel man ten nine

וּבְאַנְשֵׁי אַבְנֵר שְׁלֹשׁ־ מֵאוֹת וְשִׁשִּׁים אִישׁ מֵתוּ׃ (32) וַיִּשְׂאוּ
and-they-took (32) they-died man and-sixty hundreds three-of Abner and-of-men-of

the spot. And every man
stopped when he came to the
place where Asahel had fallen
and died.
24But Joab and Abishai pursued Abner, and as the sun
was setting, they came to the
hill of Ammah, near Giah on
the way to the wasteland of
Gibeon. 25Then the men of
Benjamin rallied behind Abner. They formed themselves
into a group and took their
stand on top of a hill.
26Abner called out to Joab,
"Must the sword devour forever? Don't you realize that
this will end in bitterness?
How long before you order
your men to stop pursuing
their brothers?"
27Joab answered, "As surely
as God lives, if you had not
spoken, the men would have
continued the pursuit of their
brothers until morning.[c]"
28So Joab blew the trumpet,
and all the men came to a halt;
they no longer pursued Israel,
nor did they fight anymore.
29All that night Abner and
his men marched through the
Arabah. They crossed the Jordan, continued through the
whole Bithron[d] and came to
Mahanaim.
30Then Joab returned from
pursuing Abner and assem-
bled all his men. Besides
Asahel, nineteen of David's
men were found missing.
31But David's men had killed
three hundred and sixty Benjamites who were with Abner.

[c]27 Or *spoken this morning, the men would not have taken up the pursuit of their brothers;* or *spoken, the men would have given up the pursuit of their brothers by morning*

[d]29 Or *morning;* or *ravine;* the meaning of the Hebrew for this word is uncertain.

°23 ק תחתיו

אֶת־עֲשָׂהאֵל וַיִּקְבְּרֻהוּ בְּקֶבֶר אָבִיו אֲשֶׁר בֵּית לָחֶם
Lehem Beth that father-of-him in-tomb-of and-they-buried-him Asahel ***

וַיֵּלְכוּ כָל־ הַלַּיְלָה יוֹאָב וַאֲנָשָׁיו וַיֵּאֹר לָהֶם
to-them and-he-dawned and-men-of-him Joab the-night all-of then-they-marched

בְּחֶבְרוֹן׃ וַתְּהִי הַמִּלְחָמָה אֲרֻכָּה בֵּין בֵּית שָׁאוּל וּבֵין
and-between Saul house-of between long the-war and-she-was (3:1) at-Hebron

בֵּית דָּוִד וְדָוִד הֹלֵךְ וְחָזֵק וּבֵית שָׁאוּל
Saul while-house-of and-he-was-strong growing and-David David house-of

הֹלְכִים וְדַלִּים׃ וַיִּלְּדוּ לְדָוִד בָנִים בְּחֶבְרוֹן
in-Hebron sons to-David and-they-were-born (2) and-ones-weak ones-growing

וַיְהִי בְכוֹרוֹ אַמְנוֹן לַאֲחִינֹעַם הַיִּזְרְעֵאלִת׃
the-Jezreelite of-Ahinoam Amnon firstborn-of-him and-he-was

וּמִשְׁנֵהוּ כִלְאָב לַאֲבִיגַל אֵשֶׁת נָבָל הַכַּרְמְלִי
the-Carmelite Nabal widow-of of-Abigail Kileab and-second-of-him (3)

וְהַשְּׁלִשִׁי אַבְשָׁלוֹם בֶּן־ מַעֲכָה בַּת־ תַּלְמַי מֶלֶךְ גְּשׁוּר׃
Geshur king-of Talmai daughter-of Maacah son-of Absalom and-the-third

וְהָרְבִיעִי אֲדֹנִיָּה בֶן־ חַגִּית וְהַחֲמִישִׁי שְׁפַטְיָה בֶן־
son-of Shephatiah and-the-fifth Haggith son-of Adonijah and-the-fourth (4)

אֲבִיטָל׃ וְהַשִּׁשִּׁי יִתְרְעָם לְעֶגְלָה אֵשֶׁת דָּוִד אֵלֶּה יֻלְּדוּ
they-were-born these David wife-of of-Eglah Ithream and-the-sixth (5) Abital

לְדָוִד בְּחֶבְרוֹן׃ וַיְהִי בִּהְיוֹת הַמִּלְחָמָה בֵּין בֵּית שָׁאוּל
Saul house-of between the-war while-to-be and-he-was (6) in-Hebron to-David

וּבֵין בֵּית דָּוִד וְאַבְנֵר הָיָה מִתְחַזֵּק בְּבֵית
in-house-of strengthening-himself he-was now-Abner David house-of and-between

שָׁאוּל׃ וּלְשָׁאוּל פִּלֶגֶשׁ וּשְׁמָהּ רִצְפָּה בַת־ אַיָּה
Aiah daughter-of Rizpah and-name-of-her concubine now-to-Saul (7) Saul

וַיֹּאמֶר אֶל־ אַבְנֵר מַדּוּעַ בָּאתָה אֶל־ פִּילֶגֶשׁ אָבִי׃
father-of-me concubine-of into you-went why? Abner to and-he-said

וַיִּחַר לְאַבְנֵר מְאֹד עַל־ דִּבְרֵי אִישׁ־ בֹּשֶׁת וַיֹּאמֶר
and-he-said Bosheth Ish words-of because-of very to-Abner and-he-angered (8)

הֲרֹאשׁ כֶּלֶב אָנֹכִי אֲשֶׁר לִיהוּדָה הַיּוֹם אֶעֱשֶׂה־ חֶסֶד עִם־ בֵּית ׀ שָׁאוּל
Saul house-of to loyalty I-show the-day to-Judah that I dog head-of?

אָבִיךָ אֶל־ אֶחָיו וְאֶל־ מֵרֵעֵהוּ וְלֹא הִמְצִיתִךָ
I-gave-you and-not friend-of-him and-to brothers-of-him to father-of-you

בְּיַד־ דָּוִד וַתִּפְקֹד עָלַי עֲוֺן הָאִשָּׁה הַיּוֹם׃
the-day the-woman offense-of against-me but-you-accuse David into-hand-of

כֹּה־ יַעֲשֶׂה אֱלֹהִים לְאַבְנֵר וְכֹה יֹסִיף לוֹ כִּי
if-not to-him may-he-be-severe and-so with-Abner God may-he-deal so (9)

32They took Asahel and buried
him in his father's tomb at
Bethlehem. Then Joab and his
men marched all night and arrived at Hebron by daybreak.
3 The war between the
house of Saul and the
house of David lasted a long
time. David grew stronger and
stronger, while the house of
Saul grew weaker and weaker.
2Sons were born to David in
Hebron:
His firstborn was Am-
non the son of Ahinoam
of Jezreel;
3his second, Kileab the
son of Abigail the widow
of Nabal of Carmel;
the third, Absalom the
son of Maacah daughter
of Talmai king of Geshur;
4the fourth, Adonijah the
son of Haggith;
the fifth, Shephatiah the
son of Abital;
5and the sixth, Ithream
the son of David's wife
Eglah.
These were born to Da-
vid in Hebron.

Abner Goes Over to David

6During the war between
the house of Saul and the
house of David, Abner had
been strengthening his own
position in the house of Saul.
7Now Saul had had a concubine named Rizpah daughter
of Aiah. And Ish-Bosheth said
to Abner, "Why did you sleep
with my father's concubine?"
8Abner was very angry be-
cause of what Ish-Bosheth
said and he answered, "Am I
a dog's head—on Judah's side?
This very day I am loyal to the
house of your father Saul and
to his family and friends. I
haven't handed you over to
David. Yet now you accuse me
of an offense involving this
woman! 9May God deal with
Abner, be it ever so severely, if

°2 ק ויולדו
°3 ק לאביגיל

כַּאֲשֶׁר נִשְׁבַּע יְהוָה לְדָוִד כִּי־ כֵן אֶעֱשֶׂה־ לּוֹ׃ לְהַעֲבִיר
to-transfer (10) for-him I-do so if-not to-David Yahweh he-swore just-as

הַמַּמְלָכָה מִבֵּית שָׁאוּל וּלְהָקִים אֶת־ כִּסֵּא דָוִד עַל־
over David throne-of *** and-to-establish Saul from-house-of the-kingdom

יִשְׂרָאֵל וְעַל־ יְהוּדָה מִדָּן וְעַד־ בְּאֵר שָׁבַע׃ וְלֹא־ יָכֹל
he-dared and-not (11) Sheba Beer even-to from-Dan Judah and-over Israel

עוֹד לְהָשִׁיב אֶת־ אַבְנֵר דָּבָר מִיִּרְאָתוֹ אֹתוֹ׃ וַיִּשְׁלַח
then-he-sent (12) him because-to-fear-him word Abner *** to-return again

אַבְנֵר מַלְאָכִים ׀ אֶל־ דָּוִד תַּחְתָּו לֵאמֹר לְמִי־ אָרֶץ לֵאמֹר
to-say land to-whom? to-say on-behalf-of-him David to messengers Abner

כָּרְתָה בְרִיתְךָ אִתִּי וְהִנֵּה יָדִי עִמָּךְ לְהָסֵב
to-bring with-you hand-of-me and-see! with-me agreement-of-you you-make

אֵלֶיךָ אֶת־ כָּל־ יִשְׂרָאֵל׃ וַיֹּאמֶר טוֹב אֲנִי אֶכְרֹת אִתְּךָ
with-you I-will-make I good and-he-said (13) Israel all-of *** to-you

בְּרִית אַךְ דָּבָר אֶחָד אָנֹכִי שֹׁאֵל מֵאִתְּךָ לֵאמֹר לֹא־ תִרְאֶה
you-will-see not to-say from-with-you demanding I one thing but agreement

אֶת־ פָּנַי כִּי ׀ אִם־ לִפְנֵי הֱבִיאֲךָ אֵת מִיכַל בַּת־ שָׁאוּל
Saul daughter-of Michal *** to-bring-you before if unless faces-of-me ***

בְּבֹאֲךָ לִרְאוֹת אֶת־ פָּנָי׃ וַיִּשְׁלַח דָּוִד מַלְאָכִים
messengers David then-he-sent (14) faces-of-me *** to-see when-to-come-you

אֶל־אִישׁ־ בֹּשֶׁת בֶּן־ שָׁאוּל לֵאמֹר תְּנָה אֶת־ אִשְׁתִּי אֶת־ מִיכַל אֲשֶׁר
whom Michal *** wife-of-me *** give! to-demand Saul son-of Bosheth Ish to

אֵרַשְׂתִּי לִי בְּמֵאָה עָרְלוֹת פְּלִשְׁתִּים׃ וַיִּשְׁלַח
so-he-gave-order (15) Philistines foreskins-of for-hundred to-me I-betrothed

אִישׁ בֹּשֶׁת וַיִּקָּחֶהָ מֵעִם אִישׁ מֵעִם פַּלְטִיאֵל בֶּן־
son-of Paltiel from-with husband from-with and-he-had-taken-her Bosheth Ish

לָוִשׁ׃ וַיֵּלֶךְ אִתָּהּ אִישָׁהּ הָלוֹךְ וּבָכֹה אַחֲרֶיהָ
behind-her and-to-weep to-go husband-of-her with-her but-he-went (16) Laish

עַד־ בַּחֻרִים וַיֹּאמֶר אֵלָיו אַבְנֵר לֵךְ שׁוּב וַיָּשֹׁב׃
so-he-went-back go-back! go! Abner to-him then-he-said Bahurim to

וּדְבַר־ אַבְנֵר הָיָה עִם־ זִקְנֵי יִשְׂרָאֵל לֵאמֹר גַּם־
indeed to-say Israel elders-of with he-was Abner then-conference-of (17)

תְּמוֹל גַּם־ שִׁלְשֹׁם הֱיִיתֶם מְבַקְשִׁים אֶת־ דָּוִד לְמֶלֶךְ עֲלֵיכֶם׃
over-you as-king David *** ones-wanting you-were before and yesterday

וְעַתָּה עֲשׂוּ כִּי יְהוָה אָמַר אֶל־ דָּוִד לֵאמֹר בְּיַד ׀ דָּוִד
David by-hand-of to-say David to he-promised Yahweh for do! so-now (18)

עַבְדִּי הוֹשִׁיעַ אֶת־ עַמִּי יִשְׂרָאֵל מִיַּד פְּלִשְׁתִּים
Philistines from-hand-of Israel people-of-me *** he-will-rescue servant-of-me

I do not do for David what the
LORD promised him on oath
10and transfer the kingdom
from the house of Saul and
establish David's throne over
Israel and Judah from Dan to
Beersheba." 11Ish-Bosheth did
not dare to say another word
to Abner, because he was
afraid of him.
12Then Abner sent messen-
gers on his behalf to say to David, "Whose land is it? Make
an agreement with me, and I
will help you bring all Israel
over to you."
13"Good," said David. "I will
make an agreement with you.
But I demand one thing of
you: Do not come into my
presence unless you bring Michal daughter of Saul when
you come to see me." 14Then
David sent messengers to Ish-
Bosheth son of Saul, demanding, "Give me my wife Mi-
chal, whom I betrothed to myself for the price of a hundred
Philistine foreskins."
15So Ish-Bosheth gave orders
and had her taken away from
her husband Paltiel son of Laish. 16Her husband, however,
went with her, weeping behind her all the way to Bahurim. Then Abner said to him,
"Go back home!" So he went
back.
17Abner conferred with the
elders of Israel and said, "For
some time you have wanted to
make David your king. 18Now
do it! For the LORD promised
David, 'By my servant David I
will rescue my people Israel

°12 ק תחתיו
°15 ק ליש

וּמִיַּד כָּל־ אֹיְבֵיהֶם׃ וַיְדַבֵּר גַּם־ אַבְנֵר
Abner also and-he-spoke (19) being-enemies-of-them all-of and-from-hand-of

בְּאָזְנֵי בִנְיָמִין וַיֵּלֶךְ גַּם־ אַבְנֵר לְדַבֵּר בְּאָזְנֵי דָוִד
David in-ears-of to-tell Abner also then-he-went Benjamin in-ears-of

בְּחֶבְרוֹן אֵת כָּל־ אֲשֶׁר־ טוֹב בְּעֵינֵי יִשְׂרָאֵל וּבְעֵינֵי כָּל־
whole-of and-in-eyes-of Israel in-eyes-of good that all *** at-Hebron

בֵּית בִּנְיָמִן׃ וַיָּבֹא אַבְנֵר אֶל־ דָּוִד חֶבְרוֹן וְאִתּוֹ
and-with-him Hebron David to Abner when-he-came (20) Benjamin house-of

עֶשְׂרִים אֲנָשִׁים וַיַּעַשׂ דָּוִד לְאַבְנֵר וְלַאֲנָשִׁים אֲשֶׁר־ אִתּוֹ מִשְׁתֶּה׃
feast with-him who and-for-the-men for-Abner David then-he-prepared men twenty

וַיֹּאמֶר אַבְנֵר אֶל־ דָּוִד אָקוּמָה ׀ וְאֵלֵכָה וְאֶקְבְּצָה
and-let-me-assemble and-let-me-go let-me-rise David to Abner then-he-said (21)

אֶל־ אֲדֹנִי הַמֶּלֶךְ אֶת־ כָּל־ יִשְׂרָאֵל וְיִכְרְתוּ אִתְּךָ בְּרִית
compact with-you so-they-may-make Israel all-of *** the-king lord-of-me for

וּמָלַכְתָּ בְּכֹל אֲשֶׁר־ תְּאַוֶּה נַפְשֶׁךָ וַיְשַׁלַּח* דָּוִד
David so-he-sent-away heart-of-you she-desires that over-all and-you-may-rule

אֶת־אַבְנֵר וַיֵּלֶךְ בְּשָׁלוֹם׃ וְהִנֵּה עַבְדֵי דָוִד וְיוֹאָב בָּא
returning and-Joab David men-of then-see! (22) in-peace and-he-went Abner ***

מֵהַגְּדוּד וְשָׁלָל רָב עִמָּם הֵבִיאוּ וְאַבְנֵר אֵינֶנּוּ
not-he but-Abner they-brought with-them great-deal and-plunder from-the-raid

עִם־ דָּוִד בְּחֶבְרוֹן כִּי שִׁלְּחוֹ וַיֵּלֶךְ בְּשָׁלוֹם׃ וְיוֹאָב
when-Joab (23) in-peace and-he-went he-sent-away-him for in-Hebron David with

וְכָל־ הַצָּבָא אֲשֶׁר־ אִתּוֹ בָּאוּ וַיַּגִּדוּ לְיוֹאָב לֵאמֹר
to-say to-Joab then-they-told they-arrived with-him who the-army and-all-of

בָּא־ אַבְנֵר בֶּן־ נֵר אֶל־ הַמֶּלֶךְ וַיְשַׁלְּחֵהוּ וַיֵּלֶךְ
and-he-went and-he-sent-away-him the-king to Ner son-of Abner he-came

בְּשָׁלוֹם׃ וַיָּבֹא יוֹאָב אֶל־ הַמֶּלֶךְ וַיֹּאמֶר מֶה עָשִׂיתָה הִנֵּה־
look! you-did what? and-he-said the-king to Joab so-he-went (24) in-peace

בָא אַבְנֵר אֵלֶיךָ לָמָּה־ זֶּה שִׁלַּחְתּוֹ וַיֵּלֶךְ הָלוֹךְ׃ יָדַעְתָּ
you-know (25) to-go and-he-went you-let-go-him this why? to-you Abner he-came

אֶת־אַבְנֵר בֶּן־ נֵר כִּי לְפַתֹּתְךָ בָּא וְלָדַעַת אֶת־
*** and-to-observe he-came to-deceive-you that Ner son-of Abner ***

מוֹצָאֲךָ וְאֶת־ מְבוֹאֶךָ° וְלָדַעַת אֵת כָּל־ אֲשֶׁר אַתָּה עֹשֶׂה׃
doing you that all *** and-to-find-out coming-of-you and going-of-you

וַיֵּצֵא יוֹאָב מֵעִם דָּוִד וַיִּשְׁלַח מַלְאָכִים אַחֲרֵי אַבְנֵר
Abner after messengers and-he-sent David from-with Joab then-he-left (26)

וַיָּשִׁבוּ אֹתוֹ מִבּוֹר הַסִּרָה וְדָוִד לֹא יָדָע׃
he-knew not but-David the-Sirah from-well-of him and-they-brought-back

from the hand of the Philistines and from the hand of all
their enemies.' "
19 Abner also spoke to the
Benjamites in person. Then he
went to Hebron to tell David
everything that Israel and the
whole house of Benjamin
wanted to do. 20 When Abner,
who had twenty men with
him, came to David at He-
bron, David prepared a feast
for him and his men. 21 Then
Abner said to David, "Let me
go at once and assemble all Israel for my lord the king, so
that they may make a compact
with you, and that you may
rule over all that your heart desires." So David sent Abner
away, and he went in peace.

Joab Murders Abner

22 Just then David's men and
Joab returned from a raid and
brought with them a great deal
of plunder. But Abner was no
longer with David in Hebron,
because David had sent him
away, and he had gone in
peace. 23 When Joab and all the
soldiers with him arrived, he
was told that Abner son of Ner
had come to the king and that
the king had sent him away
and that he had gone in peace.
24 So Joab went to the king
and said, "What have you
done? Look, Abner came to
you. Why did you let him go?
Now he is gone! 25 You know
Abner son of Ner; he came to
deceive you and observe your
movements and find out
everything you are doing."
26 Joab then left David and
sent messengers after Abner,
and they brought him back
from the well of Sirah. But David did not know it. 27 Now

*21 Most mss have no *dagesh* in the *yod* (וַיְ).

°25 ק מובאך

וַיָּשָׁב אַבְנֵר חֶבְרוֹן וַיַּטֵּהוּ יוֹאָב אֶל־תּוֹךְ
midst-of into Joab then-he-took-aside-him Hebron Abner when-he-returned (27)

הַשַּׁעַר לְדַבֵּר אִתּוֹ בַּשֶּׁלִי וַיַּכֵּהוּ שָׁם
there and-he-stabbed-him in-the-private with-him to-speak the-gateway

הַחֹמֶשׁ וַיָּמָת בְּדַם עֲשָׂה־אֵל אָחִיו׃ וַיִּשְׁמַע
when-he-heard (28) brother-of-him Asahel for-blood-of and-he-died the-stomach

דָּוִד מֵאַחֲרֵי כֵן וַיֹּאמֶר נָקִי אָנֹכִי וּמַמְלַכְתִּי מֵעִם
from-before and-kingdom-of-me I innocent then-he-said this from-after David

יְהוָה עַד־עוֹלָם מִדְּמֵי אַבְנֵר בֶּן־נֵר׃ יָחֻלוּ
may-they-fall (29) Ner son-of Abner concerning-bloods-of forever to Yahweh

עַל־רֹאשׁ יוֹאָב וְאֶל כָּל־בֵּית אָבִיו וְאַל־
and-not father-of-him house-of all-of and-upon Joab head-of upon

יִכָּרֵת מִבֵּית יוֹאָב זָב וּמְצֹרָע
or-one-being-leprous running-sore Joab from-house-of may-he-be-cut-off

וּמַחֲזִיק בַּפֶּלֶךְ וְנֹפֵל בַּחֶרֶב וַחֲסַר־לָחֶם׃
food or-lack-of by-the-sword or-one-falling on-the-crutch or-one-leaning

וְיוֹאָב וַאֲבִישַׁי אָחִיו הָרְגוּ לְאַבְנֵר עַל אֲשֶׁר
that because to-Abner they-murdered brother-of-him and-Abishai now-Joab (30)

הֵמִית אֶת־עֲשָׂהאֵל אֲחִיהֶם בְּגִבְעוֹן בַּמִּלְחָמָה׃ וַיֹּאמֶר
then-he-said (31) in-the-battle at-Gibeon brother-of-them Asahel *** he-killed

דָּוִד אֶל־יוֹאָב וְאֶל־כָּל־הָעָם אֲשֶׁר־אִתּוֹ קִרְעוּ בִגְדֵיכֶם
clothes-of-you tear! with-him who the-people all-of and-to Joab to David

וְחִגְרוּ שַׂקִּים וְסִפְדוּ לִפְנֵי אַבְנֵר וְהַמֶּלֶךְ דָּוִד
David and-the-king Abner in-front-of and-mourn! sackcloths and-put-on!

הֹלֵךְ אַחֲרֵי הַמִּטָּה׃ וַיִּקְבְּרוּ אֶת־אַבְנֵר בְּחֶבְרוֹן וַיִּשָּׂא*
and-he-raised in-Hebron Abner *** and-they-buried (32) the-bier behind walking

הַמֶּלֶךְ אֶת־קוֹלוֹ וַיֵּבְךְּ אֶל־קֶבֶר אַבְנֵר וַיִּבְכּוּ כָּל־
all-of and-they-wept Abner tomb-of at and-he-wept voice-of-him *** the-king

הָעָם׃ וַיְקֹנֵן הַמֶּלֶךְ אֶל־אַבְנֵר וַיֹּאמַר הַכְמוֹת
as-death-of? and-he-said Abner for the-king and-he-sang-lament (33) the-people

נָבָל יָמוּת אַבְנֵר׃ יָדֶךָ לֹא־אֲסֻרוֹת וְרַגְלֶיךָ
and-feet-of-you ones-being-bound not hand-of-you Abner should-he-die lawless

לֹא־לִנְחֻשְׁתַּיִם הֻגָּשׁוּ כִּנְפוֹל לִפְנֵי בְנֵי־עַוְלָה נָפָלְתָּ
you-fell wickedness men-of before as-to-fall they-were-held in-fetters not

וַיֹּסִפוּ כָל־הָעָם לִבְכּוֹת עָלָיו׃ וַיָּבֹא כָל־
all-of then-he-came (35) over-him to-weep the-people all-of and-they-repeated

הָעָם לְהַבְרוֹת אֶת־דָּוִד לֶחֶם בְּעוֹד הַיּוֹם וַיִּשָּׁבַע
but-he-took-oath the-day while-still food David *** to-urge-to-eat the-people

when Abner returned to Hebron, Joab took him aside into the gateway, as though to speak with him privately. And there, to avenge the blood of his brother Asahel, Joab stabbed him in the stomach, and he died.

28Later, when David heard about this, he said, "I and my kingdom are forever innocent before the LORD concerning the blood of Abner son of Ner.
29May his blood fall upon the head of Joab and upon all his father's house! May Joab's house never be without someone who has a running sore or leprosy[c] or who leans on a crutch or who falls by the sword or who lacks food."

30(Joab and his brother Abishai murdered Abner because he had killed their brother Asahel in the battle at Gibeon.)

31Then David said to Joab and all the people with him, "Tear your clothes and put on sackcloth and walk in mourning in front of Abner." King David himself walked behind
the bier. 32They buried Abner
in Hebron, and the king wept aloud at Abner's tomb. All the people wept also.

33The king sang this lament for Abner:

"Should Abner have died
as the lawless die?
34 Your hands were not
bound,
your feet were not
fettered.
You fell as one falls before
wicked men."

And all the people wept over him again.

35Then they all came and urged David to eat something while it was still day; but David took an oath, saying,

[c]29 The Hebrew word was used for various diseases affecting the skin—not necessarily leprosy.

*32 Most mss have *dagesh* in the *yod* (יּ).

דָּוִד לֵאמֹר כֹּה יַעֲשֶׂה־ לִּי אֱלֹהִים וְכֹה יֹסִיף כִּי אִם־
indeed if may-he-be-severe and-so God with-me may-he-deal so to-say David

לִפְנֵי בוֹא־ הַשֶּׁמֶשׁ אֶטְעַם־ לֶחֶם אוֹ כָל־ מְאוּמָה׃ וְכָל־
and-all-of (36) thing any-of or bread I-taste the-sun to-set before

הָעָם הִכִּירוּ וַיִּיטַב בְּעֵינֵיהֶם כְּכֹל אֲשֶׁר
that as-all in-eyes-of-them and-he-was-pleasing they-took-note the-people

עָשָׂה הַמֶּלֶךְ בְּעֵינֵי כָל־ הָעָם טוֹב׃ וַיֵּדְעוּ
so-they-knew (37) pleasant the-people all-of in-eyes-of the-king he-did

כָל־ הָעָם וְכָל־ יִשְׂרָאֵל בַּיּוֹם הַהוּא כִּי לֹא הָיְתָה
she-was not that the-that on-the-day Israel and-all-of the-people all-of

מֵהַמֶּלֶךְ לְהָמִית אֶת־ אַבְנֵר בֶּן־ נֵר׃ וַיֹּאמֶר הַמֶּלֶךְ אֶל־
to the-king then-he-said (38) Ner son-of Abner *** to-murder from-the-king

עֲבָדָיו הֲלוֹא תֵדְעוּ כִּי־ שַׂר וְגָדוֹל נָפַל הַיּוֹם
the-day he-fell and-great-man prince that you-realize not? men-of-him

הַזֶּה בְּיִשְׂרָאֵל׃ וְאָנֹכִי הַיּוֹם רַךְ וּמָשׁוּחַ מֶלֶךְ
king though-being-anointed weak the-day and-I (39) in-Israel the-this

וְהָאֲנָשִׁים הָאֵלֶּה בְּנֵי צְרוּיָה קָשִׁים מִמֶּנִּי יְשַׁלֵּם
may-he-repay more-than-I ones-strong Zeruiah sons-of the-these and-the-men

יְהוָה לְעֹשֵׂה הָרָעָה כְּרָעָתוֹ׃ וַיִּשְׁמַע בֶּן־ שָׁאוּל
Saul son-of when-he-heard (4:1) as-evil-of-him the-evil to-one-doing Yahweh

כִּי מֵת אַבְנֵר בְּחֶבְרוֹן וַיִּרְפּוּ יָדָיו וְכָל־ יִשְׂרָאֵל
Israel and-all-of hands-of-him then-they-fell in-Hebron Abner he-died that

נִבְהָלוּ׃ וּשְׁנֵי אֲנָשִׁים שָׂרֵי־ גְדוּדִים הָיוּ
they-were raiding-bands leaders-of men now-two-of (2) they-became-alarmed

בֶן־ שָׁאוּל שֵׁם הָאֶחָד בַּעֲנָה וְשֵׁם הַשֵּׁנִי רֵכָב בְּנֵי רִמּוֹן
Rimmon sons-of Recab the-other and-name-of Baanah the-one name-of Saul son-of

הַבְּאֶרֹתִי* מִבְּנֵי בִנְיָמִן כִּי גַּם־ בְּאֵרוֹת תֵּחָשֵׁב עַל־
in she-is-considered Beeroth indeed now Benjamin from-sons-of the-Beerothite

בִּנְיָמִן׃ וַיִּבְרְחוּ הַבְּאֵרֹתִים גִּתָּיְמָה וַיִּהְיוּ־ שָׁם
there and-they-live to-Gittaim the-Beerothites for-they-fled (3) Benjamin

גָּרִים עַד הַיּוֹם הַזֶּה׃ וְלִיהוֹנָתָן בֶּן־ שָׁאוּל בֵּן
son Saul son-of now-to-Jonathan (4) the-this the-day to ones-being-aliens

נְכֵה רַגְלָיִם בֶּן־ חָמֵשׁ שָׁנִים הָיָה בְּבֹא שְׁמֻעַת שָׁאוּל
Saul news-of when-to-come he-was years five son-of both-feet lame-of

וִיהוֹנָתָן מִיִּזְרְעֶאל וַתִּשָּׂאֵהוּ אֹמַנְתּוֹ וַתָּנֹס
and-she-fled one-nursing-him and-she-picked-up-him from-Jezreel and-Jonathan

וַיְהִי בְּחָפְזָהּ לָנוּס וַיִּפֹּל וַיִּפָּסֵחַ
and-he-became-crippled then-he-fell to-leave as-to-hurry-her but-he-was

"May God deal with me, be it ever so severely, if I taste bread or anything else before the sun sets!"

[36]All the people took note and were pleased; indeed, everything the king did pleased them. [37]So on that day all the people and all Israel knew that the king had no part in the murder of Abner son of Ner.

[38]Then the king said to his men, "Do you not realize that a prince and a great man has fallen in Israel this day? [39]And today, though I am the anointed king, I am weak, and these sons of Zeruiah are too strong for me. May the LORD repay the evildoer according to his evil deeds!"

Ish-Bosheth Murdered

4 When Ish-Bosheth son of Saul heard that Abner had died in Hebron, he lost courage, and all Israel became alarmed. [2]Now Saul's son had two men who were leaders of raiding bands. One was named Baanah and the other Recab; they were sons of Rimmon the Beerothite from the tribe of Benjamin—Beeroth is considered part of Benjamin, [3]because the people of Beeroth fled to Gittaim and have lived there as aliens to this day.

[4](Jonathan son of Saul had a son who was lame in both feet. He was five years old when the news about Saul and Jonathan came from Jezreel. His nurse picked him up and fled, but as she hurried to

*2 Most mss have *tsere* under the *aleph* (הַבְּאֵ).

וּשְׁמוֹ מְפִיבֹשֶׁת׃ וַיֵּלְכוּ בְּנֵי־ רִמּוֹן הַבְּאֵרֹתִי
the-Beerothite Rimmon sons-of now-they-set-out (5) Mephibosheth and-name-of-him

רֵכָב וּבַעֲנָה וַיָּבֹאוּ כְּחֹם הַיּוֹם אֶל־ בֵּית אִישׁ בֹּשֶׁת
Bosheth Ish house-of at the-day in-heat-of and-they-arrived and-Baanah Recab

וְהוּא שֹׁכֵב אֵת מִשְׁכַּב הַצָּהֳרָיִם׃ וְהֵנָּה בָּאוּ עַד־
into they-went and-to-there (6) the-noonday rest-of *** resting while-he

תּוֹךְ הַבַּיִת לֹקְחֵי חִטִּים וַיַּכֻּהוּ אֶל־
in and-they-stabbed-him wheats ones-getting-of the-house inner-part-of

הַחֹמֶשׁ וְרֵכָב וּבַעֲנָה אָחִיו נִמְלָטוּ׃
they-slipped-away brother-of-him and-Baanah then-Racab the-stomach

וַיָּבֹאוּ הַבַּיִת וְהוּא־ שֹׁכֵב עַל־ מִטָּתוֹ בַּחֲדַר
in-room-of bed-of-him on lying while-he the-house now-they-entered (7)

מִשְׁכָּבוֹ וַיַּכֻּהוּ וַיְמִתֻהוּ וַיָּסִירוּ אֶת־
*** and-they-cut-off and-they-killed-him and-they-stabbed-him bed-of-him

רֹאשׁוֹ וַיִּקְחוּ אֶת־ רֹאשׁוֹ וַיֵּלְכוּ דֶּרֶךְ הָעֲרָבָה
the-Arabah way-of and-they-traveled head-of-him *** and-they-took head-of-him

כָּל־ הַלָּיְלָה׃ וַיָּבִאוּ אֶת־ רֹאשׁ אִישׁ־ בֹּשֶׁת אֶל־ דָּוִד
David to Bosheth Ish head-of *** and-they-brought (8) the-night all-of

חֶבְרוֹן וַיֹּאמְרוּ אֶל־ הַמֶּלֶךְ הִנֵּה־ רֹאשׁ אִישׁ־ בֹּשֶׁת בֶּן־ שָׁאוּל
Saul son-of Bosheth Ish head-of see! the-king to and-they-said Hebron

אֹיִבְךָ אֲשֶׁר בִּקֵּשׁ אֶת־ נַפְשֶׁךָ וַיִּתֵּן יְהוָה
Yahweh now-he-gave life-of-you *** he-sought who being-enemy-of-you

לַאדֹנִי הַמֶּלֶךְ נְקָמוֹת הַיּוֹם הַזֶּה מִשָּׁאוּל
against-Saul the-this the-day vengeances the-king to-lord-of-me

וּמִזַּרְעוֹ׃ וַיַּעַן דָּוִד אֶת־ רֵכָב | וְאֶת־ בַּעֲנָה
Baanah and Recab *** David and-he-answered (9) and-against-offspring-of-him

אָחִיו בְּנֵי רִמּוֹן הַבְּאֵרֹתִי וַיֹּאמֶר לָהֶם חַי־
life-of to-them and-he-said the-Beerothite Rimmon sons-of brother-of-him

יְהוָה אֲשֶׁר־ פָּדָה אֶת־ נַפְשִׁי מִכָּל־ צָרָה׃ כִּי
when (10) trouble from-all-of life-of-me *** he-delivered who Yahweh

הַמַּגִּיד לִי לֵאמֹר הִנֵּה־ מֵת שָׁאוּל וְהוּא־ הָיָה
he-was and-he Saul he-is-dead see! to-say to-me the-one-telling

כִמְבַשֵּׂר בְּעֵינָיו וָאֹחֲזָה בוֹ
onto-him then-I-seized in-eyes-of-him like-one-bringing-good-news

וָאֶהְרְגֵהוּ בְצִקְלָג אֲשֶׁר לְתִתִּי־ לוֹ בְּשֹׂרָה׃ אַף
much-more (11) good-news to-him to-reward-me that in-Ziklag and-I-killed-him

כִּי־ אֲנָשִׁים רְשָׁעִים הָרְגוּ אֶת־ אִישׁ־ צַדִּיק בְּבֵיתוֹ עַל־
on in-house-of-him innocent man *** they-killed wicked-ones men when

leave, he fell and became crippled. His name was Me-
phibosheth.)
5Now Recab and Baanah,
the sons of Rimmon the Beerothite, set out for the house of
Ish-Bosheth, and they arrived
there in the heat of the day
while he was taking his noon-
day rest. 6They went into the
inner part of the house as if to
get some wheat, and they
stabbed him in the stomach.
Then Recab and his brother
Baanah slipped away.
7They had gone into the
house while he was lying on
the bed in his bedroom. After
they stabbed and killed him,
they cut off his head. Taking it
with them, they traveled all
night by way of the Arabah.
8They brought the head of Ish-
Bosheth to David at Hebron
and said to the king, "Here is
the head of Ish-Bosheth son of
Saul, your enemy, who tried to
take your life. This day the
LORD has avenged my lord the
king against Saul and his
offspring."
9David answered Recab and
his brother Baanah, the sons
of Rimmon the Beerothite,
"As surely as the LORD lives,
who has delivered me out of
all trouble, 10when a man told
me, 'Saul is dead,' and thought
he was bringing good news, I
seized him and put him to
death in Ziklag. That was the
reward I gave him for his
news! 11How much more—
when wicked men have killed
an innocent man in his own

מִשְׁכָּבוֹ וְעַתָּה הֲלוֹא אֲבַקֵּשׁ אֶת־ דָּמוֹ מִיֶּדְכֶם
from-hand-of-you blood-of-him *** I-should-demand not? then-now bed-of-him

וּבִעַרְתִּי אֶתְכֶם מִן־ הָאָרֶץ׃ וַיְצַו דָּוִד אֶת־ הַנְּעָרִים
the-men *** David so-he-ordered (12) the-earth from you and-I-remove

וַיַּהַרְגוּם וַיְקַצְּצוּ אֶת־ יְדֵיהֶם וְאֶת־ רַגְלֵיהֶם
feet-of-them and hands-of-them *** and-they-cut-off and-they-killed-them

וַיִּתְלוּ עַל־ הַבְּרֵכָה בְּחֶבְרוֹן וְאֵת רֹאשׁ אִישׁ־ בֹּשֶׁת לָקָחוּ
they-took Bosheth Ish head-of but in-Hebron the-pool by and-they-hung

וַיִּקְבְּרוּ בְקֶבֶר־ אַבְנֵר בְּחֶבְרוֹן׃ וַיָּבֹאוּ כָּל־
all-of and-they-came (5:1) at-Hegron Abner in-tomb-of and-they-buried

שִׁבְטֵי יִשְׂרָאֵל אֶל־ דָּוִד חֶבְרוֹנָה וַיֹּאמְרוּ לֵאמֹר הִנְנוּ עַצְמְךָ
bone-of-you see-us! to-say and-they-said at-Hebron David to Israel tribes-of

וּבְשָׂרְךָ אֲנָחְנוּ׃ גַּם־ אֶתְמוֹל גַּם־ שִׁלְשׁוֹם בִּהְיוֹת שָׁאוּל מֶלֶךְ
king Saul while-to-be before and yesterday now (2) we and-flesh-of-you

עָלֵינוּ אַתָּה הָיִיתָה °מוֹצִיא °וְהַמֵּבִי אֶת־ יִשְׂרָאֵל
Israel *** and-the-one-leading-in the-one-leading-out you-were you over-us

וַיֹּאמֶר יְהוָה לְךָ אַתָּה תִרְעֶה אֶת־ עַמִּי אֶת־ יִשְׂרָאֵל
Israel *** people-of-me *** you-will-sheperd you to-you Yahweh and-he-said

וְאַתָּה תִּהְיֶה לְנָגִיד עַל־ יִשְׂרָאֵל׃ וַיָּבֹאוּ כָּל־
all-of when-they-came (3) Israel over as-ruler you-will-become and-you

זִקְנֵי יִשְׂרָאֵל אֶל־ הַמֶּלֶךְ חֶבְרוֹנָה וַיִּכְרֹת לָהֶם הַמֶּלֶךְ דָּוִד
David the-king with-them then-he-made at-Hebron the-king to Israel elders-of

בְּרִית בְּחֶבְרוֹן לִפְנֵי יְהוָה וַיִּמְשְׁחוּ אֶת־ דָּוִד לְמֶלֶךְ עַל־
over as-king David *** and-they-anointed Yahweh before at-Hebron compact

יִשְׂרָאֵל׃ בֶּן־ שְׁלֹשִׁים שָׁנָה דָּוִד בְּמָלְכוֹ אַרְבָּעִים שָׁנָה
year forty when-to-become-king-him David year thirty son-of (4) Israel

מָלָךְ׃ בְּחֶבְרוֹן מָלַךְ עַל־ יְהוּדָה שֶׁבַע שָׁנִים וְשִׁשָּׁה חֳדָשִׁים
months and-six years seven Judah over he-reigned in-Hebron (5) he-reigned

וּבִירוּשָׁלַםִ מָלַךְ שְׁלֹשִׁים וְשָׁלֹשׁ שָׁנָה עַל כָּל־ יִשְׂרָאֵל
Israel all-of over year and-three thirty he-reigned and-in-Jerusalem

וִיהוּדָה׃ וַיֵּלֶךְ הַמֶּלֶךְ וַאֲנָשָׁיו יְרוּשָׁלַםִ אֶל־
against Jerusalem and-men-of-him the-king then-he-marched (6) and-Judah

הַיְבֻסִי יוֹשֵׁב הָאָרֶץ וַיֹּאמֶר לְדָוִד לֵאמֹר לֹא־ תָבוֹא
you-will-get-in not to-say to-David and-he-said the-land living-of the-Jebusite

הֵנָּה כִּי אִם־ הֱסִירְךָ הַעִוְרִים וְהַפִּסְחִים
and-the-lame-ones the-blind-ones he-can-ward-off-you even for to-here

לֵאמֹר לֹא־ יָבוֹא דָוִד הֵנָּה׃ וַיִּלְכֹּד דָּוִד אֵת
*** David but-he-captured (7) to-here David he-can-get-in not to-think

house and on his own bed—
should I not now demand his
blood from your hand and rid
the earth of you!"
12So David gave an order to
his men, and they killed them.
They cut off their hands and
feet and hung the bodies by
the pool in Hebron. But they
took the head of Ish-Bosheth
and buried it in Abner's tomb
at Hebron.

David Becomes King Over Israel

5 All the tribes of Israel
came to David at Hebron
and said, "We are your own
flesh and blood. 2In the past,
while Saul was king over us,
you were the one who led Israel on their military campaigns.
And the LORD said to you, 'You
will shepherd my people Israel, and you will become their
ruler.' "
3When all the elders of Israel
had come to King David at
Hebron, the king made a compact with them at Hebron before the LORD, and they
anointed David king over Israel.
4David was thirty years old
when he became king, and he
reigned forty years. 5In Hebron he reigned over Judah
seven years and six months,
and in Jerusalem he reigned
over all Israel and Judah
thirty-three years.

David Conquers Jerusalem

6The king and his men
marched to Jerusalem to attack
the Jebusites, who lived there.
The Jebusites said to David,
"You will not get in here; even
the blind and the lame can
ward you off." They thought,
"David cannot get in here."
7Nevertheless, David captured

°2a ק היית המוציא
°2b ק והמביא

מְצֻדַת צִיּוֹן הִיא עִיר דָּוִד׃ וַיֹּאמֶר דָּוִד בַּיּוֹם הַהוּא
the-that on-the-day David and-he-said (8) David City-of that Zion fortress-of

כָּל־ מַכֵּה יְבֻסִי וְיִגַּע בַּצִּנּוֹר
through-the-water-shaft then-he-must-reach Jebusite one-conquering any-of

וְאֶת־ הַפִּסְחִים וְאֶת־ הַעִוְרִים שְׂנֻאֵו נֶפֶשׁ דָּוִד עַל־ כֵּן
this for David life-of being-enemies-of the-blind-ones and the-lame-ones both

יֹאמְרוּ עִוֵּר וּפִסֵּחַ לֹא יָבוֹא אֶל־ הַבָּיִת׃ וַיֵּשֶׁב
then-he-resided (9) the-palace into he-will-enter not and-lame blind they-say

דָּוִד בַּמְּצֻדָה וַיִּקְרָא־ לָהּ עִיר דָּוִד וַיִּבֶן דָּוִד
David and-he-built-up David City-of to-her and-he-called in-the-fortress David

סָבִיב מִן־ הַמִּלּוֹא וָבָיְתָה׃ וַיֵּלֶךְ דָּוִד הָלוֹךְ
to-increase David and-he-continued (10) and-inward the-terrace from around

וְגָדוֹל וַיהוָה אֱלֹהֵי צְבָאוֹת עִמּוֹ׃ וַיִּשְׁלַח חִירָם מֶלֶךְ־
king-of Hiram now-he-sent (11) with-him Hosts God-of for-Yahweh and-powerful

צֹר מַלְאָכִים אֶל־ דָּוִד וַעֲצֵי אֲרָזִים וְחָרָשֵׁי עֵץ וְחָרָשֵׁי
and-carvers-of wood and-carvers-of cedars and-logs-of David to messengers Tyre

אֶבֶן קִיר וַיִּבְנוּ־ בַיִת לְדָוִד׃ וַיֵּדַע דָּוִד כִּי־
that David and-he-knew (12) for-David palace and-they-built wall stone-of

הֱכִינוֹ יְהוָה לְמֶלֶךְ עַל־ יִשְׂרָאֵל וְכִי נִשֵּׂא
he-exalted and-that Israel over as-king Yahweh he-established-him

מַמְלַכְתּוֹ בַּעֲבוּר עַמּוֹ יִשְׂרָאֵל׃ וַיִּקַּח דָּוִד עוֹד
more David and-he-took (13) Israel people-of-him for-sake-of kingdom-of-him

פִּלַגְשִׁים וְנָשִׁים מִירוּשָׁלַםִ אַחֲרֵי בֹּאוֹ מֵחֶבְרוֹן
from-Hebron to-leave-him after in-Jerusalem and-wives concubines

וַיִּוָּלְדוּ עוֹד לְדָוִד בָּנִים וּבָנוֹת׃ וְאֵלֶּה שְׁמוֹת
names-of and-these (14) and-daughters sons to-David more and-they-were-born

הַיִּלֹּדִים לוֹ בִּירוּשָׁלָםִ שַׁמּוּעַ וְשׁוֹבָב וְנָתָן וּשְׁלֹמֹה׃
and-Solomon and-Nathan and-Shobab Shammua in-Jerusalem to-him the-ones-born

וְיִבְחָר וֶאֱלִישׁוּעַ וָנֶפֶג וְיָפִיעַ׃ וֶאֱלִישָׁמָע וְאֶלְיָדָע
and-Eliada and-Elishama (16) and-Japhia and-Nepheg and-Elishua and-Ibhar (15)

וֶאֱלִיפָלֶט׃ וַיִּשְׁמְעוּ פְלִשְׁתִּים כִּי־ מָשְׁחוּ אֶת־ דָּוִד
David *** they-anointed that Philistines when-they-heard (17) and-Eliphelet

לְמֶלֶךְ עַל־ יִשְׂרָאֵל וַיַּעֲלוּ כָל־ פְּלִשְׁתִּים לְבַקֵּשׁ אֶת־
*** to-search-for Philistines all-of then-they-went-up Israel over as-king

דָּוִד וַיִּשְׁמַע דָּוִד וַיֵּרֶד אֶל־ הַמְּצוּדָה׃ וּפְלִשְׁתִּים
now-Philistines (18) the-stronghold to and-he-went-down David but-he-heard David

בָּאוּ וַיִּנָּטְשׁוּ בְּעֵמֶק רְפָאִים׃ וַיִּשְׁאַל דָּוִד
David and-he-inquired (19) Rephaim in-Valley-of and-they-spread-out they-came

°8 ק שנאי

the fortress of Zion, the City of David.

[8]On that day, David said, "Anyone who conquers the Jebusites will have to use the water shaft[f] to reach those 'lame and blind' who are David's enemies.[g]" That is why they say, "The 'blind and lame' will not enter the palace."

[9]David then took up residence in the fortress and called it the City of David. He built up the area around it, from the supporting terraces[h] inward. [10]And he became more and more powerful, because the LORD God Almighty was with him.

[11]Now Hiram king of Tyre sent messengers to David, along with cedar logs and carpenters and stonemasons, and they built a palace for David. [12]And David knew that the LORD had established him as king over Israel and had exalted his kingdom for the sake of his people Israel.

[13]After he left Hebron, David took more concubines and wives in Jerusalem, and more sons and daughters were born to him. [14]These are the names of the children born to him there: Shammua, Shobab, Nathan, Solomon, [15]Ibhar, Elishua, Nepheg, Japhia, [16]Elishama, Eliada and Eliphelet.

David Defeats the Philistines

[17]When the Philistines heard that David had been anointed king over Israel, they went up in full force to search for him, but David heard about it and went down to the stronghold. [18]Now the Philistines had come and spread out in the Valley of Rephaim; [19]so David

f8 Or use scaling hooks
g8 Or are hated by David *h9 Or the Millo*

בַּיהוָה֙ לֵאמֹ֔ר הַאֶֽעֱלֶה֙ אֶל־ פְּלִשְׁתִּ֔ים הֲתִתְּנֵ֖ם
will-you-give-them? Philistines against shall-I-go? to-ask of-Yahweh

בְּיָדִ֑י וַיֹּ֨אמֶר יְהוָ֤ה אֶל־ דָּוִד֙ עֲלֵ֔ה כִּֽי־ נָתֹ֥ן אֶתֵּ֛ן
I-will-give to-give for go! David to Yahweh and-he-answered into-hand-of-me

אֶת־ הַפְּלִשְׁתִּ֖ים בְּיָדֶֽךָ׃ וַיָּבֹ֨א דָוִ֜ד בְּבַֽעַל־ פְּרָצִים֙
Perazim to-Baal David so-he-went (20) into-hand-of-you the-Philistines ***

וַיַּכֵּ֣ם שָׁם֮ דָּוִד֒ וַיֹּ֗אמֶר פָּרַ֨ץ יְהוָ֧ה אֶת־
against Yahweh he-broke-out and-he-said David there and-he-defeated-them

אֹיְבַ֛י לְפָנַ֖י כְּפֶ֣רֶץ מָ֑יִם עַל־ כֵּ֗ן קָרָ֛א
he-called this for waters as-breaking-out-of before-me being-enemies-of-me

שֵׁם־ הַמָּק֥וֹם הַה֖וּא בַּ֥עַל פְּרָצִֽים׃ וַיַּעַזְבוּ־ שָׁ֖ם אֶת־
*** there and-they-abandoned (21) Perazim Baal the-that the-place name-of

עֲצַבֵּיהֶ֑ם וַיִּשָּׂאֵ֥ם דָּוִ֖ד וַאֲנָשָֽׁיו׃ וַיֹּסִ֥פוּ
and-they-repeated (22) and-men-of-him David and-he-carried-off-them idols-of-them

ע֥וֹד פְּלִשְׁתִּ֖ים לַעֲל֑וֹת וַיִּנָּטְשׁ֖וּ בְּעֵ֥מֶק רְפָאִֽים׃
Rephaim in-Valley-of and-they-spread-out to-come-up Philistines again

וַיִּשְׁאַ֤ל דָּוִד֙ בַּֽיהוָ֔ה וַיֹּ֖אמֶר לֹ֣א תַעֲלֶ֑ה הָסֵב֙
circle! you-go-up not and-he-answered of-Yahweh David so-he-inquired (23)

אֶל־ אַחֲרֵיהֶ֔ם וּבָ֥אתָ לָהֶ֖ם מִמּ֥וּל בְּכָאִֽים׃
balsam-trees in-front-of against-them and-you-attack behind-them to

וִיהִ֗י בְּשָׁמְעֲךָ֞ אֶת־ ק֤וֹל צְעָדָה֙ בְּרָאשֵׁ֣י
in-tops-of marching sound-of *** as-to-hear-you and-he-will-be (24)

הַבְּכָאִ֔ים אָ֖ז תֶּחֱרָ֑ץ כִּ֣י אָ֗ז יָצָ֤א יְהוָה֙ לְפָנֶ֔יךָ
before-you Yahweh he-went-out then for you-move-quickly then the-balsam-trees

לְהַכּ֖וֹת בְּמַחֲנֵ֥ה פְלִשְׁתִּֽים׃ וַיַּ֤עַשׂ דָּוִד֙ כֵּ֔ן כַּאֲשֶׁ֥ר
just-as this David so-he-did (25) Philistines against-camp-of to-strike

צִוָּ֖הוּ יְהוָ֑ה וַיַּךְ֙ אֶת־ פְּלִשְׁתִּ֔ים מִגֶּ֖בַע עַד־
to from-Geba Philitines *** and-he-struck Yahweh he-commanded-him

בֹּאֲךָ֥ גָֽזֶר׃ וַיֹּ֨סֶף ע֥וֹד דָּוִ֛ד אֶת־ כָּל־
all-of *** David again and-he-brought-together (6:1) Gezer to-go-you

בָּח֥וּר בְּיִשְׂרָאֵ֖ל שְׁלֹשִׁ֥ים אָֽלֶף׃ וַיָּ֣קָם ׀ וַיֵּ֣לֶךְ דָּוִ֗ד
David and-he-set-out and-he-rose (2) thousand thirty from-Israel being-chosen

וְכָל־ הָעָם֙ אֲשֶׁ֣ר אִתּ֔וֹ מִֽבַּעֲלֵ֖י יְהוּדָ֑ה לְהַעֲל֣וֹת מִשָּׁ֗ם
from-there to-bring-up Judah from-Baale-of with-him who the-people and-all-of

אֵ֚ת אֲר֣וֹן הָאֱלֹהִ֔ים אֲשֶׁר־ נִקְרָ֣א שֵׁ֗ם שֵׁ֣ם יְהוָ֧ה צְבָא֛וֹת
Hosts Yahweh-of name-of Name he-is-called which the-God ark-of ***

יֹשֵׁ֥ב הַכְּרֻבִ֖ים עָלָֽיו׃ וַיַּרְכִּ֜בוּ אֶת־ אֲר֤וֹן הָאֱלֹהִים֙
the-God ark-of *** and-they-set (3) on-him the-cherubim being-enthroned-of

inquired of the LORD, "Shall I
go and attack the Philistines?
Will you hand them over to
me?"
The LORD answered him,
"Go, for I will surely hand the
Philistines over to you."
[20]So David went to Baal
Perazim, and there he de-
feated them. He said, "As waters break out, the LORD has
broken out against my enemies before me." So that place
was called Baal Perazim.[i] [21]The
Philistines abandoned their
idols there, and David and his
men carried them off.
[22]Once more the Philistines
came up and spread out in the
Valley of Rephaim; [23]so David
inquired of the LORD, and he
answered, "Do not go straight
up, but circle around behind
them and attack them in front
of the balsam trees. [24]As soon
as you hear the sound of
marching in the tops of the
balsam trees, move quickly,
because that will mean the
LORD has gone out in front of
you to strike the Philistine
army." [25]So David did as the
LORD commanded him, and he
struck down the Philistines all
the way from Gibeon[j] to Gezer.

The Ark Brought to Jerusalem

6 David again brought to-
gether out of Israel chosen
men, thirty thousand in all.
[2]He and all his men set out
from Baalah of Judah[k] to bring
up from there the ark of God,
which is called by the Name,[l]
the name of the LORD Al-
mighty, who is enthroned between the cherubim that are
on the ark. [3]They set the ark of

[i]20 *Baal Perazim* means *the lord who breaks out.*
[j]25 Septuagint (see also 1 Chron. 14:16); Hebrew *Geba*
[k]2 That is, Kiriath Jearim; Hebrew *Baale Judah*, a variant of *Baalah of Judah*
[l]2 Hebrew; Septuagint and Vulgate do not have *the Name.*

°24 ק כשמעך

אֶל־עֲגָלָה חֲדָשָׁה וַיִּשָּׂאֻהוּ מִבֵּית אֲבִינָדָב אֲשֶׁר בַּגִּבְעָה
on-the-hill which Abinadab from-house-of and-they-brought-him new cart on

וְעֻזָּא וְאַחְיוֹ בְּנֵי אֲבִינָדָב נֹהֲגִים אֶת־ הָעֲגָלָה חֲדָשָׁה׃
new the-cart *** ones-guiding Abinadab sons-of and-Ahio and-Uzzah

וַיִּשָּׂאֻהוּ מִבֵּית אֲבִינָדָב אֲשֶׁר בַּגִּבְעָה עִם אֲרוֹן
ark-of with on-the-hill which Abinadab from-house-of and-they-brought-him (4)

הָאֱלֹהִים וְאַחְיוֹ הֹלֵךְ לִפְנֵי הָאָרוֹן׃ וְדָוִד ׀ וְכָל־
and-whole-of now-David (5) the-ark in-front-of walking and-Ahio the-God

בֵּית יִשְׂרָאֵל מְשַׂחֲקִים לִפְנֵי יְהוָה בְּכֹל עֲצֵי
instruments-of with-all-of Yahweh before ones-celebrating Israel house-of

בְרוֹשִׁים וּבְכִנֹּרוֹת וּבִנְבָלִים וּבְתֻפִּים וּבִמְנַעַנְעִים
and-with-sistrums and-with-tambourines and-with-lyres and-with-harps pines

וּבְצֶלְצֶלִים׃ וַיָּבֹאוּ עַד־ גֹּרֶן נָכוֹן וַיִּשְׁלַח
then-he-reached Nacon threshing-floor-of to when-they-came (6) and-with-cymbals

עֻזָּא אֶל־ אֲרוֹן הָאֱלֹהִים וַיֹּאחֶז בּוֹ כִּי שָׁמְטוּ הַבָּקָר׃
the-ox they-stumbled for onto-him and-he-held the-God ark-of to Uzzah

וַיִּחַר־ אַף יְהוָה בְּעֻזָּה וַיַּכֵּהוּ שָׁם
there and-he-struck-down-him against-Uzzah Yahweh anger-of and-he-burned (7)

הָאֱלֹהִים עַל־ הַשַּׁל וַיָּמָת שָׁם עִם אֲרוֹן הָאֱלֹהִים׃
the-God ark-of beside there and-he-died the-irreverent-act because-of the-God

וַיִּחַר לְדָוִד עַל אֲשֶׁר פָּרַץ יְהוָה פֶּרֶץ
breaking-out Yahweh he-broke-out that because to-David and-he-angered (8)

בְּעֻזָּה וַיִּקְרָא לַמָּקוֹם הַהוּא פֶּרֶץ עֻזָּה עַד הַיּוֹם
the-day to Uzzah Perez the-that to-the-place so-he-called against-Uzzah

הַזֶּה׃ וַיִּרָא דָוִד אֶת־ יְהוָה בַּיּוֹם הַהוּא וַיֹּאמֶר
and-he-said the-that on-the-day Yahweh *** David and-he-feared (9) the-this

אֵיךְ יָבוֹא אֵלַי אֲרוֹן יְהוָה׃ וְלֹא־ אָבָה דָוִד
David he-was-willing and-not (10) Yahweh ark-of to-me can-he-come how?

לְהָסִיר אֵלָיו אֶת־ אֲרוֹן יְהוָה עַל־ עִיר דָּוִד וַיַּטֵּהוּ דָוִד
David so-he-took-him David City-of in Yahweh ark-of *** with-him to-take

בֵּית עֹבֵד־ אֱדוֹם הַגִּתִּי׃ וַיֵּשֶׁב אֲרוֹן יְהוָה בֵּית
house-of Yahweh ark-of and-he-remained (11) the-Gittite Edom Obed house-of

עֹבֵד אֱדֹם הַגִּתִּי שְׁלֹשָׁה חֳדָשִׁים וַיְבָרֶךְ יְהוָה אֶת־ עֹבֵד אֱדֹם וְאֶת
and Edom Obed *** Yahweh and-he-blessed months three the-Gittite Edom Obed

כָּל־ בֵּיתוֹ׃ וַיֻּגַּד לַמֶּלֶךְ דָּוִד לֵאמֹר
to-say David to-the-king now-he-was-told (12) household-of-him entire-of

בֵּרַךְ יְהוָה אֶת־ בֵּית עֹבֵד אֱדֹם וְאֶת־כָּל־אֲשֶׁר־ לוֹ בַּעֲבוּר
because-of to-him that all and Edom Obed household-of *** Yahweh he-blessed

God on a new cart and
brought it from the house of
Abinadab, which was on the
hill. Uzzah and Ahio, sons of
Abinadab, were guiding the
new cart [4]with the ark of God
on it,[m] and Ahio was walking
in front of it. [5]David and the
whole house of Israel were
celebrating with all their
might before the LORD, with
songs[n] and with harps, lyres,
tambourines, sistrums and
cymbals.
[6]When they came to the
threshing floor of Nacon, Uzzah reached out and took hold
of the ark of God, because the
oxen stumbled. [7]The LORD's
anger burned against Uzzah
because of his irreverent act;
therefore God struck him
down and he died there beside
the ark of God.
[8]Then David was angry because the LORD's wrath had
broken out against Uzzah, and
to this day that place is called
Perez Uzzah.[o]
[9]David was afraid of the
LORD that day and said, "How
can the ark of the LORD ever
come to me?" [10]He was not
willing to take the ark of the
LORD to be with him in the
City of David. Instead, he took
it aside to the house of Obed-
Edom the Gittite. [11]The ark of
the LORD remained in the
house of Obed-Edom the Gittite for three months, and the
LORD blessed him and his entire household.
[12]Now King David was told,
"The LORD has blessed the
household of Obed-Edom and
everything he has, because of

[m]3,4 Some Septuagint manuscripts; Hebrew *cart [4]and they brought it with the ark of God from the house of Abinadab, which was on the hill*
[n]5 See Septuagint and 1 Chronicles 13:8; Hebrew *celebrating before the LORD with all kinds of instruments made of pine*
[o]8 *Perez Uzzah* means *outbreak against Uzzah.*

אֲרוֹן הָאֱלֹהִים וַיֵּלֶךְ דָּוִד וַיַּעַל אֶת־ אֲרוֹן הָאֱלֹהִים
the-God ark-of *** and-he-brought-up David so-he-went-down the-God ark-of

מִבֵּית עֹבֵד אֱדֹם עִיר דָּוִד בְּשִׂמְחָה׃ וַיְהִי כִּי
when and-he-was (13) with-rejoicing David City-of Edom Obed from-house-of

צָעֲדוּ נֹשְׂאֵי אֲרוֹן־ יְהוָה שִׁשָּׁה צְעָדִים וַיִּזְבַּח שׁוֹר
bull then-he-sacrificed steps six Yahweh ark-of ones-carrying-of they-walked

וּמְרִיא׃ וְדָוִד מְכַרְכֵּר בְּכָל־ עֹז לִפְנֵי יְהוָה
Yahweh before might with-all-of dancing and-David (14) and-fattened-calf

וְדָוִד חָגוּר אֵפוֹד בָּד׃ וְדָוִד וְכָל־ בֵּית יִשְׂרָאֵל
Israel house-of and-entire-of and-David (15) linen ephod wearing now-David

מַעֲלִים אֶת־ אֲרוֹן יְהוָה בִּתְרוּעָה וּבְקוֹל שׁוֹפָר׃
trumpet and-with-sound-of with-shout Yaheh ark-of *** ones-bringing-up

וְהָיָה אֲרוֹן יְהוָה בָּא עִיר דָּוִד וּמִיכַל בַּת־
daughter-of and-Michal David City-of entering Yahweh ark-of and-he-was (16)

שָׁאוּל נִשְׁקְפָה ׀ בְּעַד הַחַלּוֹן וַתֵּרֶא אֶת־ הַמֶּלֶךְ דָּוִד מְפַזֵּז
leaping David the-king *** when-she-saw the-window from watching Saul

וּמְכַרְכֵּר לִפְנֵי יְהוָה וַתִּבֶז לוֹ בְּלִבָּהּ׃
in-heart-of-her at-him then-she-despised Yahweh before and-dancing

וַיָּבִאוּ אֶת־ אֲרוֹן יְהוָה וַיַּצִּגוּ אֹתוֹ בִּמְקוֹמוֹ
in-place-of-him him and-they-set Yahweh ark-of *** and-they-brought (17)

בְּתוֹךְ הָאֹהֶל אֲשֶׁר נָטָה־ לוֹ דָּוִד וַיַּעַל דָּוִד
David and-he-sacrificed David for-him he-pitched that the-tent inside-of

עֹלוֹת לִפְנֵי יְהוָה וּשְׁלָמִים׃ וַיְכַל
when-he-finished (18) and-fellowship-offerings Yahweh before burnt-offerings

דָּוִד מֵהַעֲלוֹת הָעוֹלָה וְהַשְּׁלָמִים
and-the-fellowship-offerings the-burnt-offering from-to-sacrifice David

וַיְבָרֶךְ אֶת־ הָעָם בְּשֵׁם יְהוָה צְבָאוֹת׃ וַיְחַלֵּק
then-he-gave (19) Hosts Yahweh-of in-name-of the-people *** then-he-blessed

לְכָל־ הָעָם לְכָל־ הֲמוֹן יִשְׂרָאֵל לְמֵאִישׁ וְעַד־ אִשָּׁה
woman even-to to-both-man Israel crowd-of in-whole-of the-people to-each-of

לְאִישׁ חַלַּת לֶחֶם אַחַת וְאֶשְׁפָּר אֶחָד וַאֲשִׁישָׁה אֶחָת וַיֵּלֶךְ
and-he-went one and-raisin-cake one and-date-cake one bread loaf-of to-each

כָּל־ הָעָם אִישׁ לְבֵיתוֹ׃ וַיָּשָׁב דָּוִד לְבָרֵךְ
to-bless David when-he-returned (20) to-home-of-him each the-people all-of

אֶת־ בֵּיתוֹ וַתֵּצֵא מִיכַל בַּת־ שָׁאוּל לִקְרַאת דָּוִד
David to-meet Saul daughter-of Michal then-she-came-out household-of-him ***

וַתֹּאמֶר מַה־ נִּכְבַּד הַיּוֹם מֶלֶךְ יִשְׂרָאֵל אֲשֶׁר
when Israel king-of the-day he-distinguished-himself how! and-she-said

the ark of God." So David
went down and brought up
the ark of God from the house
of Obed-Edom to the City of
David with rejoicing. [13]When
those who were carrying the
ark of the LORD had taken six
steps, he sacrificed a bull and a
fattened calf. [14]David, wearing
a linen ephod, danced before
the LORD with all his might,
[15]while he and the entire
house of Israel brought up the
ark of the LORD with shouts
and the sound of trumpets.
[16]As the ark of the LORD was
entering the City of David,
Michal daughter of Saul
watched from a window. And
when she saw King David
leaping and dancing before
the LORD, she despised him in
her heart.
[17]They brought the ark of the
LORD and set it in its place inside the tent that David had
pitched for it, and David sacrificed burnt offerings and fellowship offerings[p] before the
LORD. [18]After he had finished
sacrificing the burnt offerings
and fellowship offerings, he
blessed the people in the name
of the LORD Almighty. [19]Then
he gave a loaf of bread, a cake
of dates and a cake of raisins
to each person in the whole
crowd of Israelites, both men
and women. And all the
people went to their homes.
[20]When David returned
home to bless his household,
Michal daughter of Saul came
out to meet him and said,
"How the king of Israel has
distinguished himself today,

[p]17 Traditionally *peace offerings;* also in verse 18

נִגְלָה הַיּוֹם לְעֵינֵי אַמְהוֹת עֲבָדָיו כְּהִגָּלוֹת
as-to-disrobe servants-of-him slave-girls-of before-eyes-of the-day he-disrobed

נִגְלוֹת אַחַד הָרֵקִים׃ וַיֹּאמֶר דָּוִד אֶל־מִיכַל לִפְנֵי
before Michal to David and-he-said (21) the-vulgar-fellows one-of to-disrobe

יְהוָה אֲשֶׁר בָּחַר־בִּי מֵאָבִיךְ וּמִכָּל־
or-rather-than-all-of rather-than-father-of-you to-me he-chose who Yahweh

בֵּיתוֹ לְצַוֹּת אֹתִי נָגִיד עַל־עַם יְהוָה עַל־יִשְׂרָאֵל
Israel over Yahweh people-of over ruler me to-appoint house-of-him

וְשִׂחַקְתִּי לִפְנֵי יְהוָה׃ וּנְקַלֹּתִי עוֹד
more and-I-will-become-undignified (22) Yahweh before and-I-will-celebrate

מִזֹּאת וְהָיִיתִי שָׁפָל בְּעֵינָי וְעִם־הָאֲמָהוֹת אֲשֶׁר
whom the-slave-girls but-by in-eyes-of-me humiliated and-I-will-be than-this

אָמַרְתְּ עִמָּם אִכָּבֵדָה׃ וּלְמִיכַל בַּת־שָׁאוּל לֹא־
not Saul daughter-of and-to-Michal (23) I-will-be-honored by-them you-spoke

הָיָה לָהּ יָלֶד עַד יוֹם מוֹתָהּ׃ וַיְהִי כִּי־
after and-he-was (7:1) death-of-her day-of until child to-her he-was

יָשַׁב הַמֶּלֶךְ בְּבֵיתוֹ וַיהוָה הֵנִיחַ־לוֹ מִסָּבִיב
at-around to-him he-gave-rest and-Yahweh in-palace-of-him the-king he-settled

מִכָּל־אֹיְבָיו׃ וַיֹּאמֶר הַמֶּלֶךְ אֶל־נָתָן
Nathan to the-king then-he-said (2) being-enemies-of-him from-all-of

הַנָּבִיא רְאֵה נָא אָנֹכִי יוֹשֵׁב בְּבֵית אֲרָזִים וַאֲרוֹן הָאֱלֹהִים
the-God while-ark-of cedars in-palace-of living I now! see! the-prophet

יֹשֵׁב בְּתוֹךְ הַיְרִיעָה׃ וַיֹּאמֶר נָתָן אֶל־הַמֶּלֶךְ כֹּל אֲשֶׁר
that all the-king to Nathan and-he-replied (3) the-tent inside-of remaining

בִּלְבָבְךָ לֵךְ עֲשֵׂה כִּי יְהוָה עִמָּךְ׃ וַיְהִי בַּלַּיְלָה
in-the-night and-he-was (4) with-you Yahweh for do! go-ahead! in-heart-of-you

הַהוּא וַיְהִי דְּבַר־יְהוָה אֶל־נָתָן לֵאמֹר׃ לֵךְ וְאָמַרְתָּ
and-you-tell go! (5) to-say Nathan to Yahweh word-of then-he-came the-that

אֶל־עַבְדִּי אֶל־דָּוִד כֹּה אָמַר יְהוָה הַאַתָּה תִּבְנֶה־לִּי
for-me will-you-build you? Yahweh he-says this David to servant-of-me to

בַיִת לְשִׁבְתִּי׃ כִּי לֹא יָשַׁבְתִּי בְּבַיִת לְמִיּוֹם הַעֲלֹתִי אֶת־
*** to-bring-me at-from-day in-house I-dwelt not for (6) to-dwell-me house

בְּנֵי יִשְׂרָאֵל מִמִּצְרַיִם וְעַד הַיּוֹם הַזֶּה וָאֶהְיֶה מִתְהַלֵּךְ בְּאֹהֶל
in-tent moving and-I-was the-this the-day even-to from-Egypt Israel sons-of

וּבְמִשְׁכָּן׃ בְּכֹל אֲשֶׁר־הִתְהַלַּכְתִּי בְּכָל־בְּנֵי יִשְׂרָאֵל
Israel sons-of with-all-of I-moved that in-everywhere (7) and-in-dwelling

הֲדָבָר דִּבַּרְתִּי אֶת־אַחַד שִׁבְטֵי יִשְׂרָאֵל אֲשֶׁר צִוִּיתִי לִרְעוֹת אֶת־
*** to-shepherd I-commanded whom Israel rulers-of one-of *** I-said word?

disrobing in the sight of the
slave girls of his servants as
any vulgar fellow would!"
21David said to Michal, "It
was before the LORD, who
chose me rather than your father or anyone from his house
when he appointed me ruler
over the LORD's people Israel—
I will celebrate before the
LORD. 22I will become even
more undignified than this,
and I will be humiliated in my
own eyes. But by these slave
girls you spoke of, I will be
held in honor."
23And Michal daughter of
Saul had no children to the
day of her death.

God's Promise to David

7 After the king was settled
in his palace and the LORD
had given him rest from all his
enemies around him, 2he said
to Nathan the prophet, "Here
I am, living in a palace of cedar, while the ark of God remains in a tent."
3Nathan replied to the king,
"Whatever you have in mind,
go ahead and do it, for the
LORD is with you."
4That night the word of the
LORD came to Nathan, saying:

5"Go and tell my servant
David, 'This is what the
LORD says: Are you the one
to build me a house to dwell
in? 6I have not dwelt in a
house from the day I
brought the Israelites up
out of Egypt to this day. I
have been moving from
place to place with a tent as
my dwelling. 7Wherever I
have moved with all the Israelites, did I ever say to
any of their rulers whom I
commanded to shepherd

עַמִּי אֶת־יִשְׂרָאֵל לֵאמֹר לָמָּה לֹא־בְנִיתֶם לִי בֵּית אֲרָזִים׃

cedars house-of for-me you-built not why? to-say Israel *** people-of-me

וְעַתָּה כֹּה־תֹאמַר לְעַבְדִּי לְדָוִד כֹּה אָמַר יְהוָה

Yahweh-of he-says this to-David to-servant-of-me you-tell this then-now (8)

צְבָאוֹת אֲנִי לְקַחְתִּיךָ מִן־הַנָּוֶה מֵאַחַר הַצֹּאן לִהְיוֹת נָגִיד עַל־

over ruler to-be the-flock from-after the-pasture from I-took-you I Hosts

עַמִּי עַל־יִשְׂרָאֵל׃ וָאֶהְיֶה עִמְּךָ בְּכֹל אֲשֶׁר הָלַכְתָּ

you-went that in-everywhere with-you and-I-was (9) Israel over people-of-me

וָאַכְרִתָה אֶת־כָּל־אֹיְבֶיךָ מִפָּנֶיךָ וְעָשִׂתִי

now-I-will-make from-before-you being-enemies-of-you all-of *** and-I-cut-off

לְךָ שֵׁם גָּדוֹל כְּשֵׁם הַגְּדֹלִים אֲשֶׁר בָּאָרֶץ׃

of-the-earth who the-great-ones like-name-of great name of-you

וְשַׂמְתִּי מָקוֹם לְעַמִּי לְיִשְׂרָאֵל וּנְטַעְתִּיו

and-I-will-plant-him for-Israel for-people-of-me place and-I-will-provide (10)

וְשָׁכַן תַּחְתָּיו וְלֹא יִרְגַּז עוֹד וְלֹא־

and-not longer he-will-be-disturbed and-not place-of-him so-he-can-stay

יֹסִיפוּ בְנֵי־עַוְלָה לְעַנּוֹתוֹ כַּאֲשֶׁר בָּרִאשׁוֹנָה׃

at-the-beginning just-as to-oppress-him wickedness sons-of they-will-continue

וּלְמִן־הַיּוֹם אֲשֶׁר צִוִּיתִי שֹׁפְטִים עַל־עַמִּי

people-of-me over ones-leading I-appointed when the-day and-at-from (11)

יִשְׂרָאֵל וַהֲנִיחֹתִי לְךָ מִכָּל־אֹיְבֶיךָ

being-enemies-of-you from-all-of to-you and-I-will-give-rest Israel

וְהִגִּיד לְךָ יְהוָה כִּי־בַיִת יַעֲשֶׂה־לְּךָ יְהוָה׃

Yahweh for-you he-will-establish house that Yahweh to-you and-he-declares

כִּי ׀ יִמְלְאוּ יָמֶיךָ וְשָׁכַבְתָּ אֶת־אֲבֹתֶיךָ

fathers-of-you with and-you-rest days-of-you they-are-over when (12)

וַהֲקִימֹתִי אֶת־זַרְעֲךָ אַחֲרֶיךָ אֲשֶׁר יֵצֵא

he-will-come who after-you offspring-of-you *** then-I-will-raise-up

מִמֵּעֶיךָ וַהֲכִינֹתִי אֶת־מַמְלַכְתּוֹ׃ הוּא

he (13) kingdom-of-him *** and-I-will-establish from-bodies-of-you

יִבְנֶה־בַּיִת לִשְׁמִי וְכֹנַנְתִּי אֶת־כִּסֵּא

throne-of *** and-I-will-establish for-Name-of-me house he-will-build

מַמְלַכְתּוֹ עַד־עוֹלָם׃ אֲנִי אֶהְיֶה־לּוֹ לְאָב וְהוּא יִהְיֶה־

he-will-be and-he as-father to-him I-will-be I (14) forever to kingdom-of-him

לִּי לְבֵן אֲשֶׁר בְּהַעֲוֺתוֹ וְהֹכַחְתִּיו בְּשֵׁבֶט אֲנָשִׁים

men with-rod-of then-I-will-punish-him when-to-do-wrong-him when as-son to-me

וּבְנִגְעֵי בְּנֵי אָדָם׃ וְחַסְדִּי לֹא־יָסוּר

he-will-be-taken not but-love-of-me (15) man sons-of and-with-floggings-of

my people Israel, "Why have you not built me a house of cedar?" '

8 "Now then, tell my servant David, 'This is what the LORD Almighty says: I took you from the pasture and from following the flock to be ruler over my people Israel. 9 I have been with you wherever you have gone, and I have cut off all your enemies from before you. Now I will make your name great, like the names of the greatest men of the earth. 10 And I will provide a place for my people Israel and will plant them so that they can have a home of their own and no longer be disturbed. Wicked people will not oppress them anymore, as they did at the beginning 11 and have done ever since the time I appointed leaders[q] over my people Israel. I will also give you rest from all your enemies.

" 'The LORD declares to you that the LORD himself will establish a house for you: 12 When your days are over and you rest with your fathers, I will raise up your offspring to succeed you, who will come from your own body, and I will establish his kingdom. 13 He is the one who will build a house for my Name, and I will establish the throne of his kingdom forever. 14 I will be his father, and he will be my son. When he does wrong, I will punish him with the rod of men, with floggings inflicted by men. 15 But my love will

q11 Traditionally *judges*

מִמֶּנּוּ כַּאֲשֶׁר הֲסִרֹתִי מֵעִם שָׁאוּל אֲשֶׁר הֲסִרֹתִי מִלְּפָנֶיךָ׃
from-before-you I-removed whom Saul from-with I-took just-as from-him

וְנֶאְמַן בֵּיתְךָ וּמַמְלַכְתְּךָ עַד־ עוֹלָם לְפָנֶיךָ
before-you forever to and-kingdom-of-you house-of-you and-he-will-endure (16)

כִּסְאֲךָ יִהְיֶה נָכוֹן עַד־ עוֹלָם׃ כְּכֹל
as-all-of (17) forever to being-established he-will-be throne-of-you

הַדְּבָרִים הָאֵלֶּה וּכְכֹל הַחִזָּיוֹן הַזֶּה כֵּן דִּבֶּר
he-reported so the-this the-revelation and-as-all-of the-these the-words

נָתָן אֶל־ דָּוִד׃ וַיָּבֹא הַמֶּלֶךְ דָּוִד וַיֵּשֶׁב לִפְנֵי יְהוָה
Yahweh before and-he-sat David the-king then-he-went-in (18) David to Nathan

וַיֹּאמֶר מִי אָנֹכִי אֲדֹנָי יְהוִה וּמִי בֵיתִי כִּי הֲבִיאֹתַנִי
you-brought-me that family-of-me and-what? Yahweh Lord I who? and-he-said

עַד־ הֲלֹם׃ וַתִּקְטַן עוֹד זֹאת בְּעֵינֶיךָ אֲדֹנָי יְהוִה
Yahweh Lord in-eyes-of-you this still if-she-was-small (19) this-far to

וַתְּדַבֵּר גַּם אֶל־ בֵּית־ עַבְדְּךָ לְמֵרָחוֹק וְזֹאת
now-this about-in-future servant-of-you house-of of also then-you-spoke

תּוֹרַת הָאָדָם אֲדֹנָי יְהוִה׃ וּמַה־ יּוֹסִיף דָּוִד עוֹד
more David can-he-add now-what? (20) Yahweh Lord the-man usual-dealing-of

לְדַבֵּר אֵלֶיךָ וְאַתָּה יָדַעְתָּ אֶת־ עַבְדְּךָ אֲדֹנָי יְהוִה׃ בַּעֲבוּר
for-sake-of (21) Yahweh Lord servant-of-you *** you-know for-you to-you to-say

דְּבָרְךָ וּכְלִבְּךָ עָשִׂיתָ אֵת כָּל־ הַגְּדוּלָּה
the-great-thing all-of *** you-did and-according-to-will-of-you word-of-you

הַזֹּאת לְהוֹדִיעַ אֶת־ עַבְדֶּךָ׃ עַל־ כֵּן גָּדַלְתָּ אֲדֹנָי
Lord you-are-great this for (22) servant-of-you *** to-make-known the-this

יְהוִה כִּי־ אֵין כָּמוֹךָ וְאֵין אֱלֹהִים זוּלָתֶךָ בְּכֹל אֲשֶׁר־ שָׁמַעְנוּ
we-heard that as-all but-you God and-no like-you no-one for Yahweh

בְּאָזְנֵינוּ׃ וּמִי כְעַמְּךָ כְּיִשְׂרָאֵל גּוֹי אֶחָד
one nation like-Israel like-people-of-you and-who? (23) with-ears-of-us

בָּאָרֶץ אֲשֶׁר הָלְכוּ־ אֱלֹהִים לִפְדּוֹת־ לוֹ לְעָם וְלָשׂוּם
and-to-make as-people for-him to-redeem God they-went-out that on-the-earth

לוֹ שֵׁם וְלַעֲשׂוֹת לָכֶם הַגְּדוּלָּה וְנֹרָאוֹת
and-things-being-wonders the-great-thing for-you and-to-perform name for-him

לְאַרְצֶךָ מִפְּנֵי עַמְּךָ אֲשֶׁר פָּדִיתָ לְּךָ
for-you you-redeemed whom people-of-you from-before for-land-of-you

מִמִּצְרַיִם גּוֹיִם וֵאלֹהָיו׃ וַתְּכוֹנֵן לְךָ אֶת־
*** for-you and-you-established (24) and-gods-of-him nations from-Egypt

עַמְּךָ יִשְׂרָאֵל ׀ לְךָ לְעָם עַד־ עוֹלָם וְאַתָּה יְהוָה הָיִיתָ
you-became Yahweh and-you forever to as-people for-you Israel people-of-you

never be taken away from him, as I took it away from Saul, whom I removed from before you. [16]Your house and your kingdom will endure forever before me[r]; your throne will be established forever.' "

[17]Nathan reported to David all the words of this entire revelation.

David's Prayer

[18]Then King David went in and sat before the LORD, and he said:

"Who am I, O Sovereign LORD, and what is my family, that you have brought me this far? [19]And as if this were not enough in your sight, O Sovereign LORD, you have also spoken about the future of the house of your servant. Is this your usual way of dealing with man, O Sovereign LORD?

[20]"What more can David say to you? For you know your servant, O Sovereign LORD. [21]For the sake of your word and according to your will, you have done this great thing and made it known to your servant.

[22]"How great you are, O Sovereign LORD! There is no one like you, and there is no God but you, as we have heard with our own ears. [23]And who is like your people Israel—the one nation on earth that God went out to redeem as a people for himself, and to make a name for himself, and to perform great and awesome wonders by driving out nations and their gods from before your people, whom you redeemed from Egypt?[s] [24]You have established your people Israel as your very own forever, and you, O LORD, have become

[r]16 Some Hebrew manuscripts and Septuagint; most Hebrew manuscripts *you*
[s]23 See Septuagint and 1 Chronicles 17:21; Hebrew *wonders for your land and before your people, whom you redeemed from Egypt, from the nations and their gods*

לָהֶם לֵאלֹהִים׃ וְעַתָּה יְהוָה אֱלֹהִים הַדָּבָר אֲשֶׁר דִּבַּרְתָּ עַל־
concerning you-made that the-promise God Yahweh and-now (25) as-God for-them

עַבְדְּךָ וְעַל־ בֵּיתוֹ הָקֵם עַד־ עוֹלָם וַעֲשֵׂה כַּאֲשֶׁר
just-as and-do! forever to keep! house-of-him and-concerning servant-of-you

דִּבַּרְתָּ׃ וְיִגְדַּל שִׁמְךָ עַד־ עוֹלָם לֵאמֹר יְהוָה
Yahweh-of to-say forever to name-of-you so-he-will-be-great (26) you-promised

צְבָאוֹת אֱלֹהִים עַל־ יִשְׂרָאֵל וּבֵית עַבְדְּךָ דָוִד יִהְיֶה
he-will-be David servant-of-you and-house-of Israel over God Hosts

נָכוֹן לְפָנֶיךָ׃ כִּי־ אַתָּה יְהוָה צְבָאוֹת אֱלֹהֵי יִשְׂרָאֵל
Israel God-of Hosts Yahweh-of you now (27) before-you being-established

גָּלִיתָה אֶת־ אֹזֶן עַבְדְּךָ לֵאמֹר בַּיִת אֶבְנֶה־ לָּךְ
for-you I-will-build house to-say servant-of-you ear-of to you-revealed

עַל־ כֵּן מָצָא עַבְדְּךָ אֶת־ לִבּוֹ לְהִתְפַּלֵּל אֵלֶיךָ אֶת־
*** to-you to-offer courage-of-him *** servant-of-you he-found this for

הַתְּפִלָּה הַזֹּאת׃ וְעַתָּה ׀ אֲדֹנָי יְהוִה אַתָּה־ הוּא הָאֱלֹהִים וּדְבָרֶיךָ
and-words-of-you the-God he you Yahweh Lord and-now (28) the-this the-prayer

יִהְיוּ אֱמֶת וַתְּדַבֵּר אֶל־ עַבְדְּךָ אֶת־ הַטּוֹבָה הַזֹּאת׃
the-this the-good *** servant-of-you to and-you-promised trustworthy they-are

וְעַתָּה הוֹאֵל וּבָרֵךְ אֶת־ בֵּית עַבְדְּךָ לִהְיוֹת
to-continue servant-of-you house-of *** and-bless! be-pleased! and-now (29)

לְעוֹלָם לְפָנֶיךָ כִּי־ אַתָּה אֲדֹנָי יְהוִה דִּבַּרְתָּ וּמִבִּרְכָתְךָ
and-with-blessing-of-you you-spoke Yahweh Lord you for before-you to-forever

יְבֹרַךְ בֵּית־ עַבְדְּךָ לְעוֹלָם׃ וַיְהִי אַחֲרֵי־
after and-he-was (8:1) to-forever servant-of-you house-of he-will-be-blessed

כֵן וַיַּךְ דָּוִד אֶת־ פְּלִשְׁתִּים וַיַּכְנִיעֵם וַיִּקַּח
and-he-took and-he-subdued-them Philistines *** David then-he-defeated this

דָּוִד אֶת־ מֶתֶג הָאַמָּה מִיַּד פְּלִשְׁתִּים׃ וַיַּךְ אֶת־
*** and-he-defeated (2) Philistines from-hand-of the-Ammah Metheg-of *** David

מוֹאָב וַיְמַדְּדֵם בַּחֶבֶל הַשְׁכֵּב אוֹתָם אַרְצָה
on-ground them to-make-lie-down with-the-cord and-he-measured-them Moab

וַיְמַדֵּד שְׁנֵי־ חֲבָלִים לְהָמִית וּמְלֹא הַחֶבֶל לְהַחֲיוֹת
to-let-live the-length and-fullness-of to-kill lengths two-of and-he-measured

וַתְּהִי מוֹאָב לְדָוִד לַעֲבָדִים נֹשְׂאֵי מִנְחָה׃
tribute ones-bringing-of as-subjects to-David Moab so-she-became

וַיַּךְ דָּוִד אֶת־ הֲדַדְעֶזֶר בֶּן־ רְחֹב מֶלֶךְ צוֹבָה בְּלֶכְתּוֹ
when-to-go-him Zobah king-of Rehob son-of Hadadezer *** David and-he-fought (3)

לְהָשִׁיב יָדוֹ בִּנְהַר־ ׃ וַיִּלְכֹּד דָּוִד
David and-he-captured (4) *Euphrates along-River-of control-of-him to-restore

their God.

[25]"And now, LORD God, keep forever the promise you have made concerning your servant and his house. Do as you promised, [26]so that your name will be great forever. Then men will say, 'The LORD Almighty is God over Israel!' And the house of your servant David will be established before you.

[27]"O LORD Almighty, God of Israel, you have revealed this to your servant, saying, 'I will build a house for you.' So your servant has found courage to offer you this prayer. [28]O Sovereign LORD, you are God! Your words are trustworthy, and you have given this good promise to your servant. [29]Now be pleased to bless the house of your servant, that it may continue forever in your sight; for you, O Sovereign LORD, have spoken, and with your blessing the house of your servant will be blessed forever."

David's Victories

8 In the course of time, David defeated the Philistines and subdued them, and he took Metheg Ammah from the control of the Philistines.

[2]David also defeated the Moabites. He made them lie down on the ground and measured them off with a length of cord. Every two lengths of them were put to death, and the third length was allowed to live. So the Moabites became subject to David and brought tribute.

[3]Moreover, David fought Hadadezer son of Rehob, king of Zobah, when he went to restore his control along the Euphrates River. [4]David captured a thousand of his chariots, seven thousand

[f]4 Septuagint (see also 1 Chron. 18:4); Hebrew *captured seventeen hundred of his charioteers*

*3 Many mss include פרת, *Euphrates*, or include the reading as a marginal *Qere*.

מִמֶּנּוּ אֶלֶף וּשְׁבַע־ מֵאוֹת פָּרָשִׁים וְעֶשְׂרִים אֶלֶף אִישׁ
man thousand and-twenty charioteers hundreds and-seven-of thousand from-him

רַגְלִי וַיְעַקֵּר דָּוִד אֶת־ כָּל־ הָרֶכֶב וַיּוֹתֵר
but-he-left the-chariot-horse all-of *** David and-he-hamstrung foot-soldier

מִמֶּנּוּ מֵאָה רָכֶב׃ וַתָּבֹא אֲרַם דַּמֶּשֶׂק לַעְזֹר
to-help Damascus Aram-of when-she-came (5) chariot-horse hundred from-him

לַהֲדַדְעֶזֶר מֶלֶךְ צוֹבָה וַיַּךְ דָּוִד בַּאֲרָם עֶשְׂרִים־ וּשְׁנַיִם
and-two twenty of-Aram David then-he-struck-down Zobah king-of to-Hadadezer

אֶלֶף אִישׁ׃ וַיָּשֶׂם דָּוִד נְצִבִים בַּאֲרַם דַּמֶּשֶׂק וַתְּהִי
and-she-became Damascus in-Aram-of garrisons David and-he-put (6) man thousand

אֲרָם לְדָוִד לַעֲבָדִים נוֹשְׂאֵי מִנְחָה וַיֹּשַׁע יְהוָה
Yahweh and-he-gave-victory tribute ones-bringing-of as-subjects to-David Aram

אֶת־ דָּוִד בְּכֹל אֲשֶׁר הָלָךְ׃ וַיִּקַּח דָּוִד אֵת שִׁלְטֵי
shields-of *** David and-he-took (7) he-went that in-everywhere David to

הַזָּהָב אֲשֶׁר הָיוּ אֶל עַבְדֵי הֲדַדְעָזֶר וַיְבִיאֵם יְרוּשָׁלָםִ׃
Jerusalem and-he-brought-them Hadadezer officers-of to they-were that the-gold

וּמִבֶּטַח וּמִבֵּרֹתַי עָרֵי הֲדַדְעָזֶר לָקַח הַמֶּלֶךְ
the-king he-took Hadadezer towns-of and-from-Berothai and-from-Betah (8)

דָּוִד נְחֹשֶׁת הַרְבֵּה מְאֹד׃ וַיִּשְׁמַע תֹּעִי מֶלֶךְ חֲמָת כִּי
that Hamath king-of Toi when-he-heard (9) very to-be-great bronze David

הִכָּה דָוִד אֵת כָּל־ חֵיל הֲדַדְעָזֶר׃ וַיִּשְׁלַח תֹּעִי
Toi then-he-sent (10) Hadadezer army-of entire-of *** David he-defeated

אֶת־ יוֹרָם־ בְּנוֹ אֶל־ הַמֶּלֶךְ־ דָּוִד לִשְׁאָל־ לוֹ לְשָׁלוֹם
for-peace to-him to-greet David the-king to son-of-him Joram ***

וּלְבָרְכוֹ עַל אֲשֶׁר נִלְחַם בַּהֲדַדְעֶזֶר
against-Hadadezer he-fought that because and-to-congratulate-him

וַיַּכֵּהוּ כִּי־ אִישׁ מִלְחֲמוֹת תֹּעִי הָיָה הֲדַדְעָזֶר וּבְיָדוֹ
and-in-hand-of-him Hadadezer he-was Toi wars-of man-of for and-he-defeated-him

הָיוּ כְּלֵי־ כֶסֶף וּכְלֵי־ זָהָב וּכְלֵי נְחֹשֶׁת׃
bronze and-articles-of gold and-articles-of silver articles-of they-were

גַּם־ אֹתָם הִקְדִּישׁ הַמֶּלֶךְ דָּוִד לַיהוָה עִם־ הַכֶּסֶף
the-silver with to-Yahweh David the-king he-dedicated them also (11)

וְהַזָּהָב אֲשֶׁר הִקְדִּישׁ מִכָּל־ הַגּוֹיִם אֲשֶׁר כִּבֵּשׁ׃
he-subdued that the-nations from-all-of he-dedicated that and-the-gold

מֵאֲרָם וּמִמּוֹאָב וּמִבְּנֵי עַמּוֹן וּמִפְּלִשְׁתִּים
and-from-Philistines Ammon and-from-sons-of and-from-Moab from-Aram (12)

וּמֵעֲמָלֵק וּמִשְּׁלַל הֲדַדְעֶזֶר בֶּן־ רְחֹב מֶלֶךְ צוֹבָה׃
Zobah king-of Rehob son-of Hadadezer and-from-plunder-of and-from-Amalek

charioteers[t] and twenty thousand foot soldiers. He hamstrung all but a hundred of the chariot horses.
5When the Arameans of Damascus came to help Hadadezer king of Zobah, David struck down twenty-two thousand of them.
6He put garrisons in the Aramean kingdom of Damascus, and the Arameans became subject to him and brought tribute. The LORD gave David victory everywhere he went.
7David took the gold shields that belonged to the officers of Hadadezer and brought them to Jerusalem.
8From Tebah[u] and Berothai, towns that belonged to Hadadezer, King David took a great quantity of bronze.
9When Tou[v] king of Hamath heard that David had defeated the entire army of Hadadezer,
10he sent his son Joram[w] to King David to greet him and congratulate him on his victory in battle over Hadadezer, who had been at war with Tou. Joram brought with him articles of silver and gold and bronze.
11King David dedicated these articles to the LORD, as he had done with the silver and gold from all the nations he had subdued:
12Edom[x] and Moab, the Ammonites and the Philistines, and Amalek. He also dedicated the plunder taken from Hadadezer son of Rehob, king of Zobah.

[u]8 See some Septuagint manuscripts (see also 1 Chron. 18:8); Hebrew *Betah*
[v]9 Hebrew *Toi*, a variant of *Tou*; also in verse 10
[w]10 A variant of *Hadoram*
[x]12 Some Hebrew manuscripts, Septuagint and Syriac (see also 1 Chron. 18:11); most Hebrew manuscripts *Aram*

וַיַּעַשׂ דָּוִד שֵׁם בְּשֻׁבוֹ מֵהַכּוֹתוֹ אֶת־
*** from-to-strike-down-him when-to-return-him name David and-he-made (13)

אֲרָם בְּגֵיא־מֶלַח שְׁמוֹנָה עָשָׂר אָלֶף׃ וַיָּשֶׂם בֶּאֱדוֹם
throughout-Edom and-he-put (14) thousand ten eight Salt in-Valley-of Aram

נְצִבִים בְּכָל־אֱדוֹם שָׂם נְצִבִים וַיְהִי כָל־אֱדוֹם עֲבָדִים
subjects Edom all-of and-he-became garrisons he-put Edom in-all-of garrisons

לְדָוִד וַיּוֹשַׁע יְהוָה אֶת־דָּוִד בְּכֹל אֲשֶׁר הָלָךְ׃
he-went that in-everywhere David to Yahweh and-he-gave-victory to-David

וַיִּמְלֹךְ דָּוִד עַל־כָּל־יִשְׂרָאֵל וַיְהִי דָוִד עֹשֶׂה מִשְׁפָּט
justice doing David and-he-was Israel all-of over David and-he-reigned (15)

וּצְדָקָה לְכָל־עַמּוֹ׃ וְיוֹאָב בֶּן־צְרוּיָה עַל־הַצָּבָא
the-army over Zeruiah son-of and-Joab (16) people-of-him for-all-of and-right

וִיהוֹשָׁפָט בֶּן־אֲחִילוּד מַזְכִּיר׃ וְצָדוֹק בֶּן־אֲחִיטוּב
Ahitub son-of and-Zadok (17) one-recording Ahilud son-of and-Jehoshaphat

וַאֲחִימֶלֶךְ בֶּן־אֶבְיָתָר כֹּהֲנִים וּשְׂרָיָה סוֹפֵר׃
one-being-secretary and-Seraiah priests Abiathar son-of and-Ahimelech

וּבְנָיָהוּ בֶּן־יְהוֹיָדָע וְהַכְּרֵתִי וְהַפְּלֵתִי
and-the-Pelethites and-the-Kerethites Jehoiada son-of and-Benaiah (18)

וּבְנֵי דָוִד כֹּהֲנִים הָיוּ׃ וַיֹּאמֶר דָּוִד הֲכִי
indeed? David and-he-asked (9:1) they-were royal-advisers David and-sons-of

יֶשׁ־עוֹד אֲשֶׁר נוֹתַר לְבֵית שָׁאוּל וְאֶעֱשֶׂה עִמּוֹ חֶסֶד
kindness to-him that-I-can-show Saul of-house-of he-is-left who still is-he

בַּעֲבוּר יְהוֹנָתָן׃ וּלְבֵית שָׁאוּל עֶבֶד וּשְׁמוֹ
and-name-of-him servant Saul now-of-household-of (2) Jonathan for-sake-of

צִיבָא וַיִּקְרְאוּ־לוֹ אֶל־דָּוִד וַיֹּאמֶר הַמֶּלֶךְ אֵלָיו הַאַתָּה צִיבָא
Ziba you? to-him the-king and-he-said David to to-him and-they-called Ziba

וַיֹּאמֶר עַבְדֶּךָ׃ וַיֹּאמֶר הַמֶּלֶךְ הַאֶפֶס עוֹד אִישׁ
one still not? the-king and-he-asked (3) servant-of-you and-he-replied

לְבֵית שָׁאוּל וְאֶעֱשֶׂה עִמּוֹ חֶסֶד אֱלֹהִים וַיֹּאמֶר צִיבָא
Ziba and-he-answered God kindness-of to-him that-I-can-show Saul of-house-of

אֶל־הַמֶּלֶךְ עוֹד בֵּן לִיהוֹנָתָן נְכֵה רַגְלָיִם׃ וַיֹּאמֶר־
and-he-asked (4) both-feet crippled-of of-Jonathan son still the-king to

לוֹ הַמֶּלֶךְ אֵיפֹה הוּא וַיֹּאמֶר צִיבָא אֶל־הַמֶּלֶךְ הִנֵּה־הוּא בֵּית
house-of he see! the-king to Ziba and-he-answered he where? the-king to-him

מָכִיר בֶּן־עַמִּיאֵל בְּלוֹ דְבָר׃ וַיִּשְׁלַח הַמֶּלֶךְ דָּוִד
David the-king so-he-sent (5) Debar in-Lo Ammiel son-of Makir

וַיִּקָּחֵהוּ מִבֵּית מָכִיר בֶּן־עַמִּיאֵל מִלּוֹ דְבָר׃
Debar from-Lo Ammiel son-of Makir from-house-of and-he-had-brought-him

13 And David became famous
after he returned from striking
down eighteen thousand
Edomites[y] in the Valley of
Salt.
14 He put garrisons throughout Edom, and all the Edomites became subject to David.
The LORD gave David victory
everywhere he went.

David's Officials

15 David reigned over all Israel, doing what was just and
right for all his people. 16 Joab
son of Zeruiah was over the
army; Jehoshaphat son of Ahilud was recorder; 17 Zadok son
of Ahitub and Ahimelech son
of Abiathar were priests; Seraiah was secretary; 18 Benaiah
son of Jehoiada was over the
Kerethites and Pelethites; and
David's sons were royal advisers.[z]

David and Mephibosheth

9 David asked, "Is there
anyone still left of the
house of Saul to whom I can
show kindness for Jonathan's
sake?"
2 Now there was a servant of
Saul's household named Ziba.
They called him to appear before David, and the king said
to him, "Are you Ziba?"
"Your servant," he replied.
3 The king asked, "Is there no
one still left of the house of
Saul to whom I can show
God's kindness?"
Ziba answered the king,
"There is still a son of Jonathan; he is crippled in both
feet."
4 "Where is he?" the king
asked.
Ziba answered, "He is at the
house of Makir son of Ammiel
in Lo Debar."
5 So King David had him
brought from Lo Debar, from
the house of Makir son of Ammiel.

[y] *13* A few Hebrew manuscripts, Septuagint and Syriac (see also 1 Chron. 18:12); most Hebrew manuscripts *Aram* (that is, Arameans)
[z] *18* Or *were priests*

וַיָּבֹא מְפִיבֹשֶׁת בֶּן־ יְהוֹנָתָן בֶּן־ שָׁאוּל אֶל־ דָּוִד

David to Saul son-of Jonathan son-of Mephibosheth when-he-came (6)

וַיִּפֹּל עַל־ פָּנָיו וַיִּשְׁתָּחוּ וַיֹּאמֶר דָּוִד מְפִיבֹשֶׁת

Mephibosheth David and-he-said and-he-paid-honor faces-of-him on then-he-fell

וַיֹּאמֶר הִנֵּה עַבְדֶּךָ׃ וַיֹּאמֶר לוֹ דָוִד אַל־ תִּירָא

you-fear not David to-him and-he-said (7) servant-of-you see! and-he-replied

כִּי עָשֹׂה אֶעֱשֶׂה עִמְּךָ חֶסֶד בַּעֲבוּר יְהוֹנָתָן אָבִיךָ

father-of-you Jonathan for-sake-of kindness to-you I-will-show to-show for

וַהֲשִׁבֹתִי לְךָ אֶת־ כָּל־ שְׂדֵה שָׁאוּל אָבִיךָ וְאַתָּה

and-you father-of-you Saul land-of all-of *** to-you and-I-will-restore

תֹּאכַל לֶחֶם עַל־ שֻׁלְחָנִי תָּמִיד׃ וַיִּשְׁתַּחוּ וַיֹּאמֶר מֶה

what? and-he-said and-he-bowed (8) always table-of-me at food you-will-eat

עַבְדֶּךָ כִּי פָנִיתָ אֶל־ הַכֶּלֶב הַמֵּת אֲשֶׁר כָּמוֹנִי׃

like-me that the-dead the-dog to you-notice that servant-of-you

וַיִּקְרָא הַמֶּלֶךְ אֶל־ צִיבָא נַעַר שָׁאוּל וַיֹּאמֶר אֵלָיו

to-him and-he-said Saul servant-of Ziba to the-king then-he-summoned (9)

כֹּל אֲשֶׁר הָיָה לְשָׁאוּל וּלְכָל־ בֵּיתוֹ נָתַתִּי לְבֶן־

to-son-of I-gave family-of-him and-to-all-of to-Saul he-was that all

אֲדֹנֶיךָ׃ וְעָבַדְתָּ לּוֹ אֶת־הָאֲדָמָה אַתָּה וּבָנֶיךָ

and-sons-of-you you the-land *** for-him and-you-shall-farm (10) masters-of-you

וַעֲבָדֶיךָ וְהֵבֵאתָ וְהָיָה לְבֶן־ אֲדֹנֶיךָ

masters-of-you for-son-of so-he-may-be and-you-bring-in and-servants-of-you

לֶּחֶם וַאֲכָלוֹ וּמְפִיבֹשֶׁת בֶּן־ אֲדֹנֶיךָ

masters-of-you son-of and-Mephibosheth and-he-may-eat-him provision

יֹאכַל תָּמִיד לֶחֶם עַל־ שֻׁלְחָנִי וּלְצִיבָא חֲמִשָּׁה עָשָׂר בָּנִים וְעֶשְׂרִים

and-twenty sons ten five now-to-Ziba table-of-me at food always he-will-eat

עֲבָדִים׃ וַיֹּאמֶר צִיבָא אֶל־ הַמֶּלֶךְ כְּכֹל אֲשֶׁר יְצַוֶּה

he-commands that as-all the-king to Ziba then-he-said (11) servants

אֲדֹנִי הַמֶּלֶךְ אֶת־ עַבְדּוֹ כֵּן יַעֲשֶׂה עַבְדֶּךָ

servant-of-you he-will-do so servant-of-him *** the-king master-of-me

וּמְפִיבֹשֶׁת אֹכֵל עַל־ שֻׁלְחָנִי כְּאַחַד מִבְּנֵי הַמֶּלֶךְ׃

the-king of-sons-of like-one table-of-me at eating so-Mephibosheth

וְלִמְפִיבֹשֶׁת בֵּן־ קָטָן וּשְׁמוֹ מִיכָא וְכֹל

and-every-of Mica and-name-of-him young son now-to-Mephibosheth (12)

מוֹשַׁב בֵּית־ צִיבָא עֲבָדִים לִמְפִיבֹשֶׁת׃ וּמְפִיבֹשֶׁת

and-Mephibosheth (13) of-Mephibosheth servants Ziba household-of member-of

יֹשֵׁב בִּירוּשָׁלִַם כִּי עַל־ שֻׁלְחַן הַמֶּלֶךְ תָּמִיד הוּא אֹכֵל וְהוּא

and-he eating he always the-king table-of at because in-Jerusalem living

6When Mephibosheth son of
Jonathan, the son of Saul,
came to David, he bowed
down to pay him honor.
David said, "Me-
phibosheth!"
"Your servant," he replied.
7"Don't be afraid," David
said to him, "for I will surely
show you kindness for the
sake of your father Jonathan. I
will restore to you all the land
that belonged to your grandfather Saul, and you will always eat at my table."
8Mephibosheth bowed
down and said, "What is your
servant, that you should notice a dead dog like me?"
9Then the king summoned
Ziba, Saul's servant, and said
to him, "I have given your
master's grandson everything
that belonged to Saul and his
family. 10You and your sons
and your servants are to farm
the land for him and bring in
the crops, so that your master's grandson may be provided for. And Mephibosheth,
grandson of your master, will
always eat at my table." (Now
Ziba had fifteen sons and
twenty servants.)
11Then Ziba said to the king,
"Your servant will do whatever my lord the king commands his servant to do." So
Mephibosheth ate at David's[a]
table like one of the king's
sons.
12Mephibosheth had a
young son named Mica, and
all the members of Ziba's
household were servants of
Mephibosheth. 13And Me-
phibosheth lived in Jerusalem,
because he always ate at the

[a]11 Septuagint; Hebrew *my*

פִּסֵּחַ שְׁתֵּי רַגְלָיו׃ וַיְהִי אַחֲרֵי־ כֵן וַיָּמָת
then-he-died this after and-he-was (10:1) feet-of-him both-of crippled

מֶלֶךְ בְּנֵי עַמּוֹן וַיִּמְלֹךְ חָנוּן בְּנוֹ תַּחְתָּיו׃
in-place-of-him son-of-him Hanun and-he-became-king Ammon sons-of king-of

וַיֹּאמֶר דָּוִד אֶעֱשֶׂה־ חֶסֶד׀ עִם־ חָנוּן בֶּן־ נָחָשׁ כַּאֲשֶׁר
just-as Nahash son-of Hanun to kindness I-will-show David and-he-thought (2)

עָשָׂה אָבִיו עִמָּדִי חֶסֶד וַיִּשְׁלַח דָּוִד לְנַחֲמוֹ
to-console-him David so-he-sent kindness to-me father-of-him he-showed

בְּיַד־ עֲבָדָיו אֶל־ אָבִיו וַיָּבֹאוּ עַבְדֵי
men-of when-they-came father-of-him concerning delegates-of-him by-hand-of

דָוִד אֶרֶץ בְּנֵי עַמּוֹן׃ וַיֹּאמְרוּ שָׂרֵי בְנֵי־ עַמּוֹן אֶל־
to Ammon sons-of nobles-of then-they-said (3) Ammon sons-of land-of David

חָנוּן אֲדֹנֵיהֶם הַמְכַבֵּד דָּוִד אֶת־ אָבִיךָ בְּעֵינֶיךָ כִּי־
because in-eyes-of-you father-of-you *** David honoring? lords-of-them Hanun

שָׁלַח לְךָ מְנַחֲמִים הֲלוֹא בַּעֲבוּר חֲקוֹר אֶת־ הָעִיר
the-city *** to-explore in-order not? ones-expressing-sympathy to-you he-sends

וּלְרַגְּלָהּ וּלְהָפְכָהּ שָׁלַח דָּוִד אֶת־ עֲבָדָיו אֵלֶיךָ׃
to-you men-of-him *** David he-sent and-to-overthrow-her and-to-spy-out-her

וַיִּקַּח חָנוּן אֶת־ עַבְדֵי דָוִד וַיְגַלַּח אֶת־ חֲצִי
half-of *** and-he-shaved-off David men-of *** Hanun so-he-seized (4)

זְקָנָם וַיִּכְרֹת אֶת־ מַדְוֵיהֶם בַּחֵצִי עַד שְׁתוֹתֵיהֶם
buttocks-of-them at in-middle garments-of-them *** and-he-cut-off beard-of-them

וַיְשַׁלְּחֵם׃ וַיַּגִּדוּ לְדָוִד וַיִּשְׁלַח לִקְרָאתָם
to-meet-them then-he-sent to-David when-they-told (5) and-he-sent-away-them

כִּי־ הָיוּ הָאֲנָשִׁים נִכְלָמִים מְאֹד וַיֹּאמֶר הַמֶּלֶךְ
the-king and-he-said greatly ones-being-humiliated the-men they-were for

שְׁבוּ בִירֵחוֹ עַד־ יְצַמַּח זְקַנְכֶם וְשַׁבְתֶּם׃
then-you-come-back beard-of-you he-grows till at-Jericho stay!

וַיִּרְאוּ בְּנֵי עַמּוֹן כִּי נִבְאֲשׁוּ בְּדָוִד
to-David they-became-stench that Ammon sons-of when-they-realized (6)

וַיִּשְׁלְחוּ בְנֵי־ עַמּוֹן וַיִּשְׂכְּרוּ אֶת־ אֲרַם בֵּית־ רְחוֹב וְאֶת־
and Rehob Beth Aram-of *** and-they-hired Ammon sons-of then-they-sent

אֲרַם צוֹבָא עֶשְׂרִים אֶלֶף רַגְלִי וְאֶת־ מֶלֶךְ מַעֲכָה אֶלֶף אִישׁ
man thousand Maacah king-of and foot-soldier thousand twenty Zobah Aram-of

וְאִישׁ טוֹב שְׁנֵים־עָשָׂר אֶלֶף אִישׁ׃ וַיִּשְׁמַע דָּוִד וַיִּשְׁלַח אֶת־
*** then-he-sent David when-he-heard (7) man thousand ten two Tob and-man-of

יוֹאָב וְאֵת כָּל־ הַצָּבָא הַגִּבֹּרִים׃ וַיֵּצְאוּ בְּנֵי
sons-of and-they-came-out (8) the-fighting-men the-army entire-of and Joab

king's table, and he was crippled in both feet.

David Defeats the Ammonites

10 In the course of time, the king of the Ammonites died, and his son Hanun succeeded him as king.
2David thought, "I will show kindness to Hanun son of Nahash, just as his father showed kindness to me." So David sent a delegation to express his sympathy to Hanun concerning his father.

When David's men came to the land of the Ammonites,
3the Ammonite nobles said to Hanun their lord, "Do you think David is honoring your father by sending men to you to express sympathy? Hasn't David sent them to you to explore the city and spy it out and overthrow it?"
4So Hanun seized David's men, shaved off half of each man's beard, cut off their garments in the middle at the buttocks, and sent them away.

5When David was told about this, he sent messengers to meet the men, for they were greatly humiliated. The king said, "Stay at Jericho till your beards have grown, and then come back."

6When the Ammonites realized that they had become a stench in David's nostrils, they hired twenty thousand Aramean foot soldiers from Beth Rehob and Zobah, as well as the king of Maacah with a thousand men, and also twelve thousand men from Tob.

7On hearing this, David sent Joab out with the entire army of fighting men.
8The Ammonites came out and drew up

עַמּ֗וֹן וַיַּֽעַרְכוּ֙ מִלְחָמָ֔ה פֶּ֖תַח הַשָּׁ֑עַר וַאֲרַ֞ם

and-Aram-of the-gate entrance-of battle-formation and-they-drew-up Ammon

צוֹבָ֨א וּרְח֜וֹב וְאִ֥ישׁ־ט֛וֹב וּמַעֲכָ֖ה לְבַדָּ֥ם בַּשָּׂדֶֽה׃

in-the-open-country by-themselves and-Maacah Tob and-man-of and-Rehob Zobah

וַיַּ֣רְא יוֹאָ֗ב כִּֽי־הָיְתָ֤ה אֵלָיו֙ פְּנֵ֣י הַמִּלְחָמָ֔ה מִפָּנִ֖ים

in-front the-battle lines-of to-him she-was that Joab and-he-saw (9)

וּמֵאָח֑וֹר וַיִּבְחַ֗ר מִכֹּל֙ בְּחוּרֵ֣י בִּישְׂרָאֵ֔ל°

Israel ones-being-chosen-of from-all-of so-he-selected and-at-behind

וַֽיַּעֲרֹ֖ךְ לִקְרַ֥את אֲרָֽם׃ וְאֵת֙ יֶ֣תֶר הָעָ֔ם נָתַ֕ן בְּיַ֖ד

under-hand-of he-put the-people rest-of and (10) Aram to-meet and-he-deployed

אַבְשַׁ֣י אָחִ֑יו וַֽיַּעֲרֹ֔ךְ לִקְרַ֖את בְּנֵ֥י עַמּֽוֹן׃ וַיֹּ֗אמֶר

and-he-said (11) Ammon sons-of to-meet and-he-deployed brother-of-him Abishai

אִם־תֶּחֱזַ֤ק אֲרָם֙ מִמֶּ֔נִּי וְהָיִ֥תָה לִּ֖י לִֽישׁוּעָ֑ה

for-rescue to-me then-you-must-come more-than-me Aram she-is-strong if

וְאִם־בְּנֵ֤י עַמּוֹן֙ יֶחֱזְק֣וּ* מִמְּךָ֔ וְהָלַכְתִּ֖י לְהוֹשִׁ֥יעַ

to-rescue then-I-will-come more-than-you they-are-strong Ammon sons-of but-if

לָֽךְ׃ חֲזַ֤ק וְנִתְחַזַּק֙ בְּעַד־עַמֵּ֔נוּ וּבְעַ֖ד

and-for people-of-us for and-let-us-fight-bravely be-strong! (12) to-you

עָרֵ֣י אֱלֹהֵ֑ינוּ וַֽיהוָ֔ה יַעֲשֶׂ֖ה הַטּ֥וֹב בְּעֵינָֽיו׃

in-eyes-of-him the-good he-will-do and-Yahweh God-of-us cities-of

וַיִּגַּ֣שׁ יוֹאָ֗ב וְהָעָם֙ אֲשֶׁ֣ר עִמּ֔וֹ לַמִּלְחָמָ֖ה בַּאֲרָ֑ם

with-Aram to-the-fight with-him who and-the-troop Joab then-he-advanced (13)

וַיָּנֻ֖סוּ מִפָּנָֽיו׃ וּבְנֵ֧י עַמּ֣וֹן רָא֗וּ כִּי־נָ֣ס

he-fled that they-saw Ammon when-sons-of (14) from-before-him and-they-fled

אֲרָ֔ם וַיָּנֻ֙סוּ֙ מִפְּנֵ֣י אֲבִישַׁ֔י וַיָּבֹ֖אוּ הָעִ֑יר

the-city and-they-went-inside Abishai from-before then-they-fled Aram

וַיָּ֣שָׁב יוֹאָ֗ב מֵעַל֙ בְּנֵ֣י עַמּ֔וֹן וַיָּבֹ֖א יְרוּשָׁלִָֽם׃

Jerusalem and-he-came Ammon sons-of from-against Joab so-he-returned

וַיַּ֣רְא אֲרָ֔ם כִּ֥י נִגַּ֖ף לִפְנֵ֣י יִשְׂרָאֵ֑ל וַיֵּאָסְפ֖וּ

then-they-regrouped Israel before he-was-routed that Aram after-he-saw (15)

יָֽחַד׃ וַיִּשְׁלַ֣ח הֲדַדְעֶ֗זֶר וַיֹּצֵ֤א אֶת־אֲרָם֙ אֲשֶׁר֙ מֵעֵ֣בֶר

at-beyond who Aram *** and-he-had-brought Hadadezer and-he-sent (16) together

הַנָּהָ֔ר וַיָּבֹ֖אוּ חֵילָ֑ם וְשׁוֹבַ֛ךְ שַׂר־צְבָ֥א הֲדַדְעֶ֖זֶר

Hadadezer army-of commander-of and-Shobach Helam and-they-went the-River

לִפְנֵיהֶֽם׃ וַיֻּגַּ֣ד לְדָוִ֗ד וַיֶּאֱסֹ֤ף אֶת־כָּל־יִשְׂרָאֵל֙

Israel all-of *** then-he-gathered to-David when-he-was-told (17) before-them

וַיַּעֲבֹ֣ר אֶת־הַיַּרְדֵּ֔ן וַיָּבֹ֖א חֵלָ֑אמָה וַיַּעַרְכ֣וּ אֲרָ֗ם

Aram and-they-formed-line to-Helam and-he-went the-Jordan *** and-he-crossed

in battle formation at the entrance to their city gate, while
the Arameans of Zobah and
Rehob and the men of Tob
and Maacah were by them-
selves in the open country.
[9]Joab saw that there were
battle lines in front of him and
behind him; so he selected
some of the best troops in Israel and deployed them against
the Arameans. [10]He put the
rest of the men under the command of Abishai his brother
and deployed them against
the Ammonites. [11]Joab said,
"If the Arameans are too
strong for me, then you are to
come to my rescue; but if the
Ammonites are too strong for
you, then I will come to rescue
you. [12]Be strong and let us fight
bravely for our people and the
cities of our God. The LORD
will do what is good in his
sight."
[13]Then Joab and the troops
with him advanced to fight
the Arameans, and they fled
before him. [14]When the Ammonites saw that the Ara-
means were fleeing, they fled
before Abishai and went inside the city. So Joab returned
from fighting the Ammonites
and came to Jerusalem.
[15]After the Arameans saw
that they had been routed by
Israel, they regrouped. [16]Hada-
dezer had Arameans brought
from beyond the River[b]; they
went to Helam, with Shobach
the commander of Hadade-
zer's army leading them.
[17]When David was told of
this, he gathered all Israel,
crossed the Jordan and went to
Helam. The Arameans formed

[b]16 That is, the Euphrates

*11 Most mss have *segol* under the *beth* (יֶחֱ).

°9 ק ישראל

לִקְרַאת דָּוִד וַיִּלָּחֲמוּ עִמּוֹ׃ וַיָּנָס אֲרָם מִפְּנֵי
from-before Aram but-he-fled (18) against-him and-they-fought David to-meet

יִשְׂרָאֵל וַיַּהֲרֹג דָּוִד מֵאֲרָם שְׁבַע מֵאוֹת רֶכֶב וְאַרְבָּעִים
and-forty charioteer hundreds seven-of from-Aram David and-he-killed Israel

אֶלֶף פָּרָשִׁים וְאֵת שׁוֹבַךְ שַׂר־ צְבָאוֹ הִכָּה
he-struck-down army-of-him commander-of Shobach and horsemen thousand

וַיָּמָת שָׁם׃ וַיִּרְאוּ כָל־ הַמְּלָכִים עַבְדֵי הֲדַדְעֶזֶר
Hadadezer vassals-of the-kings all-of when-they-saw (19) there and-he-died

כִּי נִגְּפוּ לִפְנֵי יִשְׂרָאֵל וַיַּשְׁלִמוּ אֶת־ יִשְׂרָאֵל
Israel with then-they-made-peace Israel before they-were-defeated that

וַיַּעַבְדוּם וַיִּרְאוּ אֲרָם לְהוֹשִׁיעַ עוֹד אֶת־
*** anymore to-help Aram so-they-were-afraid and-they-became-subject-to-them

בְּנֵי עַמּוֹן׃ וַיְהִי לִתְשׁוּבַת הַשָּׁנָה לְעֵת ׀ צֵאת
to-go-off at-time-of the-year in-spring-of and-he-was (11:1) Ammon sons-of

הַמַּלְאכִים* וַיִּשְׁלַח דָּוִד אֶת־ יוֹאָב וְאֶת־ עֲבָדָיו עִמּוֹ וְאֶת־ כָּל־
whole-of and with-him men-of-him and Joab *** David then-he-sent the-kings

יִשְׂרָאֵל וַיַּשְׁחִתוּ אֶת־ בְּנֵי עַמּוֹן וַיָּצֻרוּ עַל־ רַבָּה
Rabbah against and-they-besieged Ammon sons-of *** and-they-destroyed Israel

וְדָוִד יוֹשֵׁב בִּירוּשָׁלִָם׃ וַיְהִי ׀ לְעֵת הָעֶרֶב
the-evening at-time-of and-he-was (2) in-Jerusalem remaining but-David

וַיָּקָם דָּוִד מֵעַל מִשְׁכָּבוֹ וַיִּתְהַלֵּךְ עַל־ גַּג בֵּית־
palace-of roof-of on and-he-walked bed-of-him from-on David then-he-got-up

הַמֶּלֶךְ וַיַּרְא אִשָּׁה רֹחֶצֶת מֵעַל הַגָּג וְהָאִשָּׁה טוֹבַת
beautiful-of now-the-woman the-roof from-on bathing woman and-he-saw the-king

מַרְאֶה מְאֹד׃ וַיִּשְׁלַח דָּוִד וַיִּדְרֹשׁ לָאִשָּׁה
about-the-woman and-he-found-out David and-he-sent (3) very appearance

וַיֹּאמֶר הֲלוֹא־ זֹאת בַּת־ שֶׁבַע בַּת־ אֱלִיעָם אֵשֶׁת אוּרִיָּה הַחִתִּי׃
the-Hittite Uriah wife-of Eliam daughter-of Sheba Bath this not? and-he-said

וַיִּשְׁלַח דָּוִד מַלְאָכִים וַיִּקָּחֶהָ וַתָּבוֹא אֵלָיו
to-him and-she-came and-he-got-her messengers David then-he-sent (4)

וַיִּשְׁכַּב עִמָּהּ וְהִיא מִתְקַדֶּשֶׁת מִטֻּמְאָתָהּ
from-uncleanness-of-her purifying-herself now-she with-her and-he-slept

וַתָּשָׁב אֶל־ בֵּיתָהּ׃ וַתַּהַר הָאִשָּׁה וַתִּשְׁלַח
and-she-sent the-woman and-she-conceived (5) home-of-her to then-she-went-back

וַתַּגֵּד לְדָוִד וַתֹּאמֶר הָרָה אָנֹכִי׃ וַיִּשְׁלַח דָּוִד אֶל־יוֹאָב
Joab to David so-he-sent (6) I pregnant and-she-said to-David and-she-told

שְׁלַח אֵלַי אֶת־ אוּרִיָּה הַחִתִּי וַיִּשְׁלַח יוֹאָב אֶת־ אוּרִיָּה אֶל־ דָּוִד׃
David to Uriah *** Joab and-he-sent the-Hittite Uriah *** to-me send!

their battle lines to meet David and fought against him.
[18]But they fled before Israel,
and David killed seven hundred of their charioteers and
forty thousand of their foot
soldiers.[c] He also struck down
Shobach the commander of
their army, and he died there.
[19]When all the kings who were
vassals of Hadadezer saw that
they had been defeated by Israel, they made peace with the
Israelites and became subject
to them.

So the Arameans were
afraid to help the Ammonites
anymore.

David and Bathsheba

11 In the spring, at the
time when kings go off
to war, David sent Joab out
with the king's men and the
whole Israelite army. They destroyed the Ammonites and
besieged Rabbah. But David
remained in Jerusalem.

[2]One evening David got up
from his bed and walked
around on the roof of the palace. From the roof he saw a
woman bathing. The woman
was very beautiful, [3]and David sent someone to find out
about her. The man said,
"Isn't this Bathsheba, the
daughter of Eliam and the
wife of Uriah the Hittite?"
[4]Then David sent messengers
to get her. She came to him,
and he slept with her. (She
had purified herself from her
uncleanness.) Then[d] she went
back home. [5]The woman conceived and sent word to David, saying, "I am pregnant."

[6]So David sent this word to
Joab: "Send me Uriah the Hittite." And Joab sent him to

[c]18 Some Septuagint manuscripts (see also 1 Chron. 19:18); Hebrew *horsemen*

[d]4 Or *with her. When she purified herself from her uncleanness,*

*1 Some mss have *sheva* under the *mem* and *qamets* under the *lamed* (הַמְּלָא׳); some mss spell the form without *aleph* (לכים–); others have a note about the unnecessary *aleph*.

וַיָּבֹא אוּרִיָּה אֵלָיו וַיִּשְׁאַל דָּוִד לִשְׁלוֹם יוֹאָב
Joab about-welfare-of David then-he-asked to-him Uriah when-he-came (7)

וְלִשְׁלוֹם הָעָם וְלִשְׁלוֹם הַמִּלְחָמָה׃ וַיֹּאמֶר
then-he-said (8) the-war and-about-welfare-of the-people and-about-welfare-of

דָּוִד לְאוּרִיָּה רֵד לְבֵיתְךָ וּרְחַץ רַגְלֶיךָ וַיֵּצֵא
so-he-left feet-of-you and-wash! to-house-of-you go-down! to-Uriah David

אוּרִיָּה מִבֵּית הַמֶּלֶךְ וַתֵּצֵא אַחֲרָיו מַשְׂאַת הַמֶּלֶךְ׃
the-king gift-of after-him and-she-went the-king from-palace-of Uriah

וַיִּשְׁכַּב אוּרִיָּה פֶּתַח בֵּית הַמֶּלֶךְ אֵת כָּל־ עַבְדֵי
servants-of all-of with the-king palace-of entrance-of Uriah but-he-slept (9)

אֲדֹנָיו וְלֹא יָרַד אֶל־ בֵּיתוֹ׃ וַיַּגִּדוּ
when-they-told (10) house-of-him to he-went-down and-not masters-of-him

לְדָוִד לֵאמֹר לֹא־ יָרַד אוּרִיָּה אֶל־ בֵּיתוֹ וַיֹּאמֶר דָּוִד
David then-he-asked home-of-him to Uriah he-went-down not to-say to-David

אֶל־אוּרִיָּה הֲלוֹא מִדֶּרֶךְ אַתָּה בָא מַדּוּעַ לֹא־ יָרַדְתָּ אֶל־ בֵּיתֶךָ׃
home-of-you to you-went-down not why? coming you from-distance not? Uriah to

וַיֹּאמֶר אוּרִיָּה אֶל־ דָּוִד הָאָרוֹן וְיִשְׂרָאֵל וִיהוּדָה יֹשְׁבִים
ones-staying and-Judah and-Israel the-ark David to Uriah and-he-said (11)

בַּסֻּכּוֹת וַאדֹנִי יוֹאָב וְעַבְדֵי אֲדֹנִי עַל־ פְּנֵי
surfaces-of on lord-of-me and-men-of Joab and-master-of-me in-the-tents

הַשָּׂדֶה חֹנִים וַאֲנִי אָבוֹא אֶל־ בֵּיתִי לֶאֱכֹל וְלִשְׁתּוֹת
and-to-drink to-eat house-of-me to could-I-go now-I ones-camping the-field

וְלִשְׁכַּב עִם־ אִשְׁתִּי חַיֶּךָ וְחֵי נַפְשֶׁךָ אִם־ אֶעֱשֶׂה
I-will-do not self-of-you and-life-of life-of-you wife-of-me with and-to-lie

אֶת־ הַדָּבָר הַזֶּה׃ וַיֹּאמֶר דָּוִד אֶל־אוּרִיָּה שֵׁב בָּזֶה גַּם־
also at-here stay! Uriah to David then-he-said (12) the-this the-thing ***

הַיּוֹם וּמָחָר אֲשַׁלְּחֶךָּ וַיֵּשֶׁב אוּרִיָּה בִּירוּשָׁלִַם
in-Jerusalem Uriah so-he-remained I-will-send-back-you and-tomorrow the-day

בַּיּוֹם הַהוּא וּמִמָּחֳרָת׃ וַיִּקְרָא־ לוֹ דָוִד
David to-him and-he-invited (13) and-on-next-day the-that on-the-day

וַיֹּאכַל לְפָנָיו וַיֵּשְׁתְּ וַיְשַׁכְּרֵהוּ וַיֵּצֵא
but-he-went-out and-he-made-drunk-him and-he-drank before-him and-he-ate

בָעֶרֶב לִשְׁכַּב בְּמִשְׁכָּבוֹ עִם־ עַבְדֵי אֲדֹנָיו וְאֶל־
and-to masters-of-him servants-of among on-mat-of-him to-sleep in-the-evening

בֵּיתוֹ לֹא יָרָד׃ וַיְהִי בַבֹּקֶר וַיִּכְתֹּב דָּוִד
David then-he-wrote in-the-morning and-he-was (14) he-went not home-of-him

סֵפֶר אֶל־יוֹאָב וַיִּשְׁלַח בְּיַד אוּרִיָּה׃ וַיִּכְתֹּב בַּסֵּפֶר
in-the-letter and-he-wrote (15) Uriah by-hand-of and-he-sent Joab to letter

David. [7]When Uriah came to
him, David asked him how
Joab was, how the soldiers
were and how the war was going. [8]Then David said to
Uriah, "Go down to your
house and wash your feet." So
Uriah left the palace, and a gift
from the king was sent after
him. [9]But Uriah slept at the entrance to the palace with all
his master's servants and did
not go down to his house.

[10]When David was told,
"Uriah did not go home," he
asked him, "Haven't you just
come from a distance? Why
didn't you go home?"

[11]Uriah said to David, "The
ark and Israel and Judah are
staying in tents, and my master Joab and my lord's men are
camped in the open fields.
How could I go to my house to
eat and drink and lie with my
wife? As surely as you live, I
will not do such a thing!"

[12]Then David said to him,
"Stay here one more day, and
tomorrow I will send you
back." So Uriah remained in
Jerusalem that day and the
next. [13]At David's invitation,
he ate and drank with him,
and David made him drunk.
But in the evening Uriah went
out to sleep on his mat among
his master's servants; he did
not go home.

[14]In the morning David
wrote a letter to Joab and sent
it with Uriah. [15]In it he wrote,

[e]21 Also known as *Jerub-Baal* (that is, Gideon)

לֵאמֹר הָבוּ אֶת־אוּרִיָּה אֶל־ מוּל פְּנֵי הַמִּלְחָמָה הַחֲזָקָה וְשַׁבְתֶּם
then-you-withdraw the-fierce the-battle faces-of front in Uriah *** put! to-say

מֵאַחֲרָיו וְנִכָּה וָמֵת׃ וַיְהִי
and-he-was (16) and-he-will-die so-he-will-be-struck-down from-behind-him

בִּשְׁמוֹר יוֹאָב אֶל־ הָעִיר וַיִּתֵּן אֶת־אוּרִיָּה אֶל־ הַמָּקוֹם
the-place at Uriah *** then-he-put the-city against Joab while-to-besiege

אֲשֶׁר יָדַע כִּי אַנְשֵׁי־ חַיִל שָׁם׃ וַיֵּצְאוּ אַנְשֵׁי
men-of when-they-came-out (17) there strength defenders-of that he-knew where

הָעִיר וַיִּלָּחֲמוּ אֶת־יוֹאָב וַיִּפֹּל מִן־ הָעָם מֵעַבְדֵי דָוִד
David from-men-of the-army from then-he-fell Joab *** and-they-fought the-city

וַיָּמָת גַּם אוּרִיָּה הַחִתִּי׃ וַיִּשְׁלַח יוֹאָב וַיַּגֵּד לְדָוִד
to-David and-he-told Joab and-he-sent (18) the-Hittite Uriah also and-he-died

אֶת־ כָּל־ דִּבְרֵי הַמִּלְחָמָה׃ וַיְצַו אֶת־ הַמַּלְאָךְ
the-messenger *** and-he-instructed (19) the-battle accounts-of all-of ***

לֵאמֹר כְּכַלּוֹתְךָ אֵת כָּל־ דִּבְרֵי הַמִּלְחָמָה לְדַבֵּר אֶל־
to to-tell the-battle accounts-of all-of *** when-to-finish-you to-say

הַמֶּלֶךְ׃ וְהָיָה אִם־ תַּעֲלֶה חֲמַת הַמֶּלֶךְ וְאָמַר
and-he-says the-king anger-of she-flares-up if and-he-will-be (20) the-king

לְךָ מַדּוּעַ נִגַּשְׁתֶּם אֶל־ הָעִיר לְהִלָּחֵם הֲלוֹא יְדַעְתֶּם אֵת אֲשֶׁר־
that *** you-know not? to-fight the-city to you-got-close why? to-you

יֹרוּ מֵעַל הַחוֹמָה׃ מִי־ הִכָּה אֶת־ אֲבִימֶלֶךְ בֶּן־
son-of Abimelech *** he-killed who? (21) the-wall from-on they-shoot

יְרֻבֶּשֶׁת הֲלוֹא־אִשָּׁה הִשְׁלִיכָה עָלָיו פֶּלַח רֶכֶב מֵעַל הַחוֹמָה
the-wall from-on millstone half-of on-him she-threw woman not? Jerub-Besheth

וַיָּמָת בְּתֵבֵץ לָמָּה נִגַּשְׁתֶּם אֶל־ הַחוֹמָה וְאָמַרְתָּ גַּם
also then-you-say the-wall to you-got-close why? in-Thebez so-he-died

עַבְדְּךָ אוּרִיָּה הַחִתִּי מֵת׃ וַיֵּלֶךְ הַמַּלְאָךְ
the-messenger so-he-set-out (22) he-is-dead the-Hittite Uriah servant-of-you

וַיָּבֹא וַיַּגֵּד לְדָוִד אֵת כָּל־ אֲשֶׁר שְׁלָחוֹ יוֹאָב׃
Joab he-sent-him that all *** to-David then-he-told when-he-arrived

וַיֹּאמֶר הַמַּלְאָךְ אֶל־ דָּוִד כִּי־ גָבְרוּ עָלֵינוּ
over-us they-overpowered indeed David to the-messenger and-he-said (23)

הָאֲנָשִׁים וַיֵּצְאוּ אֵלֵינוּ הַשָּׂדֶה וַנִּהְיֶה עֲלֵיהֶם עַד־
to upon-them but-we-were the-open against-us and-they-came-out the-men

פֶּתַח הַשָּׁעַר׃ וַיֹּרְאוּ הַמּוֹרְאִים אֶל־
at the-ones-being-archers then-they-shot (24) the-gate entrance-of

עֲבָדֶךָ מֵעַל הַחוֹמָה וַיָּמוּתוּ מֵעַבְדֵי הַמֶּלֶךְ וְגַם
and-also the-king from-men-of and-they-died the-wall from-on servant-of-you

"Put Uriah in the front line where the fighting is fiercest. Then withdraw from him so he will be struck down and die."

[16]So while Joab had the city under siege, he put Uriah at a place where he knew the strongest defenders were. [17]When the men of the city came out and fought against Joab, some of the men in David's army fell; moreover, Uriah the Hittite was dead.

[18]Joab sent David a full account of the battle. [19]He instructed the messenger: "When you have finished giving the king this account of the battle, [20]the king's anger may flare up, and he may ask you, 'Why did you get so close to the city to fight? Didn't you know they would shoot arrows from the wall? [21]Who killed Abimelech son of Jerub-Besheth[c]? Didn't a woman throw an upper millstone on him from the wall, so that he died in Thebez? Why did you get so close to the wall?' If he asks you this, then say to him, 'Also, your servant Uriah the Hittite is dead.' "

[22]The messenger set out, and when he arrived he told David everything Joab had sent him to say. [23]The messenger said to David, "The men overpowered us and came out against us in the open, but we drove them back to the entrance to the city gate. [24]Then the archers shot arrows at your servants from the wall, and some

°24a ק וירו
°24b ק המורים

עַבְדְּךָ אוּרִיָּה הַחִתִּי מֵת׃ וַיֹּאמֶר דָּוִד אֶל־
to David and-he-told (25) he-is-dead the-Hittite Uriah servant-of-you

הַמַּלְאָךְ כֹּה־ תֹאמַר אֶל־ יוֹאָב אַל־ יֵרַע בְּעֵינֶיךָ אֶת־
*** in-eyes-of-you let-him-be-evil not Joab to you-say this the-messenger

הַדָּבָר הַזֶּה כִּי־ כָזֹה וְכָזֶה תֹּאכַל הֶחָרֶב
the-sword she-devours so-as-that-one as-this-one for the-this the-thing

הַחֲזֵק מִלְחַמְתְּךָ אֶל־ הָעִיר וְהָרְסָהּ וְחַזְּקֵהוּ׃
so-encourage-him! and-destroy-her! the-city against attack-of-you press!

וַתִּשְׁמַע אֵשֶׁת אוּרִיָּה כִּי־ מֵת אוּרִיָּה אִישָׁהּ
husband-of-her Uriah he-was-dead that Uriah wife-of when-she-heard (26)

וַתִּסְפֹּד עַל־ בַּעְלָהּ׃ וַיַּעֲבֹר הָאֵבֶל
the-mourning-time when-he-was-over (27) husband-of-her for then-she-mourned

וַיִּשְׁלַח דָּוִד וַיַּאַסְפָהּ אֶל־ בֵּיתוֹ וַתְּהִי־
and-she-became house-of-him to and-he-had-brought-her David then-he-sent

לוֹ לְאִשָּׁה וַתֵּלֶד לוֹ בֵּן וַיֵּרַע הַדָּבָר אֲשֶׁר־
that the-thing but-he-was-displeasing son to-him and-she-bore as-wife to-him

עָשָׂה דָוִד בְּעֵינֵי יְהוָה׃ וַיִּשְׁלַח יְהוָה אֶת־ נָתָן אֶל־ דָּוִד
David to Nathan *** Yahweh and-he-sent (12:1) Yahweh in-eyes-of David he-did

וַיָּבֹא אֵלָיו וַיֹּאמֶר לוֹ שְׁנֵי אֲנָשִׁים הָיוּ בְּעִיר אֶחָת
certain in-town they-were men two-of to-him then-he-said to-him when-he-came

אֶחָד עָשִׁיר וְאֶחָד רָאשׁ׃ לְעָשִׁיר הָיָה צֹאן וּבָקָר הַרְבֵּה
to-be-many and-cattle sheep he-was to-rich (2) being-poor and-other rich one

מְאֹד׃ וְלָרָשׁ אֵין־ כֹּל כִּי אִם־ כִּבְשָׂה אַחַת קְטַנָּה
little one ewe-lamb except only anything not but-to-the-being-poor (3) very

אֲשֶׁר קָנָה וַיְחַיֶּהָ וַתִּגְדַּל עִמּוֹ וְעִם־
and-with with-him and-she-grew-up and-he-raised-her he-bought that

בָּנָיו יַחְדָּו מִפִּתּוֹ תֹאכַל וּמִכֹּסוֹ
and-from-cup-of-him she-ate from-food-of-him together children-of-him

תִשְׁתֶּה וּבְחֵיקוֹ תִשְׁכָּב וַתְּהִי־ לוֹ כְּבַת׃
like-daughter to-him and-she-was she-slept and-on-chest-of-him she-drank

וַיָּבֹא הֵלֶךְ לְאִישׁ הֶעָשִׁיר וַיַּחְמֹל לָקַחַת
to-take but-he-refrained the-rich to-man traveller now-he-came (4)

מִצֹּאנוֹ וּמִבְּקָרוֹ לַעֲשׂוֹת לָאֹרֵחַ
for-the-one-travelling to-prepare or-from-cattle-of-him from-sheep-of-him

הַבָּא־ לוֹ וַיִּקַּח אֶת־ כִּבְשַׂת הָאִישׁ הָרָאשׁ
the-one-being-poor the-man ewe-lamb-of *** so-he-took to-him the-one-coming

וַיַּעֲשֶׂהָ לָאִישׁ הַבָּא אֵלָיו׃ וַיִּחַר־
and-he-burned (5) to-him the-one-coming for-the-man and-he-prepared-her

of the king's men died. Moreover, your servant Uriah the
Hittite is dead."

[25]David told the messenger,
"Say this to Joab: 'Don't let
this upset you; the sword de-
vours one as well as another.
Press the attack against the
city and destroy it.' Say this to
encourage Joab."

[26]When Uriah's wife heard
that her husband was dead,
she mourned for him. [27]After
the time of mourning was
over, David had her brought
to his house, and she became
his wife and bore him a son.
But the thing David had done
displeased the LORD.

Nathan Rebukes David

12 The LORD sent Nathan
to David. When he
came to him, he said, "There
were two men in a certain
town, one rich and the other
poor. [2]The rich man had a very
large number of sheep and cattle, [3]but the poor man had
nothing except one little ewe
lamb he had bought. He raised
it, and it grew up with him
and his children. It shared his
food, drank from his cup and
even slept in his arms. It was
like a daughter to him.

[4]"Now a traveler came to the
rich man, but the rich man re-
frained from taking one of his
own sheep or cattle to prepare
a meal for the traveler who
had come to him. Instead, he
took the ewe lamb that belonged to the poor man and
prepared it for the one who
had come to him."

אַף דָּוִד בָּאִישׁ מְאֹד וַיֹּאמֶר אֶל־ נָתָן חַי־ יְהוָה
Yahweh life-of Nathan to and-he-said very against-the-man David anger-of

כִּי בֶן־ מָוֶת הָאִישׁ הָעֹשֶׂה זֹאת׃ וְאֶת־הַכִּבְשָׂה יְשַׁלֵּם
he-must-pay-for the-lamb and (6) this the-one-doing the-man death son-of indeed

אַרְבַּעְתָּיִם עֵקֶב אֲשֶׁר עָשָׂה אֶת־ הַדָּבָר הַזֶּה וְעַל אֲשֶׁר לֹא־
not that and-because the-this the-thing *** he-did that because four-times

חָמָל׃ וַיֹּאמֶר נָתָן אֶל־ דָּוִד אַתָּה הָאִישׁ כֹּה־ אָמַר יְהוָה
Yahweh he-says this the-man you David to Nathan then-he-said (7) he-had-pity

אֱלֹהֵי יִשְׂרָאֵל אָנֹכִי מְשַׁחְתִּיךָ לְמֶלֶךְ עַל־ יִשְׂרָאֵל וְאָנֹכִי הִצַּלְתִּיךָ
I-delivered-you and-I Israel over as-king I-anointed-you I Israel God-of

מִיַּד שָׁאוּל׃ וָאֶתְּנָה לְךָ אֶת־ בֵּית אֲדֹנֶיךָ וְאֶת־
and masters-of-you house-of *** to-you and-I-gave (8) Saul from-hand-of

נְשֵׁי אֲדֹנֶיךָ בְּחֵיקֶךָ וָאֶתְּנָה לְךָ אֶת־ בֵּית יִשְׂרָאֵל
Israel house-of *** to-you and-I-gave into-arm-of-you masters-of-you wives-of

וִיהוּדָה וְאִם־ מְעָט וְאֹסִפָה לְּךָ כָּהֵנָּה וְכָהֵנָּה׃
and-as-those as-these to-you then-I-would-give too-little and-if and-Judah

מַדּוּעַ בָּזִיתָ ׀ אֶת־ דְּבַר יְהוָה לַעֲשׂוֹת הָרַע בְּעֵינָו אֵת
*** in-eyes-of-me the-evil to-do Yahweh word-of *** you-despised why? (9)

אוּרִיָּה הַחִתִּי הִכִּיתָ בַחֶרֶב וְאֶת־ אִשְׁתּוֹ לָקַחְתָּ
you-took wife-of-him and with-the-sword you-struck-down the-Hittite Uriah

לְּךָ לְאִשָּׁה וְאֹתוֹ הָרַגְתָּ בְּחֶרֶב בְּנֵי עַמּוֹן׃ וְעַתָּה
so-now (10) Ammon sons-of with-sword-of you-killed and-him as-wife for-you

לֹא־ תָסוּר חֶרֶב מִבֵּיתְךָ עַד־ עוֹלָם עֵקֶב כִּי
that because forever to from-house-of-you sword she-will-depart not

בְזִתָנִי וַתִּקַּח אֶת־ אֵשֶׁת אוּרִיָּה הַחִתִּי לִהְיוֹת לְךָ
for-you to-be the-Hittite Uriah wife-of *** and-you-took you-despised-me

לְאִשָּׁה׃ כֹּה ׀ אָמַר יְהוָה הִנְנִי מֵקִים עָלֶיךָ רָעָה
calamity on-you bringing see-I! Yahweh he-says this (11) as-wife

מִבֵּיתֶךָ וְלָקַחְתִּי אֶת־ נָשֶׁיךָ לְעֵינֶיךָ
before-eyes-of-you wives-of-you *** and-I-will-take from-household-of-you

וְנָתַתִּי לְרֵעֶיךָ וְשָׁכַב עִם־ נָשֶׁיךָ
wives-of-you with and-he-will-lie to-one-close-of-you and-I-will-give

לְעֵינֵי הַשֶּׁמֶשׁ הַזֹּאת׃ כִּי אַתָּה עָשִׂיתָ בַסָּתֶר וַאֲנִי
but-I in-the-secret you-did you indeed (12) the-this the-sun before-eyes-of

אֶעֱשֶׂה אֶת־ הַדָּבָר הַזֶּה נֶגֶד כָּל־ יִשְׂרָאֵל וְנֶגֶד הַשָּׁמֶשׁ׃
the-sun and-before Israel all-of before the-this the-thing *** I-will-do

וַיֹּאמֶר דָּוִד אֶל־ נָתָן חָטָאתִי לַיהוָה וַיֹּאמֶר
and-he-replied against-Yahweh I-sinned Nathan to David then-he-said (13)

5 David burned with anger against the man and said to Nathan, "As surely as the LORD lives, the man who did this deserves to die! 6 He must pay for that lamb four times over, because he did such a thing and had no pity."

7 Then Nathan said to David, "You are the man! This is what the LORD, the God of Israel, says: 'I anointed you king over Israel, and I delivered you from the hand of Saul. 8 I gave your master's house to you, and your master's wives into your arms. I gave you the house of Israel and Judah. And if all this had been too little, I would have given you even more. 9 Why did you despise the word of the LORD by doing what is evil in his eyes? You struck down Uriah the Hittite with the sword and took his wife to be your own. You killed him with the sword of the Ammonites. 10 Now, therefore, the sword will never depart from your house, because you despised me and took the wife of Uriah the Hittite to be your own.'

11 "This is what the LORD says: 'Out of your own household I am going to bring calamity upon you. Before your very eyes I will take your wives and give them to one who is close to you, and he will lie with your wives in broad daylight. 12 You did it in secret, but I will do this thing in broad daylight before all Israel.'"

13 Then David said to Nathan, "I have sinned against the LORD."

°9 ק בעיני

נָתָן אֶל־דָּוִד גַּם־יְהוָה הֶעֱבִיר חַטָּאתְךָ לֹא תָמוּת׃ אֶפֶס
but (14) you-will-die not sin-of-you he-took-away Yahweh also David to Nathan

כִּי־נִאֵץ נִאַצְתָּ אֶת־אֹיְבֵי
being-enemies-of *** you-made-show-contempt to-make-show-contempt because

יְהוָה בַּדָּבָר הַזֶּה גַּם הַבֵּן הַיִּלּוֹד לְךָ מוֹת
to-die to-you the-one-born the-son indeed the-this by-the-thing Yahweh

יָמוּת׃ וַיֵּלֶךְ נָתָן אֶל־בֵּיתוֹ וַיִּגֹּף יְהוָה
Yahweh then-he-struck home-of-him to Nathan after-he-went (15) he-will-die

אֶת־הַיֶּלֶד אֲשֶׁר יָלְדָה אֵשֶׁת־אוּרִיָּה לְדָוִד וַיֵּאָנַשׁ׃
and-he-became-ill to-David Uriah wife-of she-bore whom the-child ***

וַיְבַקֵּשׁ דָּוִד אֶת־הָאֱלֹהִים בְּעַד הַנָּעַר וַיָּצָם דָּוִד
David and-he-fasted the-child for the-God with David and-he-pleaded (16)

צוֹם וּבָא וְלָן וְשָׁכַב אָרְצָה׃ וַיָּקֻמוּ
and-they-stood (17) on-ground and-he-lay and-he-spent-night and-he-went fast

זִקְנֵי בֵיתוֹ עָלָיו לַהֲקִימוֹ מִן־הָאָרֶץ וְלֹא
but-not the-ground from to-get-up-him beside-him household-of-him elders-of

אָבָה וְלֹא־בָרָא אִתָּם לָחֶם׃ וַיְהִי בַּיּוֹם הַשְּׁבִיעִי
the-seventh on-the-day and-he-was (18) food with-them he-ate and-not he-would

וַיָּמָת הַיֶּלֶד וַיִּרְאוּ עַבְדֵי דָוִד לְהַגִּיד לוֹ ׀
to-him to-tell David servants-of and-they-were-afraid the-child then-he-died

כִּי־מֵת הַיֶּלֶד כִּי אָמְרוּ הִנֵּה בִהְיוֹת הַיֶּלֶד חַי
alive the-child while-to-be see! they-thought for the-child he-was-dead that

דִּבַּרְנוּ אֵלָיו וְלֹא־שָׁמַע בְּקוֹלֵנוּ וְאֵיךְ נֹאמַר
can-we-tell so-how? to-voice-of-us he-listened but-not to-him we-spoke

אֵלָיו מֵת הַיֶּלֶד וְעָשָׂה רָעָה׃ וַיַּרְא
and-he-noticed (19) desperate-thing for-he-may-do the-child he-is-dead to-him

דָּוִד כִּי עֲבָדָיו מִתְלַחֲשִׁים וַיָּבֶן דָּוִד כִּי
that David and-he-realized ones-whispering servants-of-him that David

מֵת הַיֶּלֶד וַיֹּאמֶר דָּוִד אֶל־עֲבָדָיו הֲמֵת
is-he-dead? servants-of-him to David so-he-asked the-child he-was-dead

הַיֶּלֶד וַיֹּאמְרוּ מֵת׃ וַיָּקָם דָּוִד מֵהָאָרֶץ
from-the-ground David then-he-got-up (20) he-is-dead and-they-replied the-child

וַיִּרְחַץ וַיָּסֶךְ וַיְחַלֵּף שִׂמְלֹתָו וַיָּבֹא
and-he-went clothes-of-him and-he-changed and-he-put-on-lotion and-he-washed

בֵּית־יְהוָה וַיִּשְׁתָּחוּ וַיָּבֹא אֶל־בֵּיתוֹ וַיִּשְׁאַל
and-he-requested house-of-him to then-he-went and-he-worshiped Yahweh house-of

וַיָּשִׂימוּ לוֹ לֶחֶם וַיֹּאכַל׃ וַיֹּאמְרוּ עֲבָדָיו
servants-of-him and-they-asked (21) and-he-ate food to-him and-they-served

Nathan replied, "The LORD
has taken away your sin. You
are not going to die. [14]But because by doing this you have
made the enemies of the LORD
show utter contempt,[f] the son
born to you will die."
[15]After Nathan had gone
home, the LORD struck the
child that Uriah's wife had
borne to David, and he
became ill. [16]David pleaded
with God for the child. He
fasted and went into his house
and spent the nights lying on
the ground. [17]The elders of his
household stood beside him to
get him up from the ground,
but he refused, and he would
not eat any food with them.
[18]On the seventh day the
child died. David's servants
were afraid to tell him that the
child was dead, for they
thought, "While the child was
still living, we spoke to David
but he would not listen to us.
How can we tell him the child
is dead? He may do something
desperate."
[19]David noticed that his servants were whispering among
themselves and he realized the
child was dead. "Is the child
dead?" he asked.
"Yes," they replied, "he is
dead."
[20]Then David got up from
the ground. After he had
washed, put on lotions and
changed his clothes, he went
into the house of the LORD and
worshiped. Then he went to
his own house, and at his request they served him food,
and he ate.
[21]His servants asked him,

[f]14 Masoretic Text; an ancient Hebrew scribal tradition *this you have shown utter contempt for the LORD*

°20 ק שמלתיו

אֵלָיו מֶה־ הַדָּבָר הַזֶּה אֲשֶׁר עָשִׂיתָה בַּעֲבוּר הַיֶּלֶד חַי
alive the-child for-sake-of you-act that the-this the-way why? to-him

צַמְתָּ וַתֵּבְךְּ וְכַאֲשֶׁר מֵת הַיֶּלֶד קַמְתָּ וַתֹּאכַל
and-you-eat you-get-up the-child he-is-dead but-just-as and-you-wept you-fasted

לָחֶם׃ וַיֹּאמֶר בְּעוֹד הַיֶּלֶד חַי צַמְתִּי וָאֶבְכֶּה כִּי
for and-I-wept I-fasted alive the-child while-still and-he-answered (22) food

אָמַרְתִּי מִי יוֹדֵעַ יְחַנַּנִי° יְהוָה וְחַי
and-he-may-live Yahweh now-he-may-be-gracious-to-me knowing who? I-thought

הַיָּלֶד׃ וְעַתָּה ׀ מֵת לָמָּה זֶּה אֲנִי צָם הַאוּכַל לַהֲשִׁיבוֹ
to-bring-back-him can-I? fasting I then why? he-is-dead but-now (23) the-child

עוֹד אֲנִי הֹלֵךְ אֵלָיו וְהוּא לֹא־ יָשׁוּב אֵלָי׃ וַיְנַחֵם
then-he-comforted (24) to-me he-will-return not but-he to-him going I again

דָּוִד אֵת בַּת־ שֶׁבַע אִשְׁתּוֹ וַיָּבֹא אֵלֶיהָ וַיִּשְׁכַּב עִמָּהּ
with-her and-he-lay to-her and-he-went wife-of-him Sheba Bath *** David

וַתֵּלֶד בֵּן וַיִּקְרָא° אֶת־ שְׁמוֹ שְׁלֹמֹה וַיהוָה
and-Yahweh Solomon name-of-him *** and-she-called son and-she-bore

אֲהֵבוֹ׃ וַיִּשְׁלַח בְּיַד נָתָן הַנָּבִיא וַיִּקְרָא אֶת־
*** and-he-called the-prophet Nathan by-hand-of so-he-sent (25) he-loved-him

שְׁמוֹ יְדִידְיָהּ בַּעֲבוּר יְהוָה׃ וַיִּלָּחֶם יוֹאָב בְּרַבַּת
against-Rabbah-of Joab now-he-fought (26) Yahweh because-of Jedidiah name-of-him

בְּנֵי עַמּוֹן וַיִּלְכֹּד אֶת־ עִיר הַמְּלוּכָה׃ וַיִּשְׁלַח
then-he-sent (27) the-royal citadel-of *** and-he-captured Ammon sons-of

יוֹאָב מַלְאָכִים אֶל־דָּוִד וַיֹּאמֶר נִלְחַמְתִּי בְרַבָּה גַּם־ לָכַדְתִּי אֶת־
*** I-took also against-Rabbah I-fought and-he-said David to messengers Joab

עִיר הַמָּיִם׃ וְעַתָּה אֱסֹף אֶת־ יֶתֶר הָעָם וַחֲנֵה
and-besiege! the-troop rest-of *** muster! and-now (28) the-waters city-of

עַל־ הָעִיר וְלָכְדָהּ פֶּן־ אֶלְכֹּד אֲנִי אֶת־ הָעִיר
the-city *** I I-will-take otherwise and-capture-her! the-city against

וְנִקְרָא שְׁמִי עָלֶיהָ׃ וַיֶּאֱסֹף דָּוִד אֶת־ כָּל־
entire-of *** David so-he-mustered (29) to-her name-of-me and-he-will-be-called

הָעָם וַיֵּלֶךְ רַבָּתָה וַיִּלָּחֶם בָּהּ וַיִּלְכְּדָהּ׃
and-he-captured-her against-her and-he-attacked to-Rabbah and-he-went the-army

וַיִּקַּח אֶת־ עֲטֶרֶת־ מַלְכָּם מֵעַל רֹאשׁוֹ
head-of-him from-on king-of-them crown-of *** and-he-took (30)

וּמִשְׁקָלָהּ כִּכַּר זָהָב וְאֶבֶן יְקָרָה וַתְּהִי עַל־ רֹאשׁ
head-of on and-she-was precious and-stone gold talent-of and-weight-of-her

דָּוִד וּשְׁלַל הָעִיר הוֹצִיא הַרְבֵּה מְאֹד׃ וְאֶת־ הָעָם
the-people and (31) very to-be-great he-took the-city and-plunder-of David

"Why are you acting this way? While the child was alive, you fasted and wept, but now that the child is dead, you get up and eat!"

22He answered, "While the child was still alive, I fasted and wept. I thought, 'Who knows? The LORD may be gracious to me and let the child live.'
23But now that he is dead, why should I fast? Can I bring him back again? I will go to him, but he will not return to me."

24Then David comforted his wife Bathsheba, and he went to her and lay with her. She gave birth to a son, and they named him Solomon. The LORD loved him;
25and because the LORD loved him, he sent word through Nathan the prophet to name him Jedidiah.[g]

26Meanwhile Joab fought against Rabbah of the Ammonites and captured the royal citadel.
27Joab then sent messengers to David, saying, "I have fought against Rabbah and taken its water supply.
28Now muster the rest of the troops and besiege the city and capture it. Otherwise I will take the city, and it will be named after me."

29So David mustered the entire army and went to Rabbah, and attacked and captured it.
30He took the crown from the head of their king[h]—its weight was a talent[i] of gold, and it was set with precious stones—and it was placed on David's head. He took a great quantity of plunder from the city
31and

g25 *Jedidiah* means *loved by the LORD.*
h30 Or *of Milcom* (that is, Molech)
i30 That is, about 75 pounds (about 34 kilograms)

°22 ק וחנני
°24 ק ותקרא

אֲשֶׁר־ בָּהּ הוֹצִיא וַיָּשֶׂם בַּמְּגֵרָה וּבַחֲרִצֵי
and-to-picks-of to-the-saw and-he-consigned he-brought-out in-her who

הַבַּרְזֶל וּבְמַגְזְרֹת הַבַּרְזֶל וְהֶעֱבִיר אוֹתָם בַּמַּלְכֵּן
at-the-brickmaking them and-he-made-work the-iron and-to-axes-of the-iron

וְכֵן יַעֲשֶׂה לְכֹל עָרֵי בְנֵי־ עַמּוֹן וַיָּשָׁב דָּוִד
David then-he-returned Ammon sons-of towns-of to-all-of he-did and-this

וְכָל־ הָעָם יְרוּשָׁלִָם׃ וַיְהִי אַחֲרֵי־ כֵן וּלְאַבְשָׁלוֹם
that-to-Absalom this after and-he-was (13:1) Jerusalem the-army and-entire-of

בֶּן־ דָּוִד אָחוֹת יָפָה וּשְׁמָהּ תָּמָר וַיֶּאֱהָבֶהָ אַמְנוֹן
Amnon and-he-loved-her Tamar and-name-of-her beautiful sister David son-of

בֶּן־ דָּוִד׃ וַיֵּצֶר לְאַמְנוֹן לְהִתְחַלּוֹת בַּעֲבוּר
an-account-of to-be-ill to-Amnon and-he-became-frustrating (2) David son-of

תָּמָר אֲחֹתוֹ כִּי בְתוּלָה הִיא וַיִּפָּלֵא בְּעֵינֵי אַמְנוֹן
Amnon in-eyes-of and-he-was-impossible she virgin for sister-of-him Tamar

לַעֲשׂוֹת לָהּ מְאוּמָה׃ וּלְאַמְנוֹן רֵעַ וּשְׁמוֹ יוֹנָדָב בֶּן־
son-of Jonadab and-name-of-him friend now-to-Amnon (3) anything to-her to-do

שִׁמְעָה אֲחִי דָוִד וְיוֹנָדָב אִישׁ חָכָם מְאֹד׃ וַיֹּאמֶר לוֹ
to-him and-he-asked (4) very shrewd man now-Jonadab David brother-of Shimeah

מַדּוּעַ אַתָּה כָּכָה דַּל בֶּן־ הַמֶּלֶךְ בַּבֹּקֶר בַּבֹּקֶר הֲלוֹא
not? in-the-morning in-the-morning the-king son-of haggard so you why?

תַּגִּיד לִי וַיֹּאמֶר לוֹ אַמְנוֹן אֶת־ תָּמָר אֲחוֹת אַבְשָׁלֹם
Absalom sister-of Tamar *** Amnon to-him and-he-said to-me you-tell

אָחִי אֲנִי אֹהֵב׃ וַיֹּאמֶר לוֹ יְהוֹנָדָב שְׁכַב עַל־ מִשְׁכָּבְךָ
bed-of-you in lie! Jonadab to-him and-he-said (5) loving I brother-of-me

וְהִתְחָל וּבָא אָבִיךָ לִרְאוֹתֶךָ וְאָמַרְתָּ אֵלָיו
to him then-you-say to-see-you father-of-you when-he-comes and-act-ill!

תָּבֹא נָא תָמָר אֲחוֹתִי וְתַבְרֵנִי לֶחֶם
food and-let-her-feed-me sister-of-me Tamar now! let-her-come

וְעָשְׂתָה לְעֵינַי אֶת־ הַבִּרְיָה לְמַעַן אֲשֶׁר אֶרְאֶה
I-may-watch *** so-that the-food *** before-eyes-of-me and-let-her-prepare

וְאָכַלְתִּי מִיָּדָהּ׃ וַיִּשְׁכַּב אַמְנוֹן וַיִּתְחָל
and-he-acted-ill Amnon so-he-lay-down (6) from-hand-of-her then-I-may-eat

וַיָּבֹא הַמֶּלֶךְ לִרְאֹתוֹ וַיֹּאמֶר אַמְנוֹן אֶל־ הַמֶּלֶךְ תָּבוֹא־
let-her-come the-king to Amnon then-he-said to-see-him the-king when-he-came

נָא תָמָר אֲחֹתִי וּתְלַבֵּב לְעֵינַי שְׁתֵּי
two-of before-eyes-of-me and-let-her-make-bread sister-of-me Tamar now!

לְבִבוֹת וְאֶבְרֶה מִיָּדָהּ׃ וַיִּשְׁלַח דָּוִד אֶל־ תָּמָר
Tamar to David so-he-sent (7) from-hand-of-her so-I-may-eat breads

brought out the people who were there, consigning them to labor with saws and with iron picks and axes, and he made them work at brickmaking.[k] He did this to all the Ammonite towns. Then David and his entire army returned to Jerusalem.

Amnon and Tamar

13 In the course of time, Amnon son of David fell in love with Tamar, the beautiful sister of Absalom son of David.
[2]Amnon became frustrated to the point of illness on account of his sister Tamar, for she was a virgin, and it seemed impossible for him to do anything to her.
[3]Now Amnon had a friend named Jonadab son of Shimeah, David's brother. Jonadab was a very shrewd man. [4]He asked Amnon, "Why do you, the king's son, look so haggard morning after morning? Won't you tell me?"
Amnon said to him, "I'm in love with Tamar, my brother Absalom's sister."
[5]"Go to bed and pretend to be ill," Jonadab said. "When your father comes to see you, say to him, 'I would like my sister Tamar to come and give me something to eat. Let her prepare the food in my sight so I may watch her and then eat it from her hand.' "
[6]So Amnon lay down and pretended to be ill. When the king came to see him, Amnon said to him, "I would like my sister Tamar to come and make some special bread in my sight, so I may eat from her hand."
[7]David sent word to Tamar

[k]31 The meaning of the Hebrew for this clause is uncertain.

°31 ק במלבן

הַבַּיְתָה לֵאמֹר לְכִי נָא בֵּית אַמְנוֹן אָחִיךְ וַעֲשִׂי־
and-prepare! brother-of-you Amnon house-of now! go! to-say at-the-palace

לוֹ הַבִּרְיָה׃ וַתֵּלֶךְ תָּמָר בֵּית אַמְנוֹן אָחִיהָ וְהוּא
and-he brother-of-her Amnon house-of Tamar so-she-went (8) the-food for-him

שֹׁכֵב וַתִּקַּח אֶת־ הַבָּצֵק וַתָּלוֹשׁ וַתְּלַבֵּב
and-she-made-bread and-she-kneaded the-dough *** and-she-took lying-down

לְעֵינָיו וַתְּבַשֵּׁל אֶת־הַלְּבִבוֹת׃ וַתִּקַּח אֶת־ הַמַּשְׂרֵת
the-pan *** then-she-took (9) the-breads *** and-she-baked before-eyes-of-him

וַתִּצֹק לְפָנָיו וַיְמָאֵן לֶאֱכוֹל וַיֹּאמֶר אַמְנוֹן הוֹצִיאוּ
send-out! Amnon and-he-said to-eat but-he-refused before-him and-she-served

כָל־ אִישׁ מֵעָלַי וַיֵּצְאוּ כָל־ אִישׁ מֵעָלָיו׃
from-with-him person every-of so-they-left from-with-me person every-of

וַיֹּאמֶר אַמְנוֹן אֶל־ תָּמָר הָבִיאִי הַבִּרְיָה הַחֶדֶר וְאֶבְרֶה
so-I-may-eat the-bedroom the-food bring! Tamar to Amnon then-he-said (10)

מִיָּדֵךְ וַתִּקַּח תָּמָר אֶת־ הַלְּבִבוֹת אֲשֶׁר עָשָׂתָה
she-prepared that the-breads *** Tamar and-she-took from-hand-of-you

וַתָּבֵא לְאַמְנוֹן אָחִיהָ הֶחָדְרָה׃ וַתַּגֵּשׁ
when-she-took (11) in-the-bedroom brother-of-her to-Amnon and-she-brought

אֵלָיו לֶאֱכֹל וַיַּחֲזֶק־ בָּהּ וַיֹּאמֶר לָהּ בּוֹאִי שִׁכְבִי
come-to-bed! come! to-her and-he-said onto-her then-he-grabbed to-eat to-him

עִמִּי אֲחוֹתִי׃ וַתֹּאמֶר לוֹ אַל־ אָחִי אַל־
not brother-of-me no to-him and-she-said (12) sister-of-me with-me

תְּעַנֵּנִי כִּי לֹא־ יֵעָשֶׂה כֵן בְּיִשְׂרָאֵל אַל־ תַּעֲשֵׂה אֶת־
*** you-do not in-Israel such he-should-be-done not for you-force-me

הַנְּבָלָה הַזֹּאת׃ וַאֲנִי אָנָה אוֹלִיךְ אֶת־ חֶרְפָּתִי
disgrace-of-me *** could-I-get-rid where? and-I (13) the-this the-wicked-thing

וְאַתָּה תִּהְיֶה כְּאַחַד הַנְּבָלִים בְּיִשְׂרָאֵל וְעַתָּה דַּבֶּר־
speak! so-now in-Israel the-wicked-fools like-one-of you-would-be and-you

נָא אֶל־הַמֶּלֶךְ כִּי לֹא יִמְנָעֵנִי מִמֶּךָּ׃ וְלֹא אָבָה
he-wanted but-not (14) from-you he-will-keep-me not for the-king to now!

לִשְׁמֹעַ בְּקוֹלָהּ וַיֶּחֱזַק מִמֶּנָּה וַיְעַנֶּהָ
and-he-raped-her than-her and-he-was-stronger to-voice-of-her to-listen

וַיִּשְׁכַּב אֹתָהּ׃ וַיִּשְׂנָאֶהָ אַמְנוֹן שִׂנְאָה גְּדוֹלָה מְאֹד כִּי
in-fact very intense hatred Amnon then-he-hated-her (15) her and-he-lay-with

גְדוֹלָה הַשִּׂנְאָה אֲשֶׁר שְׂנֵאָהּ מֵאַהֲבָה אֲשֶׁר אֲהֵבָהּ
he-loved-her which than-love he-hated-her which the-hatred greater

וַיֹּאמֶר־ לָהּ אַמְנוֹן קוּמִי לֵכִי׃ וַתֹּאמֶר לוֹ אַל־
no to-him and-she-said (16) get-out! get-up! Amnon to-her and-he-said

at the palace: "Go to the house
of your brother Amnon and
prepare some food for him."
8So Tamar went to the house
of her brother Amnon, who
was lying down. She took
some dough, kneaded it, made
the bread in his sight and
baked it. 9Then she took the
pan and served him the bread,
but he refused to eat.

"Send everyone out of
here," Amnon said. So everyone left him. 10Then Amnon
said to Tamar, "Bring the food
here into my bedroom so I
may eat from your hand."
And Tamar took the bread she
had prepared and brought it to
her brother Amnon in his
bedroom. 11But when she took
it to him to eat, he grabbed her
and said, "Come to bed with
me, my sister."

12"Don't, my brother!" she
said to him. "Don't force me.
Such a thing should not be
done in Israel! Don't do this
wicked thing. 13What about
me? Where could I get rid of
my disgrace? And what about
you? You would be like one of
the wicked fools in Israel.
Please speak to the king; he
will not keep me from being
married to you." 14But he
refused to listen to her, and
since he was stronger than
she, he raped her.

15Then Amnon hated her
with intense hatred. In fact,
he hated her more than he had
loved her. Amnon said to her,
"Get up and get out!"

16"No!" she said to him.

°8 ק ותלש

אוֹדֹת הָרָעָה הַגְּדוֹלָה הַזֹּאת מֵאַחֶרֶת אֲשֶׁר־עָשִׂיתָ עִמִּי
to-me you-did that more-than-other the-this the-great the-wrong causes-of

לְשַׁלְּחֵנִי וְלֹא אָבָה לִשְׁמֹעַ לָהּ׃ וַיִּקְרָא אֶת־
*** and-he-called (17) to-her to-listen he-wanted but-not to-send-away-me

נַעֲרוֹ מְשָׁרְתוֹ וַיֹּאמֶר שִׁלְחוּ־נָא אֶת־זֹאת
this-woman *** now! send-out! and-he-said one-attending-him servant-of-him

מֵעָלַי הַחוּצָה וּנְעֹל הַדֶּלֶת אַחֲרֶיהָ׃ וְעָלֶיהָ
now-on-her (18) after-her the-door and-bolt! to-the-outside from-with-me

כְּתֹנֶת פַּסִּים כִּי כֵן תִּלְבַּשְׁןָ בְנוֹת־הַמֶּלֶךְ הַבְּתוּלֹת
the-virgins the-king daughters-of they-wore this for ornaments robe-of

מְעִילִים וַיֹּצֵא אוֹתָהּ מְשָׁרְתוֹ הַחוּץ וְנָעַל
and-he-bolted the-outside one-attending-him her and-he-put-out garments

הַדֶּלֶת אַחֲרֶיהָ׃ וַתִּקַּח תָּמָר אֵפֶר עַל־רֹאשָׁהּ וּכְתֹנֶת
and-robe-of head-of-her on ash Tamar and-she-put (19) after-her the-door

הַפַּסִּים אֲשֶׁר עָלֶיהָ קָרָעָה וַתָּשֶׂם יָדָהּ עַל־רֹאשָׁהּ
head-of-her on hand-of-her and-she-put she-tore on-her that the-ornaments

וַתֵּלֶךְ הָלוֹךְ וְזָעָקָה׃ וַיֹּאמֶר אֵלֶיהָ אַבְשָׁלוֹם אָחִיהָ
brother-of-her Absalom to-her and-he-said (20) and-she-wept to-go and-she-went

הַאֲמִינוֹן אָחִיךְ הָיָה עִמָּךְ וְעַתָּה אֲחוֹתִי הַחֲרִישִׁי
be-quiet! sister-of-me and-now with-you was-he brother-of-you Amnon?

אָחִיךְ הוּא אַל־תָּשִׁיתִי אֶת־לִבֵּךְ לַדָּבָר הַזֶּה
the-this to-the-thing heart-of-you *** you-take not he brother-of-you

וַתֵּשֶׁב תָּמָר וְשֹׁמֵמָה בֵּית אַבְשָׁלוֹם אָחִיהָ׃
brother-of-her Absalom house-of and-being-desolate Tamar and-she-lived

וְהַמֶּלֶךְ דָּוִד שָׁמַע אֵת כָּל־הַדְּבָרִים הָאֵלֶּה
the-these the-things all-of *** he-heard David when-the-king (21)

וַיִּחַר לוֹ מְאֹד׃ וְלֹא־דִבֶּר אַבְשָׁלוֹם עִם־אַמְנוֹן
Amnon to Absalom he-said-word and-not (22) very to-him then-he-was-furious

לְמֵרָע וְעַד־טוֹב כִּי־שָׂנֵא אַבְשָׁלוֹם אֶת־אַמְנוֹן עַל־דְּבַר אֲשֶׁר
that reason-of for Amnon *** Absalom he-hated for good even-to to-from-bad

עִנָּה אֵת תָּמָר אֲחֹתוֹ׃ וַיְהִי לִשְׁנָתַיִם יָמִים
days after-two-years and-he-was (23) sister-of-him Tamar *** he-disgraced

וַיִּהְיוּ גֹזְזִים לְאַבְשָׁלוֹם בְּבַעַל חָצוֹר אֲשֶׁר עִם־אֶפְרָיִם
Ephraim near that Hazor at-Baal for-Absalom ones-sheepshearing when-they-were

וַיִּקְרָא אַבְשָׁלוֹם לְכָל־בְּנֵי הַמֶּלֶךְ׃ וַיָּבֹא אַבְשָׁלוֹם
Absalom and-he-went (24) the-king sons-of to-all-of Absalom then-he-invited

אֶל־הַמֶּלֶךְ וַיֹּאמֶר הִנֵּה־נָא גֹזְזִים לְעַבְדֶּךָ יֵלֶךְ־
will-he-come for-servant-of-you ones-shearing now! see! and-he-said the-king to

"Sending me away would be a
greater wrong than what you
have already done to me."
But he refused to listen to
her. 17He called his personal
servant and said, "Get this
woman out of here and bolt
the door after her." 18So his
servant put her out and bolted
the door after her. She was
wearing a richly ornamented[l]
robe, for this was the kind of
garment the virgin daughters
of the king wore. 19Tamar put
ashes on her head and tore the
ornamented[m] robe she was
wearing. She put her hand on
her head and went away,
weeping aloud as she went.
20Her brother Absalom said
to her, "Has that Amnon, your
brother, been with you? Be
quiet now, my sister; he is
your brother. Don't take this
thing to heart." And Tamar
lived in her brother Absalom's
house, a desolate woman.
21When King David heard
all this, he was furious. 22Absa-
lom never said a word to Amnon, either good or bad; he
hated Amnon because he had
disgraced his sister Tamar.

Absalom Kills Amnon

23Two years later, when Absalom's sheepshearers were at
Baal Hazor near the border of
Ephraim, he invited all the
king's sons to come there.
24Absalom went to the king
and said, "Your servant has
had shearers come. Will the

[l]18 The meaning of the Hebrew for this phrase is uncertain.
[m]19 The meaning of the Hebrew for this word is uncertain.

נָא הַמֶּלֶךְ וַעֲבָדָיו עִם־ עַבְדֶּךָ׃ וַיֹּאמֶר
and-he-replied (25) servant-of-you with and-officials-of-him the-king now!

הַמֶּלֶךְ אֶל־אַבְשָׁלוֹם אַל־ בְּנִי אַל־ נָא נֵלֵךְ כֻּלָּנוּ וְלֹא
so-not all-of-us we-should-go now! not son-of-me no Absalom to the-king

נִכְבַּד עָלֶיךָ וַיִּפְרָץ־ בּוֹ וְלֹא־ אָבָה לָלֶכֶת
to-go he-wanted but-not to-him although-he-urged to-you we-would-be-burden

וַיְבָרְכֵהוּ׃ וַיֹּאמֶר אַבְשָׁלוֹם וָלֹא יֵלֶךְ־ נָא אִתָּנוּ
with-us now! let-him-come if-not Absalom then-he-said (26) but-he-blessed-him

אַמְנוֹן אָחִי וַיֹּאמֶר לוֹ הַמֶּלֶךְ לָמָּה יֵלֵךְ עִמָּךְ׃
with-you should-he-go why? the-king-to-him and-he-asked brother-of-me Amnon

וַיִּפְרָץ־ בּוֹ אַבְשָׁלוֹם וַיִּשְׁלַח אִתּוֹ אֶת־ אַמְנוֹן וְאֵת כָּל־
all-of and Amnon *** with-him so-he-sent Absalom to-him but-he-urged (27)

בְּנֵי הַמֶּלֶךְ׃ וַיְצַו אַבְשָׁלוֹם אֶת־ נְעָרָיו לֵאמֹר רְאוּ נָא
now! see! to-say men-of-him *** Absalom and-he-ordered (28) the-king sons-of

כְּטוֹב לֵב־ אַמְנוֹן בַּיַּיִן וְאָמַרְתִּי אֲלֵיכֶם הַכּוּ
strike-down! to-you and-I-say from-the-wine Amnon spirit-of when-to-be-high

אֶת־ אַמְנוֹן וַהֲמִתֶּם אֹתוֹ אַל־ תִּירָאוּ הֲלוֹא כִּי אָנֹכִי צִוִּיתִי אֶתְכֶם
you I-ordered I indeed not? you-be-afraid not him then-you-kill Amnon ***

חִזְקוּ וִהְיוּ לִבְנֵי־ חָיִל׃ וַיַּעֲשׂוּ נַעֲרֵי אַבְשָׁלוֹם
Absalom men-of so-they-did (29) bravery as-sons-of and-be! be-strong!

לְאַמְנוֹן כַּאֲשֶׁר צִוָּה אַבְשָׁלוֹם וַיָּקֻמוּ ׀ כָּל־ בְּנֵי הַמֶּלֶךְ
the-king sons-of all-of then-they-got-up Absalom he-ordered just-as to-Amnon

וַיִּרְכְּבוּ אִישׁ עַל־ פִּרְדּוֹ וַיָּנֻסוּ׃ וַיְהִי הֵמָּה
they whle-he-was (30) and-they-fled mule-of-him on each and-they-mounted

בַדֶּרֶךְ וְהַשְּׁמֻעָה בָּאָה אֶל־ דָּוִד לֵאמֹר הִכָּה אַבְשָׁלוֹם
Absalom he-struck-down to-say David to she-came then-the-report on-the-way

אֶת־ כָּל־ בְּנֵי הַמֶּלֶךְ* וְלֹא־ נוֹתַר מֵהֶם אֶחָד׃ וַיָּקָם
and-he-stood-up (31) one of-them he-is-left and-not the-king sons-of all-of ***

הַמֶּלֶךְ וַיִּקְרַע אֶת־ בְּגָדָיו וַיִּשְׁכַּב אַרְצָה וְכָל־
and-all-of on-ground and-he-lay clothes-of-him *** and-he-tore the-king

עֲבָדָיו נִצָּבִים קְרֻעֵי בְגָדִים׃ וַיַּעַן
but-he-said (32) clothes ones-being-torn-of ones-standing servants-of-him

יוֹנָדָב ׀ בֶּן־ שִׁמְעָה אֲחִי־ דָוִד וַיֹּאמֶר אַל־ יֹאמַר
he-should-think not and-he-said David brother-of Shimeah son-of Jonadab

אֲדֹנִי אֵת כָּל־ הַנְּעָרִים בְּנֵי־ הַמֶּלֶךְ הֵמִיתוּ כִּי־ אַמְנוֹן
Amnon only they-killed the-king sons-of the-princes all-of *** lord-of-me

לְבַדּוֹ מֵת כִּי־ עַל־ פִּי אַבְשָׁלוֹם הָיְתָה שׂוּמָה מִיּוֹם
from-day intention she-was Absalom mouth-of on for he-is-dead by-himself

king and his officials please join me?"
25 "No, my son," the king replied. "All of us should not go; we would only be a burden to you." Although Absalom urged him, he still refused to go, but gave him his blessing.
26 Then Absalom said, "If not, please let my brother Amnon come with us."

The king asked him, "Why should he go with you?"
27 But Absalom urged him, so he sent with him Amnon and the rest of the king's sons.
28 Absalom ordered his men, "Listen! When Amnon is in high spirits from drinking wine and I say to you, 'Strike Amnon down,' then kill him. Don't be afraid. Have not I given you this order? Be strong and brave."
29 So Absalom's men did to Amnon what Absalom had ordered. Then all the king's sons got up, mounted their mules and fled.
30 While they were on their way, the report came to David: "Absalom has struck down all the king's sons; not one of them is left."
31 The king stood up, tore his clothes and lay down on the ground; and all his servants stood by with their clothes torn.
32 But Jonadab son of Shimeah, David's brother, said, "My lord should not think that they killed all the princes; only Amnon is dead. This has been Absalom's expressed intention ever since the day

*30 Most mss have *sheva* in the *kaph* (ךְ).

עַנֹּתוֹ אֵת תָּמָר אֲחֹתוֹ׃ וְעַתָּה אַל־ יָשֵׂם אֲדֹנִי
lord-of-me he-should-take not so-now (33) sister-of-him Tamar *** to-rape-him

הַמֶּלֶךְ אֶל־ לִבּוֹ דָּבָר לֵאמֹר כָּל־ בְּנֵי הַמֶּלֶךְ מֵתוּ
they-are-dead the-king sons-of all-of to-say report heart-of-him to the-king

כִּי־ אִם־ אַמְנוֹן לְבַדּוֹ מֵת׃ וַיִּבְרַח אַבְשָׁלוֹם וַיִּשָּׂא
and-he-lifted Absalom and-he-fled (34) he-is-dead by-himself Amnon only for

הַנַּעַר הַצֹּפֶה אֶת־ עֵינָו וַיַּרְא וְהִנֵּה עַם־
people and-see! and-he-looked eyes-of-him *** the-one-standing-watch the-man

רַב הֹלְכִים מִדֶּרֶךְ אַחֲרָיו מִצַּד הָהָר׃ וַיֹּאמֶר
and-he-said (35) the-hill on-side-of west-of-him on-road ones-coming many

יוֹנָדָב אֶל־הַמֶּלֶךְ הִנֵּה בְנֵי־ הַמֶּלֶךְ בָּאוּ כִּדְבַר עַבְדְּךָ
servant-of-you as-word-of they-come the-king sons-of see! the-king to Jonadab

כֵּן הָיָה׃ וַיְהִי ׀ כְּכַלֹּתוֹ לְדַבֵּר וְהִנֵּה בְנֵי־
sons-of then-see! to-speak as-to-finish-him and-he-was (36) he-happened so

הַמֶּלֶךְ בָּאוּ וַיִּשְׂאוּ קוֹלָם וַיִּבְכּוּ וְגַם־
and-also and-they-wailed voice-of-them and-they-lifted they-came the-king

הַמֶּלֶךְ וְכָל־ עֲבָדָיו בָּכוּ בְּכִי גָּדוֹל מְאֹד׃
very bitter weeping they-wept servants-of-him and-all-of the-king

וְאַבְשָׁלוֹם בָּרַח וַיֵּלֶךְ אֶל־תַּלְמַי בֶּן־ עַמִּיחוּר מֶלֶךְ גְּשׁוּר
Geshur king-of Ammihud son-of Talmai to and-he-went he-fled and-Absalom (37)

וַיִּתְאַבֵּל עַל־ בְּנוֹ כָּל־ הַיָּמִים׃ וְאַבְשָׁלוֹם בָּרַח
he-fled and-Absalom (38) the-days all-of son-of-him for but-he-mourned

וַיֵּלֶךְ גְּשׁוּר וַיְהִי־ שָׁם שָׁלֹשׁ שָׁנִים׃ וַתְּכַל דָּוִד
David *and-she-longed (39) years three there and-he-stayed Geshur and-he-went

הַמֶּלֶךְ לָצֵאת אֶל־אַבְשָׁלוֹם כִּי־ נִחַם עַל־ אַמְנוֹן כִּי־ מֵת׃
he-died that Amnon concerning he-was-consoled for Absalom to to-go the-king

וַיֵּדַע יוֹאָב בֶּן־ צְרֻיָה כִּי־ לֵב הַמֶּלֶךְ עַל־אַבְשָׁלוֹם׃
Absalom for the-king heart-of that Zeruiah son-of Joab and-he-knew (14:1)

וַיִּשְׁלַח יוֹאָב תְּקוֹעָה וַיִּקַּח מִשָּׁם אִשָּׁה חֲכָמָה
wise woman from-there and-he-had-brought to-Tekoa Joab so-he-sent (2)

וַיֹּאמֶר אֵלֶיהָ הִתְאַבְּלִי־ נָא וְלִבְשִׁי־ נָא בִגְדֵי־ אֵבֶל
mourning clothes-of now! and-dress! now! pretend-to-mourn! to-her and-he-said

וְאַל־ תָּסוּכִי שֶׁמֶן וְהָיִית כְּאִשָּׁה זֶה יָמִים רַבִּים מִתְאַבֶּלֶת עַל־
for grieving many days this like-woman and-you-act lotion you-use and-not

מֵת׃ וּבָאת אֶל־ הַמֶּלֶךְ וְדִבַּרְתְּ אֵלָיו כַּדָּבָר הַזֶּה
the-this as-the-word to-him and-you-speak the-king to then-you-go (3) dead

וַיָּשֶׂם יוֹאָב אֶת־הַדְּבָרִים בְּפִיהָ׃ וַתֹּאמֶר הָאִשָּׁה
the-woman when-she-spoke (4) in-mouth-of-her the-words *** Joab and-he-put

Amnon raped his sister Tamar. [33]My lord the king should not be concerned about the report that all the king's sons are dead. Only Amnon is dead."

[34]Meanwhile, Absalom had fled.

Now the man standing watch looked up and saw many people on the road west of him, coming down the side of the hill. The watchman went and told the king, "I see men in the direction of Horonaim, on the side of the hill."[n]

[35]Jonadab said to the king, "See, the king's sons are here; it has happened just as your servant said."

[36]As he finished speaking, the king's sons came in, wailing loudly. The king, too, and all his servants wept very bitterly.

[37]Absalom fled and went to Talmai son of Ammihud, the king of Geshur. But King David mourned for his son every day.

[38]After Absalom fled and went to Geshur, he stayed there three years. [39]And the spirit of the king[o] longed to go to Absalom, for he was consoled concerning Amnon's death.

Absalom Returns to Jerusalem

14 Joab son of Zeruiah knew that the king's heart longed for Absalom. [2]So Joab sent someone to Tekoa and had a wise woman brought from there. He said to her, "Pretend you are in mourning. Dress in mourning clothes, and don't use any cosmetic lotions. Act like a woman who has spent many days grieving for the dead. [3]Then go to the king and speak these words to him." And Joab put the words in her mouth.

[4]When the woman from

[n]34 Septuagint; Hebrew does not have this sentence.
[o]39 Some Septuagint manuscripts; Hebrew *But the spirit of David the king*

*39 Apparently the feminine subject, *spirit*, evident in some versions, has dropped out of text.

°34 ק עיניו
°37 ק עמיהוד

הַתְּקֹעִית אֶל־הַמֶּלֶךְ וַתִּפֹּל עַל־ אַפֶּיהָ אַרְצָה וַתִּשְׁתָּחוּ
and-she-honored to-ground faces-of-her on then-she-fell the-king to the-Tekoaite

וַתֹּאמֶר הוֹשִׁעָה הַמֶּלֶךְ׃ וַיֹּאמֶר־ לָהּ הַמֶּלֶךְ מַה־ לָּךְ
to-you what? the-king to-her and-he-asked (5) the-king help! and-she-said

וַתֹּאמֶר אֲבָל אִשָּׁה־ אַלְמָנָה אָנִי וַיָּמָת אִישִׁי׃
husband-of-me and-he-is-dead I widow woman indeed and-she-said

וּלְשִׁפְחָתְךָ שְׁנֵי בָנִים וַיִּנָּצוּ שְׁנֵיהֶם בַּשָּׂדֶה
in-the-field two-of-them and-they-fought sons two-of and-to-servant-of-you (6)

וְאֵין מַצִּיל בֵּינֵיהֶם וַיַּכּוּ הָאֶחָד אֶת־ הָאֶחָד
the-other *** the-one and-he-struck-him between-them one-separating and-not

וַיָּמֶת אֹתוֹ׃ וְהִנֵּה קָמָה כָל־ הַמִּשְׁפָּחָה עַל־
against the-clan whole-of she-rose-up now-see! (7) him and-he-killed

שִׁפְחָתֶךָ וַיֹּאמְרוּ תְּנִי ׀ אֶת־ מַכֵּה אָחִיו
brother-of-him one-striking-down *** hand-over! and-they-say servant-of-you

וּנְמִתֵהוּ בְּנֶפֶשׁ אָחִיו אֲשֶׁר הָרָג וְנַשְׁמִידָה
and-we-will-get-rid he-killed whom brother-of-him for-life-of so-we-may-kill-him

גַּם אֶת־ הַיּוֹרֵשׁ וְכִבּוּ אֶת־ גַּחַלְתִּי אֲשֶׁר
that burning-coal-of-me *** and-they-will-put-out the-one-being-heir *** also

נִשְׁאָרָה לְבִלְתִּי שׁוֹם־ לְאִישִׁי שֵׁם וּשְׁאֵרִית עַל־ פְּנֵי
faces-of on or-descendant name to-husband-of-me to-leave not being-left

הָאֲדָמָה׃ וַיֹּאמֶר הַמֶּלֶךְ אֶל־ הָאִשָּׁה לְכִי לְבֵיתֵךְ וַאֲנִי
and-I to-home-of-you go! the-woman to the-king and-he-said (8) the-earth

אֲצַוֶּה עָלָיִךְ׃ וַתֹּאמֶר הָאִשָּׁה הַתְּקוֹעִית אֶל־ הַמֶּלֶךְ
the-king to the-Tekoaite the-woman but-she-said (9) for-you I-will-issue-order

עָלַי אֲדֹנִי הַמֶּלֶךְ הֶעָוֹן וְעַל־ בֵּית אָבִי וְהַמֶּלֶךְ
and-the-king father-of-me family-of and-on the-blame the-king lord-of-me on-me

וְכִסְאוֹ נָקִי׃ וַיֹּאמֶר הַמֶּלֶךְ הַמְדַבֵּר
the-one-saying the-king and-he-replied (10) without-guilt and-throne-of-him

אֵלַיִךְ וַהֲבֵאתוֹ אֵלַי וְלֹא־ יֹסִיף עוֹד לָגַעַת
to-bother again he-will-repeat and-not to-me then-bring-him! to-you

בָּךְ׃ וַתֹּאמֶר יִזְכָּר־ נָא הַמֶּלֶךְ אֶת־ יְהוָה
Yahweh *** the-king now! let-him-invoke and-she-said (11) against-you

אֱלֹהֶיךָ מֵהַרְבִּית גֹּאֵל הַדָּם לְשַׁחֵת וְלֹא
so-not to-destroy the-blood one-avenging-of from-to-add God-of-you

יַשְׁמִידוּ אֶת־ בְּנִי וַיֹּאמֶר חַי־ יְהוָה אִם־ יִפֹּל
he-will-fall not Yahweh life-of and-he-said son-of-me *** they-will-destroy

מִשַּׂעֲרַת בִּנֵךְ אָרְצָה׃ וַתֹּאמֶר הָאִשָּׁה תְּדַבֶּר־
let-her-speak the-woman then-she-said (12) to-ground son-of-you from-hair-of

°7 ק שים
°11 ק מהרבת

Tekoa went[p] to the king, she
fell with her face to the ground
to pay him honor, and she
said, "Help me, O king!"
5The king asked her, "What
is troubling you?"
She said, "I am indeed a
widow; my husband is dead.
6I your servant had two sons.
They got into a fight with each
other in the field, and no one
was there to separate them.
One struck the other and
killed him. 7Now the whole
clan has risen up against your
servant; they say, 'Hand over
the one who struck his brother
down, so that we may put him
to death for the life of his
brother whom he killed; then
we will get rid of the heir as
well.' They would put out the
only burning coal I have left,
leaving my husband neither
name nor descendant on the
face of the earth."
8The king said to the
woman, "Go home, and I will
issue an order in your behalf."
9But the woman from Tekoa
said to him, "My lord the king,
let the blame rest on me and
on my father's family, and let
the king and his throne be
without guilt."
10The king replied, "If anyone says anything to you,
bring him to me, and he will
not bother you again."
11She said, "Then let the
king invoke the LORD his God
to prevent the avenger of
blood from adding to the destruction, so that my son will
not be destroyed."
"As surely as the LORD
lives," he said, "not one hair
of your son's head will fall to
the ground."
12Then the woman said, "Let

[p]4 Many Hebrew manuscripts, Septuagint, Vulgate and Syriac; most Hebrew manuscripts *spoke*

נָא שִׁפְחָתְךָ אֶל־ אֲדֹנִי הַמֶּלֶךְ דָּבָר וַיֹּאמֶר דַּבֵּרִי׃

speak! and-he-replied word the-king lord-of-me to servant-of-you now!

וַתֹּאמֶר הָאִשָּׁה וְלָמָּה חָשַׁבְתָּה כָּזֹאת עַל־ עַם

people-of against like-this you-devised then-why? the-woman and-she-said (13)

אֱלֹהִים וּמִדַּבֵּר הַמֶּלֶךְ הַדָּבָר הַזֶּה כְּאָשֵׁם לְבִלְתִּי

not as-conviction the-this the-thing the-king and-when-to-say God

הָשִׁיב הַמֶּלֶךְ אֶת־ נִדְּחוֹ׃ כִּי־ מוֹת

to-die for (14) one-being-banished-of-him *** the-king to-bring-back

נָמוּת וְכַמַּיִם הַנִּגָּרִים אַרְצָה אֲשֶׁר לֹא

not which on-ground the-ones-being-spilled and-like-the-waters we-must-die

יֵאָסֵפוּ וְלֹא־ יִשָּׂא אֱלֹהִים נֶפֶשׁ וְחָשַׁב מַחֲשָׁבוֹת

ways but-he-devises life God he-takes-away but-not they-can-be-recovered

לְבִלְתִּי יִדַּח מִמֶּנּוּ נִדָּח׃ וְעַתָּה אֲשֶׁר־

that and-now (15) one-being-banished from-him he-remains-estranged so-not

בָּאתִי לְדַבֵּר אֶל־ הַמֶּלֶךְ אֲדֹנִי אֶת־ הַדָּבָר הַזֶּה כִּי

for the-this the-word *** lord-of-me the-king to to-say I-came

יֵרְאֻנִי הָעָם וַתֹּאמֶר שִׁפְחָתְךָ אֲדַבְּרָה־

I-will-speak servant-of-you and-she-thought the-people they-make-afraid-me

נָּא אֶל־הַמֶּלֶךְ אוּלַי יַעֲשֶׂה הַמֶּלֶךְ אֶת־ דְּבַר אֲמָתוֹ׃

servant-of-him request-of *** the-king he-will-do perhaps the-king to now!

כִּי יִשְׁמַע הַמֶּלֶךְ לְהַצִּיל אֶת־ אֲמָתוֹ מִכַּף

from-hand-of servant-of-him *** to-deliver the-king he-will-agree perhaps (16)

הָאִישׁ לְהַשְׁמִיד אֹתִי וְאֶת־ בְּנִי יַחַד מִנַּחֲלַת אֱלֹהִים׃

God from-inheritance-of together son-of-me and me to-cut-off the-man

וַתֹּאמֶר שִׁפְחָתְךָ יִהְיֶה־ נָּא דְּבַר־ אֲדֹנִי הַמֶּלֶךְ

the-king lord-of-me word-of now! may-he-be servant-of-you now-she-says (17)

לִמְנוּחָה כִּי׀ כְּמַלְאַךְ הָאֱלֹהִים כֵּן אֲדֹנִי הַמֶּלֶךְ לִשְׁמֹעַ הַטּוֹב

the-good to-discern the-king lord-of-me so the-God like-angel-of for as-rest

וְהָרָע וַיהוָה אֱלֹהֶיךָ יְהִי עִמָּךְ׃ וַיַּעַן

then-he-answered (18) with-you may-he-be God-of-you and-Yahweh and-the-evil

הַמֶּלֶךְ וַיֹּאמֶר אֶל־ הָאִשָּׁה אַל־ נָא תְכַחֲדִי מִמֶּנִּי דָּבָר אֲשֶׁר אָנֹכִי

I that answer from-me you-keep now! not the-woman and-he-said the-king

שֹׁאֵל אֹתָךְ וַתֹּאמֶר הָאִשָּׁה יְדַבֶּר־ נָא אֲדֹנִי הַמֶּלֶךְ׃

the-king lord-of-me now! let-him-speak the-woman and-she-said you asking

וַיֹּאמֶר הַמֶּלֶךְ הֲיַד יוֹאָב אִתָּךְ בְּכָל־ זֹאת

this in-all-of with-you Joab hand-of? the-king and-he-asked (19)

וַתַּעַן הָאִשָּׁה וַתֹּאמֶר חֵי־ נַפְשְׁךָ אֲדֹנִי

lord-of-me self-of-you life-of and-she-said the-woman and-she-answered

your servant speak a word to
my lord the king."
"Speak," he replied.
[13]The woman said, "Why
then have you devised a thing
like this against the people of
God? When the king says this,
does he not convict himself,
for the king has not brought
back his banished son? [14]Like
water spilled on the ground,
which cannot be recovered, so
we must die. But God does not
take away life; instead, he de-
vises ways so that a banished
person may not remain es-
tranged from him.
[15]"And now I have come to
say this to my lord the king
because the people have made
me afraid. Your servant
thought, 'I will speak to the
king; perhaps he will do what
his servant asks. [16]Perhaps the
king will agree to deliver his
servant from the hand of the
man who is trying to cut off
both me and my son from the
inheritance God gave us.'
[17]"And now your servant
says, 'May the word of my lord
the king bring me rest, for my
lord the king is like an angel of
God in discerning good and
evil. May the LORD your God
be with you.'"
[18]Then the king said to the
woman, "Do not keep from
me the answer to what I am
going to ask you."
"Let my lord the king
speak," the woman said.
[19]The king asked, "Isn't the
hand of Joab with you in all
this?"
The woman answered, "As
surely as you live, my lord the

הַמֶּלֶךְ אִם־ אִשׁ ׀ לְהֵמִין וּלְהַשְׂמִיל מִכֹּל אֲשֶׁר־ דִּבֶּר
he-says that from-anything or-to-turn-left to-turn-right he-is not the-king

אֲדֹנִי הַמֶּלֶךְ כִּי־ עַבְדְּךָ יוֹאָב הוּא צִוָּנִי וְהוּא
and-he he-instructed-me he Joab servant-of-you indeed the-king lord-of-me

שָׂם בְּפִי שִׁפְחָתְךָ אֵת כָּל־ הַדְּבָרִים הָאֵלֶּה׃
the-these the-words all-of *** servant-of-you into-mouth-of he-put

לְבַעֲבוּר סַבֵּב אֶת־ פְּנֵי הַדָּבָר עָשָׂה עַבְדְּךָ
servant-of-you he-did the-situation faces-of *** to-change in-order-to (20)

יוֹאָב אֶת־ הַדָּבָר הַזֶּה וַאדֹנִי חָכָם כְּחָכְמַת מַלְאַךְ
angel-of like-wisdom-of wise and-lord-of-me the-this the-thing *** Joab

הָאֱלֹהִים לָדַעַת אֶת־ כָּל־ אֲשֶׁר בָּאָרֶץ׃ וַיֹּאמֶר הַמֶּלֶךְ אֶל־
to the-king and-he-said (21) in-the-land that everything *** to-know the-God

יוֹאָב הִנֵּה־ נָא עָשִׂיתִי אֶת־ הַדָּבָר הַזֶּה וְלֵךְ הָשֵׁב אֶת־
*** bring-back! now-go! the-this the-thing *** I-will-do-now! see! Joab

הַנַּעַר אֶת־אַבְשָׁלוֹם׃ וַיִּפֹּל יוֹאָב אֶל־ פָּנָיו אַרְצָה
to-ground faces-of-him on Joab and-he-fell (22) Absalom *** the-young-man

וַיִּשְׁתַּחוּ וַיְבָרֶךְ אֶת־ הַמֶּלֶךְ וַיֹּאמֶר יוֹאָב הַיּוֹם
the-day Joab and-he-said the-king *** and-he-blessed and-he-paid-honor

יָדַע עַבְדְּךָ כִּי־ מָצָאתִי חֵן בְּעֵינֶיךָ אֲדֹנִי
lord-of-me on-eyes-of-you favor I-found that servant-of-you he-knows

הַמֶּלֶךְ אֲשֶׁר־ עָשָׂה הַמֶּלֶךְ אֶת־ דְּבַר עַבְדֶּו׃
servant-of-you request-of *** the-king he-granted that the-king

וַיָּקָם יוֹאָב וַיֵּלֶךְ גְּשׁוּרָה וַיָּבֵא אֶת־אַבְשָׁלוֹם
Absalom *** and-he-brought-back to-Geshur and-he-went Joab then-he-rose (23)

יְרוּשָׁלָם׃ וַיֹּאמֶר הַמֶּלֶךְ יִסֹּב אֶל־ בֵּיתוֹ וּפָנַי
and-faces-of-me house-of-him to he-must-go the-king but-he-said (24) Jerusalem

לֹא יִרְאֶה וַיִּסֹּב אַבְשָׁלוֹם אֶל־ בֵּיתוֹ וּפְנֵי הַמֶּלֶךְ
the-king and-faces-of house-of-him to Absalom so-he-went he-must-see not

לֹא רָאָה׃ וּכְאַבְשָׁלוֹם לֹא־ הָיָה אִישׁ־ יָפֶה בְּכָל־יִשְׂרָאֵל
Israel in-all-of handsome man-of he-was not now-as-Absalom (25) he-saw not

לְהַלֵּל מְאֹד מִכַּף רַגְלוֹ וְעַד קָדְקֳדוֹ לֹא־ הָיָה
he-was not head-of-him even-to foot-of-him from-sole-of highly to-praise

בוֹ מוּם׃ וּבְגַלְּחוֹ אֶת־ רֹאשׁוֹ וְהָיָה מִקֵּץ
from-end-of and-he-was head-of-him *** and-when-to-cut-him (26) blemish on-him

יָמִים ׀ לַיָּמִים אֲשֶׁר יְגַלֵּחַ כִּי־ כָבֵד עָלָיו וְגִלְּחוֹ
then-he-cut-him on-him heavy when he-would-cut that to-the-days days

וְשָׁקַל אֶת־ שְׂעַר רֹאשׁוֹ מָאתַיִם שְׁקָלִים בְּאֶבֶן
by-standard-of shekels two-hundreds head-of-him hair-of *** and-he-would-weigh

king, no one can turn to the
right or to the left from anything my lord the king says.
Yes, it was your servant Joab
who instructed me to do this
and who put all these words
into the mouth of your servant. 20 Your servant Joab did
this to change the present
situation. My lord has wisdom
like that of an angel of God—
he knows everything that
happens in the land."
21 The king said to Joab,
"Very well, I will do it. Go,
bring back the young man Absalom."
22 Joab fell with his face to the
ground to pay him honor, and
he blessed the king. Joab said,
"Today your servant knows
that he has found favor in
your eyes, my lord the king,
because the king has granted
his servant's request."
23 Then Joab went to Geshur
and brought Absalom back to
Jerusalem. 24 But the king said,
"He must go to his own house;
he must not see my face." So
Absalom went to his own
house and did not see the face
of the king.
25 In all Israel there was not a
man so highly praised for his
handsome appearance as Absalom. From the top of his
head to the sole of his foot
there was no blemish in him.
26 Whenever he cut the hair of
his head—he used to cut his
hair from time to time when it
became too heavy for him—he
would weigh it, and its weight
was two hundred shekels[q] by
the royal standard.

[q]26 That is, about 5 pounds (about 2.3 kilograms)

°22 ק עבדך

הַמֶּלֶךְ׃ וַיִּוָּלְדוּ לְאַבְשָׁלוֹם שְׁלוֹשָׁה בָנִים וּבַת אַחַת
one and-daughter sons three to-Absalom and-they-were-born (27) the-king

וּשְׁמָהּ תָּמָר הִיא הָיְתָה אִשָּׁה יְפַת מַרְאֶה׃
appearance beautiful-of woman she-became she Tamar and-name-of-her

וַיֵּשֶׁב אַבְשָׁלוֹם בִּירוּשָׁלַםִ שְׁנָתַיִם יָמִים וּפְנֵי הַמֶּלֶךְ
the-king and-faces-of days two-years in-Jerusalem Absalom and-he-lived (28)

לֹא רָאָה׃ וַיִּשְׁלַח אַבְשָׁלוֹם אֶל־יוֹאָב לִשְׁלֹחַ אֹתוֹ אֶל־הַמֶּלֶךְ וְלֹא
but-not the-king to him to-send Joab for Absalom then-he-sent (29) he-saw not

אָבָה לָבוֹא אֵלָיו וַיִּשְׁלַח עוֹד שֵׁנִית וְלֹא אָבָה לָבוֹא׃
to-come he-wanted but-not second again so-he-sent to-him to-come he-wanted

וַיֹּאמֶר אֶל־ עֲבָדָיו רְאוּ חֶלְקַת יוֹאָב אֶל־ יָדִי
hand-of-me at Joab field-of look! servants-of-him to then-he-said (30)

וְלוֹ־ שָׁם שְׂעֹרִים לְכוּ וְהוֹצִתִּיהָ בָאֵשׁ וַיַּצִּתוּ
so-they-set-on-fire with-fire and-set-on-fire-her! go! barleys there and-to-him

עַבְדֵי אַבְשָׁלוֹם אֶת־הַחֶלְקָה בָּאֵשׁ׃ וַיָּקָם יוֹאָב וַיָּבֹא
and-he-went Joab then-he-rose (31) with-fire the-field *** Absalom servants-of

אֶל־ אַבְשָׁלוֹם הַבָּיְתָה וַיֹּאמֶר אֵלָיו לָמָּה הֵצִיתוּ
they-set-on-fire why? to-him and-he-said at-the-house Absalom to

עֲבָדֶךָ אֶת־ הַחֶלְקָה אֲשֶׁר־ לִי בָּאֵשׁ׃ וַיֹּאמֶר אַבְשָׁלוֹם
Absalom and-he-said (32) with-fire to-me that the-field *** servant-of-you

אֶל־יוֹאָב הִנֵּה שָׁלַחְתִּי אֵלֶיךָ ׀ לֵאמֹר בֹּא הֵנָּה וְאֶשְׁלְחָה אֹתְךָ אֶל־
to you so-I-can-send to-here come! to-say to-you I-sent see! Joab to

הַמֶּלֶךְ לֵאמֹר לָמָּה בָּאתִי מִגְּשׁוּר טוֹב לִי עֹד אֲנִי־שָׁם וְעַתָּה
and-now there I still for-me better from-Geshur I-came why? to-say the-king

אֶרְאֶה פְּנֵי הַמֶּלֶךְ וְאִם־ יֶשׁ־ בִּי עָוֺן וֶהֱמִתָנִי׃
then-let-him-kill-me guilt in-me there-is and-if the-king faces-of I-would-see

וַיָּבֹא יוֹאָב אֶל־ הַמֶּלֶךְ וַיַּגֶּד־ לוֹ וַיִּקְרָא אֶל־
to then-he-summoned to-him and-he-told the-king to Joab so-he-went (33)

אַבְשָׁלוֹם וַיָּבֹא אֶל־ הַמֶּלֶךְ וַיִּשְׁתַּחוּ לוֹ עַל־ אַפָּיו
faces-of-him on before-him and-he-bowed the-king to and-he-came Absalom

אַרְצָה לִפְנֵי הַמֶּלֶךְ וַיִּשַּׁק הַמֶּלֶךְ לְאַבְשָׁלוֹם׃ וַיְהִי
and-he-was (15:1) on-Absalom the-king and-he-kissed the-king before to-ground

מֵאַחֲרֵי כֵּן וַיַּעַשׂ לוֹ אַבְשָׁלוֹם מֶרְכָּבָה וְסֻסִים וַחֲמִשִּׁים
and-fifty and-horses chariot Absalom for-him that-he-provided this at-after

אִישׁ רָצִים לְפָנָיו׃ וְהִשְׁכִּים אַבְשָׁלוֹם וְעָמַד עַל־
by and-he-stood Absalom and-he-got-up (2) ahead-of-him ones-running man

יַד דֶּרֶךְ הַשָּׁעַר וַיְהִי כָּל־ הָאִישׁ אֲשֶׁר־ יִהְיֶה־ לוֹ־
to-him he-was who the-person any-of and-he-was the-gate road-of side-of

27 Three sons and a daughter
were born to Absalom. The
daughter's name was Tamar,
and she became a beautiful
woman.
28 Absalom lived two years in
Jerusalem without seeing the
king's face. 29 Then Absalom
sent for Joab in order to send
him to the king, but Joab
refused to come to him. So he
sent a second time, but he
refused to come. 30 Then he
said to his servants, "Look,
Joab's field is next to mine,
and he has barley there. Go
and set it on fire." So Absalom's servants set the field on
fire.
31 Then Joab did go to Absalom's house and he said to
him, "Why have your ser-
vants set my field on fire?"
32 Absalom said to Joab,
"Look, I sent word to you and
said, 'Come here so I can send
you to the king to ask, "Why
have I come from Geshur? It
would be better for me if I
were still there!"' Now then, I
want to see the king's face,
and if I am guilty of anything,
let him put me to death."
33 So Joab went to the king
and told him this. Then the
king summoned Absalom,
and he came in and bowed
down with his face to the
ground before the king. And
the king kissed Absalom.

Absalom's Conspiracy

15 In the course of time,
Absalom provided
himself with a chariot and
horses and with fifty men to
run ahead of him. 2 He would
get up early and stand by the
side of the road leading to the
city gate. Whenever anyone

°30 ק והציתוה

רִיב לָבוֹא אֶל־ הַמֶּלֶךְ לַמִּשְׁפָּט וַיִּקְרָא אַבְשָׁלוֹם
Absalom then-he-called for-the-decision the-king before to-place complaint

אֵלָיו וַיֹּאמֶר אֵי־ מִזֶּה עִיר אַתָּה וַיֹּאמֶר מֵאַחַד
from-one-of and-he-answered you town from-there where? and-he-said to-him

שִׁבְטֵי־ יִשְׂרָאֵל עַבְדֶּךָ׃ וַיֹּאמֶר אֵלָיו אַבְשָׁלוֹם רְאֵה
look! Absalom to-him then-he-said (3) servant-of-you Israel tribes-of

דְבָרֶךָ טוֹבִים וּנְכֹחִים וְשֹׁמֵעַ אֵין־ לְךָ מֵאֵת
from for-you not but-one-hearing and-proper-ones valid-ones claim-of-you

הַמֶּלֶךְ׃ וַיֹּאמֶר אַבְשָׁלוֹם מִי־ יְשִׂמֵנִי שֹׁפֵט
one-judging he-appointed-me if-only Absalom and-he-said (4) the-king

בָּאָרֶץ וְעָלַי יָבוֹא כָּל־ אִישׁ אֲשֶׁר־ יִהְיֶה־ לּוֹ־
to-him he-is who person every-of he-could-come then-to-me in-the-land

רִיב וּמִשְׁפָּט וְהִצְדַּקְתִּיו׃ וְהָיָה
and-he-was (5) then-I-would-bring-justice-to-him or-case complaint

בִּקְרָב־ אִישׁ לְהִשְׁתַּחֲוֹת לוֹ וְשָׁלַח אֶת־ יָדוֹ
hand-of-him *** then-he-reached-out before-him to-bow anyone when-to-approach

וְהֶחֱזִיק לוֹ וְנָשַׁק לוֹ׃ וַיַּעַשׂ אַבְשָׁלוֹם
Absalom and-he-behaved (6) on-him and-he-kissed of-him and-he-took-hold

כַּדָּבָר הַזֶּה לְכָל־ יִשְׂרָאֵל אֲשֶׁר־ יָבֹאוּ לַמִּשְׁפָּט אֶל־
to for-the-justice they-came who Israel to-all-of the-this in-the-way

הַמֶּלֶךְ וַיְגַנֵּב אַבְשָׁלוֹם אֶת־ לֵב אַנְשֵׁי יִשְׂרָאֵל׃ וַיְהִי
and-he-was (7) Israel men-of heart-of *** Absalom so-he-stole the-king

מִקֵּץ אַרְבָּעִים שָׁנָה וַיֹּאמֶר אַבְשָׁלוֹם אֶל־ הַמֶּלֶךְ אֵלֲכָה נָּא
now! let-me-go the-king to Absalom then-he-said year forty at-end-of

וַאֲשַׁלֵּם* אֶת־ נִדְרִי אֲשֶׁר־ נָדַרְתִּי לַיהוָה בְּחֶבְרוֹן׃ כִּי־
for (8) to-Hebron to-Yahweh I-made that vow-of-me *** and-let-me-fulfill

נֶדֶר נָדַר עַבְדְּךָ בְּשִׁבְתִּי בִגְשׁוּר בַּאֲרָם לֵאמֹר אִם־
if to-say in-Aram at-Geshur while-to-live-me servant-of-you he-made vow

יָשׁיב° יְשִׁיבֵנִי יְהוָה יְרוּשָׁלַםִ וְעָבַדְתִּי אֶת־
*** then-I-will-worship Jerusalem Yahweh he-takes-back-me to-take-back

יְהוָה׃ וַיֹּאמֶר־ לוֹ הַמֶּלֶךְ לֵךְ בְּשָׁלוֹם וַיָּקָם וַיֵּלֶךְ
and-he-went so-he-rose in-peace go! the-king to-him and-he-said (9) Yahweh

חֶבְרוֹנָה׃ וַיִּשְׁלַח אַבְשָׁלוֹם מְרַגְּלִים בְּכָל־
through-all-of ones-bringing-message Absalom then-he-sent (10) to-Hebron

שִׁבְטֵי יִשְׂרָאֵל לֵאמֹר כְּשָׁמְעֲכֶם אֶת־ קוֹל הַשֹּׁפָר וַאֲמַרְתֶּם
then-you-say the-trumpet sound-of *** as-to-hear-you to-say Israel tribes-of

מָלַךְ אַבְשָׁלוֹם בְּחֶבְרוֹן׃ וְאֶת־ אַבְשָׁלוֹם הָלְכוּ
they-accompanied Absalom and-with (11) in-Hebron Absalom he-is-king

came with a complaint to be
placed before the king for a
decision, Absalom would call
out to him, "What town are
you from?" He would answer,
"Your servant is from one of
the tribes of Israel." [3]Then Absalom would say to him,
"Look, your claims are valid
and proper, but there is no
representative of the king to
hear you." [4]And Absalom
would add, "If only I were appointed judge in the land!
Then everyone who has a
complaint or case could come
to me and I would see that he
gets justice."
[5]Also, whenever anyone approached him to bow down
before him, Absalom would
reach out his hand, take hold
of him and kiss him. [6]Absalom
behaved in this way toward
all the Israelites who came to
the king asking for justice, and
so he stole the hearts of the
men of Israel.
[7]At the end of four[r] years,
Absalom said to the king, "Let
me go to Hebron and fulfill a
vow I made to the LORD.
[8]While your servant was living at Geshur in Aram, I made
this vow: 'If the LORD takes me
back to Jerusalem, I will worship the LORD in Hebron.[s]' "
[9]The king said to him, "Go
in peace." So he went to Hebron.
[10]Then Absalom sent secret
messengers throughout the
tribes of Israel to say, "As soon
as you hear the sound of the
trumpets, then say, 'Absalom
is king in Hebron.' " [11]Two
hundred men from Jerusalem
had accompanied Absalom.

[r]7 Some Septuagint manuscripts, Syriac and Josephus; Hebrew *forty*
[s]8 Some Septuagint manuscripts; Hebrew does not have *in Hebron.*

***7 Most mss have the accent *darga* (וַאֲשַׁלֵּם).**

°8 ק ישוב

מָאתַיִם אִישׁ מִירוּשָׁלִַם קְרֻאִים וְהֹלְכִים
and-ones-going ones-being-invited from-Jerusalem man two-hundreds

לְתֻמָּם וְלֹא יָדְעוּ כָּל־ דָּבָר׃ וַיִּשְׁלַח אַבְשָׁלוֹם
Absalom and-he-sent (12) matter any-of they-knew and-not in-innocence-of-them

אֶת־ אֲחִיתֹפֶל הַגִּילֹנִי יוֹעֵץ דָּוִד מֵעִירוֹ
from-town-of-him David one-counselling-of the-Gilonite Ahithophel ***

מִגִּלֹה בְּזָבְחוֹ אֶת־ הַזְּבָחִים וַיְהִי הַקֶּשֶׁר
the-conspiracy and-he-became the-sacrifices *** while-to-offer-him from-Giloh

אַמִּץ וְהָעָם הוֹלֵךְ וָרָב אֶת־ אַבְשָׁלוֹם׃ וַיָּבֹא
and-he-came (13) Absalom with and-great increasing and-the-people strong

הַמַּגִּיד אֶל־ דָּוִד לֵאמֹר הָיָה לֶב־ אִישׁ יִשְׂרָאֵל אַחֲרֵי
with Israel man-of heart-of he-is to-say David to the-one-bringing-message

אַבְשָׁלוֹם׃ וַיֹּאמֶר דָּוִד לְכָל־ עֲבָדָיו אֲשֶׁר־ אִתּוֹ
with-him who officials-of-him to-all-of David then-he-said (14) Absalom

בִירוּשָׁלִַם קוּמוּ וְנִבְרָחָה כִּי לֹא־ תִהְיֶה־ לָּנוּ פְלֵיטָה
escape for-us she-will-be not or now-we-must-flee come! in-Jerusalem

מִפְּנֵי אַבְשָׁלֹם מַהֲרוּ לָלֶכֶת פֶּן־ יְמַהֵר
he-will-move-quickly or to-leave be-immediate! Absalom from-before

וְהִשִּׂגֻנוּ וְהִדִּיחַ עָלֵינוּ אֶת־ הָרָעָה וְהִכָּה
and-he-will-put the-ruin *** on-us and-he-will-bring and-he-will-overtake-us

הָעִיר לְפִי־ חָרֶב׃ וַיֹּאמְרוּ עַבְדֵי־ הַמֶּלֶךְ אֶל־
to the-king officials-of and-they-answered (15) sword to-edge-of the-city

הַמֶּלֶךְ כְּכֹל אֲשֶׁר־ יִבְחַר אֲדֹנִי הַמֶּלֶךְ הִנֵּה עֲבָדֶיךָ׃
servants-of-you see! the-king lord-of-me he-chooses that as-all the-king

וַיֵּצֵא הַמֶּלֶךְ וְכָל־ בֵּיתוֹ בְּרַגְלָיו
at-feet-of-him household-of-him and-entire-of the-king and-he-set-out (16)

וַיַּעֲזֹב הַמֶּלֶךְ אֵת עֶשֶׂר נָשִׁים פִּלַגְשִׁים לִשְׁמֹר הַבָּיִת׃
the-palace to-take-care-of concubines women ten *** the-king but-he-left

וַיֵּצֵא הַמֶּלֶךְ וְכָל־ הָעָם בְּרַגְלָיו
at-feet-of-him the-people and-all-of the-king so-he-set-out (17)

וַיַּעַמְדוּ בֵּית הַמֶּרְחָק׃ וְכָל־ עֲבָדָיו עֹבְרִים
ones-passing men-of-him and-all-of (18) the-distance place-of and-they-halted

עַל־ יָדוֹ וְכָל־ הַכְּרֵתִי וְכָל־ הַפְּלֵתִי וְכָל־
and-all-of the-Pelethite and-all-of the-Kerethite and-all-of hand-of-him under

הַגִּתִּים שֵׁשׁ־ מֵאוֹת אִישׁ אֲשֶׁר־ בָּאוּ בְרַגְלוֹ מִגַּת
from-Gath at-feet-of-him they-came who man hundreds six the-Gittites

עֹבְרִים עַל־ פְּנֵי הַמֶּלֶךְ׃ וַיֹּאמֶר הַמֶּלֶךְ אֶל־ אִתַּי
Ittai to the-king and-he-said (19) the-king faces-of before ones-marching

They had been invited as guests and went quite innocently, knowing nothing about the matter.
[12]While Absalom was offering sacrifices, he also sent for Ahithophel the Gilonite, David's counselor, to come from Giloh, his home town. And so the conspiracy gained strength, and Absalom's following kept on increasing.

David Flees

[13]A messenger came and told David, "The hearts of the men of Israel are with Absalom."

[14]Then David said to all his officials who were with him in Jerusalem, "Come! We must flee, or none of us will escape from Absalom. We must leave immediately, or he will move quickly to overtake us and bring ruin upon us and put the city to the sword."

[15]The king's officials answered him, "Your servants are ready to do whatever our lord the king chooses."

[16]The king set out, with his entire household following him; but he left ten concubines to take care of the palace.
[17]So the king set out, with all the people following him, and they halted at a place some distance away.
[18]All his men marched past him, along with all the Kerethites and Pelethites; and all the six hundred Gittites who had accompanied him from Gath marched before the king.

[19]The king said to Ittai the

הגתי למה תלך גם־ אתה אתנו שוב ושב עם־ המלך
the-king with and-stay! go-back! with-us you indeed you-go why? the-Gittite

כי־ נכרי אתה וגם־ גלה אתה למקומך׃
from-homeland-of-you you one-being-exiled and-also you foreigner for

תמול | בואך והיום אנועך° עמנו ללכת
to-go with-us shall-I-make-wander-you and-the-day to-come-you yesterday (20)

ואני הולך על אשר־אני הולך שוב והשב את־ אחיך
countrymen-of-you *** and-take! go-back! going I where to going when-I

עמך חסד ואמת׃ ויען אתי את־ המלך
the-king *** Ittai but-he-replied (21) and-faithfulness kindness with-you

ויאמר חי־ יהוה וחי אדני המלך כי אם־
*whether indeed the-king lord-of-me and-life-of Yahweh life-of and-he-said

במקום אשר יהיה־ שם | אדני המלך אם־ למות אם־
or for-death whether the-king lord-of-me there he-may-be where in-place-of

לחיים כי־ שם יהיה עבדך׃ ויאמר דוד אל־
to David and-he-said (22) servant-of-you he-will-be there indeed for-lives

אתי לך ועבר ויעבר אתי הגתי וכל־
and-all-of the-Gittite Ittai so-he-marched-on and-march-on! go! Ittai

אנשיו וכל־ הטף אשר אתו׃ וכל־ הארץ
the-country and-whole-of (23) with-him that the-family and-all-of men-of-him

בוכים קול גדול וכל־ העם עברים והמלך
and-the-king ones-passing-by the-people as-all-of loud voice ones-weeping

עבר בנחל קדרון וכל־ העם עברים על־
toward ones-moving-on the-people and-all-of Kidron over-Valley-of crossing

פני־ דרך את־ המדבר׃ והנה גם־ צדוק וכל־ הלוים
the-Levites and-all-of Zadok also and-see! (24) the-desert *** road surfaces-of

אתו נשאים את־ ארון ברית האלהים ויצקו את־
*** and-they-set-down the-God covenant-of ark-of *** ones-carrying with-him

ארון האלהים ויעל אביתר עד־ תם כל־ העם
the-people all-of to-finish until Abiathar and-he-sacrificed the-God ark-of

לעבור מן־ העיר׃ ויאמר המלך לצדוק השב את־
*** take-back! to-Zadok the-king then-he-said (25) the-city from to-leave

ארון האלהים העיר אם־אמצא חן בעיני יהוה והשבני
then-he-will-return-me Yahweh in-eyes-of favor I-find if the-city the-God ark-of

והראני אתו ואת־ נוהו׃ ואם כה יאמר לא
not he-says this but-if (26) dwelling-of-him and him and-he-will-let-see-me

חפצתי בך הנני יעשה־ לי כאשר טוב בעיניו׃
in-eyes-of-him good just-as to-me let-him-do see-I! with-you I-am-pleased

Gittite, "Why should you come along with us? Go back and stay with King Absalom. You are a foreigner, an exile from your homeland. [20]You came only yesterday. And today shall I make you wander about with us, when I do not know where I am going? Go back, and take your countrymen. May kindness and faithfulness be with you."

[21]But Ittai replied to the king, "As surely as the LORD lives, and as my lord the king lives, wherever my lord the king may be, whether it means life or death, there will your servant be."

[22]David said to Ittai, "Go ahead, march on." So Ittai the Gittite marched on with all his men and the families that were with him.

[23]The whole countryside wept aloud as all the people passed by. The king also crossed the Kidron Valley, and all the people moved on toward the desert.

[24]Zadok was there, too, and all the Levites who were with him were carrying the ark of the covenant of God. They set down the ark of God, and Abiathar offered sacrifices[t] until all the people had finished leaving the city.

[25]Then the king said to Zadok, "Take the ark of God back into the city. If I find favor in the LORD's eyes, he will bring me back and let me see it and his dwelling place again. [26]But if he says, 'I am not pleased with you,' then I am ready; let him do to me whatever seems good to him."

[t]24 Or *Abiathar went up*

*21 Most mss eliminate this word from the text in a *Qere* reading or omit it without a note.

°20 ק אניעך

וַיֹּאמֶר הַמֶּלֶךְ אֶל־צָדוֹק הַכֹּהֵן הֲרוֹאֶה אַתָּה שֻׁבָה הָעִיר
the-city go-back! you seer? the-priest Zadok to the-king and-he-said (27)

בְּשָׁלוֹם וַאֲחִימַעַץ בִּנְךָ וִיהוֹנָתָן בֶּן־אֶבְיָתָר שְׁנֵי
two-of Abiathar son-of and-Jonathan son-of-you and-Ahimaaz in-peace

בְנֵיכֶם אִתְּכֶם׃ רְאוּ אָנֹכִי מִתְמַהְמֵהַּ בְּעַבְרוֹת° הַמִּדְבָּר עַד בּוֹא
to-come until the-desert at-fords-of waiting I see! (28) with-you sons-of-you

דָבָר מֵעִמָּכֶם לְהַגִּיד לִי׃ וַיָּשֶׁב צָדוֹק וְאֶבְיָתָר
and-Abiathar Zadok so-he-took-back (29) to-me to-inform from-with-you word

אֶת־אֲרוֹן הָאֱלֹהִים יְרוּשָׁלָםִ וַיֵּשְׁבוּ שָׁם׃ וְדָוִד עֹלֶה
going-up but-David (30) there and-they-stayed Jerusalem the-God ark-of ***

בְמַעֲלֵה הַזֵּיתִים עֹלֶה ׀ וּבוֹכֶה וְרֹאשׁ לוֹ חָפוּי
being-covered on-him and-head and-weeping going the-Olives on-Mount-of

וְהוּא הֹלֵךְ יָחֵף וְכָל־הָעָם אֲשֶׁר־אִתּוֹ חָפוּ אִישׁ
each they-covered with-him who the-people and-all-of barefoot walking and-he

רֹאשׁוֹ וְעָלוּ עָלֹה וּבָכֹה׃ וְדָוִד הִגִּיד
he-told now-David (31) and-to-weep to-go-up and-they-went-up head-of-him

לֵאמֹר אֲחִיתֹפֶל בַּקֹּשְׁרִים עִם־אַבְשָׁלוֹם וַיֹּאמֶר דָּוִד
David so-he-prayed Absalom with among-the-ones-conspiring Ahithophel to-say

סַכֶּל־נָא אֶת־עֲצַת אֲחִיתֹפֶל יְהוָה׃ וַיְהִי דָוִד
David when-he-was (32) Yahweh Ahithophel counsel-of *** now! turn-foolish!

בָּא עַד־הָרֹאשׁ אֲשֶׁר־יִשְׁתַּחֲוֶה שָׁם לֵאלֹהִים וְהִנֵּה לִקְרָאתוֹ
to-meet-him then-see! to-God there he-worshiped where the-summit at arriving

חוּשַׁי הָאַרְכִּי קָרוּעַ כֻּתָּנְתּוֹ וַאֲדָמָה עַל־רֹאשׁוֹ׃
head-of-him on and-dust robe-of-him being-torn the-Arkite Hushai

וַיֹּאמֶר לוֹ דָּוִד אִם עָבַרְתָּ אִתִּי וְהָיִתָ עָלַי
to-me then-you-will-be with-me you-go if David to-him and-he-said (33)

לְמַשָּׂא׃ וְאִם־הָעִיר תָּשׁוּב וְאָמַרְתָּ לְאַבְשָׁלוֹם
to-Absalom and-you-say you-return the-city but-if (34) as-burden

עַבְדְּךָ אֲנִי הַמֶּלֶךְ אֶהְיֶה עֶבֶד אָבִיךָ וַאֲנִי מֵאָז
in-past also-I father-of-you servant-of I-will-be the-king I servant-of-you

וְעַתָּה וַאֲנִי עַבְדֶּךָ וְהֵפַרְתָּה לִי אֵת עֲצַת
advice-of *** for-me then-you-can-frustrate servant-of-you also-I but-now

אֲחִיתֹפֶל׃ וַהֲלוֹא עִמְּךָ שָׁם צָדוֹק וְאֶבְיָתָר הַכֹּהֲנִים
the-priests and-Abiathar Zadok there with-you and-not? (35) Ahithophel

וְהָיָה כָּל־הַדָּבָר אֲשֶׁר תִּשְׁמַע מִבֵּית הַמֶּלֶךְ תַּגִּיד
you-tell the-king in-palace-of you-hear that the-thing any-of and-he-will-be

לְצָדוֹק וּלְאֶבְיָתָר הַכֹּהֲנִים׃ הִנֵּה־שָׁם עִמָּם שְׁנֵי
two-of with-them there see! (36) the-priests and-to-Abiathar to-Zadok

[27]The king also said to Zadok
the priest, "Aren't you a seer?
Go back to the city in peace,
with your son Ahimaaz and
Jonathan son of Abiathar. You
and Abiathar take your two
sons with you. [28]I will wait at
the fords in the desert until
word comes from you to inform me." [29]So Zadok and
Abiathar took the ark of God
back to Jerusalem and stayed
there.

[30]But David continued up
the Mount of Olives, weeping
as he went; his head was
covered and he was barefoot.
All the people with him
covered their heads too and
were weeping as they went
up. [31]Now David had been
told, "Ahithophel is among
the conspirators with Absalom." So David prayed, "O
LORD, turn Ahithophel's counsel into foolishness."

[32]When David arrived at the
summit, where people used to
worship God, Hushai the Arkite was there to meet him, his
robe torn and dust on his
head. [33]David said to him, "If
you go with me, you will be a
burden to me. [34]But if you return to the city and say to Absalom, 'I will be your servant,
O king; I was your father's servant in the past, but now I will
be your servant,' then you can
help me by frustrating Ahithophel's advice. [35]Won't the
priests Zadok and Abiathar be
there with you? Tell them anything you hear in the king's

°28 ק בערבות

בְנֵיהֶם אֲחִימַעַץ לְצָדוֹק וִיהוֹנָתָן לְאֶבְיָתָר וּשְׁלַחְתֶּם
and-you-send of-Abiathar and-Jonathan of-Zadok Ahimaaz sons-of-them

בְּיָדָם אֵלַי כָּל־ דָּבָר אֲשֶׁר תִּשְׁמָעוּ׃ וַיָּבֹא חוּשַׁי
Hushai so-he-arrived (37) you-hear that thing any-of to-me by-hand-of-them

רֵעֶה דָוִד הָעִיר וְאַבְשָׁלֹם יָבֹא יְרוּשָׁלִָם׃ וְדָוִד
when-David (16:1) Jerusalem he-entered and-Absalom the-city David friend-of

עָבַר מְעַט מֵהָרֹאשׁ וְהִנֵּה צִיבָא נַעַר מְפִי־ בֹשֶׁת
Bosheth Mephi steward-of Ziba then-see! from-the-summit little he-went-beyond

לִקְרָאתוֹ וְצֶמֶד חֲמֹרִים חֲבֻשִׁים וַעֲלֵיהֶם מָאתַיִם
two-hundreds and-on-them ones-being-saddled donkeys and-string-of to-meet-him

לֶחֶם וּמֵאָה צִמּוּקִים וּמֵאָה קַיִץ וְנֵבֶל יָיִן׃
wine and-skin-of fig-cake and-hundred raisin-cakes and-hundred bread

וַיֹּאמֶר הַמֶּלֶךְ אֶל־צִיבָא מָה־ אֵלֶּה לָּךְ וַיֹּאמֶר צִיבָא
Ziba and-he-answered with-you these why? Ziba to the-king and-he-asked (2)

הַחֲמוֹרִים לְבֵית־ הַמֶּלֶךְ לִרְכֹּב וְלַהַלֶּחֶם° וְהַקַּיִץ
and-the-fruit and-the-bread to-ride the-king for-household-of the-donkeys

לֶאֱכוֹל הַנְּעָרִים וְהַיַּיִן לִשְׁתּוֹת הַיָּעֵף בַּמִּדְבָּר׃
in-the-desert the-one-exhausted to-refresh and-the-wine the-men to-eat

וַיֹּאמֶר הַמֶּלֶךְ וְאַיֵּה בֶּן־ אֲדֹנֶיךָ וַיֹּאמֶר צִיבָא
Ziba and-he-said masters-of-you son-of and-where? the-king then-he-asked (3)

אֶל־הַמֶּלֶךְ הִנֵּה יוֹשֵׁב בִּירוּשָׁלִַם כִּי אָמַר הַיּוֹם יָשִׁיבוּ
they-will-give-back the-day he-thinks for in-Jerusalem staying see! the-king to

לִי בֵּית יִשְׂרָאֵל אֵת מַמְלְכוּת אָבִי׃ וַיֹּאמֶר הַמֶּלֶךְ
the-king then-he-said (4) father-of-me kingdom-of *** Israel house-of to-me

לְצִבָא הִנֵּה לְךָ כֹּל אֲשֶׁר לִמְפִי־ בֹשֶׁת וַיֹּאמֶר צִיבָא הִשְׁתַּחֲוֵיתִי
I-humbly-bow Ziba and-he-said Bosheth to-Mephi that all to-you see! to-Ziba

אֶמְצָא־ חֵן בְּעֵינֶיךָ אֲדֹנִי הַמֶּלֶךְ׃ וּבָא
as-he-approached (5) the-king lord-of-me in-eyes-of-you favor may-I-find

הַמֶּלֶךְ דָּוִד עַד־ בַּחוּרִים וְהִנֵּה מִשָּׁם אִישׁ יוֹצֵא מִמִּשְׁפַּחַת
from-clan-of coming-out man from-there then-see! Bahurim to David the-king

בֵּית־ שָׁאוּל וּשְׁמוֹ שִׁמְעִי בֶּן־ גֵּרָא יֹצֵא יָצוֹא
to-come-out coming-out Gera son-of Shimei and-name-of-him Saul house-of

וּמְקַלֵּל׃ וַיְסַקֵּל בָּאֲבָנִים אֶת־ דָּוִד וְאֶת־ כָּל־ עַבְדֵי
officials-of all-of and David *** with-the-stones and-he-pelted (6) and-cursing

הַמֶּלֶךְ דָּוִד וְכָל־ הָעָם וְכָל־ הַגִּבֹּרִים מִימִינוֹ
on-right-of-him the-guards and-all-of the-troop though-all-of David the-king

וּמִשְּׂמֹאלוֹ׃ וְכֹה־ אָמַר שִׁמְעִי בְּקַלְלוֹ צֵא
get-out! as-to-curse-him Shimei he-said and-this (7) and-on-left-of-him

°2 ק והלחם

palace. 36 Their two sons, Ahimaaz son of Zadok and Jonathan son of Abiathar, are there with them. Send them to me with anything you hear."

37 So David's friend Hushai arrived at Jerusalem as Absalom was entering the city.

David and Ziba

16 When David had gone a short distance beyond the summit, there was Ziba, the steward of Mephibosheth, waiting to meet him. He had a string of donkeys saddled and loaded with two hundred loaves of bread, a hundred cakes of raisins, a hundred cakes of figs and a skin of wine.

2 The king asked Ziba, "Why have you brought these?"

Ziba answered, "The donkeys are for the king's household to ride on, the bread and fruit are for the men to eat, and the wine is to refresh those who become exhausted in the desert."

3 The king then asked, "Where is your master's grandson?"

Ziba said to him, "He is staying in Jerusalem, because he thinks, 'Today the house of Israel will give me back my grandfather's kingdom.' "

4 Then the king said to Ziba, "All that belonged to Mephibosheth is now yours."

"I humbly bow," Ziba said. "May I find favor in your eyes, my lord the king."

Shimei Curses David

5 As King David approached Bahurim, a man from the same clan as Saul's family came out from there. His name was Shimei son of Gera, and he cursed as he came out. 6 He pelted David and all the king's officials with stones, though all the troops and the special guard were on David's right and left. 7 As he cursed, Shimei said, "Get out, get out,

צֵא אִישׁ הַדָּמִים וְאִישׁ הַבְּלִיָּעַל׃ הֵשִׁיב עָלֶיךָ
to-you he-repaid (8) the-worthless and-man-of the-bloods man-of get-out!

יְהוָה כֹּל ׀ דְּמֵי בֵית־ שָׁאוּל אֲשֶׁר מָלַכְתָּ תַּחְתָּו
in-place-of-him you-reigned who Saul household-of bloods-of all-of Yahweh

וַיִּתֵּן יְהוָה אֶת־ הַמְּלוּכָה בְּיַד אַבְשָׁלוֹם בְּנֶךָ
son-of-you Absalom into-hand-of the-kingdom *** Yahweh and-he-handed

וְהִנְּךָ בְּרָעָתֶךָ כִּי אִישׁ דָּמִים אָתָּה׃ וַיֹּאמֶר אֲבִישַׁי
Abishai then-he-said (9) you bloods man-of for in-ruin-of-you and-see-you!

בֶן־ צְרוּיָה אֶל־ הַמֶּלֶךְ לָמָּה יְקַלֵּל הַכֶּלֶב הַמֵּת הַזֶּה
the-this the-dead the-dog should-he-curse why? the-king to Zeruiah son-of

אֶת־ אֲדֹנִי הַמֶּלֶךְ אֶעְבְּרָה־ נָּא וְאָסִירָה אֶת־ רֹאשׁוֹ׃
head-of-him *** and-let-me-cut-off now! let-me-go-over the-king lord-of-me ***

וַיֹּאמֶר הַמֶּלֶךְ מַה־ לִּי וְלָכֶם בְּנֵי צְרֻיָה כֹּי
so Zeruiah sons-of and-to-you to-me what? the-king but-he-said (10)

יְקַלֵּל וְכִּי יְהוָה אָמַר לוֹ קַלֵּל אֶת־ דָּוִד וּמִי יֹאמַר
he-can-ask and-who? David *** curse! to-him he-said Yahweh if he-may-curse

מַדּוּעַ עָשִׂיתָה כֵּן׃ וַיֹּאמֶר דָּוִד אֶל־ אֲבִישַׁי וְאֶל־ כָּל־
all-of and-to Abishai to David then-he-said (11) this you-do why?

עֲבָדָיו הִנֵּה בְנִי אֲשֶׁר־ יָצָא מִמֵּעַי מְבַקֵּשׁ אֶת־
*** seeking from-flesh-of-me he-came who son-of-me see! officials-of-him

נַפְשִׁי וְאַף כִּי־ עַתָּה בֶּן־הַיְמִינִי הַנִּחוּ לוֹ
to-him leave-alone! the-Benjamite now indeed and-more life-of-me

וִיקַלֵּל כִּי אָמַר־ לוֹ יְהוָה׃ אוּלַי יִרְאֶה יְהוָה
Yahweh he-will-see perhaps (12) Yahweh to-him he-told for and-let-him-curse

בְּעֵוֹנִי וְהֵשִׁיב יְהוָה לִי טוֹבָה תַּחַת קִלְלָתוֹ
curse-of-him for good to-me Yahweh and-he-will-repay to-distress-of-me

הַיּוֹם הַזֶּה׃ וַיֵּלֶךְ דָּוִד וַאֲנָשָׁיו בַּדָּרֶךְ
along-the-road and-men-of-him David so-he-went (13) the-this the-day

וְשִׁמְעִי הֹלֵךְ בְּצֵלַע הָהָר לְעֻמָּתוֹ הָלוֹךְ וַיְקַלֵּל
and-he-cursed to-go at-opposite-of-him the-hill along-side-of going and-Shimei

וַיְסַקֵּל בָּאֲבָנִים לְעֻמָּתוֹ וְעִפַּר בֶּעָפָר׃
with-the-dirt and-he-showered at-side-of-him with-the-stones and-he-pelted

וַיָּבֹא הַמֶּלֶךְ וְכָל־ הָעָם אֲשֶׁר־ אִתּוֹ עֲיֵפִים
ones-exhausted with-him who the-people and-all-of the-king and-he-arrived (14)

וַיִּנָּפֵשׁ שָׁם׃ וְאַבְשָׁלוֹם וְכָל־ הָעָם אִישׁ
man-of the-people and-all-of now-Absalom (15) there and-he-refreshed-himself

יִשְׂרָאֵל בָּאוּ יְרוּשָׁלִָם וַאֲחִיתֹפֶל אִתּוֹ׃ וַיְהִי כַּאֲשֶׁר־
just-then and-he-was (16) with-him and-Ahithophel Jerusalem they-came Israel

you man of blood, you scoundrel! 8The LORD has repaid you
for all the blood you shed in
the household of Saul, in
whose place you have reigned.
The LORD has handed the
kingdom over to your son Absalom. You have come to ruin
because you are a man of
blood!"
9Then Abishai son of Zeruiah said to the king, "Why
should this dead dog curse my
lord the king? Let me go over
and cut off his head."
10But the king said, "What
do you and I have in common,
you sons of Zeruiah? If he is
cursing because the LORD said
to him, 'Curse David,' who
can ask, 'Why do you do
this?' "
11David then said to Abishai
and all his officials, "My son,
who is of my own flesh, is trying to take my life. How much
more, then, this Benjamite!
Leave him alone; let him
curse, for the LORD has told
him to. 12It may be that the
LORD will see my distress and
repay me with good for the
cursing I am receiving today."
13So David and his men continued along the road while
Shimei was going along the
hillside opposite him, cursing
as he went and throwing
stones at him and showering
him with dirt. 14The king and
all the people with him arrived at their destination exhausted. And there he re-
freshed himself.

The Advice of Hushai and Ahithophel

15Meanwhile, Absalom and
all the men of Israel came to
Jerusalem, and Ahithophel
was with him. 16Then Hushai

°8 ק תחתיו
°10a ק כה
°10b ק כי
°12 ק בעיני

בָּא חוּשַׁי הָאַרְכִּי רֵעֶה דָוִד אֶל־אַבְשָׁלוֹם וַיֹּאמֶר חוּשַׁי אֶל־
to Hushai and-he-said Absalom to David friend-of the-Arkite Hushai he-went

אַבְשָׁלֹם יְחִי הַמֶּלֶךְ יְחִי הַמֶּלֶךְ׃ וַיֹּאמֶר אַבְשָׁלוֹם
Absalom and-he-asked (17) the-king may-he-live the-king may-he-live Absalom

אֶל־חוּשַׁי זֶה חַסְדְּךָ אֶת־רֵעֶךָ לָמָּה לֹא־הָלַכְתָּ אֶת־
with you-went not why? friend-of-you for love-of-you this Hushai to

רֵעֶךָ׃ וַיֹּאמֶר חוּשַׁי אֶל־אַבְשָׁלֹם לֹא° כִּי אֲשֶׁר בָּחַר יְהוָה
Yahweh he-chose whom for no Absalom to Hushai and-he-said (18) friend-of-you

וְהָעָם הַזֶּה וְכָל־אִישׁ יִשְׂרָאֵל לֹא אֶהְיֶה וְאִתּוֹ
and-with-him I-will-be to-him Israel man-of and-all-of the-this and-the-people

אֵשֵׁב׃ וְהַשֵּׁנִית לְמִי אֲנִי אֶעֱבֹד הֲלוֹא לִפְנֵי
before not? I-should-serve I to-whom? and-the-further (19) I-will-remain

בְנוֹ כַּאֲשֶׁר עָבַדְתִּי לִפְנֵי אָבִיךָ כֵּן אֶהְיֶה לְפָנֶיךָ׃
before-you I-will-be so father-of-you before I-served just-as son-of-him

וַיֹּאמֶר אַבְשָׁלוֹם אֶל־אֲחִיתֹפֶל הָבוּ לָכֶם עֵצָה מַה־נַּעֲשֶׂה׃
should-we-do what? advice for-you give! Ahithophel to Absalom and-he-said (20)

וַיֹּאמֶר אֲחִיתֹפֶל אֶל־אַבְשָׁלֹם בּוֹא אֶל־פִּלַגְשֵׁי אָבִיךָ
father-of-you concubines-of into go! Absalom to Ahithophel and-he-answered (21)

אֲשֶׁר הִנִּיחַ לִשְׁמוֹר הַבָּיִת וְשָׁמַע כָּל־יִשְׂרָאֵל כִּי־
that Israel all-of then-he-will-hear the-palace to-care-for he-left whom

נִבְאַשְׁתָּ אֶת־אָבִיךָ וְחָזְקוּ
and-they-will-become-strong father-of-you *** you-made-yourself-stench

יְדֵי כָּל־אֲשֶׁר אִתָּךְ׃ וַיַּטּוּ לְאַבְשָׁלוֹם הָאֹהֶל עַל־
on the-tent for-Absalom so-they-pitched (22) with-you who all hands-of

הַגָּג וַיָּבֹא אַבְשָׁלוֹם אֶל־פִּלַגְשֵׁי אָבִיו לְעֵינֵי
before-eyes-of father-of-him concubines-of into Absalom and-he-went the-roof

כָּל־יִשְׂרָאֵל׃ וַעֲצַת אֲחִיתֹפֶל אֲשֶׁר יָעַץ בַּיָּמִים הָהֵם
the-those in-the-days he-gave that Ahithophel now-advice-of (23) Israel all-of

כַּאֲשֶׁר יִשְׁאַל־ * בִּדְבַר הָאֱלֹהִים כֵּן כָּל־עֲצַת אֲחִיתֹפֶל
Ahithophel advice-of all-of so the-God of-word-of * he-inquired like-that

גַּם־לְדָוִד גַּם לְאַבְשָׁלֹם׃ וַיֹּאמֶר אֲחִיתֹפֶל אֶל־אַבְשָׁלֹם
Absalom to Ahithophel and-he-said (17:1) to-Absalom and to-David both

אֶבְחֲרָה נָּא שְׁנֵים־עָשָׂר אֶלֶף אִישׁ וְאָקוּמָה וְאֶרְדְּפָה
and-let-me-pursue and-let-me-rise man thousand ten two now! let-me-choose

אַחֲרֵי־דָוִד הַלָּיְלָה׃ וְאָבוֹא עָלָיו וְהוּא יָגֵעַ
weary while-he against-him and-let-me-attack (2) the-night David after

וּרְפֵה יָדַיִם וְהַחֲרַדְתִּי אֹתוֹ וְנָס כָּל־הָעָם
the-people all-of and-he-will-flee him and-I-will-terrify hands and-weak-of

the Arkite, David's friend,
went to Absalom and said to
him, "Long live the king! Long
live the king!"
[17]Absalom asked Hushai, "Is
this the love you show your
friend? Why didn't you go
with your friend?"
[18]Hushai said to Absalom,
"No, the one chosen by the
LORD, by these people, and by
all the men of Israel—his I will
be, and I will remain with
him. [19]Furthermore, whom
should I serve? Should I not
serve the son? Just as I served
your father, so I will serve
you."
[20]Absalom said to Ahithophel, "Give us your advice.
What should we do?"
[21]Ahithophel answered, "Lie
with your father's concubines
whom he left to take care of
the palace. Then all Israel will
hear that you have made yourself a stench in your father's
nostrils, and the hands of
everyone with you will be
strengthened." [22]So they
pitched a tent for Absalom on
the roof, and he lay with his
father's concubines in the
sight of all Israel.
[23]Now in those days the advice Ahithophel gave was like
that of one who inquires of
God. That was how both David and Absalom regarded all
of Ahithophel's advice.

17 Ahithophel said to Ab-
salom, "I would[u]
choose twelve thousand men
and set out tonight in pursuit
of David. [2]I would[v] attack him
when he is weary and weak. I
would[v] strike him with terror,
and then all the people with
him will flee. I would[v] strike

[u]1 Or *Let me* [v]2 Or *will*

*23 Many mss have אִישׁ, *one* (*man*), as a *Qere* reading.

°18 ק לו

אֲשֶׁר־ אִתּוֹ וְהִכֵּיתִי אֶת־ הַמֶּלֶךְ לְבַדּוֹ׃
by-himself the-king *** and-I-will-strike-down with-him who

וְאָשִׁיבָה כָל־ הָעָם אֵלֶיךָ כְּשׁוּב הַכֹּל
the-whole as-to-return to-you the-people all-of and-I-will-bring-back (3)

הָאִישׁ אֲשֶׁר אַתָּה מְבַקֵּשׁ כָּל־ הָעָם יִהְיֶה שָׁלוֹם׃
unharmed he-will-be the-people all-of seeking you whom the-man

וַיִּשַׁר הַדָּבָר בְּעֵינֵי אַבְשָׁלֹם וּבְעֵינֵי כָּל־
all-of and-in-eyes-of Absalom in-eyes-of the-plan and-he-was-good (4)

זִקְנֵי יִשְׂרָאֵל׃ וַיֹּאמֶר אַבְשָׁלוֹם קְרָא נָא גַּם לְחוּשַׁי
to-Hushai also now! summon! Absalom but-he-said (5) Israel elders-of

הָאַרְכִּי וְנִשְׁמְעָה מַה־ בְּפִיו גַּם־ הוּא׃ וַיָּבֹא
when-he-came (6) he also in-mouth-of-him what so-we-can-hear the-Arkite

חוּשַׁי אֶל־אַבְשָׁלוֹם וַיֹּאמֶר אַבְשָׁלוֹם אֵלָיו לֵאמֹר כַּדָּבָר הַזֶּה
the-this as-the-advice to-say to-him Absalom then-he-said Absalom to Hushai

דִּבֶּר אֲחִיתֹפֶל הֲנַעֲשֶׂה אֶת־ דְּבָרוֹ אִם־ אַיִן אַתָּה דַבֵּר׃
give-opinion! you not if saying-of-him *** should-we-do? Ahithophel he-spoke

וַיֹּאמֶר חוּשַׁי אֶל־אַבְשָׁלוֹם לֹא־טוֹבָה הָעֵצָה אֲשֶׁר־יָעַץ אֲחִיתֹפֶל
Ahithophel he-gave that the-advice good not Absalom to Hushai and-he-replied (7)

בַּפַּעַם הַזֹּאת׃ וַיֹּאמֶר חוּשַׁי אַתָּה יָדַעְתָּ אֶת־ אָבִיךָ
father-of-you *** you-know you Hushai and-he-said (8) the-this at-the-time

וְאֶת־ אֲנָשָׁיו כִּי גִבֹּרִים הֵמָּה וּמָרֵי נֶפֶשׁ הֵמָּה כְּדֹב
as-bear they spirit and-ones-fierce-of they fighters that men-of-him and

שַׁכּוּל בַּשָּׂדֶה וְאָבִיךָ אִישׁ מִלְחָמָה וְלֹא
and-not fight man-of and-father-of-you in-the-wild robbed-of-cubs

יָלִין אֶת־ הָעָם׃ הִנֵּה עַתָּה הוּא־ נֶחְבָּא בְּאַחַת
in-one-of hiding he now see! (9) the-troop with he-will-spend-night

הַפְּחָתִים אוֹ בְּאַחַד הַמְּקוֹמֹת וְהָיָה כִּנְפֹל בָּהֶם
of-them when-to-fall and-he-will-be the-places in-one-of or the-caves

בַּתְּחִלָּה וְשָׁמַע הַשֹּׁמֵעַ וְאָמַר הָיְתָה מַגֵּפָה
slaughter she-was then-he-will-say the-one-hearing when-he-hears at-the-first

בָּעָם אֲשֶׁר אַחֲרֵי אַבְשָׁלֹם׃ וְהוּא גַם־ בֶּן־ חַיִל אֲשֶׁר
who bravery son-of even then-he (10) Absalom after who among-the-troop

לִבּוֹ כְּלֵב הָאַרְיֵה הִמֵּס יִמָּס כִּי־ יֹדֵעַ כָּל־
all-of knowing for he-will-melt to-melt the-lion like-heart-of heart-of-him

יִשְׂרָאֵל כִּי־ גִבּוֹר אָבִיךָ וּבְנֵי־ חַיִל אֲשֶׁר אִתּוֹ׃ כִּי
so (11) with-him who bravery and-sons-of father-of-you fighter that Israel

יָעַצְתִּי הֵאָסֹף יֵאָסֵף עָלֶיךָ כָל־ יִשְׂרָאֵל מִדָּן
from-Dan Israel all-of to-you let-him-be-gathered to-be-gathered I-advise

down only the king [3]and bring all the people back to you. The death of the man you seek will mean the return of all; all the people will be unharmed." [4]This plan seemed good to Absalom and to all the elders of Israel.

[5]But Absalom said, "Summon also Hushai the Arkite, so we can hear what he has to say." [6]When Hushai came to him, Absalom said, "Ahithophel has given this advice. Should we do what he says? If not, give us your opinion."

[7]Hushai replied to Absalom, "The advice Ahithophel has given is not good this time. [8]You know your father and his men; they are fighters, and as fierce as a wild bear robbed of her cubs. Besides, your father is an experienced fighter; he will not spend the night with the troops. [9]Even now, he is hidden in a cave or some other place. If he should attack your troops first,[w] whoever hears about it will say, 'There has been a slaughter among the troops who follow Absalom.' [10]Then even the bravest soldier, whose heart is like the heart of a lion, will melt with fear, for all Israel knows that your father is a fighter and that those with him are brave.

[11]"So I advise you: Let all Israel, from Dan to Beersheba—

[w]9 Or *When some of the men fall at the first attack*

וְעַד־ בְּאֵר שֶׁבַע כַּחוֹל אֲשֶׁר־עַל־ הַיָּם לָרֹב וּפָנֶיךָ
and-faces-of-you in-the-number the-sea by that as-the-sand Sheba Beer even-to

הֹלְכִים בַּקְרָב׃ וּבָאנוּ אֵלָיו בְּאַחַת
at-one-of against-him then-we-will-go (12) into-the-battle ones-leading

הַמְּקוֹמֹת אֲשֶׁר נִמְצָא שָׁם וְנַחְנוּ עָלָיו כַּאֲשֶׁר יִפֹּל הַטַּל
the-dew he-settles just-as on-him and-we there he-is-found where the-places

עַל־הָאֲדָמָה וְלֹא־ נוֹתַר בּוֹ וּבְכָל־ הָאֲנָשִׁים אֲשֶׁר־
who the-men or-of-any-of of-him he-will-be-left-alive and-not the-ground on

אִתּוֹ גַּם־אֶחָד׃ וְאִם־אֶל־ עִיר יֵאָסֵף וְהִשִּׂיאוּ
then-they-will-bring he-withdraws city to and-if (13) one even with-him

כָל־ יִשְׂרָאֵל אֶל־ הָעִיר הַהִיא חֲבָלִים וְסָחַבְנוּ אֹתוֹ עַד־ הַנַּחַל
the-valley to him and-we-will-drag ropes the-that the-city to Israel all-of

עַד אֲשֶׁר־ לֹא־ נִמְצָא שָׁם גַּם־צְרוֹר׃ וַיֹּאמֶר אַבְשָׁלוֹם
Absalom and-he-said (14) piece even there he-can-be-found not when until

וְכָל־ אִישׁ יִשְׂרָאֵל טוֹבָה עֲצַת חוּשַׁי הָאַרְכִּי מֵעֲצַת
than-advice-of the-Arkite Hushai advice-of better Israel man-of and-all-of

אֲחִיתֹפֶל וַיהוָה צִוָּה לְהָפֵר אֶת־ עֲצַת אֲחִיתֹפֶל
Ahithophel advice-of *** to-frustrate he-determined for-Yahweh Ahithophel

הַטּוֹבָה לְבַעֲבוּר הָבִיא יְהוָה אֶל־ אַבְשָׁלוֹם אֶת־ הָרָעָה׃
the-disaster *** Absalom on Yahweh to-bring in-order-to the-good

וַיֹּאמֶר חוּשַׁי אֶל־ צָדוֹק וְאֶל־ אֶבְיָתָר הַכֹּהֲנִים כָּזֹאת
as-such the-priests Abiathar and-to Zadok to Hushai then-he-told (15)

וְכָזֹאת יָעַץ אֲחִיתֹפֶל אֶת־אַבְשָׁלֹם וְאֵת זִקְנֵי יִשְׂרָאֵל וְכָזֹאת
but-as-so Israel elders-of and Absalom *** Ahithophel he-advised and-as-such

וְכָזֹאת יָעַצְתִּי אָנִי׃ וְעַתָּה שִׁלְחוּ מְהֵרָה וְהַגִּידוּ לְדָוִד
to-David and-tell! immediately send! and-now (16) I I-advised and-as-so

לֵאמֹר אַל־ תָּלֶן הַלַּיְלָה בְּעַרְבוֹת הַמִּדְבָּר וְגַם
but-indeed the-desert at-fords-of the-night you-spend-night not to-say

עָבוֹר תַּעֲבוֹר פֶּן יְבֻלַּע לַמֶּלֶךְ
to-the-king he-will-be-swallowed-up or you-cross-over to-cross-over

וּלְכָל־ הָעָם אֲשֶׁר אִתּוֹ׃ וִיהוֹנָתָן וַאֲחִימַעַץ
and-Ahimaaz now-Jonathan (17) with-him who the-people and-to-all-of

עֹמְדִים בְּעֵין־ רֹגֵל וְהָלְכָה הַשִּׁפְחָה וְהִגִּידָה
and-she-informed the-servant-girl and-she-went Rogel at-En ones-staying

לָהֶם וְהֵם יֵלְכוּ וְהִגִּידוּ לַמֶּלֶךְ דָּוִד כִּי לֹא
not for David to-the-king and-they-would-tell they-would-go so-they to-them

יוּכְלוּ לְהֵרָאוֹת לָבוֹא הָעִירָה׃ וַיַּרְא אֹתָם נַעַר
young-man them but-he-saw (18) into-the-city to-enter to-be-seen they-could

as numerous as the sand on
the seashore—be gathered to
you, with you yourself leading
them into battle. [12]Then we
will attack him wherever he
may be found, and we will fall
on him as dew settles on the
ground. Neither he nor any of
his men will be left alive. [13]If
he withdraws into a city, then
all Israel will bring ropes to
that city, and we will drag it
down to the valley until not
even a piece of it can be
found."
[14]Absalom and all the men of
Israel said, "The advice of Hushai the Arkite is better than
that of Ahithophel." For the
LORD had determined to frus-
trate the good advice of Ahithophel in order to bring disaster on Absalom.
[15]Hushai told Zadok and
Abiathar, the priests, "Ahithophel has advised Absalom
and the elders of Israel to do
such and such, but I have advised them to do so and so.
[16]Now send a message
immediately and tell David,
'Do not spend the night at the
fords in the desert; cross over
without fail, or the king and
all the people with him will be
swallowed up.' "
[17]Jonathan and Ahimaaz
were staying at En Rogel. A
servant girl was to go and inform them, and they were to
go and tell King David, for
they could not risk being seen
entering the city. [18]But a
young man saw them and told

°12 ק באחד

וַיַּגֵּד לְאַבְשָׁלֹם וַיֵּלְכוּ שְׁנֵיהֶם מְהֵרָה וַיָּבֹאוּ | אֶל־
to and-they-went quickly two-of-them so-they-left to-Absalom and-he-told

בֵּית־ אִישׁ בְּבַחוּרִים וְלוֹ בְאֵר בַּחֲצֵרוֹ וַיֵּרְדוּ
and-they-went-down in-courtyard-of-him well and-to-him in-Bahurim man house-of

שָׁם׃ וַתִּקַּח הָאִשָּׁה וַתִּפְרֹשׂ אֶת־ הַמָּסָךְ עַל־
over the-covering *** and-she-spread the-wife and-she-took (19) there

פְּנֵי הַבְּאֵר וַתִּשְׁטַח עָלָיו הָרִפוֹת וְלֹא
and-not the-grains over-him and-she-scattered the-well openings-of

נוֹדַע דָּבָר׃ וַיָּבֹאוּ עַבְדֵי אַבְשָׁלוֹם אֶל־ הָאִשָּׁה
the-woman to Absalom men-of when-they-came (20) matter he-was-known

הַבַּיְתָה וַיֹּאמְרוּ אַיֵּה אֲחִימַעַץ וִיהוֹנָתָן וַתֹּאמֶר
and-she-answered and-Jonathan Ahimaaz where? then-they-asked at-the-house

לָהֶם הָאִשָּׁה עָבְרוּ מִיכַל הַמָּיִם וַיְבַקְשׁוּ
and-they-searched the-waters brook-of they-crossed-over the-woman to-them

וְלֹא מָצָאוּ וַיָּשֻׁבוּ יְרוּשָׁלָםִ׃ וַיְהִי | אַחֲרֵי
after and-he-was (21) Jerusalem so-they-returned they-found but-not

לֶכְתָּם וַיַּעֲלוּ מֵהַבְּאֵר וַיֵּלְכוּ וַיַּגִּדוּ
and-they-informed and-they-went from-the-well then-they-climbed-up to-go-them

לַמֶּלֶךְ דָּוִד וַיֹּאמְרוּ אֶל־ דָּוִד קוּמוּ וְעִבְרוּ מְהֵרָה אֶת־
*** at-once and-cross! set-out! David to and-they-said David to-the-king

הַמַּיִם כִּי־ כָכָה יָעַץ עֲלֵיכֶם אֲחִיתֹפֶל׃ וַיָּקָם
so-he-set-out (22) Ahithophel against-you he-advised such for the-waters

דָּוִד וְכָל־ הָעָם אֲשֶׁר אִתּוֹ וַיַּעַבְרוּ אֶת־ הַיַּרְדֵּן
the-Jordan *** and-they-crossed with-him who the-people and-all-of David

עַד־ אוֹר הַבֹּקֶר עַד־אַחַד לֹא נֶעְדָּר אֲשֶׁר לֹא־ עָבַר אֶת־
*** he-crossed not who he-was-left not one even the-morning light-of by

הַיַּרְדֵּן׃ וַאֲחִיתֹפֶל רָאָה כִּי לֹא נֶעֶשְׂתָה עֲצָתוֹ
advice-of-him she-was-followed not that he-saw when-Ahithophel (23) the-Jordan

וַיַּחֲבֹשׁ אֶת־ הַחֲמוֹר וַיָּקָם וַיֵּלֶךְ אֶל־ בֵּיתוֹ
house-of-him to and-he-went and-he-set-out the-donkey *** then-he-saddled

אֶל־ עִירוֹ וַיְצַו אֶל־ בֵּיתוֹ וַיֵּחָנַק
then-he-hanged-himself house-of-him to and-he-put-in-order town-of-him in

וַיָּמָת וַיִּקָּבֵר בְּקֶבֶר אָבִיו׃ וְדָוִד בָּא
he-went now-David (24) father-of-him in-tomb-of and-he-was-buried so-he-died

מַחֲנָיְמָה וְאַבְשָׁלֹם עָבַר אֶת־ הַיַּרְדֵּן הוּא וְכָל־ אִישׁ
man-of and-all-of he the-Jordan *** he-crossed and-Absalom to-Mahanaim

יִשְׂרָאֵל עִמּוֹ׃ וְאֶת־עֲמָשָׂא שָׂם אַבְשָׁלֹם תַּחַת יוֹאָב עַל־
over Joab in-place-of Absalom he-appointed Amasa and (25) with-him Israel

Absalom. So the two of them
left quickly and went to the
house of a man in Bahurim.
He had a well in his courtyard,
and they climbed down into
it. [19]His wife took a covering
and spread it out over the
opening of the well and scattered grain over it. No one
knew anything about it.
[20]When Absalom's men
came to the woman at the
house, they asked, "Where are
Ahimaaz and Jonathan?"
The woman answered them,
"They crossed over the
brook."[x] The men searched
but found no one, so they returned to Jerusalem.
[21]After the men had gone,
the two climbed out of the well
and went to inform King David. They said to him, "Set out
and cross the river at once; A-
hithophel has advised such
and such against you." [22]So
David and all the people with
him set out and crossed the
Jordan. By daybreak, no one
was left who had not crossed
the Jordan.
[23]When Ahithophel saw that
his advice had not been followed, he saddled his donkey
and set out for his house in his
home town. He put his house
in order and then hanged
himself. So he died and was
buried in his father's tomb.
[24]David went to Mahanaim,
and Absalom crossed the Jordan with all the men of Israel.
[25]Absalom had appointed
Amasa over the army in place

[x]20 Or *"They passed by the sheep pen toward the water."*

הַצָּבָא וַעֲמָשָׂא בֶן־ אִישׁ וּשְׁמוֹ יִתְרָא הַיִּשְׂרְאֵלִי אֲשֶׁר־
who the-Israelite Ithra and-name-of-him man son-of now-Amasa the-army

בָּא אֶל־ אֲבִיגַל בַּת־ נָחָשׁ אֲחוֹת צְרוּיָה אֵם יוֹאָב׃
Joab mother-of Zeruiah sister-of Nahash daughter-of Abigal into he-went

וַיִּחַן יִשְׂרָאֵל וְאַבְשָׁלֹם אֶרֶץ הַגִּלְעָד׃ וַיְהִי
and-he-was (27) the-Gilead land-of and-Absalom Israel and-he-camped (26)

כְּבוֹא דָוִד מַחֲנָיְמָה וְשֹׁבִי בֶן־ נָחָשׁ מֵרַבַּת בְּנֵי־
sons-of from-Rabbah-of Nahash son-of then-Shobi to-Mahanaim David when-to-come

עַמּוֹן וּמָכִיר בֶּן־ עַמִּיאֵל מִלֹּא דְבָר וּבַרְזִלַּי הַגִּלְעָדִי
the-Gileadite and-Barzillai Debar from-Lo Ammiel son-of and-Makir Ammon

מֵרֹגְלִים׃ מִשְׁכָּב וְסַפּוֹת וּכְלִי יוֹצֵר
one-making-pottery and-articles-of and-bowls bedding (28) from-Rogelim

וְחִטִּים וּשְׂעֹרִים וְקֶמַח וְקָלִי וּפוֹל וַעֲדָשִׁים
and-lentils and-bean and-roasted-grain and-flour and-barleys and-wheats

וְקָלִי׃ וּדְבַשׁ וְחֶמְאָה וְצֹאן וּשְׁפוֹת בָּקָר
cow and-cheese-of and-sheep and-curd and-honey (29) and-roasted-grain

הִגִּישׁוּ לְדָוִד וְלָעָם אֲשֶׁר־ אִתּוֹ לֶאֱכוֹל כִּי אָמְרוּ
they-said for to-eat with-him who and-for-the-people for-David they-brought

הָעָם רָעֵב וְעָיֵף וְצָמֵא בַּמִּדְבָּר׃ וַיִּפְקֹד
and-he-mustered (18:1) in-the-desert and-thirsty and-tired hungry the-people

דָּוִד אֶת־ הָעָם אֲשֶׁר אִתּוֹ וַיָּשֶׂם עֲלֵיהֶם שָׂרֵי
commanders-of over-them and-he-appointed with-him who the-people *** David

אֲלָפִים וְשָׂרֵי מֵאוֹת׃ וַיְשַׁלַּח דָּוִד אֶת־ הָעָם
the-troop *** David and-he-sent-out (2) hundreds and-commanders-of thousands

הַשְּׁלִשִׁית בְּיַד־ יוֹאָב וְהַשְּׁלִשִׁית בְּיַד אֲבִישַׁי בֶן־
son-of Abishai under-hand-of and-the-third Joab under-hand-of the-third

צְרוּיָה אֲחִי יוֹאָב וְהַשְּׁלִשִׁת בְּיַד אִתַּי הַגִּתִּי
the-Gittite Ittai under-hand-of and-the-third Joab brother-of Zeruiah

וַיֹּאמֶר הַמֶּלֶךְ אֶל־ הָעָם יָצֹא אֵצֵא גַּם־ אָנִי
I even I-will-march-out to-march-out the-troop to the-king and-he-told

עִמָּכֶם׃ וַיֹּאמֶר הָעָם לֹא תֵצֵא כִּי אִם־ נֹס
to-flee if for you-must-go-out not the-people but-he-said (3) with-you

נָנוּס לֹא־ יָשִׂימוּ אֵלֵינוּ לֵב וְאִם־ יָמֻתוּ חֶצְיֵנוּ לֹא־
not half-of-us they-die even-if heart to-us they-will-set not we-must-flee

יָשִׂימוּ אֵלֵינוּ לֵב כִּי־ עַתָּה כָמֹנוּ עֲשָׂרָה אֲלָפִים וְעַתָּה טוֹב כִּי־
that better so-now thousands ten like-us now for heart to-us they-will-set

תִהְיֶה־ לָּנוּ מֵעִיר לַעְזִיר׃ וַיֹּאמֶר אֲלֵיהֶם הַמֶּלֶךְ
the-king to-them and-he-answered (4) to-give-help from-city for-us you-be

°3 ק לעזור

of Joab. Amasa was the son of
a man named Jether,[y] an Israelite[z] who had married Abigail,[a] the daughter of Nahash
and sister of Zeruiah the
mother of Joab. 26The Israelites
and Absalom camped in the
land of Gilead.
27When David came to
Mahanaim, Shobi son of Nahash from Rabbah of the Ammonites, and Makir son of
Ammiel from Lo Debar, and
Barzillai the Gileadite from
Rogelim 28brought bedding
and bowls and articles of pot-
tery. They also brought wheat
and barley, flour and roasted
grain, beans and lentils,[b]
29honey and curds, sheep, and
cheese from cows' milk for David and his people to eat. For
they said, "The people have
become hungry and tired and
thirsty in the desert."

Absalom's Death

18 David mustered the
men who were with
him and appointed over them
commanders of thousands
and commanders of hundreds.
2David sent the troops out—a
third under the command of
Joab, a third under Joab's
brother Abishai son of Zeruiah, and a third under Ittai the
Gittite. The king told the
troops, "I myself will surely
march out with you."
3But the men said, "You
must not go out; if we are
forced to flee, they won't care
about us. Even if half of us die,
they won't care; but you are
worth ten thousand of us.[c] It
would be better now for you to
give us support from the city."
4The king answered, "I will

[y]25 Hebrew *Ithra,* a variant of *Jether*
[z]25 Hebrew and some Septuagint manuscripts; other Septuagint manuscripts (see also 1 Chron. 2:17) *Ishmaelite* or *Jezreelite*
[a]25 Hebrew *Abigal,* a variant of *Abigail*
[b]28 Most Septuagint manuscripts and Syriac; Hebrew *lentils, and roasted grain*
[c]3 Two Hebrew manuscripts, some Septuagint manuscripts and Vulgate; most Hebrew manuscripts *care; for now there are ten thousand like us*

אֲשֶׁר־ יִיטַב בְּעֵינֵיכֶם אֶעֱשֶׂה וַיַּעֲמֹד הַמֶּלֶךְ אֶל ־יַד
side-of at the-king so-he-stood I-will-do in-eyes-of-you he-is-good what

הַשַּׁעַר וְכָל־ הָעָם יָצְאוּ לְמֵאוֹת וְלַאֲלָפִים׃
and-in-thousands in-hundreds they-marched-out the-people while-all-of the-gate

(5) וַיְצַו הַמֶּלֶךְ אֶת־ יוֹאָב וְאֶת־ אֲבִישַׁי וְאֶת־ אִתַּי לֵאמֹר
to-say Ittai and Abishai and Joab *** the-king and-he-commanded (5)

לְאַט־ לִי לַנַּעַר לְאַבְשָׁלוֹם וְכָל־ הָעָם
the-troop and-all-of with-Absalom with-the-young-man for-me for-gentleness

שָׁמְעוּ בְּצַוֺּת הַמֶּלֶךְ אֶת־ כָּל־ הַשָּׂרִים עַל־ דְּבַר
matter-of about the-commanders each-of *** the-king when-to-order they-heard

אַבְשָׁלוֹם׃ (6) וַיֵּצֵא הָעָם הַשָּׂדֶה לִקְרַאת יִשְׂרָאֵל
Israel to-fight the-field the-army and-he-marched-out (6) Absalom

וַתְּהִי הַמִּלְחָמָה בְּיַעַר אֶפְרָיִם׃ (7) וַיִּנָּגְפוּ שָׁם
there and-they-were-defeated (7) Ephraim in-forest-of the-battle and-she-was

עַם יִשְׂרָאֵל לִפְנֵי עַבְדֵי דָוִד וַתְּהִי־ שָׁם הַמַּגֵּפָה גְדוֹלָה
great the-casualty there and-she-was David men-of before Israel army-of

בַּיּוֹם הַהוּא עֶשְׂרִים אָלֶף׃ (8) וַתְּהִי־ שָׁם הַמִּלְחָמָה
the-battle there and-she-was (8) thousand twenty the-that on-the-day

נָפֹצֶית[°] עַל־ פְּנֵי כָל־ הָאָרֶץ וַיֶּרֶב
and-he-was-greater the-country whole-of surfaces-of over being-spread

הַיַּעַר לֶאֱכֹל בָּעָם מֵאֲשֶׁר אָכְלָה הַחֶרֶב
the-sword she-consumed than-what of-the-people to-consune the-forest

בַּיּוֹם הַהוּא׃ (9) וַיִּקָּרֵא אַבְשָׁלוֹם לִפְנֵי עַבְדֵי דָוִד וְאַבְשָׁלוֹם
now-Absalom David men-of by Absalom and-he-was-met (9) the-that on-the-day

רֹכֵב עַל־ הַפֶּרֶד וַיָּבֹא הַפֶּרֶד תַּחַת שׂוֹבֶךְ הָאֵלָה הַגְּדוֹלָה
the-large the-oak branch-of under the-mule and-he-went the-mule on riding

וַיֶּחֱזַק רֹאשׁוֹ בָאֵלָה וַיֻּתַּן בֵּין הַשָּׁמַיִם
the-skies between and-he-was-left in-the-oak head-of-him and-he-was-caught

וּבֵין הָאָרֶץ וְהַפֶּרֶד אֲשֶׁר־ תַּחְתָּיו עָבָר׃
he-went-on under-him that while-the-mule the-ground and-between

(10) וַיַּרְא אִישׁ אֶחָד וַיַּגֵּד לְיוֹאָב וַיֹּאמֶר הִנֵּה רָאִיתִי אֶת־
*** I-saw see! and-he-said to-Joab then-he-told one man when-he-saw (10)

אַבְשָׁלֹם תָּלוּי בָּאֵלָה׃ (11) וַיֹּאמֶר יוֹאָב לָאִישׁ הַמַּגִּיד
the-one-telling to-the-man Joab and-he-said (11) in-the-oak hanging Absalom

לוֹ וְהִנֵּה רָאִיתָ וּמַדּוּעַ לֹא־ הִכִּיתוֹ שָׁם אַרְצָה
to-ground there you-struck-down-him not so-why? you-saw now-what! to-him

וְעָלַי לָתֶת לְךָ עֲשָׂרָה כֶסֶף וַחֲגֹרָה אֶחָת׃ (12) וַיֹּאמֶר
but-he-said (12) one and-belt-of-warrior silver ten to-you to-give then-upon-me

do whatever seems best to you."

So the king stood beside the gate while all the men marched out in units of hundreds and of thousands. [5]The king commanded Joab, Abishai and Ittai, "Be gentle with the young man Absalom for my sake." And all the troops heard the king giving orders concerning Absalom to each of the commanders.

[6]The army marched into the field to fight Israel, and the battle took place in the forest of Ephraim. [7]There the army of Israel was defeated by David's men, and the casualties that day were great—twenty thousand men. [8]The battle spread out over the whole countryside, and the forest claimed more lives that day than the sword.

[9]Now Absalom happened to meet David's men. He was riding his mule, and as the mule went under the thick branches of a large oak, Absalom's head got caught in the tree. He was left hanging in midair, while the mule he was riding kept on going.

[10]When one of the men saw this, he told Joab, "I just saw Absalom hanging in an oak tree."

[11]Joab said to the man who had told him this, "What! You saw him? Why didn't you strike him to the ground right there? Then I would have had to give you ten shekels[d] of silver and a warrior's belt."

[d]11 That is, about 4 ounces (about 115 grams)

°8 ק נפוצת

הָאִישׁ אֶל־יוֹאָב וְלֹא אָנֹכִי שֹׁקֵל עַל־ כַּפַּי אֶלֶף כֶּסֶף לֹא־
not silver thousand hands-of-me into weighing I even-if Joab to the-man

אֶשְׁלַח יָדִי אֶל־ בֶּן־ הַמֶּלֶךְ כִּי בְאָזְנֵינוּ צִוָּה
he-commanded in-ears-of-us for the-king son-of against hand-of-me I-would-lift

הַמֶּלֶךְ אֹתְךָ וְאֶת־ אֲבִישַׁי וְאֶת־אִתַּי לֵאמֹר שִׁמְרוּ־ מִי בַּנַּעַר
to-the-young-man whoever protect! to-say Ittai and Abishai and you the-king

בְּאַבְשָׁלוֹם׃ אוֹ־עָשִׂיתִי בְנַפְשׁוֹ שֶׁקֶר וְכָל־ דָּבָר
thing and-any-of treacherously against-life-of-me I-acted if (13) to-Absalom

לֹא־ יִכָּחֵד מִן־ הַמֶּלֶךְ וְאַתָּה תִּתְיַצֵּב מִנֶּגֶד׃
from-before you-would-keep-distance then-you the-king from he-is-hidden not

וַיֹּאמֶר יוֹאָב לֹא־ כֵן אֹחִילָה לְפָנֶיךָ וַיִּקַּח שְׁלֹשָׁה
three so-he-took before-you I-will-wait like-this not Joab and-he-said (14)

שְׁבָטִים בְּכַפּוֹ וַיִּתְקָעֵם בְּלֵב אַבְשָׁלוֹם עוֹדֶנּוּ
while-he Absalom into-heart-of and-he-plunged-them in-hand-of-him javelins

חַי בְּלֵב הָאֵלָה׃ וַיָּסֹבּוּ עֲשָׂרָה נְעָרִים נֹשְׂאֵי
ones-bearing-of men ten and-they-surrounded (15) the-oak in-heart-of alive

כְּלֵי יוֹאָב וַיַּכּוּ אֶת־ אַבְשָׁלוֹם וַיְמִיתֻהוּ׃
and-they-killed-him Absalom *** and-they-struck Joab armors-of

וַיִּתְקַע יוֹאָב בַּשֹּׁפָר וַיָּשָׁב הָעָם
the-troop and-he-stopped on-the-trumpet Joab then-he-sounded (16)

מִרְדֹף אַחֲרֵי יִשְׂרָאֵל כִּי־ חָשַׂךְ יוֹאָב אֶת־ הָעָם׃ וַיִּקְחוּ
and-they-took (17) the-troop *** Joab he-halted for Israel after from-to-pursue

אֶת־ אַבְשָׁלוֹם וַיַּשְׁלִיכוּ אֹתוֹ בַיַּעַר אֶל־ הַפַּחַת הַגָּדוֹל
the-big the-pit into in-the-forest him and-they-threw Absalom ***

וַיַּצִּבוּ עָלָיו גַּל־ אֲבָנִים גָּדוֹל מְאֹד וְכָל־ יִשְׂרָאֵל נָסוּ
they-fled Israel and-all-of very large rocks heap-of over-him and-they-piled

אִישׁ לְאֹהָלוֹ׃ וְאַבְשָׁלֹם לָקַח וַיַּצֶּב־ לוֹ
to-himself and-he-erected he-took now-Absalom (18) to-homes-of-him each

בְחַיָּו אֶת־ מַצֶּבֶת אֲשֶׁר בְּעֵמֶק־ הַמֶּלֶךְ כִּי אָמַר אֵין־
not he-thought for the-King in-Valley-of that pillar *** during-lives-of-him

לִי בֵן בַּעֲבוּר הַזְכִּיר שְׁמִי וַיִּקְרָא לַמַּצֶּבֶת
to-the-pillar so-he-named name-of-me to-carry-on-memory in-order-to son to-me

עַל־ שְׁמוֹ וַיִּקָּרֵא לָהּ יַד אַבְשָׁלֹם עַד הַיּוֹם
the-day to Absalom Monument-of to-her and-he-is-called name-of-him after

הַזֶּה׃ וַאֲחִימַעַץ בֶּן־ צָדוֹק אָמַר אָרוּצָה נָּא
now! let-me-run he-said Zadok son-of now-Ahimaaz (19) the-this

וַאֲבַשְּׂרָה אֶת־ הַמֶּלֶךְ כִּי־ שְׁפָטוֹ יְהוָה מִיַּד
from-hand-of Yahweh he-delivered-him that the-king *** and-let-me-take-news

12But the man replied, "Even
if a thousand shekels[f] were
weighed out into my hands, I
would not lift my hand
against the king's son. In our
hearing the king commanded
you and Abishai and Ittai,
'Protect the young man Absalom for my sake.[g]' 13And if I
had put my life in jeop-
ardy[h]—and nothing is hidden
from the king—you would
have kept your distance from
me."
14Joab said, "I'm not going to
wait like this for you." So he
took three javelins in his hand
and plunged them into Absalom's heart while Absalom
was still alive in the oak tree.
15And ten of Joab's armor-
bearers surrounded Absalom,
struck him and killed him.
16Then Joab sounded the
trumpet, and the troops
stopped pursuing Israel, for
Joab halted them. 17They took
Absalom, threw him into a big
pit in the forest and piled up a
large heap of rocks over him.
Meanwhile, all the Israelites
fled to their homes.
18During his lifetime Absalom had taken a pillar and
erected it in the King's Valley
as a monument to himself, for
he thought, "I have no son to
carry on the memory of my
name." He named the pillar
after himself, and it is called
Absalom's Monument to this
day.

David Mourns

19Now Ahimaaz son of
Zadok said, "Let me run and
take the news to the king that
the LORD has delivered him

f12 That is, about 25 pounds (about 11 kilograms)
g12 A few Hebrew manuscripts, Septuagint, Vulgate and Syriac; most Hebrew manuscripts may be translated *Absalom, whoever you may be.*
h13 Or *Otherwise, if I had acted treacherously toward him*

°12 ק ולו
°13 ק בנפשי
°17 ק לאהליו

אֹיְבָיו׃ וַיֹּאמֶר לוֹ יוֹאָב לֹא אִישׁ בְּשֹׂרָה אַתָּה הַיּוֹם
the-day you news man-of not Joab to-him and-he-told (20) being-enemies-of-him

הַזֶּה וּבִשַּׂרְתָּ בְּיוֹם אַחֵר וְהַיּוֹם הַזֶּה לֹא
not the-this but-the-day another on-day now-you-may-take-news the-this

תְבַשֵּׂר כִּי־ עַל * בֶּן־ הַמֶּלֶךְ מֵת׃ וַיֹּאמֶר
then-he-said (21) he-is-dead the-king son-of * for because you-take-news

יוֹאָב לַכּוּשִׁי לֵךְ הַגֵּד לַמֶּלֶךְ אֲשֶׁר רָאִיתָה וַיִּשְׁתַּחוּ כוּשִׁי
Cushite and-he-bowed you-saw what to-the-king tell! go! to-the-Cushite Joab

לְיוֹאָב וַיָּרֹץ׃ וַיֹּסֶף עוֹד אֲחִימַעַץ בֶּן־ צָדוֹק
Zadok son-of Ahimaaz again and-he-repeated (22) and-he-ran-off before-Joab

וַיֹּאמֶר אֶל־יוֹאָב וִיהִי מָה אָרֻצָה־ נָּא גַם־ אָנִי אַחֲרֵי
after I also now! let-me-run whatever now-may-he-be Joab to and-he-said

הַכּוּשִׁי וַיֹּאמֶר יוֹאָב לָמָּה־ זֶּה אַתָּה רָץ בְּנִי וּלְכָה
for-to-you son-of-me running you this why? Joab but-he-replied the-Cushite

אֵין־בְּשׂוֹרָה מֹצֵאת׃ וִיהִי־ מָה אָרוּץ וַיֹּאמֶר לוֹ
to-him so-he-said I-would-run whatever now-may-he-be (23) bringing news not

רוּץ וַיָּרָץ אֲחִימַעַץ דֶּרֶךְ הַכִּכָּר וַיַּעֲבֹר אֶת־ הַכּוּשִׁי׃
the-Cushite *** and-he-outran the-plain way-of Ahimaaz then-he-ran run!

וְדָוִד יוֹשֵׁב בֵּין־ שְׁנֵי הַשְּׁעָרִים וַיֵּלֶךְ
and-he-went-up the-gates two-of between sitting now-David (24)

הַצֹּפֶה אֶל־ גַּג הַשַּׁעַר אֶל־ הַחוֹמָה וַיִּשָּׂא אֶת־
*** and-he-raised the-wall by the-gateway roof-of to the-one-watching

עֵינָיו וַיַּרְא וְהִנֵּה־ אִישׁ רָץ לְבַדּוֹ׃ וַיִּקְרָא
and-he-called (25) by-himself running man and-see! and-he-looked eyes-of-him

הַצֹּפֶה וַיַּגֵּד לַמֶּלֶךְ וַיֹּאמֶר הַמֶּלֶךְ אִם־
if the-king and-he-said to-the-king and-he-reported the-one-watching

לְבַדּוֹ בְּשׂוֹרָה בְּפִיו וַיֵּלֶךְ הָלוֹךְ וְקָרֵב׃
even-close to-come and-he-came in-mouth-of-him good-news by-himself

וַיַּרְא הַצֹּפֶה אִישׁ־ אַחֵר רָץ וַיִּקְרָא
and-he-called running another man the-one-watching then-he-saw (26)

הַצֹּפֶה אֶל־ הַשֹּׁעֵר וַיֹּאמֶר הִנֵּה־ אִישׁ רָץ לְבַדּוֹ
by-himself running man look! and-he-said the-gatekeeper to the-one-watching

וַיֹּאמֶר הַמֶּלֶךְ גַּם־ זֶה מְבַשֵּׂר׃ וַיֹּאמֶר
and-he-said (27) one-bringing-good-news he also the-king and-he-said

הַצֹּפֶה אֲנִי רֹאֶה אֶת־ מְרוּצַת הָרִאשׁוֹן כִּמְרֻצַת אֲחִימַעַץ בֶּן־
son-of Ahimaaz running-of the-first running-of *** seeing I the-one-watching

צָדוֹק וַיֹּאמֶר הַמֶּלֶךְ אִישׁ־ טוֹב זֶה וְאֶל־ בְּשׂוֹרָה טוֹבָה יָבוֹא׃
he-comes good news and-with this good man the-king and-he-said Zadok

from the hand of his enemies."

[20]"You are not the one to take the news today," Joab told him. "You may take the news another time, but you must not do so today, because the king's son is dead."

[21]Then Joab said to a Cushite, "Go, tell the king what you have seen." The Cushite bowed down before Joab and ran off.

[22]Ahimaaz son of Zadok again said to Joab, "Come what may, please let me run behind the Cushite."

But Joab replied, "My son, why do you want to go? You don't have any news that will bring you a reward."

[23]He said, "Come what may, I want to run."

So Joab said, "Run!" Then Ahimaaz ran by way of the plain[i] and outran the Cushite.

[24]While David was sitting between the inner and outer gates, the watchman went up to the roof of the gateway by the wall. As he looked out, he saw a man running alone. [25]The watchman called out to the king and reported it.

The king said, "If he is alone, he must have good news." And the man came closer and closer.

[26]Then the watchman saw another man running, and he called down to the gatekeeper, "Look, another man running alone!"

The king said, "He must be bringing good news, too."

[27]The watchman said, "It seems to me that the first one runs like Ahimaaz son of Zadok."

"He's a good man," the king said. "He comes with good news."

[i]23 That is, the plain of the Jordan

*21 Many mss have כן, *this*, as a *Qere* to be read with the *tsere* under על.

וַיִּקְרָא אֲחִימַעַץ וַיֹּאמֶר אֶל־ הַמֶּלֶךְ שָׁלוֹם וַיִּשְׁתַּחוּ
and-he-bowed well the-king to and-he-said Ahimaaz then-he-called (28)

לַמֶּלֶךְ לְאַפָּיו אָרְצָה וַיֹּאמֶר בָּרוּךְ יְהוָה
Yahweh being-praised and-he-said to-ground on-faces-of-him before-the-king

אֱלֹהֶיךָ אֲשֶׁר סִגַּר אֶת־ הָאֲנָשִׁים אֲשֶׁר־ נָשְׂאוּ אֶת־ יָדָם
hand-of-them *** they-lifted who the-men *** he-delivered-up who God-of-you

בַּאדֹנִי הַמֶּלֶךְ׃ וַיֹּאמֶר הַמֶּלֶךְ שָׁלוֹם לַנַּעַר
to-the-young-man safe the-king and-he-asked (29) the-king against-lord-of-me

לְאַבְשָׁלוֹם וַיֹּאמֶר אֲחִימַעַץ רָאִיתִי הֶהָמוֹן הַגָּדוֹל לִשְׁלֹחַ
to-send the-great the-confusion I-saw Ahimaaz and-he-answered to-Absalom

אֶת־ עֶבֶד הַמֶּלֶךְ יוֹאָב וְאֶת־ עַבְדֶּךָ וְלֹא יָדַעְתִּי מָה׃
what I-knew but-not servant-of-you and Joab the-king servant-of ***

וַיֹּאמֶר הַמֶּלֶךְ סֹב הִתְיַצֵּב כֹּה וַיִּסֹּב
so-he-stepped-aside here and-wait! stand-aside! the-king and-he-said (30)

וַיַּעֲמֹד׃ וְהִנֵּה הַכּוּשִׁי בָּא וַיֹּאמֶר הַכּוּשִׁי
the-Cushite and-he-said arriving the-Cushite then-see! (31) and-he-stood

יִתְבַּשֵּׂר אֲדֹנִי הַמֶּלֶךְ כִּי־ שְׁפָטְךָ יְהוָה הַיּוֹם
the-day Yahweh he-delivered-you for the-king lord-of-me may-he-hear-good-news

מִיַּד כָּל־ הַקָּמִים עָלֶיךָ׃ וַיֹּאמֶר הַמֶּלֶךְ
the-king and-he-asked (32) against-you the-ones-rising all-of from-hand-of

אֶל־ הַכּוּשִׁי הֲשָׁלוֹם לַנַּעַר לְאַבְשָׁלוֹם וַיֹּאמֶר הַכּוּשִׁי
the-Cushite and-he-replied to-Absalom to-the-young-man safe? the-Cushite to

יִהְיוּ כַנַּעַר אֹיְבֵי אֲדֹנִי הַמֶּלֶךְ
the-king lord-of-me being-enemies-of like-the-young-man may-they-be

וְכֹל אֲשֶׁר־ קָמוּ עָלֶיךָ לְרָעָה׃ וַיִּרְגַּז הַמֶּלֶךְ
the-king and-he-was-shaken *(19:1) to-harm against-you they-rise who and-all

וַיַּעַל עַל־ עֲלִיַּת הַשַּׁעַר וַיֵּבְךְּ וְכֹה ׀ אָמַר
he-said and-this and-he-wept the-gateway upper-room-of to and-he-went-up

בְּלֶכְתּוֹ בְּנִי אַבְשָׁלוֹם בְּנִי בְנִי אַבְשָׁלוֹם מִי־ יִתֵּן
he-would-grant who? Absalom son-of-me son-of-me Absalom son-of-me as-to-go-him

מוּתִי אֲנִי תַחְתֶּיךָ אַבְשָׁלוֹם בְּנִי בְנִי׃ וַיֻּגַּד
and-he-was-told (2) son-of-me son-of-me Absalom instead-of-you I to-die-me

לְיוֹאָב הִנֵּה הַמֶּלֶךְ בֹּכֶה וַיִּתְאַבֵּל עַל־ אַבְשָׁלֹם׃ וַתְּהִי
and-she-turned (3) Absalom for and-he-mourns weeping the-king see! to-Joab

הַתְּשֻׁעָה בַּיּוֹם הַהוּא לְאֵבֶל לְכָל־ הָעָם כִּי־
for the-army for-all-of into-mourning the-that on-the-day the-victory

שָׁמַע הָעָם בַּיּוֹם הַהוּא לֵאמֹר נֶעֱצַב הַמֶּלֶךְ עַל־
for the-king he-grieves to-say the-that on-the-day the-troop he-heard

[28]Then Ahimaaz called out to
the king, "All is well!" He
bowed down before the king
with his face to the ground
and said, "Praise be to the
LORD your God! He has de-
livered up the men who lifted
their hands against my lord
the king."
[29]The king asked, "Is the
young man Absalom safe?"
Ahimaaz answered, "I saw
great confusion just as Joab
was about to send the king's
servant and me, your servant,
but I don't know what it was."
[30]The king said, "Stand aside
and wait here." So he stepped
aside and stood there.
[31]Then the Cushite arrived
and said, "My lord the king,
hear the good news! The LORD
has delivered you today from
all who rose up against you."
[32]The king asked the Cushite, "Is the young man Absalom safe?"
The Cushite replied, "May
the enemies of my lord the
king and all who rise up to
harm you be like that young
man."
[33]The king was shaken. He
went up to the room over the
gateway and wept. As he
went, he said: "O my son Absalom! My son, my son Absalom! If only I had died instead
of you—O Absalom, my son,
my son!"
19 Joab was told, "The
king is weeping and
mourning for Absalom." [2]And
for the whole army the victory
that day was turned into
mourning, because on that
day the troops heard it said,
"The king is grieving for his

**1* The Hebrew numeration of chapter 19 begins with verse 33 of chapter 18 in English; thus, there is a one-verse discrepancy throughout chapter 18.

בְּנוֹ׃ וַיִּתְגַּנֵּב הָעָם בַּיּוֹם הַהוּא לָבוֹא הָעִיר
the-city to-enter the-that on-the-day the-people and-he-stole-in (4) son-of-him

כַּאֲשֶׁר יִתְגַּנֵּב הָעָם הַנִּכְלָמִים בְּנוּסָם
when-to-flee-them the-ones-being-ashamed the-people he-steals-in just-as

בַּמִּלְחָמָה׃ וְהַמֶּלֶךְ לָאַט אֶת־ פָּנָיו וַיִּזְעַק
and-he-cried faces-of-him *** he-covered and-the-king (5) from-the-battle

הַמֶּלֶךְ קוֹל גָּדוֹל בְּנִי אַבְשָׁלוֹם אַבְשָׁלוֹם בְּנִי בְּנִי׃
son-of-me son-of-me Absalom Absalom son-of-me loud voice the-king

וַיָּבֹא יוֹאָב אֶל־ הַמֶּלֶךְ הַבָּיִת וַיֹּאמֶר הֹבַשְׁתָּ
you-humiliated and-he-said the-house the-king into Joab then-he-went (6)

הַיּוֹם אֶת־ פְּנֵי כָל־ עֲבָדֶיךָ הַמְמַלְּטִים אֶת־ נַפְשְׁךָ
life-of-you *** the-ones-saving men-of-you all-of faces-of *** the-day

הַיּוֹם וְאֵת נֶפֶשׁ בָּנֶיךָ וּבְנֹתֶיךָ וְנֶפֶשׁ נָשֶׁיךָ
wives-of-you and-life-of and-daughters-of-you sons-of-you life-of and the-day

וְנֶפֶשׁ פִּלַגְשֶׁיךָ׃ לְאַהֲבָה אֶת־ שֹׂנְאֶיךָ וְלִשְׂנֹא
and-to-hate ones-hating-you *** to-love (7) concubines-of-you and-life-of

אֶת־ אֹהֲבֶיךָ כִּי ׀ הִגַּדְתָּ הַיּוֹם כִּי אֵין לְךָ שָׂרִים
commanders to-you nothing that the-day you-made-clear for ones-loving-you ***

וַעֲבָדִים כִּי ׀ יָדַעְתִּי הַיּוֹם כִּי °לֹא אַבְשָׁלוֹם חַי וְכֻלָּנוּ הַיּוֹם
the-day and-all-of-us alive Absalom if that the-day I-see indeed and-men

מֵתִים כִּי־ אָז יָשָׁר בְּעֵינֶיךָ׃ וְעַתָּה קוּם צֵא
go-out! rise! and-now (8) in-eyes-of-you pleasing then that ones-dead

וְדַבֵּר עַל־ לֵב עֲבָדֶיךָ כִּי בַיהוָה נִשְׁבַּעְתִּי כִּי־ אֵינְךָ יוֹצֵא
going-out not-you if I-swear by-Yahweh for men-of-you heart-of to and-speak!

אִם־ יָלִין אִישׁ אִתְּךָ הַלַּיְלָה וְרָעָה לְךָ זֹאת מִכָּל־
than-all-of this for-you and-worse the-night with-you man he-will-remain not

הָרָעָה אֲשֶׁר־ בָּאָה עָלֶיךָ מִנְּעֻרֶיךָ עַד־ עָתָּה׃
now till from-youths-of-you upon-you she-came that the-calamity

וַיָּקָם הַמֶּלֶךְ וַיֵּשֶׁב בַּשַּׁעַר וּלְכָל־ הָעָם
the-people and-to-all-of in-the-gateway and-he-sat the-king so-he-got-up (9)

הִגִּידוּ לֵאמֹר הִנֵּה הַמֶּלֶךְ יוֹשֵׁב בַּשַּׁעַר וַיָּבֹא כָל־
all-of and-he-came in-the-gateway sitting the-king see! to-say they-told

הָעָם לִפְנֵי הַמֶּלֶךְ וְיִשְׂרָאֵל נָס אִישׁ לְאֹהָלָיו׃
to-homes-of-him each he-fled now-Israel the-king before the-people

וַיְהִי כָל־ הָעָם נָדוֹן בְּכָל־ שִׁבְטֵי יִשְׂרָאֵל
Israel tribes-of through-all-of arguing the-people all-of and-he-was (10)

לֵאמֹר הַמֶּלֶךְ הִצִּילָנוּ ׀ מִכַּף אֹיְבֵינוּ וְהוּא
and-he being-enemies-of-us from-hand-of he-delivered-us the-king to-say

son." [3]The men stole into the
city that day as men steal in
who are ashamed when they
flee from battle. [4]The king
covered his face and cried
aloud, "O my son Absalom! O
Absalom, my son, my son!"
[5]Then Joab went into the
house to the king and said,
"Today you have humiliated
all your men, who have just
saved your life and the lives of
your sons and daughters and
the lives of your wives and
concubines. [6]You love those
who hate you and hate those
who love you. You have made
it clear today that the commanders and their men mean
nothing to you. I see that you
would be pleased if Absalom
were alive today and all of us
were dead. [7]Now go out and
encourage your men. I swear
by the LORD that if you don't
go out, not a man will be left
with you by nightfall. This
will be worse for you than all
the calamities that have come
upon you from your youth till
now."
[8]So the king got up and took
his seat in the gateway. When
the men were told, "The king
is sitting in the gateway,"
they all came before him.

David Returns to Jerusalem

Meanwhile, the Israelites
had fled to their homes.
[9]Throughout the tribes of Israel, the people were all arguing
with each other, saying, "The
king delivered us from the
hand of our enemies; he is the

*See the note on page 307.

°7 ק לו

מִלְטָנוּ מִכַּף פְּלִשְׁתִּים וְעַתָּה בָּרַח מִן־ הָאָרֶץ
the-country from he-fled but-now Philistines from-hand-of he-rescued-us

מֵעַל אַבְשָׁלוֹם׃ וְאַבְשָׁלוֹם אֲשֶׁר מָשַׁחְנוּ עָלֵינוּ מֵת
he-died over-us we-anointed whom and-Absalom (11) Absalom because-of

בַּמִּלְחָמָה וְעַתָּה לָמָה אַתֶּם מַחֲרִשִׁים לְהָשִׁיב אֶת־ הַמֶּלֶךְ׃
the-king *** to-bring-back ones-saying-nothing you why? so-now in-the-battle

וְהַמֶּלֶךְ דָּוִד שָׁלַח אֶל־ צָדוֹק וְאֶל־ אֶבְיָתָר הַכֹּהֲנִים לֵאמֹר
to-say the-priests Abiathar and-to Zadok to he-sent David now-the-king

דַּבְּרוּ אֶל־ זִקְנֵי יְהוּדָה לֵאמֹר לָמָּה תִהְיוּ אַחֲרֹנִים לְהָשִׁיב
to-bring-back last-ones should-you-be why? to-say Judah elders-of to ask!

אֶת־ הַמֶּלֶךְ אֶל־ בֵּיתוֹ וּדְבַר כָּל־ יִשְׂרָאֵל בָּא אֶל־
to he-reached Israel all-of since-word-of palace-of-him to the-king ***

הַמֶּלֶךְ אֶל־ בֵּיתוֹ׃ אַחַי אַתֶּם עַצְמִי וּבְשָׂרִי
and-flesh-of-me bone-of-me you brothers-of-me (13) residence-of-him at the-king

אַתֶּם וְלָמָּה תִהְיוּ אַחֲרֹנִים לְהָשִׁיב אֶת־ הַמֶּלֶךְ׃
the-king *** to-bring-back last-ones should-you-be so-why? you

וְלַעֲמָשָׂא תֹּמְרוּ הֲלוֹא עַצְמִי וּבְשָׂרִי אַתָּה כֹּה יַעֲשֶׂה־
may-he-deal so you and-flesh-of-me bone-of-me not? you-say and-to-Amasa (14)

לִּי אֱלֹהִים וְכֹה יוֹסִיף אִם־ לֹא שַׂר־ צָבָא תִּהְיֶה
you-are army commander-of not if may-he-be-severe and-so God with-me

לְפָנַי כָּל־ הַיָּמִים תַּחַת יוֹאָב׃ וַיַּט אֶת־ לְבַב
heart-of *** and-he-won-over (15) Joab in-place-of the-days all-of before-me

כָּל־ אִישׁ־ יְהוּדָה כְּאִישׁ אֶחָד וַיִּשְׁלְחוּ אֶל־ הַמֶּלֶךְ שׁוּב אַתָּה
you return! the-king to and-they-sent one as-man Judah man-of all-of

וְכָל־ עֲבָדֶיךָ׃ וַיָּשָׁב הַמֶּלֶךְ וַיָּבֹא עַד־
as-far-as and-he-went the-king then-he-returned (16) men-of-you and-all-of

הַיַּרְדֵּן וִיהוּדָה בָּא הַגִּלְגָּלָה לָלֶכֶת לִקְרַאת הַמֶּלֶךְ
the-king to-meet to-go-out to-the-Gilgal he-came now-Judah the-Jordan

לְהַעֲבִיר אֶת־ הַמֶּלֶךְ אֶת־ הַיַּרְדֵּן׃ וַיְמַהֵר שִׁמְעִי בֶן־
son-of Shimei and-he-hurried (17) the-Jordan *** the-king *** to-bring-across

גֵּרָא בֶן־הַיְמִינִי אֲשֶׁר מִבַּחוּרִים וַיֵּרֶד עִם־ אִישׁ יְהוּדָה
Judah man-of with and-he-went-down from-Bahurim who the-Benjamite Gera

לִקְרַאת הַמֶּלֶךְ דָּוִד׃ וְאֶלֶף אִישׁ עִמּוֹ מִבִּנְיָמִן וְצִיבָא
and-Ziba from-Benjamin with-him man and-thousand (18) David the-king to-meet

נַעַר בֵּית שָׁאוּל וַחֲמֵשֶׁת עָשָׂר בָּנָיו וְעֶשְׂרִים
and-twenty sons-of-him ten and-five-of Saul household-of steward-of

עֲבָדָיו אִתּוֹ וְצָלְחוּ הַיַּרְדֵּן לִפְנֵי הַמֶּלֶךְ׃
the-king before the-Jordan and-they-rushed with-him servants-of-him

one who rescued us from the
hand of the Philistines. But
now he has fled the country
because of Absalom; [10]and Absalom, whom we anointed to
rule over us, has died in battle.
So why do you say nothing
about bringing the king
back?"

[11]King David sent this message to Zadok and Abiathar,
the priests: "Ask the elders of
Judah, 'Why should you be the
last to bring the king back to
his palace, since what is being
said throughout Israel has
reached the king at his quarters? [12]You are my brothers,
my own flesh and blood. So
why should you be the last to
bring back the king?' [13]And
say to Amasa, 'Are you not my
own flesh and blood? May
God deal with me, be it ever so
severely, if from now on you
are not the commander of my
army in place of Joab.' "

[14]He won over the hearts of
all the men of Judah as though
they were one man. They sent
word to the king, "Return, you
and all your men." [15]Then the
king returned and went as far
as the Jordan.

Now the men of Judah had
come to Gilgal to go out and
meet the king and bring him
across the Jordan. [16]Shimei
son of Gera, the Benjamite
from Bahurim, hurried down
with the men of Judah to meet
King David. [17]With him were
a thousand Benjamites, along
with Ziba, the steward of
Saul's household, and his
fifteen sons and twenty servants. They rushed to the Jordan, where the king was.

*See the note on page 307.

וְעָבְרָה הָעֲבָרָה לַעֲבִיר אֶת־ בֵּית הַמֶּלֶךְ וְלַעֲשׂוֹת
and-to-do the-king household-of *** to-take-over the-ford and-she-crossed (19)

הַטּוֹב בְּעֵינָו וְשִׁמְעִי בֶן־ גֵּרָא נָפַל לִפְנֵי הַמֶּלֶךְ
the-king before he-fell Gera son-of and-Shimei in-eyes-of-him the-good

בְּעָבְרוֹ בַּיַּרְדֵּן׃ וַיֹּאמֶר אֶל־ הַמֶּלֶךְ אַל־
not the-king to and-he-said (20) over-the-Jordan when-to-cross-him

יַחֲשָׁב־ לִי אֲדֹנִי עָוֺן וְאַל־ תִּזְכֹּר אֵת אֲשֶׁר
how *** you-remember and-not guilt lord-of-me against-me may-he-hold

הֶעֱוָה עַבְדְּךָ בַּיּוֹם אֲשֶׁר־ יָצָא אֲדֹנִי־ הַמֶּלֶךְ
the-king lord-of-me he-left that on-the-day servant-of-you he-did-wrong

מִירוּשָׁלִָם לָשׂוּם הַמֶּלֶךְ אֶל־ לִבּוֹ׃ כִּי יָדַע
he-knows for (21) heart-of-him to the-king to-take from-Jerusalem

עַבְדְּךָ כִּי אֲנִי חָטָאתִי וְהִנֵּה־ בָאתִי הַיּוֹם רִאשׁוֹן לְכָל־
of-whole-of first the-day I-came but-see! I-sinned I that servant-of-you

בֵּית יוֹסֵף לָרֶדֶת לִקְרַאת אֲדֹנִי הַמֶּלֶךְ׃ וַיַּעַן
then-he-replied (22) the-king lord-of-me to-meet to-come-down Joseph house-of

אֲבִישַׁי בֶּן־ צְרוּיָה וַיֹּאמֶר הֲתַחַת זֹאת לֹא יוּמַת שִׁמְעִי
Shimei he-should-be-killed not this for? and-he-said Zeruiah son-of Abishai

כִּי קִלֵּל אֶת־ מְשִׁיחַ יְהוָה׃ וַיֹּאמֶר דָּוִד מַה־ לִּי
to-me what? David and-he-replied (23) Yahweh anointed-of *** he-cursed for

וְלָכֶם בְּנֵי צְרוּיָה כִּי־ תִהְיוּ־ לִי הַיּוֹם לְשָׂטָן הַיּוֹם
the-day as-adversary the-day to-me you-became for Zeruiah sons-of and-to-you

יוּמַת אִישׁ בְּיִשְׂרָאֵל כִּי הֲלוֹא יָדַעְתִּי כִּי הַיּוֹם
the-day that I-know not? indeed in-Israel anyone should-he-be-killed

אֲנִי־מֶלֶךְ עַל־יִשְׂרָאֵל׃ וַיֹּאמֶר הַמֶּלֶךְ אֶל־ שִׁמְעִי לֹא תָמוּת
you-shall-die not Shimei to the-king so-he-said (24) Israel over king I

וַיִּשָּׁבַע לוֹ הַמֶּלֶךְ׃ וּמְפִבֹשֶׁת בֶּן־ שָׁאוּל
Saul son-of and-Mephibosheth (25) the-king to-him and-he-promised-on-oath

יָרַד לִקְרַאת הַמֶּלֶךְ וְלֹא־ עָשָׂה רַגְלָיו וְלֹא־
and-not feet-of-him he-took-care and-not the-king to-meet he-went-down

עָשָׂה שְׂפָמוֹ וְאֶת־ בְּגָדָיו לֹא כִבֵּס לְמִן־ הַיּוֹם
the-day at-from washed not clothes-of-him and mustache-of-him he-trimmed

לֶכֶת הַמֶּלֶךְ עַד־ הַיּוֹם אֲשֶׁר־ בָּא בְשָׁלוֹם׃ וַיְהִי
and-he-was (26) in-safety he-returned that the-day until the-king to-leave

כִּי־ בָא יְרוּשָׁלִַם לִקְרַאת הַמֶּלֶךְ וַיֹּאמֶר לוֹ הַמֶּלֶךְ לָמָּה
why? the-king to-him and-he-asked the-king to-meet Jerusalem he-left when

לֹא־ הָלַכְתָּ עִמִּי מְפִיבֹשֶׁת׃ וַיֹּאמֶר אֲדֹנִי הַמֶּלֶךְ
the-king lord-of-me and-he-said (27) Mephibosheth with-me you-went not

18They crossed at the ford to
take the king's household over
and to do whatever he wished.
When Shimei son of Gera
crossed the Jordan, he fell
prostrate before the king 19and
said to him, "May my lord not
hold me guilty. Do not remember how your servant did
wrong on the day my lord the
king left Jerusalem. May the
king put it out of his mind.
20For I your servant know that
I have sinned, but today I
have come here as the first of
the whole house of Joseph to
come down and meet my lord
the king."
21Then Abishai son of Zeruiah said, "Shouldn't Shimei be
put to death for this? He
cursed the LORD's anointed."
22David replied, "What do
you and I have in common,
you sons of Zeruiah? This day
you have become my adver-
saries! Should anyone be put
to death in Israel today? Do I
not know that today I am king
over Israel?" 23So the king said
to Shimei, "You shall not die."
And the king promised him
on oath.
24Mephibosheth, Saul's
grandson, also went down to
meet the king. He had not tak-
en care of his feet or trimmed
his mustache or washed his
clothes from the day the king
left until the day he returned
safely. 25When he came from
Jerusalem to meet the king, the
king asked him, "Why didn't
you go with me, Me-
phibosheth?"
26He said, "My lord the king,

*See the note on page 307.

°19 ק בעיניו

עַבְדִּי רִמָּנִי כִּי־ אָמַר עַבְדְּךָ אֶחְבְּשָׁה־
I-will-have-saddled servant-of-you he-said for he-betrayed-me servant-of-me

לִּי הַחֲמוֹר וְאֶרְכַּב עָלֶיהָ וְאֵלֵךְ אֶת־ הַמֶּלֶךְ כִּי פִּסֵּחַ
lame for the-king with so-I-can-go on-her and-I-will-ride the-donkey for-me

עַבְדֶּךָ: (28) וַיְרַגֵּל בְּעַבְדְּךָ אֶל־ אֲדֹנִי
lord-of-me to against-servant-of-you and-he-slandered (28) servant-of-you

הַמֶּלֶךְ וַאדֹנִי הַמֶּלֶךְ כְּמַלְאַךְ הָאֱלֹהִים וַעֲשֵׂה הַטּוֹב
the-good so-do! the-God like-angel-of the-king and-lord-of-me the-king

בְּעֵינֶיךָ: (29) כִּי לֹא הָיָה כָּל־ בֵּית אָבִי
father-of-me descendant-of any-of he-was not for (29) in-eyes-of-you

כִּי אִם־ אַנְשֵׁי־ מָוֶת לַאדֹנִי הַמֶּלֶךְ וַתָּשֶׁת אֶת־
*** but-you-gave-place the-king from-lord-of-me death men-of only except

עַבְדְּךָ בְּאֹכְלֵי שֻׁלְחָנֶךָ וּמַה־ יֶּשׁ־ לִי
to-me there-is so-what? table-of-you with-ones-eating-of servant-of-you

עוֹד צְדָקָה וְלִזְעֹק עוֹד אֶל־ הַמֶּלֶךְ: (30) וַיֹּאמֶר לוֹ
to-him and-he-said (30) the-king to any-more that-to-appeal right any-more

הַמֶּלֶךְ לָמָּה תְּדַבֵּר עוֹד דְּבָרֶיךָ אָמַרְתִּי אַתָּה וְצִיבָא תַּחְלְקוּ
you-divide and-Ziba you I-order words-of-you more you-speak why? the-king

אֶת־הַשָּׂדֶה: (31) וַיֹּאמֶר מְפִיבֹשֶׁת אֶל־ הַמֶּלֶךְ גַּם אֶת־ הַכֹּל
the-whole *** indeed the-king to Mephibosheth and-he-said (31) the-field ***

יִקָּח אַחֲרֵי אֲשֶׁר־ בָּא אֲדֹנִי הַמֶּלֶךְ† בְּשָׁלוֹם אֶל־
at in-safety the-king lord-of-me he-arrived when after let-him-take

בֵּיתוֹ: (32) וּבַרְזִלַּי הַגִּלְעָדִי יָרַד מֵרֹגְלִים
from-Rogelim he-came-down the-Gileadite and-Barzillai (32) home-of-him

וַיַּעֲבֹר אֶת־ הַמֶּלֶךְ הַיַּרְדֵּן לְשַׁלְּחוֹ אֶת־ בַּיַּרְדֵּן°:
the-Jordan *** to-send-him the-Jordan the-king with and-he-crossed

(33) וּבַרְזִלַּי זָקֵן מְאֹד בֶּן־ שְׁמֹנִים שָׁנָה וְהוּא־ כִלְכַּל
he-provided and-he year eighty son-of very he-was-old now-Barzillai (33)

אֶת־ הַמֶּלֶךְ בְּשִׁיבָתוֹ בְמַחֲנַיִם כִּי־ אִישׁ גָּדוֹל הוּא מְאֹד:
very he wealthy man for in-Mahanaim during-stay-of-him the-king ***

(34) וַיֹּאמֶר הַמֶּלֶךְ אֶל־ בַּרְזִלַּי אַתָּה עֲבֹר אִתִּי
with-me cross-over! you Barzillai to the-king and-he-said (34)

וְכִלְכַּלְתִּי אֹתְךָ עִמָּדִי בִּירוּשָׁלָםִ: (35) וַיֹּאמֶר בַּרְזִלַּי
Barzillai but-he-answered (35) in-Jerusalem with-me you and-I-will-provide

אֶל־ הַמֶּלֶךְ כַּמָּה יְמֵי שְׁנֵי חַיַּי כִּי־ אֶעֱלֶה
I-should-go-up that lives-of-me years-of days-of like-the-what? the-king to

אֶת־ הַמֶּלֶךְ יְרוּשָׁלָםִ: (36) בֶּן־ שְׁמֹנִים שָׁנָה אָנֹכִי הַיּוֹם הַאֵדַע |
can-I-tell? the-day I year eighty son-of (36) Jerusalem the-king with

since I your servant am lame,
I said, 'I will have my donkey
saddled and will ride on it, so
I can go with the king.' But
Ziba my servant betrayed me.
27And he has slandered your
servant to my lord the king.
My lord the king is like an angel of God; so do whatever
pleases you. 28All my grandfather's descendants deserved
nothing but death from my
lord the king, but you gave
your servant a place among
those who sat at your table. So
what right do I have to make
any more appeals to the
king?"
29The king said to him,
"Why say more? I order you
and Ziba to divide the fields."
30Mephibosheth said to the
king, "Let him take everything, now that my lord the
king has arrived home safely."
31Barzillai the Gileadite also
came down from Rogelim to
cross the Jordan with the king
and to send him on his way
from there. 32Now Barzillai
was a very old man, eighty
years of age. He had provided
for the king during his stay in
Mahanaim, for he was a very
wealthy man. 33The king said
to Barzillai, "Cross over with
me and stay with me in
Jerusalem, and I will provide
for you."
34But Barzillai answered the
king, "How many more years
will I live, that I should go up
to Jerusalem with the king? 35I
am now eighty years old. Can

*See the note on page 307.

†31 Most mss have *sheva* in the *kaph* (ךְ).

°32 ק הירדן

בֵּין־ טוֹב לְרָע אִם־ יִטְעַם עַבְדְּךָ אֶת־ אֲשֶׁר אֹכַל וְאֶת־
or I-eat what *** servant-of-you can-he-taste or from-bad good between

אֲשֶׁר אֶשְׁתֶּה אִם־ אֶשְׁמַע עוֹד בְּקוֹל שָׁרִים וְשָׁרוֹת
and-women-singing men-singing to-voice-of still can-I-hear or I-drink what

וְלָמָּה יִהְיֶה עַבְדְּךָ עוֹד לְמַשָּׂא אֶל־ אֲדֹנִי הַמֶּלֶךְ׃
the-king lord-of-me to as-burden more servant-of-you should-he-be so-why?

כִּמְעַט יַעֲבֹר עַבְדְּךָ אֶת־ הַיַּרְדֵּן אֶת־ הַמֶּלֶךְ
the-king with the-Jordan *** servant-of-you he-will-cross just-little (37)

וְלָמָּה יִגְמְלֵנִי הַמֶּלֶךְ הַגְּמוּלָה הַזֹּאת׃ יָשָׁב־
let-him-return (38) the-this the-reward the-king should-he-reward-me but-why?

נָא עַבְדְּךָ וְאָמֻת בְּעִירִי עִם קֶבֶר אָבִי
father-of-me tomb-of near in-town-of-me so-I-may-die servant-of-you now!

וְאִמִּי וְהִנֵּה ׀ עַבְדְּךָ כִמְהָם יַעֲבֹר עִם־
with let-him-cross-over Kimham servant-of-you but-see! and-mother-of-me

אֲדֹנִי הַמֶּלֶךְ וַעֲשֵׂה־ לוֹ אֵת אֲשֶׁר־ טוֹב בְּעֵינֶיךָ׃
in-eyes-of-you good what *** for-him and-do! the-king lord-of-me

וַיֹּאמֶר הַמֶּלֶךְ אִתִּי יַעֲבֹר כִּמְהָם וַאֲנִי אֶעֱשֶׂה־
I-will-do and-I Kimham he-shall-cross-over with-me the-king and-he-said (39)

לּוֹ אֶת־ הַטּוֹב בְּעֵינֶיךָ וְכֹל אֲשֶׁר־ תִּבְחַר עָלַי אֶעֱשֶׂה־
I-will-do from-me you-desire that and-all in-eyes-of-you the-good *** for-him

לָּךְ׃ וַיַּעֲבֹר כָּל־ הָעָם אֶת־ הַיַּרְדֵּן וְהַמֶּלֶךְ
then-the-king the-Jordan *** the-people all-of so-he-crossed (40) for-you

עָבָר וַיִּשַּׁק הַמֶּלֶךְ לְבַרְזִלַּי וַיְבָרְכֵהוּ
and-he-blessed-him to-Barzillai the-king and-he-kissed he-crossed-over

וַיָּשָׁב לִמְקֹמוֹ׃ וַיַּעֲבֹר הַמֶּלֶךְ הַגִּלְגָּלָה
to-the-Gilgal the-king when-he-crossed (41) to-home-of-him and-he-returned

וְכִמְהָן עָבַר עִמּוֹ וְכָל־ עַם יְהוּדָה וַיֶּעֶבְרוּ° אֶת־
*** they-took-over Judah troop-of and-all-of with-him he-crossed then-Kimham

הַמֶּלֶךְ וְגַם חֲצִי עַם יִשְׂרָאֵל׃ וְהִנֵּה כָּל־ אִישׁ
man-of all-of then-see! (42) Israel troop-of half-of and-also the-king

יִשְׂרָאֵל בָּאִים אֶל־ הַמֶּלֶךְ† וַיֹּאמְרוּ אֶל־ הַמֶּלֶךְ מַדּוּעַ גְּנָבוּךָ
they-stole-you why? the-king to and-they-said the-king to ones-coming Israel

אַחֵינוּ אִישׁ יְהוּדָה וַיַּעֲבִרוּ אֶת־ הַמֶּלֶךְ וְאֶת־
and the-king *** and-they-brought-across Judah man-of brothers-of-us

בֵּיתוֹ אֶת־ הַיַּרְדֵּן וְכָל־ אַנְשֵׁי דָוִד עִמּוֹ׃
with-him David men-of and-all-of the-Jordan *** household-of-him

וַיַּעַן כָּל־ אִישׁ יְהוּדָה עַל־ אִישׁ יִשְׂרָאֵל כִּי־ קָרוֹב
close because Israel man-of to Judah man-of all-of and-he-answered (43)

I tell the difference between
what is good and what is not?
Can your servant taste what
he eats and drinks? Can I still
hear the voices of men and
women singers? Why should
your servant be an added burden to my lord the king?
[36]Your servant will cross over
the Jordan with the king for a
short distance, but why
should the king reward me in
this way? [37]Let your servant
return, that I may die in my
own town near the tomb of
my father and mother. But
here is your servant Kimham.
Let him cross over with my
lord the king. Do for him
whatever pleases you."
[38]The king said, "Kimham
shall cross over with me, and I
will do for him whatever
pleases you. And anything
you desire from me I will do
for you."
[39]So all the people crossed
the Jordan, and then the king
crossed over. The king kissed
Barzillai and gave him his
blessing, and Barzillai returned to his home.
[40]When the king crossed
over to Gilgal, Kimham
crossed with him. All the
troops of Judah and half the
troops of Israel had taken the
king over.
[41]Soon all the men of Israel
were coming to the king and
saying to him, "Why did our
brothers, the men of Judah,
steal the king away and bring
him and his household across
the Jordan, together with all
his men?"
[42]All the men of Judah answered the men of Israel, "We

*See the note on page 307.

†42 Most mss have *sheva* in the *kaph* (ךְ).

°41 ק העבירו

הַמֶּלֶךְ אֵלַי וְלָמָּה זֶּה חָרָה לְךָ עַל־ הַדָּבָר הַזֶּה
the-this the-thing about to-you he-angers this now-why? to-us the-king

הֶאָכוֹל אָכַלְנוּ מִן־ הַמֶּלֶךְ אִם־ נִשֵּׂאת נִשָּׂא לָנוּ׃ וַיַּעַן
then-he-answered (44) for-us we-took anything or the-king from we-ate to-eat?

אִישׁ־ יִשְׂרָאֵל אֶת־ אִישׁ יְהוּדָה וַיֹּאמֶר עֶשֶׂר־ יָדוֹת לִי בַמֶּלֶךְ
in-the-king to-me shares ten and-he-said Judah man-of *** Israel man-of

וְגַם־ בְּדָוִד אֲנִי מִמְּךָ וּמַדּוּעַ הֱקִלֹּתַנִי†
you-treat-with-contempt-me so-why? more-than-you I to-David and-besides

וְלֹא־ הָיָה דְבָרִי רִאשׁוֹן לִי לְהָשִׁיב אֶת־ מַלְכִּי
king-of-me *** to-bring-back to-me first word-of-me he-was now-not

וַיִּקֶשׁ דְּבַר־ אִישׁ יְהוּדָה מִדְּבַר אִישׁ יִשְׂרָאֵל׃
Israel man-of more-than-word-of Judah man-of response-of but-he-was-harsh

וְשָׁם נִקְרָא אִישׁ בְּלִיַּעַל וּשְׁמוֹ שֶׁבַע בֶּן־
son-of Sheba and-name-of-him troublemaker man-of he-happened now-there (20:1)

בִּכְרִי אִישׁ יְמִינִי וַיִּתְקַע בַּשֹּׁפָר וַיֹּאמֶר אֵין־
not and-he-shouted on-the-trumpet and-he-sounded ††Jamite man-of Bicri

לָנוּ חֵלֶק בְּדָוִד וְלֹא נַחֲלָה־ לָנוּ בְּבֶן־ יִשַׁי אִישׁ לְאֹהָלָיו
to-tent-of-him each Jesse in-son-of to-us part and-not in-David share to-us

יִשְׂרָאֵל׃ וַיַּעַל כָּל־ אִישׁ יִשְׂרָאֵל מֵאַחֲרֵי דָוִד אַחֲרֵי שֶׁבַע
Sheba after David from-after Israel man-of all-of so-he-deserted (2) Israel

בֶּן־ בִּכְרִי וְאִישׁ יְהוּדָה דָּבְקוּ בְמַלְכָּם מִן־ הַיַּרְדֵּן
the-Jordan from by-king-of-them they-stayed Judah but-man-of Bicri son-of

וְעַד־ יְרוּשָׁלִָם׃ וַיָּבֹא דָוִד אֶל־ בֵּיתוֹ יְרוּשָׁלִַם
Jerusalem palace-of-him to David when-he-returned (3) Jerusalem even-to

וַיִּקַּח הַמֶּלֶךְ אֵת עֶשֶׂר־ נָשִׁים ׀ פִּלַגְשִׁים אֲשֶׁר הִנִּיחַ לִשְׁמֹר
to-take-care-of he-left whom concubines women ten *** the-king then-he-took

הַבַּיִת וַיִּתְּנֵם בֵּית־ מִשְׁמֶרֶת וַיְכַלְכְּלֵם וַאֲלֵיהֶם
but-into-them and-he-provided-for-them guard house-of and-he-put-them the-palace

לֹא־ בָא וַתִּהְיֶינָה צְרֻרוֹת עַד־ יוֹם מֻתָן
death-of-them day-of till ones-being-confined and-they-were he-went not

אַלְמְנוּת חַיּוּת׃ וַיֹּאמֶר הַמֶּלֶךְ אֶל־ עֲמָשָׂא הַזְעֶק־ לִי אֶת־
*** to-me summon! Amasa to the-king then-he-said (4) living widowhood-of

אִישׁ־ יְהוּדָה שְׁלֹשֶׁת יָמִים וְאַתָּה פֹּה עֲמֹד׃ וַיֵּלֶךְ עֲמָשָׂא
Amasa when-he-went (5) be! here and-you days three-of Judah man-of

לְהַזְעִיק אֶת־יְהוּדָה וַיּיחֶר° מִן־ הַמּוֹעֵד אֲשֶׁר יְעָדוֹ׃
he-set-for-him that the-time than then-he-took-longer Judah *** to-summon

וַיֹּאמֶר דָּוִד אֶל־אֲבִישַׁי עַתָּה יֵרַע לָנוּ שֶׁבַע בֶּן־ בִּכְרִי
Bicri son-of Sheba to-us he-will-harm now Abishai to David and-he-said (6)

did this because the king is closely related to us. Why are you angry about it? Have we eaten any of the king's provisions? Have we taken anything for ourselves?"
43Then the men of Israel answered the men of Judah, "We have ten shares in the king; and besides, we have a greater claim on David than you have. So why do you treat us with contempt? Were we not the first to speak of bringing back our king?"
But the men of Judah responded even more harshly than the men of Israel.

Sheba Rebels Against David

20 Now a troublemaker named Sheba son of Bicri, a Benjamite, happened to be there. He sounded the trumpet and shouted,

"We have no share in David,
no part in Jesse's son!
Every man to his tent, O Israel!"

2So all the men of Israel deserted David to follow Sheba son of Bicri. But the men of Judah stayed by their king all the way from the Jordan to Jerusalem.
3When David returned to his palace in Jerusalem, he took the ten concubines he had left to take care of the palace and put them in a house under guard. He provided for them, but did not lie with them. They were kept in confinement till the day of their death, living as widows.
4Then the king said to Amasa, "Summon the men of Judah to come to me within three days, and be here yourself."
5But when Amasa went to summon Judah, he took longer than the time the king had set for him.
6David said to Abishai, "Now Sheba son of Bicri will

*See the note on page 307.

†44 Most mss have *hateph pathah* under the *he* (הֲ).

††1 That is, *Benjamite*.

°5 ק ויחר

מִן־ אַבְשָׁלוֹם אַתָּה קַח אֶת־עַבְדֵי אֲדֹנֶיךָ וּרְדֹף אַחֲרָיו
after-him and-pursue! masters-of-you men-of *** take! you Absalom more-than

פֶּן־ מָצָא לוֹ עָרִים בְּצֻרוֹת וְהִצִּיל
and-he-will-escape ones-being-fortified cities for-him he-will-find or

עֵינֵנוּ׃ וַיֵּצְאוּ אַחֲרָיו אַנְשֵׁי יוֹאָב וְהַכְּרֵתִי
and-the-Kerethite Joab men-of after-him so-he-went-out (7) eye-of-us

וְהַפְּלֵתִי וְכָל־ הַגִּבֹּרִים וַיֵּצְאוּ מִירוּשָׁלַםִ
from-Jerusalem and-they-marched-out the-warriors and-all-of and-the-Pelethite

לִרְדֹּף אַחֲרֵי שֶׁבַע בֶּן־ בִּכְרִי׃ הֵם עִם־ הָאֶבֶן הַגְּדוֹלָה אֲשֶׁר
that the-great the-rock at they (8) Bicri son-of Sheba after to-pursue

בְּגִבְעוֹן וַעֲמָשָׂא בָּא לִפְנֵיהֶם וְיוֹאָב חָגוּר ׀ מִדּוֹ
military-tunic-of-him wearing now-Joab before-them he-came and-Amasa in-Gibeon

לְבֻשׁוֹ וְעָלָו חֲגוֹר חֶרֶב מְצֻמֶּדֶת עַל־ מָתְנָיו
waists-of-him at being-strapped dagger belt-of and-over-him clothing-of-him

בְּתַעְרָהּ וְהוּא יָצָא וַתִּפֹּל׃ וַיֹּאמֶר
and-he-said (9) then-she-dropped-out he-stepped-forward as-he in-sheath-of-her

יוֹאָב לַעֲמָשָׂא הֲשָׁלוֹם אַתָּה אָחִי וַתֹּחֶז יַד־ יְמִין
right-of hand-of then-she-grabbed brother-of-me you well? to-Amasa Joab

יוֹאָב בִּזְקַן עֲמָשָׂא לִנְשָׁק־ לוֹ׃ וַעֲמָשָׂא לֹא־ נִשְׁמַר
he-was-on-guard not and-Amasa (10) on-him to-kiss Amasa on-beard-of Joab

בַּחֶרֶב ׀ אֲשֶׁר בְּיַד־ יוֹאָב וַיַּכֵּהוּ בָהּ אֶל־
into with-her and-he-stabbed-him Joab in-hand-of that against-the-sword

הַחֹמֶשׁ וַיִּשְׁפֹּךְ מֵעָיו אַרְצָה וְלֹא־ שָׁנָה
he-did-again and-not on-ground intestines-of-him and-he-spilled-out the-belly

לוֹ וַיָּמֹת וְיוֹאָב וַאֲבִישַׁי אָחִיו רָדַף אַחֲרֵי
after he-pursued brother-of-him and-Abishai then-Joab and-he-died to-him

שֶׁבַע בֶּן־ בִּכְרִי׃ וְאִישׁ עָמַד עָלָיו מִנַּעֲרֵי יוֹאָב
Joab from-men-of beside-him he-stood and-man (11) Bicri son-of Sheba

וַיֹּאמֶר מִי אֲשֶׁר חָפֵץ בְּיוֹאָב וּמִי אֲשֶׁר־ לְדָוִד אַחֲרֵי יוֹאָב׃
Joab after for-David ever and-who to-Joab he-favors ever who and-he-said

וַעֲמָשָׂא מִתְגֹּלֵל בַּדָּם בְּתוֹךְ הַמְסִלָּה וַיַּרְא
and-he-saw the-road in-middle-of in-the-blood wallowing and-Amasa (12)

הָאִישׁ כִּי־ עָמַד כָּל־ הָעָם וַיַּסֵּב אֶת־ עֲמָשָׂא מִן־
from Amasa *** and-he-dragged the-troop all-of he-halted that the-man

הַמְסִלָּה הַשָּׂדֶה וַיַּשְׁלֵךְ עָלָיו בֶּגֶד כַּאֲשֶׁר רָאָה
he-realized as-soon-as garment over-him and-he-threw the-field the-road

כָּל־ הַבָּא עָלָיו וְעָמָד׃ כַּאֲשֶׁר הֹגָה
he-removed as-soon-as (13) then-he-stopped to-him the-one-coming every-of

do us more harm than Absalom did. Take your master's
men and pursue him, or he
will find fortified cities and escape from us." 7So Joab's men
and the Kerethites and Pelethites and all the mighty warriors went out under the command of Abishai. They
marched out from Jerusalem to
pursue Sheba son of Bicri.
8While they were at the great
rock in Gibeon, Amasa came
to meet them. Joab was wearing his military tunic, and
strapped over it at his waist
was a belt with a dagger in its
sheath. As he stepped forward, it dropped out of its
sheath.
9Joab said to Amasa, "How
are you, my brother?" Then
Joab took Amasa by the beard
with his right hand to kiss
him. 10Amasa was not on his
guard against the dagger in
Joab's hand, and Joab plunged
it into his belly, and his intes-
tines spilled out on the
ground. Without being
stabbed again, Amasa died.
Then Joab and his brother Abishai pursued Sheba son of
Bicri.
11One of Joab's men stood
beside Amasa and said,
"Whoever favors Joab, and
whoever is for David, let him
follow Joab!" 12Amasa lay wallowing in his blood in the
middle of the road, and the
man saw that all the troops
came to a halt there. When he
realized that everyone who
came up to Amasa stopped, he
dragged him from the road
into a field and threw a garment over him. 13After Amasa
had been removed from the

°8 ק ועליו

מן־ המסלה עבר כל־ איש אחרי יואב לרדף אחרי שבע בן־
son-of Sheba after to-pursue Joab with man every-of he-went-on the-road from

בכרי׃ ויעבר בכל־ שבטי ישראל אבלה ובית
even-Beth to-Abel Israel tribes-of through-all-of and-he-passed (14) Bicri

מעכה וכל־ הברים ויקלהו° ויבאו אף־
also and-they-followed and-they-gathered the-Berites and-all-of Maacah

אחריו׃ ויבאו ויצרו עליו באבלה בית
Beth in-Abel against-him and-they-besieged and-they-came (15) after-him

המעכה וישפכו סללה אל־ העיר ותעמד
and-she-stood the-city up-to siege-ramp and-they-built the-Maacah

בחל וכל־ העם אשר את־ יואב
Joab with that the-troop and-all-of against-the-outer-fortification

משחיתם להפיל החומה׃ ותקרא אשה חכמה מן־
from wise woman and-she-called (16) the-wall to-bring-down ones-battering

העיר שמעו שמעו אמרו־ נא אל־יואב קרב עד־ הנה ואדברה
so-I-can-speak here to come! Joab to now! tell! listen! listen! the-city

אליך׃ ויקרב אליה ותאמר האשה האתה יואב
Joab you? the-woman and-she-asked toward-her and-he-went (17) to-you

ויאמר אני ותאמר לו שמע דברי אמתך
servant-of-you words-of listen! to-him and-she-said I and-he-answered

ויאמר שמע אנכי׃ ותאמר דבר ידברו לאמר
they-said to-say to-say and-she-spoke (18) I listening and-he-said

בראשנה לאמר שאל ישאלו באבל וכן התמו׃
they-settled and-so at-Abel they-get-answer to-get-answer to-say in-the-past

אנכי שלמי אמוני ישראל אתה מבקש
trying you Israel ones-being-faithful-of ones-being-peaceful-of I (19)

להמית עיר ואם בישראל למה תבלע נחלת
inheritance-of would-you-swallow why? in-Israel and-mother city to-destroy

יהוה׃ ויען יואב ויאמר חלילה חלילה לי אם־
if from-me far-be-it! far-be-it! and-he-said Joab and-he-replied (20) Yahweh

אבלע ואם־ אשחית׃ לא־ כן הדבר כי איש מהר
from-hill-country-of man but the-case this not (21) I-destroy or-if I-swallow-up

אפרים שבע בן־ בכרי שמו נשא ידו במלך
against-the-king hand-of-him he-lifted name-of-him Bicri son-of Sheba Ephraim

בדוד תנו־ אתו לבדו ואלכה מעל
from-against and-I-will-withdraw by-himself him hand-over! against-David

העיר ותאמר האשה אל־יואב הנה ראשו משלך אליך
to-you being-thrown head-of-him see! Joab to the-woman and-she-said the-city

°14 ק ויקהלו

road, all the men went on with
Joab to pursue Sheba son of
Bicri.
14Sheba passed through all
the tribes of Israel to Abel Beth
Maacah[j] and through the entire region of the Berites, who
gathered together and followed him. 15All the troops
with Joab came and besieged
Sheba in Abel Beth Maacah.
They built a siege ramp up to
the city, and it stood against
the outer fortifications. While
they were battering the wall to
bring it down, 16a wise woman
called from the city, "Listen!
Listen! Tell Joab to come here
so I can speak to him." 17He
went toward her, and she
asked, "Are you Joab?"
"I am," he answered.
She said, "Listen to what
your servant has to say."
"I'm listening," he said.
18She continued, "Long ago
they used to say, 'Get your answer at Abel,' and that settled
it. 19We are the peaceful and
faithful in Israel. You are trying to destroy a city that is a
mother in Israel. Why do you
want to swallow up the LORD's
inheritance?"
20"Far be it from me!" Joab
replied, "Far be it from me to
swallow up or destroy! 21That
is not the case. A man named
Sheba son of Bicri, from the
hill country of Ephraim, has
lifted up his hand against the
king, against David. Hand
over this one man, and I'll
withdraw from the city."
The woman said to Joab,

j14 Or *Abel, even Beth Maacah*; also in verse 15

בְּעַד הַחוֹמָה׃ וַתָּבוֹא הָאִשָּׁה אֶל־ כָּל־ הָעָם
the-people all-of to the-woman then-she-went (22) the-wall from

בְּחָכְמָתָהּ וַיִּכְרְתוּ אֶת־ רֹאשׁ שֶׁבַע בֶּן־ בִּכְרִי
Bicri son-of Sheba head-of *** and-they-cut-off with-wise-advice-of-her

וַיַּשְׁלִכוּ אֶל־ יוֹאָב וַיִּתְקַע בַּשּׁוֹפָר וַיָּפֻצוּ
and-they-dispersed on-the-trumpet so-he-sounded Joab to and-they-threw

מֵעַל־ הָעִיר אִישׁ לְאֹהָלָיו וְיוֹאָב שָׁב יְרוּשָׁלַםִ
Jerusalem he-went-back and-Joab to-homes-of-him each the-city from-against

אֶל־הַמֶּלֶךְ׃ וְיוֹאָב אֶל כָּל־ הַצָּבָא יִשְׂרָאֵל וּבְנָיָה בֶּן־
son-of and-Benaiah Israel the-army entire-of over now-Joab (23) the-king to

יְהוֹיָדָע עַל־ הַכְּרֵי וְעַל־ הַפְּלֵתִי׃ וַאֲדֹרָם עַל־
over and-Adoram (24) the-Pelethite and-over the-Kerethite over Jehoiada

הַמַּס וִיהוֹשָׁפָט בֶּן־ אֲחִילוּד הַמַּזְכִּיר׃
the-one-recording Ahilud son-of and-Jehoshaphat the-forced-labor

וּשְׁיָא סֹפֵר וְצָדוֹק וְאֶבְיָתָר כֹּהֲנִים׃ וְגַם עִירָא
Ira and-also (26) priests and-Abiathar and-Zadok secretary and-Sheva (25)

הַיָּאִרִי הָיָה כֹהֵן לְדָוִד׃ וַיְהִי רָעָב בִּימֵי דָוִד
David in-days-of famine and-he-was (21:1) to-David priest he-was the-Jairite

שָׁלֹשׁ שָׁנִים שָׁנָה אַחֲרֵי שָׁנָה וַיְבַקֵּשׁ דָּוִד אֶת־ פְּנֵי יְהוָה
Yahweh faces-of *** David so-he-sought year after year years three

וַיֹּאמֶר יְהוָה אֶל־ שָׁאוּל וְאֶל־ בֵּית הַדָּמִים
the-bloods house-of and-on-account-of Saul on-account-of Yahweh and-he-said

עַל־ אֲשֶׁר־ הֵמִית אֶת־ הַגִּבְעֹנִים׃ וַיִּקְרָא הַמֶּלֶךְ
the-king and-he-summoned (2) the-Gibeonites *** he-killed that because

לַגִּבְעֹנִים וַיֹּאמֶר אֲלֵיהֶם וְהַגִּבְעֹנִים לֹא מִבְּנֵי
from-sons-of not now-the-Gibeonites to-them and-he-spoke to-the-Gibeonites

יִשְׂרָאֵל הֵמָּה כִּי אִם־ מִיֶּתֶר הָאֱמֹרִי וּבְנֵי יִשְׂרָאֵל
Israel and-sons-of the-Amorite from-survivor-of rather but they Israel

נִשְׁבְּעוּ לָהֶם וַיְבַקֵּשׁ שָׁאוּל לְהַכֹּתָם בְּקַנֹּאתוֹ
in-zeal-of-him to-annihilate-them Saul but-he-tried to-them they-swore

לִבְנֵי־ יִשְׂרָאֵל וִיהוּדָה׃ וַיֹּאמֶר דָּוִד אֶל־ הַגִּבְעֹנִים מָה
what? the-Gibeonites to David and-he-asked (3) and-Judah Israel for-sons-of

אֶעֱשֶׂה לָכֶם וּבַמָּה אֲכַפֵּר וּבָרְכוּ אֶת־
*** so-bless! shall-I-make-amends and-by-the-how? for-you shall-I-do

נַחֲלַת יְהוָה׃ וַיֹּאמְרוּ לוֹ הַגִּבְעֹנִים אֵין־ לִי
to-us not the-Gibeonites to-him and-they-answered (4) Yahweh inheritance-of

כֶּסֶף וְזָהָב עִם־ שָׁאוּל וְעִם־ בֵּיתוֹ וְאֵין־ לָנוּ אִישׁ לְהָמִית
to-kill anyone to-us and-not family-of-him or-from Saul from or-gold silver

"His head will be thrown to you from the wall."

[22]Then the woman went to all the people with her wise advice, and they cut off the head of Sheba son of Bicri and threw it to Joab. So he sounded the trumpet, and his men dispersed from the city, each returning to his home. And Joab went back to the king in Jerusalem.

[23]Joab was over Israel's entire army; Benaiah son of Jehoiada was over the Kerethites and Pelethites; [24]Adoniram[k] was in charge of forced labor; Jehoshaphat son of Ahilud was recorder; [25]Sheva was secretary; Zadok and Abiathar were priests; [26]and Ira the Jairite was David's priest.

The Gibeonites Avenged

21 During the reign of David, there was a famine for three successive years; so David sought the face of the LORD. The LORD said, "It is on account of Saul and his blood-stained house; it is because he put the Gibeonites to death."

[2]The king summoned the Gibeonites and spoke to them. (Now the Gibeonites were not a part of Israel but were survivors of the Amorites; the Israelites had sworn to ⌞spare⌟ them, but Saul in his zeal for Israel and Judah had tried to annihilate them.) [3]David asked the Gibeonites, "What shall I do for you? How shall I make amends so that you will bless the LORD's inheritance?"

[4]The Gibeonites answered him, "We have no right to demand silver or gold from Saul or his family, nor do we have the right to put anyone in Israel to death."

[k]24 Septuagint (see also 1 Kings 4:6 and 5:14); Hebrew *Adoram*

°23 ק הכרתי
°25 ק ושוא
°4 ק לנו

בְּיִשְׂרָאֵל וַיֹּאמֶר מָה־ אַתֶּם אֹמְרִים אֶעֱשֶׂה לָכֶם׃
for-you I-should-do ones-asking you what? and-he-asked in-Israel

וַיֹּאמְרוּ אֶל־ הַמֶּלֶךְ הָאִישׁ אֲשֶׁר כִּלָּנוּ וַאֲשֶׁר
and-who he-destroyed-us who the-man the-king to and-they-answered (5)

דִּמָּה־ לָנוּ נִשְׁמַדְנוּ מֵהִתְיַצֵּב בְּכָל־ גְּבֻל
place-of in-any-of from-to-have-place he-decimated-us against-us he-plotted

יִשְׂרָאֵל׃ יֻנְתַּן־° לָנוּ שִׁבְעָה אֲנָשִׁים מִבָּנָיו
from-sons-of-him men seven to-us let-him-be-given (6) Israel

וְהוֹקַעֲנוּם לַיהוָה בְּגִבְעַת שָׁאוּל בְּחִיר יְהוָה
Yahweh chosen-of Saul at-Gibeah-of before-Yahweh and-let-them-expose-them

וַיֹּאמֶר הַמֶּלֶךְ אֲנִי אֶתֵּן׃ וַיַּחְמֹל הַמֶּלֶךְ עַל־ מְפִיבֹשֶׁת
Mephibosheth to the-king and-he-spared (7) I-will-give I the-king so-he-said

בֶּן־ יְהוֹנָתָן בֶּן־ שָׁאוּל עַל־ שְׁבֻעַת יְהוָה אֲשֶׁר בֵּינֹתָם
between-them that Yahweh oath-of because-of Saul son-of Jonathan son-of

בֵּין דָּוִד וּבֵין יְהוֹנָתָן בֶּן־ שָׁאוּל׃ וַיִּקַּח הַמֶּלֶךְ אֶת־
*** the-king but-he-took (8) Saul son-of Jonathan and-between David between

שְׁנֵי בְּנֵי רִצְפָּה בַת־ אַיָּה אֲשֶׁר יָלְדָה לְשָׁאוּל אֶת־ אַרְמֹנִי
Armoni *** to-Saul she-bore whom Aiah daughter-of Rizpah sons-of two-of

וְאֶת־ מְפִבֹשֶׁת וְאֶת־ חֲמֵשֶׁת בְּנֵי מִיכַל בַּת־ שָׁאוּל אֲשֶׁר יָלְדָה
she-bore whom Saul daughter-of Michal sons-of five-of and Mephibosheth and

לְעַדְרִיאֵל בֶּן־ בַּרְזִלַּי הַמְּחֹלָתִי׃ וַיִּתְּנֵם בְּיַד
into-hand-of and-he-gave-them (9) the-Meholathite Barzillai son-of to-Adriel

הַגִּבְעֹנִים וַיֹּקִיעֻם בָּהָר לִפְנֵי יְהוָה וַיִּפְּלוּ
and-they-fell Yahweh before on-the-hill and-they-exposed-them the-Gibeonites

שְׁבַעְתָּים° יָחַד וְהֵם° הֻמְתוּ בִּימֵי קָצִיר
harvest in-days-of they-were-killed now-they together seven-of-them

בָּרִאשֹׁנִים תְּחִלַּת° קְצִיר שְׂעֹרִים׃ וַתִּקַּח
and-she-took (10) barleys harvest-of at-beginning-of during-the-first-ones

רִצְפָּה בַת־ אַיָּה אֶת־ הַשַּׂק וַתַּטֵּהוּ לָהּ אֶל־
on for-her and-she-spread-out-him the-sackcloth *** Aiah daughter-of Rizpah

הַצּוּר מִתְּחִלַּת קָצִיר עַד נִתַּךְ־ מַיִם עֲלֵיהֶם מִן־
from on-them rains he-poured-down till harvest from-beginning-of the-rock

הַשָּׁמָיִם וְלֹא־ נָתְנָה עוֹף הַשָּׁמַיִם לָנוּחַ עֲלֵיהֶם יוֹמָם וְאֶת־
or by-day on-them to-touch the-skies bird-of she-let and-not the-heavens

חַיַּת הַשָּׂדֶה לָיְלָה׃ וַיֻּגַּד לְדָוִד אֵת אֲשֶׁר־ עָשְׂתָה
she-did what *** to-David when-he-was-told (11) night the-field animal-of

רִצְפָּה בַת־ אַיָּה פִּלֶגֶשׁ שָׁאוּל׃ וַיֵּלֶךְ דָּוִד וַיִּקַּח
and-he-took David then-he-went (12) Saul concubine-of Aiah daughter-of Rizpah

"What do you want me to do
for you?" David asked.
[5]They answered the king,
"As for the man who de-
stroyed us and plotted against
us so that we have been deci-
mated and have no place anywhere in Israel, [6]let seven of
his male descendants be given
to us to be killed and exposed
before the LORD at Gibeah of
Saul—the Lord's chosen one."
So the king said, "I will give
them to you."
[7]The king spared Me-
phibosheth son of Jonathan,
the son of Saul, because of the
oath before the LORD between
David and Jonathan son of
Saul. [8]But the king took Armoni and Mephibosheth, the
two sons of Aiah's daughter
Rizpah, whom she had borne
to Saul, together with the five
sons of Saul's daughter
Merab,[l] whom she had borne
to Adriel son of Barzillai the
Meholathite. [9]He handed
them over to the Gibeonites,
who killed and exposed them
on a hill before the LORD. All
seven of them fell together;
they were put to death during
the first days of the harvest,
just as the barley harvest was
beginning.
[10]Rizpah daughter of Aiah
took sackcloth and spread it
out for herself on a rock. From
the beginning of the harvest
till the rain poured down from
the heavens on the bodies, she
did not let the birds of the air
touch them by day or the wild
animals by night. [11]When David was told what Aiah's
daughter Rizpah, Saul's concubine, had done, [12]he went

[l]8 Two Hebrew manuscripts, some Septuagint manuscripts and Syriac (see also 1 Samuel 18:19); most Hebrew and Septuagint manuscripts *Michal*

°6 ק יתן
°9a ק שבעתם
°9b ק והמה
°9c ק בתחלת

אֶת־עַצְמוֹת שָׁאוּל וְאֶת־עַצְמוֹת יְהוֹנָתָן בְּנוֹ מֵאֵת בַּעֲלֵי יָבֵישׁ
Jabesh citizens-of from son-of-him Jonathan bones-of and Saul bones-of ***

גִּלְעָד אֲשֶׁר גָּנְבוּ אֹתָם מֵרְחֹב בֵּית־שַׁן אֲשֶׁר
where Shan Beth from-square-of them they-secretly-took who Gilead

תְּלָוּם° שָׁם° הַפְּלִשְׁתִּים בְּיוֹם הַכּוֹת פְּלִשְׁתִּים אֶת־שָׁאוּל
Saul *** Philistines to-strike on-day Philistines at-there they-hung-them

בַּגִּלְבֹּעַ׃ וַיַּעַל מִשָּׁם אֶת־עַצְמוֹת שָׁאוּל וְאֶת־עַצְמוֹת
bones-of and Saul bones-of *** from-there and-he-brought-up (13) on-the-Gilboa

יְהוֹנָתָן בְּנוֹ וַיַּאַסְפוּ אֶת־עַצְמוֹת הַמּוּקָעִים׃
the-ones-being-exposed bones-of *** and-they-gathered son-of-him Jonathan

וַיִּקְבְּרוּ אֶת־עַצְמוֹת־שָׁאוּל וִיהוֹנָתָן־בְּנוֹ בְּאֶרֶץ
in-land-of son-of-him and-Jonathan Saul bones-of *** and-they-buried (14)

בִּנְיָמִן בְּצֵלָע בְּקֶבֶר קִישׁ אָבִיו וַיַּעֲשׂוּ כֹּל אֲשֶׁר־
that all and-they-did father-of-him Kish in-tomb-of at-Zela Benjamin

צִוָּה הַמֶּלֶךְ וַיֵּעָתֵר אֱלֹהִים לָאָרֶץ אַחֲרֵי־כֵן׃
that after for-the-land God and-he-answered-prayer the-king he-commanded

וַתְּהִי־עוֹד מִלְחָמָה לַפְּלִשְׁתִּים אֶת־יִשְׂרָאֵל
Israel against with-the-Philistines battle again and-she-was (15)

וַיֵּרֶד דָּוִד וַעֲבָדָיו עִמּוֹ וַיִּלָּחֲמוּ אֶת־
against and-they-fought with-him and-men-of-him David and-he-went-down

פְּלִשְׁתִּים וַיָּעַף דָּוִד׃ וְיִשְׁבּוֹ° בְּנֹב אֲשֶׁר׀
who Benob and-Ishbi (16) David and-he-became-exhausted Philistines

בִּילִידֵי הָרָפָה וּמִשְׁקַל קֵינוֹ שְׁלֹשׁ מֵאוֹת
hundreds three-of spearhead-of-him and-weight-of the-Rapha of-descendants-of

מִשְׁקַל נְחֹשֶׁת וְהוּא חָגוּר חֲדָשָׁה וַיֹּאמֶר לְהַכּוֹת אֶת־דָּוִד׃
David *** to-kill and-he-said new being-armed and-he bronze weight-of

וַיַּעֲזָר־לוֹ אֲבִישַׁי בֶּן־צְרוּיָה וַיַּךְ אֶת־
*** and-he-struck-down Zeruiah son-of Abishai to-him but-he-rescued (17)

הַפְּלִשְׁתִּי וַיְמִיתֵהוּ אָז נִשְׁבְּעוּ אַנְשֵׁי־דָוִד לוֹ לֵאמֹר
to-say to-him David men-of they-swore then and-he-killed-him the-Philistine

לֹא־תֵצֵא עוֹד אִתָּנוּ לַמִּלְחָמָה וְלֹא תְכַבֶּה אֶת־
*** you-extinguish so-not to-the-battle with-us again you-will-go-out not

נֵר יִשְׂרָאֵל׃ וַיְהִי אַחֲרֵי־כֵן וַתְּהִי־עוֹד הַמִּלְחָמָה
the-battle again then-she-was this after and-he-was (18) Israel lamp-of

בְּגוֹב עִם־פְּלִשְׁתִּים אָז הִכָּה סִבְּכַי הַחֻשָׁתִי אֶת־סַף
Saph *** the-Hushathite Sibbecai he-killed then Philistines with at-Gob

אֲשֶׁר בִּילִדֵי הָרָפָה׃ וַתְּהִי־עוֹד הַמִּלְחָמָה בְּגוֹב
at-Gob the-battle again and-she-was (19) the-Rapha of-descendants-of who

and took the bones of Saul and
his son Jonathan from the citizens of Jabesh Gilead. (They
had taken them secretly from
the public square at Beth
Shan, where the Philistines
had hung them after they
struck Saul down on Gilboa.)
13David brought the bones of
Saul and his son Jonathan
from there, and the bones of
those who had been killed and
exposed were gathered up.
14They buried the bones of
Saul and his son Jonathan in
the tomb of Saul's father Kish,
at Zela in Benjamin, and did
everything the king com-
manded. After that, God answered prayer in behalf of the
land.

Wars Against the Philistines

15Once again there was a
battle between the Philistines
and Israel. David went down
with his men to fight against
the Philistines, and he became
exhausted. 16And Ishbi-Benob,
one of the descendants of
Rapha, whose bronze spear-
head weighed three hundred
shekels[m] and who was armed
with a new ⸤sword⸥, said he
would kill David. 17But Abishai son of Zeruiah came to
David's rescue; he struck the
Philistine down and killed
him. Then David's men swore
to him, saying, "Never again
will you go out with us to battle, so that the lamp of Israel
will not be extinguished."
18In the course of time, there
was another battle with the
Philistines, at Gob. At that

[m]16 That is, about 7 1/2 pounds (about 3.5 kilograms)

°12a ק תלאום
°12b ק שמה פלשתים
°16 ק וישבי

עִם־ פְּלִשְׁתִּים וַיַּךְ אֶלְחָנָן בֶּן־ יַעְרֵי אֹרְגִים בֵּית הַלַּחְמִי
the-Bethlehemite Oregim Jaare son-of Elhanan and-he-killed Philistines with

אֵת גָּלְיָת הַגִּתִּי וְעֵץ חֲנִיתוֹ כִּמְנוֹר אֹרְגִים׃
ones-weaving like-rod-of spear-of-him and-shaft-of the-Gittite Goliath ***

וַתְּהִי־ עוֹד מִלְחָמָה בְּגַת וַיְהִי ׀ אִישׁ מָדִין וְאֶצְבְּעֹת
and-fingers-of huge man and-he-was at-Gath battle again and-she-was (20)

יָדָיו וְאֶצְבְּעוֹת רַגְלָיו שֵׁשׁ וָשֵׁשׁ עֶשְׂרִים וְאַרְבַּע מִסְפָּר
total and-four twenty and-six six feet-of-him and-toes-of hands-of-him

וְגַם־ הוּא יֻלַּד לְהָרָפָה׃ וַיְחָרֵף אֶת־יִשְׂרָאֵל
Israel *** when-he-taunted (21) from-the-Rapha he-was-descended he and-also

וַיַּכֵּהוּ יְהוֹנָתָן בֶּן־ שִׁמְעֵי אֲחִי דָוִד׃ אֶת־אַרְבַּעַת
four-of *** (22) David brother-of Shimeah son-of Jonathan then-he-killed-him

אֵלֶּה יֻלְּדוּ לְהָרָפָה בְּגַת וַיִּפְּלוּ בְיַד־
at-hand-of and-they-fell in-Gath from-the-Rapha they-were-descended these

דָּוִד וּבְיַד עֲבָדָיו׃ וַיְדַבֵּר דָּוִד לַיהוָה אֶת־
*** to-Yahweh David and-he-sang (22:1) men-of-him and-at-hand-of David

דִּבְרֵי הַשִּׁירָה הַזֹּאת בְּיוֹם הִצִּיל יְהוָה אֹתוֹ מִכַּף כָּל־
all-of from-hand-of him Yahweh he-delivered on-day the-this the-song words-of

אֹיְבָיו וּמִכַּף שָׁאוּל׃ וַיֹּאמַר יְהוָה סַלְעִי
rock-of-me Yahweh and-he-said (2) Saul and-from-hand-of being-enemies-of-him

וּמְצֻדָתִי וּמְפַלְטִי־ לִי׃ אֱלֹהֵי צוּרִי
rock-of-me God-of (3) for-me and-one-delivering-me and-fortress-of-me

אֶחֱסֶה־ בּוֹ מָגִנִּי וְקֶרֶן יִשְׁעִי מִשְׂגַּבִּי
stronghold-of-me salvation-of-me and-horn-of shield-of-me in-him I-take-refuge

וּמְנוּסִי מֹשִׁעִי מֵחָמָס תֹּשִׁעֵנִי׃ מְהֻלָּל
being-praised (4) you-save-me from-violence one-saving-me and-refuge-of-me

אֶקְרָא יְהוָה וּמֵאֹיְבַי אִוָּשֵׁעַ׃ כִּי
indeed (5) I-am-saved and-from-being-enemies-of-me Yahweh I-call

אֲפָפֻנִי מִשְׁבְּרֵי־ מָוֶת נַחֲלֵי בְלִיַּעַל
destruction torrents-of death waves-of they-swirled-around-me

יְבַעֲתֻנִי׃ חֶבְלֵי שְׁאוֹל סַבֻּנִי
they-coiled-around-me Sheol cords-of (6) they-overwhelmed-me

קִדְּמֻנִי מֹקְשֵׁי־ מָוֶת׃ בַּצַּר־ לִי אֶקְרָא יְהוָה
Yahweh I-called of-me in-the-distress (7) death snares-of they-confronted-me

וְאֶל־ אֱלֹהַי אֶקְרָא וַיִּשְׁמַע מֵהֵיכָלוֹ קוֹלִי
voice-of-me from-temple-of-him and-he-heard I-called-out God-of-me and-to

וְשַׁוְעָתִי בְּאָזְנָיו׃ וַתִּגְעַשׁ וַתִּרְעַשׁ הָאָרֶץ
the-earth and-she-quaked and-she-trembled (8) in-ears-of-him and-cry-of-me

time Sibbecai the Hushathite
killed Saph, one of the descendants of Rapha.
19 In another battle with the
Philistines at Gob, Elhanan
son of Jaare-Oregim[n] the
Bethlehemite killed Goliath[o]
the Gittite, who had a spear
with a shaft like a weaver's
rod.
20 In still another battle,
which took place at Gath,
there was a huge man with six
fingers on each hand and six
toes on each foot—twenty-
four in all. He also was descended from Rapha.
21 When
he taunted Israel, Jonathan
son of Shimeah, David's
brother, killed him.
22 These four were descendants of Rapha in Gath, and
they fell at the hands of David
and his men.

David's Song of Praise

22 David sang to the LORD
the words of this song
when the LORD delivered him
from the hand of all his enemies and from the hand of
Saul.
2 He said:

"The LORD is my rock, my
fortress and my
deliverer;
3 my God is my rock, in
whom I take refuge,
my shield and the horn[p]
of my salvation.
He is my stronghold, my
refuge and my savior—
from violent men you
save me.
4 I call to the LORD, who is
worthy of praise,
and I am saved from my
enemies.

5 "The waves of death
swirled about me;
the torrents of
destruction
overwhelmed me.
6 The cords of the grave[q]
coiled around me;
the snares of death
confronted me.
7 In my distress I called to
the LORD;
I called out to my God.
From his temple he heard
my voice;
my cry came to his ears.

8 "The earth trembled and
quaked,

[n]19 Or *son of Jair the weaver*
[o]19 Hebrew and Septuagint; 1 Chronicles 20:5 *son of Jair killed Lahmi the brother of Goliath*
[p]3 *Horn* here symbolizes strength.
[q]6 Hebrew *Sheol*

°20 ק מדון
°21 ק שמעה
°8 ק ויתגעש

מוֹסְדוֹת הַשָּׁמַיִם יִרְגָּזוּ וַיִּתְגָּעֲשׁוּ כִּי־ חָרָה
he-angered because and-they-trembled they-shook the-heavens foundations-of

לוֹ׃ (9) עָלָה עָשָׁן בְּאַפּוֹ וְאֵשׁ מִפִּיו
from-mouth-of-him and-fire from-nostril-of-him smoke he-rose (9) to-him

תֹּאכֵל גֶּחָלִים בָּעֲרוּ מִמֶּנּוּ׃ (10) וַיֵּט שָׁמַיִם
heavens and-he-parted (10) from-him they-burned coals she-consumed

וַיֵּרַד וַעֲרָפֶל תַּחַת רַגְלָיו׃ (11) וַיִּרְכַּב עַל־
on and-he-mounted (11) feet-of-him under and-dark-cloud and-he-came-down

כְּרוּב וַיָּעֹף וַיֵּרָא עַל־ כַּנְפֵי־ רוּחַ׃ (12) וַיָּשֶׁת
and-he-made (12) wind wings-of on and-he-appeared and-he-flew cherub

חֹשֶׁךְ סְבִיבֹתָיו סֻכּוֹת חַשְׁרַת־ מַיִם עָבֵי שְׁחָקִים׃
dark-clouds clouds-of waters mass-of canopies around-him darkness

(13) מִנֹּגַהּ נֶגְדּוֹ בָּעֲרוּ גַּחֲלֵי־ אֵשׁ׃
lightning bolts-of they-blazed presence-of-him from-brightness-of (13)

(14) יַרְעֵם מִן־ שָׁמַיִם יְהוָה וְעֶלְיוֹן יִתֵּן
he-resounded and-Most-High Yahweh heavens from he-thundered (14)

קוֹלוֹ׃ (15) וַיִּשְׁלַח חִצִּים וַיְפִיצֵם בָּרָק
lightning-bolt and-he-scattered-them arrows and-he-shot (15) voice-of-him

וַיָּהְמֹם׃ (16) וַיֵּרָאוּ אֲפִקֵי יָם יִגָּלוּ
they-were-laid-bare sea valleys-of and-they-were-exposed (16) and-he-routed

מֹסְדוֹת תֵּבֵל בְּגַעֲרַת יְהוָה מִנִּשְׁמַת רוּחַ אַפּוֹ׃
nostril-of-him breath-of at-blast-of Yahweh at-rebuke-of earth foundations-of

(17) יִשְׁלַח מִמָּרוֹם יִקָּחֵנִי יַמְשֵׁנִי מִמַּיִם
from-waters he-drew-out-me he-took-hold-of-me from-on-high he-reached (17)

רַבִּים׃ (18) יַצִּילֵנִי מֵאֹיְבִי עָז
powerful from-being-enemy-of-me he-rescued-me (18) deep-ones

מִשֹּׂנְאַי כִּי אָמְצוּ מִמֶּנִּי׃ (19) יְקַדְּמֻנִי
they-confronted-me (19) for-me they-were-too-strong for from-ones-hating-me

בְּיוֹם אֵידִי וַיְהִי יְהוָה מִשְׁעָן לִי׃
to-me support Yahweh but-he-was disaster-of-me in-day-of

(20) וַיֹּצֵא לַמֶּרְחָב אֹתִי יְחַלְּצֵנִי כִּי־
because he-rescued-me me to-the-spacious-place and-he-brought-out (20)

חָפֵץ בִּי׃ (21) יִגְמְלֵנִי יְהוָה כְּצִדְקָתִי
as-righteousness-of-me Yahweh he-dealt-with-me (21) in-me he-delighted

כְּבֹר יָדַי יָשִׁיב לִי׃ (22) כִּי שָׁמַרְתִּי דַּרְכֵי
ways-of I-kept for (22) to-me he-rewarded hands-of-me as-cleanness-of

יְהוָה וְלֹא רָשַׁעְתִּי מֵאֱלֹהָי׃ (23) כִּי כָל־ מִשְׁפָּטוֹ
laws-of-him all-of indeed (23) from-God-of-me I-did-evil and-not Yahweh

the foundations of the
heavens[r] shook;
they trembled because he
was angry.
9Smoke rose from his
nostrils;
consuming fire came
from his mouth,
burning coals blazed out
of it.
10He parted the heavens and
came down;
dark clouds were under
his feet.
11He mounted the cherubim
and flew;
he soared[s] on the wings
of the wind.
12He made darkness his
canopy around him—
the dark[t] rain clouds of
the sky.
13Out of the brightness of
his presence
bolts of lightning blazed
forth.
14The LORD thundered from
heaven;
the voice of the Most
High resounded.
15He shot arrows and
scattered ⌞the enemies⌟,
bolts of lightning and
routed them.
16The valleys of the sea were
exposed
and the foundations of
the earth laid bare
at the rebuke of the LORD,
at the blast of breath
from his nostrils.

17"He reached down from on
high and took hold of
me;
he drew me out of deep
waters.
18He rescued me from my
powerful enemy,
from my foes, who were
too strong for me.
19They confronted me in the
day of my disaster,
but the LORD was my
support.
20He brought me out into a
spacious place;
he rescued me because
he delighted in me.

21"The LORD has dealt with
me according to my
righteousness;
according to the
cleanness of my hands
he has rewarded me.
22For I have kept the ways of
the LORD;
I have not done evil by
turning from my God.

r8 Hebrew; Vulgate and Syriac (see also Psalm 18:7) *mountains*
s11 Many Hebrew manuscripts (see also Psalm 18:10); most Hebrew manuscripts *appeared*
t12 Septuagint and Vulgate (see also Psalm 18:11); Hebrew *massed*

°15 ק ויהם °23 ק משפטיו

לְנֶגְדִּי וְחֻקֹּתָיו לֹא־ אָסוּר מִמֶּנָּה׃ וָאֶהְיֶה
and-I-was (24) from-her I-turned-away not and-decrees-of-him at-before-me

תָמִים לוֹ וָאֶשְׁתַּמְּרָה מֵעֲוֹנִי׃ וַיָּשֶׁב
and-he-rewarded (25) from-sin-of-me and-I-kept-myself before-him blameless

יְהוָה לִי כְּצִדְקָתִי כְּבֹרִי לְנֶגֶד עֵינָיו׃
eyes-of-him at-before as-cleanness-of-me as-righteousness-of-me to-me Yahweh

עִם־ חָסִיד תִּתְחַסָּד עִם־ גִּבּוֹר תָּמִים
blameless man-of to you-show-yourself-faithful faithful to (26)

תִּתַּמָּם׃ עִם־ נָבָר תִּתָּבָר
you-show-yourself-pure one-being-pure to (27) you-show-yourself-blameless

וְעִם־ עִקֵּשׁ תִּתַּפָּל׃ וְאֶת־ עַם עָנִי תּוֹשִׁיעַ
you-save humble people-of and (28) you-show-yourself-shrewd crooked but-to

וְעֵינֶיךָ עַל־ רָמִים תַּשְׁפִּיל׃ כִּי־ אַתָּה
you indeed (29) you-bring-low ones-being-haughty on but-eyes-of-you

נֵירִי יְהוָה וַיהוָה יַגִּיהַּ חָשְׁכִּי׃ כִּי
indeed (30) darkness-of-me he-makes-light and-Yahweh Yahweh lamp-of-me

בְכָה אָרוּץ גְּדוּד בֵּאלֹהַי אֲדַלֶּג־ שׁוּר׃ הָאֵל
the-God (31) wall I-can-scale with-God-of-me troop I-can-advance with-you

תָּמִים דַּרְכּוֹ אִמְרַת יְהוָה צְרוּפָה מָגֵן הוּא לְכֹל
to-all-of he shield being-flawless Yahweh word-of way-of-him perfect

הַחֹסִים בּוֹ׃ כִּי מִי־ אֵל מִבַּלְעֲדֵי יְהוָה וּמִי צוּר
Rock and-who? Yahweh besides God who? for (32) in-him the-ones-taking-refuge

מִבַּלְעֲדֵי אֱלֹהֵינוּ׃ הָאֵל מָעוּזִּי חָיִל וַיַּתֵּר תָּמִים
perfect and-he-makes strong refuge-of-me the-God (33) God-of-us besides

°דַּרְכּוֹ׃ מְשַׁוֶּה °רַגְלָיו כָּאַיָּלוֹת וְעַל בָּמוֹתַי
heights-of-me and-on like-the-deer feet-of-me one-making (34) way-of-me

יַעֲמִדֵנִי׃ מְלַמֵּד יָדַי לַמִּלְחָמָה
for-the-battle hands-of-me one-training (35) he-makes-stand-me

וְנִחַת קֶשֶׁת־ נְחוּשָׁה זְרֹעֹתָי׃ וַתִּתֶּן־ לִי מָגֵן
shield-of to-me and-you-give (36) arms-of-me bronze bow-of and-he-can-bend

יִשְׁעֶךָ וַעֲנֹתְךָ תַּרְבֵּנִי׃ תַּרְחִיב
you-broaden (37) you-make-great-me and-to-stoop-down-you victory-of-you

צַעֲדִי תַּחְתֵּנִי וְלֹא מָעֲדוּ קַרְסֻלָּי׃ אֶרְדְּפָה
I-pursued (38) ankles-of-me they-turn so-not beneath-me path-of-me

אֹיְבַי וָאַשְׁמִידֵם וְלֹא אָשׁוּב עַד־
till I-turned-back and-not and-I-crushed-them being-enemies-of-me

כַּלּוֹתָם׃ וָאֲכַלֵּם וָאֶמְחָצֵם וְלֹא
so-not and-I-crushed-them and-I-destroyed-them (39) to-destroy-them

23 All his laws are before me;
I have not turned away
from his decrees.
24 I have been blameless
before him
and have kept myself
from sin.
25 The LORD has rewarded me
according to my
righteousness,
according to my
cleanness[u] in his sight.

26 "To the faithful you show
yourself faithful,
to the blameless you
show yourself
blameless,
27 to the pure you show
yourself pure,
but to the crooked you
show yourself shrewd.
28 You save the humble,
but your eyes are on the
haughty to bring them
low.
29 You are my lamp, O LORD;
the LORD turns my
darkness into light.
30 With your help I can
advance against a
troop[v];
with my God I can scale
a wall.

31 "As for God, his way is
perfect;
the word of the LORD is
flawless.
He is a shield
for all who take refuge in
him.
32 For who is God besides the
LORD?
And who is the Rock
except our God?
33 It is God who arms me
with strength[w]
and makes my way
perfect.
34 He makes my feet like the
feet of a deer;
he enables me to stand
on the heights.
35 He trains my hands for
battle;
my arms can bend a bow
of bronze.
36 You give me your shield of
victory;
you stoop down to make
me great.
37 You broaden the path
beneath me,
so that my ankles do not
turn.

38 "I pursued my enemies
and crushed them;
I did not turn back till
they were destroyed.

[u]25 Hebrew; Septuagint and Vulgate (see also Psalm 18:24) *to the cleanness of my hands*
[v]30 Or *can run through a barricade*
[w]33 Dead Sea Scrolls, some Septuagint manuscripts, Vulgate and Syriac (see also Psalm 18:32); Masoretic Text *who is my strong refuge*

°33 ק דרכי °34 ק רגלי

יְקוּמוּן וַיִּפְּלוּ תַּחַת רַגְלָי׃ וַתַּזְרֵנִי
and-you-armed-me (40) feet-of-me beneath and-they-fell they-could-rise

חַיִל לַמִּלְחָמָה תַּכְרִיעַ קָמַי תַּחְתֵּנִי׃
beneath-me adversaries-of-me you-made-bow for-the-battle strength

וְאֹיְבַי תַּתָּה לִּי עֹרֶף מְשַׂנְאַי
ones-hating-me back to-me you-made-turn and-being-enemies-of-me (41)

וָאַצְמִיתֵם׃ יִשְׁעוּ וְאֵין מֹשִׁיעַ אֶל־ יְהוָה
Yahweh to saving but-no-one they-cried-for-help (42) also-I-destroyed-them

וְלֹא עָנָם׃ וְאֶשְׁחָקֵם כַּעֲפַר־ אָרֶץ
earth like-dust-of and-I-beat-them (43) he-answered-them but-not

כְּטִיט־ חוּצוֹת אֲדִקֵּם אֶרְקָעֵם׃ וַתְּפַלְּטֵנִי
and-you-delivered-me (44) I-trampled-them I-pounded-them streets like-mud-of

מֵרִיבֵי עַמִּי תִּשְׁמְרֵנִי לְרֹאשׁ גּוֹיִם עַם לֹא־
not people nations as-head-of you-preserved-me people-of-me from-attacks-of

יָדַעְתִּי יַעַבְדֻנִי׃ בְּנֵי נֵכָר יִתְכַּחֲשׁוּ־
they-come-cringing foreigner sons-of (45) they-are-subject-to-me I-know

לִי לִשְׁמוֹעַ אֹזֶן יִשָּׁמְעוּ לִי׃ בְּנֵי נֵכָר יִבֹּלוּ
they-lose-heart foreigner sons-of (46) to-me they-obey ear to-hear to-me

וְיַחְגְּרוּ מִמִּסְגְּרוֹתָם׃ חַי־ יְהוָה
Yahweh life-of (47) from-strongholds-of-them and-they-arm-themselves

וּבָרוּךְ צוּרִי וְיָרֻם אֱלֹהֵי צוּר
Rock-of God-of and-may-he-be-exalted Rock-of-me and-being-praised

יִשְׁעִי׃ הָאֵל הַנֹּתֵן נְקָמֹת לִי וּמוֹרִיד
and-one-putting to-me vengeances the-one-giving the-God (48) Savior-of-me

עַמִּים תַּחְתֵּנִי׃ וּמוֹצִיאִי מֵאֹיְבָי
from-being-enemies-of-me and-one-setting-free-me (49) under-me nations

וּמִקָּמַי תְּרוֹמְמֵנִי מֵאִישׁ חֲמָסִים תַּצִּילֵנִי׃
you-rescued-me violences from-man-of you-exalted-me and-above-foes-of-me

עַל־ כֵּן אוֹדְךָ יְהוָה בַּגּוֹיִם וּלְשִׁמְךָ
and-to-name-of-you among-the-nations Yahweh I-will-praise-you this for (50)

אֲזַמֵּר׃ מִגְדּוֹל יְשׁוּעוֹת מַלְכּוֹ וְעֹשֶׂה־
and-showing king-of-him victories-of greatness-of (51) I-will-sing-praise

חֶסֶד לִמְשִׁיחוֹ לְדָוִד וּלְזַרְעוֹ
and-to-descendant-of-him to-David to-anointed-of-him unfailing-kindness

עַד־ עוֹלָם׃ וְאֵלֶּה דִּבְרֵי דָוִד הָאַחֲרֹנִים נְאֻם דָּוִד
David oracle-of the-last-ones David words-of and-these (23:1) forever to

בֶּן־ יִשַׁי וּנְאֻם הַגֶּבֶר הֻקַם עָל מְשִׁיחַ אֱלֹהֵי
God-of anointed-of above he-was-exalted the-man and-oracle-of Jesse son-of

39 I crushed them completely,
and they could not
rise;
they fell beneath my feet.
40 You armed me with
strength for battle;
you made my adversaries
bow at my feet.
41 You made my enemies turn
their backs in flight,
and I destroyed my foes.
42 They cried for help, but
there was no one to
save them—
to the LORD, but he did
not answer.
43 I beat them as fine as the
dust of the earth;
I pounded and trampled
them like mud in the
streets.

44 "You have delivered me
from the attacks of my
people;
you have preserved me
as the head of nations.
People I did not know are
subject to me,
45 and foreigners come
cringing to me;
as soon as they hear me,
they obey me.
46 They all lose heart;
they come trembling[x]
from their strongholds.

47 "The LORD lives! Praise be
to my Rock!
Exalted be God, the Rock,
my Savior!
48 He is the God who avenges
me,
who puts the nations
under me,
49 who sets me free from
my enemies.
You exalted me above my
foes;
from violent men you
rescued me.
50 Therefore I will praise you,
O LORD, among the
nations;
I will sing praises to your
name.
51 He gives his king great
victories;
he shows unfailing
kindness to his
anointed,
to David and his
descendants forever."

The Last Words of David

23 These are the last
words of David:

"The oracle of David son of
Jesse,
the oracle of the man
exalted by the Most
High,
the man anointed by the
God of Jacob,
Israel's singer of songs[y]:

x46 See Septuagint, Vulgate and Psalm 18:45; Masoretic Text *they arm themselves*
y1 Or *Israel's beloved singer*

יַעֲקֹב וּנְעִים זְמִרוֹת יִשְׂרָאֵל׃ רוּחַ יְהוָה דִּבֶּר־ בִּי
through-me he-spoke Yahweh Spirit-of (2) Israel songs-of and-singer-of Jacob

וּמִלָּתוֹ עַל־ לְשׁוֹנִי׃ אָמַר אֱלֹהֵי יִשְׂרָאֵל לִי דִבֶּר
he-said to-me Israel God-of he-spoke (3) tongue-of-me on and-word-of-him

צוּר יִשְׂרָאֵל מוֹשֵׁל בָּאָדָם צַדִּיק מוֹשֵׁל יִרְאַת
fear-of one-ruling righteousness over-the-man one-ruling Israel Rock-of

אֱלֹהִים׃ וּכְאוֹר בֹּקֶר יִזְרַח־ שָׁמֶשׁ בֹּקֶר לֹא עָבוֹת
clouds without morning sun he-rises morning and-as-light-of (4) God

מִנֹּגַהּ מִמָּטָר דֶּשֶׁא מֵאָרֶץ׃ כִּי־ לֹא־ כֵן
right not indeed (5) from-earth grass after-rain like-brightness

בֵּיתִי עִם־ אֵל כִּי בְרִית עוֹלָם שָׂם לִי
with-me he-made everlasting covenant-of indeed God with house-of-me

עֲרוּכָה בַכֹּל וּשְׁמֻרָה כִּי־ כָל־ יִשְׁעִי
salvation-of-me all-of indeed and-being-secured in-the-whole being-arranged

וְכָל־ חֵפֶץ כִּי־ לֹא יַצְמִיחַ׃ וּבְלִיַּעַל
but-evil (6) he-will-bring-to-fruition not indeed desire and-every-of

כְּקוֹץ מֻנָד כֻּלָּהַם כִּי־ לֹא בְיָד יִקָּחוּ׃
they-are-gathered with-hand not that all-of-them being-cast-aside like-thorn

וְאִישׁ יִגַּע בָּהֶם יִמָּלֵא בַרְזֶל וְעֵץ חֲנִית
spear or-shaft-of iron he-is-used on-them he-touches and-whoever (7)

וּבָאֵשׁ שָׂרוֹף יִשָּׂרְפוּ בַּשָּׁבֶת׃ אֵלֶּה שְׁמוֹת
names-of these (8) in-the-place they-are-burned to-burn and-with-fire

הַגִּבֹּרִים אֲשֶׁר לְדָוִד יֹשֵׁב בַּשֶּׁבֶת תַּחְכְּמֹנִי ׀ רֹאשׁ הַשָּׁלִשִׁי
the-three chief-of Tahkemonite Basshebeth Josheb of-David who the-mighty-men

הוּא עֲדִינוֹ הָעֶצְנוֹ עַל־ שְׁמֹנֶה מֵאוֹת חָלָל בְּפַעַם אֶחָד׃
one in-encounter killed hundreds eight against the-Eznite Adino he

וְאַחֲרָו אֶלְעָזָר בֶּן־ דֹּדַי* בֶּן־ אֲחֹחִי בִּשְׁלֹשָׁה
of-three Ahohi son-of *Dodai son-of Eleazar and-next-to-him (9)

גִבֹּרִים עִם־ דָּוִד בְּחָרְפָם בַּפְּלִשְׁתִּים
against-the-Philistines when-to-taunt-them David with the-mighty-men

נֶאֶסְפוּ־ שָׁם לַמִּלְחָמָה וַיַּעֲלוּ אִישׁ יִשְׂרָאֵל׃
Israel man-of then-they-retreated for-the-battle there they-gathered

הוּא קָם וַיַּךְ בַּפְּלִשְׁתִּים עַד ׀ כִּי־
when until against-the-Philistines and-he-struck he-stood he (10)

יָגְעָה יָדוֹ וַתִּדְבַּק יָדוֹ אֶל־ הַחֶרֶב
the-sword to hand-of-him and-she-froze hand-of-him she-grew-tired

וַיַּעַשׂ יְהוָה תְּשׁוּעָה גְדוֹלָה בַּיּוֹם הַהוּא וְהָעָם
and-the-troop the-that on-the-day great victory Yahweh and-he-brought

[2]"The Spirit of the LORD
spoke through me;
his word was on my
tongue.
[3]The God of Israel spoke,
the Rock of Israel said to
me:
'When one rules over men
in righteousness,
when he rules in the fear
of God,
[4]he is like the light of
morning at sunrise
on a cloudless morning,
like the brightness after
rain
that brings the grass
from the earth.'

[5]"Is not my house right
with God?
Has he not made with
me an everlasting
covenant,
arranged and secured in
every part?
Will he not bring to
fruition my salvation
and grant me my every
desire?
[6]But evil men are all to be
cast aside like thorns,
which are not gathered
with the hand.
[7]Whoever touches thorns
uses a tool of iron or the
shaft of a spear;
they are burned up
where they lie."

David's Mighty Men

[8]These are the names of David's mighty men:
Josheb-Basshebeth,[z] a Tahkemonite,[a] was chief of the
Three; he raised his spear
against eight hundred men,
whom he killed[b] in one encounter.
[9]Next to him was Eleazar
son of Dodai the Ahohite. As
one of the three mighty men,
he was with David when they
taunted the Philistines gathered ⌊at Pas Dammim⌋[c] for battle. Then the men of Israel retreated, [10]but he stood his
ground and struck down the
Philistines till his hand grew
tired and froze to the sword.
The LORD brought about a

[z]8 Hebrew; Septuagint suggests *Ish-Bosheth*, that is, *Esh-Baal* (see also 1 Chron. 11:11 *Jashobeam*).
[a]8 Probably a variant of Hacmonite
[b]8 Some Septuagint manuscripts (see also 1 Chron. 11:11); Hebrew and other Septuagint manuscripts *Three; it was Adino the Eznite who killed eight hundred men*
[c]9 See 1 Chronicles 11:13; Hebrew *gathered there.*

*9 The NIV transliterates the *Kethib* form; the *Qere* reads *Dodo* or *uncle-of-him*.

°8a ק העצני °8b ק אחת
°9a ק ואחריו °9b ק דדו
°9c ק הגברים

יָשֻׁבוּ אַחֲרָיו אַךְ־לְפַשֵּׁט׃ וְאַחֲרָיו שַׁמָּא בֶן־אָגֵא

Agee son-of Shammah and-next-to-him (11) to-strip only to-him they-returned

הָרָרִי וַיֵּאָסְפוּ פְלִשְׁתִּים לַחַיָּה וַתְּהִי־שָׁם

there and-she-was as-the-group Philistines when-they-banded-together Hararite

חֶלְקַת הַשָּׂדֶה מְלֵאָה עֲדָשִׁים וְהָעָם נָס מִפְּנֵי

from-before he-fled and-the-troop lentils full the-field portion-of

פְלִשְׁתִּים׃ וַיִּתְיַצֵּב בְּתוֹךְ־הַחֶלְקָה וַיַּצִּילֶהָ

and-he-defended-her the-field in-middle-of but-he-took-stand (12) Philistines

וַיַּךְ אֶת־פְּלִשְׁתִּים וַיַּעַשׂ יְהוָה תְּשׁוּעָה גְדוֹלָה׃

great victory Yahweh and-he-brought Philistines *** and-he-struck-down

וַיֵּרְדוּ שְׁלֹשִׁים מֵהַשְּׁלֹשִׁים רֹאשׁ וַיָּבֹאוּ אֶל־

during and-they-went chief of-the-thirty three and-they-came-down (13)

קָצִיר אֶל־דָּוִד אֶל־מְעָרַת עֲדֻלָּם וְחַיַּת פְּלִשְׁתִּים חֹנָה

camping Philistines and-band-of Adullam cave-of at David to harvest

בְּעֵמֶק רְפָאִים׃ וְדָוִד אָז בַּמְּצוּדָה וּמַצַּב

and-garrison-of in-the-stronghold then and-David (14) Rephaim in-Valley-of

פְּלִשְׁתִּים אָז בֵּית לָחֶם׃ וַיִּתְאַוֶּה דָוִד וַיֹּאמַר מִי

who? and-he-said David and-he-longed (15) Lehem Beth then Philistines

יַשְׁקֵנִי מַיִם מִבֹּאר בֵּית־לֶחֶם אֲשֶׁר בַּשָּׁעַר׃

near-the-gate that Lehem Beth from-well-of waters he-will-get-drink-for-me

וַיִּבְקְעוּ שְׁלֹשֶׁת הַגִּבֹּרִים בְּמַחֲנֵה פְלִשְׁתִּים

Philistines through-line-of the-mighty-men three-of so-they-broke (16)

וַיִּשְׁאֲבוּ־מַיִם מִבֹּאר בֵּית־לֶחֶם אֲשֶׁר בַּשַּׁעַר

near-the-gate that Lehem Beth from-well-of waters and-they-drew

וַיִּשְׂאוּ וַיָּבִאוּ אֶל־דָּוִד וְלֹא אָבָה לִשְׁתּוֹתָם

to-drink-them he-would but-not David to and-they-brought and-they-carried

וַיַּסֵּךְ אֹתָם לַיהוָה׃ וַיֹּאמֶר חָלִילָה לִּי

from-me far-be-it! and-he-said (17) before-Yahweh them but-he-poured-out

יְהוָה מֵעֲשֹׂתִי זֹאת הֲדַם הָאֲנָשִׁים הַהֹלְכִים בְּנַפְשׁוֹתָם

at-lives-of-them the-ones-going the-men blood-of? this from-to-do-me Yahweh

וְלֹא אָבָה לִשְׁתּוֹתָם אֵלֶּה עָשׂוּ שְׁלֹשֶׁת הַגִּבֹּרִים׃

the-mighty-men three-of they-did these to-drink-them he-would and-not

וַאֲבִישַׁי אֲחִי ׀ יוֹאָב בֶּן־צְרוּיָה הוּא רֹאשׁ הַשְּׁלֹשִׁי וְהוּא

and-he the-Three chief-of he Zeruiah son-of Joab brother-of and-Abishai (18)

עוֹרֵר אֶת־חֲנִיתוֹ עַל־שְׁלֹשׁ מֵאוֹת חָלָל וְלוֹ־

so-to-him killed hundreds three-of against spear-of-him *** one-raising

שֵׁם בַּשְּׁלֹשָׁה׃ מִן־הַשְּׁלֹשָׁה הֲכִי נִכְבָּד

being-honored indeed? the-Three more-than (19) among-the-Three name

great victory that day. The
troops returned to Eleazar, but
only to strip the dead.
11 Next to him was Shammah
son of Agee the Hararite.
When the Philistines banded
together at a place where there
was a field full of lentils, Israel's troops fled from them.
12 But Shammah took his stand
in the middle of the field. He
defended it and struck the
Philistines down, and the
LORD brought about a great
victory.
13 During harvest time, three
of the thirty chief men came
down to David at the cave of
Adullam, while a band of Philistines was encamped in the
Valley of Rephaim. 14 At that
time David was in the stronghold, and the Philistine garri-
son was at Bethlehem. 15 David
longed for water and said,
"Oh, that someone would get
me a drink of water from the
well near the gate of Bethlehem!" 16 So the three mighty
men broke through the Philistine lines, drew water from
the well near the gate of Bethlehem and carried it back to
David. But he refused to drink
it; instead, he poured it out before the LORD. 17 "Far be it from
me, O LORD, to do this!" he
said. "Is it not the blood of
men who went at the risk of
their lives?" And David would
not drink it.
Such were the exploits of the
three mighty men.
18 Abishai the brother of Joab
son of Zeruiah was chief of the
Three.[d] He raised his spear
against three hundred men,
whom he killed, and so he
became as famous as the
Three. 19 Was he not held in
greater honor than the Three?

[d] 18 Most Hebrew manuscripts (see also 1 Chron. 11:20); two Hebrew manuscripts and Syriac *Thirty*

°13 ק שלשה

°18 ק השלשה

וַיְהִי לָהֶם לְשָׂר וְעַד־ הַשְּׁלֹשָׁה לֹא־ בָא׃
he-came not the-Three though-among as-commander to-them and-he-became

(20) וּבְנָיָהוּ בֶן־ יְהוֹיָדָע בֶּן־ אִישׁ־ חַי° רַב־ פְּעָלִים
exploits great-of valor man-of son-of Jehoiada son-of and-Benaiah (20)

מִקַּבְצְאֵל הוּא הִכָּה אֵת שְׁנֵי אֲרִאֵל מוֹאָב וְהוּא
and-he Moab best-man-of two-of *** he-struck-down he from-Kabzeel

יָרַד וְהִכָּה אֶת־ הָאֲרִיָּה° בְּתוֹךְ הַבֹּאר בְּיוֹם הַשָּׁלֶג׃
the-snow on-day-of the-pit inside-of the-lion *** and-he-killed he-went-down

(21) וְהוּא־ הִכָּה אֶת־ אִישׁ מִצְרִי אֲשֶׁר° מַרְאֶה וּבְיַד
though-in-hand-of huge man-of Egyptian man *** he-struck-down and-he (21)

הַמִּצְרִי חֲנִית וַיֵּרֶד אֵלָיו בַּשָּׁבֶט וַיִּגְזֹל אֶת־
*** and-he-snatched with-the-club against-him and-he-went spear the-Egyptian

הַחֲנִית מִיַּד הַמִּצְרִי וַיַּהַרְגֵהוּ בַּחֲנִיתוֹ׃
with-spear-of-him and-he-killed-him the-Egyptian from-hand-of the-spear

(22) אֵלֶּה עָשָׂה בְּנָיָהוּ בֶּן־ יְהוֹיָדָע וְלוֹ־ שֵׁם בִּשְׁלֹשָׁה
among-three name and-to-him Jehoiada son-of Benaiah he-did these (22)

הַגִּבֹּרִים׃ (23) מִן־ הַשְּׁלֹשִׁים נִכְבָּד וְאֶל־ הַשְּׁלֹשָׁה
the-Three though-among being-honored the-Thirty more-than (23) the-mighty-men

לֹא־ בָא וַיְשִׂמֵהוּ דָוִד אֶל־ מִשְׁמַעְתּוֹ׃
bodyguard-of-him over David and-he-put-in-charge-him he-came not

(24) עֲשָׂה־ אֵל אֲחִי־ יוֹאָב בַּשְּׁלֹשִׁים אֶלְחָנָן בֶּן־ דֹּדוֹ בֵּית לָחֶם׃
Lehem Beth Dodo son-of Elhanan among-the-Thirty Joab brother-of El Asah (24)

(25) שַׁמָּה הַחֲרֹדִי אֱלִיקָא הַחֲרֹדִי׃ (26) חֶלֶץ הַפַּלְטִי עִירָא
Ira the-Paltite Helez (26) the-Harodite Elika the-Harodite Shammah (25)

בֶן־ עִקֵּשׁ הַתְּקוֹעִי׃ (27) אֲבִיעֶזֶר הָעַנְּתֹתִי מְבֻנַּי
Mebunnai the-Anathothite Abiezer (27) the-Tekoaite Ikkesh son-of

הַחֻשָׁתִי׃ (28) צַלְמוֹן הָאֲחֹחִי מַהְרַי הַנְּטֹפָתִי׃ (29) חֵלֶב
Heleb (29) the-Netophathite Maharai the-Ahohite Zalmon (28) the-Hushathite

בֶּן־ בַּעֲנָה הַנְּטֹפָתִי אִתַּי בֶּן־ רִיבַי מִגִּבְעַת בְּנֵי
sons-of from-Gibeah-of Ribai son-of Ithai the-Netophathite Baanah son-of

בִנְיָמִן׃ (30) בְּנָיָהוּ פִּרְעָתֹנִי הִדַּי מִנַּחֲלֵי גָעַשׁ׃ (31) אֲבִי־ עַלְבוֹן
Albon Abi (31) Gaash from-ravines-of Hiddai Pirathonite Benaiah (30) Benjamin

הָעַרְבָתִי עַזְמָוֶת הַבַּרְחֻמִי׃ (32) אֶלְיַחְבָּא הַשַּׁעַלְבֹנִי בְּנֵי
sons-of the-Shaalbonite Eliahba (32) the-Barhumite Azmaveth the-Arbathite

יָשֵׁן יְהוֹנָתָן׃ (33) שַׁמָּה הַהֲרָרִי אֲחִיאָם בֶּן־ שָׁרָר הָאֲרָרִי׃
Hararite Sharar son-of Ahiam the-Hararite Shammah (33) Jonathan Jashen

(34) אֱלִיפֶלֶט בֶּן־ אֲחַסְבַּי בֶּן־ הַמַּעֲכָתִי אֱלִיעָם בֶּן־ אֲחִיתֹפֶל
Ahithophel son-of Eliam the-Maacathite son-of Ahasbai son-of Eliphelet (34)

He became their commander,
even though he was not included among them.
[20]Benaiah son of Jehoiada
was a valiant fighter from
Kabzeel, who performed great
exploits. He struck down two
of Moab's best men. He also
went down into a pit on a
snowy day and killed a lion.
[21]And he struck down a huge
Egyptian. Although the Egyptian had a spear in his hand,
Benaiah went against him
with a club. He snatched the
spear from the Egyptian's
hand and killed him with his
own spear. [22]Such were the exploits of Benaiah son of Jehoiada; he too was as famous as
the three mighty men. [23]He
was held in greater honor
than any of the Thirty, but he
was not included among the
Three. And David put him in
charge of his bodyguard.

[24]Among the Thirty were:
Asahel the brother of
Joab,
Elhanan son of Dodo
from Bethlehem,
[25]Shammah the Harodite,
Elika the Harodite,
[26]Helez the Paltite,
Ira son of Ikkesh from
Tekoa,
[27]Abiezer from Anathoth,
Mebunnai[e] the Husha-
thite,
[28]Zalmon the Ahohite,
Maharai the Netopha-
thite,
[29]Heled[f] son of Baanah
the Netophathite,
Ithai son of Ribai from
Gibeah of Benjamin,
[30]Benaiah the Pirathon-
ite,
Hiddai[g] from the ra-
vines of Gaash,
[31]Abi-Albon the Arbath-
ite,
Azmaveth the Barhu-
mite,
[32]Eliahba the
Shaalbonite,
the sons of Jashen,
Jonathan [33]son of[h]
Shammah the Hara-
rite,
Ahiam son of Sharar[i]
the Hararite,
[34]Eliphelet son of Ahasbai the Maacathite,

[e]27 Hebrew; some Septuagint manuscripts (see also 1 Chron. 11:29) *Sibbecai*
[f]29 Some Hebrew manuscripts and Vulgate (see also 1 Chron. 11:30); most Hebrew manuscripts *Heleb*
[g]30 Hebrew; some Septuagint manuscripts (see also 1 Chron. 11:32) *Hurai*
[h]33 Some Septuagint manuscripts (see also 1 Chron. 11:34); Hebrew does not have *son of.*
[i]33 Hebrew; some Septuagint manuscripts (see also 1 Chron. 11:35) *Sacar*

°20a ק חיל °20b ק הארי
°21 ק איש

הַגִּלֹנִֽי׃ °חֶצְרוֹ הַכַּרְמְלִי פַּעֲרַי הָאַרְבִּֽי׃ יִגְאָל בֶּן־
son-of Igal (36) the-Arbite Paarai the-Carmelite *Hezro (35) the-Gilonite

נָתָן מִצֹּבָה בָּנִי הַגָּדִֽי׃ צֶלֶק הָעַמֹּנִי נַחְרַי
Naharai the-Ammonite Zelek (37) †Haggadi son-of† from-Zobah Nathan

הַבְּאֵרֹתִי °נֹשְׂאֵי כְּלֵי יוֹאָב בֶּן־ צְרֻיָֽה׃ עִירָא הַיִּתְרִי
the-Ithrite Ira (38) Zeruiah son-of Joab armors-of one-bearing the-Beerothite

גָּרֵב הַיִּתְרִֽי׃ אוּרִיָּה הַחִתִּי כֹּל שְׁלֹשִׁים וְשִׁבְעָֽה׃
and-seven thirty total-of the-Hittite Uriah (39) the-Ithrite Gareb

וַיֹּסֶף אַף־ יְהוָה לַחֲרוֹת בְּיִשְׂרָאֵל וַיָּסֶת
and-he-incited against-Israel to-burn Yahweh anger-of and-he-repeated (24:1)

אֶת־ דָּוִד בָּהֶם לֵאמֹר לֵךְ מְנֵה אֶת־ יִשְׂרָאֵל וְאֶת־יְהוּדָֽה׃ וַיֹּאמֶר
so-he-said (2) Judah and Israel *** count! go! to-say against-them David ***

הַמֶּלֶךְ אֶל־ יוֹאָב ׀ שַׂר־ הַחַיִל אֲשֶׁר־ אִתּוֹ שׁוּט־ נָא בְּכָל־
through-all-of now! go! with-him who the-army commander-of Joab to the-king

שִׁבְטֵי יִשְׂרָאֵל מִדָּן וְעַד־ בְּאֵר שֶׁבַע וּפִקְדוּ אֶת־ הָעָם
the-people *** and-enroll! Sheba Beer even-to from-Dan Israel tribes-of

וְיָדַעְתִּי אֵת מִסְפַּר הָעָֽם׃ וַיֹּאמֶר יוֹאָב אֶל־ הַמֶּלֶךְ
the-king to Joab but-he-replied (3) the-people number-of *** so-I-may-know

וְיוֹסֵף יְהוָה אֱלֹהֶיךָ אֶל־ הָעָם כָּהֵם ׀ וְכָהֵם
and-as-they as-they the-troop to God-of-you Yahweh now-may-he-multiply

מֵאָה פְעָמִים וְעֵינֵי אֲדֹנִי־ הַמֶּלֶךְ רֹאוֹת וַאדֹנִי
but-lord-of-me ones-seeing the-king lord-of-me and-eyes-of times hundred

הַמֶּלֶךְ לָמָּה חָפֵץ בַּדָּבָר הַזֶּֽה׃ וַיֶּחֱזַק דְּבַר־
word-of but-he-overruled (4) the-this for-the-thing he-wants why? the-king

הַמֶּלֶךְ אֶל־ יוֹאָב וְעַל שָׂרֵי הֶחָיִל וַיֵּצֵא יוֹאָב
Joab so-he-left the-army commanders-of and-over Joab over the-king

וְשָׂרֵי הַחַיִל לִפְנֵי הַמֶּלֶךְ לִפְקֹד אֶת־ הָעָם
the-people *** to-enroll the-king presences-of the-army and-commanders-of

אֶת־יִשְׂרָאֵֽל׃ וַיַּעַבְרוּ אֶת־ הַיַּרְדֵּן וַיַּחֲנוּ בַעֲרוֹעֵר
near-Aroer and-they-camped the-Jordan *** and-they-crossed (5) Israel ***

הָעִיר אֲשֶׁר בְּתוֹךְ־ הַנַּחַל הַגָּד וְאֶל־ יַעְזֵֽר׃
Jazer and-to the-Gad the-gorge in-midst-of that the-town south-of

וַיָּבֹאוּ הַגִּלְעָדָה וְאֶל־ אֶרֶץ תַּחְתִּים חָדְשִׁי וַיָּבֹאוּ
and-they-went Hodshi Tahtim region-of and-to to-the-Gilead and-they-went (6)

דָּנָה יַּעַן וְסָבִיב אֶל־ צִידוֹן׃ וַיָּבֹאוּ מִבְצַר־ צֹר
Tyre fortress-of then-they-went (7) Sidon toward and-around Jaan to-Dan

וְכָל־ עָרֵי הַחִוִּי וְהַכְּנַעֲנִי וַיֵּצְאוּ אֶל־ נֶגֶב
Negev-of to and-they-went and-the-Canaanite the-Hivite towns-of and-all-of

Eliam son of Ahithophel the Gilonite,
35 Hezro the Carmelite,
Paarai the Arbite,
36 Igal son of Nathan from Zobah,
the son of Hagri,[j]
37 Zelek the Ammonite,
Naharai the Beerothite,
the armor-bearer of Joab son of Zeruiah,
38 Ira the Ithrite,
Gareb the Ithrite
39 and Uriah the Hittite.
There were thirty-seven in all.

David Counts the Fighting Men

24 Again the anger of the LORD burned against Israel, and he incited David against them, saying, "Go and count Israel and Judah."
2 So the king said to Joab and the army commanders[k] with him, "Go throughout the tribes of Israel from Dan to Beersheba and enroll the fighting men, so that I may know how many there are."
3 But Joab replied to the king, "May the LORD your God multiply the troops a hundred times over, and may the eyes of my lord the king see it. But why does my lord the king want to do such a thing?"
4 The king's word, however, overruled Joab and the army commanders; so they left the presence of the king to enroll the fighting men of Israel.
5 After crossing the Jordan, they camped near Aroer, south of the town in the gorge, and then went through Gad and on to Jazer. 6 They went to Gilead and the region of Tahtim Hodshi, and on to Dan Jaan and around toward Sidon. 7 Then they went toward the fortress of Tyre and all the towns of the Hivites and Canaanites. Finally, they went on to Beersheba in the Negev of Judah.

j36 Some Septuagint manuscripts (see also 1 Chron. 11:38); Hebrew *Haggadi*
k2 Septuagint (see also verse 4 and 1 Chron. 21:2); Hebrew *Joab the army commander*

*35 The NIV transliterates the *Kethib* Form; the *Qere* reads *Hezrai*.

†36 The NIV translates here in harmony with 1 Chronicles 11:38; the forms as written are the proper name *Bani the-Gadite*.

°35 ק חצרי
°37 ק נשא

יְהוּדָה בְּאֵר שָׁבַע׃ וַיָּשֻׁטוּ בְּכָל־ הָאָרֶץ וַיָּבֹאוּ
then-they-came the-land through-entire-of and-they-went (8) Sheba Beer Judah

מִקְצֵה תִשְׁעָה חֳדָשִׁים וְעֶשְׂרִים יוֹם יְרוּשָׁלִָם׃ וַיִּתֵּן יוֹאָב אֶת־
*** Joab and-he-reported (9) Jerusalem day and-twenty months nine at-end-of

מִסְפַּר מִפְקַד־ הָעָם אֶל־ הַמֶּלֶךְ וַתְּהִי יִשְׂרָאֵל שְׁמֹנֶה מֵאוֹת
hundreds eight Israel and-she-was the-king to the-people list-of number-of

אֶלֶף אִישׁ־ חַיִל שֹׁלֵף חֶרֶב וְאִישׁ יְהוּדָה חֲמֵשׁ־ מֵאוֹת
hundreds five-of Judah and-man-of sword handling ability man-of thousand

אֶלֶף אִישׁ׃ וַיַּךְ לֵב־ דָּוִד אֹתוֹ אַחֲרֵי־ כֵן סָפַר
he-counted this after him David conscience-of and-he-struck (10) man thousand

אֶת־ הָעָם וַיֹּאמֶר דָּוִד אֶל־ יְהוָה חָטָאתִי מְאֹד אֲשֶׁר עָשִׂיתִי
I-did what greatly I-sinned Yahweh to David and-he-said the-people ***

וְעַתָּה יְהוָה הַעֲבֶר־ נָא אֶת־ עֲוֺן עַבְדְּךָ כִּי נִסְכַּלְתִּי
I-was-foolish for servant-of-you guilt-of *** now! take-away! Yahweh and-now

מְאֹד׃ וַיָּקָם דָּוִד בַּבֹּקֶר וּדְבַר־ יְהוָה הָיָה אֶל־
to he-came Yahweh and-word-of in-the-morning David and-he-got-up (11) very

גָּד הַנָּבִיא חֹזֵה דָוִד לֵאמֹר׃ הָלוֹךְ וְדִבַּרְתָּ אֶל־ דָּוִד כֹּה
this David to and-you-tell to-go (12) to-say David seer-of the-prophet Gad

אָמַר יְהוָה שָׁלֹשׁ אָנֹכִי נוֹטֵל עָלֶיךָ בְּחַר־ לְךָ אַחַת־ מֵהֶם
of-them one for-you choose! to-you giving I three Yahweh he-says

וְאֶעֱשֶׂה־ לָּךְ׃ וַיָּבֹא־ גָד אֶל־ דָּוִד וַיַּגֶּד־ לוֹ
to-him and-he-told David to Gad so-he-went (13) to-you and-I-will-do

וַיֹּאמֶר לוֹ הֲתָבוֹא לְךָ שֶׁבַע שָׁנִים ׀ רָעָב ׀ בְּאַרְצֶךָ
in-land-of-you famine years seven upon-you shall-she-come? to-him and-he-said

אִם־ שְׁלֹשָׁה חֳדָשִׁים נֻסְךָ לִפְנֵי־ צָרֶיךָ וְהוּא רֹדְפֶךָ
pursuing-you while-he enemies-of-you before to-flee-you months three or

וְאִם־ הֱיוֹת שְׁלֹשֶׁת יָמִים דֶּבֶר בְּאַרְצֶךָ עַתָּה דַּע וּרְאֵה מָה־
how? and-decide! think! now in-land-of-you plague days three-of to-be or-if

אָשִׁיב שֹׁלְחִי דָּבָר׃ וַיֹּאמֶר דָּוִד אֶל־ גָּד צַר־
distress Gad to David and-he-said (14) answer one-sending-me should-I-bring

לִי מְאֹד נִפְּלָה־ נָּא בְיַד־ יְהוָה כִּי־ רַבִּים רַחֲמָו°
mercies-of-him great-ones for Yahweh into-hand-of now! let-us-fall deep to-me

וּבְיַד־ אָדָם אַל־ אֶפֹּלָה׃ וַיִּתֵּן יְהוָה דֶּבֶר בְּיִשְׂרָאֵל
on-Israel plague Yahweh so-he-sent (15) let-me-fall not man but-into-hand-of

מֵהַבֹּקֶר וְעַד־ עֵת מוֹעֵד וַיָּמָת מִן־ הָעָם
the-people from and-he-died designated time-of even-to from-the-morning

מִדָּן וְעַד־ בְּאֵר שֶׁבַע שִׁבְעִים אֶלֶף אִישׁ׃ וַיִּשְׁלַח
when-he-stretched (16) man thousand seventy Sheba Beer even-to from-Dan

°14 ק רחמיו

[8]After they had gone through the entire land, they came back to Jerusalem at the end of nine months and twenty days.

[9]Joab reported the number of the fighting men to the king: In Israel there were eight hundred thousand able-bodied men who could handle a sword, and in Judah five hundred thousand.

[10]David was conscience-stricken after he had counted the fighting men, and he said to the LORD, "I have sinned greatly in what I have done. Now, O LORD, I beg you, take away the guilt of your servant. I have done a very foolish thing."

[11]Before David got up the next morning, the word of the LORD had come to Gad the prophet, David's seer: [12]"Go and tell David, 'This is what the LORD says: I am giving you three options. Choose one of them for me to carry out against you.'"

[13]So Gad went to David and said to him, "Shall there come upon you three[l] years of famine in your land? Or three months of fleeing from your enemies while they pursue you? Or three days of plague in your land? Now then, think it over and decide how I should answer the one who sent me."

[14]David said to Gad, "I am in deep distress. Let us fall into the hands of the LORD, for his mercy is great; but do not let me fall into the hands of men."

[15]So the LORD sent a plague on Israel from that morning until the end of the time designated, and seventy thousand of the people from Dan to Beersheba died. [16]When the

[l]13 Some Septuagint manuscripts (see also 1 Chron. 21:12); Hebrew *seven*

יָדוֹ הַמַּלְאָךְ ׀ יְרוּשָׁלַםִ לְשַׁחֲתָהּ וַיִּנָּחֶם יְהוָה
Yahweh then-he-was-grieved to-destroy-her Jerusalem the-angel hand-of-him

אֶל־ הָרָעָה וַיֹּאמֶר לַמַּלְאָךְ הַמַּשְׁחִית
the-one-afflicting to-the-angel and-he-said the-calamity because-of

בָּעָם רַב עַתָּה הֶרֶף יָדֶךָ וּמַלְאַךְ יְהוָה
Yahweh now-angel-of hand-of-you withdraw! now enough against-the-people

הָיָה עִם־ גֹּרֶן הָאֲוַרְנָה הַיְבֻסִי׃ וַיֹּאמֶר דָּוִד
David and-he-said (17) the-Jebusite the-Araunah threshing-floor-of at he-was

אֶל־ יְהוָה בִּרְאֹתוֹ ׀ אֶת־ הַמַּלְאָךְ ׀ הַמַּכֶּה בָעָם
against-the-people the-one-striking the-angel *** when-to-see-him Yahweh to

וַיֹּאמֶר הִנֵּה אָנֹכִי חָטָאתִי וְאָנֹכִי הֶעֱוֵיתִי וְאֵלֶּה הַצֹּאן מֶה
what? the-sheep and-these I-did-wrong and-I I-sinned I see! and-he-said

עָשׂוּ תְּהִי נָא יָדְךָ בִּי וּבְבֵית אָבִי׃
father-of-me and-upon-house-of upon-me hand-of-you now! let-her-fall they-did

וַיָּבֹא־ גָד אֶל־ דָּוִד בַּיּוֹם הַהוּא וַיֹּאמֶר לוֹ עֲלֵה
go-up! to-him and-he-said the-that on-the-day David to Gad and-he-went (18)

הָקֵם לַיהוָה מִזְבֵּחַ בְּגֹרֶן אֲרַנְיָה הַיְבֻסִי׃
the-Jebusite Araunah on-threshing-floor-of altar to-Yahweh build!

וַיַּעַל דָּוִד כִּדְבַר־ גָּד כַּאֲשֶׁר צִוָּה יְהוָה׃
Yahweh he-commanded just-as Gad as-word-of David so-he-went-up (19)

וַיַּשְׁקֵף אֲרַוְנָה וַיַּרְא אֶת־ הַמֶּלֶךְ וְאֶת־ עֲבָדָיו
men-of-him and the-king *** and-he-saw Araunah when-he-looked (20)

עֹבְרִים עָלָיו וַיֵּצֵא אֲרַוְנָה וַיִּשְׁתַּחוּ לַמֶּלֶךְ
before-the-king and-he-bowed Araunah then-he-went-out toward-him ones-coming

אַפָּיו אָרְצָה׃ וַיֹּאמֶר אֲרַוְנָה מַדּוּעַ בָּא אֲדֹנִי־
lord-of-me he-comes why? Araunah and-he-said (21) to-ground faces-of-him

הַמֶּלֶךְ אֶל־ עַבְדּוֹ וַיֹּאמֶר דָּוִד לִקְנוֹת מֵעִמְּךָ אֶת־
*** from-with-you to-buy David and-he-answered servant-of-him to the-king

הַגֹּרֶן לִבְנוֹת מִזְבֵּחַ לַיהוָה וְתֵעָצַר הַמַּגֵּפָה
the-plague so-she-may-be-stopped to-Yahweh altar to-build the-threshing-floor

מֵעַל הָעָם׃ וַיֹּאמֶר אֲרַוְנָה אֶל־ דָּוִד יִקַּח
let-him-take David to Araunah and-he-said (22) the-people from-on

וְיַעַל אֲדֹנִי הַמֶּלֶךְ הַטּוֹב בְּעֵינָו רְאֵה הַבָּקָר
the-ox see! in-eyes-of-him the-good the-king lord-of-me and-let-him-offer

לָעֹלָה וְהַמֹּרִגִּים וּכְלֵי הַבָּקָר
the-ox and-yokes-of and-the-threshing-sledges for-the-burnt-offering

לָעֵצִים׃ הַכֹּל נָתַן אֲרַוְנָה הַמֶּלֶךְ לַמֶּלֶךְ
to-the-king the-king Araunah he-gives the-whole (23) for-the-woods

angel stretched out his hand to
destroy Jerusalem, the LORD
was grieved because of the
calamity and said to the angel
who was afflicting the people,
"Enough! Withdraw your
hand." The angel of the LORD
was then at the threshing floor
of Araunah the Jebusite.
[17]When David saw the angel
who was striking down the
people, he said to the LORD, "I
am the one who has sinned
and done wrong. These are
but sheep. What have they
done? Let your hand fall upon
me and my family."

David Builds an Altar

[18]On that day Gad went to
David and said to him, "Go up
and build an altar to the LORD
on the threshing floor of Araunah the Jebusite." [19]So David
went up, as the LORD had commanded through Gad. [20]When
Araunah looked and saw the
king and his men coming
toward him, he went out and
bowed down before the king
with his face to the ground.
[21]Araunah said, "Why has
my lord the king come to his
servant?"
"To buy your threshing
floor," David answered, "so I
can build an altar to the LORD,
that the plague on the people
may be stopped."
[22]Araunah said to David,
"Let my lord the king take
whatever pleases him and
offer it up. Here are oxen for
the burnt offering, and here
are threshing sledges and ox
yokes for the wood. [23]O king,
Araunah gives all this to the

°*16* ק הארונה
°*18* ק ארונה
°*22* ק בעיניו

וַיֹּ֤אמֶר אֲרַוְנָה֙ אֶל־ הַמֶּ֔לֶךְ יְהוָ֥ה אֱלֹהֶ֖יךָ יִרְצֶֽךָ׃

may-he-accept-you God-of-you Yahweh the-king to Araunah and-he-said

(24) וַיֹּ֨אמֶר הַמֶּ֜לֶךְ אֶל־ אֲרַ֗וְנָה לֹ֤א כִּֽי־ קָנ֨וֹ אֶקְנֶ֤ה

I-will-buy to-buy indeed no Araunah to the-king but-he-replied (24)

מֵאוֹתְךָ֙ בִּמְחִ֔יר וְלֹ֧א אַעֲלֶ֛ה לַיהוָ֥ה אֱלֹהַ֖י

God-of-me to-Yahweh I-will-sacrifice for-not for-price from-you

עֹל֣וֹת חִנָּ֑ם וַיִּ֨קֶן דָּוִ֤ד אֶת־ הַגֹּ֙רֶן֙

the-threshing-floor *** David so-he-bought without-cost burnt-offerings

וְאֶת־ הַבָּקָ֔ר בְּכֶ֖סֶף שְׁקָלִ֥ים חֲמִשִּֽׁים׃ (25) וַיִּ֨בֶן שָׁ֤ם דָּוִד֙ מִזְבֵּ֙חַ֙

altar David there and-he-built (25) fifty shekels with-silver the-ox and

לַֽיהוָ֔ה וַיַּ֥עַל עֹל֖וֹת וּשְׁלָמִ֑ים

and-fellowship-offerings burnt-offerings and-he-sacrificed to-Yahweh

וַיֵּעָתֵ֤ר יְהוָה֙ לָאָ֔רֶץ וַתֵּעָצַ֥ר

and-she-was-stopped in-behalf-of-the-land Yahweh and-he-answered-prayer

הַמַּגֵּפָ֖ה מֵעַ֥ל יִשְׂרָאֵֽל׃

Israel from-on the-plague

king." Araunah also said to him, "May the LORD your God accept you."

24But the king replied to
Araunah, "No, I insist on paying you for it. I will not sacrifice to the LORD my God burnt offerings that cost me nothing."

So David bought the threshing floor and the oxen and paid fifty shekels[m] of silver for
them. 25David built an altar to
the LORD there and sacrificed burnt offerings and fellowship offerings.[n] Then the LORD answered prayer in behalf of the land, and the plague on Israel was stopped.

[m]24 That is, about 1 1/4 pounds (about 0.6 kilogram)

[n]25 Traditionally *peace offerings*

וְהַמֶּלֶךְ דָּוִד זָקֵן בָּא בַּיָּמִים
in-the-days he-was-advanced he-was-old David now-the-king (1)

וַיְכַסֻּהוּ בַּבְּגָדִים וְלֹא יִחַם לוֹ׃
for-him he-was-warm but-not with-the-garments and-they-covered-him

וַיֹּאמְרוּ לוֹ עֲבָדָיו יְבַקְשׁוּ לַאדֹנִי
for-lord-of-me let-them-look-for servants-of-him to-him so-they-said (2)

הַמֶּלֶךְ נַעֲרָה בְתוּלָה וְעָמְדָה לִפְנֵי הַמֶּלֶךְ וּתְהִי־
and-she-may-be the-king before so-she-may-attend virgin young-woman the-king

לוֹ סֹכֶנֶת וְשָׁכְבָה בְחֵיקֶךָ וְחַם
so-he-may-be-warm at-side-of-you and-she-can-lie one-caring for-him

לַאדֹנִי הַמֶּלֶךְ׃ וַיְבַקְשׁוּ נַעֲרָה יָפָה בְּכֹל
through-all-of beautiful girl then-they-searched (3) the-king for-lord-of-me

גְּבוּל יִשְׂרָאֵל וַיִּמְצְאוּ אֶת־ אֲבִישַׁג הַשּׁוּנַמִּית וַיָּבִאוּ
and-they-brought the-Shunammite Abishag *** and-they-found Israel territory-of

אֹתָהּ לַמֶּלֶךְ׃ וְהַנַּעֲרָה יָפָה עַד־ מְאֹד וַתְּהִי
and-she-was very-much to beautiful and-the-girl (4) to-the-king her

לַמֶּלֶךְ סֹכֶנֶת וַתְּשָׁרְתֵהוּ וְהַמֶּלֶךְ לֹא יְדָעָהּ׃
he-knew-her not but-the-king and-she-waited-on-him one-caring for-the-king

וַאֲדֹנִיָּה בֶן־ חַגִּית מִתְנַשֵּׂא לֵאמֹר אֲנִי אֶמְלֹךְ
I-will-be-king I to-say putting-himself-forward Haggith son-of now-Adonijah (5)

וַיַּעַשׂ לוֹ רֶכֶב וּפָרָשִׁים וַחֲמִשִּׁים אִישׁ רָצִים
ones-running man and-fifty and-horses chariot for-him and-he-got-ready

לְפָנָיו׃ וְלֹא־ עֲצָבוֹ אָבִיו מִיָּמָיו
in-days-of-him father-of-him he-interfered-with-him and-not (6) ahead-of-him

לֵאמֹר מַדּוּעַ כָּכָה עָשִׂיתָ וְגַם־ הוּא טוֹב־ תֹּאַר מְאֹד וְאֹתוֹ יָלְדָה
she-bore and-him very form handsome-of he now-also you-behave so why? to-ask

אַחֲרֵי אַבְשָׁלוֹם׃ וַיִּהְיוּ דְבָרָיו עִם יוֹאָב בֶּן־ צְרוּיָה
Zeruiah son-of Joab with words-of-him and-they-were (7) Absalom after

וְעִם אֶבְיָתָר הַכֹּהֵן וַיַּעְזְרוּ אַחֲרֵי אֲדֹנִיָּה׃ וְצָדוֹק
but-Zadok (8) Adonijah to and-they-gave-support the-priest Abiathar and-with

הַכֹּהֵן וּבְנָיָהוּ בֶּן־ יְהוֹיָדָע וְנָתָן הַנָּבִיא וְשִׁמְעִי
and-Shimei the-prophet and-Nathan Jehoiada son-of and-Benaiah the-priest

וְרֵעִי וְהַגִּבּוֹרִים אֲשֶׁר לְדָוִד לֹא הָיוּ עִם־ אֲדֹנִיָּהוּ׃
Adonijah with they-were not to-David that and-the-special-guards and-Rei

וַיִּזְבַּח אֲדֹנִיָּהוּ צֹאן וּבָקָר וּמְרִיא עִם אֶבֶן
Stone-of at and-fattened-calf and-cattle sheep Adonijah then-he-sacrificed (9)

הַזֹּחֶלֶת אֲשֶׁר־ אֵצֶל עֵין רֹגֵל וַיִּקְרָא אֶת־ כָּל־ אֶחָיו
brothers-of-him all-of *** and-he-invited Rogel En near that the-Zoheleth

Adonijah Sets Himself Up as King

1 When King David was old
and well advanced in
years, he could not keep warm
even when they put covers
over him. [2]So his servants said
to him, "Let us look for a
young virgin to attend the
king and take care of him. She
can lie beside him so that our
lord the king may keep
warm."
[3]Then they searched
throughout Israel for a beautiful girl and found Abishag, a
Shunammite, and brought her
to the king. [4]The girl was very
beautiful; she took care of the
king and waited on him, but
the king had no intimate relations with her.
[5]Now Adonijah, whose
mother was Haggith, put himself forward and said, "I will
be king." So he got chariots
and horses[a] ready, with fifty
men to run ahead of him. [6](His
father had never interfered
with him by asking, "Why do
you behave as you do?" He
was also very handsome and
was born next after Absalom.)
[7]Adonijah conferred with
Joab son of Zeruiah and with
Abiathar the priest, and they
gave him their support. [8]But
Zadok the priest, Benaiah son
of Jehoiada, Nathan the
prophet, Shimei and Rei[b] and
David's special guard did not
join Adonijah.
[9]Adonijah then sacrificed
sheep, cattle and fattened
calves at the Stone of Zoheleth
near En Rogel. He invited all
his brothers, the king's sons,

[a]5 Or *charioteers* [b]8 Or *and his friends*

בְּנֵי הַמֶּלֶךְ וּלְכָל־ אַנְשֵׁי יְהוּדָה עַבְדֵי הַמֶּלֶךְ׃ וְאֶת־
but (10) the-king officials-of Judah men-of and-to-all-of the-king sons-of

נָתָן הַנָּבִיא וּבְנָיָהוּ וְאֶת־ הַגִּבּוֹרִים וְאֶת־ שְׁלֹמֹה אָחִיו
brother-of-him Solomon or the-special-guards or or-Benaiah the-prophet Nathan

לֹא קָרָא׃ וַיֹּאמֶר נָתָן אֶל־ בַּת־ שֶׁבַע אֵם־ שְׁלֹמֹה
Solomon mother-of Sheba Bath to Nathan then-he-asked (11) he-invited not

לֵאמֹר הֲלוֹא שָׁמַעַתְּ כִּי מָלַךְ אֲדֹנִיָּהוּ בֶן־ חַגִּית
Haggith son-of Adonijah he-became-king that you-heard not? to-say

וַאֲדֹנֵינוּ דָוִד לֹא יָדָע׃ וְעַתָּה לְכִי אִיעָצֵךְ נָא
now! let-me-advise-you come! so-now (12) he-knows not David and-lords-of-us

עֵצָה וּמַלְּטִי אֶת־ נַפְשֵׁךְ וְאֶת־ נֶפֶשׁ בְּנֵךְ שְׁלֹמֹה׃ לְכִי
come! (13) Solomon son-of-you life-of and life-of-you *** and-save! advice

וּבֹאִי ׀ אֶל־ הַמֶּלֶךְ דָּוִד וְאָמַרְתְּ אֵלָיו הֲלֹא־אַתָּה אֲדֹנִי הַמֶּלֶךְ
the-king lord-of-me you not? to-him and-you-say David the-king to and-go!

נִשְׁבַּעְתָּ לַאֲמָתְךָ לֵאמֹר כִּי־ שְׁלֹמֹה בְנֵךְ יִמְלֹךְ
he-shall-be-king son-of-you Solomon surely to-say to-servant-of-you you-swore

אַחֲרַי וְהוּא יֵשֵׁב עַל־ כִּסְאִי וּמַדּוּעַ מָלַךְ אֲדֹנִיָהוּ׃*
Adonijah he-became-king then-why? throne-of-me on he-will-sit and-he after-me

הִנֵּה עוֹדָךְ מְדַבֶּרֶת שָׁם עִם־ הַמֶּלֶךְ וַאֲנִי אָבוֹא אַחֲרַיִךְ
after-you I-will-come-in then-I the-king to there talking still-you see! (14)

וּמִלֵּאתִי אֶת־ דְּבָרָיִךְ׃ וַתָּבֹא בַת־ שֶׁבַע† אֶל־הַמֶּלֶךְ
the-king to Sheba Bath so-she-went (15) words-of-you *** and-I-will-confirm

הַחַדְרָה וְהַמֶּלֶךְ זָקֵן מְאֹד וַאֲבִישַׁג הַשּׁוּנַמִּית מְשָׁרַת
attending the-Shunammite and-Abishag very he-was-old and-the-king in-the-room

אֶת־הַמֶּלֶךְ׃ וַתִּקֹּד בַּת־ שֶׁבַע וַתִּשְׁתַּחוּ לַמֶּלֶךְ
before-the-king and-she-knelt Sheba Bath and-she-bowed (16) the-king to

וַיֹּאמֶר הַמֶּלֶךְ מַה־ לָּךְ׃ וַתֹּאמֶר לוֹ אֲדֹנִי
lord-of-me to-him and-she-said (17) to-you what? the-king and-he-asked

אַתָּה נִשְׁבַּעְתָּ בַּיהוָה אֱלֹהֶיךָ לַאֲמָתֶךָ כִּי־ שְׁלֹמֹה
Solomon surely to-servant-of-you God-of-you by-Yahweh you-swore you

בְנֵךְ יִמְלֹךְ אַחֲרָי וְהוּא יֵשֵׁב עַל־ כִּסְאִי׃
throne-of-me on he-will-sit and-he after-me he-shall-be-king son-of-you

וְעַתָּה הִנֵּה אֲדֹנִיָּה מָלָךְ וְעַתָּה אֲדֹנִי הַמֶּלֶךְ לֹא
not the-king lord-of-me and-now he-became-king Adonijah see! but-now (18)

יָדָעְתָּ׃ וַיִּזְבַּח שׁוֹר וּמְרִיא־ וְצֹאן
and-sheep and-fattened-calf cattle and-he-sacrificed (19) you-know

לָרֹב וַיִּקְרָא לְכָל־ בְּנֵי הַמֶּלֶךְ וּלְאֶבְיָתָר
and-to-Abiathar the-king sons-of to-all-of and-he-invited to-great-number

and all the men of Judah who were royal officials, [10]but he did not invite Nathan the prophet or Benaiah or the special guard or his brother Solomon.

[11]Then Nathan asked Bathsheba, Solomon's mother, "Have you not heard that Adonijah, the son of Haggith, has become king without our lord David's knowing it? [12]Now then, let me advise you how you can save your own life and the life of your son Solomon. [13]Go in to King David and say to him, 'My lord the king, did you not swear to me your servant: "Surely Solomon your son shall be king after me, and he will sit on my throne"? Why then has Adonijah become king?' [14]While you are still there talking to the king, I will come in and confirm what you have said."

[15]So Bathsheba went to see the aged king in his room, where Abishag the Shunammite was attending him. [16]Bathsheba bowed low and knelt before the king.

"What is it you want?" the king asked.

[17]She said to him, "My lord, you yourself swore to me your servant by the LORD your God: 'Solomon your son shall be king after me, and he will sit on my throne.' [18]But now Adonijah has become king, and you, my lord the king, do not know about it. [19]He has sacrificed great numbers of cattle, fattened calves, and sheep, and has invited all the king's sons, Abiathar the

******13* Most mss have *dagesh* in the *yod* (יָּהוּ—).

†*15* Most mss have *pathah* under the *beth* (שֶׁבַע).

הַכֹּהֵן וּלְיֹאָב שַׂר הַצָּבָא וְלִשְׁלֹמֹה עַבְדְּךָ
servant-of-you but-to-Solomon the-army commander-of and-to-Joab the-priest

לֹא קָרָא׃ וְאַתָּה אֲדֹנִי הַמֶּלֶךְ עֵינֵי כָל־יִשְׂרָאֵל עָלֶיךָ
on-you Israel all-of eyes-of the-king lord-of-me and-you (20) he-invited not

לְהַגִּיד לָהֶם מִי יֵשֵׁב עַל־כִּסֵּא אֲדֹנִי־הַמֶּלֶךְ אַחֲרָיו׃
after-him the-king lord-of-me throne-of on he-will-sit who to-them to-tell

וְהָיָה כִּשְׁכַב אֲדֹנִי־הַמֶּלֶךְ עִם־אֲבֹתָיו
fathers-of-him with the-king lord-of-me when-to-lie or-he-will-be (21)

וְהָיִיתִי אֲנִי וּבְנִי שְׁלֹמֹה חַטָּאִים׃ וְהִנֵּה עוֹדֶנָּה
still-she and-see! (22) criminals Solomon and-son-of-me I then-I-will-be

מְדַבֶּרֶת עִם־הַמֶּלֶךְ וְנָתָן הַנָּבִיא בָּא׃ וַיַּגִּידוּ
and-they-told (23) he-arrived the-prophet then-Nathan the-king with speaking

לַמֶּלֶךְ לֵאמֹר הִנֵּה נָתָן הַנָּבִיא וַיָּבֹא לִפְנֵי הַמֶּלֶךְ
the-king before so-he-went the-prophet Nathan see! to-say to-the-king

וַיִּשְׁתַּחוּ לַמֶּלֶךְ עַל־אַפָּיו אָרְצָה׃ וַיֹּאמֶר
and-he-said (24) to-ground faces-of-him on before-the-king and-he-bowed

נָתָן אֲדֹנִי הַמֶּלֶךְ אַתָּה אָמַרְתָּ אֲדֹנִיָּהוּ יִמְלֹךְ
he-shall-be-king Adonijah you-declared you the-king lord-of-me Nathan

אַחֲרָי וְהוּא יֵשֵׁב עַל־כִּסְאִי׃ כִּי ׀ יָרַד הַיּוֹם
the-day he-went-down for (25) throne-of-me on he-will-sit and-he after-me

וַיִּזְבַּח שׁוֹר וּמְרִיא־ וְצֹאן לָרֹב
to-great-number and-sheep and-fattened-calf cattle and-he-sacrificed

וַיִּקְרָא לְכָל־ בְּנֵי הַמֶּלֶךְ וּלְשָׂרֵי הַצָּבָא
the-army and-to-commanders-of the-king sons-of to-all-of and-he-invited

וּלְאֶבְיָתָר הַכֹּהֵן וְהִנָּם אֹכְלִים וְשֹׁתִים
and-ones-drinking ones-eating and-see-they! the-priest and-to-Abiathar

לְפָנָיו וַיֹּאמְרוּ יְחִי הַמֶּלֶךְ אֲדֹנִיָּהוּ׃ וְלִי אֲנִי־
I but-to-me (26) Adonijah the-king may-he-live and-they-say with-him

עַבְדֶּךָ וּלְצָדֹק הַכֹּהֵן וְלִבְנָיָהוּ בֶן־ יְהוֹיָדָע
Jehoiada son-of and-to-Benaiah the-priest and-to-Zadok servant-of-you

וְלִשְׁלֹמֹה עַבְדְּךָ לֹא קָרָא׃ אִם מֵאֵת אֲדֹנִי
lord-of-me from indeed? (27) he-invited not servant-of-you and-to-Solomon

הַמֶּלֶךְ נִהְיָה הַדָּבָר הַזֶּה וְלֹא הוֹדַעְתָּ אֶת־
*** you-let-know and-not the-this the-thing he-was-done the-king

עֲבָדֶיךָ° מִי יֵשֵׁב עַל־ כִּסֵּא אֲדֹנִי־ הַמֶּלֶךְ אַחֲרָיו׃
after-him the-king lord-of-me throne-of on he-would-sit who servant-of-you

וַיַּעַן הַמֶּלֶךְ דָּוִד וַיֹּאמֶר קִרְאוּ־ לִי לְבַת־ שָׁבַע
Sheba to-Bath to-me call! and-he-said David the-king then-he-answered (28)

priest and Joab the com-
mander of the army, but he
has not invited Solomon your
servant. 20My lord the king,
the eyes of all Israel are on
you, to learn from you who
will sit on the throne of my
lord the king after him. 21Oth-
erwise, as soon as my lord the
king is laid to rest with his fathers, I and my son Solomon
will be treated as criminals."
22While she was still
speaking with the king, Nathan the prophet arrived.
23And they told the king, "Nathan the prophet is here." So
he went before the king and
bowed with his face to the
ground.
24Nathan said, "Have you,
my lord the king, declared that
Adonijah shall be king after
you, and that he will sit on
your throne? 25Today he has
gone down and sacrificed
great numbers of cattle, fattened calves, and sheep. He
has invited all the king's sons,
the commanders of the army
and Abiathar the priest. Right
now they are eating and
drinking with him and saying, 'Long live King Adonijah!' 26But me your servant,
and Zadok the priest, and Benaiah son of Jehoiada, and
your servant Solomon he did
not invite. 27Is this something
my lord the king has done
without letting his servants
know who should sit on the
throne of my lord the king after him?"

David Makes Solomon King

28Then King David said,
"Call in Bathsheba." So she

°27 ק עבדך

וַתָּבֹא לִפְנֵי הַמֶּלֶךְ וַֽתַּעֲמֹד לִפְנֵי הַמֶּלֶךְ׃
the-king before and-she-stood the-king into-presences-of so-she-came

וַיִּשָּׁבַע הַמֶּלֶךְ וַיֹּאמַר חַי־ יְהוָה אֲשֶׁר־ פָּדָה
he-delivered who Yahweh life-of and-he-said the-king and-he-took-oath (29)

אֶת־ נַפְשִׁי מִכָּל־ צָרָה׃ כִּי כַּאֲשֶׁר נִשְׁבַּעְתִּי לָךְ
to-you I-swore just-as surely (30) trouble from-every-of life-of-me ***

בַּיהוָה אֱלֹהֵי יִשְׂרָאֵל לֵאמֹר כִּי־ שְׁלֹמֹה בְנֵךְ יִמְלֹךְ
he-shall-be-king son-of-you Solomon surely to-say Israel God-of by-Yahweh

אַחֲרַי וְהוּא יֵשֵׁב עַל־ כִּסְאִי תַּחְתָּי כִּי כֵּן
this surely in-place-of-me throne-of-me on he-will-sit and-he after-me

אֶעֱשֶׂה הַיּוֹם הַזֶּה׃ וַתִּקֹּד בַּת־ שֶׁבַע אַפַּיִם
faces Sheba Bath then-she-bowed (31) the-this the-day I-will-carry-out

אֶרֶץ וַתִּשְׁתַּחוּ לַמֶּלֶךְ וַתֹּאמֶר יְחִי אֲדֹנִי
lord-of-me may-he-live and-she-said before-the-king and-she-knelt ground

הַמֶּלֶךְ דָּוִד לְעֹלָם׃ וַיֹּאמֶר ׀ הַמֶּלֶךְ דָּוִד קִרְאוּ־ לִי
to-me call! David the-king and-he-said (32) to-forever David the-king

לְצָדוֹק הַכֹּהֵן וּלְנָתָן הַנָּבִיא וְלִבְנָיָהוּ בֶּן־ יְהוֹיָדָע
Jehoiada son-of and-to-Benaiah the-prophet and-to-Nathan the-priest to-Zadok

וַיָּבֹאוּ לִפְנֵי הַמֶּלֶךְ׃ וַיֹּאמֶר הַמֶּלֶךְ לָהֶם קְחוּ
take! to-them the-king and-he-said (33) the-king before and-they-came

עִמָּכֶם אֶת־ עַבְדֵי אֲדֹנֵיכֶם וְהִרְכַּבְתֶּם אֶת־ שְׁלֹמֹה בְנִי עַל־
on son-of-me Solomon *** and-you-set lords-of-you servants-of *** with-you

הַפִּרְדָּה אֲשֶׁר־ לִי וְהוֹרַדְתֶּם אֹתוֹ אֶל־ גִּחוֹן׃ וּמָשַׁח
and-he-will-anoint (34) Gihon to him and-you-take-down to-me that the-mule

אֹתוֹ שָׁם צָדוֹק הַכֹּהֵן וְנָתָן הַנָּבִיא לְמֶלֶךְ עַל־ יִשְׂרָאֵל
Israel over as-king the-prophet and-Nathan the-priest Zadok there him

וּתְקַעְתֶּם בַּשּׁוֹפָר וַאֲמַרְתֶּם יְחִי הַמֶּלֶךְ שְׁלֹמֹה׃
Solomon the-king may-he-live and-you-shout on-the-trumpet and-you-blow

וַעֲלִיתֶם אַחֲרָיו וּבָא וְיָשַׁב עַל־
on and-he-shall-sit and-he-shall-come with-him then-you-go-up (35)

כִּסְאִי וְהוּא יִמְלֹךְ תַּחְתָּי וְאֹתוֹ צִוִּיתִי לִהְיוֹת
to-be I-appointed now-him in-place-of-me he-shall-reign and-he throne-of-me

נָגִיד עַל־ יִשְׂרָאֵל וְעַל־ יְהוּדָה׃ וַיַּעַן בְּנָיָהוּ בֶן־ יְהוֹיָדָע
Jehoiada son-of Benaiah and-he-answered (36) Judah and-over Israel over ruler

אֶת־ הַמֶּלֶךְ וַיֹּאמֶר ׀ אָמֵן כֵּן יֹאמַר יְהוָה אֱלֹהֵי אֲדֹנִי
lord-of-me God-of Yahweh may-he-declare so amen! and-he-said the-king ***

הַמֶּלֶךְ׃ כַּאֲשֶׁר הָיָה יְהוָה עִם־ אֲדֹנִי הַמֶּלֶךְ כֵּן יְהִי
may-he-be so the-king lord-of-me with Yahweh he-was just-as (37) the-king

came into the king's presence
and stood before him.
[29]The king then took an
oath: "As surely as the LORD
lives, who has delivered me
out of every trouble, [30]I will
surely carry out today what I
swore to you by the LORD, the
God of Israel: Solomon your
son shall be king after me, and
he will sit on my throne in my
place."
[31]Then Bathsheba bowed
low with her face to the
ground and, kneeling before
the king, said, "May my lord
King David live forever!"
[32]King David said, "Call in
Zadok the priest, Nathan the
prophet and Benaiah son of
Jehoiada." When they came
before the king, [33]he said to
them: "Take your lord's servants with you and set Solomon my son on my own mule
and take him down to Gihon.
[34]There have Zadok the priest
and Nathan the prophet
anoint him king over Israel.
Blow the trumpet and shout,
'Long live King Solomon!'
[35]Then you are to go up with
him, and he is to come and sit
on my throne and reign in my
place. I have appointed him
ruler over Israel and Judah."
[36]Benaiah son of Jehoiada
answered the king, "Amen!
May the LORD, the God of my
lord the king, so declare it. [37]As
the LORD was with my lord the

°37 ק יהיה

עִם־ שְׁלֹמֹה וִֽיגַדֵּל אֶת־ כִּסְאוֹ מִכִּסֵּא
more-than-throne-of throne-of-him *** and-may-he-make-great Solomon with

אֲדֹנִי הַמֶּלֶךְ דָּוִֽד׃ וַיֵּרֶד צָדוֹק הַכֹּהֵן וְנָתָן
and-Nathan the-priest Zadok so-he-went-down (38) David the-king lord-of-me

הַנָּבִיא וּבְנָיָהוּ בֶן־ יְהוֹיָדָע וְהַכְּרֵתִי וְהַפְּלֵתִי
and-the-Pelethite and-the-Kerethite Jehoiada son-of and-Benaiah the-prophet

וַיַּרְכִּבוּ אֶת־ שְׁלֹמֹה עַל־ פִּרְדַּת הַמֶּלֶךְ דָּוִד וַיֹּלִכוּ אֹתוֹ
him and-they-escorted David the-king donkey-of on Solomon *** and-they-put

עַל־ גִּחֽוֹן׃ וַיִּקַּח צָדוֹק הַכֹּהֵן אֶת־ קֶרֶן הַשֶּׁמֶן מִן־ הָאֹהֶל
the-tent from the-oil horn-of *** the-priest Zadok and-he-took (39) Gihon to

וַיִּמְשַׁח אֶת־ שְׁלֹמֹה וַֽיִּתְקְעוּ בַּשּׁוֹפָר וַיֹּֽאמְרוּ
and-they-shouted on-the-trumpet then-they-sounded Solomon *** and-he-anointed

כָּל־ הָעָם יְחִי הַמֶּלֶךְ שְׁלֹמֹֽה׃ וַיַּעֲלוּ כָל־
all-of and-they-went-up (40) Solomon the-king may-he-live the-people all-of

הָעָם אַחֲרָיו וְהָעָם מְחַלְּלִים בַּחֲלִלִים וּשְׂמֵחִים
and-ones-joyful on-flutes ones-playing and-the-people after-him the-people

שִׂמְחָה גְדוֹלָה וַתִּבָּקַע הָאָרֶץ בְּקוֹלָֽם׃ וַיִּשְׁמַע
and-he-heard (41) with-sound-of-them the-ground so-she-shook great joy

אֲדֹנִיָּהוּ וְכָל־ הַקְּרֻאִים אֲשֶׁר אִתּוֹ וְהֵם כִּלּוּ
they-finished and-they with-him who the-ones-being-invited and-all-of Adonijah

לֶאֱכֹל וַיִּשְׁמַע יוֹאָב אֶת־ קוֹל הַשּׁוֹפָר וַיֹּאמֶר מַדּוּעַ
what? then-he-asked the-trumpet sound-of *** Joab when-he-heard to-feast

קוֹל־ הַקִּרְיָה הוֹמָֽה׃ עוֹדֶנּוּ מְדַבֵּר וְהִנֵּה יוֹנָתָן בֶּן־
son-of Jonathan and-see! speaking still-he (42) noise the-city sound-of

אֶבְיָתָר הַכֹּהֵן בָּא וַיֹּאמֶר אֲדֹנִיָּהוּ בֹּא כִּי אִישׁ חַיִל
worthy man-of for come! Adonijah and-he-said he-arrived the-priest Abiathar

אַתָּה וְטוֹב תְּבַשֵּֽׂר׃ וַיַּעַן יוֹנָתָן וַיֹּאמֶר
and-he-said Jonathan and-he-answered (43) you-bring-news and-good you

לַאֲדֹנִיָּהוּ אֲבָל אֲדֹנֵינוּ הַמֶּֽלֶךְ־ דָּוִד הִמְלִיךְ אֶת־ שְׁלֹמֹֽה׃
Solomon *** he-made-king David the-king lord-of-us no! to-Adonijah

וַיִּשְׁלַח אִתּֽוֹ־ הַמֶּלֶךְ אֶת־ צָדוֹק הַכֹּהֵן וְאֶת־ נָתָן
Nathan and the-priest Zadok *** the-king with-him and-he-sent (44)

הַנָּבִיא וּבְנָיָהוּ בֶּן־ יְהוֹיָדָע וְהַכְּרֵתִי וְהַפְּלֵתִי
and-the-Pelethite and-the-Kerethite Jehoiada son-of and-Benaiah the-prophet

וַיַּרְכִּבוּ אֹתוֹ עַל פִּרְדַּת הַמֶּֽלֶךְ׃ וַיִּמְשְׁחוּ אֹתוֹ צָדוֹק
Zadok him and-they-anointed (45) the-king mule-of on him and-they-put

הַכֹּהֵן וְנָתָן הַנָּבִיא לְמֶלֶךְ בְּגִחוֹן וַיַּעֲלוּ מִשָּׁם
from-there and-they-went-up at-Gihon as-king the-prophet and-Nathan the-priest

king, so may he be with Solomon to make his throne even
greater than the throne of my
lord King David!"
[38]So Zadok the priest, Nathan the prophet, Benaiah son
of Jehoiada, the Kerethites
and the Pelethites went down
and put Solomon on King David's mule and escorted him to
Gihon. [39]Zadok the priest took
the horn of oil from the sacred
tent and anointed Solomon.
Then they sounded the trumpet and all the people shouted,
"Long live King Solomon!"
[40]And all the people went up
after him, playing flutes and
rejoicing greatly, so that the
ground shook with the sound.
[41]Adonijah and all the guests
who were with him heard it as
they were finishing their
feast. On hearing the sound of
the trumpet, Joab asked,
"What's the meaning of all the
noise in the city?"
[42]Even as he was speaking,
Jonathan son of Abiathar the
priest arrived. Adonijah said,
"Come in. A worthy man like
you must be bringing good
news."
[43]"Not at all!" Jonathan answered. "Our lord King David
has made Solomon king. [44]The
king has sent with him Zadok
the priest, Nathan the
prophet, Benaiah son of Jehoiada, the Kerethites and the
Pelethites, and they have put
him on the king's mule, [45]and
Zadok the priest and Nathan
the prophet have anointed
him king at Gihon. From there
they have gone up cheering,

שְׂמֵחִ֔ים וַתֵּהֹ֖ם הַקִּרְיָ֑ה ה֥וּא הַקּ֖וֹל אֲשֶׁ֥ר שְׁמַעְתֶּֽם׃
you-hear that the-noise that the-city and-she-resounds ones-cheerful

(46) וְגַם֙ יָשַׁ֣ב שְׁלֹמֹ֔ה עַ֖ל כִּסֵּ֥א הַמְּלוּכָֽה׃ (47) וְגַם־ בָּ֜אוּ
they-came and-also (47) the-royal throne-of on Solomon he-sat and-more (46)

עַבְדֵ֣י הַמֶּ֗לֶךְ לְ֠בָרֵךְ אֶת־ אֲדֹנֵ֜ינוּ הַמֶּ֣לֶךְ דָּוִד֮ לֵאמֹר֒
to-say David the-king lords-of-us *** to-congratulate the-king officials-of

יֵיטֵ֨ב אֱלֹהֶ֜יךָ אֶת־ שֵׁ֤ם שְׁלֹמֹה֙ מִשְּׁמֶ֔ךָ
more-than-name-of-you Solomon name-of *** God may-he-make-famous

וִֽיגַדֵּ֥ל אֶת־ כִּסְא֖וֹ מִכִּסְאֶ֑ךָ וַיִּשְׁתַּ֥חוּ
and-he-bowed more-than-throne-of-you throne-of-him *** and-may-he-make-great

הַמֶּ֖לֶךְ עַל־הַמִּשְׁכָּֽב׃ (48) וְגַם־ כָּ֖כָה אָמַ֣ר הַמֶּ֑לֶךְ בָּר֨וּךְ יְהוָ֜ה
Yahweh being-praised the-king he-said this and-also (48) the-bed in the-king

אֱלֹהֵ֣י יִשְׂרָאֵ֗ל אֲשֶׁ֨ר נָתַ֥ן הַיּ֛וֹם יֹשֵׁ֥ב עַל־ כִּסְאִ֖י וְעֵינַ֥י
and-eyes-of-me throne-of-me on one-sitting the-day he-gave who Israel God-of

רֹאֽוֹת׃ (49) וַיֶּֽחֶרְדוּ֙ וַיָּקֻ֔מוּ כָּל־
all-of and-they-rose and-they-were-alarmed (49) ones-seeing

הַקְּרֻאִ֖ים אֲשֶׁ֣ר לַאֲדֹנִיָּ֑הוּ וַיֵּלְכ֖וּ אִ֥ישׁ לְדַרְכּֽוֹ׃
on-way-of-him each and-they-dispersed with-Adonijah who the-ones-being-invited

(50) וַאֲדֹ֣נִיָּ֔הוּ יָרֵ֖א מִפְּנֵ֣י שְׁלֹמֹ֑ה וַיָּ֙קָם֙ וַיֵּ֔לֶךְ
and-he-went and-he-rose Solomon from-before he-feared but-Adonijah (50)

וַֽיַּחֲזֵ֖ק בְּקַרְנ֥וֹת הַמִּזְבֵּֽחַ׃ (51) וַיֻּגַּ֨ד לִשְׁלֹמֹ֜ה
to-Solomon then-he-was-told (51) the-altar of-horns-of and-he-took-hold

לֵאמֹ֗ר הִנֵּה֙ אֲדֹ֣נִיָּ֔הוּ יָרֵ֖א אֶת־ הַמֶּ֣לֶךְ שְׁלֹמֹ֑ה וְהִנֵּה֩ אָחַ֨ז
he-clings and-see! Solomon the-king *** he-fears Adonijah see! to-say

בְּקַרְנ֤וֹת הַמִּזְבֵּ֙חַ֙ לֵאמֹ֔ר יִשָּֽׁבַֽע־ לִ֨י כַיּ֜וֹם הַמֶּ֣לֶךְ שְׁלֹמֹ֗ה
Solomon the-king as-the-day to-me let-him-swear to-say the-altar to-horns-of

אִם־ יָמִ֥ית אֶת־ עַבְדּ֖וֹ בֶּחָֽרֶב׃ (52) וַיֹּ֣אמֶר
and-he-replied (52) with-the-sword servant-of-him *** he-will-kill not

שְׁלֹמֹ֔ה אִ֚ם יִהְיֶ֣ה לְבֶן־ חַ֔יִל לֹא־ יִפֹּ֥ל מִשַּׂעֲרָת֖וֹ
from-hair-of-him he-will-fall not worthiness as-son-of he-is if Solomon

אָ֑רְצָה וְאִם־ רָעָ֥ה תִמָּצֵא־ ב֖וֹ וָמֵֽת׃ (53) וַיִּשְׁלַ֞ח
then-he-sent (53) then-he-will-die in-him she-is-found evil but-if to-ground

הַמֶּ֣לֶךְ שְׁלֹמֹ֗ה וַיֹּרִדֻ֙הוּ֙ מֵעַ֣ל הַמִּזְבֵּ֔חַ וַיָּבֹ֕א
and-he-came the-altar from-on and-they-brought-down-him Solomon the-king

וַיִּשְׁתַּ֖חוּ לַמֶּ֣לֶךְ שְׁלֹמֹ֑ה וַיֹּֽאמֶר־ ל֥וֹ שְׁלֹמֹ֖ה לֵ֥ךְ
go! Solomon to-him and-he-said Solomon before-the-king and-he-bowed

לְבֵיתֶֽךָ׃ (2:1) וַיִּקְרְב֥וּ יְמֵֽי־ דָוִ֖ד לָמ֑וּת וַיְצַ֛ו
then-he-charged to-die David days-of when-they-drew-near (2:1) to-home-of-you

and the city resounds with it.
That's the noise you hear.
[46]Moreover, Solomon has tak-
en his seat on the royal throne.
[47]Also, the royal officials have
come to congratulate our lord
King David, saying, 'May
your God make Solomon's
name more famous than yours
and his throne greater than
yours!' And the king bowed in
worship on his bed [48]and said,
'Praise be to the LORD, the God
of Israel, who has allowed my
eyes to see a successor on my
throne today.' "
[49]At this, all Adonijah's
guests rose in alarm and dispersed. [50]But Adonijah, in fear
of Solomon, went and took
hold of the horns of the altar.
[51]Then Solomon was told,
"Adonijah is afraid of King
Solomon and is clinging to the
horns of the altar. He says, 'Let
King Solomon swear to me today that he will not put his
servant to death with the
sword.' "
[52]Solomon replied, "If he
shows himself to be a worthy
man, not a hair of his head
will fall to the ground; but if
evil is found in him, he will
die." [53]Then King Solomon
sent men, and they brought
him down from the altar. And
Adonijah came and bowed
down to King Solomon, and
Solomon said, "Go to your
home."

David's Charge to Solomon

2 When the time drew near
for David to die, he gave a

[c]6 Hebrew *Sheol*; also in verse 9

°47 ק אלהים

אֶת־ שְׁלֹמֹה בְנוֹ לֵאמֹר׃ אָנֹכִי הֹלֵךְ בְּדֶרֶךְ כָּל־ הָאָרֶץ
the-earth all-of on-way-of going I (2) to-say son-of-him Solomon ***

וְחָזַקְתָּ וְהָיִיתָ לְאִישׁ׃ וְשָׁמַרְתָּ אֶת־ מִשְׁמֶרֶת ׀
requirement-of *** and-you-observe (3) as-man and-you-be so-you-be-strong

יְהוָה אֱלֹהֶיךָ לָלֶכֶת בִּדְרָכָיו לִשְׁמֹר חֻקֹּתָיו
decrees-of-him to-keep in-ways-of-him to-walk God-of-you Yahweh

מִצְוֹתָיו וּמִשְׁפָּטָיו וְעֵדְוֹתָיו כַּכָּתוּב
as-the-being-written and-requirements-of-him and-laws-of-him commands-of-him

בְּתוֹרַת מֹשֶׁה לְמַעַן תַּשְׂכִּיל אֵת כָּל־אֲשֶׁר תַּעֲשֶׂה וְאֵת כָּל־
everywhere and you-do that all *** you-may-prosper so-that Moses in-Law-of

אֲשֶׁר תִּפְנֶה שָׁם׃ לְמַעַן יָקִים יְהוָה אֶת־ דְּבָרוֹ אֲשֶׁר
that promise-of-him *** Yahweh he-may-keep so-that (4) there you-go that

דִּבֶּר עָלַי לֵאמֹר אִם־ יִשְׁמְרוּ בָנֶיךָ אֶת־ דַּרְכָּם
way-of-them *** descendants-of-you they-watch if to-say to-me he-promised

לָלֶכֶת לְפָנַי בֶּאֱמֶת בְּכָל־ לְבָבָם וּבְכָל־
and-with-all-of heart-of-them with-all-of in-faith before-me to-walk

נַפְשָׁם לֵאמֹר לֹא־ יִכָּרֵת לְךָ אִישׁ מֵעַל כִּסֵּא
throne-of from-on man of-you he-will-be-cut-off not to-say soul-of-them

יִשְׂרָאֵל׃ וְגַם אַתָּה יָדַעְתָּ אֵת אֲשֶׁר־עָשָׂה לִי יוֹאָב בֶּן־ צְרוּיָה
Zeruiah son-of Joab to-me he-did what *** you-know you now-also (5) Israel

אֲשֶׁר עָשָׂה לִשְׁנֵי־ שָׂרֵי צִבְאוֹת יִשְׂרָאֵל לְאַבְנֵר בֶּן־ נֵר
Ner son-of to-Abner Israel armies-of commanders-of to-two-of he-did what

וְלַעֲמָשָׂא בֶן־ יֶתֶר וַיַּהַרְגֵם וַיָּשֶׂם דְּמֵי־ מִלְחָמָה
battle bloods-of and-he-shed that-he-killed-them Jether son-of and-to-Amasa

בְּשָׁלֹם וַיִּתֵּן דְּמֵי מִלְחָמָה בַּחֲגֹרָתוֹ אֲשֶׁר
that on-belts-of-him battle bloods-of and-he-put in-peacetime

בְּמָתְנָיו וּבְנַעֲלוֹ אֲשֶׁר בְּרַגְלָיו׃ וְעָשִׂיתָ
so-you-deal (6) on-feet-of-him that and-on-sandal-of-him around-waists-of-him

כְּחָכְמָתֶךָ וְלֹא־ תוֹרֵד שֵׂיבָתוֹ בְּשָׁלֹם שְׁאֹל׃
Sheol in-peace gray-head-of-him you-let-go-down but-not as-wisdom-of-you

וְלִבְנֵי בַרְזִלַּי הַגִּלְעָדִי תַּעֲשֶׂה־ חֶסֶד וְהָיוּ
and-let-them-be kindness you-show the-Gileadite Barzillai but-to-sons-of (7)

בְּאֹכְלֵי שֻׁלְחָנֶךָ כִּי־ כֵן קָרְבוּ אֵלַי
by-me they-stood-by indeed for table-of-you among-ones-eating-of

בְּבָרְחִי מִפְּנֵי אַבְשָׁלוֹם אָחִיךָ׃ וְהִנֵּה עִמְּךָ
with-you and-see! (8) brother-of-you Absalom from-before when-to-flee-me

שִׁמְעִי בֶן־ גֵּרָא בֶן־הַיְמִינִי מִבַּחֻרִים וְהוּא קִלְלַנִי קְלָלָה
curse he-cursed-me and-he from-Bahurim the-Benjamite Gera son-of Shimei

charge to Solomon his son.
2 "I am about to go the way of
all the earth," he said. "So be
strong, show yourself a man,
3 and observe what the LORD
your God requires: Walk in his
ways, and keep his decrees
and commands, his laws and
requirements, as written in
the Law of Moses, so that you
may prosper in all you do and
wherever you go, 4 and that the
LORD may keep his promise to
me: 'If your descendants
watch how they live, and if
they walk faithfully before me
with all their heart and soul,
you will never fail to have a
man on the throne of Israel.'
5 "Now you yourself know
what Joab son of Zeruiah did
to me—what he did to the two
commanders of Israel's armies, Abner son of Ner and
Amasa son of Jether. He killed
them, shedding their blood in
peacetime as if in battle, and
with that blood stained the
belt around his waist and the
sandals on his feet. 6 Deal with
him according to your wisdom, but do not let his gray
head go down to the grave[c] in
peace.
7 "But show kindness to the
sons of Barzillai of Gilead and
let them be among those who
eat at your table. They stood
by me when I fled from your
brother Absalom.
8 "And remember, you have
with you Shimei son of Gera,
the Benjamite from Bahurim,
who called down bitter curses

נִמְרֶצֶת בְּיוֹם לֶכְתִּי מַחֲנָיִם וְהוּא־ יָרַד לִקְרָאתִי
to-meet-me he-came-down when-he Mahanaim to-go-me on-day being-bitter

הַיַּרְדֵּן וָאֶשָּׁבַע לוֹ בַיהוָה לֵאמֹר אִם־ אֲמִיתְךָ
I-will-kill-you not to-say by-Yahweh to-him then-I-swore the-Jordan

בֶּחָרֶב׃ (9) וְעַתָּה אַל־ תְּנַקֵּהוּ כִּי אִישׁ חָכָם אָתָּה
you wise man for you-consider-innocent-him not but-now (9) with-the-sword

וְיָדַעְתָּ אֵת אֲשֶׁר תַּעֲשֶׂה־ לּוֹ וְהוֹרַדְתָּ אֶת־
*** and-you-bring-down to-him you-must-do what *** and-you-will-know

שֵׂיבָתוֹ בְּדָם שְׁאוֹל׃ (10) וַיִּשְׁכַּב דָּוִד עִם־ אֲבֹתָיו
fathers-of-him with David then-he-rested (10) Sheol in-blood gray-head-of-him

וַיִּקָּבֵר בְּעִיר דָּוִד׃ (11) וְהַיָּמִים אֲשֶׁר מָלַךְ דָּוִד
David he-reigned that and-the-days (11) David in-City-of and-he-was-buried

עַל־יִשְׂרָאֵל אַרְבָּעִים שָׁנָה בְּחֶבְרוֹן מָלַךְ שֶׁבַע שָׁנִים וּבִירוּשָׁלִַם
and-in-Jerusalem years seven he-reigned in-Hebron year forty Israel over

מָלַךְ שְׁלֹשִׁים וְשָׁלֹשׁ שָׁנִים׃ (12) וּשְׁלֹמֹה יָשַׁב עַל־ כִּסֵּא דָּוִד
David throne-of on he-sat so-Solomon (12) years and-three thirty he-reigned

אָבִיו וַתִּכֹּן מַלְכֻתוֹ מְאֹד׃ (13) וַיָּבֹא
now-he-went (13) firmly kingdom-of-him and-she-was-established father-of-him

אֲדֹנִיָּהוּ בֶן־ חַגֵּית* אֶל־ בַּת־ שֶׁבַע אֵם־ שְׁלֹמֹה וַתֹּאמֶר
and-she-asked Solomon mother-of Sheba Bath to Hagith son-of Adonijah

הֲשָׁלוֹם בֹּאֶךָ וַיֹּאמֶר שָׁלוֹם׃ (14) וַיֹּאמֶר דָּבָר
word then-he-said (14) peacefully and-he-answered to-come-you peacefully?

לִי אֵלָיִךְ וַתֹּאמֶר דַּבֵּר׃ (15) וַיֹּאמֶר אַתְּ יָדַעַתְּ כִּי־ לִי
to-me that you-know you and-he-said (15) speak! and-she-replied to-you of-me

הָיְתָה הַמְּלוּכָה וְעָלַי שָׂמוּ כָל־ יִשְׂרָאֵל פְּנֵיהֶם
faces-of-them Israel all-of they-turned and-to-me the-kingdom she-was

לִמְלֹךְ וַתִּסֹּב הַמְּלוּכָה וַתְּהִי לְאָחִי כִּי
for to-brother-of-me and-she-went the-kingdom but-she-changed to-be-king

מֵיְהוָה הָיְתָה לּוֹ׃ (16) וְעַתָּה שְׁאֵלָה אַחַת אָנֹכִי שֹׁאֵל מֵאִתָּךְ
from-with-you asking I one request and-now (16) to-him she-came from-Yahweh

אַל־ תָּשִׁבִי אֶת־ פָּנָי וַתֹּאמֶר אֵלָיו דַּבֵּר׃ (17) וַיֹּאמֶר
so-he-said (17) speak! to-him and-she-said faces-of-me *** you-refuse not

אִמְרִי־ נָא לִשְׁלֹמֹה הַמֶּלֶךְ כִּי לֹא־ יָשִׁיב אֶת־ פָּנָיִךְ
faces-of-you *** he-will-refuse not for the-king to-Solomon now! ask!

וְיִתֶּן־ לִי אֶת־ אֲבִישַׁג הַשּׁוּנַמִּית לְאִשָּׁה׃ (18) וַתֹּאמֶר
and-she-replied (18) as-wife the-Shunammite Abishag *** to-me so-he-gives

בַּת־ שֶׁבַע טוֹב אָנֹכִי אֲדַבֵּר עָלֶיךָ אֶל־ הַמֶּלֶךְ׃ (19) וַתָּבֹא
when-she-went (19) the-king to for-you I-will-speak I very-well Sheba Bath

on me the day I went to Mahanaim. When he came down to
meet me at the Jordan, I swore
to him by the LORD: 'I will not
put you to death by the
sword.' 9But now, do not consider him innocent. You are a
man of wisdom; you will
know what to do to him. Bring
his gray head down to the
grave in blood."
10Then David rested with his
fathers and was buried in the
City of David. 11He had
reigned forty years over Israel—seven years in Hebron and
thirty-three in Jerusalem. 12So
Solomon sat on the throne of
his father David, and his rule
was firmly established.

Solomon's Throne Established

13Now Adonijah, the son of
Haggith, went to Bathsheba,
Solomon's mother. Bathsheba
asked him, "Do you come
peacefully?"
He answered, "Yes, peace-
fully." 14Then he added, "I
have something to say to
you."
"You may say it," she re-
plied.
15"As you know," he said,
"the kingdom was mine. All
Israel looked to me as their
king. But things changed, and
the kingdom has gone to my
brother; for it has come to him
from the LORD. 16Now I have
one request to make of you. Do
not refuse me."
"You may make it," she
said.
17So he continued, "Please
ask King Solomon—he will
not refuse you—to give me
Abishag the Shunammite as
my wife."
18"Very well," Bathsheba replied, "I will speak to the king
for you."
19When Bathsheba went to

*13 Most mss have *bireq* under the *gimel* (חַגִּית).

בַּת־שֶׁבַע אֶל־הַמֶּלֶךְ שְׁלֹמֹה לְדַבֶּר־לוֹ עַל־אֲדֹנִיָּהוּ וַיָּקָם
and-he-stood-up Adonijah for to-him to-speak Solomon the-king to Sheba Bath

הַמֶּלֶךְ לִקְרָאתָהּ וַיִּשְׁתַּחוּ לָהּ וַיֵּשֶׁב עַל־כִּסְאוֹ
throne-of-him on and-he-sat to-her and-he-bowed to-meet-her the-king

וַיָּשֶׂם כִּסֵּא לְאֵם הַמֶּלֶךְ וַתֵּשֶׁב לִימִינוֹ׃
at-right-of-him and-she-sat the-king for-mother-of throne and-he-had-brought

וַתֹּאמֶר שְׁאֵלָה אַחַת קְטַנָּה אָנֹכִי שֹׁאֶלֶת מֵאִתָּךְ אַל־תָּשֶׁב
you-refuse not from-with-you asking I small one request and-she-said (20)

אֶת־פָּנָי וַיֹּאמֶר־לָהּ הַמֶּלֶךְ שַׁאֲלִי אִמִּי כִּי לֹא־
not for mother-of-me ask! the-king to-her and-he-replied faces-of-me ***

אָשִׁיב אֶת־פָּנָיִךְ׃ וַתֹּאמֶר יֻתַּן אֶת־אֲבִישַׁג
Abishag *** let-him-be-given so-she-said (21) faces-of-you *** I-will-refuse

הַשֻּׁנַמִּית לַאֲדֹנִיָּהוּ אָחִיךָ לְאִשָּׁה׃ וַיַּעַן
and-he-answered (22) as-wife brother-of-you to-Adonijah the-Shunammite

הַמֶּלֶךְ שְׁלֹמֹה וַיֹּאמֶר לְאִמּוֹ וְלָמָה אַתְּ שֹׁאֶלֶת אֶת־
*** requesting you now-why? to-mother-of-him and-he-said Solomon the-king

אֲבִישַׁג הַשֻּׁנַמִּית לַאֲדֹנִיָּהוּ וְשַׁאֲלִי־לוֹ אֶת־הַמְּלוּכָה כִּי
for the-kingdom *** for-him now-request! for-Adonijah the-Shunammite Abishag

הוּא אָחִי הַגָּדוֹל מִמֶּנִּי וְלוֹ וּלְאֶבְיָתָר הַכֹּהֵן
the-priest and-for-Abiathar and-for-him than-me the-older brother-of-me he

וּלְיוֹאָב בֶּן־צְרוּיָה׃ וַיִּשָּׁבַע הַמֶּלֶךְ שְׁלֹמֹה בַּיהוָה
by-Yahweh Solomon the-king then-he-swore (23) Zeruiah son-of and-for-Joab

לֵאמֹר כֹּה יַעֲשֶׂה־לִּי אֱלֹהִים וְכֹה יוֹסִיף כִּי
if-not may-he-be-severe and-so God with-me may-he-deal so to-say

בְנַפְשׁוֹ דִּבֶּר אֲדֹנִיָּהוּ אֶת־הַדָּבָר הַזֶּה׃ וְעַתָּה
and-now (24) the-this the-request *** Adonijah he-pays with-life-of-him

חַי־יְהוָה אֲשֶׁר הֱכִינַנִי וַיּוֹשִׁיבִינִי עַל־כִּסֵּא דָּוִד
David throne-of on and-he-made-sit-me he-established-me who Yahweh life-of

אָבִי וַאֲשֶׁר עָשָׂה־לִי בַּיִת כַּאֲשֶׁר דִּבֵּר כִּי
indeed he-promised just-as dynasty for-me he-founded and-who father-of-me

הַיּוֹם יוּמַת אֲדֹנִיָּהוּ׃ וַיִּשְׁלַח הַמֶּלֶךְ שְׁלֹמֹה
Solomon the-king so-he-gave-order (25) Adonijah he-shall-die the-day

בְּיַד בְּנָיָהוּ בֶן־יְהוֹיָדָע וַיִּפְגַּע־בּוֹ וַיָּמֹת׃
and-he-died against-him and-he-struck Jehoiada son-of Benaiah to-hand-of

וּלְאֶבְיָתָר הַכֹּהֵן אָמַר הַמֶּלֶךְ עֲנָתֹת לֵךְ עַל־
to go-back! Anathoth the-king he-said the-priest and-to-Abiathar (26)

שָׂדֶיךָ כִּי אִישׁ מָוֶת אָתָּה וּבַיּוֹם הַזֶּה לֹא
not the-this but-on-the-day you death man-of indeed fields-of-you

King Solomon to speak to him
for Adonijah, the king stood
up to meet her, bowed down
to her and sat down on his
throne. He had a throne
brought for the king's mother,
and she sat down at his right
hand.
20"I have one small request
to make of you," she said. "Do
not refuse me."
The king replied, "Make it,
my mother; I will not refuse
you."
21So she said, "Let Abishag
the Shunammite be given in
marriage to your brother
Adonijah."
22King Solomon answered
his mother, "Why do you request Abishag the Shunam-
mite for Adonijah? You might
as well request the kingdom
for him—after all, he is my older brother—yes, for him and
for Abiathar the priest and
Joab son of Zeruiah!"
23Then King Solomon swore
by the LORD: "May God deal
with me, be it ever so severely,
if Adonijah does not pay with
his life for this request! 24And
now, as surely as the LORD
lives—he who has established
me securely on the throne of
my father David and has
founded a dynasty for me as
he promised—Adonijah shall
be put to death today!" 25So
King Solomon gave orders to
Benaiah son of Jehoiada, and
he struck down Adonijah and
he died.
26To Abiathar the priest the
king said, "Go back to your
fields in Anathoth. You deserve to die, but I will not put
you to death now, because you

*24 Most mss have *tsere* under the *beth* and no *yod* after the *beth* (—בֵנִי).

°24 ק ויושיבני

אֲמִיתֶךָ כִּי־ נָשָׂאתָ אֶת־ אֲרוֹן אֲדֹנָי יְהוִה לִפְנֵי דָּוִד
David before Yahweh Lord ark-of *** you-carried for I-will-kill-you

אָבִי וְכִי הִתְעַנִּיתָ בְּכֹל אֲשֶׁר־ הִתְעַנָּה
he-had-hardship that in-all you-shared-hardship and-for father-of-me

אָבִי׃ וַיְגָרֶשׁ שְׁלֹמֹה אֶת־ אֶבְיָתָר מִהְיוֹת כֹּהֵן
priest from-to-be Abiathar *** Solomon so-he-removed (27) father-of-me

לַיהוָה לְמַלֵּא אֶת־ דְּבַר יְהוָה אֲשֶׁר דִּבֶּר עַל־ בֵּית עֵלִי
Eli house-of about he-spoke that Yahweh word-of *** to-fulfill of-Yahweh

בְּשִׁלֹה׃ וְהַשְּׁמֻעָה בָּאָה עַד־יוֹאָב כִּי יוֹאָב נָטָה אַחֲרֵי
with he-conspired Joab now Joab to she-reached when-the-news (28) at-Shiloh

אֲדֹנִיָּה וְאַחֲרֵי אַבְשָׁלוֹם לֹא נָטָה וַיָּנָס יוֹאָב אֶל־ אֹהֶל
tent-of to Joab then-he-fled he-conspired not Absalom but-with Adonijah

יְהוָה וַיַּחֲזֵק בְּקַרְנוֹת הַמִּזְבֵּחַ׃ וַיֻּגַּד
when-he-was-told (29) the-altar of-horns-of and-he-took-hold Yahweh

לַמֶּלֶךְ שְׁלֹמֹה כִּי נָס יוֹאָב אֶל־ אֹהֶל יְהוָה וְהִנֵּה אֵצֶל
beside and-see! Yahweh tent-of to Joab he-fled that Solomon to-the-king

הַמִּזְבֵּחַ וַיִּשְׁלַח שְׁלֹמֹה אֶת־ בְּנָיָהוּ בֶן־ יְהוֹיָדָע לֵאמֹר לֵךְ
go! to-say Jehoiada son-of Benaiah *** Solomon then-he-ordered the-altar

פְּגַע־ בּוֹ׃ וַיָּבֹא בְנָיָהוּ אֶל־ אֹהֶל יְהוָה
Yahweh tent-of into Benaiah so-he-entered (30) against-him strike!

וַיֹּאמֶר אֵלָיו כֹּה־ אָמַר הַמֶּלֶךְ צֵא וַיֹּאמֶר ׀ לֹא כִּי
for no but-he-answered come-out! the-king he-says this to-him and-he-said

פֹה אָמוּת וַיָּשֶׁב בְּנָיָהוּ אֶת־ הַמֶּלֶךְ דָּבָר לֵאמֹר כֹּה־ דִבֶּר
he-said this to-say report the-king *** Benaiah and-he-sent I-will-die here

יוֹאָב וְכֹה עָנָנִי׃ וַיֹּאמֶר לוֹ הַמֶּלֶךְ עֲשֵׂה
do! the-king to-him then-he-commanded (31) he-answered-me and-this Joab

כַּאֲשֶׁר דִּבֶּר וּפְגַע־ בּוֹ וּקְבַרְתּוֹ וַהֲסִירֹתָ ׀
so-you-clear and-you-bury-him against-him and-strike! he-says just-as

דְּמֵי חִנָּם אֲשֶׁר שָׁפַךְ יוֹאָב מֵעָלַי וּמֵעַל
and-from-against from-against-me Joab he-shed that innocent bloods-of

בֵּית אָבִי׃ וְהֵשִׁיב יְהוָה אֶת־ דָּמוֹ עַל־
on blood-of-him *** Yahweh and-he-will-repay (32) father-of-me house-of

רֹאשׁוֹ אֲשֶׁר פָּגַע בִּשְׁנֵי־ אֲנָשִׁים צַדִּקִים וְטֹבִים
and-ones-good ones-upright men against-two-of he-attacked because head-of-him

מִמֶּנּוּ וַיַּהַרְגֵם בַּחֶרֶב וְאָבִי דָוִד לֹא
not David and-father-of-me with-the-sword and-he-killed-them more-than-him

יָדָע אֶת־אַבְנֵר בֶּן־ נֵר שַׂר־ צְבָא יִשְׂרָאֵל וְאֶת־עֲמָשָׂא בֶן־
son-of Amasa and Israel army-of commander-of Ner son-of Abner *** he-knew

carried the ark of the Sovereign Lord before my father
David and shared all my father's hardships."
27So Solomon removed Abiathar from
the priesthood of the Lord,
fulfilling the word the Lord
had spoken at Shiloh about
the house of Eli.
28When the news reached
Joab, who had conspired with
Adonijah though not with
Absalom, he fled to the tent of
the Lord and took hold of the
horns of the altar.
29King Solomon was told that Joab had
fled to the tent of the Lord and
was beside the altar. Then
Solomon ordered Benaiah son
of Jehoiada, "Go, strike him
down!"
30So Benaiah entered the
tent of the Lord and said to
Joab, "The king says, 'Come
out!' "

But he answered, "No, I will
die here."

Benaiah reported to the
king, "This is how Joab answered me."
31Then the king commanded
Benaiah, "Do as he says.
Strike him down and bury
him, and so clear me and my
father's house of the guilt of
the innocent blood that Joab
shed.
32The Lord will repay
him for the blood he shed, because without the knowledge
of my father David he attacked
two men and killed them with
the sword. Both of them—
Abner son of Ner, commander
of Israel's army, and Amasa
son of Jether, commander of
Judah's army—were better
men and more upright than

יֶתֶר שַׂר־ צְבָא יְהוּדָה׃ (33) וְשָׁבוּ דְמֵיהֶם
bloods-of-them and-may-they-rest (33) Judah army-of commander-of Jether

בְּרֹאשׁ יוֹאָב וּבְרֹאשׁ זַרְעוֹ לְעֹלָם וּלְדָוִד
but-on-David to-forever descendant-of-him and-on-head-of Joab on-head-of

וּלְזַרְעוֹ וּלְבֵיתוֹ וּלְכִסְאוֹ יִהְיֶה
may-he-be and-on-throne-of-him and-on-house-of-him and-on-descendant-of-him

שָׁלוֹם עַד־ עוֹלָם מֵעִם יְהוָה׃ (34) וַיַּעַל בְּנָיָהוּ בֶּן־ יְהוֹיָדָע
Jehoiada son-of Benaiah so-he-went-up (34) Yahweh from-with forever to peace

וַיִּפְגַּע־ בּוֹ וַיְמִתֵהוּ וַיִּקָּבֵר בְּבֵיתוֹ
in-tomb-of-him and-he-was-buried and-he-killed-him against-him and-he-struck

בַּמִּדְבָּר׃ (35) וַיִּתֵּן הַמֶּלֶךְ אֶת־ בְּנָיָהוּ בֶן־ יְהוֹיָדָע
Jehoiada son-of Benaiah *** the-king and-he-put (35) in-the-desert

תַּחְתָּיו עַל־ הַצָּבָא וְאֶת־ צָדוֹק הַכֹּהֵן נָתַן הַמֶּלֶךְ
the-king he-put the-priest Zadok and the-army over in-place-of-him

תַּחַת אֶבְיָתָר׃ (36) וַיִּשְׁלַח הַמֶּלֶךְ וַיִּקְרָא לְשִׁמְעִי
for-Shimei and-he-called the-king then-he-sent (36) Abiathar in-place-of

וַיֹּאמֶר לוֹ בְּנֵה־ לְךָ בַיִת בִּירוּשָׁלַםִ וְיָשַׁבְתָּ שָׁם
there and-you-live in-Jerusalem house for-you build! to-him and-he-said

וְלֹא־ תֵצֵא מִשָּׁם אָנֶה וָאָנָה׃ (37) וְהָיָה ׀ בְּיוֹם
on-day for-he-will-be (37) or-to-there to-here from-there you-go but-not

צֵאתְךָ וְעָבַרְתָּ אֶת־ נַחַל קִדְרוֹן יָדֹעַ תֵּדַע
you-can-be-sure to-be-sure Kidron Valley-of *** and-you-cross to-leave-you

כִּי מוֹת תָּמוּת דָּמְךָ יִהְיֶה בְרֹאשֶׁךָ׃
on-head-of-you he-will-be blood-of-you you-will-die to-die that

(38) וַיֹּאמֶר שִׁמְעִי לַמֶּלֶךְ טוֹב הַדָּבָר כַּאֲשֶׁר דִּבֶּר
he-said just-as the-word good to-the-king Shimei and-he-answered (38)

אֲדֹנִי הַמֶּלֶךְ כֵּן יַעֲשֶׂה עַבְדֶּךָ וַיֵּשֶׁב שִׁמְעִי
Shimei and-he-stayed servant-of-you he-will-do so the-king lord-of-me

בִּירוּשָׁלַםִ יָמִים רַבִּים׃ (39) וַיְהִי מִקֵּץ שָׁלֹשׁ שָׁנִים וַיִּבְרְחוּ
then-they-ran-off days three at-end-of but-he-was (39) many days in-Jerusalem

שְׁנֵי־ עֲבָדִים לְשִׁמְעִי אֶל־ אָכִישׁ בֶּן־ מַעֲכָה מֶלֶךְ גַּת וַיַּגִּידוּ
and-they-told Gath king-of Maacah son-of Achish to of-Shimei slaves two-of

לְשִׁמְעִי לֵאמֹר הִנֵּה עֲבָדֶיךָ בְּגַת׃ (40) וַיָּקָם שִׁמְעִי
Shimei so-he-rose (40) in-Gath slaves-of-you see! to-say to-Shimei

וַיַּחֲבֹשׁ אֶת־ חֲמֹרוֹ וַיֵּלֶךְ גַּתָה אֶל־ אָכִישׁ לְבַקֵּשׁ
to-search-for Achish to to-Gath and-he-went donkey-of-him *** and-he-saddled

אֶת־ עֲבָדָיו וַיֵּלֶךְ שִׁמְעִי וַיָּבֵא אֶת־ עֲבָדָיו
slaves-of-him *** and-he-brought-back Shimei so-he-went slaves-of-him ***

he. [33]May the guilt of their blood rest on the head of Joab and his descendants forever. But on David and his descendants, his house and his throne, may there be the LORD's peace forever."

[34]So Benaiah son of Jehoiada went up and struck down Joab and killed him, and he was buried on his own land[d] in the desert. [35]The king put Benaiah son of Jehoiada over the army in Joab's position and replaced Abiathar with Zadok the priest.

[36]Then the king sent for Shimei and said to him, "Build yourself a house in Jerusalem and live there, but do not go anywhere else. [37]The day you leave and cross the Kidron Valley, you can be sure you will die; your blood will be on your own head."

[38]Shimei answered the king, "What you say is good. Your servant will do as my lord the king has said." And Shimei stayed in Jerusalem for a long time.

[39]But three years later, two of Shimei's slaves ran off to Achish son of Maacah, king of Gath, and Shimei was told, "Your slaves are in Gath." [40]At this, he saddled his donkey and went to Achish at Gath in search of his slaves. So Shimei went away and brought the slaves back from Gath.

[d]34 Or *buried in his tomb*

מִגַּת׃ וַיֻּגַּד לִשְׁלֹמֹה כִּֽי־ הָלַךְ שִׁמְעִי מִירוּשָׁלַ͏ִם
from-Jerusalem Shimei he-went that to-Solomon when-he-was-told (41) from-Gath

גַּת וַיָּשֹׁב׃ וַיִּשְׁלַח הַמֶּלֶךְ וַיִּקְרָא לְשִׁמְעִי
to-Shimei and-he-called the-king then-he-summoned (42) and-he-returned Gath

וַיֹּאמֶר אֵלָיו הֲלוֹא הִשְׁבַּעְתִּיךָ בַיהוָה וָאָעִד בְּךָ
to-you and-I-warned by-Yahweh I-made-swear-you not? to-him and-he-said

לֵאמֹר בְּיוֹם צֵאתְךָ וְהָלַכְתָּ אָנֶה וָאָנָה יָדֹעַ
to-be-sure or-to-there to-here and-you-go to-leave-you on-day to-say

תֵּדַע כִּי מוֹת תָּמוּת וַתֹּאמֶר אֵלַי טוֹב הַדָּבָר
the-word good to-me and-you-said you-will-die to-die that you-can-be-sure

שָׁמָעְתִּי׃ וּמַדּוּעַ לֹא שָׁמַרְתָּ אֵת שְׁבֻעַת יְהוָה וְאֶת־ הַמִּצְוָה
the-command and Yahweh oath-of *** you-kept not then-why? (43) I-will-obey

אֲשֶׁר־צִוִּיתִי עָלֶיךָ׃ וַיֹּאמֶר הַמֶּלֶךְ אֶל־שִׁמְעִי אַתָּה יָדַעְתָּ אֵת
*** you-know you Shimei to the-king and-he-said (44) to-you I-gave that

כָּל־ הָרָעָה אֲשֶׁר יָדַע לְבָבְךָ אֲשֶׁר עָשִׂיתָ לְדָוִד אָבִי
father-of-me to-David you-did that heart-of-you he-knows that the-wrong all-of

וְהֵשִׁיב יְהוָה אֶת־ רָעָתְךָ בְּרֹאשֶׁךָ׃ וְהַמֶּלֶךְ
but-the-king (45) on-head-of-you wrongdoing-of-you *** Yahweh now-he-will-repay

שְׁלֹמֹה בָּרוּךְ וְכִסֵּא דָוִד יִהְיֶה נָכוֹן לִפְנֵי
before being-secure he-will-remain David and-throne-of being-blessed Solomon

יְהוָה עַד־עוֹלָם׃ וַיְצַו הַמֶּלֶךְ אֶת־ בְּנָיָהוּ בֶּן־ יְהוֹיָדָע
Jehoiada son-of Benaiah *** the-king then-he-ordered (46) forever to Yahweh

וַיֵּצֵא וַיִּפְגַּע־ בּוֹ וַיָּמֹת וְהַמַּמְלָכָה
and-the-kingdom and-he-died against-him and-he-struck and-he-went-out

נָכוֹנָה בְּיַד־ שְׁלֹמֹה׃ וַיִּתְחַתֵּן שְׁלֹמֹה אֶת־
with Solomon and-he-made-alliance (3:1) Solomon in-hand-of being-established

פַּרְעֹה מֶלֶךְ מִצְרָיִם וַיִּקַּח אֶת־ בַּת־ פַּרְעֹה וַיְבִיאֶהָ
and-he-brought-her Pharaoh daughter-of *** and-he-married Egypt king-of Pharaoh

אֶל־ עִיר דָּוִד עַד כַּלֹּתוֹ לִבְנוֹת אֶת־ בֵּיתוֹ וְאֶת־ בֵּית
temple-of and palace-of-him *** to-build to-finish-him until David City-of to

יְהוָה וְאֶת־חוֹמַת יְרוּשָׁלַ͏ִם סָבִיב׃ רַק הָעָם מְזַבְּחִים
ones-sacrificing the-people however (2) around Jerusalem wall-of and Yahweh

בַּבָּמוֹת כִּי לֹא־ נִבְנָה בַיִת לְשֵׁם יְהוָה עַד
at Yahweh for-Name-of temple he-was-built not for at-the-high-places

הַיָּמִים הָהֵם׃ וַיֶּאֱהַב שְׁלֹמֹה אֶת־ יְהוָה לָלֶכֶת
to-walk Yahweh *** Solomon and-he-showed-love (3) the-those the-days

בְּחֻקּוֹת דָּוִד אָבִיו רַק בַּבָּמוֹת הוּא מְזַבֵּחַ
sacrificing he at-the-high-places except father-of-him David in-statutes-of

41When Solomon was told
that Shimei had gone from
Jerusalem to Gath and had returned, 42the king summoned
Shimei and said to him, "Did
I not make you swear by the
LORD and warn you, 'On the
day you leave to go anywhere
else, you can be sure you will
die'? At that time you said to
me, 'What you say is good. I
will obey.' 43Why then did you
not keep your oath to the LORD
and obey the command I gave
you?"
44The king also said to
Shimei, "You know in your
heart all the wrong you did to
my father David. Now the
LORD will repay you for your
wrongdoing. 45But King Solomon will be blessed, and David's throne will remain secure before the LORD forever."
46Then the king gave the order to Benaiah son of Jehoiada, and he went out and
struck Shimei down and killed
him.
The kingdom was now
firmly established in Solomon's hands.

Solomon Asks for Wisdom

3 Solomon made an alliance
with Pharaoh king of
Egypt and married his daughter. He brought her to the City
of David until he finished
building his palace and the
temple of the LORD, and the
wall around Jerusalem. 2The
people, however, were still
sacrificing at the high places,

וּמַקְטִיר׃ וַיֵּלֶךְ הַמֶּלֶךְ גִּבְעֹנָה לִזְבֹּחַ שָׁם כִּי
for there to-sacrifice to-Gibeon the-king and-he-went (4) and-burning-incense

הִיא הַבָּמָה הַגְּדוֹלָה אֶלֶף עֹלוֹת יַעֲלֶה שְׁלֹמֹה
Solomon he-offered burnt-offerings thousand the-important the-high-place that

עַל הַמִּזְבֵּחַ הַהוּא׃ בְּגִבְעוֹן נִרְאָה יְהוָה אֶל־שְׁלֹמֹה בַּחֲלוֹם
in-dream-of Solomon to Yahweh he-appeared at-Gibeon (5) the-that the-altar on

הַלָּיְלָה וַיֹּאמֶר אֱלֹהִים שְׁאַל מָה אֶתֶּן־לָךְ׃ וַיֹּאמֶר
and-he-said (6) to-you I-should-give whatever ask! God and-he-said the-night

שְׁלֹמֹה אַתָּה עָשִׂיתָ עִם־עַבְדְּךָ דָוִד אָבִי חֶסֶד גָּדוֹל
great kindness father-of-me David servant-of-you to you-showed you Solomon

כַּאֲשֶׁר הָלַךְ לְפָנֶיךָ בֶּאֱמֶת וּבִצְדָקָה
and-in-righteousness in-faithfulness before-you he-walked because-that

וּבְיִשְׁרַת לֵבָב עִמָּךְ וַתִּשְׁמָר־לוֹ אֶת־הַחֶסֶד
the-kindness *** to-him and-you-continued with-you heart and-in-uprightness-of

הַגָּדוֹל הַזֶּה וַתִּתֶּן־לוֹ בֵן יֹשֵׁב עַל־כִּסְאוֹ
throne-of-him on sitting son to-him and-you-gave the-this the-great

כַּיּוֹם הַזֶּה׃ וְעַתָּה יְהוָה אֱלֹהָי אַתָּה הִמְלַכְתָּ אֶת־
*** you-made-king you God-of-me Yahweh and-now (7) the-this as-the-day

עַבְדְּךָ תַּחַת דָּוִד אָבִי וְאָנֹכִי נַעַר קָטֹן לֹא אֵדַע
I-know not little child but-I father-of-me David in-place-of servant-of-you

צֵאת וָבֹא׃ וְעַבְדְּךָ בְּתוֹךְ עַמְּךָ אֲשֶׁר בָּחָרְתָּ
you-chose whom people-of-you among and-servant-of-you (8) or-to-come to-go

עַם־רָב אֲשֶׁר לֹא־יִמָּנֶה וְלֹא יִסָּפֵר מֵרֹב׃
for-number he-can-be-numbered and-not he-can-be-counted not who great people

וְנָתַתָּ לְעַבְדְּךָ לֵב שֹׁמֵעַ לִשְׁפֹּט אֶת־עַמְּךָ
people-of-you *** to-govern discerning heart to-servant-of-you so-you-give (9)

לְהָבִין בֵּין־טוֹב לְרָע כִּי מִי יוּכַל לִשְׁפֹּט אֶת־
*** to-govern he-is-able who? for from-wrong right between to-distinguish

עַמְּךָ הַכָּבֵד הַזֶּה׃ וַיִּיטַב הַדָּבָר
the-thing and-he-was-pleasing (10) the-this the-great people-of-you

בְּעֵינֵי אֲדֹנָי כִּי שָׁאַל שְׁלֹמֹה אֶת־הַדָּבָר הַזֶּה׃ וַיֹּאמֶר
so-he-said (11) the-this the-thing *** Solomon he-asked that Lord in-eyes-of

אֱלֹהִים אֵלָיו יַעַן אֲשֶׁר שָׁאַלְתָּ אֶת־הַדָּבָר הַזֶּה וְלֹא־שָׁאַלְתָּ
you-asked and-not the-this the-thing *** you-asked that since to-him God

לְּךָ יָמִים רַבִּים וְלֹא־שָׁאַלְתָּ לְּךָ עֹשֶׁר וְלֹא שָׁאַלְתָּ נֶפֶשׁ
life-of you-asked and-not wealth for-you you-asked and-not many days for-you

אֹיְבֶיךָ וְשָׁאַלְתָּ לְּךָ הָבִין לִשְׁמֹעַ מִשְׁפָּט׃
justice to-administer to-discern for-you but-you-asked being-enemies-of-you

because a temple had not yet
been built for the Name of the
LORD. [3]Solomon showed his
love for the LORD by walking
according to the statutes of his
father David, except that he
offered sacrifices and burned
incense on the high places.
[4]The king went to Gibeon to
offer sacrifices, for that was
the most important high
place, and Solomon offered a
thousand burnt offerings on
that altar. [5]At Gibeon the LORD
appeared to Solomon during
the night in a dream, and God
said, "Ask for whatever you
want me to give you."
[6]Solomon answered, "You
have shown great kindness to
your servant, my father David, because he was faithful to
you and righteous and upright
in heart. You have continued
this great kindness to him and
have given him a son to sit on
his throne this very day.
[7]"Now, O LORD my God, you
have made your servant king
in place of my father David.
But I am only a little child and
do not know how to carry out
my duties. [8]Your servant is
here among the people you
have chosen, a great people,
too numerous to count or
number. [9]So give your servant
a discerning heart to govern
your people and to distinguish
between right and wrong. For
who is able to govern this
great people of yours?"
[10]The Lord was pleased that
Solomon had asked for this.
[11]So God said to him, "Since
you have asked for this and
not for long life or wealth for
yourself, nor have asked for
the death of your enemies but
for discernment in adminis-
tering justice, [12]I will do what

הִנֵּה עָשִׂיתִי כִּדְבָרֶיךָ הִנֵּה ׀ נָתַתִּי לְךָ לֵב חָכָם
wise heart to-you I-will-give see! as-requests-of-you I-will-do see! (12)

וְנָבוֹן אֲשֶׁר כָּמוֹךָ לֹא־ הָיָה לְפָנֶיךָ וְאַחֲרֶיךָ לֹא־
not or-after-you before-you he-was not like-you that and-discerning

יָקוּם כָּמוֹךָ׃ וְגַם אֲשֶׁר לֹא־ שָׁאַלְתָּ נָתַתִּי לָךְ
to-you I-will-give you-asked not what and-more (13) like-you he-will-rise

גַּם־ עֹשֶׁר גַּם־ כָּבוֹד אֲשֶׁר לֹא־ הָיָה כָמוֹךָ אִישׁ בַּמְּלָכִים
among-the-kings anyone like-you he-will-be not that honor and wealth both

כָּל־ יָמֶיךָ׃ וְאִם ׀ תֵּלֵךְ בִּדְרָכַי לִשְׁמֹר חֻקַּי
statutes-of-me to-obey in-ways-of-me you-walk and-if (14) days-of-you all-of

וּמִצְוֺתַי כַּאֲשֶׁר הָלַךְ דָּוִיד אָבִיךָ וְהַאֲרַכְתִּי
then-I-will-make-long father-of-you David he-walked just-as and-commands-of-me

אֶת־ יָמֶיךָ׃ וַיִּקַץ שְׁלֹמֹה וְהִנֵּה חֲלוֹם וַיָּבוֹא
and-he-returned dream and-see! Solomon then-he-awoke (15) days-of-you ***

יְרוּשָׁלִַם וַיַּעֲמֹד ׀ לִפְנֵי ׀ אֲרוֹן בְּרִית־ אֲדֹנָי וַיַּעַל
and-he-sacrificed Lord covenant-of ark-of before and-he-stood Jerusalem

עֹלוֹת וַיַּעַשׂ שְׁלָמִים וַיַּעַשׂ מִשְׁתֶּה
feast then-he-gave fellowship-offerings and-he-offered burnt-offerings

לְכָל־ עֲבָדָיו׃ אָז תָּבֹאנָה שְׁתַּיִם נָשִׁים זֹנוֹת
being-prostitutes women two they-came now (16) courtiers-of-him for-all-of

אֶל־ הַמֶּלֶךְ וַתַּעֲמֹדְנָה לְפָנָיו׃ וַתֹּאמֶר הָאִשָּׁה הָאַחַת
the-one the-woman and-she-said (17) before-him and-they-stood the-king to

בִּי אֲדֹנִי אֲנִי וְהָאִשָּׁה הַזֹּאת יֹשְׁבֹת בְּבַיִת אֶחָד
same in-house ones-living the-this and-the-woman I lord-of-me oh!

וָאֵלֵד עִמָּהּ בַּבָּיִת׃ וַיְהִי בַּיּוֹם הַשְּׁלִישִׁי
the-third on-the-day and-he-was (18) in-the-house with-her and-I-had-baby

לְלִדְתִּי וַתֵּלֶד גַּם־ הָאִשָּׁה הַזֹּאת וַאֲנַחְנוּ יַחְדָּו
alone and-we the-this the-woman also then-she-had-baby to-give-birth-me

אֵין־ זָר אִתָּנוּ בַּבַּיִת זוּלָתִי שְׁתַּיִם־אֲנַחְנוּ בַּבָּיִת׃
in-the-house we two but in-the-house with-us one-being-stranger not

וַיָּמָת בֶּן־ הָאִשָּׁה הַזֹּאת לָיְלָה אֲשֶׁר שָׁכְבָה עָלָיו׃
on-him she-lay because night the-this the-woman son-of and-he-died (19)

וַתָּקָם בְּתוֹךְ הַלַּיְלָה וַתִּקַּח אֶת־ בְּנִי
son-of-me *** and-she-took the-night in-middle-of so-she-got-up (20)

מֵאֶצְלִי וַאֲמָתְךָ יְשֵׁנָה וַתַּשְׁכִּיבֵהוּ
and-she-put-him she-was-asleep while-servant-of-you from-beside-me

בְּחֵיקָהּ וְאֶת־ בְּנָהּ הַמֵּת הִשְׁכִּיבָה בְחֵיקִי׃
by-breast-of-me she-put the-dead son-of-her and by-breast-of-her

you have asked. I will give you a wise and discerning heart, so that there will never have been anyone like you, nor will there ever be. [13]Moreover, I will give you what you have not asked for—both riches and honor—so that in your lifetime you will have no equal among kings. [14]And if you walk in my ways and obey my statutes and commands as David your father did, I will give you a long life." [15]Then Solomon awoke—and he realized it had been a dream.

He returned to Jerusalem, stood before the ark of the Lord's covenant and sacrificed burnt offerings and fellowship offerings.[c] Then he gave a feast for all his court.

A Wise Ruling

[16]Now two prostitutes came to the king and stood before him. [17]One of them said, "My lord, this woman and I live in the same house. I had a baby while she was there with me. [18]The third day after my child was born, this woman also had a baby. We were alone; there was no one in the house but the two of us.

[19]"During the night this woman's son died because she lay on him. [20]So she got up in the middle of the night and took my son from my side while I your servant was asleep. She put him by her breast and put her dead son by

[c]15 Traditionally *peace offerings*

וָאָקֻם בַּבֹּקֶר לְהֵינִיק אֶת־ בְּנִי וְהִנֵּה־ מֵת
dead and-see! son-of-me *** to-nurse in-the-morning and-I-got-up (21)

וָאֶתְבּוֹנֵן אֵלָיו בַּבֹּקֶר וְהִנֵּה לֹא־ הָיָה בְנִי
son-of-me he-was not then-see! in-the-morning at-him when-I-looked-closely

אֲשֶׁר יָלָדְתִּי׃ וַתֹּאמֶר הָאִשָּׁה הָאַחֶרֶת לֹא כִי בְּנִי הַחַי
the-living son-of-me so not the-other the-woman and-she-said (22) I-bore whom

וּבְנֵךְ הַמֵּת וְזֹאת אֹמֶרֶת לֹא כִי בְּנֵךְ הַמֵּת
the-dead son-of-you so not insisting but-this-one the-dead and-son-of-you

וּבְנִי הֶחָי וַתְּדַבֵּרְנָה לִפְנֵי הַמֶּלֶךְ׃ וַיֹּאמֶר
and-he-said (23) the-king before so-they-argued the-living and-son-of-me

הַמֶּלֶךְ זֹאת אֹמֶרֶת זֶה־ בְּנִי הַחַי וּבְנֵךְ הַמֵּת
the-dead and-son-of-you the-living son-of-me this saying this-one the-king

וְזֹאת אֹמֶרֶת לֹא כִי בְּנֵךְ הַמֵּת וּבְנִי הֶחָי׃
the-living and-son-of-me the-dead son-of-you so not saying while-that-one

וַיֹּאמֶר הַמֶּלֶךְ קְחוּ לִי־ חָרֶב וַיָּבִאוּ הַחֶרֶב
the-sword so-they-brought sword to-me bring! the-king then-he-said (24)

לִפְנֵי הַמֶּלֶךְ׃ וַיֹּאמֶר הַמֶּלֶךְ גִּזְרוּ אֶת־ הַיֶּלֶד הַחַי
the-living the-child *** cut! the-king then-he-ordered (25) the-king before

לִשְׁנָיִם וּתְנוּ אֶת־ הַחֲצִי לְאַחַת וְאֶת־ הַחֲצִי לְאֶחָת׃ וַתֹּאמֶר
and-she-said (26) to-other the-half and to-one the-half *** and-give! in-two

הָאִשָּׁה אֲשֶׁר־ בְּנָהּ הַחַי אֶל־ הַמֶּלֶךְ כִּי־ נִכְמְרוּ
they-were-warmed for the-king to the-living son-of-her who the-woman

רַחֲמֶיהָ עַל־ בְּנָהּ וַתֹּאמֶר ׀ בִּי אֲדֹנִי תְּנוּ־
give! lord-of-me please! and-she-said son-of-her for compassions-of-her

לָהּ אֶת־ הַיָּלוּד הַחַי וְהָמֵת אַל־ תְּמִיתֻהוּ
you-kill-him not but-to-kill the-living the-one-being-born *** to-her

וְזֹאת אֹמֶרֶת גַּם־ לִי גַּם־ לָךְ לֹא יִהְיֶה גְּזֹרוּ׃
cut-in-two! he-shall-be not to-you also to-me also saying but-that-one

וַיַּעַן הַמֶּלֶךְ וַיֹּאמֶר תְּנוּ־ לָהּ אֶת־ הַיָּלוּד
the-one-being-born *** to-her give! and-he-said the-king then-he-ruled (27)

הַחַי וְהָמֵת לֹא תְמִיתֻהוּ הִיא אִמּוֹ׃ וַיִּשְׁמְעוּ
when-they-heard (28) mother-of-him she you-kill-him not and-to-kill the-living

כָל־ יִשְׂרָאֵל אֶת־ הַמִּשְׁפָּט אֲשֶׁר שָׁפַט הַמֶּלֶךְ וַיִּרְאוּ
then-they-were-in-awe the-king he-gave that the-verdict *** Israel all-of

מִפְּנֵי הַמֶּלֶךְ כִּי רָאוּ כִּי־ חָכְמַת אֱלֹהִים בְּקִרְבּוֹ
in-inside-of-him God wisdom-of that they-saw because the-king from-before

לַעֲשׂוֹת מִשְׁפָּט׃ וַיְהִי הַמֶּלֶךְ שְׁלֹמֹה מֶלֶךְ עַל־ כָּל־
all-of over ruler Solomon the-king so-he-was (4:1) justice to-administer

my breast. 21 The next morning, I got up to nurse my son—
and he was dead! But when I
looked at him closely in the
morning light, I saw that it
wasn't the son I had borne."
22 The other woman said,
"No! The living one is my son;
the dead one is yours."
But the first one insisted,
"No! The dead one is yours;
the living one is mine." And
so they argued before the king.
23 The king said, "This one
says, 'My son is alive and your
son is dead,' while that one
says, 'No! Your son is dead
and mine is alive.' "
24 Then the king said, "Bring
me a sword." So they brought
a sword for the king. 25 He then
gave an order: "Cut the living
child in two and give half to
one and half to the other."
26 The woman whose son
was alive was filled with compassion for her son and said to
the king, "Please, my lord,
give her the living baby! Don't
kill him!"
But the other said, "Neither
I nor you shall have him. Cut
him in two!"
27 Then the king gave his ruling: "Give the living baby to
the first woman. Do not kill
him; she is his mother."
28 When all Israel heard the
verdict the king had given,
they held the king in awe, because they saw that he had
wisdom from God to adminis-
ter justice.

Solomon's Officials and Governors

4 So King Solomon ruled
over all Israel. 2 And these

יִשְׂרָאֵל׃ וְאֵלֶּה הַשָּׂרִים אֲשֶׁר־ לוֹ עֲזַרְיָהוּ בֶן־ צָדוֹק
Zadok son-of Azariah to-him who the-chief-officials and-these (2) Israel

הַכֹּהֵן׃ אֱלִיחֹרֶף וַאֲחִיָּה בְּנֵי שִׁישָׁא סֹפְרִים יְהוֹשָׁפָט
Jehoshaphat secretaries Shisha sons-of and-Ahijah Elihoreph (3) the-priest

בֶּן־ אֲחִילוּד הַמַּזְכִּיר׃ וּבְנָיָהוּ בֶן־ יְהוֹיָדָע עַל־
over Jehoiada son-of and-Benaiah (4) the-one-recording Ahilud son-of

הַצָּבָא וְצָדוֹק וְאֶבְיָתָר כֹּהֲנִים׃ וַעֲזַרְיָהוּ בֶן־ נָתָן עַל־
over Nathan son-of and-Azariah (5) priests and-Abiathar and-Zadok the-army

הַנִּצָּבִים וְזָבוּד בֶּן־ נָתָן כֹּהֵן רֵעֶה
personal-adviser-of priest Nathan son-of and-Zabud the-ones-being-officers

הַמֶּלֶךְ׃ וַאֲחִישָׁר עַל־ הַבָּיִת וַאֲדֹנִירָם בֶּן־ עַבְדָּא עַל־
over Abda son-of and-Adoniram the-palace over and-Abishar (6) the-king

הַמַּס׃ וְלִשְׁלֹמֹה שְׁנֵים־ עָשָׂר נִצָּבִים עַל־ כָּל־
all-of over ones-governing ten two and-to-Solomon (7) the-forced-labor

יִשְׂרָאֵל וְכִלְכְּלוּ אֶת־ הַמֶּלֶךְ וְאֶת־ בֵּיתוֹ חֹדֶשׁ
month house-of-him and the-king *** and-they-supplied-provision Israel

בַּשָּׁנָה יִהְיֶה עַל־ אֶחָד לְכַלְכֵּל׃ וְאֵלֶּה שְׁמוֹתָם
names-of-them and-these (8) to-provide the-each for he-was in-the-year

בֶּן־ חוּר בְּהַר אֶפְרָיִם׃ בֶּן־ דֶּקֶר בְּמָקַץ וּבְשַׁעַלְבִים
and-in-Shaalbim in-Makaz Deker Ben (9) Ephraim in-hill-country-of Hur Ben

וּבֵית שֶׁמֶשׁ וְאֵילוֹן בֵּית חָנָן׃ בֶּן־ חֶסֶד בָּאֲרֻבּוֹת לוֹ
to-him in-the-Arubboth Hesed Ben (10) Hanan Beth and-Elon Shemesh and-Beth

שֹׂכֹה וְכָל־ אֶרֶץ חֵפֶר׃ בֶּן־ אֲבִינָדָב כָּל־ נָפַת דֹּאר טָפַת
Taphath Dor Naphoth all-of Abinadab Ben (11) Hepher land-of and-all-of Socoh

בַּת־ שְׁלֹמֹה הָיְתָה לּוֹ לְאִשָּׁה׃ בַּעֲנָא בֶּן־ אֲחִילוּד תַּעְנַךְ
Taanach Ahilud son-of Baana (12) as-wife to-him she-was Solomon daughter-of

וּמְגִדּוֹ וְכָל־ בֵּית שְׁאָן אֲשֶׁר אֵצֶל צָרְתַנָה מִתַּחַת לְיִזְרְעֶאל
to-Jezreel at-below to-Zarethan next that Shan Beth and-all-of and-Megiddo

מִבֵּית שְׁאָן עַד אָבֵל מְחוֹלָה עַד מֵעֵבֶר לְיָקְמְעָם׃ בֶּן־ גֶּבֶר
Geber Ben (13) to-Jokmeam at-across to Meholath Abel to Shan from-Beth

בְּרָמֹת גִּלְעָד לוֹ חַוֺּת יָאִיר בֶּן־ מְנַשֶּׁה אֲשֶׁר בַּגִּלְעָד
in-the-Gilead that Manasseh son-of Jair settlements-of to-him Gilead in-Ramoth

לוֹ חֶבֶל אַרְגֹּב אֲשֶׁר בַּבָּשָׁן שִׁשִּׁים עָרִים גְּדֹלוֹת חוֹמָה
wall large-ones cities sixty in-the-Bashan that Argob district-of to-him

וּבְרִיחַ נְחֹשֶׁת׃ אֲחִינָדָב בֶּן־ עִדֹּא מַחֲנָיְמָה׃ אֲחִימַעַץ
Ahimaaz (15) in-Mahanaim Iddo son-of Ahinadab (14) bronze and-gate-bar-of

בְּנַפְתָּלִי גַּם־ הוּא לָקַח אֶת־ בָּשְׂמַת בַּת־ שְׁלֹמֹה לְאִשָּׁה׃
as-wife Solomon daughter-of Basemath *** he-took he also in-Naphtali

°7 ק האחד

were his chief officials:

Azariah son of Zadok—the priest;
[3]Elihoreph and Ahijah, sons of Shisha—secretaries;
Jehoshaphat son of Ahilud—recorder;
[4]Benaiah son of Jehoiada—commander in chief;
Zadok and Abiathar—priests;
[5]Azariah son of Nathan—in charge of the district officers;
Zabud son of Nathan—a priest and personal adviser to the king;
[6]Ahishar—in charge of the palace;
Adoniram son of Abda—in charge of forced labor.

[7]Solomon also had twelve district governors over all Israel, who supplied provisions for the king and the royal household. Each one had to provide supplies for one month in the year. [8]These are their names:

Ben-Hur—in the hill country of Ephraim;
[9]Ben-Deker—in Makaz, Shaalbim, Beth Shemesh and Elon Bethhanan;
[10]Ben-Hesed—in Arubboth (Socoh and all the land of Hepher were his);
[11]Ben-Abinadab—in Naphoth Dor[f] (he was married to Taphath daughter of Solomon);
[12]Baana son of Ahilud—in Taanach and Megiddo, and in all of Beth Shan next to Zarethan below Jezreel, from Beth Shan to Abel Meholah across to Jokmeam;
[13]Ben-Geber—in Ramoth Gilead (the settlements of Jair son of Manasseh in Gilead were his, as well as the district of Argob in Bashan and its sixty large walled cities with bronze gate bars);
[14]Ahinadab son of Iddo—in Mahanaim;
[15]Ahimaaz—in Naphtali (he had married Basemath daughter of Solomon);

[f]11 Or *in the heights of Dor*

בַּעֲנָא בֶּן־ חוּשַׁי בְּאָשֵׁר וּבְעָלוֹת׃ יְהוֹשָׁפָט בֶּן־
son-of Jehoshaphat (17) and-in-Aloth in-Asher Hushai son-of Baana (16)

פָּרוּחַ בְּיִשָּׂשכָר†׃ שִׁמְעִי בֶן־ אֵלָא בְּבִנְיָמִן׃ גֶּבֶר בֶּן־ אֻרִי
Uri son-of Geber (19) in-Benjamin Ela son-of Shimei (18) in-Issachar Paruah

בְּאֶרֶץ גִּלְעָד אֶרֶץ סִיחוֹן ׀ מֶלֶךְ הָאֱמֹרִי וְעוֹג מֶלֶךְ
king-of and-Og the-Amorite king-of Sihon country-of Gilead in-land-of

הַבָּשָׁן וּנְצִיב אֶחָד אֲשֶׁר בָּאָרֶץ׃ יְהוּדָה וְיִשְׂרָאֵל
and-Israel Judah (20) over-the-district that only and-governor the-Bashan

רַבִּים כַּחוֹל אֲשֶׁר־ עַל־ הַיָּם לָרֹב אֹכְלִים
ones-eating in-number the-sea by that as-the-sand ones-numerous

וְשֹׁתִים וּשְׂמֵחִים׃ וּשְׁלֹמֹה הָיָה מוֹשֵׁל
ruling he-was and-Solomon *(5:1[21]) and-ones-happy and-ones-drinking

בְּכָל־ הַמַּמְלָכוֹת מִן־ הַנָּהָר אֶרֶץ פְּלִשְׁתִּים וְעַד
and-as-far-as Philistines land-of the-River from the-kingdoms over-all-of

גְּבוּל מִצְרָיִם מַגִּשִׁים מִנְחָה וְעֹבְדִים אֶת־ שְׁלֹמֹה כָּל־
all-of Solomon *** and-ones-serving tribute ones-bringing Egypt border-of

יְמֵי חַיָּיו׃ וַיְהִי לֶחֶם־ שְׁלֹמֹה לְיוֹם אֶחָד
one for-day Solomon provision-of and-he-was (2[22]) lives-of-him days-of

שְׁלֹשִׁים כֹּר סֹלֶת וְשִׁשִּׁים כֹּר קָמַח׃ עֲשָׂרָה בָקָר בְּרִאִים
ones-stall-fed cattle ten (3[23]) meal cor and-sixty fine-flour cor thirty

וְעֶשְׂרִים בָּקָר רְעִי וּמֵאָה צֹאן לְבַד מֵאַיָּל
from-deer apart-from sheep and-hundred pasture-fed cattle and-twenty

וּצְבִי וְיַחְמוּר וּבַרְבֻּרִים אֲבוּסִים׃ כִּי־ הוּא רֹדֶה ׀
ruling he for (4[24]) ones-being-choice and-fowls and-roebuck and-gazelle

בְּכָל־ עֵבֶר הַנָּהָר מִתִּפְסַח וְעַד־ עַזָּה בְּכָל־
over-all-of Gaza even-to from-Tiphsah the-River west-of over-all-of

מַלְכֵי עֵבֶר הַנָּהָר וְשָׁלוֹם הָיָה לוֹ מִכָּל־ עֲבָרָיו
sides-of-him on-all-of to-him he-was and-peace the-River west-of kingdoms-of

מִסָּבִיב׃ וַיֵּשֶׁב יְהוּדָה וְיִשְׂרָאֵל לָבֶטַח אִישׁ תַּחַת
under each in-safety and-Israel Judah and-he-lived (5[25]) at-around

גַּפְנוֹ וְתַחַת תְּאֵנָתוֹ מִדָּן וְעַד־ בְּאֵר שָׁבַע כֹּל יְמֵי
days-of all-of Sheba Beer even-to from-Dan fig-of-him and-under vine-of-him

שְׁלֹמֹה׃ וַיְהִי לִשְׁלֹמֹה אַרְבָּעִים אֶלֶף אֻרְוֹת סוּסִים
horses stalls-of thousand forty to-Solomon and-he-was (6[26]) Solomon

לְמֶרְכָּבוֹ וּשְׁנֵים־ עָשָׂר אֶלֶף פָּרָשִׁים׃ וְכִלְכְּלוּ
and-they-provided (7[27]) horses thousand ten and-two for-chariot-of-him

הַנִּצָּבִים הָאֵלֶּה אֶת־ הַמֶּלֶךְ שְׁלֹמֹה וְאֵת כָּל־
all-of and Solomon the-king *** the-these the-ones-being-officers

16 Baana son of Hushai—in
Asher and in Aloth;
17 Jehoshaphat son of Paruah—in Issachar;
18 Shimei son of Ela—in Benjamin;
19 Geber son of Uri—in Gilead
(the country of Sihon
king of the Amorites and
the country of Og king of
Bashan). He was the only
governor over the district.

Solomon's Daily Provisions

20 The people of Judah and Israel were as numerous as the
sand on the seashore; they ate,
they drank and they were
happy. 21 And Solomon ruled
over all the kingdoms from the
River[g] to the land of the Philistines, as far as the border of
Egypt. These countries
brought tribute and were Solomon's subjects all his life.
22 Solomon's daily provisions
were thirty cors[h] of fine flour
and sixty cors[i] of meal, 23 ten
head of stall-fed cattle, twenty
of pasture-fed cattle and a
hundred sheep and goats, as
well as deer, gazelles, roebucks
and choice fowl. 24 For he ruled
over all the kingdoms west of
the River, from Tiphsah to
Gaza, and had peace on all
sides. 25 During Solomon's lifetime Judah and Israel, from
Dan to Beersheba, lived in
safety, each man under his
own vine and fig tree.
26 Solomon had four[j] thousand stalls for chariot horses,
and twelve thousand horses.[k]
27 The district officers, each
in his month, supplied provisions for King Solomon and

[g] 21 That is, the Euphrates; also in verse 24
[h] 22 That is, probably about 185 bushels (about 6.6 kiloliters)
[i] 22 That is, probably about 375 bushels (about 13.2 kiloliters)
[j] 26 Some Septuagint manuscripts (see also 2 Chron. 9:25); Hebrew *forty*
[k] 26 Or *charioteers*

*The Hebrew numeration of chapter 5 begins with verse 21 of chapter 4 in English. The number in brackets indicates the English numeration.

†17 Most mss have *dagesh* in the *sin* (בְּיִשָּׂ).

הַקָּרֵב אֶל־ שֻׁלְחַן הַמֶּלֶךְ־ שְׁלֹמֹה אִישׁ חָדְשׁוֹ לֹא יְעַדְּרוּ
they-lacked not month-of-him each Solomon the-king table-of to the-one-near

דָּבָר׃ וְהַשְּׂעֹרִים וְהַתֶּבֶן לַסּוּסִים
for-the-horses and-the-straw and-the-barleys (8[28]) thing

וְלָרֶכֶשׁ יָבִאוּ אֶל־ הַמָּקוֹם אֲשֶׁר יִהְיֶה־ שָּׁם אִישׁ
each there he-was where the-place to they-brought and-for-the-chariot-horse

כְּמִשְׁפָּטוֹ׃ וַיִּתֵּן אֱלֹהִים חָכְמָה לִשְׁלֹמֹה וּתְבוּנָה
and-insight to-Solomon wisdom God and-he-gave (9[29]) as-quota-of-him

הַרְבֵּה מְאֹד וְרֹחַב לֵב כַּחוֹל אֲשֶׁר עַל־ שְׂפַת
shore-of on that as-the-sand understanding and-breadth-of very to-be-great

הַיָּם׃ וַתֵּרֶב חָכְמַת שְׁלֹמֹה מֵחָכְמַת
more-than-wisdom-of Solomon wisdom-of and-she-was-great (10[30]) the-sea

כָּל־ בְּנֵי־ קֶדֶם וּמִכֹּל חָכְמַת מִצְרָיִם׃ וַיֶּחְכַּם
and-he-was-wise (11[31]) Egypt wisdom-of and-more-than-all-of East men-of all-of

מִכָּל־ הָאָדָם מֵאֵיתָן הָאֶזְרָחִי וְהֵימָן וְכַלְכֹּל
and-Calcol and-Heman the-Ezrahite more-than-Ethan the-man more-than-any-of

וְדַרְדַּע בְּנֵי מָחוֹל וַיְהִי־ שְׁמוֹ בְכָל־ הַגּוֹיִם סָבִיב׃
around the-nations to-all-of name-of-him and-he-was Mahol sons-of and-Darda

וַיְדַבֵּר שְׁלֹשֶׁת אֲלָפִים מָשָׁל וַיְהִי שִׁירוֹ חֲמִשָּׁה
five song-of-him and-he-was proverb thousands three-of and-he-spoke (12[32])

וָאָלֶף׃ וַיְדַבֵּר עַל־ הָעֵצִים מִן־ הָאֶרֶז אֲשֶׁר
that the-cedar from the-plants about and-he-described (13[33]) and-thousand

בַּלְּבָנוֹן וְעַד הָאֵזוֹב אֲשֶׁר יֹצֵא בַּקִּיר וַיְדַבֵּר
and-he-taught from-the-wall growing that the-hyssop even-to of-the-Lebanon

עַל־ הַבְּהֵמָה וְעַל־ הָעוֹף וְעַל־ הָרֶמֶשׂ וְעַל־ הַדָּגִים׃
the-fishes and-about the-reptile and-about the-bird and-about the-animal about

וַיָּבֹאוּ מִכָּל - הָעַמִּים לִשְׁמֹעַ אֵת חָכְמַת
wisdom-of *** to-listen the-nations from-all-of and-they-came (14[34])

שְׁלֹמֹה מֵאֵת כָּל־ מַלְכֵי הָאָרֶץ אֲשֶׁר שָׁמְעוּ אֶת־ חָכְמָתוֹ׃
wisdom-of-him *** they-heard who the-world kings-of all-of from Solomon

וַיִּשְׁלַח חִירָם מֶלֶךְ־ צוֹר אֶת־ עֲבָדָיו אֶל־ שְׁלֹמֹה כִּי
when Solomon to envoys-of-him *** Tyre king-of Hiram and-he-sent (15[1])

שָׁמַע כִּי אֹתוֹ מָשְׁחוּ לְמֶלֶךְ תַּחַת אָבִיהוּ כִּי
for father-of-him in-place-of as-king they-anointed him that he-heard

אֹהֵב הָיָה חִירָם לְדָוִד כָּל־ הַיָּמִים׃ וַיִּשְׁלַח
and-he-sent (16[2]) the-days all-of with-David Hiram he-was being-friendly

שְׁלֹמֹה אֶל־חִירָם לֵאמֹר׃ אַתָּה יָדַעְתָּ אֶת־ דָּוִד אָבִי כִּי
that father-of-me David *** you-know you (17[3]) to-say Hiram to Solomon

all who came to the king's table. They saw to it that nothing was lacking. [28]They also brought to the proper place their quotas of barley and straw for the chariot horses and the other horses.

Solomon's Wisdom

[29]God gave Solomon wisdom and very great insight, and a breadth of understanding as measureless as the sand on the seashore. [30]Solomon's wisdom was greater than the wisdom of all the men of the East, and greater than all the wisdom of Egypt. [31]He was wiser than any other man, including Ethan the Ezrahite—wiser than Heman, Calcol and Darda, the sons of Mahol. And his fame spread to all the surrounding nations. [32]He spoke three thousand proverbs and his songs numbered a thousand and five. [33]He described plant life, from the cedar of Lebanon to the hyssop that grows out of walls. He also taught about animals and birds, reptiles and fish. [34]Men of all nations came to listen to Solomon's wisdom, sent by all the kings of the world, who had heard of his wisdom.

Preparations for Building the Temple

5 When Hiram king of Tyre heard that Solomon had been anointed king to succeed his father David, he sent his envoys to Solomon, because he had always been on friendly terms with David. [2]Solomon sent back this message to Hiram:

[3]"You know that because

*See the note on page 346.

לֹא יָכֹל לִבְנוֹת בַּיִת לְשֵׁם יְהוָה אֱלֹהָיו מִפְּנֵי הַמִּלְחָמָה
the-war because-of God-of-him Yahweh for-Name-of temple to-build he-could not

אֲשֶׁר סְבָבֻהוּ עַד תֵּת־ יְהוָה אֹתָם תַּחַת כַּפּוֹת רַגְלָו׃
feet-of-him soles-of under them Yahweh to-put until they-surrounded-him that

(18[4]) וְעַתָּה הֵנִיחַ יְהוָה אֱלֹהַי לִי מִסָּבִיב אֵין שָׂטָן
adversary no at-around to-me God-of-me Yahweh he-gave-peace but-now (18[4])

וְאֵין פֶּגַע רָע׃ (19[5]) וְהִנְנִי אֹמֵר לִבְנוֹת בַּיִת
temple to-build intending so-see-I! (19[5]) disaster incident-of and-no

לְשֵׁם יְהוָה אֱלֹהָי כַּאֲשֶׁר ׀ דִּבֶּר יְהוָה אֶל־ דָּוִד אָבִי
father-of-me David to Yahweh he-told just-as God-of-me Yahweh for-Name-of

לֵאמֹר בִּנְךָ אֲשֶׁר אֶתֵּן תַּחְתֶּיךָ עַל־ כִּסְאֶךָ הוּא־
he throne-of-you on in-place-of-you I-will-put whom son-of-you to-say

יִבְנֶה הַבַּיִת לִשְׁמִי׃ (20[6]) וְעַתָּה צַוֵּה
give-order! so-now (20[6]) for-Name-of-me the-temple he-will-build

וְיִכְרְתוּ־ לִי אֲרָזִים מִן־ הַלְּבָנוֹן וַעֲבָדַי יִהְיוּ עִם־
with they-will-be and-men-of-me the-Lebanon from cedars for-me so-they-cut

עֲבָדֶיךָ וּשְׂכַר עֲבָדֶיךָ אֶתֵּן לְךָ כְּכֹל אֲשֶׁר תֹּאמֵר
you-say that as-all to-you I-will-pay men-of-you and-wage-of men-of-you

כִּי ׀ אַתָּה יָדַעְתָּ כִּי אֵין בָּנוּ אִישׁ יֹדֵעַ לִכְרָת־ עֵצִים
timbers to-fell being-skilled man among-us not that you-know you for

כַּצִּדֹנִים׃ (21[7]) וַיְהִי כִּשְׁמֹעַ חִירָם אֶת־ דִּבְרֵי שְׁלֹמֹה
Solomon words-of *** Hiram when-to-hear and-he-was (21[7]) as-the-Sidonians

וַיִּשְׂמַח מְאֹד וַיֹּאמֶר בָּרוּךְ יְהוָה הַיּוֹם אֲשֶׁר
who the-day Yahweh being-praised and-he-said greatly then-he-was-pleased

נָתַן לְדָוִד בֵּן חָכָם עַל־ הָעָם הָרָב הַזֶּה׃ (22[8]) וַיִּשְׁלַח
so-he-sent (22[8]) the-this the-great the-nation over wise son to-David he-gave

חִירָם אֶל־שְׁלֹמֹה לֵאמֹר שָׁמַעְתִּי אֵת אֲשֶׁר־שָׁלַחְתָּ אֵלָי אֲנִי אֶעֱשֶׂה אֶת־
*** I-will-do I to-me you-sent what *** I-received to-say Solomon to Hiram

כָּל־ חֶפְצְךָ בַּעֲצֵי אֲרָזִים וּבַעֲצֵי בְרוֹשִׁים׃ (23[9]) עֲבָדַי
men-of-me (23[9]) pines and-in-logs-of cedars in-logs-of desire-of-you all-of

יֹרִדוּ מִן־ הַלְּבָנוֹן יָמָּה וַאֲנִי אֲשִׂימֵם דֹּבְרוֹת
rafts I-will-float-them and-I to-sea the-Lebanon from they-will-haul-down

בַּיָּם עַד־ הַמָּקוֹם אֲשֶׁר־ תִּשְׁלַח אֵלַי וְנִפַּצְתִּים שָׁם
there and-I-will-separate-them to-me you-specify that the-place to by-the-sea

וְאַתָּה תִשָּׂא וְאַתָּה תַּעֲשֶׂה אֶת־ חֶפְצִי לָתֵת לֶחֶם
food-of to-provide wish-of-me *** you-grant and-you you-take-away and-you

בֵּיתִי׃ (24[10]) וַיְהִי חִירוֹם נֹתֵן לִשְׁלֹמֹה עֲצֵי אֲרָזִים
cedars logs-of to-Solomon supplying Hiram so-he-was (24[10]) household-of-me

of the wars waged against
my father David from all
sides, he could not build a
temple for the Name of the
LORD his God until the LORD
put his enemies under his
feet. [4]But now the LORD my
God has given me peace on
every side, and there is no
adversary or disaster. [5]I intend, therefore, to build a
temple for the Name of the
LORD my God, as the LORD
told my father David, when
he said, 'Your son whom I
will put on the throne in
your place will build the
temple for my Name.'
[6]"So give orders that cedars of Lebanon be cut for
me. My men will work with
yours, and I will pay you
for your men whatever
wages you set. You know
that we have no one so
skilled in felling timber as
the Sidonians."

[7]When Hiram heard Solo-
mon's message, he was greatly
pleased and said, "Praise be to
the LORD today, for he has giv-
en David a wise son to rule
over this great nation."
[8]So Hiram sent word to Solomon:

"I have received the mes-
sage you sent me and will
do all you want in pro-
viding the cedar and pine
logs. [9]My men will haul
them down from Lebanon
to the sea, and I will float
them in rafts by sea to the
place you specify. There I
will separate them and you
can take them away. And
you are to grant my wish
by providing food for my
royal household."

[10]In this way Hiram kept
Solomon supplied with all the

*See the note on page 346.

°17 ק רגלי

וַעֲצֵי בְרוֹשִׁים כָּל־חֶפְצוֹ׃ וּשְׁלֹמֹה נָתַן לְחִירָם
to-Hiram he-gave and-Solomon (25[11]) desire-of-him all-of pines and-logs-of

עֶשְׂרִים אֶלֶף כֹּר חִטִּים מַכֹּלֶת לְבֵיתוֹ וְעֶשְׂרִים כֹּר שֶׁמֶן
olive-oil cor and-twenty for-household-of-him food wheats cor thousand twenty

כָּתִית כֹּה־יִתֵּן שְׁלֹמֹה לְחִירָם שָׁנָה בְשָׁנָה׃ וַיהוָה
and-Yahweh (26[12]) after-year year for-Hiram Solomon he-did so pressed

נָתַן חָכְמָה לִשְׁלֹמֹה כַּאֲשֶׁר דִּבֶּר־לוֹ וַיְהִי שָׁלֹם
peace and-he-was to-him he-promised just-as to-Solomon wisdom he-gave

בֵּין חִירָם וּבֵין שְׁלֹמֹה וַיִּכְרְתוּ בְרִית שְׁנֵיהֶם׃
two-of-them treaty and-they-made Solomon and-between Hiram between

וַיַּעַל הַמֶּלֶךְ שְׁלֹמֹה מַס מִכָּל־יִשְׂרָאֵל
Israel from-all-of laborer Solomon the-king and-he-conscripted (27[13])

וַיְהִי הַמַּס שְׁלֹשִׁים אֶלֶף אִישׁ׃ וַיִּשְׁלָחֵם
and-he-sent-off-them (28[14]) man thousand thirty the-laborer and-he-was

לְבָנוֹנָה עֲשֶׂרֶת אֲלָפִים בַּחֹדֶשׁ חֲלִיפוֹת חֹדֶשׁ יִהְיוּ בַלְּבָנוֹן
in-the-Lebanon they-were month shifts in-the-month thousands ten-of to-Lebanon

שְׁנַיִם חֳדָשִׁים בְּבֵיתוֹ וַאֲדֹנִירָם עַל־הַמַּס׃ וַיְהִי
and-he-was (29[15]) the-forced-labor over and-Adoniram at-home-of-him months two

לִשְׁלֹמֹה שִׁבְעִים אֶלֶף נֹשֵׂא סַבָּל וּשְׁמֹנִים אֶלֶף חֹצֵב
stone-cutting thousand and-eighty burden carrying thousand seventy to-Solomon

בָּהָר׃ לְבַד מִשָּׂרֵי הַנִּצָּבִים
the-ones-being-appointed from-foremen-of apart-from (30[16]) in-the-hill

לִשְׁלֹמֹה אֲשֶׁר עַל־הַמְּלָאכָה שְׁלֹשֶׁת אֲלָפִים וּשְׁלֹשׁ מֵאוֹת
hundreds and-three-of thousands three-of the-project over who to-Solomon

הָרֹדִים בָּעָם הָעֹשִׂים בַּמְּלָאכָה׃
on-the-project the-ones-working over-the-people the-ones-supervising

וַיְצַו הַמֶּלֶךְ וַיַּסִּעוּ אֲבָנִים גְּדֹלוֹת אֲבָנִים
stones large-ones stones and-they-removed the-king and-he-commanded (31[17])

יְקָרוֹת לְיַסֵּד הַבָּיִת אַבְנֵי גָזִית׃
dressed stones-of the-temple to-provide-foundation quality-ones

וַיִּפְסְלוּ בֹּנֵי שְׁלֹמֹה וּבֹנֵי
and-ones-being-craftsmen-of Solomon ones-being-craftsmen-of and-they-cut (32[18])

חִירוֹם וְהַגִּבְלִים וַיָּכִינוּ הָעֵצִים וְהָאֲבָנִים לִבְנוֹת
to-build and-the-stones the-timbers and-they-prepared and-the-Gebalites Hiram

הַבָּיִת׃ וַיְהִי בִשְׁמוֹנִים שָׁנָה וְאַרְבַּע מֵאוֹת שָׁנָה לְצֵאת
to-come-out year hundreds and-four year in-eighty and-he-was (6:1) the-temple

בְּנֵי־יִשְׂרָאֵל מֵאֶרֶץ־מִצְרַיִם בַּשָּׁנָה הָרְבִיעִית בְּחֹדֶשׁ זִו
Ziv in-month-of the-fourth in-the-year Egypt from-land-of Israel sons-of

cedar and pine logs he wanted, 11 and Solomon gave Hiram
twenty thousand cors[l] of
wheat as food for his
household, in addition to
twenty thousand baths[m] [n] of
pressed olive oil. Solomon
continued to do this for Hiram
year after year. 12 The LORD
gave Solomon wisdom, just as
he had promised him. There
were peaceful relations between Hiram and Solomon,
and the two of them made a
treaty.

13 King Solomon conscripted
laborers from all Israel—thirty
thousand men. 14 He sent them
off to Lebanon in shifts of ten
thousand a month, so that
they spent one month in
Lebanon and two months at
home. Adoniram was in
charge of the forced labor.
15 Solomon had seventy thousand carriers and eighty thousand stonecutters in the hills,
16 as well as thirty-three hundred[o] foremen who super-
vised the project and directed
the workmen. 17 At the king's
command they removed from
the quarry large blocks of
quality stone to provide a
foundation of dressed stone
for the temple. 18 The craftsmen
of Solomon and Hiram and
the men of Gebal[p] cut and prepared the timber and stone for
the building of the temple.

Solomon Builds the Temple

6 In the four hundred and
eightieth[q] year after the
Israelites had come out of
Egypt, in the fourth year of

[l]11 That is, probably about 125,000 bushels (about 4,400 kiloliters)
[m]11 Septuagint (see also 2 Chron. 2:10); Hebrew *twenty cors*
[n]11 That is, about 115,000 gallons (about 440 kiloliters)
[o]16 Hebrew; some Septuagint manuscripts (see also 2 Chron. 2:2, 18) *thirty-six hundred*
[p]18 That is, Byblos
[q]1 Hebrew; Septuagint *four hundred and fortieth*

*See the note on page 346.

הוּא הַחֹדֶשׁ הַשֵּׁנִי לִמְלֹךְ שְׁלֹמֹה עַל־ יִשְׂרָאֵל וַיִּבֶן
then-he-built Israel over Solomon to-reign the-second the-month this

הַבַּיִת לַיהוָה׃ (2) וְהַבַּיִת אֲשֶׁר בָּנָה הַמֶּלֶךְ שְׁלֹמֹה
Solomon the-king he-built that and-the-temple (2) of-Yahweh the-temple

לַיהוָה שִׁשִּׁים־ אַמָּה אָרְכּוֹ וְעֶשְׂרִים רָחְבּוֹ וּשְׁלֹשִׁים
and-thirty width-of-him and-twenty length-of-him cubit sixty for-Yahweh

אַמָּה קוֹמָתוֹ׃ (3) וְהָאוּלָם עַל־ פְּנֵי הֵיכַל הַבַּיִת
the-temple main-hall-of front-of at and-the-portico (3) height-of-him cubit

עֶשְׂרִים אַמָּה אָרְכּוֹ עַל־ פְּנֵי רֹחַב הַבָּיִת עֶשֶׂר בָּאַמָּה
by-the-cubit ten the-temple width-of front-of at length-of-him cubit twenty

רָחְבּוֹ עַל־ פְּנֵי הַבָּיִת׃ (4) וַיַּעַשׂ לַבָּיִת
in-the-temple and-he-made (4) the-temple front-of at projection-of-him

חַלּוֹנֵי שְׁקֻפִים אֲטֻמִים׃ (5) וַיִּבֶן עַל־ קִיר
wall-of against and-he-built (5) ones-being-narrow clerestories windows-of

הַבַּיִת יָצוֹעַ° סָבִיב אֶת־ קִירוֹת הַבַּיִת סָבִיב לַהֵיכָל
of-the-main-hall around the-building walls-of *** around side-room the-building

וְלַדְּבִיר וַיַּעַשׂ צְלָעוֹת סָבִיב׃ (6) הַיָּצוֹעַ°
the-floor (6) around structures and-he-made and-of-the-inner-sanctuary

הַתַּחְתֹּנָה חָמֵשׁ בָּאַמָּה רָחְבָּהּ וְהַתִּיכֹנָה שֵׁשׁ בָּאַמָּה
by-the-cubit six and-the-middle width-of-her by-the-cubit five the-lowest

רָחְבָּהּ וְהַשְּׁלִישִׁית שֶׁבַע בָּאַמָּה רָחְבָּהּ כִּי
indeed width-of-her by-the-cubit seven and-the-third width-of-her

מִגְרָעוֹת נָתַן לַבַּיִת סָבִיב חוּצָה לְבִלְתִּי אֲחֹז
to-insert not at-outside around on-the-temple he-made offset-ledges

בְּקִירוֹת־ הַבָּיִת׃ (7) וְהַבַּיִת בְּהִבָּנֹתוֹ אֶבֶן־ שְׁלֵמָה
dressed block when-to-be-built-him and-the-temple (7) the-temple in-walls-of

מַסָּע נִבְנָה וּמַקָּבוֹת וְהַגַּרְזֶן כָּל־ כְּלִי בַרְזֶל לֹא־
not iron tool-of any-of and-the-chisel and-hammers being-used quarry

נִשְׁמַע בַּבַּיִת בְּהִבָּנֹתוֹ׃ (8) פֶּתַח הַצֵּלָע
the-floor entrance-of (8) when-to-be-built-him at-the-temple he-was-heard

הַתִּיכֹנָה אֶל־ כֶּתֶף הַבַּיִת הַיְמָנִית וּבְלוּלִּים יַעֲלוּ עַל־
to they-went-up and-on-stairs the-south the-temple side-of on the-middle

הַתִּיכֹנָה וּמִן־ הַתִּיכֹנָה אֶל־ הַשְּׁלִשִׁים׃ (9) וַיִּבֶן אֶת־
*** so-he-built (9) the-third-ones to the-middle and-from the-middle

הַבַּיִת וַיְכַלֵּהוּ וַיִּסְפֹּן אֶת־ הַבַּיִת גֵּבִים וּשְׂדֵרֹת
and-planks beams the-temple *** and-he-roofed and-he-completed-him the-temple

בָּאֲרָזִים׃ (10) וַיִּבֶן אֶת־ הַיָּצוֹעַ° עַל־ כָּל־ הַבַּיִת
the-temple all-of along the-side-room *** and-he-built (10) of-the-cedars

Solomon's reign over Israel, in
the month of Ziv, the second
month, he began to build the
temple of the LORD.
[2]The temple that King Solomon built for the LORD was
sixty cubits long, twenty wide
and thirty high.[r] [3]The portico
at the front of the main hall of
the temple extended the width
of the temple, that is twenty
cubits,[s] and projected ten cubits[t] from the front of the temple. [4]He made narrow clerestо-
ry windows in the temple.
[5]Against the walls of the main
hall and inner sanctuary he
built a structure around the
building, in which there were
side rooms. [6]The lowest floor
was five cubits[u] wide, the
middle floor six cubits[v] and
the third floor seven.[w] He
made offset ledges around the
outside of the temple so that
nothing would be inserted
into the temple walls.
[7]In building the temple, only
blocks dressed at the quarry
were used, and no hammer,
chisel or any other iron tool
was heard at the temple site
while it was being built.
[8]The entrance to the lowest[x]
floor was on the south side of
the temple; a stairway led up
to the middle level and from
there to the third. [9]So he built
the temple and completed it,
roofing it with beams and cedar planks. [10]And he built the

[r]2 That is, about 90 feet (about 27 meters) long and 30 feet (about 9 meters) wide and 45 feet (about 13.5 meters) high
[s]3 That is, about 30 feet (about 9 meters)
[t]3 That is, about 15 feet (about 4.5 meters)
[u]6 That is, about 7 1/2 feet (about 2.3 meters)
[v]6 That is, about 9 feet (about 2.7 meters)
[w]6 That is, about 10 1/2 feet (about 3.1 meters)
[x]8 Septuagint; Hebrew *middle*

°5 ק יציע
°6 ק היציע
°10 ק היציע

חָמֵשׁ אַמּוֹת קוֹמָתוֹ וַיֶּאֱחֹז אֶת־ הַבַּיִת בַּעֲצֵי אֲרָזִים׃
cedars by-beams-of the-temple *** and-he-attached height-of-him cubits five

וַיְהִי דְּבַר־ יְהוָה אֶל־ שְׁלֹמֹה לֵאמֹר׃ הַבַּיִת הַזֶּה
the-this the-temple (12) to-say Solomon to Yahweh word-of and-he-came (11)

אֲשֶׁר־אַתָּה בֹנֶה אִם־ תֵּלֵךְ בְּחֻקֹּתַי וְאֶת־ מִשְׁפָּטַי
regulations-of-me and in-decrees-of-me you-follow if building you that

תַּעֲשֶׂה וְשָׁמַרְתָּ אֶת־ כָּל־ מִצְוֺתַי לָלֶכֶת בָּהֶם
to-them to-obey commands-of-me all-of *** and-you-keep you-carry-out

וַהֲקִמֹתִי אֶת־ דְּבָרִי אִתָּךְ אֲשֶׁר דִּבַּרְתִּי אֶל־ דָּוִד
David to I-gave that through-you promise-of-me *** then-I-will-fulfill

אָבִיךָ׃ וְשָׁכַנְתִּי בְּתוֹךְ בְּנֵי יִשְׂרָאֵל וְלֹא אֶעֱזֹב
I-will-abandon and-not Israel sons-of among and-I-will-live (13) father-of-you

אֶת־ עַמִּי יִשְׂרָאֵל׃ וַיִּבֶן שְׁלֹמֹה אֶת־ הַבַּיִת
the-temple *** Solomon so-he-built (14) Israel people-of-me ***

וַיְכַלֵּהוּ׃ וַיִּבֶן אֶת־ קִירוֹת הַבַּיִת מִבַּיְתָה
at-interior the-temple walls-of *** and-he-lined (15) and-he-completed-him

בְּצַלְעוֹת אֲרָזִים מִקַּרְקַע הַבַּיִת עַד־ קִירוֹת הַסִּפֻּן
the-ceiling rafters-of to the-temple from-floor-of cedars with-boards-of

צִפָּה עֵץ מִבָּיִת וַיְצַף אֶת־ קַרְקַע הַבַּיִת
the-temple floor-of *** and-he-covered at-interior wood he-paneled

בְּצַלְעוֹת בְּרוֹשִׁים׃ וַיִּבֶן אֶת־עֶשְׂרִים אַמָּה °מִיַּרְכּוֹתֵי
at-rear-parts-of cubit twenty *** and-he-partitioned (16) pines with-planks-of

הַבַּיִת בְּצַלְעוֹת אֲרָזִים מִן־ הַקַּרְקַע עַד־הַקִּירוֹת וַיִּבֶן
and-he-formed the-ceilings to the-floor from cedars with-boards-of the-temple

לוֹ מִבַּיִת לִדְבִיר לְקֹדֶשׁ הַקֳּדָשִׁים׃
the-Holy-Places for-Holy-of for-inner-sanctuary within-temple for-him

וְאַרְבָּעִים בָּאַמָּה הָיָה הַבָּיִת הוּא הַהֵיכָל
the-main-hall this the-room he-was by-the-cubit and-forty (17)

לִפְנָי*׃ וְאֶרֶז אֶל־ הַבַּיִת פְּנִימָה מִקְלַעַת פְּקָעִים
gourds carved-of at-inside the-temple in and-cedar (18) *in-front-of-me

וּפְטוּרֵי צִצִּים הַכֹּל אֶרֶז אֵין אֶבֶן נִרְאָה׃
he-was-seen stone no cedar the-whole flowers and-ones-being-opened-of

וּדְבִיר בְּתוֹךְ־ הַבַּיִת מִפְּנִימָה הֵכִין לְתִתֵּן†
†to-set he-prepared at-inside the-temple within and-inner-sanctuary (19)

שָׁם אֶת־ אֲרוֹן בְּרִית יְהוָה׃ וְלִפְנֵי הַדְּבִיר
the-inner-sanctuary and-front-of (20) Yahweh covenant-of ark-of *** there

עֶשְׂרִים אַמָּה אֹרֶךְ וְעֶשְׂרִים אַמָּה רֹחַב וְעֶשְׂרִים אַמָּה קוֹמָתוֹ
height-of-him cubit and-twenty width cubit and-twenty length cubit twenty

side rooms all along the temple. The height of each was
five cubits,[y] and they were attached to the temple by beams
of cedar.
11 The word of the LORD came
to Solomon: 12 "As for this temple you are building, if you follow my decrees, carry out my
regulations and keep all my
commands and obey them, I
will fulfill through you the
promise I gave to David your
father. 13 And I will live among
the Israelites and will not
abandon my people Israel."
14 So Solomon built the temple and completed it. 15 He
lined its interior walls with cedar boards, paneling them
from the floor of the temple to
the ceiling, and covered the
floor of the temple with planks
of pine. 16 He partitioned off
twenty cubits[z] at the rear of
the temple with cedar boards
from floor to ceiling to form
within the temple an inner
sanctuary, the Most Holy
Place. 17 The main hall in front
of this room was forty cubits[a]
long. 18 The inside of the temple was cedar, carved with
gourds and open flowers.
Everything was cedar; no
stone was to be seen.
19 He prepared the inner
sanctuary within the temple
to set the ark of the covenant
of the LORD there. 20 The inner
sanctuary was twenty cubits
long, twenty wide and twenty

[y] *10* That is, about 7 1/2 feet (about 2.3 meters); also in verse 24
[z] *16* That is, about 30 feet (about 9 meters)
[a] *17* That is, about 60 feet (about 18 meters)

**17* Pointed with *tsere* instead of *qamets* (לִפְנֵי), this would read simply *in-front*.

†19 This form should probably be read (לָתֵת), as in the *Ketbib-Qere* of 17:14.

°*16* ק מירכתי

וַיְצַפֵּהוּ זָהָב סָגוּר וַיְצַף מִזְבֵּחַ אָרֶז׃ וַיְצַף
and-he-covered (21) cedar altar and-he-overlaid pure gold and-he-overlaid-him

שְׁלֹמֹה אֶת־ הַבַּיִת מִפְּנִימָה זָהָב סָגוּר וַיְעַבֵּר בְּרַתִּיקוֹת
with-chains-of and-he-extended pure gold at-inside the-temple *** Solomon

זָהָב לִפְנֵי הַדְּבִיר וַיְצַפֵּהוּ זָהָב׃ וְאֶת־ כָּל־
whole-of so (22) gold and-he-overlaid-him the-inner-sanctuary front-of gold

הַבַּיִת צִפָּה זָהָב עַד־ תֹּם כָּל־ הַבַּיִת
the-interior whole-of to-be-finished until gold he-overlaid the-interior

וְכָל־ הַמִּזְבֵּחַ אֲשֶׁר־ לַדְּבִיר צִפָּה זָהָב׃ וַיַּעַשׂ
and-he-made (23) gold he-overlaid to-the-sanctuary that the-altar and-whole-of

בַּדְּבִיר שְׁנֵי כְרוּבִים עֲצֵי־ שָׁמֶן עֶשֶׂר אַמּוֹת קוֹמָתוֹ׃
height-of-him cubits ten olive woods-of cherubim pair-of in-the-inner-sanctuary

וְחָמֵשׁ אַמּוֹת כְּנַף הַכְּרוּב הָאֶחָת וְחָמֵשׁ אַמּוֹת כְּנַף
wing-of cubits and-five the-first the-cherub wing-of cubits and-five (24)

הַכְּרוּב הַשֵּׁנִית עֶשֶׂר אַמּוֹת מִקְצוֹת כְּנָפָיו וְעַד־ קְצוֹת
tips-of even-to wings-of-him from-tips cubits ten the-other the-cherub

כְּנָפָיו׃ וְעֶשֶׂר בָּאַמָּה הַכְּרוּב הַשֵּׁנִי מִדָּה אַחַת
identical size the-second the-cherub by-the-cubit and-ten (25) wings-of-him

וְקֶצֶב אֶחָד לִשְׁנֵי הַכְּרֻבִים׃ קוֹמַת הַכְּרוּב
the-cherub height-of (26) the-cherubim for-two-of identical and-shape

הָאֶחָד עֶשֶׂר בָּאַמָּה וְכֵן הַכְּרוּב הַשֵּׁנִי׃ וַיִּתֵּן
and-he-placed (27) the-second the-cherub and-same by-the-cubit ten the-first

אֶת־ הַכְּרוּבִים בְּתוֹךְ ׀ הַבַּיִת הַפְּנִימִי וַיִּפְרְשׂוּ אֶת־
*** and-they-spread-out the-innermost the-temple inside-of the-cherubim ***

כַּנְפֵי הַכְּרֻבִים וַתִּגַּע כְּנַף־ הָאֶחָד בַּקִּיר וּכְנַף
and-wing-of on-the-wall the-one wing-of and-she-touched the-cherubim wings-of

הַכְּרוּב הַשֵּׁנִי נֹגַעַת בַּקִּיר הַשֵּׁנִי וְכַנְפֵיהֶם אֶל־
in and-wings-of-them the-other on-the-wall touching the-other the-cherub

תּוֹךְ הַבַּיִת נֹגְעֹת כָּנָף אֶל־ כָּנָף׃ וַיְצַף אֶת־
*** and-he-overlaid (28) wing to wing ones-touching the-room middle-of

הַכְּרוּבִים זָהָב׃ וְאֵת כָּל־ קִירוֹת הַבַּיִת מֵסַב ׀ קָלַע
he-carved around the-temple walls-of all-of and (29) gold the-cherubim

פִּתּוּחֵי מִקְלְעוֹת כְּרוּבִים וְתִמֹּרֹת וּפְטוּרֵי
and-ones-being-open-of and-palm-trees cherubim carvings-of engravings-of

צִצִּים מִלִּפְנִים וְלַחִיצוֹן׃ וְאֶת־ קַרְקַע הַבַּיִת צִפָּה
he-covered the-temple floor-of and (30) and-on-the-outside on-inside flowers

זָהָב לִפְנִימָה וְלַחִיצוֹן׃ וְאֵת פֶּתַח הַדְּבִיר
the-inner-sanctuary entrance-of and (31) and-on-the-outside on-inside gold

high.[b] He overlaid the inside
with pure gold, and he also
overlaid the altar of cedar.
21Solomon covered the inside
of the temple with pure gold,
and he extended gold chains
across the front of the inner
sanctuary, which was overlaid
with gold. 22So he overlaid the
whole interior with gold. He
also overlaid with gold the altar that belonged to the inner
sanctuary.
23In the inner sanctuary he
made a pair of cherubim of olive wood, each ten cubits[c]
high. 24One wing of the first
cherub was five cubits long,
and the other wing five cubits—ten cubits from wing tip
to wing tip. 25The second
cherub also measured ten cubits, for the two cherubim
were identical in size and
shape. 26The height of each
cherub was ten cubits. 27He
placed the cherubim inside
the innermost room of the
temple, with their wings
spread out. The wing of one
cherub touched one wall,
while the wing of the other
touched the other wall, and
their wings touched each other in the middle of the room.
28He overlaid the cherubim
with gold.
29On the walls all around the
temple, in both the inner and
outer rooms, he carved cherubim, palm trees and open
flowers. 30He also covered the
floors of both the inner and
outer rooms of the temple with
gold.
31For the entrance of the inner sanctuary he made doors

[b]20 That is, about 30 feet (about 9 meters) long, wide and high
[c]23 That is, about 15 feet (about 4.5 meters)

°21 ק ברתוקות

עָשָׂה דַּלְתוֹת עֲצֵי־שָׁמֶן הָאַיִל מְזוּזוֹת חֲמִשִׁית׃ וּשְׁתֵּי
and-two-of (32) five-sided jambs the-lintel olive woods-of doors-of he-made

דַּלְתוֹת עֲצֵי־שֶׁמֶן וְקָלַע עֲלֵיהֶם מִקְלְעוֹת כְּרוּבִים
cherubim carvings-of on-them and-he-carved olive woods-of doors-of

וְתִמֹרוֹת וּפְטוּרֵי צִצִּים וְצִפָּה זָהָב
gold and-he-overlaid flowers and-ones-being-open-of and-palm-trees

וַיָּרֶד עַל־הַכְּרוּבִים וְעַל־הַתִּמֹרוֹת אֶת־הַזָּהָב׃
the-gold *** the-palm-trees and-over the-cherubim over and-he-beat

וְכֵן עָשָׂה לְפֶתַח הַהֵיכָל מְזוּזוֹת עֲצֵי־שָׁמֶן
olive woods-of jambs-of the-main-hall for-entrance-of he-made and-same (33)

מֵאֵת רְבִעִית׃ וּשְׁתֵּי דַלְתוֹת עֲצֵי בְרוֹשִׁים שְׁנֵי צְלָעִים
leaves two-of pines woods-of doors-of and-two-of (34) four-sided from

הַדֶּלֶת הָאַחַת גְּלִילִים וּשְׁנֵי קְלָעִים הַדֶּלֶת
the-door leaves and-two-of ones-turning-in-sockets the-one the-door

הַשֵּׁנִית גְּלִילִים׃ וְקָלַע כְּרוּבִים וְתִמֹרוֹת
and-palm-trees cherubim and-he-carved (35) ones-turning-in-sockets the-other

וּפְטֻרֵי צִצִּים וְצִפָּה זָהָב מְיֻשָּׁר עַל־
over being-even gold and-he-overlaid flowers and-ones-being-open-of

הַמְּחֻקֶּה׃ וַיִּבֶן אֶת־הֶחָצֵר הַפְּנִימִית שְׁלֹשָׁה טוּרֵי
courses-of three the-inner the-courtyard *** and-he-built (36) the-carving

גָזִית וְטוּר כְּרֻתֹת אֲרָזִים׃ בַּשָּׁנָה
in-the-year (37) cedars ones-being-trimmed-of and-course-of dressed-stone

הָרְבִיעִית יֻסַּד בֵּית יְהוָה בְּיֶרַח זִו׃ וּבַשָּׁנָה
and-in-the-year (38) Ziv in-month-of Yahweh temple-of he-was-founded the-fourth

הָאַחַת עֶשְׂרֵה בְּיֶרַח בּוּל הוּא הַחֹדֶשׁ הַשְּׁמִינִי כָּלָה הַבַּיִת
the-temple he-finished the-eighth the-month this Bul in-month-of ten the-one

לְכָל־דְּבָרָיו וּלְכָל־מִשְׁפָּטָו וַיִּבְנֵהוּ
and-he-built-him specifications-of-him and-in-all-of details-of-him in-all-of

שֶׁבַע שָׁנִים׃ וְאֶת־בֵּיתוֹ בָּנָה שְׁלֹמֹה שְׁלֹשׁ עֶשְׂרֵה שָׁנָה
year ten three-of Solomon he-built palace-of-him but (7:1) years seven

וַיְכַל אֶת־כָּל־בֵּיתוֹ׃ וַיִּבֶן אֶת־בֵּית
Palace-of *** and-he-built (2) palace-of-him all-of *** then-he-completed

יַעַר הַלְּבָנוֹן מֵאָה אַמָּה אָרְכּוֹ וַחֲמִשִּׁים אַמָּה רָחְבּוֹ
width-of-him cubit and-fifty length-of-him cubit hundred the-Lebanon Forest-of

וּשְׁלֹשִׁים אַמָּה קוֹמָתוֹ עַל אַרְבָּעָה טוּרֵי עַמּוּדֵי אֲרָזִים
cedars columns-of rows-of four with height-of-him cubit and-thirty

וּכְרֻתוֹת אֲרָזִים עַל־הָעַמּוּדִים׃ וְסָפֻן
and-being-roofed (3) the-columns on cedars and-ones-being-trimmed-of

of olive wood with five-sided
jambs. [32]And on the two olive
wood doors he carved cherubim, palm trees and open
flowers, and overlaid the
cherubim and palm trees with
beaten gold. [33]In the same way
he made four-sided jambs of
olive wood for the entrance to
the main hall. [34]He also made
two pine doors, each having
two leaves that turned in sockets. [35]He carved cherubim,
palm trees and open flowers
on them and overlaid them
with gold hammered evenly
over the carvings.
[36]And he built the inner
courtyard of three courses of
dressed stone and one course
of trimmed cedar beams.
[37]The foundation of the temple of the LORD was laid in the
fourth year, in the month of
Ziv. [38]In the eleventh year in
the month of Bul, the eighth
month, the temple was
finished in all its details according to its specifications.
He had spent seven years
building it.

Solomon Builds His Palace

7 It took Solomon thirteen
years, however, to com-
plete the construction of his
palace. [2]He built the Palace of
the Forest of Lebanon a hundred cubits long, fifty wide
and thirty high,[d] with four
rows of cedar columns supporting trimmed cedar beams.
[3]It was roofed with cedar

[d]2 That is, about 150 feet (about 46 meters) long, 75 feet (about 23 meters) wide and 45 feet (about 13.5 meters) high

°38 ק משפטיו

בָּאֶרֶז מִמַּעַל עַל־ הַצְּלָעֹת אֲשֶׁר עַל־ הָעַמּוּדִים אַרְבָּעִים וַחֲמִשָּׁה
and-five forty the-columns on that the-beams over at-above with-the-cedar

חֲמִשָּׁה עָשָׂר הַטּוּר׃ וּשְׁקֻפִים שְׁלֹשָׁה טוּרִים וּמֶחֱזָה אֶל־מֶחֱזָה שָׁלֹשׁ פְּעָמִים׃
times three face to and-face sets three and-windows (4) the-row ten five

וְכָל־ הַפְּתָחִים וְהַמְּזוּזוֹת רְבֻעִים שָׁקֶף וּמוּל
and-front frame ones-rectangular and-the-jambs the-doorways and-all-of (5)

מֶחֱזָה אֶל־מֶחֱזָה שָׁלֹשׁ פְּעָמִים׃ וְאֵת אוּלָם הָעַמּוּדִים עָשָׂה חֲמִשִּׁים
fifty he-made the-pillars colonnade-of and (6) times three face to face

אַמָּה אָרְכּוֹ וּשְׁלֹשִׁים אַמָּה רָחְבּוֹ וְאוּלָם עַל־ פְּנֵיהֶם
front-of-them at and-portico width-of-him cubit and-thirty length-of-him cubit

וְעַמֻּדִים וְעָב עַל־ פְּנֵיהֶם׃ וְאוּלָם הַכִּסֵּא
the-throne and-hall-of (7) front-of-them at and-overhanging-roof and-pillars

אֲשֶׁר יִשְׁפָּט־ שָׁם אֻלָם הַמִּשְׁפָּט עָשָׂה וְסָפוּן
and-being-covered he-built the-Justice Hall-of there he-judged where

בָּאֶרֶז מֵהַקַּרְקַע עַד־ הַקַּרְקָע׃ וּבֵיתוֹ אֲשֶׁר־
where and-palace-of-him (8) the-floor to from-the-floor with-the-cedar

יֵשֶׁב שָׁם חָצֵר הָאַחֶרֶת מִבֵּית לָאוּלָם
of-the-hall from-building-of the-one-back courtyard there he-lived

כַּמַּעֲשֶׂה הַזֶּה הָיָה וּבַיִת יַעֲשֶׂה לְבַת־ פַּרְעֹה
Pharaoh for-daughter-of he-made and-palace he-was the-this like-the-design

אֲשֶׁר לָקַח שְׁלֹמֹה כָּאוּלָם הַזֶּה׃ כָּל־ אֵלֶּה אֲבָנִים
stones these all-of (9) the-this like-the-hall Solomon he-married whom

יְקָרֹת כְּמִדֹּת גָּזִית מְגֹרָרוֹת בַּמְּגֵרָה מִבַּיִת
inside with-the-saw ones-being-trimmed cutting as-sizes-of high-grade-ones

וּמִחוּץ וּמִמַּסָּד עַד־ הַטְּפָחוֹת וּמִחוּץ עַד־ הֶחָצֵר
the-courtyard to and-outside the-eaves to and-from-foundation and-outside

הַגְּדוֹלָה׃ וּמְיֻסָּד אֲבָנִים יְקָרוֹת אֲבָנִים גְּדֹלוֹת
large-ones stones quality-ones stones and-being-founded (10) the-great

אַבְנֵי עֶשֶׂר אַמּוֹת וְאַבְנֵי שְׁמֹנֶה אַמּוֹת׃ וּמִלְמַעְלָה אֲבָנִים
stones and-at-above (11) cubits eight and-stones-of cubits ten stones-of

יְקָרוֹת כְּמִדּוֹת גָּזִית וָאָרֶז׃ וְחָצֵר הַגְּדוֹלָה
the-great and-courtyard (12) and-cedar cutting as-sizes-of high-grade-ones

סָבִיב שְׁלֹשָׁה טוּרִים גָּזִית וְטוּר כְּרֻתֹת אֲרָזִים
cedars ones-being-trimmed-of and-course dressed-stone courses three surrounded

וְלַחֲצַר בֵּית־ יְהוָה הַפְּנִימִית וּלְאֻלָם הַבָּיִת׃
the-temple and-to-portico-of the-inner Yahweh temple-of also-to-courtyard-of

וַיִּשְׁלַח הַמֶּלֶךְ שְׁלֹמֹה וַיִּקַּח אֶת־ חִירָם מִצֹּר׃
from-Tyre Hiram * and-he-brought Solomon the-king and-he-sent (13)**

above the beams that rested
on the columns—forty-five
beams, fifteen to a row. 4 Its
windows were placed high in
sets of three, facing each other.
5 All the doorways had rectan-
gular frames; they were in the
front part in sets of three, facing each other.[e]
6 He made a colonnade fifty
cubits long and thirty wide.[f]
In front of it was a portico,
and in front of that were pillars and an overhanging roof.
7 He built the throne hall, the
Hall of Justice, where he was
to judge, and he covered it
with cedar from floor to ceiling.[g] 8 And the palace in which
he was to live, set farther back,
was similar in design. Solomon also made a palace like
this hall for Pharaoh's daughter, whom he had married.
9 All these structures, from
the outside to the great courtyard and from foundation to
eaves, were made of blocks of
high-grade stone cut to size
and trimmed with a saw on
their inner and outer faces.
10 The foundations were laid
with large stones of good quality, some measuring ten cubits[h] and some eight.[i] 11 Above
were high-grade stones, cut to
size, and cedar beams. 12 The
great courtyard was surrounded by a wall of three courses of
dressed stone and one course
of trimmed cedar beams, as
was the inner courtyard of the
temple of the LORD with its
portico.

The Temple's Furnishings

13 King Solomon sent to Tyre
and brought Huram,[j] 14 whose

[e] 5 The meaning of the Hebrew for this verse is uncertain.
[f] 6 That is, about 75 feet (about 23 meters) long and 45 feet (about 13.5 meters) wide
[g] 7 Vulgate and Syriac; Hebrew *floor*
[h] 10 That is, about 15 feet (about 4.5 meters)
[i] 10 That is, about 12 feet (about 3.6 meters)
[j] 13 Hebrew *Hiram*, a variant of *Huram*; also in verses 40 and 45

בֶּן־ אִשָּׁה אַלְמָנָה הוּא מִמַּטֵּה נַפְתָּלִי וְאָבִיו אִישׁ־

man and-father-of-him Naphtali from-tribe-of he widow woman son-of (14)

צֹרִי חֹרֵשׁ נְחֹשֶׁת וַיִּמָּלֵא אֶת־ הַחָכְמָה וְאֶת־ הַתְּבוּנָה

the-experience and the-skill *** and-he-was-filled bronze one-crafting Tyrian

וְאֶת־ הַדַּעַת לַעֲשׂוֹת כָּל־מְלָאכָה בַּנְּחֹשֶׁת וַיָּבוֹא אֶל־ הַמֶּלֶךְ

the-king to and-he-came with-the-bronze work all-of to-do the-knowledge and

שְׁלֹמֹה וַיַּעַשׂ אֶת־ כָּל־ מְלַאכְתּוֹ׃ וַיָּצַר אֶת־ שְׁנֵי

two-of *** and-he-cast (15) work-of-him all-of *** and-he-did Solomon

הָעַמּוּדִים נְחֹשֶׁת שְׁמֹנֶה עֶשְׂרֵה אַמָּה קוֹמַת הָעַמּוּד הָאֶחָד וְחוּט

and-line the-each the-pillar height-of cubit ten eight bronze the-pillars

שְׁתֵּים־עֶשְׂרֵה אַמָּה יָסֹב אֶת־ הָעַמּוּד הַשֵּׁנִי׃ וּשְׁתֵּי

and-two-of (16) the-second the-pillar *** he-went-around cubit ten two

כֹתָרֹת עָשָׂה לָתֵת עַל־ רָאשֵׁי הָעַמּוּדִים מֻצַק נְחֹשֶׁת חָמֵשׁ

five bronze being-cast-of the-pillars tops-of on to-set he-made capitals

אַמּוֹת קוֹמַת הַכֹּתֶרֶת הָאֶחָת וְחָמֵשׁ אַמּוֹת קוֹמַת הַכֹּתֶרֶת

the-capital height-of cubits and-five the-one the-capital height-of cubits

הַשֵּׁנִית׃ שְׂבָכִים מַעֲשֵׂה שְׂבָכָה גְּדִלִים מַעֲשֵׂה שַׁרְשְׁרוֹת לַכֹּתָרֹת

on-the-capitals chains work-of festoons net work-of networks (17) the-second

אֲשֶׁר עַל־ רֹאשׁ הָעַמּוּדִים שִׁבְעָה לַכֹּתֶרֶת הָאֶחָת וְשִׁבְעָה

and-seven the-one for-the-capital seven the-pillars top-of on that

לַכֹּתֶרֶת הַשֵּׁנִית׃ וַיַּעַשׂ אֶת־הָעַמּוּדִים וּשְׁנֵי טוּרִים

rows and-two-of the-pillars *** and-he-made (18) the-second for-the-capital

סָבִיב עַל־ הַשְּׂבָכָה הָאֶחָת לְכַסּוֹת אֶת־ הַכֹּתָרֹת אֲשֶׁר עַל־

on that the-capitals *** to-decorate the-each the-network on encircling

רֹאשׁ הָרִמֹּנִים וְכֵן עָשָׂה לַכֹּתֶרֶת הַשֵּׁנִית׃

the-second for-the-capital he-did and-same the-pomegranates top-of

וְכֹתָרֹת אֲשֶׁר עַל־ רֹאשׁ הָעַמּוּדִים מַעֲשֵׂה שׁוּשַׁן בָּאוּלָם

in-the-portico lily shape-of the-pillars top-of on that and-capitals (19)

אַרְבַּע אַמּוֹת׃ וְכֹתָרֹת עַל־ שְׁנֵי הָעַמּוּדִים גַּם־ מִמַּעַל

at-above indeed the-pillars both-of on and-capitals (20) cubits four

מִלְּעֻמַּת הַבֶּטֶן אֲשֶׁר לְעֵבֶר ‑שְׂבָכָה וְהָרִמּוֹנִים

and-the-pomegranates the-network at-next-to that the-bowl-shape at-close-of

מָאתַיִם טֻרִים סָבִיב עַל הַכֹּתֶרֶת הַשֵּׁנִית׃ וַיָּקֶם אֶת־

*** and-he-erected (21) the-second the-capital on around rows two-hundreds

הָעַמֻּדִים לְאֻלָם הַהֵיכָל וַיָּקֶם אֶת־ הָעַמּוּד הַיְמָנִי

the-south the-pillar *** and-he-erected the-temple at-portico-of the-pillars

וַיִּקְרָא אֶת־ שְׁמוֹ יָכִין וַיָּקֶם אֶת־ הָעַמּוּד הַשְּׂמָאלִי

the-north the-pillar *** and-he-erected Jakin name-of-him *** and-he-called

mother was a widow from the tribe of Naphtali and whose father was a man of Tyre and a craftsman in bronze. Huram was highly skilled and experienced in all kinds of bronze work. He came to King Solomon and did all the work assigned to him.

[15]He cast two bronze pillars, each eighteen cubits high and twelve cubits around,[m] by line. [16]He also made two capitals of cast bronze to set on the tops of the pillars; each capital was five cubits[n] high. [17]A network of interwoven chains festooned the capitals on top of the pillars, seven for each capital. [18]He made pomegranates in two rows[o] encircling each network to decorate the capitals on top of the pillars.[p] He did the same for each capital. [19]The capitals on top of the pillars in the portico were in the shape of lilies, four cubits[r] high. [20]On the capitals of both pillars, above the bowl-shaped part next to the network, were the two hundred pomegranates in rows all around. [21]He erected the pillars at the portico of the temple. The pillar to the south he named Jakin[s] and

[m]15 That is, about 27 feet (about 8.1 meters) high and 18 feet (about 5.4 meters) around

[n]16 That is, about 7 1/2 feet (about 2.3 meters); also in verse 23

[o]18 Two Hebrew manuscripts and Septuagint; most Hebrew manuscripts *made the pillars, and there were two rows*

[p]18 Many Hebrew manuscripts and Syriac; most Hebrew manuscripts *pomegranates*

[r]19 That is, about 6 feet (about 1.8 meters); also in verse 38

[s]21 *Jakin* probably means *he establishes.*

°20 ק השבכה

וַיִּקְרָא אֶת־ שְׁמוֹ בֹּעַז׃ וְעַל רֹאשׁ הָעַמּוּדִים מַעֲשֵׂה
shape-of the-pillars top-of and-on (22) Boaz name-of-him *** and-he-called

שׁוֹשָׁן וַתִּתֹּם מְלֶאכֶת הָעַמּוּדִים׃ וַיַּעַשׂ אֶת־ הַיָּם
the-Sea *** and-he-made (23) the-pillars work-of so-she-was-completed lily

מוּצָק עֶשֶׂר בָּאַמָּה מִשְּׂפָתוֹ עַד־ שְׂפָתוֹ עָגֹל ׀ סָבִיב
around circular rim-of-him to from-rim-of-him by-the-cubit ten being-cast

וְחָמֵשׁ בָּאַמָּה קוֹמָתוֹ וְקָוֹה° שְׁלֹשִׁים בָּאַמָּה
by-the-cubit thirty and-line height-of-him by-the-cubit and-five

יָסֹב אֹתוֹ סָבִיב׃ וּפְקָעִים מִתַּחַת לִשְׂפָתוֹ ׀ סָבִיב
around to-rim-of-him at-below and-gourds (24) around him he-measured-around

סֹבְבִים אֹתוֹ עֶשֶׂר בָּאַמָּה מַקִּפִים אֶת־ הַיָּם סָבִיב
around the-Sea *** ones-encircling to-the-cubit ten him ones-encircling

שְׁנֵי טוּרִים הַפְּקָעִים יְצֻקִים בִּיצֻקָתוֹ׃ עֹמֵד עַל־ שְׁנֵי
two-of on standing (25) with-casting-of-him ones-cast the-gourds rows two-of

עָשָׂר בָּקָר שְׁלֹשָׁה פֹנִים ׀ צָפוֹנָה וּשְׁלֹשָׁה פֹנִים ׀ יָמָּה וּשְׁלֹשָׁה ׀
and-three to-west ones-facing and-three to-north ones-facing three bull ten

פֹּנִים נֶגְבָּה וּשְׁלֹשָׁה פֹּנִים מִזְרָחָה וְהַיָּם עֲלֵיהֶם
on-them and-the-Sea to-east ones-facing and-three to-south ones-facing

מִלְמָעְלָה וְכָל־ אֲחֹרֵיהֶם בָּיְתָה׃ וְעָבְיוֹ
and-thickness-of-him (26) toward-center hindquarters-of-them and-all-of at-on-top

טֶפַח וּשְׂפָתוֹ כְּמַעֲשֵׂה שְׂפַת־ כּוֹס פֶּרַח שׁוֹשָׁן
lily blossom-of cup rim-of like-shape-of and-rim-of-him handbreadth

אַלְפַּיִם בַּת יָכִיל׃ וַיַּעַשׂ אֶת־ הַמְּכֹנוֹת עֶשֶׂר
ten the-movable-stands *** and-he-made (27) he-held bath two-thousands

נְחֹשֶׁת אַרְבַּע בָּאַמָּה אֹרֶךְ הַמְּכוֹנָה הָאֶחָת וְאַרְבַּע בָּאַמָּה
by-the-cubit and-four the-each the-stand length-of by-the-cubit four bronze

רָחְבָּהּ וְשָׁלֹשׁ בָּאַמָּה קוֹמָתָהּ׃ וְזֶה מַעֲשֵׂה
make-up-of and-this (28) height-of-her by-the-cubit and-three width-of-her

הַמְּכוֹנָה מִסְגְּרֹת לָהֶם וּמִסְגְּרֹת בֵּין הַשְׁלַבִּים׃ וְעַל־
and-on (29) the-uprights between and-side-panels to-them side-panels the-stand

הַמִּסְגְּרוֹת אֲשֶׁר ׀ בֵּין הַשְׁלַבִּים אֲרָיוֹת ׀ בָּקָר וּכְרוּבִים וְעַל־
and-on and-cherubim bull lions the-uprights between that the-side-panels

הַשְׁלַבִּים כֵּן מִמָּעַל וּמִתַּחַת לַאֲרָיוֹת וְלַבָּקָר לֹיוֹת
wreaths and-to-the-bull to-the-lions and-at-below at-above same the-uprights

מַעֲשֵׂה מוֹרָד׃ וְאַרְבָּעָה אוֹפַנֵּי נְחֹשֶׁת לַמְּכוֹנָה הָאַחַת
the-each for-the-stand bronze wheels-of and-four (30) hammer work-of

וְסַרְנֵי נְחֹשֶׁת וְאַרְבָּעָה פַעֲמֹתָיו כְּתֵפֹת לָהֶם מִתַּחַת לַכִּיֹּר
to-the-basin at-below to-them supports feet-of-him and-four bronze and-axles-of

the one to the north Boaz.[t] [22]The capitals on top were in the shape of lilies. And so the work on the pillars was completed.

[23]He made the Sea of cast metal, circular in shape, measuring ten cubits[u] from rim to rim and five cubits high. It took a line of thirty cubits[v] to measure around it. [24]Below the rim, gourds encircled it—ten to a cubit. The gourds were cast in two rows in one piece with the Sea.

[25]The Sea stood on twelve bulls, three facing north, three facing west, three facing south and three facing east. The Sea rested on top of them, and their hindquarters were toward the center. [26]It was a handbreadth in thickness, and its rim was like the rim of a cup, like a lily blossom. It held two thousand baths.[w]

[27]He also made ten movable stands of bronze; each was four cubits long, four wide and three high.[x] [28]This is how the stands were made: They had side panels attached to uprights. [29]On the panels between the uprights were lions, bulls and cherubim—and on the uprights as well. Above and below the lions and bulls were wreaths of hammered work. [30]Each stand had four bronze wheels with bronze axles, and each had a basin resting on four supports, cast with

[t]21 *Boaz* probably means *in him is strength.*
[u]23 That is, about 15 feet (about 4.5 meters)
[v]23 That is, about 45 feet (about 13.5 meters)
[w]26 That is, probably about 11,500 gallons (about 44 kiloliters); the Septuagint does not have this sentence.
[x]27 That is, about 6 feet (about 1.8 meters) long and wide and about 4 1/2 feet (about 1.3 meters) high

°23 ק וקו

הַכְּתֵפֹת יְצֻקוֹת מֵעֵבֶר אִישׁ לֹיוֹת׃ (31) וּפִיהוּ
and-opening-of-him (31) wreaths each on-side-of ones-cast the-supports

מִבֵּית לַכֹּתֶרֶת וָמַעְלָה בָּאַמָּה וּפִיהָ עָגֹל
round and-opening-of-her at-the-cubit and-above of-the-stand on-inside-of

מַעֲשֵׂה־ כֵן אַמָּה וַחֲצִי הָאַמָּה וְגַם־ עַל־ פִּיהָ
opening-of-her around and-also the-cubit and-half-of cubit base work-of

מִקְלָעוֹת וּמִסְגְּרֹתֵיהֶם מְרֻבָּעוֹת לֹא עֲגֻלּוֹת׃ (32) וְאַרְבַּעַת
and-four-of (32) ones-round not ones-being-square and-panels-of-them engravings

הָאוֹפַנִּים לְמִתַּחַת לַמִּסְגְּרוֹת וִידוֹת הָאוֹפַנִּים בַּמְּכֹנָה
on-the-stand the-wheels and-axles-of to-the-panels at-under the-wheels

וְקוֹמַת הָאוֹפַן הָאֶחָד אַמָּה וַחֲצִי הָאַמָּה׃
the-cubit and-half-of cubit the-each the-wheel and-diameter-of

(33) וּמַעֲשֵׂה הָאוֹפַנִּים כְּמַעֲשֵׂה אוֹפַן הַמֶּרְכָּבָה יְדוֹתָם
axles-of-them the-chariot wheel-of like-make-of the-wheels and-make-of (33)

וְגַבֵּיהֶם וְחִשֻּׁקֵיהֶם וְחִשֻּׁרֵיהֶם הַכֹּל מוּצָק׃
being-cast the-whole and-hubs-of-them and-spokes-of-them and-rims-of-them

(34) וְאַרְבַּע כְּתֵפוֹת אֶל אַרְבַּע פִּנּוֹת הַמְּכֹנָה הָאֶחָת מִן־ הַמְּכֹנָה
the-stand from the-each the-stand corners four on handles and-four (34)

כְּתֵפֶיהָ׃ (35) וּבְרֹאשׁ הַמְּכוֹנָה חֲצִי הָאַמָּה קוֹמָה
height the-cubit half-of the-stand and-at-top-of (35) projections-of-her

עָגֹל ׀ סָבִיב וְעַל רֹאשׁ הַמְּכֹנָה יְדֹתֶיהָ וּמִסְגְּרֹתֶיהָ
and-panels-of-her supports-of-her the-stand top-of and-on around circle

מִמֶּנָּה׃ (36) וַיְפַתַּח עַל־ הַלֻּחֹת יְדֹתֶיהָ וְעַל
and-on supports-of-her the-surfaces on and-he-engraved (36) from-her

וּמִסְגְּרֹתֶיהָ° כְּרוּבִים אֲרָיוֹת וְתִמֹרֹת כְּמַעַר־ אִישׁ וְלֹיוֹת
and-wreaths each as-space-of and-palm-trees lions cherubim panels-of-her

סָבִיב׃ (37) כָּזֹאת עָשָׂה אֵת עֶשֶׂר הַמְּכֹנוֹת מוּצָק אֶחָד מִדָּה אַחַת
identical size same mold the-stands ten *** he-made as-this (37) around

קֶצֶב אֶחָד לְכֻלָּהְנָה׃ (38) וַיַּעַשׂ עֲשָׂרָה כִיֹּרוֹת נְחֹשֶׁת
bronze basins-of ten then-he-made (38) for-all-of-them identical shape

אַרְבָּעִים בַּת יָכִיל ׀ הַכִּיּוֹר הָאֶחָד אַרְבַּע בָּאַמָּה הַכִּיּוֹר הָאֶחָד
the-each the-basin by-the-cubit four the-each the-basin he-held bath forty

כִּיּוֹר אֶחָד עַל־ הַמְּכוֹנָה הָאַחַת לְעֶשֶׂר הַמְּכֹנוֹת׃ (39) וַיִּתֵּן אֶת־
*** and-he-placed (39) the-stands for-ten the-each the-stand on one basin

הַמְּכֹנוֹת חָמֵשׁ עַל־ כֶּתֶף הַבַּיִת מִיָּמִין וְחָמֵשׁ עַל־ כֶּתֶף הַבַּיִת
the-temple side-of at and-five at-south the-temple side-of on five the-stands

מִשְּׂמֹאלוֹ וְאֶת־ הַיָּם נָתַן מִכֶּתֶף הַבַּיִת הַיְמָנִית
the-south the-temple on-side-of he-placed the-Sea and at-north-of-him

wreaths on each side. [31]On the inside of the stand there was an opening that had a circular frame one cubit[y] deep. This opening was round, and with its basework it measured a cubit and a half.[z] Around its opening there was engraving. The panels of the stands were square, not round. [32]The four wheels were under the panels, and the axles of the wheels were attached to the stand. The diameter of each wheel was a cubit and a half. [33]The wheels were made like chariot wheels; the axles, rims, spokes and hubs were all of cast metal.

[34]Each stand had four handles, one on each corner, projecting from the stand. [35]At the top of the stand there was a circular band half a cubit[a] deep. The supports and panels were attached to the top of the stand. [36]He engraved cherubim, lions and palm trees on the surfaces of the supports and on the panels, in every available space, with wreaths all around. [37]This is the way he made the ten stands. They were all cast in the same molds and were identical in size and shape.

[38]He then made ten bronze basins, each holding forty baths[b] and measuring four cubits across, one basin to go on each of the ten stands. [39]He placed five of the stands on the south side of the temple and five on the north. He placed the Sea on the south side, at

[y]31 That is, about 1 1/2 feet (about 0.5 meter)
[z]31 That is, about 2 1/4 feet (about 0.7 meter); also in verse 32
[a]35 That is, about 3/4 foot (about 0.2 meter)
[b]38 That is, about 230 gallons (about 880 liters)

°36 ק מסגרתיה

קֵדְמָה מִמּוּל נֶגֶב׃ וַיַּעַשׂ חִירוֹם אֶת־ הַכִּיֹּרוֹת וְאֶ
.d the-basins *** Hiram and-he-made (40) south at-corner-of at-east

הַיָּעִים וְאֶת־ הַמִּזְרָקוֹת וַיְכַל חִירָם לַעֲשׂוֹת אֶת־ כָּל־
all-of *** to-do Hiram so-he-finished the-sprinkling-bowls and the-shovels

הַמְּלָאכָה אֲשֶׁר עָשָׂה לַמֶּלֶךְ שְׁלֹמֹה בֵּית יְהוָה׃
Yahweh temple-of Solomon for-the-king he-undertook that the-work

עַמֻּדִים שְׁנַיִם וְגֻלֹּת הַכֹּתָרֹת אֲשֶׁר־עַל־רֹאשׁ הָעַמֻּדִים שְׁתָּיִם
two the-pillars top-of on that the-capitals and-bowls-of two pillars (41)

וְהַשְּׂבָכוֹת שְׁתַּיִם לְכַסּוֹת אֶת־ שְׁתֵּי גֻּלֹּת הַכֹּתָרֹת אֲשֶׁר עַל־
on that the-capitals bowls-of two-of *** to-decorate two and-the-networks

רֹאשׁ הָעַמּוּדִים׃ וְאֶת־ הָרִמֹּנִים אַרְבַּע מֵאוֹת לִשְׁתֵּי
for-two-of hundreds four the-pomegranates and (42) the-pillars top-of

הַשְּׂבָכוֹת שְׁנֵי־ טוּרִים רִמֹּנִים לַשְּׂבָכָה הָאֶחָת לְכַסּוֹת
to-decorate the-each for-the-network pomegranates rows two-of the-networks

אֶת־ שְׁתֵּי גֻּלֹּת הַכֹּתָרֹת אֲשֶׁר עַל־ פְּנֵי הָעַמּוּדִים׃ וְאֶת־
and (43) the-pillars tops-of on that the-capitals bowls-of two-of ***

הַמְּכֹנוֹת עֶשֶׂר וְאֶת־ הַכִּיֹּרֹת עֲשָׂרָה עַל־הַמְּכֹנוֹת׃ וְאֶת־ הַיָּם הָאֶחָד
the-one the-Sea and (44) the-stands on ten the-basins and ten the-stands

וְאֶת־הַבָּקָר שְׁנֵים־עָשָׂר תַּחַת הַיָּם׃ וְאֶת־ הַסִּירוֹת וְאֶת־ הַיָּעִים
the-shovels and the-pots and (45) the-Sea under ten two the-bull and

וְאֶת־ הַמִּזְרָקוֹת וְאֵת כָּל־ הַכֵּלִים הָאֹהֶל° אֲשֶׁר עָשָׂה חִירָם
Hiram he-made that the-these the-objects all-of and the-sprinkling-bowls and

לַמֶּלֶךְ שְׁלֹמֹה בֵּית יְהוָה נְחֹשֶׁת מְמֹרָט׃ בְּכִכַּר
in-plain-of (46) being-burnished bronze Yahweh temple-of Solomon for-the-king

הַיַּרְדֵּן יְצָקָם הַמֶּלֶךְ בְּמַעֲבֵה הָאֲדָמָה בֵּין סֻכּוֹת
Succoth between the-ground in-clay-of the-king he-cast-them the-Jordan

וּבֵין צָרְתָן׃ וַיַּנַּח שְׁלֹמֹה אֶת־ כָּל־ הַכֵּלִים
the-things all-of *** Solomon and-he-left (47) Zarethan and-between

מֵרֹב מְאֹד מְאֹד לֹא נֶחְקַר מִשְׁקַל הַנְּחֹשֶׁת׃
the-bronze weight-of he-was-determined not many many for-number

וַיַּעַשׂ שְׁלֹמֹה אֵת כָּל־ הַכֵּלִים אֲשֶׁר בֵּית יְהוָה
Yahweh temple-of that the-furnishings all-of *** Solomon and-he-made (48)

אֵת מִזְבַּח הַזָּהָב וְאֶת־ הַשֻּׁלְחָן אֲשֶׁר עָלָיו לֶחֶם הַפָּנִים
the-Presences bread-of on-him that the-table and the-gold altar-of ***

זָהָב׃ וְאֶת־ הַמְּנֹרוֹת חָמֵשׁ מִיָּמִין וְחָמֵשׁ מִשְּׂמֹאול לִפְנֵי
in-front-of on-left and-five on-right five the-lampstands and (49) gold

הַדְּבִיר זָהָב סָגוּר וְהַפֶּרַח וְהַנֵּרֹת וְהַמֶּלְקַחַיִם*
and-the-tongs and-the-lamps and-the-floral-work pure gold the-inner-sanctuary

the southeast corner of the temple. [40]He also made the basins and shovels and sprinkling bowls.

So Huram finished all the work he had undertaken for King Solomon in the temple of the LORD:

[41]the two pillars;
the two bowl-shaped capitals on top of the pillars;
the two sets of network decorating the two bowl-shaped capitals on top of the pillars;
[42]the four hundred pomegranates for the two sets of network (two rows of pomegranates for each network, decorating the bowl-shaped capitals on top of the pillars);
[43]the ten stands with their ten basins;
[44]the Sea and the twelve bulls under it;
[45]the pots, shovels and sprinkling bowls.

All these objects that Huram made for King Solomon for the temple of the LORD were of burnished bronze. [46]The king had them cast in clay molds in the plain of the Jordan between Succoth and Zarethan. [47]Solomon left all these things unweighed, because there were so many; the weight of the bronze was not determined.

[48]Solomon also made all the furnishings that were in the LORD's temple:

the golden altar;
the golden table on which was the bread of the Presence;
[49]the lampstands of pure gold (five on the right and five on the left, in front of the inner sanctuary);
the gold floral work and lamps and tongs;

*49 Most mss have *qamets* under the *qoph* (קָ).

°45 ק האלה

זָהָב׃ (50) וְהַסִּפּוֹת וְהַמְזַמְּרוֹת וְהַמִּזְרָקוֹת
and-the-sprinkling-bowls and-the-wick-trimmers and-the-dishes (50) gold

וְהַכַּפּוֹת וְהַמַּחְתּוֹת זָהָב סָגוּר וְהַפֹּתוֹת לְדַלְתוֹת
for-doors-of and-the-sockets pure gold and-the-censers and-the-ladles

הַבַּיִת הַפְּנִימִי לְקֹדֶשׁ הַקֳּדָשִׁים לְדַלְתֵי הַבַּיִת
the-temple for-doors-of the-Holy-Places for-Holy-of the-innermost the-room

לַהֵיכָל זָהָב׃ (51) וַתִּשְׁלַם כָּל־ הַמְּלָאכָה אֲשֶׁר
that the-work all-of when-she-was-finished (51) gold for-the-main-hall

עָשָׂה הַמֶּלֶךְ שְׁלֹמֹה בֵּית יְהוָה וַיָּבֵא שְׁלֹמֹה אֶת־
*** Solomon then-he-brought-in Yahweh temple-of Solomon the-king he-did

קָדְשֵׁי ׀ דָּוִד אָבִיו אֶת־ הַכֶּסֶף וְאֶת־ הַזָּהָב וְאֶת־
and the-gold and the-silver *** father-of-him David dedicated-things-of

הַכֵּלִים נָתַן בְּאֹצְרוֹת בֵּית יְהוָה׃ (8:1) אָז
then (8:1) Yahweh temple-of in-treasuries-of he-placed the-furnishings

יַקְהֵל שְׁלֹמֹה אֶת־ זִקְנֵי יִשְׂרָאֵל אֶת־ כָּל־ רָאשֵׁי הַמַּטּוֹת
the-tribes heads-of all-of *** Israel elders-of *** Solomon he-summoned

נְשִׂיאֵי הָאָבוֹת לִבְנֵי יִשְׂרָאֵל אֶל־ הַמֶּלֶךְ שְׁלֹמֹה יְרוּשָׁלָם
Jerusalem Solomon the-king to Israel of-sons-of the-families chiefs-of

לְהַעֲלוֹת אֶת־ אֲרוֹן בְּרִית־ יְהוָה מֵעִיר דָּוִד הִיא צִיּוֹן׃
Zion this David from-City-of Yahweh covenant-of ark-of *** to-bring-up

(2) וַיִּקָּהֲלוּ אֶל־ הַמֶּלֶךְ שְׁלֹמֹה כָּל־ אִישׁ יִשְׂרָאֵל בְּיֶרַח
in-month-of Israel man-of all-of Solomon the-king to and-they-came-together (2)

הָאֵתָנִים בֶּחָג הוּא הַחֹדֶשׁ הַשְּׁבִיעִי׃ (3) וַיָּבֹאוּ
when-they-arrived (3) the-seventh the-month this in-the-festival the-Ethanim

כֹּל זִקְנֵי יִשְׂרָאֵל וַיִּשְׂאוּ הַכֹּהֲנִים אֶת־ הָאָרוֹן׃
the-ark *** the-priests then-they-took-up Israel elders-of all-of

(4) וַיַּעֲלוּ אֶת־ אֲרוֹן יְהוָה וְאֶת־ אֹהֶל מוֹעֵד וְאֶת־ כָּל־
all-of and Meeting Tent-of and Yahweh ark-of *** and-they-brought-up (4)

כְּלֵי הַקֹּדֶשׁ אֲשֶׁר בָּאֹהֶל וַיַּעֲלוּ אֹתָם
them and-they-carried-up in-the-Tent that the-sacred furnishings-of

הַכֹּהֲנִים וְהַלְוִיִּם׃ (5) וְהַמֶּלֶךְ שְׁלֹמֹה וְכָל־ עֲדַת
assembly-of and-entire-of Solomon and-the-king (5) the-Levites the-priests

יִשְׂרָאֵל הַנּוֹעָדִים עָלָיו אִתּוֹ לִפְנֵי הָאָרוֹן מְזַבְּחִים
ones-sacrificing the-ark before with-him about-him the-ones-gathering Israel

צֹאן וּבָקָר אֲשֶׁר לֹא־ יִסָּפְרוּ וְלֹא יִמָּנוּ
they-could-be-counted and-not they-could-be-recorded not that and-cattle sheep

מֵרֹב׃ (6) וַיָּבִאוּ הַכֹּהֲנִים אֶת־ אֲרוֹן בְּרִית־ יְהוָה
Yahweh covenant-of ark-of *** the-priests then-they-brought (6) for-number

50 the pure gold dishes, wick trimmers, sprinkling bowls, ladles and censers;
and the gold sockets for the doors of the innermost room, the Most Holy Place, and also for the doors of the main hall of the temple.

51 When all the work King Solomon had done for the temple of the LORD was finished, he brought in the things his father David had dedicated—the silver and gold and the furnishings—and he placed them in the treasuries of the LORD's temple.

The Ark Brought to the Temple

8 Then King Solomon summoned into his presence at Jerusalem the elders of Israel, all the heads of the tribes and the chiefs of the Israelite families, to bring up the ark of the LORD's covenant from Zion, the City of David.
2 All the men of Israel came together to King Solomon at the time of the festival in the month of Ethanim, the seventh month.
3 When all the elders of Israel had arrived, the priests took up the ark,
4 and they brought up the ark of the LORD and the Tent of Meeting and all the sacred furnishings in it. The priests and Levites carried them up,
5 and King Solomon and, with him, the entire assembly of Israel that had gathered about him were before the ark, sacrificing so many sheep and cattle that they could not be recorded or counted.
6 The priests then brought the ark of the LORD's covenant

אֶל־מְקוֹמוֹ אֶל־דְּבִיר הַבַּיִת אֶל־קֹדֶשׁ הַקֳּדָשִׁים
the-Holy-Places Holy-of to the-temple inner-sanctuary-of in place-of-him to

אֶל־תַּחַת כַּנְפֵי הַכְּרוּבִים׃ כִּי הַכְּרוּבִים פֹּרְשִׂים כְּנָפַיִם
wings ones-spreading the-cherubim for (7) the-cherubim wings-of beneath at

אֶל־מְקוֹם הָאָרוֹן וַיָּסֹכּוּ הַכְּרֻבִים עַל־הָאָרוֹן וְעַל־
and-over the-ark over the-cherubim and-they-overshadow the-ark place-of over

בַּדָּיו מִלְמָעְלָה׃ וַיַּאֲרִכוּ הַבַּדִּים וַיֵּרָאוּ
so-they-could-be-seen the-poles and-they-were-long (8) at-above poles-of-him

רָאשֵׁי הַבַּדִּים מִן־הַקֹּדֶשׁ עַל־פְּנֵי הַדְּבִיר וְלֹא
but-not the-inner-sanctuary front-of at the-Holy-Place from the-poles ends-of

יֵרָאוּ הַחוּצָה וַיִּהְיוּ שָׁם עַד הַיּוֹם הַזֶּה׃
the-this the-day to there and-they-are from-the-outside they-could-be-seen

אֵין בָּאָרוֹן רַק שְׁנֵי לֻחוֹת הָאֲבָנִים אֲשֶׁר הִנִּחַ
he-placed that the-stones tablets-of two-of except in-the-ark nothing (9)

שָׁם מֹשֶׁה בְּחֹרֵב אֲשֶׁר כָּרַת יְהוָה עִם־בְּנֵי יִשְׂרָאֵל
Israel sons-of with Yahweh he-made-covenant where at-Horeb Moses there

בְּצֵאתָם מֵאֶרֶץ מִצְרָיִם׃ וַיְהִי בְּצֵאת
when-to-withdraw and-he-was (10) Egypt from-land-of after-to-come-out-them

הַכֹּהֲנִים מִן־הַקֹּדֶשׁ וְהֶעָנָן מָלֵא אֶת־בֵּית
temple-of *** he-filled then-the-cloud the-Holy-Place from the-priests

יְהוָה׃ וְלֹא־יָכְלוּ הַכֹּהֲנִים לַעֲמֹד לְשָׁרֵת מִפְּנֵי
because-of to-serve to-stand the-priests they-could and-not (11) Yahweh

הֶעָנָן כִּי־מָלֵא כְבוֹד־יְהוָה אֶת־בֵּית יְהוָה׃ אָז
then (12) Yahweh temple-of *** Yahweh glory-of he-filled for the-cloud

אָמַר שְׁלֹמֹה יְהוָה אָמַר לִשְׁכֹּן בָּעֲרָפֶל׃ בָּנֹה
to-build (13) in-the-dark-cloud to-dwell he-said Yahweh Solomon he-said

בָנִיתִי בֵּית זְבֻל לָךְ מָכוֹן לְשִׁבְתְּךָ עוֹלָמִים׃
forevers to-dwell-you place for-you magnificence temple-of I-built

וַיַּסֵּב הַמֶּלֶךְ אֶת־פָּנָיו וַיְבָרֶךְ אֵת כָּל־
whole-of *** and-he-blessed faces-of-him *** the-king and-he-turned (14)

קְהַל יִשְׂרָאֵל וְכָל־קְהַל יִשְׂרָאֵל עֹמֵד׃ וַיֹּאמֶר
then-he-said (15) standing Israel assembly-of while-all-of Israel assembly-of

בָּרוּךְ יְהוָה אֱלֹהֵי יִשְׂרָאֵל אֲשֶׁר דִּבֶּר בְּפִיו אֵת
*** with-mouth-of-him he-promised who Israel God-of Yahweh being-praised

דָּוִד אָבִי וּבְיָדוֹ מִלֵּא לֵאמֹר׃ מִן־הַיּוֹם
the-day since (16) to-say he-fulfilled and-with-hand-of-him father-of-me David

אֲשֶׁר הוֹצֵאתִי אֶת־עַמִּי אֶת־יִשְׂרָאֵל מִמִּצְרַיִם לֹא־בָחַרְתִּי בְּעִיר
to-city I-chose not from-Egypt Israel *** people-of-me *** I-brought that

to its place in the inner sanctuary of the temple, the Most
Holy Place, and put it beneath
the wings of the cherubim.
7 The cherubim spread their
wings over the place of the ark
and overshadowed the ark
and its carrying poles. 8 These
poles were so long that their
ends could be seen from the
Holy Place in front of the inner sanctuary, but not from
outside the Holy Place; and
they are still there today.
9 There was nothing in the ark
except the two stone tablets
that Moses had placed in it at
Horeb, where the LORD made a
covenant with the Israelites
after they came out of Egypt.
10 When the priests with-
drew from the Holy Place, the
cloud filled the temple of the
LORD. 11 And the priests could
not perform their service because of the cloud, for the glory of the LORD filled his temple.
12 Then Solomon said, "The
LORD has said that he would
dwell in a dark cloud; 13 I have
indeed built a magnificent
temple for you, a place for you
to dwell forever."
14 While the whole assembly
of Israel was standing there,
the king turned around and
blessed them. 15 Then he said:

"Praise be to the LORD,
the God of Israel, who with
his own hand has fulfilled
what he promised with his
own mouth to my father
David. For he said, 16 'Since
the day I brought my
people Israel out of Egypt, I
have not chosen a city in

מִכֹּל שִׁבְטֵי יִשְׂרָאֵל לִבְנוֹת בַּיִת לִהְיוֹת שְׁמִי שָׁם וָאֶבְחַר
but-I-chose there Name-of-me to-be temple to-build Israel tribes-of in-any-of

בְּדָוִד לִהְיוֹת עַל־ עַמִּי יִשְׂרָאֵל׃ וַיְהִי עִם־ לְבַב דָּוִד
David heart-of in and-he-was (17) Israel people-of-me over to-be to-David

אָבִי לִבְנוֹת בַּיִת לְשֵׁם יְהוָה אֱלֹהֵי יִשְׂרָאֵל׃ וַיֹּאמֶר
but-he-said (18) Israel God-of Yahweh for-Name-of temple to-build father-of-me

יְהוָה אֶל־ דָּוִד אָבִי יַעַן אֲשֶׁר הָיָה עִם־ לְבָבְךָ לִבְנוֹת
to-build heart-of-you in he-was that because father-of-me David to Yahweh

בַּיִת לִשְׁמִי הֱטִיבֹתָ כִּי הָיָה עִם־ לְבָבֶךָ׃ רַק
nevertheless (19) heart-of-you in he-was for you-did-well for-Name-of-me temple

אַתָּה לֹא תִבְנֶה הַבָּיִת כִּי אִם־ בִּנְךָ הַיֹּצֵא
the-one-coming son-of-you rather but the-temple you-will-build not you

מֵחֲלָצֶיךָ הוּא־ יִבְנֶה הַבַּיִת לִשְׁמִי׃ וַיָּקֶם
and-he-kept (20) for-Name-of-me the-temple he-will-build he from-loins-of-you

יְהוָה אֶת־ דְּבָרוֹ אֲשֶׁר דִּבֵּר וָאָקֻם תַּחַת דָּוִד
David after and-I-succeeded he-made that promise-of-him *** Yahweh

אָבִי וָאֵשֵׁב עַל־ כִּסֵּא יִשְׂרָאֵל כַּאֲשֶׁר דִּבֶּר יְהוָה
Yahweh he-promised just-as Israel throne-of on and-I-sit father-of-me

וָאֶבְנֶה הַבַּיִת לְשֵׁם יְהוָה אֱלֹהֵי יִשְׂרָאֵל׃ וָאָשִׂם
and-I-provided (21) Israel God-of Yahweh for-Name-of the-temple and-I-built

שָׁם מָקוֹם לָאָרוֹן אֲשֶׁר־ שָׁם בְּרִית יְהוָה אֲשֶׁר כָּרַת עִם־
with he-made that Yahweh covenant-of there where for-the-ark place there

אֲבֹתֵינוּ בְּהוֹצִיאוֹ אֹתָם מֵאֶרֶץ מִצְרָיִם׃ וַיַּעֲמֹד
then-he-stood (22) Egypt from-land-of them when-to-bring-out-him fathers-of-us

שְׁלֹמֹה לִפְנֵי מִזְבַּח יְהוָה נֶגֶד כָּל־ קְהַל יִשְׂרָאֵל
Israel assembly-of whole-of in-front-of Yahweh altar-of before Solomon

וַיִּפְרֹשׂ כַּפָּיו הַשָּׁמָיִם׃ וַיֹּאמַר יְהוָה אֱלֹהֵי
God-of Yahweh and-he-said (23) the-heavens hands-of-him and-he-spread-out

יִשְׂרָאֵל אֵין־כָּמוֹךָ אֱלֹהִים בַּשָּׁמַיִם מִמַּעַל וְעַל־ הָאָרֶץ מִתָּחַת
at-below the-earth or-on at-above in-the-heavens God like-you not Israel

שֹׁמֵר הַבְּרִית וְהַחֶסֶד לַעֲבָדֶיךָ הַהֹלְכִים
the-ones-walking with-servants-of-you and-the-love the-covenant keeping

לְפָנֶיךָ בְּכָל־ לִבָּם׃ אֲשֶׁר שָׁמַרְתָּ לְעַבְדְּךָ
to-servant-of-you you-kept who (24) heart-of-them with-whole-of before-you

דָּוִד אָבִי אֵת אֲשֶׁר־ דִּבַּרְתָּ לוֹ וַתְּדַבֵּר
and-you-promised to-him you-promised what *** father-of-me David

בְּפִיךָ וּבְיָדְךָ מִלֵּאתָ כַּיּוֹם הַזֶּה׃
the-this as-the-day you-fulfilled and-with-hand-of-you with-mouth-of-you

any tribe of Israel to have a
temple built for my Name
to be there, but I have chosen David to rule my people
Israel.'
17 "My father David had it
in his heart to build a temple for the Name of the
LORD, the God of Israel.
18 But the LORD said to my
father David, 'Because it
was in your heart to build a
temple for my Name, you
did well to have this in
your heart. 19 Nevertheless,
you are not the one to build
the temple, but your son,
who is your own flesh and
blood—he is the one who
will build the temple for my
Name.'
20 "The LORD has kept the
promise he made: I have
succeeded David my father
and now I sit on the throne
of Israel, just as the LORD
promised, and I have built
the temple for the Name of
the LORD, the God of Israel.
21 I have provided a place
there for the ark, in which
is the covenant of the LORD
that he made with our fa-
thers when he brought
them out of Egypt."

Solomon's Prayer of Dedication

22 Then Solomon stood be-
fore the altar of the LORD in
front of the whole assembly of
Israel, spread out his hands
toward heaven 23 and said:

"O LORD, God of Israel,
there is no God like you in
heaven above or on earth
below—you who keep your
covenant of love with your
servants who continue
wholeheartedly in your
way. 24 You have kept your
promise to your servant
David my father; with your
mouth you have promised
and with your hand you
have fulfilled it—as it is today.

וְעַתָּ֞ה יְהוָ֣ה ׀ אֱלֹהֵ֣י יִשְׂרָאֵ֗ל שְׁמֹר֩ לְעַבְדְּךָ֨ דָוִ֜ד אָבִ֗י
father-of-me David for-servant-of-you keep! Israel God-of Yahweh and-now (25)

אֵת֩ אֲשֶׁ֨ר דִּבַּ֤רְתָּ לּוֹ֙ לֵאמֹ֔ר לֹֽא־ יִכָּרֵ֨ת לְךָ֥ אִ֙ישׁ
man of-you he-shall-be-cut-off not to-say to-him you-promised what ***

מִלְּפָנַ֔י יֹשֵׁ֖ב עַל־ כִּסֵּ֣א יִשְׂרָאֵ֑ל רַ֠ק אִם־ יִשְׁמְר֨וּ
they-are-careful if only Israel throne-of on sitting from-before-me

בָ֜נֶיךָ אֶת־ דַּרְכָּ֗ם לָלֶ֙כֶת֙ לְפָנַ֔י כַּאֲשֶׁ֥ר הָלַ֖כְתָּ לְפָנָֽי׃
before-me you-walked just-as before-me to-walk way-of-them *** sons-of-you

וְעַתָּ֕ה אֱלֹהֵ֖י יִשְׂרָאֵ֑ל יֵאָ֤מֶן נָא֙ דְּבָ֣רְיךָ֔ אֲשֶׁ֣ר
that word-of-you now! let-him-come-true Israel God-of and-now (26)

דִּבַּ֔רְתָּ לְעַבְדְּךָ֖ דָּוִ֥ד אָבִֽי׃ כִּ֚י הַֽאֻמְנָ֔ם
really? but (27) father-of-me David to-servant-of-you you-promised

יֵשֵׁ֥ב אֱלֹהִ֖ים עַל־הָאָ֑רֶץ הִ֠נֵּה הַשָּׁמַ֜יִם וּשְׁמֵ֤י הַשָּׁמַ֙יִם֙
the-heavens and-heavens-of the-heavens see! the-earth on God will-he-dwell

לֹ֣א יְכַלְכְּל֔וּךָ אַ֕ף כִּֽי־ הַבַּ֥יִת הַזֶּ֖ה אֲשֶׁ֥ר
that the-this the-temple indeed how-much-less they-can-contain-you not

בָּנִֽיתִי׃ וּפָנִ֜יתָ אֶל־ תְּפִלַּ֧ת עַבְדְּךָ֛ וְאֶל־
and-to servant-of-you prayer-of to yet-you-give-attention (28) I-built

תְּחִנָּת֖וֹ יְהוָ֣ה אֱלֹהָ֑י לִשְׁמֹ֤עַ אֶל־ הָֽרִנָּה֙ וְאֶל־ הַתְּפִלָּ֔ה
the-prayer and-to the-cry to to-hear God-of-me Yahweh mercy-plea-of-him

אֲשֶׁ֧ר עַבְדְּךָ֛ מִתְפַּלֵּ֥ל לְפָנֶ֖יךָ הַיּֽוֹם׃ לִהְי֨וֹת
to-be (29) the-day in-presences-of-you praying servant-of-you that

עֵינֶ֜ךָ פְתֻחֹ֗ת אֶל־ הַבַּ֤יִת הַזֶּה֙ לַ֣יְלָה וָי֔וֹם אֶל־
toward and-day night the-this the-temple toward ones-being-open eye-of-you

הַמָּק֔וֹם אֲשֶׁ֣ר אָמַ֔רְתָּ יִהְיֶ֥ה שְׁמִ֖י שָׁ֑ם לִשְׁמֹ֙עַ֙ אֶל־ הַתְּפִלָּ֔ה
the-prayer to to-hear there Name-of-me he-shall-be you-said which the-place

אֲשֶׁ֚ר יִתְפַּלֵּ֣ל עַבְדְּךָ֔ אֶל־ הַמָּק֖וֹם הַזֶּֽה׃ וְשָׁמַעְתָּ֞ אֶל־
to and-you-hear (30) the-this the-place toward servant-of-you he-prays that

תְּחִנַּ֤ת עַבְדְּךָ֙ וְעַמְּךָ֣ יִשְׂרָאֵ֔ל אֲשֶׁ֥ר יִֽתְפַּלְל֖וּ אֶל־
toward they-pray when Israel and-people-of-you servant-of-you prayer-of

הַמָּק֣וֹם הַזֶּ֑ה וְ֠אַתָּה תִּשְׁמַ֞ע אֶל־ מְק֤וֹם שִׁבְתְּךָ֙ אֶל־
from to-dwell-you place-of from you-hear and-you the-this the-place

הַשָּׁמַ֔יִם וְשָׁמַעְתָּ֖ וְסָלָֽחְתָּ׃ אֵ֣ת אֲשֶׁ֤ר יֶחֱטָא אִישׁ֙
man he-wrongs when *** (31) then-you-forgive when-you-hear the-heavens

לְרֵעֵ֔הוּ וְנָֽשָׁא־ ב֥וֹ אָלָ֖ה לְהַאֲלֹת֑וֹ וּבָ֗א
and-he-comes to-take-oath-him oath on-him and-he-takes to-neighbor-of-him

אָלָ֔ה לִפְנֵ֥י מִֽזְבַּחֲךָ֖ בַּבַּ֥יִת הַזֶּֽה׃ וְאַתָּ֣ה ׀
then-you (32) the-this in-the-temple altar-of-you before he-swears-oath

[25]"Now LORD, God of Is-
rael, keep for your servant
David my father the prom-
ises you made to him when
you said, 'You shall never
fail to have a man to sit before me on the throne of Israel, if only your sons are
careful in all they do to
walk before me as you have
done.' [26]And now, O God of
Israel, let your word that
you promised your servant
David my father come true.
[27]"But will God really
dwell on earth? The heav-
ens, even the highest heav-
en, cannot contain you.
How much less this temple
I have built! [28]Yet give attention to your servant's
prayer and his plea for
mercy, O LORD my God.
Hear the cry and the prayer
that your servant is praying
in your presence this day.
[29]May your eyes be open
toward this temple night
and day, this place of
which you said, 'My Name
shall be there,' so that you
will hear the prayer your
servant prays toward this
place. [30]Hear the supplication of your servant and of
your people Israel when
they pray toward this place.
Hear from heaven, your
dwelling place, and when
you hear, forgive.
[31]"When a man wrongs
his neighbor and is re-
quired to take an oath and
he comes and swears the
oath before your altar in
this temple, [32]then hear

°26 ק דברך

תִּשְׁמַע הַשָּׁמַיִם וְעָשִׂיתָ וְשָׁפַטְתָּ אֶת־ עֲבָדֶיךָ לְהַרְשִׁיעַ
to-condemn servants-of-you *** and-you-judge and-you-act the-heavens you-hear

רָשָׁע לָתֵת דַּרְכּוֹ בְּרֹאשׁוֹ וּלְהַצְדִּיק צַדִּיק
innocent and-to-declare-innocent on-head-of-him way-of-him to-bring guilty

לָתֶת לוֹ כְּצִדְקָתוֹ׃ (33) בְּהִנָּגֵף עַמְּךָ
people-of-you when-to-be-defeated (33) as-innocence-of-him for-him to-establish

יִשְׂרָאֵל לִפְנֵי אוֹיֵב אֲשֶׁר יֶחֶטְאוּ־ לָךְ וְשָׁבוּ
when-they-turn-back against-you they-sinned because being-enemy before Israel

אֵלֶיךָ וְהוֹדוּ אֶת־ שְׁמֶךָ וְהִתְפַּלְלוּ וְהִתְחַנְּנוּ
and-they-make-supplication and-they-pray name-of-you *** and-they-confess to-you

אֵלֶיךָ בַּבַּיִת הַזֶּה׃ (34) וְאַתָּה תִּשְׁמַע הַשָּׁמַיִם
the-heavens you-hear then-you (34) the-this in-the-temple to-you

וְסָלַחְתָּ לְחַטַּאת עַמְּךָ יִשְׂרָאֵל וַהֲשֵׁבֹתָם אֶל־
to and-you-bring-back-them Israel people-of-you to-sin-of and-you-forgive

הָאֲדָמָה אֲשֶׁר נָתַתָּ לַאֲבוֹתָם׃ (35) בְּהֵעָצֵר שָׁמַיִם
heavens when-to-be-shut-up (35) to-fathers-of-them you-gave that the-land

וְלֹא־ יִהְיֶה מָטָר כִּי יֶחֶטְאוּ־ לָךְ וְהִתְפַּלְלוּ אֶל־
toward when-they-pray against-you they-sinned because rain he-is and-not

הַמָּקוֹם הַזֶּה וְהוֹדוּ אֶת־ שְׁמֶךָ וּמֵחַטָּאתָם
and-from-sin-of-them name-of-you *** and-they-confess the-this the-place

יְשׁוּבוּן כִּי תַעֲנֵם׃ (36) וְאַתָּה ׀ תִּשְׁמַע הַשָּׁמַיִם
the-heavens you-hear then-you (36) you-afflicted-them because they-turn

וְסָלַחְתָּ לְחַטַּאת עֲבָדֶיךָ וְעַמְּךָ יִשְׂרָאֵל כִּי
indeed Israel and-people-of-you servants-of-you to-sin-of and-you-forgive

תוֹרֵם אֶת־ הַדֶּרֶךְ הַטּוֹבָה אֲשֶׁר יֵלְכוּ־ בָהּ
in-her they-should-walk that the-right the-way *** you-teach-them

וְנָתַתָּה מָטָר עַל־ אַרְצְךָ אֲשֶׁר־ נָתַתָּה לְעַמְּךָ
to-people-of-you you-gave that land-of-you on rain and-you-send

לְנַחֲלָה׃ (37) רָעָב כִּי־ יִהְיֶה בָאָרֶץ דֶּבֶר כִּי־ יִהְיֶה
he-comes when plague on-the-land he-comes when famine (37) for-inheritance

שִׁדָּפוֹן יֵרָקוֹן אַרְבֶּה חָסִיל כִּי יִהְיֶה כִּי יָצַר־ לוֹ
against-him he-besieges when he-comes when grasshopper locust mildew blight

אֹיְבוֹ בְּאֶרֶץ שְׁעָרָיו כָּל־ נֶגַע כָּל־ מַחֲלָה׃
disease any-of disaster any-of gates-of-him in-land-of being-enemy-of-him

(38) כָּל־ תְּפִלָּה כָל־ תְּחִנָּה אֲשֶׁר תִהְיֶה לְכָל־ הָאָדָם
the-person from-any-of she-comes that plea any-of prayer any-of (38)

לְכֹל עַמְּךָ יִשְׂרָאֵל אֲשֶׁר יֵדְעוּן אִישׁ נֶגַע
affliction-of each they-are-aware who Israel people-of-you from-any-of

from heaven and act. Judge
between your servants,
condemning the guilty and
bringing down on his own
head what he has done. Declare the innocent not
guilty, and so establish his
innocence.
33"When your people Is-
rael have been defeated by
an enemy because they
have sinned against you,
and when they turn back to
you and confess your
name, praying and making
supplication to you in this
temple, 34then hear from
heaven and forgive the sin
of your people Israel and
bring them back to the land
you gave to their fathers.
35"When the heavens are
shut up and there is no rain
because your people have
sinned against you, and
when they pray toward this
place and confess your
name and turn from their
sin because you have
afflicted them, 36then hear
from heaven and forgive
the sin of your servants,
your people Israel. Teach
them the right way to live,
and send rain on the land
you gave your people for an
inheritance.
37"When famine or
plague comes to the land, or
blight or mildew, locusts or
grasshoppers, or when an
enemy besieges them in
any of their cities, whatever disaster or disease
may come, 38and when a
prayer or plea is made by
any of your people Israel—
each one aware of the

לְבָבוֹ וּפָרַשׂ כַּפָּיו אֶל־ הַבַּיִת הַזֶּה׃
heart-of-him and-he-spreads-out hands-of-him toward the-temple the-this

(39) וְאַתָּה תִּשְׁמַע הַשָּׁמַיִם מְכוֹן שִׁבְתֶּךָ וְסָלַחְתָּ
(39) then-you you-hear the-heavens place-of to-dwell-you and-you-forgive

וְעָשִׂיתָ וְנָתַתָּ לָאִישׁ כְּכָל־ דְּרָכָיו אֲשֶׁר תֵּדַע
and-you-act and-you-deal with-the-each as-all-of ways-of-him since you-know

אֶת־ לְבָבוֹ כִּֽי־ אַתָּה יָדַעְתָּ לְבַדְּךָ אֶת־ לְבַב כָּל־ בְּנֵי
*** heart-of-him for you you-know by-yourself *** heart-of all-of sons-of

הָאָדָם׃ (40) לְמַעַן יִרָאוּךָ כָּל־ הַיָּמִים אֲשֶׁר־ הֵם חַיִּים
the-man (40) so-that they-will-fear-you all-of the-days that they ones-alive

עַל־ פְּנֵי הָאֲדָמָה אֲשֶׁר נָתַתָּה לַאֲבֹתֵינוּ׃ (41) וְגַם אֶל־
on faces-of the-land that you-gave to-fathers-of-us (41) and-also for

הַנָּכְרִי אֲשֶׁר לֹא־ מֵעַמְּךָ יִשְׂרָאֵל הוּא וּבָא מֵאֶרֶץ
the-foreigner who not from-people-of-you Israel he but-he-came from-land

רְחוֹקָה לְמַעַן שְׁמֶךָ׃ (42) כִּי יִשְׁמְעוּן אֶת־ שִׁמְךָ
distant because-of name-of-you (42) for they-will-hear *** name-of-you

הַגָּדוֹל וְאֶת־ יָדְךָ הַחֲזָקָה וּזְרֹעֲךָ הַנְּטוּיָה
the-great and hand-of-you the-mighty and-arm-of-you the-being-outstretched

וּבָא וְהִתְפַּלֵּל אֶל־ הַבַּיִת הַזֶּה׃ (43) אַתָּה תִּשְׁמַע
when-he-comes and-he-prays toward the-temple the-this (43) you you-hear

הַשָּׁמַיִם מְכוֹן שִׁבְתֶּךָ וְעָשִׂיתָ כְּכֹל אֲשֶׁר־ יִקְרָא אֵלֶיךָ
the-heavens place-of to-dwell-you and-you-do as-all that he-asks of-you

הַנָּכְרִי לְמַעַן יֵדְעוּן כָּל־ עַמֵּי הָאָרֶץ אֶת־
the-foreigner so-that they-may-know all-of peoples-of the-earth ***

שְׁמֶךָ לְיִרְאָה אֹתְךָ כְּעַמְּךָ יִשְׂרָאֵל וְלָדַעַת כִּי־ שִׁמְךָ
name-of-you to-fear you as-people-of-you Israel and-to-know that Name-of-you

נִקְרָא עַל־ הַבַּיִת הַזֶּה אֲשֶׁר בָּנִיתִי׃ (44) כִּי־ יֵצֵא
he-is-called on the-house the-this that I-built (44) when he-goes-out

עַמְּךָ לַמִּלְחָמָה עַל־ אֹיְבוֹ בַּדֶּרֶךְ אֲשֶׁר
people-of-you to-the-war against being-enemy-of-him in-the-way that

תִּשְׁלָחֵם וְהִתְפַּלְלוּ אֶל־ יְהוָה דֶּרֶךְ הָעִיר אֲשֶׁר בָּחַרְתָּ
you-send-them and-they-pray to Yahweh direction-of the-city that you-chose

בָּהּ וְהַבַּיִת אֲשֶׁר־ בָּנִתִי לִשְׁמֶךָ׃ (45) וְשָׁמַעְתָּ
to-her and-the-temple that I-built for-Name-of-you (45) then-you-hear

הַשָּׁמַיִם אֶת־ תְּפִלָּתָם וְאֶת־ תְּחִנָּתָם וְעָשִׂיתָ מִשְׁפָּטָם׃
the-heavens *** prayer-of-them and plea-of-them and-you-uphold cause-of-them

(46) כִּי יֶחֶטְאוּ־ לָךְ כִּי אֵין אָדָם אֲשֶׁר לֹא־ יֶחֱטָא וְאָנַפְתָּ
(46) when they-sin against-you for no person who not he-sins and-you-are-angry

afflictions of his own heart,
and spreading out his
hands toward this temple—
39then hear from heaven,
your dwelling place. For-
give and act; deal with each
man according to all he
does, since you know his
heart (for you alone know
the hearts of all men), 40so
that they will fear you all
the time they live in the
land you gave our fathers.
41"As for the foreigner
who does not belong to
your people Israel but has
come from a distant land
because of your name—
42for men will hear of your
great name and your
mighty hand and your out-
stretched arm—when he
comes and prays toward
this temple, 43then hear
from heaven, your dwell-
ing place, and do whatever
the foreigner asks of you, so
that all the peoples of the
earth may know your name
and fear you, as do your
own people Israel, and may
know that this house I have
built bears your Name.
44"When your people go
to war against their ene-
mies, wherever you send
them, and when they pray
to the LORD toward the city
you have chosen and the
temple I have built for your
Name, 45then hear from
heaven their prayer and
their plea, and uphold their
cause.
46"When they sin against
you—for there is no one
who does not sin—and you
become angry with them

בָּם וּנְתַתָּם לִפְנֵי אוֹיֵב וְשָׁבוּם

and-they-take-captive-them being-enemy over-to and-you-give-them with-them

שֹׁבֵיהֶם אֶל־ אֶרֶץ הָאוֹיֵב רְחוֹקָה אוֹ קְרוֹבָה׃

near or far-away the-one-being-enemy land-of to ones-being-captive-of-them

וְהֵשִׁיבוּ אֶל־ לִבָּם בָּאָרֶץ אֲשֶׁר נִשְׁבּוּ־

they-are-held-captive where in-the-land heart-of-them in and-they-change (47)

שָׁם וְשָׁבוּ ׀ וְהִתְחַנְּנוּ אֵלֶיךָ בְּאֶרֶץ שֹׁבֵיהֶם

ones-conquering-them in-land-of with-you and-they-plead and-they-repent there

לֵאמֹר חָטָאנוּ וְהֶעֱוִינוּ רָשָׁעְנוּ׃ וְשָׁבוּ

and-they-turn (48) and-we-acted-wickedly and-we-did-wrong we-sinned to-say

אֵלֶיךָ בְּכָל־ לְבָבָם וּבְכָל־ נַפְשָׁם בְּאֶרֶץ

in-land-of soul-of-them and-with-all-of heart-of-them with-all-of to-you

אֹיְבֵיהֶם אֲשֶׁר־ שָׁבוּ אֹתָם וְהִתְפַּלְלוּ אֵלֶיךָ

to-you and-they-pray them they-captured who ones-being-enemies-of-them

דֶּרֶךְ אַרְצָם אֲשֶׁר נָתַתָּה לַאֲבוֹתָם הָעִיר אֲשֶׁר

that the-city to-fathers-of-them you-gave that land-of-them direction-of

בָּחַרְתָּ וְהַבַּיִת אֲשֶׁר־ בָּנִיתָ לִשְׁמֶךָ׃ וְשָׁמַעְתָּ

then-you-hear (49) for-Name-of-you I-built that and-the-temple you-chose

הַשָּׁמַיִם מְכוֹן שִׁבְתְּךָ אֶת־ תְּפִלָּתָם וְאֶת־ תְּחִנָּתָם

plea-of-them and prayer-of-them *** to-dwell-you place-of the-heavens

וְעָשִׂיתָ מִשְׁפָּטָם׃ וְסָלַחְתָּ לְעַמְּךָ אֲשֶׁר

who to-people-of-you and-you-forgive (50) cause-of-them and-you-uphold

חָטְאוּ־ לָךְ וּלְכָל־ פִּשְׁעֵיהֶם אֲשֶׁר פָּשְׁעוּ־

they-committed that offenses-of-them and-to-all-of against-you they-sinned

בָךְ וּנְתַתָּם לְרַחֲמִים לִפְנֵי שֹׁבֵיהֶם

ones-conquering-them before into-mercies and-you-give-them against-you

וְרִחֲמוּם׃ כִּי־ עַמְּךָ וְנַחֲלָתְךָ הֵם

they and-inheritance-of-you people-of-you for (51) so-they-show-mercy-to-them

אֲשֶׁר הוֹצֵאתָ מִמִּצְרַיִם מִתּוֹךְ כּוּר הַבַּרְזֶל׃ לִהְיוֹת

to-be (52) the-iron furnace-of from-midst-of from-Egypt you-brought whom

עֵינֶיךָ פְתֻחוֹת אֶל־ תְּחִנַּת עַבְדְּךָ וְאֶל־ תְּחִנַּת

plea-of and-to servant-of-you plea-of to ones-being-open eyes-of-you

עַמְּךָ יִשְׂרָאֵל לִשְׁמֹעַ אֲלֵיהֶם בְּכֹל קָרְאָם אֵלֶיךָ׃ כִּי־

for (53) to-you to-cry-them in-all to-them to-listen Israel people-of-you

אַתָּה הִבְדַּלְתָּם לְךָ לְנַחֲלָה מִכֹּל עַמֵּי

nations-of from-all-of as-inheritance for-you you-singled-out-them you

הָאָרֶץ כַּאֲשֶׁר דִּבַּרְתָּ בְּיַד ׀ מֹשֶׁה עַבְדְּךָ

servant-of-you Moses by-hand-of you-declared just-as the-earth

°48 ק בניתי

and give them over to the
enemy, who takes them
captive to his own land, far
away or near; [47]and if they
have a change of heart in
the land where they are
held captive, and repent
and plead with you in the
land of their conquerors
and say, 'We have sinned,
we have done wrong, we
have acted wickedly'; [48]and
if they turn back to you
with all their heart and soul
in the land of their enemies
who took them captive,
and pray to you toward the
land you gave their fathers,
toward the city you have
chosen and the temple I
have built for your Name;
[49]then from heaven, your
dwelling place, hear their
prayer and their plea, and
uphold their cause. [50]And
forgive your people, who
have sinned against you;
forgive all the offenses they
have committed against
you, and cause their con-
querors to show them
mercy; [51]for they are your
people and your inheri-
tance, whom you brought
out of Egypt, out of that
iron-smelting furnace.

[52]"May your eyes be open
to your servant's plea and
to the plea of your people
Israel, and may you listen
to them whenever they cry
out to you. [53]For you sin-
gled them out from all the
nations of the world to be
your own inheritance, just
as you declared through
your servant Moses when

בְּהוֹצִיאֲךָ אֶת־ אֲבֹתֵינוּ מִמִּצְרַיִם אֲדֹנָי יְהוִה׃ וַיְהִי ׀
and-he-was (54) Yahweh Lord from-Egypt fathers-of-us *** when-to-bring-you

כְּכַלּוֹת שְׁלֹמֹה לְהִתְפַּלֵּל אֶל־ יְהוָה אֵת כָּל־ הַתְּפִלָּה
the-prayer all-of *** Yahweh to to-pray Solomon when-to-finish

וְהַתְּחִנָּה הַזֹּאת קָם מִלִּפְנֵי מִזְבַּח יְהוָה
Yahweh altar-of from-before he-rose the-this and-the-supplication

מִכְּרֹעַ עַל־ בִּרְכָּיו וְכַפָּיו פְּרֻשׂוֹת
ones-being-spread-out and-hands-of-him knees-of-him on from-to-kneel

הַשָּׁמָיִם׃ וַיַּעֲמֹד וַיְבָרֶךְ אֵת כָּל־ קְהַל יִשְׂרָאֵל
Israel assembly-of whole-of *** and-he-blessed and-he-stood (55) the-heavens

קוֹל גָּדוֹל לֵאמֹר׃ בָּרוּךְ יְהוָה אֲשֶׁר נָתַן מְנוּחָה לְעַמּוֹ
to-people-of-him rest he-gave who Yahweh being-praised (56) to-say loud voice

יִשְׂרָאֵל כְּכֹל אֲשֶׁר דִּבֵּר לֹא־ נָפַל דָּבָר אֶחָד מִכֹּל דְּבָרוֹ
promise-of-him of-all-of one word he-failed not he-promised that as-all Israel

הַטּוֹב אֲשֶׁר דִּבֶּר בְּיַד מֹשֶׁה עַבְדּוֹ׃ יְהִי
may-he-be (57) servant-of-him Moses by-hand-of he-promised that the-good

יְהוָה אֱלֹהֵינוּ עִמָּנוּ כַּאֲשֶׁר הָיָה עִם־ אֲבֹתֵינוּ אַל־
not fathers-of-us with he-was just-as with-us God-of-us Yahweh

יַעַזְבֵנוּ וְאַל־ יִטְּשֵׁנוּ׃ לְהַטּוֹת לְבָבֵנוּ אֵלָיו
to-him heart-of-us to-turn (58) may-he-forsake-us and-not may-he-leave-us

לָלֶכֶת בְּכָל־ דְּרָכָיו וְלִשְׁמֹר מִצְוֺתָיו וְחֻקָּיו
and-decrees-of-him commands-of-him to-keep ways-of-him in-all-of to-walk

וּמִשְׁפָּטָיו אֲשֶׁר צִוָּה אֶת־ אֲבֹתֵינוּ׃ וְיִהְיוּ
and-may-they-be (59) fathers-of-us *** he-gave that and-regulations-of-him

דְבָרַי אֵלֶּה אֲשֶׁר הִתְחַנַּנְתִּי לִפְנֵי יְהוָה קְרֹבִים אֶל־ יְהוָה אֱלֹהֵינוּ
God-of-us Yahweh to ones-near Yahweh before I-prayed which these words-of-me

יוֹמָם וָלָיְלָה לַעֲשׂוֹת ׀ מִשְׁפַּט עַבְדּוֹ וּמִשְׁפַּט עַמּוֹ
people-of-him and-cause-of servant-of-him cause-of to-uphold and-night by-day

יִשְׂרָאֵל דְּבַר־ יוֹם בְּיוֹמוֹ׃ לְמַעַן דַּעַת כָּל־ עַמֵּי
peoples-of all-of to-know so-that (60) in-day-of-him day need-of Israel

הָאָרֶץ כִּי יְהוָה הוּא הָאֱלֹהִים אֵין עוֹד׃ וְהָיָה לְבַבְכֶם
heart-of-you but-he-must-be (61) other no the-God he Yahweh that the-earth

שָׁלֵם עִם יְהוָה אֱלֹהֵינוּ לָלֶכֶת בְּחֻקָּיו וְלִשְׁמֹר
and-to-obey by-decrees-of-him to-live God-of-us Yahweh to fully-committed

מִצְוֺתָיו כַּיּוֹם הַזֶּה׃ וְהַמֶּלֶךְ וְכָל־ יִשְׂרָאֵל
Israel and-all-of then-the-king (62) the-this as-the-day commands-of-him

עִמּוֹ זֹבְחִים זֶבַח לִפְנֵי יְהוָה׃ וַיִּזְבַּח שְׁלֹמֹה
Solomon and-he-offered (63) Yahweh before sacrifice ones-offering with-him

you, O Sovereign LORD,
brought our fathers out of
Egypt."

54When Solomon had
finished all these prayers and
supplications to the LORD, he
rose from before the altar of
the LORD, where he had been
kneeling with his hands
spread out toward heaven.
55He stood and blessed the
whole assembly of Israel in a
loud voice, saying:

56"Praise be to the LORD,
who has given rest to his
people Israel just as he
promised. Not one word
has failed of all the good
promises he gave through
his servant Moses. 57May
the LORD our God be with
us as he was with our fa-
thers; may he never leave
or forsake us. 58May he turn
our hearts to him, to walk
in all his ways and to keep
the commands, decrees and
regulations he gave our fathers. 59And may these
words of mine, which I
have prayed before the
LORD, be near to the LORD
our God day and night, that
he may uphold the cause of
his servant and the cause of
his people Israel according
to each day's need, 60so that
all the peoples of the earth
may know that the LORD is
God and that there is no
other. 61But your hearts
must be fully committed to
the LORD our God, to live by
his decrees and obey his
commands, as at this time."

The Dedication of the Temple

62Then the king and all Israel
with him offered sacrifices before the LORD. 63Solomon

אֶת זֶבַח הַשְּׁלָמִים אֲשֶׁר זָבַח לַיהוָה בָּקָר
cattle to-Yahweh he-offered which the-fellowship-offerings sacrifice-of ***

עֶשְׂרִים וּשְׁנַיִם אֶלֶף וְצֹאן מֵאָה וְעֶשְׂרִים אָלֶף וַיַּחְנְכוּ
so-they-dedicated thousand and-twenty hundred and-sheep thousand and-two twenty

אֶת־ בֵּית יְהוָה הַמֶּלֶךְ וְכָל־ בְּנֵי יִשְׂרָאֵל׃ בַּיּוֹם
on-the-day (64) Israel sons-of and-all-of the-king Yahweh temple-of ***

הַהוּא קִדַּשׁ הַמֶּלֶךְ אֶת־ תּוֹךְ הֶחָצֵר אֲשֶׁר לִפְנֵי
in-front-of that the-courtyard middle-of *** the-king he-consecrated the-same

בֵית־ יְהוָה כִּי־ עָשָׂה שָׁם אֶת־ הָעֹלָה וְאֶת־
and the-burnt-offering *** there he-offered for Yahweh temple-of

הַמִּנְחָה וְאֵת חֶלְבֵי הַשְּׁלָמִים כִּי־ מִזְבַּח
altar-of for the-fellowship-offerings fat-parts-of and the-grain-offering

הַנְּחֹשֶׁת אֲשֶׁר לִפְנֵי יְהוָה קָטֹן מֵהָכִיל אֶת־ הָעֹלָה וְאֶת־
and the-burnt-offering *** than-to-hold smaller Yahweh before that the-bronze

הַמִּנְחָה וְאֵת חֶלְבֵי הַשְּׁלָמִים׃ וַיַּעַשׂ
so-he-observed (65) the-fellowship-offerings fat-parts-of and the-grain-offering

שְׁלֹמֹה בָעֵת־ הַהִיא ׀ אֶת־ הֶחָג וְכָל־ יִשְׂרָאֵל עִמּוֹ
with-him Israel and-all-of the-festival *** the-that at-the-time Solomon

קָהָל גָּדוֹל מִלְּבוֹא חֲמָת ׀ עַד־ נַחַל מִצְרַיִם לִפְנֵי יְהוָה אֱלֹהֵינוּ
God-of-us Yahweh before Egypt Wadi-of to Hamath from-Lebo vast assembly

שִׁבְעַת יָמִים וְשִׁבְעַת יָמִים אַרְבָּעָה עָשָׂר יוֹם׃ בַּיּוֹם הַשְּׁמִינִי
the-eighth on-the-day (66) day ten four days and-seven-of days seven-of

שִׁלַּח אֶת־ הָעָם וַיְבָרְכוּ אֶת־ הַמֶּלֶךְ וַיֵּלְכוּ
then-they-went the-king *** and-they-blessed the-people *** he-sent-away

לְאָהֳלֵיהֶם שְׂמֵחִים וְטוֹבֵי לֵב עַל כָּל־ הַטּוֹבָה
the-good all-of for heart and-ones-glad-of ones-joyful to-homes-of-them

אֲשֶׁר עָשָׂה יְהוָה לְדָוִד עַבְדּוֹ וּלְיִשְׂרָאֵל עַמּוֹ׃
people-of-him and-for-Israel servant-of-him for-David Yahweh he-did that

וַיְהִי כְּכַלּוֹת שְׁלֹמֹה לִבְנוֹת אֶת־ בֵּית־ יְהוָה וְאֶת־
and Yahweh temple-of *** to-build Solomon when-to-finish and-he-was (9:1)

בֵּית הַמֶּלֶךְ וְאֵת כָּל־ חֵשֶׁק שְׁלֹמֹה אֲשֶׁר חָפֵץ לַעֲשׂוֹת׃
to-do he-desired that Solomon desire-of all-of and the-king palace-of

וַיֵּרָא יְהוָה אֶל־ שְׁלֹמֹה שֵׁנִית כַּאֲשֶׁר נִרְאָה
he-appeared just-as second-time Solomon to Yahweh then-he-appeared (2)

אֵלָיו בְּגִבְעוֹן׃ וַיֹּאמֶר יְהוָה אֵלָיו שָׁמַעְתִּי אֶת־ תְּפִלָּתְךָ
prayer-of-you *** I-heard to-him Yahweh and-he-said (3) at-Gibeon to-him

וְאֶת־ תְּחִנָּתְךָ אֲשֶׁר הִתְחַנַּנְתָּה לְפָנַי הִקְדַּשְׁתִּי אֶת־ הַבַּיִת
the-temple *** I-consecrated before-me you-prayed that plea-of-you and

offered a sacrifice of fellowship offerings[c] to the LORD: twenty-two thousand cattle and a hundred and twenty thousand sheep and goats. So the king and all the Israelites dedicated the temple of the LORD.

[64]On that same day the king consecrated the middle part of the courtyard in front of the temple of the LORD, and there he offered burnt offerings, grain offerings and the fat of the fellowship offerings, because the bronze altar before the LORD was too small to hold the burnt offerings, the grain offerings and the fat of the fellowship offerings.

[65]So Solomon observed the festival at that time, and all Israel with him—a vast assembly, people from Lebo[d] Hamath to the Wadi of Egypt. They celebrated it before the LORD our God for seven days and seven days more, fourteen days in all. [66]On the following day he sent the people away. They blessed the king and then went home, joyful and glad in heart for all the good the LORD had done for his servant David and his people Israel.

The LORD Appears to Solomon

9 When Solomon had finished building the temple of the LORD and the royal palace, and had achieved all he had desired to do, [2]the LORD appeared to him a second time, as he had appeared to him at Gibeon. [3]The LORD said to him:

"I have heard the prayer and plea you have made before me; I have consecrated this temple, which

[c]63 Traditionally *peace offerings;* also in verse 64
[d]65 Or *from the entrance to*

הַזֶּה אֲשֶׁר בָּנִתָה לָשׂוּם־ שְׁמִי שָׁם עַד־ עוֹלָם וְהָיוּ

and-they-will-be forever to there Name-of-me to-put you-built which the-this

עֵינַי וְלִבִּי שָׁם כָּל־ הַיָּמִים׃ וְאַתָּה אִם־ תֵּלֵךְ

you-walk if and-you (4) the-days all-of there and-heart-of-me eyes-of-me

לְפָנַי כַּאֲשֶׁר הָלַךְ דָּוִד אָבִיךָ בְּתָם־ לֵבָב

heart in-integrity-of father-of-you David he-walked just-as before-me

וּבְיֹשֶׁר לַעֲשׂוֹת כְּכֹל אֲשֶׁר צִוִּיתִיךָ חֻקַּי

decrees-of-me I-command-you that as-all to-do and-in-uprightness

וּמִשְׁפָּטַי תִּשְׁמֹר׃ וַהֲקִמֹתִי אֶת־ כִּסֵּא

throne-of *** then-I-will-establish (5) you-observe and-judgments-of-me

מַמְלַכְתְּךָ עַל־ יִשְׂרָאֵל לְעֹלָם כַּאֲשֶׁר דִּבַּרְתִּי עַל־ דָּוִד

David to I-promised just-as to-forever Israel over kingdom-of-you

אָבִיךָ לֵאמֹר לֹא־ יִכָּרֵת לְךָ אִישׁ מֵעַל כִּסֵּא

throne-of from-on man of-you he-shall-be-cut-off not to-say father-of-you

יִשְׂרָאֵל׃ אִם־ שׁוֹב תְּשֻׁבוּן אַתֶּם וּבְנֵיכֶם מֵאַחֲרַי וְלֹא

and-not from-after-me or-sons-of-you you you-turn to-turn if (6) Israel

תִשְׁמְרוּ מִצְוֺתַי חֻקֹּתַי אֲשֶׁר נָתַתִּי לִפְנֵיכֶם וַהֲלַכְתֶּם

and-you-go before-you I-gave that decrees-of-me commands-of-me you-observe

וַעֲבַדְתֶּם אֱלֹהִים אֲחֵרִים וְהִשְׁתַּחֲוִיתֶם לָהֶם׃ וְהִכְרַתִּי

then-I-will-cut-off (7) to-them and-you-worship other-ones gods and-you-serve

אֶת־יִשְׂרָאֵל מֵעַל פְּנֵי הָאֲדָמָה אֲשֶׁר נָתַתִּי לָהֶם וְאֶת־ הַבַּיִת

the-temple and to-them I-gave that the-land surfaces-of from-on Israel ***

אֲשֶׁר הִקְדַּשְׁתִּי לִשְׁמִי אֲשַׁלַּח מֵעַל פָּנָי

faces-of-me from-before I-will-reject for-Name-of-me I-consecrated that

וְהָיָה יִשְׂרָאֵל לְמָשָׁל וְלִשְׁנִינָה בְּכָל־

among-all-of and-as-object-of-ridicule as-byword Israel then-he-will-become

הָעַמִּים׃ וְהַבַּיִת הַזֶּה יִהְיֶה עֶלְיוֹן כָּל־ עֹבֵר

passing every-of imposing he-is the-this though-the-temple (8) the-peoples

עָלָיו יִשֹּׁם וְשָׁרָק וְאָמְרוּ עַל־ מֶה

why? for and-they-will-say and-he-will-scoff he-will-be-appalled by-him

עָשָׂה יְהוָה כָּכָה לָאָרֶץ הַזֹּאת וְלַבַּיִת הַזֶּה׃

the-this and-to-the-temple the-this to-the-land such Yahweh he-did

וְאָמְרוּ עַל אֲשֶׁר עָזְבוּ אֶת־ יְהוָה אֱלֹהֵיהֶם

God-of-them Yahweh *** they-forsook that because and-they-will-answer (9)

אֲשֶׁר הוֹצִיא אֶת־ אֲבֹתָם מֵאֶרֶץ מִצְרַיִם וַיַּחֲזִקוּ

and-they-embraced Egypt from-land-of fathers-of-them *** he-brought who

בֵּאלֹהִים אֲחֵרִים וַיִּשְׁתַּחֲוֻ לָהֶם וַיַּעַבְדֻם עַל־ כֵּן

this for and-they-served-them to-them and-they-worshiped other-ones on-gods

you have built, by putting
my Name there forever. My
eyes and my heart will always be there.
4 "As for you, if you walk
before me in integrity of
heart and uprightness, as
David your father did, and
do all I command and ob-
serve my decrees and laws,
5 I will establish your royal
throne over Israel forever,
as I promised David your
father when I said, 'You
shall never fail to have a
man on the throne of Israel.'
6 "But if you[e] or your sons
turn away from me and do
not observe the commands
and decrees I have given
you[e] and go off to serve
other gods and worship
them, 7 then I will cut off Israel from the land I have
given them and will reject
this temple I have conse-
crated for my Name. Israel
will then become a byword
and an object of ridicule
among all peoples. 8 And
though this temple is now
imposing, all who pass by
will be appalled and will
scoff and say, 'Why has the
LORD done such a thing to
this land and to this temple?' 9 People will answer,
'Because they have forsak-
en the LORD their God, who
brought their fathers out of
Egypt, and have embraced
other gods, worshiping and
serving them—that is why

[e]6 The Hebrew is plural.

°9 ק וישתחוו

הֵבִיא יְהוָה עֲלֵיהֶם אֵת כָּל־ הָרָעָה הַזֹּאת׃ וַיְהִי
and-he-was (10) the-this the-disaster all-of *** God-of-them Yahweh he-brought

מִקְצֵה עֶשְׂרִים שָׁנָה אֲשֶׁר־ בָּנָה שְׁלֹמֹה אֶת־ שְׁנֵי הַבָּתִּים אֶת־
*** the-buildings two-of *** Solomon he-built when year twenty at-end-of

בֵּית יְהוָה וְאֶת־ בֵּית הַמֶּלֶךְ׃ חִירָם מֶלֶךְ־ צֹר נִשָּׂא
he-supplied Tyre king-of Hiram (11) the-king palace-of and Yahweh temple-of

אֶת־ שְׁלֹמֹה בַּעֲצֵי אֲרָזִים וּבַעֲצֵי בְרוֹשִׁים וּבַזָּהָב
and-with-the-gold pines and-with-woods-of cedars with-woods-of Solomon ***

לְכָל־ חֶפְצוֹ אָז יִתֵּן הַמֶּלֶךְ שְׁלֹמֹה לְחִירָם עֶשְׂרִים עִיר
town twenty to-Hiram Solomon the-king he-gave then want-of-him as-all-of

בְּאֶרֶץ הַגָּלִיל׃ וַיֵּצֵא חִירָם מִצֹּר לִרְאוֹת אֶת־ הֶעָרִים
the-towns *** to-see from-Tyre Hiram but-he-went (12) the-Galilee in-land-of

אֲשֶׁר נָתַן־ לוֹ שְׁלֹמֹה וְלֹא יָשְׁרוּ בְּעֵינָיו׃
in-eyes-of-him they-were-pleasant but-not Solomon to-him he-gave that

וַיֹּאמֶר מָה הֶעָרִים הָאֵלֶּה אֲשֶׁר־ נָתַתָּה לִּי אָחִי
brother-of-me to-me you-gave that the-these the-towns what? and-he-asked (13)

וַיִּקְרָא לָהֶם אֶרֶץ כָּבוּל עַד הַיּוֹם הַזֶּה׃ וַיִּשְׁלַח
now-he-sent (14) the-this the-day to Cabul Land-of to-them and-he-called

חִירָם לַמֶּלֶךְ מֵאָה וְעֶשְׂרִים כִּכַּר זָהָב׃ וְזֶה דְבַר־
account-of now-this (15) gold talent-of and-twenty hundred to-the-king Hiram

הַמַּס אֲשֶׁר־ הֶעֱלָה ׀ הַמֶּלֶךְ שְׁלֹמֹה לִבְנוֹת אֶת־ בֵּית
temple-of *** to-build Solomon the-king he-conscripted that the-forced-labor

יְהוָה וְאֶת־ בֵּיתוֹ וְאֶת־ הַמִּלּוֹא וְאֵת חוֹמַת יְרוּשָׁלָם
Jerusalem wall-of and the-supporting-terrace and palace-of-him and Yahweh

וְאֶת־ חָצֹר וְאֶת־ מְגִדּוֹ וְאֶת־ גָּזֶר׃ פַּרְעֹה מֶלֶךְ־ מִצְרַיִם עָלָה
he-attacked Egypt king-of Pharaoh (16) Gezer and Megiddo and Hazor and

וַיִּלְכֹּד אֶת־ גֶּזֶר וַיִּשְׂרְפָהּ בָּאֵשׁ וְאֶת־ הַכְּנַעֲנִי
the-Canaanite and with-fire and-he-burned-her Gezer *** and-he-captured

הַיֹּשֵׁב בָּעִיר הָרָג וַיִּתְּנָהּ שִׁלֻּחִים
wedding-gifts then-he-gave-her he-killed in-the-city the-one-inhabiting

לְבִתּוֹ אֵשֶׁת שְׁלֹמֹה׃ וַיִּבֶן שְׁלֹמֹה אֶת־ גֶּזֶר וְאֶת־
and Gezer *** Solomon and-he-rebuilt (17) Solomon wife-of to-daughter-of-him

בֵּית חֹרֹן תַּחְתּוֹן׃ וְאֶת־ בַּעֲלָת וְאֶת־ תַּ°מֹר בַּמִּדְבָּר בָּאָרֶץ׃
within-the-land in-the-desert Tadmor and Baalath and (18) Lower Horon Beth

וְאֵת כָּל־ עָרֵי הַמִּסְכְּנוֹת אֲשֶׁר הָיוּ לִשְׁלֹמֹה וְאֵת עָרֵי
towns-of and to-Solomon they-were that the-stores cities-of all-of and (19)

הָרֶכֶב וְאֵת עָרֵי הַפָּרָשִׁים וְאֵת ׀ חֵשֶׁק שְׁלֹמֹה אֲשֶׁר חָשַׁק
he-desired that Solomon desire-of and the-horses towns-of and the-chariot

the Lord brought all this
disaster on them.' "

Solomon's Other Activities

10At the end of twenty years,
during which Solomon built
these two buildings—the temple of the Lord and the royal
palace— 11King Solomon gave
twenty towns in Galilee to
Hiram king of Tyre, because
Hiram had supplied him with
all the cedar and pine and gold
he wanted. 12But when Hiram
went from Tyre to see the
towns that Solomon had given
him, he was not pleased with
them. 13"What kind of towns
are these you have given me,
my brother?" he asked. And
he called them the Land of
Cabul,[f] a name they have to
this day. 14Now Hiram had
sent to the king 120 talents[g] of
gold.

15Here is the account of the
forced labor King Solomon
conscripted to build the Lord's
temple, his own palace, the
supporting terraces,[h] the wall
of Jerusalem, and Hazor,
Megiddo and Gezer. 16(Pharaoh king of Egypt had at-
tacked and captured Gezer. He
had set it on fire. He killed its
Canaanite inhabitants and
then gave it as a wedding gift
to his daughter, Solomon's
wife. 17And Solomon rebuilt
Gezer.) He built up Lower Beth
Horon, 18Baalath, and Tadmor[i] in the desert, within his
land, 19as well as all his store
cities and the towns for his
chariots and for his
horses[j]—whatever he desired

f13 *Cabul* sounds like the Hebrew for *good-for-nothing*.
g14 That is, about 4 1/2 tons (about 4 metric tons)
h15 Or *the Millo;* also in verse 24
i18 The Hebrew may also be read *Tamar.*
j19 Or *charioteers*

°18 ק תדמר

לִבְנ֥וֹת בִּירוּשָׁלַ֙͏ִם֙ וּבַלְּבָנ֔וֹן וּבְכֹ֖ל אֶ֥רֶץ
territory-of and-through-all-of and-in-the-Lebanon in-Jerusalem to-build

מֶמְשַׁלְתּֽוֹ׃ כָּל־ הָעָ֗ם הַנּוֹתָ֞ר מִן־ הָֽאֱמֹרִ֜י
the-Amorite from the-one-being-left the-people all-of (20) rule-of-him

הַחִתִּ֤י הַפְּרִזִּי֙ הַחִוִּ֣י וְהַיְבוּסִ֔י אֲשֶׁ֛ר לֹֽא־ מִבְּנֵ֥י
from-sons-of not who and-the-Jebusite the-Hivite the-Perizzite the-Hittite

יִשְׂרָאֵ֖ל הֵֽמָּה׃ בְּנֵיהֶ֗ם אֲשֶׁ֨ר נֹתְר֤וּ אַחֲרֵיהֶם֙ בָּאָ֔רֶץ
in-the-land after-them they-remained who descendants-of-them (21) they Israel

אֲשֶׁ֛ר לֹא־ יָכְל֥וּ בְּנֵ֥י יִשְׂרָאֵ֖ל לְהַחֲרִימָ֑ם וַיַּעֲלֵ֤ם
now-he-conscripted-them to-exterminate-them Israel sons-of they-could not who

שְׁלֹמֹה֙ לְמַס־ עֹבֵ֔ד עַ֖ד הַיּ֥וֹם הַזֶּֽה׃ וּמִבְּנֵי֙
but-from-sons-of (22) the-this the-day to being-slave to-forced-labor-of Solomon

יִשְׂרָאֵ֔ל לֹא־ נָתַ֥ן שְׁלֹמֹ֖ה עָ֑בֶד כִּי־ הֵ֞ם אַנְשֵׁ֣י הַמִּלְחָמָ֗ה וַעֲבָדָיו֙
and-officials-of-him the-fight men-of they for slave Solomon he-made not Israel

וְשָׂרָ֣יו וְשָׁלִשָׁ֔יו וְשָׂרֵ֥י רִכְבּ֖וֹ
chariot-of-him and-commanders-of and-captains-of-him and-officers-of-him

וּפָרָשָֽׁיו׃ אֵ֣לֶּה ׀ שָׂרֵ֣י הַנִּצָּבִ֗ים אֲשֶׁ֤ר עַל־
over who the-ones-being-officials chiefs-of these (23) and-charioteers-of-him

הַמְּלָאכָה֙ לִשְׁלֹמֹ֔ה חֲמִשִּׁ֖ים וַחֲמֵ֣שׁ מֵא֑וֹת הָרֹדִ֣ים
the-ones-supervising hundreds and-five-of fifty of-Solomon the-project

בָּעָ֔ם הָעֹשִׂ֖ים בַּמְּלָאכָֽה׃ אַ֣ךְ בַּת־ פַּרְעֹ֗ה
Pharaoh daughter-of also (24) in-the-work the-ones-doing over-the-people

עָֽלְתָה֙ מֵעִ֣יר דָּוִ֔ד אֶל־ בֵּיתָ֖הּ אֲשֶׁ֣ר בָּֽנָה־ לָ֑הּ אָ֖ז
then for-her he-built that palace-of-her to David from-City-of she-came-up

בָּנָ֥ה אֶת־ הַמִּלּֽוֹא׃ וְהֶעֱלָ֣ה שְׁלֹמֹ֡ה שָׁלֹ֣שׁ
three Solomon and-he-sacrificed (25) the-supporting-terrace *** he-built

פְּעָמִ֣ים בַּשָּׁנָ֡ה עֹלוֹת֩ וּשְׁלָמִ֨ים עַל־ הַמִּזְבֵּ֜חַ אֲשֶׁ֣ר
that the-altar on and-fellowship-offerings burnt-offerings in-the-year times

בָּנָ֣ה לַיהוָ֗ה וְהַקְטֵ֣יר אִתּ֔וֹ אֲשֶׁ֖ר לִפְנֵ֣י יְהוָ֑ה
Yahweh before that with-him and-he-burned-incense for-Yahweh he-built

וְשִׁלַּ֖ם אֶת־ הַבָּֽיִת׃ וָאֳנִ֡י עָשָׂה֩ הַמֶּ֨לֶךְ שְׁלֹמֹ֜ה
Solomon the-king he-built and-ship (26) the-temple *** so-he-fulfilled

בְּעֶצְיוֹן־ גֶּ֨בֶר אֲשֶׁ֜ר אֶת־ אֵל֗וֹת עַל־שְׂפַ֛ת יַם־ ס֖וּף בְּאֶ֥רֶץ אֱדֽוֹם׃
Edom in-land-of Reed Sea-of shore-of on Elath near that Geber at-Ezion

וַיִּשְׁלַ֨ח חִירָ֤ם בָּֽאֳנִי֙ אֶת־ עֲבָדָ֔יו אַנְשֵׁ֣י אֳנִיּ֔וֹת יֹדְעֵ֖י
ones-knowing-of ships men-of men-of-him *** to-fleet Hiram and-he-sent (27)

הַיָּ֑ם עִ֖ם עַבְדֵ֣י שְׁלֹמֹֽה׃ וַיָּבֹ֣אוּ אוֹפִ֔ירָה וַיִּקְח֣וּ
and-they-brought to-Ophir and-they-sailed (28) Solomon men-of with the-sea

to build in Jerusalem, in Lebanon and throughout all the territory he ruled.

20 All the people left from the Amorites, Hittites, Perizzites, Hivites and Jebusites (these peoples were not Israelites),
21 that is, their descendants remaining in the land, whom the Israelites could not exterminate[k]—these Solomon conscripted for his slave labor force, as it is to this day.
22 But Solomon did not make slaves of any of the Israelites; they were his fighting men, his government officials, his officers, his captains, and the commanders of his chariots and charioteers.
23 They were also the chief officials in charge of Solomon's projects—550 officials supervising the men who did the work.

24 After Pharaoh's daughter had come up from the City of David to the palace Solomon had built for her, he constructed the supporting terraces.

25 Three times a year Solomon sacrificed burnt offerings and fellowship offerings[l] on the altar he had built for the LORD, burning incense before the LORD along with them, and so fulfilled the temple obligations.

26 King Solomon also built ships at Ezion Geber, which is near Elath in Edom, on the shore of the Red Sea.[m]
27 And Hiram sent his men—sailors who knew the sea—to serve in the fleet with Solomon's men.
28 They sailed to Ophir and

[k] *21* The Hebrew term refers to the irrevocable giving over of things or persons to the LORD, often by totally destroying them.
[l] *25* Traditionally *peace offerings*
[m] *26* Hebrew *Yam Suph*; that is, Sea of Reeds

מִשָּׁם זָהָב אַרְבַּע־מֵאוֹת וְעֶשְׂרִים כִּכָּר וַיָּבִאוּ אֶל־ הַמֶּלֶךְ
the-king to and-they-delivered talent and-twenty hundreds four gold from-there

שְׁלֹמֹה׃ וּמַלְכַּת־ שְׁבָא שֹׁמַעַת אֶת־ שֵׁמַע שְׁלֹמֹה לְשֵׁם
to-name-of Solomon fame-of *** hearing Sheba when-queen-of (10:1) Solomon

יְהוָה וַתָּבֹא לְנַסֹּתוֹ בְּחִידוֹת׃ וַתָּבֹא
and-she-arrived (2) with-hard-questions to-test-him then-she-came Yahweh

יְרוּשָׁלַמָה בְּחַיִל כָּבֵד מְאֹד גְּמַלִּים נֹשְׂאִים בְּשָׂמִים וְזָהָב
and-gold spices ones-carrying camels very great with-caravan at-Jerusalem

רַב־ מְאֹד וְאֶבֶן יְקָרָה וַתָּבֹא אֶל־ שְׁלֹמֹה וַתְּדַבֵּר אֵלָיו
with-him and-she-talked Solomon to and-she-came precious and-stone very much

אֵת כָּל־אֲשֶׁר הָיָה עִם־ לְבָבָהּ׃ וַיַּגֶּד־ לָהּ שְׁלֹמֹה אֶת־
*** Solomon to-her and-he-answered (3) mind-of-her on he-was that all ***

כָּל־ דְּבָרֶיהָ לֹא־ הָיָה דָּבָר נֶעְלָם מִן־ הַמֶּלֶךְ אֲשֶׁר
that the-king for being-too-hard question he-was not questions-of-her all-of

לֹא הִגִּיד לָהּ׃ וַתֵּרֶא מַלְכַּת־ שְׁבָא אֵת כָּל־ חָכְמַת
wisdom-of all-of *** Sheba queen-of when-she-saw (4) to-her he-explained not

שְׁלֹמֹה וְהַבַּיִת אֲשֶׁר בָּנָה׃ וּמַאֲכַל שֻׁלְחָנוֹ
table-of-him and-food-of (5) he-built that and-the-palace Solomon

וּמוֹשַׁב עֲבָדָיו וּמַעֲמַד מְשָׁרְתָו°
ones-attending-him and-station-of officials-of-him and-seating-of

וּמַלְבֻּשֵׁיהֶם וּמַשְׁקָיו וְעֹלָתוֹ אֲשֶׁר
that and-burnt-offering-of-him and-cupbearers-of-him and-robes-of-them

יַעֲלֶה בֵּית יְהוָה וְלֹא־ הָיָה בָהּ עוֹד רוּחַ׃
breath longer in-her he-was then-not Yahweh temple-of he-offered

וַתֹּאמֶר אֶל־ הַמֶּלֶךְ אֱמֶת הָיָה הַדָּבָר אֲשֶׁר שָׁמַעְתִּי
I-heard that the-report he-was true the-king to and-she-said (6)

בְּאַרְצִי עַל־ דְּבָרֶיךָ וְעַל־ חָכְמָתֶךָ׃
wisdom-of-you and-about achievements-of-you about in-country-of-me

וְלֹא־ הֶאֱמַנְתִּי לַדְּבָרִים עַד אֲשֶׁר־ בָּאתִי וַתִּרְאֶינָה
and-they-saw I-came when until in-the-things I-believed but-not (7)

עֵינַי וְהִנֵּה לֹא־ הֻגַּד־ לִי הַחֵצִי הוֹסַפְתָּ חָכְמָה
wisdom you-exceeded the-half to-me he-was-told not and-see! eyes-of-me

וָטוֹב אֶל־ הַשְּׁמוּעָה אֲשֶׁר שָׁמַעְתִּי׃ אַשְׁרֵי אֲנָשֶׁיךָ
men-of-you happinesses-of (8) I-heard that the-report beyond and-wealth

אַשְׁרֵי עֲבָדֶיךָ אֵלֶּה הָעֹמְדִים לְפָנֶיךָ תָּמִיד
continually before-you the-ones-standing these officials-of-you happinesses-of

הַשֹּׁמְעִים אֶת־ חָכְמָתֶךָ׃ יְהִי יְהוָה אֱלֹהֶיךָ
God-of-you Yahweh may-he-be (9) wisdom-of-you *** the-ones-hearing

°5 ק משרתיו

brought back 420 talents[n] of
gold, which they delivered to
King Solomon.

The Queen of Sheba Visits Solomon

10 When the queen of
Sheba heard about the
fame of Solomon and his relation to the name of the LORD,
she came to test him with hard
questions. 2 Arriving at Jerusalem with a very great cara-
van—with camels carrying
spices, large quantities of gold,
and precious stones—she
came to Solomon and talked
with him about all that she
had on her mind. 3 Solomon
answered all her questions;
nothing was too hard for the
king to explain to her. 4 When
the queen of Sheba saw all the
wisdom of Solomon and the
palace he had built, 5 the food
on his table, the seating of his
officials, the attending servants in their robes, his cup-
bearers, and the burnt
offerings he made at[o] the temple of the LORD, she was overwhelmed.
6 She said to the king, "The
report I heard in my own
country about your achievements and your wisdom is
true. 7 But I did not believe
these things until I came and
saw with my own eyes. In-
deed, not even half was told
me; in wisdom and wealth
you have far exceeded the report I heard. 8 How happy your
men must be! How happy
your officials, who continually
stand before you and hear
your wisdom! 9 Praise be to the

[n]28 That is, about 16 tons (about 14.5 metric tons)
[o]5 Or *the ascent by which he went up to*

בָּרוּךְ אֲשֶׁר חָפֵץ בְּךָ לְתִתְּךָ עַל־ כִּסֵּא יִשְׂרָאֵל
Israel throne-of on to-place-you in-you he-delighted who being-praised

בְּאַהֲבַת יְהוָה אֶת־ יִשְׂרָאֵל לְעֹלָם וַיְשִׂימְךָ לְמֶלֶךְ
as-king and-he-made-you to-forever Israel *** Yahweh because-to-love

לַעֲשׂוֹת מִשְׁפָּט וּצְדָקָה׃ וַתִּתֵּן לַמֶּלֶךְ מֵאָה
hundred to-the-king and-she-gave (10) and-righteousness justice to-maintain

וְעֶשְׂרִים ׀ כִּכַּר זָהָב וּבְשָׂמִים הַרְבֵּה מְאֹד וְאֶבֶן יְקָרָה
precious and-stone very to-be-many and-spices gold talent-of and-twenty

לֹא־ בָא כַבֹּשֶׂם הַהוּא עוֹד לָרֹב אֲשֶׁר־ נָתְנָה
she-gave that in-quantity again the-this like-the-spice he-came never

מַלְכַּת־ שְׁבָא לַמֶּלֶךְ שְׁלֹמֹה׃ וְגַם אֳנִי חִירָם אֲשֶׁר־
that Hiram ship-of and-also (11) Solomon to-the-king Sheba queen-of

נָשָׂא זָהָב מֵאוֹפִיר הֵבִיא מֵאֹפִיר עֲצֵי אַלְמֻגִּים הַרְבֵּה
to-be-great almugs woods-of from-Ophir he-brought from-Ophir gold he-brought

מְאֹד וְאֶבֶן יְקָרָה׃ וַיַּעַשׂ הַמֶּלֶךְ אֶת־ עֲצֵי הָאַלְמֻגִּים
the-almugs woods-of *** the-king and-he-made (12) precious and-stone very

מִסְעָד לְבֵית־ יְהוָה וּלְבֵית הַמֶּלֶךְ וְכִנֹּרוֹת וּנְבָלִים
and-lyres and-harps the-king and-for-palace-of Yahweh for-temple-of support

לַשָּׁרִים לֹא בָא־ כֵן עֲצֵי אַלְמֻגִּים וְלֹא
and-never almugs woods-of so-much he-came never for-the-ones-making-music

נִרְאָה עַד הַיּוֹם הַזֶּה׃ וְהַמֶּלֶךְ שְׁלֹמֹה נָתַן לְמַלְכַּת־
to-queen-of he-gave Solomon and-the-king (13) the-this the-day to he-was-seen

שְׁבָא אֶת־ כָּל־ חֶפְצָהּ אֲשֶׁר שָׁאָלָה מִלְּבַד אֲשֶׁר נָתַן־
he-gave what besides she-asked-for that desire-of-her all-of *** Sheba

לָהּ כְּיַד הַמֶּלֶךְ שְׁלֹמֹה וַתֵּפֶן וַתֵּלֶךְ
and-she-returned then-she-left Solomon the-king as-hand-of to-her

לְאַרְצָהּ הִיא וַעֲבָדֶיהָ׃ וַיְהִי מִשְׁקַל הַזָּהָב
the-gold weight-of and-he-was (14) and-servants-of-her she to-country-of-her

אֲשֶׁר־ בָּא לִשְׁלֹמֹה בְּשָׁנָה אֶחָת שֵׁשׁ מֵאוֹת שִׁשִּׁים וָשֵׁשׁ כִּכַּר
talent-of and-six sixty hundreds six each in-year to-Solomon he-came that

זָהָב׃ לְבַד מֵאַנְשֵׁי הַתָּרִים וּמִסְחַר
and-revenue-of the-ones-being-merchants from-men-of besides (15) gold

הָרֹכְלִים וְכָל־ מַלְכֵי הָעֶרֶב וּפַחוֹת הָאָרֶץ׃
the-land and-governors-of the-Arab kings-of and-all-of the-ones-trading

וַיַּעַשׂ הַמֶּלֶךְ שְׁלֹמֹה מָאתַיִם צִנָּה זָהָב שָׁחוּט
being-hammered gold shield two-hundreds Solomon the-king and-he-made (16)

שֵׁשׁ־ מֵאוֹת זָהָב יַעֲלֶה עַל־ הַצִּנָּה הָאֶחָת׃ וּשְׁלֹשׁ־ מֵאוֹת
hundreds and-three-of (17) the-each the-shield into he-went gold hundreds six

LORD your God, who has delighted in you and placed you on the throne of Israel. Because of the LORD's eternal love for Israel, he has made you king, to maintain justice and righteousness."

10 And she gave the king 120 talents[p] of gold, large quantities of spices, and precious stones. Never again were so many spices brought in as those the queen of Sheba gave to King Solomon.

11 (Hiram's ships brought gold from Ophir; and from there they brought great cargoes of almugwood[r] and precious stones. 12 The king used the almugwood to make supports for the temple of the LORD and for the royal palace, and to make harps and lyres for the musicians. So much almugwood has never been imported or seen since that day.)

13 King Solomon gave the queen of Sheba all she desired and asked for, besides what he had given her out of his royal bounty. Then she left and returned with her retinue to her own country.

Solomon's Splendor

14 The weight of the gold that Solomon received yearly was 666 talents,[s] 15 not including the revenues from merchants and traders and from all the Arabian kings and the governors of the land.

16 King Solomon made two hundred large shields of hammered gold; six hundred bekas[t] of gold went into each shield. 17 He also made three

[p] *10* That is, about 4 1/2 tons (about 4 metric tons)
[r] *11* Probably a variant of *algumwood;* also in verse 12
[s] *14* That is, about 25 tons (about 23 metric tons)
[t] *16* That is, about 7 1/2 pounds (about 3.5 kilograms)

מָגִנִּים זָהָב שָׁחוּט שְׁלֹשֶׁת מָנִים זָהָב יַעֲלֶה עַל־הַמָּגֵן
the-shield into he-went gold minas three-of being-hammered gold small-shields

הָאֶחָת וַיִּתְּנֵם הַמֶּלֶךְ בֵּית יַעַר הַלְּבָנוֹן׃
the-Lebanon Forest-of Palace-of the-king and-he-put-them the-each

וַיַּעַשׂ הַמֶּלֶךְ כִּסֵּא־שֵׁן גָּדוֹל וַיְצַפֵּהוּ זָהָב
gold and-he-overlaid-them great ivory throne-of the-king then-he-made (18)

מוּפָז׃ שֵׁשׁ מַעֲלוֹת לַכִּסֵּה וְרֹאשׁ־עָגֹל לַכִּסֵּה
on-the-throne rounded and-top to-the-throne steps six-of (19) being-fine

מֵאַחֲרָיו וְיָדֹת מִזֶּה וּמִזֶּה אֶל־מְקוֹם
place-of at and-on-that-side on-this-side and-armrests on-backs-of-him

הַשָּׁבֶת וּשְׁנַיִם אֲרָיוֹת עֹמְדִים אֵצֶל הַיָּדוֹת׃ וּשְׁנַיִם עָשָׂר
ten and-two (20) the-armrests beside ones-standing lions and-two the-seat

אֲרָיִים עֹמְדִים שָׁם עַל־שֵׁשׁ הַמַּעֲלוֹת מִזֶּה וּמִזֶּה לֹא־
not and-on-that-end on-this-end the-steps six-of on there ones-standing lions

נַעֲשָׂה כֵן לְכָל־מַמְלָכוֹת׃ וְכֹל כְּלֵי מַשְׁקֵה
drinking-of goblets-of and-all-of (21) kingdoms for-any-of like he-was-made

הַמֶּלֶךְ שְׁלֹמֹה זָהָב וְכֹל כְּלֵי בֵּית־יַעַר הַלְּבָנוֹן
the-Lebanon Forest-of Palace-of articles-of and-all-of gold Solomon the-king

זָהָב סָגוּר אֵין כֶּסֶף לֹא נֶחְשָׁב בִּימֵי שְׁלֹמֹה
Solomon in-days-of being-considered not silver nothing-of pure gold

לִמְאוּמָה׃ כִּי אֳנִי תַרְשִׁישׁ לַמֶּלֶךְ בַּיָּם עִם אֳנִי
ship-of with at-the-sea to-the-king Tarshish ship-of indeed (22) as-anything

חִירָם אַחַת לְשָׁלֹשׁ שָׁנִים תָּבוֹא ׀ אֳנִי תַרְשִׁישׁ נֹשְׂאֵת זָהָב
gold carrying Tarshish ship-of she-returned years in-three once Hiram

וָכֶסֶף שֶׁנְהַבִּים וְקֹפִים וְתֻכִּיִּים׃ וַיִּגְדַּל הַמֶּלֶךְ
the-king and-he-was-great (23) and-baboons and-apes ivories and-silver

שְׁלֹמֹה מִכֹּל מַלְכֵי הָאָרֶץ לְעֹשֶׁר וּלְחָכְמָה׃
and-in-wisdom in-wealth the-earth kings-of more-than-all-of Solomon

וְכָל־הָאָרֶץ מְבַקְשִׁים אֶת־פְּנֵי שְׁלֹמֹה לִשְׁמֹעַ אֶת־
*** to-hear Solomon faces-of *** ones-seeking the-earth and-all-of (24)

חָכְמָתוֹ אֲשֶׁר־נָתַן אֱלֹהִים בְּלִבּוֹ׃ וְהֵמָּה מְבִאִים
ones-bringing and-they (25) in-heart-of-him God he-put that wisdom-of-him

אִישׁ מִנְחָתוֹ כְּלֵי כֶסֶף וּכְלֵי זָהָב וּשְׂלָמוֹת וְנֵשֶׁק
and-weapon and-robes gold and-articles-of silver articles-of gift-of-him each

וּבְשָׂמִים סוּסִים וּפְרָדִים דְּבַר־שָׁנָה בְּשָׁנָה׃ וַיֶּאֱסֹף
and-he-accumulated (26) after-year year event-of and-mules horses and-spices

שְׁלֹמֹה רֶכֶב וּפָרָשִׁים וַיְהִי־לוֹ אֶלֶף וְאַרְבַּע־מֵאוֹת
hundreds and-four thousand to-him and-he-was and-horses chariot Solomon

hundred small shields of hammered gold, with three minas[u]
of gold in each shield. The
king put them in the Palace of
the Forest of Lebanon.
18 Then the king made a great
throne inlaid with ivory and
overlaid with fine gold. 19 The
throne had six steps, and its
back had a rounded top. On
both sides of the seat were
armrests, with a lion standing
beside each of them. 20 Twelve
lions stood on the six steps,
one at either end of each step.
Nothing like it had ever been
made for any other kingdom.
21 All King Solomon's goblets
were gold, and all the
household articles in the Palace of the Forest of Lebanon
were pure gold. Nothing was
made of silver, because silver
was considered of little value
in Solomon's days. 22 The king
had a fleet of trading ships[v] at
sea along with the ships of
Hiram. Once every three years
it returned carrying gold, silver and ivory, and apes and
baboons.
23 King Solomon was greater
in riches and wisdom than all
the other kings of the earth.
24 The whole world sought
audience with Solomon to
hear the wisdom God had put
in his heart. 25 Year after year,
everyone who came brought a
gift—articles of silver and
gold, robes, weapons and
spices, and horses and mules.
26 Solomon accumulated
chariots and horses; he had
fourteen hundred chariots and

[u]17 That is, about 3 3/4 pounds (about 1.7 kilograms)
[v]22 Hebrew *of ships of Tarshish*

רכב ושנים־ עשר אלף פרשים וינחם בערי הרכב
chariot and-two ten thousand horses and-he-kept-them in-cities-of the-chariot

ועם־ המלך בירושלם׃ וַיִּתֵּן המלך את־ הכסף
and-with the-king in-Jerusalem (27) and-he-made the-king *** the-silver

בירושלם כאבנים ואת הארזים נתן כשקמים
in-Jerusalem as-the-stones and the-cedars he-made as-the-sycamore-fig-trees

אשר־ בשפלה לרב׃ ומוצא הסוסים אשר
that in-the-foothill in-number (28) and-importing-of the-horses that

לשלמה ממצרים ומקוה סחרי המלך
to-Solomon from-Egypt and-from-Kue ones-being-merchants-of the-king

יקחו מקוה במחיר׃ ותעלה ותצא
they-purchased from-Kue for-price (29) and-she-came-up and-she-came-out

מרכבה ממצרים בשש מאות כסף וסוס בחמשים ומאה
chariot from-Egypt for-six hundreds silver and-horse for-fifty and-hundred

וכן לכל־ מלכי החתים ולמלכי ארם בידם
and-so to-all-of kings-of the-Hittites and-to-kings-of Aram to-hand-of-them

יצאו׃ והמלך שלמה אהב נשים נכריות רבות
they-exported (11:1) but-the-king Solomon he-loved women foreign-ones many

ואת־ בת־ פרעה מואביות עמניות אדמית צדנית חתית׃
besides daughter-of Pharaoh Moabites Ammonites Edomites Sidonians Hittites

מן־ הגוים אשר אמר־ יהוה אל־ בני ישראל לא־ תבאו
(2) from the-nations which he-told Yahweh to sons-of Israel not you-must-go

בהם והם לא־ יבאו בכם אכן יטו את־
into-them and-they not they-must-come into-you because they-will-turn ***

לבבכם אחרי אלהיהם בהם דבק שלמה לאהבה׃
heart-of-you after gods-of-them to-them he-held-fast Solomon in-love

ויהי־ לו נשים שרות שבע מאות ופלגשים
(3) and-he-was to-him wives royal-ones seven-of hundreds and-concubines

שלש מאות ויטו נשיו את־ לבו׃
three-of hundreds and-they-led-astray wives-of-him *** heart-of-him

ויהי לעת זקנת שלמה נשיו הטו את־
(4) and-he-was at-time-of old-age-of Solomon wives-of-him they-turned ***

לבבו אחרי אלהים אחרים ולא־ היה לבבו שלם
heart-of-him after gods other-ones and-not he-was heart-of-him fully-devoted

עם־ יהוה אלהיו כלבב דויד אביו׃ וילך
to Yahweh God-of-him as-heart-of David father-of-him (5) and-he-followed

שלמה אחרי עשתרת אלהי צדנים ואחרי מלכם שקץ
Solomon after Ashtoreth gods-of Sidonians and-after Milcom detestable-one-of

twelve thousand horses,[w] which he kept in the chariot cities and also with him in Jerusalem. [27]The king made silver as common in Jerusalem as stones, and cedar as plentiful as sycamore-fig trees in the foothills. [28]Solomon's horses were imported from Egypt[x] and from Kue[y]—the royal merchants purchased them from Kue. [29]They imported a chariot from Egypt for six hundred shekels[z] of silver, and a horse for a hundred and fifty.[a] They also exported them to all the kings of the Hittites and of the Arameans.

Solomon's Wives

11 King Solomon, however, loved many foreign women besides Pharaoh's daughter—Moabites, Ammonites, Edomites, Sidonians and Hittites. [2]They were from nations about which the LORD had told the Israelites, "You must not intermarry with them, because they will surely turn your hearts after their gods." Nevertheless, Solomon held fast to them in love. [3]He had seven hundred wives of royal birth and three hundred concubines, and his wives led him astray. [4]As Solomon grew old, his wives turned his heart after other gods, and his heart was not fully devoted to the LORD his God, as the heart of David his father had been. [5]He followed Ashtoreth the goddess of the Sidonians, and Molech[b] the detestable god of

[w]26 Or *charioteers*
[x]28 Or possibly *Muzur*, a region in Cilicia; also in verse 29
[y]28 Probably *Cilicia*
[z]29 That is, about 15 pounds (about 7 kilograms)
[a]29 That is, about 3 3/4 pounds (about 1.7 kilograms)
[b]5 Hebrew *Milcom*; also in verse 33

עַמֹּנִים׃ וַיַּעַשׂ שְׁלֹמֹה הָרַע בְּעֵינֵי יְהוָה וְלֹא
and-not Yahweh in-eyes-of the-evil Solomon so-he-did (6) Ammonites

מִלֵּא אַחֲרֵי יְהוָה כְּדָוִד אָבִיו׃ אָז יִבְנֶה
he-built then (7) father-of-him as-David Yahweh after he-was-complete

שְׁלֹמֹה בָּמָה לִכְמוֹשׁ שִׁקֻּץ מוֹאָב בָּהָר אֲשֶׁר עַל־
to that on-the-hill Moab detestable-one-of for-Chemosh high-place Solomon

פְּנֵי יְרוּשָׁלָםִ וּלְמֹלֶךְ שִׁקֻּץ בְּנֵי עַמּוֹן׃
Ammon sons-of detestable-one-of and-for-Molech Jerusalem east-of

וְכֵן עָשָׂה לְכָל־ נָשָׁיו הַנָּכְרִיּוֹת מַקְטִירוֹת
ones-burning-incense the-foreign-ones wives-of-him for-all-of he-did and-same (8)

וּמְזַבְּחוֹת לֵאלֹהֵיהֶן׃ וַיִּתְאַנַּף יְהוָה
Yahweh and-he-became-angry (9) to-gods-of-them and-ones-offering-sacrifices

בִּשְׁלֹמֹה כִּי־ נָטָה לְבָבוֹ מֵעִם יְהוָה אֱלֹהֵי
God-of Yahweh from-with heart-of-him he-turned-away because with-Solomon

יִשְׂרָאֵל הַנִּרְאָה אֵלָיו פַּעֲמָיִם׃ וְצִוָּה אֵלָיו עַל־
about to-him though-he-commanded (10) twice to-him who-he-appeared Israel

הַדָּבָר הַזֶּה לְבִלְתִּי־ לֶכֶת אַחֲרֵי אֱלֹהִים אֲחֵרִים וְלֹא שָׁמַר אֵת
*** he-kept but-not other-ones gods after to-follow not the-this the-thing

אֲשֶׁר־ צִוָּה יְהוָה׃ וַיֹּאמֶר יְהוָה לִשְׁלֹמֹה יַעַן אֲשֶׁר
that since to-Solomon Yahweh so-he-said (11) Yahweh he-commanded what

הָיְתָה־ זֹּאת עִמָּךְ וְלֹא שָׁמַרְתָּ בְּרִיתִי וְחֻקֹּתַי
and-decrees-of-me covenant-of-me you-kept and-not with-you this she-was

אֲשֶׁר צִוִּיתִי עָלֶיךָ קָרֹעַ אֶקְרַע אֶת־ הַמַּמְלָכָה
the-kingdom *** I-will-tear-away to-tear-away to-you I-commanded which

מֵעָלֶיךָ וּנְתַתִּיהָ לְעַבְדֶּךָ׃ אַךְ־
nevertheless (12) to-subordinate-of-you and-I-will-give-her from-on-you

בְּיָמֶיךָ לֹא אֶעֱשֶׂנָּה לְמַעַן דָּוִד אָבִיךָ מִיַּד
from-hand-of father-of-you David for-sake-of I-will-do-her not in-days-of-you

בִּנְךָ אֶקְרָעֶנָּה׃ רַק אֶת־ כָּל־ הַמַּמְלָכָה לֹא
not the-kingdom whole-of *** yet (13) I-will-tear-her son-of-you

אֶקְרָע שֵׁבֶט אֶחָד אֶתֵּן לִבְנֶךָ לְמַעַן דָּוִד
David for-sake-of to-son-of-you I-will-give one tribe I-will-tear-away

עַבְדִּי וּלְמַעַן יְרוּשָׁלַםִ אֲשֶׁר בָּחָרְתִּי׃ וַיָּקֶם
then-he-raised-up (14) I-chose which Jerusalem and-for-sake-of servant-of-me

יְהוָה שָׂטָן לִשְׁלֹמֹה אֵת הֲדַד הָאֲדֹמִי מִזֶּרַע הַמֶּלֶךְ
the-king from-line-of the-Edomite Hadad *** against-Solomon adversary Yahweh

הוּא בֶּאֱדוֹם׃ וַיְהִי בִּהְיוֹת דָּוִד אֶת־ אֱדוֹם בַּעֲלוֹת יוֹאָב
Joab when-to-go-up Edom against David when-to-be and-he-was (15) in-Edom he

the Ammonites. [6]So Solomon
did evil in the eyes of the
LORD; he did not follow the
LORD completely, as David his
father had done.

[7]On a hill east of Jerusalem,
Solomon built a high place for
Chemosh the detestable god of
Moab, and for Molech the detestable god of the Ammonites.
[8]He did the same for all
his foreign wives, who burned
incense and offered sacrifices
to their gods.

[9]The LORD became angry
with Solomon because his
heart had turned away from
the LORD, the God of Israel,
who had appeared to him
twice. [10]Although he had forbidden Solomon to follow other gods, Solomon did not keep
the LORD's command. [11]So the
LORD said to Solomon, "Since
this is your attitude and you
have not kept my covenant
and my decrees, which I commanded you, I will most certainly tear the kingdom away
from you and give it to one of
your subordinates. [12]Nevertheless, for the sake of David
your father, I will not do it
during your lifetime. I will
tear it out of the hand of your
son. [13]Yet I will not tear the
whole kingdom from him, but
will give him one tribe for the
sake of David my servant and
for the sake of Jerusalem,
which I have chosen."

Solomon's Adversaries

[14]Then the LORD raised up
against Solomon an adversary, Hadad the Edomite,
from the royal line of Edom.
[15]Earlier when David was
fighting with Edom, Joab the

שַׂר הַצָּבָא לְקַבֵּר אֶת־ הַחֲלָלִים וַיַּךְ כָּל־
all-of then-he-struck-down the-dead-ones *** to-bury the-army commander-of

זָכָר בֶּאֱדוֹם׃ כִּי שֵׁשֶׁת חֳדָשִׁים יָשַׁב־ שָׁם יוֹאָב וְכָל־ יִשְׂרָאֵל
Israel and-all-of Joab there he-stayed months six-of for (16) in-Edom man

עַד־ הִכְרִית כָּל־ זָכָר בֶּאֱדוֹם׃ וַיִּבְרַח אֲדַד הוּא וַאֲנָשִׁים
and-men he Hadad but-he-fled (17) in-Edom man all-of he-destroyed until

אֲדֹמִיִּים מֵעַבְדֵי אָבִיו אִתּוֹ לָבוֹא מִצְרַיִם וַהֲדַד נַעַר
boy now-Hadad Egypt to-go with-him father-of-him from-officials-of Edomites

קָטָן׃ וַיָּקֻמוּ מִמִּדְיָן וַיָּבֹאוּ פָּארָן וַיִּקְחוּ
then-they-took Paran and-they-went from-Midian and-they-set-out (18) small

אֲנָשִׁים עִמָּם מִפָּארָן וַיָּבֹאוּ מִצְרַיִם אֶל־פַּרְעֹה מֶלֶךְ־מִצְרַיִם
Egypt king-of Pharaoh to Egypt and-they-went from-Paran with-them men

וַיִּתֶּן־ לוֹ בַיִת וְלֶחֶם אָמַר לוֹ וְאֶרֶץ נָתַן
he-gave and-land from-him he-provided and-food house to-him and-he-gave

לוֹ׃ וַיִּמְצָא הֲדַד חֵן בְּעֵינֵי פַרְעֹה מְאֹד וַיִּתֶּן־
so-he-gave great Pharaoh in-eyes-of favor Hadad and-he-found (19) to-him

לוֹ אִשָּׁה אֶת־ אֲחוֹת אִשְׁתּוֹ אֲחוֹת תַּחְפְּנֵיס הַגְּבִירָה׃
the-queen Tahpenes sister-of wife-of-him sister-of *** wife to-him

וַתֵּלֶד לוֹ אֲחוֹת תַּחְפְּנֵיס אֵת גְּנֻבַת בְּנוֹ
son-of-him Genubath *** Tahpenes sister-of to-him and-she-bore (20)

וַתִּגְמְלֵהוּ תַחְפְּנֵס בְּתוֹךְ בֵּית פַּרְעֹה וַיְהִי
and-he-was Pharaoh palace-of inside-of Tahpenes and-she-brought-up-him

גְנֻבַת בֵּית פַּרְעֹה בְּתוֹךְ בְּנֵי פַרְעֹה׃ וַהֲדַד
and-Hadad (21) Pharaoh children-of in-among Pharaoh palace-of Genubath

שָׁמַע בְּמִצְרַיִם כִּי־ שָׁכַב דָּוִד עִם־ אֲבֹתָיו וְכִי־
and-that fathers-of-him with David he-rested that in-Egypt he-heard

מֵת יוֹאָב שַׂר־ הַצָּבָא וַיֹּאמֶר הֲדַד אֶל־ פַּרְעֹה
Pharaoh to Hadad then-he-said the-army commander-of Joab he-was-dead

שַׁלְּחֵנִי וְאֵלֵךְ אֶל־ אַרְצִי׃ וַיֹּאמֶר לוֹ פַּרְעֹה
Pharaoh to-him and-he-asked (22) country-of-me to so-I-may-return let-go-me!

כִּי מָה־ אַתָּה חָסֵר עִמִּי וְהִנְּךָ מְבַקֵּשׁ לָלֶכֶת אֶל־
to to-go-back wanting so-see-you! with-me lacking you what? indeed

אַרְצֶךָ וַיֹּאמֶר ׀ לֹא כִּי שַׁלֵּחַ תְּשַׁלְּחֵנִי׃
you-let-go-me to-let-go but nothing and-he-replied country-of-you

וַיָּקֶם אֱלֹהִים לוֹ שָׂטָן אֶת־ רְזוֹן בֶּן־ אֶלְיָדָע אֲשֶׁר
who Eliada son-of Rezon *** adversary against-him God and-he-raised-up (23)

בָּרַח מֵאֵת הֲדַדְעֶזֶר מֶלֶךְ־ צוֹבָה אֲדֹנָיו׃ וַיִּקְבֹּץ
and-he-gathered (24) masters-of-him Zobah king-of Hadadezer from he-fled

commander of the army, who
had gone up to bury the dead,
had struck down all the men
in Edom. 16Joab and all the Israelites stayed there for six
months, until they had destroyed all the men in Edom.
17But Hadad, still only a boy,
fled to Egypt with some
Edomite officials who had
served his father. 18They set
out from Midian and went to
Paran. Then taking men from
Paran with them, they went to
Egypt, to Pharaoh king of
Egypt, who gave Hadad a
house and land and provided
him with food.
19Pharaoh was so pleased
with Hadad that he gave him
a sister of his own wife,
Queen Tahpenes, in marriage.
20The sister of Tahpenes bore
him a son named Genubath,
whom Tahpenes brought up
in the royal palace. There
Genubath lived with Phar-
aoh's own children.
21While he was in Egypt,
Hadad heard that David rested with his fathers and that
Joab the commander of the
army was also dead. Then
Hadad said to Pharaoh, "Let
me go, that I may return to my
own country."
22"What have you lacked
here that you want to go back
to your own country?" Pharaoh asked.
"Nothing," Hadad replied,
"but do let me go!"
23And God raised up against
Solomon another adversary,
Rezon son of Eliada, who had
fled from his master, Hadadezer king of Zobah. 24He gathered men around him and

עָלָיו אֲנָשִׁים וַיְהִי שַׂר־ גְּדוּד בַּהֲרֹג דָּוִד
David when-to-destroy rebel-band leader-of and-he-became men around-him

אֹתָם וַיֵּלְכוּ דַמֶּשֶׂק וַיֵּשְׁבוּ בָהּ וַיִּמְלְכוּ
and-they-took-control in-her and-they-settled Damascus and-they-went them

בְּדַמָּשֶׂק׃ וַיְהִי שָׂטָן לְיִשְׂרָאֵל כָּל־ יְמֵי שְׁלֹמֹה
Solomon days-of all-of to-Israel adversary and-he-was (25) over-Damascus

וְאֶת־ הָרָעָה אֲשֶׁר הֲדָד וַיָּקָץ בְּיִשְׂרָאֵל וַיִּמְלֹךְ
and-he-ruled toward-Israel and-he-was-hostile Hadad that the-trouble plus

עַל־אֲרָם׃ וְיָרָבְעָם בֶּן־ נְבָט אֶפְרָתִי מִן־ הַצְּרֵדָה
the-Zeredah from Ephraimite Nebat son-of and-Jeroboam (26) Aram in

וְשֵׁם אִמּוֹ צְרוּעָה אִשָּׁה אַלְמָנָה עֶבֶד לִשְׁלֹמֹה
of-Solomon official widow woman Zeruah mother-of-him and-name-of

וַיָּרֶם יָד בַּמֶּלֶךְ׃ וְזֶה הַדָּבָר אֲשֶׁר־ הֵרִים
he-raised how the-account and-this (27) against-the-king hand and-he-raised

יָד בַּמֶּלֶךְ שְׁלֹמֹה בָּנָה אֶת־ הַמִּלּוֹא סָגַר
he-filled the-supporting-terrace *** he-built Solomon against-the-king hand

אֶת־פֶּרֶץ עִיר דָּוִד אָבִיו׃ וְהָאִישׁ יָרָבְעָם גִּבּוֹר חָיִל
standing man-of Jeroboam now-the-man (28) father-of-him David city-of gap ***

וַיַּרְא שְׁלֹמֹה אֶת־ הַנַּעַר כִּי־ עֹשֵׂה מְלָאכָה הוּא וַיַּפְקֵד
then-he-put-in-charge he work doing that the-young-man *** Solomon when-he-saw

אֹתוֹ לְכָל־ סֵבֶל בֵּית יוֹסֵף׃ וַיְהִי בָּעֵת
about-the-time and-he-was (29) Joseph house-of labor-force of-whole-of him

הַהִיא וְיָרָבְעָם יָצָא מִירוּשָׁלָםִ וַיִּמְצָא אֹתוֹ אֲחִיָּה
Ahijah him and-he-met from-Jerusalem he-went-out now-Jeroboam the-this

הַשִּׁילֹנִי הַנָּבִיא בַּדֶּרֶךְ וְהוּא מִתְכַּסֶּה בְּשַׂלְמָה חֲדָשָׁה
new with-cloak being-clothed and-he on-the-way the-prophet the-Shilonite

וּשְׁנֵיהֶם לְבַדָּם בַּשָּׂדֶה׃ וַיִּתְפֹּשׂ אֲחִיָּה
Ahijah and-he-took-hold (30) in-the-country by-themselves and-two-of-them

בַּשַּׂלְמָה הַחֲדָשָׁה אֲשֶׁר עָלָיו וַיִּקְרָעֶהָ שְׁנֵים עָשָׂר קְרָעִים׃
pieces ten two and-he-tore-her on-him that the-new on-the-cloak

וַיֹּאמֶר לְיָרָבְעָם קַח־ לְךָ עֲשָׂרָה קְרָעִים כִּי כֹה אָמַר
he-says this for pieces ten for-you take! to-Jeroboam then-he-said (31)

יְהוָה אֱלֹהֵי יִשְׂרָאֵל הִנְנִי קֹרֵעַ אֶת־ הַמַּמְלָכָה מִיַּד שְׁלֹמֹה
Solomon from-hand-of the-kingdom *** tearing see-I! Israel God-of Yahweh

וְנָתַתִּי לְךָ אֵת עֲשָׂרָה הַשְּׁבָטִים׃ וְהַשֵּׁבֶט הָאֶחָד
the-one but-the-tribe (32) the-tribes ten *** to-you and-I-will-give

יִהְיֶה־ לּוֹ לְמַעַן ׀ עַבְדִּי דָוִד וּלְמַעַן יְרוּשָׁלַםִ
Jerusalem and-for-sake-of David servant-of-me for-sake-of for-him he-will-be

became the leader of a band of rebels when David destroyed the forces[d] ⌞of Zobah⌟; the rebels went to Damascus, where they settled and took control. 25Rezon was Israel's adversary as long as Solomon lived, adding to the trouble caused by Hadad. So Rezon ruled in Aram and was hostile toward Israel.

Jeroboam Rebels Against Solomon

26Also, Jeroboam son of Nebat rebelled against the king. He was one of Solomon's officials, an Ephraimite from Zeredah, and his mother was a widow named Zeruah.

27Here is the account of how he rebelled against the king: Solomon had built the supporting terraces[e] and had filled in the gap in the wall of the city of David his father. 28Now Jeroboam was a man of standing, and when Solomon saw how well the young man did his work, he put him in charge of the whole labor force of the house of Joseph.

29About that time Jeroboam was going out of Jerusalem, and Ahijah the prophet of Shiloh met him on the way, wearing a new cloak. The two of them were alone out in the country, 30and Ahijah took hold of the new cloak he was wearing and tore it into twelve pieces. 31Then he said to Jeroboam, "Take ten pieces for yourself, for this is what the LORD, the God of Israel, says: 'See, I am going to tear the kingdom out of Solomon's hand and give you ten tribes. 32But for the sake of my servant David and the city of

[d]24 Hebrew *destroyed them*
[e]27 Or *the Millo*

הָעִיר אֲשֶׁר בָּחַרְתִּי בָהּ מִכֹּל שִׁבְטֵי יִשְׂרָאֵל׃ יַעַן ׀ אֲשֶׁר
that because (33) Israel tribes-of from-all-of to-her I-choose which the-city

עֲזָבוּנִי וַיִּשְׁתַּחֲווּ לְעַשְׁתֹּרֶת אֱלֹהֵי צִדֹנִין לִכְמוֹשׁ
to-Chemosh Sidonian gods-of to-Ashtoreth and-they-worshiped they-forsook-me

אֱלֹהֵי מוֹאָב וּלְמִלְכֹּם אֱלֹהֵי בְנֵי־ עַמּוֹן וְלֹא־ הָלְכוּ
they-walked and-not Ammon sons-of gods-of and-to-Milcom Moab gods-of

בִדְרָכַי לַעֲשׂוֹת הַיָּשָׁר בְּעֵינַי וְחֻקֹּתַי וּמִשְׁפָּטַי
or-laws-of-me or-statutes-of-me in-eyes-of-me the-right to-do in-ways-of-me

כְּדָוִד אָבִיו׃ וְלֹא־ אֶקַּח אֶת־ כָּל־ הַמַּמְלָכָה
the-kingdom whole-of *** I-will-take but-not (34) father-of-him as-David

מִיָּדוֹ כִּי ׀ נָשִׂיא אֲשִׁתֶנּוּ כֹּל יְמֵי חַיָּיו
lives-of-him days-of all-of I-made-him ruler because from-hand-of-him

לְמַעַן דָּוִד עַבְדִּי אֲשֶׁר בָּחַרְתִּי אֹתוֹ אֲשֶׁר שָׁמַר
he-observed who him I-chose whom servant-of-me David for-sake-of

מִצְוֹתַי וְחֻקֹּתָי׃ וְלָקַחְתִּי הַמְּלוּכָה
the-kingdom so-I-will-take (35) and-statutes-of-me commands-of-me

מִיַּד בְּנוֹ וּנְתַתִּיהָ לְּךָ אֵת עֲשֶׂרֶת הַשְּׁבָטִים׃
the-tribes ten-of *** to-you and-I-will-give-her son-of-him from-hand-of

וְלִבְנוֹ אֶתֵּן שֵׁבֶט־ אֶחָד לְמַעַן הֱיוֹת־ נִיר לְדָוִיד־
for-David lamp to-be so-that one tribe I-will-give and-to-son-of-him (36)

עַבְדִּי כָּל־ הַיָּמִים ׀ לְפָנַי בִּירוּשָׁלִַם הָעִיר אֲשֶׁר בָּחַרְתִּי
I-chose which the-city in-Jerusalem before-me the-days all-of servant-of-me

לִי לָשׂוּם שְׁמִי שָׁם׃ וְאֹתְךָ אֶקַּח וּמָלַכְתָּ
and-you-will-rule I-will-take but-you (37) there Name-of-me to-put for-me

בְּכֹל אֲשֶׁר־ תְּאַוֶּה נַפְשֶׁךָ וְהָיִיתָ מֶּלֶךְ עַל־יִשְׂרָאֵל׃
Israel over king and-you-will-be heart-of-you she-desires that over-all

וְהָיָה אִם־ תִּשְׁמַע אֶת־ כָּל־ אֲשֶׁר אֲצַוֶּךָ וְהָלַכְתָּ
and-you-walk I-command-you that all *** you-do if and-he-will-be (38)

בִדְרָכַי וְעָשִׂיתָ הַיָּשָׁר בְּעֵינַי לִשְׁמוֹר חֻקּוֹתַי
statutes-of-me to-keep in-eyes-of-me the-right and-you-do in-ways-of-me

וּמִצְוֹתַי כַּאֲשֶׁר עָשָׂה דָּוִד עַבְדִּי וְהָיִיתִי עִמָּךְ
with-you and-I-will-be servant-of-me David he-did just-as and-commands-of-me

וּבָנִיתִי לְךָ בַיִת־ נֶאֱמָן כַּאֲשֶׁר בָּנִיתִי לְדָוִד
for-David I-built just-as enduring dynasty for-you and-I-will-build

וְנָתַתִּי לְךָ אֶת־ יִשְׂרָאֵל׃ וַאעַנֶּה* אֶת־ זֶרַע
descendant-of *** and-I-will-humble (39) Israel *** to-you and-I-will-give

דָּוִד לְמַעַן זֹאת אַךְ לֹא כָל־ הַיָּמִים׃ וַיְבַקֵּשׁ שְׁלֹמֹה
Solomon and-he-tried (40) the-days all-of not but this because-of David

Jerusalem, which I have chosen out of all the tribes of Israel, he will have one tribe. [33]I will do this because they have[g] forsaken me and worshiped Ashtoreth the goddess of the Sidonians, Chemosh the god of the Moabites, and Molech[h] the god of the Ammonites, and have not walked in my ways, nor done what is right in my eyes, nor kept my statutes and laws as David, Solomon's father, did.

[34]" 'But I will not take the whole kingdom out of Solomon's hand; I have made him ruler all the days of his life for the sake of David my servant, whom I chose and who observed my commands and statutes. [35]I will take the kingdom from his son's hands and give you ten tribes. [36]I will give one tribe to his son so that David my servant may always have a lamp before me in Jerusalem, the city where I chose to put my Name. [37]However, as for you, I will take you, and you will rule over all that your heart desires; you will be king over Israel. [38]If you do whatever I command you and walk in my ways and do what is right in my eyes by keeping my statutes and commands, as David my servant did, I will be with you. I will build you a dynasty as enduring as the one I built for David and will give Israel to you. [39]I will humble David's descendants because of this, but not forever.' "

[g]33 Hebrew; Septuagint, Vulgate and Syriac *because he has*
[h]33 Hebrew *Milcom*

**39* Most mss have the Qere form (ועָנה), though the *kethib* form should probably remain, with *hateph pathah* under the *aleph* (וַאֲעַנֶּה).

לְהָמִית אֶת־ יָרָבְעָם וַיָּקָם יָרָבְעָם וַיִּבְרַח מִצְרַיִם אֶל־ שִׁישַׁק

Shishak to Egypt and-he-fled Jeroboam but-he-got-up Jeroboam *** to-kill

מֶלֶךְ־ מִצְרַיִם וַיְהִי בְמִצְרַיִם עַד־ מוֹת שְׁלֹמֹה׃ וְיֶתֶר

and-rest-of (41) Solomon death-of until in-Egypt and-he-stayed Egypt king-of

דִּבְרֵי שְׁלֹמֹה וְכָל־ אֲשֶׁר עָשָׂה וְחָכְמָתוֹ הֲלוֹא־ הֵם

they not? and-wisdom-of-him he-did that and-all Solomon events-of

כְּתֻבִים עַל־ סֵפֶר דִּבְרֵי שְׁלֹמֹה׃ וְהַיָּמִים אֲשֶׁר

that and-the-days (42) Solomon annals-of book-of in ones-being-written

מָלַךְ שְׁלֹמֹה בִירוּשָׁלַםִ עַל־ כָּל־ יִשְׂרָאֵל אַרְבָּעִים שָׁנָה׃

year forty Israel all-of over in-Jerusalem Solomon he-reigned

וַיִּשְׁכַּב שְׁלֹמֹה עִם־ אֲבֹתָיו וַיִּקָּבֵר בְּעִיר

in-city-of and-he-was-buried fathers-of-him with Solomon then-he-rested (43)

דָּוִד אָבִיו וַיִּמְלֹךְ רְחַבְעָם בְּנוֹ תַּחְתָּיו׃

in-place-of-him son-of-him Rehoboam and-he-became-king father-of-him David

וַיֵּלֶךְ רְחַבְעָם שְׁכֶם כִּי שְׁכֶם בָּא כָל־ יִשְׂרָאֵל

Israel all-of he-went Shechem for Shechem Rehoboam and-he-went (12:1)

לְהַמְלִיךְ אֹתוֹ׃ וַיְהִי כִּשְׁמֹעַ ׀ יָרָבְעָם בֶּן־ נְבָט וְהוּא

now-he Nebat son-of Jeroboam when-to-hear and-he-was (2) him to-make-king

עוֹדֶנּוּ בְמִצְרַיִם אֲשֶׁר בָּרַח מִפְּנֵי הַמֶּלֶךְ שְׁלֹמֹה וַיֵּשֶׁב

and-he-remained Solomon the-king from-before he-fled where in-Egypt still-he

יָרָבְעָם בְּמִצְרָיִם׃ וַיִּשְׁלְחוּ וַיִּקְרְאוּ־ לוֹ וַיָּבֹאוּ

and-he-went for-him and-they-called so-they-sent (3) in-Egypt Jeroboam

יָרָבְעָם וְכָל־ קְהַל יִשְׂרָאֵל וַיְדַבְּרוּ אֶל־ רְחַבְעָם לֵאמֹר׃

to-say Rehoboam to and-they-said Israel assembly-of and-whole-of Jeroboam

אָבִיךָ הִקְשָׁה אֶת־ עֻלֵּנוּ וְאַתָּה עַתָּה הָקֵל

lighten! now but-you yoke-of-us *** he-made-heavy father-of-you (4)

מֵעֲבֹדַת אָבִיךָ הַקָּשָׁה וּמֵעֻלּוֹ הַכָּבֵד אֲשֶׁר־

that the-heavy and-from-yoke-of-him the-harsh father-of-you from-labor-of

נָתַן עָלֵינוּ וְנַעַבְדֶךָּ׃ וַיֹּאמֶר אֲלֵיהֶם לְכוּ עֹד

for go-away! to-them and-he-answered (5) and-we-will-serve-you on-us he-put

שְׁלֹשָׁה יָמִים וְשׁוּבוּ אֵלָי וַיֵּלְכוּ הָעָם׃

the-people so-they-went-away to-me then-come-back! days three

וַיִּוָּעַץ הַמֶּלֶךְ רְחַבְעָם אֶת־ הַזְּקֵנִים אֲשֶׁר־ הָיוּ

they-were who the-elders with Rehoboam the-king then-he-consulted (6)

עֹמְדִים אֶת־ פְּנֵי שְׁלֹמֹה אָבִיו בִּהְיֹתוֹ חַי לֵאמֹר

to-say alive while-to-be-him father-of-him Solomon before *** ones-serving

אֵיךְ אַתֶּם נוֹעָצִים לְהָשִׁיב אֶת־ הָעָם־ הַזֶּה דָבָר׃

answer the-this the-people *** to-return ones-advising you how?

°3 ק ויבא

40Solomon tried to kill Jeroboam, but Jeroboam fled to Egypt, to Shishak the king, and stayed there until Solomon's death.

Solomon's Death

41As for the other events of Solomon's reign—all he did and the wisdom he displayed—are they not written in the book of the annals of Solomon? 42Solomon reigned in Jerusalem over all Israel forty years. 43Then he rested with his fathers and was buried in the city of David his father. And Rehoboam his son succeeded him as king.

Israel Rebels Against Rehoboam

12 Rehoboam went to Shechem, for all the Israelites had gone there to make him king. 2When Jeroboam son of Nebat heard this (he was still in Egypt, where he had fled from King Solomon), he returned from[i] Egypt. 3So they sent for Jeroboam, and he and the whole assembly of Israel went to Rehoboam and said to him: 4"Your father put a heavy yoke on us, but now lighten the harsh labor and the heavy yoke he put on us, and we will serve you."

5Rehoboam answered, "Go away for three days and then come back to me." So the people went away.

6Then King Rehoboam consulted the elders who had served his father Solomon during his lifetime. "How would you advise me to answer these people?" he asked.

i2 Or *he remained in*

(7) וַיְדַבְּרו֯ אֵלָיו לֵאמֹר אִם־הַיּוֹם תִּהְיֶה־עֶבֶד לָעָם
to-the-people servant you-will-be the-day if to-say to-him and-they-replied (7)

הַזֶּה וַעֲבַדְתָּם וַעֲנִיתָם וְדִבַּרְתָּ אֲלֵיהֶם
to-them and-you-speak and-you-answer-them and-you-serve-them the-this

דְּבָרִים טוֹבִים וְהָיוּ לְךָ עֲבָדִים כָּל־הַיָּמִים׃
the-days all-of servants to-you then-they-will-be favorable-ones answers

(8) וַיַּעֲזֹב אֶת־עֲצַת הַזְּקֵנִים אֲשֶׁר יְעָצֻהוּ וַיִּוָּעַץ
and-he-consulted they-gave-him that the-elders advice-of *** but-he-rejected (8)

אֶת־הַיְלָדִים אֲשֶׁר גָּדְלוּ אִתּוֹ אֲשֶׁר הָעֹמְדִים
the-ones-serving who with-him they-grew-up who the-young-men ***

לְפָנָיו׃ (9) וַיֹּאמֶר אֲלֵיהֶם מָה אַתֶּם נוֹעָצִים וְנָשִׁיב
that-we-should-give ones-advising you what? to-them and-he-asked (9) before-him

דָּבָר אֶת־הָעָם הַזֶּה אֲשֶׁר דִּבְּרוּ אֵלַי לֵאמֹר הָקֵל מִן־
from lighten! to-say to-me they-say who the-this the-people *** answer

הָעֹל אֲשֶׁר־נָתַן אָבִיךָ עָלֵינוּ׃ (10) וַיְדַבְּרוּ אֵלָיו
to-him and-they-replied (10) on-us father-of-you he-put that the-yoke

הַיְלָדִים אֲשֶׁר גָּדְלוּ אִתּוֹ לֵאמֹר כֹּה־תֹאמַר לָעָם
to-the-people you-tell this to-say with-him they-grew-up who the-young-men

הַזֶּה אֲשֶׁר דִּבְּרוּ אֵלֶיךָ לֵאמֹר אָבִיךָ הִכְבִּיד אֶת־
*** he-made-heavy father-of-you to-say to-you they-said who the-this

עֻלֵּנוּ וְאַתָּה הָקֵל מֵעָלֵינוּ כֹּה תְּדַבֵּר אֲלֵיהֶם
to-them you-tell this from-yoke-of-us you-make-light but-you yoke-of-us

קָטָנִּי עָבָה מִמָּתְנֵי אָבִי׃ (11) וְעַתָּה
and-now (11) father-of-me more-than-waists-of he-is-thick little-one-of-me

אָבִי הֶעְמִיס עֲלֵיכֶם עֹל כָּבֵד וַאֲנִי אוֹסִיף עַל־עֻלְּכֶם
yoke-of-you to I-will-add but-I heavy yoke on-you he-laid father-of-me

אָבִי יִסַּר אֶתְכֶם בַּשּׁוֹטִים וַאֲנִי אֲיַסֵּר אֶתְכֶם
you I-will-scourge but-I with-the-whips you he-scourged father-of-me

בָּעַקְרַבִּים׃ (12) וַיָּבוֹ֯ יָרָבְעָם וְכָל־הָעָם אֶל־
to the-people and-all-of Jeroboam and-he-returned (12) with-the-scorpions

רְחַבְעָם בַּיּוֹם הַשְּׁלִישִׁי כַּאֲשֶׁר דִּבֶּר הַמֶּלֶךְ לֵאמֹר שׁוּבוּ
come-back! to-say the-king he-said just-as the-third on-the-day Rehoboam

אֵלַי בַּיּוֹם הַשְּׁלִישִׁי׃ (13) וַיַּעַן הַמֶּלֶךְ אֶת־הָעָם
the-people *** the-king and-he-answered (13) the-third on-the-day to-me

קָשָׁה וַיַּעֲזֹב אֶת־עֲצַת הַזְּקֵנִים אֲשֶׁר יְעָצֻהוּ׃
they-gave-him that the-elders advice-of *** and-he-rejected harshly

(14) וַיְדַבֵּר אֲלֵיהֶם כַּעֲצַת הַיְלָדִים לֵאמֹר אָבִי
father-of-me to-say the-young-men as-advice-of to-them and-he-spoke (14)

[7]They replied, "If today you
will be a servant to these
people and serve them and
give them a favorable answer,
they will always be your servants."
[8]But Rehoboam rejected the
advice the elders gave him
and consulted the young men
who had grown up with him
and were serving him. [9]He
asked them, "What is your advice? How should we answer
these people who say to me,
'Lighten the yoke your father
put on us'?"
[10]The young men who had
grown up with him replied,
"Tell these people who have
said to you, 'Your father put a
heavy yoke on us, but make
our yoke lighter'—tell them,
'My little finger is thicker than
my father's waist. [11]My father
laid on you a heavy yoke; I
will make it even heavier. My
father scourged you with
whips; I will scourge you with
scorpions.' "
[12]Three days later Jeroboam
and all the people returned to
Rehoboam, as the king had
said, "Come back to me in
three days." [13]The king answered the people harshly. Re-
jecting the advice given him
by the elders, [14]he followed the
advice of the young men and
said, "My father made your

°7 ק וידברו
°12 ק ויבוא

הִכְבִּיד אֶת־ עֻלְּכֶם וַאֲנִי אֹסִיף עַל־ עֻלְּכֶם אָבִי
father-of-me yoke-of-you to I-will-add but-I yoke-of-you *** he-made-heavy

יִסַּר אֶתְכֶם בַּשּׁוֹטִים וַאֲנִי אֲיַסֵּר אֶתְכֶם בָּעַקְרַבִּים׃
with-the-scorpions you I-will-scourge but-I with-the-whips you he-scourged

וְלֹא־ שָׁמַע הַמֶּלֶךְ אֶל־ הָעָם כִּי־ הָיְתָה סִבָּה
turn-of-events she-was for the-people to the-king he-listened so-not (15)

מֵעִם יְהוָה לְמַעַן הָקִים אֶת־ דְּבָרוֹ אֲשֶׁר דִּבֶּר יְהוָה
Yahweh he-spoke that word-of-him *** to-fulfill in-order-to Yahweh from-with

בְּיַד אֲחִיָּה הַשִּׁלֹנִי אֶל־ יָרָבְעָם בֶּן־ נְבָט׃ וַיַּרְא
when-he-saw (16) Nebat son-of Jeroboam to the-Shilonite Ahijah by-hand-of

כָּל־ יִשְׂרָאֵל כִּי לֹא־ שָׁמַע הַמֶּלֶךְ אֲלֵיהֶם וַיָּשִׁבוּ הָעָם
the-people then-they-gave to-them the-king he-listened not that Israel all-of

אֶת־הַמֶּלֶךְ דָּבָר ׀ לֵאמֹר מַה־ לָּנוּ חֵלֶק בְּדָוִד וְלֹא־ נַחֲלָה בְּבֶן־
in-son-of part and-not in-David share to-us what? to-say answer the-king ***

יִשַׁי לְאֹהָלֶיךָ יִשְׂרָאֵל עַתָּה רְאֵה בֵיתְךָ דָּוִד וַיֵּלֶךְ
so-he-went David house-of-you look-after! now Israel to-tents-of-you Jesse

יִשְׂרָאֵל לְאֹהָלָיו׃ וּבְנֵי יִשְׂרָאֵל הַיֹּשְׁבִים בְּעָרֵי
in-towns-of the-ones-living Israel but-sons-of (17) to-homes-of-him Israel

יְהוּדָה וַיִּמְלֹךְ עֲלֵיהֶם רְחַבְעָם׃ וַיִּשְׁלַח הַמֶּלֶךְ רְחַבְעָם
Rehoboam the-king and-he-sent-out (18) Rehoboam over-them and-he-ruled Judah

אֶת־אֲדֹרָם אֲשֶׁר עַל־ הַמַּס וַיִּרְגְּמוּ כָל־ יִשְׂרָאֵל בּוֹ
on-him Israel all-of but-they-stoned the-forced-labor over who Adoram ***

אֶבֶן וַיָּמֹת וְהַמֶּלֶךְ רְחַבְעָם הִתְאַמֵּץ לַעֲלוֹת בַּמֶּרְכָּבָה
into-the-chariot to-get-up he-managed Rehoboam but-the-king and-he-died stone

לָנוּס יְרוּשָׁלִָם׃ וַיִּפְשְׁעוּ יִשְׂרָאֵל בְּבֵית דָּוִד עַד
to David against-house-of Israel so-they-rebelled (19) Jerusalem to-escape

הַיּוֹם הַזֶּה׃ וַיְהִי כִּשְׁמֹעַ כָּל־ יִשְׂרָאֵל כִּי־ שָׁב
he-returned that Israel all-of when-to-hear and-he-was (20) the-this the-day

יָרָבְעָם וַיִּשְׁלְחוּ וַיִּקְרְאוּ אֹתוֹ אֶל־ הָעֵדָה וַיַּמְלִיכוּ
and-they-made-king the-assembly to him and-they-called then-they-sent Jeroboam

אֹתוֹ עַל־ כָּל־ יִשְׂרָאֵל לֹא הָיָה אַחֲרֵי בֵית־ דָּוִד זוּלָתִי שֵׁבֶט־
tribe-of except David house-of after he-was not Israel all-of over him

יְהוּדָה לְבַדּוֹ׃ וַיָּבֹאו° רְחַבְעָם יְרוּשָׁלִַם וַיַּקְהֵל אֶת־
*** then-he-mustered Jerusalem Rehoboam when-he-arrived (21) by-himself Judah

כָּל־ בֵּית יְהוּדָה וְאֶת־ שֵׁבֶט בִּנְיָמִן מֵאָה וּשְׁמֹנִים אֶלֶף
thousand and-eighty hundred Benjamin tribe-of and Judah house-of whole-of

בָּחוּר עֹשֵׂה מִלְחָמָה לְהִלָּחֵם עִם־ בֵּית יִשְׂרָאֵל לְהָשִׁיב אֶת־
*** to-regain Israel house-of against to-make-war fight doing being-chosen

yoke heavy; I will make it even heavier. My father scourged you with whips; I will scourge you with scorpions." 15So the king did not listen to the people, for this turn of events was from the LORD, to fulfill the word the LORD had spoken to Jeroboam son of Nebat through Ahijah the Shilonite.

16When all Israel saw that the king refused to listen to them, they answered the king:

"What share do we have in David,
what part in Jesse's son?
To your tents, O Israel!
Look after your own house, O David!"

So the Israelites went home.
17But as for the Israelites who were living in the towns of Judah, Rehoboam still ruled over them.

18King Rehoboam sent out Adoniram,[j] who was in charge of forced labor, but all Israel stoned him to death. King Rehoboam, however, managed to get into his chariot and escape to Jerusalem.
19So Israel has been in rebellion against the house of David to this day.

20When all the Israelites heard that Jeroboam had returned, they sent and called him to the assembly and made him king over all Israel. Only the tribe of Judah remained loyal to the house of David.

21When Rehoboam arrived in Jerusalem, he mustered the whole house of Judah and the tribe of Benjamin—a hundred and eighty thousand fighting men—to make war against the house of Israel and to regain

j18 Some Septuagint manuscripts and Syriac (see also 1 Kings 4:6 and 5:14); Hebrew *Adoram*

°21 ויבא ק

הַמְּלוּכָה לִרְחַבְעָם בֶּן־ שְׁלֹמֹה׃ וַיְהִי דְּבַר הָאֱלֹהִים
the-God word-of but-he-came (22) Solomon son-of for-Rehoboam the-kingdom

אֶל־שְׁמַעְיָה אִישׁ־ הָאֱלֹהִים לֵאמֹר׃ אֱמֹר אֶל־רְחַבְעָם בֶּן־ שְׁלֹמֹה
Solomon son-of Rehoboam to say! (23) to-say the-God man-of Shemaiah to

מֶלֶךְ יְהוּדָה וְאֶל־ כָּל־ בֵּית יְהוּדָה וּבִנְיָמִין וְיֶתֶר
and-rest-of and-Benjamin Judah house-of whole-of and-to Judah king-of

הָעָם לֵאמֹר׃ כֹּה אָמַר יְהוָה לֹא־ תַעֲלוּ וְלֹא־ תִלָּחֲמוּן
you-fight and-not you-go-up not Yahweh he-says this (24) to-say the-people

עִם־ אֲחֵיכֶם בְנֵי־ יִשְׂרָאֵל שׁוּבוּ אִישׁ לְבֵיתוֹ כִּי
for to-home-of-him each go-back! Israel sons-of brothers-of-you against

מֵאִתִּי נִהְיָה הַדָּבָר הַזֶּה וַיִּשְׁמְעוּ אֶת־ דְּבַר יְהוָה
Yahweh word-of *** so-they-obeyed the-this the-thing he-is-done from-with-me

וַיָּשֻׁבוּ לָלֶכֶת כִּדְבַר יְהוָה׃ וַיִּבֶן יָרָבְעָם
Jeroboam then-he-fortified (25) Yahweh as-order-of to-go and-they-returned

אֶת־ שְׁכֶם בְּהַר אֶפְרַיִם וַיֵּשֶׁב בָּהּ וַיֵּצֵא
and-he-went-out in-her and-he-lived Ephraim in-hill-country-of Shechem ***

מִשָּׁם וַיִּבֶן אֶת־ פְּנוּאֵל׃ וַיֹּאמֶר יָרָבְעָם
Jeroboam and-he-thought (26) Penuel *** and-he-built-up from-there

בְּלִבּוֹ עַתָּה תָּשׁוּב הַמַּמְלָכָה לְבֵית דָּוִד׃ אִם־
if (27) David to-house-of the-kingdom she-will-revert now in-heart-of-him

יַעֲלֶה ׀ הָעָם הַזֶּה לַעֲשׂוֹת זְבָחִים בְּבֵית־ יְהוָה
Yahweh at-temple-of sacrifices to-offer the-this the-people he-goes-up

בִירוּשָׁלַםִ וְשָׁב לֵב הָעָם הַזֶּה אֶל־ אֲדֹנֵיהֶם
lords-of-them to the-this the-people heart-of then-he-will-return in-Jerusalem

אֶל־ רְחַבְעָם מֶלֶךְ יְהוּדָה וַהֲרָגֻנִי וְשָׁבוּ אֶל־
to and-they-will-return and-they-will-kill-me Judah king-of Rehoboam to

רְחַבְעָם מֶלֶךְ־ יְהוּדָה׃ וַיִּוָּעַץ הַמֶּלֶךְ וַיַּעַשׂ שְׁנֵי
two-of and-he-made the-king and-he-sought-advice (28) Judah king-of Rehoboam

עֶגְלֵי זָהָב וַיֹּאמֶר אֲלֵהֶם רַב־ לָכֶם מֵעֲלוֹת יְרוּשָׁלַםִ
Jerusalem from-to-go-up for-you too-much to-them and-he-said gold calves-of

הִנֵּה אֱלֹהֶיךָ יִשְׂרָאֵל אֲשֶׁר הֶעֱלוּךָ מֵאֶרֶץ מִצְרָיִם׃
Egypt from-land-of they-brought-up-you who Israel gods-of-you here!

וַיָּשֶׂם אֶת־ הָאֶחָד בְּבֵית־ אֵל וְאֶת־ הָאֶחָד נָתַן בְּדָן׃
in-Dan he-set-up the-other and El in-Beth the-one *** and-he-set-up (29)

וַיְהִי הַדָּבָר הַזֶּה לְחַטָּאת וַיֵּלְכוּ הָעָם לִפְנֵי
before the-people and-they-went as-sin the-this the-thing and-he-became (30)

הָאֶחָד עַד־ דָּן׃ וַיַּעַשׂ אֶת־ בֵּית בָּמוֹת
high-places shrine-of *** and-he-built (31) Dan as-far-as the-one

the kingdom for Rehoboam
son of Solomon.
22But this word of God came
to Shemaiah the man of God:
23"Say to Rehoboam son of
Solomon king of Judah, to the
whole house of Judah and
Benjamin, and to the rest of
the people, 24'This is what the
LORD says: Do not go up to
fight against your brothers,
the Israelites. Go home, every
one of you, for this is my doing.' " So they obeyed the
word of the LORD and went
home again, as the LORD had
ordered.

Golden Calves at Bethel and Dan

25Then Jeroboam fortified
Shechem in the hill country of
Ephraim and lived there.
From there he went out and
built up Peniel.[k]
26Jeroboam thought to himself, "The kingdom will now
likely revert to the house of
David. 27If these people go up
to offer sacrifices at the temple
of the LORD in Jerusalem, they
will again give their allegiance
to their lord, Rehoboam king
of Judah. They will kill me and
return to King Rehoboam."
28After seeking advice, the
king made two golden calves.
He said to the people, "It is too
much for you to go up to
Jerusalem. Here are your gods,
O Israel, who brought you up
out of Egypt." 29One he set up
in Bethel, and the other in
Dan. 30And this thing became
a sin; the people went even as
far as Dan to worship the one
there.
31Jeroboam built shrines on
high places and appointed

[k]25 Hebrew *Penuel*, a variant of *Peniel*

וַיַּעַשׂ כֹּהֲנִים מִקְצוֹת הָעָם אֲשֶׁר לֹא־הָיוּ
they-were not who the-people from-ends-of priests and-he-appointed

מִבְּנֵי לֵוִי׃ וַיַּעַשׂ יָרָבְעָם ׀ חָג בַּחֹדֶשׁ
in-the-month festival Jeroboam and-he-instituted (32) Levi from-sons-of

הַשְּׁמִינִי בַּחֲמִשָּׁה־עָשָׂר יוֹם ׀ לַחֹדֶשׁ כֶּחָג ׀ אֲשֶׁר בִּיהוּדָה
in-Judah that like-festival of-the-month day ten on-five the-eighth

וַיַּעַל עַל־הַמִּזְבֵּחַ כֵּן עָשָׂה בְּבֵית־אֵל לְזַבֵּחַ לָעֲגָלִים
to-the-calves to-sacrifice El in-Beth he-did this the-altar on and-he-offered

אֲשֶׁר־עָשָׂה וְהֶעֱמִיד בְּבֵית אֵל אֶת־כֹּהֲנֵי הַבָּמוֹת אֲשֶׁר
that the-high-places priests-of *** El at-Beth and-he-installed he-made that

עָשָׂה׃ וַיַּעַל עַל־הַמִּזְבֵּחַ ׀ אֲשֶׁר־עָשָׂה בְּבֵית־אֵל בַּחֲמִשָּׁה
on-five El at-Beth he-made that the-altar on and-he-offered (33) he-made

עָשָׂר יוֹם בַּחֹדֶשׁ הַשְּׁמִינִי בַּחֹדֶשׁ אֲשֶׁר־בָּדָא °מִלִּבד
by-himself he-chose that in-the-month the-eighth of-the-month day ten

וַיַּעַשׂ חָג לִבְנֵי יִשְׂרָאֵל וַיַּעַל עַל־הַמִּזְבֵּחַ
the-altar to and-he-went-up Israel for-sons-of festival so-he-instituted

לְהַקְטִיר׃ וְהִנֵּה ׀ אִישׁ אֱלֹהִים בָּא מִיהוּדָה בִּדְבַר
by-word-of from-Judah coming God man-of then-see! (13:1) to-make-offering

יְהוָה אֶל־בֵּית־אֵל וְיָרָבְעָם עֹמֵד עַל־הַמִּזְבֵּחַ לְהַקְטִיר׃
to-make-offering the-altar by standing and-Jeroboam El Beth to Yahweh

וַיִּקְרָא עַל־הַמִּזְבֵּחַ בִּדְבַר יְהוָה וַיֹּאמֶר מִזְבֵּחַ
altar and-he-said Yahweh by-word-of the-altar against and-he-cried-out (2)

מִזְבֵּחַ כֹּה אָמַר יְהוָה הִנֵּה־בֵן נוֹלָד לְבֵית־דָּוִד יֹאשִׁיָּהוּ
Josiah David to-house-of being-born son see! Yahweh he-says this altar

שְׁמוֹ וְזָבַח עָלֶיךָ אֶת־כֹּהֲנֵי הַבָּמוֹת
the-high-places priests-of *** on-you and-he-will-sacrifice name-of-him

הַמַּקְטִרִים עָלֶיךָ וְעַצְמוֹת אָדָם יִשְׂרְפוּ עָלֶיךָ׃
on-you they-will-burn human and-bones-of on-you the-ones-making-offerings

וְנָתַן בַּיּוֹם הַהוּא מוֹפֵת לֵאמֹר זֶה הַמּוֹפֵת אֲשֶׁר
that the-sign this to-say sign the-that on-the-day and-he-gave (3)

דִּבֶּר יְהוָה הִנֵּה הַמִּזְבֵּחַ נִקְרָע וְנִשְׁפַּךְ
and-he-will-be-poured-out being-split-apart the-altar see! Yahweh he-declared

הַדֶּשֶׁן אֲשֶׁר־עָלָיו׃ וַיְהִי כִשְׁמֹעַ הַמֶּלֶךְ אֶת־דְּבַר אִישׁ־
man-of word-of *** the-king when-to-hear and-he-was (4) on-him that the-ash

הָאֱלֹהִים אֲשֶׁר קָרָא עַל־הַמִּזְבֵּחַ בְּבֵית־אֵל וַיִּשְׁלַח
and-he-stretched-out El at-Beth the-altar against he-cried-out that the-God

יָרָבְעָם אֶת־יָדוֹ מֵעַל הַמִּזְבֵּחַ לֵאמֹר ׀ תִּפְשֻׂהוּ וַתִּיבַשׁ
but-she-shriveled seize-him! to-say the-altar from-on hand-of-him *** Jeroboam

°33 ק מלבו

priests from all sorts of people,
even though they were not Levites. [32]He instituted a festival
on the fifteenth day of the
eighth month, like the festival
held in Judah, and offered sacrifices on the altar. This he did
in Bethel, sacrificing to the
calves he had made. And at
Bethel he also installed priests
at the high places he had
made. [33]On the fifteenth day
of the eighth month, a month
of his own choosing, he
offered sacrifices on the altar
he had built at Bethel. So he
instituted the festival for the
Israelites and went up to the
altar to make offerings.

The Man of God From Judah

13 By the word of the
LORD a man of God
came from Judah to Bethel, as
Jeroboam was standing by the
altar to make an offering. [2]He
cried out against the altar by
the word of the LORD: "O altar,
altar! This is what the LORD
says: 'A son named Josiah will
be born to the house of David.
On you he will sacrifice the
priests of the high places who
now make offerings here, and
human bones will be burned
on you.' " [3]That same day the
man of God gave a sign: "This
is the sign the LORD has declared: The altar will be split
apart and the ashes on it will
be poured out."
[4]When King Jeroboam heard
what the man of God cried out
against the altar at Bethel, he
stretched out his hand from
the altar and said, "Seize
him!" But the hand he

יָדוֹ אֲשֶׁר שָׁלַח עָלָיו וְלֹא יָכֹל לַהֲשִׁיבָה
to-pull-back-her he-could so-not toward-him he-stretched that hand-of-him

אֵלָיו׃ וְהַמִּזְבֵּחַ נִקְרָע וַיִּשָּׁפֵךְ הַדֶּשֶׁן
the-ash and-he-was-poured-out he-was-split-apart and-the-altar (5) to-him

מִן־הַמִּזְבֵּחַ כַּמּוֹפֵת אֲשֶׁר נָתַן אִישׁ הָאֱלֹהִים בִּדְבַר יְהוָה׃
Yahweh by-word-of the-God man-of he-gave that as-the-sign the-altar from

וַיַּעַן הַמֶּלֶךְ וַיֹּאמֶר ׀ אֶל־אִישׁ הָאֱלֹהִים חַל־נָא
now! intercede! the-God man-of to and-he-said the-king then-he-replied (6)

אֶת־פְּנֵי יְהוָה אֱלֹהֶיךָ וְהִתְפַּלֵּל בַּעֲדִי וְתָשֹׁב
so-she-may-be-restored on-behalf-of-me and-pray! God-of-you Yahweh before ***

יָדִי אֵלָי וַיְחַל אִישׁ־הָאֱלֹהִים אֶת־פְּנֵי יְהוָה
Yahweh before *** the-God man-of so-he-interceded to-me hand-of-me

וַתָּשָׁב יַד־הַמֶּלֶךְ אֵלָיו וַתְּהִי כְּבָרִאשֹׁנָה׃
as-before and-she-became to-him the-king hand-of and-she-was-restored

וַיְדַבֵּר הַמֶּלֶךְ אֶל־אִישׁ הָאֱלֹהִים בֹּאָה־אִתִּי הַבַּיְתָה
to-the-home with-me come! the-God man-of to the-king and-he-said (7)

וּסְעָדָה וְאֶתְּנָה לְךָ מַתָּת׃ וַיֹּאמֶר אִישׁ־הָאֱלֹהִים
the-God man-of but-he-answered (8) gift to-you and-I-will-give and-eat!

אֶל־הַמֶּלֶךְ אִם־תִּתֶּן־לִי אֶת־חֲצִי בֵיתֶךָ לֹא אָבֹא
I-would-go not house-of-you half-of *** to-me you-gave if the-king to

עִמָּךְ וְלֹא־אֹכַל לֶחֶם וְלֹא אֶשְׁתֶּה־מַּיִם בַּמָּקוֹם
at-the-place waters I-would-drink and-not bread I-would-eat and-not with-you

הַזֶּה׃ כִּי־כֵן ׀ צִוָּה אֹתִי בִּדְבַר יְהוָה לֵאמֹר לֹא־
not to-say Yahweh by-word-of me he-commanded thus for (9) the-this

תֹאכַל לֶחֶם וְלֹא תִשְׁתֶּה־מָּיִם וְלֹא תָשׁוּב
you-must-return and-not waters you-must-drink and-not bread you-must-eat

בַּדֶּרֶךְ אֲשֶׁר הָלָכְתָּ׃ וַיֵּלֶךְ בְּדֶרֶךְ אַחֵר וְלֹא־שָׁב
he-returned and-not another by-road so-he-went (10) you-came that by-the-way

בַּדֶּרֶךְ אֲשֶׁר בָּא בָהּ אֶל־בֵּית־אֵל׃ וְנָבִיא אֶחָד זָקֵן
old certain now-prophet (11) El Beth to on-her he-came that by-the-way

יֹשֵׁב בְּבֵית־אֵל וַיָּבוֹא בְנוֹ וַיְסַפֶּר־לוֹ אֶת־כָּל־
all-of *** to-him and-he-told son-of-him and-he-came El in-Beth living

הַמַּעֲשֶׂה אֲשֶׁר־עָשָׂה אִישׁ־הָאֱלֹהִים ׀ הַיּוֹם בְּבֵית־אֵל אֶת־הַדְּבָרִים אֲשֶׁר
that the-things *** El in-Beth the-day the-God man-of he-did that the-deed

דִּבֶּר אֶל־הַמֶּלֶךְ וַיְסַפְּרוּם לַאֲבִיהֶם׃ וַיְדַבֵּר
and-he-asked (12) to-father-of-them and-they-told-them the-king to he-said

אֲלֵהֶם אֲבִיהֶם אֵי־זֶה הַדֶּרֶךְ הָלָךְ וַיִּרְאוּ
and-they-showed he-went the-way this where? father-of-them to-them

stretched out toward the man
shriveled up, so that he could
not pull it back. 5Also, the altar
was split apart and its ashes
poured out according to the
sign given by the man of God
by the word of the LORD.
6Then the king said to the
man of God, "Intercede with
the LORD your God and pray
for me that my hand may be
restored." So the man of God
interceded with the LORD, and
the king's hand was restored
and became as it was before.
7The king said to the man of
God, "Come home with me
and have something to eat,
and I will give you a gift."
8But the man of God an-
swered the king, "Even if you
were to give me half your
possessions, I would not go
with you, nor would I eat
bread or drink water here. 9For
I was commanded by the
word of the LORD: 'You must
not eat bread or drink water or
return by the way you came.' "
10So he took another road and
did not return by the way he
had come to Bethel.
11Now there was a certain
old prophet living in Bethel,
whose sons came and told him
all that the man of God had
done there that day. They also
told their father what he had
said to the king. 12Their father
asked them, "Which way did
he go?" And his sons showed

בָּנָיו אֶת־הַדֶּרֶךְ אֲשֶׁר הָלַךְ אִישׁ הָאֱלֹהִים אֲשֶׁר־בָּא מִיהוּדָה׃
from-Judah he-came who the-God man-of he-went that the-road *** sons-of-him

וַיֹּאמֶר אֶל־בָּנָיו חִבְשׁוּ־לִי הַחֲמוֹר וַיַּחְבְּשׁוּ־
and-they-saddled the-donkey for-me saddle! sons-of-him to so-he-said (13)

לוֹ הַחֲמוֹר וַיִּרְכַּב עָלָיו׃ וַיֵּלֶךְ אַחֲרֵי אִישׁ
man-of after and-he-rode (14) on-him and-he-mounted the-donkey for-him

הָאֱלֹהִים וַיִּמְצָאֵהוּ יֹשֵׁב תַּחַת הָאֵלָה וַיֹּאמֶר אֵלָיו
to-him and-he-asked the-oak-tree under sitting and-he-found-him the-God

הַאַתָּה אִישׁ־הָאֱלֹהִים אֲשֶׁר־בָּאתָ מִיהוּדָה וַיֹּאמֶר אָנִי׃ וַיֹּאמֶר
so-he-said (15) I and-he-replied from-Judah you-came who the-God man-of you?

אֵלָיו לֵךְ אִתִּי הַבָּיְתָה וֶאֱכֹל לָחֶם׃ וַיֹּאמֶר לֹא אוּכַל
I-can not and-he-said (16) bread and-eat! to-the-home with-me come! to-him

לָשׁוּב אִתָּךְ וְלָבוֹא אִתָּךְ וְלֹא־אֹכַל לֶחֶם וְלֹא־
and-not bread I-can-eat and-not with-you and-to-go with-you to-turn-back

אֶשְׁתֶּה אִתְּךָ מַיִם בַּמָּקוֹם הַזֶּה׃ כִּי־דָבָר אֵלַי
to-me he-told for (17) the-this in-the-place waters with-you I-can-drink

בִּדְבַר יְהוָה לֹא־תֹאכַל לֶחֶם וְלֹא־תִשְׁתֶּה שָׁם מָיִם
waters there you-must-drink and-not bread you-must-eat not Yahweh by-word-of

לֹא־תָשׁוּב לָלֶכֶת בַּדֶּרֶךְ אֲשֶׁר־הָלַכְתָּ בָּהּ׃ וַיֹּאמֶר
and-he-answered (18) on-her you-came that by-the-way to-go you-must-return not

לוֹ גַּם־אֲנִי נָבִיא כָּמוֹךָ וּמַלְאָךְ דִּבֶּר אֵלַי בִּדְבַר יְהוָה
Yahweh by-word-of to-me he-said and-angel as-you prophet I also to-him

לֵאמֹר הֲשִׁבֵהוּ אִתְּךָ אֶל־בֵּיתֶךָ וְיֹאכַל לֶחֶם
bread so-may-he-eat house-of-you to with-you bring-back-him! to-say

וְיֵשְׁתְּ מָיִם כִּחֵשׁ לוֹ׃ וַיָּשָׁב אִתּוֹ
with-him so-he-returned (19) to-him he-lied waters and-he-may-drink

וַיֹּאכַל לֶחֶם בְּבֵיתוֹ וַיֵּשְׁתְּ מָיִם׃ וַיְהִי הֵם
they and-he-was (20) waters and-he-drank in-house-of-him bread and-he-ate

יֹשְׁבִים אֶל־הַשֻּׁלְחָן וַיְהִי דְּבַר־יְהוָה אֶל־הַנָּבִיא אֲשֶׁר
who the-prophet to Yahweh word-of and-he-came the-table at ones-sitting

הֱשִׁיבוֹ׃ וַיִּקְרָא אֶל־אִישׁ הָאֱלֹהִים אֲשֶׁר־בָּא
he-came who the-God man-of to and-he-cried-out (21) he-brought-back-him

מִיהוּדָה לֵאמֹר כֹּה אָמַר יְהוָה יַעַן כִּי מָרִיתָ פִּי יְהוָה
Yahweh word-of you-defied that because Yahweh he-says this to-say from-Judah

וְלֹא שָׁמַרְתָּ אֶת־הַמִּצְוָה אֲשֶׁר צִוְּךָ יְהוָה אֱלֹהֶיךָ׃
God-of-you Yahweh he-commanded-you that the-command *** you-kept and-not

וַתָּשָׁב וַתֹּאכַל לֶחֶם וַתֵּשְׁתְּ מַיִם בַּמָּקוֹם
in-the-place waters and-you-drank bread and-you-ate and-you-came-back (22)

him which road the man of
God from Judah had taken.
13So he said to his sons, "Saddle the donkey for me." And
when they had saddled the
donkey for him, he mounted it
14and rode after the man of
God. He found him sitting under an oak tree and asked,
"Are you the man of God who
came from Judah?"
"I am," he replied.
15So the prophet said to him,
"Come home with me and
eat."
16The man of God said, "I
cannot turn back and go with
you, nor can I eat bread or
drink water with you in this
place. 17I have been told by the
word of the LORD: 'You must
not eat bread or drink water
there or return by the way you
came.' "
18The old prophet answered,
"I too am a prophet, as you
are. And an angel said to me
by the word of the LORD:
'Bring him back with you to
your house so that he may eat
bread and drink water.' " (But
he was lying to him.) 19So the
man of God returned with
him and ate and drank in his
house.
20While they were sitting at
the table, the word of the LORD
came to the old prophet who
had brought him back. 21He
cried out to the man of God
who had come from Judah,
"This is what the LORD says:
'You have defied the word of
the LORD and have not kept
the command the LORD your
God gave you. 22You came
back and ate bread and drank
water in the place where he

אֲשֶׁר דִּבֶּר אֵלֶיךָ אַל־ תֹּאכַל לֶחֶם וְאַל־ תֵּשְׁתְּ מָיִם לֹא־
not waters you-drink and-not bread you-eat not to-you he-told where

תָבוֹא נִבְלָתְךָ אֶל־ קֶבֶר אֲבֹתֶיךָ׃ (23) וַיְהִי אַחֲרֵי
after and-he-was (23) fathers-of-you tomb-of into body-of-you she-will-go

אָכְלוֹ לֶחֶם וְאַחֲרֵי שְׁתוֹתוֹ וַיַּחֲבָשׁ־ לוֹ הַחֲמוֹר
the-donkey for-him then-he-saddled to-drink-him and-after bread to-eat-him

לַנָּבִיא אֲשֶׁר הֱשִׁיבוֹ׃ (24) וַיֵּלֶךְ וַיִּמְצָאֵהוּ
and-he-met-him and-he-went (24) he-brought-back-him who by-the-prophet

אַרְיֵה בַּדֶּרֶךְ וַיְמִיתֵהוּ וַתְּהִי נִבְלָתוֹ מֻשְׁלֶכֶת
being-thrown-down body-of-him and-she-was and-he-killed-him on-the-road lion

בַּדֶּרֶךְ וְהַחֲמוֹר עֹמֵד אֶצְלָהּ וְהָאַרְיֵה עֹמֵד אֵצֶל
beside standing and-the-lion beside-her standing and-the-donkey on-the-road

הַנְּבֵלָה׃ (25) וְהִנֵּה אֲנָשִׁים עֹבְרִים וַיִּרְאוּ אֶת־ הַנְּבֵלָה
the-body *** and-they-saw ones-passing-by people then-see! (25) the-body

מֻשְׁלֶכֶת בַּדֶּרֶךְ וְאֶת־ הָאַרְיֵה עֹמֵד אֵצֶל הַנְּבֵלָה
the-body beside standing the-lion and on-the-road being-thrown-down

וַיָּבֹאוּ וַיְדַבְּרוּ בָעִיר אֲשֶׁר הַנָּבִיא הַזָּקֵן יֹשֵׁב
living the-old the-prophet where in-the-city and-they-reported and-they-went

בָּהּ׃ (26) וַיִּשְׁמַע הַנָּבִיא אֲשֶׁר הֱשִׁיבוֹ מִן־
from he-brought-back-him who the-prophet when-he-heard (26) in-her

הַדֶּרֶךְ וַיֹּאמֶר אִישׁ הָאֱלֹהִים הוּא אֲשֶׁר מָרָה אֶת־ פִּי יְהוָה
Yahweh word-of *** he-defied who he the-God man-of then-he-said the-journey

וַיִּתְּנֵהוּ יְהוָה לָאַרְיֵה וַיִּשְׁבְּרֵהוּ וַיְמִתֵהוּ
and-he-killed-him and-he-mauled-him to-the-lion Yahweh and-he-gave-him

כִּדְבַר יְהוָה אֲשֶׁר דִּבֶּר־ לוֹ׃ (27) וַיְדַבֵּר אֶל־ בָּנָיו
sons-of-him to and-he-said (27) to-him he-warned that Yahweh as-word-of

לֵאמֹר חִבְשׁוּ־ לִי אֶת־ הַחֲמוֹר וַיַּחֲבֹשׁוּ׃ (28) וַיֵּלֶךְ
then-he-went-out (28) so-they-saddled the-donkey *** for-me saddle! to-say

וַיִּמְצָא אֶת־ נִבְלָתוֹ מֻשְׁלֶכֶת בַּדֶּרֶךְ וַחֲמוֹר
and-donkey on-the-road being-thrown-down body-of-him *** and-he-found

וְהָאַרְיֵה עֹמְדִים אֵצֶל הַנְּבֵלָה לֹא־ אָכַל הָאַרְיֵה אֶת־ הַנְּבֵלָה
the-body *** the-lion he-ate not the-body beside ones-standing and-the-lion

וְלֹא שָׁבַר אֶת־ הַחֲמוֹר׃ (29) וַיִּשָּׂא הַנָּבִיא אֶת־
*** the-prophet so-he-picked-up (29) the-donkey *** he-mauled and-not

נִבְלַת אִישׁ־ הָאֱלֹהִים וַיַּנִּחֵהוּ אֶל־ הַחֲמוֹר וַיְשִׁיבֵהוּ
and-he-brought-back-him the-donkey on and-he-laid-him the-God man-of body-of

וַיָּבֹא אֶל־ עִיר הַנָּבִיא הַזָּקֵן לִסְפֹּד וּלְקָבְרוֹ׃
and-to-bury-him to-mourn the-old the-prophet city-of to and-he-brought

told you not to eat or drink.
Therefore your body will not
be buried in the tomb of your
fathers.' "
23When the man of God had
finished eating and drinking,
the prophet who had brought
him back saddled his donkey
for him. 24As he went on his
way, a lion met him on the
road and killed him, and his
body was thrown down on the
road, with both the donkey
and the lion standing beside
it. 25Some people who passed
by saw the body thrown down
there, with the lion standing
beside the body, and they
went and reported it in the
city where the old prophet
lived.
26When the prophet who
had brought him back from
his journey heard of it, he
said, "It is the man of God
who defied the word of the
LORD. The LORD has given him
over to the lion, which has
mauled him and killed him, as
the word of the LORD had
warned him."
27The prophet said to his
sons, "Saddle the donkey for
me," and they did so. 28Then
he went out and found the
body thrown down on the
road, with the donkey and the
lion standing beside it. The
lion had neither eaten the
body nor mauled the donkey.
29So the prophet picked up the
body of the man of God, laid it
on the donkey, and brought it
back to his own city to mourn
for him and bury him. 30Then

וַיַּנַּח אֶת־ נִבְלָתוֹ בְּקִבְרוֹ וַיִּסְפְּדוּ עָלָיו
over-him and-they-mourned in-tomb-of-him body-of-him *** then-he-laid (30)

הוֹי אָחִי׃ וַיְהִי אַחֲרֵי קָבְרוֹ אֹתוֹ וַיֹּאמֶר אֶל־
to then-he-said him to-bury-him after and-he-was (31) brother-of-me oh!

בָּנָיו לֵאמֹר בְּמוֹתִי וּקְבַרְתֶּם אֹתִי בַּקֶּבֶר אֲשֶׁר
where in-the-grave me then-you-bury when-to-die-me to-say sons-of-him

אִישׁ הָאֱלֹהִים קָבוּר בּוֹ אֵצֶל עַצְמֹתָיו הַנִּיחוּ אֶת־ עַצְמֹתָי׃
bones-of-me *** lay! bones-of-him beside in-him being-buried the-God man-of

כִּי הָיֹה יִהְיֶה הַדָּבָר אֲשֶׁר קָרָא בִּדְבַר
by-word-of he-declared that the-message he-will-come-true to-come-true for (32)

יְהוָה עַל־ הַמִּזְבֵּחַ אֲשֶׁר בְּבֵית־ אֵל וְעַל כָּל־ בָּתֵּי
shrines-of all-of and-against El in-Beth that the-altar against Yahweh

הַבָּמוֹת אֲשֶׁר בְּעָרֵי שֹׁמְרוֹן׃ אַחַר הַדָּבָר הַזֶּה לֹא־
not the-this the-event after (33) Samaria in-towns-of that the-high-places

שָׁב יָרָבְעָם מִדַּרְכּוֹ הָרָעָה וַיָּשָׁב וַיַּעַשׂ
and-he-appointed but-he-returned the-evil from-way-of-him Jeroboam he-changed

מִקְצוֹת הָעָם כֹּהֲנֵי בָמוֹת הֶחָפֵץ יְמַלֵּא
he-consecrated the-one-wanting high-places priests-of the-people from-ends-of

אֶת־ יָדוֹ וִיהִי כֹּהֲנֵי בָמוֹת׃ וַיְהִי
and-he-became (34) high-places priests-of so-he-became hand-of-him ***

בַּדָּבָר הַזֶּה לְחַטַּאת בֵּית יָרָבְעָם וּלְהַכְחִיד
and-to-bring-down Jeroboam house-of as-sin-of the-this in-the-thing

וּלְהַשְׁמִיד מֵעַל פְּנֵי הָאֲדָמָה׃ בָּעֵת הַהִיא
the-that at-the-time (14:1) the-earth faces-of from-on and-to-destroy

חָלָה אֲבִיָּה בֶן־ יָרָבְעָם׃ וַיֹּאמֶר יָרָבְעָם לְאִשְׁתּוֹ
to-wife-of-him Jeroboam and-he-said (2) Jeroboam son-of Abijah he-becme-ill

קוּמִי נָא וְהִשְׁתַּנִּית וְלֹא יֵדְעוּ כִּי־ אַתִּי אֵשֶׁת
wife-of you that they-will-recognize so-not and-disguise-yourself! now! go!

יָרָבְעָם וְהָלַכְתְּ שִׁלֹה הִנֵּה־ שָׁם אֲחִיָּה הַנָּבִיא הוּא־ דִבֶּר עָלַי
to-me he-told he the-prophet Ahijah there see! Shiloh then-you-go Jeroboam

לְמֶלֶךְ עַל־ הָעָם הַזֶּה׃ וְלָקַחַתְּ בְּיָדֵךְ עֲשָׂרָה לֶחֶם
bread ten in-hand-of-you and-you-take (3) the-this the-people over as-king

וְנִקֻּדִים וּבַקְבֻּק דְּבַשׁ וּבָאת אֵלָיו הוּא יַגִּיד לָךְ מַה־
what to-you he-will-tell he to-him and-you-go honey and-jar-of and-cakes

יִהְיֶה לַנָּעַר׃ וַתַּעַשׂ כֵּן אֵשֶׁת יָרָבְעָם וַתָּקָם
and-she-got-up Jeroboam wife-of so and-she-did (4) to-the-boy he-will-happen

וַתֵּלֶךְ שִׁלֹה וַתָּבֹא בֵּית אֲחִיָּה וַאֲחִיָּהוּ לֹא־ יָכֹל
he-could not now-Ahijah Ahijah house-of and-she-came Shiloh and-she-went

°2 ק את

he laid the body in his own tomb, and they mourned over him and said, "Oh, my brother!"

[31]After burying him, he said to his sons, "When I die, bury me in the grave where the man of God is buried; lay my bones beside his bones. [32]For the message he declared by the word of the LORD against the altar in Bethel and against all the shrines on the high places in the towns of Samaria will certainly come true."

[33]Even after this, Jeroboam did not change his evil ways, but once more appointed priests for the high places from all sorts of people. Anyone who wanted to become a priest he consecrated for the high places. [34]This was the sin of the house of Jeroboam that led to its downfall and to its destruction from the face of the earth.

Ahijah's Prophecy Against Jeroboam

14 At that time Abijah son of Jeroboam became ill, [2]and Jeroboam said to his wife, "Go, disguise yourself, so you won't be recognized as the wife of Jeroboam. Then go to Shiloh. Ahijah the prophet is there—the one who told me I would be king over this people. [3]Take ten loaves of bread with you, some cakes and a jar of honey, and go to him. He will tell you what will happen to the boy." [4]So Jeroboam's wife did what he said and went to Ahijah's house in Shiloh.

Now Ahijah could not see;

לִרְאוֹת כִּי קָמוּ עֵינָיו מִשֵּׂיבוֹ׃ וַיהוָה
but-Yahweh (5) because-of-age-of-him eyes-of-him they-were-gone for to-see

אָמַר אֶל־אֲחִיָּהוּ הִנֵּה אֵשֶׁת יָרָבְעָם בָּאָה לִדְרֹשׁ דָּבָר מֵעִמְּךָ
from-with-you word to-ask coming Jeroboam wife-of see! Ahijah to he-told

אֶל־בְּנָהּ כִּי־חֹלֶה הוּא כָּזֹה וְכָזֶה תְּדַבֵּר אֵלֶיהָ
to-her you-answer and-as-such as-such he being-ill for son-of-her about

וִיהִי כְבֹאָהּ וְהִיא מִתְנַכֵּרָה׃ וַיְהִי
and-he-was (6) being-someone-else then-she when-to-arrive-her and-he-will-be

כִשְׁמֹעַ אֲחִיָּהוּ אֶת־קוֹל רַגְלֶיהָ בָּאָה בַפֶּתַח וַיֹּאמֶר
and-he-said to-the-door coming feet-of-her sound-of *** Ahijah when-to-hear

בֹּאִי אֵשֶׁת יָרָבְעָם לָמָּה זֶּה אַתְּ מִתְנַכֵּרָה וְאָנֹכִי שָׁלוּחַ אֵלַיִךְ
to-you being-sent now-I pretending you this why? Jeroboam wife-of come-in!

קָשָׁה׃ לְכִי אִמְרִי לְיָרָבְעָם כֹּה־אָמַר יְהוָה אֱלֹהֵי יִשְׂרָאֵל יַעַן
because Israel God-of Yahweh he-says this to-Jeroboam tell! go! (7) bad-news

אֲשֶׁר הֲרִימֹתִיךָ מִתּוֹךְ הָעָם וָאֶתֶּנְךָ נָגִיד עַל
over leader and-I-made-you the-people from-among I-raised-up-you that

עַמִּי יִשְׂרָאֵל׃ וָאֶקְרַע אֶת־הַמַּמְלָכָה מִבֵּית דָּוִד
David from-house-of the-kingdom *** and-I-tore (8) Israel people-of-me

וָאֶתְּנֶהָ לָךְ וְלֹא־הָיִיתָ כְּעַבְדִּי דָוִד אֲשֶׁר שָׁמַר
he-kept who David like-servant-of-me you-were but-not to-you and-I-gave-her

מִצְוֹתַי וַאֲשֶׁר־הָלַךְ אַחֲרַי בְּכָל־לִבּוֹ לַעֲשׂוֹת
to-do heart-of-him with-all-of after-me he-followed and-who commands-of-me

רַק הַיָּשָׁר בְּעֵינָי׃ וַתָּרַע לַעֲשׂוֹת מִכֹּל אֲשֶׁר־
who more-than-all to-do and-you-did-evil (9) in-eyes-of-me the-right only

הָיוּ לְפָנֶיךָ וַתֵּלֶךְ וַתַּעֲשֶׂה־לְּךָ אֱלֹהִים אֲחֵרִים
other-ones gods for-you and-you-made and-you-went before-you they-lived

וּמַסֵּכוֹת לְהַכְעִיסֵנִי וְאֹתִי הִשְׁלַכְתָּ אַחֲרֵי גַוֶּךָ׃
back-of-you behind you-thrust and-me to-make-angry-me and-metal-idols

לָכֵן הִנְנִי מֵבִיא רָעָה אֶל־בֵּית יָרָבְעָם וְהִכְרַתִּי
and-I-will-cut-off Jeroboam house-of on disaster bringing see-I! therefore (10)

לְיָרָבְעָם מַשְׁתִּין בְּקִיר עָצוּר וְעָזוּב בְּיִשְׂרָאֵל
in-Israel or-being-free being-slave against-wall one-urinating from-Jeroboam

וּבִעַרְתִּי אַחֲרֵי בֵית־יָרָבְעָם כַּאֲשֶׁר יְבַעֵר הַגָּלָל עַד־
until the-dung he-burns just-as Jeroboam house-of after and-I-will-burn

תֻּמּוֹ׃ הַמֵּת לְיָרָבְעָם בָּעִיר יֹאכְלוּ הַכְּלָבִים
the-dogs they-will-eat in-the-city of-Jeroboam the-dead (11) to-be-gone-him

וְהַמֵּת בַּשָּׂדֶה יֹאכְלוּ עוֹף הַשָּׁמַיִם כִּי יְהוָה
Yahweh for the-airs bird-of they-will-eat in-the-country and-the-dead

his sight was gone because of
his age. 5But the LORD had told
Ahijah, "Jeroboam's wife is
coming to ask you about her
son, for he is ill, and you are to
give her such and such an answer. When she arrives, she
will pretend to be someone
else."
6So when Ahijah heard the
sound of her footsteps at the
door, he said, "Come in, wife
of Jeroboam. Why this pre-
tense? I have been sent to you
with bad news. 7Go, tell Jeroboam that this is what the
LORD, the God of Israel, says: 'I
raised you up from among the
people and made you a leader
over my people Israel. 8I tore
the kingdom away from the
house of David and gave it to
you, but you have not been
like my servant David, who
kept my commands and fol-
lowed me with all his heart,
doing only what was right in
my eyes. 9You have done more
evil than all who lived before
you. You have made for yourself other gods, idols made of
metal; you have provoked me
to anger and thrust me behind
your back.
10" 'Because of this, I am going to bring disaster on the
house of Jeroboam. I will cut
off from Jeroboam every last
male in Israel—slave or free. I
will burn up the house of Jeroboam as one burns dung, until
it is all gone. 11Dogs will eat
those belonging to Jeroboam
who die in the city, and the
birds of the air will feed on
those who die in the country.
The LORD has spoken!'

[l]14 The meaning of the Hebrew for this sentence is uncertain.
[m]15 That is, the Euphrates
[n]15 That is, symbols of the goddess Asherah; here and elsewhere in 1 Kings

דִּבֵּר׃ וְאַתְּ קוּמִי לְכִי לְבֵיתֵךְ בְּבֹאָה
when-to-enter to-home-of-you go-back! get-up! now-you (12) he-spoke

רַגְלַיִךְ הָעִירָה וּמֵת הַיָּלֶד׃ וְסָפְדוּ־
and-they-will-mourn (13) the-boy then-he-will-die into-the-city feet-of-you

לוֹ כָל־ יִשְׂרָאֵל וְקָבְרוּ אֹתוֹ כִּי־ זֶה לְבַדּוֹ
by-himself this-one indeed him and-they-will-bury Israel all-of for-him

יָבֹא לְיָרָבְעָם אֶל־ קָבֶר יַעַן נִמְצָא־ בוֹ דָּבָר טוֹב אֶל־
to good thing in-him he-was-found because tomb into of-Jeroboam he-will-go

יְהוָה אֱלֹהֵי יִשְׂרָאֵל בְּבֵית יָרָבְעָם׃ וְהֵקִים יְהוָה
Yahweh and-he-will-raise-up (14) Jeroboam in-house-of Israel God-of Yahweh

לוֹ מֶלֶךְ עַל־ יִשְׂרָאֵל אֲשֶׁר יַכְרִית אֶת־ בֵּית יָרָבְעָם זֶה
this Jeroboam house-of *** he-will-cut-off who Israel over king for-him

הַיּוֹם וּמֶה גַּם־ עָתָּה׃ וְהִכָּה יְהוָה אֶת־ יִשְׂרָאֵל
Israel *** Yahweh and-he-will-strike (15) now indeed now-what? the-day

כַּאֲשֶׁר יָנוּד הַקָּנֶה בַּמַּיִם וְנָתַשׁ אֶת־ יִשְׂרָאֵל
Israel *** and-he-will-uproot in-the-waters the-reed he-sways just-as

מֵעַל הָאֲדָמָה הַטּוֹבָה הַזֹּאת אֲשֶׁר נָתַן לַאֲבוֹתֵיהֶם
to-fathers-of-them he-gave that the-this the-good the-land from-on

וְזֵרָם מֵעֵבֶר לַנָּהָר יַעַן אֲשֶׁר עָשׂוּ אֶת־
*** they-made that because to-the-River at-beyond and-he-will-scatter-them

אֲשֵׁרֵיהֶם מַכְעִיסִים אֶת־ יְהוָה׃ וְיִתֵּן
and-he-will-give-up (16) Yahweh *** ones-making-angry Asherah-poles-of-them

אֶת־ יִשְׂרָאֵל בִּגְלַל חַטֹּאות יָרָבְעָם אֲשֶׁר חָטָא וַאֲשֶׁר
and-that he-committed that Jeroboam sins-of on-account-of Israel ***

הֶחֱטִיא אֶת־ יִשְׂרָאֵל׃ וַתָּקָם אֵשֶׁת יָרָבְעָם
Jeroboam wife-of then-she-got-up (17) Israel *** he-caused-to-commit

וַתֵּלֶךְ וַתָּבֹא תִרְצָתָה הִיא בָּאָה בְסַף־ הַבַּיִת
the-house over-threshold-of stepping she to-Tirzah and-she-went and-she-left

וְהַנַּעַר מֵת׃ וַיִּקְבְּרוּ אֹתוֹ וַיִּסְפְּדוּ־ לוֹ כָּל־
all-of for-him and-they-mourned him and-they-buried (18) he-died and-the-boy

יִשְׂרָאֵל כִּדְבַר יְהוָה אֲשֶׁר דִּבֶּר בְּיַד־ עַבְדּוֹ אֲחִיָּהוּ
Ahijah servant-of-him by-hand-of he-said that Yahweh as-word-of Israel

הַנָּבִיא׃ וְיֶתֶר דִּבְרֵי יָרָבְעָם אֲשֶׁר נִלְחַם וַאֲשֶׁר
and-how he-warred how Jeroboam events-of and-rest-of (19) the-prophet

מָלָךְ הִנָּם כְּתוּבִים עַל־ סֵפֶר דִּבְרֵי הַיָּמִים
the-days annals-of book-of in ones-being-written see-they! he-ruled

לְמַלְכֵי יִשְׂרָאֵל׃ וְהַיָּמִים אֲשֶׁר מָלַךְ יָרָבְעָם עֶשְׂרִים וּשְׁתַּיִם
and-two twenty Jeroboam he-reigned that and-the-days (20) Israel of-kings-of

12"As for you, go back home.
When you set foot in your city,
the boy will die. 13All Israel
will mourn for him and bury
him. He is the only one belonging to Jeroboam who will
be buried, because he is the
only one in the house of Jeroboam in whom the LORD, the
God of Israel, has found anything good.
14"The LORD will raise up for
himself a king over Israel who
will cut off the family of Jeroboam. This is the day! What?
Yes, even now.[l] 15And the
LORD will strike Israel, so that
it will be like a reed swaying
in the water. He will uproot
Israel from this good land that
he gave to their forefathers
and scatter them beyond the
River,[m] because they provoked
the LORD to anger by making
Asherah poles.[n] 16And he will
give Israel up because of the
sins Jeroboam has committed
and has caused Israel to commit."
17Then Jeroboam's wife got
up and left and went to Tirzah.
As soon as she stepped over
the threshold of the house, the
boy died. 18They buried him,
and all Israel mourned for him
as the LORD had said through
his servant the prophet Ahijah.
19The other events of Jeroboam's reign, his wars and
how he ruled, are written in
the book of the annals of the
kings of Israel. 20He reigned
for twenty-two years and then

שָׁנָה וַיִּשְׁכַּב עִם־ אֲבֹתָיו וַיִּמְלֹךְ נָדָב בְּנוֹ
son-of-him Nadab and-he-became-king fathers-of-him with then-he-rested year

תַּחְתָּיו׃ (21) וּרְחַבְעָם בֶּן־ שְׁלֹמֹה מָלַךְ בִּיהוּדָה בֶּן־
son-of in-Judah he-was-king Solomon son-of and-Rehoboam (21) on-place-of-him

אַרְבָּעִים וְאַחַת שָׁנָה רְחַבְעָם בְּמָלְכוֹ וּשְׁבַע עֶשְׂרֵה
ten and-seven-of when-to-become-king-him Rehoboam year and-one forty

שָׁנָה ׀ מָלַךְ בִּירוּשָׁלַםִ הָעִיר אֲשֶׁר־ בָּחַר יְהוָה לָשׂוּם אֶת־
*** to-put Yahweh he-chose which the-city in-Jerusalem he-reigned year

שְׁמוֹ שָׁם מִכֹּל שִׁבְטֵי יִשְׂרָאֵל וְשֵׁם אִמּוֹ
mother-of-him and-name-of Israel tribes-of from-all-of there Name-of-him

נַעֲמָה הָעַמֹּנִית׃ (22) וַיַּעַשׂ יְהוּדָה הָרַע בְּעֵינֵי יְהוָה
Yahweh in-eyes-of the-evil Judah and-he-did (22) the-Ammonite Naamah

וַיְקַנְאוּ אֹתוֹ מִכֹּל אֲשֶׁר עָשׂוּ אֲבֹתָם
fathers-of-them they-did that more-than-all him and-they-made-jealous

בְּחַטֹּאתָם אֲשֶׁר חָטָאוּ׃ (23) וַיִּבְנוּ גַם־ הֵמָּה לָהֶם
for-them they indeed and-they-set-up (23) they-committed that by-sin-of-them

בָּמוֹת וּמַצֵּבוֹת וַאֲשֵׁרִים עַל כָּל־ גִּבְעָה גְבֹהָה
high hill every-of on and-Asherah-poles and-sacred-stones high-places

וְתַחַת כָּל־ עֵץ רַעֲנָן׃ (24) וְגַם־ קָדֵשׁ הָיָה
he-was male-prostitute and-even (24) spreading tree every-of and-under

בָאָרֶץ עָשׂוּ כְּכֹל הַתּוֹעֲבֹת הַגּוֹיִם אֲשֶׁר
that the-nations the-detestable-practices-of as-all-of they-did in-the-land

הוֹרִישׁ יְהוָה מִפְּנֵי בְּנֵי יִשְׂרָאֵל׃ (25) וַיְהִי בַּשָּׁנָה
in-the-year and-he-was (25) Israel sons-of from-before Yahweh he-drove-out

הַחֲמִישִׁית לַמֶּלֶךְ רְחַבְעָם עָלָה שׁוֹשַׁק מֶלֶךְ־ מִצְרַיִם עַל־
against Egypt king-of Shishak he-attacked Rehoboam of-the-king the-fifth

יְרוּשָׁלָםִ׃ (26) וַיִּקַּח אֶת־ אֹצְרוֹת בֵּית־ יְהוָה וְאֶת־
and Yahweh temple-of treasures-of *** and-he-carried-off (26) Jerusalem

אוֹצְרוֹת בֵּית הַמֶּלֶךְ וְאֶת־ הַכֹּל לָקָח וַיִּקַּח אֶת־ כָּל־
all-of *** and-he-took he-took the-whole and the-king palace-of treasures-of

מָגִנֵּי הַזָּהָב אֲשֶׁר עָשָׂה שְׁלֹמֹה׃ (27) וַיַּעַשׂ הַמֶּלֶךְ רְחַבְעָם
Rehoboam the-king so-he-made (27) Solomon he-made that the-gold shields-of

תַּחְתָּם מָגִנֵּי נְחֹשֶׁת וְהִפְקִיד עַל־ יַד שָׂרֵי
commanders-of hand-of under and-he-assigned bronze shields-of in-place-of-them

הָרָצִים הַשֹּׁמְרִים פֶּתַח בֵּית הַמֶּלֶךְ׃
the-king palace-of entrance-of the-ones-being-on-duty the-ones-guarding

(28) וַיְהִי מִדֵּי־ בֹא הַמֶּלֶךְ בֵּית יְהוָה יִשָּׂאוּם
they-bore-them Yahweh temple-of the-king to-come as-often-as and-he-was (28)

°25 ק שישק

rested with his fathers. And
Nadab his son succeeded him
as king.

Rehoboam King of Judah

21Rehoboam son of Solomon
was king in Judah. He was
forty-one years old when he
became king, and he reigned
seventeen years in Jerusalem,
the city the LORD had chosen
out of all the tribes of Israel in
which to put his Name. His
mother's name was Naamah;
she was an Ammonite.
22Judah did evil in the eyes
of the LORD. By the sins they
committed they stirred up his
jealous anger more than their
fathers had done. 23They also
set up for themselves high
places, sacred stones and
Asherah poles on every high
hill and under every spreading tree. 24There were even
male shrine prostitutes in the
land; the people engaged in all
the detestable practices of the
nations the LORD had driven
out before the Israelites.
25In the fifth year of King
Rehoboam, Shishak king of
Egypt attacked Jerusalem. 26He
carried off the treasures of the
temple of the LORD and the
treasures of the royal palace.
He took everything, including
all the gold shields Solomon
had made. 27So King Reho-
boam made bronze shields to
replace them and assigned
these to the commanders of
the guard on duty at the entrance to the royal palace.
28Whenever the king went to
the LORD's temple, the guards

הָרָצִים וֶהֱשִׁיבוּם אֶל־ תָּא הָרָצִים׃
the-ones-guarding room-of to then-they-returned-them the-ones-guarding

וְיֶתֶר דִּבְרֵי רְחַבְעָם וְכָל־ אֲשֶׁר עָשָׂה הֲלֹא־הֵמָּה
they not? he-did that and-all Rehoboam events-of and-rest-of (29)

כְּתוּבִים עַל־ סֵפֶר דִּבְרֵי הַיָּמִים לְמַלְכֵי יְהוּדָה׃
Judah of-kings-of the-days annals-of book-of in ones-being-written

וּמִלְחָמָה הָיְתָה בֵין־ רְחַבְעָם וּבֵין יָרָבְעָם כָּל־הַיָּמִים׃
the-days all-of Jeroboam and-between Rehoboam between she-was and-warfare (30)

וַיִּשְׁכַּב רְחַבְעָם עִם־ אֲבֹתָיו וַיִּקָּבֵר עִם־
with and-he-was-buried fathers-of-him with Rehoboam and-he-rested (31)

אֲבֹתָיו בְּעִיר דָּוִד וְשֵׁם אִמּוֹ נַעֲמָה הָעַמֹּנִית
the-Ammonite Naamah mother-of-him and-name-of David in-City-of fathers-of-him

וַיִּמְלֹךְ אֲבִיָּם בְּנוֹ תַּחְתָּיו׃ וּבִשְׁנַת
and-in-years-of (15:1) in-place-of-him son-of-him Abijam and-he-became-king

שְׁמֹנֶה עֶשְׂרֵה לַמֶּלֶךְ יָרָבְעָם בֶּן־ נְבָט מָלַךְ אֲבִיָּם עַל־יְהוּדָה׃
Judah over Abijam he-became-king Nebat son-of Jeroboam of-the-king ten eight

שָׁלֹשׁ שָׁנִים מָלַךְ בִּירוּשָׁלָ͏ִם וְשֵׁם אִמּוֹ מַעֲכָה
Maacah mother-of-him and-name-of in-Jerusalem he-reigned years three (2)

בַּת־ אֲבִישָׁלוֹם׃ וַיֵּלֶךְ בְּכָל־ חַטֹּאות אָבִיו
father-of-him sins-of in-all-of and-he-walked (3) Abishalom daughter-of

אֲשֶׁר־עָשָׂה לְפָנָיו וְלֹא־ הָיָה לְבָבוֹ שָׁלֵם עִם־ יְהוָה
Yahweh to fully-devoted heart-of-him he-was and-not before-him he-did that

אֱלֹהָיו כִּלְבַב דָּוִד אָבִיו׃ כִּי לְמַעַן
for-sake-of nevertheless (4) forefather-of-him David as-heart-of God-of-him

דָּוִד נָתַן יְהוָה אֱלֹהָיו לוֹ נִיר בִּירוּשָׁלָ͏ִם לְהָקִים אֶת־
*** to-raise-up in-Jerusalem lamp to-him God-of-him Yahweh he-gave David

בְּנוֹ אַחֲרָיו וּלְהַעֲמִיד אֶת־ יְרוּשָׁלָ͏ִם׃ אֲשֶׁר עָשָׂה דָוִד
Dvaid he-did for (5) Jerusalem *** and-to-make-strong after-him son-of-him

אֶת־ הַיָּשָׁר בְּעֵינֵי יְהוָה וְלֹא־ סָר מִכֹּל אֲשֶׁר־
that from-anything he-turned and-not Yahweh in-eyes-of the-right ***

צִוָּהוּ כֹּל יְמֵי חַיָּיו רַק בִּדְבַר אוּרִיָּה
Uriah in-case-of except lives-of-him days-of all-of he-commanded-him

הַחִתִּי׃ וּמִלְחָמָה הָיְתָה בֵין־ רְחַבְעָם וּבֵין יָרָבְעָם כָּל־
all-of Jeroboam and-between Rehoboam between she-was and-war (6) the-Hittite

יְמֵי חַיָּיו׃ וְיֶתֶר דִּבְרֵי אֲבִיָּם וְכָל־ אֲשֶׁר עָשָׂה
he-did that and-all Abijam events-of and-rest-of (7) lives-of-him days-of

הֲלוֹא־הֵם כְּתוּבִים עַל־ סֵפֶר דִּבְרֵי הַיָּמִים לְמַלְכֵי יְהוּדָה
Judah of-kings-of the-days annals-of book-of in ones-being-written they not?

bore the shields, and afterward they returned them to
the guardroom.
29As for the other events of
Rehoboam's reign, and all he
did, are they not written in the
book of the annals of the kings
of Judah? 30There was continu-
al warfare between Rehoboam
and Jeroboam. 31And Reho-
boam rested with his fathers
and was buried with them in
the City of David. His
mother's name was Naamah;
she was an Ammonite. And
Abijah[n] his son succeeded
him as king.

Abijah King of Judah

15 In the eighteenth year
of the reign of Jero-
boam son of Nebat, Abijah[o]
became king of Judah, 2and he
reigned in Jerusalem three
years. His mother's name was
Maacah daughter of Abishalom.[p]
3He committed all the sins
his father had done before
him; his heart was not fully
devoted to the LORD his God,
as the heart of David his
forefather had been. 4Never-
theless, for David's sake the
LORD his God gave him a lamp
in Jerusalem by raising up a
son to succeed him and by
making Jerusalem strong. 5For
David had done what was
right in the eyes of the LORD
and had not failed to keep any
of the LORD's commands all
the days of his life—except in
the case of Uriah the Hittite.
6There was war between
Rehoboam[q] and Jeroboam
throughout ⌊Abijah's⌋ lifetime.
7As for the other events of
Abijah's reign, and all he did,
are they not written in the
book of the annals of the kings

[n]*31* Some Hebrew manuscripts and Septuagint (see also 2 Chron 12:16); most Hebrew manuscripts *Abijam*
[o]*1* Some Hebrew manuscripts and Septuagint (see also 2 Chron 12:16); most Hebrew manuscripts *Abijam;* also in verse 7 and 8
[p]*2* A variant of *Absalom;* also in verse 10
[q]*6* Most Hebrew manuscripts; some Hebrew manuscripts and Syriac *Abijam* (that is, Abijah)

וּמִלְחָמָה הָיְתָה בֵּין אֲבִיָּם וּבֵין יָרָבְעָם׃ וַיִּשְׁכַּב אֲבִיָּם
Abijam and-he-rested (8) Jeroboam and-between Abijam between she-was and-war

עִם־ אֲבֹתָיו וַיִּקְבְּרוּ אֹתוֹ בְּעִיר דָּוִד וַיִּמְלֹךְ
and-he-became-king David in-City-of him and-they-buried fathers-of-him with

אָסָא בְנוֹ תַּחְתָּיו׃ וּבִשְׁנַת עֶשְׂרִים לְיָרָבְעָם מֶלֶךְ
king-of of-Jeroboam twenty and-in-year-of (9) in-place-of-him son-of-him Asa

יִשְׂרָאֵל מָלַךְ אָסָא מֶלֶךְ יְהוּדָה׃ וְאַרְבָּעִים וְאַחַת שָׁנָה
year and-one and-forty (10) Judah king-of Asa he-became-king Israel

מָלַךְ בִּירוּשָׁלִַם וְשֵׁם אִמּוֹ מַעֲכָה בַּת־
daughter-of Maacah mother-of-him and-name-of in-Jerusalem he-reigned

אֲבִישָׁלוֹם׃ וַיַּעַשׂ אָסָא הַיָּשָׁר בְּעֵינֵי יְהוָה כְּדָוִד
as-David Yahweh in-eyes-of the-right Asa and-he-did (11) Abishalom

אָבִיו׃ וַיַּעֲבֵר הַקְּדֵשִׁים מִן־ הָאָרֶץ
the-land from the-male-prostitutes and-he-expelled (12) father-of-him

וַיָּסַר אֶת־ כָּל־ הַגִּלֻּלִים אֲשֶׁר עָשׂוּ אֲבֹתָיו׃
fathers-of-him they-made that the-idols all-of *** and-he-got-rid

וְגַם ׀ אֶת־ מַעֲכָה אִמּוֹ וַיְסִרֶהָ מִגְּבִירָה
from-queen-mother also-he-deposed-her mother-of-him Maacah *** and-even (13)

אֲשֶׁר־ עָשְׂתָה מִפְלֶצֶת לָאֲשֵׁרָה וַיִּכְרֹת אָסָא אֶת־
*** Asa and-he-cut-down to-the-Asherah repulsive-pole she-made because

מִפְלַצְתָּהּ וַיִּשְׂרֹף בְּנַחַל קִדְרוֹן׃ וְהַבָּמוֹת
but-the-high-places (14) Kidron in-Valley-of and-he-burned repulsive-pole-of-her

לֹא־ סָרוּ רַק לְבַב־ אָסָא הָיָה שָׁלֵם עִם־ יְהוָה
Yahweh to fully-committed he-was Asa heart-of however they-removed not

כָּל־ יָמָיו׃ וַיָּבֵא אֶת־ קָדְשֵׁי אָבִיו
father-of-him dedicated-things-of *** and-he-brought (15) days-of-him all-of

וְקָדְשָׁו בֵּית יְהוָה כֶּסֶף וְזָהָב וְכֵלִים׃
and-articles and-gold silver Yahweh temple-of *and-dedicated-things-of-him

וּמִלְחָמָה הָיְתָה בֵּין אָסָא וּבֵין בַּעְשָׁא מֶלֶךְ־ יִשְׂרָאֵל כָּל־
all-of Israel king-of Baasha and-between Asa between she-was and-war (16)

יְמֵיהֶם׃ וַיַּעַל בַּעְשָׁא מֶלֶךְ־ יִשְׂרָאֵל עַל־ יְהוּדָה
Judah against Israel king-of Baasha and-he-went-up (17) days-of-them

וַיִּבֶן אֶת־ הָרָמָה לְבִלְתִּי תֵּת יֹצֵא וָבָא
or-one-entering one-leaving to-allow not the-Ramah *** and-he-fortified

לְאָסָא מֶלֶךְ יְהוּדָה׃ וַיִּקַּח אָסָא אֶת־ כָּל־ הַכֶּסֶף וְהַזָּהָב
and-the-gold the-silver all-of *** Asa then-he-took (18) Judah king-of to-Asa

הַנּוֹתָרִים ׀ בְּאוֹצְרוֹת בֵּית־ יְהוָה וְאֶת־ אוֹצְרוֹת
treasuries-of and Yahweh temple-of in-treasuries-of the-ones-being-left

of Judah? There was war between Abijah and Jeroboam.
[8]And Abijah rested with his
fathers and was buried in the
City of David. And Asa his
son succeeded him as king.

Asa King of Judah

[9]In the twentieth year of
Jeroboam king of Israel, Asa
became king of Judah, [10]and
he reigned in Jerusalem forty-
one years. His grandmother's
name was Maacah daughter of
Abishalom.
[11]Asa did what was right in
the eyes of the LORD, as his father David had done. [12]He ex-
pelled the male shrine prostitutes from the land and got rid
of all the idols his fathers had
made. [13]He even deposed his
grandmother Maacah from
her position as queen mother,
because she had made a repul-
sive Asherah pole. Asa cut the
pole down and burned it in
the Kidron Valley. [14]Although
he did not remove the high
places, Asa's heart was fully
committed to the LORD all his
life. [15]He brought into the temple of the LORD the silver and
gold and the articles that he
and his father had dedicated.
[16]There was war between
Asa and Baasha king of Israel
throughout their reigns. [17]Ba-
asha king of Israel went up
against Judah and fortified
Ramah to prevent anyone
from leaving or entering the
territory of Asa king of Judah.
[18]Asa then took all the silver
and gold that was left in the
treasuries of the LORD's temple

15 This translation follows the NIV in rendering the *Ketbib* form rather than the *Qere, and-dedicated-things-of.

°15 ק וקדשי

בֵּית מֶלֶךְ° וַיִּתְּנֵם בְּיַד־ עֲבָדָיו
officials-of-him into-hand-of and-he-entrusted-them the-king palace-of

וַיִּשְׁלָחֵם הַמֶּלֶךְ אָסָא אֶל־בֶּן־ הֲדַד בֶּן־ טַבְרִמֹּן בֶּן־ חֶזְיוֹן
Hezion son-of Tabrimmon son-of Hadad Ben to Asa the-king and-he-sent-them

מֶלֶךְ אֲרָם הַיֹּשֵׁב בְּדַמֶּשֶׂק לֵאמֹר׃ בְּרִית בֵּינִי
between-me treaty (19) to-say in-Damascus the-one-ruling Aram king-of

וּבֵינֶךָ בֵּין אָבִי וּבֵין אָבִיךָ הִנֵּה שָׁלַחְתִּי
I-send see! father-of-you and-between father-of-me between and-between-you

לְךָ שֹׁחַד כֶּסֶף וְזָהָב לֵךְ הָפֵרָה אֶת־ בְּרִיתְךָ אֶת־ בַּעְשָׁא
Baasha with treaty-of-you *** break! come! and-gold silver gift-of to-you

מֶלֶךְ־ יִשְׂרָאֵל וְיַעֲלֶה מֵעָלָי׃ וַיִּשְׁמַע בֶּן־
Ben and-he-agreed (20) from-against-me so-he-will-withdraw Israel king-of

הֲדַד אֶל־ הַמֶּלֶךְ אָסָא וַיִּשְׁלַח אֶת־ שָׂרֵי הַחֲיָלִים אֲשֶׁר־ לוֹ
to-him that the-forces commanders-of *** and-he-sent Asa the-king with Hadad

עַל־ עָרֵי יִשְׂרָאֵל וַיַּךְ אֶת־עִיּוֹן וְאֶת־דָּן וְאֵת אָבֵל בֵּית־מַעֲכָה
Maacah Beth Abel and Dan and Ijon *** and-he-conquered Israel towns-of against

וְאֵת כָּל־ כִּנְּרוֹת עַל כָּל־ אֶרֶץ נַפְתָּלִי׃ וַיְהִי כִּשְׁמֹעַ
when-to-hear and-he-was (21) Naphtali land-of all-of with Kinnereth all-of and

בַּעְשָׁא וַיֶּחְדַּל מִבְּנוֹת אֶת־ הָרָמָה וַיֵּשֶׁב בְּתִרְצָה׃
to-Tirzah and-he-withdrew the-Ramah *** from-to-build then-he-stopped Baasha

וְהַמֶּלֶךְ אָסָא הִשְׁמִיעַ אֶת־ כָּל־ יְהוּדָה אֵין נָקִי
exempt no-one Judah all-of *** he-issued-order Asa then-the-king (22)

וַיִּשְׂאוּ אֶת־ אַבְנֵי הָרָמָה וְאֶת־ עֵצֶיהָ אֲשֶׁר
that timbers-of-her and the-Ramah stones-of *** and-they-carried-away

בָּנָה בַּעְשָׁא וַיִּבֶן בָּם הַמֶּלֶךְ אָסָא אֶת־ גֶּבַע בִּנְיָמִן
Benjamin Geba-of *** Asa the-king with-them and-he-built-up Baasha he-used

וְאֶת־ הַמִּצְפָּה׃ וְיֶתֶר כָּל־ דִּבְרֵי־ אָסָא וְכָל־
and-all-of Asa events-of all-of and-rest-of (23) the-Mizpah and

גְּבוּרָתוֹ וְכָל־ אֲשֶׁר עָשָׂה וְהֶעָרִים אֲשֶׁר בָּנָה הֲלֹא־
not? he-built that and-the-cities he-did that and-all achievement-of-him

הֵמָּה כְתוּבִים עַל־ סֵפֶר דִּבְרֵי הַיָּמִים לְמַלְכֵי יְהוּדָה
Judah of-kings-of the-days annals-of book-of in ones-being-written they

רַק לְעֵת זִקְנָתוֹ חָלָה אֶת־ רַגְלָיו׃
feet-of-him *** he-became-diseased old-age-of-him at-time-of however

וַיִּשְׁכַּב אָסָא עִם־ אֲבֹתָיו וַיִּקָּבֵר עִם־
with and-he-was-buried fathers-of-him with Asa then-he-rested (24)

אֲבֹתָיו בְּעִיר דָּוִד אָבִיו וַיִּמְלֹךְ יְהוֹשָׁפָט
Jehoshaphat and-he-became-king father-of-him David in-City-of fathers-of-him

and of his own palace. He entrusted it to his officials and sent them to Ben-Hadad son of Tabrimmon, the son of Hezion, the king of Aram, who was ruling in Damascus.
19 "Let there be a treaty between me and you," he said, "as there was between my father and your father. See, I am sending you a gift of silver and gold. Now break your treaty with Baasha king of Israel so he will withdraw from me."
20 Ben-Hadad agreed with King Asa and sent the commanders of his forces against the towns of Israel. He conquered Ijon, Dan, Abel Beth-maacah and all Kinnereth in addition to Naphtali.
21 When Baasha heard this, he stopped building Ramah and withdrew to Tirzah.
22 Then King Asa issued an order to all Judah—no one was exempt—and they carried away from Ramah the stones and timber Baasha had been using there. With them King Asa built up Geba in Benjamin, and also Mizpah.
23 As for all the other events of Asa's reign, all his achievements, all he did and the cities he built, are they not written in the book of the annals of the kings of Judah? In his old age, however, his feet became diseased.
24 Then Asa rested with his fathers and was buried with them in the city of his father David. And Jehoshaphat his son succeeded him as king.

°18 ק המלך

בְּנוֹ תַּחְתָּיו׃ וְנָדָב בֶּן־ יָרָבְעָם מָלַךְ עַל־
over he-became-king Jeroboam son-of and-Nadab (25) in-place-of-him son-of-him

יִשְׂרָאֵל בִּשְׁנַת שְׁתַּיִם לְאָסָא מֶלֶךְ יְהוּדָה וַיִּמְלֹךְ עַל־יִשְׂרָאֵל
Israel over and-he-reigned Judah king-of of-Asa two in-year-of Israel

שְׁנָתָיִם׃ וַיַּעַשׂ הָרַע בְּעֵינֵי יְהוָה וַיֵּלֶךְ בְּדֶרֶךְ
in-way-of and-he-walked Yahweh in-eyes-of the-evil and-he-did (26) two-years

אָבִיו וּבְחַטָּאתוֹ אֲשֶׁר הֶחֱטִיא אֶת־יִשְׂרָאֵל׃
Israel *** he-caused-to-commit which and-in-sin-of-him father-of-him

וַיִּקְשֹׁר עָלָיו בַּעְשָׁא בֶן־ אֲחִיָּה לְבֵית יִשָּׂשכָר
Issachar of-house-of Ahijah son-of Baasha against-him and-he-plotted (27)

וַיַּכֵּהוּ בַעְשָׁא בְּגִבְּתוֹן אֲשֶׁר לַפְּלִשְׁתִּים וְנָדָב
and-Nadab of-the-Philistines that at-Gibbethon Baasha and-he-struck-down-him

וְכָל־ יִשְׂרָאֵל צָרִים עַל־ גִּבְּתוֹן׃ וַיְמִתֵהוּ
and-he-killed-him (28) Gibbethon against ones-besieging Israel and-all-of

בַעְשָׁא בִּשְׁנַת שָׁלֹשׁ לְאָסָא מֶלֶךְ יְהוּדָה וַיִּמְלֹךְ
and-he-became-king Judah king-of of-Asa three in-year-of Baasha

תַּחְתָּיו׃ וַיְהִי כְמָלְכוֹ הִכָּה אֶת־ כָּל־
whole-of *** he-killed as-to-reign-him and-he-was (29) in-place-of-him

בֵּית יָרָבְעָם לֹא־הִשְׁאִיר כָּל־ נְשָׁמָה לְיָרָבְעָם עַד־ הִשְׁמִדוֹ
he-destroyed-him but to-Jeroboam breath any-of he-left not Jeroboam family-of

כִּדְבַר יְהוָה אֲשֶׁר דִּבֶּר בְּיַד־ עַבְדּוֹ אֲחִיָּה הַשִּׁילֹנִי׃
the-Shilonite Ahijah servant-of-him by-hand-of he-gave that Yahweh as-word-of

עַל־ חַטֹּאות יָרָבְעָם אֲשֶׁר חָטָא וַאֲשֶׁר הֶחֱטִיא
he-caused-to-commit and-that he-committed that Jeroboam sins-of because-of (30)

אֶת־יִשְׂרָאֵל בְּכַעְסוֹ אֲשֶׁר הִכְעִיס אֶת־ יְהוָה אֱלֹהֵי
God-of Yahweh *** he-provoked-to-anger for in-provocation-of-him Israel ***

יִשְׂרָאֵל׃ וְיֶתֶר דִּבְרֵי נָדָב וְכָל־ אֲשֶׁר עָשָׂה הֲלֹא־ הֵם
they not? he-did that and-all Nadab events-of and-rest-of (31) Israel

כְּתוּבִים עַל־ סֵפֶר דִּבְרֵי הַיָּמִים לְמַלְכֵי יִשְׂרָאֵל׃
Israel of-kings-of the-days annals-of book-of in ones-being-written

וּמִלְחָמָה הָיְתָה בֵּין אָסָא וּבֵין בַּעְשָׁא מֶלֶךְ־יִשְׂרָאֵל כָּל־
all-of Israel king-of Baasha and-between Asa between she-was and-war (32)

יְמֵיהֶם׃ בִּשְׁנַת שָׁלֹשׁ לְאָסָא מֶלֶךְ יְהוּדָה מָלַךְ
he-became-king Judah king-of of-Asa three in-year-of (33) days-of-them

בַּעְשָׁא בֶן־ אֲחִיָּה עַל־ כָּל־יִשְׂרָאֵל בְּתִרְצָה עֶשְׂרִים וְאַרְבַּע שָׁנָה׃
year and-four twenty in-Tirzah Israel all-of over Ahijah son-of Baasha

וַיַּעַשׂ הָרַע בְּעֵינֵי יְהוָה וַיֵּלֶךְ בְּדֶרֶךְ יָרָבְעָם
Jeroboam in-way-of and-he-walked Yahweh in-eyes-of the-evil and-he-did (34)

Nadab King of Israel

25Nadab son of Jeroboam
became king of Israel in the
second year of Asa king of
Judah, and he reigned over Israel two years. 26He did evil in
the eyes of the LORD, walking
in the ways of his father and
in his sin, which he had
caused Israel to commit.
27Baasha son of Ahijah of the
house of Issachar plotted
against him, and he struck
him down at Gibbethon, a
Philistine town, while Nadab
and all Israel were besieging
it. 28Baasha killed Nadab in the
third year of Asa king of Judah
and succeeded him as king.
29As soon as he began to
reign, he killed Jeroboam's
whole family. He did not leave
Jeroboam anyone that
breathed, but destroyed them
all, according to the word of
the LORD given through his
servant Ahijah the Shilonite—
30because of the sins Jeroboam
had committed and had
caused Israel to commit, and
because he provoked the LORD,
the God of Israel, to anger.
31As for the other events of
Nadab's reign, and all he did,
are they not written in the
book of the annals of the kings
of Israel? 32There was war between Asa and Baasha king of
Israel throughout their reigns.

Baasha King of Israel

33In the third year of Asa
king of Judah, Baasha son of
Ahijah became king of all Israel in Tirzah, and he reigned
twenty-four years. 34He did
evil in the eyes of the LORD,
walking in the ways of Jeroboam and in his sin, which he

וּבְחַטָּאתוֹ אֲשֶׁר הֶחֱטִיא אֶת־ יִשְׂרָאֵל׃ וַיְהִי
then-he-came (16:1) Israel *** he-caused-to-commit which and-in-sin-of-him

דְבַר־ יְהוָה אֶל־ יֵהוּא בֶן־ חֲנָנִי עַל־בַּעְשָׁא לֵאמֹר׃ יַעַן אֲשֶׁר
that because (2) to-say Baasha against Hanani son-of Jehu to Yahweh word-of

הֲרִימֹתִיךָ מִן־ הֶעָפָר וָאֶתֶּנְךָ נָגִיד עַל עַמִּי יִשְׂרָאֵל
Israel people-of-me over leader and-I-made-you the-dust from I-lifted-up-you

וַתֵּלֶךְ׀ בְּדֶרֶךְ יָרָבְעָם וַתַּחֲטִא אֶת־ עַמִּי
people-of-me *** and-you-caused-to-sin Jeroboam in-way-of but-you-walked

יִשְׂרָאֵל לְהַכְעִיסֵנִי בְּחַטֹּאתָם׃ הִנְנִי מַבְעִיר אַחֲרֵי
after consuming see-I! (3) by-sins-of-them to-provoke-to-anger-me Israel

בַעְשָׁא וְאַחֲרֵי בֵיתוֹ וְנָתַתִּי אֶת־ בֵּיתְךָ כְּבֵית
like-house-of house-of-you *** and-I-will-make house-of-him and-after Baasha

יָרָבְעָם בֶּן־ נְבָט׃ הַמֵּת לְבַעְשָׁא בָּעִיר יֹאכְלוּ
they-will-eat in-the-city of-Baasha the-dead (4) Nebat son-of Jeroboam

הַכְּלָבִים וְהַמֵּת לוֹ בַּשָּׂדֶה יֹאכְלוּ עוֹף הַשָּׁמָיִם׃
the-airs bird-of they-will-eat in-the-field of-him and-the-dead the-dogs

וְיֶתֶר דִּבְרֵי בַעְשָׁא וַאֲשֶׁר עָשָׂה וּגְבוּרָתוֹ הֲלֹא־
not? and-achievement-of-him he-did and-what Baasha events-of and-rest-of (5)

הֵם כְּתוּבִים עַל־ סֵפֶר דִּבְרֵי הַיָּמִים לְמַלְכֵי יִשְׂרָאֵל׃
Israel of-kings-of the-days annals-of book-of in ones-being-written they

וַיִּשְׁכַּב בַּעְשָׁא עִם־ אֲבֹתָיו וַיִּקָּבֵר בְּתִרְצָה
in-Tirzah and-he-was-buried fathers-of-him with Baasha then-he-rested (6)

וַיִּמְלֹךְ אֵלָה בְנוֹ תַּחְתָּיו׃ וְגַם בְּיַד־
by-hand-of and-also (7) in-place-of-him son-of-him Elah and-he-became-king

יֵהוּא בֶן־ חֲנָנִי הַנָּבִיא דְּבַר־ יְהוָה הָיָה אֶל־בַּעְשָׁא וְאֶל־
and-to Baasha to he-came Yahweh word-of the-prophet Hanani son-of Jehu

בֵּיתוֹ וְעַל כָּל־ הָרָעָה׀ אֲשֶׁר־ עָשָׂה׀ בְּעֵינֵי יְהוָה
Yahweh in-eyes-of he-did that the-evil all-of and-because-of house-of-him

לְהַכְעִיסוֹ בְּמַעֲשֵׂה יָדָיו לִהְיוֹת כְּבֵית
like-house-of to-become hands-of-him by-deed-of to-provoke-to-anger-him

יָרָבְעָם וְעַל אֲשֶׁר־ הִכָּה אֹתוֹ׃ בִּשְׁנַת עֶשְׂרִים וָשֵׁשׁ
and-six twenty in-year-of (8) him he-destroyed that and-because Jeroboam

שָׁנָה לְאָסָא מֶלֶךְ יְהוּדָה מָלַךְ אֵלָה בֶן־ בַּעְשָׁא עַל־יִשְׂרָאֵל
Israel over Baasha son-of Elah he-became-king Judah king-of of-Asa year

בְּתִרְצָה שְׁנָתָיִם׃ וַיִּקְשֹׁר עָלָיו עַבְדּוֹ זִמְרִי
Zimri official-of-him against-him and-he-plotted (9) two-years in-Tirzah

שַׂר מַחֲצִית הָרָכֶב וְהוּא בְתִרְצָה שֹׁתֶה שִׁכּוֹר בֵּית
home-of drunk drinking in-Tirzah now-he the-chariot half-of commander-of

had caused Israel to commit.
16 Then the word of the
LORD came to Jehu son
of Hanani against Baasha: [2]"I
lifted you up from the dust
and made you leader of my
people Israel, but you walked
in the ways of Jeroboam and
caused my people Israel to sin
and to provoke me to anger by
their sins. [3]So I am about to
consume Baasha and his
house, and I will make your
house like that of Jeroboam
son of Nebat. [4]Dogs will eat
those belonging to Baasha
who die in the city, and the
birds of the air will feed on
those who die in the country."
[5]As for the other events of
Baasha's reign, what he did
and his achievements, are
they not written in the book of
the annals of the kings of Israel? [6]Baasha rested with his fathers and was buried in Tirzah. And Elah his son succeeded him as king.
[7]Moreover, the word of the
LORD came through the
prophet Jehu son of Hanani to
Baasha and his house, because
of all the evil he had done in
the eyes of the LORD, provoking him to anger by the things
he did, and becoming like the
house of Jeroboam—and also
because he destroyed it.

Elah King of Israel

[8]In the twenty-sixth year of
Asa king of Judah, Elah son of
Baasha became king of Israel,
and he reigned in Tirzah two
years.
[9]Zimri, one of his officials,
who had command of half his
chariots, plotted against him.
Elah was in Tirzah at the time,
getting drunk in the home of

אַרְצָא אֲשֶׁר עַל־הַבַּיִת בְּתִרְצָה׃ וַיָּבֹא זִמְרִי וַיַּכֵּהוּ
and-he-struck-him Zimri and-he-came-in (10) at-Tirzah the-palace over who Arza

וַיְמִיתֵהוּ בִּשְׁנַת עֶשְׂרִים וָשֶׁבַע לְאָסָא מֶלֶךְ יְהוּדָה
Judah king-of of-Asa and-seven twenty in-year-of and-he-killed-him

וַיִּמְלֹךְ תַּחְתָּיו׃ וַיְהִי בְמָלְכוֹ
when-to-reign-him and-he-was (11) in-place-of-him and-he-became-king

כְּשִׁבְתּוֹ עַל־ כִּסְאוֹ הִכָּה אֶת־ כָּל־ בֵּית בַּעְשָׁא לֹא־
not Baasha family-of entire-of *** he-killed throne-of-him on as-to-sit-him

הִשְׁאִיר לוֹ מַשְׁתִּין בְּקִיר וְגֹאֲלָיו
or-ones-being-relatives-of-him against-wall one-urinating of-him he-spared

וְרֵעֵהוּ׃ וַיַּשְׁמֵד זִמְרִי אֵת כָּל־ בֵּית בַּעְשָׁא
Baasha family-of whole-of *** Zimri so-he-destroyed (12) of-friend-of-him

כִּדְבַר יְהוָה אֲשֶׁר דִּבֶּר אֶל־ בַּעְשָׁא בְּיַד יֵהוּא הַנָּבִיא׃
the-prophet Jehu by-hand-of Baasha against he-spoke that Yahweh as-word-of

אֶל כָּל־ חַטֹּאות בַּעְשָׁא וְחַטֹּאות אֵלָה בְנוֹ אֲשֶׁר
that son-of-him Elah and-sins-of Baasha sins-of all-of because-of (13)

חָטְאוּ וַאֲשֶׁר הֶחֱטִיאוּ אֶת־ יִשְׂרָאֵל לְהַכְעִיס
to-provoke-to-anger Israel *** they-caused-to-commit and-that they-committed

אֶת־ יְהוָה אֱלֹהֵי יִשְׂרָאֵל בְּהַבְלֵיהֶם׃ וְיֶתֶר דִּבְרֵי
events-of and-rest-of (14) by-worthless-ones-them Israel God-of Yahweh ***

אֵלָה וְכָל־ אֲשֶׁר עָשָׂה הֲלוֹא־הֵם כְּתוּבִים עַל־ סֵפֶר דִּבְרֵי
annals-of book-of in ones-being-written they not? he-did that and-all Elah

הַיָּמִים לְמַלְכֵי יִשְׂרָאֵל׃ בִּשְׁנַת עֶשְׂרִים וָשֶׁבַע שָׁנָה לְאָסָא
of-Asa year and-seven twenty in-year-of (15) Israel of-kings-of the-days

מֶלֶךְ יְהוּדָה מָלַךְ זִמְרִי שִׁבְעַת יָמִים בְּתִרְצָה וְהָעָם
and-the-army in-Tirzah days seven-of Zimri he-reigned Judah king-of

חֹנִים עַל־ גִּבְּתוֹן אֲשֶׁר לַפְּלִשְׁתִּים׃ וַיִּשְׁמַע
when-he-heard (16) of-the-Philistines that Gibbethon near ones-camping

הָעָם הַחֹנִים לֵאמֹר קָשַׁר זִמְרִי וְגַם הִכָּה אֶת־
*** he-murdered and-also Zimri he-plotted to-say the-ones-camping the-army

הַמֶּלֶךְ וַיַּמְלִכוּ כָל־ יִשְׂרָאֵל אֶת־עָמְרִי שַׂר־ צָבָא עַל־
over army commander-of Omri *** Israel all-of then-they-made-king the-king

יִשְׂרָאֵל בַּיּוֹם הַהוּא בַּמַּחֲנֶה׃ וַיַּעֲלֶה עָמְרִי וְכָל־
and-all-of Omri then-he-withdrew (17) in-the-camp the-that on-the-day Israel

יִשְׂרָאֵל עִמּוֹ מִגִּבְּתוֹן וַיָּצֻרוּ עַל־ תִּרְצָה׃ וַיְהִי
and-he-was (18) Tirzah to and-they-laid-siege from-Gibbethon with-him Israel

כִּרְאוֹת זִמְרִי כִּי־ נִלְכְּדָה הָעִיר וַיָּבֹא אֶל־ אַרְמוֹן
citadel-of into then-he-went the-city she-was-taken that Zimri when-to-see

Arza, the man in charge of the
palace at Tirzah. 10Zimri came
in, struck him down and killed
him in the twenty-seventh
year of Asa king of Judah.
Then he succeeded him as
king.
11As soon as he began to
reign and was seated on the
throne, he killed off Baasha's
whole family. He did not
spare a single male, whether
relative or friend. 12So Zimri
destroyed the whole family of
Baasha, in accordance with
the word of the LORD spoken
against Baasha through the
prophet Jehu— 13because of all
the sins Baasha and his son
Elah had committed and had
caused Israel to commit, so
that they provoked the LORD,
the God of Israel to anger by
their worthless idols.
14As for the other events of
Elah's reign, and all he did, are
they not written in the book of
the annals of the kings of Israel?

Zimri King of Israel

15In the twenty-seventh year
of Asa king of Judah, Zimri
reigned in Tirzah seven days.
The army was encamped near
Gibbethon, a Philistine town.
16When the Israelites in the
camp heard that Zimri had
plotted against the king and
murdered him, they pro-
claimed Omri, the com-
mander of the army, king over
Israel that very day there in
the camp. 17Then Omri and all
the Israelites with him withdrew from Gibbethon and laid
siege to Tirzah. 18When Zimri
saw that the city was taken, he
went into the citadel of the

בֵּית־ הַמֶּלֶךְ וַיִּשְׂרֹף עָלָיו אֶת־ בֵּית־ מֶלֶךְ בָּאֵשׁ
with-fire king palace-of *** around-him and-he-set-fire the-king palace-of

וַיָּמֹת׃ עַל־ חַטֹּאתָו אֲשֶׁר חָטָא לַעֲשׂוֹת הָרַע
the-evil to-do he-committed that sins-of-him because-of (19) so-he-died

בְּעֵינֵי יְהוָה לָלֶכֶת בְּדֶרֶךְ יָרָבְעָם וּבְחַטָּאתוֹ אֲשֶׁר
that and-in-sin-of-him Jeroboam in-way-of to-walk Yahweh in-eyes-of

עָשָׂה לְהַחֲטִיא אֶת־ יִשְׂרָאֵל׃ וְיֶתֶר דִּבְרֵי זִמְרִי
Zimri events-of and-rest-of (20) Israel *** to-cause-to-commit he-committed

וְקִשְׁרוֹ אֲשֶׁר קָשָׁר הֲלֹא־ הֵם כְּתוּבִים עַל־
in ones-being-written they not? he-rebelled that and-rebellion-of-him

סֵפֶר דִּבְרֵי הַיָּמִים לְמַלְכֵי יִשְׂרָאֵל׃ אָז יֵחָלֵק הָעָם
the-people he-was-split then (21) Israel of-kings-of the-days annals-of book-of

יִשְׂרָאֵל לַחֵצִי חֲצִי הָעָם הָיָה אַחֲרֵי תִבְנִי בֶן־ גִּינַת
Ginath son-of Tibni after he-was the-people half-of in-two Israel

לְהַמְלִיכוֹ וְהַחֵצִי אַחֲרֵי עָמְרִי׃ וַיֶּחֱזַק הָעָם
the-people but-he-was-stronger (22) Omri after and-the-half to-make-king-him

אֲשֶׁר אַחֲרֵי עָמְרִי אֶת־ הָעָם אֲשֶׁר אַחֲרֵי תִּבְנִי בֶן־ גִּינַת וַיָּמָת
so-he-died Ginath son-of Tibni after who the-people than Omri after who

תִּבְנִי וַיִּמְלֹךְ עָמְרִי׃ בִּשְׁנַת שְׁלֹשִׁים וְאַחַת שָׁנָה לְאָסָא
of-Asa year and-one thirty in-year-of (23) Omri and-he-became-king Tibni

מֶלֶךְ יְהוּדָה מָלַךְ עָמְרִי עַל־יִשְׂרָאֵל שְׁתֵּים עֶשְׂרֵה שָׁנָה בְּתִרְצָה
in-Tirzah year ten two Israel over Omri he-became-king Judah king-of

מָלַךְ שֵׁשׁ־ שָׁנִים׃ וַיִּקֶן אֶת־ הָהָר שֹׁמְרוֹן מֵאֶת שֶׁמֶר
Shemer from Samaria the-hill *** and-he-bought (24) years six he-reigned

בְּכִכְּרַיִם כָּסֶף וַיִּבֶן אֶת־ הָהָר וַיִּקְרָא אֶת־ שֵׁם
name-of *** and-he-called the-hill on and-he-built silver for-two-talents

הָעִיר אֲשֶׁר בָּנָה עַל שֶׁם־ שֶׁמֶר אֲדֹנֵי הָהָר שֹׁמְרוֹן׃
Samaria the-hill owners-of Shemer name-of after he-built that the-city

וַיַּעֲשֶׂה עָמְרִי הָרַע בְּעֵינֵי יְהוָה וַיָּרַע מִכֹּל
more-than-all and-he-sinned Yahweh in-eyes-of the-evil Omri but-he-did (25)

אֲשֶׁר לְפָנָיו׃ וַיֵּלֶךְ בְּכָל־ דֶּרֶךְ יָרָבְעָם בֶּן־ נְבָט
Nebat son-of Jeroboam way-of in-all-of and-he-walked (26) before-him who

וּבְחַטֹּאתָיו אֲשֶׁר הֶחֱטִיא אֶת־ יִשְׂרָאֵל לְהַכְעִיס
to-provoke-to-anger Israel *** he-caused-to-commit which and-in-sin-of-him

אֶת־ יְהוָה אֱלֹהֵי יִשְׂרָאֵל בְּהַבְלֵיהֶם׃ וְיֶתֶר דִּבְרֵי
events-of and-rest-of (27) by-worthless-ones-of-them Israel God-of Yahweh ***

עָמְרִי אֲשֶׁר עָשָׂה וּגְבוּרָתוֹ אֲשֶׁר עָשָׂה הֲלֹא־ הֵם
they not? he-did that and-achievement-of-him he-did what Omri

royal palace and set the palace on fire around him. So he died,
19 because of the sins he had committed, doing evil in the eyes of the LORD and walking in the ways of Jeroboam and in the sin he had committed and had caused Israel to commit.
20 As for the other events of Zimri's reign, and the rebellion he carried out, are they not written in the book of the annals of the kings of Israel?

Omri King of Israel

21 Then the people of Israel were split into two factions; half supported Tibni son of Ginath for king, and the other half supported Omri.
22 But Omri's followers proved stronger than those of Tibni son of Ginath. So Tibni died and Omri became king.
23 In the thirty-first year of Asa king of Judah, Omri became king of Israel, and he reigned twelve years, six of them in Tirzah.
24 He bought the hill of Samaria from Shemer for two talents[r] of silver and built a city on the hill, calling it Samaria, after Shemer, the name of the former owner of the hill.
25 But Omri did evil in the eyes of the LORD and sinned more than all those before him.
26 He walked in all the ways of Jeroboam son of Nebat and in his sin, which he had caused Israel to commit, so that they provoked the LORD, the God of Israel, to anger by their worthless idols.
27 As for the other events of Omri's reign, what he did and the things he achieved, are

[r]24 That is, about 150 pounds (about 70 kilograms)

*26 Most mss end this verse with *soph pasuq* (:).

°19 ק חטאתיו

°26 ק ובחטאתו

כְּתוּבִים עַל־ סֵפֶר דִּבְרֵי הַיָּמִים לְמַלְכֵי יִשְׂרָאֵל׃
Israel of-kings-of the-days annals-of book-of in ones-being-written

וַיִּשְׁכַּב עָמְרִי עִם־ אֲבֹתָיו וַיִּקָּבֵר בְּשֹׁמְרוֹן
in-Samaria and-he-was-buried fathers-of-him with Omri and-he-rested (28)

וַיִּמְלֹךְ אַחְאָב בְּנוֹ תַּחְתָּיו׃ וְאַחְאָב בֶּן־ עָמְרִי
Omri son-of and-Ahab (29) in-place-of-him son-of-him Ahab and-he-became-king

מָלַךְ עַל־יִשְׂרָאֵל בִּשְׁנַת שְׁלֹשִׁים וּשְׁמֹנֶה שָׁנָה לְאָסָא מֶלֶךְ
king-of of-Asa year and-eight thirty in-year-of Israel over he-became-king

יְהוּדָה וַיִּמְלֹךְ אַחְאָב בֶּן־ עָמְרִי עַל־יִשְׂרָאֵל בְּשֹׁמְרוֹן עֶשְׂרִים וּשְׁתַּיִם
and-two twenty in-Samaria Israel over Omri son-of Ahab and-he-reigned Judah

שָׁנָה׃ וַיַּעַשׂ אַחְאָב בֶּן־ עָמְרִי הָרַע בְּעֵינֵי יְהוָה מִכֹּל
more-than-all Yahweh in-eyes-of the-evil Omri son-of Ahab and-he-did (30) year

אֲשֶׁר לְפָנָיו׃ וַיְהִי הֲנָקֵל לֶכְתּוֹ בְּחַטֹּאות יָרָבְעָם
Jeroboam in-sins-of to-walk-him being-trivial? and-he-was (31) before-him who

בֶּן־ נְבָט וַיִּקַּח אִשָּׁה אֶת־ אִיזֶבֶל בַּת־ אֶתְבַּעַל מֶלֶךְ
king-of Ethbaal daughter-of Jezebel *** wife but-he-took Nebat son-of

צִידֹנִים וַיֵּלֶךְ וַיַּעֲבֹד אֶת־ הַבַּעַל וַיִּשְׁתַּחוּ לוֹ׃
to-him and-he-worshiped the-Baal *** and-he-served and-he-went Sidonians

וַיָּקֶם מִזְבֵּחַ לַבָּעַל בֵּית הַבַּעַל אֲשֶׁר בָּנָה
he-built that the-Baal temple-of to-the-Baal altar and-he-set-up (32)

בְּשֹׁמְרוֹן׃ וַיַּעַשׂ אַחְאָב אֶת־ הָאֲשֵׁרָה וַיּוֹסֶף אַחְאָב
Ahab and-he-added the-Asherah-pole *** Ahab and-he-made (33) in-Samaria

לַעֲשׂוֹת לְהַכְעִיס אֶת־ יְהוָה אֱלֹהֵי יִשְׂרָאֵל מִכֹּל מַלְכֵי
kings-of more-than-all-of Israel God-of Yahweh *** to-provoke-to-anger to-do

יִשְׂרָאֵל אֲשֶׁר הָיוּ לְפָנָיו׃ בְּיָמָיו בָּנָה חִיאֵל
Hiel he-rebuilt in-days-of-him (34) before-him they-were who Israel

בֵּית הָאֱלִי אֶת־ יְרִיחֹה בַּאֲבִירָם בְּכֹרוֹ יִסְּדָהּ
he-founded-her firstborn-of-him with-Abiram Jericho *** the-Bethelite

וּבִשְׂגִיב° צְעִירוֹ הִצִּיב דְּלָתֶיהָ כִּדְבַר יְהוָה אֲשֶׁר
that Yahweh as-word-of gates-of-her he-set-up youngest-of-him and-with-Segub

דִּבֶּר בְּיַד יְהוֹשֻׁעַ בִּן־ נוּן׃ וַיֹּאמֶר אֵלִיָּהוּ הַתִּשְׁבִּי
the-Tishbite Elijah now-he-said (17:1) Nun son-of Joshua by-hand-of he-spoke

מִתֹּשָׁבֵי גִלְעָד אֶל־אַחְאָב חַי־ יְהוָה אֱלֹהֵי יִשְׂרָאֵל אֲשֶׁר עָמַדְתִּי
I-serve whom Israel God-of Yahweh life-of Ahab to Gilead from-Tishbe-of

לְפָנָיו אִם־ יִהְיֶה הַשָּׁנִים הָאֵלֶּה טַל וּמָטָר כִּי אִם־
if except or-rain dew the-these the-years he-will-be not before-him

לְפִי דְבָרִי׃ וַיְהִי דְבַר־ יְהוָה אֵלָיו לֵאמֹר׃
to-say to-him Yahweh word-of then-he-came (2) word-of-me at-mouth-of

they not written in the book of
the annals of the kings of Israel? 28Omri rested with his fathers and was buried in Samaria. And Ahab his son succeeded him as king.

Ahab Becomes King of Israel

29In the thirty-eighth year of
Asa king of Judah, Ahab son
of Omri became king of Israel,
and he reigned in Samaria
over Israel twenty-two years.
30Ahab son of Omri did more
evil in the eyes of the LORD
than any of those before him.
31He not only considered it
trivial to commit the sins of
Jeroboam son of Nebat, but he
also married Jezebel daughter
of Ethbaal king of the Sidonians, and began to serve Baal
and worship him. 32He set up
an altar for Baal in the temple
of Baal that he built in Samaria. 33Ahab also made an
Asherah pole and did more to
provoke the LORD, the God of
Israel, to anger than did all the
kings of Israel before him.
34In Ahab's time, Hiel of
Bethel rebuilt Jericho. He laid
its foundations at the cost of
his firstborn son Abiram, and
he set up its gates at the cost of
his youngest son Segub, in accordance with the word of the
LORD spoken by Joshua son of
Nun.

Elijah Fed by Ravens

17 Now Elijah the Tish-
bite, from Tishbe[s] in
Gilead, said to Ahab, "As the
LORD, the God of Israel, lives,
whom I serve, there will be
neither dew nor rain in the
next few years except at my
word."
2Then the word of the LORD

[s]1 Or *Tishbite, of the settlers*

°34 ק ובשגוב

לֵךְ מִזֶּה וּפָנִיתָ לְּךָ קֵדְמָה וְנִסְתַּרְתָּ בְּנַחַל

in-Ravine-of and-you-hide to-east to-you and-you-turn from-here leave! (3)

כְּרִית אֲשֶׁר עַל־ פְּנֵי הַיַּרְדֵּן׃ וְהָיָה מֵהַנַּחַל

from-the-brook and-he-will-be (4) the-Jordan east-of to that Kerith

תִּשְׁתֶּה וְאֶת־ הָעֹרְבִים צִוִּיתִי לְכַלְכֶּלְךָ שָׁם׃ וַיֵּלֶךְ

so-he-went (5) there to-feed-you I-ordered the-ravens and you-will-drink

וַיַּעַשׂ כִּדְבַר יְהוָה וַיֵּלֶךְ וַיֵּשֶׁב בְּנַחַל כְּרִית

Kerith at-Ravine-of and-he-stayed and-he-went Yahweh as-word-of and-he-did

אֲשֶׁר עַל־ פְּנֵי הַיַּרְדֵּן׃ וְהָעֹרְבִים מְבִאִים לוֹ לֶחֶם

bread to-him ones-bringing and-the-ravens (6) the-Jordan east-of at that

וּבָשָׂר בַּבֹּקֶר וְלֶחֶם וּבָשָׂר בָּעָרֶב וּמִן־ הַנַּחַל

the-brook and-from in-the-evening and-meat and-bread in-the-morning and-meat

יִשְׁתֶּה׃ וַיְהִי מִקֵּץ יָמִים וַיִּיבַשׁ הַנָּחַל כִּי

because the-brook then-he-dried-up days at-end-of and-he-was (7) he-drank

לֹא־ הָיָה גֶשֶׁם בָּאָרֶץ׃ וַיְהִי דְבַר־ יְהוָה אֵלָיו לֵאמֹר׃

to-say to-him Yahweh word-of then-he-came (8) on-the-land rain he-was not

קוּם לֵךְ צָרְפַתָה אֲשֶׁר לְצִידוֹן וְיָשַׁבְתָּ שָׁם הִנֵּה צִוִּיתִי

I-commanded see! there and-you-stay of-Sidon that to-Zarephath go! rise! (9)

שָׁם אִשָּׁה אַלְמָנָה לְכַלְכְּלֶךָ׃ וַיָּקָם ׀ וַיֵּלֶךְ צָרְפַתָה

to-Zarephath and-he-went so-he-rose (10) to-supply-you widow woman there

וַיָּבֹא אֶל־ פֶּתַח הָעִיר וְהִנֵּה־ שָׁם אִשָּׁה אַלְמָנָה מְקֹשֶׁשֶׁת

gathering widow woman there then-see! the-town gate-of to when-he-came

עֵצִים וַיִּקְרָא אֵלֶיהָ וַיֹּאמַר קְחִי־ נָא לִי מְעַט־ מַיִם

waters little-of to-me now! bring! and-he-said to-her and-he-called sticks

בַּכְּלִי וְאֶשְׁתֶּה׃ וַתֵּלֶךְ לָקַחַת וַיִּקְרָא אֵלֶיהָ

to-her and-he-called to-get and-she-went (11) so-I-may-drink in-the-jar

וַיֹּאמַר לִקְחִי־ נָא לִי פַּת־ לֶחֶם בְּיָדֵךְ׃ וַתֹּאמֶר

and-she-said (12) in-hand-of-you bread piece-of to-me now! bring! and-he-said

חַי־ יְהוָה אֱלֹהֶיךָ אִם־ יֶשׁ־ לִי מָעוֹג כִּי אִם־ מְלֹא

fullness-of only but bread to-me there-is not God-of-you Yahweh life-of

כַף־ קֶמַח בַּכַּד וּמְעַט־ שֶׁמֶן בַּצַּפָּחַת וְהִנְנִי מְקֹשֶׁשֶׁת

gathering and-see-I! in-the-jug oil and-little-of in-the-jar flour hand-of

שְׁנַיִם עֵצִים וּבָאתִי וַעֲשִׂיתִיהוּ לִי וְלִבְנִי

and-for-son-of-me for-me and-I-will-make-him then-I-will-go sticks two

וַאֲכַלְנֻהוּ וָמָתְנוּ׃ וַיֹּאמֶר אֵלֶיהָ אֵלִיָּהוּ אַל־ תִּירְאִי

you-fear not Elijah to-her and-he-said (13) and-we-may-die so-we-may-eat-him

בֹּאִי עֲשִׂי כִדְבָרֵךְ אַךְ עֲשִׂי־ לִי מִשָּׁם עֻגָה קְטַנָּה בָרִאשֹׁנָה

at-the-first small cake from-there for-me make! but as-word-of-you do! go!

came to Elijah: [3]"Leave here, turn eastward and hide in the Kerith Ravine, east of the Jordan. [4]You will drink from the brook, and I have ordered the ravens to feed you there."

[5]So he did what the LORD had told him. He went to the Kerith Ravine, east of the Jordan, and stayed there. [6]The ravens brought him bread and meat in the morning and bread and meat in the evening, and he drank from the brook.

The Widow at Zarephath

[7]Some time later the brook dried up because there had been no rain in the land. [8]Then the word of the LORD came to him: [9]"Go at once to Zarephath of Sidon and stay there. I have commanded a widow in that place to supply you with food." [10]So he went to Zarephath. When he came to the town gate, a widow was there gathering sticks. He called to her and asked, "Would you bring me a little water in a jar so I may have a drink?" [11]As she was going to get it, he called, "And bring me, please, a piece of bread."

[12]"As surely as the LORD your God lives," she replied, "I don't have any bread—only a handful of flour in a jar and a little oil in a jug. I am gathering a few sticks to take home and make a meal for myself and my son, that we may eat it—and die."

[13]Elijah said to her, "Don't be afraid. Go home and do as you have said. But first make a small cake of bread for me from what you have and bring

וְהוֹצֵאתְ* לִי וְלָךְ וְלִבְנֵךְ תַּעֲשִׂי בָּאַחֲרֹנָה׃
at-the-afterward you-make and-for-son-of-you then-for-you to-me and-you-bring

כִּי כֹה אָמַר יְהוָה אֱלֹהֵי יִשְׂרָאֵל כַּד הַקֶּמַח לֹא
not the-flour jar-of Israel God-of Yahweh he-says this for (14)

תִכְלָה וְצַפַּחַת הַשֶּׁמֶן לֹא תֶחְסָר עַד יוֹם °תֵּתֶּן־
to-give day until she-will-run-dry not the-oil and-jug-of she-will-be-used-up

יְהוָה גֶּשֶׁם עַל־ פְּנֵי הָאֲדָמָה׃ וַתֵּלֶךְ וַתַּעֲשֶׂה כִּדְבַר
as-word-of and-she-did so-she-went (15) the-land surfaces-of on rain Yahweh

אֵלִיָּהוּ וַתֹּאכַל °הוא־ °וָהִיא וּבֵיתָהּ יָמִים׃ כַּד הַקֶּמַח
the-flour jar-of (16) days and-family-of-her and-he she and-she-ate Elijah

לֹא כָלָתָה וְצַפַּחַת הַשֶּׁמֶן לֹא חָסֵר כִּדְבַר יְהוָה
Yahweh as-word-of he-ran-dry not the-oil and-jug-of she-was-used-up not

אֲשֶׁר דִּבֶּר בְּיַד אֵלִיָּהוּ׃ וַיְהִי אַחַר הַדְּבָרִים הָאֵלֶּה
the-these the-things after and-he-was (17) Elijah by-hand-of he-spoke that

חָלָה בֶּן־ הָאִשָּׁה בַּעֲלַת הַבָּיִת וַיְהִי חָלְיוֹ
illness-of-him and-he-became the-house owner-of the-woman son-of he-became-ill

חָזָק מְאֹד עַד אֲשֶׁר לֹא־ נוֹתְרָה־ בּוֹ נְשָׁמָה׃ וַתֹּאמֶר אֶל־
to and-she-said (18) breath in-him she-remained not when until very worse

אֵלִיָּהוּ מַה־ לִּי וָלָךְ אִישׁ הָאֱלֹהִים בָּאתָ אֵלַי לְהַזְכִּיר אֶת־
*** to-remind to-me you-came the-God man-of and-to-you to-me what? Elijah

עֲוֹנִי וּלְהָמִית אֶת־ בְּנִי׃ וַיֹּאמֶר אֵלֶיהָ תְּנִי־ לִי
to-me give! to-her and-he-replied (19) son-of-me *** and-to-kill sin-of-me

אֶת־ בְּנֵךְ וַיִּקָּחֵהוּ מֵחֵיקָהּ וַיַּעֲלֵהוּ אֶל־
to and-he-carried-him from-bosom-of-her and-he-took-him son-of-you ***

הָעֲלִיָּה אֲשֶׁר־ הוּא יֹשֵׁב שָׁם וַיַּשְׁכִּבֵהוּ עַל־ מִטָּתוֹ׃
bed-of-him on and-he-laid-him there staying he where the-upper-room

וַיִּקְרָא אֶל־ יְהוָה וַיֹּאמַר יְהוָה אֱלֹהָי הֲגַם עַל־
upon also? God-of-me Yahweh and-he-said Yahweh to then-he-cried-out (20)

הָאַלְמָנָה אֲשֶׁר־אֲנִי מִתְגּוֹרֵר עִמָּהּ הֲרֵעוֹתָ לְהָמִית אֶת־ בְּנָהּ׃
son-of-her *** to-kill you-brought-evil with-her staying I whom the-widow

וַיִּתְמֹדֵד עַל־ הַיֶּלֶד שָׁלֹשׁ פְּעָמִים וַיִּקְרָא אֶל־ יְהוָה
Yahweh to and-he-cried times three the-boy on then-he-stretched-out (21)

וַיֹּאמַר יְהוָה אֱלֹהָי תָּשָׁב נָא נֶפֶשׁ־ הַיֶּלֶד הַזֶּה
the-this the-boy life-of now! let-her-return God-of-me Yahweh and-he-said

עַל־ קִרְבּוֹ׃ וַיִּשְׁמַע יְהוָה בְּקוֹל אֵלִיָּהוּ וַתָּשָׁב
and-she-returned Elijah to-cry-of Yahweh and-he-heard (22) body-of-him to

נֶפֶשׁ־ הַיֶּלֶד עַל־ קִרְבּוֹ וַיֶּחִי׃ וַיִּקַּח אֵלִיָּהוּ
Elijah then-he-picked-up (23) and-he-lived body-of-him to the-boy life-of

it to me, and then make something for yourself and your
son. [14]For this is what the
LORD, the God of Israel, says:
'The jar of flour will not be
used up and the jug of oil will
not run dry until the day the
LORD gives rain on the land.' "
[15]She went away and did as
Elijah had told her. So there
was food every day for Elijah
and for the woman and her
family. [16]For the jar of flour
was not used up and the jug of
oil did not run dry, in keeping
with the word of the LORD
spoken by Elijah.
[17]Some time later the son of
the woman who owned the
house became ill. He grew
worse and worse, and finally
stopped breathing. [18]She said
to Elijah, "What do you have
against me, man of God? Did
you come to remind me of my
sin and kill my son?"
[19]"Give me your son," Elijah
replied. He took him from her
arms, carried him to the upper
room where he was staying,
and laid him on his bed.
[20]Then he cried out to the
LORD, "O LORD my God, have
you brought tragedy also upon
this widow I am staying with,
by causing her son to die?"
[21]Then he stretched himself
out on the boy three times and
cried to the LORD, "O LORD my
God, let this boy's life return
to him!"
[22]The LORD heard Elijah's
cry, and the boy's life returned
to him, and he lived. [23]Elijah

*13 Most mss have no *sheva* under the *tav* (תְ—).

°14 ק תת
°15a ק היא
°15b ק והוא

אֶת־ הַיֶּלֶד וַיֹּרִדֵהוּ מִן־ הָעֲלִיָּה הַבַּיְתָה

into-the-house the-upper-room from and-he-carried-down-him the-child ***

וַֽיִּתְּנֵהוּ לְאִמּוֹ וַיֹּאמֶר אֵלִיָּהוּ רְאִי חַי בְּנֵךְ׃

son-of-you alive look! Elijah and-he-said to-mother-of-him and-he-gave-him

וַתֹּאמֶר הָאִשָּׁה אֶל־אֵלִיָּהוּ עַתָּה זֶה יָדַעְתִּי כִּי אִישׁ אֱלֹהִים

God man-of that I-know this now Elijah to the-woman then-she-said (24)

אַתָּה וּדְבַר־ יְהוָה בְּפִיךָ אֱמֶת׃ וַיְהִי יָמִים רַבִּים

many days and-he-was (18:1) truth from-mouth-of-you Yahweh and-word-of you

וּדְבַר־ יְהוָה הָיָה אֶל־אֵלִיָּהוּ בַּשָּׁנָה הַשְּׁלִישִׁית לֵאמֹר לֵךְ

go! to-say the-third in-the-year Elijah to he-came Yahweh and-word-of

הֵרָאֵה אֶל־אַחְאָב וְאֶתְּנָה מָטָר עַל־ פְּנֵי הָאֲדָמָה׃

the-land surfaces-of on rain and-I-will-send Ahab to present-yourself!

וַיֵּלֶךְ אֵלִיָּהוּ לְהֵרָאוֹת אֶל־אַחְאָב וְהָרָעָב חָזָק

severe now-the-famine Ahab to to-present-himself Elijah so-he-went (2)

בְּשֹׁמְרוֹן׃ וַיִּקְרָא אַחְאָב אֶל־עֹבַדְיָהוּ אֲשֶׁר עַל־ הַבָּיִת

the-palace over who Obadiah to Ahab and-he-summoned (3) in-Samaria

וְעֹבַדְיָהוּ הָיָה יָרֵא אֶת־ יְהוָה מְאֹד׃ וַיְהִי בְּהַכְרִית

while-to-kill and-he-was (4) devoutly Yahweh *** fearing he-was now-Obadiah

אִיזֶבֶל אֵת נְבִיאֵי יְהוָה וַיִּקַּח עֹבַדְיָהוּ מֵאָה נְבִאִים

prophets hundred Obadiah then-he-took Yahweh prophets-of *** Jezebel

וַיַּחְבִּיאֵם חֲמִשִּׁים אִישׁ בַּמְּעָרָה וְכִלְכְּלָם לֶחֶם וָמָיִם׃

and-waters food and-he-supplied-them in-the-cave each fifty and-he-hid-them

וַיֹּאמֶר אַחְאָב אֶל־עֹבַדְיָהוּ לֵךְ בָּאָרֶץ אֶל־ כָּל־ מַעְיְנֵי

springs-of all-of to through-the-land go! Obadiah to Ahab and-he-said (5)

הַמַּיִם וְאֶל כָּל־ הַנְּחָלִים אוּלַי ׀ נִמְצָא חָצִיר

grass we-can-find perhaps the-valleys all-of and-to the-waters

וּנְחַיֶּה סוּס וָפֶרֶד וְלוֹא נַכְרִית מֵהַבְּהֵמָה׃

from-the-animal we-must-kill so-not and-mule horse and-we-can-keep-alive

וַיְחַלְּקוּ לָהֶם אֶת־ הָאָרֶץ לַעֲבָר־ בָּהּ אַחְאָב

Ahab through-her to-cover the-land *** between-them so-they-divided (6)

הָלַךְ בְּדֶרֶךְ אֶחָד לְבַדּוֹ וְעֹבַדְיָהוּ הָלַךְ בְּדֶרֶךְ־ אֶחָד

another in-direction he-went and-Obadiah by-himself one in-direction he-went

לְבַדּוֹ׃ וַיְהִי עֹבַדְיָהוּ בַּדֶּרֶךְ וְהִנֵּה אֵלִיָּהוּ לִקְרָאתוֹ

to-meet-him Elijah and-see! on-the-way Obadiah and-he-was (7) by-himself

וַיַּכִּרֵהוּ וַיִּפֹּל עַל־ פָּנָיו וַיֹּאמֶר הַאַתָּה זֶה

this you? and-he-said faces-of-him on and-he-bowed and-he-recognized-him

אֲדֹנִי אֵלִיָּהוּ׃ וַיֹּאמֶר לוֹ אָנִי לֵךְ אֱמֹר לַאדֹנֶיךָ

to-masters-of-you tell! go! I to-him and-he-replied (8) Elijah lord-of-me

picked up the child and carried him down from the room into the house. He gave him to his mother and said, "Look, your son is alive!"

[24]Then the woman said to Elijah, "Now I know that you are a man of God and that the word of the LORD from your mouth is the truth."

Elijah and Obadiah

18 After a long time, in the third year, the word of the LORD came to Elijah: "Go and present yourself to Ahab, and I will send rain on the land." [2]So Elijah went to present himself to Ahab.

Now the famine was severe in Samaria, [3]and Ahab had summoned Obadiah, who was in charge of his palace. (Obadiah was a devout believer in the LORD. [4]While Jezebel was killing off the LORD's prophets, Obadiah had taken a hundred prophets and hidden them in two caves, fifty in each, and had supplied them with food and water.) [5]Ahab had said to Obadiah, "Go through the land to all the springs and valleys. Maybe we can find some grass to keep the horses and mules alive so we will not have to kill any of our animals." [6]So they divided the land they were to cover, Ahab going in one direction and Obadiah in another.

[7]As Obadiah was walking along, Elijah met him. Obadiah recognized him, bowed down to the ground, and said, "Is it really you, my lord Elijah?"

[8]"Yes," he replied. "Go tell

הִנֵּה אֵלִיָּהוּ׃ (9) וַיֹּאמֶר מֶה חָטָאתִי כִּי־אַתָּה נֹתֵן אֶת־
*** handing you that I-did-wrong what? and-he-said (9) Elijah see!

עַבְדְּךָ בְּיַד־אַחְאָב לַהֲמִיתֵנִי׃ (10) חַי ׀ יְהוָה אֱלֹהֶיךָ
God-of-you Yahweh life-of (10) to-kill-me Ahab into-hand-of servant-of-you

אִם־יֶשׁ־גּוֹי וּמַמְלָכָה אֲשֶׁר לֹא־שָׁלַח אֲדֹנִי שָׁם
there master-of-me he-sent not where or-kingdom nation there-is not

לְבַקֶּשְׁךָ וְאָמְרוּ אָיִן וְהִשְׁבִּיעַ אֶת־הַמַּמְלָכָה
the-kingdom *** and-he-made-swear he-is-not and-they-said to-look-for-you

וְאֶת־הַגּוֹי כִּי לֹא יִמְצָאֶכָּה׃ (11) וְעַתָּה אַתָּה אֹמֵר לֵךְ
go! telling you but-now (11) he-could-find-you not that the-nation and

אֱמֹר לַאדֹנֶיךָ הִנֵּה אֵלִיָּהוּ׃ (12) וְהָיָה אֲנִי ׀ אֵלֵךְ
I-will-leave I and-he-will-be (12) Elijah see! to-masters-of-you say!

מֵאִתָּךְ וְרוּחַ יְהוָה ׀ יִשָּׂאֲךָ עַל אֲשֶׁר לֹא־אֵדָע
I-know not where to he-may-carry-you Yahweh and-Spirit-of from-with-you

וּבָאתִי לְהַגִּיד לְאַחְאָב וְלֹא יִמְצָאֲךָ וַהֲרָגָנִי
then-he-will-kill-me he-finds-you and-not to-Ahab to-tell if-I-go

וְעַבְדְּךָ יָרֵא אֶת־יְהוָה מִנְּעֻרָי׃ (13) הֲלֹא־
not? (13) from-youths-of-me Yahweh *** worshiping yet-servant-of-you

הֻגַּד לַאדֹנִי אֵת אֲשֶׁר־עָשִׂיתִי בַּהֲרֹג אִיזֶבֶל אֵת
*** Jezebel while-to-kill I-did what *** to-lord-of-me he-was-told

נְבִיאֵי יְהוָה וָאַחְבִּא מִנְּבִיאֵי יְהוָה מֵאָה אִישׁ חֲמִשִּׁים
fifty man hundred Yahweh from-prophets-of and-I-hid Yahweh prophets-of

חֲמִשִּׁים אִישׁ בַּמְּעָרָה וָאֲכַלְכְּלֵם לֶחֶם וָמָיִם׃ (14) וְעַתָּה
but-now (14) and-waters food and-I-supplied-them in-the-cave each fifty

אַתָּה אֹמֵר לֵךְ אֱמֹר לַאדֹנֶיךָ הִנֵּה אֵלִיָּהוּ וַהֲרָגָנִי׃
and-he-will-kill-me Elijah see! to-masters-of-you say! go! telling you

(15) וַיֹּאמֶר אֵלִיָּהוּ חַי יְהוָה צְבָאוֹת אֲשֶׁר עָמַדְתִּי לְפָנָיו
before-him I-serve whom Hosts Yahweh-of life-of Elijah and-he-said (15)

כִּי הַיּוֹם אֵרָאֶה אֵלָיו׃ (16) וַיֵּלֶךְ עֹבַדְיָהוּ לִקְרַאת
to-meet Obadiah so-he-went (16) to-him I-will-present-myself the-day surely

אַחְאָב וַיַּגֶּד־לוֹ וַיֵּלֶךְ אַחְאָב לִקְרַאת אֵלִיָּהוּ׃ (17) וַיְהִי
and-he-was (17) Elijah to-meet Ahab and-he-went to-him and-he-told Ahab

כִּרְאוֹת אַחְאָב אֶת־אֵלִיָּהוּ וַיֹּאמֶר אַחְאָב אֵלָיו הַאַתָּה זֶה עֹכֵר
one-troubling that you? to-him Ahab then-he-said Elijah *** Ahab when-to-see

יִשְׂרָאֵל׃ (18) וַיֹּאמֶר לֹא עָכַרְתִּי אֶת־יִשְׂרָאֵל כִּי אִם־אַתָּה
you rather but Israel *** I-troubled not and-he-said (18) Israel

וּבֵית אָבִיךָ בַּעֲזָבְכֶם אֶת־מִצְוֹת יְהוָה
Yahweh commands-of *** when-to-abandon-you father-of-you and-family-of

your master, 'Elijah is here.' "
9"What have I done wrong,"
asked Obadiah, "that you are
handing your servant over to
Ahab to be put to death? 10As
surely as the LORD your God
lives, there is not a nation or
kingdom where my master
has not sent someone to look
for you. And whenever a nation or kingdom claimed you
were not there, he made them
swear they could not find you.
11But now you tell me to go to
my master and say, 'Elijah is
here.' 12I don't know where
the Spirit of the LORD may carry you when I leave you. If I go
and tell Ahab and he doesn't
find you, he will kill me. Yet I
your servant have worshiped
the LORD since my youth.
13Haven't you heard, my lord,
what I did while Jezebel was
killing the prophets of the
LORD? I hid a hundred of the
LORD's prophets in two caves,
fifty in each, and supplied
them with food and water.
14And now you tell me to go to
my master and say, 'Elijah is
here.' He will kill me!"
15Elijah said, "As the LORD
Almighty lives, whom I serve,
I will surely present myself to
Ahab today."

Elijah on Mount Carmel

16So Obadiah went to meet
Ahab and told him, and Ahab
went to meet Elijah. 17When
he saw Elijah, he said to him,
"Is that you, you troubler of
Israel?"
18"I have not made trouble
for Israel," Elijah replied. "But
you and your father's family
have. You have abandoned
the LORD's commands and

וַתֵּלֶךְ אַחֲרֵי הַבְּעָלִים׃ וְעַתָּה שְׁלַח קְבֹץ אֵלַי אֶת־
*** to-me gather! summon! and-now (19) the-Baals after and-you-followed

כָּל־יִשְׂרָאֵל אֶל־הַר הַכַּרְמֶל וְאֶת־נְבִיאֵי הַבַּעַל אַרְבַּע מֵאוֹת
hundreds four the-Baal prophets-of and the-Carmel Mount-of on Israel all-of

וַחֲמִשִּׁים וּנְבִיאֵי הָאֲשֵׁרָה אַרְבַּע מֵאוֹת אֹכְלֵי שֻׁלְחַן
table-of ones-eating-of hundreds four the-Asherah and-prophets-of and-fifty

אִיזָבֶל׃ וַיִּשְׁלַח אַחְאָב בְּכָל־בְּנֵי יִשְׂרָאֵל וַיִּקְבֹּץ
and-he-assembled Israel sons-of through-all-of Ahab so-he-sent (20) Jezebel

אֶת־הַנְּבִיאִים אֶל־הַר הַכַּרְמֶל׃ וַיִּגַּשׁ אֵלִיָּהוּ אֶל־
before Elijah and-he-went (21) the-Carmel Mount-of on the-prophets ***

כָּל־הָעָם וַיֹּאמֶר עַד־מָתַי אַתֶּם פֹּסְחִים עַל־שְׁתֵּי
two-of between ones-wavering you when? until and-he-said the-people all-of

הַסְּעִפִּים אִם־יְהוָה הָאֱלֹהִים לְכוּ אַחֲרָיו וְאִם־הַבַּעַל לְכוּ
follow! the-Baal but-if after-him follow! the-God Yahweh if the-opinions

אַחֲרָיו וְלֹא־עָנוּ הָעָם אֹתוֹ דָּבָר׃ וַיֹּאמֶר אֵלִיָּהוּ
Elijah then-he-said (22) anything him the-people they-said but-not after-him

אֶל־הָעָם אֲנִי נוֹתַרְתִּי נָבִיא לַיהוָה לְבַדִּי וּנְבִיאֵי
but-prophets-of by-myself of-Yahweh prophet I-am-left I the-people to

הַבַּעַל אַרְבַּע־מֵאוֹת וַחֲמִשִּׁים אִישׁ׃ וְיִתְּנוּ־לָנוּ שְׁנַיִם פָּרִים
bulls two for-us now-you-get (23) man and-fifty hundreds four the-Baal

וְיִבְחֲרוּ לָהֶם הַפָּר הָאֶחָד וִינַתְּחֻהוּ
and-let-them-cut-up-him the-one the-bull for-them and-let-them-choose

וְיָשִׂימוּ עַל־הָעֵצִים וְאֵשׁ לֹא יָשִׂימוּ וַאֲנִי אֶעֱשֶׂה ׀
I-will-prepare and-I let-them-set not but-fire the-woods on and-let-them-put

אֶת־הַפָּר הָאֶחָד וְנָתַתִּי עַל־הָעֵצִים וְאֵשׁ לֹא אָשִׂים׃
I-will-set not but-fire the-woods on and-I-will-put the-other the-bull ***

וּקְרָאתֶם בְּשֵׁם אֱלֹהֵיכֶם וַאֲנִי אֶקְרָא בְשֵׁם־
on-name-of I-will-call and-I gods-of-you on-name-of then-you-call (24)

יְהוָה וְהָיָה הָאֱלֹהִים אֲשֶׁר־יַעֲנֶה בָאֵשׁ הוּא הָאֱלֹהִים
the-God he by-fire he-answers who the-God and-he-will-be Yahweh

וַיַּעַן כָּל־הָעָם וַיֹּאמְרוּ טוֹב הַדָּבָר׃
the-word good and-they-said the-people all-of and-they-replied

וַיֹּאמֶר אֵלִיָּהוּ לִנְבִיאֵי הַבַּעַל בַּחֲרוּ לָכֶם הַפָּר
the-bull for-you choose! the-Baal to-prophets-of Elijah then-he-said (25)

הָאֶחָד וַעֲשׂוּ רִאשֹׁנָה כִּי אַתֶּם הָרַבִּים וְקִרְאוּ בְּשֵׁם אֱלֹהֵיכֶם
gods-of-you on-name-of and-call! the-many you since first and-prepare! the-one

וְאֵשׁ לֹא תָשִׂימוּ׃ וַיִּקְחוּ אֶת־הַפָּר אֲשֶׁר־נָתַן לָהֶם
to-them he-gave that the-bull *** so-they-took (26) you-set not but-fire

have followed the Baals.
19Now summon the people
from all over Israel to meet me
on Mount Carmel. And bring
the four hundred and fifty
prophets of Baal and the four
hundred prophets of Asherah,
who eat at Jezebel's table."
20So Ahab sent word
throughout all Israel and assembled the prophets on
Mount Carmel. 21Elijah went
before the people and said,
"How long will you waver between two opinions? If the
LORD is God, follow him; but if
Baal is God, follow him."
But the people said nothing.
22Then Elijah said to them,
"I am the only one of the
LORD's prophets left, but Baal
has four hundred and fifty
prophets. 23Get two bulls for
us. Let them choose one for
themselves, and let them cut it
into pieces and put it on the
wood but not set fire to it. I
will prepare the other bull and
put it on the wood but not set
fire to it. 24Then you call on the
name of your god, and I will
call on the name of the LORD.
The god who answers by fire—
he is God."
Then all the people said,
"What you say is good."
25Elijah said to the prophets
of Baal, "Choose one of the
bulls and prepare it first, since
there are so many of you. Call
on the name of your god, but
do not light the fire." 26So they
took the bull given them and

ויעשו ויקראו בשם־ הבעל מהבקר
from-the-morning the-Baal on-name-of and-they-called and-they-prepared

ועד־ הצהרים לאמר הבעל עננו ואין קול ואין ענה
answering and-no response but-no answer-us! the-Baal to-say the-noon and-till

ויפסחו על־ המזבח אשר עשה : (27) ויהי בצהרים
at-the-noon and-he-was (27) he-made that the-altar around and-they-danced

ויהתל בהם אליהו ויאמר קראו בקול־ גדול כי־
surely loud with-voice shout! and-he-said Elijah against-them then-he-taunted

אלהים הוא כי שיח וכי־ שיג לו וכי־ דרך לו
to-him travel or-perhaps to-him busy or-perhaps thoughtful perhaps he God

אולי ישן הוא ויקץ: (28) ויקראו בקול גדול
loud with-voice so-they-shouted (28) and-he-must-awaken he sleeping maybe

ויתגדדו כמשפטם בחרבות וברמחים
and-with-the-spears with-the-swords as-custom-of-them and-they-slashed-themselves

עד־ שפך־ דם עליהם: (29) ויהי כעבר הצהרים
the-midday as-to-pass and-he-was (29) on-them blood to-flow until

ויתנבאו עד לעלות המנחה ואין־ קול
response but-no the-evening-sacrifice to-offer until and-they-prophesied

ואין־ ענה ואין קשב : (30) ויאמר אליהו לכל־
to-all-of Elijah then-he-said (30) attention and-no answering and-no

העם גשו אלי ויגשו כל־ העם אליו וירפא
and-he-repaired to-him the-people all-of then-they-came to-me come! the-people

את־ מזבח יהוה ההרוס: (31) ויקח אליהו שתים
two Elijah then-he-took (31) the-one-being-in-ruins Yahweh altar-of ***

עשרה אבנים כמספר שבטי בני־ יעקב אשר היה דבר־
word-of he-came whom Jacob sons-of tribes-of as-number-of stones ten

יהוה אליו לאמר ישראל יהיה שמך: (32) ויבנה את־
*** and-he-built (32) name-of-you he-shall-be Israel to-say to-him Yahweh

האבנים מזבח בשם יהוה ויעש תעלה כבית
as-container-of trench and-he-dug Yahweh in-name-of altar the-stones

סאתים זרע סביב למזבח: (33) ויערך את־ העצים
the-woods *** and-he-arranged (33) to-the-altar around seed two-seahs

וינתח את־ הפר וישם על־ העצים: *(34) ויאמר
then-he-said *(34) the-woods on and-he-laid the-bull *** and-he-cut-up

מלאו ארבעה כדים מים ויצקו על־ העלה ועל־ העצים
the-woods and-on the-offering on and-pour! waters jars four fill!

ויאמר שנו וישנו ויאמר שלשו
do-third-time! and-he-ordered and-they-did-again do-again! and-he-said

prepared it.
Then they called on the
name of Baal from morning
till noon. "O Baal, answer us!"
they shouted. But there was no
response; no one answered.
And they danced around the
altar they had made.
27At noon Elijah began to
taunt them. "Shout louder!"
he said. "Surely he is a god!
Perhaps he is deep in thought,
or busy, or traveling. Maybe
he is sleeping and must be
awakened." 28So they shouted
louder and slashed themselves
with swords and spears, as
was their custom, until their
blood flowed. 29Midday
passed, and they continued
their frantic prophesying until
the time for the evening sacrifice. But there was no response, no one answered, no
one paid attention.
30Then Elijah said to all the
people, "Come here to me."
They came to him, and he repaired the altar of the LORD,
which was in ruins. 31Elijah
took twelve stones, one for
each of the tribes descended
from Jacob, to whom the word
of the LORD had come, saying,
"Your name shall be Israel."
32With the stones he built an
altar in the name of the LORD,
and he dug a trench around it
large enough to hold two
seahs[f] of seed. 33He arranged
the wood, cut the bull into
pieces and laid it on the wood.
Then he said to them, "Fill
four large jars with water and
pour it on the offering and on
the wood."
34"Do it again," he said, and
they did it again.
"Do it a third time," he ordered, and they did it the third

[f]32 That is, probably about 13 quarts (about 15 liters)

*34 Verse 34 in Hebrew begins in the middle of verse 33 in English.

וַיְשַׁלֵּשׁוּ׃ וַיֵּלְכוּ הַמַּיִם סָבִיב לַמִּזְבֵּחַ
to-the-altar around the-waters and-they-ran (35) and-they-did-third-time

וְגַם אֶת־ הַתְּעָלָה מִלֵּא־ מָיִם׃ וַיְהִי ׀ בַּעֲלוֹת
when-to-offer and-he-was (36) waters he-filled the-trench *** and-even

הַמִּנְחָה וַיִּגַּשׁ אֵלִיָּהוּ הַנָּבִיא וַיֹּאמַר
and-he-prayed the-prophet Elijah then-he-stepped-forward the-sacrifice

יְהוָה אֱלֹהֵי אַבְרָהָם יִצְחָק וְיִשְׂרָאֵל הַיּוֹם יִוָּדַע כִּי־אַתָּה
you that let-him-be-known the-day and-Israel Isaac Abraham God-of Yahweh

אֱלֹהִים בְּיִשְׂרָאֵל וַאֲנִי עַבְדֶּךָ °וּבִדְבָרְיךָ עָשִׂיתִי אֵת כָּל־
all-of *** I-did and-at-command-of-you servant-of-you and-I in-Israel God

הַדְּבָרִים הָאֵלֶּה׃ עֲנֵנִי יְהוָה עֲנֵנִי וְיֵדְעוּ
so-they-will-know answer-me! Yahweh answer-me! (37) the-these the-things

הָעָם הַזֶּה כִּי־ אַתָּה יְהוָה הָאֱלֹהִים וְאַתָּה הֲסִבֹּתָ אֶת־
*** you-will-turn and-you the-God Yahweh you that the-this the-people

לִבָּם אֲחֹרַנִּית׃ וַתִּפֹּל אֵשׁ־ יְהוָה וַתֹּאכַל אֶת־
*** and-she-burned-up Yahweh fire-of then-she-fell (38) back heart-of-them

הָעֹלָה וְאֶת־ הָעֵצִים וְאֶת־ הָאֲבָנִים וְאֶת־ הֶעָפָר וְאֶת־ הַמַּיִם אֲשֶׁר־
that the-waters and the-soil and the-stones and the-woods and the-sacrifice

בַּתְּעָלָה לִחֵכָה׃ וַיַּרְא כָּל־ הָעָם וַיִּפְּלוּ
then-they-fell the-people all-of when-he-saw (39) she-licked-up in-the-trench

עַל־ פְּנֵיהֶם וַיֹּאמְרוּ יְהוָה הוּא הָאֱלֹהִים יְהוָה הוּא הָאֱלֹהִים׃
the-God he Yahweh the-God he Yahweh and-they-said faces-of-them on

וַיֹּאמֶר אֵלִיָּהוּ לָהֶם תִּפְשׂוּ ׀ אֶת־ נְבִיאֵי הַבַּעַל אִישׁ
anyone the-Baal prophets-of *** seize! to-them Elijah then-he-commanded (40)

אַל־ יִמָּלֵט מֵהֶם וַיִּתְפְּשׂוּם וַיּוֹרִדֵם
and-he-brought-down-them and-they-seized-them from-them let-him-get-away not

אֵלִיָּהוּ אֶל־ נַחַל קִישׁוֹן וַיִּשְׁחָטֵם שָׁם׃ וַיֹּאמֶר
and-he-said (41) there and-he-slaughtered-them Kishon Valley-of to Elijah

אֵלִיָּהוּ לְאַחְאָב עֲלֵה אֱכֹל וּשְׁתֵה כִּי־ קוֹל הֲמוֹן הַגָּשֶׁם׃
the-rain heaviness-of sound-of for and-drink! eat! go! to-Ahab Elijah

וַיַּעֲלֶה אַחְאָב לֶאֱכֹל וְלִשְׁתּוֹת וְאֵלִיָּהוּ עָלָה אֶל־
to he-climbed but-Elijah and-to-drink to-eat Ahab so-he-went-off (42)

רֹאשׁ הַכַּרְמֶל וַיִּגְהַר אַרְצָה וַיָּשֶׂם פָּנָיו בֵּין
between faces-of-him and-he-put to-ground and-he-bent-down the-Carmel top-of

°בִּרְכָּו׃ וַיֹּאמֶר אֶל־ נַעֲרוֹ עֲלֵה־ נָא הַבֵּט דֶּרֶךְ־
direction-of look! now! go! servant-of-him to and-he-told (43) knees-of-him

יָם וַיַּעַל וַיַּבֵּט וַיֹּאמֶר אֵין מְאוּמָה
anything there-is-not and-he-said and-he-looked and-he-went-up sea

°36 ק ובדברך
°42 ק ברכיו

time. [35]The water ran down
around the altar and even
filled the trench.
[36]At the time of sacrifice, the
prophet Elijah stepped forward and prayed: "O LORD,
God of Abraham, Isaac and Israel, let it be known today that
you are God in Israel and that
I am your servant and have
done all these things at your
command. [37]Answer me, O
LORD, answer me, so these
people will know that you, O
LORD, are God, and that you
are turning their hearts back
again."
[38]Then the fire of the LORD
fell and burned up the sacrifice, the wood, the stones
and the soil, and also licked up
the water in the trench.
[39]When all the people saw
this, they fell prostrate and
cried, "The LORD, he is God!
The LORD—he is God!"
[40]Then Elijah commanded
them, "Seize the prophets of
Baal. Don't let anyone get
away!" They seized them, and
Elijah had them brought
down to the Kishon Valley
and slaughtered there.
[41]And Elijah said to Ahab,
"Go, eat and drink, for there is
the sound of a heavy rain."
[42]So Ahab went off to eat and
drink, but Elijah climbed to
the top of Carmel, bent down
to the ground and put his face
between his knees.
[43]"Go and look toward the
sea," he told his servant. And
he went up and looked.
"There is nothing there," he
said.

וַיֹּאמֶר שֻׁב שֶׁבַע פְּעָמִים׃ וַיְהִי בַּשְּׁבִעִית וַיֹּאמֶר
then-he-said on-the-seventh and-he-was (44) times seven go-back! and-he-said

הִנֵּה־עָב קְטַנָּה כְּכַף־אִישׁ עֹלָה מִיָּם וַיֹּאמֶר עֲלֵה אֱמֹר אֶל־
to tell! go! so-he-said from-sea rising man as-hand-of small cloud see!

אַחְאָב אֱסֹר וָרֵד וְלֹא יַעַצָרְכָה* הַגָּשֶׁם׃ וַיְהִי ׀
and-he-was (45) the-rain he-stops-you so-not and-go-down! hitch-up! Ahab

עַד־כֹּה וְעַד־כֹּה וְהַשָּׁמַיִם הִתְקַדְּרוּ עָבִים וְרוּחַ
and-wind clouds they-grew-black then-the-skies that and-while this while

וַיְהִי גֶּשֶׁם גָּדוֹל וַיִּרְכַּב אַחְאָב וַיֵּלֶךְ יִזְרְעֶאלָה׃
to-Jezreel and-he-went Ahab and-he-rode heavy rain and-he-came

וְיַד־יְהוָה הָיְתָה אֶל־אֵלִיָּהוּ וַיְשַׁנֵּס
and-he-tucked-in-cloak Elijah upon she-came Yahweh and-hand-of (46)

מָתְנָיו וַיָּרָץ לִפְנֵי אַחְאָב עַד־בֹּאֲכָה יִזְרְעֶאלָה׃
to-Jezreel to-go-you to Ahab ahead-of and-he-ran loins-of-him

וַיַּגֵּד אַחְאָב לְאִיזֶבֶל אֵת כָּל־אֲשֶׁר עָשָׂה אֵלִיָּהוּ וְאֵת כָּל־אֲשֶׁר
how all and Elijah he-did that all *** to-Jezebel Ahab now-he-told (19:1)

הָרַג אֶת־כָּל־הַנְּבִיאִים בֶּחָרֶב׃ וַתִּשְׁלַח אִיזֶבֶל
Jezebel so-she-sent (2) with-the-sword the-prophets all-of *** he-killed

מַלְאָךְ אֶל־אֵלִיָּהוּ לֵאמֹר כֹּה־יַעֲשׂוּן אֱלֹהִים וְכֹה יוֹסִפוּן
may-they-be-severe and-so gods may-they-deal so to-say Elijah to messenger

כִּי־כָעֵת מָחָר אָשִׂים אֶת־נַפְשְׁךָ כְּנֶפֶשׁ אַחַד מֵהֶם׃
of-them one as-life-of life-of-you *** I-make tomorrow by-the-time if-not

וַיַּרְא וַיָּקָם וַיֵּלֶךְ אֶל־נַפְשׁוֹ וַיָּבֹא
when-he-came life-of-him for and-he-ran and-he-got-up and-he-was-afraid (3)

בְּאֵר שֶׁבַע אֲשֶׁר לִיהוּדָה וַיַּנַּח אֶת־נַעֲרוֹ שָׁם׃ וְהוּא־
while-he (4) there servant-of-him *** then-he-left in-Judah that Sheba Beer

הָלַךְ בַּמִּדְבָּר דֶּרֶךְ יוֹם וַיָּבֹא וַיֵּשֶׁב תַּחַת
under and-he-sat and-he-came day journey-of into-the-desert he-went

רֹתֶם אֶחָת° וַיִּשְׁאַל אֶת־נַפְשׁוֹ לָמוּת וַיֹּאמֶר ׀ רַב עַתָּה
now enough and-he-said to-die life-of-him *** and-he-prayed one broom-tree

יְהוָה קַח נַפְשִׁי כִּי־לֹא־טוֹב אָנֹכִי מֵאֲבֹתָי׃ וַיִּשְׁכַּב
then-he-lay (5) than-ancestors-of-me I better not for life-of-me take! Yahweh

וַיִּישַׁן תַּחַת רֹתֶם אֶחָד וְהִנֵּה־זֶה מַלְאָךְ נֹגֵעַ בּוֹ
on-him touching angel there and-see! one broom-tree under and-he-fell-asleep

וַיֹּאמֶר לוֹ קוּם אֱכוֹל׃ וַיַּבֵּט וְהִנֵּה מְרַאֲשֹׁתָיו
by-heads-of-him and-see! and-he-looked (6) eat! get-up! to-him and-he-said

עֻגַת רְצָפִים וְצַפַּחַת מָיִם וַיֹּאכַל וַיֵּשְׁתְּ וַיָּשָׁב
and-he-returned and-he-drank and-he-ate waters and-jar-of coals-baked cake-of

Seven times Elijah said, "Go
back."
44The seventh time the servant reported, "A cloud as
small as a man's hand is rising
from the sea."
So Elijah said, "Go and tell
Ahab, 'Hitch up your chariot
and go down before the rain
stops you.' "
45Meanwhile, the sky grew
black with clouds, the wind
rose, a heavy rain came on
and Ahab rode off to Jezreel.
46The power of the LORD came
upon Elijah and, tucking his
cloak into his belt, he ran
ahead of Ahab all the way to
Jezreel.

Elijah Flees to Horeb

19 Now Ahab told Jezebel
everything Elijah had
done and how he had killed all
the prophets with the sword.
2So Jezebel sent a messenger to
Elijah to say, "May the gods
deal with me, be it ever so
severely, if by this time tomorrow I do not make your life
like that of one of them."
3Elijah was afraid[u] and ran
for his life. When he came to
Beersheba in Judah, he left his
servant there, 4while he himself went a day's journey into
the desert. He came to a broom
tree, sat down under it and
prayed that he might die. "I
have had enough, LORD," he
said. "Take my life; I am no
better than my ancestors."
5Then he lay down under the
tree and fell asleep.
All at once an angel touched
him and said, "Get up and
eat." 6He looked around, and
there by his head was a cake of
bread baked over hot coals,
and a jar of water. He ate and
drank and then lay down
again.

[u]3 Or *Elijah saw*

*44 Most mss have *hateph pathah* under the *ayin* (יַעְצָ־).

°4 ק אחד

וַיִּשְׁכָּֽב׃ וַיָּשָׁב מַלְאַךְ יְהוָה ׀ שֵׁנִית וַיִּגַּע־
and-he-touched second Yahweh angel-of and-he-came-back (7) and-he-lay-down

בּוֹ וַיֹּאמֶר קוּם אֱכֹל כִּי רַב מִמְּךָ הַדָּֽרֶךְ׃
the-journey for-you too-much for eat! get-up! and-he-said on-him

וַיָּקָם וַיֹּאכַל וַיִּשְׁתֶּה וַיֵּלֶךְ בְּכֹחַ ׀
in-strength-of and-he-traveled and-he-drank and-he-ate so-he-got-up (8)

הָאֲכִילָה הַהִיא אַרְבָּעִים יוֹם וְאַרְבָּעִים לַיְלָה עַד הַר הָאֱלֹהִים חֹרֵֽב׃
Horeb the-God mountain-of until night and-forty day forty the-that the-food

וַיָּבֹא־ שָׁם אֶל־ הַמְּעָרָה וַיָּלֶן שָׁם וְהִנֵּה
and-see! there and-he-spent-night the-cave into there and-he-went (9)

דְבַר־ יְהוָה אֵלָיו וַיֹּאמֶר לוֹ מַה־ לְּךָ פֹה אֵלִיָּֽהוּ׃
Elijah here to-you what? to-him and-he-said to-him Yahweh word-of

וַיֹּאמֶר קַנֹּא קִנֵּאתִי לַיהוָה ׀ אֱלֹהֵי צְבָאוֹת כִּֽי־
for Hosts God-of for-Yahweh I-was-zealous to-be-zealous and-he-replied (10)

עָזְבוּ בְרִיתְךָ בְּנֵי יִשְׂרָאֵל אֶת־ מִזְבְּחֹתֶיךָ הָרָסוּ
they-broke-down altars-of-you *** Israel sons-of covenant-of-you they-rejected

וְאֶת־ נְבִיאֶיךָ הָרְגוּ בֶחָרֶב וָאִוָּתֵר אֲנִי לְבַדִּי
by-myself I and-I-am-left with-the-sword they-killed prophets-of-you and

וַיְבַקְשׁוּ אֶת־ נַפְשִׁי לְקַחְתָּֽהּ׃ וַיֹּאמֶר צֵא וְעָמַדְתָּ
and-you-stand go! and-he-said (11) to-take-her life-of-me *** and-they-seek

בָהָר לִפְנֵי יְהוָה וְהִנֵּה יְהוָה עֹבֵר וְרוּחַ
then-wind passing-by Yahweh for-see! Yahweh in-presences-of on-the-mountain

גְּדוֹלָה וְחָזָק מְפָרֵק הָרִים וּמְשַׁבֵּר סְלָעִים לִפְנֵי יְהוָה
Yahweh before rocks and-shattering mountains tearing-apart and-powerful great

לֹא בָרוּחַ יְהוָה וְאַחַר הָרוּחַ רַעַשׁ לֹא בָרַעַשׁ
in-the-earthquake not earthquake the-wind and-after Yahweh in-the-wind not

יְהוָֽה׃ וְאַחַר הָרַעַשׁ אֵשׁ לֹא בָאֵשׁ יְהוָה וְאַחַר
and-after Yahweh in-the-fire not fire the-earthquake and-after (12) Yahweh

הָאֵשׁ קוֹל דְּמָמָה דַקָּֽה׃ וַיְהִי ׀ כִּשְׁמֹעַ אֵלִיָּהוּ
Elijah when-to-hear and-he-was (13) gentle whisper voice the-fire

וַיָּלֶט פָּנָיו בְּאַדַּרְתּוֹ וַיֵּצֵא וַיַּעֲמֹד
and-he-stood and-he-went-out with-cloak-of-him faces-of-him then-he-covered

פֶּתַח הַמְּעָרָה וְהִנֵּה אֵלָיו קוֹל וַיֹּאמֶר מַה־ לְּךָ פֹּה
here to-you what? and-he-said voice to-him then-see! the-cave mouth-of

אֵלִיָּֽהוּ׃ וַיֹּאמֶר קַנֹּא קִנֵּאתִי לַיהוָה ׀ אֱלֹהֵי
God-of for-Yahweh I-was-zealous to-be-zealous and-he-replied (14) Elijah

צְבָאוֹת כִּֽי־ עָזְבוּ בְרִיתְךָ בְּנֵי יִשְׂרָאֵל אֶת־ מִזְבְּחֹתֶיךָ
altars-of-you *** Israel sons-of covenant-of-you they-rejected for Hosts

7The angel of the LORD came
back a second time and
touched him and said, "Get up
and eat, for the journey is too
much for you." 8So he got up
and ate and drank.
Strengthened by that food, he
traveled forty days and forty
nights until he reached Horeb,
the mountain of God. 9There
he went into a cave and spent
the night.

The LORD Appears to Elijah

And the word of the LORD
came to him: "What are you
doing here, Elijah?"
10He replied, "I have been
very zealous for the LORD God
Almighty. The Israelites have
rejected your covenant, broken down your altars, and put
your prophets to death with
the sword. I am the only one
left, and now they are trying
to kill me too."
11The LORD said, "Go out and
stand on the mountain in the
presence of the LORD, for the
LORD is about to pass by."
Then a great and powerful
wind tore the mountains apart
and shattered the rocks before
the LORD, but the LORD was not
in the wind. After the wind
there was an earthquake, but
the LORD was not in the earthquake. 12After the earthquake
came a fire, but the LORD was
not in the fire. And after the
fire came a gentle whisper.
13When Elijah heard it, he
pulled his cloak over his face
and went out and stood at the
mouth of the cave.
Then a voice said to him,
"What are you doing here, Elijah?"
14He replied, "I have been
very zealous for the LORD God
Almighty. The Israelites have
rejected your covenant, broken down your altars, and put

הָרָסוּ וְאֶת־ נְבִיאֶיךָ הָרְגוּ בֶחָרֶב וָאִוָּתֵר
and-I-am-left with-the-sword they-killed prophets-of-you and they-broke-down

אֲנִי לְבַדִּי וַיְבַקְשׁוּ אֶת־ נַפְשִׁי לְקַחְתָּהּ׃ וַיֹּאמֶר יְהוָה
Yahweh and-he-said (15) to-take-her life-of-me *** and-they-seek by-myself I

אֵלָיו לֵךְ שׁוּב לְדַרְכְּךָ מִדְבַּרָה דַמָּשֶׂק וּבָאתָ
when-you-arrive Damascus to-Desert-of on-way-of-you go-back! go! to-him

וּמָשַׁחְתָּ אֶת־ חֲזָאֵל לְמֶלֶךְ עַל־ אֲרָם׃ וְאֵת יֵהוּא בֶן־ נִמְשִׁי
Nimshi son-of Jehu and (16) Aram over as-king Hazael *** then-you-anoint

תִּמְשַׁח לְמֶלֶךְ עַל־יִשְׂרָאֵל וְאֶת־אֱלִישָׁע בֶּן־ שָׁפָט מֵאָבֵל מְחוֹלָה
Meholah from-Abel Shaphat son-of Elisha and Israel over as-king you-anoint

תִּמְשַׁח לְנָבִיא תַּחְתֶּיךָ׃ וְהָיָה הַנִּמְלָט
the-one-escaping and-he-will-be (17) in-place-of-you as-prophet you-anoint

מֵחֶרֶב חֲזָאֵל יָמִית יֵהוּא וְהַנִּמְלָט מֵחֶרֶב
from-sword-of and-the-one-escaping Jehu he-will-kill Hazael from-sword-of

יֵהוּא יָמִית אֱלִישָׁע׃ וְהִשְׁאַרְתִּי בְיִשְׂרָאֵל שִׁבְעַת אֲלָפִים
thousands seven-of in-Israel yet-I-reserve (18) Elisha he-will-kill Jehu

כָּל־ הַבִּרְכַּיִם אֲשֶׁר לֹא־ כָרְעוּ לַבַּעַל וְכָל־ הַפֶּה אֲשֶׁר
that the-mouth and-all-of to-the-Baal they-bowed not that the-knees all-of

לֹא־ נָשַׁק לוֹ׃ וַיֵּלֶךְ מִשָּׁם וַיִּמְצָא אֶת־אֱלִישָׁע
Elisha *** and-he-found from-there so-he-went (19) on-him he-kissed not

בֶּן־ שָׁפָט וְהוּא חֹרֵשׁ שְׁנֵים־עָשָׂר צְמָדִים לְפָנָיו וְהוּא בִּשְׁנֵים
with-two and-he before-him yokes ten two plowing now-he Shaphat son-of

הֶעָשָׂר וַיַּעֲבֹר אֵלִיָּהוּ אֵלָיו וַיַּשְׁלֵךְ אַדַּרְתּוֹ אֵלָיו׃
around-him cloak-of-him and-he-threw to-him Elijah and-he-went-up the-ten

וַיַּעֲזֹב אֶת־ הַבָּקָר וַיָּרָץ אַחֲרֵי אֵלִיָּהוּ וַיֹּאמֶר אֶשְּׁקָה־
let-me-kiss and-he-said Elijah after and-he-ran the-ox *** then-he-left (20)

נָּא לְאָבִי וּלְאִמִּי וְאֵלְכָה אַחֲרֶיךָ
after-you then-I-will-come and-on-mother-of-me on-father-of-me now!

וַיֹּאמֶר לוֹ לֵךְ שׁוּב כִּי מֶה־עָשִׂיתִי לָךְ׃ וַיָּשָׁב
so-he-went-back (21) to-you I-did what? for go-back! go! to-him and-he-replied

מֵאַחֲרָיו וַיִּקַּח אֶת־ צֶמֶד הַבָּקָר וַיִּזְבָּחֵהוּ
and-he-slaughtered-him the-ox yoke-of *** and-he-took from-after-him

וּבִכְלִי הַבָּקָר בִּשְּׁלָם הַבָּשָׂר וַיִּתֵּן לָעָם
to-the-people and-he-gave the-meat he-cooked-them the-ox and-with-equipment-of

וַיֹּאכֵלוּ וַיָּקָם וַיֵּלֶךְ אַחֲרֵי אֵלִיָּהוּ וַיְשָׁרְתֵהוּ׃
and-he-attended-him Elijah after and-he-followed then-he-set-out and-they-ate

וּבֶן־ הֲדַד מֶלֶךְ־ אֲרָם קָבַץ אֶת־ כָּל־ חֵילוֹ
army-of-him entire-of *** he-mustered Aram king-of Hadad now-Ben (20:1)

your prophets to death with
the sword. I am the only one
left, and now they are trying
to kill me too."
15 The LORD said to him, "Go
back the way you came, and
go to the Desert of Damascus.
When you get there, anoint
Hazael king over Aram. 16 Also,
anoint Jehu son of Nimshi
king over Israel, and anoint
Elisha son of Shaphat from
Abel Meholah to succeed you
as prophet. 17 Jehu will put to
death any who escape the
sword of Hazael, and Elisha
will put to death any who escape the sword of Jehu. 18 Yet I
reserve seven thousand in Israel—all whose knees have not
bowed down to Baal and all
whose mouths have not kissed
him."

The Call of Elisha

19 So Elijah went from there
and found Elisha son of Shaphat. He was plowing with
twelve yoke of oxen, and he
himself was driving the
twelfth pair. Elijah went up to
him and threw his cloak
around him. 20 Elisha then left
his oxen and ran after Elijah.
"Let me kiss my father and
mother good-by," he said,
"and then I will come with
you."
"Go back," Elijah replied.
"What have I done to you?"
21 So Elisha left him and
went back. He took his yoke of
oxen and slaughtered them.
He burned the plowing equipment to cook the meat and
gave it to the people, and they
ate. Then he set out to follow
Elijah and became his attendant.

Ben-Hadad Attacks Samaria

20 Now Ben-Hadad king
of Aram mustered his
entire army. Accompanied by

וּשְׁלֹשִׁים וּשְׁנַיִם מֶלֶךְ אִתּוֹ וְסוּס וָרָכֶב וַיַּעַל
and-he-went-up and-chariot and-horse with-him king and-two and-thirty

וַיָּצַר עַל־ שֹׁמְרוֹן וַיִּלָּחֶם בָּהּ׃ וַיִּשְׁלַח
and-he-sent (2) against-her and-he-attacked Samaria against and-he-besieged

מַלְאָכִים אֶל־אַחְאָב מֶלֶךְ־יִשְׂרָאֵל הָעִירָה׃ וַיֹּאמֶר לוֹ כֹּה
this to-him and-he-said *(3) into-the-city Israel king-of Ahab to messengers

אָמַר בֶּן־ הֲדַד כַּסְפְּךָ וּזְהָבְךָ לִי־ הוּא וְנָשֶׁיךָ
and-wives-of-you he to-me and-gold-of-you silver-of-you Hadad Ben he-says

וּבָנֶיךָ הַטּוֹבִים לִי־ הֵם׃ וַיַּעַן מֶלֶךְ־יִשְׂרָאֵל
Israel king-of and-he-answered (4) they to-me the-best-ones and-sons-of-you

וַיֹּאמֶר כִּדְבָרְךָ אֲדֹנִי הַמֶּלֶךְ לְךָ אֲנִי וְכָל־ אֲשֶׁר־ לִי׃
to-me that and-all I to-you the-king lord-of-me as-word-of-you and-he-said

וַיָּשֻׁבוּ הַמַּלְאָכִים וַיֹּאמְרוּ כֹּה־ אָמַר בֶּן־ הֲדַד
Hadad Ben he-says this and-they-said the-messengers and-they-came-again (5)

לֵאמֹר כִּי־ שָׁלַחְתִּי אֵלֶיךָ לֵאמֹר כַּסְפְּךָ וּזְהָבְךָ
and-gold-of-you silver-of-you to-demand to-you I-sent indeed to-say

וְנָשֶׁיךָ וּבָנֶיךָ לִי תִתֵּן׃ כִּי | אִם־ כָּעֵת
at-the-time rather but (6) you-give to-me and-sons-of-you and-wives-of-you

מָחָר אֶשְׁלַח אֶת־ עֲבָדַי אֵלֶיךָ וְחִפְּשׂוּ אֶת־
*** and-they-will-search to-you officials-of-me *** I-will-send tomorrow

בֵּיתְךָ וְאֵת בָּתֵּי עֲבָדֶיךָ וְהָיָה כָּל־ מַחְמַד
value-of any-of and-he-will-be officials-of-you houses-of and palace-of-you

עֵינֶיךָ יָשִׂימוּ בְיָדָם וְלָקָחוּ׃
and-they-will-take in-hand-of-them they-will-seize eyes-of-you

וַיִּקְרָא מֶלֶךְ־יִשְׂרָאֵל לְכָל־ זִקְנֵי הָאָרֶץ וַיֹּאמֶר
and-he-said the-land elders-of to-all-of Israel king-of and-he-summoned (7)

דְּעוּ־ נָא וּרְאוּ כִּי רָעָה זֶה מְבַקֵּשׁ כִּי־ שָׁלַח אֵלַי
to-me he-sent when looking-for this-man trouble that and-see! now! know!

לְנָשַׁי וּלְבָנַי וּלְכַסְפִּי וְלִזְהָבִי
and-for-gold-of-me and-for-silver-of-me and-for-sons-of-me for-wives-of-me

וְלֹא מָנַעְתִּי מִמֶּנּוּ׃ וַיֹּאמְרוּ אֵלָיו כָּל־ הַזְּקֵנִים
the-elders all-of to-him and-they-answered (8) from-him I-refused then-not

וְכָל־ הָעָם אַל־ תִּשְׁמַע וְלוֹא תֹאבֶה׃ וַיֹּאמֶר
so-he-replied (9) you-agree and-not you-listen not the-people and-all-of

לְמַלְאֲכֵי בֶן־ הֲדַד אִמְרוּ לַאדֹנִי הַמֶּלֶךְ כֹּל אֲשֶׁר־שָׁלַחְתָּ
you-sent that all the-king to-lord-of-me tell! Hadad Ben to-messengers-of

אֶל־ עַבְדְּךָ בָרִאשֹׁנָה אֶעֱשֶׂה וְהַדָּבָר הַזֶּה לֹא אוּכַל
I-can not the-this but-the-demand I-will-do at-the-first servant-of-you to

thirty-two kings with their horses and chariots, he went up and besieged Samaria and attacked it. [2]He sent messengers into the city to Ahab king of Israel, saying, "This is what Ben-Hadad says: [3]'Your silver and gold are mine, and the best of your wives and children are mine.' "

[4]The king of Israel answered, "Just as you say, my lord the king. I and all I have are yours."

[5]The messengers came again and said, "This is what Ben-Hadad says: 'I sent to demand your silver and gold, your wives and your children. [6]But about this time tomorrow I am going to send my officials to search your palace and the houses of your officials. They will seize everything you value and carry it away.' "

[7]The king of Israel summoned all the elders of the land and said to them, "See how this man is looking for trouble! When he sent for my wives and my children, my silver and my gold, I did not refuse him."

[8]The elders and the people all answered, "Don't listen to him or agree to his demands."

[9]So he replied to Ben-Hadad's messengers, "Tell my lord the king, 'Your servant will do all you demanded the first time, but this demand I

*3 Verse 3 in Hebrew begins in the middle of verse 2 in English.

לַעֲשׂוֹת וַיֵּלְכוּ הַמַּלְאָכִים וַיְשִׁבֻהוּ דָּבָר׃
answer and-they-took-back-him the-messengers and-they-left to-meet

(10) וַיִּשְׁלַח אֵלָיו בֶּן־ הֲדַד וַיֹּאמֶר כֹּה־ יַעֲשׂוּן לִי
with-me may-they-deal so and-he-said Hadad Ben to-him then-he-sent (10)

אֱלֹהִים וְכֹה יֹסִפוּ אִם־ יִשְׂפֹּק עֲפַר שֹׁמְרוֹן לִשְׁעָלִים
for-handfuls Samaria dust-of he-is-enough if may-they-be-severe and-so gods

לְכָל־ הָעָם אֲשֶׁר בְּרַגְלָי׃ (11) וַיַּעַן מֶלֶךְ־יִשְׂרָאֵל
Israel king-of and-he-answered (11) at-feet-of-me who the-people for-all-of

וַיֹּאמֶר דַּבְּרוּ אַל־ יִתְהַלֵּל חֹגֵר כִּמְפַתֵּחַ׃
like-one-taking-off one-putting-on-armor he-should-boast not tell! and-he-said

(12) וַיְהִי כִּשְׁמֹעַ אֶת־ הַדָּבָר הַזֶּה וְהוּא שֹׁתֶה
drinking then-he the-this the-message *** when-to-hear and-he-was (12)

הוּא וְהַמְּלָכִים בַּסֻּכּוֹת וַיֹּאמֶר אֶל־ עֲבָדָיו שִׂימוּ
prepare! men-of-him to and-he-ordered in-the-tents and-the-kings he

וַיָּשִׂימוּ עַל־ הָעִיר׃ (13) וְהִנֵּה נָבִיא אֶחָד נִגַּשׁ אֶל־
to he-came one prophet then-see! (13) the-city against so-they-prepared

אַחְאָב מֶלֶךְ־יִשְׂרָאֵל וַיֹּאמֶר כֹּה אָמַר יְהוָה הֲרָאִיתָ אֵת כָּל־
all-of *** you-see? Yahweh he-says this and-he-announced Israel king-of Ahab

הֶהָמוֹן הַגָּדוֹל הַזֶּה הִנְנִי נֹתְנוֹ בְיָדְךָ הַיּוֹם
the-day into-hand-of-you giving-him see-I! the-this the-vast the-army

וְיָדַעְתָּ כִּי־ אֲנִי יְהוָה׃ (14) וַיֹּאמֶר אַחְאָב בְּמִי
by-whom? Ahab and-he-asked (14) Yahweh I that then-you-will-know

וַיֹּאמֶר כֹּה־ אָמַר יְהוָה בְּנַעֲרֵי שָׂרֵי הַמְּדִינוֹת
the-provinces commanders-of by-young-men-of Yahweh he-says this and-he-replied

וַיֹּאמֶר מִי־ יֶאְסֹר הַמִּלְחָמָה וַיֹּאמֶר אָתָּה׃
you and-he-answered the-battle he-will-start who? and-he-asked

(15) וַיִּפְקֹד אֶת־ נַעֲרֵי שָׂרֵי הַמְּדִינוֹת
the-provinces commanders-of young-men-of *** so-he-summoned (15)

וַיִּהְיוּ מָאתַיִם שְׁנַיִם וּשְׁלֹשִׁים וְאַחֲרֵיהֶם פָּקַד אֶת־
*** he-assembled and-after-them and-thirty two two-hundreds and-they-were

כָּל־ הָעָם כָּל־ בְּנֵי יִשְׂרָאֵל שִׁבְעַת אֲלָפִים׃ (16) וַיֵּצְאוּ
and-they-set-out (16) thousands seven-of Israel sons-of all-of the-people all-of

בַּצָּהֳרָיִם וּבֶן־ הֲדַד שֹׁתֶה שִׁכּוֹר בַּסֻּכּוֹת הוּא וְהַמְּלָכִים
and-the-kings he in-the-tents drunken drinking Hadad while-Ben at-the-noon

שְׁלֹשִׁים־וּשְׁנַיִם מֶלֶךְ עֹזֵר אֹתוֹ׃ (17) וַיֵּצְאוּ נַעֲרֵי
young-men-of and-they-went-out (17) with-him allying king and-two thirty

שָׂרֵי הַמְּדִינוֹת בָּרִאשֹׁנָה וַיִּשְׁלַח בֶּן־ הֲדַד
Hadad Ben and-he-dispatched at-the-first the-provinces commanders-of

cannot meet.' " They left and
took the answer back to Ben-
Hadad.
10Then Ben-Hadad sent an-
other message to Ahab: "May
the gods deal with me, be it
ever so severely, if enough
dust remains in Samaria to
give each of my men a handful."
11The king of Israel an-
swered, "Tell him: 'One who
puts on his armor should not
boast like one who takes it
off.' "
12Ben-Hadad heard this
message while he and the
kings were drinking in their
tents,[v] and he ordered his
men: "Prepare to attack." So
they prepared to attack the
city.

Ahab Defeats Ben-Hadad

13Meanwhile a prophet came
to Ahab king of Israel and announced, "This is what the
LORD says: 'Do you see this
vast army? I will give it into
your hand today, and then
you will know that I am the
LORD.' "
14"But who will do this?"
asked Ahab.
The prophet replied, "This is
what the LORD says: 'The
young officers of the provincial commanders will do it.' "
"And who will start the battle?" he asked.
The prophet answered,
"You will."
15So Ahab summoned the
young officers of the provincial commanders, 232 men.
Then he assembled the rest of
the Israelites, 7,000 in all.
16They set out at noon while
Ben-Hadad and the 32 kings
allied with him were in their
tents getting drunk. 17The
young officers of the provincial commanders went out
first.

[v]12 Or *in Succoth*; also in verse 16

וַיַּגִּידוּ לוֹ לֵאמֹר אֲנָשִׁים יָצְאוּ מִשֹּׁמְרוֹן׃ וַיֹּאמֶר

and-he-said (18) from-Samaria they-advance men to-say to-him and-they-reported

אִם־ לְשָׁלוֹם יָצָאוּ תִּפְשׂוּם חַיִּים וְאִם לְמִלְחָמָה

for-war and-if ones-alive you-take-them they-come-out for-peace if

יָצְאוּ חַיִּים תִּפְשׂוּם׃ וְאֵלֶּה יָצְאוּ מִן־

from they-marched-out and-these (19) you-take-them ones-alive they-come-out

הָעִיר נַעֲרֵי שָׂרֵי הַמְּדִינוֹת וְהַחַיִל אֲשֶׁר אַחֲרֵיהֶם׃

behind-them who and-the-army the-provinces commanders-of young-men-of the-city

וַיַּכּוּ אִישׁ אִישׁוֹ וַיָּנֻסוּ אֲרָם

Aram and-they-fled opponent-of-him each and-they-struck-down (20)

וַיִּרְדְּפֵם יִשְׂרָאֵל וַיִּמָּלֵט בֶּן־ הֲדַד מֶלֶךְ אֲרָם עַל־ סוּס

horse on Aram king-of Hadad Ben but-he-escaped Israel and-he-pursued-them

וּפָרָשִׁים׃ וַיֵּצֵא מֶלֶךְ יִשְׂרָאֵל וַיַּךְ אֶת־

*** and-he-overpowered Israel king-of and-he-advanced (21) with-horsemen

הַסּוּס וְאֶת־ הָרֶכֶב וְהִכָּה בַאֲרָם מַכָּה גְדוֹלָה׃

heavy loss on-Aram and-he-inflicted-loss the-chariot and the-horse

וַיִּגַּשׁ הַנָּבִיא אֶל־ מֶלֶךְ יִשְׂרָאֵל וַיֹּאמֶר לוֹ לֵךְ

go! to-him and-he-said Israel king-of to the-prophet and-he-came (22)

הִתְחַזַּק וְדַע וּרְאֵה אֵת אֲשֶׁר־ תַּעֲשֶׂה כִּי לִתְשׁוּבַת

at-return-of for you-must-do what *** and-see! and-know! strengthen-yourself!

הַשָּׁנָה מֶלֶךְ אֲרָם עֹלֶה עָלֶיךָ׃ וְעַבְדֵי מֶלֶךְ־

king-of and-officials-of (23) against-you attacking Aram king-of the-year

אֲרָם אָמְרוּ אֵלָיו אֱלֹהֵי הָרִים אֱלֹהֵיהֶם עַל־ כֵּן חָזְקוּ

they-are-strong this for gods-of-them hills gods-of to-him they-advised Aram

מִמֶּנּוּ וְאוּלָם נִלָּחֵם אִתָּם בַּמִּישׁוֹר אִם־ לֹא

surely then on-the-plain with-them we-fight but-if more-than-us

נֶחֱזַק מֵהֶם׃ וְאֶת־ הַדָּבָר הַזֶּה עֲשֵׂה הָסֵר

remove! do! the-this the-thing and (24) more-than-they we-will-be-strong

הַמְּלָכִים אִישׁ מִמְּקֹמוֹ וְשִׂים פַּחוֹת תַּחְתֵּיהֶם׃

in-place-of-them officers and-put from-command-of-him each the-kings

וְאַתָּה תִמְנֶה־ לְךָ | חַיִל כַּחַיִל הַנֹּפֵל

the-one-being-lost like-the-army army for-you you-must-raise and-you (25)

מֵאוֹתָךְ וְסוּס כַּסּוּס | וְרֶכֶב כָּרֶכֶב וְנִלָּחֲמָה

so-we-can-fight like-the-chariot and-chariot like-the-horse and-horse from-you

אוֹתָם בַּמִּישׁוֹר אִם־ לֹא נֶחֱזַק מֵהֶם וַיִּשְׁמַע

and-he-listened more-than-they we-will-be-strong surely then on-the-plain them

לְקֹלָם וַיַּעַשׂ כֵּן׃ וַיְהִי לִתְשׁוּבַת

at-return-of and-he-was (26) accordingly and-he-acted to-voice-of-them

Now Ben-Hadad had dis-
patched scouts, who reported,
"Men are advancing from Samaria."
[18]He said, "If they have
come out for peace, take them
alive; if they have come out for
war, take them alive."
[19]The young officers of the
provincial commanders
marched out of the city with
the army behind them [20]and
each one struck down his opponent. At that, the Arameans
fled, with the Israelites in pursuit. But Ben-Hadad king of
Aram escaped on horseback
with some of his horsemen.
[21]The king of Israel advanced
and overpowered the horses
and chariots and inflicted
heavy losses on the Arameans.
[22]Afterward, the prophet
came to the king of Israel and
said, "Strengthen your position and see what must be
done, because next spring the
king of Aram will attack you
again."
[23]Meanwhile, the officials of
the king of Aram advised him,
"Their gods are gods of the
hills. That is why they were
too strong for us. But if we
fight them on the plains, surely we will be stronger than
they. [24]Do this: Remove all the
kings from their commands
and replace them with other
officers. [25]You must also raise
an army like the one you lost—
horse for horse and chariot for
chariot—so we can fight Israel
on the plains. Then surely we
will be stronger than they."
He agreed with them and acted accordingly.

הַשָּׁנָה וַיִּפְקֹד בֶּן־הֲדַד אֶת־אֲרָם וַיַּעַל אֲפֵקָה
to-Aphek and-he-went-up Aram *** Hadad Ben then-he-mustered the-year

לַמִּלְחָמָה עִם־יִשְׂרָאֵל׃ וּבְנֵי יִשְׂרָאֵל הָתְפָּקְדוּ
they-were-mustered Israel and-sons-of (27) Israel against to-the-fight

וְכָלְכְּלוּ וַיֵּלְכוּ לִקְרָאתָם וַיַּחֲנוּ
and-they-camped to-meet-them and-they-marched-out and-they-were-provided

בְנֵי־יִשְׂרָאֵל נֶגְדָּם כִּשְׁנֵי חֲשִׂפֵי עִזִּים וַאֲרָם
while-Aram goats small-flocks-of like-two-of opposite-them Israel sons-of

מִלְאוּ אֶת־הָאָרֶץ׃ וַיִּגַּשׁ אִישׁ הָאֱלֹהִים
the-God man-of and-he-came-up (28) the-countryside *** they-covered

וַיֹּאמֶר אֶל־מֶלֶךְ יִשְׂרָאֵל וַיֹּאמֶר כֹּה־אָמַר יְהוָה יַעַן אֲשֶׁר
that because Yahweh he-says this and-he-said Israel king-of to and-he-told

אָמְרוּ אֲרָם אֱלֹהֵי הָרִים יְהוָה וְלֹא־אֱלֹהֵי עֲמָקִים הוּא וְנָתַתִּי
then-I-will-give he valleys God-of and-not Yahweh hills God-of Aram they-think

אֶת־כָּל־הֶהָמוֹן הַגָּדוֹל הַזֶּה בְּיָדֶךָ וִידַעְתֶּם
and-you-will-know into-hand-of-you the-this the-vast the-army all-of ***

כִּי־אֲנִי יְהוָה׃ וַיַּחֲנוּ אֵלֶּה נֹכַח אֵלֶּה שִׁבְעַת יָמִים
days seven-of those opposite these and-they-camped (29) Yahweh I that

וַיְהִי ׀ בַּיּוֹם הַשְּׁבִיעִי וַתִּקְרַב הַמִּלְחָמָה
the-battle then-she-was-joined the-seventh on-the-day and-he-was

וַיַּכּוּ בְנֵי־יִשְׂרָאֵל אֶת־אֲרָם מֵאָה־אֶלֶף
thousand hundred Aram *** Israel sons-of and-they-inflicted-casualties

רַגְלִי בְּיוֹם אֶחָד׃ וַיָּנֻסוּ הַנּוֹתָרִים ׀ אֲפֵקָה
to-Aphek the-ones-remaining and-they-escaped (30) one on-day foot-soldier

אֶל־הָעִיר וַתִּפֹּל הַחוֹמָה עַל־עֶשְׂרִים וְשִׁבְעָה אֶלֶף אִישׁ
man thousand and-seven twenty on the-wall and-she-collapsed the-city to

הַנּוֹתָרִים וּבֶן־הֲדַד נָס וַיָּבֹא אֶל־הָעִיר חֶדֶר
room the-city into and-he-went he-fled Hadad and-Ben the-ones-remaining

בְּחָדֶר׃ וַיֹּאמְרוּ אֵלָיו עֲבָדָיו הִנֵּה־נָא שָׁמַעְנוּ כִּי
that we-heard now! look! officials-of-him to-him and-they-said (31) in-room

מַלְכֵי בֵּית יִשְׂרָאֵל כִּי־מַלְכֵי חֶסֶד הֵם נָשִׂימָה נָּא שַׂקִּים
sackcloths now! let-us-put they mercy kings-of that Israel house-of kings-of

בְּמָתְנֵינוּ וַחֲבָלִים בְּרֹאשֵׁנוּ וְנֵצֵא אֶל־מֶלֶךְ
king-of to and-let-us-go around-head-of-us and-ropes around-waists-of-us

יִשְׂרָאֵל אוּלַי יְחַיֶּה אֶת־נַפְשֶׁךָ׃ וַיַּחְגְּרוּ שַׂקִּים
sackcloths so-they-wore (32) life-of-you *** he-will-spare perhaps Israel

בְּמָתְנֵיהֶם וַחֲבָלִים בְּרָאשֵׁיהֶם וַיָּבֹאוּ אֶל־מֶלֶךְ
king-of to and-they-went around-heads-of-them and-ropes around-waists-of-them

26 The next spring Ben-
Hadad mustered the Ara-
means and went up to Aphek
to fight against Israel.
27 When
the Israelites were also mustered and given provisions,
they marched out to meet
them. The Israelites camped
opposite them like two small
flocks of goats, while the Arameans covered the countryside.
28 The man of God came up
and told the king of Israel,
"This is what the LORD says:
'Because the Arameans think
the LORD is a god of the hills
and not a god of the valleys, I
will deliver this vast army into
your hands, and you will
know that I am the LORD.' "
29 For seven days they
camped opposite each other,
and on the seventh day the
battle was joined. The Israelites inflicted a hundred thousand casualties on the Aramean foot soldiers in one day.
30 The rest of them escaped to
the city of Aphek, where the
wall collapsed on twenty-sev-
en thousand of them. And
Ben-Hadad fled to the city and
hid in an inner room.
31 His officials said to him,
"Look, we have heard that the
kings of the house of Israel are
merciful. Let us go to the king
of Israel with sackcloth
around our waists and ropes
around our heads. Perhaps he
will spare your life."
32 Wearing sackcloth around
their waists and ropes around
their heads, they went to the

יִשְׂרָאֵל וַיֹּאמְרוּ עַבְדְּךָ בֶן־הֲדַד אָמַר תְּחִי־נָא
now! let-her-live he-says Hadad Ben servant-of-you and-they-said Israel

נַפְשִׁי וַיֹּאמֶר הַעוֹדֶנּוּ חַי אָחִי הוּא׃ וְהָאֲנָשִׁים
and-the-men (33) he brother-of-me alive still-he? and-he-answered life-of-me

יְנַחֲשׁוּ וַיְמַהֲרוּ *וַיַּחְלְטוּ הֲמִמֶּנּוּ*
whether-from-him and-they-picked-up and-they-were-quick they-took-as-good-sign

וַיֹּאמְרוּ אָחִיךָ בֶן־הֲדַד וַיֹּאמֶר בֹּאוּ קָחֻהוּ וַיֵּצֵא
when-he-came get-him! go! and-he-said Hadad Ben brother-of-you and-they-said

אֵלָיו בֶּן־הֲדַד וַיַּעֲלֵהוּ עַל־הַמֶּרְכָּבָה׃ וַיֹּאמֶר
and-he-said (34) the-chariot into then-he-brought-up-him Hadad Ben to-him

אֵלָיו הֶעָרִים אֲשֶׁר־לָקַח־אָבִי מֵאֵת אָבִיךָ אָשִׁב
I-will-return father-of-you from father-of-me he-took that the-cities to-him

וְחוּצוֹת תָּשִׂים לְךָ בְדַמֶּשֶׂק כַּאֲשֶׁר־שָׂם
he-set-up just-as in-Damascus for-you you-may-set-up and-market-areas

אָבִי בְּשֹׁמְרוֹן וַאֲנִי בַּבְּרִית אֲשַׁלְּחֶךָּ וַיִּכְרָת־
so-he-made I-will-set-free-you in-the-treaty and-I in-Samaria father-of-me

לוֹ בְרִית וַיְשַׁלְּחֵהוּ׃ וְאִישׁ אֶחָד מִבְּנֵי הַנְּבִיאִים
the-prophets of-sons-of one and-man (35) and-he-let-go-him treaty with-him

אָמַר אֶל־רֵעֵהוּ בִּדְבַר יְהוָה הַכֵּינִי נָא וַיְמָאֵן
but-he-refused now! strike-me! Yahweh by-word-of companion-of-him to he-said

הָאִישׁ לְהַכֹּתוֹ׃ וַיֹּאמֶר לוֹ יַעַן אֲשֶׁר לֹא־שָׁמַעְתָּ
you-obeyed not that because to-him so-he-said (36) to-strike-him the-man

בְּקוֹל יְהוָה הִנְּךָ הוֹלֵךְ מֵאִתִּי וְהִכְּךָ
and-he-will-kill-you from-with-me leaving see-you! Yahweh to-voice-of

הָאַרְיֵה וַיֵּלֶךְ מֵאֶצְלוֹ וַיִּמְצָאֵהוּ הָאַרְיֵה וַיַּכֵּהוּ׃
and-he-killed-him the-lion and-he-found-him from-with-him and-he-went the-lion

וַיִּמְצָא אִישׁ אַחֵר וַיֹּאמֶר הַכֵּינִי נָא וַיַּכֵּהוּ
so-he-struck-him now! strike-me! and-he-said another man and-he-found (37)

הָאִישׁ הַכֵּה וּפָצֹעַ׃ וַיֵּלֶךְ הַנָּבִיא וַיַּעֲמֹד
and-he-stood the-prophet then-he-went (38) and-to-wound to-strike the-man

לַמֶּלֶךְ עַל־הַדָּרֶךְ וַיִּתְחַפֵּשׂ בָּאֲפֵר עַל־
over with-the-headband and-he-disguised-himself the-road by for-the-king

עֵינָיו׃ וַיְהִי הַמֶּלֶךְ עֹבֵר וְהוּא צָעַק אֶל־
to he-called-out and-he passing-by the-king and-he-was (39) eyes-of-him

הַמֶּלֶךְ וַיֹּאמֶר עַבְדְּךָ | יָצָא בְקֶרֶב־הַמִּלְחָמָה וְהִנֵּה־
and-see! the-battle into-thick-of he-went servant-of-you and-he-said the-king

אִישׁ סָר וַיָּבֵא אֵלַי אִישׁ וַיֹּאמֶר שְׁמֹר אֶת־הָאִישׁ הַזֶּה
the-this the-man *** guard! and-he-said man to-me and-he-brought coming man

king of Israel and said, "Your servant Ben-Hadad says: 'Please let me live.' "

The king answered, "Is he still alive? He is my brother."
33The men took this as a
good sign and were quick to pick up his word. "Yes, your brother Ben-Hadad!" they said.

"Go and get him," the king said. When Ben-Hadad came out, Ahab had him come up into his chariot.
34"I will return the cities my
father took from your father," Ben-Hadad offered. "You may set up your own market areas in Damascus, as my father did in Samaria."

⌞Ahab said,⌟ "On the basis of a treaty I will set you free." So he made a treaty with him, and let him go.

A Prophet Condemns Ahab

35By the word of the LORD
one of the sons of the prophets said to his companion, "Strike me with your weapon," but the man refused.
36So the prophet said, "Be-
cause you have not obeyed the LORD, as soon as you leave me a lion will kill you." And after the man went away, a lion found him and killed him.
37The prophet found another
man and said, "Strike me, please." So the man struck him and wounded him.
38Then the prophet went and
stood by the road waiting for the king. He disguised himself with his headband down over
his eyes. 39As the king passed
by, the prophet called out to him, "Your servant went into the thick of the battle, and someone came to me with a captive and said, 'Guard this

*33 Many Western mss emend this *Ketbib* form with the *Qere* (וּהָ מִ־), *and-they-picked-up-her from-him*, which is the *Ketbib* in some Eastern mss.

אִם־ הִפָּקֵד יִפָּקֵד וְהָיְתָה נַפְשְׁךָ תַּחַת נַפְשׁוֹ
life-of-him for life-of-you then-she-will-be he-is-missing to-be-missing if

אוֹ כִכַּר־ כֶּסֶף תִּשְׁקוֹל׃ וַיְהִי עַבְדְּךָ עֹשֶׂה
being-busy servant-of-you and-he-was (40) you-must-pay silver talent-of or

הֵנָּה וָהֵנָּה וְהוּא אֵינֶנּוּ וַיֹּאמֶר אֵלָיו מֶלֶךְ־ יִשְׂרָאֵל כֵּן
that Israel king-of to-him and-he-said not-he and-he and-at-there at-here

מִשְׁפָּטֶךָ אַתָּה חָרָצְתָּ׃ וַיְמַהֵר וַיָּסַר אֶת־
*** and-he-removed then-he-was-quick (41) you-pronounced you sentence-of-you

הָאֲפֵר מֵעַל° עֵינָיו וַיַּכֵּר אֹתוֹ מֶלֶךְ יִשְׂרָאֵל כִּי
that Israel king-of him and-he-recognized eyes-of-him from-over the-headband

מֵהַנְּבִאִים הוּא׃ וַיֹּאמֶר אֵלָיו כֹּה אָמַר יְהוָה יַעַן
because Yahweh he-says this to-him and-he-said (42) he from-the-prophets

שִׁלַּחְתָּ אֶת־ אִישׁ־ חֶרְמִי מִיָּד וְהָיְתָה נַפְשְׁךָ
life-of-you then-she-shall-be from-hand determined-to-die man *** you-set-free

תַּחַת נַפְשׁוֹ וְעַמְּךָ תַּחַת עַמּוֹ׃ וַיֵּלֶךְ מֶלֶךְ־
king-of and-he-went (43) people-of-him for and-people-of-you life-of-him for

יִשְׂרָאֵל עַל־ בֵּיתוֹ סַר וְזָעֵף וַיָּבֹא שֹׁמְרוֹנָה׃
to-Samaria and-he-went and-angry sullen palace-of-him to Israel

וַיְהִי אַחַר הַדְּבָרִים הָאֵלֶּה כֶּרֶם הָיָה לְנָבוֹת
to-Naboth he-was vineyard the-these the-things after and-he-was (21:1)

הַיִּזְרְעֵאלִי אֲשֶׁר בְּיִזְרְעֶאל אֵצֶל הֵיכַל אַחְאָב מֶלֶךְ שֹׁמְרוֹן׃
Samaria king-of Ahab palace-of close-to in-Jezreel that the-Jezreelite

וַיְדַבֵּר אַחְאָב אֶל־ נָבוֹת ׀ לֵאמֹר ׀ תְּנָה־ לִּי אֶת־ כַּרְמְךָ
vineyard-of-you *** to-me give! to-say Naboth to Ahab and-he-said (2)

וִיהִי־ לִי לְגַן־ יָרָק כִּי הוּא קָרוֹב אֵצֶל
next-to close he since vegetable as-garden-of for-me and-let-him-be

בֵּיתִי וְאֶתְּנָה לְךָ תַּחְתָּיו כֶּרֶם טוֹב
better vineyard in-exchange-for-him to-you and-I-will-give palace-of-me

מִמֶּנּוּ אִם טוֹב בְּעֵינֶיךָ אֶתְּנָה־ לְךָ כֶסֶף מְחִיר זֶה׃
this value-of silver to-you I-will-give in-eyes-of-you good or than-he

וַיֹּאמֶר נָבוֹת אֶל־ אַחְאָב חָלִילָה לִּי מֵיְהוָה
from-Yahweh from-me far-be-it! Ahab to Naboth but-he-replied (3)

מִתִּתִּי אֶת־ נַחֲלַת אֲבֹתַי לָךְ׃ וַיָּבֹא אַחְאָב
Ahab so-he-went (4) to-you fathers-of-me inheritance-of *** from-to-give-me

אֶל־ בֵּיתוֹ סַר וְזָעֵף עַל־ הַדָּבָר אֲשֶׁר־ דִּבֶּר אֵלָיו
to-him he-said that the-word because-of and-angry sullen home-of-him to

נָבוֹת הַיִּזְרְעֵאלִי וַיֹּאמֶר לֹא־ אֶתֵּן לְךָ אֶת־ נַחֲלַת
inheritance-of *** to-you I-will-give not and-he-said the-Jezreelite Naboth

man. If he is missing, it will be
your life for his life, or you
must pay a talent[w] of silver.'
40While your servant was busy
here and there, the man disappeared."
"That is your sentence," the
king of Israel said. "You have
pronounced it yourself."
41Then the prophet quickly
removed the headband from
his eyes, and the king of Israel
recognized him as one of the
prophets. 42He said to the king,
"This is what the LORD says:
'You have set free a man I had
determined should die.[x]
Therefore it is your life for his
life, your people for his
people.' " 43Sullen and angry,
the king of Israel went to his
palace in Samaria.

Naboth's Vineyard

21 Some time later there
was an incident in-
volving a vineyard belonging
to Naboth the Jezreelite. The
vineyard was in Jezreel, close
to the palace of Ahab king of
Samaria. 2Ahab said to
Naboth, "Let me have your
vineyard to use for a vegetable
garden, since it is close to my
palace. In exchange I will give
you a better vineyard or, if you
prefer, I will pay you whatever
it is worth."
3But Naboth replied, "The
LORD forbid that I should give
you the inheritance of my fathers."

w39 That is, about 75 pounds (about 34 kilograms)
x42 The Hebrew term refers to the irrevocable giving over of things or persons to the LORD, often by totally destroying them.

°41 ק מעלי

אֲבֹתָי וַיִּשְׁכַּב עַל־ מִטָּתוֹ וַיַּסֵּב אֶת־ פָּנָיו וְלֹא־
and-not faces-of-him *** and-he-turned bed-of-him on and-he-lay fathers-of-me

אָכַל לָחֶם׃ וַתָּבֹא אֵלָיו אִיזֶבֶל אִשְׁתּוֹ וַתְּדַבֵּר אֵלָיו
to-him and-she-asked wife-of-him Jezebel to-him and-she-came (5) food he-ate

מַה־ זֶּה רוּחֲךָ סָרָה וְאֵינְךָ אֹכֵל לָחֶם׃ וַיְדַבֵּר
and-he-answered (6) food eating and-not-you sullen spirit-of-you this what?

אֵלֶיהָ כִּי־ אֲדַבֵּר אֶל־ נָבוֹת הַיִּזְרְעֵאלִי וָאֹמַר לוֹ תְּנָה־ לִּי
to-me sell! to-him and-I-said the-Jezreelite Naboth to I-spoke because to-her

אֶת־ כַּרְמְךָ בְּכֶסֶף אוֹ אִם־ חָפֵץ אַתָּה אֶתְּנָה־ לְךָ
to-you I-will-give you he-pleases if or for-silver vineyard-of-you ***

כֶּרֶם תַּחְתָּיו וַיֹּאמֶר לֹא־ אֶתֵּן לְךָ אֶת־ כַּרְמִי׃
vineyard-of-me *** to-you I-will-give not but-he-said in-place-of-him vineyard

וַתֹּאמֶר אֵלָיו אִיזֶבֶל אִשְׁתּוֹ אַתָּה עַתָּה תַּעֲשֶׂה מְלוּכָה עַל־יִשְׂרָאֵל
Israel over king you-act now you wife-of-him Jezebel to-him and-she-said (7)

קוּם אֱכָל־ לֶחֶם וְיִטַב לִבֶּךָ אֲנִי אֶתֵּן לְךָ
for-you I-will-get I heart-of-you and-let-him-cheer-up food eat! get-up!

אֶת־ כֶּרֶם נָבוֹת הַיִּזְרְעֵאלִי׃ וַתִּכְתֹּב סְפָרִים בְּשֵׁם
in-name-of letters so-she-wrote (8) the-Jezreelite Naboth vineyard-of ***

אַחְאָב וַתַּחְתֹּם בְּחֹתָמוֹ וַתִּשְׁלַח הַסְּפָרִים אֶל־ הַזְּקֵנִים*
the-elders to letters and-she-sent with-seal-of-him and-she-sealed Ahab

וְאֶל־ הַחֹרִים אֲשֶׁר בְּעִירוֹ הַיֹּשְׁבִים אֶת־ נָבוֹת׃
Naboth with the-ones-living in-city-of-him who the-nobles and-to

וַתִּכְתֹּב בַּסְּפָרִים לֵאמֹר קִרְאוּ־ צוֹם וְהוֹשִׁיבוּ אֶת־ נָבוֹת
Naboth *** and-seat! fast proclaim! to-say in-the-letters and-she-wrote (9)

בְּרֹאשׁ הָעָם׃ וְהוֹשִׁיבוּ שְׁנַיִם אֲנָשִׁים בְּנֵי־ בְלִיַּעַל נֶגְדּוֹ
opposite-him scoundrel sons-of men two but-seat! (10) the-people at-head-of

וִיעִדֻהוּ לֵאמֹר בֵּרַכְתָּ אֱלֹהִים וָמֶלֶךְ
and-king God you-cursed to-say and-they-shall-testify-against-him

וְהוֹצִיאֻהוּ וְסִקְלֻהוּ וְיָמֹת׃ וַיַּעֲשׂוּ אַנְשֵׁי
men-of and-they-did (11) so-he-dies and-stone-him! then-take-out-him!

עִירוֹ הַזְּקֵנִים וְהַחֹרִים אֲשֶׁר הַיֹּשְׁבִים בְּעִירוֹ
in-city-of-him the-ones-living who and-the-nobles the-elders city-of-him

כַּאֲשֶׁר שָׁלְחָה אֲלֵיהֶם אִיזָבֶל כַּאֲשֶׁר כָּתוּב בַּסְּפָרִים
in-the-letters being-written just-as Jezebel to-them she-directed just-as

אֲשֶׁר שָׁלְחָה אֲלֵיהֶם׃ קָרְאוּ צוֹם וְהֹשִׁיבוּ אֶת־ נָבוֹת
Naboth *** and-they-seated fast they-proclaimed (12) to-them she-sent that

בְּרֹאשׁ הָעָם׃ וַיָּבֹאוּ שְׁנֵי הָאֲנָשִׁים בְּנֵי־ בְלִיַּעַל
scoundrel sons-of the-men two-of then-they-came (13) the-people at-head-of

[4]So Ahab went home, sullen
and angry because Naboth the
Jezreelite had said, "I will not
give you the inheritance of my
fathers." He lay on his bed
sulking and refused to eat.
[5]His wife Jezebel came in
and asked him, "Why are you
so sullen? Why won't you
eat?"
[6]He answered her, "Because
I said to Naboth the Jezreelite,
'Sell me your vineyard; or if
you prefer, I will give you another vineyard in its place.'
But he said, 'I will not give you
my vineyard.' "
[7]Jezebel his wife said, "Is
this how you act as king over
Israel? Get up and eat! Cheer
up. I'll get you the vineyard of
Naboth the Jezreelite."
[8]So she wrote letters in
Ahab's name, placed his seal
on them, and sent them to the
elders and nobles who lived in
Naboth's city with him. [9]In
those letters she wrote:

> "Proclaim a day of fasting and seat Naboth in a prominent place among the people. [10]But seat two scoundrels opposite him and have them testify that he has cursed both God and the king. Then take him out and stone him to death."

[11]So the elders and nobles
who lived in Naboth's city did
as Jezebel directed in the letters she had written to them.
[12]They proclaimed a fast and
seated Naboth in a prominent
place among the people.
[13]Then two scoundrels came

*8 Most mss have *dagesh* in the *zayin* (הַזְּ).

°8 ק ספרים

וישבו נגדו ויעדהו אנשי הבליעל
the-scoundrel men-of and-they-testified-against-him opposite-him and-they-sat

את־ נבות נגד העם לאמר ברך נבות אלהים ומלך
and-king God Naboth he-cursed to-say the-people before Naboth ***

ויצאהו מחוץ לעיר ויסקלהו באבנים
with-the-stones and-they-stoned-him of-the-city outside and-they-took-him

וימת׃ וישלחו אל־ איזבל לאמר סקל נבות
Naboth he-was-stoned to-say Jezebel to and-they-sent (14) so-he-died

וימת׃ ויהי כשמע איזבל כי־ סקל
he-was-stoned that Jezebel when-to-hear and-he-was (15) and-he-is-dead

נבות וימת ותאמר איזבל אל־אחאב קום רש את־
*** possess! get-up! Ahab to Jezebel then-she-said and-he-died Naboth

כרם ׀ נבות היזרעאלי אשר מאן לתת־ לך בכסף
for-silver to-you to-sell he-refused that the-Jezreelite Naboth vineyard-of

כי אין נבות חי כי־ מת׃ ויהי כשמע אחאב כי
that Ahab when-to-hear and-he-was (16) dead but alive Naboth not for

מת נבות ויקם אחאב לרדת אל־ כרם נבות
Naboth vineyard-of to to-go-down Ahab then-he-got-up Naboth he-was-dead

היזרעאלי לרשתו׃ ויהי דבר־ יהוה אל־ אליהו
Elijah to Yahweh word-of then-he-came (17) to-possess-him the-Jezreelite

התשבי לאמר׃ קום רד לקראת אחאב מלך־ישראל
Israel king-of Ahab to-meet go-down! get-up! (18) to-say the-Tishbite

אשר בשמרון הנה בכרם נבות אשר־ ירד שם לרשתו׃
to-possess-him there he-went where Naboth in-vineyard-of see! in-Samaria who

ודברת אליו לאמר כה אמר יהוה הרצחת וגם־
and-also you-murdered? Yahweh he-says this to-say to-him and-you-say (19)

ירשת ודברת אליו לאמר כה אמר יהוה
Yahweh he-says this to-say to-him then-you-say you-seized-property

במקום אשר לקקו הכלבים את־ דם נבות ילקו
they-will-lick-up Naboth blood-of *** the-dogs they-licked-up where in-place

הכלבים את־ דמך גם־ אתה׃ ויאמר אחאב אל־אליהו
Elijah to Ahab and-he-said (20) you also blood-of-you *** the-dogs

המצאתני איבי ויאמר מצאתי יען התמכרך
to-sell-you because I-found and-he-answered being-enemy-of-me you-found-me?

לעשות הרע בעיני יהוה׃ הנני מבי° אליך רעה
disaster on-you bringing see-I! (21) Yahweh in-eyes-of the-evil to-do

ובערתי אחריך והכרתי לאחאב משתין
one-urinating from-Ahab and-I-will-cut-off after-you and-I-will-consume

and sat opposite him and
brought charges against
Naboth before the people, saying, "Naboth has cursed both
God and the king." So they
took him outside the city and
stoned him to death. [14]Then
they sent word to Jezebel:
"Naboth has been stoned and
is dead."
[15]As soon as Jezebel heard
that Naboth had been stoned
to death, she said to Ahab,
"Get up and take possession of
the vineyard of Naboth the
Jezreelite that he refused to sell
you. He is no longer alive, but
dead." [16]When Ahab heard
that Naboth was dead, he got
up and went down to take
possession of Naboth's vineyard.
[17]Then the word of the LORD
came to Elijah the Tishbite:
[18]"Go down to meet Ahab king
of Israel, who rules in Samaria. He is now in Naboth's
vineyard, where he has gone
to take possession of it. [19]Say
to him, 'This is what the LORD
says: Have you not murdered
a man and seized his property?' Then say to him, 'This is
what the LORD says: In the
place where dogs licked up
Naboth's blood, dogs will lick
up your blood—yes, yours!' "
[20]Ahab said to Elijah, "So
you have found me, my enemy!"
"I have found you," he answered, "because you have
sold yourself to do evil in the
eyes of the LORD. [21]'I am going
to bring disaster on you. I will
consume your descendants
and cut off from Ahab every

°21 ק מביא

בְּקִיר וְעָצוּר וְעָזוּב בְּיִשְׂרָאֵל׃ וְנָתַתִּי
and-I-will-make (22) in-Israel or-being-free and-being-slave against-wall

אֶת־ בֵּיתְךָ כְּבֵית יָרָבְעָם בֶּן־ נְבָט וּכְבֵית בַּעְשָׁא
Baasha and-like-house-of Nebat son-of Jeroboam like-house-of house-of-you ***

בֶן־ אֲחִיָּה אֶל־ הַכַּעַס אֲשֶׁר הִכְעַסְתָּ וַתַּחֲטִא
and-you-caused-to-sin you-provoked-anger that the-anger for Ahijah son-of

אֶת־יִשְׂרָאֵל׃ וְגַם־ לְאִיזֶבֶל דִּבֶּר יְהוָה לֵאמֹר הַכְּלָבִים
the-dogs to-say Yahweh he-speaks about-Jezebel and-also (23) Israel ***

יֹאכְלוּ אֶת־ אִיזֶבֶל בְּחֵל יִזְרְעֶאל׃ הַמֵּת לְאַחְאָב
of-Ahab the-dead (24) Jezreel by-wall-of Jezebel *** they-will-devour

בָּעִיר יֹאכְלוּ הַכְּלָבִים וְהַמֵּת בַּשָּׂדֶה יֹאכְלוּ
they-will-eat in-the-country and-the-dead the-dogs they-will-eat in-the-city

עוֹף הַשָּׁמָיִם׃ רַק לֹא־ הָיָה כְאַחְאָב אֲשֶׁר הִתְמַכֵּר לַעֲשׂוֹת
to-do he-sold-himself who like-Ahab he-was not indeed (25) the-airs bird-of

הָרַע בְּעֵינֵי יְהוָה אֲשֶׁר־ הֵסַתָּה אֹתוֹ אִיזֶבֶל אִשְׁתּוֹ׃
wife-of-him Jezebel him she-urged-on whom Yahweh in-eyes-of the-evil

וַיַּתְעֵב מְאֹד לָלֶכֶת אַחֲרֵי הַגִּלֻּלִים כְּכֹל אֲשֶׁר עָשׂוּ
they-did that like-all the-idols after to-go very and-he-behaved-vilely (26)

הָאֱמֹרִי אֲשֶׁר הוֹרִישׁ יְהוָה מִפְּנֵי בְּנֵי יִשְׂרָאֵל׃
Israel sons-of from-before Yahweh he-drove-out whom the-Amorite

וַיְהִי כִשְׁמֹעַ אַחְאָב אֶת־ הַדְּבָרִים הָאֵלֶּה וַיִּקְרַע
then-he-tore the-these the-words *** Ahab when-to-hear and-he-was (27)

בְּגָדָיו וַיָּשֶׂם־ שַׂק עַל־ בְּשָׂרוֹ וַיָּצוֹם וַיִּשְׁכַּב
and-he-lay and-he-fasted body-of-him on sackcloth and-he-put clothes-of-him

בַּשָּׂק וַיְהַלֵּךְ אַט׃ וַיְהִי דְּבַר־ יְהוָה אֶל־
to Yahweh word-of then-he-came (28) meekly and-he-walked in-the-sackcloth

אֵלִיָּהוּ הַתִּשְׁבִּי לֵאמֹר׃ הֲרָאִיתָ כִּי־ נִכְנַע אַחְאָב
Ahab he-humbled-himself how you-noticed? (29) to-say the-Tishbite Elijah

מִלְּפָנָי יַעַן כִּי־ נִכְנַע מִפָּנַי לֹא־ אָבִי
I-will-bring not from-before-me he-humbled-himself that because from-before-me

הָרָעָה בְּיָמָיו בִּימֵי בְנוֹ אָבִיא הָרָעָה
the-disaster I-will-bring son-of-him in-days-of in-days-of-him the-disaster

עַל־ בֵּיתוֹ׃ וַיֵּשְׁבוּ שָׁלֹשׁ שָׁנִים אֵין מִלְחָמָה בֵּין
between war there-was-no years three and-they-remained (22:1) house-of-him on

אֲרָם וּבֵין יִשְׂרָאֵל׃ וַיְהִי בַּשָּׁנָה הַשְּׁלִישִׁית וַיֵּרֶד
he-went-down the-third in-the-year but-he-was (2) Israel and-between Aram

יְהוֹשָׁפָט מֶלֶךְ־ יְהוּדָה אֶל־ מֶלֶךְ יִשְׂרָאֵל׃ וַיֹּאמֶר מֶלֶךְ־יִשְׂרָאֵל
Israel king-of and-he-said (3) Israel king-of to Judah king-of Jehoshaphat

°29 ק אביא

last male in Israel—slave or
free. 22I will make your house
like that of Jeroboam son of
Nebat and that of Baasha son
of Ahijah, because you have
provoked me to anger and
have caused Israel to sin.'
23"And also concerning Jezebel the LORD says: 'Dogs will
devour Jezebel by the wall of[y]
Jezreel.'
24"Dogs will eat those belonging to Ahab who die in
the city, and the birds of the
air will feed on those who die
in the country."
25(There was never a man
like Ahab, who sold himself to
do evil in the eyes of the LORD,
urged on by Jezebel his wife.
26He behaved in the vilest
manner by going after idols,
like the Amorites the LORD
drove out before Israel.)
27When Ahab heard these
words, he tore his clothes, put
on sackcloth and fasted. He
lay in sackcloth and went
around meekly.
28Then the word of the LORD
came to Elijah the Tishbite:
29"Have you noticed how
Ahab has humbled himself
before me? Because he has
humbled himself, I will not
bring this disaster in his day,
but I will bring it on his house
in the days of his son."

Micaiah Prophesies Against Ahab

22 For three years there
was no war between
Aram and Israel. 2But in the
third year Jehoshaphat king of
Judah went down to see the
king of Israel. 3The king of Israel had said to his officials,

[y]23 Most Hebrew manuscripts; a few Hebrew manuscripts, Vulgate and Syriac (see also 2 Kings 9:26) *the plot of ground at*

אֶל־ עֲבָדָיו הַיְדַעְתֶּם כִּי־ לָנוּ רָמֹת גִּלְעָד וַאֲנַחְנוּ
yet-we Gilead Ramoth to-us that you-know? officials-of-him to

מַחְשִׁים מִקַּחַת אֹתָהּ מִיַּד מֶלֶךְ אֲרָם׃
Aram king-of from-hand-of her from-to-retake ones-doing-nothing

וַיֹּאמֶר אֶל־ יְהוֹשָׁפָט הֲתֵלֵךְ אִתִּי לַמִּלְחָמָה רָמֹת גִּלְעָד
Gilead Ramoth to-the-fight with-me will-you-go? Jehoshaphat to so-he-asked (4)

וַיֹּאמֶר יְהוֹשָׁפָט אֶל־ מֶלֶךְ יִשְׂרָאֵל כָּמוֹנִי כָמוֹךָ כְּעַמִּי
so-people-of-me as-you so-me Israel king-of to Jehoshaphat and-he-replied

כְעַמֶּךָ כְּסוּסַי כְּסוּסֶיךָ׃ וַיֹּאמֶר יְהוֹשָׁפָט
Jehoshaphat but-he-said (5) as-horses-of-you so-horses-of-me as-people-of-you

אֶל־ מֶלֶךְ יִשְׂרָאֵל דְּרָשׁ־ נָא כַיּוֹם אֶת־ דְּבַר יְהוָה׃
Yahweh counsel-of *** as-the-day now! seek! Israel king-of to

וַיִּקְבֹּץ מֶלֶךְ־ יִשְׂרָאֵל אֶת־ הַנְּבִיאִים כְּאַרְבַּע מֵאוֹת אִישׁ
man hundreds about-four the-prophets *** Israel king-of so-he-gathered (6)

וַיֹּאמֶר אֲלֵהֶם הַאֵלֵךְ עַל־ רָמֹת גִּלְעָד לַמִּלְחָמָה אִם־
or to-the-war Gilead Ramoth against shall-I-go? to-them and-he-asked

אֶחְדָּל וַיֹּאמְרוּ עֲלֵה וְיִתֵּן אֲדֹנָי בְּיַד
into-hand-of Lord for-he-will-give go! and-they-answered shall-I-refrain

הַמֶּלֶךְ׃ וַיֹּאמֶר יְהוֹשָׁפָט הַאֵין פֹּה נָבִיא לַיהוָה עוֹד
still of-Yahweh prophet here not? Jehoshaphat but-he-asked (7) the-king

וְנִדְרְשָׁה מֵאוֹתוֹ׃ וַיֹּאמֶר מֶלֶךְ־ יִשְׂרָאֵל ׀ אֶל־ יְהוֹשָׁפָט
Jehoshaphat to Israel king-of and-he-answered (8) of-him that-we-can-inquire

עוֹד אִישׁ־ אֶחָד לִדְרֹשׁ אֶת־ יְהוָה מֵאֹתוֹ וַאֲנִי שְׂנֵאתִיו כִּי
because I-hate-him but-I through-him Yahweh *** to-inquire one man still

לֹא־ יִתְנַבֵּא עָלַי טוֹב כִּי אִם־ רָע מִיכָיְהוּ בֶּן־ יִמְלָה
Imlah son-of Micaiah bad rather but good about-me he-prophesies not

וַיֹּאמֶר יְהוֹשָׁפָט אַל־ יֹאמַר הַמֶּלֶךְ כֵּן׃ וַיִּקְרָא
so-he-called (9) that the-king he-should-say not Jehoshaphat and-he-replied

מֶלֶךְ יִשְׂרָאֵל אֶל־ סָרִיס אֶחָד וַיֹּאמֶר מַהֲרָה מִיכָיְהוּ בֶן־
son-of Micaiah bring-at-once! and-he-said one official *** Israel king-of

יִמְלָה׃ וּמֶלֶךְ יִשְׂרָאֵל וִיהוֹשָׁפָט מֶלֶךְ־ יְהוּדָה יֹשְׁבִים
ones-sitting Judah king-of and-Jehoshaphat Israel and-king-of (10) Imlah

אִישׁ עַל־ כִּסְאוֹ מְלֻבָּשִׁים בְּגָדִים בְּגֹרֶן פֶּתַח
entrance-of at-threshing-floor robes ones-being-dressed throne-of-him on each

שַׁעַר שֹׁמְרוֹן וְכָל־ הַנְּבִיאִים מִתְנַבְּאִים לִפְנֵיהֶם׃
before-them ones-prophesying the-prophets and-all-of Samaria gate-of

וַיַּעַשׂ לוֹ צִדְקִיָּה בֶן־ כְּנַעֲנָה קַרְנֵי בַרְזֶל וַיֹּאמֶר
and-he-said iron horns-of Kenaanah son-of Zedekiah for-him now-he-made (11)

"Don't you know that Ramoth
Gilead belongs to us and yet
we are doing nothing to retake
it from the king of Aram?"
[4]So he asked Jehoshaphat,
"Will you go with me to fight
against Ramoth Gilead?"
Jehoshaphat replied to the
king of Israel, "I am as you are,
my people as your people, my
horses as your horses." [5]But Jehoshaphat also said to the
king of Israel, "First seek the
counsel of the LORD."
[6]So the king of Israel
brought together the pro-
phets—about four hundred
men—and asked them, "Shall
I go to war against Ramoth
Gilead, or shall I refrain?"
"Go," they answered, "for
the Lord will give it into the
king's hand."
[7]But Jehoshaphat asked, "Is
there not a prophet of the LORD
here whom we can inquire
of?"
[8]The king of Israel answered
Jehoshaphat, "There is still
one man through whom we
can inquire of the LORD, but I
hate him because he never
prophesies anything good
about me, but always bad. He
is Micaiah son of Imlah."
"The king should not say
that," Jehoshaphat replied.
[9]So the king of Israel called
one of his officials and said,
"Bring Micaiah son of Imlah
at once."
[10]Dressed in their royal
robes, the king of Israel and
Jehoshaphat king of Judah
were sitting on their thrones
at the threshing floor by the
entrance of the gate of Samaria, with all the prophets
prophesying before them.
[11]Now Zedekiah son of Kenaanah had made iron horns and

כֹּה־אָמַר יְהוָה בְּאֵלֶּה תְּנַגַּח אֶת־אֲרָם עַד־כַּלֹּתָם׃
to-destroy-them until Aram *** you-will-gore with-these Yahweh he-says this

וְכָל־ הַנְּבִאִים נִבְּאִים כֵּן לֵאמֹר עֲלֵה רָמֹת
Ramoth attack! to-say same ones-prophesying the-prophets and-all-of (12)

גִּלְעָד וְהַצְלַח וְנָתַן יְהוָה בְּיַד הַמֶּלֶךְ׃
the-king into-hand-of Yahweh for-he-will-give and-be-victorious! Gilead

וְהַמַּלְאָךְ אֲשֶׁר־הָלַךְ ׀ לִקְרֹא מִיכָיְהוּ דִּבֶּר אֵלָיו לֵאמֹר
to-say to-him he-said Micaiah to-summon he-went who and-the-messenger (13)

הִנֵּה־נָא דִּבְרֵי הַנְּבִיאִים פֶּה־אֶחָד טוֹב אֶל־הַמֶּלֶךְ
the-king for success one mouth the-prophets words-of now! look!

יְהִי־נָא דְבָרְךָ כִּדְבַר אַחַד מֵהֶם וְדִבַּרְתָּ טּוֹב׃
favorably and-you-speak with-them one as-word word-of-you now! let-him-be

וַיֹּאמֶר מִיכָיְהוּ חַי־יְהוָה כִּי אֶת־אֲשֶׁר יֹאמַר יְהוָה אֵלַי
to-me Yahweh he-tells what *** only Yahweh life-of Micaiah but-he-said (14)

אֹתוֹ אֲדַבֵּר׃ וַיָּבוֹא אֶל־הַמֶּלֶךְ וַיֹּאמֶר הַמֶּלֶךְ
the-king then-he-asked the-king at when-he-arrived (15) I-can-tell him

אֵלָיו מִיכָיְהוּ הֲנֵלֵךְ אֶל־רָמֹת גִּלְעָד לַמִּלְחָמָה אִם־
or to-the-war Gilead Ramoth against shall-we-go? Micaiah to-him

נֶחְדָּל וַיֹּאמֶר אֵלָיו עֲלֵה וְהַצְלַח
and-be-victorious! attack! to-him and-he-answered shall-we-refrain

וְנָתַן יְהוָה בְּיַד הַמֶּלֶךְ׃ וַיֹּאמֶר אֵלָיו
to-him but-he-said (16) the-king into-hand-of Yahweh for-he-will-give

הַמֶּלֶךְ עַד־כַּמֶּה פְעָמִים אֲנִי מַשְׁבִּעֶךָ אֲשֶׁר לֹא־תְדַבֵּר
you-tell not that making-swear-you I times as-the-how-many? to the-king

אֵלַי רַק־אֱמֶת בְּשֵׁם יְהוָה׃ וַיֹּאמֶר רָאִיתִי אֶת־כָּל־
all-of *** I-saw then-he-answered (17) Yahweh in-name-of truth only to-me

יִשְׂרָאֵל נְפֹצִים אֶל־הֶהָרִים כַּצֹּאן אֲשֶׁר אֵין־לָהֶם
to-them not that like-the-sheep the-hills on ones-being-scattered Israel

רֹעֶה וַיֹּאמֶר יְהוָה לֹא־אֲדֹנִים לָאֵלֶּה יָשׁוּבוּ אִישׁ־
each let-them-go to-these masters not Yahweh and-he-said one-shepherding

לְבֵיתוֹ בְּשָׁלוֹם׃ וַיֹּאמֶר מֶלֶךְ־יִשְׂרָאֵל אֶל־יְהוֹשָׁפָט הֲלוֹא
not? Jehoshaphat to Israel king-of and-he-said (18) in-peace to-home-of-him

אָמַרְתִּי אֵלֶיךָ לוֹא־יִתְנַבֵּא עָלַי טוֹב כִּי אִם־רָע׃ וַיֹּאמֶר
and-he-said (19) bad only but good about-me he-prophesies not to-you I-told

לָכֵן שְׁמַע דְּבַר־יְהוָה רָאִיתִי אֶת־יְהוָה יֹשֵׁב עַל־כִּסְאוֹ
throne-of-him on sitting Yahweh *** I-saw Yahweh word-of hear! therefore

וְכָל־ צְבָא הַשָּׁמַיִם עֹמֵד עָלָיו מִימִינוֹ
on-right-of-him around-him standing the-heavens host-of and-all-of

he declared, "This is what the LORD says: 'With these you will gore the Arameans until they are destroyed.' "
12All the other prophets were prophesying the same thing. "Attack Ramoth Gilead and be victorious," they said, "for the LORD will give it into the king's hand."
13The messenger who had gone to summon Micaiah said to him, "Look, as one man the other prophets are predicting success for the king. Let your word agree with theirs, and speak favorably."
14But Micaiah said, "As surely as the LORD lives, I can tell him only what the LORD tells me."
15When he arrived, the king asked him, "Micaiah, shall we go to war against Ramoth Gilead, or shall I refrain?"
"Attack and be victorious," he answered, "for the LORD will give it into the king's hand."
16The king said to him, "How many times must I make you swear to tell me nothing but the truth in the name of the LORD?"
17Then Micaiah answered, "I saw all Israel scattered on the hills like sheep without a shepherd, and the LORD said, 'These people have no master. Let each one go home in peace.' "
18The king of Israel said to Jehoshaphat, "Didn't I tell you that he never prophesies anything good about me, but only bad?"
19Micaiah continued, "Therefore hear the word of the LORD: I saw the LORD sitting on his throne with all the host of heaven standing around him on his right and

°13 ק דברך

וּמִשְּׂמֹאלוֹ׃ וַיֹּאמֶר יְהוָה מִי יְפַתֶּה אֶת־אַחְאָב
Ahab *** he-will-lure who? Yahweh and-he-said (20) and-on-left-of-him

וְיַעַל וְיִפֹּל בְּרָמֹת גִּלְעָד וַיֹּאמֶר זֶה בְּכֹה
as-such this and-he-suggested Gilead at-Ramoth and-he-falls so-he-attacks

וְזֶה אֹמֵר בְּכֹה׃ וַיֵּצֵא הָרוּחַ וַיַּעֲמֹד
and-he-stood the-spirit and-he-came-forward (21) as-such suggesting and-that

לִפְנֵי יְהוָה וַיֹּאמֶר אֲנִי אֲפַתֶּנּוּ וַיֹּאמֶר יְהוָה אֵלָיו
to-him Yahweh and-he-asked I-will-lure-him I and-he-said Yahweh before

בַּמָּה׃ וַיֹּאמֶר אֵצֵא וְהָיִיתִי רוּחַ שֶׁקֶר
lying spirit and-I-will-be I-will-go-out and-he-said (22) by-the-how?

בְּפִי כָּל־ נְבִיאָיו וַיֹּאמֶר תְּפַתֶּה וְגַם־
and-also you-will-lure and-he-said prophets-of-him all-of in-mouth-of

תּוּכָל צֵא וַעֲשֵׂה־ כֵן׃ וְעַתָּה הִנֵּה נָתַן יְהוָה רוּחַ
spirit Yahweh he-put see! so-now (23) this and-do! go! you-will-succeed

שֶׁקֶר בְּפִי כָּל־ נְבִיאֶיךָ אֵלֶּה וַיהוָה דִּבֶּר
he-decreed and-Yahweh these prophets-of-you all-of in-mouth-of lying

עָלֶיךָ רָעָה׃ וַיִּגַּשׁ צִדְקִיָּהוּ בֶן־ כְּנַעֲנָה וַיַּכֶּה
and-he-slapped Kenaanah son-of Zedekiah then-he-went-up (24) disaster for-you

אֶת־מִיכָיְהוּ עַל־ הַלֶּחִי וַיֹּאמֶר אֵי־ זֶה עָבַר רוּחַ־ יְהוָה
Yahweh spirit-of he-went this where? and-he-asked the-cheek on Micaiah ***

מֵאִתִּי לְדַבֵּר אוֹתָךְ׃ וַיֹּאמֶר מִיכָיְהוּ הִנְּךָ
see-you! Micaiah and-he-replied (25) to-you to-speak from-with-me

רֹאֶה בַּיּוֹם הַהוּא אֲשֶׁר תָּבֹא חֶדֶר בְּחֶדֶר לְהֵחָבֵה׃
to-hide in-room room you-go when the-that on-the-day finding-out

וַיֹּאמֶר מֶלֶךְ יִשְׂרָאֵל קַח אֶת־ מִיכָיְהוּ וַהֲשִׁיבֵהוּ אֶל־
to and-send-back-him! Micaiah *** take! Israel king-of then-he-ordered (26)

אָמֹן שַׂר־ הָעִיר וְאֶל־ יוֹאָשׁ בֶּן־ הַמֶּלֶךְ׃ וְאָמַרְתָּ כֹּה
this and-you-say (27) the-king son-of Joash and-to the-city ruler-of Amon

אָמַר הַמֶּלֶךְ שִׂימוּ אֶת־ זֶה בֵּית הַכֶּלֶא וְהַאֲכִילֻהוּ
and-give-to-eat-him! the-prison house-of this-one *** put! the-king he-says

לֶחֶם לַחַץ וּמַיִם לַחַץ עַד בֹּאִי בְשָׁלוֹם׃ וַיֹּאמֶר
and-he-said (28) in-safety to-return-me until scanty and-waters scanty bread

מִיכָיְהוּ אִם־ שׁוֹב תָּשׁוּב בְּשָׁלוֹם לֹא־ דִבֶּר יְהוָה בִּי
through-me Yahweh he-spoke not in-safety you-return to-return if Micaiah

וַיֹּאמֶר שִׁמְעוּ עַמִּים כֻּלָּם׃ וַיַּעַל מֶלֶךְ־
king-of so-he-went-up (29) all-of-them peoples mark-words! then-he-said

יִשְׂרָאֵל וִיהוֹשָׁפָט* מֶלֶךְ־ יְהוּדָה רָמֹת גִּלְעָד׃ וַיֹּאמֶר מֶלֶךְ
king-of and-he-said (30) Gilead Ramoth Judah king-of and-Jehoshaphat Israel

*29 Most mss have *hireq* under the *vav* (וִיהוֹ).

on his left. 20 And the LORD
said, 'Who will lure Ahab into
attacking Ramoth Gilead and
going to his death there?'
"One suggested this, and
another that. 21 Finally, a spirit
came forward, stood before
the LORD and said, 'I will lure
him.'
22 " 'By what means?' the
LORD asked.
" 'I will go out and be a lying
spirit in the mouths of all his
prophets,' he said.
" 'You will succeed in luring
him,' said the LORD. 'Go and
do it.'
23 "So now the LORD has put a
lying spirit in the mouths of
all these prophets of yours.
The LORD has decreed disaster
for you."
24 Then Zedekiah son of
Kenaanah went up and
slapped Micaiah in the face.
"Which way did the spirit
from[z] the LORD go when he
went from me to speak to
you?" he asked.
25 Micaiah replied, "You will
find out on the day you go to
hide in an inner room."
26 The king of Israel then ordered, "Take Micaiah and
send him back to Amon the
ruler of the city and to Joash
the king's son 27 and say, 'This
is what the king says: Put this
fellow in prison and give him
nothing but bread and water
until I return safely.' "
28 Micaiah declared, "If you
ever return safely, the LORD
has not spoken through me."
Then he added, "Mark my
words, all you people!"

Ahab Killed at Ramoth Gilead

29 So the king of Israel and Jehoshaphat king of Judah went
up to Ramoth Gilead. 30 The

z24 Or *Spirit of*

יִשְׂרָאֵל אֶל־יְהוֹשָׁפָט הִתְחַפֵּשׂ וָבֹא בַּמִּלְחָמָה

into-the-battle and-he-will-enter he-will-disguise-himself Jehoshaphat to Israel

וְאַתָּה לְבַשׁ בְּגָדֶיךָ וַיִּתְחַפֵּשׂ מֶלֶךְ יִשְׂרָאֵל וַיָּבוֹא

and-he-went Israel king-of so-he-disguised-himself robes-of-you wear! but-you

בַּמִּלְחָמָה׃ וּמֶלֶךְ אֲרָם צִוָּה אֶת־שָׂרֵי

commanders-of *** he-ordered Aram now-king-of (31) into-the-battle

הָרֶכֶב אֲשֶׁר־לוֹ שְׁלֹשִׁים וּשְׁנַיִם לֵאמֹר לֹא תִּלָּחֲמוּ אֶת־קָטֹן וְאֶת־

or small *** you-fight not to-say and-two thirty to-him that the-chariot

גָּדוֹל כִּי אִם־אֶת־מֶלֶךְ יִשְׂרָאֵל לְבַדּוֹ׃ וַיְהִי כִּרְאוֹת

when-to-see and-he-was (32) by-himself Israel king-of *** only except great

שָׂרֵי הָרֶכֶב אֶת־יְהוֹשָׁפָט וְהֵמָּה אָמְרוּ אַךְ

surely they-thought then-they Jehoshaphat *** the-chariot commanders-of

מֶלֶךְ־יִשְׂרָאֵל הוּא וַיָּסֻרוּ עָלָיו לְהִלָּחֵם וַיִּזְעַק

but-he-cried-out to-attack against-him so-they-turned this Israel king-of

יְהוֹשָׁפָט׃ וַיְהִי כִּרְאוֹת שָׂרֵי הָרֶכֶב כִּי־לֹא־

not that the-chariot commanders-of when-to-see then-he-was (33) Jehoshaphat

מֶלֶךְ יִשְׂרָאֵל הוּא וַיָּשׁוּבוּ מֵאַחֲרָיו׃ וְאִישׁ מָשַׁךְ

he-drew but-someone (34) from-after-him then-they-turned he Israel king-of

בַּקֶּשֶׁת לְתֻמּוֹ וַיַּכֶּה אֶת־מֶלֶךְ יִשְׂרָאֵל בֵּין

between Israel king-of *** and-he-hit at-random-of-him on-the-bow

הַדְּבָקִים וּבֵין הַשִּׁרְיָן וַיֹּאמֶר לְרַכָּבוֹ

to-chariot-driver-of-him and-he-told the-armor and-between the-sections

הֲפֹךְ יָדְךָ וְהוֹצִיאֵנִי מִן־הַמַּחֲנֶה כִּי הָחֳלֵיתִי׃

I-am-wounded for the-fight from and-get-out-me! hand-of-you turn-around!

וַתַּעֲלֶה הַמִּלְחָמָה בַּיּוֹם הַהוּא וְהַמֶּלֶךְ הָיָה

he-was and-the-king the-that through-the-day the-battle and-she-raged (35)

מָעֳמָד בַּמֶּרְכָּבָה נֹכַח אֲרָם וַיָּמָת בָּעֶרֶב

in-the-evening and-he-died Aram facing in-the-chariot being-propped-up

וַיִּצֶק דַּם־הַמַּכָּה אֶל־חֵיק הָרָכֶב׃ וַיַּעֲבֹר

and-he-spread (36) the-chariot floor-of onto the-wound blood-of and-he-ran

הָרִנָּה בַּמַּחֲנֶה כְּבֹא הַשֶּׁמֶשׁ לֵאמֹר אִישׁ אֶל־עִירוֹ

town-of-him to each to-say the-sun as-to-set through-the-army the-cry

וְאִישׁ אֶל־אַרְצוֹ׃ וַיָּמָת הַמֶּלֶךְ וַיָּבוֹא שֹׁמְרוֹן

Samaria and-he-went the-king so-he-died (37) land-of-him to and-each

וַיִּקְבְּרוּ אֶת־הַמֶּלֶךְ בְּשֹׁמְרוֹן׃ וַיִּשְׁטֹף אֶת־הָרֶכֶב

the-chariot *** and-he-washed (38) in-Samaria the-king *** and-they-buried

עַל ׀ בְּרֵכַת שֹׁמְרוֹן וַיָּלֹקּוּ הַכְּלָבִים אֶת־דָּמוֹ

blood-of-him *** the-dogs and-they-licked-up Samaria pool-of in

king of Israel said to Jehoshaphat, "I will enter the battle in
disguise, but you wear your
royal robes." So the king of Israel disguised himself and
went into battle.
[31]Now the king of Aram had
ordered his thirty-two chariot
commanders, "Do not fight
with anyone, small or great,
except the king of Israel."
[32]When the chariot commanders saw Jehoshaphat, they
thought, "Surely this is the
king of Israel." So they turned
to attack him, but when Jehoshaphat cried out, [33]the
chariot commanders saw that
he was not the king of Israel
and stopped pursuing him.
[34]But someone drew his bow
at random and hit the king of
Israel between the sections of
his armor. The king told his
chariot driver, "Wheel around
and get me out of the fighting.
I've been wounded." [35]All day
long the battle raged, and the
king was propped up in his
chariot facing the Arameans.
The blood from his wound ran
onto the floor of the chariot,
and that evening he died. [36]As
the sun was setting, a cry
spread through the army:
"Every man to his town;
everyone to his land!"
[37]So the king died and was
brought to Samaria, and they
buried him there. [38]They
washed the chariot at a pool in
Samaria (where the prostitutes
bathed)[a] and the dogs licked
up his blood, as the word of

[a]38 Or *Samaria and cleaned the weapons*

וְהַזֹּנוֹת רָחָצוּ כִּדְבַר יְהוָה אֲשֶׁר
that Yahweh as-word-of they-bathed and-the-ones-being-prostitutes

דִּבֵּר׃ וְיֶתֶר דִּבְרֵי אַחְאָב וְכָל־ אֲשֶׁר עָשָׂה וּבֵית
and-palace-of he-did that and-all Ahab events-of and-rest-of (39) he-declared

הַשֵּׁן אֲשֶׁר בָּנָה וְכָל־ הֶעָרִים אֲשֶׁר בָּנָה הֲלוֹא־
not? he-fortified that the-cities and-all-of he-built that the-ivory

הֵם כְּתוּבִים עַל־ סֵפֶר דִּבְרֵי הַיָּמִים לְמַלְכֵי יִשְׂרָאֵל׃
Israel of-kings-of the-days annals-of book-of in ones-being-written they

וַיִּשְׁכַּב אַחְאָב עִם־ אֲבֹתָיו וַיִּמְלֹךְ אֲחַזְיָהוּ
Ahaziah and-he-became-king fathers-of-him with Ahab and-he-rested (40)

בְנוֹ תַּחְתָּיו׃ וִיהוֹשָׁפָט בֶּן־ אָסָא מָלַךְ
he-became-king Asa son-of now-Jehoshaphat (41) in-place-of-him son-of-him

עַל־ יְהוּדָה בִּשְׁנַת אַרְבַּע לְאַחְאָב מֶלֶךְ יִשְׂרָאֵל׃ יְהוֹשָׁפָט בֶּן־
son-of Jehoshaphat (42) Israel king-of of-Ahab four in-year-of Judah over

שְׁלֹשִׁים וְחָמֵשׁ שָׁנָה בְּמָלְכוֹ וְעֶשְׂרִים וְחָמֵשׁ שָׁנָה
year and-five and-twenty when-to-become-king-him year and-five thirty

מָלַךְ בִּירוּשָׁלִָם וְשֵׁם אִמּוֹ עֲזוּבָה בַּת־
daughter-of Azubah mother-of-him and-name-of in-Jerusalem he-reigned

שִׁלְחִי׃ וַיֵּלֶךְ בְּכָל־ דֶּרֶךְ אָסָא אָבִיו לֹא־ סָר
he-strayed not father-of-him Asa way-of in-all-of and-he-walked (43) Shilhi

מִמֶּנּוּ לַעֲשׂוֹת הַיָּשָׁר בְּעֵינֵי יְהוָה׃ אַךְ הַבָּמוֹת
the-high-places however *(44) Yahweh in-eyes-of the-right to-do from-him

לֹא־ סָרוּ עוֹד הָעָם מְזַבְּחִים
and-ones-offering-sacrifices the-people still they-were-removed not

וּמְקַטְּרִים בַּבָּמוֹת׃ וַיַּשְׁלֵם
and-he-was-at-peace (45) at-the-high-places and-ones-burning-incense

יְהוֹשָׁפָט עִם־ מֶלֶךְ יִשְׂרָאֵל׃ וְיֶתֶר דִּבְרֵי יְהוֹשָׁפָט
Jehoshaphat events-of and-rest-of (46) Israel king-of with Jehoshaphat

וּגְבוּרָתוֹ אֲשֶׁר־ עָשָׂה וַאֲשֶׁר נִלְחָם הֲלֹא־ הֵם
they not? he-fought and-how he-did that and-achievement-of-him

כְּתוּבִים עַל־ סֵפֶר דִּבְרֵי הַיָּמִים לְמַלְכֵי יְהוּדָה׃
Judah of-kings-of the-days annals-of book-of in ones-being-written

וְיֶתֶר הַקָּדֵשׁ אֲשֶׁר נִשְׁאַר בִּימֵי אָסָא
Asa from-days-of he-remained who the-male-prostitute and-rest-of (47)

אָבִיו בִּעֵר מִן־ הָאָרֶץ׃ וּמֶלֶךְ אֵין בֶּאֱדוֹם
in-Edom there-was-not and-king (48) the-land from he-rid father-of-him

נִצָּב מֶלֶךְ׃ יְהוֹשָׁפָט עָשָׂר אֳנִיּוֹת תַּרְשִׁישׁ לָלֶכֶת
to-go Tarshish ships-of he-built Jehoshaphat (49) ruler one-being-appointed

the Lord had declared.
[39]As for the other events of
Ahab's reign, including all he
did, the palace he built and inlaid with ivory, and the cities
he fortified, are they not written in the book of the annals
of the kings of Israel? [40]Ahab
rested with his fathers. And
Ahaziah his son succeeded
him as king.

Jehoshaphat King of Judah

[41]Jehoshaphat son of Asa
became king of Judah in the
fourth year of Ahab king of Israel. [42]Jehoshaphat was thirty-
five years old when he became
king, and he reigned in
Jerusalem twenty-five years.
His mother's name was Azubah daughter of Shilhi. [43]In
everything he walked in the
ways of his father Asa and did
not stray from them; he did
what was right in the eyes of
the Lord. The high places,
however, were not removed,
and the people continued to
offer sacrifices and burn incense there. [44]Jehoshaphat was
also at peace with the king of
Israel.
[45]As for the other events of
Jehoshaphat's reign, the
things he achieved and his
military exploits, are they not
written in the book of the annals of the kings of Judah?
[46]He rid the land of the rest of
the male shrine prostitutes
who remained there even after the reign of his father Asa.
[47]There was then no king in
Edom; a deputy ruled.
[48]Now Jehoshaphat built a
fleet of trading ships[h] to go to

[h]48 Hebrew *of ships of Tarshish*

*44 Verse 44 in Hebrew begins in the middle of verse 43 in English and creates a one-verse discrepancy through the rest of the chapter.

°49 ק עשה

אוֹפִ֫ירָה לַזָּהָב וְלֹא הָלָךְ כִּי־ נִשְׁבְּרָה אֳנִיּוֹת

ships they-were-wrecked for he-sailed but-not for-the-gold to-Ophir

בְּעֶצְיוֹן גָּבֶר׃ אָז אָמַר אֲחַזְיָהוּ בֶן־ אַחְאָב אֶל־ יְהוֹשָׁפָט

Jehoshaphat to Ahab son-of Ahaziah he-said then (50) Geber at-Ezion

יֵלְכוּ עֲבָדַי עִם־ עֲבָדֶיךָ בָּאֳנִיּוֹת וְלֹא אָבָה

he-allowed but-not in-the-ships men-of-you with men-of-me let-them-sail

יְהוֹשָׁפָט׃ וַיִּשְׁכַּב יְהוֹשָׁפָט עִם־ אֲבֹתָיו

fathers-of-him with Jehoshaphat then-he-rested (51) Jehoshaphat

וַיִּקָּבֵר עִם־ אֲבֹתָיו בְּעִיר דָּוִד אָבִיו

father-of-him David in-City-of fathers-of-him with and-he-was-buried

וַיִּמְלֹךְ יְהוֹרָם בְּנוֹ תַּחְתָּיו׃ אֲחַזְיָהוּ בֶן־

son-of Ahaziah (52) in-place-of-him son-of-him Jehoram and-he-became-king

אַחְאָב מָלַךְ עַל־ יִשְׂרָאֵל בְּשֹׁמְרוֹן בִּשְׁנַת שְׁבַע עֶשְׂרֵה

ten seven-of in-year-of in-Samaria Israel over he-became-king Ahab

לִיהוֹשָׁפָט מֶלֶךְ יְהוּדָה וַיִּמְלֹךְ עַל־ יִשְׂרָאֵל שְׁנָתָיִם׃

two-years Israel over and-he-reigned Judah king-of of-Jehoshaphat

וַיַּעַשׂ הָרַע בְּעֵינֵי יְהוָה וַיֵּלֶךְ בְּדֶרֶךְ

in-way-of and-he-walked Yahweh in-eyes-of the-evil and-he-did (53)

אָבִיו וּבְדֶרֶךְ אִמּוֹ וּבְדֶרֶךְ יָרָבְעָם בֶּן־

son-of Jeroboam and-in-way-of mother-of-him and-in-way-of father-of-him

נְבָט אֲשֶׁר הֶחֱטִיא אֶת־יִשְׂרָאֵל׃ וַיַּעֲבֹד אֶת־ הַבַּעַל

the-Baal *** and-he-served (54) Israel *** he-caused-to-sin who Nebat

וַיִּשְׁתַּחֲוֶה לוֹ וַיַּכְעֵס אֶת־ יְהוָה אֱלֹהֵי יִשְׂרָאֵל

Israel God-of Yahweh *** and-he-provoked-to-anger to-him and-he-worshiped

כְּכֹל אֲשֶׁר־ עָשָׂה אָבִיו׃

father-of-him he-did that as-all

Ophir for gold, but they never
set sail—they were wrecked at
Ezion Geber. 49At that time
Ahaziah son of Ahab said to
Jehoshaphat, "Let my men sail
with your men," but Jehoshaphat refused.
50Then Jehoshaphat rested
with his fathers and was buried with them in the city of
David his father. And Jehoram
his son succeeded him.

Ahaziah King of Israel

51Ahaziah son of Ahab
became king of Israel in Samaria in the seventeenth year
of Jehoshaphat king of Judah,
and he reigned over Israel two
years. 52He did evil in the eyes
of the LORD, because he
walked in the ways of his father and mother and in the
ways of Jeroboam son of
Nebat, who caused Israel to
sin. 53He served and wor-
shiped Baal and provoked the
LORD, the God of Israel, to anger, just as his father had
done.

*See the note on page 422.

°49 ק נשברו

וַיִּפְשַׁע מוֹאָב בְּיִשְׂרָאֵל אַחֲרֵי מוֹת אַחְאָב׃ וַיִּפֹּל
now-he-fell (2) Ahab death-of after against-Israel Moab and-he-rebelled (1)

אֲחַזְיָה בְּעַד הַשְּׂבָכָה בַּעֲלִיָּתוֹ אֲשֶׁר בְּשֹׁמְרוֹן
in-Samaria that of-upper-room-of-him the-lattice-work through Ahaziah

וַיָּחַל וַיִּשְׁלַח מַלְאָכִים וַיֹּאמֶר אֲלֵהֶם לְכוּ דִרְשׁוּ
consult! go! to-them and-he-said messengers so-he-sent and-he-was-injured

בְּבַעַל זְבוּב אֱלֹהֵי עֶקְרוֹן אִם־ אֶחְיֶה מֵחֳלִי זֶה׃
this from-injury I-will-recover whether Ekron gods-of Zebub with-Baal

וּמַלְאַךְ יְהוָה דִּבֶּר אֶל־אֵלִיָּה הַתִּשְׁבִּי קוּם עֲלֵה לִקְרַאת
to-meet go-up! rise! the-Tishbite Elijah to he-said Yahweh but-angel-of (3)

מַלְאֲכֵי מֶלֶךְ־ שֹׁמְרוֹן וְדַבֵּר אֲלֵהֶם הֲמִבְּלִי אֵין־
there-is-no because-not? of-them and-ask! Samaria king-of messengers-of

אֱלֹהִים בְּיִשְׂרָאֵל אַתֶּם הֹלְכִים לִדְרֹשׁ בְּבַעַל זְבוּב אֱלֹהֵי עֶקְרוֹן׃
Ekron gods-of Zebub with-Baal to-consult ones-going you in-Israel God

וְלָכֵן כֹּה־ אָמַר יְהוָה הַמִּטָּה אֲשֶׁר־ עָלִיתָ שָּׁם לֹא־
not there you-lie that the-bed Yahweh he-says this now-therefore (4)

תֵרֵד מִמֶּנָּה כִּי מוֹת תָּמוּת וַיֵּלֶךְ אֵלִיָּה׃
Elijah so-he-went you-will-die to-die for from-her you-will-leave

וַיָּשׁוּבוּ הַמַּלְאָכִים אֵלָיו וַיֹּאמֶר אֲלֵיהֶם מַה־ זֶּה
this why? to-them then-he-asked to-him the-messengers when-they-returned (5)

שַׁבְתֶּם׃ וַיֹּאמְרוּ אֵלָיו אִישׁ ׀ עָלָה לִקְרָאתֵנוּ וַיֹּאמֶר
and-he-said to-meet-us he-came man to-him and-they-replied (6) you-came-back

אֵלֵינוּ לְכוּ שׁוּבוּ אֶל־ הַמֶּלֶךְ אֲשֶׁר־ שָׁלַח אֶתְכֶם וְדִבַּרְתֶּם אֵלָיו כֹּה
this to-him and-you-tell you he-sent who the-king to go-back! go! to-us

אָמַר יְהוָה הֲמִבְּלִי אֵין־ אֱלֹהִים בְּיִשְׂרָאֵל אַתָּה שֹׁלֵחַ לִדְרֹשׁ
to-consult sending you in-Israel God there-is-no because-not? Yahweh he-says

בְּבַעַל זְבוּב אֱלֹהֵי עֶקְרוֹן לָכֵן הַמִּטָּה אֲשֶׁר־ עָלִיתָ שָּׁם לֹא־
not there you-lie that the-bed therefore Ekron gods-of Zebub with-Baal

תֵרֵד מִמֶּנָּה כִּי־ מוֹת תָּמוּת׃ וַיְדַבֵּר אֲלֵהֶם
to-them and-he-asked (7) you-will-die to-die for from-her you-will-leave

מֶה מִשְׁפַּט הָאִישׁ אֲשֶׁר עָלָה לִקְרַאתְכֶם וַיְדַבֵּר אֲלֵיכֶם אֶת־
*** to-you and-he-told to-meet-you he-came who the-man kind-of what?

הַדְּבָרִים הָאֵלֶּה׃ וַיֹּאמְרוּ אֵלָיו אִישׁ בַּעַל שֵׂעָר
hair-garment owner-of man-of to-him and-they-replied (8) the-these the-things

וְאֵזוֹר עוֹר אָזוּר בְּמָתְנָיו וַיֹּאמַר אֵלִיָּה
Elijah and-he-said around-waists-of-him being-tied leather and-belt-of

הַתִּשְׁבִּי הוּא׃ וַיִּשְׁלַח אֵלָיו שַׂר־ חֲמִשִּׁים וַחֲמִשָּׁיו
with-fifty-of-him fifty captain-of to-him then-he-sent (9) that the-Tishbite

The LORD's Judgment on Ahaziah

1 After Ahab's death, Moab
rebelled against Israel.
2Now Ahaziah had fallen
through the lattice of his upper room in Samaria and in-
jured himself. So he sent messengers, saying to them, "Go
and consult Baal-Zebub, the
god of Ekron, to see if I will
recover from this injury."
3But the angel of the LORD
said to Elijah the Tishbite, "Go
up and meet the messengers of
the king of Samaria and ask
them, 'Is it because there is no
God in Israel that you are going off to consult Baal-Zebub,
the god of Ekron?' 4Therefore
this is what the LORD says:
'You will not leave the bed you
are lying on. You will certainly
die!' " So Elijah went.
5When the messengers re-
turned to the king, he asked
them, "Why have you come
back?"
6"A man came to meet us,"
they replied. "And he said to
us, 'Go back to the king who
sent you and tell him, "This is
what the LORD says: Is it because there is no God in Israel
that you are sending men to
consult Baal-Zebub, the god of
Ekron? Therefore you will not
leave the bed you are lying on.
You will certainly die!" ' "
7The king asked them,
"What kind of man was it
who came to meet you and
told you this?"
8They replied, "He was a
man with a garment of hair
and a leather belt around his
waist."
The king said, "That was
Elijah the Tishbite."
9Then he sent to Elijah a captain with his company of fifty

וַיַּעַל אֵלָיו וְהִנֵּה יֹשֵׁב עַל־רֹאשׁ הָהָר וַיְדַבֵּר אֵלָיו
to-him and-he-said the-hill top-of on sitting and-see! to-him and-he-went-up

אִישׁ הָאֱלֹהִים הַמֶּלֶךְ דִּבֶּר רֵדָה׃ וַיַּעֲנֶה אֵלִיָּהוּ
Elijah and-he-answered (10) come-down! he-says the-king the-God man-of

וַיְדַבֵּר אֶל־שַׂר הַחֲמִשִּׁים וְאִם־אִישׁ אֱלֹהִים אָנִי תֵּרֶד
may-she-come-down I God man-of now-if the-fifty captain-of to and-he-said

אֵשׁ מִן־הַשָּׁמַיִם וְתֹאכַל אֹתְךָ וְאֶת־חֲמִשֶּׁיךָ וַתֵּרֶד
then-she-fell fifty-of-you and you and-may-she-consume the-heavens from fire

אֵשׁ מִן־הַשָּׁמַיִם וַתֹּאכַל אֹתוֹ וְאֶת־חֲמִשָּׁיו׃ וַיָּשָׁב
and-he-returned (11) fifty-of-him and him and-she-consumed the-heavens from fire

וַיִּשְׁלַח אֵלָיו שַׂר־חֲמִשִּׁים אַחֵר וַחֲמִשָּׁיו וַיַּעַן
and-he-answered with-fifty-of-him another fifty captain-of to-him and-he-sent

וַיְדַבֵּר אֵלָיו אִישׁ הָאֱלֹהִים כֹּה־אָמַר הַמֶּלֶךְ מְהֵרָה רֵדָה׃
come-down! hurry! the-king he-says this the-God man-of to-him and-he-said

וַיַּעַן אֵלִיָּה וַיְדַבֵּר אֲלֵיהֶם אִם־אִישׁ הָאֱלֹהִים אָנִי
I the-God man-of if to-them and-he-said Elijah and-he-replied (12)

תֵּרֶד אֵשׁ מִן־הַשָּׁמַיִם וְתֹאכַל אֹתְךָ וְאֶת־
and you and-may-she-consume the-heavens from fire may-she-come-down

חֲמִשֶּׁיךָ וַתֵּרֶד אֵשׁ־אֱלֹהִים מִן־הַשָּׁמַיִם וַתֹּאכַל אֹתוֹ
him and-she-consumed the-heavens from God fire-of then-she-fell fifty-of-you

וְאֶת־חֲמִשָּׁיו׃ וַיָּשָׁב וַיִּשְׁלַח שַׂר־חֲמִשִּׁים שְׁלִשִׁים
third-ones fifty captain-of and-he-sent so-he-returned (13) fifty-of-him and

וַחֲמִשָּׁיו וַיַּעַל וַיָּבֹא שַׂר־הַחֲמִשִּׁים הַשְּׁלִישִׁי
the-third the-fifty captain-of and-he-came and-he-went-up with-fifty-of-him

וַיִּכְרַע עַל־בִּרְכָּיו לְנֶגֶד אֵלִיָּהוּ וַיִּתְחַנֵּן אֵלָיו
to-him and-he-begged Elijah at-before knees-of-him on and-he-knelt

וַיְדַבֵּר אֵלָיו אִישׁ הָאֱלֹהִים תִּיקַר־נָא נַפְשִׁי
life-of-me now! let-her-be-respected the-God man-of to-him and-he-said

וְנֶפֶשׁ עֲבָדֶיךָ אֵלֶּה חֲמִשִּׁים בְּעֵינֶיךָ׃ הִנֵּה יָרְדָה
she-fell see! (14) in-eyes-of-you fifty these servants-of-you and-life-of

אֵשׁ מִן־הַשָּׁמַיִם וַתֹּאכַל אֶת־שְׁנֵי שָׂרֵי הַחֲמִשִּׁים
the-fifty captains-of two-of *** and-she-consumed the-heavens from fire

הָרִאשֹׁנִים וְאֶת־חֲמִשֵּׁיהֶם וְעַתָּה תִּיקַר נַפְשִׁי
life-of-me let-her-be-respected but-now fifty-of-them and the-first-ones

בְּעֵינֶיךָ׃ וַיְדַבֵּר מַלְאַךְ יְהוָה אֶל־אֵלִיָּהוּ רֵד אוֹתוֹ
with-him go-down! Elijah to Yahweh angel-of and-he-said (15) in-eyes-of-you

אַל־תִּירָא מִפָּנָיו וַיָּקָם וַיֵּרֶד אוֹתוֹ אֶל־
to with-him and-he-went-down so-he-got-up because-of-him you-be-afraid not

men. The captain went up to
Elijah, who was sitting on the
top of a hill, and said to him,
"Man of God, the king says,
'Come down!' "
10 Elijah answered the captain, "If I am a man of God,
may fire come down from
heaven and consume you and
your fifty men!" Then fire fell
from heaven and consumed
the captain and his men.
11 At this the king sent to Elijah another captain with his
fifty men. The captain said to
him, "Man of God, this is
what the king says, 'Come
down at once!' "
12 "If I am a man of God," Elijah replied, "may fire come
down from heaven and con-
sume you and your fifty men!"
Then the fire of God fell from
heaven and consumed him
and his fifty men.
13 So the king sent a third
captain with his fifty men.
This third captain went up
and fell on his knees before
Elijah. "Man of God," he
begged, "please have respect
for my life and the lives of
these fifty men, your servants!
14 See, fire has fallen from
heaven and consumed the
first two captains and all their
men. But now have respect for
my life!"
15 The angel of the LORD said
to Elijah, "Go down with him;
do not be afraid of him." So
Elijah got up and went down
with him to the king.

הַמֶּֽלֶךְ׃ וַיְדַבֵּר אֵלָיו כֹּה־אָמַר יְהוָה יַעַן אֲשֶׁר־שָׁלַחְתָּ
you-sent that because Yahweh he-says this to-him and-he-told (16) the-king

מַלְאָכִים לִדְרֹשׁ בְּבַעַל זְבוּב אֱלֹהֵי עֶקְרוֹן הֲמִבְּלִי אֵין־
there-is-no because-not Ekron gods-of Zebub with-Baal to-consult messengers

אֱלֹהִים בְּיִשְׂרָאֵל לִדְרֹשׁ בִּדְבָרוֹ לָכֵן הַמִּטָּה אֲשֶׁר־עָלִיתָ
you-lie that the-bed therefore with-word-of-him to-consult in-Israel God

שָּׁם לֹא־תֵרֵד מִמֶּנָּה כִּי־מוֹת תָּמוּת׃ וַיָּמָת
so-he-died (17) you-will-die to-die for from-her you-will-leave not there

כִּדְבַר יְהוָה ׀ אֲשֶׁר־דִּבֶּר אֵלִיָּהוּ וַיִּמְלֹךְ יְהוֹרָם
Jehoram and-he-became-king Elijah he-spoke that Yahweh as-word-of

תַּחְתָּיו בִּשְׁנַת שְׁתַּיִם לִיהוֹרָם בֶּן־יְהוֹשָׁפָט מֶלֶךְ יְהוּדָה
Judah king-of Jehoshaphat son-of of-Jehoram two in-year-of in-place-of-him

כִּי לֹא־הָיָה לוֹ בֵּן׃ וְיֶתֶר דִּבְרֵי אֲחַזְיָהוּ אֲשֶׁר עָשָׂה
he-did what Ahaziah events-of and-rest-of (18) son to-him he-was not because

הֲלֹא־הֵמָּה כְתוּבִים עַל־סֵפֶר דִּבְרֵי הַיָּמִים לְמַלְכֵי יִשְׂרָאֵל׃
Israel of-kings-of the-days annals-of book-of in ones-being-written they not?

וַיְהִי בְּהַעֲלוֹת יְהוָה אֶת־אֵלִיָּהוּ בַּסְעָרָה הַשָּׁמָיִם
the-heavens in-the-whirlwind Elijah *** Yahweh when-to-take and-he-was (2:1)

וַיֵּלֶךְ אֵלִיָּהוּ וֶאֱלִישָׁע מִן־הַגִּלְגָּל׃ וַיֹּאמֶר אֵלִיָּהוּ אֶל־
to Elijah and-he-said (2) the-Gilgal from and-Elisha Elijah then-he-went

אֱלִישָׁע שֵׁב־נָא פֹה כִּי יְהוָה שְׁלָחַנִי עַד־בֵּית־אֵל וַיֹּאמֶר אֱלִישָׁע
Elisha but-he-said El Beth to he-sent-me Yahweh for here now! stay! Elisha

חַי־יְהוָה וְחֵי־נַפְשְׁךָ אִם־אֶעֶזְבֶךָּ וַיֵּרְדוּ
so-they-went-down I-will-leave-you not soul-of-you and-life-of Yahweh life-of

בֵּית־אֵל׃ וַיֵּצְאוּ בְנֵי־הַנְּבִיאִים אֲשֶׁר־בֵּית־אֵל אֶל־אֱלִישָׁע
Elisha to El Beth who the-prophets sons-of and-they-came-out (3) El Beth

וַיֹּאמְרוּ אֵלָיו הֲיָדַעְתָּ כִּי הַיּוֹם יְהוָה לֹקֵחַ אֶת־
*** taking Yahweh the-day that do-you-know? to-him and-they-asked

אֲדֹנֶיךָ מֵעַל רֹאשֶׁךָ וַיֹּאמֶר גַּם־אֲנִי יָדַעְתִּי
I-know I indeed and-he-replied head-of-you from-over masters-of-you

הֶחֱשׁוּ׃ וַיֹּאמֶר לוֹ אֵלִיָּהוּ אֱלִישָׁע ׀ שֵׁב־נָא פֹה כִּי
for here now! stay! Elisha Elijah to-him then-he-said (4) do-not-speak!

יְהוָה שְׁלָחַנִי יְרִיחוֹ וַיֹּאמֶר חַי־יְהוָה וְחֵי־
and-life-of Yahweh life-of and-he-replied Jericho he-sent-me Yahweh

נַפְשְׁךָ אִם־אֶעֶזְבֶךָּ וַיָּבֹאוּ יְרִיחוֹ׃ וַיִּגְּשׁוּ
and-they-went-up (5) Jericho so-they-went I-will-leave-you not soul-of-you

בְנֵי־הַנְּבִיאִים אֲשֶׁר־בִּירִיחוֹ אֶל־אֱלִישָׁע וַיֹּאמְרוּ אֵלָיו
to-him and-they-asked Elisha to in-Jericho who the-prophets sons-of

16 He told the king, "This is
what the LORD says: Is it because there is no God in Israel
for you to consult that you
have sent messengers to consult Baal-Zebub, the god of Ekron? Because you have done
this, you will never leave the
bed you are lying on. You will
certainly die!" 17 So he died, according to the word of the
LORD that Elijah had spoken.
Because Ahaziah had no
son, Joram[a] succeeded him as
king in the second year of Jehoram son of Jehoshaphat
king of Judah. 18 As for all the
other events of Ahaziah's
reign, and what he did, are
they not written in the book of
the annals of the kings of Israel?

Elijah Taken Up to Heaven

2 When the LORD was about
to take Elijah up to heaven
in a whirlwind, Elijah and Elisha were on their way from
Gilgal. 2 Elijah said to Elisha,
"Stay here; the LORD has sent
me to Bethel."
But Elisha said, "As surely
as the LORD lives and as you
live, I will not leave you." So
they went down to Bethel.
3 The company of the prophets at Bethel came out to Elisha
and asked, "Do you know that
the LORD is going to take your
master from you today?"
"Yes, I know," Elisha re-
plied, "but do not speak of it."
4 Then Elijah said to him,
"Stay here, Elisha; the LORD
has sent me to Jericho."
And he replied, "As surely
as the LORD lives and as you
live, I will not leave you." So
they went to Jericho.
5 The company of the prophets at Jericho went up to Elisha

[a]17 Hebrew *Jehoram*, a variant of *Joram*

הֲיָדַעְתָּ כִּי הַיּוֹם יְהוָה לֹקֵחַ אֶת־ אֲדֹנֶיךָ מֵעַל
from-over masters-of-you *** taking Yahweh the-day that do-you-know?

רֹאשֶׁךָ וַיֹּאמֶר גַּם־ אֲנִי יָדַעְתִּי הֶחֱשׁוּ׃ וַיֹּאמֶר
then-he-said (6) do-not-speak! I-know I indeed and-he-replied head-of-you

לוֹ אֵלִיָּהוּ שֵׁב־ נָא פֹה כִּי יְהוָה שְׁלָחַנִי הַיַּרְדֵּנָה
to-the-Jordan he-sent-me Yahweh for here now! stay! Elijah to-him

וַיֹּאמֶר חַי־ יְהוָה וְחֵי־ נַפְשְׁךָ אִם־ אֶעֶזְבֶךָּ
I-will-leave-you not soul-of-you and-life-of Yahweh life-of and-he-replied

וַיֵּלְכוּ שְׁנֵיהֶם׃ וַחֲמִשִּׁים אִישׁ מִבְּנֵי הַנְּבִיאִים
the-prophets of-sons-of man and-fifty (7) two-of-them so-they-walked-on

הָלְכוּ וַיַּעַמְדוּ מִנֶּגֶד מֵרָחוֹק וּשְׁנֵיהֶם עָמְדוּ
they-stopped and-two-of-them at-distance at-facing and-they-stood they-went

עַל־ הַיַּרְדֵּן׃ וַיִּקַּח אֵלִיָּהוּ אֶת־ אַדַּרְתּוֹ וַיִּגְלֹם
and-he-rolled-up cloak-of-him *** Elijah and-he-took (8) the-Jordan at

וַיַּכֶּה אֶת־ הַמַּיִם וַיֵּחָצוּ הֵנָּה וָהֵנָּה
and-to-there to-here and-they-divided the-waters *** and-he-struck

וַיַּעַבְרוּ שְׁנֵיהֶם בֶּחָרָבָה׃ וַיְהִי
and-he-was (9) on-the-dry-ground two-of-them and-they-crossed-over

כְעָבְרָם וְאֵלִיָּהוּ אָמַר אֶל־אֱלִישָׁע שְׁאַל מָה אֶעֱשֶׂה־
can-I-do what? tell! Elisha to he-said then-Elijah when-to-cross-over-them

לָּךְ בְּטֶרֶם אֶלָּקַח מֵעִמָּךְ וַיֹּאמֶר אֱלִישָׁע
Elisha and-he-replied from-with-you I-am-taken at-before for-you

וִיהִי־ נָא פִּי־ שְׁנַיִם בְּרוּחֲךָ אֵלָי׃ וַיֹּאמֶר
and-he-said (10) for-me of-spirit-of-you double portion-of now! now-let-him-be

הִקְשִׁיתָ לִשְׁאוֹל אִם־תִּרְאֶה אֹתִי לֻקָּח מֵאִתָּךְ יְהִי־
he-will-be from-with-you he-is-taken me you-see if to-ask you-made-difficult

לְךָ כֵן וְאִם־ אַיִן לֹא יִהְיֶה׃ וַיְהִי הֵמָּה הֹלְכִים
ones-walking they and-he-was (11) he-will-be not not but-if this for-you

הָלוֹךְ וְדַבֵּר וְהִנֵּה רֶכֶב־ אֵשׁ וְסוּסֵי אֵשׁ
fire and-horses-of fire chariot-of and-see! and-to-talk to-walk

וַיַּפְרִדוּ בֵּין שְׁנֵיהֶם וַיַּעַל אֵלִיָּהוּ בַּסְּעָרָה
in-the-whirlwind Elijah and-he-went-up two-of-them between and-they-separated

הַשָּׁמָיִם׃ וֶאֱלִישָׁע רֹאֶה וְהוּא מְצַעֵק אָבִי ׀ אָבִי
father-of-me father-of-me crying-out and-he seeing and-Elisha (12) the-heavens

רֶכֶב יִשְׂרָאֵל וּפָרָשָׁיו וְלֹא רָאָהוּ עוֹד
any-more he-saw-him and-not and-horses-of-him Israel chariot-of

וַיַּחֲזֵק בִּבְגָדָיו וַיִּקְרָעֵם לִשְׁנַיִם קְרָעִים׃
pieces into-two and-he-tore-them of-clothes-of-him then-he-took-hold

and asked him, "Do you know that the LORD is going to take your master from you today?"
"Yes, I know," he replied, "but do not speak of it."
6 Then Elijah said to him, "Stay here; the LORD has sent me to the Jordan."
And he replied, "As surely as the LORD lives and as you live, I will not leave you." So the two of them walked on.
7 Fifty men of the company of the prophets went and stood at a distance, facing the place where Elijah and Elisha had stopped at the Jordan.
8 Elijah took his cloak, rolled it up and struck the water with it. The water divided to the right and to the left, and the two of them crossed over on dry ground.
9 When they had crossed, Elijah said to Elisha, "Tell me, what can I do for you before I am taken from you?"
"Let me inherit a double portion of your spirit," Elisha replied.
10 "You have asked a difficult thing," Elijah said, "yet if you see me when I am taken from you, it will be yours—otherwise not."
11 As they were walking along and talking together, suddenly a chariot of fire and horses of fire appeared and separated the two of them, and Elijah went up to heaven in a whirlwind.
12 Elisha saw this and cried out, "My father! My father! The chariots and horsemen of Israel!" And Elisha saw him no more. Then he took hold of his own clothes and tore them apart.

וַיָּרֶם אֶת־ אַדֶּרֶת אֵלִיָּהוּ אֲשֶׁר נָפְלָה מֵעָלָיו
from-on-him she-fell that Elijah cloak-of *** and-he-picked-up (13)

וַיָּשָׁב וַיַּעֲמֹד עַל־ שְׂפַת הַיַּרְדֵּן׃ וַיִּקַּח אֶת־
*** then-he-took (14) the-Jordan bank-of on and-he-stood and-he-went-back

אַדֶּרֶת אֵלִיָּהוּ אֲשֶׁר־ נָפְלָה מֵעָלָיו וַיַּכֶּה אֶת־ הַמַּיִם
the-waters *** and-he-struck from-on-him she-fell that Elijah cloak-of

וַיֹּאמַר אַיֵּה יְהוָה אֱלֹהֵי אֵלִיָּהוּ אַף־הוּא ׀ וַיַּכֶּה אֶת־ הַמַּיִם
the-waters *** when-he-struck he also Elijah God-of Yahweh where? and-he-said

וַיֵּחָצוּ הֵנָּה וָהֵנָּה וַיַּעֲבֹר אֱלִישָׁע׃
Elisha and-he-crossed-over and-to-there to-here then-they-divided

וַיִּרְאֻהוּ בְנֵי־ הַנְּבִיאִים אֲשֶׁר־ בִּירִיחוֹ מִנֶּגֶד
at-facing from-Jericho who the-prophets sons-of and-they-watched-him (15)

וַיֹּאמְרוּ נָחָה רוּחַ אֵלִיָּהוּ עַל־אֱלִישָׁע וַיָּבֹאוּ לִקְרָאתוֹ
to-meet-him and-they-went Elisha on Elijah spirit-of she-rests and-they-said

וַיִּשְׁתַּחֲווּ־ לוֹ אָרְצָה׃ וַיֹּאמְרוּ אֵלָיו הִנֵּה־ נָא
now! look! to-him and-they-said (16) to-ground before-him and-they-bowed

יֵשׁ־ אֶת־ עֲבָדֶיךָ חֲמִשִּׁים אֲנָשִׁים בְּנֵי־ חַיִל יֵלְכוּ נָא
now! let-them-go ability sons-of men fifty servants-of-you with there-is

וִיבַקְשׁוּ אֶת־ אֲדֹנֶיךָ פֶּן־ נְשָׂאוֹ רוּחַ
Spirit-of he-picked-up-him perhaps masters-of-you *** and-let-them-look-for

יְהוָה וַיַּשְׁלִכֵהוּ בְּאַחַד הֶהָרִים אוֹ בְּאַחַת הַגֵּיאָוֹת
the-valleys in-one-of or the-mountains on-one-of and-he-set-down-him Yahweh

וַיֹּאמֶר לֹא תִשְׁלָחוּ׃ וַיִּפְצְרוּ־ בוֹ עַד־
until with-him but-they-persisted (17) you-send not but-he-replied

בֹּשׁ וַיֹּאמֶר שְׁלָחוּ וַיִּשְׁלְחוּ חֲמִשִּׁים אִישׁ וַיְבַקְשׁוּ
and-they-searched man fifty and-they-sent send! so-he-said to-be-ashamed

שְׁלֹשָׁה־יָמִים וְלֹא מְצָאֻהוּ׃ וַיָּשֻׁבוּ אֵלָיו וְהוּא
now-he to-him when-they-returned (18) they-found-him but-not days three

יֹשֵׁב בִּירִיחוֹ וַיֹּאמֶר אֲלֵהֶם הֲלוֹא־אָמַרְתִּי אֲלֵיכֶם אַל־ תֵּלֵכוּ׃
you-go not to-you I-told not? to-them then-he-said in-Jericho staying

וַיֹּאמְרוּ אַנְשֵׁי הָעִיר אֶל־אֱלִישָׁע הִנֵּה־ נָא מוֹשַׁב הָעִיר
the-city situation-of now! look! Elisha to the-city men-of and-they-said (19)

טוֹב כַּאֲשֶׁר אֲדֹנִי רֹאֶה וְהַמַּיִם רָעִים וְהָאָרֶץ
and-the-land bad-ones but-the-waters seeing lord-of-me just-as good

מְשַׁכָּלֶת׃ וַיֹּאמֶר קְחוּ־ לִי צְלֹחִית חֲדָשָׁה וְשִׂימוּ שָׁם
there and-put! new bowl to-me bring! and-he-said (20) being-unproductive

מֶלַח וַיִּקְחוּ אֵלָיו׃ וַיֵּצֵא אֶל־ מוֹצָא הַמַּיִם
the-waters spring-of to then-he-went-out (21) to-him so-they-brought salt

°16 ק הגאיות

[13]He picked up the cloak that
had fallen from Elijah and
went back and stood on the
bank of the Jordan. [14]Then he
took the cloak that had fallen
from him and struck the water
with it. "Where now is the
LORD, the God of Elijah?" he
asked. When he struck the
water, it divided to the right
and to the left, and he crossed
over.

[15]The company of the prophets from Jericho, who were
watching, said, "The spirit of
Elijah is resting on Elisha."
And they went to meet him
and bowed to the ground before him. [16]"Look," they said,
"we your servants have fifty
able men. Let them go and
look for your master. Perhaps
the Spirit of the LORD has
picked him up and set him
down on some mountain or in
some valley."

"No," Elisha replied, "do
not send them."

[17]But they persisted until he
was too ashamed to refuse. So
he said, "Send them." And
they sent fifty men, who
searched for three days but did
not find him. [18]When they returned to Elisha, who was
staying in Jericho, he said to
them, "Didn't I tell you not to
go?"

Healing of the Water

[19]The men of the city said to
Elisha, "Look, our lord, this
town is well situated, as you
can see, but the water is bad
and the land is unproductive."

[20]"Bring me a new bowl," he
said, "and put salt in it." So
they brought it to him.

[21]Then he went out to the

וַיַּשְׁלֶךְ־ שָׁם מֶלַח וַיֹּאמֶר כֹּה־ אָמַר יְהוָה רִפִּאתִי
I-healed Yahweh he-says this and-he-said salt there and-he-threw

לַמַּיִם הָאֵלֶּה לֹא־ יִהְיֶה מִשָּׁם עוֹד מָוֶת
death again from-there he-will-be not the-these to-the-waters

וּמְשַׁכָּלֶת׃ (22) וַיֵּרָפוּ הַמַּיִם עַד הַיּוֹם
the-day to the-waters and-they-are-wholesome (22) or-being-unproductive

הַזֶּה כִּדְבַר אֱלִישָׁע אֲשֶׁר דִּבֵּר׃ (23) וַיַּעַל מִשָּׁם
from-there and-he-went-up (23) he-spoke that Elisha as-word-of the-this

בֵּית־ אֵל וְהוּא ׀ עֹלֶה בַדֶּרֶךְ וּנְעָרִים קְטַנִּים יָצְאוּ
they-came-out young-ones and-youths along-the-road walking and-he El Beth

מִן־ הָעִיר וַיִּתְקַלְּסוּ־ בוֹ וַיֹּאמְרוּ לוֹ עֲלֵה קֵרֵחַ
baldhead go-up! to-him and-they-said at-him and-they-jeered the-town from

עֲלֵה קֵרֵחַ׃ (24) וַיִּפֶן אַחֲרָיו וַיִּרְאֵם
and-he-looked-at-them behind-him and-he-turned (24) baldhead go-up!

וַיְקַלְלֵם בְּשֵׁם יְהוָה וַתֵּצֶאנָה שְׁתַּיִם דֻּבִּים מִן־
from bears two then-they-came-out Yahweh in-name-of and-he-cursed-them

הַיַּעַר וַתְּבַקַּעְנָה מֵהֶם אַרְבָּעִים וּשְׁנֵי יְלָדִים׃ (25) וַיֵּלֶךְ
and-he-went-on (25) youths and-two-of forty of-them and-they-mauled the-wood

מִשָּׁם אֶל־ הַר הַכַּרְמֶל וּמִשָּׁם שָׁב שֹׁמְרוֹן׃
Samaria he-returned and-from-there the-Carmel Mount-of to from-there

(3:1) וִיהוֹרָם בֶּן־ אַחְאָב מָלַךְ עַל־יִשְׂרָאֵל בְּשֹׁמְרוֹן בִּשְׁנַת
in-year-of in-Samaria Israel over he-became-king Ahab son-of now-Jehoram (3:1)

שְׁמֹנֶה עֶשְׂרֵה לִיהוֹשָׁפָט מֶלֶךְ יְהוּדָה וַיִּמְלֹךְ שְׁתֵּים־עֶשְׂרֵה שָׁנָה׃
year ten two and-he-reigned Judah king-of of-Jehoshaphat ten eight

(2) וַיַּעֲשֶׂה הָרַע בְּעֵינֵי יְהוָה רַק לֹא כְּאָבִיו
as-father-of-him not but Yahweh in-eyes-of the-evil and-he-did (2)

וּכְאִמּוֹ וַיָּסַר אֶת־ מַצְּבַת הַבַּעַל אֲשֶׁר עָשָׂה
he-made that the-Baal sacred-stone-of *** and-he-got-rid and-as-mother-of-him

אָבִיו׃ (3) רַק בְּחַטֹּאות יָרָבְעָם בֶּן־ נְבָט אֲשֶׁר־
which Nebat son-of Jeroboam to-sins-of nevertheless (3) father-of-him

הֶחֱטִיא אֶת־יִשְׂרָאֵל דָּבֵק לֹא־ סָר מִמֶּנָּה׃ (4) וּמֵישַׁע
now-Mesha (4) from-her he-turned not he-clung Israel *** he-caused-to-sin

מֶלֶךְ־ מוֹאָב הָיָה נֹקֵד וְהֵשִׁיב לְמֶלֶךְ־ יִשְׂרָאֵל מֵאָה־
hundred Israel to-king-of and-he-supplied sheep-raiser he-was Moab king-of

אֶלֶף כָּרִים וּמֵאָה אֶלֶף אֵילִים צָמֶר׃ (5) וַיְהִי כְּמוֹת
when-to-die but-he-was (5) wool rams thousand and-hundred lambs thousand

אַחְאָב וַיִּפְשַׁע מֶלֶךְ־ מוֹאָב בְּמֶלֶךְ יִשְׂרָאֵל׃ (6) וַיֵּצֵא
so-he-set-out (6) Israel against-king-of Moab king-of then-he-rebelled Ahab

spring and threw the salt into
it, saying, "This is what the
LORD says: 'I have healed this
water. Never again will it
cause death or make the land
unproductive.' " 22And the
water has remained whole-
some to this day, according to
the word Elisha had spoken.

Elisha Is Jeered

23From there Elisha went up
to Bethel. As he was walking
along the road, some youths
came out of the town and
jeered at him. "Go on up, you
baldhead!" they said. "Go on
up, you baldhead!" 24He
turned around, looked at them
and called down a curse on
them in the name of the LORD.
Then two bears came out of
the woods and mauled forty-
two of the youths. 25And he
went on to Mount Carmel and
from there returned to Samaria.

Moab Revolts

3 Joram[b] son of Ahab
became king of Israel in
Samaria in the eighteenth
year of Jehoshaphat king of
Judah, and he reigned twelve
years. 2He did evil in the eyes
of the LORD, but not as his father and mother had done. He
got rid of the sacred stone of
Baal that his father had made.
3Nevertheless he clung to the
sins of Jeroboam son of Nebat,
which he had caused Israel to
commit; he did not turn away
from them.
4Now Mesha king of Moab
raised sheep, and he had to
supply the king of Israel with
a hundred thousand lambs
and with the wool of a hundred thousand rams. 5But after
Ahab died, the king of Moab
rebelled against the king of Israel. 6So at that time King

[b]1 Hebrew *Jehoram,* a variant of *Joram;* also in verse 6

הַמֶּלֶךְ יְהוֹרָם בַּיּוֹם הַהוּא מִשֹּׁמְרוֹן וַיִּפְקֹד אֶת־ כָּל־
all-of *** and-he-mobilized from-Samaria the-that on-the-day Jehoram the-king

יִשְׂרָאֵל׃ וַיֵּלֶךְ וַיִּשְׁלַח אֶל־ יְהוֹשָׁפָט מֶלֶךְ־ יְהוּדָה לֵאמֹר
to-say Judah king-of Jehoshaphat to and-he-sent and-he-went (7) Israel

מֶלֶךְ מוֹאָב פָּשַׁע בִּי הֲתֵלֵךְ אִתִּי אֶל־ מוֹאָב
Moab against with-me will-you-go? against-me he-rebelled Moab king-of

לַמִּלְחָמָה וַיֹּאמֶר אֶעֱלֶה כָּמוֹנִי כָמוֹךָ כְּעַמִּי
so-people-of-me as-you so-me I-will-go and-he-replied to-the-fight

כְעַמֶּךָ כְּסוּסַי כְּסוּסֶיךָ׃ וַיֹּאמֶר אֵי־
where? and-he-asked (8) as-horses-of-you so-horses-of-me as-people-of-you

זֶה הַדֶּרֶךְ נַעֲלֶה וַיֹּאמֶר דֶּרֶךְ מִדְבַּר אֱדוֹם׃
Edom Desert-of route-of and-he-answered we-shall-attack the-route this

וַיֵּלֶךְ מֶלֶךְ יִשְׂרָאֵל וּמֶלֶךְ־ יְהוּדָה וּמֶלֶךְ אֱדוֹם
Edom and-king-of Judah and-king-of Israel king-of so-he-set-out (9)

וַיָּסֹבּוּ דֶּרֶךְ שִׁבְעַת יָמִים וְלֹא־ הָיָה מַיִם
waters he-was and-not days seven-of journey-of and-they-marched-around

לַמַּחֲנֶה וְלַבְּהֵמָה אֲשֶׁר בְּרַגְלֵיהֶם׃ וַיֹּאמֶר
and-he-exclaimed (10) at-feet-of-them that or-for-the-animal for-the-army

מֶלֶךְ יִשְׂרָאֵל אֲהָהּ כִּי־ קָרָא יְהוָה לִשְׁלֹשֶׁת הַמְּלָכִים הָאֵלֶּה
the-these the-kings to-three-of Yahweh he-called indeed what! Israel king-of

לָתֵת אוֹתָם בְּיַד־ מוֹאָב׃ וַיֹּאמֶר יְהוֹשָׁפָט הַאֵין
is-there-not? Jehoshaphat but-he-asked (11) Moab into-hand-of them to-give

פֹּה נָבִיא לַיהוָה וְנִדְרְשָׁה אֶת־ יְהוָה מֵאוֹתוֹ
through-him Yahweh *** that-we-may-inquire of-Yahweh prophet here

וַיַּעַן אֶחָד מֵעַבְדֵי מֶלֶךְ־ יִשְׂרָאֵל וַיֹּאמֶר פֹּה אֱלִישָׁע
Elisha here and-he-said Israel king-of of-officers-of one and-he-answered

בֶּן־ שָׁפָט אֲשֶׁר־ יָצַק מַיִם עַל־ יְדֵי אֵלִיָּהוּ׃ וַיֹּאמֶר
then-he-said (12) Elijah hands-of on waters he-poured who Shaphat son-of

יְהוֹשָׁפָט יֵשׁ אוֹתוֹ דְּבַר־ יְהוָה וַיֵּרְדוּ אֵלָיו מֶלֶךְ
king-of to-him so-they-went-down Yahweh word-of with-him there-is Jehoshaphat

יִשְׂרָאֵל וִיהוֹשָׁפָט וּמֶלֶךְ אֱדוֹם׃ וַיֹּאמֶר אֱלִישָׁע אֶל־ מֶלֶךְ
king-of to Elisha and-he-said (13) Edom and-king-of and-Jehoshaphat Israel

יִשְׂרָאֵל מַה־ לִּי וָלָךְ לֵךְ אֶל־ נְבִיאֵי אָבִיךָ וְאֶל־
and-to father-of-you prophets-of to go! and-to-you to-me what? Israel

נְבִיאֵי אִמֶּךָ וַיֹּאמֶר לוֹ מֶלֶךְ יִשְׂרָאֵל אַל כִּי־
for no Israel king-of to-him and-he-answered mother-of-you prophets-of

קָרָא יְהוָה לִשְׁלֹשֶׁת הַמְּלָכִים הָאֵלֶּה לָתֵת אוֹתָם בְּיַד־
into-hand-of them to-give the-these the-kings to-three-of Yahweh he-called

Joram set out from Samaria
and mobilized all Israel. 7He
also sent this message to Jehoshaphat king of Judah: "The
king of Moab has rebelled
against me. Will you go with
me to fight against Moab?"
"I will go with you," he replied. "I am as you are, my
people as your people, my
horses as your horses."
8"By what route shall we attack?" he asked.
"Through the Desert of
Edom," he answered.
9So the king of Israel set out
with the king of Judah and the
king of Edom. After a round-
about march of seven days,
the army had no more water
for themselves or for the animals with them.
10"What!" exclaimed the
king of Israel. "Has the LORD
called us three kings together
only to hand us over to
Moab?"
11But Jehoshaphat asked, "Is
there no prophet of the LORD
here, that we may inquire of
the LORD through him?"
An officer of the king of Israel answered, "Elisha son of
Shaphat is here. He used to
pour water on the hands of
Elijah.[c]"
12Jehoshaphat said, "The
word of the LORD is with him."
So the king of Israel and Jehoshaphat and the king of
Edom went down to him.
13Elisha said to the king of
Israel, "What do we have to do
with each other? Go to the
prophets of your father and
the prophets of your mother."
"No," the king of Israel answered, "because it was the
LORD who called us three kings
together to hand us over to

c11 That is, he was Elijah's personal servant.

*9 Most mss have *sheva* in the *kaph* (ךְ).

מוֹאָב׃ וַיֹּאמֶר אֱלִישָׁע חַי־ יְהוָה צְבָאוֹת אֲשֶׁר עָמַדְתִּי לְפָנָיו
before-him I-serve whom Hosts Yahweh-of life-of Elisha and-he-said (14) Moab

כִּי לוּלֵי פְּנֵי יְהוֹשָׁפָט מֶלֶךְ־ יְהוּדָה אֲנִי נֹשֵׂא אִם־
not respecting I Judah king-of Jehoshaphat presences-of if-not indeed

אַבִּיט אֵלֶיךָ וְאִם־ אֶרְאֶךָּ׃ וְעַתָּה קְחוּ־ לִי
to-me bring! but-now (15) I-would-notice-you and-not at-you I-would-look

מְנַגֵּן וְהָיָה כְּנַגֵּן הַמְנַגֵּן וַתְּהִי
then-she-came the-one-playing-harp while-to-play and-he-was one-playing-harp

עָלָיו יַד־ יְהוָה׃ וַיֹּאמֶר כֹּה אָמַר יְהוָה עָשֹׂה
to-make Yahweh he-says this and-he-said (16) Yahweh hand-of upon-him

הַנַּחַל הַזֶּה גֵּבִים ׀ גֵּבִים׃ כִּי־ כֹה ׀ אָמַר יְהוָה לֹא־
not Yahweh he-says this for (17) ditches ditches the-this the-valley

תִרְאוּ רוּחַ וְלֹא־ תִרְאוּ גֶשֶׁם וְהַנַּחַל הַהוּא
the-this yet-the-valley rain you-will-see and-not wind you-will-see

יִמָּלֵא מָיִם וּשְׁתִיתֶם אַתֶּם וּמִקְנֵיכֶם
and-cattle-of-you you and-you-will-drink waters he-will-be-filled

וּבְהֶמְתְּכֶם׃ וְנָקַל זֹאת בְּעֵינֵי יְהוָה וְנָתַן
and-he-will-give Yahweh in-eyes-of this and-he-is-easy (18) and-animal-of-you

אֶת־ מוֹאָב בְּיֶדְכֶם׃ וְהִכִּיתֶם כָּל־ עִיר
city-of every-of and-you-will-overthrow (19) into-hand-of-you Moab ***

מִבְצָר וְכָל־ עִיר מִבְחוֹר וְכָל־ עֵץ טוֹב
good tree and-every-of major town-of and-every-of fortification

תַּפִּילוּ וְכָל־ מַעְיְנֵי־ מַיִם תִּסְתֹּמוּ וְכֹל
and-every-of you-will-stop-up waters springs-of and-all-of you-will-cut-down

הַחֶלְקָה הַטּוֹבָה תַּכְאִבוּ בָּאֲבָנִים׃ וַיְהִי
and-he-was (20) with-the-stones you-will-ruin the-good the-field

בַבֹּקֶר כַּעֲלוֹת הַמִּנְחָה וְהִנֵּה־ מַיִם בָּאִים
ones-flowing waters then-see! the-sacrifice when-to-offer in-the-morning

מִדֶּרֶךְ אֱדוֹם וַתִּמָּלֵא הָאָרֶץ אֶת־ הַמָּיִם׃ וְכָל־
now-all-of (21) waters *** the-land and-she-was-filled Edom from-direction-of

מוֹאָב שָׁמְעוּ כִּי־ עָלוּ הַמְּלָכִים לְהִלָּחֶם בָּם וַיִּצָּעֲקוּ
and-they-called against-them to-fight the-kings they-came that they-heard Moab

מִכֹּל חֹגֵר חֲגֹרָה וָמַעְלָה וַיַּעַמְדוּ עַל־ הַגְּבוּל׃
the-border on and-they-stationed and-upward arm bearing from-every-of

וַיַּשְׁכִּימוּ בַבֹּקֶר וְהַשֶּׁמֶשׁ זָרְחָה עַל־ הַמָּיִם
the-waters on she-shined then-the-sun in-the-morning when-they-got-up (22)

וַיִּרְאוּ מוֹאָב מִנֶּגֶד אֶת־ הַמַּיִם אֲדֻמִּים כַּדָּם׃
like-the-blood ones-red the-waters *** at-across Moab and-they-saw

Moab."
[14]Elisha said, "As surely as
the LORD Almighty lives,
whom I serve, if I did not have
respect for the presence of Jehoshaphat king of Judah, I
would not look at you or even
notice you. [15]But now bring
me a harpist."
While the harpist was playing, the hand of the LORD
came upon Elisha [16]and he
said, "This is what the LORD
says: Make this valley full of
ditches. [17]For this is what the
LORD says: You will see neither
wind nor rain, yet this valley
will be filled with water, and
you, your cattle and your other
animals will drink. [18]This is an
easy thing in the eyes of the
LORD; he will also hand Moab
over to you. [19]You will overthrow every fortified city and
every major town. You will cut
down every good tree, stop up
all the springs, and ruin every
good field with stones."
[20]The next morning, about
the time for offering the sacrifice, there it was—water
flowing from the direction of
Edom! And the land was filled
with water.
[21]Now all the Moabites had
heard that the kings had come
to fight against them; so every
man, young and old, who
could bear arms was called up
and stationed on the border.
[22]When they got up early in
the morning, the sun was
shining on the water. To the
Moabites across the way, the
water looked red—like blood.

וַיֹּאמְרוּ דָּם זֶה הָחֳרֵב נֶחֶרְבוּ הַמְּלָכִים
the-kings they-fought to-fight that blood and-they-said (23)

וַיַּכּוּ אִישׁ אֶת־ רֵעֵהוּ וְעַתָּה לַשָּׁלָל מוֹאָב׃
Moab to-the-plunder and-now fellow-of-him *** each and-they-slaughtered

וַיָּבֹאוּ אֶל־ מַחֲנֵה יִשְׂרָאֵל וַיָּקֻמוּ יִשְׂרָאֵל וַיַּכּוּ
and-they-fought Israel then-they-rose-up Israel camp-of to when-they-came (24)

אֶת־ מוֹאָב וַיָּנֻסוּ מִפְּנֵיהֶם וַיַּבּוּ־ בָהּ
into-her and-they-invaded from-before-them so-they-fled Moab ***

וְהַכּוֹת אֶת־ מוֹאָב׃ וְהֶעָרִים יַהֲרֹסוּ וְכָל־
and-every-of they-destroyed and-the-towns (25) Moab *** and-to-slaughter

חֶלְקָה טוֹבָה יַשְׁלִיכוּ אִישׁ־ אַבְנוֹ וּמִלְאוּהָ וְכָל־
and-every-of so-they-covered-her stone-of-him man they-threw good field

מַעְיַן־ מַיִם יִסְתֹּמוּ וְכָל־ עֵץ־ טוֹב יַפִּילוּ עַד־
until they-cut-down good tree and-every-of they-stopped-up waters spring-of

הִשְׁאִיר אֲבָנֶיהָ בַּקִּיר חֲרֶשֶׂת* וַיָּסֹבּוּ הַקַּלָּעִים
the-slingers but-they-surrounded Hareseth in-the-Kir stones-of-her he-left

וַיַּכּוּהָ׃ וַיַּרְא מֶלֶךְ מוֹאָב כִּי־ חָזַק
he-prevailed that Moab king-of when-he-saw (26) and-they-attacked-her

מִמֶּנּוּ הַמִּלְחָמָה וַיִּקַּח אוֹתוֹ שְׁבַע־ מֵאוֹת אִישׁ שֹׁלֵף
drawing man hundreds seven-of with-him then-he-took the-battle against-him

חֶרֶב לְהַבְקִיעַ אֶל־ מֶלֶךְ אֱדוֹם וְלֹא יָכֹלוּ׃ וַיִּקַּח
then-he-took (27) they-could but-not Edom king-of to to-break-through sword

אֶת־ בְּנוֹ הַבְּכוֹר אֲשֶׁר־ יִמְלֹךְ תַּחְתָּיו
in-place-of-him he-would-become-king who the-firstborn son-of-him ***

וַיַּעֲלֵהוּ עֹלָה עַל־ הַחֹמָה וַיְהִי קֶצֶף־ גָּדוֹל עַל־
against great fury and-he-was the-wall on sacrifice and-he-offered-him

יִשְׂרָאֵל וַיִּסְעוּ מֵעָלָיו וַיָּשֻׁבוּ לָאָרֶץ׃
to-the-land and-they-returned from-against-him so-they-withdrew Israel

וְאִשָּׁה אַחַת מִנְּשֵׁי בְנֵי־ הַנְּבִיאִים צָעֲקָה אֶל־
to she-cried-out the-prophets sons-of from-wives-of one now-woman (4:1)

אֱלִישָׁע לֵאמֹר עַבְדְּךָ אִישִׁי מֵת וְאַתָּה יָדַעְתָּ כִּי
that you-know and-you he-is-dead husband-of-me servant-of-you to-say Elisha

עַבְדְּךָ הָיָה יָרֵא אֶת־ יְהוָה וְהַנֹּשֶׁה בָּא
coming but-the-one-being-creditor Yahweh *** revering he-was servant-of-you

לָקַחַת אֶת־ שְׁנֵי יְלָדַי לוֹ לַעֲבָדִים׃ וַיֹּאמֶר אֵלֶיהָ
to-her and-he-replied (2) as-slaves to-him boys-of-me two-of *** to-take

אֱלִישָׁע מָה אֶעֱשֶׂה־ לָּךְ הַגִּידִי לִי מַה־ יֶּשׁ־ לָכִי בַּבָּיִת
in-the-house to-you is-there what? to-me tell! for-you can-I-do what? Elisha

23"That's blood!" they said.
"Those kings must have
fought and slaughtered each
other. Now to the plunder,
Moab!"
24But when the Moabites
came to the camp of Israel, the
Israelites rose up and fought
them until they fled. And the
Israelites invaded the land
and slaughtered the Moabites.
25They destroyed the towns,
and each man threw a stone
on every good field until it was
covered. They stopped up all
the springs and cut down
every good tree. Only Kir
Hareseth was left with its
stones in place, but men
armed with slings surrounded
it and attacked it as well.
26When the king of Moab
saw that the battle had gone
against him, he took with him
seven hundred swordsmen to
break through to the king of
Edom, but they failed. 27Then
he took his firstborn son, who
was to succeed him as king,
and offered him as a sacrifice
on the city wall. The fury
against Israel was great; they
withdrew and returned to
their own land.

The Widow's Oil

4 The wife of a man from
the company of the
prophets cried out to Elisha,
"Your servant my husband is
dead, and you know that he
revered the LORD. But now his
creditor is coming to take my
two boys as his slaves."
2Elisha replied to her, "How
can I help you? Tell me, what
do you have in your house?"

*25 Some mss have *shin* for *sin* (שׁת).

°24 ק ויכו

°2 ק לך

ותאמר אין לשפחתך כל בבית כי אם־
only except in-the-house all-of to-servant-of-you nothing and-she-said

אסוך שמן׃ ויאמר לכי שאלי־ לך כלים מן־ החוץ מאת
from the-area from jars for-you ask! go! and-he-said (3) oil flask-of

כל־ שכנכי° כלים רקים אל־ תמעיטי׃ ובאת
then-you-go (4) you-get-few not empty-ones jars neighbors-of-you all-of

וסגרת הדלת בעדך ובעד־ בניך ויצקת על
in and-you-pour sons-of-you and-behind behind-you the-door and-you-shut

כל־ הכלים האלה והמלא תסיעי׃ ותלך
so-she-left (5) you-put-aside and-the-one-filled the-these the-jars all-of

מאתו ותסגר הדלת בעדה ובעד בניה הם
they sons-of-her and-behind behind-her the-door and-she-shut from-with-him

מגשים אליה והיא מיצקת°׃ ויהי כמלאת הכלים
the-jars when-to-be-full and-he-was (6) pouring and-she to-her ones-bringing

ותאמר אל־ בנה הגישה אלי עוד כלי ויאמר אליה
to-her but-he-replied jar another to-me bring! son-of-her to then-she-said

אין עוד כלי ויעמד השמן׃ ותבא ותגד
and-she-told then-she-went (7) the-oil then-he-stopped jar another not

לאיש האלהים ויאמר לכי מכרי את־ השמן ושלמי את־ נשיכי°
debts-of-you *** and-pay! the-oil *** sell! go! and-he-said the-God to-man-of

ואת בניכי° תחיי בנותר׃ ויהי
and-he-was (8) on-the-being-left you-can-live and-sons-of-you and-you

היום ויעבר אלישע אל־ שונם ושם אשה גדולה ותחזק־
and-she-urged well-to-do woman and-there Shunem to Elisha then-he-went the-day

בו לאכל־לחם ויהי מדי עברו יסר שמה
at-there he-stopped to-come-by-him at-times-of so-he-was meal to-eat with-him

לאכל־לחם׃ ותאמר אל־ אישה הנה־ נא ידעתי כי איש
man-of that I-know now! see! husband-of-her to and-she-said (9) meal to-eat

אלהים קדוש הוא עבר עלינו תמיד׃ נעשה־ נא עלית־ קיר
roof upper-room-of now! let-us-make (10) often to-us coming he holy God

קטנה ונשים לו שם מטה ושלחן וכסא ומנורה
and-lamp and-chair and-table bed there for-him and-let-us-put small

והיה בבאו אלינו יסור שמה׃ ויהי
and-he-was (11) at-there he-can-stay to-us when-to-come-him and-he-will-be

היום ויבא שמה ויסר אל־ העליה וישכב־ שמה׃
at-there and-he-lay the-room to and-he-went to-there then-he-came the-day

ויאמר אל־ גחזי נערו קרא לשונמית הזאת
the-this to-the-Shunnamite call! servant-of-him Gehazi to and-he-said (12)

"Your servant has nothing there at all," she said, "except a little oil."

[3]Elisha said, "Go around and ask all your neighbors for empty jars. Don't ask for just a few. [4]Then go inside and shut the door behind you and your sons. Pour oil into all the jars, and as each is filled, put it to one side."

[5]She left him and afterward shut the door behind her and her sons. They brought the jars to her and she kept pouring. [6]When all the jars were full, she said to her son, "Bring me another one."

But he replied, "There is not a jar left." Then the oil stopped flowing.

[7]She went and told the man of God, and he said, "Go, sell the oil and pay your debts. You and your sons can live on what is left."

The Shunammite's Son Restored to Life

[8]One day Elisha went to Shunem. And a well-to-do woman was there, who urged him to stay for a meal. So whenever he came by, he stopped there to eat. [9]She said to her husband, "I know that this man who often comes our way is a holy man of God. [10]Let's make a small room on the roof and put in it a bed and a table, a chair and a lamp for him. Then he can stay there whenever he comes to us."

[11]One day when Elisha came, he went up to his room and lay down there. [12]He said to his servant Gehazi, "Call

°3 ק שכניך
°5 ק מוצקת
°7a ק נשיך
°7b ק ובניך

וַיִּקְרָא־ לָהּ וַתַּעֲמֹד לְפָנָיו׃ וַיֹּאמֶר לוֹ אֱמָר־
tell! to-him and-he-said (13) before-him and-she-stood to-her so-he-called

נָא אֵלֶיהָ הִנֵּה חָרַדְתְּ | אֵלֵינוּ אֶת־ כָּל־ הַחֲרָדָה הַזֹּאת
the-this the-care all-of *** for-us you-went-to-trouble see! to-her! now!

מֶה לַעֲשׂוֹת לָךְ הֲיֵשׁ לְדַבֶּר־ לָךְ אֶל־ הַמֶּלֶךְ אוֹ אֶל־ שַׂר
commander-of to or the-king to for-you to-speak is-there? for-you to-do what?

הַצָּבָא וַתֹּאמֶר בְּתוֹךְ עַמִּי אָנֹכִי יֹשָׁבֶת׃ וַיֹּאמֶר
and-he-asked (14) having-home I people-of-me among and-she-replied the-army

וּמֶה לַעֲשׂוֹת לָהּ וַיֹּאמֶר גֵּיחֲזִי אֲבָל בֵּן אֵין־ לָהּ
to-her there-is-not son well Gehazi and-he-said for-her to-do now-what?

וְאִישָׁהּ זָקֵן׃ וַיֹּאמֶר קְרָא־ לָהּ וַיִּקְרָא־
so-he-called to-her call! then-he-said (15) he-is-old and-husband-of-her

לָהּ וַתַּעֲמֹד בַּפָּתַח׃ וַיֹּאמֶר לַמּוֹעֵד הַזֶּה
the-this at-the-season and-he-said (16) in-the-doorway and-she-stood to-her

כָּעֵת חַיָּה אַתְּי חֹבֶקֶת בֵּן וַתֹּאמֶר אַל־ אֲדֹנִי אִישׁ הָאֱלֹהִים
the-God man-of lord-of-me no but-she-said son holding you spring at-time-of

אַל־ תְּכַזֵּב בְּשִׁפְחָתֶךָ׃ וַתַּהַר הָאִשָּׁה
the-woman but-she-became-pregnant (17) to-servant-of-you you-mislead not

וַתֵּלֶד בֵּן לַמּוֹעֵד הַזֶּה כָּעֵת חַיָּה אֲשֶׁר־ דִּבֶּר
he-told as the-spring at-time-of the-that at-the-season son and-she-bore

אֵלֶיהָ אֱלִישָׁע׃ וַיִּגְדַּל הַיָּלֶד וַיְהִי הַיּוֹם וַיֵּצֵא
then-he-went-out the-day and-he-was the-child and-he-grew (18) Elisha to-her

אֶל־ אָבִיו אֶל־ הַקֹּצְרִים׃ וַיֹּאמֶר אֶל־ אָבִיו
father-of-him to and-he-said (19) the-ones-reaping to father-of-him to

רֹאשִׁי | רֹאשִׁי וַיֹּאמֶר אֶל־ הַנַּעַר שָׂאֵהוּ אֶל־ אִמּוֹ׃
mother-of-him to carry-him! the-servant to and-he-told head-of-me head-of-me

וַיִּשָּׂאֵהוּ וַיְבִיאֵהוּ אֶל־ אִמּוֹ וַיֵּשֶׁב עַל־
on and-he-sat mother-of-him to and-he-carried-him so-he-lifted-him (20)

בִּרְכֶּיהָ עַד־ הַצָּהֳרַיִם וַיָּמֹת׃ וַתַּעַל וַתַּשְׁכִּבֵהוּ
and-she-laid-him then-she-went-up (21) then-he-died the-noon until knees-of-her

עַל־ מִטַּת אִישׁ הָאֱלֹהִים וַתִּסְגֹּר בַּעֲדוֹ וַתֵּצֵא׃
and-she-went-out behind-him then-she-shut the-God man-of bed-of on

וַתִּקְרָא אֶל־ אִישָׁהּ וַתֹּאמֶר שִׁלְחָה נָא לִי אֶחָד
one to-me now! send! and-she-said husband-of-her to and-she-called (22)

מִן־ הַנְּעָרִים וְאַחַת הָאֲתֹנוֹת וְאָרוּצָה עַד־ אִישׁ
man-of to so-I-can-go-quickly the-donkeys and-one-of the-servants from

הָאֱלֹהִים וְאָשׁוּבָה׃ וַיֹּאמֶר מַדּוּעַ אַתְּי הֹלַכְתִּי אֵלָיו הַיּוֹם
the-day to-him going you why? and-he-asked (23) and-I-can-return the-God

the Shunammite." So he called
her, and she stood before him.
13 Elisha said to him, "Tell her,
'You have gone to all this trouble for us. Now what can be
done for you? Can we speak
on your behalf to the king or
the commander of the
army?' "
She replied, "I have a home
among my own people."
14 "What can be done for
her?" Elisha asked.
Gehazi said, "Well, she has
no son and her husband is
old."
15 Then Elisha said, "Call
her." So he called her, and she
stood in the doorway.
16 "About this time next year,"
Elisha said, "you will hold a
son in your arms."
"No, my lord," she objected.
"Don't mislead your servant,
O man of God!"
17 But the woman became
pregnant, and the next year
about that same time she gave
birth to a son, just as Elisha
had told her.
18 The child grew, and one
day he went out to his father,
who was with the reapers.
19 "My head! My head!" he said
to his father.
His father told a servant,
"Carry him to his mother."
20 After the servant had lifted
him up and carried him to his
mother, the boy sat on her lap
until noon, and then he died.
21 She went up and laid him on
the bed of the man of God,
then shut the door and went
out.
22 She called her husband
and said, "Please send me one
of the servants and a donkey
so I can go to the man of God
quickly and return."
23 "Why go to him today?" he

°16 ק את
°23a ק את
°23b ק הלכת

לֹא־ חֹדֶשׁ וְלֹא שַׁבָּת וַתֹּאמֶר שָׁלוֹם׃ וַתַּחֲבֹשׁ
and-she-saddled (24) all-right and-she-said Sabbath and-not New-Moon not

הָאָתוֹן וַתֹּאמֶר אֶל־ נַעֲרָהּ נְהַג וָלֵךְ אַל־ תַּעֲצָר־
you-slow-down not and-go! lead-on! servant-of-her to and-she-said the-donkey

לִי לִרְכֹּב כִּי אִם־אָמַרְתִּי לָךְ׃ וַתֵּלֶךְ וַתָּבוֹא אֶל־
to and-she-came so-she-set-out (25) to-you I-tell if except to-ride for-me

אִישׁ הָאֱלֹהִים אֶל־ הַר הַכַּרְמֶל וַיְהִי כִּרְאוֹת אִישׁ־הָאֱלֹהִים
the-God man-of when-to-see and-he-was the-Carmel Mount-of at the-God man-of

אֹתָהּ מִנֶּגֶד וַיֹּאמֶר אֶל־ גֵּיחֲזִי נַעֲרוֹ הִנֵּה הַשּׁוּנַמִּית
the-Shunnamite look! servant-of-him Gehazi to then-he-said in-distance her

הַלָּז׃ עַתָּה רוּץ־ נָא לִקְרָאתָהּ וֶאֱמָר־ לָהּ הֲשָׁלוֹם לָךְ
with-you all-right? of-her and-ask! to-meet-her now! run! now (26) the-that

הֲשָׁלוֹם לְאִישֵׁךְ הֲשָׁלוֹם לַיָּלֶד וַתֹּאמֶר
and-she-said with-the-child all-right? with-husband-of-you all-right?

שָׁלוֹם׃ וַתָּבֹא אֶל־ אִישׁ הָאֱלֹהִים אֶל־ הָהָר
the-mountain at the-God man-of to when-she-reached (27) all-right

וַתַּחֲזֵק בְּרַגְלָיו וַיִּגַּשׁ גֵּיחֲזִי לְהָדְפָהּ
to-push-away-her Gehazi and-he-came-over of-feet-of-him then-she-took-hold

וַיֹּאמֶר אִישׁ הָאֱלֹהִים הַרְפֵּה־ לָהּ כִּי־ נַפְשָׁהּ מָרָה־
she-is-bitter spirit-of-her for to-her leave-alone! the-God man-of but-he-said

לָהּ וַיהוָה הֶעְלִים מִמֶּנִּי וְלֹא הִגִּיד לִי׃ וַתֹּאמֶר
and-she-said (28) to-me he-told and-not from-me he-hid but-Yahweh to-her

הֲשָׁאַלְתִּי בֵן מֵאֵת אֲדֹנִי הֲלֹא אָמַרְתִּי לֹא תַשְׁלֶה אֹתִי׃
me you-raise-hope not I-told not? lord-of-me from son did-I-ask?

וַיֹּאמֶר לְגֵיחֲזִי חֲגֹר מָתְנֶיךָ וְקַח מִשְׁעַנְתִּי
staff-of-me and-take! waists-of-you tuck-cloak! to-Gehazi and-he-said (29)

בְּיָדְךָ וָלֵךְ כִּי־ תִמְצָא אִישׁ לֹא תְבָרְכֶנּוּ וְכִי־
and-if you-greet-him not anyone you-meet if and-run! in-hand-of-you

יְבָרֶכְךָ אִישׁ לֹא תַעֲנֶנּוּ וְשַׂמְתָּ מִשְׁעַנְתִּי עַל־ פְּנֵי
faces-of on staff-of-me then-you-lay you-answer-him not anyone he-greets-you

הַנָּעַר׃ וַתֹּאמֶר אֵם הַנַּעַר חַי־ יְהוָה וְחֵי־
and-life-of Yahweh life-of the-child mother-of but-she-said (30) the-boy

נַפְשְׁךָ אִם־ אֶעֶזְבֶךָּ וַיָּקָם וַיֵּלֶךְ אַחֲרֶיהָ׃
after-her and-he-followed so-he-got-up I-will-leave-you not soul-of-you

וְגֵחֲזִי עָבַר לִפְנֵיהֶם וַיָּשֶׂם אֶת־ הַמִּשְׁעֶנֶת עַל־
on the-staff *** and-he-laid ahead-of-them he-went-on and-Gehazi (31)

פְּנֵי הַנַּעַר וְאֵין קוֹל וְאֵין קָשֶׁב
response and-there-was-no sound but-there-was-no the-boy faces-of

asked. "It's not the New Moon or the Sabbath."

"It's all right," she said.

24She saddled the donkey and said to her servant, "Lead on; don't slow down for me unless I tell you." 25So she set
out and came to the man of God at Mount Carmel.

When he saw her in the distance, the man of God said to his servant Gehazi, "Look! There's the Shunammite!
26Run to meet her and ask her, 'Are you all right? Is your husband all right? Is your child all right?' "

"Everything is all right," she said.

27When she reached the man of God at the mountain, she took hold of his feet. Gehazi came over to push her away, but the man of God said, "Leave her alone! She is in bitter distress, but the LORD has hidden it from me and has not told me why."

28"Did I ask you for a son, my lord?" she said. "Didn't I tell you, 'Don't raise my hopes'?"

29Elisha said to Gehazi, "Tuck your cloak into your belt, take my staff in your hand and run. If you meet anyone, do not greet him, and if anyone greets you, do not answer. Lay my staff on the boy's face."

30But the child's mother said, "As surely as the LORD lives and as you live, I will not leave you." So he got up and followed her.

31Gehazi went on ahead and laid the staff on the boy's face, but there was no sound or response. So Gehazi went back

וַיָּשָׁב לִקְרָאתוֹ וַיַּגֶּד־ לוֹ לֵאמֹר לֹא הֵקִיץ הַנָּעַר׃
the-boy he-awoke not to-say to-him and-he-told to-meet-him so-he-went-back

וַיָּבֹא אֱלִישָׁע הַבָּיְתָה וְהִנֵּה הַנַּעַר מֵת מֻשְׁכָּב
lying he-was-dead the-boy then-see! to-the-house Elisha when-he-reached (32)

עַל־ מִטָּתוֹ׃ וַיָּבֹא וַיִּסְגֹּר הַדֶּלֶת בְּעַד שְׁנֵיהֶם
two-of-them behind the-door and-he-shut and-he-went-in (33) couch-of-him on

וַיִּתְפַּלֵּל אֶל־ יְהוָה׃ וַיַּעַל וַיִּשְׁכַּב עַל־ הַיֶּלֶד
the-boy upon and-he-lay then-he-got-on (34) Yahweh to and-he-prayed

וַיָּשֶׂם פִּיו עַל־ פִּיו וְעֵינָיו עַל־ עֵינָיו
eyes-of-him to and-eyes-of-him mouth-of-him to mouth-of-him and-he-put

וְכַפָּיו עַל־ כַּפָּו° וַיִּגְהַר עָלָיו וַיָּחָם
and-he-grew-warm upon-him and-he-stretched-out hands-of-him to and-hands-of-him

בְּשַׂר הַיָּלֶד׃ וַיָּשָׁב וַיֵּלֶךְ בַּבַּיִת אַחַת
once in-the-room and-he-walked and-he-turned-away (35) the-boy body-of

הֵנָּה וְאַחַת הֵנָּה וַיַּעַל וַיִּגְהַר עָלָיו
upon-him and-he-stretched-out then-he-got-on to-there and-once to-here

וַיְזוֹרֵר הַנַּעַר עַד־ שֶׁבַע פְּעָמִים וַיִּפְקַח הַנַּעַר אֶת־ עֵינָיו׃
eyes-of-him *** the-boy and-he-opened times seven to the-boy and-he-sneezed

וַיִּקְרָא אֶל־ גֵּיחֲזִי וַיֹּאמֶר קְרָא אֶל־ הַשּׁוּנַמִּית הַזֹּאת
the-this the-Shunnamite to call! and-he-said Gehazi to and-he-summoned (36)

וַיִּקְרָאֶהָ וַתָּבוֹא אֵלָיו וַיֹּאמֶר שְׂאִי בְנֵךְ׃
son-of-you take! and-he-said to-him and-she-came and-he-called-her

וַתָּבֹא וַתִּפֹּל עַל־ רַגְלָיו וַתִּשְׁתַּחוּ אָרְצָה
to-ground and-she-bowed feet-of-him at and-she-fell and-she-came-in (37)

וַתִּשָּׂא אֶת־ בְּנָהּ וַתֵּצֵא׃ וֶאֱלִישָׁע שָׁב
he-returned and-Elisha (38) and-she-went-out son-of-her *** then-she-took

הַגִּלְגָּלָה וְהָרָעָב בָּאָרֶץ וּבְנֵי הַנְּבִיאִים
the-prophets and-sons-of in-the-region and-the-famine to-the-Gilgal

יֹשְׁבִים לְפָנָיו וַיֹּאמֶר לְנַעֲרוֹ שְׁפֹת הַסִּיר
the-pot put-on! to-servant-of-him and-he-said before-him ones-sitting

הַגְּדוֹלָה וּבַשֵּׁל נָזִיד לִבְנֵי הַנְּבִיאִים׃ וַיֵּצֵא אֶחָד
one and-he-went-out (39) the-prophets for-sons-of stew and-cook! the-large

אֶל־ הַשָּׂדֶה לְלַקֵּט אֹרֹת וַיִּמְצָא גֶּפֶן שָׂדֶה וַיְלַקֵּט
and-he-gathered field vine-of and-he-found herbs to-gather the-field into

מִמֶּנּוּ פַּקֻּעֹת שָׂדֶה מְלֹא בִגְדוֹ וַיָּבֹא
when-he-returned cloak-of-him fullness-of field gourds-of from-him

וַיְפַלַּח אֶל־ סִיר הַנָּזִיד כִּי־ לֹא יָדָעוּ׃ וַיִּצְקוּ
and-they-poured (40) they-knew not though the-stew pot-of into then-he-cut-up

to meet Elisha and told him,
"The boy has not awakened."
32When Elisha reached the
house, there was the boy lying
dead on his couch. 33He went
in, shut the door on the two of
them and prayed to the LORD.
34Then he got on the bed and
lay upon the boy, mouth to
mouth, eyes to eyes, hands to
hands. As he stretched himself
out upon him, the boy's body
grew warm. 35Elisha turned
away and walked back and
forth in the room and then got
on the bed and stretched out
upon him once more. The boy
sneezed seven times and
opened his eyes.
36Elisha summoned Gehazi
and said, "Call the Shunammite." And he did. When she
came, he said, "Take your
son." 37She came in, fell at his
feet and bowed to the ground.
Then she took her son and
went out.

Death in the Pot

38Elisha returned to Gilgal
and there was a famine in that
region. While the company of
the prophets was meeting
with him, he said to his servant, "Put on the large pot and
cook some stew for these
men."
39One of them went out into
the fields to gather herbs and
found a wild vine. He gathered some of its gourds and
filled the fold of his cloak.
When he returned, he cut
them up into the pot of stew,
though no one knew what

°34 ק כפיו

וְהֵמָּה מֵהַנָּזִיד כְּאָכְלָם וַיְהִי לֶאֱכוֹל לַאֲנָשִׁים
then-they from-the-stew as-to-eat-them but-he-was to-eat for-the-men

וְלֹא הָאֱלֹהִים אִישׁ בַּסִּיר מָוֶת וַיֹּאמְרוּ צָעָקוּ
and-not the-God man-of in-the-pot death and-they-said they-cried-out

הַסִּיר אֶל־ וַיַּשְׁלֵךְ קֶמַח וּקְחוּ־ וַיֹּאמֶר (41) לֶאֱכֹל׃ יָכְלוּ
the-pot into and-he-put flour now-get! and-he-said (41) to-eat they-could

רָע דָּבָר הָיָה וְלֹא וְיֹאכֵלוּ לָעָם צַק וַיֹּאמֶר
harmful anything he-was and-not so-they-eat to-the-people serve! and-he-said

לְאִישׁ וַיָּבֵא שָׁלִשָׁה מִבַּעַל בָּא וְאִישׁ (42) בַּסִּיר׃
to-man-of and-he-brought Shalishah from-Baal he-came now-man (42) in-the-pot

וְכַרְמֶל שְׂעֹרִים לֶחֶם עֶשְׂרִים־ בִּכּוּרִים לֶחֶם הָאֱלֹהִים
and-new-grain barleys loaf-of twenty first-fruits bread-of the-God

וַיֹּאמֶר (43) וְיֹאכֵלוּ׃ לָעָם תֵּן וַיֹּאמֶר בְּצִקְלֹנוֹ
and-he-asked (43) so-they-eat to-the-people give! and-he-said in-bag-of-him

תֵּן וַיֹּאמֶר אִישׁ מֵאָה לִפְנֵי זֶה אֶתֵּן מָה מְשָׁרְתוֹ
give! but-he-answered man hundred before this can-I-set how? one-serving-him

וְהוֹתֵר׃ אָכֹל יְהוָה אָמַר כֹה כִּי וְיֹאכְלוּ לָעָם
and-to-be-left-over to-eat Yahweh he-says this for so-they-eat to-the-people

כִּדְבַר וַיּוֹתִרוּ וַיֹּאכְלוּ לִפְנֵיהֶם וַיִּתֵּן (44)
as-word-of and-they-had-left-over and-they-ate before-them then-he-set (44)

גָּדוֹל אִישׁ הָיָה אֲרָם מֶלֶךְ־ צְבָא שַׂר־ וְנַעֲמָן (5:1) יְהוָה׃
great man he-was Aram king-of army-of commander-of now-Naaman (5:1) Yahweh

בוֹ כִּי־ פָנִים וּנְשֻׂא אֲדֹנָיו לִפְנֵי
through-him because faces and-being-regarded-of masters-of-him before

חַיִל גִּבּוֹר הָיָה וְהָאִישׁ לַאֲרָם תְּשׁוּעָה יְהוָה נָתַן־
valiant soldier he-was and-the-man to-Aram victory Yahweh he-gave

וַיִּשְׁבּוּ גְדוּדִים יָצְאוּ וַאֲרָם (2) מְצֹרָע׃
and-they-took-captive bands they-went-out and-Aram (2) having-leprosy

נַעֲמָן׃ אֵשֶׁת לִפְנֵי וַתְּהִי קְטַנָּה נַעֲרָה יִשְׂרָאֵל מֵאֶרֶץ
Naaman wife-of before and-she-was young girl Israel from-land-of

הַנָּבִיא לִפְנֵי אֲדֹנִי אַחֲלֵי גְּבִרְתָּהּ אֶל־ וַתֹּאמֶר (3)
the-prophet before master-of-me if-only mistress-of-her to and-she-said (3)

וַיָּבֹא (4) מִצָּרַעְתּוֹ׃ אֹתוֹ יֶאֱסֹף אָז בְּשֹׁמְרוֹן אֲשֶׁר
and-he-went (4) of-leprosy-of-him him he-would-cure then in-Samaria who

הַנַּעֲרָה דִּבְּרָה וְכָזֹאת כָּזֹאת לֵאמֹר לַאדֹנָיו וַיַּגֵּד
the-girl she-said and-as-that as-this to-say to-masters-of-him and-he-told

בֹּא לֶךְ־ אֲרָם מֶלֶךְ־ וַיֹּאמֶר (5) יִשְׂרָאֵל׃ מֵאֶרֶץ אֲשֶׁר
go! leave! Aram king-of and-he-replied (5) Israel from-land-of who

they were. [40]The stew was
poured out for the men, but as
they began to eat it, they cried
out, "O man of God, there is
death in the pot!" And they
could not eat it.
[41]Elisha said, "Get some
flour." He put it into the pot
and said, "Serve it to the
people to eat." And there was
nothing harmful in the pot.

Feeding of a Hundred

[42]A man came from Baal
Shalishah, bringing the man
of God twenty loaves of barley
bread baked from the first ripe
grain, along with some heads
of new grain. "Give it to the
people to eat," Elisha said.
[43]"How can I set this before
a hundred men?" his servant
asked.
But Elisha answered, "Give
it to the people to eat. For this
is what the LORD says: 'They
will eat and have some left
over.' " [44]Then he set it before
them, and they ate and had
some left over, according to
the word of the LORD.

Naaman Healed of Leprosy

5 Now Naaman was com-
mander of the army of the
king of Aram. He was a great
man in the sight of his master
and highly regarded, because
through him the LORD had giv-
en victory to Aram. He was a
valiant soldier, but he had leprosy.[d]
[2]Now bands from Aram had
gone out and had taken captive a young girl from Israel,
and she served Naaman's
wife. [3]She said to her mistress,
"If only my master would see
the prophet who is in Samaria!
He would cure him of his leprosy."
[4]Naaman went to his master
and told him what the girl
from Israel had said. [5]"By all
means, go," the king of Aram

[d]1 The Hebrew word was used for various diseases affecting the skin—not necessarily leprosy.

וְאֶשְׁלְחָה סֵפֶר אֶל־ מֶלֶךְ יִשְׂרָאֵל וַיֵּלֶךְ וַיִּקַּח בְּיָדוֹ
in-hand-of-him and-he-took so-he-left Israel king-of to letter and-I-will-send

עֶשֶׂר כִּכְּרֵי־ כֶסֶף וְשֵׁשֶׁת אֲלָפִים זָהָב וְעֶשֶׂר חֲלִיפוֹת בְּגָדִים׃
clothings sets-of and-ten gold thousands and-six-of silver talents-of ten

וַיָּבֵא הַסֵּפֶר אֶל־ מֶלֶךְ יִשְׂרָאֵל לֵאמֹר וְעַתָּה כְּבוֹא
as-to-come and-now to-say Israel king-of to the-letter and-he-took (6)

הַסֵּפֶר הַזֶּה אֵלֶיךָ הִנֵּה שָׁלַחְתִּי אֵלֶיךָ אֶת־ נַעֲמָן עַבְדִּי
servant-of-me Naaman *** to-you I-send see! to-you the-this the-letter

וַאֲסַפְתּוֹ מִצָּרַעְתּוֹ׃ וַיְהִי כִּקְרֹא מֶלֶךְ־
king-of as-to-read and-he-was (7) of-leprosy-of-him so-you-may-cure-him

יִשְׂרָאֵל אֶת־ הַסֵּפֶר וַיִּקְרַע בְּגָדָיו וַיֹּאמֶר הַאֱלֹהִים אָנִי
I God? and-he-said robes-of-him then-he-tore the-letter *** Israel

לְהָמִית וּלְהַחֲיוֹת כִּי־ זֶה שֹׁלֵחַ אֵלַי לֶאֱסֹף אִישׁ
someone to-cure to-me sending this-one that and-to-bring-to-life to-kill

מִצָּרַעְתּוֹ כִּי אַךְ־ דְּעוּ־ נָא וּרְאוּ כִּי־ מִתְאַנֶּה הוּא
he picking-quarrel that and-see! now! know! indeed so of-leprosy-of-him

לִי׃ וַיְהִי כִּשְׁמֹעַ ׀ אֱלִישָׁע אִישׁ־ הָאֱלֹהִים כִּי־ קָרַע
he-tore that the-God man-of Elisha when-to-hear and-he-was (8) with-me

מֶלֶךְ־ יִשְׂרָאֵל אֶת־ בְּגָדָיו וַיִּשְׁלַח אֶל־ הַמֶּלֶךְ לֵאמֹר לָמָּה
why? to-say the-king to then-he-sent robes-of-him *** Israel king-of

קָרַעְתָּ בְּגָדֶיךָ יָבֹא־ נָא אֵלַי וְיֵדַע כִּי
that and-he-will-know to-me now! have-him-come robes-of-you you-tore

יֵשׁ נָבִיא בְּיִשְׂרָאֵל׃ וַיָּבֹא נַעֲמָן בְּסוּסָו
with-horses-of-him Naaman so-he-went (9) in-Israel prophet there-is

וּבְרִכְבּוֹ וַיַּעֲמֹד פֶּתַח־ הַבַּיִת לֶאֱלִישָׁע׃
of-Elisha the-house door-of and-he-stopped and-with-chariot-of-him

וַיִּשְׁלַח אֵלָיו אֱלִישָׁע מַלְאָךְ לֵאמֹר הָלוֹךְ וְרָחַצְתָּ שֶׁבַע־
seven and-you-wash to-go to-say messenger Elisha to-him and-he-sent (10)

פְּעָמִים בַּיַּרְדֵּן וְיָשֹׁב בְּשָׂרְךָ לְךָ וּטְהָר׃
and-be-clean! to-you flesh-of-you and-he-will-be-restored in-the-Jordan times

וַיִּקְצֹף נַעֲמָן וַיֵּלַךְ וַיֹּאמֶר הִנֵּה אָמַרְתִּי
I-thought see! and-he-said and-he-went-away Naaman but-he-became-angry (11)

אֵלַי ׀ יֵצֵא יָצוֹא וְעָמַד וְקָרָא
and-he-would-call and-he-would-stand to-come-out he-would-come-out to-me

בְּשֵׁם־ יְהוָה אֱלֹהָיו וְהֵנִיף יָדוֹ אֶל־ הַמָּקוֹם
the-spot over hand-of-him and-he-would-wave God-of-him Yahweh on-name-of

וְאָסַף הַמְּצֹרָע׃ הֲלֹא טוֹב אֲבָנָה וּפַרְפַּר
and-Pharpar Abana better not? (12) the-part-being-leprous and-he-would-cure

replied. "I will send a letter to the king of Israel." So Naaman left, taking with him ten talents[e] of silver, six thousand shekels[f] of gold and ten sets of clothing. [6]The letter that he took to the king of Israel read: "With this letter I am sending my servant Naaman to you so that you may cure him of his leprosy."

[7]As soon as the king of Israel read the letter, he tore his robes and said, "Am I God? Can I kill and bring back to life? Why does this fellow send someone to me to be cured of his leprosy? See how he is trying to pick a quarrel with me!"

[8]When Elisha the man of God heard that the king of Israel had torn his robes, he sent him this message: "Why have you torn your robes? Have the man come to me and he will know that there is a prophet in Israel." [9]So Naaman went with his horses and chariots and stopped at the door of Elisha's house. [10]Elisha sent a messenger to say to him, "Go, wash yourself seven times in the Jordan, and your flesh will be restored and you will be cleansed."

[11]But Naaman went away angry and said, "I thought that he would surely come out to me and stand and call on the name of the LORD his God, wave his hand over the spot and cure me of my leprosy. [12]Are not Abana and Pharpar,

[e]5 That is, about 750 pounds (about 340 kilograms)
[f]5 That is, about 150 pounds (about 70 kilograms)

°9 ק בסוסיו
°12 ק אמנה

נַהֲרוֹת דַּמֶּשֶׂק מִכֹּל מֵימֵי יִשְׂרָאֵל הֲלֹא־ אֶרְחַץ בָּהֶם
in-them I-could-wash not? Israel waters-of than-all-of Damascus rivers-of

וְטָהָרְתִּי וַיִּפֶן וַיֵּלֶךְ בְּחֵמָה׃ וַיִּגְּשׁוּ
and-they-went (13) in-rage and-he-went-off so-he-turned and-I-would-be-cleansed

עֲבָדָיו וַיְדַבְּרוּ אֵלָיו וַיֹּאמְרוּ אָבִי דָּבָר גָּדוֹל
great thing father-of-me and-they-said to-him and-they-spoke servants-of-him

הַנָּבִיא דִּבֶּר אֵלֶיךָ הֲלוֹא תַעֲשֶׂה וְאַף כִּי־ אָמַר
he-tells when then-how-much-more you-would-do not? to-you he-told the-prophet

אֵלֶיךָ רְחַץ וּטְהָר׃ וַיֵּרֶד וַיִּטְבֹּל בַּיַּרְדֵּן
in-the-Jordan and-he-dipped so-he-went-down (14) and-be-cleansed! wash! to-you

שֶׁבַע פְּעָמִים כִּדְבַר אִישׁ הָאֱלֹהִים וַיָּשָׁב בְּשָׂרוֹ
flesh-of-him and-he-was-restored the-God man-of as-word-of times seven

כִּבְשַׂר נַעַר קָטֹן וַיִּטְהָר׃ וַיָּשָׁב אֶל־ אִישׁ
man-of to then-he-went-back (15) and-he-became-clean young boy as-flesh-of

הָאֱלֹהִים הוּא וְכָל־ מַחֲנֵהוּ וַיָּבֹא וַיַּעֲמֹד לְפָנָיו
before-him and-he-stood and-he-went attendant-of-him and-all-of he the-God

וַיֹּאמֶר הִנֵּה־ נָא יָדַעְתִּי כִּי אֵין אֱלֹהִים בְּכָל־ הָאָרֶץ כִּי
except the-world in-all-of God there-is-no that I-know now! see! and-he-said

אִם־בְּיִשְׂרָאֵל וְעַתָּה קַח־ נָא בְרָכָה מֵאֵת עַבְדֶּךָ׃ וַיֹּאמֶר
but-he-said (16) servant-of-you from gift now! accept! and-now in-Israel only

חַי־ יְהוָה אֲשֶׁר־ עָמַדְתִּי לְפָנָיו אִם־ אֶקָּח וַיִּפְצַר־
and-he-urged I-will-accept not before-him I-serve whom Yahweh life-of

בּוֹ לָקַחַת וַיְמָאֵן׃ וַיֹּאמֶר נַעֲמָן וָלֹא
if-not Naaman and-he-said (17) but-he-refused to-accept with-him

יֻתַּן־ נָא לְעַבְדְּךָ מַשָּׂא צֶמֶד־ פְּרָדִים אֲדָמָה כִּי לוֹא־
not for earth mules pair-of load-of servant-of-you now! let-him-be-given

יַעֲשֶׂה עוֹד עַבְדְּךָ עֹלָה וָזֶבַח לֵאלֹהִים
to-gods or-sacrifice burnt-offering servant-of-you again he-will-make

אֲחֵרִים כִּי אִם־ לַיהוָה׃ לַדָּבָר הַזֶּה יִסְלַח
may-he-forgive the-this to-the-thing (18) to-Yahweh only except other-ones

יְהוָה לְעַבְדֶּךָ בְּבוֹא אֲדֹנִי בֵית־ רִמּוֹן
Rimmon temple-of master-of-me when-to-enter to-servant-of-you Yahweh

לְהִשְׁתַּחֲוֺת שָׁמָּה וְהוּא ׀ נִשְׁעָן עַל־ יָדִי וְהִשְׁתַּחֲוֵיתִי בֵּית
temple-of and-I-bow arm-of-me on leaning and-he at-there to-bow-down

רִמֹּן בְּהִשְׁתַּחֲוָיָתִי בֵּית רִמֹּן יִסְלַח־ נא* יְהוָה
Yahweh now! may-he-forgive Rimmon temple-of when-to-bow-down-me Rimmon

לְעַבְדְּךָ בַּדָּבָר הַזֶּה׃ וַיֹּאמֶר לוֹ לֵךְ לְשָׁלוֹם
in-peace go! to-him and-he-said (19) the-this for-the-thing to-servant-of-you

the rivers of Damascus, better
than any of the waters of Israel? Couldn't I wash in them
and be cleansed?" So he
turned and went off in a rage.
13 Naaman's servants went to
him and said, "My father, if
the prophet had told you to do
some great thing, would you
not have done it? How much
more, then, when he tells you,
'Wash and be cleansed'!" 14 So
he went down and dipped
himself in the Jordan seven
times, as the man of God had
told him, and his flesh was restored and became clean like
that of a young boy.
15 Then Naaman and all his
attendants went back to the
man of God. He stood before
him and said, "Now I know
that there is no God in all the
world except in Israel. Please
accept now a gift from your
servant."
16 The prophet answered,
"As surely as the LORD lives,
whom I serve, I will not accept
a thing." And even though
Naaman urged him, he
refused.
17 "If you will not," said Naaman, "please let me, your servant, be given as much earth
as a pair of mules can carry, for
your servant will never again
make burnt offerings and sacrifices to any other god but the
LORD. 18 But may the LORD forgive your servant for this one
thing: When my master enters
the temple of Rimmon to bow
down and he is leaning on my
arm and I bow there also—
when I bow down in the temple of Rimmon, may the LORD
forgive your servant for this."
19 "Go in peace," Elisha said.

*18 Many mss omit this word or indicate in the *Qere* that it is not to be read.

וַיֵּלֶךְ מֵאִתּוֹ כִּבְרַת־ אָרֶץ׃ וַיֹּאמֶר גֵּיחֲזִי נַעַר
servant-of Gehazi and-he-said (20) land distance-of from-with-him so-he-went

אֱלִישָׁע אִישׁ־ הָאֱלֹהִים הִנֵּה ׀ חָשַׂךְ אֲדֹנִי אֶת־ נַעֲמָן הָאֲרַמִּי
the-Aramean Naaman *** master-of-me he-was-easy see! the-God man-of Elisha

הַזֶּה מִקַּחַת מִיָּדוֹ אֵת אֲשֶׁר־ הֵבִיא חַי־ יְהוָה
Yahweh life-of he-brought what *** from-hand-of-him from-to-accept the-this

כִּי־ אִם־ רַצְתִּי אַחֲרָיו וְלָקַחְתִּי מֵאִתּוֹ מְאוּמָה׃
something from-with-him and-I-will-get after-him I-will-run indeed that

וַיִּרְדֹּף גֵּיחֲזִי אַחֲרֵי נַעֲמָן וַיִּרְאֶה נַעֲמָן רָץ אַחֲרָיו
after-him running Naaman when-he-saw Naaman after Gehazi so-he-pursued (21)

וַיִּפֹּל מֵעַל הַמֶּרְכָּבָה לִקְרָאתוֹ וַיֹּאמֶר הֲשָׁלוֹם׃
all-right? and-he-asked to-meet-him the-chariot from-on then-he-got-down

וַיֹּאמֶר ׀ שָׁלוֹם אֲדֹנִי שִׁלְּחַנִי לֵאמֹר הִנֵּה עַתָּה זֶה
here now see! to-say he-sent-me master-of-me all-right and-he-answered (22)

בָּאוּ אֵלַי שְׁנֵי־ נְעָרִים מֵהַר אֶפְרַיִם מִבְּנֵי
from-sons-of Ephraim from-hill-country-of young-men two-of to-me they-came

הַנְּבִיאִים תְּנָה־ נָּא לָהֶם כִּכַּר־ כֶּסֶף וּשְׁתֵּי חֲלִפוֹת בְּגָדִים׃
clothes sets-of and-two-of silver talent-of to-them now! give! the-prophets

וַיֹּאמֶר נַעֲמָן הוֹאֵל קַח כִּכָּרָיִם וַיִּפְרָץ־ בּוֹ
with-him and-he-urged two-talents take! be-willing! Naaman and-he-said (23)

וַיָּצַר כִּכְּרַיִם כֶּסֶף בִּשְׁנֵי חֲרִטִים וּשְׁתֵּי חֲלִפוֹת בְּגָדִים
clothes sets-of and-two-of bags in-two-of silver two-talents then-he-tied-up

וַיִּתֵּן אֶל־ שְׁנֵי נְעָרָיו וַיִּשְׂאוּ לְפָנָיו׃
ahead-of-him and-they-carried servants-of-him two-of to and-he-gave

וַיָּבֹא אֶל־ הָעֹפֶל וַיִּקַּח מִיָּדָם וַיִּפְקֹד
and-he-put-away from-hand-of-them then-he-took the-hill to when-he-came (24)

בַּבָּיִת וַיְשַׁלַּח אֶת־ הָאֲנָשִׁים וַיֵּלֵכוּ׃ וְהוּא־
then-he (25) and-they-left the-men *** then-he-sent-away in-the-house

בָא וַיַּעֲמֹד אֶל־ אֲדֹנָיו וַיֹּאמֶר אֵלָיו אֱלִישָׁע
Elisha to-him and-he-asked masters-of-him before and-he-stood he-went-in

מֵאַ֯ן גֵּחֲזִי וַיֹּאמֶר לֹא־ הָלַךְ עַבְדְּךָ אָנֶה
to-here servant-of-you he-went not and-he-answered Gehazi from-where?

וָאָנָה׃ וַיֹּאמֶר אֵלָיו לֹא־ לִבִּי הָלַךְ כַּאֲשֶׁר
as-when he-went spirit-of-me not to-him but-he-said (26) or-to-there

הָפַךְ־ אִישׁ מֵעַל מֶרְכַּבְתּוֹ לִקְרָאתֶךָ הַעֵת לָקַחַת אֶת־
*** to-take time? to-meet-you chariot-of-him from-on man he-got-down

הַכֶּסֶף וְלָקַחַת בְּגָדִים וְזֵיתִים וּכְרָמִים וְצֹאן וּבָקָר
or-herd or-flock or-vineyards or-olive-groves clothes or-to-accept the-silver

After Naaman had traveled some distance, [20]Gehazi, the servant of Elisha the man of God, said to himself, "My master was too easy on Naaman, this Aramean, by not accepting from him what he brought. As surely as the LORD lives, I will run after him and get something from him."

[21]So Gehazi hurried after Naaman. When Naaman saw him running toward him, he got down from the chariot to meet him. "Is everything all right?" he asked.

[22]"Everything is all right," Gehazi answered. "My master sent me to say, 'Two young men from the company of the prophets have just come to me from the hill country of Ephraim. Please give them a talent[g] of silver and two sets of clothing.' "

[23]"By all means, take two talents," said Naaman. He urged Gehazi to accept them, and then tied up the two talents of silver in two bags, with two sets of clothing. He gave them to two of his servants, and they carried them ahead of Gehazi. [24]When Gehazi came to the hill, he took the things from the servants and put them away in the house. He sent the men away and they left. [25]Then he went in and stood before his master Elisha.

"Where have you been, Gehazi?" Elisha asked.

"Your servant didn't go anywhere," Gehazi answered.

[26]But Elisha said to him, "Was not my spirit with you when the man got down from his chariot to meet you? Is this the time to take money, or to accept clothes, olive groves, vineyards, flocks, herds, or

g22 That is, about 75 pounds (about 34 kilograms)

°25 ק מאין

וַעֲבָדִים וּשְׁפָחוֹת׃ וְצָרַעַת נַעֲמָן תִּדְבַּק־
she-will-cling Naaman now-leprosy-of (27) or-maidservants or-menservants

בְּךָ וּבְזַרְעֲךָ* לְעוֹלָם וַיֵּצֵא מִלְּפָנָיו
from-presences-of-him then-he-went to-forever and-to-descendant-of-you to-you

מְצֹרָע כַּשָּׁלֶג׃ וַיֹּאמְרוּ בְנֵי־ הַנְּבִיאִים אֶל־אֱלִישָׁע
Elisha to the-prophets sons-of and-they-said (6:1) as-the-snow being-leprous

הִנֵּה־ נָא הַמָּקוֹם אֲשֶׁר אֲנַחְנוּ יֹשְׁבִים שָׁם לְפָנֶיךָ צַר מִמֶּנּוּ׃
for-us too-small before-you there ones-sitting we where the-place now! look!

נֵלְכָה־ נָּא עַד־ הַיַּרְדֵּן וְנִקְחָה מִשָּׁם אִישׁ קוֹרָה אֶחָת
one pole each from-there and-let-us-get the-Jordan to now! let-us-go (2)

וְנַעֲשֶׂה־ לָּנוּ שָׁם מָקוֹם לָשֶׁבֶת שָׁם וַיֹּאמֶר לֵכוּ׃
go! and-he-said there to-live place there for-us and-let-us-build

וַיֹּאמֶר הָאֶחָד הוֹאֶל נָא וְלֵךְ אֶת־ עֲבָדֶיךָ
servants-of-you with and-come! now! be-willing! the-one then-he-said (3)

וַיֹּאמֶר אֲנִי אֵלֵךְ׃ וַיֵּלֶךְ אִתָּם וַיָּבֹאוּ
and-they-went with-them and-he-went (4) I-will-go I and-he-replied

הַיַּרְדֵּנָה וַיִּגְזְרוּ הָעֵצִים׃ וַיְהִי הָאֶחָד מַפִּיל
cutting-down the-one and-he-was (5) the-trees and-they-cut-down to-the-Jordan

הַקּוֹרָה וְאֶת־ הַבַּרְזֶל נָפַל אֶל־ הַמָּיִם וַיִּצְעַק וַיֹּאמֶר
and-he-said and-he-cried-out the-waters into he-fell the-iron and the-tree

אֲהָהּ אֲדֹנִי וְהוּא שָׁאוּל׃ וַיֹּאמֶר אִישׁ־ הָאֱלֹהִים
the-God man-of and-he-asked (6) being-borrowed now-he lord-of-me oh!

אָנָה נָפָל וַיַּרְאֵהוּ אֶת־ הַמָּקוֹם וַיִּקְצָב־ עֵץ
stick then-he-cut the-place *** when-he-showed-him he-fell at-where?

וַיַּשְׁלֶךְ־ שָׁמָּה וַיָּצֶף הַבַּרְזֶל׃ וַיֹּאמֶר הָרֶם
lift-out! and-he-said (7) the-iron and-he-made-float at-there and-he-threw

לָךְ וַיִּשְׁלַח יָדוֹ וַיִּקָּחֵהוּ׃ וּמֶלֶךְ אֲרָם
Aram now-king-of (8) and-he-took-him hand-of-him then-he-reached-out to-you

הָיָה נִלְחָם בְּיִשְׂרָאֵל וַיִּוָּעַץ אֶל־ עֲבָדָיו לֵאמֹר אֶל־
in to-say officers-of-him with and-he-conferred with-Israel warring he-was

מְקוֹם פְּלֹנִי אַלְמֹנִי תַּחֲנֹתִי׃ וַיִּשְׁלַח אִישׁ הָאֱלֹהִים אֶל־ מֶלֶךְ
king-of to the-God man-of and-he-sent (9) camp-of-me such such place-of

יִשְׂרָאֵל לֵאמֹר הִשָּׁמֶר מֵעֲבֹר הַמָּקוֹם הַזֶּה כִּי־ שָׁם אֲרָם
Aram there for the-that the-place of-to-pass beware! to-say Israel

נְחִתִּים׃ וַיִּשְׁלַח מֶלֶךְ יִשְׂרָאֵל אֶל־ הַמָּקוֹם אֲשֶׁר אָמַר־
he-told that the-place to Israel king-of and-he-sent (10) ones-going-down

לוֹ אִישׁ־ הָאֱלֹהִים וְהִזְהִירֹה° וְנִשְׁמַר שָׁם לֹא אַחַת
once not there so-he-was-on-guard and-he-warned-him the-God man-of to-him

menservants and maidservants? [27]Naaman's leprosy will cling to you and to your descendants forever." Then Gehazi went from Elisha's presence and he was leprous, as white as snow.

An Axhead Floats

6 The company of the prophets said to Elisha, "Look, the place where we meet with you is too small for us. [2]Let us go to the Jordan, where each of us can get a pole; and let us build a place there for us to live."

And he said, "Go."

[3]Then one of them said, "Won't you please come with your servants?"

"I will," Elisha replied. [4]And he went with them.

They went to the Jordan and began to cut down trees. [5]As one of them was cutting down a tree, the iron axhead fell into the water. "Oh, my lord," he cried out, "it was borrowed!"

[6]The man of God asked, "Where did it fall?" When he showed him the place, Elisha cut a stick and threw it there, and made the iron float. [7]"Lift it out," he said. Then the man reached out his hand and took it.

Elisha Traps Blinded Arameans

[8]Now the king of Aram was at war with Israel. After conferring with his officers, he said, "I will set up my camp in such and such a place."

[9]The man of God sent word to the king of Israel: "Beware of passing that place, because the Arameans are going down there." [10]So the king of Israel checked on the place indicated by the man of God. Time and again Elisha warned the king, so that he was on his guard in such places.

*27 Most mss have the accent *tiphha* (ךָ֖).

°*10* ק והזהירו

וְלֹא שְׁתָּיִם׃ (11) וַיִּסָּעֵר לֵב מֶלֶךְ־אֲרָם עַל־הַדָּבָר
the-thing over Aram king-of heart-of and-he-was-enraged (11) twice and-not

הַזֶּה וַיִּקְרָא אֶל־עֲבָדָיו וַיֹּאמֶר אֲלֵיהֶם הֲלוֹא תַּגִּידוּ
you-tell not? to-them and-he-said officers-of-him to and-he-summoned the-this

לִי מִי מִשֶּׁלָּנוּ אֶל־מֶלֶךְ יִשְׂרָאֵל׃ (12) וַיֹּאמֶר אַחַד
one and-he-said (12) Israel king-of with from-who-of-us who? to-me

מֵעֲבָדָיו לוֹא אֲדֹנִי הַמֶּלֶךְ כִּי־אֱלִישָׁע הַנָּבִיא אֲשֶׁר
who the-prophet Elisha but the-king lord-of-me none from-officers-of-him

בְּיִשְׂרָאֵל יַגִּיד לְמֶלֶךְ יִשְׂרָאֵל אֶת־הַדְּבָרִים אֲשֶׁר תְּדַבֵּר בַּחֲדַר
in-room-of-you you-speak that the-words *** Israel to-king-of he-tells in-Israel

מִשְׁכָּבֶךָ׃ (13) וַיֹּאמֶר לְכוּ וּרְאוּ אֵיכֹה הוּא וְאֶשְׁלַח
so-I-can-send he where and-find-out! go! and-he-ordered (13) sleep-of-you

וְאֶקָּחֵהוּ וַיֻּגַּד־לוֹ לֵאמֹר הִנֵּה בְדֹתָן׃
in-Dothan see! to-say to-him and-he-was-reported and-I-can-capture-him

(14) וַיִּשְׁלַח־שָׁמָּה סוּסִים וְרֶכֶב וְחַיִל כָּבֵד וַיָּבֹאוּ
and-they-went strong and-force and-chariot horses to-there then-he-sent (14)

לַיְלָה וַיַּקִּפוּ עַל־הָעִיר׃ (15) וַיַּשְׁכֵּם מְשָׁרֵת
one-serving when-he-got-up (15) the-city around and-they-surrounded night

אִישׁ הָאֱלֹהִים לָקוּם וַיֵּצֵא וְהִנֵּה־חַיִל סוֹבֵב אֶת־
*** surrounding army then-see! and-he-went-out to-rise the-God man-of

הָעִיר וְסוּס וָרֶכֶב וַיֹּאמֶר נַעֲרוֹ אֵלָיו אֲהָהּ
oh! to-him servant-of-him and-he-asked and-chariot and-horse the-city

אֲדֹנִי אֵיכָה נַעֲשֶׂה׃ (16) וַיֹּאמֶר אַל־תִּירָא כִּי
for you-be-afraid not and-he-answered (16) shall-we-do what? lord-of-me

רַבִּים אֲשֶׁר אִתָּנוּ מֵאֲשֶׁר אוֹתָם׃ (17) וַיִּתְפַּלֵּל אֱלִישָׁע
Elisha and-he-prayed (17) with-them more-than-who with-us who ones-many

וַיֹּאמַר יְהוָה פְּקַח־נָא אֶת־עֵינָיו וְיִרְאֶה וַיִּפְקַח
then-he-opened so-may-he-see eyes-of-him *** now! open! Yahweh and-he-said

יְהוָה אֶת־עֵינֵי הַנַּעַר וַיַּרְא וְהִנֵּה הָהָר מָלֵא
being-full the-hill and-see! and-he-looked the-servant eyes-of *** Yahweh

סוּסִים וְרֶכֶב אֵשׁ סְבִיבֹת אֱלִישָׁע׃ (18) וַיֵּרְדוּ
and-they-came-down (18) Elisha ones-around fire and-chariot-of horses

אֵלָיו וַיִּתְפַּלֵּל אֱלִישָׁע אֶל־יְהוָה וַיֹּאמַר הַךְ־נָא אֶת־
*** now! strike! and-he-said Yahweh to Elisha and-he-prayed toward-him

הַגּוֹי־הַזֶּה בַּסַּנְוֵרִים וַיַּכֵּם בַּסַּנְוֵרִים
with-the-blindnesses so-he-struck-them with-the-blindnesses the-this the-people

כִּדְבַר אֱלִישָׁע׃ (19) וַיֹּאמֶר אֲלֵהֶם אֱלִישָׁע לֹא זֶה הַדֶּרֶךְ
the-road this not Elisha to-them and-he-told (19) Elisha as-request-of

11This enraged the king of
Aram. He summoned his
officers and demanded of
them, "Will you not tell me
which of us is on the side of
the king of Israel?"
12"None of us, my lord the
king," said one of his officers,
"but Elisha, the prophet who
is in Israel, tells the king of Israel the very words you speak
in your bedroom."
13"Go, find out where he is,"
the king ordered, "so I can
send men and capture him."
The report came back: "He is
in Dothan." 14Then he sent
horses and chariots and a
strong force there. They went
by night and surrounded the
city.
15When the servant of the
man of God got up and went
out early the next morning, an
army with horses and chariots
had surrounded the city. "Oh,
my lord, what shall we do?"
the servant asked.
16"Don't be afraid," the
prophet answered. "Those
who are with us are more than
those who are with them."
17And Elisha prayed, "O
LORD, open his eyes so he may
see." Then the LORD opened
the servant's eyes, and he
looked and saw the hills full of
horses and chariots of fire all
around Elisha.
18As the enemy came down
toward him, Elisha prayed to
the LORD, "Strike these people
with blindness." So he struck
them with blindness, as Elisha
had asked.
19Elisha told them, "This is
not the road and this is not the

וְלֹא זֶה הָעִיר לְכוּ אַחֲרַי וְאוֹלִיכָה אֶתְכֶם אֶל־הָאִישׁ
the-man to you and-I-will-lead after-me follow! the-city this and-not

אֲשֶׁר תְּבַקֵּשׁוּן וַיֹּלֶךְ אוֹתָם שֹׁמְרוֹנָה׃ וַיְהִי כְּבֹאָם
as-to-enter-them and-he-was (20) to-Samaria them and-he-led you-look-for whom

שֹׁמְרוֹן וַיֹּאמֶר אֱלִישָׁע יְהוָה פְּקַח אֶת־עֵינֵי־אֵלֶּה וְיִרְאוּ
so-they-can-see these eyes-of *** open! Yahweh Elisha then-he-said Samaria

וַיִּפְקַח יְהוָה אֶת־עֵינֵיהֶם וַיִּרְאוּ וְהִנֵּה בְּתוֹךְ
inside-of and-see! and-they-looked eyes-of-them *** Yahweh then-he-opened

שֹׁמְרוֹן׃ וַיֹּאמֶר מֶלֶךְ־יִשְׂרָאֵל אֶל־אֱלִישָׁע כִּרְאֹתוֹ אוֹתָם
them when-to-see-him Elisha to Israel king-of and-he-asked (21) Samaria

הַאַכֶּה אַכֶּה אָבִי׃ וַיֹּאמֶר לֹא תַכֶּה
you-kill not and-he-answered (22) father-of-me shall-I-kill shall-I-kill?

הַאֲשֶׁר שָׁבִיתָ בְּחַרְבְּךָ וּבְקַשְׁתְּךָ אַתָּה מַכֶּה
killing you and-with-bow-of-you with-sword-of-you you-captured whom?

שִׂים לֶחֶם וָמַיִם לִפְנֵיהֶם וְיֹאכְלוּ וְיִשְׁתּוּ
and-they-may-drink so-they-may-eat before-them and-waters food set!

וְיֵלְכוּ אֶל־אֲדֹנֵיהֶם׃ וַיִּכְרֶה לָהֶם
for-them then-he-gave-feast (23) masters-of-them to then-they-may-go-back

כֵּרָה גְדוֹלָה וַיֹּאכְלוּ וַיִּשְׁתּוּ וַיְשַׁלְּחֵם וַיֵּלְכוּ
and-they-returned and-he-sent-away-them and-they-drank and-they-ate great feast

אֶל־אֲדֹנֵיהֶם וְלֹא־יָסְפוּ עוֹד גְּדוּדֵי אֲרָם לָבוֹא
to-raid Aram bands-of again they-repeated and-not masters-of-them to

בְּאֶרֶץ יִשְׂרָאֵל׃ וַיְהִי אַחֲרֵי־כֵן וַיִּקְבֹּץ בֶּן־הֲדַד
Hadad Ben then-he-mobilized this after and-he-was (24) Israel in-territory-of

מֶלֶךְ־אֲרָם אֶת־כָּל־מַחֲנֵהוּ וַיַּעַל וַיָּצַר
and-he-laid-siege and-he-marched-up army-of-him entire-of *** Aram king-of

עַל־שֹׁמְרוֹן׃ וַיְהִי רָעָב גָּדוֹל בְּשֹׁמְרוֹן וְהִנֵּה צָרִים
ones-laying-siege and-see! in-Samaria great famine and-he-was (25) Samaria to

עָלֶיהָ עַד הֱיוֹת רֹאשׁ־חֲמוֹר בִּשְׁמֹנִים כֶּסֶף וְרֹבַע הַקַּב
the-cab and-fourth-of silver for-eighty donkey head-of to-be until to-them

°חִרְיוֹנִים בַּחֲמִשָּׁה־כָסֶף׃ וַיְהִי מֶלֶךְ יִשְׂרָאֵל עֹבֵר עַל־
on passing-by Israel king-of and-he-was (26) silver for-five dung-of-doves

הַחֹמָה וְאִשָּׁה צָעֲקָה אֵלָיו לֵאמֹר הוֹשִׁיעָה אֲדֹנִי הַמֶּלֶךְ׃
the-king lord-of-me help! to-say to-him she-cried and-woman the-wall

וַיֹּאמֶר אַל־יוֹשִׁעֵךְ יְהוָה מֵאַיִן אוֹשִׁיעֵךְ
I-can-help-you from-where? Yahweh he-helps-you not and-he-replied (27)

הֲמִן־הַגֹּרֶן אוֹ מִן־הַיָּקֶב׃ וַיֹּאמֶר־לָהּ
to-her then-he-asked (28) the-winepress from or the-threshing-floor from?

°25 ק דביונים

city. Follow me, and I will lead
you to the man you are looking for." And he led them to
Samaria.
20After they entered the city,
Elisha said, "LORD, open the
eyes of these men so they can
see." Then the LORD opened
their eyes and they looked,
and there they were, inside
Samaria.
21When the king of Israel
saw them, he asked Elisha,
"Shall I kill them, my father?
Shall I kill them?"
22"Do not kill them," he answered. "Would you kill men
you have captured with your
own sword or bow? Set food
and water before them so that
they may eat and drink and
then go back to their master."
23So he prepared a great feast
for them, and after they had
finished eating and drinking,
he sent them away, and they
returned to their master. So
the bands from Aram stopped
raiding Israel's territory.

Famine in Besieged Samaria

24Some time later, Ben-
Hadad king of Aram mobi-
lized his entire army and
marched up and laid siege to
Samaria. 25There was a great
famine in the city; the siege
lasted so long that a donkey's
head sold for eighty shekels[h]
of silver, and a fourth of a cab[i]
of seed pods[j] for five shekels.[k]
26As the king of Israel was
passing by on the wall, a
woman cried to him, "Help
me, my lord the king!"
27The king replied, "If the
LORD does not help you, where
can I get help for you? From
the threshing floor? From the
winepress?" 28Then he asked

[h]25 That is, about 2 pounds (about 1 kilogram)
[i]25 That is, probably about 1/2 pint (about 0.3 liter)
[j]25 Or *of dove's dung*
[k]25 That is, about 2 ounces (about 55 grams)

הַמֶּלֶךְ מַה־ לָּךְ וַתֹּאמֶר הָאִשָּׁה הַזֹּאת אָמְרָה אֵלַי
to-me she-said the-this the-woman and-she-answered to-you what? the-king

תְּנִי אֶת־ בְּנֵךְ וְנֹאכְלֶנּוּ הַיּוֹם וְאֶת־ בְּנִי נֹאכַל
we-will-eat son-of-me and the-day so-we-may-eat-him son-of-you *** give-up!

מָחָר׃ (29) וַנְּבַשֵּׁל אֶת־ בְּנִי וַנֹּאכְלֵהוּ וָאֹמַר אֵלֶיהָ
to-her and-I-said and-we-ate-him son-of-me *** so-we-cooked (29) tomorrow

בַּיּוֹם הָאַחֵר תְּנִי אֶת־ בְּנֵךְ וְנֹאכְלֶנּוּ וַתַּחְבִּא
but-she-hid so-we-may-eat-him son-of-you *** give-up! the-next on-the-day

אֶת־ בְּנָהּ׃ (30) וַיְהִי כִשְׁמֹעַ הַמֶּלֶךְ אֶת־ דִּבְרֵי הָאִשָּׁה
the-woman words-of *** the-king when-to-hear and-he-was (30) son-of-her ***

וַיִּקְרַע אֶת־ בְּגָדָיו וְהוּא עֹבֵר עַל־ הַחֹמָה וַיַּרְא
and-he-looked the-wall on going-along and-he robes-of-him *** then-he-tore

הָעָם וְהִנֵּה הַשַּׂק עַל־ בְּשָׂרוֹ מִבָּיִת׃ (31) וַיֹּאמֶר
and-he-said (31) underneath body-of-him on the-sackcloth and-see! the-people

כֹּה־ יַעֲשֶׂה־ לִּי אֱלֹהִים וְכֹה יוֹסִף אִם־ יַעֲמֹד רֹאשׁ
head-of he-remains if may-he-be-severe and-so God with-me may-he-deal so

אֱלִישָׁע בֶּן־ שָׁפָט עָלָיו הַיּוֹם׃ (32) וֶאֱלִישָׁע יֹשֵׁב בְּבֵיתוֹ
in-house-of-him sitting now-Elisha (32) the-day on-him Shaphat son-of Elisha

וְהַזְּקֵנִים יֹשְׁבִים אִתּוֹ וַיִּשְׁלַח אִישׁ מִלְּפָנָיו
at-ahead-of-him man and-he-sent with-him ones-sitting and-the-elders

בְּטֶרֶם יָבֹא הַמַּלְאָךְ אֵלָיו וְהוּא ׀ אָמַר אֶל־ הַזְּקֵנִים
the-elders to he-said then-he to-him the-messenger he-arrived but-before

הַרְּאִיתֶם כִּי־ שָׁלַח בֶּן־ הַמְרַצֵּחַ הַזֶּה לְהָסִיר אֶת־
*** to-cut-off the-this the-one-murdering son-of he-sends how you-see?

רֹאשִׁי רְאוּ ׀ כְּבֹא הַמַּלְאָךְ סִגְרוּ הַדֶּלֶת וּלְחַצְתֶּם
and-you-hold-shut the-door shut! the-messenger when-to-come look! head-of-me

אֹתוֹ בַּדֶּלֶת הֲלוֹא קוֹל רַגְלֵי אֲדֹנָיו אַחֲרָיו׃
behind-him masters-of-him feet-of sound-of not? with-the-door him

(33) עוֹדֶנּוּ מְדַבֵּר עִמָּם וְהִנֵּה הַמַּלְאָךְ יֹרֵד אֵלָיו
to-him coming-down the-messenger then-see! to-them talking while-he (33)

וַיֹּאמֶר הִנֵּה־ זֹאת הָרָעָה מֵאֵת יְהוָה מָה־ אוֹחִיל לַיהוָה
for-Yahweh should-I-wait why? Yahweh from the-disaster this see! and-he-said

עוֹד׃ (7:1) וַיֹּאמֶר אֱלִישָׁע שִׁמְעוּ דְּבַר־ יְהוָה כֹּה ׀ אָמַר יְהוָה
Yahweh he-says this Yahweh word-of hear! Elisha and-he-said (7:1) longer

כָּעֵת ׀ מָחָר סְאָה־ סֹלֶת בְּשֶׁקֶל וְסָאתַיִם שְׂעֹרִים
barleys and-two-seahs for-shekel flour seah tomorrow about-the-time

בְּשֶׁקֶל בְּשַׁעַר שֹׁמְרוֹן׃ (2) וַיַּעַן הַשָּׁלִישׁ אֲשֶׁר־ לַמֶּלֶךְ
by-the-king who the-officer and-he-answered (2) Samaria at-gate-of for-shekel

her, "What's the matter?"
She answered, "This
woman said to me, 'Give up
your son so we may eat him
today, and tomorrow we'll eat
my son.' 29So we cooked my
son and ate him. The next day
I said to her, 'Give up your son
so we may eat him,' but she
had hidden him."
30When the king heard the
woman's words, he tore his
robes. As he went along the
wall, the people looked, and
there, underneath, he had
sackcloth on his body. 31He
said, "May God deal with me,
be it ever so severely, if the
head of Elisha son of Shaphat
remains on his shoulders today!"
32Now Elisha was sitting in
his house, and the elders were
sitting with him. The king
sent a messenger ahead, but
before he arrived, Elisha said
to the elders, "Don't you see
how this murderer is sending
someone to cut off my head?
Look, when the messenger
comes, shut the door and hold
it shut against him. Is not the
sound of his master's footsteps
behind him?"
33While he was still talking
to them, the messenger came
down to him. And ⌊the king⌋
said, "This disaster is from the
LORD. Why should I wait for
the LORD any longer?"
7 Elisha said, "Hear the
word of the LORD. This is
what the LORD says: About
this time tomorrow, a seah[l] of
flour will sell for a shekel[m] and
two seahs[n] of barley for a
shekel at the gate of Samaria."
2The officer on whose arm

[l]1 That is, probably about 7 quarts (about 7.3 liters); also in verses 16 and 18
[m]1 That is, about 2/5 ounce (about 11 grams); also in verses 16 and 18
[n]1 That is, probably about 13 quarts (about 15 liters); also in verses 16 and 18

נִשְׁעָן עַל־ יָדוֹ אֶת־ אִישׁ הָאֱלֹהִים וַיֹּאמַר הִנֵּה יְהוָה עֹשֶׂה
opening Yahweh look! and-he-said the-God man-of *** arm-of-him on leaning

אֲרֻבּוֹת בַּשָּׁמַיִם הֲיִהְיֶה הַדָּבָר הַזֶּה וַיֹּאמֶר
and-he-answered the-this the-thing could-he-happen? of-the-heavens floodgates

הִנְּכָה רֹאֶה בְּעֵינֶיךָ וּמִשָּׁם לֹא תֹאכֵל׃ וְאַרְבָּעָה
now-four (3) you-will-eat not but-from-there with-eyes-of-you seeing see-you!

אֲנָשִׁים הָיוּ מְצֹרָעִים פֶּתַח הַשָּׁעַר וַיֹּאמְרוּ אִישׁ
each and-they-said the-gate entrance-of ones-being-leprous they-were men

אֶל־ רֵעֵהוּ מָה אֲנַחְנוּ יֹשְׁבִים פֹּה עַד־ מָתְנוּ׃ אִם־אָמַרְנוּ
we-say if (4) we-die until here ones-staying we why? fellow-of-him to

נָבוֹא הָעִיר וְהָרָעָב בָּעִיר וָמַתְנוּ שָׁם
there and-we-will-die in-the-city then-the-famine the-city we-will-go-into

וְאִם־ יָשַׁבְנוּ פֹה וָמָתְנוּ וְעַתָּה לְכוּ וְנִפְּלָה אֶל־
at and-let-us-surrender go! so-now then-we-will-die here we-stay and-if

מַחֲנֵה אֲרָם אִם־ יְחַיֻּנוּ נִחְיֶה וְאִם־ יְמִיתֻנוּ וָמָתְנוּ׃
then-we-will-die they-kill-us and-if we-will-live they-spare-us if Aram camp-of

וַיָּקֻמוּ בַנֶּשֶׁף לָבוֹא אֶל־ מַחֲנֵה אֲרָם וַיָּבֹאוּ עַד־
to when-they-reached Aram camp-of to to-go at-the-dusk and-they-got-up (5)

קְצֵה מַחֲנֵה אֲרָם וְהִנֵּה אֵין־ שָׁם אִישׁ׃ וַאדֹנָי
for-Lord (6) man there there-was-not then-see! Aram camp-of edge-of

הִשְׁמִיעַ אֶת־ מַחֲנֵה אֲרָם קוֹל רֶכֶב קוֹל סוּס קוֹל
sound-of horse sound-of chariot sound-of Aram camp-of *** he-caused-to-hear

חַיִל גָּדוֹל וַיֹּאמְרוּ אִישׁ אֶל־ אָחִיו הִנֵּה שָׂכַר־ עָלֵינוּ
against-us he-hired look! fellow-of-him to each so-they-said great army

מֶלֶךְ יִשְׂרָאֵל אֶת־ מַלְכֵי הַחִתִּים וְאֶת־ מַלְכֵי מִצְרַיִם לָבוֹא
to-attack Egypt kings-of and the-Hittites kings-of *** Israel king-of

עָלֵינוּ׃ וַיָּקוּמוּ וַיָּנוּסוּ בַנֶּשֶׁף וַיַּעַזְבוּ
and-they-abandoned into-the-dusk and-they-fled so-they-got-up (7) against-us

אֶת־ אָהֳלֵיהֶם וְאֶת־ סוּסֵיהֶם וְאֶת־ חֲמֹרֵיהֶם הַמַּחֲנֶה כַּאֲשֶׁר־
just-as the-camp donkeys-of-them and horses-of-them and tents-of-them ***

הִיא וַיָּנֻסוּ אֶל־ נַפְשָׁם׃ וַיָּבֹאוּ הַמְצֹרָעִים
the-ones-having-leprosy and-they-reached (8) life-of-them for and-they-ran she

הָאֵלֶּה עַד־ קְצֵה הַמַּחֲנֶה וַיָּבֹאוּ אֶל־ אֹהֶל אֶחָד וַיֹּאכְלוּ
and-they-ate one tent into and-they-went the-camp edge-of to the-these

וַיִּשְׁתּוּ וַיִּשְׂאוּ מִשָּׁם כֶּסֶף וְזָהָב וּבְגָדִים
and-clothes and-gold silver from-there and-they-carried and-they-drank

וַיֵּלְכוּ וַיַּטְמִנוּ וַיָּשֻׁבוּ וַיָּבֹאוּ אֶל־ אֹהֶל
tent into and-they-went and-they-returned and-they-hid and-they-went-off

the king was leaning said to the man of God, "Look, even if the LORD should open the floodgates of the heavens, could this happen?"

"You will see it with your own eyes," answered Elisha, "but you will not eat any of it!"

The Siege Lifted

3Now there were four men
with leprosy[a] at the entrance
of the city gate. They said to
each other, "Why stay here
until we die? 4If we say, 'We'll
go into the city'—the famine is
there, and we will die. And if
we stay here, we will die. So
let's go over to the camp of the
Arameans and surrender. If
they spare us, we live; if they
kill us, then we die."
5At dusk they got up and
went to the camp of the Arameans. When they reached
the edge of the camp, not a
man was there, 6for the Lord
had caused the Arameans to
hear the sound of chariots and
horses and a great army, so
that they said to one another,
"Look, the king of Israel has
hired the Hittite and Egyptian
kings to attack us!" 7So they
got up and fled in the dusk and
abandoned their tents and
their horses and donkeys.
They left the camp as it was
and ran for their lives.
8The men who had leprosy
reached the edge of the camp
and entered one of the tents.
They ate and drank, and carried away silver, gold and
clothes, and went off and hid
them. They returned and entered another tent and took

[a]3 The Hebrew word is used for various diseases affecting the skin—not necessarily leprosy; also in verse 8.

אַחֵר וַיִּשְׂאוּ מִשָּׁם וַיֵּלְכוּ וַיַּטְמִנוּ׃ וַיֹּאמְרוּ
then-they-said (9) and-they-hid and-they-went from-there and-they-took another

אִישׁ אֶל־ רֵעֵהוּ לֹא־ כֵן׀ אֲנַחְנוּ עֹשִׂים הַיּוֹם הַזֶּה יוֹם־
day-of the-this the-day ones-doing we right not fellow-of-him to each

בְּשֹׂרָה הוּא וַאֲנַחְנוּ מַחְשִׁים וְחִכִּינוּ עַד־ אוֹר
light-of until if-we-wait ones-keeping-silent and-we he good-news

הַבֹּקֶר וּמְצָאָנוּ עָוֺן וְעַתָּה לְכוּ וְנָבֹאָה
and-let-us-go go! so-now punishment then-he-will-overtake-us the-morning

וְנַגִּידָה בֵּית הַמֶּלֶךְ׃ וַיָּבֹאוּ וַיִּקְרְאוּ אֶל־
to and-they-called so-they-went (10) the-king palace-of and-let-us-report

שֹׁעֵר הָעִיר וַיַּגִּידוּ לָהֶם לֵאמֹר בָּאנוּ אֶל־ מַחֲנֵה
camp-of into we-went to-say to-them and-they-told the-city gatekeeper-of

אֲרָם וְהִנֵּה אֵין־ שָׁם אִישׁ וְקוֹל אָדָם כִּי אִם־
only except anyone or-sound-of man there there-was-not and-see! Aram

הַסּוּס אָסוּר וְהַחֲמוֹר אָסוּר וְאֹהָלִים כַּאֲשֶׁר־
just-as and-tents being-tethered and-the-donkey being-tethered the-horse

הֵמָּה׃ וַיִּקְרָא הַשֹּׁעֲרִים וַיַּגִּידוּ בֵּית הַמֶּלֶךְ
the-king palace-of and-they-reported the-gatekeepers and-he-shouted (11) they

פְּנִימָה׃ וַיָּקָם הַמֶּלֶךְ לַיְלָה וַיֹּאמֶר אֶל־ עֲבָדָיו
officers-of-him to and-he-said night the-king and-he-got-up (12) at-inside

אַגִּידָה־ נָּא לָכֶם אֵת אֲשֶׁר־ עָשׂוּ לָנוּ אֲרָם יָדְעוּ כִּי־
that they-know Aram to-us they-did what *** to-you now! I-will-tell

רְעֵבִים אֲנָחְנוּ וַיֵּצְאוּ מִן־ הַמַּחֲנֶה לְהֵחָבֵה בַהַשָּׂדֶה לֵאמֹר
to-think in-the-field to-hide the-camp from so-they-left we ones-starving

כִּי־ יֵצְאוּ מִן־ הָעִיר וְנִתְפְּשֵׂם חַיִּים
ones-alive then-we-will-take-them the-city from they-will-come-out surely

וְאֶל־ הָעִיר נָבֹא׃ וַיַּעַן אֶחָד מֵעֲבָדָיו
of-officers-of-him one and-he-answered (13) we-will-go the-city and-into

וַיֹּאמֶר וְיִקְחוּ־ נָא חֲמִשָּׁה מִן־ הַסּוּסִים הַנִּשְׁאָרִים
the-ones-being-left the-horses from five now! now-let-them-take and-he-said

אֲשֶׁר נִשְׁאֲרוּ־ בָהּ הִנָּם כְּכָל־ הֶהָמוֹן יִשְׂרָאֵל אֲשֶׁר נִשְׁאֲרוּ־
they-are-left who Israel rest-of as-all-of see-they! in-her they-are-left that

בָהּ הִנָּם כְּכָל־ הֲמוֹן יִשְׂרָאֵל אֲשֶׁר־ תָּמּוּ וְנִשְׁלְחָה
now-let-us-send they-are-doomed who Israel rest-of as-all-of see-they! in-her

וְנִרְאֶה׃ וַיִּקְחוּ שְׁנֵי רֶכֶב סוּסִים וַיִּשְׁלַח
and-he-sent horses chariot-of two-of so-they-selected (14) and-let-us-find-out

הַמֶּלֶךְ אַחֲרֵי מַחֲנֵה־ אֲרָם לֵאמֹר לְכוּ וּרְאוּ׃ וַיֵּלְכוּ
and-they-followed (15) and-find-out! go! to-say Aram army-of after the-king

some things from it and hid
them also.
[9]Then they said to each other, "We're not doing right.
This is a day of good news and
we are keeping it to ourselves.
If we wait until daylight, punishment will overtake us. Let's
go at once and report this to
the royal palace."
[10]So they went and called out
to the city gatekeepers and
told them, "We went into the
Aramean camp and not a man
was there—not a sound of
anyone—only tethered horses
and donkeys, and the tents left
just as they were." [11]The gatekeepers shouted the news, and
it was reported within the palace.
[12]The king got up in the
night and said to his officers,
"I will tell you what the Arameans have done to us. They
know we are starving; so they
have left the camp to hide in
the countryside, thinking,
'They will surely come out,
and then we will take them
alive and get into the city.' "
[13]One of his officers answered, "Have some men take
five of the horses that are left
in the city. Their plight will be
like that of all the Israelites left
here—yes, they will only be
like all these Israelites who are
doomed. So let us send them to
find out what happened."
[14]So they selected two chariots with their horses, and the
king sent them after the Aramean army. He commanded
the drivers, "Go and find out
what has happened." [15]They

°12 ק בשדה
°13 ק המון

אַחֲרֵיהֶם עַד־הַיַּרְדֵּן וְהִנֵּה כָל־הַדֶּרֶךְ מְלֵאָה בְגָדִים
clothes full the-road whole-of and-see! the-Jordan as-far-as after-them

וְכֵלִים אֲשֶׁר־הִשְׁלִיכוּ אֲרָם בְּהֶחָפְזָם וַיָּשֻׁבוּ
so-they-returned when-to-flee-them Aram they-threw-down that and-equipments

הַמַּלְאָכִים וַיַּגִּדוּ לַמֶּלֶךְ׃ וַיֵּצֵא הָעָם
the-people then-he-went-out (16) to-the-king and-they-reported the-messengers

וַיָּבֹזּוּ אֵת מַחֲנֵה אֲרָם וַיְהִי סְאָה־סֹלֶת בְּשֶׁקֶל
for-shekel flour seah so-he-was Aram camp-of *** and-they-plundered

וְסָאתַיִם שְׂעֹרִים בְּשֶׁקֶל כִּדְבַר יְהוָה׃ וְהַמֶּלֶךְ
now-the-king (17) Yahweh as-word-of for-shekel barleys and-two-seahs

הִפְקִיד אֶת־הַשָּׁלִישׁ אֲשֶׁר־נִשְׁעָן עַל־יָדוֹ עַל־הַשַּׁעַר
the-gate over arm-of-him on leaning whom the-officer *** he-put-in-charge

וַיִּרְמְסֻהוּ הָעָם בַּשַּׁעַר וַיָּמֹת כַּאֲשֶׁר
just-as and-he-died in-the-gateway the-people and-they-trampled-him

דִּבֶּר אִישׁ הָאֱלֹהִים אֲשֶׁר דִּבֶּר בְּרֶדֶת הַמֶּלֶךְ אֵלָיו׃
to-him the-king when-to-come-down he-foretold who the-God man-of he-foretold

וַיְהִי כְּדַבֵּר אִישׁ הָאֱלֹהִים אֶל־הַמֶּלֶךְ לֵאמֹר סָאתַיִם
two-seahs to-say the-king to the-God man-of as-to-say and-he-happened (18)

שְׂעֹרִים בְּשֶׁקֶל וּסְאָה־סֹלֶת בְּשֶׁקֶל יִהְיֶה כָּעֵת
about-the-time he-will-be for-shekel flour and-seah for-shekel barleys

מָחָר בְּשַׁעַר שֹׁמְרוֹן׃ וַיַּעַן הַשָּׁלִישׁ אֶת־אִישׁ
man-of *** the-officer and-he-answered (19) Samaria at-gate-of tomorrow

הָאֱלֹהִים וַיֹּאמַר וְהִנֵּה יְהוָה עֹשֶׂה אֲרֻבּוֹת בַּשָּׁמַיִם
of-the-heavens floodgates opening Yahweh now-look! and-he-said the-God

הֲיִהְיֶה כַּדָּבָר הַזֶּה וַיֹּאמֶר הִנְּךָ רֹאֶה
seeing see-you! and-he-replied the-this as-the-thing could-he-happen?

בְּעֵינֶיךָ וּמִשָּׁם לֹא תֹאכֵל׃ וַיְהִי־לוֹ
to-him and-he-happened (20) you-will-eat not but-from-there with-eyes-of-you

כֵּן וַיִּרְמְסוּ אֹתוֹ הָעָם בַּשַּׁעַר וַיָּמֹת׃
so-he-died in-the-gateway the-people him for-they-trampled exactly

וֶאֱלִישָׁע דִּבֶּר אֶל־הָאִשָּׁה אֲשֶׁר־הֶחֱיָה אֶת־בְּנָהּ
son-of-her *** he-restored-to-life whom the-woman to he-said now-Elisha (8:1)

לֵאמֹר קוּמִי וּלְכִי אַתְּי וּבֵיתֵךְ וְגוּרִי בַּאֲשֶׁר
at-where and-stay! and-family-of-you you and-go-away! get-up! to-say

תָּגוּרִי כִּי־קָרָא יְהוָה לָרָעָב וְגַם־בָּא
he-will-come and-also for-the-famine Yahweh he-decreed for you-can-stay

אֶל־הָאָרֶץ שֶׁבַע שָׁנִים׃ וַתָּקָם הָאִשָּׁה וַתַּעַשׂ כִּדְבַר
as-word-of and-she-did the-woman so-she-got-up (2) years seven the-land onto

°15 ק בחפזם
°1 ק את

followed them as far as the Jordan, and they found the whole
road strewn with the clothing
and equipment the Arameans
had thrown away in their
headlong flight. So the messengers returned and reported
to the king. 16Then the people
went out and plundered the
camp of the Arameans. So a
seah of flour sold for a shekel,
and two seahs of barley sold
for a shekel, as the LORD had
said.
17Now the king had put the
officer on whose arm he
leaned in charge of the gate,
and the people trampled him
in the gateway, and he died,
just as the man of God had
foretold when the king came
down to his house. 18It happened as the man of God had
said to the king: "About this
time tomorrow, a seah of flour
will sell for a shekel and two
seahs of barley for a shekel at
the gate of Samaria."
19The officer had said to the
man of God, "Look, even if the
LORD should open the floodgates of the heavens, could
this happen?" The man of God
had replied, "You will see it
with your own eyes, but you
will not eat any of it!" 20And
that is exactly what happened
to him, for the people trampled him in the gateway, and
he died.

The Shunammite's Land Restored

8 Now Elisha had said to
the woman whose son he
had restored to life, "Go away
with your family and stay for
a while wherever you can, because the LORD has decreed a
famine in the land that will
last seven years." 2The woman
proceeded to do as the man of

אִישׁ הָאֱלֹהִים וַתֵּלֶךְ הִיא וּבֵיתָהּ וַתָּגָר
and-she-stayed and-family-of-her she and-she-went-away the-God man-of

בְּאֶרֶץ־ פְּלִשְׁתִּים שֶׁבַע שָׁנִים׃ (3) וַיְהִי מִקְצֵה שֶׁבַע שָׁנִים
years seven at-end-of and-he-was (3) years seven Philistines in-land-of

וַתָּשָׁב הָאִשָּׁה מֵאֶרֶץ פְּלִשְׁתִּים וַתֵּצֵא לִצְעֹק
to-beg and-she-went Philistines from-land-of the-woman then-she-came-back

אֶל־ הַמֶּלֶךְ אֶל־ בֵּיתָהּ וְאֶל־ שָׂדָהּ׃ (4) וְהַמֶּלֶךְ מְדַבֵּר
talking and-the-king (4) land-of-her and-for house-of-her for the-king to

אֶל־ גֵּחֲזִי נַעַר אִישׁ־ הָאֱלֹהִים לֵאמֹר סַפְּרָה־ נָּא לִי אֵת כָּל־
all-of *** to-me now! tell! to-say the-God man-of servant-of Gehazi to

הַגְּדֹלוֹת אֲשֶׁר־ עָשָׂה אֱלִישָׁע׃ (5) וַיְהִי הוּא מְסַפֵּר לַמֶּלֶךְ
to-the-king telling he and-he-was (5) Elisha he-did that the-great-things

אֵת אֲשֶׁר־ הֶחֱיָה אֶת־ הַמֵּת וְהִנֵּה הָאִשָּׁה אֲשֶׁר־
whom the-woman then-see! the-dead *** he-restored-to-life how ***

הֶחֱיָה אֶת־ בְּנָהּ צֹעֶקֶת אֶל־ הַמֶּלֶךְ עַל־ בֵּיתָהּ
house-of-her for the-king to begging son-of-her *** he-restored-to-life

וְעַל־ שָׂדָהּ וַיֹּאמֶר גֵּחֲזִי אֲדֹנִי הַמֶּלֶךְ זֹאת הָאִשָּׁה
the-woman this the-king lord-of-me Gehazi and-he-said land-of-her and-for

וְזֶה־ בְּנָהּ אֲשֶׁר־ הֶחֱיָה אֱלִישָׁע׃ (6) וַיִּשְׁאַל הַמֶּלֶךְ
the-king and-he-asked (6) Elisha he-restored-to-life whom son-of-her and-this

לָאִשָּׁה וַתְּסַפֶּר־ לוֹ וַיִּתֶּן־ לָהּ הַמֶּלֶךְ סָרִיס
official the-king to-her then-he-assigned to-him and-she-told to-the-woman

אֶחָד לֵאמֹר הָשֵׁיב אֶת־ כָּל־ אֲשֶׁר־ לָהּ וְאֵת כָּל־ תְּבוּאֹת הַשָּׂדֶה
the-land income-of all-of and to-her that all *** give-back! to-say one

מִיּוֹם עָזְבָה אֶת־ הָאָרֶץ וְעַד־ עָתָּה׃ (7) וַיָּבֹא אֱלִישָׁע דַּמֶּשֶׂק
Damascus Elisha now-he-went (7) now and-to the-land *** she-left from-day

וּבֶן־ הֲדַד מֶלֶךְ־ אֲרָם חֹלֶה וַיֻּגַּד־ לוֹ לֵאמֹר בָּא
he-came to-say to-him when-he-was-told being-ill Aram king-of Hadad and-Ben

אִישׁ הָאֱלֹהִים עַד־ הֵנָּה׃ (8) וַיֹּאמֶר הַמֶּלֶךְ אֶל־ חֲזָהאֵל קַח
take! Hazael to the-king and-he-said (8) to-here to the-God man-of

בְּיָדְךָ מִנְחָה וְלֵךְ לִקְרַאת אִישׁ הָאֱלֹהִים וְדָרַשְׁתָּ אֶת־
*** and-you-consult the-God man-of to-meet and-go! gift in-hand-of-you

יְהוָה מֵאוֹתוֹ לֵאמֹר הַאֶחְיֶה מֵחֳלִי זֶה׃ (9) וַיֵּלֶךְ
so-he-went (9) this from-illness will-I-recover? to-ask through-him Yahweh

חֲזָאֵל לִקְרָאתוֹ וַיִּקַּח מִנְחָה בְיָדוֹ וְכָל־ טוּב
finery-of and-all-of in-hand-of-him gift and-he-took to-meet-him Hazael

דַּמֶּשֶׂק מַשָּׂא אַרְבָּעִים גָּמָל וַיָּבֹא וַיַּעֲמֹד לְפָנָיו וַיֹּאמֶר
and-he-said before-him and-he-stood and-he-went camel forty load-of Damascus

God said. She and her family
went away and stayed in the
land of the Philistines seven
years.
3At the end of the seven
years she came back from the
land of the Philistines and
went to the king to beg for her
house and land. 4The king was
talking to Gehazi, the servant
of the man of God, and had
said, "Tell me about all the
great things Elisha has done."
5Just as Gehazi was telling the
king how Elisha had restored
the dead to life, the woman
whose son Elisha had brought
back to life came to beg the
king for her house and land.
Gehazi said, "This is the
woman, my lord the king, and
this is her son whom Elisha
restored to life." 6The king
asked the woman about it, and
she told him.
Then he assigned an official
to her case and said to him,
"Give back everything that
belonged to her, including all
the income from her land from
the day she left the country
until now."

Hazael Murders Ben-Hadad

7Elisha went to Damascus,
and Ben-Hadad king of Aram
was ill. When the king was
told, "The man of God has
come all the way up here," 8he
said to Hazael, "Take a gift
with you and go to meet the
man of God. Consult the LORD
through him; ask him, 'Will I
recover from this illness?' "
9Hazael went to meet Elisha,
taking with him as a gift forty
camel-loads of all the finest
wares of Damascus. He went
in and stood before him, and

בִּנְךָ בֶן־הֲדַד מֶלֶךְ־אֲרָם שְׁלָחַנִי אֵלֶיךָ לֵאמֹר הַאֶחְיֶה
will-I-recover? to-ask to-you he-sent-me Aram king-of Hadad Ben son-of-you

מֵחֳלִי זֶה׃ וַיֹּאמֶר אֵלָיו אֱלִישָׁע לֵךְ אֱמָר־לֹא*
*to-him say! go! Elisha to-him and-he-answered (10) this from-illness

חָיֹה תִחְיֶה וְהִרְאַנִי יְהוָה כִּי־מוֹת
to-die that Yahweh but-he-revealed-to-me you-will-recover to-recover

יָמוּת׃ וַיַּעֲמֵד אֶת־פָּנָיו וַיָּשֶׂם עַד־
until and-he-stared faces-of-him *** and-he-set (11) he-will-die

בֹּשׁ וַיֵּבְךְּ אִישׁ הָאֱלֹהִים׃ וַיֹּאמֶר חֲזָאֵל מַדּוּעַ
why? Hazael then-he-asked (12) the-God man-of then-he-wept to-be-ashamed

אֲדֹנִי בֹכֶה וַיֹּאמֶר כִּי־יָדַעְתִּי אֵת אֲשֶׁר־תַּעֲשֶׂה
you-will-do that *** I-know because and-he-answered weeping lord-of-me

לִבְנֵי יִשְׂרָאֵל רָעָה מִבְצְרֵיהֶם תְּשַׁלַּח בָּאֵשׁ
with-fire you-will-set fortified-places-of-them harm Israel to-sons-of

וּבַחֻרֵיהֶם בַּחֶרֶב תַּהֲרֹג וְעֹלְלֵיהֶם
and-children-of-them you-will-kill with-the-sword and-young-men-of-them

תְּרַטֵּשׁ וְהָרֹתֵיהֶם תְּבַקֵּעַ׃
you-will-rip-open and-pregnant-women-of-them you-will-dash-to-ground

וַיֹּאמֶר חֲזָהאֵל כִּי מָה עַבְדְּךָ הַכֶּלֶב כִּי יַעֲשֶׂה
he-could-do indeed the-dog servant-of-you how? indeed Hazael and-he-said (13)

הַדָּבָר הַגָּדוֹל הַזֶּה וַיֹּאמֶר אֱלִישָׁע הִרְאַנִי יְהוָה אֹתְךָ
you Yahweh he-showed-me Elisha and-he-answered the-this the-great the-feat

מֶלֶךְ עַל־אֲרָם׃ וַיֵּלֶךְ ׀ מֵאֵת אֱלִישָׁע וַיָּבֹא אֶל־אֲדֹנָיו
masters-of-him to and-he-returned Elisha from then-he-left (14) Aram over king

וַיֹּאמֶר לוֹ מָה־אָמַר לְךָ אֱלִישָׁע וַיֹּאמֶר אָמַר
he-told and-he-replied Elisha to-you he-said what? to-him when-he-asked

לִי חָיֹה תִחְיֶה׃ וַיְהִי מִמָּחֳרָת וַיִּקַּח
then-he-took on-next-day but-he-was (15) you-will-recover to-recover to-me

הַמַּכְבֵּר וַיִּטְבֹּל בַּמַּיִם וַיִּפְרֹשׂ עַל־פָּנָיו
faces-of-him over and-he-spread in-the-waters and-he-soaked the-cloth

וַיָּמֹת וַיִּמְלֹךְ חֲזָהאֵל תַּחְתָּיו׃ וּבִשְׁנַת חָמֵשׁ
five in-year-of (16) in-place-of-him Hazael and-he-became-king and-he-died

לְיוֹרָם בֶּן־אַחְאָב מֶלֶךְ יִשְׂרָאֵל וִיהוֹשָׁפָט מֶלֶךְ יְהוּדָה
Judah king-of when-Jehoshaphat Israel king-of Ahab son-of of-Joram

מָלַךְ יְהוֹרָם בֶּן־יְהוֹשָׁפָט מֶלֶךְ יְהוּדָה׃ בֶּן־שְׁלֹשִׁים
thirty son-of (17) Judah king-of Jehoshaphat son-of Jehoram he-became-king

וּשְׁתַּיִם שָׁנָה הָיָה בְמָלְכוֹ וּשְׁמֹנֶה שָׁנָה מָלַךְ
he-reigned years and-eight when-to-become-king-him he-was year and-two

said, "Your son Ben-Hadad king of Aram has sent me to ask, 'Will I recover from this illness?' "
[10]Elisha answered, "Go and say to him, 'You will certainly recover'; but[p] the LORD has revealed to me that he will in fact die."
[11]He stared at him with a fixed gaze until Hazael felt ashamed. Then the man of God began to weep.
[12]"Why is my lord weeping?" asked Hazael.
"Because I know the harm you will do to the Israelites," he answered. "You will set fire to their fortified places, kill their young men with the sword, dash their little children to the ground, and rip open their pregnant women."
[13]Hazael said, "How could your servant, a mere dog, accomplish such a feat?"
"The LORD has shown me that you will become king of Aram," answered Elisha.
[14]Then Hazael left Elisha and returned to his master. When Ben-Hadad asked, "What did Elisha say to you?" Hazael replied, "He told me that you would certainly
recover." [15]But the next day he took a thick cloth, soaked it in water and spread it over the king's face, so that he died. Then Hazael succeeded him as king.

Jehoram King of Judah

[16]In the fifth year of Joram son of Ahab king of Israel, when Jehoshaphat was king of Judah, Jehoram son of Jehoshaphat began his reign as king of Judah.
[17]He was thirty-two years old when he became king, and he reigned in

[p]10 The Hebrew may also be read *Go and say, 'You will certainly not recover,' for.*

*10 The *Kethib* form reads *not;* the *Qere* reads *to-him.*

°10 ק לו

°17 ק שנים

בִּירוּשָׁלִָם׃ וַיֵּלֶךְ בְּדֶרֶךְ ׀ מַלְכֵי יִשְׂרָאֵל כַּאֲשֶׁר עָשׂוּ
they-did just-as Israel kings-of in-way-of and-he-walked (18) in-Jerusalem

בֵּית אַחְאָב כִּי בַת־אַחְאָב הָיְתָה־לּוֹ לְאִשָּׁה וַיַּעַשׂ
and-he-did as-wife to-him she-was Ahab daughter-of for Ahab house-of

הָרַע בְּעֵינֵי יְהוָה׃ וְלֹא־אָבָה יְהוָה לְהַשְׁחִית
to-destroy Yahweh he-was-willing but-not (19) Yahweh in-eyes-of the-evil

אֶת־יְהוּדָה לְמַעַן דָּוִד עַבְדּוֹ כַּאֲשֶׁר אָמַר־לוֹ
to-him he-promised just-as servant-of-him David for-sake-of Judah ***

לָתֵת לוֹ נִיר לְבָנָיו כָּל־הַיָּמִים׃
the-days all-of for-descendants-of-him lamp for-him to-maintain

בְּיָמָיו פָּשַׁע אֱדוֹם מִתַּחַת יַד־יְהוּדָה וַיַּמְלִכוּ
and-they-set-king Judah hand-of from-under Edom he-rebelled in-days-of-him (20)

עֲלֵיהֶם מֶלֶךְ׃ וַיַּעֲבֹר יוֹרָם צָעִירָה וְכָל־הָרֶכֶב עִמּוֹ
with-him the-chariot and-all-of to-Zair Joram so-he-went (21) king over-them

וַיְהִי־הוּא קָם לַיְלָה וַיַּכֶּה אֶת־אֱדוֹם הַסֹּבֵיב
the-one-surrounding Edom *** and-he-broke-through night he-rose he and-he-was

אֵלָיו וְאֵת שָׂרֵי הָרֶכֶב וַיָּנָס הָעָם לְאֹהָלָיו׃
to-homes-of-him the-army but-he-fled the-chariot commanders-of and around-him

וַיִּפְשַׁע אֱדוֹם מִתַּחַת יַד־יְהוּדָה עַד הַיּוֹם הַזֶּה אָז
then the-this the-day to Judah hand-of from-under Edom and-he-rebels (22)

תִּפְשַׁע לִבְנָה בָּעֵת הַהִיא׃ וְיֶתֶר דִּבְרֵי יוֹרָם
Joram events-of and-rest-of (23) the-same at-the-time Libnah she-revolted

וְכָל־אֲשֶׁר עָשָׂה הֲלוֹא־הֵם כְּתוּבִים עַל־סֵפֶר דִּבְרֵי
annals-of book-of in ones-being-written they not? he-did that and-all

הַיָּמִים לְמַלְכֵי יְהוּדָה׃ וַיִּשְׁכַּב יוֹרָם עִם־אֲבֹתָיו
fathers-of-him with Joram and-he-rested (24) Judah of-kings-of the-days

וַיִּקָּבֵר עִם־אֲבֹתָיו בְּעִיר דָּוִד וַיִּמְלֹךְ
and-he-became-king David in-City-of fathers-of-him with and-he-was-buried

אֲחַזְיָהוּ בְנוֹ תַּחְתָּיו׃ בִּשְׁנַת שְׁתֵּים־עֶשְׂרֵה שָׁנָה לְיוֹרָם
of-Joram year ten two in-year-of (25) in-place-of-him son-of-him Ahaziah

בֶּן־אַחְאָב מֶלֶךְ יִשְׂרָאֵל מָלַךְ אֲחַזְיָהוּ בֶן־יְהוֹרָם מֶלֶךְ
king-of Jehoram son-of Ahaziah he-became-king Israel king-of Ahab son-of

יְהוּדָה׃ בֶּן־עֶשְׂרִים וּשְׁתַּיִם שָׁנָה אֲחַזְיָהוּ בְּמָלְכוֹ
when-to-become-king-him Ahaziah year and-two twenty son-of (26) Judah

וְשָׁנָה אַחַת מָלַךְ בִּירוּשָׁלִָם וְשֵׁם אִמּוֹ עֲתַלְיָהוּ
Athaliah mother-of-him and-name-of in-Jerusalem he-reigned one and-year

בַּת־עָמְרִי מֶלֶךְ יִשְׂרָאֵל׃ וַיֵּלֶךְ בְּדֶרֶךְ בֵּית אַחְאָב
Ahab house-of in-way-of and-he-walked (27) Israel king-of Omri daughter-of

Jerusalem eight years. [18]He
walked in the ways of the
kings of Israel, as the house of
Ahab had done, for he married a daughter of Ahab. He
did evil in the eyes of the
LORD. [19]Nevertheless, for the
sake of his servant David, the
LORD was not willing to destroy Judah. He had promised
to maintain a lamp for David
and his descendants forever.
[20]In the time of Jehoram,
Edom rebelled against Judah
and set up its own king. [21]So
Jehoram[q] went to Zair with all
his chariots. The Edomites
surrounded him and his chariot commanders, but he rose
up and broke through by
night; his army, however, fled
back home. [22]To this day
Edom has been in rebellion
against Judah. Libnah revolted at the same time.
[23]As for the other events of
Jehoram's reign, and all he
did, are they not written in the
book of the annals of the kings
of Judah? [24]Jehoram rested
with his fathers and was buried with them in the City of
David. And Ahaziah his son
succeeded him as king.

Ahaziah King of Judah

[25]In the twelfth year of
Joram son of Ahab king of Israel, Ahaziah son of Jehoram
king of Judah began to reign.
[26]Ahaziah was twenty-two
years old when he became
king, and he reigned in
Jerusalem one year. His
mother's name was Athaliah,
a granddaughter of Omri king
of Israel. [27]He walked in the
ways of the house of Ahab and

[q]21 Hebrew *Joram*, a variant of *Jehoram*; also in verses 23 and 24

וַיַּעַשׂ הָרַע בְּעֵינֵי יְהוָה כְּבֵית אַחְאָב כִּי חֲתַן
son-in-law-of for Ahab as-house-of Yahweh in-eyes-of the-evil and-he-did

בֵּית־אַחְאָב הוּא׃ וַיֵּלֶךְ אֶת־יוֹרָם בֶּן־אַחְאָב לַמִּלְחָמָה עִם־
against to-the-war Ahab son-of Joram with and-he-went (28) he Ahab house-of

חֲזָהאֵל מֶלֶךְ־אֲרָם בְּרָמֹת גִּלְעָד וַיַּכּוּ אֲרַמִּים אֶת־יוֹרָם׃
Joram *** Arameans and-they-wounded Gilead at-Ramoth Aram king-of Hazael

וַיָּשָׁב יוֹרָם הַמֶּלֶךְ לְהִתְרַפֵּא בְיִזְרְעֶאל מִן־הַמַּכִּים
the-wounds from in-Jezreel to-recover the-king Joram so-he-returned (29)

אֲשֶׁר יַכֻּהוּ אֲרַמִּים בָּרָמָה בְּהִלָּחֲמוֹ אֶת־
*** when-to-fight-him at-the-Ramah Arameans they-inflicted-on-him that

חֲזָהאֵל מֶלֶךְ אֲרָם וַאֲחַזְיָהוּ בֶן־יְהוֹרָם מֶלֶךְ יְהוּדָה יָרַד
he-went-down Judah king-of Jehoram son-of then-Ahaziah Aram king-of Hazael

לִרְאוֹת אֶת־יוֹרָם בֶּן־אַחְאָב בְּיִזְרְעֶאל כִּי־חֹלֶה הוּא׃ וֶאֱלִישָׁע
now-Elisha (9:1) he being-wounded for to-Jezreel Ahab son-of Joram *** to-see

הַנָּבִיא קָרָא לְאַחַד מִבְּנֵי הַנְּבִיאִים וַיֹּאמֶר לוֹ
to-him and-he-said the-prophets from-sons-of to-one he-summoned the-prophet

חֲגֹר מָתְנֶיךָ וְקַח פַּךְ הַשֶּׁמֶן הַזֶּה בְּיָדֶךָ
in-hand-of-you the-this the-oil flask-of and-take! belts-of-you tuck-in-cloak!

וְלֵךְ רָמֹת גִּלְעָד׃ וּבָאתָ שָׁמָּה וּרְאֵה־שָׁם יֵהוּא בֶן־
son-of Jehu there then-look! to-there when-you-get (2) Gilead Ramoth and-go!

יְהוֹשָׁפָט בֶּן־נִמְשִׁי וּבָאתָ וַהֲקֵמֹתוֹ מִתּוֹךְ*
from-among and-you-get-away-him and-you-go Nimshi son-of Jehoshaphat

אֶחָיו וְהֵבֵיאתָ אֹתוֹ חֶדֶר בְּחָדֶר׃ וְלָקַחְתָּ פַךְ־
flask-of then-you-take (3) in-room room him and-you-take companions-of-him

הַשֶּׁמֶן וְיָצַקְתָּ עַל־רֹאשׁוֹ וְאָמַרְתָּ כֹּה־אָמַר יְהוָה
Yahweh he-says this and-you-declare head-of-him on and-you-pour the-oil

מְשַׁחְתִּיךָ לְמֶלֶךְ אֶל־יִשְׂרָאֵל וּפָתַחְתָּ הַדֶּלֶת וְנַסְתָּה וְלֹא
and-not and-you-run the-door then-you-open Israel over as-king I-anoint-you

תְחַכֶּה׃ וַיֵּלֶךְ הַנַּעַר הַנַּעַר הַנָּבִיא רָמֹת
Ramoth the-prophet the-young-man the-young-man so-he-went (4) you-delay

גִּלְעָד׃ וַיָּבֹא וְהִנֵּה שָׂרֵי הַחַיִל יֹשְׁבִים
ones-sitting the-army officers-of then-see! when-he-arrived (5) Gilead

וַיֹּאמֶר דָּבָר לִי אֵלֶיךָ הַשָּׂר וַיֹּאמֶר יֵהוּא אֶל־
for Jehu and-he-asked the-commander for-you with-me message and-he-said

מִי מִכֻּלָּנוּ וַיֹּאמֶר אֵלֶיךָ הַשָּׂר׃ וַיָּקָם
and-he-got-up (6) the-commander for-you and-he-replied of-all-of-us whom?

וַיָּבֹא הַבַּיְתָה וַיִּצֹק הַשֶּׁמֶן אֶל־רֹאשׁוֹ
head-of-him on the-oil then-he-poured into-the-house and-he-went

did evil in the eyes of the
LORD, as the house of Ahab
had done, for he was related
by marriage to Ahab's family.
28Ahaziah went with Joram
son of Ahab to war against
Hazael king of Aram at
Ramoth Gilead. The Ara-
means wounded Joram; 29so
King Joram returned to Jezreel
to recover from the wounds
the Arameans had inflicted on
him at Ramoth[r] in his battle
with Hazael king of Aram.
Then Ahaziah son of Je-
horam king of Judah went
down to Jezreel to see Joram
son of Ahab, because he had
been wounded.

Jehu Anointed King of Israel

9 The prophet Elisha sum-
moned a man from the
company of the prophets and
said to him, "Tuck your cloak
into your belt, take this flask of
oil with you and go to Ramoth
Gilead. 2When you get there,
look for Jehu son of Jehoshaphat, the son of Nimshi. Go to
him, get him away from his
companions and take him
into an inner room. 3Then take
the flask and pour the oil on
his head and declare, 'This is
what the LORD says: I anoint
you king over Israel.' Then
open the door and run; don't
delay!"
4So the young man, the
prophet, went to Ramoth Gilead. 5When he arrived, he
found the army officers sitting
together. "I have a message for
you, commander," he said.
"For which of us?" asked
Jehu.
"For you, commander," he
replied.
6Jehu got up and went into
the house. Then the prophet
poured the oil on Jehu's head

[r]29 Hebrew *Ramah*, a variant of *Ramoth*

*2 Most mss have *sheva* in the *kaph* (ךְ—).

וַיֹּאמֶר לוֹ כֹּה־ אָמַר יְהוָה אֱלֹהֵי יִשְׂרָאֵל מְשַׁחְתִּיךָ
I-anoint-you Israel God-of Yahweh he-says this to-him and-he-declared

לְמֶלֶךְ אֶל־ עַם יְהוָה אֶל־יִשְׂרָאֵל׃ (7) וְהִכִּיתָה אֶת־
*** and-you-must-destroy (7) Israel over Yahweh people-of over as-king

בֵּית אַחְאָב אֲדֹנֶיךָ וְנִקַּמְתִּי דְּמֵי ׀ עֲבָדַי
servants-of-me bloods-of and-I-will-avenge masters-of-you Ahab house-of

הַנְּבִיאִים וּדְמֵי כָּל־ עַבְדֵי יְהוָה מִיַּד אִיזָבֶל׃
Jezebel by-hand-of Yahweh servants-of all-of and-bloods-of the-prophets

(8) וְאָבַד כָּל־ בֵּית אַחְאָב וְהִכְרַתִּי לְאַחְאָב
from-Ahab and-I-will-cut-off Ahab house-of whole-of and-he-will-perish (8)

מַשְׁתִּין בְּקִיר וְעָצוּר וְעָזוּב בְּיִשְׂרָאֵל׃
in-Israel or-being-free and-being-slave against-wall one-urinating

(9) וְנָתַתִּי אֶת־ בֵּית אַחְאָב כְּבֵית יָרָבְעָם בֶּן־ נְבָט
Nebat son-of Jeroboam like-house-of Ahab house-of *** and-I-will-make (9)

וּכְבֵית בַּעְשָׁא בֶן־ אֲחִיָּה׃ (10) וְאֶת־ אִיזֶבֶל יֹאכְלוּ
they-will-devour Jezebel and (10) Ahijah son-of Baasha and-like-house-of

הַכְּלָבִים בְּחֵלֶק יִזְרְעֶאל וְאֵין קֹבֵר וַיִּפְתַּח
then-he-opened burying and-no-one Jezreel on-plot-of-ground-of the-dogs

הַדֶּלֶת וַיָּנֹס׃ (11) וְיֵהוּא יָצָא אֶל־ עַבְדֵי אֲדֹנָיו
masters-of-him officers-of to he-went-out when-Jehu (11) and-he-ran the-door

וַיֹּאמֶר לוֹ הֲשָׁלוֹם מַדּוּעַ בָּא־ הַמְשֻׁגָּע הַזֶּה
the-this the-one-being-mad he-came why? all-right? to-him then-they-asked

אֵלֶיךָ וַיֹּאמֶר אֲלֵיהֶם אַתֶּם יְדַעְתֶּם אֶת־ הָאִישׁ וְאֶת־ שִׂיחוֹ׃
saying-of-him and the-man *** you-know you to-them and-he-replied to-you

(12) וַיֹּאמְרוּ שֶׁקֶר הַגֶּד־ נָא לָנוּ וַיֹּאמֶר כָּזֹאת וְכָזֹאת
and-as-that as-this and-he-said to-us now! tell! not-true and-they-said (12)

אָמַר אֵלַי לֵאמֹר כֹּה אָמַר יְהוָה מְשַׁחְתִּיךָ לְמֶלֶךְ אֶל־יִשְׂרָאֵל׃
Israel over as-king I-anoint-you Yahweh he-says this to-say to-me he-told

(13) וַיְמַהֲרוּ וַיִּקְחוּ אִישׁ בִּגְדוֹ וַיָּשִׂימוּ
and-they-spread cloak-of-him each and-they-took and-they-hurried (13)

תַּחְתָּיו אֶל־ גֶּרֶם הַמַּעֲלוֹת וַיִּתְקְעוּ בַּשּׁוֹפָר וַיֹּאמְרוּ
and-they-said on-the-trumpet then-they-blew the-steps bare-part-of on under-him

מָלַךְ יֵהוּא׃ (14) וַיִּתְקַשֵּׁר יֵהוּא בֶּן־ יְהוֹשָׁפָט בֶּן־ נִמְשִׁי
Nimshi son-of Jehoshaphat son-of Jehu so-he-conspired (14) Jehu he-is-king

אֶל־ יוֹרָם וְיוֹרָם הָיָה שֹׁמֵר בְּרָמֹת גִּלְעָד הוּא וְכָל־
and-all-of he Gilead at-Ramoth defending he-was now-Joram Joram against

יִשְׂרָאֵל מִפְּנֵי חֲזָאֵל מֶלֶךְ־ אֲרָם׃ (15) וַיָּשָׁב יְהוֹרָם הַמֶּלֶךְ
the-king Jehoram but-he-returned (15) Aram king-of Hazael from-before Israel

and declared, "This is what the LORD, the God of Israel, says: 'I anoint you king over the LORD's people Israel.
7You are to destroy the house of Ahab your master, and I will avenge the blood of my servants the prophets and the blood of all the LORD's servants shed by Jezebel.
8The whole house of Ahab will perish. I will cut off from Ahab every last male in Israel—slave or free.
9I will make the house of Ahab like the house of Jeroboam son of Nebat and like the house of Baasha son of Ahijah.
10As for Jezebel, dogs will devour her on the plot of ground at Jezreel, and no one will bury her.'" Then he opened the door and ran.

11When Jehu went out to his fellow officers, one of them asked him, "Is everything all right? Why did this madman come to you?"

"You know the man and the sort of things he says," Jehu replied.

12"That's not true!" they said. "Tell us."

Jehu said, "Here is what he told me: 'This is what the LORD says: I anoint you king over Israel.'"

13They hurried and took their cloaks and spread them under him on the bare steps. Then they blew the trumpet and shouted, "Jehu is king!"

Jehu Kills Joram and Ahaziah

14So Jehu son of Jehoshaphat, the son of Nimshi, conspired against Joram. (Now Joram and all Israel had been defending Ramoth Gilead against Hazael king of Aram,
15but King Joram[s] had returned to Jezreel to recover

[s]15 Hebrew *Jehoram*, a variant of *Joram*; also in verses 17 and 21-24

לְהִתְרַפֵּא בִּיזְרְעֶאל מִן־ הַמַּכִּים אֲשֶׁר יַכֻּהוּ אֲרַמִּים
Arameans they-inflicted-on-him that the-wounds from in-Jezreel to-recover

בְּהִלָּחֲמוֹ אֶת־ חֲזָאֵל מֶלֶךְ אֲרָם וַיֹּאמֶר יֵהוּא אִם־ יֵשׁ
this-is if Jehu and-he-said Aram king-of Hazael *** when-to-fight-him

נַפְשְׁכֶם אַל־ יֵצֵא פָלִיט מִן־ הָעִיר לָלֶכֶת לְגִּיד
to-tell-news to-go the-city from escapee let-him-slip-out not feeling-of-you

בְּיִזְרְעֶאל׃ וַיִּרְכַּב יֵהוּא וַיֵּלֶךְ יִזְרְעֶאלָה כִּי
because to-Jezreel and-he-went Jehu then-he-got-into-chariot (16) in-Jezreel

יוֹרָם שֹׁכֵב שָׁמָּה וַאֲחַזְיָה מֶלֶךְ יְהוּדָה יָרַד לִרְאוֹת
to-see he-went-down Judah king-of and-Ahaziah at-there resting Joram

אֶת־ יוֹרָם׃ וְהַצֹּפֶה עֹמֵד עַל־ הַמִּגְדָּל בְּיִזְרְעֶאל
in-Jezreel the-tower on standing and-the-one-looking-out (17) Joram ***

וַיַּרְא אֶת־ שִׁפְעַת יֵהוּא בְּבֹאוֹ וַיֹּאמֶר
then-he-called-out when-to-approach-him Jehu troop-of *** when-he-saw

שִׁפְעַת אֲנִי רֹאֶה וַיֹּאמֶר יְהוֹרָם קַח רַכָּב וּשְׁלַח לִקְרָאתָם
to-meet-them and-send! horseman get! Jehoram and-he-ordered seeing I troop-of

וְיֹאמַר הֲשָׁלוֹם׃ וַיֵּלֶךְ רֹכֵב הַסּוּס לִקְרָאתוֹ
to-meet-him the-horse one-riding so-he-went (18) peace? and-he-shall-ask

וַיֹּאמֶר כֹּה־ אָמַר הַמֶּלֶךְ הֲשָׁלוֹם וַיֹּאמֶר יֵהוּא מַה־ לְּךָ
to-you what? Jehu and-he-replied peace? the-king he-says this and-he-said

וּלְשָׁלוֹם סֹב אֶל־ אַחֲרָי וַיַּגֵּד הַצֹּפֶה
the-one-looking-out and-he-reported behind-me at fall-in! and-to-peace

לֵאמֹר בָּא־ הַמַּלְאָךְ עַד־ הֵם וְלֹא־ שָׁב׃ וַיִּשְׁלַח
so-he-sent (19) he-came-back but-not them to the-messenger he-reached to-say

רֹכֵב סוּס שֵׁנִי וַיָּבֹא אֲלֵהֶם וַיֹּאמֶר כֹּה־ אָמַר
he-says this then-he-said to-them when-he-came second horse one-riding

הַמֶּלֶךְ שָׁלוֹם וַיֹּאמֶר יֵהוּא מַה־ לְּךָ וּלְשָׁלוֹם סֹב אֶל־
at fall-in! and-to-peace to-you what? Jehu and-he-replied peace the-king

אַחֲרָי׃ וַיַּגֵּד הַצֹּפֶה לֵאמֹר בָּא עַד־
to he-reached to-say the-one-looking-out and-he-reported (20) behind-me

אֲלֵיהֶם וְלֹא־ שָׁב וְהַמִּנְהָג כְּמִנְהַג יֵהוּא בֶן־
son-of Jehu like-driving-of and-the-driving he-came-back but-not with-them

נִמְשִׁי כִּי בְשִׁגָּעוֹן יִנְהָג׃ וַיֹּאמֶר יְהוֹרָם אֱסֹר
hitch-up! Jehoram and-he-ordered (21) he-drives like-madman for Nimshi

וַיֶּאְסֹר רִכְבּוֹ וַיֵּצֵא יְהוֹרָם מֶלֶךְ־ יִשְׂרָאֵל
Israel king-of Jehoram then-he-rode-out chariot-of-him when-he-hitched-up

וַאֲחַזְיָהוּ מֶלֶךְ־ יְהוּדָה אִישׁ בְּרִכְבּוֹ וַיֵּצְאוּ לִקְרַאת
to-meet and-they-rode-out in-chariot-of-him each Judah king-of and-Ahaziah

from the wounds the Arameans had inflicted on him in the battle with Hazael king of Aram.) Jehu said, "If this is the way you feel, don't let anyone slip out of the city to go and tell the news in Jezreel."
[16]Then he got into his chariot and rode to Jezreel, because Joram was resting there and Ahaziah king of Judah had gone down to see him.
[17]When the lookout standing on the tower in Jezreel saw Jehu's troops approaching, he called out, "I see some troops coming."

"Get a horseman," Joram ordered. "Send him to meet them and ask, 'Do you come in peace?' "
[18]The horseman rode off to meet Jehu and said, "This is what the king says: 'Do you come in peace?' "

"What do you have to do with peace?" Jehu replied. "Fall in behind me."

The lookout reported, "The messenger has reached them, but he isn't coming back."
[19]So the king sent out a second horseman. When he came to them he said, "This is what the king says: 'Do you come in peace?' "

Jehu replied, "What do you have to do with peace? Fall in behind me."
[20]The lookout reported, "He has reached them, but he isn't coming back either. The driving is like that of Jehu son of Nimshi—he drives like a madman."
[21]"Hitch up my chariot," Joram ordered. And when it was hitched up, Joram king of Israel and Ahaziah king of Judah rode out, each in his own chariot, to meet Jehu.

*15 Most mss have *sheva* under the *beth* and *hireq* under the *yod* (בְּיִ).

°15 ק להגיד

יֵהוּא וַיִּמְצָאֻהוּ בְּחֶלְקַת נָבוֹת הַיִּזְרְעֵאלִי׃
the-Jezreelite Naboth at-plot-of-ground-of and-they-met-him Jehu

וַיְהִי כִּרְאוֹת יְהוֹרָם אֶת־יֵהוּא וַיֹּאמֶר הֲשָׁלוֹם יֵהוּא
Jehu peace? then-he-asked Jehu *** Jehoram when-to-see and-he-was (22)

וַיֹּאמֶר מָה הַשָּׁלוֹם עַד־זְנוּנֵי אִיזֶבֶל אִמְּךָ
mother-of-you Jezebel idolatries-of as-long-as the-peace how? and-he-replied

וּכְשָׁפֶיהָ הָרַבִּים׃ וַיַּהֲפֹךְ יְהוֹרָם
Jehoram and-he-turned-about (23) the-many-ones and-witchcrafts-of-her

יָדָיו וַיָּנָס וַיֹּאמֶר אֶל־אֲחַזְיָהוּ מִרְמָה אֲחַזְיָה׃
Ahaziah treachery Ahaziah to and-he-called-out and-he-fled hands-of-him

וְיֵהוּא מִלֵּא יָדוֹ בַקֶּשֶׁת וַיַּךְ אֶת־יְהוֹרָם
Jehoram *** and-he-shot on-the-bow hand-of-him he-drew then-Jehu (24)

בֵּין זְרֹעָיו וַיֵּצֵא הַחֵצִי מִלִּבּוֹ
from-heart-of-him the-arrow and-he-came-out shoulders-of-him between

וַיִּכְרַע בְּרִכְבּוֹ׃ וַיֹּאמֶר אֶל־בִּדְקַר שָׁלִשֹׁה
officer-of-him Bidkar to and-he-said (25) in-chariot-of-him and-he-slumped

שָׂא הַשְׁלִכֵהוּ בְּחֶלְקַת שְׂדֵה נָבוֹת הַיִּזְרְעֵאלִי כִּי־
for the-Jezreelite Naboth field-of in-portion-of throw-him! pick-up!

זְכֹר אֲנִי וָאַתָּה אֵת רֹכְבִים צְמָדִים אַחֲרֵי אַחְאָב אָבִיו
father-of-him Ahab behind ones-together ones-riding with and-you I remember!

וַיהוָה נָשָׂא עָלָיו אֶת־הַמַּשָּׂא הַזֶּה׃ אִם־
surely (26) the-this the-prophecy *** about-him he-prophesied when-Yahweh

לֹא אֶת־דְּמֵי נָבוֹת וְאֶת־דְּמֵי בָנָיו רָאִיתִי אֶמֶשׁ
yesterday I-saw sons-of-him bloods-of and Naboth bloods-of *** indeed

נְאֻם־יְהוָה וְשִׁלַּמְתִּי לְךָ בַּחֶלְקָה
for-the-plot-of-ground to-you and-I-will-make-pay Yahweh declaration-of

הַזֹּאת נְאֻם־יְהוָה וְעַתָּה שָׂא הַשְׁלִכֵהוּ בַּחֶלְקָה
on-the-plot throw-him! pick-up! so-now Yahweh declaration-of the-this

כִּדְבַר יְהוָה׃ וַאֲחַזְיָה מֶלֶךְ־יְהוּדָה רָאָה וַיָּנָס
then-he-fled he-saw Judah king-of when-Ahaziah (27) Yahweh as-word-of

דֶּרֶךְ בֵּית הַגָּן וַיִּרְדֹּף אַחֲרָיו יֵהוּא וַיֹּאמֶר גַּם־אֹתוֹ
him also and-he-shouted Jehu after-him and-he-chased Haggan Beth road-of

הַכֻּהוּ אֶל־הַמֶּרְכָּבָה בְּמַעֲלֵה־גוּר אֲשֶׁר אֶת־יִבְלְעָם וַיָּנָס
but-he-escaped Ibleam near that Gur on-way-up-of the-chariot in kill-him!

מְגִדּוֹ וַיָּמָת שָׁם׃ וַיַּרְכִּבוּ אֹתוֹ עֲבָדָיו
servants-of-him him and-they-took-by-chariot (28) there and-he-died Megiddo

יְרוּשָׁלְַמָה וַיִּקְבְּרוּ אֹתוֹ בִקְבֻרָתוֹ עִם־אֲבֹתָיו
fathers-of-him with in-tomb-of-him him and-they-buried to-Jerusalem

They met him at the plot of ground that had belonged to Naboth the Jezreelite.
22When Joram saw Jehu he asked, "Have you come in peace, Jehu?"

"How can there be peace," Jehu replied, "as long as all the idolatry and witchcraft of your mother Jezebel abound?"

23Joram turned about and fled, calling out to Ahaziah, "Treachery, Ahaziah!"

24Then Jehu drew his bow and shot Joram between the shoulders. The arrow pierced his heart and he slumped down in his chariot.
25Jehu said to Bidkar, his chariot officer, "Pick him up and throw him on the field that belonged to Naboth the Jezreelite. Remember how you and I were riding together in chariots behind Ahab his father when the LORD made this prophecy about him:
26'Yesterday I saw the blood of Naboth and the blood of his sons, declares the LORD, and I will surely make you pay for it on this plot of ground, declares the LORD.'[t] Now then, pick him up and throw him on that plot, in accordance with the word of the LORD."

27When Ahaziah king of Judah saw what had happened, he fled up the road to Beth Haggan.[u] Jehu chased him, shouting, "Kill him too!" They wounded him in his chariot on the way up to Gur near Ibleam, but he escaped to Megiddo and died there.
28His servants took him by chariot to Jerusalem and buried him with his fathers in his tomb in

[t]26 See 1 Kings 21:19.
[u]27 *Or fled by way of the garden house*

°25 ק שלשו

בְּעִיר דָּוִד׃ וּבִשְׁנַת אַחַת עֶשְׂרֵה שָׁנָה לְיוֹרָם בֶּן־
son-of of-Joram year ten-of one-of now-in-year-of (29) David in-City-of

אַחְאָב מָלַךְ אֲחַזְיָה עַל־יְהוּדָה׃ וַיָּבוֹא יֵהוּא יִזְרְעֶאלָה
to-Jezreel Jehu then-he-went (30) Judah over Ahaziah he-became-king Ahab

וְאִיזֶבֶל שָׁמְעָה וַתָּשֶׂם בַּפּוּךְ עֵינֶיהָ
eyes-of-her with-the-paint then-she-prepared she-heard when-Jezebel

וַתֵּיטֶב אֶת־רֹאשָׁהּ וַתַּשְׁקֵף בְּעַד הַחַלּוֹן׃
the-window out-of and-she-looked hair-of-her *** and-she-made-good

וְיֵהוּא בָּא בַשַּׁעַר וַתֹּאמֶר הֲשָׁלוֹם זִמְרִי
Zimri peace? and-she-asked through-the-gate he-entered and-Jehu (31)

הֹרֵג אֲדֹנָיו׃ וַיִּשָּׂא פָנָיו אֶל־הַחַלּוֹן
the-window to faces-of-him and-he-lifted (32) masters-of-him one-murdering

וַיֹּאמֶר מִי אִתִּי מִי וַיַּשְׁקִיפוּ אֵלָיו שְׁנַיִם שְׁלֹשָׁה
three two at-him and-they-looked-down who? with-me who? and-he-called-out

סָרִיסִים׃ וַיֹּאמֶר שִׁמְטֻהוּ וַיִּשְׁמְטוּהָ
so-they-threw-down-her throw-down-her! and-he-said (33) eunuchs

וַיִּז מִדָּמָהּ אֶל־הַקִּיר וְאֶל־הַסּוּסִים
the-horses and-on the-wall on from-blood-of-her and-he-spattered

וַיִּרְמְסֶנָּה׃ וַיָּבֹא וַיֹּאכַל וַיֵּשְׁתְּ וַיֹּאמֶר
and-he-said and-he-drank and-he-ate then-he-went-in (34) and-he-trampled-her

פִּקְדוּ־נָא אֶת־הָאֲרוּרָה הַזֹּאת וְקִבְרוּהָ כִּי
for and-bury-her! the-that the-woman-being-cursed *** now! take-care!

בַת־מֶלֶךְ הִיא׃ וַיֵּלְכוּ לְקָבְרָהּ וְלֹא־מָצְאוּ
they-found then-nothing to-bury-her when-they-went (35) she king daughter-of

בָהּ כִּי אִם־הַגֻּלְגֹּלֶת וְהָרַגְלַיִם וְכַפּוֹת הַיָּדָיִם׃
the-hands and-palms-of and-the-feet the-skull only except of-her

וַיָּשֻׁבוּ וַיַּגִּידוּ לוֹ וַיֹּאמֶר דְּבַר־יְהוָה
Yahweh word-of and-she-said to-him and-they-told and-they-went-back (36)

הוּא אֲשֶׁר דִּבֶּר בְּיַד־עַבְדּוֹ אֵלִיָּהוּ הַתִּשְׁבִּי לֵאמֹר
to-say the-Tishbite Elijah servant-of-him by-hand-of he-spoke that this

בְּחֵלֶק יִזְרְעֶאל יֹאכְלוּ הַכְּלָבִים אֶת־בְּשַׂר אִיזָבֶל׃
Jezebel flesh-of *** the-dogs they-will-devour Jezreel on-plot-of-ground-of

וְהָיְתָ נִבְלַת אִיזֶבֶל כְּדֹמֶן עַל־פְּנֵי הַשָּׂדֶה
the-ground surfaces-of on like-refuse Jezebel body-of and-she-will-be (37)

בְּחֵלֶק יִזְרְעֶאל אֲשֶׁר לֹא־יֹאמְרוּ זֹאת אִיזָבֶל׃ וּלְאַחְאָב
now-to-Ahab (10:1) Jezebel this they-will-say not that Jezreel at-plot-of

שִׁבְעִים בָּנִים בְּשֹׁמְרוֹן וַיִּכְתֹּב יֵהוּא סְפָרִים וַיִּשְׁלַח שֹׁמְרוֹן אֶל־
to Samaria and-he-sent letters Jehu so-he-wrote in-Samaria sons seventy

the City of David. 29(In the eleventh year of Joram son of Ahab, Ahaziah had become king of Judah.)

Jezebel Killed

30Then Jehu went to Jezreel. When Jezebel heard about it, she painted her eyes, arranged her hair and looked out of a window. 31As Jehu entered the gate, she asked, "Have you come in peace, Zimri, you murderer of your master?"[v]

32He looked up at the window and called out, "Who is on my side? Who?" Two or three eunuchs looked down at him. 33"Throw her down!" Jehu said. So they threw her down, and some of her blood spattered the wall and the horses as they trampled her underfoot.

34Jehu went in and ate and drank. "Take care of that cursed woman," he said, "and bury her, for she was a king's daughter." 35But when they went out to bury her, they found nothing except her skull, her feet and her hands. 36They went back and told Jehu, who said, "This is the word of the LORD that he spoke through his servant Elijah the Tishbite: On the plot of ground at Jezreel dogs will devour Jezebel's flesh.[w] 37Jezebel's body will be like refuse on the ground in the plot at Jezreel, so that no one will be able to say, 'This is Jezebel.' "

Ahab's Family Killed

10 Now there were in Samaria seventy sons of the house of Ahab. So Jehu wrote letters and sent them to

v31 Or *"Did Zimri have peace, who murdered his master?"*
w36 See 1 Kings 21:23.

°33 ק שמטוה
°37 ק והיתה

שָׂרֵי יִזְרְעֶאל הַזְּקֵנִים וְאֶל־ הָאֹמְנִים אַחְאָב לֵאמֹר׃
to-say Ahab the-ones-guarding and-to the-elders Jezreel officials-of

(2) וְעַתָּה כְּבֹא הַסֵּפֶר הַזֶּה אֲלֵיכֶם וְאִתְּכֶם בְּנֵי
sons-of since-with-you to-you the-this the-letter as-to-reach and-now (2)

אֲדֹנֵיכֶם וְאִתְּכֶם הָרֶכֶב וְהַסּוּסִים וְעִיר מִבְצָר
fortified and-city and-the-horses the-chariot and-with-you masters-of-you

וְהַנָּשֶׁק׃ (3) וּרְאִיתֶם הַטּוֹב וְהַיָּשָׁר מִבְּנֵי
from-sons-of and-the-worthy the-good now-you-choose (3) and-the-weapon

אֲדֹנֵיכֶם וְשַׂמְתֶּם עַל־ כִּסֵּא אָבִיו וְהִלָּחֲמוּ עַל־
for then-fight! father-of-him throne-of on and-you-set masters-of-you

בֵּית אֲדֹנֵיכֶם׃ (4) וַיִּרְאוּ מְאֹד מְאֹד וַיֹּאמְרוּ
and-they-said very very but-they-were-terrified (4) masters-of-you house-of

הִנֵּה שְׁנֵי הַמְּלָכִים לֹא עָמְדוּ לְפָנָיו וְאֵיךְ נַעֲמֹד
can-we-resist so-how? before-him they-could-resist not the-kings two-of see!

אֲנָחְנוּ׃ (5) וַיִּשְׁלַח אֲשֶׁר־ עַל־ הַבַּיִת וַאֲשֶׁר עַל־ הָעִיר וְהַזְּקֵנִים
and-the-elders the-city over and-who the-palace over who so-he-sent (5) we

וְהָאֹמְנִים אֶל־ יֵהוּא ׀ לֵאמֹר עֲבָדֶיךָ אֲנַחְנוּ וְכֹל אֲשֶׁר־
that and-all we servants-of-you to-say Jehu to and-the-ones-guarding

תֹּאמַר אֵלֵינוּ נַעֲשֶׂה לֹא־ נַמְלִיךְ אִישׁ הַטּוֹב
the-good anyone we-will-appoint-as-king not we-will-do to-us you-say

בְּעֵינֶיךָ עֲשֵׂה׃ (6) וַיִּכְתֹּב אֲלֵיהֶם סֵפֶר ׀ שֵׁנִית לֵאמֹר אִם־ לִי
to-me if to-say second letter to-them then-he-wrote (6) do! in-eyes-of-you

אַתֶּם וּלְקֹלִי ׀ אַתֶּם שֹׁמְעִים קְחוּ אֶת־ רָאשֵׁי אַנְשֵׁי בְנֵי־
sons-of men-of heads-of *** take! ones-obeying you and-to-voice-of-me you

אֲדֹנֵיכֶם וּבֹאוּ אֵלַי כָּעֵת מָחָר יִזְרְעֶאלָה וּבְנֵי
now-sons-of in-Jezreel tomorrow by-the-time to-me and-come! masters-of-you

הַמֶּלֶךְ שִׁבְעִים אִישׁ אֶת־ גְּדֹלֵי הָעִיר מְגַדְּלִים אוֹתָם׃
them ones-rearing the-city leading-men-of with man seventy the-king

(7) וַיְהִי כְּבֹא הַסֵּפֶר אֲלֵיהֶם וַיִּקְחוּ אֶת־ בְּנֵי
sons-of *** then-they-took to-them the-letter when-to-arrive and-he-was (7)

הַמֶּלֶךְ וַיִּשְׁחֲטוּ שִׁבְעִים אִישׁ וַיָּשִׂימוּ אֶת־ רָאשֵׁיהֶם
heads-of-them *** and-they-put man seventy and-they-slaughtered the-king

בַּדּוּדִים וַיִּשְׁלְחוּ אֵלָיו יִזְרְעֶאלָה׃ (8) וַיָּבֹא
when-he-arrived (8) in-Jezreel to-him and-they-sent in-the-baskets

הַמַּלְאָךְ וַיַּגֶּד־ לוֹ לֵאמֹר הֵבִיאוּ רָאשֵׁי בְנֵי־
sons-of heads-of they-brought to-say to-him then-he-told the-messenger

הַמֶּלֶךְ וַיֹּאמֶר שִׂימוּ אֹתָם שְׁנֵי צִבֻּרִים פֶּתַח הַשַּׁעַר
the-city-gate entrance-of piles two-of them put! then-he-ordered the-king

Samaria: to the officials of Jezreel,[x] to the elders and to the
guardians of Ahab's children.
He said, 2"As soon as this letter reaches you, since your
master's sons are with you
and you have chariots and
horses, a fortified city and
weapons, 3choose the best and
most worthy of your master's
sons and set him on his father's throne. Then fight for
your master's house."
4But they were terrified and
said, "If two kings could not
resist him, how can we?"
5So the palace administrator,
the city governor, the elders
and the guardians sent this
message to Jehu: "We are your
servants and we will do anything you say. We will not appoint anyone as king; you do
whatever you think best."
6Then Jehu wrote them a
second letter, saying, "If you
are on my side and will obey
me, take the heads of your
master's sons and come to me
in Jezreel by this time tomorrow."
Now the royal princes, seventy of them, were with the
leading men of the city, who
were rearing them. 7When the
letter arrived, these men took
the princes and slaughtered all
seventy of them. They put
their heads in baskets and
sent them to Jehu in Jezreel.
8When the messenger arrived,
he told Jehu, "They have
brought the heads of the
princes."
Then Jehu ordered, "Put
them in two piles at the entrance of the city gate until

[x]1 Hebrew; some Septuagint manuscripts and Vulgate *of the city*

עַד־הַבֹּֽקֶר׃ (9) וַיְהִי בַבֹּקֶר וַיֵּצֵא וַֽיַּעֲמֹד
and-he-stood then-he-went-out in-the-morning and-he-was (9) the-morning until

וַיֹּאמֶר אֶל־כָּל־הָעָם צַדִּקִים אַתֶּם הִנֵּה אֲנִי קָשַׁרְתִּי
I-conspired I see! you ones-innocent the-people all-of to and-he-said

עַל־אֲדֹנִי וָאֶהַרְגֵהוּ וּמִי הִכָּה אֶת־כָּל־אֵֽלֶּה׃
these all-of *** he-killed but-who? and-I-killed-him master-of-me against

(10) דְּעוּ אֵפוֹא כִּי לֹא יִפֹּל מִדְּבַר יְהוָה אַרְצָה אֲשֶׁר־
that to-ground Yahweh from-word-of he-will-fall not that then know! (10)

דִּבֶּר יְהוָה עַל־בֵּית אַחְאָב וַיהוָה עָשָׂה אֵת אֲשֶׁר
what *** he-did for-Yahweh Ahab house-of against Yahweh he-spoke

דִּבֶּר בְּיַד עַבְדּוֹ אֵלִיָּֽהוּ׃ (11) וַיַּךְ יֵהוּא אֵת
*** Jehu so-he-killed (11) Elijah servant-of-him by-hand-of he-promised

כָּל־הַנִּשְׁאָרִים לְבֵית־אַחְאָב בְּיִזְרְעֶאל וְכָל־
and-all-of in-Jezreel Ahab of-house-of the-ones-remaining all-of

גְּדֹלָיו וּמְיֻדָּעָיו וְכֹהֲנָיו עַד־בִּלְתִּי הִשְׁאִיר־
he-left not until and-priests-of-him and-ones-knowing-him chief-men-of-him

לוֹ שָׂרִֽיד׃ (12) וַיָּקָם וַיָּבֹא וַיֵּלֶךְ שֹׁמְרוֹן הוּא
he Samaria and-he-went and-he-set-out then-he-got-up (12) survivor to-him

בֵּית־עֵקֶד הָרֹעִים בַּדָּֽרֶךְ׃ (13) וְיֵהוּא מָצָא אֶת־
*** he-met and-Jehu (13) on-the-way the-Ones-Shepherding Eked-of Beth

אֲחֵי אֲחַזְיָהוּ מֶלֶךְ־יְהוּדָה וַיֹּאמֶר מִי אַתֶּם וַיֹּאמְרוּ
and-they-said you who? and-he-asked Judah king-of Ahaziah relatives-of

אֲחֵי אֲחַזְיָהוּ אֲנַחְנוּ וַנֵּרֶד לִשְׁלוֹם בְּנֵי־הַמֶּלֶךְ
the-king families-of for-greeting-of and-we-came-down we Ahaziah relatives-of

וּבְנֵי הַגְּבִירָֽה׃ (14) וַיֹּאמֶר תִּפְשׂוּם חַיִּים
ones-alive take-them! and-he-ordered (14) the-queen-mother and-families-of

וַיִּתְפְּשׂוּם חַיִּים וַֽיִּשְׁחָטוּם אֶל־בּוֹר בֵּית־עֵקֶד
Eked Beth well-of by and-they-slaughtered-them ones-alive so-they-took-them

אַרְבָּעִים וּשְׁנַיִם אִישׁ וְלֹא־הִשְׁאִיר אִישׁ מֵהֶֽם׃ (15) וַיֵּלֶךְ
and-he-left (15) of-them anyone he-left-survivor and-not man and-two forty

מִשָּׁם וַיִּמְצָא אֶת־יְהוֹנָדָב בֶּן־רֵכָב לִקְרָאתוֹ
to-meet-him Recab son-of Jehonadab *** and-he-came-upon from-there

וַֽיְבָרְכֵהוּ וַיֹּאמֶר אֵלָיו הֲיֵשׁ אֶת־לְבָבְךָ יָשָׁר
in-accord heart-of-you *** is-there? to-him and-he-said and-he-greeted-him

כַּאֲשֶׁר לְבָבִי עִם־לְבָבֶךָ וַיֹּאמֶר יְהוֹנָדָב יֵשׁ
there-is Jehonadab and-he-said heart-of-you with heart-of-me just-as

וָיֵשׁ תְּנָה אֶת־יָדֶךָ וַיִּתֵּן יָדוֹ וַיַּעֲלֵהוּ
and-he-helped-up-him hand-of-him so-he-gave hand-of-you *** give! if-there-is

morning."
9The next morning Jehu
went out. He stood before all
the people and said, "You are
innocent. It was I who conspired against my master and
killed him, but who killed all
these? 10Know then, that not a
word the LORD has spoken
against the house of Ahab will
fail. The LORD has done what
he promised through his servant Elijah." 11So Jehu killed
everyone in Jezreel who remained of the house of Ahab,
as well as all his chief men, his
close friends and his priests,
leaving him no survivor.
12Jehu then set out and went
toward Samaria. At Beth Eked
of the Shepherds, 13he met
some relatives of Ahaziah
king of Judah and asked,
"Who are you?"
They said, "We are relatives
of Ahaziah, and we have come
down to greet the families of
the king and of the queen
mother."
14"Take them alive!" he ordered. So they took them alive
and slaughtered them by the
well of Beth Eked—forty-two
men. He left no survivor.
15After he left there, he came
upon Jehonadab son of Recab,
who was on his way to meet
him. Jehu greeted him and
said, "Are you in accord with
me, as I am with you?"
"I am," Jehonadab an-
swered.
"If so," said Jehu, "give me
your hand." So he did, and
Jehu helped him up into the

אֵלָיו אֶל־הַמֶּרְכָּבָה׃ (16) וַיֹּאמֶר לְכָה אִתִּי וּרְאֵה
and-see! with-me come! and-he-said (16) the-chariot into to-him

בְּקִנְאָתִי לַיהוָה וַיַּרְכִּבוּ אֹתוֹ בְּרִכְבּוֹ׃
in-chariot-of-him him then-he-had-ride for-Yahweh to-zeal-of-me

(17) וַיָּבֹא שֹׁמְרוֹן וַיַּךְ אֶת־כָּל־הַנִּשְׁאָרִים
the-ones-being-left all-of *** then-he-killed Samaria when-he-came (17)

לְאַחְאָב בְּשֹׁמְרוֹן עַד־הִשְׁמִידוֹ כִּדְבַר יְהוָה אֲשֶׁר דִּבֶּר
he-spoke that Yahweh as-word-of he-destroyed-him until in-Samaria of-Ahab

אֶל־אֵלִיָּהוּ׃ (18) וַיִּקְבֹּץ יֵהוּא אֶת־כָּל־הָעָם
the-people all-of *** Jehu then-he-brought-together (18) Elijah to

וַיֹּאמֶר אֲלֵהֶם אַחְאָב עָבַד אֶת־הַבַּעַל מְעָט יֵהוּא יַעַבְדֶנּוּ
he-will-serve-him Jehu little the-Baal *** he-served Ahab to-them and-he-said

הַרְבֵּה׃ (19) וְעַתָּה כָל־נְבִיאֵי הַבַּעַל כָּל־עֹבְדָיו
ones-ministering-him all-of the-Baal prophets-of all-of so-now (19) to-be-much

וְכָל־כֹּהֲנָיו קִרְאוּ אֵלַי אִישׁ אַל־יִפָּקֵד כִּי
because let-him-be-missing not anyone to-me summon! priests-of-him and-all-of

זֶבַח גָּדוֹל לִי לַבַּעַל כֹּל אֲשֶׁר־יִפָּקֵד לֹא יִחְיֶה
he-will-live not he-is-missing who anyone for-the-Baal by-me great sacrifice

וְיֵהוּא עָשָׂה בְעָקְבָּה לְמַעַן הַאֲבִיד אֶת־עֹבְדֵי
ones-ministering-of *** to-destroy in-order on-deception he-acted but-Jehu

הַבָּעַל׃ (20) וַיֹּאמֶר יֵהוּא קַדְּשׁוּ עֲצָרָה לַבַּעַל
for-the-Baal assembly set-apart! Jehu and-he-said (20) the-Baal

וַיִּקְרָאוּ׃ (21) וַיִּשְׁלַח יֵהוּא בְּכָל־יִשְׂרָאֵל וַיָּבֹאוּ
and-they-came Israel through-all-of Jehu then-he-sent (21) so-they-proclaimed

כָּל־עֹבְדֵי הַבַּעַל וְלֹא־נִשְׁאַר אִישׁ אֲשֶׁר לֹא־בָא
he-came not who one he-was-left and-not the-Baal ones-ministering-of all-of

וַיָּבֹאוּ בֵּית הַבַּעַל וַיִּמָּלֵא בֵית־הַבַּעַל פֶּה
end the-Baal temple-of so-he-was-full the-Baal temple-of and-they-entered

לָפֶה׃ (22) וַיֹּאמֶר לַאֲשֶׁר עַל־הַמֶּלְתָּחָה הוֹצֵא לְבוּשׁ לְכֹל
for-all-of robe bring! the-wardrobe over to-whom and-he-said (22) to-end

עֹבְדֵי הַבָּעַל וַיֹּצֵא לָהֶם הַמַּלְבּוּשׁ׃
the-robe for-them so-he-brought-out the-Baal ones-ministering-of

(23) וַיָּבֹא יֵהוּא וִיהוֹנָדָב בֶּן־רֵכָב בֵּית הַבָּעַל
the-Baal temple-of Recab son-of and-Jehonadab Jehu then-he-went (23)

וַיֹּאמֶר לְעֹבְדֵי הַבַּעַל חַפְּשׂוּ וּרְאוּ פֶּן־
not and-see! look-around! the-Baal to-ones-ministering-of and-he-said

יֶשׁ־פֹּה עִמָּכֶם מֵעַבְדֵי יְהוָה כִּי אִם־עֹבְדֵי
ones-ministering-of only but Yahweh from-servants-of with-you here there-is

chariot. 16Jehu said, "Come
with me and see my zeal for
the LORD." Then he had him
ride along in his chariot.
17When Jehu came to Sa-
maria, he killed all who were
left there of Ahab's family; he
destroyed them, according to
the word of the LORD spoken
to Elijah.

Ministers of Baal Killed

18Then Jehu brought all the
people together and said to
them, "Ahab served Baal a little; Jehu will serve him much.
19Now summon all the prophets of Baal, all his ministers
and all his priests. See that no
one is missing, because I am
going to hold a great sacrifice
for Baal. Anyone who fails to
come will no longer live." But
Jehu was acting deceptively in
order to destroy the ministers
of Baal.
20Jehu said, "Call an assembly in honor of Baal." So they
proclaimed it. 21Then he sent
word throughout Israel, and
all the ministers of Baal came;
not one stayed away. They
crowded into the temple of
Baal until it was full from one
end to the other. 22And Jehu
said to the keeper of the wardrobe, "Bring robes for all the
ministers of Baal." So he
brought out robes for them.
23Then Jehu and Jehonadab
son of Recab went into the
temple of Baal. Jehu said to the
ministers of Baal, "Look
around and see that no servants of the LORD are here
with you—only ministers of

הַבַּעַל לְבַדָּם׃ (24) וַיָּבֹאוּ לַעֲשׂוֹת זְבָחִים
sacrifices to-make so-they-went-in (24) by-themselves the-Baal

וְעֹלוֹת וְיֵהוּא שָׂם־ לוֹ בַחוּץ שְׁמֹנִים אִישׁ
man eighty at-the-outside for-him he-posted now-Jehu and-burnt-offerings

וַיֹּאמֶר הָאִישׁ אֲשֶׁר־ יִמָּלֵט מִן־ הָאֲנָשִׁים אֲשֶׁר אֲנִי מֵבִיא עַל־
in placing I whom the-men from he-lets-escape who the-one and-he-said

יְדֵיכֶם נַפְשׁוֹ תַּחַת נַפְשׁוֹ׃ (25) וַיְהִי כְּכַלֹּתוֹ ׀
as-to-finish-him and-he-was (25) life-of-him for life-of-him hands-of-you

לַעֲשׂוֹת הָעֹלָה וַיֹּאמֶר יֵהוּא לָרָצִים
to-the-ones-guarding Jehu then-he-ordered the-burnt-offering to-make

וְלַשָּׁלִשִׁים בֹּאוּ הַכּוּם אִישׁ אַל־ יֵצֵא
he-must-escape not anyone kill-them! go-in! and-to-the-officers

וַיַּכּוּם לְפִי־ חָרֶב וַיַּשְׁלִכוּ הָרָצִים
the-ones-guarding and-they-threw-out sword with-edge-of so-they-cut-down-them

וְהַשָּׁלִשִׁים וַיֵּלְכוּ עַד־ עִיר בֵּית־ הַבָּעַל׃
the-Baal temple-of inner-shrine-of into then-they-went and-the-officers

(26) וַיֹּצִאוּ אֶת־ מַצְּבוֹת בֵּית־ הַבַּעַל
the-Baal temple-of sacred-stones-of *** and-they-brought-out (26)

וַיִּשְׂרְפוּהָ׃ (27) וַיִּתְּצוּ אֵת מַצְּבַת הַבָּעַל
the-Baal sacred-stone-of *** and-they-demolished (27) and-they-burned-her

וַיִּתְּצוּ אֶת־ בֵּית הַבַּעַל וַיְשִׂמֻהוּ לְמַחֲרָאוֹת*
*as-latrines and-they-used-him the-Baal temple-of *** and-they-tore-down

עַד־הַיּוֹם׃ (28) וַיַּשְׁמֵד יֵהוּא אֶת־ הַבַּעַל מִיִּשְׂרָאֵל׃ (29) רַק
however (29) from-Israel the-Baal *** Jehu so-he-destroyed (28) the-day to

חֲטָאֵי יָרָבְעָם בֶּן־ נְבָט אֲשֶׁר הֶחֱטִיא אֶת־יִשְׂרָאֵל לֹא־
not Israel *** he-caused-to-commit which Nebat son-of Jeroboam sins-of

סָר יֵהוּא מֵאַחֲרֵיהֶם עֶגְלֵי הַזָּהָב אֲשֶׁר בֵּית־אֵל
El Beth that the-gold calves-of from-after-them Jehu he-turned-away

וַאֲשֶׁר בְּדָן׃ (30) וַיֹּאמֶר יְהוָה אֶל־יֵהוּא יַעַן אֲשֶׁר־ הֱטִיבֹתָ
you-did-well that because Jehu to Yahweh and-he-said (30) at-Dan and-that

לַעֲשׂוֹת הַיָּשָׁר בְּעֵינַי כְּכֹל אֲשֶׁר בִּלְבָבִי עָשִׂיתָ
you-did in-mind-of-me that as-all in-eyes-of-me the-right to-accomplish

לְבֵית אַחְאָב בְּנֵי רְבִעִים יֵשְׁבוּ לְךָ עַל־ כִּסֵּא
throne-of on of-you they-will-sit fourth-ones sons-of Ahab to-house-of

יִשְׂרָאֵל׃ (31) וְיֵהוּא לֹא שָׁמַר לָלֶכֶת בְּתוֹרַת־ יְהוָה אֱלֹהֵי־
God-of Yahweh to-law-of to-keep he-was-careful not yet-Jehu (31) Israel

יִשְׂרָאֵל בְּכָל־ לְבָבוֹ לֹא סָר מֵעַל חַטֹּאות יָרָבְעָם
Jeroboam sins-of away-from he-turned not heart-of-him with-all-of Israel

Baal." [24]So they went in to
make sacrifices and burnt
offerings. Now Jehu had posted eighty men outside with
this warning: "If one of you
lets any of the men I am placing in your hands escape, it
will be your life for his life."
[25]As soon as Jehu had
finished making the burnt
offering, he ordered the
guards and officers: "Go in
and kill them; let no one escape." So they cut them down
with the sword. The guards
and officers threw the bodies
out and then entered the inner
shrine of the temple of Baal.
[26]They brought the sacred
stone out of the temple of Baal
and burned it. [27]They demolished the sacred stone of Baal
and tore down the temple of
Baal, and people have used it
for a latrine to this day.
[28]So Jehu destroyed Baal
worship in Israel. [29]However,
he did not turn away from the
sins of Jeroboam son of Nebat,
which he had caused Israel to
commit—the worship of the
golden calves at Bethel and
Dan.
[30]The LORD said to Jehu, "Because you have done well in
accomplishing what is right in
my eyes and have done to the
house of Ahab all I had in
mind to do, your descendants
will sit on the throne of Israel
to the fourth generation."
[31]Yet Jehu was not careful to
keep the law of the LORD, the
God of Israel, with all his
heart. He did not turn away
from the sins of Jeroboam,

*27 The *Qere for-going-out,* is a less graphic word than the *Ketbib.*

°27 ק למוצאות

אֲשֶׁר הֶחֱטִיא אֶת־ יִשְׂרָאֵל׃ בַּיָּמִים הָהֵם הֵחֵל
he-began the-those in-the-days (32) Israel *** he-caused-to-commit which

יְהוָה לְקַצּוֹת בְּיִשְׂרָאֵל וַיַּכֵּם חֲזָאֵל בְּכָל־
through-all-of Hazael and-he-overpowered-them of-Israel to-reduce-size Yahweh

גְּבוּל יִשְׂרָאֵל׃ מִן־ הַיַּרְדֵּן מִזְרַח הַשֶּׁמֶשׁ אֵת כָּל־ אֶרֶץ
land-of all-of *** the-sun rise-of the-Jordan from (33) Israel territory-of

הַגִּלְעָד הַגָּדִי וְהָרְאוּבֵנִי* וְהַמְנַשִּׁי מֵעֲרֹעֵר אֲשֶׁר
that from-Aroer and-the-Manassite and-the-Reubenite the-Gadite the-Gilead

עַל־ נַחַל אַרְנֹן וְהַגִּלְעָד וְהַבָּשָׁן׃ וְיֶתֶר דִּבְרֵי
events-of and-rest-of (34) and-the-Bashan and-the-Gilead Arnon Gorge-of by

יֵהוּא וְכָל־ אֲשֶׁר עָשָׂה וְכָל־ גְּבוּרָתוֹ הֲלוֹא־ הֵם
they not? achievement-of-him and-all-of he-did that and-all Jehu

כְּתוּבִים עַל־ סֵפֶר דִּבְרֵי הַיָּמִים לְמַלְכֵי יִשְׂרָאֵל׃
Israel of-kings-of the-days annals-of book-of in ones-being-written

וַיִּשְׁכַּב יֵהוּא עִם־ אֲבֹתָיו וַיִּקְבְּרוּ אֹתוֹ בְּשֹׁמְרוֹן
in-Samaria him and-they-buried fathers-of-him with Jehu and-he-rested (35)

וַיִּמְלֹךְ יְהוֹאָחָז בְּנוֹ תַּחְתָּיו׃ וְהַיָּמִים
and-the-days (36) in-place-of-him son-of-him Jehoahaz and-he-became-king

אֲשֶׁר מָלַךְ יֵהוּא עַל־ יִשְׂרָאֵל עֶשְׂרִים וּשְׁמֹנֶה־ שָׁנָה בְּשֹׁמְרוֹן׃
in-Samaria year and-eight twenty Israel over Jehu he-reigned that

וַעֲתַלְיָה אֵם אֲחַזְיָהוּ וְרָאֲתָה° כִּי מֵת בְּנָהּ
son-of-her he-was-dead that she-saw Ahaziah mother-of when-Athaliah (11:1)

וַתָּקָם וַתְּאַבֵּד אֵת כָּל־ זֶרַע הַמַּמְלָכָה׃
the-royal family-of whole-of *** and-she-destroyed then-she-proceeded

וַתִּקַּח יְהוֹשֶׁבַע בַּת־ הַמֶּלֶךְ־ יוֹרָם אֲחוֹת אֲחַזְיָהוּ אֶת־
*** Ahaziah sister-of Joram the-king daughter-of Jehosheba but-she-took (2)

יוֹאָשׁ בֶּן־ אֲחַזְיָה וַתִּגְנֹב אֹתוֹ מִתּוֹךְ בְּנֵי־ הַמֶּלֶךְ
the-king sons-of from-among him and-she-stole-away Ahaziah son-of Joash

הַמְּמוֹתָתִים° אֹתוֹ וְאֶת־ מֵינִקְתּוֹ בַּחֲדַר הַמִּטּוֹת
the-beds in-room-of one-nursing-him and him the-ones-being-murdered

וַיַּסְתִּרוּ אֹתוֹ מִפְּנֵי עֲתַלְיָהוּ וְלֹא הוּמָת׃ וַיְהִי
and-he-was (3) he-was-killed so-not Athaliah from-before him and-they-hid

אִתָּהּ בֵּית יְהוָה מִתְחַבֵּא שֵׁשׁ שָׁנִים וַעֲתַלְיָה מֹלֶכֶת עַל־
over ruling while-Athaliah years six hiding Yahweh temple-of with-her

הָאָרֶץ׃ וּבַשָּׁנָה הַשְּׁבִיעִית שָׁלַח יְהוֹיָדָע וַיִּקַּח ׀ אֶת־
*** and-he-got Jehoiada he-sent the-seventh and-in-the-year (4) the-land

שָׂרֵי הַמֵּאיוֹת° לַכָּרִי וְלָרָצִים
and-for-the-ones-guarding for-the-Carite the-hundreds commanders-of

which he had caused Israel to commit.

[32]In those days the LORD began to reduce the size of Israel. Hazael overpowered the Israelites throughout their territory [33]east of the Jordan in all the land of Gilead (the region of Gad, Reuben and Manasseh), from Aroer by the Arnon Gorge through Gilead to Bashan.

[34]As for the other events of Jehu's reign, all he did, and all his achievements, are they not written in the book of the annals of the kings of Israel?

[35]Jehu rested with his fathers and was buried in Samaria. And Jehoahaz his son succeeded him as king. [36]The time that Jehu reigned over Israel in Samaria was twenty-eight years.

Athaliah and Joash

11 When Athaliah the mother of Ahaziah saw that her son was dead, she proceeded to destroy the whole royal family. [2]But Jehosheba, the daughter of King Jehoram[y] and sister of Ahaziah, took Joash son of Ahaziah and stole him away from among the royal princes who were about to be murdered. She put him and his nurse in a bedroom to hide him from Athaliah; so he was not killed. [3]He remained hidden with his nurse at the temple of the LORD for six years while Athaliah ruled the land.

[4]In the seventh year Jehoiada sent for the commanders of units of a hundred, the Carites and the guards and had

[y]2 Hebrew *Joram*, a variant of *Jehoram*

*33 Most mss have *dagesh* in the *vav* and no *qibbuts* under the *resh* (רֻאוּ־).

°1 ק ראתה
°2 ק המומתים
°4 ק המאות

וַיָּבֵא אֹתָם אֵלָיו בֵּית יְהוָה וַיִּכְרֹת לָהֶם בְּרִית
covenant with-them and-he-made Yahweh temple-of to-him them and-he-brought

וַיַּשְׁבַּע אֹתָם בְּבֵית יְהוָה וַיַּרְא אֹתָם אֶת־
*** them then-he-showed Yahweh at-temple-of them and-he-put-under-oath

בֶּן־ הַמֶּלֶךְ׃ וַיְצַוֵּם לֵאמֹר זֶה הַדָּבָר אֲשֶׁר
that the-thing this to-say and-he-commanded-them (5) the-king son-of

תַּעֲשׂוּן הַשְּׁלִשִׁית מִכֶּם בָּאֵי הַשַּׁבָּת
the-Sabbath ones-going-on-duty-of of-you the-third you-must-do

וְשֹׁמְרֵי מִשְׁמֶרֶת בֵּית הַמֶּלֶךְ׃ וְהַשְּׁלִשִׁית
and-the-third (6) the-king palace-of guard-of and-ones-guarding-of

בְּשַׁעַר סוּר וְהַשְּׁלִשִׁית בַּשַּׁעַר אַחַר הָרָצִים
the-ones-guarding behind at-the-gate and-the-third Sur at-Gate-of

וּשְׁמַרְתֶּם אֶת־ מִשְׁמֶרֶת הַבַּיִת מַסָּח׃ וּשְׁתֵּי הַיָּדוֹת
the-companies and-two-of (7) in-turn the-temple guard-of *** and-you-guard

בָּכֶם כֹּל יֹצְאֵי הַשַּׁבָּת וְשָׁמְרוּ אֶת־
*** then-they-must-guard the-Sabbath ones-going-off-duty-of all-of of-you

מִשְׁמֶרֶת בֵּית־ יְהוָה אֶל־ הַמֶּלֶךְ׃ . וְהִקַּפְתֶּם עַל־
by and-you-station-yourselves (8) the-king for Yahweh temple-of guard-of

הַמֶּלֶךְ סָבִיב אִישׁ וְכֵלָיו בְּיָדוֹ וְהַבָּא
and-the-one-approaching in-hand-of-him with-weapons-of-him each around the-king

אֶל־ הַשְּׂדֵרוֹת יוּמָת וִהְיוּ אֶת־ הַמֶּלֶךְ בְּצֵאתוֹ
when-to-go-him the-king with and-stay! he-must-be-killed the-ranks to

וּבְבֹאוֹ׃ וַיַּעֲשׂוּ שָׂרֵי הַמֵּאיוֹת כְּכֹל אֲשֶׁר־
that as-all the-hundreds commanders-of and-they-did (9) and-when-to-come-him

צִוָּה יְהוֹיָדָע הַכֹּהֵן וַיִּקְחוּ אִישׁ אֶת־ אֲנָשָׁיו
men-of-him *** each and-they-took the-priest Jehoiada he-ordered

בָּאֵי הַשַּׁבָּת עִם יֹצְאֵי הַשַּׁבָּת
the-Sabbath ones-going-off-duty-of with the-Sabbath ones-going-on-duty-of

וַיָּבֹאוּ אֶל־ יְהוֹיָדָע הַכֹּהֵן׃ וַיִּתֵּן הַכֹּהֵן
the-priest then-he-gave (10) the-priest Jehoiada to and-they-came

לְשָׂרֵי הַמֵּאיוֹת אֶת־ הַחֲנִית וְאֶת־ הַשְּׁלָטִים אֲשֶׁר לַמֶּלֶךְ
to-the-king that the-shields and the-spear *** the-hundreds to-commanders-of

דָּוִד אֲשֶׁר בְּבֵית יְהוָה׃ וַיַּעַמְדוּ הָרָצִים
the-ones-guarding and-they-stationed (11) Yahweh in-temple-of that David

אִישׁ ׀ וְכֵלָיו בְּיָדוֹ מִכֶּתֶף הַבַּיִת הַיְמָנִית
the-south the-temple from-side-of in-hand-of-him with-weapons-of-him each

עַד־ כֶּתֶף הַבַּיִת הַשְּׂמָאלִית לַמִּזְבֵּחַ וְלַבָּיִת עַל־
by and-near-the-temple near-the-altar the-north the-temple side-of to

°9 ק המאות
°10 ק המאות

them brought to him at the
temple of the LORD. He made a
covenant with them and put
them under oath at the temple
of the LORD. Then he showed
them the king's son. [5]He commanded them, saying, "This
is what you are to do: You who
are in the three companies
that are going on duty on the
Sabbath—a third of you guarding the royal palace, [6]a third at
the Sur Gate, and a third at the
gate behind the guard, who
take turns guarding the temple— [7]and you who are in the
other two companies that nor-
mally go off Sabbath duty are
all to guard the temple for the
king. [8]Station yourselves
around the king, each man
with his weapon in his hand.
Anyone who approaches your
ranks[z] must be put to death.
Stay close to the king
wherever he goes."
[9]The commanders of units of
a hundred did just as Jehoiada
the priest ordered. Each one
took his men—those who were
going on duty on the Sabbath
and those who were going off
duty—and came to Jehoiada
the priest. [10]Then he gave the
commanders the spears and
shields that had belonged to
King David and that were in
the temple of the LORD. [11]The
guards, each with his weapon
in his hand, stationed themselves around the king—near
the altar and the temple, from
the south side to the north side
of the temple.

[z]8 Or *approaches the precincts*

הַמֶּלֶךְ סָבִיב׃ (12) וַיּוֹצִא אֶת־ בֶּן־ הַמֶּלֶךְ וַיִּתֵּן
and-he-put the-king son-of *** and-he-brought-out (12) around the-king

עָלָיו אֶת־ הַנֵּזֶר וְאֶת־ הָעֵדוּת וַיַּמְלִכוּ אֹתוֹ
him and-they-proclaimed-king the-covenant and the-crown *** on-him

וַיִּמְשָׁחֻהוּ וַיַּכּוּ־ כָף וַיֹּאמְרוּ יְחִי
may-he-live and-they-shouted hand and-they-clapped and-they-anointed-him

הַמֶּלֶךְ׃ (13) וַתִּשְׁמַע עֲתַלְיָה אֶת־ קוֹל הָרָצִין
the-ones-guarding noise-of *** Athaliah when-she-heard (13) the-king

הָעָם וַתָּבֹא אֶל־ הָעָם בֵּית יְהוָה׃ (14) וַתֵּרֶא
and-she-looked (14) Yahweh temple-of the-people to then-she-went the-people

וְהִנֵּה הַמֶּלֶךְ עֹמֵד עַל־ הָעַמּוּד כַּמִּשְׁפָּט וְהַשָּׂרִים
and-the-officers as-the-custom the-pillar by standing the-king and-see!

וְהַחֲצֹצְרוֹת אֶל־ הַמֶּלֶךְ וְכָל־ עַם הָאָרֶץ שָׂמֵחַ
rejoicing the-land people-of and-all-of the-king beside and-the-trumpeters

וְתֹקֵעַ בַּחֲצֹצְרוֹת וַתִּקְרַע עֲתַלְיָה אֶת־ בְּגָדֶיהָ
robes-of-her *** Athaliah then-she-tore on-the-trumpets and-blowing

וַתִּקְרָא קֶשֶׁר קָשֶׁר׃ (15) וַיְצַו יְהוֹיָדָע הַכֹּהֵן
the-priest Jehoiada then-he-ordered (15) treason treason and-she-called-out

אֶת־ שָׂרֵי הַמֵּאוֹת° פְּקֻדֵי הַחַיִל וַיֹּאמֶר
and-he-said the-troop ones-being-in-charge-of the-hundreds commanders-of ***

אֲלֵיהֶם הוֹצִיאוּ אֹתָהּ אֶל־ מִבֵּית לַשְּׂדֵרֹת וְהַבָּא
and-the-one-following of-the-ranks outside-of to her bring-out! to-them

אַחֲרֶיהָ הָמֵת בֶּחָרֶב כִּי אָמַר הַכֹּהֵן אַל־ תּוּמַת
she-must-be-killed not the-priest he-said for with-the-sword to-kill after-her

בֵּית יְהוָה׃ (16) וַיָּשִׂמוּ לָהּ יָדַיִם וַתָּבוֹא דֶּרֶךְ־
place-of as-she-reached hands on-her so-they-laid (16) Yahweh temple-of

מְבוֹא הַסּוּסִים בֵּית הַמֶּלֶךְ וַתּוּמַת שָׁם׃
there and-she-was-killed the-king palace-of the-horses entrance-of

(17) וַיִּכְרֹת יְהוֹיָדָע אֶת־ הַבְּרִית בֵּין יְהוָה וּבֵין
and-between Yahweh between the-covenant *** Jehoiada then-he-made (17)

הַמֶּלֶךְ וּבֵין הָעָם לִהְיוֹת לְעָם לַיהוָה וּבֵין
and-between of-Yahweh as-people to-be the-people and-between the-king

הַמֶּלֶךְ וּבֵין הָעָם׃ (18) וַיָּבֹאוּ כָל־ עַם הָאָרֶץ
the-land people-of all-of and-they-went (18) the-people and-between the-king

בֵּית־ הַבַּעַל וַיִּתְּצֻהוּ אֶת־ מִזְבְּחֹתָו° וְאֶת־ צְלָמָיו
idols-of-him and altars-of-him *** and-they-tore-down-him the-Baal temple-of

שִׁבְּרוּ הֵיטֵב וְאֵת מַתָּן כֹּהֵן הַבַּעַל הָרְגוּ לִפְנֵי
in-front-of they-killed the-Baal priest-of Mattan and to-do-well they-smashed

[12]Jehoiada brought out the
king's son and put the crown
on him; he presented him
with a copy of the covenant
and proclaimed him king.
They anointed him, and the
people clapped their hands
and shouted, "Long live the
king!"
[13]When Athaliah heard the
noise made by the guards and
the people, she went to the
people at the temple of the
LORD. [14]She looked and there
was the king, standing by the
pillar, as the custom was. The
officers and the trumpeters
were beside the king, and all
the people of the land were rejoicing and blowing trumpets.
Then Athaliah tore her robes
and called out, "Treason! Treason!"
[15]Jehoiada the priest ordered
the commanders of units of a
hundred, who were in charge
of the troops: "Bring her out
between the ranks[a] and put to
the sword anyone who fol-
lows her." For the priest had
said, "She must not be put to
death in the temple of the
LORD." [16]So they seized her as
she reached the place where
the horses enter the palace
grounds, and there she was
put to death.
[17]Jehoiada then made a covenant between the LORD and
the king and people that they
would be the LORD's people.
He also made a covenant between the king and the people.
[18]All the people of the land
went to the temple of Baal and
tore it down. They smashed
the altars and idols to pieces
and killed Mattan the priest of
Baal in front of the altars.

[a]15 *Or out from the precincts*

°15 ק המאות
°18 ק מזבחתיו

הַמִּזְבְּחֹת וַיָּשֶׂם הַכֹּהֵן פְּקֻדּוֹת עַל־ בֵּית יְהוָה׃
Yahweh temple-of at guards the-priest then-he-posted the-altars

(19) וַיִּקַּח אֶת־ שָׂרֵי הַמֵּאוֹת וְאֶת־ הַכָּרִי וְאֶת־
and the-Carite and the-hundreds commanders-of *** and-he-took (19)

הָרָצִים וְאֵת | כָּל־ עַם הָאָרֶץ וַיֹּרִידוּ אֶת־
*** and-they-brought-down the-land people-of all-of and the-ones-guarding

הַמֶּלֶךְ מִבֵּית יְהוָה וַיָּבוֹאוּ דֶּרֶךְ† ־שַׁעַר הָרָצִים
the-ones-guarding gate-of way-of and-they-went Yahweh from-temple-of the-king

בֵּית הַמֶּלֶךְ וַיֵּשֶׁב עַל־ כִּסֵּא הַמְּלָכִים׃
the-kings throne-of on then-he-took-place the-king palace-of

(20) וַיִּשְׂמַח כָּל־ עַם־ הָאָרֶץ וְהָעִיר שָׁקָטָה
she-was-quiet and-the-city the-land people-of all-of and-he-rejoiced (20)

וְאֶת־ עֲתַלְיָהוּ הֵמִיתוּ בַחֶרֶב בֵּית °מֶּלֶךְ׃ *(12:1) בֶּן־
son-of *(12:1) the-king palace-of with-the-sword they-killed Athaliah and

שֶׁבַע שָׁנִים יְהוֹאָשׁ בְּמָלְכוֹ׃ (2) בִּשְׁנַת־ שֶׁבַע לְיֵהוּא
of-Jehu seven in-year-of (2) when-to-reign-him Jehoash years seven

מָלַךְ יְהוֹאָשׁ וְאַרְבָּעִים שָׁנָה מָלַךְ בִּירוּשָׁלָ͏ִם וְשֵׁם
and-name-of in-Jerusalem he-reigned year and-forty Jehoash he-became-king

אִמּוֹ צִבְיָה מִבְּאֵר שָׁבַע׃ (3) וַיַּעַשׂ יְהוֹאָשׁ הַיָּשָׁר
the-right Jehoash and-he-did (3) Sheba from-Beer Zibiah mother-of-him

בְּעֵינֵי יְהוָה כָּל־ יָמָיו אֲשֶׁר הוֹרָהוּ יְהוֹיָדָע
Jehoiada he-instructed-him that days-of-him all-of Yahweh in-eyes-of

הַכֹּהֵן׃ (4) רַק הַבָּמוֹת לֹא־ סָרוּ עוֹד הָעָם
the-people still they-removed not the-high-places however (4) the-priest

מְזַבְּחִים וּמְקַטְּרִים בַּבָּמוֹת׃
at-the-high-places and-ones-burning-incense ones-offering-sacrifices

(5) וַיֹּאמֶר יְהוֹאָשׁ אֶל־ הַכֹּהֲנִים כֹּל° כֶּסֶף הַקֳּדָשִׁים
the-sacred-offerings money-of all-of the-priests to Jehoash and-he-said (5)

אֲשֶׁר־ יוּבָא בֵית־ יְהוָה כֶּסֶף עוֹבֵר אִישׁ כֶּסֶף
money-of man passing-by-of money-of Yahweh temple-of he-is-brought that

נַפְשׁוֹת עֶרְכּוֹ כָּל־ כֶּסֶף אֲשֶׁר יַעֲלֶה עַל לֶב־ אִישׁ
man heart-of from he-comes that money all-of value-of-him persons-of

לְהָבִיא בֵּית יְהוָה׃ (6) יִקְחוּ לָהֶם הַכֹּהֲנִים אִישׁ
each the-priests for-them let-them-receive (6) Yahweh temple-of to-bring

מֵאֵת מַכָּרוֹ וְהֵם יְחַזְּקוּ אֶת־ בֶּדֶק הַבַּיִת
the-temple damage-of *** let-them-repair and-they treasurer-of-him from

לְכֹל אֲשֶׁר־ יִמָּצֵא שָׁם בָּדֶק׃ (7) וַיְהִי בִּשְׁנַת עֶשְׂרִים
twenty by-year-of but-he-was (7) damage there he-is-found that for-all

Then Jehoiada the priest
posted guards at the temple of
the LORD. [19]He took with him
the commanders of hundreds,
the Carites, the guards and all
the people of the land, and together they brought the king
down from the temple of the
LORD and went into the palace,
entering by way of the gate of
the guards. The king then took
his place on the royal throne,
[20]and all the people of the land
rejoiced. And the city was quiet, because Athaliah had been
slain with the sword at the
palace.
[21]Joash[b] was seven years old
when he began to reign.

Joash Repairs the Temple

12 In the seventh year of
Jehu, Joash[c] became
king, and he reigned in
Jerusalem forty years. His
mother's name was Zibiah;
she was from Beersheba.
[2]Joash did what was right in
the eyes of the LORD all the
years Jehoiada the priest instructed him. [3]The high places,
however, were not removed;
the people continued to offer
sacrifices and burn incense
there.
[4]Joash said to the priests,
"Collect all the money that is
brought as sacred offerings to
the temple of the LORD—the
money collected in the census,
the money received from personal vows and the money
brought voluntarily to the
temple. [5]Let every priest re-
ceive the money from one of
the treasurers, and let it be
used to repair whatever damage is found in the temple."
[6]But by the twenty-third

[b]21 Hebrew *Jehoash*, a variant of *Joash*
[c]1 Hebrew *Jehoash*, a variant of *Joash*; also in verses 2, 4, 6, 7 and 18

*The Hebrew numeration of chapter 12 begins with verse 21 of chapter 11 in English; thus, there is a one-verse discrepancy throughout chapter 12.

†19 Most mss have *sheva* in the *kaph* (ךְ־).

°20 ק המלך

וּשְׁלֹשׁ שָׁנָה לַמֶּלֶךְ יְהוֹאָשׁ לֹא־ חִזְּקוּ הַכֹּהֲנִים אֶת־
*** the-priests they-repaired not Jehoash of-the-king year and-three

בֶּדֶק הַבָּיִת׃ (8) וַיִּקְרָא הַמֶּלֶךְ יְהוֹאָשׁ לִיהוֹיָדָע
for-Jehoiada Jehoash the-king so-he-summoned (8) the-temple damage-of

הַכֹּהֵן וְלַכֹּהֲנִים וַיֹּאמֶר אֲלֵהֶם מַדּוּעַ אֵינְכֶם
not-you why? to-them and-he-asked and-for-the-priests the-priest

מְחַזְּקִים אֶת־ בֶּדֶק הַבָּיִת וְעַתָּה אַל־ תִּקְחוּ־ כֶסֶף מֵאֵת
from money you-take not and-now the-temple damage-of *** ones-repairing

מַכָּרֵיכֶם כִּי־ לְבֶדֶק הַבַּיִת תִּתְּנֻהוּ׃
you-hand-over-him the-temple for-damage-of but treasuries-of-you

(9) וַיֵּאֹתוּ הַכֹּהֲנִים לְבִלְתִּי קְחַת־ כֶּסֶף מֵאֵת הָעָם וּלְבִלְתִּי
and-not the-people from money to-collect not the-priests and-they-agreed (9)

חַזֵּק אֶת־ בֶּדֶק הַבָּיִת׃ (10) וַיִּקַּח יְהוֹיָדָע הַכֹּהֵן
the-priest Jehoiada and-he-took (10) the-temple damage-of *** to-repair

אֲרוֹן אֶחָד וַיִּקֹּב חֹר בְּדַלְתּוֹ וַיִּתֵּן אֹתוֹ אֵצֶל הַמִּזְבֵּחַ
the-altar next-to him and-he-placed in-lid-of-him hole and-he-bored one chest

בְּיָמִין° בְּבוֹא־ אִישׁ בֵּית יְהוָה וְנָתְנוּ־ שָׁמָּה הַכֹּהֲנִים
the-priests at-there and-they-put Yahweh temple-of one as-to-enter on-right

שֹׁמְרֵי הַסַּף אֶת־ כָּל־ הַכֶּסֶף הַמּוּבָא
the-one-being-brought the-money all-of *** the-entrance ones-guarding-of

בֵית־ יְהוָה׃ (11) וַיְהִי כִּרְאוֹתָם כִּי־ רַב הַכֶּסֶף
the-money large-amount that when-to-see-them and-he-was (11) Yahweh temple-of

בָּאָרוֹן וַיַּעַל סֹפֵר הַמֶּלֶךְ וְהַכֹּהֵן הַגָּדוֹל
the-high and-the-priest the-king secretary-of then-he-came in-the-chest

וַיָּצֻרוּ וַיִּמְנוּ אֶת־ הַכֶּסֶף הַנִּמְצָא
the-one-being-brought the-money *** and-they-counted and-they-bagged

בֵית־ יְהוָה׃ (12) וְנָתְנוּ אֶת־ הַכֶּסֶף הַמְתֻכָּן
the-one-being-determined the-money *** and-they-gave (12) Yahweh temple-of

עַל־ יְדֵי° עֹשֵׂי הַמְּלָאכָה הַפְּקֻדִים° בֵּית
temple-of the-ones-being-appointed the-work ones-supervising-of hands-of into

יְהוָה וַיּוֹצִיאֻהוּ לְחָרָשֵׁי הָעֵץ וְלַבֹּנִים
and-to-the-ones-building the-wood to-ones-cutting-of and-they-paid-him Yahweh

הָעֹשִׂים בֵּית יְהוָה׃ (13) וְלַגֹּדְרִים
and-to-the-ones-being-masons (13) Yahweh temple-of the-ones-working

וּלְחֹצְבֵי הָאֶבֶן וְלִקְנוֹת עֵצִים וְאַבְנֵי
and-stones-of timbers and-to-purchase the-stone and-to-ones-cutting-of

מַחְצֵב לְחַזֵּק אֶת־ בֶּדֶק בֵּית־ יְהוָה וּלְכֹל אֲשֶׁר־ יֵצֵא
he-paid that and-for-all Yahweh temple-of damage-of *** to-repair dressed

year of King Joash the priests
still had not repaired the temple. [7]Therefore King Joash
summoned Jehoiada the priest
and the other priests and
asked them, "Why aren't you
repairing the damage done to
the temple? Take no more
money from your treasurers,
but hand it over for repairing
the temple." [8]The priests
agreed that they would not
collect any more money from
the people and that they
would not repair the temple
themselves.
[9]Jehoiada the priest took a
chest and bored a hole in its
lid. He placed it beside the altar, on the right side as one
enters the temple of the LORD.
The priests who guarded the
entrance put into the chest all
the money that was brought to
the temple of the LORD.
[10]Whenever they saw that
there was a large amount of
money in the chest, the royal
secretary and the high priest
came, counted the money that
had been brought into the
temple of the LORD and put it
into bags. [11]When the amount
had been determined, they
gave the money to the men appointed to supervise the work
on the temple. With it they
paid those who worked on the
temple of the LORD—the carpenters and builders, [12]the masons and stonecutters. They
purchased timber and dressed
stone for the repair of the temple of the LORD, and met all the

*See the note on page 463.

°10 ק מימין
°12a ק ידי
°12b ק המפקדים

עַל־ הַבַּיִת לְחָזְקָה׃ אַךְ לֹא יֵעָשֶׂה בֵּית יְהוָה
Yahweh temple-of he-was-made not however (14) to-repair the-temple for

סִפּוֹת כֶּסֶף מְזַמְּרוֹת מִזְרָקוֹת חֲצֹצְרוֹת כָּל־ כְּלִי
article-of any-of trumpets sprinkling-bowls wick-trimmers silver basins-of

זָהָב וּכְלִי־ כָסֶף מִן־ הַכֶּסֶף הַמּוּבָא בֵית־
temple-of the-one-being-brought the-money from silver or-article-of gold

יְהוָה׃ כִּי־ לְעֹשֵׂי הַמְּלָאכָה יִתְּנֻהוּ וְחִזְּקוּ־
and-they-repaired they-paid-him the-work to-ones-doing-of for (15) Yahweh

בוֹ אֶת־ בֵּית יְהוָה׃ וְלֹא יְחַשְּׁבוּ אֶת־
*** they-required-to-account and-not (16) Yahweh temple-of *** with-him

הָאֲנָשִׁים אֲשֶׁר יִתְּנוּ אֶת־ הַכֶּסֶף עַל־ יָדָם לָתֵת לְעֹשֵׂי
to-ones-doing-of to-pay hand-of-them into the-money *** they-gave whom the-men

הַמְּלָאכָה כִּי בֶאֱמֻנָה הֵם עֹשִׂים׃ כֶּסֶף אָשָׁם
guilt-offering money-of (17) ones-acting they in-honesty because the-work

וְכֶסֶף חַטָּאוֹת לֹא יוּבָא בֵּית יְהוָה לַכֹּהֲנִים
for-the-priests Yahweh temple-of he-was-brought not sin-offerings and-money-of

יִהְיוּ׃ אָז יַעֲלֶה חֲזָאֵל מֶלֶךְ אֲרָם וַיִּלָּחֶם עַל־
against and-he-attacked Aram king-of Hazael he-went-up then (18) they-were

גַּת וַיִּלְכְּדָהּ וַיָּשֶׂם חֲזָאֵל פָּנָיו לַעֲלוֹת עַל־
against to-attack faces-of-him Hazael then-he-turned and-he-captured-her Gath

יְרוּשָׁלָםִ׃ וַיִּקַּח יְהוֹאָשׁ מֶלֶךְ־ יְהוּדָה אֵת כָּל־ הַקֳּדָשִׁים
the-sacred-objects all-of *** Judah king-of Jehoash but-he-took (19) Jerusalem

אֲשֶׁר־ הִקְדִּישׁוּ יְהוֹשָׁפָט וִיהוֹרָם וַאֲחַזְיָהוּ אֲבֹתָיו
fathers-of-him and-Ahaziah and-Jehoram Jehoshaphat they-dedicated that

מַלְכֵי יְהוּדָה וְאֶת־ קֳדָשָׁיו וְאֵת כָּל־ הַזָּהָב הַנִּמְצָא
the-being-found the-gold all-of and dedicated-gifts-of-him and Judah kings-of

בְּאֹצְרוֹת בֵּית־ יְהוָה וּבֵית הַמֶּלֶךְ וַיִּשְׁלַח
and-he-sent the-king and-palace-of Yahweh temple-of in-treasuries-of

לַחֲזָאֵל מֶלֶךְ אֲרָם וַיַּעַל מֵעַל יְרוּשָׁלָםִ׃ וְיֶתֶר
and-rest-of (20) Jerusalem from-against and-he-withdrew Aram king-of to-Hazael

דִּבְרֵי יוֹאָשׁ וְכָל־ אֲשֶׁר עָשָׂה הֲלוֹא־ הֵם כְּתוּבִים עַל־ סֵפֶר
book-of in ones-being-written they not? he-did that and-all Joash events-of

דִּבְרֵי הַיָּמִים לְמַלְכֵי יְהוּדָה׃ וַיָּקֻמוּ עֲבָדָיו
officials-of-him and-they-rose (21) Judah of-kings-of the-days annals-of

וַיִּקְשְׁרוּ־ קָשֶׁר וַיַּכּוּ אֶת־ יוֹאָשׁ בֵּית מִלֹּא
Millo Beth Joash *** and-they-assassinated conspiracy and-they-conspired

הַיֹּרֵד סִלָּא׃ וְיוֹזָבָד בֶּן־ שִׁמְעָת וִיהוֹזָבָד
and-Jehozabad Shimeath son-of and-Jozabad (22) Silla the-one-going-down

other expenses of restoring the
temple.
13The money brought into
the temple was not spent for
making silver basins, wick
trimmers, sprinkling bowls,
trumpets or any other articles
of gold or silver for the temple
of the LORD; 14it was paid to the
workmen, who used it to repair the temple. 15They did not
require an accounting from
those to whom they gave the
money to pay the workers, because they acted with complete honesty. 16The money
from the guilt offerings and
sin offerings was not brought
into the temple of the LORD; it
belonged to the priests.
17About this time Hazael
king of Aram went up and attacked Gath and captured it.
Then he turned to attack
Jerusalem. 18But Joash king of
Judah took all the sacred objects dedicated by his fathers—
Jehoshaphat, Jehoram and
Ahaziah, the kings of Judah—
and the gifts he himself had
dedicated and all the gold
found in the treasuries of the
temple of the LORD and of the
royal palace, and he sent them
to Hazael king of Aram, who
then withdrew from Jerusalem.
19As for the other events of
the reign of Joash, and all he
did, are they not written in the
book of the annals of the kings
of Judah? 20His officials conspired against him and assassinated him at Beth Millo, on
the road down to Silla. 21The
officials who murdered him
were Jozabad son of Shimeath

*See the note on page 463.

בֶּן־ שֹׁמֵר ׀ עֲבָדָיו הִכֻּהוּ וַיָּמֹת וַיִּקְבְּרוּ
and-they-buried and-he-died they-murdered-him officials-of-him Shomer son-of

אֹתוֹ עִם־ אֲבֹתָיו בְּעִיר דָּוִד וַיִּמְלֹךְ אֲמַצְיָה
Amaziah and-he-became-king David in-City-of fathers-of-him with him

בְּנוֹ תַּחְתָּיו׃ בִּשְׁנַת עֶשְׂרִים וְשָׁלֹשׁ שָׁנָה לְיוֹאָשׁ
of-Joash year and-three twenty in-year-of (13:1) in-place-of-him son-of-him

בֶּן־ אֲחַזְיָהוּ מֶלֶךְ יְהוּדָה מָלַךְ יְהוֹאָחָז בֶּן־ יֵהוּא עַל־יִשְׂרָאֵל
Israel over Jehu son-of Jehoahaz he-became-king Judah king-of Ahaziah son-of

בְּשֹׁמְרוֹן שְׁבַע עֶשְׂרֵה שָׁנָה׃ וַיַּעַשׂ הָרַע בְּעֵינֵי יְהוָה
Yahweh in-eyes-of the-evil and-he-did (2) year ten seven-of in-Samaria

וַיֵּלֶךְ אַחַר חַטֹּאת יָרָבְעָם בֶּן־ נְבָט אֲשֶׁר־ הֶחֱטִיא
he-caused-to-commit which Nebat son-of Jeroboam sins-of after and-he-followed

אֶת־יִשְׂרָאֵל לֹא־ סָר מִמֶּנָּה׃ וַיִּחַר־ אַף יְהוָה
Yahweh anger-of so-he-burned (3) from-her he-turned-away not Israel ***

בְּיִשְׂרָאֵל וַיִּתְּנֵם בְּיַד ׀ חֲזָאֵל מֶלֶךְ־ אֲרָם
Aram king-of Hazael under-power-of and-he-kept-them against-Israel

וּבְיַד בֶּן־ הֲדַד בֶּן־ חֲזָאֵל כָּל־ הַיָּמִים׃ וַיְחַל
then-he-sought (4) the-days all-of Hazael son-of Hadad Ben and-under-power-of

יְהוֹאָחָז אֶת־ פְּנֵי יְהוָה וַיִּשְׁמַע אֵלָיו יְהוָה כִּי רָאָה אֶת־
*** he-saw for Yahweh to-him and-he-listened Yahweh faces-of *** Jehoahaz

לַחַץ יִשְׂרָאֵל כִּי־ לָחַץ אֹתָם מֶלֶךְ אֲרָם׃ וַיִּתֵּן
and-he-provided (5) Aram king-of them he-oppressed that Israel oppression-of

יְהוָה לְיִשְׂרָאֵל מוֹשִׁיעַ וַיֵּצְאוּ מִתַּחַת יַד־ אֲרָם
Aram power-of from-under and-they-escaped one-delivering for-Israel Yahweh

וַיֵּשְׁבוּ בְנֵי־ יִשְׂרָאֵל בְּאָהֳלֵיהֶם כִּתְמוֹל שִׁלְשׁוֹם׃ אַךְ
but (6) before as-yesterday in-homes-of-them Israel sons-of so-they-lived

לֹא־ סָרוּ מֵחַטֹּאות בֵּית־ יָרָבְעָם אֲשֶׁר־ הֶחֱטִי
he-caused-to-commit which Jeroboam house-of from-sins-of they-turned-away not

אֶת־ יִשְׂרָאֵל בָּהּ הָלָךְ וְגַם הָאֲשֵׁרָה עָמְדָה בְּשֹׁמְרוֹן׃
in-Samaria she-stood the-Asherah-pole and-also he-continued in-her Israel ***

כִּי לֹא הִשְׁאִיר לִיהוֹאָחָז עָם כִּי אִם־ חֲמִשִּׁים פָּרָשִׁים וַעֲשָׂרָה
and-ten horsemen fifty only except army to-Jehoahaz he-left not for (7)

רֶכֶב וַעֲשֶׂרֶת אֲלָפִים רַגְלִי כִּי אִבְּדָם מֶלֶךְ אֲרָם
Aram king-of he-destroyed-them for foot-soldier thousands and-ten-of chariot

וַיְשִׂמֵם כֶּעָפָר לָדֻשׁ׃ וְיֶתֶר דִּבְרֵי יְהוֹאָחָז
Jehoahaz events-of and-rest-of (8) to-thresh like-the-dust and-he-made-them

וְכָל־ אֲשֶׁר עָשָׂה וּגְבוּרָתוֹ הֲלוֹא־ הֵם כְּתוּבִים עַל־
in ones-being-written they not? and-achievement-of-him he-did that and-all

and Jehozabad son of Shomer.
He died and was buried with
his fathers in the City of David. And Amaziah his son succeeded him as king.

Jehoahaz King of Israel

13 In the twenty-third
year of Joash son of
Ahaziah king of Judah, Jehoahaz son of Jehu became king
of Israel in Samaria, and he
reigned seventeen years. [2]He
did evil in the eyes of the LORD
by following the sins of Jeroboam son of Nebat, which he
had caused Israel to commit,
and he did not turn away from
them. [3]So the LORD's anger
burned against Israel, and for
a long time he kept them under the power of Hazael king
of Aram and Ben-Hadad his
son.
[4]Then Jehoahaz sought the
LORD's favor, and the LORD listened to him, for he saw how
severely the king of Aram was
oppressing Israel. [5]The LORD
provided a deliverer for Israel,
and they escaped from the
power of Aram. So the Israelites lived in their own homes
as they had before. [6]But they
did not turn away from the
sins of the house of Jeroboam,
which he had caused Israel to
commit; they continued in
them. Also, the Asherah pole[d]
remained standing in Sa-
maria.
[7]Nothing had been left of
the army of Jehoahaz except
fifty horsemen, ten chariots
and ten thousand foot soldiers, for the king of Aram had
destroyed the rest and made
them like the dust at threshing
time.
[8]As for the other events of
the reign of Jehoahaz, all he
did and his achievements, are
they not written in the book of

[d]6 That is, a symbol of the goddess Asherah; here and elsewhere in 2 Kings

*See the note on page 463.

°6 ק החטיא

סֵפֶר דִּבְרֵי הַיָּמִים לְמַלְכֵי יִשְׂרָאֵל׃ וַיִּשְׁכַּב יְהוֹאָחָז
Jehoahaz and-he-rested (9) Israel of-kings-of the-days annals-of book-of

עִם־ אֲבֹתָיו וַיִּקְבְּרֻהוּ בְּשֹׁמְרוֹן וַיִּמְלֹךְ יוֹאָשׁ
Joash and-he-became-king in-Samaria and-they-buried-him fathers-of-him with

בְּנוֹ תַּחְתָּיו׃ בִּשְׁנַת שְׁלֹשִׁים וָשֶׁבַע שָׁנָה לְיוֹאָשׁ
of-Joash year and-seven thirty in-year-of (10) in-place-of-him son-of-him

מֶלֶךְ יְהוּדָה מָלַךְ יְהוֹאָשׁ בֶּן־ יְהוֹאָחָז עַל־ יִשְׂרָאֵל בְּשֹׁמְרוֹן
in-Samaria Israel over Jehoahaz son-of Jehoash he-became-king Judah king-of

שֵׁשׁ עֶשְׂרֵה שָׁנָה׃ וַיַּעֲשֶׂה הָרַע בְּעֵינֵי יְהוָה לֹא סָר
he-turned-away not Yahweh in-eyes-of the-evil and-he-did (11) year ten six-of

מִכָּל־ חַטֹּאות יָרָבְעָם בֶּן־ נְבָט אֲשֶׁר־ הֶחֱטִיא אֶת־ יִשְׂרָאֵל
Israel *** he-caused-to-sin which Nebat son-of Jeroboam sins-of from-any-of

בָּהּ הָלָךְ׃ וְיֶתֶר דִּבְרֵי יוֹאָשׁ וְכָל־ אֲשֶׁר עָשָׂה
he-did that and-all Joash events-of and-rest-of (12) he-continued in-her

וּגְבוּרָתוֹ אֲשֶׁר נִלְחַם עִם אֲמַצְיָה מֶלֶךְ־ יְהוּדָה הֲלוֹא־
not? Judah king-of Amaziah against he-warred when and-achievement-of-him

הֵם כְּתוּבִים עַל־ סֵפֶר דִּבְרֵי הַיָּמִים לְמַלְכֵי יִשְׂרָאֵל׃
Israel of-kings-of the-days annals-of book-of in ones-being-written they

וַיִּשְׁכַּב יוֹאָשׁ עִם־ אֲבֹתָיו וְיָרָבְעָם יָשַׁב עַל־
on he-sat and-Jeroboam fathers-of-him with Joash and-he-rested (13)

כִּסְאוֹ וַיִּקָּבֵר יוֹאָשׁ בְּשֹׁמְרוֹן עִם מַלְכֵי יִשְׂרָאֵל׃
Israel kings-of with in-Samaria Joash and-he-was-buried throne-of-him

וֶאֱלִישָׁע חָלָה אֶת־ חָלְיוֹ אֲשֶׁר יָמוּת בּוֹ
from-him he-would-die which illness-of-him *** he-suffered now-Elisha (14)

וַיֵּרֶד אֵלָיו יוֹאָשׁ מֶלֶךְ־ יִשְׂרָאֵל וַיֵּבְךְּ עַל־ פָּנָיו
faces-of-him over and-he-wept Israel king-of Joash to-him and-he-went-down

וַיֹּאמַר אָבִי | אָבִי רֶכֶב יִשְׂרָאֵל וּפָרָשָׁיו׃
and-horsemen-of-him Israel chariot-of father-of-me father-of-me and-he-cried

וַיֹּאמֶר לוֹ אֱלִישָׁע קַח קֶשֶׁת וְחִצִּים וַיִּקַּח אֵלָיו קֶשֶׁת
bow for-him so-he-got and-arrows bow get! Elisha to-him and-he-said (15)

וְחִצִּים׃ וַיֹּאמֶר | לְמֶלֶךְ יִשְׂרָאֵל הַרְכֵּב יָדְךָ עַל־ הַקֶּשֶׁת
the-bow on hand-of-you place! Israel to-king-of and-he-said (16) and-arrows

וַיַּרְכֵּב יָדוֹ וַיָּשֶׂם אֱלִישָׁע יָדָיו עַל־ יְדֵי
hands-of on hands-of-him Elisha then-he-put hand-of-him when-he-placed

הַמֶּלֶךְ׃ וַיֹּאמֶר פְּתַח הַחַלּוֹן קֵדְמָה וַיִּפְתָּח וַיֹּאמֶר
and-he-said and-he-opened to-east the-window open! and-he-said (17) the-king

אֱלִישָׁע יְרֵה וַיּוֹר וַיֹּאמֶר חֵץ־ תְּשׁוּעָה לַיהוָה
of-Yahweh victory arrow-of and-he-declared and-he-shot shoot! Elisha

the annals of the kings of Israel? 9Jehoahaz rested with his
fathers and was buried in Samaria. And Jehoash[e] his son
succeeded him as king.

Jehoash King of Israel

10In the thirty-seventh year
of Joash king of Judah, Jehoash son of Jehoahaz became
king of Israel in Samaria, and
he reigned sixteen years. 11He
did evil in the eyes of the LORD
and did not turn away from
any of the sins of Jeroboam
son of Nebat, which he had
caused Israel to commit; he
continued in them.
12As for the other events of
the reign of Jehoash, all he did
and his achievements, including his war against Amaziah
king of Judah, are they not
written in the book of the annals of the kings of Israel? 13Je-
hoash rested with his fathers,
and Jeroboam succeeded him
on the throne. Jehoash was
buried in Samaria with the
kings of Israel.
14Now Elisha was suffering
from the illness from which he
died. Jehoash king of Israel
went down to see him and
wept over him. "My father!
My father!" he cried. "The
chariots and horsemen of Israel!"
15Elisha said, "Get a bow
and some arrows," and he did
so. 16"Take the bow in your
hands," he said to the king of
Israel. When he had taken it,
Elisha put his hands on the
king's hands.
17"Open the east window,"
he said, and he opened it.
"Shoot!" Elisha said, and he
shot. "The LORD's arrow of victory, the arrow of victory over

[e]9 Hebrew *Joash*, a variant of *Jehoash*; also in verses 12-14 and 25

וְחֵץ תְּשׁוּעָה בַאֲרָם וְהִכִּיתָ אֶת־ אֲרָם בַּאֲפֵק עַד־
to at-Aphek Aram *** now-you-will-destroy over-Aram victory and-arrow-of

כַּלֵּה׃ וַיֹּאמֶר קַח הַחִצִּים וַיִּקָּח וַיֹּאמֶר
and-he-told and-he-took the-arrows take! then-he-said (18) to-be-complete

לְמֶלֶךְ־ יִשְׂרָאֵל הַךְ־ אַרְצָה וַיַּךְ שָׁלֹשׁ־ פְּעָמִים וַיַּעֲמֹד׃
and-he-stopped times three and-he-struck on-ground strike! Israel to-king-of

וַיִּקְצֹף עָלָיו אִישׁ הָאֱלֹהִים וַיֹּאמֶר לְהַכּוֹת חָמֵשׁ
five to-strike and-he-said the-God man-of with-him and-he-was-angry (19)

אוֹ־ שֵׁשׁ פְּעָמִים אָז הִכִּיתָ אֶת־ אֲרָם עַד־ כַּלֵּה
to-completely-destroy to Aram *** you-would-defeat then times six or

וְעַתָּה שָׁלֹשׁ פְּעָמִים תַּכֶּה אֶת־ אֲרָם׃ וַיָּמָת אֱלִישָׁע
Elisha and-he-died (20) Aram *** you-will-defeat times three but-now

וַיִּקְבְּרֻהוּ וּגְדוּדֵי מוֹאָב יָבֹאוּ בָאָרֶץ
into-the-country they-entered Moab now-raiders-of and-they-buried-him

בָּא שָׁנָה׃ וַיְהִי הֵם ׀ קֹבְרִים אִישׁ וְהִנֵּה רָאוּ אֶת־
*** they-saw and-see! man ones-burying they and-he-was (21) year coming-of

הַגְּדוּד וַיַּשְׁלִיכוּ אֶת־ הָאִישׁ בְּקֶבֶר אֱלִישָׁע וַיֵּלֶךְ
when-he-went Elisha into-tomb-of the-man *** so-they-threw the-band

וַיִּגַּע הָאִישׁ בְּעַצְמוֹת אֱלִישָׁע וַיְחִי וַיָּקָם
and-he-stood-up then-he-came-to-life Elisha on-bones-of the-man and-he-touched

עַל־ רַגְלָיו׃ וַחֲזָאֵל מֶלֶךְ אֲרָם לָחַץ אֶת־יִשְׂרָאֵל
Israel *** he-oppressed Aram king-of and-Hazael (22) feet-of-him on

כֹּל יְמֵי יְהוֹאָחָז׃ וַיָּחָן יְהוָה אֹתָם
to-them Yahweh but-he-was-gracious (23) Jehoahaz days-of all-of

וַיְרַחֲמֵם וַיִּפֶן אֲלֵיהֶם לְמַעַן
because-of for-them and-he-showed-concern and-he-had-compassion-for-them

בְּרִיתוֹ אֶת־ אַבְרָהָם יִצְחָק וְיַעֲקֹב וְלֹא אָבָה
he-was-willing and-not and-Jacob Isaac Abraham with covenant-of-him

הַשְׁחִיתָם וְלֹא־ הִשְׁלִיכָם מֵעַל־ פָּנָיו עַד־
to presences-of-him from-before he-banished-them and-not to-destroy-them

עַתָּה׃ וַיָּמָת חֲזָאֵל מֶלֶךְ־ אֲרָם וַיִּמְלֹךְ בֶּן־ הֲדַד
Hadad Ben and-he-became-king Aram king-of Hazael and-he-died (24) now

בְּנוֹ תַּחְתָּיו׃ וַיָּשָׁב יְהוֹאָשׁ בֶּן־ יְהוֹאָחָז
Jehoahaz son-of Jehoash then-he-returned (25) in-place-of-him son-of-him

וַיִּקַּח אֶת־ הֶעָרִים מִיַּד בֶּן־ הֲדַד בֶּן־ חֲזָאֵל אֲשֶׁר
that Hazael son-of Hadad Ben from-hand-of the-towns *** and-he-recaptured

לָקַח מִיַּד יְהוֹאָחָז אָבִיו בַּמִּלְחָמָה שָׁלֹשׁ פְּעָמִים
times three in-the-battle father-of-him Jehoahaz from-hand-of he-took

Aram!" Elisha declared. "You
will completely destroy the
Arameans at Aphek."
[18]Then he said, "Take the arrows," and the king took
them. Elisha told him, "Strike
the ground." He struck it three
times and stopped. [19]The man
of God was angry with him
and said, "You should have
struck the ground five or six
times; then you would have
defeated Aram and completely
destroyed it. But now you will
defeat it only three times."
[20]Elisha died and was buried.

Now Moabite raiders used
to enter the country every
spring. [21]Once while some Israelites were burying a man,
suddenly they saw a band of
raiders; so they threw the
man's body into Elisha's
tomb. When the body touched
Elisha's bones, the man came
to life and stood up on his feet.
[22]Hazael king of Aram oppressed Israel throughout the
reign of Jehoahaz. [23]But the
LORD was gracious to them
and had compassion and
showed concern for them because of his covenant with
Abraham, Isaac and Jacob. To
this day he has been unwilling to destroy them or banish
them from his presence.
[24]Hazael king of Aram died,
and Ben-Hadad his son succeeded him as king. [25]Then Jehoash son of Jehoahaz recap-
tured from Ben-Hadad son of
Hazael the towns he had taken

הִכָּהוּ יוֹאָשׁ וַיָּשֶׁב אֶת־ עָרֵי יִשְׂרָאֵל׃ בִּשְׁנַת
in-year-of (14:1) Israel towns-of *** so-he-recovered Joash he-defeated-him

שְׁתַּיִם לְיוֹאָשׁ בֶּן־ יוֹאָחָז מֶלֶךְ יִשְׂרָאֵל מָלַךְ אֲמַצְיָהוּ בֶן־
son-of Amaziah he-became-king Israel king-of Jehoahaz son-of of-Joash two

יוֹאָשׁ מֶלֶךְ יְהוּדָה׃ בֶּן־ עֶשְׂרִים וְחָמֵשׁ שָׁנָה הָיָה
he-was year and-five twenty son-of (2) Judah king-of Joash

בְמָלְכוֹ וְעֶשְׂרִים וָתֵשַׁע שָׁנָה מָלַךְ בִּירוּשָׁלָםִ
in-Jerusalem he-reigned year and-nine and-twenty when-to-become-king-him

וְשֵׁם אִמּוֹ יְהוֹעַדִּין מִן־ יְרוּשָׁלָםִ׃ וַיַּעַשׂ הַיָּשָׁר
the-right and-he-did (3) Jerusalem from Jehoaddin mother-of-him and-name-of

בְּעֵינֵי יְהוָה רַק לֹא כְּדָוִד אָבִיו כְּכֹל אֲשֶׁר־ עָשָׂה יוֹאָשׁ
Joash he-did that as-all father-of-him as-David not but Yahweh in-eyes-of

אָבִיו עָשָׂה׃ רַק הַבָּמוֹת לֹא־ סָרוּ עוֹד
still they-removed not the-high-places however (4) he-followed father-of-him

הָעָם מְזַבְּחִים וּמְקַטְּרִים בַּבָּמוֹת׃
at-the-high-places and-ones-burning-incense ones-offering-sacrifices the-people

וַיְהִי כַּאֲשֶׁר חָזְקָה הַמַּמְלָכָה בְּיָדוֹ וַיַּךְ
then-he-executed in-hand-of-him the-kingdom she-was-firm just-as and-he-was (5)

אֶת־ עֲבָדָיו הַמַּכִּים אֶת־ הַמֶּלֶךְ אָבִיו׃ וְאֶת־
yet (6) father-of-him the-king *** the-ones-murdering officials-of-him ***

בְּנֵי הַמַּכִּים לֹא הֵמִית כַּכָּתוּב
as-the-thing-being-written he-killed not the-ones-assassinating sons-of

בְּסֵפֶר תּוֹרַת־מֹשֶׁה אֲשֶׁר־ צִוָּה יְהוָה לֵאמֹר לֹא־ יוּמְתוּ
they-shall-be-killed not to-say Yahweh he-commanded where Moses Law-of in-Book-of

אָבוֹת עַל־ בָּנִים וּבָנִים לֹא־ יוּמְתוּ עַל־ אָבוֹת כִּי
for fathers for they-shall-be-killed not and-children children for fathers

אִם־ אִישׁ בְּחֶטְאוֹ יָמוּת׃ הוּא־ הִכָּה אֶת־אֱדוֹם
Edom *** he-defeated he (7) he-shall-be-killed for-sin-of-him each only

בְּגֵיא־ הַמֶּלַח עֲשֶׂרֶת אֲלָפִים וְתָפַשׂ אֶת־ הַסֶּלַע בַּמִּלְחָמָה
in-the-battle the-Sela *** and-he-captured thousands ten-of Salt in-Valley-of

וַיִּקְרָא אֶת־ שְׁמָהּ יָקְתְאֵל עַד הַיּוֹם הַזֶּה׃ אָז שָׁלַח
he-sent then (8) the-this the-day to Joktheel name-of-her *** and-he-called

אֲמַצְיָה מַלְאָכִים אֶל־יְהוֹאָשׁ בֶּן־ יְהוֹאָחָז בֶּן־ יֵהוּא מֶלֶךְ יִשְׂרָאֵל
Israel king-of Jehu son-of Jehoahaz son-of Jehoash to messengers Amaziah

לֵאמֹר לְכָה נִתְרָאֶה פָנִים׃ וַיִּשְׁלַח יְהוֹאָשׁ מֶלֶךְ־ יִשְׂרָאֵל אֶל־
to Israel king-of Jehoash but-he-replied (9) faces let-us-meet come! to-say

אֲמַצְיָהוּ מֶלֶךְ־ יְהוּדָה לֵאמֹר הַחוֹחַ אֲשֶׁר בַּלְּבָנוֹן שָׁלַח אֶל־
to he-sent in-the-Lebanon that the-thistle to-say Judah king-of Amaziah

°2 ק יהועדן
°6 ק יומת
°7 ק מלח

in battle from his father Jehoahaz. Three times Jehoash defeated him, and so he recovered the Israelite towns.

Amaziah King of Judah

14 In the second year of
Jehoash[f] son of Jehoa-
haz king of Israel, Amaziah
son of Joash king of Judah began to reign. [2]He was twenty-
five years old when he became
king, and he reigned in
Jerusalem twenty-nine years.
His mother's name was Je-
hoaddin; she was from Jerusalem. [3]He did what was right in
the eyes of the LORD, but not as
his father David had done. In
everything he followed the ex-
ample of his father Joash. [4]The
high places, however, were
not removed; the people continued to offer sacrifices and
burn incense there.
[5]After the kingdom was
firmly in his grasp, he executed the officials who had murdered his father the king. [6]Yet
he did not put the sons of the
assassins to death, in accordance with what is written in
the Book of the Law of Moses
where the LORD commanded:
"Fathers shall not be put to
death for their children, nor
children put to death for their
fathers; each is to die for his
own sins."[g]
[7]He was the one who de-
feated ten thousand Edomites
in the Valley of Salt and captured Sela in battle, calling it
Joktheel, the name it has to
this day.
[8]Then Amaziah sent mes-
sengers to Jehoash son of
Jehoahaz, the son of Jehu, king
of Israel, with the challenge:
"Come, meet me face to face."
[9]But Jehoash king of Israel
replied to Amaziah king of
Judah: "A thistle in Lebanon

f1 Hebrew *Joash*, a variant of *Jehoash*; also in verses 13, 23 and 27
g6 Deut. 24:16

הָאֶרֶז אֲשֶׁר בַּלְּבָנוֹן לֵאמֹר תְּנָה־אֶת־בִּתְּךָ לִבְנִי
to-son-of-me daughter-of-you *** give! to-say in-the-Lebanon that the-cedar

לְאִשָּׁה וַתַּעֲבֹר חַיַּת הַשָּׂדֶה אֲשֶׁר בַּלְּבָנוֹן
in-the-Lebanon that the-field beast-of then-she-came-along as-wife

וַתִּרְמֹס אֶת־הַחוֹחַ׃ הַכֵּה הִכִּיתָ אֶת־אֱדוֹם
Edom *** you-defeated to-defeat (10) the-thistle *** and-she-trampled

וּנְשָׂאֲךָ לִבֶּךָ הִכָּבֵד וְשֵׁב בְּבֵיתֶךָ וְלָמָּה
now-why? at-home-of-you but-stay! glory! heart-of-you and-he-lifted-you

תִתְגָּרֶה בְּרָעָה וְנָפַלְתָּה אַתָּה וִיהוּדָה עִמָּךְ׃ וְלֹא־
but-not (11) with-you and-Judah you so-you-fall for-trouble you-ask

שָׁמַע אֲמַצְיָהוּ וַיַּעַל יְהוֹאָשׁ מֶלֶךְ־יִשְׂרָאֵל וַיִּתְרָאוּ פָנִים
faces and-they-met Israel king-of Jehoash so-he-attacked Amaziah he-listened

הוּא וַאֲמַצְיָהוּ מֶלֶךְ־יְהוּדָה בְּבֵית שֶׁמֶשׁ אֲשֶׁר לִיהוּדָה׃
in-Judah that Shemesh at-Beth Judah king-of and-Amaziah he

וַיִּנָּגֶף יְהוּדָה לִפְנֵי יִשְׂרָאֵל וַיָּנֻסוּ אִישׁ לְאֹהָלָו׃
to-homes-of-him each and-they-fled Israel before Judah and-he-was-routed (12)

וְאֵת אֲמַצְיָהוּ מֶלֶךְ־יְהוּדָה בֶּן־יְהוֹאָשׁ בֶּן־אֲחַזְיָהוּ תָּפַשׂ
he-captured Ahaziah son-of Jehoash son-of Judah king-of Amaziah and (13)

יְהוֹאָשׁ מֶלֶךְ־יִשְׂרָאֵל בְּבֵית שֶׁמֶשׁ וַיָּבֹאוּ יְרוּשָׁלַםִ וַיִּפְרֹץ
and-he-broke Jerusalem then-he-went Shemesh at-Beth Israel king-of Jehoash

בְּחוֹמַת יְרוּשָׁלַםִ בְּשַׁעַר אֶפְרַיִם עַד־שַׁעַר הַפִּנָּה אַרְבַּע
four the-Corner Gate-of to Ephraim from-Gate-of Jerusalem through-wall-of

מֵאוֹת אַמָּה׃ וְלָקַח אֶת־כָּל־הַזָּהָב־וְהַכֶּסֶף וְאֵת
and and-the-silver the-gold all-of *** and-he-took (14) cubit hundreds

כָּל־הַכֵּלִים הַנִּמְצְאִים בֵּית־יְהוָה וּבְאֹצְרוֹת
and-in-treasuries-of Yahweh temple-of the-ones-being-found the-articles all-of

בֵּית הַמֶּלֶךְ וְאֵת בְּנֵי הַתַּעֲרֻבוֹת וַיָּשָׁב שֹׁמְרוֹנָה׃
to-Samaria and-he-returned the-hostages sons-of and the-king palace-of

וְיֶתֶר דִּבְרֵי יְהוֹאָשׁ אֲשֶׁר עָשָׂה וּגְבוּרָתוֹ וַאֲשֶׁר
and-how and-achievement-of-him he-did what Jehoash events-of and-rest-of (15)

נִלְחַם עִם אֲמַצְיָהוּ מֶלֶךְ־יְהוּדָה הֲלֹא־הֵם כְּתוּבִים עַל־
in ones-being-written they not? Judah king-of Amaziah against he-warred

סֵפֶר דִּבְרֵי הַיָּמִים לְמַלְכֵי יִשְׂרָאֵל׃ וַיִּשְׁכַּב יְהוֹאָשׁ
Jehoash and-he-rested (16) Israel of-kings-of the-days annals-of book-of

עִם־אֲבֹתָיו וַיִּקָּבֵר בְּשֹׁמְרוֹן עִם מַלְכֵי יִשְׂרָאֵל
Israel kings-of with in-Samaria and-he-was-buried fathers-of-him with

וַיִּמְלֹךְ יָרָבְעָם בְּנוֹ תַּחְתָּיו׃ וַיְחִי
and-he-lived (17) in-place-of-him son-of-him Jeroboam and-he-became-king

sent a message to a cedar in
Lebanon, 'Give your daughter
to my son in marriage.' Then a
wild beast in Lebanon came
along and trampled the thistle
underfoot. 10 You have indeed
defeated Edom and now you
are arrogant. Glory in your
victory, but stay at home! Why
ask for trouble and cause your
own downfall and that of
Judah also?"
11 Amaziah, however, would
not listen, so Jehoash king of
Israel attacked. He and Amaziah king of Judah faced each
other at Beth Shemesh in
Judah. 12 Judah was routed by
Israel, and every man fled to
his home. 13 Jehoash king of Israel captured Amaziah king of
Judah, the son of Joash, the
son of Ahaziah, at Beth Shemesh. Then Jehoash went to
Jerusalem and broke down the
wall of Jerusalem from the
Ephraim Gate to the Corner
Gate—a section about six hundred feet long.[h] 14 He took all
the gold and silver and all the
articles found in the temple of
the LORD and in the treasuries
of the royal palace. He also
took hostages and returned to
Samaria.
15 As for the other events of
the reign of Jehoash, what he
did and his achievements, including his war against Amaziah king of Judah, are they
not written in the book of the
annals of the kings of Israel?
16 Jehoash rested with his fathers and was buried in Samaria with the kings of Israel.
And Jeroboam his son suc-
ceeded him as king.

[h]13 Hebrew *four hundred cubits* (about 180 meters)

°12 ק לאהליו
°13 ק ויבא

אֲמַצְיָהוּ בֶן־ יוֹאָשׁ מֶלֶךְ יְהוּדָה אַחֲרֵי מוֹת יְהוֹאָשׁ בֶּן־ יְהוֹאָחָז
Jehoahaz son-of Jehoash death-of after Judah king-of Joash son-of Amaziah

מֶלֶךְ יִשְׂרָאֵל חֲמֵשׁ עֶשְׂרֵה שָׁנָה׃ וְיֶתֶר דִּבְרֵי אֲמַצְיָהוּ הֲלֹא־
not? Amaziah events-of and-rest-of (18) year ten five-of Israel king-of

הֵם כְּתוּבִים עַל־ סֵפֶר דִּבְרֵי הַיָּמִים לְמַלְכֵי יְהוּדָה׃
Judah of-kings-of the-days annals-of book-of in ones-being-written they

וַיִּקְשְׁרוּ עָלָיו קֶשֶׁר בִּירוּשָׁלַםִ וַיָּנָס
and-he-fled in-Jerusalem conspiracy against-him and-they-conspired (19)

לָכִישָׁה וַיִּשְׁלְחוּ אַחֲרָיו לָכִישָׁה וַיְמִתֻהוּ שָׁם׃
there and-they-killed-him to-Lachish after-him but-they-sent to-Lachish

וַיִּשְׂאוּ אֹתוֹ עַל־ הַסּוּסִים וַיִּקָּבֵר בִּירוּשָׁלַםִ
in-Jerusalem and-he-was-buried the-horses on him and-they-brought-back (20)

עִם־ אֲבֹתָיו בְּעִיר דָּוִד׃ וַיִּקְחוּ כָּל־ עַם
people-of all-of then-they-took (21) David in-City-of fathers-of-him with

יְהוּדָה אֶת־ עֲזַרְיָה וְהוּא בֶּן־ שֵׁשׁ עֶשְׂרֵה שָׁנָה וַיַּמְלִכוּ אֹתוֹ
him and-they-made-king year ten six-of son-of now-he Azariah * Judah**

תַּחַת אָבִיו אֲמַצְיָהוּ׃ הוּא בָּנָה אֶת־ אֵילַת
Elath * he-rebuilt he (22) Amaziah father-of-him in-place-of**

וַיְשִׁבֶהָ לִיהוּדָה אַחֲרֵי שְׁכַב־ הַמֶּלֶךְ עִם־ אֲבֹתָיו׃
fathers-of-him with the-king to-rest after to-Judah and-he-restored-her

בִּשְׁנַת חֲמֵשׁ־עֶשְׂרֵה שָׁנָה לַאֲמַצְיָהוּ בֶן־ יוֹאָשׁ מֶלֶךְ יְהוּדָה
Judah king-of Joash son-of of-Amaziah year ten five-of in-year-of (23)

מָלַךְ יָרָבְעָם בֶּן־ יוֹאָשׁ מֶלֶךְ־ יִשְׂרָאֵל בְּשֹׁמְרוֹן אַרְבָּעִים
forty in-Samaria Israel king-of Joash son-of Jeroboam he-became-king

וְאַחַת שָׁנָה׃ וַיַּעַשׂ הָרַע בְּעֵינֵי יְהוָה לֹא סָר
he-turned-away not Yahweh in-eyes-of the-evil and-he-did (24) year and-one

מִכָּל־ חַטֹּאות יָרָבְעָם בֶּן־ נְבָט אֲשֶׁר הֶחֱטִיא אֶת־
***** he-caused-to-commit which Nebat son-of Jeroboam sins-of from-any-of**

יִשְׂרָאֵל׃ הוּא הֵשִׁיב אֶת־ גְּבוּל יִשְׂרָאֵל מִלְּבוֹא חֲמָת עַד־
to Hamath from-Lebo Israel boundary-of * he-restored he (25) Israel**

יָם הָעֲרָבָה כִּדְבַר יְהוָה אֱלֹהֵי יִשְׂרָאֵל אֲשֶׁר דִּבֶּר בְּיַד־
by-hand-of he-spoke that Israel God-of Yahweh as-word-of the-Arabah Sea-of

עַבְדּוֹ יוֹנָה בֶן־ אֲמִתַּי הַנָּבִיא אֲשֶׁר מִגַּת הַחֵפֶר׃
the-Hepher from-Gath-of who the-prophet Amittai son-of Jonah servant-of-him

כִּי־ רָאָה יְהוָה אֶת־ עֳנִי יִשְׂרָאֵל מֹרֶה מְאֹד וְאֶפֶס
and-whether very being-bitter Israel suffering-of * Yahweh he-saw for (26)**

עָצוּר וְאֶפֶס עָזוּב וְאֵין עֹזֵר לְיִשְׂרָאֵל׃ וְלֹא־
and-not (27) to-Israel helping and-no-one being-free or-whether being-slave

17Amaziah son of Joash king
of Judah lived for fifteen years
after the death of Jehoash son
of Jehoahaz king of Israel. 18As
for the other events of Amaziah's reign, are they not written in the book of the annals
of the kings of Judah?
19They conspired against
him in Jerusalem, and he fled
to Lachish, but they sent men
after him to Lachish and killed
him there. 20He was brought
back by horse and was buried
in Jerusalem with his fathers,
in the City of David.
21Then all the people of
Judah took Azariah,[i] who was
sixteen years old, and made
him king in place of his father
Amaziah. 22He was the one
who rebuilt Elath and restored
it to Judah after Amaziah rested with his fathers.

Jeroboam II King of Israel

23In the fifteenth year of
Amaziah son of Joash king of
Judah, Jeroboam son of Jehoash king of Israel became
king in Samaria, and he
reigned forty-one years. 24He
did evil in the eyes of the LORD
and did not turn away from
any of the sins of Jeroboam
son of Nebat, which he had
caused Israel to commit. 25He
was the one who restored the
boundaries of Israel from
Lebo[j] Hamath to the Sea of
the Arabah,[k] in accordance
with the word of the LORD, the
God of Israel, spoken through
his servant Jonah son of Amittai, the prophet from Gath Hepher.
26The LORD had seen how
bitterly everyone in Israel,
whether slave or free, was
suffering; there was no one to
help them. 27And since the

[i]21 Also called *Uzziah*
[j]25 Or *from the entrance to*
[k]25 That is, the Dead Sea

דִּבֶּר יְהוָה לִמְחוֹת אֶת־ שֵׁם יִשְׂרָאֵל מִתַּחַת הַשָּׁמָיִם

the-heavens from-under Israel name-of *** to-blot-out Yahweh he-said

וַיּוֹשִׁיעֵם בְּיַד יָרָבְעָם בֶּן־ יוֹאָשׁ׃ וְיֶתֶר דִּבְרֵי

events-of and-rest-of (28) Joash son-of Jeroboam by-hand-of so-he-saved-them

יָרָבְעָם וְכָל־ אֲשֶׁר עָשָׂה וּגְבוּרָתוֹ אֲשֶׁר־ נִלְחָם וַאֲשֶׁר

and-how he-fought that and-achievement-of-him he-did that and-all Jeroboam

הֵשִׁיב אֶת־ דַּמֶּשֶׂק וְאֶת־ חֲמָת לִיהוּדָה בְּיִשְׂרָאֵל הֲלֹא־ הֵם

they not? for-Israel of-Judah Hamath and Damascus *** he-recovered

כְּתוּבִים עַל־ סֵפֶר דִּבְרֵי הַיָּמִים לְמַלְכֵי יִשְׂרָאֵל׃

Israel of-kings-of the-days annals-of book-of in ones-being-written

וַיִּשְׁכַּב יָרָבְעָם עִם־ אֲבֹתָיו עִם מַלְכֵי יִשְׂרָאֵל

Israel kings-of with fathers-of-him with Jeroboam and-he-rested (29)

וַיִּמְלֹךְ זְכַרְיָה בְנוֹ תַּחְתָּיו׃ בִּשְׁנַת

in-year-of (15:1) in-place-of-him son-of-him Zechariah and-he-became-king

עֶשְׂרִים וָשֶׁבַע שָׁנָה לְיָרָבְעָם מֶלֶךְ יִשְׂרָאֵל מָלַךְ עֲזַרְיָה

Azariah he-became-king Israel king-of of-Jeroboam year and-seven twenty

בֶן־ אֲמַצְיָה מֶלֶךְ יְהוּדָה׃ בֶּן־ שֵׁשׁ עֶשְׂרֵה שָׁנָה הָיָה

he-was year ten six-of son-of (2) Judah king-of Amaziah son-of

בְמָלְכוֹ וַחֲמִשִּׁים וּשְׁתַּיִם שָׁנָה מָלַךְ בִּירוּשָׁלָםִ

in-Jerusalem he-reigned year and-two and-fifty when-to-become-king-him

וְשֵׁם אִמּוֹ יְכָלְיָהוּ מִירוּשָׁלָםִ׃ וַיַּעַשׂ הַיָּשָׁר

the-right and-he-did (3) from-Jerusalem Jecoliah mother-of-him and-name-of

בְּעֵינֵי יְהוָה כְּכֹל אֲשֶׁר־ עָשָׂה אֲמַצְיָהוּ אָבִיו׃ רַק

however (4) father-of-him Amaziah he-did that as-all Yahweh in-eyes-of

הַבָּמוֹת לֹא־ סָרוּ עוֹד הָעָם מְזַבְּחִים

ones-offering-sacrifices the-people still they-removed not the-high-places

וּמְקַטְּרִים בַּבָּמוֹת׃ וַיְנַגַּע יְהוָה אֶת־

*** Yahweh and-he-afflicted (5) at-the-high-places and-ones-burning-incense

הַמֶּלֶךְ וַיְהִי מְצֹרָע עַד־ יוֹם מֹתוֹ וַיֵּשֶׁב

and-he-lived death-of-him day-of until being-leprous and-he-was the-king

בְּבֵית הַחָפְשִׁית וְיוֹתָם בֶּן־ הַמֶּלֶךְ עַל־ הַבַּיִת שֹׁפֵט

governing the-palace over the-king son-of and-Jotham the-separate in-house-of

אֶת־ עַם הָאָרֶץ׃ וְיֶתֶר דִּבְרֵי עֲזַרְיָהוּ וְכָל־ אֲשֶׁר עָשָׂה

he-did that and-all Azariah events-of and-rest-of (6) the-land people-of ***

הֲלֹא־ הֵם כְּתוּבִים עַל־ סֵפֶר דִּבְרֵי הַיָּמִים לְמַלְכֵי יְהוּדָה׃

Judah of-kings-of the-days annals-of book-of in ones-being-written they not?

וַיִּשְׁכַּב עֲזַרְיָה עִם־ אֲבֹתָיו וַיִּקְבְּרוּ אֹתוֹ עִם־

with him and-they-buried fathers-of-him with Azariah and-he-rested (7)

LORD had not said he would
blot out the name of Israel
from under heaven, he saved
them by the hand of Jeroboam
son of Jehoash.
28 As for the other events of
Jeroboam's reign, all he did,
and his military achieve-
ments, including how he
recovered for Israel both
Damascus and Hamath,
which had belonged to
Yaudi,[l] are they not written in
the book of the annals of the
kings of Israel? 29 Jeroboam
rested with his fathers, the
kings of Israel. And Zechariah
his son succeeded him as king.

Azariah King of Judah

15 In the twenty-seventh
year of Jeroboam king
of Israel, Azariah son of Amaziah king of Judah began to
reign. 2 He was sixteen years
old when he became king, and
he reigned in Jerusalem fifty-
two years. His mother's name
was Jecoliah; she was from
Jerusalem. 3 He did what was
right in the eyes of the LORD,
just as his father Amaziah had
done. 4 The high places, however, were not removed; the
people continued to offer sacrifices and burn incense there.
5 The LORD afflicted the king
with leprosy[m] until the day he
died, and he lived in a separate house.[n] Jotham the king's
son had charge of the palace
and governed the people of
the land.
6 As for the other events of
Azariah's reign, and all he did,
are they not written in the
book of the annals of the kings
of Judah? 7 Azariah rested with
his fathers and was buried

[l] 28 Or *Judah*
[m] 5 The Hebrew word was used for various diseases affecting the skin—not necessarily leprosy.
[n] 5 Or *in a house where he was relieved of responsibility*

אֲבֹתָיו בְּעִיר דָּוִד. וַיִּמְלֹךְ יוֹתָם בְּנוֹ
son-of-him Jotham and-he-became-king David in-City-of fathers-of-him

תַּחְתָּיו׃ בִּשְׁנַת שְׁלֹשִׁים וּשְׁמֹנֶה שָׁנָה לַעֲזַרְיָהוּ מֶלֶךְ
king-of of-Azariah year and-eight thirty in-year-of (8) in-place-of-him

יְהוּדָה מָלַךְ זְכַרְיָהוּ בֶן־ יָרָבְעָם עַל־ יִשְׂרָאֵל בְּשֹׁמְרוֹן שִׁשָּׁה
six in-Samaria Israel over Jeroboam son-of Zechariah he-became-king Judah

חֳדָשִׁים׃ וַיַּעַשׂ הָרַע בְּעֵינֵי יְהוָה כַּאֲשֶׁר עָשׂוּ
they-did just-as Yahweh in-eyes-of the-evil and-he-did (9) months

אֲבֹתָיו לֹא סָר מֵחַטֹּאות יָרָבְעָם בֶּן־ נְבָט אֲשֶׁר
which Nebat son-of Jeroboam from-sins-of he-turned-away not fathers-of-him

הֶחֱטִיא אֶת־ יִשְׂרָאֵל׃ וַיִּקְשֹׁר עָלָיו שַׁלֻּם
Shallum against-him and-he-conspired (10) Israel * he-caused-to-commit**

בֶּן־ יָבֵשׁ וַיַּכֵּהוּ קָבָל־ עָם וַיְמִיתֵהוּ
and-he-assassinated-him people in-front-of and-he-attacked-him Jabesh son-of

וַיִּמְלֹךְ תַּחְתָּיו׃ וְיֶתֶר דִּבְרֵי זְכַרְיָה
Zechariah events-of and-rest-of (11) in-place-of-him and-he-became-king

הִנָּם כְּתוּבִים עַל־ סֵפֶר דִּבְרֵי הַיָּמִים לְמַלְכֵי יִשְׂרָאֵל׃
Israel of-kings-of the-days annals-of book-of in ones-being-written see-they!

הוּא דְבַר־ יְהוָה אֲשֶׁר דִּבֶּר אֶל־ יֵהוּא לֵאמֹר בְּנֵי רְבִעִים
fourth-ones sons-of to-say Jehu to he-spoke that Yahweh word-of this (12)

יֵשְׁבוּ לְךָ עַל־ כִּסֵּא יִשְׂרָאֵל וַיְהִי־ כֵן׃ שַׁלּוּם בֶּן־
son-of Shallum (13) so and-he-was Israel throne-of on of-you they-will-sit

יָבֵישׁ מָלַךְ בִּשְׁנַת שְׁלֹשִׁים וָתֵשַׁע שָׁנָה לְעֻזִיָּה מֶלֶךְ
king-of of-Uzziah year and-nine thirty in-year-of he-became-king Jabesh

יְהוּדָה וַיִּמְלֹךְ יֶרַח־ יָמִים בְּשֹׁמְרוֹן׃ וַיַּעַל מְנַחֵם
Menahem then-he-went-up (14) in-Samaria days month-of and-he-reigned Judah

בֶּן־ גָּדִי מִתִּרְצָה וַיָּבֹא שֹׁמְרוֹן וַיַּךְ אֶת־ שַׁלּוּם
Shallum * and-he-attacked Samaria and-he-went from-Tirzah Gadi son-of**

בֶּן־ יָבֵישׁ בְּשֹׁמְרוֹן וַיְמִיתֵהוּ וַיִּמְלֹךְ
and-he-became-king and-he-assassinated-him in-Samaria Jabesh son-of

תַּחְתָּיו׃ וְיֶתֶר דִּבְרֵי שַׁלּוּם וְקִשְׁרוֹ
and-conspiracy-of-him Shallum events-of and-rest-of (15) in-place-of-him

אֲשֶׁר קָשָׁר הִנָּם כְּתֻבִים עַל־ סֵפֶר דִּבְרֵי
annals-of book-of in ones-being-written see-they! he-conspired that

הַיָּמִים לְמַלְכֵי יִשְׂרָאֵל׃ אָז יַכֶּה־ מְנַחֵם אֶת־ תִּפְסַח וְאֶת־
and Tiphsah * Menahem he-attacked then (16) Israel of-kings-of the-days**

כָּל־ אֲשֶׁר־ בָּהּ וְאֶת־ גְּבוּלֶיהָ מִתִּרְצָה כִּי לֹא פָתַח
he-opened not for from-Tirzah vicinity-of-her and in-her who all

near them in the City of David. And Jotham his son succeeded him as king.

Zechariah King of Israel

[8]In the thirty-eighth year of
Azariah king of Judah, Zechariah son of Jeroboam became
king of Israel in Samaria, and
he reigned six months. [9]He did
evil in the eyes of the LORD, as
his fathers had done. He did
not turn away from the sins of
Jeroboam son of Nebat, which
he had caused Israel to commit.

[10]Shallum son of Jabesh conspired against Zechariah. He
attacked him in front of the
people,[o] assassinated him and
succeeded him as king. [11]The
other events of Zechariah's
reign are written in the book
of the annals of the kings of
Israel. [12]So the word of the
LORD spoken to Jehu was
fulfilled: "Your descendants
will sit on the throne of Israel
to the fourth generation."[p]

Shallum King of Israel

[13]Shallum son of Jabesh
became king in the thirty-
ninth year of Uzziah king of
Judah, and he reigned in Samaria one month. [14]Then
Menahem son of Gadi went
from Tirzah up to Samaria. He
attacked Shallum son of Jabesh in Samaria, assassinated
him and succeeded him as
king.

[15]The other events of Shallum's reign, and the conspiracy he led, are written in the
book of the annals of the kings
of Israel.

[16]At that time Menahem,
starting out from Tirzah, attacked Tiphsah and everyone
in the city and its vicinity, because they refused to open

[o]10 Hebrew; some Septuagint manuscripts *in Ibleam*
[p]12 2 Kings 10:30

*13 Most mss have *dagesh* in the *zayin* ('זִּ—).

וַיַּךְ אֵת כָּל־ הֶהָרוֹתֶיהָ בִּקֵּעַ׃
he-ripped-open the-pregnant-women-of-her all-of *** and-he-sacked

בִּשְׁנַת שְׁלֹשִׁים וָתֵשַׁע שָׁנָה לַעֲזַרְיָה מֶלֶךְ יְהוּדָה מָלַךְ
he-became-king Judah king-of of-Azariah year and-nine thirty in-year-of (17)

מְנַחֵם בֶּן־ גָּדִי עַל־יִשְׂרָאֵל עֶשֶׂר שָׁנִים בְּשֹׁמְרוֹן׃ וַיַּעַשׂ הָרַע
the-evil and-he-did (18) in-Samaria years ten Israel over Gadi son-of Menahem

בְּעֵינֵי יְהוָה לֹא סָר מֵעַל חַטֹּאות יָרָבְעָם בֶּן־ נְבָט
Nebat son-of Jeroboam sins-of away-from he-turned-away not Yahweh in-eyes-of

אֲשֶׁר־ הֶחֱטִיא אֶת־ יִשְׂרָאֵל כָּל־ יָמָיו׃ בָּא פוּל
Pul he-invaded (19) days-of-him all-of Israel *** he-caused-to-commit which

מֶלֶךְ־ אַשּׁוּר עַל־ הָאָרֶץ וַיִּתֵּן מְנַחֵם לְפוּל אֶלֶף כִּכַּר־
talent-of thousand to-Pul Menaham and-he-gave the-land into Assyria king-of

כֶּסֶף לִהְיוֹת יָדָיו אִתּוֹ לְהַחֲזִיק הַמַּמְלָכָה בְּיָדוֹ׃
in-hand-of-him the-kingdom to-strengthen with-him hands-of-him to-be silver

וַיֹּצֵא מְנַחֵם אֶת־ הַכֶּסֶף עַל־ יִשְׂרָאֵל עַל כָּל־ גִּבּוֹרֵי
men-of all-of from Israel from the-money *** Menahem and-he-exacted (20)

הַחַיִל לָתֵת לְמֶלֶךְ אַשּׁוּר חֲמִשִּׁים שְׁקָלִים כֶּסֶף לְאִישׁ
from-man silver shekels fifty Assyria to-king-of to-contribute the-wealth

אֶחָד וַיָּשָׁב מֶלֶךְ אַשּׁוּר וְלֹא־ עָמַד שָׁם בָּאָרֶץ׃
in-the-land there he-stayed and-not Assyria king-of so-he-withdrew each

וְיֶתֶר דִּבְרֵי מְנַחֵם וְכָל־ אֲשֶׁר עָשָׂה הֲלוֹא־ הֵם
they not? he-did that and-all Menahem events-of and-rest-of (21)

כְּתוּבִים עַל־ סֵפֶר דִּבְרֵי הַיָּמִים לְמַלְכֵי יִשְׂרָאֵל׃
Israel of-kings-of the-days annals-of book-of in ones-being-written

וַיִּשְׁכַּב מְנַחֵם עִם־ אֲבֹתָיו וַיִּמְלֹךְ פְּקַחְיָה
Pekahiah and-he-became-king fathers-of-him with Menahem and-he-rested (22)

בְּנוֹ תַּחְתָּיו׃ בִּשְׁנַת חֲמִשִּׁים שָׁנָה לַעֲזַרְיָה מֶלֶךְ
king-of of-Azariah year fifty in-year-of (23) in-place-of-him son-of-him

יְהוּדָה מָלַךְ פְּקַחְיָה בֶּן־ מְנַחֵם עַל־יִשְׂרָאֵל בְּשֹׁמְרוֹן שְׁנָתָיִם׃
two-years in-Samaria Israel over Menahem son-of Pekahiah he-became-king Judah

וַיַּעַשׂ הָרַע בְּעֵינֵי יְהוָה לֹא סָר מֵחַטֹּאות
from-sins-of he-turned-away not Yahweh in-eyes-of the-evil and-he-did (24)

יָרָבְעָם בֶּן־ נְבָט אֲשֶׁר הֶחֱטִיא אֶת־יִשְׂרָאֵל׃ וַיִּקְשֹׁר
and-he-conspired (25) Israel *** he-caused-to-commit which Nebat son-of Jeroboam

עָלָיו פֶּקַח בֶּן־ רְמַלְיָהוּ שָׁלִישׁוֹ וַיַּכֵּהוּ
and-he-assassinated-him chief-officer-of-him Remaliah son-of Pekah against-him

בְּשֹׁמְרוֹן בְּאַרְמוֹן בֵּית־ ־מֶלֶךְ אֶת־ אַרְגֹּב וְאֶת־ הָאַרְיֵה
the-Arieh and-with Argob with the-king palace-of in-citadel-of in-Samaria

their gates. He sacked Tiphsah
and ripped open all the pregnant women.

Menahem King of Israel

17In the thirty-ninth year of
Azariah king of Judah, Menahem son of Gadi became king
of Israel, and he reigned in Samaria ten years. 18He did evil
in the eyes of the LORD. During
his entire reign he did not
turn away from the sins of
Jeroboam son of Nebat, which
he had caused Israel to commit.
19Then Pul[q] king of Assyria
invaded the land, and Menahem gave him a thousand talents[r] of silver to gain his support and strengthen his own
hold on the kingdom. 20Mena-
hem exacted this money from
Israel. Every wealthy man had
to contribute fifty shekels[s] of
silver to be given to the king of
Assyria. So the king of Assyria
withdrew and stayed in the
land no longer.
21As for the other events of
Menahem's reign, and all he
did, are they not written in the
book of the annals of the kings
of Israel? 22Menahem rested
with his fathers. And Pekahiah his son succeeded him as
king.

Pekahiah King of Israel

23In the fiftieth year of Azariah king of Judah, Pekahiah
son of Menahem became king
of Israel in Samaria, and he
reigned two years. 24Pekahiah
did evil in the eyes of the
LORD. He did not turn away
from the sins of Jeroboam son
of Nebat, which he had caused
Israel to commit. 25One of his
chief officers, Pekah son of
Remaliah, conspired against

q19 Also called *Tiglath-Pileser*
r19 That is, about 37 tons (about 34 metric tons)
s20 That is, about 1 1/4 pounds (about 0.6 kilogram)

°25 ק המלך

וְעִמּוֹ חֲמִשִּׁים אִישׁ מִבְּנֵי גִלְעָדִים וַיְמִיתֵהוּ

so-he-killed-him Gileadites from-men-of man fifty and-with-him

וַיִּמְלֹךְ תַּחְתָּיו׃ (26) וְיֶתֶר דִּבְרֵי פְקַחְיָה

Pekahiah events-of and-rest-of (26) in-place-of-him and-he-became-king

וְכָל־ אֲשֶׁר עָשָׂה הִנָּם כְּתוּבִים עַל־ סֵפֶר דִּבְרֵי

annals-of book-of in ones-being-written see-they! he-did that and-all

הַיָּמִים לְמַלְכֵי יִשְׂרָאֵל׃ (27) בִּשְׁנַת חֲמִשִּׁים וּשְׁתַּיִם שָׁנָה לַעֲזַרְיָה

of-Azariah year and-two fifty in-year-of (27) Israel of-kings-of the-days

מֶלֶךְ יְהוּדָה מָלַךְ פֶּקַח בֶּן־ רְמַלְיָהוּ עַל־ יִשְׂרָאֵל בְּשֹׁמְרוֹן

in-Samaria Israel over Remaliah son-of Pekah he-became-king Judah king-of

עֶשְׂרִים שָׁנָה׃ (28) וַיַּעַשׂ הָרַע בְּעֵינֵי יְהוָה לֹא סָר

he-turned-away not Yahweh in-eyes-of the-evil and-he-did (28) year twenty

מִן־ חַטֹּאות יָרָבְעָם בֶּן־ נְבָט אֲשֶׁר הֶחֱטִיא אֶת־ יִשְׂרָאֵל׃

Israel *** he-caused-to-commit which Nebat son-of Jeroboam sins-of from

(29) בִּימֵי פֶּקַח מֶלֶךְ־ יִשְׂרָאֵל בָּא תִּגְלַת פִּלְאֶסֶר מֶלֶךְ אַשּׁוּר

Assyria king-of Pileser Tiglath he-came Israel king-of Pekah in-days-of (29)

וַיִּקַּח אֶת־ עִיּוֹן וְאֶת־אָבֵל בֵּית־מַעֲכָה וְאֶת־ יָנוֹחַ וְאֶת־ קֶדֶשׁ וְאֶת־ חָצוֹר

Hazor and Kedesh and Janoah and Maacah Beth Abel and Ijon *** and-he-took

וְאֶת־ הַגִּלְעָד וְאֶת־ הַגָּלִילָה כֹּל אֶרֶץ נַפְתָּלִי וַיַּגְלֵם

and-he-deported-them Naphtali land-of all-of to-the-Galilee and the-Gilead and

אַשּׁוּרָה׃ (30) וַיִּקְשָׁר־ קֶשֶׁר הוֹשֵׁעַ בֶּן־ אֵלָה עַל־

against Elah son-of Hoshea conspiracy then-he-conspired (30) to-Assyria

פֶּקַח בֶּן־ רְמַלְיָהוּ וַיַּכֵּהוּ וַיְמִיתֵהוּ

and-he-assassinated-him and-he-attacked-him Remaliah son-of Pekah

וַיִּמְלֹךְ תַּחְתָּיו בִּשְׁנַת עֶשְׂרִים לְיוֹתָם בֶּן־ עֻזִּיָּה*׃

Uzziah son-of of-Jotham twenty in-year-of in-place-of-him and-he-became-king

(31) וְיֶתֶר דִּבְרֵי־ פֶקַח וְכָל־ אֲשֶׁר עָשָׂה הִנָּם

see-they! he-did that and-all Pekah events-of and-rest-of (31)

כְּתוּבִים עַל־ סֵפֶר דִּבְרֵי הַיָּמִים לְמַלְכֵי יִשְׂרָאֵל׃

Israel of-kings-of the-days annals-of book-of in ones-being-written

(32) בִּשְׁנַת שְׁתַּיִם לְפֶקַח בֶּן־ רְמַלְיָהוּ מֶלֶךְ יִשְׂרָאֵל מָלַךְ

he-became-king Israel king-of Remaliah son-of of-Pekah two in-year-of (32)

יוֹתָם בֶּן־ עֻזִּיָּהוּ* מֶלֶךְ יְהוּדָה׃ (33) בֶּן־ עֶשְׂרִים וְחָמֵשׁ שָׁנָה הָיָה

he-was year and-five twenty son-of (33) Judah king-of Uzziah son-of Jotham

בְמָלְכוֹ וְשֵׁשׁ־ עֶשְׂרֵה שָׁנָה מָלַךְ בִּירוּשָׁלִַם וְשֵׁם

and-name-of in-Jerusalem he-reigned year ten and-six-of when-to-become-king-him

אִמּוֹ יְרוּשָׁא בַּת־ צָדוֹק׃ (34) וַיַּעַשׂ הַיָּשָׁר בְּעֵינֵי

in-eyes-of the-right and-he-did (34) Zadok daughter-of Jerusha mother-of-him

him. Taking fifty men of Gilead with him, he assassinated
Pekahiah, along with Argob
and Arieh, in the citadel of the
royal palace at Samaria. So
Pekah killed Pekahiah and
succeeded him as king.
26 The other events of Pekahiah's reign, and all he did,
are written in the book of the
annals of the kings of Israel.

Pekah King of Israel

27 In the fifty-second year of
Azariah king of Judah, Pekah
son of Remaliah became king
of Israel in Samaria, and he
reigned twenty years. 28 He did
evil in the eyes of the LORD. He
did not turn away from the
sins of Jeroboam son of Nebat,
which he had caused Israel to
commit.
29 In the time of Pekah king
of Israel, Tiglath-Pileser king
of Assyria came and took Ijon,
Abel Beth Maacah, Janoah,
Kedesh and Hazor. He took
Gilead and Galilee—all the
land of Naphtali—and deported the people to Assyria.
30 Then Hoshea son of Elah
conspired against Pekah son
of Remaliah. He attacked and
assassinated him, and then
succeeded him as king in the
twentieth year of Jotham son
of Uzziah.
31 As for the other events of
Pekah's reign, and all he did,
are they not written in the
book of the annals of the kings
of Israel?

Jotham King of Judah

32 In the second year of Pekah
son of Remaliah king of Israel,
Jotham son of Uzziah king of
Judah began to reign. 33 He was
twenty-five years old when he
became king, and he reigned
in Jerusalem sixteen years. His
mother's name was Jerusha
daughter of Zadok. 34 He did
what was right in the eyes of

*30,32 Most mss have *dagesh* in the *zayin* (־זִּ).

יְהוָה כְּכֹל אֲשֶׁר־ עָשָׂה עֻזִּיָּהוּ* אָבִיו עָשָׂה׃ (35) רַק
however (35) he-did father-of-him Uzziah he-did that as-all Yahweh

הַבָּמוֹת לֹא סָרוּ עוֹד הָעָם מְזַבְּחִים
ones-offering-sacrifices the-people still they-removed not the-high-places

וּמְקַטְּרִים בַּבָּמוֹת הוּא בָּנָה אֶת־ שַׁעַר
Gate-of *** he-rebuilt he at-the-high-places and-ones-burning-incense

בֵּית־ יְהוָה הָעֶלְיוֹן׃ (36) וְיֶתֶר דִּבְרֵי יוֹתָם אֲשֶׁר עָשָׂה
he-did what Jotham events-of and-rest-of (36) the-Upper Yahweh temple-of

הֲלֹא־ הֵם כְּתוּבִים עַל־ סֵפֶר דִּבְרֵי הַיָּמִים לְמַלְכֵי יְהוּדָה׃
Judah of-kings-of the-days annals-of book-of in ones-being-written they not?

(37) בַּיָּמִים הָהֵם הֵחֵל יְהוָה לְהַשְׁלִיחַ בִּיהוּדָה רְצִין
Rezin against-Judah to-send Yahweh he-began the-those in-the-days (37)

מֶלֶךְ אֲרָם וְאֵת פֶּקַח בֶּן־ רְמַלְיָהוּ׃ (38) וַיִּשְׁכַּב יוֹתָם עִם־
with Jotham and-he-rested (38) Remaliah son-of Pekah and Aram king-of

אֲבֹתָיו וַיִּקָּבֵר עִם־ אֲבֹתָיו בְּעִיר דָּוִד
David in-City-of fathers-of-him with and-he-was-buried fathers-of-him

אָבִיו וַיִּמְלֹךְ אָחָז בְּנוֹ תַּחְתָּיו׃
in-place-of-him son-of-him Ahaz and-he-became-king father-of-him

(16:1) בִּשְׁנַת שְׁבַע־ עֶשְׂרֵה שָׁנָה לְפֶקַח בֶּן־ רְמַלְיָהוּ מָלַךְ
he-became-king Remaliah son-of of-Pekah year ten seven-of in-year-of (16:1)

אָחָז בֶּן־ יוֹתָם מֶלֶךְ יְהוּדָה׃ (2) בֶּן־ עֶשְׂרִים שָׁנָה אָחָז
Ahaz year twenty son-of (2) Judah king-of Jotham son-of Ahaz

בְּמָלְכוֹ וְשֵׁשׁ־ עֶשְׂרֵה שָׁנָה מָלַךְ בִּירוּשָׁלִָם וְלֹא־
but-not in-Jerusalem he-reigned year ten and-six-of when-to-become-king-him

עָשָׂה הַיָּשָׁר בְּעֵינֵי יְהוָה אֱלֹהָיו כְּדָוִד אָבִיו׃
father-of-him like-David God-of-him Yahweh in-eyes-of the-right he-did

(3) וַיֵּלֶךְ בְּדֶרֶךְ מַלְכֵי יִשְׂרָאֵל וְגַם אֶת־ בְּנוֹ
son-of-him *** and-even Israel kings-of in-way-of and-he-walked (3)

הֶעֱבִיר בָּאֵשׁ כְּתֹעֲבוֹת הַגּוֹיִם אֲשֶׁר
that the-nations as-detestable-ways-of through-the-fire he-made-pass

הוֹרִישׁ יְהוָה אֹתָם מִפְּנֵי בְּנֵי יִשְׂרָאֵל׃ (4) וַיְזַבֵּחַ
and-he-sacrificed (4) Israel sons-of from-before them Yahweh he-drove-out

וַיְקַטֵּר בַּבָּמוֹת וְעַל־ הַגְּבָעוֹת וְתַחַת
and-under the-hilltops and-on at-the-high-places and-he-burned-incense

כָּל־ עֵץ רַעֲנָן׃ (5) אָז יַעֲלֶה רְצִין מֶלֶךְ־ אֲרָם
Aram king-of Rezin he-marched-up then (5) spreading tree-of every-of

וּפֶקַח בֶּן־ רְמַלְיָהוּ מֶלֶךְ־ יִשְׂרָאֵל יְרוּשָׁלִַם לַמִּלְחָמָה
to-the-fight Jerusalem Israel king-of Remaliah son-of and-Pekah

the LORD, just as his father Uzziah had done. [35]The high
places, however, were not
removed; the people con-
tinued to offer sacrifices and
burn incense there. Jotham rebuilt the Upper Gate of the
temple of the LORD.
[36]As for the other events of
Jotham's reign, and what he
did, are they not written in the
book of the annals of the kings
of Judah? [37](In those days the
LORD began to send Rezin
king of Aram and Pekah son of
Remaliah against Judah.) [38]Jo-
tham rested with his fathers
and was buried with them in
the City of David, the city of
his father. And Ahaz his son
succeeded him as king.

Ahaz King of Judah

16 In the seventeenth
year of Pekah son of
Remaliah, Ahaz son of Jotham
king of Judah began to reign.
[2]Ahaz was twenty years old
when he became king, and he
reigned in Jerusalem sixteen
years. Unlike David his father,
he did not do what was right
in the eyes of the LORD his
God. [3]He walked in the ways
of the kings of Israel and even
sacrificed his son in[t] the fire,
following the detestable ways
of the nations the LORD had
driven out before the Israelites. [4]He offered sacrifices and
burned incense at the high
places, on the hilltops and under every spreading tree.
[5]Then Rezin king of Aram
and Pekah son of Remaliah
king of Israel marched up to
fight against Jerusalem and

[t]3 Or *even made his son pass through*

**34* Most mss have *dagesh* in the *zayin* (זּ‑).

וַיָּצֻרוּ עַל־ אָחָז וְלֹא יָכְלוּ לְהִלָּחֵם׃
to-overpower they-could but-not Ahaz against and-they-besieged

בָּעֵת הַהִיא הֵשִׁיב רְצִין מֶלֶךְ־ אֲרָם אֶת־אֵילַת לַאֲרָם
for-Aram Elath *** Aram king-of Rezin he-recovered the-that at-the-time (6)

וַיְנַשֵּׁל אֶת־ הַיְהוּדִים מֵאֵילוֹת וַאֲרֹמִים בָּאוּ
they-moved-into and-Edomites from-Elath the-Judahites *** and-he-drove-out

אֵילַת וַיֵּשְׁבוּ שָׁם עַד הַיּוֹם הַזֶּה׃ וַיִּשְׁלַח אָחָז
Ahaz and-he-sent (7) the-this the-day to there and-they-lived Elath

מַלְאָכִים אֶל־ תְּגְלַת פְּלֶסֶר מֶלֶךְ־ אַשּׁוּר לֵאמֹר עַבְדְּךָ
servant-of-you to-say Assyria king-of Pileser Tiglath to messengers

וּבִנְךָ אָנִי עֲלֵה וְהוֹשִׁעֵנִי מִכַּף מֶלֶךְ־ אֲרָם
Aram king-of from-hand-of and-save-me! come-up! I and-vassal-of-you

וּמִכַּף מֶלֶךְ יִשְׂרָאֵל הַקּוֹמִים עָלָי׃ וַיִּקַּח
and-he-took (8) against-me the-ones-attacking Israel king-of and-from-hand-of

אָחָז אֶת־ הַכֶּסֶף וְאֶת־ הַזָּהָב הַנִּמְצָא בֵּית יְהוָה
Yahweh temple-of the-one-being-found the-gold and the-silver *** Ahaz

וּבְאֹצְרוֹת בֵּית הַמֶּלֶךְ וַיִּשְׁלַח לְמֶלֶךְ־ אַשּׁוּר שֹׁחַד׃
gift Assyria to-king-of and-he-sent the-king palace-of and-in-treasuries-of

וַיִּשְׁמַע אֵלָיו מֶלֶךְ אַשּׁוּר וַיַּעַל מֶלֶךְ אַשּׁוּר
Assyria king-of and-he-attacked Assyria king-of to-him and-he-listened (9)

אֶל־ דַּמֶּשֶׂק וַיִּתְפְּשֶׂהָ וַיַּגְלֶהָ קִירָה וְאֶת־ רְצִין
Rezin and to-Kir and-he-deported-her and-he-captured-her Damascus against

הֵמִית׃ וַיֵּלֶךְ הַמֶּלֶךְ אָחָז לִקְרַאת תִּגְלַת פִּלְאֶסֶר מֶלֶךְ־
king-of Pileser Tiglath to-meet Ahaz the-king then-he-went (10) he-killed

אַשּׁוּר דּוּמֶּשֶׂק וַיַּרְא אֶת־ הַמִּזְבֵּחַ אֲשֶׁר בְּדַמָּשֶׂק וַיִּשְׁלַח
and-he-sent in-Damascus that the-altar *** and-he-saw Damascus Assyria

הַמֶּלֶךְ אָחָז אֶל־ אוּרִיָּה הַכֹּהֵן אֶת־ דְּמוּת הַמִּזְבֵּחַ וְאֶת־ תַּבְנִיתוֹ
plan-of-him and the-altar sketch-of *** the-priest Uriah to Ahaz the-king

לְכָל־ מַעֲשֵׂהוּ׃ וַיִּבֶן אוּרִיָּה הַכֹּהֵן אֶת־
*** the-priest Uriah so-he-built (11) construction-of-him for-all-of

הַמִּזְבֵּחַ כְּכֹל אֲשֶׁר־ שָׁלַח הַמֶּלֶךְ אָחָז מִדַּמֶּשֶׂק כֵּן עָשָׂה
he-finished so from-Damascus Ahaz the-king he-sent that as-all the-altar

אוּרִיָּה הַכֹּהֵן עַד־ בּוֹא הַמֶּלֶךְ־ אָחָז מִדַּמָּשֶׂק׃ וַיָּבֹא
when-he-came (12) from-Damascus Ahaz the-king to-return before the-priest Uriah

הַמֶּלֶךְ מִדַּמֶּשֶׂק וַיַּרְא הַמֶּלֶךְ אֶת־ הַמִּזְבֵּחַ וַיִּקְרַב
then-he-approached the-altar *** the-king and-he-saw from-Damascus the-king

הַמֶּלֶךְ עַל־ הַמִּזְבֵּחַ וַיַּעַל עָלָיו׃ וַיַּקְטֵר
and-he-offered (13) on-him and-he-presented-offering the-altar to the-king

besieged Ahaz, but they could
not overpower him. [6]At that
time, Rezin king of Aram
recovered Elath for Aram by
driving out the men of Judah.
Edomites then moved into
Elath and have lived there to
this day.
[7]Ahaz sent messengers to
say to Tiglath-Pileser king of
Assyria, "I am your servant
and vassal. Come up and save
me out of the hand of the king
of Aram and of the king of Israel, who are attacking me."
[8]And Ahaz took the silver and
gold found in the temple of the
LORD and in the treasuries of
the royal palace and sent it as
a gift to the king of Assyria.
[9]The king of Assyria complied
by attacking Damascus and
capturing it. He deported its
inhabitants to Kir and put Rezin to death.
[10]Then King Ahaz went to
Damascus to meet Tiglath-
Pileser king of Assyria. He saw
an altar in Damascus and sent
to Uriah the priest a sketch of
the altar, with detailed plans
for its construction. [11]So Uriah
the priest built an altar in accordance with all the plans
that King Ahaz had sent from
Damascus and finished it before King Ahaz returned.
[12]When the king came back
from Damascus and saw the
altar, he approached it and
presented offerings[a] on it. [13]He

[a]12 Or *and went up*

°6 ק ואדמים

אֶת־ עֹלָתוֹ וְאֶת־ מִנְחָתוֹ וַיַּסֵּךְ אֶת־
*** and-he-poured-out grain-offering-of-him and burnt-offering-of-him ***

נִסְכּוֹ וַיִּזְרֹק אֶת־ דַּם־ הַשְּׁלָמִים
the-fellowship-offerings blood-of *** and-he-sprinkled drink-offering-of-him

אֲשֶׁר־ לוֹ עַל־ הַמִּזְבֵּחַ׃ (14) וְאֵת הַמִּזְבַּח הַנְּחֹשֶׁת אֲשֶׁר לִפְנֵי יְהוָה
Yahweh before that the-bronze the-altar and (14) the-altar on to-him that

וַיַּקְרֵב מֵאֵת פְּנֵי הַבַּיִת מִבֵּין הַמִּזְבֵּחַ
the-altar from-between the-temple front-of from now-he-brought

וּמִבֵּין בֵּית יְהוָה וַיִּתֵּן אֹתוֹ עַל־ יֶרֶךְ הַמִּזְבֵּחַ
the-altar side-of on him and-he-put Yahweh temple-of and-from-between

צָפוֹנָה׃ (15) וַיְצַוֵּהוּ° הַמֶּלֶךְ־ אָחָז אֶת־אוּרִיָּה הַכֹּהֵן לֵאמֹר עַל
on to-say the-priest Uriah *** Ahaz the-king then-he-ordered (15) to-north

הַמִּזְבֵּחַ הַגָּדוֹל הַקְטֵר אֶת־ עֹלַת־ הַבֹּקֶר וְאֶת־
and the-morning burnt-offering-of *** offer! the-large the-altar

מִנְחַת הָעֶרֶב וְאֶת־ עֹלַת הַמֶּלֶךְ וְאֶת־
and the-king burnt-offering-of and the-evening grain-offering-of

מִנְחָתוֹ וְאֵת עֹלַת כָּל־ עַם הָאָרֶץ
the-land people-of all-of burnt-offering-of and grain-offering-of-him

וּמִנְחָתָם וְנִסְכֵּיהֶם וְכָל־ דַּם
blood-of and-all-of and-drink-offerings-of-them and-grain-offering-of-them

עֹלָה וְכָל־ דַּם־ זֶבַח עָלָיו תִּזְרֹק וּמִזְבַּח
but-altar-of you-sprinkle on-him sacrifice blood-of and-all-of burnt-offering

הַנְּחֹשֶׁת יִהְיֶה־ לִּי לְבַקֵּר׃ (16) וַיַּעַשׂ אוּרִיָּה
Uriah and-he-did (16) to-seek-guidance for-me he-will-be the-bronze

הַכֹּהֵן כְּכֹל אֲשֶׁר־ צִוָּה הַמֶּלֶךְ אָחָז׃ (17) וַיְקַצֵּץ
and-he-took-away (17) Ahaz the-king he-ordered that as-all the-priest

הַמֶּלֶךְ אָחָז אֶת־ הַמִּסְגְּרוֹת הַמְּכֹנוֹת וַיָּסַר
and-he-removed the-movable-stands the-side-panels *** Ahaz the-king

מֵעֲלֵיהֶם וְאֶת°־ הַכִּיֹּר וְאֶת־ הַיָּם הוֹרִד מֵעַל הַבָּקָר הַנְּחֹשֶׁת
the-bronze the-bull from-on he-removed the-Sea and the-basin *** from-on-them

אֲשֶׁר תַּחְתֶּיהָ וַיִּתֵּן אֹתוֹ עַל מַרְצֶפֶת אֲבָנִים׃ (18) וְאֶת־ מֵיסַךְ°
canopy-of and (18) stones base-of on him and-he-set under-her that

הַשַּׁבָּת אֲשֶׁר־ בָּנוּ בַבַּיִת וְאֶת־ מְבוֹא הַמֶּלֶךְ
the-king entryway-of and at-the-temple they-built that the-Sabbath

הַחִיצוֹנָה הֵסֵב בֵּית יְהוָה מִפְּנֵי מֶלֶךְ אַשּׁוּר׃
Assyria king-of because-of Yahweh temple-of he-removed at-the-outside

(19) וְיֶתֶר דִּבְרֵי אָחָז אֲשֶׁר עָשָׂה הֲלֹא־ הֵם כְּתוּבִים עַל־
in ones-being-written they not? he-did what Ahaz events-of and-rest-of (19)

offered up his burnt offering
and grain offering, poured out
his drink offering, and sprinkled the blood of his fellowship offerings[v] on the altar.
14The bronze altar that stood
before the LORD he brought
from the front of the temple—
from between the new altar
and the temple of the LORD—
and put it on the north side of
the new altar.
15King Ahaz then gave these
orders to Uriah the priest: "On
the large new altar, offer the
morning burnt offering and
the evening grain offering, the
king's burnt offering and his
grain offering, and the burnt
offering of all the people of the
land, and their grain offering
and their drink offering.
Sprinkle on the altar all the
blood of the burnt offerings
and sacrifices. But I will use
the bronze altar for seeking
guidance." 16And Uriah the
priest did just as King Ahaz
had ordered.
17King Ahaz took away the
side panels and removed the
basins from the movable
stands. He removed the Sea
from the bronze bulls that supported it and set it on a stone
base. 18He took away the Sabbath canopy[w] that had been
built at the temple and
removed the royal entryway
outside the temple of the LORD,
in deference to the king of Assyria.
19As for the other events of
the reign of Ahaz, and what
he did, are they not written in

v13 Traditionally *peace offerings*
w18 Or *the dais of his throne* (see Septuagint)

°15 ק ויצוה
°17 ק את
°18 ק מוסך

סֵפֶר דִּבְרֵי הַיָּמִים לְמַלְכֵי יְהוּדָה׃ וַיִּשְׁכַּב אָחָז עִם־
with Ahaz and-he-rested (20) Judah of-kings-of the-days annals-of book-of

אֲבֹתָיו וַיִּקָּבֵר עִם־ אֲבֹתָיו בְּעִיר דָּוִד
David in-City-of fathers-of-him with and-he-was-buried fathers-of-him

וַיִּמְלֹךְ חִזְקִיָּהוּ בְנוֹ תַּחְתָּיו׃ בִּשְׁנַת
in-year-of (17:1) in-place-of-him son-of-him Hezekiah and-he-became-king

שְׁתֵּים עֶשְׂרֵה לְאָחָז מֶלֶךְ יְהוּדָה מָלַךְ הוֹשֵׁעַ בֶּן־ אֵלָה בְשֹׁמְרוֹן
in-Samaria Elah son-of Hoshea he-became-king Judah king-of of-Ahaz ten two

עַל־יִשְׂרָאֵל תֵּשַׁע שָׁנִים׃ וַיַּעַשׂ הָרַע בְּעֵינֵי יְהוָה רַק לֹא
not but Yahweh in-eyes-of the-evil and-he-did (2) years nine Israel over

כְּמַלְכֵי יִשְׂרָאֵל אֲשֶׁר הָיוּ לְפָנָיו׃ עָלָיו עָלָה
he-came-up against-him (3) before-him they-were who Israel like-kings-of

שַׁלְמַנְאֶסֶר מֶלֶךְ אַשּׁוּר וַיְהִי־ לוֹ הוֹשֵׁעַ עֶבֶד וַיָּשֶׁב
and-he-paid vassal Hoshea to-him now-he-was Assyria king-of Shalmaneser

לוֹ מִנְחָה׃ וַיִּמְצָא מֶלֶךְ־ אַשּׁוּר בְּהוֹשֵׁעַ קֶשֶׁר
traitor about-Hoshea Assyria king-of but-he-discovered (4) tribute to-him

אֲשֶׁר שָׁלַח מַלְאָכִים אֶל־סוֹא מֶלֶךְ־מִצְרַיִם וְלֹא־ הֶעֱלָה מִנְחָה לְמֶלֶךְ
to-king-of tribute he-paid and-not Egypt king-of So to envoys he-sent for

אַשּׁוּר כְּשָׁנָה בְשָׁנָה וַיַּעַצְרֵהוּ מֶלֶךְ אַשּׁוּר וַיַּאַסְרֵהוּ
and-he-imprisoned-him Assyria king-of so-he-seized-him by-year as-year Assyria

בֵּית כֶּלֶא׃ וַיַּעַל מֶלֶךְ־ אַשּׁוּר בְּכָל־ הָאָרֶץ
the-land through-entire-of Assyria king-of and-he-invaded (5) prison house-of

וַיַּעַל שֹׁמְרוֹן וַיָּצַר עָלֶיהָ שָׁלֹשׁ שָׁנִים׃ בִּשְׁנַת
in-year-of (6) years three to-her and-he-laid-siege Samaria and-he-marched

הַתְּשִׁיעִית לְהוֹשֵׁעַ לָכַד מֶלֶךְ־ אַשּׁוּר אֶת־ שֹׁמְרוֹן וַיֶּגֶל
and-he-deported Samaria *** Assyria king-of he-captured of-Hoshea the-ninth

אֶת־ יִשְׂרָאֵל אַשּׁוּרָה וַיֹּשֶׁב אֹתָם בַּחְלַח וּבְחָבוֹר נְהַר
River-of and-on-Habor in-Halah them and-he-settled to-Assyria Israel ***

גּוֹזָן וְעָרֵי מָדָי׃ וַיְהִי כִּי־ חָטְאוּ בְנֵי־
sons-of they-sinned because and-he-took-place (7) Medes and-towns-of Gozan

יִשְׂרָאֵל לַיהוָה אֱלֹהֵיהֶם הַמַּעֲלֶה אֹתָם מֵאֶרֶץ מִצְרַיִם
Egypt from-land-of them the-one-bringing-up God-of-them against-Yahweh Israel

מִתַּחַת יַד פַּרְעֹה מֶלֶךְ־ מִצְרַיִם וַיִּירְאוּ אֱלֹהִים אֲחֵרִים׃
other-ones gods and-they-worshiped Egypt king-of Pharaoh power-of from-under

וַיֵּלְכוּ בְּחֻקּוֹת הַגּוֹיִם אֲשֶׁר הוֹרִישׁ יְהוָה
Yahweh he-drove-out that the-nations after-practices-of and-they-followed (8)

מִפְּנֵי בְּנֵי יִשְׂרָאֵל וּמַלְכֵי יִשְׂרָאֵל אֲשֶׁר עָשׂוּ׃
they-introduced which Israel and-kings-of Israel sons-of from-before

the book of the annals of the
kings of Judah? 20 Ahaz rested
with his fathers and was buried with them in the City of
David. And Hezekiah his son
succeeded him as king.

Hoshea Last King of Israel

17 In the twelfth year of
Ahaz king of Judah,
Hoshea son of Elah became
king of Israel in Samaria, and
he reigned nine years. 2 He did
evil in the eyes of the LORD,
but not like the kings of Israel
who preceded him.

3 Shalmaneser king of As-
syria came up to attack Hoshea, who had been Shal-
maneser's vassal and had paid
him tribute. 4 But the king of
Assyria discovered that Hoshea was a traitor, for he had
sent envoys to So[x] king of
Egypt, and he no longer paid
tribute to the king of Assyria,
as he had done year by year.
Therefore Shalmaneser seized
him and put him in prison.
5 The king of Assyria invaded
the entire land, marched
against Samaria and laid siege
to it for three years. 6 In the
ninth year of Hoshea, the king
of Assyria captured Samaria
and deported the Israelites to
Assyria. He settled them in
Halah, in Gozan on the Habor
River and in the towns of the
Medes.

Israel Exiled Because of Sin

7 All this took place because
the Israelites had sinned
against the LORD their God,
who had brought them up out
of Egypt from under the
power of Pharaoh king of
Egypt. They worshiped other
gods 8 and followed the practices of the nations the LORD
had driven out before them, as
well as the practices which the
kings of Israel had introduced.

x4 Or *to Sais, to the; So* is possibly an abbreviation for *Osorkon.*

וַיְחַפְּאוּ בְנֵֽי־יִשְׂרָאֵל דְּבָרִים אֲשֶׁר לֹא־כֵן עַל־יְהוָה
Yahweh against right not that things Israel sons-of and-they-did-secretly (9)

אֱלֹהֵיהֶם וַיִּבְנוּ לָהֶם בָּמוֹת בְּכָל־עָרֵיהֶם
towns-of-them in-all-of high-places for-them and-they-built God-of-them

מִמִּגְדַּל נוֹצְרִים עַד־עִיר מִבְצָר׃ וַיַּצִּבוּ
and-they-set-up (10) fortified city-of to ones-watching from-tower-of

לָהֶם מַצֵּבוֹת וַאֲשֵׁרִים עַל כָּל־גִּבְעָה גְבֹהָה וְתַחַת
and-under high hill every-of on and-Asherah-poles sacred-stones for-them

כָּל־עֵץ רַעֲנָן׃ וַיְקַטְּרוּ־שָׁם בְּכָל־
at-all-of there and-they-burned-incense (11) spreading tree-of every-of

בָּמוֹת כַּגּוֹיִם אֲשֶׁר־הֶגְלָה יְהוָה מִפְּנֵיהֶם
from-before-them Yahweh he-drove-out whom as-the-nations high-places

וַֽיַּעֲשׂוּ דְּבָרִים רָעִים לְהַכְעִיס אֶת־יְהוָה׃
Yahweh *** to-provoke-to-anger wicked-ones things and-they-did

וַיַּֽעַבְדוּ הַגִּלֻּלִים אֲשֶׁר אָמַר יְהוָה לָהֶם לֹא תַעֲשׂוּ
you-shall-do not to-them Yahweh he-said that the-idols and-they-worshiped (12)

אֶת־הַדָּבָר הַזֶּה׃ וַיָּעַד יְהוָה בְּיִשְׂרָאֵל וּבִֽיהוּדָה
and-to-Judah to-Israel Yahweh and-he-warned (13) the-this the-thing ***

בְּיַד כָּל־נְבִיאֵו כָּל־חֹזֶה לֵאמֹר שֻׁבוּ מִדַּרְכֵיכֶם
from-ways-of-you turn! to-say seer all-of prophets-of all-of by-hand-of

הָֽרָעִים וְשִׁמְרוּ מִצְוֺתַי חֻקּוֹתַי כְּכָל־הַתּוֹרָה
the-Law as-entire-of decrees-of-me commands-of-me and-observe! the-evil-ones

אֲשֶׁר צִוִּיתִי אֶת־אֲבֹתֵיכֶם וַֽאֲשֶׁר שָׁלַחְתִּי אֲלֵיכֶם בְּיַד
by-hand-of to-you I-delivered and-that fathers-of-you *** I-commanded that

עֲבָדַי הַנְּבִיאִים׃ וְלֹא שָׁמֵעוּ וַיַּקְשׁוּ
and-they-made-stiff they-listened but-not (14) the-prophets servants-of-me

אֶת־עָרְפָּם כְּעֹרֶף אֲבוֹתָם אֲשֶׁר לֹא הֶֽאֱמִינוּ בַּיהוָה
in-Yahweh they-trusted not who fathers-of-them as-neck-of neck-of-them ***

אֱלֹהֵיהֶם׃ וַיִּמְאֲסוּ אֶת־חֻקָּיו וְאֶת־בְּרִיתוֹ
covenant-of-him and decrees-of-him *** and-they-rejected (15) God-of-them

אֲשֶׁר כָּרַת אֶת־אֲבוֹתָם וְאֵת עֵֽדְוֺתָיו אֲשֶׁר הֵעִיד בָּם
to-them he-warned that warnings-of-him and fathers-of-them with he-made that

וַיֵּלְכוּ אַחֲרֵי הַהֶבֶל וַיֶּהְבָּלוּ
and-they-became-worthless the-worthless-thing after and-they-followed

וְאַחֲרֵי הַגּוֹיִם אֲשֶׁר סְבִיבֹתָם אֲשֶׁר צִוָּה יְהוָה אֹתָם לְבִלְתִּי
not them Yahweh he-ordered whom ones-around-them who the-nations and-after

עֲשׂוֹת כָּהֶם׃ וַיַּעַזְבוּ אֶת־כָּל־מִצְוֺת יְהוָה אֱלֹהֵיהֶם
God-of-them Yahweh commands-of all-of *** and-they-forsook (16) as-they to-do

9The Israelites secretly did
things against the LORD their
God that were not right. From
watchtower to fortified city
they built themselves high
places in all their towns.
10They set up sacred stones
and Asherah poles on every
high hill and under every
spreading tree. 11At every high
place they burned incense, as
the nations whom the LORD
had driven out before them
had done. They did wicked
things that provoked the LORD
to anger. 12They worshiped
idols, though the LORD had
said, "You shall not do this."[y]
13The LORD warned Israel and
Judah through all his prophets
and seers: "Turn from your
evil ways. Observe my commands and decrees, in accordance with the entire Law that
I commanded your fathers to
obey and that I delivered to
you through my servants the
prophets."
14But they would not listen
and were as stiff-necked as
their fathers, who did not trust
in the LORD their God. 15They
rejected his decrees and the
covenant he had made with
their fathers and the warnings
he had given them. They followed worthless idols and
themselves became worthless.
They imitated the nations
around them although the
LORD had ordered them, "Do
not do as they do," and they
did the things the LORD had
forbidden them to do.
16They forsook all the commands of the LORD their God

y12 Exodus 20:4, 5

°13 ק נביאי

וַיַּעֲשׂוּ לָהֶם מַסֵּכָה שְׁנַיִם° עֲגָלִים וַיַּעֲשׂוּ אֲשֵׁירָה
Asherah-pole and-they-made calves two-of cast-idol for-them and-they-made

וַיִּשְׁתַּחֲווּ לְכָל־ צְבָא הַשָּׁמַיִם וַיַּעַבְדוּ אֶת־
*** and-they-worshiped the-heavens host-of to-all-of and-they-bowed-down

הַבָּעַל׃ וַיַּעֲבִירוּ אֶת־ בְּנֵיהֶם וְאֶת־ בְּנוֹתֵיהֶם
daughters-of-them and sons-of-them *** and-they-made-pass (17) the-Baal

בָּאֵשׁ וַיִּקְסְמוּ קְסָמִים וַיְנַחֵשׁוּ
and-they-practiced-sorcery divinations and-they-practiced through-the-fire

וַיִּתְמַכְּרוּ לַעֲשׂוֹת הָרַע בְּעֵינֵי יְהוָה לְהַכְעִיסוֹ׃
to-make-angry-him Yahweh in-eyes-of the-evil to-do and-they-sold-themselves

וַיִּתְאַנַּף יְהוָה מְאֹד בְּיִשְׂרָאֵל וַיְסִרֵם מֵעַל
from-before and-he-removed-them with-Israel very Yahweh so-he-was-angry (18)

פָּנָיו לֹא נִשְׁאַר רַק שֵׁבֶט יְהוּדָה לְבַדּוֹ׃ גַּם־ יְהוּדָה
Judah even (19) by-himself Judah tribe-of only he-was-left not faces-of-him

לֹא שָׁמַר אֶת־ מִצְוֺת יְהוָה אֱלֹהֵיהֶם וַיֵּלְכוּ
and-they-followed God-of-them Yahweh commands-of *** he-kept not

בְּחֻקּוֹת יִשְׂרָאֵל אֲשֶׁר עָשׂוּ׃ וַיִּמְאַס יְהוָה
Yahweh so-he-rejected (20) they-introduced that Israel after-practices-of

בְּכָל־ זֶרַע יִשְׂרָאֵל וַיְעַנֵּם וַיִּתְּנֵם בְּיַד־
into-hand-of and-he-gave-them and-he-afflicted-them Israel people-of to-all-of

שֹׁסִים עַד אֲשֶׁר הִשְׁלִיכָם מִפָּנָיו׃ כִּי־
when (21) from-presences-of-him he-thrust-them when until ones-plundering

קָרַע יִשְׂרָאֵל מֵעַל בֵּית דָּוִד וַיַּמְלִיכוּ אֶת־ יָרָבְעָם
Jeroboam *** then-they-made-king David house-of from-with Israel he-tore

בֶּן־ נְבָט וַיַּדֵּא° יָרָבְעָם אֶת־ יִשְׂרָאֵל מֵאַחֲרֵי יְהוָה
Yahweh from-after Israel *** Jeroboam and-he-enticed Nebat son-of

וְהֶחֱטֵיאָם* חֲטָאָה גְדוֹלָה׃ וַיֵּלְכוּ בְּנֵי יִשְׂרָאֵל
Israel sons-of and-they-persisted (22) great sin and-he-caused-to-sin-them

בְּכָל־ חַטֹּאות יָרָבְעָם אֲשֶׁר עָשָׂה לֹא־ סָרוּ מִמֶּנָּה׃
from-her they-turned-away not he-did that Jeroboam sins-of in-all-of

עַד אֲשֶׁר־ הֵסִיר יְהוָה אֶת־ יִשְׂרָאֵל מֵעַל פָּנָיו
presences-of-him from-before Israel *** Yahweh he-removed when until (23)

כַּאֲשֶׁר דִּבֶּר בְּיַד כָּל־ עֲבָדָיו הַנְּבִיאִים
the-prophets servants-of-him all-of by-hand-of he-warned just-as

וַיִּגֶל יִשְׂרָאֵל מֵעַל אַדְמָתוֹ אַשּׁוּרָה עַד הַיּוֹם
the-day to to-Assyria homeland-of-him from-on Israel so-he-went-into-exile

הַזֶּה׃ וַיָּבֵא מֶלֶךְ־ אַשּׁוּר מִבָּבֶל וּמִכּוּתָה
and-from-Cuthah from-Babylon Assyria king-of and-he-brought (24) the-this

and made for themselves two
idols cast in the shape of
calves, and an Asherah pole.
They bowed down to all the
starry hosts, and they worshiped Baal. 17They sacrificed
their sons and daughters in[z]
the fire. They practiced divination and sorcery and sold
themselves to do evil in the
eyes of the LORD, provoking
him to anger.
18So the LORD was very angry
with Israel and removed them
from his presence. Only the
tribe of Judah was left, 19and
even Judah did not keep the
commands of the LORD their
God. They followed the practices Israel had introduced.
20Therefore the LORD rejected
all the people of Israel; he
afflicted them and gave them
into the hands of plunderers,
until he thrust them from his
presence.
21When he tore Israel away
from the house of David, they
made Jeroboam son of Nebat
their king. Jeroboam enticed
Israel away from following the
LORD and caused them to commit a great sin. 22The Israelites
persisted in all the sins of Jeroboam and did not turn away
from them 23until the LORD
removed them from his presence, as he had warned
through all his servants the
prophets. So the people of Israel were taken from their
homeland into exile in Assyria, and they are still there.

Samaria Resettled

24The king of Assyria
brought people from Babylon,

z17 Or *They made their sons and daughters pass through*

*21 Most mss have *bireq* under the *teth* (טִ־).

°16 ק שני

°21 ק וידח

וּמֵעַוָּא וּמֵחֲמָת וּסְפַרְוָיִם וַיֹּשֶׁב בְּעָרֵי
in-towns-of and-he-settled and-Sepharvaim and-from-Hamath and-from-Avva

שֹׁמְרוֹן תַּחַת בְּנֵי יִשְׂרָאֵל וַיִּרְשׁוּ אֶת־ שֹׁמְרוֹן
Samaria *** and-they-took-over Israel sons-of in-place-of Samaria

וַיֵּשְׁבוּ בְּעָרֶיהָ׃ וַיְהִי בִּתְחִלַּת שִׁבְתָּם
to-live-them when-to-begin and-he-was (25) in-towns-of-her and-they-lived

שָׁם לֹא יָרְאוּ אֶת־ יְהוָה וַיְשַׁלַּח יְהוָה בָּהֶם אֶת־ הָאֲרָיוֹת
the-lions *** among-them Yahweh so-he-sent Yahweh *** they-worshiped not there

וַיִּהְיוּ הֹרְגִים בָּהֶם׃ וַיֹּאמְרוּ לְמֶלֶךְ אַשּׁוּר
Assyria to-king-of and-they-reported (26) of-them ones-killing and-they-were

לֵאמֹר הַגּוֹיִם אֲשֶׁר הִגְלִיתָ וַתּוֹשֶׁב בְּעָרֵי שֹׁמְרוֹן
Samaria in-towns-of and-you-resettled you-deported whom the-peoples to-say

לֹא יָדְעוּ אֶת־ מִשְׁפַּט אֱלֹהֵי הָאָרֶץ וַיְשַׁלַּח־ בָּם
among-them and-he-sent the-country gods-of requirement-of *** they-know not

אֶת־ הָאֲרָיוֹת וְהִנָּם מְמִיתִים אוֹתָם כַּאֲשֶׁר אֵינָם יֹדְעִים
ones-knowing not-they because them ones-killing and-see-they! the-lions ***

אֶת־ מִשְׁפַּט אֱלֹהֵי הָאָרֶץ׃ וַיְצַו מֶלֶךְ־ אַשּׁוּר
Assyria king-of then-he-ordered (27) the-country gods-of requirement-of ***

לֵאמֹר הֹלִיכוּ שָׁמָּה אֶחָד מֵהַכֹּהֲנִים אֲשֶׁר הִגְלִיתֶם
you-took-captive whom of-the-priests one to-there send-back! to-say

מִשָּׁם וְיֵלְכוּ וְיֵשְׁבוּ שָׁם וְיֹרֵם
and-let-him-teach-them there and-let-them-live and-let-them-go-back from-there

אֶת־ מִשְׁפַּט אֱלֹהֵי הָאָרֶץ׃ וַיָּבֹא אֶחָד מֵהַכֹּהֲנִים אֲשֶׁר
who of-the-priests one so-he-came (28) the-land gods-of requirement-of ***

הִגְלוּ מִשֹּׁמְרוֹן וַיֵּשֶׁב בְּבֵית־ אֵל וַיְהִי מוֹרֶה אֹתָם
them teaching and-he-was El in-Beth and-he-lived from-Samaria they-exiled

אֵיךְ יִירְאוּ אֶת־ יְהוָה׃ וַיִּהְיוּ עֹשִׂים גּוֹי
nation ones-making but-they-were (29) Yahweh *** they-should-worship how

גּוֹי אֱלֹהָיו וַיַּנִּיחוּ׀ בְּבֵית הַבָּמוֹת אֲשֶׁר עָשׂוּ
they-made that the-high-places in-shrine-of and-they-set-up gods-of-him nation

הַשֹּׁמְרֹנִים גּוֹי גּוֹי בְּעָרֵיהֶם אֲשֶׁר הֵם יֹשְׁבִים שָׁם׃
there ones-settling they where in-towns-of-them nation nation the-Samaritans

וְאַנְשֵׁי בָבֶל עָשׂוּ אֶת־ סֻכּוֹת בְּנוֹת וְאַנְשֵׁי־ כוּת
Cuthah and-men-of Benoth Succoth *** they-made Babylon and-men-of (30)

עָשׂוּ אֶת־ נֵרְגַל וְאַנְשֵׁי חֲמָת עָשׂוּ אֶת־ אֲשִׁימָא׃
Ashima *** they-made Hamath and-men-of Nergal *** they-made

וְהָעַוִּים עָשׂוּ נִבְחַז וְאֶת־ תַּרְתָּק וְהַסְפַרְוִים
and-the-Sepharvites Tartak and Nibhaz they-made and-the-Avvites (31)

Cuthah, Avva, Hamath and
Sepharvaim and settled them
in the towns of Samaria to replace the Israelites. They took
over Samaria and lived in its
towns. 25When they first lived
there, they did not worship
the LORD; so he sent lions
among them and they killed
some of the people. 26It was reported to the king of Assyria:
"The people you deported and
resettled in the towns of Samaria do not know what the
god of that country requires.
He has sent lions among
them, which are killing them
off, because the people do not
know what he requires."
27Then the king of Assyria
gave this order: "Have one of
the priests you took captive
from Samaria go back to live
there and teach the people
what the god of the land requires." 28So one of the priests
who had been exiled from Samaria came to live in Bethel
and taught them how to worship the LORD.
29Nevertheless, each na-
tional group made its own
gods in the several towns
where they settled, and set
them up in the shrines the
people of Samaria had made at
the high places. 30The men
from Babylon made Succoth
Benoth, the men from Cuthah
made Nergal, and the men
from Hamath made Ashima;
31the Avvites made Nibhaz

שֹׂרְפִים אֶת־ בְּנֵיהֶם בָּאֵשׁ לְאַדְרַמֶּלֶךְ וַעֲנַמֶּלֶךְ
and-Anammelech to-Adrammelech in-the-fire children-of-them *** ones-burning

אֱלֹהֵ° סְפַרְוָיִם°׃ וַיִּהְיוּ יְרֵאִים אֶת־ יְהוָה
Yahweh *** ones-worshiping and-they-were (32) Sepharvaim gods-of

וַיַּעֲשׂוּ לָהֶם מִקְצוֹתָם כֹּהֲנֵי בָמוֹת
high-places priests-of from-ends-of-them for-them but-they-appointed

וַיִּהְיוּ עֹשִׂים לָהֶם בְּבֵית הַבָּמוֹת׃
the-high-places in-shrine-of for-them ones-officiating and-they-were

אֶת־ יְהוָה הָיוּ יְרֵאִים וְאֶת־ אֱלֹהֵיהֶם הָיוּ
they-were gods-of-them but ones-worshiping they-were Yahweh *** (33)

עֹבְדִים כְּמִשְׁפַּט הַגּוֹיִם אֲשֶׁר־ הִגְלוּ אֹתָם מִשָּׁם׃
from-there them they-brought which the-nations as-custom-of ones-serving

עַד הַיּוֹם הַזֶּה הֵם עֹשִׂים כַּמִּשְׁפָּטִים הָרִאשֹׁנִים
the-former-ones in-the-practices ones-persisting they the-this the-day to (34)

אֵינָם יְרֵאִים אֶת־ יְהוָה וְאֵינָם עֹשִׂים
ones-adhering and-not-they Yahweh *** ones-worshiping not-they

כְּחֻקֹּתָם וּכְמִשְׁפָּטָם וְכַתּוֹרָה וְכַמִּצְוָה
or-to-the-command or-to-the-law or-to-ordinance-of-them to-decrees-of-them

אֲשֶׁר צִוָּה יְהוָה אֶת־ בְּנֵי יַעֲקֹב אֲשֶׁר־ שָׂם שְׁמוֹ יִשְׂרָאֵל׃
Israel name-of-him he-gave whom Jacob sons-of *** Yahweh he-gave that

וַיִּכְרֹת יְהוָה אִתָּם בְּרִית וַיְצַוֵּם לֵאמֹר
to-say then-he-commanded-them covenant with-them Yahweh when-he-made (35)

לֹא תִירְאוּ אֱלֹהִים אֲחֵרִים וְלֹא־ תִשְׁתַּחֲווּ לָהֶם וְלֹא
and-not to-them you-bow-down and-not other-ones gods you-worship not

תַעַבְדוּם וְלֹא תִזְבְּחוּ לָהֶם׃ כִּי אִם־ אֶת־ יְהוָה אֲשֶׁר
who Yahweh *** only but (36) to-them you-sacrifice and-not you-serve-them

הֶעֱלָה אֶתְכֶם מֵאֶרֶץ מִצְרַיִם בְּכֹחַ גָּדוֹל וּבִזְרוֹעַ
and-with-arm mighty with-power Egypt from-land-of you he-brought-up

נְטוּיָה אֹתוֹ תִירָאוּ וְלוֹ תִשְׁתַּחֲווּ וְלוֹ
and-to-him you-shall-bow and-to-him you-must-worship him being-outstretched

תִזְבָּחוּ׃ וְאֶת־ הַחֻקִּים וְאֶת־ הַמִּשְׁפָּטִים וְהַתּוֹרָה
and-the-law the-ordinances and the-decrees and (37) you-shall-sacrifice

וְהַמִּצְוָה אֲשֶׁר כָּתַב לָכֶם תִּשְׁמְרוּן לַעֲשׂוֹת כָּל־
all-of to-keep you-must-be-careful for-you he-wrote that and-the-command

הַיָּמִים וְלֹא תִירְאוּ אֱלֹהִים אֲחֵרִים׃ וְהַבְּרִית אֲשֶׁר־
that and-the-covenant (38) other-ones gods you-worship and-not the-days

כָּרַתִּי אִתְּכֶם לֹא תִשְׁכָּחוּ וְלֹא תִירְאוּ אֱלֹהִים אֲחֵרִים׃
other-ones gods you-worship and-not you-forget not with-you I-made

°31a ק אלהי
°31b ק ספרוים

and Tartak, and the Sepharvites burned their children in the fire as sacrifices to Adrammelech and Anammelech, the gods of Sepharvaim. [32]They worshiped the LORD, but they also appointed all sorts of their own people to officiate for them as priests in the shrines at the high places. [33]They worshiped the LORD, but they also served their own gods in accordance with the customs of the nations from which they had been brought.

[34]To this day they persist in their former practices. They neither worship the LORD nor adhere to the decrees and ordinances, the laws and commands that the LORD gave the descendants of Jacob, whom he named Israel. [35]When the LORD made a covenant with the Israelites, he commanded them: "Do not worship any other gods or bow down to them, serve them or sacrifice to them. [36]But the LORD, who brought you up out of Egypt with mighty power and outstretched arm, is the one you must worship. To him you shall bow down and to him offer sacrifices. [37]You must always be careful to keep the decrees and ordinances, the laws and commands he wrote for you. Do not worship other gods. [38]Do not forget the covenant I have made with you, and do not worship other

כִּי אִם־ אֶת־ יְהוָה אֱלֹהֵיכֶם תִּירָאוּ וְהוּא יַצִּיל
he-will-deliver and-he you-worship God-of-you Yahweh *** only rather (39)

אֶתְכֶם מִיַּד כָּל־ אֹיְבֵיכֶם׃ וְלֹא שָׁמֵעוּ כִּי
but they-listened but-not (40) being-enemies-of-you all-of from-hand-of you

אִם־ כְּמִשְׁפָּטָם הָרִאשׁוֹן הֵם עֹשִׂים׃ וַיִּהְיוּ ׀
so-they-were (41) ones-persisting they the-former as-practice-of-them rather

הַגּוֹיִם הָאֵלֶּה יְרֵאִים אֶת־ יְהוָה וְאֶת־ פְּסִילֵיהֶם הָיוּ
they-were idols-of-them and Yawheh *** ones-worshiping the-these the-nations

עֹבְדִים גַּם־ בְּנֵיהֶם ׀ וּבְנֵי בְנֵיהֶם כַּאֲשֶׁר
just-as children-of-them and-children-of children-of-them and ones-serving

עָשׂוּ אֲבֹתָם הֵם עֹשִׂים עַד הַיּוֹם הַזֶּה׃ וַיְהִי
and-he-was (18:1) the-this the-day to ones-doing they fathers-of-them they-did

בִּשְׁנַת שָׁלֹשׁ לְהוֹשֵׁעַ בֶּן־ אֵלָה מֶלֶךְ יִשְׂרָאֵל מָלַךְ חִזְקִיָּה
Hezekiah he-became-king Israel king-of Elah son-of of-Hoshea three in-year-of

בֶן־ אָחָז מֶלֶךְ יְהוּדָה׃ בֶּן־ עֶשְׂרִים וְחָמֵשׁ שָׁנָה הָיָה
he-was year and-five twenty son-of (2) Judah king-of Ahaz son-of

בְמָלְכוֹ וְעֶשְׂרִים וָתֵשַׁע שָׁנָה מָלַךְ בִּירוּשָׁלָםִ
in-Jerusalem he-reigned year and-nine and-twenty when-to-become-king-him

וְשֵׁם אִמּוֹ אֲבִי בַּת־ זְכַרְיָה׃ וַיַּעַשׂ הַיָּשָׁר
the-right and-he-did (3) Zechariah daughter-of Abi mother-of-him and-name-of

בְּעֵינֵי יְהוָה כְּכֹל אֲשֶׁר־ עָשָׂה דָּוִד אָבִיו׃ הוּא ׀ הֵסִיר
he-removed he (4) father-of-him David he-did that as-all Yahweh in-eyes-of

אֶת־ הַבָּמוֹת וְשִׁבַּר אֶת־ הַמַּצֵּבֹת וְכָרַת
and-he-cut-down the-sacred-stones *** and-he-smashed the-high-places ***

אֶת־ הָאֲשֵׁרָה וְכִתַּת נְחַשׁ הַנְּחֹשֶׁת אֲשֶׁר־ עָשָׂה מֹשֶׁה
Moses he-made that the-bronze snake-of and-he-broke-up the-Asherah-pole ***

כִּי עַד־ הַיָּמִים הָהֵמָּה הָיוּ בְנֵי־ יִשְׂרָאֵל מְקַטְּרִים
ones-burning-incense Israel sons-of they-were the-those the-days up-to for

לוֹ וַיִּקְרָא־ לוֹ נְחֻשְׁתָּן׃ בַּיהוָה אֱלֹהֵי־ יִשְׂרָאֵל בָּטָח
he-trusted Israel God-of in-Yahweh (5) Nehushtan to-him now-he-called to-him

וְאַחֲרָיו לֹא־ הָיָה כָמֹהוּ בְּכֹל מַלְכֵי יְהוּדָה וַאֲשֶׁר הָיוּ
he-was or-who Judah kings-of among-all-of like-him he-was not and-after-him

לְפָנָיו׃ וַיִּדְבַּק בַּיהוָה לֹא־ סָר מֵאַחֲרָיו
from-after-him he-turned-away not to-Yahweh and-he-held-fast (6) before-him

וַיִּשְׁמֹר מִצְוֺתָיו אֲשֶׁר־ צִוָּה יְהוָה אֶת־ מֹשֶׁה׃ וְהָיָה
and-he-was (7) Moses *** Yahweh he-gave that commands-of-him and-he-kept

יְהוָה עִמּוֹ בְּכֹל אֲשֶׁר־ יֵצֵא יַשְׂכִּיל וַיִּמְרֹד
and-he-rebelled he-was-successful he-undertook that in-all with-him Yahweh

gods. 39 Rather, worship the
LORD your God; it is he who
will deliver you from the hand
of all your enemies."
40 They would not listen,
however, but persisted in
their former practices. 41 Even
while these people were worshiping the LORD, they were
serving their idols. To this day
their children and grandchil-
dren continue to do as their
fathers did.

Hezekiah King of Judah

18 In the third year of Hoshea son of Elah king
of Israel, Hezekiah son of
Ahaz king of Judah began to
reign. 2 He was twenty-five
years old when he became
king, and he reigned in
Jerusalem twenty-nine years.
His mother's name was Abijah[a] daughter of Zechariah.
3 He did what was right in the
eyes of the LORD, just as his
father David had done. 4 He
removed the high places,
smashed the sacred stones and
cut down the Asherah poles.
He broke into pieces the
bronze snake Moses had
made, for up to that time the
Israelites had been burning
incense to it. (It was called[b]
Nehushtan.[c])
5 Hezekiah trusted in the
LORD, the God of Israel. There
was no one like him among all
the kings of Judah, either before him or after him. 6 He held
fast to the LORD and did not
cease to follow him; he kept
the commands the LORD had
given Moses. 7 And the LORD
was with him; he was successful in whatever he undertook.
He rebelled against the king of

[a]2 Hebrew *Abi*, a variant of *Abijah*
[b]4 Or *He called it*
[c]4 *Nehushtan* sounds like the Hebrew for *bronze* and *snake* and *unclean thing*.

בְּמֶלֶךְ־ אַשּׁוּר וְלֹא עֲבָדוֹ׃ הוּא־ הִכָּה אֶת־
*** he-defeated he (8) he-served-him and-not Assyria against-king-of

פְּלִשְׁתִּים עַד־ עַזָּה וְאֶת־ גְּבוּלֶיהָ מִמִּגְדַּל נוֹצְרִים
ones-watching from-tower-of territories-of-her and Gaza as-far-as Philistines

עַד־ עִיר מִבְצָר׃ וַיְהִי בַּשָּׁנָה הָרְבִיעִית לַמֶּלֶךְ
of-the-king the-fourth in-the-year and-he-was (9) fortified city-of to

חִזְקִיָּהוּ הִיא הַשָּׁנָה הַשְּׁבִיעִית לְהוֹשֵׁעַ בֶּן־ אֵלָה מֶלֶךְ יִשְׂרָאֵל
Israel king-of Elah son-of of-Hoshea the-seventh the-year this Hezekiah

עָלָה שַׁלְמַנְאֶסֶר מֶלֶךְ־ אַשּׁוּר עַל־ שֹׁמְרוֹן וַיָּצַר
and-he-laid-siege Samaria against Assyria king-of Shalmaneser he-marched

עָלֶיהָ׃ וַיִּלְכְּדֻהָ מִקְצֵה שָׁלֹשׁ שָׁנִים בִּשְׁנַת־ שֵׁשׁ
six in-year-of years three at-end-of and-they-took-her (10) to-her

לְחִזְקִיָּה הִיא שְׁנַת־ תֵּשַׁע לְהוֹשֵׁעַ מֶלֶךְ יִשְׂרָאֵל נִלְכְּדָה
she-was-captured Israel king-of of-Hoshea nine year-of this of-Hezekiah

שֹׁמְרוֹן׃ וַיֶּגֶל מֶלֶךְ־ אַשּׁוּר אֶת־ יִשְׂרָאֵל אַשּׁוּרָה
to-Assyria Israel *** Assyria king-of and-he-deported (11) Samaria

וַיַּנְחֵם בַּחְלַח וּבְחָבוֹר נְהַר גּוֹזָן וְעָרֵי
and-in-towns-of Gozan River-of and-on-Habor in-Halah and-he-settled-them

מָדָי׃ עַל ׀ אֲשֶׁר לֹא־ שָׁמְעוּ בְּקוֹל יְהוָה אֱלֹהֵיהֶם
God-of-them Yahweh to-voice-of they-obeyed not because for (12) Medes

וַיַּעַבְרוּ אֶת־ בְּרִיתוֹ אֵת כָּל־ אֲשֶׁר צִוָּה מֹשֶׁה
Moses he-commanded that all *** covenant-of-him *** but-they-violated

עֶבֶד יְהוָה וְלֹא שָׁמְעוּ וְלֹא עָשׂוּ׃
they-carried-out and-not they-listened and-not Yahweh servant-of

וּבְאַרְבַּע עֶשְׂרֵה שָׁנָה לַמֶּלֶךְ חִזְקִיָּה עָלָה סַנְחֵרִיב
Sennacherib he-attacked Hezekiah of-the-king year ten in-four-of (13)

מֶלֶךְ־ אַשּׁוּר עַל כָּל־ עָרֵי יְהוּדָה הַבְּצֻרוֹת
the-ones-being-fortified Judah cities-of all-of against Assyria king-of

וַיִּתְפְּשֵׂם׃ וַיִּשְׁלַח חִזְקִיָּה מֶלֶךְ־ יְהוּדָה אֶל־ מֶלֶךְ־
king-of to Judah king-of Hezekiah so-he-sent (14) and-he-captured-them

אַשּׁוּר ׀ לָכִישָׁה ׀ לֵאמֹר ׀ חָטָאתִי שׁוּב מֵעָלַי אֵת אֲשֶׁר־
what *** from-against-me withdraw! I-did-wrong to-say at-Lachish Assyria

תִּתֵּן עָלַי אֶשָּׂא וַיָּשֶׂם מֶלֶךְ־ אַשּׁוּר עַל־ חִזְקִיָּה
Hezekiah from Assyria king-of and-he-exacted I-will-pay of-me you-demand

מֶלֶךְ־ יְהוּדָה שְׁלֹשׁ מֵאוֹת כִּכַּר־ כֶּסֶף וּשְׁלֹשִׁים כִּכַּר זָהָב׃
gold talent-of and-thirty silver talent-of hundreds three-of Judah king-of

וַיִּתֵּן חִזְקִיָּה אֶת־ כָּל־ הַכֶּסֶף הַנִּמְצָא בֵית־
temple-of the-one-being-found the-silver all-of *** Hezekiah so-he-gave (15)

Assyria and did not serve him.
8From watchtower to fortified
city, he defeated the Philistines, as far as Gaza and its territory.
9In King Hezekiah's fourth
year, which was the seventh
year of Hoshea son of Elah
king of Israel, Shalmaneser
king of Assyria marched
against Samaria and laid siege
to it. 10At the end of three years
the Assyrians took it. So Samaria was captured in Hezekiah's sixth year, which was
the ninth year of Hoshea king
of Israel. 11The king of Assyria
deported Israel to Assyria and
settled them in Halah, in Gozan on the Habor River and in
towns of the Medes. 12This
happened because they had
not obeyed the LORD their
God, but had violated his
covenant—all that Moses the
servant of the LORD com-
manded. They neither lis-
tened to the commands nor
carried them out.
13In the fourteenth year of
King Hezekiah's reign, Sennacherib king of Assyria attacked all the fortified cities of
Judah and captured them. 14So
Hezekiah king of Judah sent
this message to the king of Assyria at Lachish: "I have done
wrong. Withdraw from me,
and I will pay whatever you
demand of me." The king of
Assyria exacted from Hezekiah king of Judah three hundred talents[d] of silver and
thirty talents[e] of gold. 15So
Hezekiah gave him all the silver that was found in the temple of the LORD and in the

[d]14 That is, about 11 tons (about 10 metric tons)
[e]14 That is, about 1 ton (about 1 metric ton)

יְהוָה וּבְאֹצְרוֹת בֵּית הַמֶּלֶךְ׃ בָּעֵת הַהִיא
the-this at-the-time (16) the-king palace-of and-in-treasuries-of Yahweh

קִצַּץ חִזְקִיָּה אֶת־ דַּלְתוֹת הֵיכַל יְהוָה וְאֶת־ הָאֹמְנוֹת
the-posts-supporting and Yahweh temple-of doors-of *** Hezekiah he-stripped

אֲשֶׁר צִפָּה חִזְקִיָּה מֶלֶךְ יְהוּדָה וַיִּתְּנֵם לְמֶלֶךְ אַשּׁוּר׃
Assyria to-king-of and-he-gave-them Judah king-of Hezekiah he-covered which

וַיִּשְׁלַח מֶלֶךְ־ אַשּׁוּר אֶת־ תַּרְתָּן וְאֶת־ רַב־ סָרִיס ׀
officer chief-of and supreme-commander *** Assyria king-of and-he-sent (17)

וְאֶת־ רַב־ שָׁקֵה מִן־ לָכִישׁ אֶל־ הַמֶּלֶךְ חִזְקִיָּהוּ בְּחֵיל
with-army Hezekiah the-king to Lachish from field-commander chief-of and

כָּבֵד יְרוּשָׁלִָם וַיַּעֲלוּ וַיָּבֹאוּ יְרוּשָׁלִַם וַיַּעֲלוּ
and-they-went-up Jerusalem and-they-came and-they-went-up Jerusalem large

וַיָּבֹאוּ וַיַּעַמְדוּ בִּתְעָלַת הַבְּרֵכָה הָעֶלְיוֹנָה אֲשֶׁר
that the-Upper the-Pool at-aqueduct-of and-they-stopped and-they-came

בִּמְסִלַּת שְׂדֵה כוֹבֵס׃ וַיִּקְרְאוּ אֶל־ הַמֶּלֶךְ
the-king for and-they-called (18) One-Washing Field-of on-road-of

וַיֵּצֵא אֲלֵהֶם אֶלְיָקִים בֶּן־ חִלְקִיָּהוּ אֲשֶׁר עַל־ הַבָּיִת וְשֶׁבְנָה
and-Shebna the-palace over who Hilkiah son-of Eliakim to-them and-he-went-out

הַסֹּפֵר וְיוֹאָח בֶּן־ אָסָף הַמַּזְכִּיר׃ וַיֹּאמֶר
and-he-said (19) the-one-recording Asaph son-of and-Joah the-secretary

אֲלֵהֶם רַב־ שָׁקֵה אִמְרוּ־ נָא אֶל־ חִזְקִיָּהוּ כֹּה־ אָמַר
he-says this Hezekiah to now! tell! field-commander chief-of to-them

הַמֶּלֶךְ הַגָּדוֹל מֶלֶךְ אַשּׁוּר מָה הַבִּטָּחוֹן הַזֶּה אֲשֶׁר
that the-this the-confidence what? Assyria king-of the-great the-king

בָּטָחְתָּ׃ אָמַרְתָּ אַךְ־ דְּבַר־ שְׂפָתַיִם עֵצָה וּגְבוּרָה
and-strength strategy lips word-of only you-speak (20) you-confiding

לַמִּלְחָמָה עַתָּה עַל־ מִי בָטַחְתָּ כִּי מָרַדְתָּ בִּי׃ עַתָּה
now (21) against-me you-rebel that you-depend whom? on now of-the-military

הִנֵּה בָטַחְתָּ לְּךָ עַל־ מִשְׁעֶנֶת הַקָּנֶה הָרָצוּץ
the-one-being-splintered the-reed staff-of on for-you you-depend look!

הַזֶּה עַל־מִצְרַיִם אֲשֶׁר יִסָּמֵךְ אִישׁ עָלָיו וּבָא בְכַפּוֹ
through-hand-of-him and-he-pierces on-him man he-leans which Egypt on the-this

וּנְקָבָהּ כֵּן פַּרְעֹה מֶלֶךְ־ מִצְרַיִם לְכָל־ הַבֹּטְחִים
the-ones-depending to-all-of Egypt king-of Pharaoh such and-he-wounds-her

עָלָיו׃ וְכִי־ תֹאמְרוּן אֵלַי אֶל־יְהוָה אֱלֹהֵינוּ בָּטָחְנוּ הֲלוֹא־הוּא
he not? we-depend God-of-us Yahweh on to-me you-say and-if (22) on-him

אֲשֶׁר הֵסִיר חִזְקִיָּהוּ אֶת־ בָּמֹתָיו וְאֶת־ מִזְבְּחֹתָיו וַיֹּאמֶר
and-he-said altars-of-him and high-places-of-him *** Hezekiah he-removed who

treasuries of the royal palace.
[16]At this time Hezekiah king
of Judah stripped off the gold
with which he had covered
the doors and doorposts of the
temple of the LORD, and gave it
to the king of Assyria.

Sennacherib Threatens Jerusalem

[17]The king of Assyria sent
his supreme commander, his
chief officer and his field commander
with a large army,
from Lachish to King Hezekiah
at Jerusalem. They came
up to Jerusalem and stopped at
the aqueduct of the Upper
Pool, on the road to the Washerman's
Field. [18]They called
for the king; and Eliakim son
of Hilkiah the palace administrator,
Shebna the secretary,
and Joah son of Asaph the
recorder went out to them.
[19]The field commander said
to them, "Tell Hezekiah:

" 'This is what the great
king, the king of Assyria,
says: On what are you basing
this confidence of
yours? [20]You say you have
strategy and military
strength—but you speak
only empty words. On
whom are you depending,
that you rebel against me?
[21]Look now, you are depending
on Egypt, that
splintered reed of a staff,
which pierces a man's
hand and wounds him if he
leans on it! Such is Pharaoh
king of Egypt to all who depend
on him. [22]And if you
say to me, "We are depending
on the LORD our
God"—isn't he the one
whose high places and altars
Hezekiah removed,

לִיהוּדָה וְלִירוּשָׁלַםִ לִפְנֵי הַמִּזְבֵּחַ הַזֶּה תִּשְׁתַּחֲווּ
you-must-worship the-this the-altar before and-to-Jerusalem to-Judah

בִּירוּשָׁלָםִ׃ וְעַתָּה הִתְעָרֶב נָא אֶת־ אֲדֹנִי אֶת־ מֶלֶךְ
king-of with master-of-me with now! make-bargain! and-now (23) in-Jerusalem

אַשּׁוּר וְאֶתְּנָה לְךָ אַלְפַּיִם סוּסִים אִם־ תּוּכַל לָתֶת
to-put you-can if horses two-thousands to-you and-I-will-give Assyria

לְךָ רֹכְבִים עֲלֵיהֶם׃ וְאֵיךְ תָּשִׁיב אֵת פְּנֵי
faces-of *** can-you-repulse now-how? (24) on-them ones-riding of-you

פַחַת אַחַד עַבְדֵי אֲדֹנִי הַקְּטַנִּים וַתִּבְטַח
though-you-depend the-least-ones master-of-me officials-of one-of officer-of

לְךָ עַל־ מִצְרַיִם לְרֶכֶב וּלְפָרָשִׁים׃ עַתָּה הֲמִבַּלְעֲדֵי יְהוָה
Yahweh apart-from? now (25) and-for-horsemen for-chariot Egypt on for-you

עָלִיתִי עַל־ הַמָּקוֹם הַזֶּה לְהַשְׁחִתוֹ יְהוָה אָמַר אֵלַי
to-me he-told Yahweh to-destroy-him the-this the-place against I-came

עֲלֵה עַל־ הָאָרֶץ הַזֹּאת וְהַשְׁחִיתָהּ׃ וַיֹּאמֶר
then-he-said (26) and-destroy-her! the-this the-country against march!

אֶלְיָקִים בֶּן־ חִלְקִיָּהוּ וְשֶׁבְנָה וְיוֹאָח אֶל־ רַב־ שָׁקֵה
field-commander chief-of to and-Joah and-Shebna Hilkiah son-of Eliakim

דַּבֶּר־ נָא אֶל־ עֲבָדֶיךָ אֲרָמִית כִּי שֹׁמְעִים אֲנָחְנוּ וְאַל־
but-not we ones-understanding since Aramaic servants-of-you to now! speak!

תְּדַבֵּר עִמָּנוּ יְהוּדִית בְּאָזְנֵי הָעָם אֲשֶׁר עַל־הַחֹמָה׃ וַיֹּאמֶר
but-he-said (27) the-wall on who the-people in-ears-of Hebrew to-us you-speak

אֲלֵיהֶם רַב־ שָׁקֵה הַעַל אֲדֹנֶיךָ וְאֵלֶיךָ שְׁלָחַנִי
he-sent-me and-to-you masters-of-you to? field-commander chief-of to-them

אֲדֹנִי לְדַבֵּר אֶת־הַדְּבָרִים הָאֵלֶּה הֲלֹא עַל־הָאֲנָשִׁים הַיֹּשְׁבִים
the-ones-sitting the-men to not? the-these the-things *** to-say master-of-me

עַל־ הַחֹמָה לֶאֱכֹל אֶת־ חֹרֵיהֶם° וְלִשְׁתּוֹת אֶת־ שֵׁינֵיהֶם°
†urines-of-them *** and-to-drink *filth-of-them *** to-eat the-wall on

עִמָּכֶם׃ וַיַּעֲמֹד רַב־ שָׁקֵה וַיִּקְרָא בְקוֹל־
with-voice and-he-called field-commander chief-of then-he-stood (28) like-you

גָּדוֹל יְהוּדִית וַיְדַבֵּר וַיֹּאמֶר שִׁמְעוּ דְּבַר־ הַמֶּלֶךְ הַגָּדוֹל מֶלֶךְ
king-of the-great the-king word-of hear! and-he-said and-he-spoke Hebrew loud

אַשּׁוּר׃ כֹּה אָמַר הַמֶּלֶךְ אַל־ יַשִּׁא לָכֶם חִזְקִיָּהוּ כִּי־
for Hezekiah to-you let-him-deceive not the-king he-says this (29) Assyria

לֹא יוּכַל לְהַצִּיל אֶתְכֶם מִיָּדוֹ׃ וְאַל־ יַבְטַח
let-him-cause-to-trust and-not (30) from-hand-of-him you to-deliver he-can not

אֶתְכֶם חִזְקִיָּהוּ אֶל־ יְהוָה לֵאמֹר הַצֵּל יַצִּילֵנוּ יְהוָה וְלֹא
and-not Yahweh he-will-deliver-us to-deliver to-say Yahweh in Hezekiah you

saying to Judah and Jerusalem, "You must worship
before this altar in Jerusalem"?
23 "'Come now, make a
bargain with my master,
the king of Assyria: I will
give you two thousand
horses, if you can put riders
on them. 24How can you re-
pulse one officer of the least
of my master's officials,
even though you are de-
pending on Egypt for
chariots and horsemen[f]?
25Furthermore, have I come
to attack and destroy this
place without word from
the LORD? The LORD himself
told me to march against
this country and destroy
it.' "

26Then Eliakim son of Hilkiah, and Shebna and Joah
said to the field commander,
"Please speak to your servants
in Aramaic, since we understand it. Don't speak to us in
Hebrew in the hearing of the
people on the wall."
27But the commander re-
plied, "Was it only to your
master and you that my master sent me to say these things,
and not to the men sitting on
the wall—who, like you, will
have to eat their own filth and
drink their own urine?"
28Then the commander
stood and called out in Hebrew: "Hear the word of the
great king, the king of Assyria!
29This is what the king says:
Do not let Hezekiah deceive
you. He cannot deliver you
from my hand. 30Do not let
Hezekiah persuade you to
trust in the LORD when he
says, 'The LORD will surely deliver us; this city will not be

[f]24 Or *charioteers*

*27a The *Qere*, *outgoing-of-them*, is a less graphic word than the *Ketbib*.

†27b The *Qere*, *waters-of feet-of-them*, is a less graphic word than the *Ketbib*.

°27a ק צואתם

°27b ק מימי רגליהם

תִּנָּתֵן אֶת־ הָעִיר הַזֹּאת בְּיַד מֶלֶךְ אַשּׁוּר׃
Assyria king-of into-hand-of the-this the-city *** she-will-be-given

אַל־ תִּשְׁמְעוּ אֶל־חִזְקִיָּהוּ כִּי כֹה אָמַר מֶלֶךְ אַשּׁוּר עֲשׂוּ־
make! Assyria king-of he-says this for Hezekiah to you-listen not (31)

אִתִּי בְרָכָה וּצְאוּ אֵלַי וְאִכְלוּ אִישׁ־ גַּפְנוֹ וְאִישׁ
and-each vine-of-him each then-eat! to-me and-come-out! peace with-me

תְּאֵנָתוֹ וּשְׁתוּ אִישׁ מֵי־ בוֹרוֹ׃ עַד־ בֹּאִי
to-come-me until (32) cistern-of-him waters-of each and-drink! fig-tree-of-him

וְלָקַחְתִּי אֶתְכֶם אֶל־ אֶרֶץ כְּאַרְצְכֶם אֶרֶץ דָּגָן וְתִירוֹשׁ אֶרֶץ
land-of and-new-wine grain land-of like-land-of-you land to you and-I-take

לֶחֶם וּכְרָמִים אֶרֶץ זֵית יִצְהָר וּדְבַשׁ וִחְיוּ וְלֹא
and-not now-live! and-honey oil olive-tree-of land-of and-vineyards bread

תָמֻתוּ וְאַל־ תִּשְׁמְעוּ אֶל־חִזְקִיָּהוּ כִּי ־יַסִּית אֶתְכֶם לֵאמֹר יְהוָה
Yahweh to-say you he-misleads for Hezekiah to you-listen and-not you-die

יַצִּילֵנוּ׃ הַהַצֵּל הִצִּילוּ אֱלֹהֵי הַגּוֹיִם אִישׁ
any the-nations gods-of they-delivered to-deliver? (33) he-will-deliver-us

אֶת־ אַרְצוֹ מִיַּד מֶלֶךְ אַשּׁוּר׃ אַיֵּה אֱלֹהֵי חֲמָת
Hamath gods-of where? (34) Assyria king-of from-hand-of land-of-him ***

וְאַרְפָּד אַיֵּה אֱלֹהֵי סְפַרְוַיִם הֵנַע וְעִוָּה כִּי־ הִצִּילוּ אֶת־
*** they-rescued indeed and-Ivvah Hena Sepharvaim gods-of where? and-Arpad

שֹׁמְרוֹן מִיָּדִי׃ מִי בְּכָל־ אֱלֹהֵי הָאֲרָצוֹת אֲשֶׁר־
who the-countries gods-of of-all-of who? (35) from-hand-of-me Samaria

הִצִּילוּ אֶת־ אַרְצָם מִיָּדִי כִּי־ יַצִּיל יְהוָה אֶת־
*** Yahweh can-he-deliver indeed from-hand-of-me land-of-them *** they-saved

יְרוּשָׁלִַם מִיָּדִי׃ וְהֶחֱרִישׁוּ הָעָם וְלֹא־
and-not the-people but-they-remained-silent (36) from-hand-of-me Jerusalem

עָנוּ אֹתוֹ דָּבָר כִּי־ מִצְוַת הַמֶּלֶךְ הִיא לֵאמֹר לֹא תַעֲנֻהוּ׃
you-answer-him not to-say this the-king command-of for word him they-replied

וַיָּבֹא אֶלְיָקִים בֶּן־ חִלְקִיָּה אֲשֶׁר־עַל־ הַבַּיִת וְשֶׁבְנָא
and-Shebna the-palace over who Hilkiah son-of Eliakim then-he-went (37)

הַסֹּפֵר וְיוֹאָח בֶּן־ אָסָף הַמַּזְכִּיר אֶל־ חִזְקִיָּהוּ
Hezekiah to the-one-recording Asaph son-of and-Joah the-secretary

קְרוּעֵי בְגָדִים וַיַּגִּדוּ לוֹ דִּבְרֵי רַב־
chief-of words-of to-him and-they-told clothes ones-being-torn-of

שָׁקֵה׃ וַיְהִי כִּשְׁמֹעַ הַמֶּלֶךְ חִזְקִיָּהוּ וַיִּקְרַע
then-he-tore Hezekiah the-king when-to-hear and-he-was (19:1) field-commander

אֶת־ בְּגָדָיו וַיִּתְכַּס בַּשָּׂק וַיָּבֹא
and-he-went-into with-the-sackcloth and-he-covered-himself clothes-of-him ***

given into the hand of the
king of Assyria.'
31 "Do not listen to Hezekiah.
This is what the king of Assyria says: Make peace with
me and come out to me. Then
every one of you will eat from
his own vine and fig tree and
drink water from his own cistern, 32 until I come and take
you to a land like your own, a
land of grain and new wine, a
land of bread and vineyards, a
land of olive trees and honey.
Choose life and not death!

"Do not listen to Hezekiah,
for he is misleading you when
he says, 'The LORD will deliver
us.' 33 Has the god of any nation ever delivered his land
from the hand of the king of
Assyria? 34 Where are the gods
of Hamath and Arpad? Where
are the gods of Sepharvaim,
Hena and Ivvah? Have they
rescued Samaria from my
hand? 35 Who of all the gods of
these countries has been able
to save his land from me? How
then can the LORD deliver
Jerusalem from my hand?"

36 But the people remained silent and said nothing in reply,
because the king had com-
manded, "Do not answer
him."

37 Then Eliakim son of Hilkiah the palace administrator,
Shebna the secretary and Joah
son of Asaph the recorder
went to Hezekiah, with their
clothes torn, and told him
what the field commander had
said.

Jerusalem's Deliverance Foretold

19 When King Hezekiah
heard this, he tore his
clothes and put on sackcloth

בֵּית יְהוָה׃ וַיִּשְׁלַח אֶת־אֶלְיָקִים אֲשֶׁר־עַל־הַבַּיִת וְשֶׁבְנָא
and-Shebna the-palace over who Eliakim *** and-he-sent (2) Yahweh temple-of

הַסֹּפֵר וְאֵת זִקְנֵי הַכֹּהֲנִים מִתְכַּסִּים בַּשַּׂקִּים
in-the-sackcloths ones-being-clothed the-priests elders-of and the-secretary

אֶל־יְשַׁעְיָהוּ הַנָּבִיא בֶּן־אָמוֹץ׃ וַיֹּאמְרוּ אֵלָיו כֹּה אָמַר
he-says this to-him and-they-told (3) Amoz son-of the-prophet Isaiah to

חִזְקִיָּהוּ יוֹם־צָרָה וְתוֹכֵחָה וּנְאָצָה הַיּוֹם הַזֶּה כִּי
as-when the-this the-day and-disgrace and-rebuke distress day-of Hezekiah

בָאוּ בָנִים עַד־מַשְׁבֵּר וְכֹחַ אַיִן לְלֵדָה׃ אוּלַי
perhaps (4) to-deliver there-is-no and-strength birth to children they-come

יִשְׁמַע יְהוָה אֱלֹהֶיךָ אֵת ׀ כָּל־דִּבְרֵי רַב־שָׁקֵה
field-commander chief-of words-of all-of *** God-of-you Yahweh he-will-hear

אֲשֶׁר שְׁלָחוֹ מֶלֶךְ־אַשּׁוּר ׀ אֲדֹנָיו לְחָרֵף אֱלֹהִים חַי
living God to-ridicule masters-of-him Assyria king-of he-sent-him whom

וְהוֹכִיחַ בַּדְּבָרִים אֲשֶׁר שָׁמַע יְהוָה אֱלֹהֶיךָ וְנָשָׂאתָ
so-you-lift God-of-you Yahweh he-heard that for-the-words and-he-will-rebuke

תְפִלָּה בְּעַד הַשְּׁאֵרִית הַנִּמְצָאָה׃ וַיָּבֹאוּ עַבְדֵי
officials-of when-they-came (5) the-one-surviving the-remnant for prayer

הַמֶּלֶךְ חִזְקִיָּהוּ אֶל־יְשַׁעְיָהוּ׃ וַיֹּאמֶר לָהֶם יְשַׁעְיָהוּ כֹּה תֹאמְרוּן
you-tell this Isaiah to-them then-he-said (6) Isaiah to Hezekiah the-king

אֶל־אֲדֹנֵיכֶם כֹּה ׀ אָמַר יְהוָה אַל־תִּירָא מִפְּנֵי הַדְּבָרִים
the-words from-before you-be-afraid not Yahweh he-says this masters-of-you to

אֲשֶׁר שָׁמַעְתָּ אֲשֶׁר גִּדְּפוּ נַעֲרֵי מֶלֶךְ־אַשּׁוּר אֹתִי׃
me Assyria king-of underlings-of they-blasphemed which you-heard that

הִנְנִי נֹתֵן בּוֹ רוּחַ וְשָׁמַע שְׁמוּעָה וְשָׁב
then-he-will-return report when-he-hears spirit in-him putting see-I! (7)

לְאַרְצוֹ וְהִפַּלְתִּיו בַּחֶרֶב בְּאַרְצוֹ׃
in-country-of-him with-the-sword and-I-will-have-cut-down-him to-country-of-him

וַיָּשָׁב רַב־שָׁקֵה וַיִּמְצָא אֶת־מֶלֶךְ
king-of *** and-he-found field-commander chief-of and-he-withdrew (8)

אַשּׁוּר נִלְחָם עַל־לִבְנָה כִּי שָׁמַע כִּי נָסַע מִלָּכִישׁ׃
from-Lachish he-left that he-heard when Libnah against fighting Assyria

וַיִּשְׁמַע אֶל־תִּרְהָקָה מֶלֶךְ־כּוּשׁ לֵאמֹר הִנֵּה יָצָא
he-marched-out see! to-say Cush king-of Tirhakah about now-he-heard (9)

לְהִלָּחֵם אִתָּךְ וַיָּשָׁב וַיִּשְׁלַח מַלְאָכִים אֶל־חִזְקִיָּהוּ
Hezekiah to messengers and-he-sent so-he-repeated against-you to-fight

לֵאמֹר׃ כֹּה תֹאמְרוּן אֶל־חִזְקִיָּהוּ מֶלֶךְ־יְהוּדָה לֵאמֹר אַל־
not to-say Judah king-of Hezekiah to you-say this (10) to-say

and went into the temple of the LORD. [2]He sent Eliakim the palace administrator, Shebna the secretary and the leading priests, all wearing sackcloth, to the prophet Isaiah son of Amoz. [3]They told him, "This is what Hezekiah says: This day is a day of distress and rebuke and disgrace, as when children come to the point of birth and there is no strength to deliver them. [4]It may be that the LORD your God will hear all the words of the field commander, whom his master, the king of Assyria, has sent to ridicule the living God, and that he will rebuke him for the words the LORD your God has heard. Therefore pray for the remnant that still survives."

[5]When King Hezekiah's officials came to Isaiah, [6]Isaiah said to them, "Tell your master, 'This is what the LORD says: Do not be afraid of what you have heard—those words with which the underlings of the king of Assyria have blasphemed me. [7]Listen! I am going to put such a spirit in him that when he hears a certain report, he will return to his own country, and there I will have him cut down with the sword.' "

[8]When the field commander heard that the king of Assyria had left Lachish, he withdrew and found the king fighting against Libnah.

[9]Now Sennacherib received a report that Tirhakah, the Cushite[g] king ⌞of Egypt⌟, was marching out to fight against him. So he again sent messengers to Hezekiah with this word: [10]"Say to Hezekiah king of Judah: Do not let the god

g9 That is, from the upper Nile region

*5 Most mss have *sheva* under the *ayin* (עְ).

†9 Most mss have *sheva* under the *kaph* (ךְ).

יַשִּׁאֲךָ אֱלֹהֶיךָ אֲשֶׁר אַתָּה בֹּטֵחַ בּוֹ לֵאמֹר לֹא
not to-say on-him depending you whom God-of-you let-him-deceive-you

תִּנָּתֵן יְרוּשָׁלַםִ בְּיַד מֶלֶךְ אַשּׁוּר׃ הִנֵּה ׀ אַתָּה שָׁמַעְתָּ
you-heard you see! (11) Assyria king-of into-hand-of Jerusalem she-will-given

אֵת אֲשֶׁר עָשׂוּ מַלְכֵי אַשּׁוּר לְכָל־ הָאֲרָצוֹת לְהַחֲרִימָם
to-destroy-them the-countries to-all-of Assyria kings-of they-did what ***

וְאַתָּה תִּנָּצֵל׃ הַהִצִּילוּ אֹתָם אֱלֹהֵי הַגּוֹיִם
the-nations gods-of them did-they-deliver? (12) will-you-be-delivered and-you

אֲשֶׁר שִׁחֲתוּ אֲבוֹתַי אֶת־ גּוֹזָן וְאֶת־ חָרָן וְרֶצֶף וּבְנֵי־
and-sons-of and-Rezeph Haran and Gozan *** fathers-of-me they-destroyed that

עֶדֶן אֲשֶׁר בִּתְלַאשָּׂר׃ אַיּוֹ מֶלֶךְ־ חֲמָת וּמֶלֶךְ אַרְפָּד
Arpad and-king-of Hamath king-of where-he? (13) in-Tel-Assar who Eden

וּמֶלֶךְ לָעִיר סְפַרְוָיִם הֵנַע וְעִוָּה׃ וַיִּקַּח חִזְקִיָּהוּ
Hezekiah and-he-received (14) or-Avvah Hena Sepharvaim of-city-of and-king

אֶת־ הַסְּפָרִים מִיַּד הַמַּלְאָכִים וַיִּקְרָאֵם וַיַּעַל
then-he-went-up and-he-read-them the-messengers from-hand-of the-letters ***

בֵּית יְהוָה וַיִּפְרְשֵׂהוּ חִזְקִיָּהוּ לִפְנֵי יְהוָה׃
Yahweh before Hezekiah and-he-spread-out-him Yahweh temple-of

וַיִּתְפַּלֵּל חִזְקִיָּהוּ לִפְנֵי יְהוָה וַיֹּאמַר יְהוָה אֱלֹהֵי יִשְׂרָאֵל
Israel God-of Yahweh and-he-said Yahweh to Hezekiah and-he-prayed (15)

יֹשֵׁב הַכְּרֻבִים אַתָּה־ הוּא הָאֱלֹהִים לְבַדְּךָ לְכֹל
over-all-of by-yourself the-God he you the-cherubim being-enthroned-of

מַמְלְכוֹת הָאָרֶץ אַתָּה עָשִׂיתָ אֶת־ הַשָּׁמַיִם וְאֶת־ הָאָרֶץ׃ הַטֵּה
give! (16) the-earth and the-heavens *** you-made you the-earth kingdoms-of

יְהוָה ׀ אָזְנְךָ וּשְׁמָע פְּקַח יְהוָה עֵינֶיךָ וּרְאֵה וּשְׁמַע
and-listen! and-see! eyes-of-you Yahweh open! and-hear! ear-of-you Yahweh

אֵת דִּבְרֵי סַנְחֵרִיב אֲשֶׁר שְׁלָחוֹ לְחָרֵף אֱלֹהִים חָי׃ אָמְנָם
truly (17) living God to-insult he-sent-him that Sennacherib words-of ***

יְהוָה הֶחֱרִיבוּ מַלְכֵי אַשּׁוּר אֶת־ הַגּוֹיִם וְאֶת־ אַרְצָם׃
land-of-them and the-nations *** Assyria kings-of they-laid-waste Yahweh

וְנָתְנוּ אֶת־ אֱלֹהֵיהֶם בָּאֵשׁ כִּי לֹא אֱלֹהִים הֵמָּה כִּי
but they gods not for into-the-fire gods-of-them *** and-they-threw (18)

אִם־ מַעֲשֵׂה יְדֵי־ אָדָם עֵץ וָאֶבֶן וַיְאַבְּדוּם׃ וְעַתָּה
so-now (19) and-they-destroyed-them and-stone wood man hands-of work-of only

יְהוָה אֱלֹהֵינוּ הוֹשִׁיעֵנוּ נָא מִיָּדוֹ וְיֵדְעוּ כָּל־
all-of so-they-may-know from-hand-of-him now! deliver-us! God-of-us Yahweh

מַמְלְכוֹת הָאָרֶץ כִּי אַתָּה יְהוָה אֱלֹהִים לְבַדֶּךָ׃ וַיִּשְׁלַח
then-he-sent (20) by-yourself God Yahweh you that the-earth kingdoms-of

you depend on deceive you when he says, 'Jerusalem will not be handed over to the king of Assyria.' 11 Surely you have heard what the kings of Assyria have done to all the countries, destroying them completely. And will you be delivered? 12 Did the gods of the nations that were destroyed by my forefathers deliver them: the gods of Gozan, Haran, Rezeph and the people of Eden who were in Tel Assar? 13 Where is the king of Hamath, the king of Arpad, the king of the city of Sepharvaim, or of Hena or Ivvah?"

Hezekiah's Prayer

14 Hezekiah received the letter from the messengers and read it. Then he went up to the temple of the LORD and spread it out before the LORD. 15 And Hezekiah prayed to the LORD: "O LORD, God of Israel, enthroned between the cherubim, you alone are God over all the kingdoms of the earth. You have made heaven and earth. 16 Give ear, O LORD, and hear; open your eyes, O LORD, and see; listen to the words Sennacherib has sent to insult the living God.

17 "It is true, O LORD, that the Assyrian kings have laid waste these nations and their lands. 18 They have thrown their gods into the fire and destroyed them, for they were not gods but only wood and stone, fashioned by men's hands. 19 Now, O LORD our God, deliver us from his hand, so that all kingdoms on earth may know that you alone, O LORD, are God."

יְשַׁעְיָהוּ בֶן־ אָמוֹץ אֶל־ חִזְקִיָּהוּ לֵאמֹר כֹּה־ אָמַר יְהוָה אֱלֹהֵי יִשְׂרָאֵל
Israel God-of Yahweh he-says this to-say Hezekiah to Amoz son-of Isaiah

אֲשֶׁר הִתְפַּלַּלְתָּ אֵלַי אֶל־ סַנְחֵרִב מֶלֶךְ־ אַשּׁוּר שָׁמַעְתִּי׃ (21) זֶה
this (21) I-heard Assyria king-of Sennacherib about to-me you-prayed what

הַדָּבָר אֲשֶׁר־ דִּבֶּר יְהוָה עָלָיו בָּזָה לְךָ לָעֲגָה
she-mocks against-you she-despises against-him Yahweh he-spoke that the-word

לְךָ בְּתוּלַת בַּת־ צִיּוֹן אַחֲרֶיךָ רֹאשׁ הֵנִיעָה בַּת
Daughter-of she-tosses head after-you Zion Daughter-of Virgin-of at-you

יְרוּשָׁלִָם׃ (22) אֶת־ מִי חֵרַפְתָּ וְגִדַּפְתָּ וְעַל־ מִי
whom? and-against and-you-blasphemed you-insulted who? *** (22) Jerusalem

הֲרִימוֹתָ קּוֹל וַתִּשָּׂא מָרוֹם עֵינֶיךָ עַל־ קְדוֹשׁ יִשְׂרָאֵל׃
Israel Holy-One-of against eyes-of-you pride and-you-lifted voice you-raised

(23) בְּיַד מַלְאָכֶיךָ חֵרַפְתָּ | אֲדֹנָי וַתֹּאמֶר בְּרֹכֶב°
with-many-of and-you-said Lord you-insulted messengers-of-you by-hand-of (23)

רִכְבִּי אֲנִי עָלִיתִי מְרוֹם הָרִים יַרְכְּתֵי לְבָנוֹן
Lebanon utmost-heights-of mountains height-of I-ascended I chariot-of-me

וָאֶכְרֹת קוֹמַת אֲרָזָיו מִבְחוֹר בְּרֹשָׁיו
pines-of-him choice-of cedars-of-him tall-one-of and-I-cut-down

וְאָבוֹאָה מְלוֹן קִצֹּה° יַעַר כַּרְמִלּוֹ׃
garden-of-him forest-of remote-part-of-him shelter-of and-I-reached

(24) אֲנִי קַרְתִּי וְשָׁתִיתִי מַיִם זָרִים וְאַחְרִב
and-I-dried-up ones-being-foreign waters and-I-drank I-dug-well I (24)

בְּכַף־ פְּעָמַי כֹּל יְאֹרֵי מָצוֹר׃ (25) הֲלֹא־ שָׁמַעְתָּ
you-heard not? (25) Egypt streams-of all-of feet-of-me with-sole-of

לְמֵרָחוֹק אֹתָהּ עָשִׂיתִי לְמִימֵי קֶדֶם וִיצַרְתִּיהָ
then-I-planned-her old at-from-days-of I-ordained her at-from-long-ago

עַתָּה הֲבֵיאתִיהָ וּתְהִי לְהַשְׁאוֹת גַּלִּים נִצִּים
ones-being-ruins piles-of-stones to-turn so-you-were I-brought-to-pass-her now

עָרִים בְּצֻרוֹת׃ (26) וְיֹשְׁבֵיהֶן קִצְרֵי־
ones-drained-of and-ones-living-of-them (26) ones-being-fortified cities

יָד חַתּוּ וַיֵּבֹשׁוּ הָיוּ עֵשֶׂב שָׂדֶה
field plant-of they-are and-they-are-put-to-shame they-are-dismayed power

וִירַק דֶּשֶׁא חֲצִיר גַּגּוֹת וּשְׁדֵפָה לִפְנֵי קָמָה׃
growing-up before and-scorched housetops grass-of grass and-tender-shoot-of

(27) וְשִׁבְתְּךָ וְצֵאתְךָ וּבֹאֲךָ יָדָעְתִּי וְאֵת הִתְרַגֶּזְךָ
to-rage-you and I-know and-to-come-you and-to-go-you but-to-stay-you (27)

אֵלָי׃ (28) יַעַן הִתְרַגֶּזְךָ אֵלַי וְשַׁאֲנַנְךָ
and-insolence-of-you against-me to-rage-you because (28) against-me

Isaiah Prophesies Sennacherib's Fall

[20]Then Isaiah son of Amoz
sent a message to Hezekiah:
"This is what the LORD, the
God of Israel, says: I have
heard your prayer concerning
Sennacherib king of Assyria.
[21]This is the word that the
LORD has spoken against him:

" 'The Virgin Daughter of
Zion
despises you and mocks
you.
The Daughter of Jerusalem
tosses her head as you
flee.
[22]Who is it you have insulted
and blasphemed?
Against whom have you
raised your voice
and lifted your eyes in
pride?
Against the Holy One of
Israel!
[23]By your messengers
you have heaped insults
on the Lord.
And you have said,
"With my many chariots
I have ascended the
heights of the
mountains,
the utmost heights of
Lebanon.
I have cut down its tallest
cedars,
the choicest of its pines.
I have reached its remotest
parts,
the finest of its forests.
[24]I have dug wells in foreign
lands
and drunk the water
there.
With the soles of my feet
I have dried up all the
streams of Egypt."
[25]" 'Have you not heard?
Long ago I ordained it.
In days of old I planned it;
now I have brought it to
pass,
that you have turned
fortified cities
into piles of stone.
[26]Their people, drained of
power,
are dismayed and put to
shame.
They are like plants in the
field,
like tender green shoots,
like grass sprouting on the
housetops,
scorched before it grows
up.
[27]" 'But I know where you
stay
and when you come and
go

°23a ק ברב
°23b ק קצו

עָלָה בְאָזְנָי וְשַׂמְתִּי חַחִי בְּאַפֶּךָ
in-nose-of-you hook-of-me and-I-will-put to-ears-of-me he-reached

וּמִתְגִּי בִּשְׂפָתֶיךָ וַהֲשִׁבֹתִיךָ בַּדֶּרֶךְ אֲשֶׁר־
that by-the-way and-I-will-make-return-you in-lips-of-you and-bit-of-me

בָּאתָ בָּהּ׃ (29) וְזֶה־ לְּךָ הָאוֹת אָכוֹל הַשָּׁנָה סָפִיחַ
growth the-year to-eat the-sign for-you and-this (29) on-her you-came

וּבַשָּׁנָה הַשֵּׁנִית סָחִישׁ וּבַשָּׁנָה הַשְּׁלִישִׁית זִרְעוּ
sow! the-third but-in-the-year aftergrowth the-second and-in-the-year

וְקִצְרוּ וְנִטְעוּ כְרָמִים וְאִכְלוּ פִּרְיָם׃ (30) וְיָסְפָה
for-she-will-repeat (30) fruit-of-them and-eat! vineyards and-plant! and-reap!

פְּלֵיטַת בֵּית־ יְהוּדָה הַנִּשְׁאָרָה שֹׁרֶשׁ לְמָטָּה וְעָשָׂה
and-he-will-bear at-below root the-one-remaining Judah house-of remnant-of

פְרִי לְמָעְלָה׃ (31) כִּי מִירוּשָׁלִַם תֵּצֵא שְׁאֵרִית וּפְלֵיטָה
and-survivor remnant she-will-come from-Jerusalem for (31) at-above fruit

מֵהַר צִיּוֹן קִנְאַת יְהוָה * תַּעֲשֶׂה־ זֹּאת׃ (32) לָכֵן
therefore (32) this she-will-accomplish * Yahweh zeal-of Zion from-Mount-of

כֹּה־ אָמַר יְהוָה אֶל־ מֶלֶךְ אַשּׁוּר לֹא יָבֹא אֶל־ הָעִיר
the-city into he-will-enter not Assyria king-of to Yahweh he-says this

הַזֹּאת וְלֹא־ יוֹרֶה שָׁם חֵץ וְלֹא־ יְקַדְּמֶנָּה
he-will-come-before-her and-not arrow here he-will-shoot and-not the-this

מָגֵן וְלֹא־ יִשְׁפֹּךְ עָלֶיהָ סֹלְלָה׃ (33) בַּדֶּרֶךְ אֲשֶׁר־
that by-the-way (33) siege-ramp against-her he-will-build and-not shield

יָבֹא בָּהּ יָשׁוּב וְאֶל־ הָעִיר הַזֹּאת לֹא יָבֹא
he-will-enter not the-this the-city and-into he-will-return on-her he-came

נְאֻם־ יְהוָה׃ (34) וְגַנּוֹתִי אֶל־ הָעִיר הַזֹּאת
the-this the-city to and-I-will-defend (34) Yahweh declaration-of

לְהוֹשִׁיעָהּ לְמַעֲנִי וּלְמַעַן דָּוִד עַבְדִּי׃ (35) וַיְהִי
and-he-was (35) servant-of-me David and-sake-of for-sake-of-me to-save-her

בַּלַּיְלָה הַהוּא וַיֵּצֵא ׀ מַלְאַךְ יְהוָה וַיַּךְ
and-he-killed Yahweh angel-of then-he-went-out the-that on-the-night

בְּמַחֲנֵה אַשּׁוּר מֵאָה שְׁמוֹנִים וַחֲמִשָּׁה אָלֶף וַיַּשְׁכִּימוּ
when-they-got-up thousand and-five eighty hundred Assyria in-camp-of

בַבֹּקֶר וְהִנֵּה כֻלָּם פְּגָרִים מֵתִים׃
ones-being-dead bodies all-of-them then-see! in-the-morning

(36) וַיִּסַּע וַיֵּלֶךְ וַיָּשָׁב סַנְחֵרִיב מֶלֶךְ־
king-of Sennacherib and-he-returned and-he-withdrew so-he-broke-camp (36)

אַשּׁוּר וַיֵּשֶׁב בְּנִינְוֵה׃ (37) וַיְהִי הוּא מִשְׁתַּחֲוֶה בֵּית ׀
temple-of worshiping he and-he-was (37) in-Nineveh and-he-stayed Assyria

and how you rage
against me.
28Because you rage against
me
and your insolence has
reached my ears,
I will put my hook in your
nose
and my bit in your
mouth,
and I will make you return
by the way you came.'

29"This will be the sign for
you, O Hezekiah:

This year you will eat what
grows by itself,
and the second year
what springs from
that.
But in the third year sow
and reap,
plant vineyards and eat
their fruit.
30Once more a remnant of
the house of Judah
will take root below and
bear fruit above.
31For out of Jerusalem will
come a remnant,
and out of Mount Zion a
band of survivors.

The zeal of the LORD Almighty
will accomplish this.

32"Therefore this is what the
LORD says concerning the king
of Assyria:

"He will not enter this city
or shoot an arrow here.
He will not come before it
with shield
or build a siege ramp
against it.
33By the way that he came
he will return;
he will not enter this
city,
declares the LORD.
34I will defend this city and
save it,
for my sake and for the
sake of David my
servant."

35That night the angel of the
LORD went out and put to
death a hundred and eighty-
five thousand men in the Assyrian camp. When the people
got up the next morning—
there were all the dead bodies!
36So Sennacherib king of Assyria broke camp and withdrew. He returned to Nineveh
and stayed there.
37One day, while he was
worshiping in the temple of

***31 Many mss have the *Qere* (צבאות), *Hosts*, from the parallel passage in Isaiah 37:32.**

נִסְרֹךְ אֱלֹהָיו וְאַדְרַמֶּלֶךְ וְשַׂרְאֶצֶר ˚ ˚ * הִכֻּהוּ
they-cut-down-him * and-Sharezer and-Adrammelech gods-of-him Nisroch

בַחֶרֶב וְהֵמָּה נִמְלְטוּ אֶרֶץ אֲרָרָט וַיִּמְלֹךְ
and-he-became-king Ararat land-of they-escaped and-they with-the-sword

אֵסַר־ חַדֹּן בְּנוֹ תַּחְתָּיו׃ בַּיָּמִים הָהֵם
the-those in-the-days (20:1) in-place-of-him son-of-him Haddon Esar

חָלָה חִזְקִיָּהוּ לָמוּת וַיָּבֹא אֵלָיו יְשַׁעְיָהוּ בֶן־ אָמוֹץ
Amoz son-of Isaiah to-him and-he-went to-die Hezekiah he-became-ill

הַנָּבִיא וַיֹּאמֶר אֵלָיו כֹּה־ אָמַר יְהוָה צַו
put-in-order! Yahweh he-says this to-him and-he-said the-prophet

לְבֵיתֶךָ כִּי מֵת אַתָּה וְלֹא תִחְיֶה׃ וַיַּסֵּב
and-he-turned (2) you-will-recover and-not you dying for to-house-of-you

אֶת־ פָּנָיו אֶל־ הַקִּיר וַיִּתְפַּלֵּל אֶל־ יְהוָה לֵאמֹר׃ אָנָּה יְהוָה
Yahweh O! (3) to-say Yahweh to and-he-prayed the-wall to faces-of-him ***

זְכָר־ נָא אֵת אֲשֶׁר הִתְהַלַּכְתִּי לְפָנֶיךָ בֶּאֱמֶת וּבְלֵבָב שָׁלֵם
whole and-with-heart in-faith before-you I-walked how *** now! remember!

וְהַטּוֹב בְּעֵינֶיךָ עָשִׂיתִי וַיֵּבְךְּ חִזְקִיָּהוּ בְּכִי גָדוֹל׃
bitter weeping Hezekiah and-he-wept I-did in-eyes-of-you and-the-good

וַיְהִי יְשַׁעְיָהוּ לֹא יָצָא הָעִיר הַתִּיכֹנָה וּדְבַר־ יְהוָה
Yahweh and-word-of the-middle court he-left not Isaiah and-he-was (4)

הָיָה אֵלָיו לֵאמֹר׃ שׁוּב וְאָמַרְתָּ אֶל־ חִזְקִיָּהוּ נְגִיד־
leader-of Hezekiah to and-you-tell go-back! (5) to-say to-him he-came

עַמִּי כֹּה־ אָמַר יְהוָה אֱלֹהֵי דָּוִד אָבִיךָ שָׁמַעְתִּי אֶת־
*** I-heard father-of-you David God-of Yahweh he-says this people-of-me

תְּפִלָּתֶךָ רָאִיתִי אֶת־ דִּמְעָתֶךָ הִנְנִי רֹפֶא לָךְ בַּיּוֹם
on-the-day to-you healing see-I! tear-of-you *** I-saw prayer-of-you

הַשְּׁלִישִׁי תַּעֲלֶה בֵּית יְהוָה׃ וְהֹסַפְתִּי עַל־ יָמֶיךָ
days-of-you to and-I-will-add (6) Yahweh temple-of you-will-go-up the-third

חֲמֵשׁ עֶשְׂרֵה שָׁנָה וּמִכַּף מֶלֶךְ־ אַשּׁוּר אַצִּילְךָ וְאֵת
and I-will-deliver-you Assyria king-of and-from-hand-of year ten five-of

הָעִיר הַזֹּאת וְגַנּוֹתִי עַל־ הָעִיר הַזֹּאת לְמַעֲנִי
for-sake-of-me the-this the-city to and-I-will-defend the-this the-city

וּלְמַעַן דָּוִד עַבְדִּי׃ וַיֹּאמֶר יְשַׁעְיָהוּ קְחוּ
prepare! Isaiah then-he-said (7) servant-of-me David and-for-sake-of

דְּבֶלֶת תְּאֵנִים וַיִּקְחוּ וַיָּשִׂימוּ עַל־ הַשְּׁחִין
the-boil to and-they-applied so-they-prepared figs poultice-of

וַיֶּחִי׃ וַיֹּאמֶר חִזְקִיָּהוּ אֶל־ יְשַׁעְיָהוּ מָה אוֹת כִּי־
that sign what? Isaiah to Hezekiah now-he-asked (8) and-he-recovered

his god Nisroch, his sons
Adrammelech and Sharezer
cut him down with the sword,
and they escaped to the land
of Ararat. And Esarhaddon his
son succeeded him as king.

Hezekiah's Illness

20 In those days Hezekiah
became ill and was at
the point of death. The
prophet Isaiah son of Amoz
went to him and said, "This is
what the LORD says: Put your
house in order, because you
will die; you will not recover."
2 Hezekiah turned his face to
the wall and prayed to the
LORD, 3 "Remember, O LORD,
how I have walked before you
faithfully and with whole-
hearted devotion and have
done what is good in your
eyes." And Hezekiah wept
bitterly.
4 Before Isaiah had left the
middle court, the word of the
LORD came to him: 5 "Go back
and tell Hezekiah, the leader
of my people, 'This is what the
LORD, the God of your father
David, says: I have heard your
prayer and seen your tears; I
will heal you. On the third day
from now you will go up to the
temple of the LORD. 6 I will add
fifteen years to your life. And
I will deliver you and this city
from the hand of the king of
Assyria. I will defend this city
for my sake and for the sake of
my servant David.' "
7 Then Isaiah said, "Prepare
a poultice of figs." They did so
and applied it to the boil, and
he recovered.
8 Hezekiah had asked Isaiah,
"What will be the sign that the

*37 Many mss have the *Qere* (בָּנָיו), *sons-of-him*, from the parallel passage in Isaiah 37:38.

°4 ק חָצֵר

יִרְפָּא יְהוָה לִי וְעָלִיתִי בַּיּוֹם הַשְּׁלִישִׁי בֵּית
temple-of the-third on-the-day and-I-will-go-up to-me Yahweh he-will-heal

יְהוָה׃ וַיֹּאמֶר יְשַׁעְיָהוּ זֶה־לְּךָ הָאוֹת מֵאֵת יְהוָה כִּי
that Yahweh from the-sign to-you this Isaiah and-he-answered (9) Yahweh

יַעֲשֶׂה יְהוָה אֶת־ הַדָּבָר אֲשֶׁר דִּבֵּר הָלַךְ
shall-he-go-forward he-promised that the-thing *** Yahweh he-will-do

הַצֵּל עֶשֶׂר מַעֲלוֹת אִם־ יָשׁוּב עֶשֶׂר מַעֲלוֹת׃ וַיֹּאמֶר יְחִזְקִיָּהוּ
Hezekiah and-he-said (10) steps ten shall-he-go-back or steps ten the-shadow

נָקֵל לַצֵּל לִנְטוֹת עֶשֶׂר מַעֲלוֹת לֹא כִּי יָשׁוּב
let-him-go-back so not steps ten to-go-forward for-the-shadow he-is-simple

הַצֵּל אֲחֹרַנִּית עֶשֶׂר מַעֲלוֹת׃ וַיִּקְרָא יְשַׁעְיָהוּ הַנָּבִיא אֶל־
upon the-prophet Isaiah then-he-called (11) steps ten backward the-shadow

יְהוָה וַיָּשֶׁב אֶת־ הַצֵּל בַּמַּעֲלוֹת אֲשֶׁר יָרְדָה
she-went-down that on-the-steps the-shadow *** and-he-made-go-back Yahweh

בְּמַעֲלוֹת אָחָז אֲחֹרַנִּית עֶשֶׂר מַעֲלוֹת׃ בָּעֵת הַהִיא שָׁלַח
he-sent the-that at-the-time (12) steps ten backward Ahaz on-steps-of

בְּרֹאדַךְ בַּלְאֲדָן בֶּן־ בַּלְאֲדָן מֶלֶךְ־ בָּבֶל סְפָרִים וּמִנְחָה אֶל־ חִזְקִיָּהוּ
Hezekiah to and-gift letters Babylon king-of Baladan son-of Baladan Merodach

כִּי שָׁמַע כִּי חָלָה חִזְקִיָּהוּ׃ וַיִּשְׁמַע עֲלֵיהֶם
to-them and-he-received (13) Hezekiah he-was-ill that he-heard because

חִזְקִיָּהוּ וַיַּרְאֵם אֶת־ כָּל־ בֵּית נְכֹתֹה אֶת־ הַכֶּסֶף
the-silver *** store-of-him house-of all-of *** and-he-showed-them Hezekiah

וְאֶת־ הַזָּהָב וְאֶת־ הַבְּשָׂמִים וְאֵת ׀ שֶׁמֶן הַטּוֹב וְאֵת בֵּית כֵּלָיו
arms-of-him house-of and the-fine oil-of and the-spices and the-gold and

וְאֵת כָּל־אֲשֶׁר נִמְצָא בְּאוֹצְרֹתָיו לֹא־ הָיָה דָבָר אֲשֶׁר לֹא־
not that thing he-was not among-treasures-of-him he-was-found that all and

הֶרְאָם חִזְקִיָּהוּ בְּבֵיתוֹ וּבְכָל־ מֶמְשַׁלְתּוֹ׃
kingdom-of-him or-in-all-of in-palace-of-him Hezekiah he-showed-them

וַיָּבֹא יְשַׁעְיָהוּ הַנָּבִיא אֶל־ הַמֶּלֶךְ חִזְקִיָּהוּ וַיֹּאמֶר
and-he-asked Hezekiah the-king to the-prophet Isaiah then-he-went (14)

אֵלָיו מָה אָמְרוּ ׀ הָאֲנָשִׁים הָאֵלֶּה וּמֵאַיִן יָבֹאוּ אֵלֶיךָ
to-you they-came and-from-where? the-those the-men they-said what? to-him

וַיֹּאמֶר חִזְקִיָּהוּ מֵאֶרֶץ רְחוֹקָה בָּאוּ מִבָּבֶל׃
from-Babylon they-came distant from-land Hezekiah and-he-replied

וַיֹּאמֶר מָה רָאוּ בְּבֵיתֶךָ וַיֹּאמֶר חִזְקִיָּהוּ אֵת
*** Hezekiah and-he-said in-palace-of-you they-saw what? and-he-said (15)

כָּל־אֲשֶׁר בְּבֵיתִי רָאוּ לֹא־ הָיָה דָבָר אֲשֶׁר לֹא־ הִרְאִיתִם
I-showed-them not that thing he-was not they-saw in-palace-of-me that all

LORD will heal me and that I will go up to the temple of the LORD on the third day from now?"

[9]Isaiah answered, "This is the LORD's sign to you that the LORD will do what he has promised: Shall the shadow go forward ten steps, or shall it go back ten steps?"

[10]"It is a simple matter for the shadow to go forward ten steps," said Hezekiah. "Rather, have it go back ten steps."

[11]Then the prophet Isaiah called upon the LORD, and the LORD made the shadow go back the ten steps it had gone down on the stairway of Ahaz.

Envoys From Babylon

[12]At that time Merodach-Baladan son of Baladan king of Babylon sent Hezekiah letters and a gift, because he had heard of Hezekiah's illness. [13]Hezekiah received the messengers and showed them all that was in his storehouses—the silver, the gold, the spices and the fine oil—his armory and everything found among his treasures. There was nothing in his palace or in all his kingdom that Hezekiah did not show them.

[14]Then Isaiah the prophet went to King Hezekiah and asked, "What did those men say, and where did they come from?"

"From a distant land," Hezekiah replied. "They came from Babylon."

[15]The prophet asked, "What did they see in your palace?"

"They saw everything in my palace," Hezekiah said. "There is nothing among my treasures that I did not show them."

13° ק נכתו

בְּאֹצְרֹתָי׃ וַיֹּאמֶר יְשַׁעְיָהוּ אֶל־חִזְקִיָּהוּ שְׁמַע דְּבַר־
word-of hear! Hezekiah to Isaiah then-he-said (16) among-treasures-of-me

יְהוָה׃ הִנֵּה יָמִים בָּאִים וְנִשָּׂא ׀ כָּל־אֲשֶׁר
that all and-he-will-be-carried-off ones-coming days see! (17) Yahweh

בְּבֵיתֶךָ וַאֲשֶׁר אָצְרוּ אֲבֹתֶיךָ עַד־הַיּוֹם הַזֶּה
the-this the-day until fathers-of-you they-stored and-that in-palace-of-you

בָּבֶלָה לֹא־יִוָּתֵר דָּבָר אָמַר יְהוָה׃ וּמִבָּנֶיךָ
and-from-sons-of-you (18) Yahweh he-says thing he-will-be-left not to-Babylon

אֲשֶׁר יֵצְאוּ מִמְּךָ אֲשֶׁר תּוֹלִיד יִקָּח°
they-will-be-taken-away you-will-father that from-you they-will-come who

וְהָיוּ סָרִיסִים בְּהֵיכַל מֶלֶךְ בָּבֶל׃ וַיֹּאמֶר
and-he-replied (19) Babylon king-of in-palace-of eunuchs and-they-will-become

חִזְקִיָּהוּ אֶל־יְשַׁעְיָהוּ טוֹב דְּבַר־יְהוָה אֲשֶׁר דִּבַּרְתָּ וַיֹּאמֶר הֲלוֹא
not? for-he-thought you-spoke that Yahweh word-of good Isaiah to Hezekiah

אִם־שָׁלוֹם וֶאֱמֶת יִהְיֶה בְיָמָי׃ וְיֶתֶר דִּבְרֵי
events-of and-rest-of (20) in-days-of-me he-will-be and-security peace indeed

חִזְקִיָּהוּ וְכָל־גְּבוּרָתוֹ וַאֲשֶׁר עָשָׂה אֶת־הַבְּרֵכָה וְאֶת־
and the-pool *** he-made and-how achievement-of-him and-all-of Hezekiah

הַתְּעָלָה וַיָּבֵא אֶת־הַמַּיִם הָעִירָה הֲלֹא־הֵם
they not? into-the-city the-waters *** and-he-brought the-tunnel

כְּתוּבִים עַל־סֵפֶר דִּבְרֵי הַיָּמִים לְמַלְכֵי יְהוּדָה׃
Judah of-kings-of the-days annals-of book-of in ones-being-written

וַיִּשְׁכַּב חִזְקִיָּהוּ עִם־אֲבֹתָיו וַיִּמְלֹךְ מְנַשֶּׁה
Manasseh and-became-king fathers-of-him with Hezekiah and-he-rested (21)

בְּנוֹ תַּחְתָּיו׃ בֶּן־שְׁתֵּים עֶשְׂרֵה שָׁנָה מְנַשֶּׁה
Manasseh year ten two son-of (21:1) in-place-of-him son-of-him

בְמָלְכוֹ וַחֲמִשִּׁים וְחָמֵשׁ שָׁנָה מָלַךְ בִּירוּשָׁלָם
in-Jerusalem he-reigned year and-five and-fifty when-to-become-king-him

וְשֵׁם אִמּוֹ חֶפְצִי־בָהּ׃ וַיַּעַשׂ הָרַע בְּעֵינֵי
in-eyes-of the-evil and-he-did (2) Bah Hephzi mother-of-him and-name-of

יְהוָה כְּתוֹעֲבֹת הַגּוֹיִם אֲשֶׁר הוֹרִישׁ יְהוָה
Yahweh he-drove-out that the-nations as-detestable-practices-of Yahweh

מִפְּנֵי בְּנֵי יִשְׂרָאֵל׃ וַיָּשָׁב וַיִּבֶן אֶת־
*** and-he-rebuilt and-he-returned (3) Israel sons-of from-before

הַבָּמוֹת אֲשֶׁר אִבַּד חִזְקִיָּהוּ אָבִיו וַיָּקֶם
and-he-erected father-of-him Hezekiah he-destroyed that the-high-places

מִזְבְּחֹת לַבַּעַל וַיַּעַשׂ אֲשֵׁרָה כַּאֲשֶׁר עָשָׂה אַחְאָב מֶלֶךְ
king-of Ahab he-did just-as Asherah-pole and-he-made to-the-Baal altars

[16]Then Isaiah said to Hezekiah, "Hear the word of the
LORD: [17]The time will surely
come when everything in
your palace, and all that your
fathers have stored up until
this day, will be carried off to
Babylon. Nothing will be left,
says the LORD. [18]And some of
your descendants, your own
flesh and blood, that will be
born to you, will be taken
away, and they will become
eunuchs in the palace of the
king of Babylon."
[19]"The word of the LORD you
have spoken is good," Hezekiah replied. For he thought,
"Will there not be peace and
security in my lifetime?"
[20]As for the other events of
Hezekiah's reign, all his
achievements and how he
made the pool and the tunnel
by which he brought water
into the city, are they not written in the book of the annals
of the kings of Judah? [21]Heze-
kiah rested with his fathers.
And Manasseh his son suc-
ceeded him as king.

Manasseh King of Judah

21 Manasseh was twelve
years old when he
became king, and he reigned
in Jerusalem fifty-five years.
His mother's name was Heph-
zibah. [2]He did evil in the eyes
of the LORD, following the detestable practices of the nations the LORD had driven out
before the Israelites. [3]He rebuilt the high places his father
Hezekiah had destroyed; he
also erected altars to Baal and
made an Asherah pole, as

°18 ק יקחו

יִשְׂרָאֵל וַיִּשְׁתַּחוּ לְכָל־ צְבָא הַשָּׁמַיִם וַיַּעֲבֹד אֹתָם׃
them and-he-worshiped the-heavens host-of to-all-of and-he-bowed Israel

וּבָנָה מִזְבְּחֹת בְּבֵית יְהוָה אֲשֶׁר אָמַר יְהוָה בִּירוּשָׁלִַם
in-Jerusalem Yahweh he-said which Yahweh in-temple-of altars and-he-built (4)

אָשִׂים אֶת־ שְׁמִי׃ וַיִּבֶן מִזְבְּחוֹת לְכָל־ צְבָא
host-of to-all-of altars and-he-built (5) Name-of-me *** I-will-put

הַשָּׁמַיִם בִּשְׁתֵּי חַצְרוֹת בֵּית־ יְהוָה׃ וְהֶעֱבִיר אֶת־
*** and-he-made-pass (6) Yahweh temple-of courts-of in-both-of the-heavens

בְּנוֹ בָּאֵשׁ וְעוֹנֵן וְנִחֵשׁ
and-he-practiced-divination and-he-practiced-sorcery through-the-fire son-of-him

וְעָשָׂה אוֹב וְיִדְּעֹנִים הִרְבָּה לַעֲשׂוֹת הָרַע בְּעֵינֵי
in-eyes-of the-evil to-do he-did-much and-spiritists medium and-he-consulted

יְהוָה לְהַכְעִיס׃ וַיָּשֶׂם אֶת־ פֶּסֶל הָאֲשֵׁרָה
the-Asherah carved-pole-of *** and-he-put (7) to-provoke-to-anger Yahweh

אֲשֶׁר עָשָׂה בַּבַּיִת אֲשֶׁר אָמַר יְהוָה אֶל־ דָּוִד וְאֶל־ שְׁלֹמֹה
Solomon and-to David to Yahweh he-said which in-the-temple he-made that

בְנוֹ בַּבַּיִת הַזֶּה וּבִירוּשָׁלִַם אֲשֶׁר בָּחַרְתִּי מִכֹּל
from-all-of I-chose which and-in-Jerusalem the-this in-the-temple son-of-him

שִׁבְטֵי יִשְׂרָאֵל אָשִׂים אֶת־ שְׁמִי לְעוֹלָם׃ וְלֹא
and-not (8) to-forever Name-of-me *** I-will-put Israel tribes-of

אֹסִיף לְהָנִיד רֶגֶל יִשְׂרָאֵל מִן־ הָאֲדָמָה אֲשֶׁר נָתַתִּי
I-gave that the-land from Israel foot-of to-make-wander I-will-repeat

לַאֲבוֹתָם רַק ׀ אִם־ יִשְׁמְרוּ לַעֲשׂוֹת כְּכֹל אֲשֶׁר צִוִּיתִים
I-commanded-them that as-all to-do they-are-careful if only to-fathers-of-them

וּלְכָל־ הַתּוֹרָה אֲשֶׁר־ צִוָּה אֹתָם עַבְדִּי מֹשֶׁה׃ וְלֹא
but-not (9) Moses servant-of-me them he-gave that the-Law and-to-whole-of

שָׁמֵעוּ וַיַּתְעֵם מְנַשֶּׁה לַעֲשׂוֹת אֶת־ הָרָע מִן־
more-than the-evil *** to-do Manasseh and-he-led-astray-them they-listened

הַגּוֹיִם אֲשֶׁר הִשְׁמִיד יְהוָה מִפְּנֵי בְּנֵי יִשְׂרָאֵל׃
Israel sons-of from-before Yahweh he-destroyed that the-nations

וַיְדַבֵּר יְהוָה בְּיַד־ עֲבָדָיו הַנְּבִיאִים לֵאמֹר׃
to-say the-prophets servants-of-him by-hand-of Yahweh and-he-spoke (10)

יַעַן אֲשֶׁר עָשָׂה מְנַשֶּׁה מֶלֶךְ־ יְהוּדָה הַתֹּעֵבוֹת
the-detestable-sins Judah king-of Manasseh he-did that because (11)

הָאֵלֶּה הֵרַע מִכֹּל אֲשֶׁר־ עָשׂוּ הָאֱמֹרִי אֲשֶׁר לְפָנָיו
before-him who the-Amorite they-did that more-than-all he-did-evil the-these

וַיַּחֲטִא גַם־ אֶת־ יְהוּדָה בְּגִלּוּלָיו׃ לָכֵן כֹּה־
this therefore (12) with-idols-of-him Judah *** also and-he-led-to-sin

Ahab king of Israel had done.
He bowed down to all the starry hosts and worshiped them.
4He built altars in the temple
of the LORD, of which the LORD
had said, "In Jerusalem I will
put my Name." 5In both courts
of the temple of the LORD, he
built altars to all the starry
hosts. 6He sacrificed his own
son in[h] the fire, practiced sorcery and divination, and consulted mediums and spiritists.
He did much evil in the eyes
of the LORD, provoking him to
anger.
7He took the carved Asherah
pole he had made and put it in
the temple, of which the LORD
had said to David and to his
son Solomon, "In this temple
and in Jerusalem, which I
have chosen out of all the
tribes of Israel, I will put my
Name forever. 8I will not again
make the feet of the Israelites
wander from the land I gave
their forefathers, if only they
will be careful to do everything I commanded them and
will keep the whole Law that
my servant Moses gave
them." 9But the people did not
listen. Manasseh led them
astray, so that they did more
evil than the nations the LORD
had destroyed before the Israelites.
10The LORD said through his
servants the prophets:
11"Manasseh king of Judah
has committed these detestable sins. He has done more
evil than the Amorites who
preceded him and has led
Judah into sin with his idols.
12Therefore this is what the

[h]6 Or *He made his own son pass through*

אָמַר יְהוָה אֱלֹהֵי יִשְׂרָאֵל הִנְנִי מֵבִיא רָעָה עַל־יְרוּשָׁלִַם וִיהוּדָה
and-Judah Jersualem on disaster bringing see-I! Israel God-of Yahweh he-says

אֲשֶׁר כָּל־ שֹׁמְעָיו° תִּצַּלְנָה שְׁתֵּי אָזְנָיו׃
ears-of-him both-of they-will-tingle one-hearing-her every-of that

(13) וְנָטִיתִי עַל־ יְרוּשָׁלִַם אֵת קָו שֹׁמְרוֹן וְאֶת־
and Samaria measuring-line-of *** Jerusalem over and-I-will-stretch (13)

מִשְׁקֹלֶת בֵּית אַחְאָב וּמָחִיתִי אֶת־ יְרוּשָׁלִַם כַּאֲשֶׁר־
just-as Jerusalem *** and-I-will-wipe-out Ahab house-of plumb-line-of

יִמְחֶה אֶת־ הַצַּלַּחַת מָחָה וְהָפַךְ עַל־ פָּנֶיהָ׃
faces-of-her on and-he-overturns he-wipes the-dish *** he-wipes

(14) וְנָטַשְׁתִּי אֵת שְׁאֵרִית נַחֲלָתִי וּנְתַתִּים
and-I-will-give-them inheritance-of-me remnant-of *** and-I-will-forsake (14)

בְּיַד אֹיְבֵיהֶם וְהָיוּ לְבַז
for-loot and-they-will-be ones-being-enemies-of-them into-hand-of

וְלִמְשִׁסָּה לְכָל־ אֹיְבֵיהֶם׃ (15) יַעַן אֲשֶׁר עָשׂוּ
they-did that because (15) ones-being-foes-of-them by-all-of and-for-plunder

אֶת־ הָרַע בְּעֵינַי וַיִּהְיוּ מַכְעִסִים אֹתִי מִן־ הַיּוֹם
the-day from me ones-making-angry and-they-were in-eyes-of-me the-evil ***

אֲשֶׁר יָצְאוּ אֲבוֹתָם מִמִּצְרַיִם וְעַד הַיּוֹם הַזֶּה׃
the-this the-day even-to from-Egypt fathers-of-them they-came-out that

(16) וְגַם דָּם נָקִי שָׁפַךְ מְנַשֶּׁה הַרְבֵּה מְאֹד עַד אֲשֶׁר־
when until very to-be-much Manasseh he-shed innocent blood and-also (16)

מִלֵּא אֶת־ יְרוּשָׁלִַם פֶּה לָפֶה לְבַד מֵחַטָּאתוֹ אֲשֶׁר הֶחֱטִיא
he-made-sin that from-sin-of-him apart to-end end Jerusalem *** he-filled

אֶת־יְהוּדָה לַעֲשׂוֹת הָרַע בְּעֵינֵי יְהוָה׃ (17) וְיֶתֶר דִּבְרֵי
events-of and-rest-of (17) Yahweh in-eyes-of the-evil to-do Judah ***

מְנַשֶּׁה וְכָל־ אֲשֶׁר עָשָׂה וְחַטָּאתוֹ אֲשֶׁר חָטָא הֲלֹא־ הֵם
they not? he-did that and-sin-of-him he-did that and-all Manasseh

כְּתוּבִים עַל־ סֵפֶר דִּבְרֵי הַיָּמִים לְמַלְכֵי יְהוּדָה׃
Judah of-kings-of the-days annals-of book-of in ones-being-written

(18) וַיִּשְׁכַּב מְנַשֶּׁה עִם־ אֲבֹתָיו וַיִּקָּבֵר בְּגַן־
in-garden-of and-he-was-buried fathers-of-him with Manasseh and-he-rested (18)

בֵּיתוֹ בְּגַן־ עֻזָּא וַיִּמְלֹךְ אָמוֹן בְּנוֹ
son-of-him Amon and-he-became-king Uzza in-garden-of palace-of-him

תַּחְתָּיו׃ (19) בֶּן־ עֶשְׂרִים וּשְׁתַּיִם שָׁנָה אָמוֹן בְּמָלְכוֹ
when-to-become-king-him Amon year and-two twenty son-of (19) in-place-of-him

וּשְׁתַּיִם שָׁנִים מָלַךְ בִּירוּשָׁלִָם וְשֵׁם אִמּוֹ מְשֻׁלֶּמֶת
Meshullemeth mother-of-him and-name-of in-Jerusalem he-reigned years and-two

°12 ק שמעה

LORD, the God of Israel, says: I
am going to bring such disaster on Jerusalem and Judah
that the ears of everyone who
hears of it will tingle.
13I will
stretch out over Jerusalem the
measuring line used against
Samaria and the plumb line
used against the house of
Ahab. I will wipe out Jerusalem as one wipes a dish, wip-
ing it and turning it upside
down.
14I will forsake the rem-
nant of my inheritance and
hand them over to their enemies. They will be looted and
plundered by all their foes,
15because they have done evil
in my eyes and have provoked
me to anger from the day their
forefathers came out of Egypt
until this day."
16Moreover, Manasseh also
shed so much innocent blood
that he filled Jerusalem from
end to end—besides the sin
that he had caused Judah to
commit, so that they did evil
in the eyes of the LORD.
17As for the other events of
Manasseh's reign, and all he
did, including the sin he committed, are they not written in
the book of the annals of the
kings of Judah?
18Manasseh
rested with his fathers and
was buried in his palace garden, the garden of Uzza. And
Amon his son succeeded him
as king.

Amon King of Judah

19Amon was twenty-two
years old when he became
king, and he reigned in
Jerusalem two years. His
mother's name was Meshul-
lemeth daughter of Haruz; she

בַּת־ חָרוּץ מִן־ יָטְבָה׃ וַיַּעַשׂ הָרַע בְּעֵינֵי יְהוָה
Yahweh in-eyes-of the-evil and-he-did (20) Jotbah from Haruz daughter-of

כַּאֲשֶׁר עָשָׂה מְנַשֶּׁה אָבִיו׃ וַיֵּלֶךְ בְּכָל־ הַדֶּרֶךְ
the-way in-all-of and-he-walked (21) father-of-him Manasseh he-did just-as

אֲשֶׁר־ הָלַךְ אָבִיו וַיַּעֲבֹד אֶת־ הַגִּלֻּלִים אֲשֶׁר עָבַד
he-worshiped that the-idols *** and-he-worshiped father-of-him he-walked that

אָבִיו וַיִּשְׁתַּחוּ לָהֶם׃ וַיַּעֲזֹב אֶת־ יְהוָה אֱלֹהֵי
God-of Yahweh *** and-he-forsook (22) to-them and-he-bowed father-of-him

אֲבֹתָיו וְלֹא הָלַךְ בְּדֶרֶךְ יְהוָה׃ וַיִּקְשְׁרוּ
and-he-conspired (23) Yahweh in-way-of he-walked and-not fathers-of-him

עַבְדֵי־ אָמוֹן עָלָיו וַיָּמִיתוּ אֶת־ הַמֶּלֶךְ
the-king *** and-they-assassinated against-him Amon officials-of

בְּבֵיתוֹ׃ וַיַּךְ עַם־ הָאָרֶץ אֵת כָּל־
all-of *** the-land people-of and-he-killed (24) in-palace-of-him

הַקֹּשְׁרִים עַל־ הַמֶּלֶךְ אָמוֹן וַיַּמְלִיכוּ עַם־
people-of and-they-make-king Amon the-king against the-ones-conspiring

הָאָרֶץ אֶת־ יֹאשִׁיָּהוּ בְנוֹ תַּחְתָּיו׃ וְיֶתֶר דִּבְרֵי
events-of and-rest-of (25) in-place-of-him son-of-him Josiah *** the-land

אָמוֹן אֲשֶׁר עָשָׂה הֲלֹא־ הֵם כְּתוּבִים עַל־ סֵפֶר דִּבְרֵי הַיָּמִים
the-days annals-of book-of in ones-being-written they not? he-did what Amon

לְמַלְכֵי יְהוּדָה׃ וַיִּקְבֹּר* אֹתוֹ בִּקְבֻרָתוֹ בְּגַן־ עֻזָּא
Uzza in-garden-of in-grave-of-him him and-he-buried (26) Judah of-kings-of

וַיִּמְלֹךְ יֹאשִׁיָּהוּ בְנוֹ תַּחְתָּיו׃ בֶּן־ שְׁמֹנֶה
eight son-of (22:1) in-place-of-him son-of-him Josiah and-he-became-king

שָׁנָה יֹאשִׁיָּהוּ בְמָלְכוֹ וּשְׁלֹשִׁים וְאַחַת שָׁנָה מָלַךְ
he-reigned year and-one and-thirty when-to-become-king-him Josiah year

בִּירוּשָׁלִָם וְשֵׁם אִמּוֹ יְדִידָה בַת־ עֲדָיָה† מִבָּצְקַת׃
from-Bozkath Adaiah daughter-of Jedidah mother-of-him and-name-of in-Jerusalem

וַיַּעַשׂ הַיָּשָׁר בְּעֵינֵי יְהוָה וַיֵּלֶךְ בְּכָל־ דֶּרֶךְ
way-of in-all-of and-he-walked Yahweh in-eyes-of the-right and-he-did (2)

דָּוִד אָבִיו וְלֹא־ סָר יָמִין וּשְׂמֹאול׃ וַיְהִי בִּשְׁמֹנֶה
in-eight and-he-was (3) or-left right he-turned and-not father-of-him David

עֶשְׂרֵה שָׁנָה לַמֶּלֶךְ יֹאשִׁיָּהוּ שָׁלַח הַמֶּלֶךְ אֶת־ שָׁפָן בֶּן־ אֲצַלְיָהוּ
Azaliah son-of Shaphan *** the-king he-sent Josiah of-the-king year ten

בֶּן־ מְשֻׁלָּם הַסֹּפֵר בֵּית יְהוָה לֵאמֹר׃ עֲלֵה אֶל־ חִלְקִיָּהוּ
Hilkiah to go-up! (4) to-say Yahweh temple-of the-secretary Meshullam son-of

הַכֹּהֵן הַגָּדוֹל וְיַתֵּם אֶת־ הַכֶּסֶף הַמּוּבָא
the-being-brought the-money *** and-let-him-get-ready the-high the-priest

was from Jotbah. [20]He did evil
in the eyes of the LORD, as his
father Manasseh had done.
[21]He walked in all the ways of
his father; he worshiped the
idols his father had wor-
shiped, and bowed down to
them. [22]He forsook the LORD,
the God of his fathers, and did
not walk in the way of the
LORD.

[23]Amon's officials conspired
against him and assassinated
the king in his palace. [24]Then
the people of the land killed all
who had plotted against King
Amon, and they made Josiah
his son king in his place.

[25]As for the other events of
Amon's reign, and what he
did, are they not written in the
book of the annals of the kings
of Judah? [26]He was buried in
his grave in the garden of
Uzza. And Josiah his son succeeded him as king.

The Book of the Law Found

22 Josiah was eight years
old when he became
king, and he reigned in
Jerusalem thirty-one years.
His mother's name was Jedidah daughter of Adaiah; she
was from Bozkath. [2]He did
what was right in the eyes of
the LORD and walked in all the
ways of his father David, not
turning aside to the right or to
the left.

[3]In the eighteenth year of
his reign, King Josiah sent the
secretary, Shaphan son of
Azaliah, the son of Meshullam, to the temple of the LORD.
He said: [4]"Go up to Hilkiah
the high priest and have him
get ready the money that has

*26 Some mss have no *sheva* under the *beth* (בֹּר־); others have no *holem* and end with *shureq* (־רוּ), *and-they-buried.*

†1 Most mss have the accent on the final syllable (עֲדָיָה).

בֵּית יְהוָה אֲשֶׁר אָסְפוּ שֹׁמְרֵי הַסַּף מֵאֵת הָעָם׃

the-people from the-door ones-keeping-of they-collected which Yahweh temple-of

וְיִתְּנָה עַל־ יַד עֹשֵׂי הַמְּלָאכָה

the-work ones-supervising-of hand-of into and-let-them-entrust-him (5)

הַמֻּפְקָדִים בבֵּית יְהוָה וְיִתְּנוּ אֹתוֹ

him and-let-them-pay Yahweh temple-of the-ones-being-appointed

לְעֹשֵׂי הַמְּלָאכָה אֲשֶׁר בְּבֵית יְהוָה לְחַזֵּק בֶּדֶק

damage-of to-repair Yahweh on-temple-of that the-work to-ones-doing-of

הַבָּיִת׃ לֶחָרָשִׁים וְלַבֹּנִים

and-to-the-ones-building to-the-carpenters (6) the-temple

וְלַגֹּדְרִים וְלִקְנוֹת עֵצִים וְאַבְנֵי מַחְצֵב

dressed and-stones-of timbers and-to-purchase and-to-the-ones-being-masons

לְחַזֵּק אֶת־ הַבָּיִת׃ אַךְ לֹא־ יֵחָשֵׁב אִתָּם הַכֶּסֶף

the-money with-them he-must-be-accounted not but (7) the-temple *** to-repair

הַנִּתָּן עַל־ יָדָם כִּי בֶאֱמוּנָה הֵם עֹשִׂים׃

ones-acting they in-faith because hand-of-them into the-one-being-entrusted

וַיֹּאמֶר חִלְקִיָּהוּ הַכֹּהֵן הַגָּדוֹל עַל־ שָׁפָן הַסֹּפֵר סֵפֶר

Book-of the-secretary Shaphan to the-high the-priest Hilkiah and-he-said (8)

הַתּוֹרָה מָצָאתִי בְּבֵית יְהוָה וַיִּתֵּן חִלְקִיָּה אֶת־ הַסֵּפֶר אֶל־

to the-book *** Hilkiah and-he-gave Yahweh in-temple-of I-found the-Law

שָׁפָן וַיִּקְרָאֵהוּ׃ וַיָּבֹא שָׁפָן הַסֹּפֵר אֶל־ הַמֶּלֶךְ

the-king to the-secretary Shaphan then-he-went (9) and-he-read-him Shaphan

וַיָּשֶׁב אֶת־ הַמֶּלֶךְ דָּבָר וַיֹּאמֶר הִתִּיכוּ עֲבָדֶיךָ

officials-of-you they-paid-out and-he-said report the-king *** and-he-gave

אֶת־ הַכֶּסֶף הַנִּמְצָא בַבַּיִת וַיִּתְּנֻהוּ עַל־

into and-they-entrusted-him in-the-temple the-one-being-found the-money ***

יַד עֹשֵׂי הַמְּלָאכָה הַמֻּפְקָדִים בֵּית יְהוָה׃

Yahweh temple-of the-ones-supervising the-work ones-doing-of hand-of

וַיַּגֵּד שָׁפָן הַסֹּפֵר לַמֶּלֶךְ לֵאמֹר סֵפֶר נָתַן

he-gave book to-say to-the-king the-secretary Shaphan then-he-informed (10)

לִי חִלְקִיָּה הַכֹּהֵן וַיִּקְרָאֵהוּ שָׁפָן לִפְנֵי הַמֶּלֶךְ׃

the-king in-presences-of Shaphan and-he-read-him the-priest Hilkiah to-me

וַיְהִי כִּשְׁמֹעַ הַמֶּלֶךְ אֶת־ דִּבְרֵי סֵפֶר הַתּוֹרָה

the-Law Book-of words-of *** the-king when-to-hear and-he-was (11)

וַיִּקְרַע אֶת־ בְּגָדָיו׃ וַיְצַו הַמֶּלֶךְ אֶת־ חִלְקִיָּה

Hilkiah *** the-king and-he-ordered (12) robes-of-him *** then-he-tore

הַכֹּהֵן וְאֶת־ אֲחִיקָם בֶּן־ שָׁפָן וְאֶת־עַכְבּוֹר בֶּן־ מִיכָיָה וְאֵת ׀ שָׁפָן

Shaphan and Micaiah son-of Acbor and Shaphat son-of Ahikam and the-priest

been brought into the temple
of the LORD, which the doorkeepers have collected from
the people. [5]Have them en-
trust it to the men appointed
to supervise the work on the
temple. And have these men
pay the workers who repair
the temple of the LORD— [6]the
carpenters, the builders and
the masons. Also have them
purchase timber and dressed
stone to repair the temple. [7]But
they need not account for the
money entrusted to them, because they are acting faithfully."
[8]Hilkiah the high priest said
to Shaphan the secretary, "I
have found the Book of the
Law in the temple of the
LORD." He gave it to Shaphan,
who read it. [9]Then Shaphan
the secretary went to the king
and reported to him: "Your
officials have paid out the
money that was in the temple
of the LORD and have entrusted it to the workers and super-
visors at the temple." [10]Then
Shaphan the secretary in-
formed the king, "Hilkiah the
priest has given me a book."
And Shaphan read from it in
the presence of the king.
[11]When the king heard the
words of the Book of the Law,
he tore his robes. [12]He gave
these orders to Hilkiah the
priest, Ahikam son of Shaphan, Acbor son of Micaiah,

°5a ק ויתנהו

°5b ק בית

הַסֹּפֵר וְאֵת עֲשָׂיָה עֶבֶד־ הַמֶּלֶךְ לֵאמֹר׃ לְכוּ דִרְשׁוּ אֶת־
*** inquire! go! (13) to-say the-king attendant-of Asaiah and the-secretary

יְהוָה בַּעֲדִי וּבְעַד־ הָעָם וּבְעַד כָּל־ יְהוּדָה עַל־ דִּבְרֵי
words-of about Judah all-of and-for the-people and-for for-me Yahweh

הַסֵּפֶר הַנִּמְצָא הַזֶּה כִּי־ גְדוֹלָה חֲמַת יְהוָה אֲשֶׁר־ הִיא
she that Yahweh anger-of great for the-this the-one-being-found the-book

נִצְּתָה בָנוּ עַל אֲשֶׁר לֹא־ שָׁמְעוּ אֲבֹתֵינוּ עַל־ דִּבְרֵי
words-of to fathers-of-us they-obeyed not that because against-us she-burns

הַסֵּפֶר הַזֶּה לַעֲשׂוֹת כְּכָל־ הַכָּתוּב עָלֵינוּ׃
about-us the-thing-being-written as-all-of to-do the-this the-book

וַיֵּלֶךְ חִלְקִיָּהוּ הַכֹּהֵן וַאֲחִיקָם וְעַכְבּוֹר וְשָׁפָן
and-Shaphan and-Acbor and-Ahikam the-priest Hilkiah and-he-went (14)

וַעֲשָׂיָה אֶל־ חֻלְדָּה הַנְּבִיאָה אֵשֶׁת ׀ שַׁלֻּם בֶּן־ תִּקְוָה בֶּן־
son-of Tikvah son-of Shallum wife-of the-prophetess Huldah to and-Asaiah

חַרְחַס שֹׁמֵר הַבְּגָדִים וְהִיא יֹשֶׁבֶת בִּירוּשָׁלִַם
in-Jerusalem living now-she the-clothes one-keeping-of Harhas

בַּמִּשְׁנֶה וַיְדַבְּרוּ אֵלֶיהָ׃ וַתֹּאמֶר אֲלֵיהֶם כֹּה־
this to-them and-she-said (15) to-her and-they-spoke in-the-Second-District

אָמַר יְהוָה אֱלֹהֵי יִשְׂרָאֵל אִמְרוּ לָאִישׁ אֲשֶׁר־ שָׁלַח אֶתְכֶם אֵלָי׃
to-me you he-sent who to-the-man tell! Israel God-of Yahweh he-says

כֹּה אָמַר יְהוָה הִנְנִי מֵבִיא רָעָה אֶל־ הַמָּקוֹם הַזֶּה
the-this the-place on disaster bringing see-I! Yahweh he-says this (16)

וְעַל־ יֹשְׁבָיו אֵת כָּל־ דִּבְרֵי הַסֵּפֶר אֲשֶׁר קָרָא מֶלֶךְ
king-of he-read that the-book words-of all-of *** ones-living-of-him and-on

יְהוּדָה׃ תַּחַת ׀ אֲשֶׁר עֲזָבוּנִי וַיְקַטְּרוּ לֵאלֹהִים
to-gods and-they-burned-incense they-forsook-me that because (17) Judah

אֲחֵרִים לְמַעַן הַכְעִיסֵנִי בְּכֹל מַעֲשֵׂה יְדֵיהֶם
hands-of-them work-of by-all-of to-anger-me in-order-to other-ones

וְנִצְּתָה חֲמָתִי בַּמָּקוֹם הַזֶּה וְלֹא
and-not the-this against-the-place anger-of-me and-she-will-burn

תִכְבֶּה׃ וְאֶל־ מֶלֶךְ יְהוּדָה הַשֹּׁלֵחַ אֶתְכֶם לִדְרֹשׁ
to-inquire you the-one-sending Judah king-of and-to (18) she-will-be-quenched

אֶת־ יְהוָה כֹּה תֹאמְרוּ אֵלָיו כֹּה־ אָמַר יְהוָה אֱלֹהֵי יִשְׂרָאֵל הַדְּבָרִים
the-words Israel God-of Yahweh he-says this to-him you-tell this Yahweh ***

אֲשֶׁר שָׁמָעְתָּ׃ יַעַן רַךְ־ לְבָבְךָ וַתִּכָּנַע ׀
and-you-humbled-self heart-of-you he-was-responsive because (19) you-heard that

מִפְּנֵי יְהוָה בְּשָׁמְעֲךָ אֲשֶׁר דִּבַּרְתִּי עַל־ הַמָּקוֹם הַזֶּה
the-this the-place against I-spoke what when-to-hear-you Yahweh from-before

Shaphan the secretary and
Asaiah the king's attendant:
13"Go and inquire of the LORD
for me and for the people and
for all Judah about what is
written in this book that has
been found. Great is the
LORD's anger that burns
against us because our fathers
have not obeyed the words of
this book; they have not acted
in accordance with all that is
written there concerning us."
14Hilkiah the priest, Ahikam, Acbor, Shaphan and
Asaiah went to speak to the
prophetess Huldah, who was
the wife of Shallum son of Tikvah, the son of Harhas, keeper
of the wardrobe. She lived in
Jerusalem, in the Second District.
15She said to them, "This is
what the LORD, the God of Israel, says: Tell the man who
sent you to me, 16'This is what
the LORD says: I am going to
bring disaster on this place
and its people, according to
everything written in the
book the king of Judah has
read. 17Because they have forsaken me and burned incense
to other gods and provoked
me to anger by all the idols
their hands have made,[i] my
anger will burn against this
place and will not be
quenched.' 18Tell the king of
Judah, who sent you to inquire of the LORD, 'This is
what the LORD, the God of Israel, says concerning the
words you heard: 19Because
your heart was responsive and
you humbled yourself before
the LORD when you heard
what I have spoken against

[i]17 Or *by everything they have done*

וְעַל־ יֹשְׁבָיו לִהְיוֹת לְשַׁמָּה וְלִקְלָלָה וַתִּקְרַע
and-you-tore and-as-curse as-waste to-become ones-living-of-him and-against

אֶת־ בְּגָדֶיךָ וַתִּבְכֶּה לְפָנָי וְגַם אָנֹכִי שָׁמַעְתִּי נְאֻם־
declaration-of I-heard I now-indeed before-me and-you-wept robes-of-you ***

יְהוָה׃ לָכֵן הִנְנִי אֹסִפְךָ עַל־ אֲבֹתֶיךָ
fathers-of-you to I-will-gather-you see-I therefore (20) Yahweh

וְנֶאֱסַפְתָּ אֶל־ קִבְרֹתֶיךָ בְּשָׁלוֹם וְלֹא־ תִרְאֶינָה
they-will-see and-not in-peace tombs-of-you in and-you-will-be-buried

עֵינֶיךָ בְּכֹל הָרָעָה אֲשֶׁר־אֲנִי מֵבִיא עַל־ הַמָּקוֹם הַזֶּה
the-this the-place on bringing I that the-disaster to-all-of eyes-of-you

וַיָּשִׁבוּ אֶת־ הַמֶּלֶךְ דָּבָר׃ וַיִּשְׁלַח הַמֶּלֶךְ
the-king then-he-called (23:1) answer the-king *** so-they-took-back

וַיַּאַסְפוּ אֵלָיו כָּל־ זִקְנֵי יְהוּדָה וִירוּשָׁלִָם׃
and-Jerusalem Judah elders-of all-of to-him and-they-came-together

וַיַּעַל הַמֶּלֶךְ בֵּית־ יְהוָה וְכָל־ אִישׁ יְהוּדָה
Judah man-of and-all-of Yahweh temple-of the-king and-he-went-up (2)

וְכָל־ יֹשְׁבֵי יְרוּשָׁלִַם אִתּוֹ וְהַכֹּהֲנִים וְהַנְּבִיאִים
and-the-prophets and-the-priests with-him Jerusalem ones-living-of and-all-of

וְכָל־ הָעָם לְמִקָּטֹן וְעַד־ גָּדוֹל וַיִּקְרָא
and-he-read greatest even-to to-from-least the-people and-all-of

בְאָזְנֵיהֶם אֶת־ כָּל־ דִּבְרֵי סֵפֶר הַבְּרִית הַנִּמְצָא
the-one-being-found the-Covenant Book-of words-of all-of *** in-ears-of-them

בְּבֵית יְהוָה׃ וַיַּעֲמֹד הַמֶּלֶךְ עַל־ הָעַמּוּד וַיִּכְרֹת
and-he-renewed the-pillar by the-king and-he-stood (3) Yahweh in-temple-of

אֶת־ הַבְּרִית לִפְנֵי יְהוָה לָלֶכֶת אַחַר יְהוָה וְלִשְׁמֹר
and-to-keep Yahweh after to-follow Yahweh in-presences-of the-covenant ***

מִצְוֹתָיו וְאֶת־ עֵדְוֹתָיו וְאֶת־ חֻקֹּתָיו בְּכָל־ לֵב
heart with-all-of decrees-of-him and regulations-of-him and commands-of-him

וּבְכָל־ נֶפֶשׁ לְהָקִים אֶת־ דִּבְרֵי הַבְּרִית הַזֹּאת
the-this the-covenant words-of *** to-confirm soul and-with-all-of

הַכְּתֻבִים עַל־ הַסֵּפֶר הַזֶּה וַיַּעֲמֹד כָּל־ הָעָם
the-people all-of then-he-pledged the-this the-book in the-ones-being-written

בַּבְּרִית׃ וַיְצַו הַמֶּלֶךְ אֶת־חִלְקִיָּהוּ הַכֹּהֵן הַגָּדוֹל
the-high the-priest Hilkiah *** the-king then-he-ordered (4) to-the-covenant

וְאֶת־ כֹּהֲנֵי הַמִּשְׁנֶה וְאֶת־ שֹׁמְרֵי הַסַּף לְהוֹצִיא
to-remove the-door ones-keeping-of and the-second priests-of and

מֵהֵיכַל יְהוָה אֵת כָּל־ הַכֵּלִים הָעֲשׂוּיִם
the-ones-being-made the-articles all-of *** Yahweh from-temple-of

this place and its people, that
they would become accursed
and laid waste, and because
you tore your robes and wept
in my presence, I have heard
you, declares the LORD.
20Therefore I will gather you to
your fathers, and you will be
buried in peace. Your eyes will
not see all the disaster I am going to bring on this place.' "
So they took her answer
back to the king.

Josiah Renews the Covenant

23 Then the king called together all the elders of
Judah and Jerusalem. 2He
went up to the temple of the
LORD with the men of Judah,
the people of Jerusalem, the
priests and the prophets—all
the people from the least to the
greatest. He read in their hearing all the words of the Book of
the Covenant, which had
been found in the temple of
the LORD. 3The king stood by
the pillar and renewed the
covenant in the presence of
the LORD—to follow the LORD
and keep his commands, regulations and decrees with all his
heart and all his soul, thus
confirming the words of the
covenant written in this book.
Then all the people pledged
themselves to the covenant.
4The king ordered Hilkiah
the high priest, the priests
next in rank and the doorkeepers to remove from the
temple of the LORD all the articles made for Baal and

לַבַּעַל וְלָאֲשֵׁרָה וּלְכֹל צְבָא הַשָּׁמָיִם
the-heavens host-of and-for-all-of and-for-the-Asherah for-the-Baal

וַיִּשְׂרְפֵם מִחוּץ לִירוּשָׁלַםִ בְּשַׁדְמוֹת קִדְרוֹן וְנָשָׂא
and-he-took Kidron in-fields-of of-Jerusalem at-outside and-he-burned-them

אֶת־ עֲפָרָם בֵּית־ אֵל׃ (5) וְהִשְׁבִּית אֶת־ הַכְּמָרִים אֲשֶׁר
whom the-pagan-priests *** and-he-did-away (5) El Beth ash-of-them ***

נָתְנוּ מַלְכֵי יְהוּדָה וַיְקַטֵּר בַּבָּמוֹת
at-the-high-places and-he-burned-incense Judah kings-of they-appointed

בְּעָרֵי יְהוּדָה וּמְסִבֵּי יְרוּשָׁלָםִ וְאֶת־ הַמְקַטְּרִים
the-ones-burning-incense and Jerusalem and-ones-around-of Judah of-towns-of

לַבַּעַל לַשֶּׁמֶשׁ וְלַיָּרֵחַ וְלַמַּזָּלוֹת וּלְכֹל
and-of-all-of and-to-the-constellations and-to-the-moon to-the-sun to-the-Baal

צְבָא הַשָּׁמָיִם׃ (6) וַיֹּצֵא אֶת־ הָאֲשֵׁרָה מִבֵּית
from-temple-of the-Asherah-pole *** and-he-took-out (6) the-heavens host-of

יְהוָה מִחוּץ לִירוּשָׁלַםִ אֶל־ נַחַל קִדְרוֹן וַיִּשְׂרֹף אֹתָהּ
her and-he-burned Kidron Valley-of to of-Jerusalem at-outside Yahweh

בְּנַחַל קִדְרוֹן וַיָּדֶק לְעָפָר וַיַּשְׁלֵךְ אֶת־ עֲפָרָהּ
dust-of-her *** and-he-scattered to-powder and-he-ground Kidron in-Valley-of

עַל־ קֶבֶר בְּנֵי הָעָם׃ (7) וַיִּתֹּץ אֶת־ בָּתֵּי
quarters-of *** and-he-tore-down (7) the-people sons-of grave-of over

הַקְּדֵשִׁים אֲשֶׁר בְּבֵית יְהוָה אֲשֶׁר הַנָּשִׁים אֹרְגוֹת
ones-weaving the-women where Yahweh in-temple-of which the-shrine-prostitutes

שָׁם בָּתִּים לָאֲשֵׁרָה׃ (8) וַיָּבֵא אֶת־ כָּל־ הַכֹּהֲנִים
the-priests all-of *** and-he-brought (8) for-Asherah garments there

מֵעָרֵי יְהוּדָה וַיְטַמֵּא אֶת־ הַבָּמוֹת אֲשֶׁר
where the-high-places *** and-he-desecrated Judah from-towns-of

קִטְּרוּ־ שָׁמָּה הַכֹּהֲנִים מִגֶּבַע עַד־ בְּאֵר שָׁבַע
Sheba Beer to from-Geba the-priests at-there they-burned-incense

וְנָתַץ אֶת־ בָּמוֹת הַשְּׁעָרִים אֲשֶׁר־ פֶּתַח שַׁעַר יְהוֹשֻׁעַ
Joshua Gate-of entrance-of that the-gates shrines *** and-he-broke-down

שַׂר־ הָעִיר אֲשֶׁר־עַל־שְׂמֹאול אִישׁ בְּשַׁעַר הָעִיר׃ (9) אַךְ לֹא
not although (9) the-city at-gate-of each left on which the-city governor-of

יַעֲלוּ כֹּהֲנֵי הַבָּמוֹת אֶל־ מִזְבַּח יְהוָה בִּירוּשָׁלָםִ כִּי
yet in-Jerusalem Yahweh altar-of at the-high-places priests-of they-served

אִם־ אָכְלוּ מַצּוֹת בְּתוֹךְ אֲחֵיהֶם׃
brothers-of-them in-among unleavened-breads they-ate indeed

(10) וְטִמֵּא אֶת־ הַתֹּפֶת אֲשֶׁר בְּגֵי בְנֵי־ הִנֹּם לְבִלְתִּי
so-not Hinnom Ben in-Valley-of which the-Topheth *** and-he-desecrated (10)

Asherah and all the starry
hosts. He burned them outside
Jerusalem in the fields of the
Kidron Valley and took the
ashes to Bethel. [5]He did away
with the pagan priests appointed by the kings of Judah
to burn incense on the high
places of the towns of Judah
and on those around Jerusalem—those who burned in-
cense to Baal, to the sun and
moon, to the constellations
and to all the starry hosts. [6]He
took the Asherah pole from
the temple of the LORD to the
Kidron Valley outside Jerusalem and burned it there. He
ground it to powder and scattered the dust over the graves
of the common people. [7]He
also tore down the quarters of
the male shrine prostitutes,
which were in the temple of
the LORD and where women
did weaving for Asherah.
[8]Josiah brought all the
priests from the towns of
Judah and desecrated the high
places, from Geba to Beersheba, where the priests had
burned incense. He broke
down the shrines[j] at the
gates—at the entrance to the
Gate of Joshua, the city governor, which is on the left of the
city gate. [9]Although the priests
of the high places did not
serve at the altar of the LORD in
Jerusalem, they ate unleavened bread with their fellow
priests.
[10]He desecrated Topheth,
which was in the Valley of
Ben Hinnom, so no one could

j8 *Or high places*

°10 ק בן

לְהַעֲבִיר אִישׁ אֶת־ בְּנוֹ וְאֶת־ בִּתּוֹ בָּאֵשׁ
through-the-fire daughter-of-him or son-of-him *** one to-make-pass-through

לַמֹּלֶךְ׃ (11) וַיַּשְׁבֵּת אֶת־ הַסּוּסִים אֲשֶׁר נָתְנוּ
they-dedicated that the-horses *** and-he-removed (11) to-the-Molech

מַלְכֵי יְהוּדָה לַשֶּׁמֶשׁ מִבֹּא בֵית־ יְהוָה אֶל־ לִשְׁכַּת
room-of near Yahweh temple-of from-to-enter to-the-sun Judah kings-of

נְתַן־ מֶלֶךְ הַסָּרִיס אֲשֶׁר בַּפַּרְוָרִים וְאֶת־ מַרְכְּבוֹת הַשֶּׁמֶשׁ
the-sun chariots-of and among-the-colonades that the-official Melech Nathan

שָׂרַף בָּאֵשׁ׃ (12) וְאֶת־הַמִּזְבְּחוֹת אֲשֶׁר עַל־ הַגָּג עֲלִיַּת אָחָז
Ahaz upper-room-of the-roof on that the-altars and (12) in-fire he-burned

אֲשֶׁר־ עָשׂוּ ׀ מַלְכֵי יְהוּדָה וְאֶת־ הַמִּזְבְּחוֹת אֲשֶׁר־ עָשָׂה מְנַשֶּׁה
Manasseh he-built that the-altars and Judah kings-of they-erected that

בִּשְׁתֵּי חַצְרוֹת בֵּית־ יְהוָה נָתַץ הַמֶּלֶךְ וַיָּרָץ
and-he-removed the-king he-pulled-down Yahweh temple-of courts-of in-two-of

מִשָּׁם וְהִשְׁלִיךְ אֶת־ עֲפָרָם אֶל־ נַחַל קִדְרוֹן׃ (13) וְאֶת־
and (13) Kidron Valley-of into rubble-of-them *** and-he-threw from-there

הַבָּמוֹת אֲשֶׁר ׀ עַל־ פְּנֵי יְרוּשָׁלַםִ אֲשֶׁר מִימִין לְהַר־
of-Hill-of on-south that Jerusalem east-of to that the-high-places

הַמַּשְׁחִית אֲשֶׁר בָּנָה שְׁלֹמֹה מֶלֶךְ־ יִשְׂרָאֵל לְעַשְׁתֹּרֶת ׀
for-Ashtoreth Israel king-of Solomon he-built that the-Corruption

שִׁקֻּץ צִידֹנִים וְלִכְמוֹשׁ שִׁקֻּץ מוֹאָב וּלְמִלְכֹּם
and-for-Milcom Moab vile-thing-of and-for-Chemosh Sidonians vile-thing-of

תּוֹעֲבַת בְּנֵי־ עַמּוֹן טִמֵּא הַמֶּלֶךְ׃ (14) וְשִׁבַּר
and-he-smashed (14) the-king he-desecrated Ammon sons-of detestable-one-of

אֶת־ הַמַּצֵּבוֹת וַיִּכְרֹת אֶת־ הָאֲשֵׁרִים וַיְמַלֵּא
and-he-covered the-Asherah-poles *** and-he-cut-down the-sacred-stones ***

אֶת־ מְקוֹמָם עַצְמוֹת אָדָם׃ (15) וְגַם אֶת־ הַמִּזְבֵּחַ אֲשֶׁר בְּבֵית־ אֵל
El at-Beth that the-altar *** and-even (15) human bones-of site-of-them ***

הַבָּמָה אֲשֶׁר עָשָׂה יָרָבְעָם בֶּן־ נְבָט אֲשֶׁר הֶחֱטִיא אֶת־
*** he-caused-to-sin who Nebat son-of Jeroboam he-made that the-high-place

יִשְׂרָאֵל גַּם אֶת־ הַמִּזְבֵּחַ הַהוּא וְאֶת־ הַבָּמָה נָתָץ
he-demolished the-high-place and the-that the-altar *** even Israel

וַיִּשְׂרֹף אֶת־ הַבָּמָה הֵדַק לְעָפָר וְשָׂרַף
and-he-burned to-powder he-ground the-high-place *** and-he-burned

אֲשֵׁרָה׃ (16) וַיִּפֶן יֹאשִׁיָּהוּ וַיַּרְא אֶת־ הַקְּבָרִים
the-tombs *** and-he-saw Josiah then-he-looked-around (16) Asherah-pole

אֲשֶׁר־ שָׁם בָּהָר וַיִּשְׁלַח וַיִּקַּח אֶת־ הָעֲצָמוֹת מִן־
from the-bones *** and-he-removed and-he-sent on-the-hillside there that

use it to sacrifice his son or
daughter in[k] the fire to Molech. 11He removed from the
entrance to the temple of the
LORD the horses that the kings
of Judah had dedicated to the
sun. They were in the court
near the room of an official
named Nathan-Melech. Josiah
then burned the chariots dedicated to the sun.
12He pulled down the altars
the kings of Judah had erected
on the roof near the upper
room of Ahaz, and the altars
Manasseh had built in the two
courts of the temple of the
LORD. He removed them from
there, smashed them to pieces
and threw the rubble into the
Kidron Valley. 13The king also
desecrated the high places that
were east of Jerusalem on the
south of the Hill of Corrup-
tion—the ones Solomon king
of Israel had built for Ashtoreth the vile goddess of the
Sidonians, for Chemosh the
vile god of Moab, and for Molech[l] the detestable god of the
people of Ammon. 14Josiah
smashed the sacred stones and
cut down the Asherah poles
and covered the sites with human bones.
15Even the altar at Bethel, the
high place made by Jeroboam
son of Nebat, who had caused
Israel to sin—even that altar
and high place he demolished.
He burned the high place and
ground it to powder, and
burned the Asherah pole also.
16Then Josiah looked around,
and when he saw the tombs
that were there on the hillside,
he had the bones removed

k10 Or *to make his son or daughter pass through*

l13 Hebrew *Milcom*

הַקְּבָרִים וַיִּשְׂרֹף עַל־הַמִּזְבֵּחַ וַיְטַמְּאֵהוּ כִּדְבַר יְהוָה
Yahweh as-word-of and-he-defiled-him the-altar on and-he-burned the-tombs

אֲשֶׁר קָרָא אִישׁ הָאֱלֹהִים אֲשֶׁר קָרָא אֶת־הַדְּבָרִים הָאֵלֶּה׃
the-these the-things *** he-foretold who the-God man-of he-proclaimed that

וַיֹּאמֶר מָה הַצִּיּוּן הַלָּז אֲשֶׁר אֲנִי רֹאֶה וַיֹּאמְרוּ
and-they-said seeing I that the-this the-tombstone what? and-he-asked (17)

אֵלָיו אַנְשֵׁי הָעִיר הַקֶּבֶר אִישׁ־הָאֱלֹהִים אֲשֶׁר־בָּא מִיהוּדָה
from-Judah he-came who the-God man-of the-tomb the-city men-of to-him

וַיִּקְרָא אֶת־הַדְּבָרִים הָאֵלֶּה אֲשֶׁר עָשִׂיתָ עַל הַמִּזְבַּח בֵּית־אֵל׃
El Beth the-altar to you-did that the-these the-things *** and-he-pronounced

וַיֹּאמֶר הַנִּיחוּ לוֹ אִישׁ אַל־יָנַע עַצְמֹתָיו
bones-of-him let-him-disturb not anyone to-him leave-alone! and-he-said (18)

וַיְמַלְּטוּ עַצְמֹתָיו אֵת עַצְמוֹת הַנָּבִיא אֲשֶׁר־בָּא מִשֹּׁמְרוֹן׃
from-Samaria he-came who the-prophet bones-of *** bones-of-him so-they-spared

וְגַם אֶת־כָּל־בָּתֵּי הַבָּמוֹת אֲשֶׁר ׀ בְּעָרֵי שֹׁמְרוֹן
Samaria in-towns-of that the-high-places shrines-of all-of *** and-also (19)

אֲשֶׁר עָשׂוּ מַלְכֵי יִשְׂרָאֵל לְהַכְעִיס הֵסִיר יֹאשִׁיָּהוּ וַיַּעַשׂ
and-he-did Josiah he-removed to-make-angry Israel kings-of they-built that

לָהֶם כְּכָל־הַמַּעֲשִׂים אֲשֶׁר עָשָׂה בְּבֵית־אֵל׃ וַיִּזְבַּח
and-he-slaughtered (20) El at-Beth he-did that the-actions as-all-of to-them

אֶת־כָּל־כֹּהֲנֵי הַבָּמוֹת אֲשֶׁר־שָׁם עַל־הַמִּזְבְּחוֹת וַיִּשְׂרֹף
and-he-burned the-altars on there who the-high-places priests-of all-of ***

אֶת־עַצְמוֹת אָדָם עֲלֵיהֶם וַיָּשָׁב יְרוּשָׁלָםִ׃ וַיְצַו
then-he-ordered (21) Jerusalem then-he-went-back on-them human bones-of ***

הַמֶּלֶךְ אֶת־כָּל־הָעָם לֵאמֹר עֲשׂוּ פֶסַח לַיהוָה
to-Yahweh Passover celebrate! to-say the-people all-of *** the-king

אֱלֹהֵיכֶם כַּכָּתוּב עַל סֵפֶר הַבְּרִית הַזֶּה׃
the-this the-Covenant Book-of in as-the-thing-being-written God-of-you

כִּי לֹא נַעֲשָׂה כַּפֶּסַח הַזֶּה מִימֵי
from-days-of the-this like-the-Passover he-was-observed not indeed (22)

הַשֹּׁפְטִים אֲשֶׁר שָׁפְטוּ אֶת־יִשְׂרָאֵל וְכֹל יְמֵי מַלְכֵי יִשְׂרָאֵל
Israel kings-of days-of nor-all-of Israel *** they-led who the-ones-judging

וּמַלְכֵי יְהוּדָה׃ כִּי אִם־בִּשְׁמֹנֶה עֶשְׂרֵה שָׁנָה לַמֶּלֶךְ יֹאשִׁיָּהוּ
Josiah of-the-king year ten in-eight indeed but (23) Judah and-kings-of

נַעֲשָׂה הַפֶּסַח הַזֶּה לַיהוָה בִּירוּשָׁלָםִ׃ וְגַם
and-also (24) in-Jerusalem to-Yahweh the-this the-Passover he-was-celebrated

אֶת־הָאֹבוֹת וְאֶת־הַיִּדְּעֹנִים וְאֶת־הַתְּרָפִים וְאֶת־הַגִּלֻּלִים
the-idols and the-household-gods and the-spiritists and the-mediums ***

from them and burned on the
altar to defile it, in accordance
with the word of the LORD proclaimed by the man of God
who foretold these things.
17 The king asked, "What is
that tombstone I see?"
The men of the city said, "It
marks the tomb of the man of
God who came from Judah
and pronounced against the
altar of Bethel the very things
you have done to it."
18 "Leave it alone," he said.
"Don't let anyone disturb his
bones." So they spared his
bones and those of the
prophet who had come from
Samaria.
19 Just as he had done at Bethel, Josiah removed and defiled
all the shrines at the high
places that the kings of Israel
had built in the towns of Samaria that had provoked the
LORD to anger. 20 Josiah slaughtered all the priests of those
high places on the altars and
burned human bones on
them. Then he went back to
Jerusalem.
21 The king gave this order to
all the people: "Celebrate the
Passover to the LORD your
God, as it is written in this
Book of the Covenant." 22 Not
since the days of the judges
who led Israel, nor throughout
the days of the kings of Israel
and the kings of Judah, had
any such Passover been observed. 23 But in the eighteenth
year of King Josiah, this Passover was celebrated to the
LORD in Jerusalem.
24 Furthermore, Josiah got rid
of the mediums and spiritists,
the household gods, the idols

וְאֵת כָּל־ הַשִּׁקֻּצִים אֲשֶׁר נִרְאוּ בְּאֶרֶץ יְהוּדָה
Judah in-land-of they-were-seen that the-detestable-things all-of and

וּבִירוּשָׁלִַם בִּעֵר יֹאשִׁיָּהוּ לְמַעַן הָקִים אֶת־ דִּבְרֵי
requirements-of *** to-fulfill in-order-to Josiah he-got-rid and-in-Jerusalem

הַתּוֹרָה הַכְּתֻבִים עַל־ הַסֵּפֶר אֲשֶׁר מָצָא חִלְקִיָּהוּ
Hilkiah he-discovered that the-book in the-ones-being-written the-law

הַכֹּהֵן בֵּית יְהוָה׃ וְכָמֹהוּ לֹא־ הָיָה לְפָנָיו מֶלֶךְ
king before-him he-was not and-like-him (25) Yahweh temple-of the-priest

אֲשֶׁר־ שָׁב אֶל־ יְהוָה בְּכָל־ לְבָבוֹ וּבְכָל־ נַפְשׁוֹ
soul-of-him and-with-all-of heart-of-him with-all-of Yahweh to he-turned who

וּבְכָל־ מְאֹדוֹ כְּכֹל תּוֹרַת מֹשֶׁה וְאַחֲרָיו לֹא־
not and-after-him Moses Law-of as-all-of strength-of-him and-with-all-of

קָם כָּמֹהוּ׃ אַךְ ׀ לֹא־ שָׁב יְהוָה מֵחֲרוֹן
from-heat-of Yahweh he-turned-away not nevertheless (26) like-him he-rose

אַפּוֹ הַגָּדוֹל אֲשֶׁר־ חָרָה אַפּוֹ בִּיהוּדָה עַל
because-of against-Judah anger-of-him he-burned which the-fierce anger-of-him

כָּל־ הַכְּעָסִים אֲשֶׁר הִכְעִיסוֹ מְנַשֶּׁה׃ וַיֹּאמֶר
so-he-said (27) Manasseh he-provoked-to-anger-him that the-provokings all-of

יְהוָה גַּם אֶת־ יְהוּדָה אָסִיר מֵעַל פָּנַי כַּאֲשֶׁר
just-as presences-of-me from-before I-will-remove Judah *** also Yahweh

הֲסִרֹתִי אֶת־יִשְׂרָאֵל וּמָאַסְתִּי אֶת־ הָעִיר הַזֹּאת אֲשֶׁר־בָּחַרְתִּי
I-chose that the-this the-city *** and-I-will-reject Israel *** I-removed

אֶת־ יְרוּשָׁלִַם וְאֶת־ הַבַּיִת אֲשֶׁר אָמַרְתִּי יִהְיֶה שְׁמִי שָׁם׃
there Name-of-me he-shall-be I-said which the-temple and Jerusalem ***

וְיֶתֶר דִּבְרֵי יֹאשִׁיָּהוּ וְכָל־ אֲשֶׁר עָשָׂה הֲלֹא־ הֵם
they not? he-did that and-all Josiah events-of and-rest-of (28)

כְּתוּבִים עַל־ סֵפֶר דִּבְרֵי הַיָּמִים לְמַלְכֵי יְהוּדָה׃
Judah of-kings-of the-days annals-of book-of in ones-being-written

בְּיָמָיו עָלָה פַרְעֹה נְכֹה מֶלֶךְ־ מִצְרַיִם עַל־ מֶלֶךְ
king-of to Egypt king-of Neco Pharaoh he-went-up in-days-of-him (29)

אַשּׁוּר עַל־ נְהַר־ פְּרָת וַיֵּלֶךְ הַמֶּלֶךְ יֹאשִׁיָּהוּ לִקְרָאתוֹ
to-meet-him Josiah the-king and-he-marched-out Euphrates River-of to Assyria

וַיְמִיתֵהוּ בִּמְגִדּוֹ כִּרְאֹתוֹ אֹתוֹ׃ וַיַּרְכִּבֻהוּ
and-they-drove-him (30) him when-to-face-him at-Megiddo but-he-killed-him

עֲבָדָיו מֵת מִמְּגִדּוֹ וַיְבִאֻהוּ יְרוּשָׁלִַם
Jerusalem and-they-brought-him from-Megiddo being-dead servants-of-him

וַיִּקְבְּרֻהוּ בִּקְבֻרָתוֹ וַיִּקַּח עַם־ הָאָרֶץ אֶת־
*** the-land people-of and-he-took in-tomb-of-him and-they-buried-him

and all the other detestable things seen in Judah and Jerusalem. This he did to fulfill the requirements of the law written in the book that Hilkiah the priest had discovered in the temple of the LORD.
[25]Neither before nor after Josiah was there a king like him who turned to the LORD as he did—with all his heart and with all his soul and with all his strength, in accordance with all the Law of Moses.

[26]Nevertheless, the LORD did not turn away from the heat of his fierce anger, which burned against Judah because of all that Manasseh had done to provoke him to anger. [27]So the LORD said, "I will remove Judah also from my presence as I removed Israel, and I will reject Jerusalem, the city I chose, and this temple, about which I said, 'There shall my Name be.'[m]"

[28]As for the other events of Josiah's reign, and all he did, are they not written in the book of the annals of the kings of Judah?

[29]While Josiah was king, Pharaoh Neco king of Egypt went up to the Euphrates River to help the king of Assyria. King Josiah marched out to meet him in battle, but Neco faced him and killed him at Megiddo. [30]Josiah's servants brought his body in a chariot from Megiddo to Jerusalem and buried him in his own tomb. And the people of the

[m]27 1 Kings 8:29

יְהוֹאָחָז בֶּן־ יֹאשִׁיָּהוּ וַיִּמְשְׁחוּ אֹתוֹ וַיַּמְלִיכוּ אֹתוֹ
him and-they-made-king him and-they-anointed Josiah son-of Jehoahaz

תַּחַת אָבִיו׃ בֶּן־ עֶשְׂרִים וְשָׁלֹשׁ שָׁנָה יְהוֹאָחָז
Jehoahaz year and-three twenty son-of (31) father-of-him in-place-of

בְּמָלְכוֹ וּשְׁלֹשָׁה חֳדָשִׁים מָלַךְ בִּירוּשָׁלָ͏ִם וְשֵׁם
and-name-of in-Jerusalem he-reigned months and-three when-to-become-king-him

אִמּוֹ חֲמוּטַל בַּת־ יִרְמְיָהוּ מִלִּבְנָה׃ וַיַּעַשׂ
and-he-did (32) from-Libnah Jeremiah daughter-of Hamutal mother-of-him

הָרַע בְּעֵינֵי יְהוָה כְּכֹל אֲשֶׁר־ עָשׂוּ אֲבֹתָיו׃
fathers-of-him they-did that as-all Yahweh in-eyes-of the-evil

וַיַּאַסְרֵהוּ פַרְעֹה נְכֹה בְרִבְלָה בְּאֶרֶץ חֲמָת בִּמְלֹךְ
from-to-reign Hamath in-land-of at-Riblah Neco Pharaoh and-he-chained-him (33)

בִּירוּשָׁלָ͏ִם וַיִּתֶּן־ עֹנֶשׁ עַל־ הָאָרֶץ מֵאָה כִכַּר־ כֶּסֶף
silver talent-of hundred the-land on levy and-he-imposed in-Jerusalem

וְכִכַּר זָהָב׃ וַיַּמְלֵךְ פַּרְעֹה נְכֹה אֶת־ אֶלְיָקִים בֶּן־
son-of Eliakim *** Neco Pharaoh and-he-made-king (34) gold and-talent-of

יֹאשִׁיָּהוּ תַּחַת יֹאשִׁיָּהוּ אָבִיו וַיַּסֵּב אֶת־ שְׁמוֹ
name-of-him *** and-he-changed father-of-him Josiah in-place-of Josiah

יְהוֹיָקִים וְאֶת־ יְהוֹאָחָז לָקָח וַיָּבֹא מִצְרַיִם וַיָּמָת שָׁם׃
there and-he-died Egypt and-he-carried-off he-took Jehoahaz but Jehoiakim

וְהַכֶּסֶף וְהַזָּהָב נָתַן יְהוֹיָקִים לְפַרְעֹה אַךְ הֶעֱרִיךְ
he-taxed but to-Pharaoh Jehoiakim he-paid and-the-gold and-the-silver (35)

אֶת־ הָאָרֶץ לָתֵת אֶת־ הַכֶּסֶף עַל־ פִּי פַרְעֹה אִישׁ
each Pharaoh demand-of at the-silver *** to-pay the-land ***

כְּעֶרְכּוֹ נָגַשׂ אֶת־ הַכֶּסֶף וְאֶת־ הַזָּהָב אֶת־ עַם
people-of *** the-gold and the-silver *** he-exacted as-assessment-of-him

הָאָרֶץ לָתֵת לְפַרְעֹה נְכֹה׃ בֶּן־ עֶשְׂרִים וְחָמֵשׁ שָׁנָה יְהוֹיָקִים
Jehoiakim year and-five twenty son-of (36) Neco to-Pharaoh to-pay the-land

בְּמָלְכוֹ וְאַחַת עֶשְׂרֵה שָׁנָה מָלַךְ בִּירוּשָׁלָ͏ִם
in-Jerusalem he-reigned year ten and-one-of when-to-become-king-him

וְשֵׁם אִמּוֹ זְבִידָּה בַת־ פְּדָיָה מִן־ רוּמָה׃
Rumah from Pedaiah daughter-of Zebidah mother-of-him and-name-of

וַיַּעַשׂ הָרַע בְּעֵינֵי יְהוָה כְּכֹל אֲשֶׁר־ עָשׂוּ אֲבֹתָיו׃
fathers-of-him they-did that as-all Yahweh in-eyes-of the-evil and-he-did (37)

בְּיָמָיו עָלָה נְבֻכַדְנֶאצַּר מֶלֶךְ בָּבֶל וַיְהִי־
and-he-was Babylon king-of Nebuchadnezzar he-invaded in-days-of-him (24:1)

לוֹ יְהוֹיָקִים עֶבֶד שָׁלֹשׁ שָׁנִים וַיָּשָׁב וַיִּמְרָד־
and-he-rebelled but-he-changed-mind years three vassal Jehoiakim to-him

land took Jehoahaz son of Josiah and anointed him and made him king in place of his father.

Jehoahaz King of Judah

[31]Jehoahaz was twenty-three years old when he became king, and he reigned in Jerusalem three months. His mother's name was Hamutal daughter of Jeremiah; she was
from Libnah. [32]He did evil in
the eyes of the LORD, just as his
fathers had done. [33]Pharaoh
Neco put him in chains at Riblah in the land of Hamath[n] so that he might not reign in Jerusalem, and he imposed on Judah a levy of a hundred talents[o] of silver and a talent[p] of
gold. [34]Pharaoh Neco made
Eliakim son of Josiah king in place of his father Josiah and changed Eliakim's name to Jehoiakim. But he took Jehoahaz and carried him off to Egypt, and there he died.
[35]Jehoiakim paid Pharaoh
Neco the silver and gold he demanded. In order to do so, he taxed the land and exacted the silver and gold from the people of the land according to their assessments.

Jehoiakim King of Judah

[36]Jehoiakim was twenty-five years old when he became king, and he reigned in Jerusalem eleven years. His mother's name was Zebidah daughter of Pedaiah; she was
from Rumah. [37]And he did evil
in the eyes of the LORD, just as his fathers had done.

24 During Jehoiakim's reign, Nebuchadnezzar king of Babylon invaded the land, and Jehoiakim became his vassal for three years. But then he changed his mind and rebelled against

[n]33 Hebrew; Septuagint (see also 2 Chron. 36:3) *Neco at Riblah in Hamath removed him*
[o]33 That is, about 3 3/4 tons (about 3.4 metric tons)
[p]33 That is, about 75 pounds (about 34 kilograms)

°33 ק ממלך
°36 ק זבודה

בּוֹ׃ (2) וַיְשַׁלַּח יְהוָה | בּוֹ אֶת־ גְּדוּדֵי כַשְׂדִּים° וְאֶת־
and Chaldeans raiders-of *** against-him Yahweh and-he-sent (2) against-him

גְּדוּדֵי אֲרָם וְאֵת | גְּדוּדֵי מוֹאָב וְאֵת גְּדוּדֵי בְנֵי־ עַמּוֹן
Ammon sons-of raiders-of and Moab raiders-of and Aram raiders-of

וַיְשַׁלְּחֵם בִּיהוּדָה לְהַאֲבִידוֹ כִּדְבַר יְהוָה אֲשֶׁר דִּבֶּר
he-proclaimed that Yahweh as-word-of to-destroy-him to-Judah and-he-sent-them

בְּיַד עֲבָדָיו הַנְּבִיאִים׃ (3) אַךְ | עַל־ פִּי יְהוָה
Yahweh command-of at surely (3) the-prophets servants-of-him by-hand-of

הָיְתָה בִּיהוּדָה לְהָסִיר מֵעַל פָּנָיו בְּחַטֹּאת
for-sins-of presences-of-him from-before to-remove to-Judah she-happened

מְנַשֶּׁה כְּכֹל אֲשֶׁר עָשָׂה׃ (4) וְגַם דַּם־ הַנָּקִי אֲשֶׁר שָׁפָךְ
he-shed that the-innocent blood-of and-also (4) he-did that as-all Manasseh

וַיְמַלֵּא אֶת־ יְרוּשָׁלִַם דָּם נָקִי וְלֹא־ אָבָה יְהוָה
Yahweh he-was-willing and-not innocent blood Jerusalem *** for-he-filled

לִסְלֹחַ׃ (5) וְיֶתֶר דִּבְרֵי יְהוֹיָקִים וְכָל־ אֲשֶׁר עָשָׂה הֲלֹא־
not? he-did that and-all Jehoiakim events-of and-rest-of (5) to-forgive

הֵם כְּתוּבִים עַל־ סֵפֶר דִּבְרֵי הַיָּמִים לְמַלְכֵי יְהוּדָה׃
Judah of-kings-of the-days annals-of book-of in ones-being-written they

(6) וַיִּשְׁכַּב יְהוֹיָקִים עִם־ אֲבֹתָיו וַיִּמְלֹךְ יְהוֹיָכִין
Jehoiachin and-he-became-king fathers-of-him with Jehoiakim and-he-rested (6)

בְּנוֹ תַּחְתָּיו׃ (7) וְלֹא־ הֹסִיף עוֹד מֶלֶךְ מִצְרַיִם
Egypt king-of again he-repeated and-not (7) in-place-of-him son-of-him

לָצֵאת מֵאַרְצוֹ כִּי־ לָקַח מֶלֶךְ בָּבֶל מִנַּחַל
from-Wadi-of Babylon king-of he-took for from-country-of-him to-march-out

מִצְרַיִם עַד־ נְהַר־ פְּרָת כֹּל אֲשֶׁר הָיְתָה לְמֶלֶךְ מִצְרָיִם׃ (8) בֶּן־
son-of (8) Egypt to-king-of she-was that all Euphrates River-of to Egypt

שְׁמֹנֶה עֶשְׂרֵה שָׁנָה יְהוֹיָכִין בְּמָלְכוֹ וּשְׁלֹשָׁה חֳדָשִׁים
months and-three when-to-become-king-him Jehoiachin year ten eight

מָלַךְ בִּירוּשָׁלִָם וְשֵׁם אִמּוֹ נְחֻשְׁתָּא בַת־
daughter-of Nehushta mother-of-him and-name-of in-Jerusalem he-reigned

אֶלְנָתָן מִירוּשָׁלִָם׃ (9) וַיַּעַשׂ הָרַע בְּעֵינֵי יְהוָה כְּכֹל
as-all Yahweh in-eyes-of the-evil and-he-did (9) from-Jerusalem Elnathan

אֲשֶׁר־ עָשָׂה אָבִיו׃ (10) בָּעֵת הַהִיא עָלָה°
they-advanced the-that at-the-time (10) father-of-him he-did that

עַבְדֵי נְבֻכַדְנֶאצַּר מֶלֶךְ־ בָּבֶל יְרוּשָׁלִָם וַתָּבֹא הָעִיר
the-city and-she-lay Jerusalem Babylon king-of Nebuchadnezzar officers-of

בַּמָּצוֹר׃ (11) וַיָּבֹא נְבוּכַדְנֶאצַּר מֶלֶךְ־ בָּבֶל עַל־ הָעִיר
the-city to Babylon king-of Nebuchadnezzar and-he-came (11) under-the-siege

Nebuchadnezzar. [2]The LORD
sent Babylonian,[q] Aramean,
Moabite and Ammonite raiders against him. He sent them
to destroy Judah, in accordance with the word of the
LORD proclaimed by his servants the prophets. [3]Surely
these things happened to
Judah according to the LORD's
command, in order to remove
them from his presence because of the sins of Manasseh
and all he had done, [4]includ-
ing the shedding of innocent
blood. For he had filled Jerusalem with innocent blood, and
the LORD was not willing to
forgive.
[5]As for the other events of
Jehoiakim's reign, and all he
did, are they not written in the
book of the annals of the kings
of Judah? [6]Jehoiakim rested
with his fathers. And Jehoiachin his son succeeded him as
king.
[7]The king of Egypt did not
march out from his own country again, because the king of
Babylon had taken all his territory, from the Wadi of Egypt
to the Euphrates River.

Jehoiachin King of Judah

[8]Jehoiachin was eighteen
years old when he became
king, and he reigned in
Jerusalem three months. His
mother's name was Nehushta
daughter of Elnathan; she was
from Jerusalem. [9]He did evil in
the eyes of the LORD, just as his
father had done.
[10]At that time the officers of
Nebuchadnezzar king of Babylon advanced on Jerusalem
and laid siege to it, [11]and
Nebuchadnezzar himself
came up to the city while his

[q]2 Or *Chaldean*

°10 ק עלו

וַעֲבָדָיו צָרִים עָלֶיהָ׃ וַיֵּצֵא
and-he-surrendered (12) against-her ones-besieging and-officers-of-him

יְהוֹיָכִין מֶלֶךְ־ יְהוּדָה עַל־ מֶלֶךְ בָּבֶל הוּא וְאִמּוֹ
and-mother-of-him he Babylon king-of to Judah king-of Jehoiachin

וַעֲבָדָיו וְשָׂרָיו וְסָרִיסָיו וַיִּקַּח אֹתוֹ
him and-he-took and-officials-of-him and-nobles-of-him and-attendants-of-him

מֶלֶךְ בָּבֶל בִּשְׁנַת שְׁמֹנֶה לְמָלְכוֹ׃ וַיּוֹצֵא מִשָּׁם
from-there and-he-removed (13) to-reign-him eight in-year-of Babylon king-of

אֶת־ כָּל־ אוֹצְרוֹת בֵּית יְהוָה וְאוֹצְרוֹת בֵּית הַמֶּלֶךְ
the-king palace-of and-treasures-of Yahweh temple-of treasures-of all-of ***

וַיְקַצֵּץ אֶת־ כָּל־ כְּלֵי הַזָּהָב אֲשֶׁר עָשָׂה שְׁלֹמֹה מֶלֶךְ־
king-of Solomon he-made that the-gold articles-of all-of *** and-he-took-away

יִשְׂרָאֵל בְּהֵיכַל יְהוָה כַּאֲשֶׁר דִּבֶּר יְהוָה׃ וְהִגְלָה
and-he-exiled (14) Yahweh he-declared just-as Yahweh for-temple-of Israel

אֶת־ כָּל־ יְרוּשָׁלִַם וְאֶת־ כָּל־ הַשָּׂרִים וְאֵת ׀ כָּל־ גִּבּוֹרֵי הַחַיִל
the-fight men-of all-of and the-officers all-of and Jerusalem all-of ***

עֲשֶׂרֶה° אֲלָפִים גּוֹלֶה וְכָל־ הֶחָרָשׁ וְהַמַּסְגֵּר לֹא
not and-the-artisan the-craftsman and-all-of being-exiled thousands ten-of

נִשְׁאַר זוּלַת דַּלַּת עַם־ הָאָרֶץ׃ וַיֶּגֶל אֶת־
*** and-he-took-captive (15) the-land people-of poor-of except he-was-left

יְהוֹיָכִין בָּבֶלָה וְאֶת־ אֵם הַמֶּלֶךְ וְאֶת־ נְשֵׁי הַמֶּלֶךְ וְאֶת־
and the-king wives-of and the-king mother-of and to-Babylon Jehoiachin

סָרִיסָיו וְאֵת אוּלֵי° הָאָרֶץ הוֹלִיךְ גּוֹלָה מִירוּשָׁלִַם
from-Jerusalem exile he-took the-land leaders-of and officials-of-him

בָּבֶלָה׃ וְאֵת כָּל־ אַנְשֵׁי הַחַיִל שִׁבְעַת אֲלָפִים
thousands seven-of the-fight men-of all-of and (16) to-Babylon

וְהֶחָרָשׁ וְהַמַּסְגֵּר אֶלֶף הַכֹּל גִּבּוֹרִים
ones-strong the-whole thousand and-the-artisan and-the-craftsman

עֹשֵׂי מִלְחָמָה וַיְבִיאֵם מֶלֶךְ־ בָּבֶל גּוֹלָה בָּבֶלָה׃
to-Babylon exile Babylon king-of and-he-took-them war ones-making-of

וַיַּמְלֵךְ מֶלֶךְ־ בָּבֶל אֶת־ מַתַּנְיָה דֹּדוֹ
uncle-of-him Mattaniah *** Babylon king-of and-he-made-king (17)

תַּחְתָּיו וַיַּסֵּב אֶת־ שְׁמוֹ צִדְקִיָּהוּ׃ בֶּן־ עֶשְׂרִים
twenty son-of (18) Zedekiah name-of-him *** and-he-changed in-place-of-him

וְאַחַת שָׁנָה צִדְקִיָּהוּ בְמָלְכוֹ וְאַחַת עֶשְׂרֵה שָׁנָה מָלַךְ
he-reigned year ten and-one-of when-to-become-king-him Zedekiah year and-one

בִּירוּשָׁלִָם וְשֵׁם אִמּוֹ חֲמִיטַל° בַּת־ יִרְמְיָהוּ
Jeremiah daughter-of Hamutal mother-of-him and-name-of in-Jerusalem

officers were besieging it.
12Jehoiachin king of Judah, his
mother, his attendants, his
nobles and his officials all surrendered to him.
In the eighth year of the
reign of the king of Babylon,
he took Jehoiachin prisoner.
13As the LORD had declared,
Nebuchadnezzar removed all
the treasures from the temple
of the LORD and from the royal
palace, and took away all the
gold articles that Solomon
king of Israel had made for the
temple of the LORD. 14He carried into exile all Jerusalem: all
the officers and fighting men,
and all the craftsmen and artisans—a total of ten thousand.
Only the poorest people of the
land were left.
15Nebuchadnezzar took
Jehoiachin captive to Babylon.
He also took from Jerusalem to
Babylon the king's mother, his
wives, his officials and the
leading men of the land. 16The
king of Babylon also deported
to Babylon the entire force of
seven thousand fighting men,
strong and fit for war, and a
thousand craftsmen and artisans. 17He made Mattaniah,
Jehoiachin's uncle, king in his
place and changed his name to
Zedekiah.

Zedekiah King of Judah

18Zedekiah was twenty-one
years old when he became
king, and he reigned in
Jerusalem eleven years. His
mother's name was Hamutal
daughter of Jeremiah; she was

°*14* ק עשרת
°*15* ק אילי
°*18* ק חמוטל

מִלִּבְנָה׃ וַיַּעַשׂ הָרַע בְּעֵינֵי יְהוָה כְּכֹל אֲשֶׁר־ עָשָׂה
he-did that as-all Yahweh in-eyes-of the-evil and-he-did (19) from-Libnah

יְהוֹיָקִים׃ כִּי ׀ עַל־ אַף יְהוָה הָיְתָה בִירוּשָׁלִַם
to-Jerusalem she-happened Yahweh anger-of because-of for (20) Jehoiachin

וּבִיהוּדָה עַד־ הִשְׁלִכוֹ אֹתָם מֵעַל פָּנָיו
presences-of-him from-before them he-thrust-him until and-to-Judah

וַיִּמְרֹד צִדְקִיָּהוּ בְּמֶלֶךְ בָּבֶל׃ וַיְהִי
so-he-was (25:1) Babylon against-king-of Zedekiah now-he-rebelled

בִשְׁנַת הַתְּשִׁיעִית לְמָלְכוֹ בַּחֹדֶשׁ הָעֲשִׂירִי בֶּעָשׂוֹר
on-the-ten the-tenth in-the-month to-reign-him the-ninth in-year-of

לַחֹדֶשׁ בָּא נְבֻכַדְנֶאצַּר מֶלֶךְ־ בָּבֶל הוּא וְכָל־
and-whole-of he Babylon king-of Nebuchadnezzar he-marched of-the-month

חֵילוֹ עַל־ יְרוּשָׁלִַם וַיִּחַן עָלֶיהָ וַיִּבְנוּ
and-they-built against-her and-he-encamped Jerusalem against army-of-him

עָלֶיהָ דָּיֵק סָבִיב׃ וַתָּבֹא הָעִיר בַּמָּצוֹר
under-the-siege the-city and-she-went (2) around siege-work against-her

עַד עַשְׁתֵּי עֶשְׂרֵה שָׁנָה לַמֶּלֶךְ צִדְקִיָּהוּ׃ בְּתִשְׁעָה לַחֹדֶשׁ
of-the-month on-nine (3) Zedekiah of-the-king year ten one-of until

וַיֶּחֱזַק הָרָעָב בָּעִיר וְלֹא־ הָיָה לֶחֶם לְעַם
for-people-of food he-was so-not in-the-city the-famine then-he-was-severe

הָאָרֶץ׃ וַתִּבָּקַע הָעִיר וְכָל־ אַנְשֵׁי
men-of and-all-of the-city then-she-was-broken-through (4) the-land

הַמִּלְחָמָה ׀ הַלַּיְלָה דֶּרֶךְ שַׁעַר ׀ בֵּין הַחֹמֹתַיִם אֲשֶׁר עַל־ גַּן
garden-of near that the-two-walls between gate way-of the-night the-war

הַמֶּלֶךְ וְכַשְׂדִּים עַל־ הָעִיר סָבִיב וַיֵּלֶךְ דֶּרֶךְ הָעֲרָבָה׃
the-Arabah way-of and-he-fled around the-city at but-Chaldeans the-king

וַיִּרְדְּפוּ חֵיל־ כַּשְׂדִּים אַחַר הַמֶּלֶךְ וַיַּשִּׂגוּ אֹתוֹ
him and-they-overtook the-king after Chaldeans army-of but-they-pursued (5)

בְּעַרְבוֹת יְרֵחוֹ וְכָל־ חֵילוֹ נָפֹצוּ מֵעָלָיו׃
from-him they-were-separated army-of-him and-all-of Jericho in-plains-of

וַיִּתְפְּשׂוּ אֶת־ הַמֶּלֶךְ וַיַּעֲלוּ אֹתוֹ אֶל־ מֶלֶךְ בָּבֶל
Babylon king-of to him and-they-took the-king *** and-they-captured (6)

רִבְלָתָה וַיְדַבְּרוּ אִתּוֹ מִשְׁפָּט׃ וְאֶת־ בְּנֵי צִדְקִיָּהוּ
Zedekiah sons-of and (7) sentence on-him and-they-pronounced at-Riblah

שָׁחֲטוּ לְעֵינָיו וְאֶת־ עֵינֵי צִדְקִיָּהוּ עִוֵּר
he-put-out Zedekiah eyes-of then before-eyes-of-him they-killed

וַיַּאַסְרֵהוּ בַנְחֻשְׁתַּיִם וַיְבִאֵהוּ בָּבֶל׃
Babylon and-he-took-him with-the-bronze-shackles and-he-bound-him

from Libnah. 19He did evil in
the eyes of the LORD, just as
Jehoiakim had done. 20It was
because of the LORD's anger
that all this happened to
Jerusalem and Judah, and in
the end he thrust them from
his presence.

The Fall of Jerusalem

Now Zedekiah rebelled
against the king of Babylon.
25 So in the ninth year of
Zedekiah's reign, on
the tenth day of the tenth
month, Nebuchadnezzar king
of Babylon marched against
Jerusalem with his whole
army. He encamped outside
the city and built siege works
all around it. 2The city was
kept under siege until the
eleventh year of King Zedekiah. 3By the ninth day of the
⌞fourth⌟[s] month the famine in
the city had become so severe
that there was no food for the
people to eat. 4Then the city
wall was broken through, and
the whole army fled at night
through the gate between the
two walls near the king's garden, though the Babylonians[t]
were surrounding the city.
They fled toward the Arabah,[u]
5but the Babylonian[v] army
pursued the king and overtook
him in the plains of Jericho.
All his soldiers were separated
from him and scattered, 6and
he was captured. He was taken
to the king of Babylon at Riblah, where sentence was pronounced on him. 7They killed
the sons of Zedekiah before
his eyes. Then they put out his
eyes, bound him with bronze
shackles and took him to Babylon.

s3 See Jeremiah 52:6.
t4 Or *Chaldeans;* also in verses 13, 25 and 26
u4 Or *the Jordan Valley*
v5 Or *Chaldean;* also in verses 10 and 24

וּבַחֹדֶשׁ הַחֲמִישִׁי בְּשִׁבְעָה לַחֹדֶשׁ הִיא שְׁנַת תְּשַׁע־
nine-of year-of this of-the-month on-seven the-fifth and-in-the-month (8)

עֶשְׂרֵה שָׁנָה לַמֶּלֶךְ נְבֻכַדְנֶאצַּר מֶלֶךְ־ בָּבֶל בָּא נְבוּזַרְאֲדָן
Nebuzaradan he-came Babylon king-of Nebuchadnezzar of-the-king year ten

רַב־ טַבָּחִים עֶבֶד מֶלֶךְ־ בָּבֶל יְרוּשָׁלִָם׃
Jerusalem Babylon king-of official-of imperial-guards commander-of

וַיִּשְׂרֹף אֶת־ בֵּית־ יְהוָה וְאֶת־ בֵּית הַמֶּלֶךְ וְאֵת כָּל־
all-of and the-king palace-of and Yahweh temple-of *** and-he-set-fire (9)

בָּתֵּי יְרוּשָׁלִַם וְאֶת־ כָּל־ בֵּית גָּדוֹל שָׂרַף בָּאֵשׁ׃
with-fire he-burned importance building-of every-of and Jerusalem houses-of

וְאֶת־ חוֹמֹת יְרוּשָׁלִַם סָבִיב נָתְצוּ כָּל־ חֵיל
army-of whole-of they-broke-down around Jerusalem walls-of and (10)

כַּשְׂדִּים אֲשֶׁר רַב־ טַבָּחִים׃ וְאֵת יֶתֶר הָעָם
the-people rest-of and (11) imperial-guards commander-of that Chaldeans

הַנִּשְׁאָרִים בָּעִיר וְאֶת־ הַנֹּפְלִים אֲשֶׁר נָפְלוּ
they-went-over who the-ones-going-over and in-the-city the-ones-remaining

עַל־ הַמֶּלֶךְ בָּבֶל וְאֵת יֶתֶר הֶהָמוֹן הֶגְלָה נְבוּזַרְאֲדָן
Nebuzaradan he-exiled the-populace rest-of and Babylon the-king-of to

רַב־ טַבָּחִים׃ וּמִדַּלַּת הָאָרֶץ הִשְׁאִיר
he-left-behind the-land but-from-poor-of (12) imperial-guards commander-of

רַב־ טַבָּחִים לְכֹרְמִים וּלְיֹגְבִים׃
and-as-ones-working-fields as-ones-working-vineyards imperial-guards commander-of

וְאֶת־ עַמּוּדֵי הַנְּחֹשֶׁת אֲשֶׁר בֵּית־ יְהוָה וְאֶת־ הַמְּכֹנוֹת
the-movable-stands and Yahweh temple-of that the-bronze pillars-of and (13)

וְאֶת־ יָם הַנְּחֹשֶׁת אֲשֶׁר בְּבֵית־ יְהוָה שִׁבְּרוּ כַשְׂדִּים
Chaldeans they-broke-up Yahweh in-temple-of that the-bronze Sea-of and

וַיִּשְׂאוּ אֶת־ נְחֻשְׁתָּם בָּבֶלָה׃ וְאֶת־ הַסִּירֹת וְאֶת־
and the-pots and (14) to-Babylon bronze-of-them *** and-they-carried

הַיָּעִים וְאֶת־ הַמְזַמְּרוֹת וְאֶת־ הַכַּפּוֹת וְאֵת כָּל־ כְּלֵי
articles-of all-of and the-ladles and the-wick-trimmers and the-shovels

הַנְּחֹשֶׁת אֲשֶׁר יְשָׁרְתוּ־ בָם לָקָחוּ׃ וְאֶת־ הַמַּחְתּוֹת וְאֶת־
and the-censers and (15) they-took with-them they-served that the-bronze

הַמִּזְרָקוֹת אֲשֶׁר זָהָב זָהָב וַאֲשֶׁר־ כֶּסֶף כֶּסֶף לָקַח
he-took-away silver silver or-that gold gold that the-sprinkling-bowls

רַב־ טַבָּחִים׃ הָעַמּוּדִים ׀ שְׁנַיִם הַיָּם הָאֶחָד
the-one the-Sea two the-pillars (16) imperial-guards commander-of

וְהַמְּכֹנוֹת אֲשֶׁר־ עָשָׂה שְׁלֹמֹה לְבֵית יְהוָה לֹא־ הָיָה
he-was not Yahweh for-temple-of Solomon he-made which and-the-movable-stands

[8]On the seventh day of the
fifth month, in the nineteenth
year of Nebuchadnezzar king
of Babylon, Nebuzaradan
commander of the imperial
guard, an official of the king of
Babylon, came to Jerusalem.
[9]He set fire to the temple of the
LORD, the royal palace and all
the houses of Jerusalem. Every
important building he burned
down. [10]The whole Babylonian army, under the com-
mander of the imperial guard,
broke down the walls around
Jerusalem. [11]Nebuzaradan the
commander of the guard carried into exile the people who
remained in the city, along
with the rest of the populace
and those who had gone over
to the king of Babylon. [12]But
the commander left behind
some of the poorest people of
the land to work the vineyards
and fields.
[13]The Babylonians broke up
the bronze pillars, the movable stands and the bronze Sea
that were at the temple of the
LORD and they carried the
bronze to Babylon. [14]They also
took away the pots, shovels,
wick trimmers, ladles and all
the bronze articles used in the
temple service. [15]The commander of the imperial guard
took away the censers and
sprinkling bowls—all that
were made of gold or silver.
[16]The bronze from the two
pillars, the Sea and the movable stands, which Solomon
had made for the temple of the
LORD, was more than could be

מִשְׁקָל לִנְחֹשֶׁת כָּל־ הַכֵּלִים הָאֵלֶּה : שְׁמֹנֶה עֶשְׂרֵה אַמָּה
cubit ten eight (17) the-these the-articles all-of of-bronze-of weight

קוֹמַת ׀ הָעַמּוּד הָאֶחָד וְכֹתֶרֶת עָלָיו ׀ נְחֹשֶׁת וְקוֹמַת
and-height-of bronze on-him and-capital the-each the-pillar height-of

הַכֹּתֶרֶת שָׁלֹשׁ אַמָּה וּשְׂבָכָה וְרִמֹּנִים עַל־ הַכֹּתֶרֶת סָבִיב
around the-capital on and-pomegranates and-network cubits three the-capital

הַכֹּל נְחֹשֶׁת וְכָאֵלֶּה לַעַמּוּד הַשֵּׁנִי עַל־ הַשְּׂבָכָה :
the-network with the-second on-the-pillar and-like-these bronze the-whole

וַיִּקַּח רַב־ טַבָּחִים אֶת־ שְׂרָיָה כֹּהֵן הָרֹאשׁ וְאֶת־
and the-chief priest-of Seraiah *** guards commander-of and-he-took (18)

צְפַנְיָהוּ כֹּהֵן מִשְׁנֶה וְאֶת־ שְׁלֹשֶׁת שֹׁמְרֵי הַסַּף :
the-door ones-keeping-of three-of and second priest-of Zephaniah

וּמִן־ הָעִיר לָקַח סָרִיס אֶחָד אֲשֶׁר־הוּא פָקִיד ׀ עַל־ אַנְשֵׁי
men-of over leader he who one officer he-took the-city and-from (19)

הַמִּלְחָמָה וַחֲמִשָּׁה אֲנָשִׁים מֵרֹאֵי פְנֵי־ הַמֶּלֶךְ אֲשֶׁר נִמְצְאוּ
they-were-found who the-king faces-of of-ones-seeing-of men and-five the-fight

בָעִיר וְאֵת הַסֹּפֵר שַׂר הַצָּבָא הַמַּצְבִּא אֶת־
*** the-one-conscripting the-host chief-of the-secretary and in-the-city

עַם הָאָרֶץ וְשִׁשִּׁים אִישׁ מֵעַם הָאָרֶץ הַנִּמְצְאִים
the-ones-being-found the-land from-people-of man and-sixty the-land people-of

בָּעִיר : וַיִּקַּח אֹתָם נְבוּזַרְאֲדָן רַב־ טַבָּחִים
guards commander-of Nebuzaradan them and-he-took (20) in-the-city

וַיֹּלֶךְ אֹתָם עַל־ מֶלֶךְ בָּבֶל רִבְלָתָה : וַיַּךְ
and-he-executed (21) at-Riblah Babylon king-of to them and-he-brought

אֹתָם מֶלֶךְ בָּבֶל וַיְמִיתֵם בְּרִבְלָה בְּאֶרֶץ חֲמָת
Hamath in-land-of at-Riblah and-he-killed-them Babylon king-of them

וַיִּגֶל יְהוּדָה מֵעַל אַדְמָתוֹ : וְהָעָם
and-the-people (22) land-of-him from-on Judah so-he-went-to-captivity

הַנִּשְׁאָר בְּאֶרֶץ יְהוּדָה אֲשֶׁר הִשְׁאִיר נְבוּכַדְנֶאצַּר
Nebuchadnezzar he-left-behind that Judah in-land-of the-one-being-left

מֶלֶךְ בָּבֶל וַיַּפְקֵד עֲלֵיהֶם אֶת־ גְּדַלְיָהוּ בֶּן־ אֲחִיקָם בֶּן־
son-of Ahikam son-of Gedeliah *** over-them then-he-appointed Babylon king-of

שָׁפָן : וַיִּשְׁמְעוּ כָל־ שָׂרֵי הַחֲיָלִים הֵמָּה וְהָאֲנָשִׁים
and-the-men they the-armies officers-of all-of when-they-heard (23) Shaphan

כִּי־ הִפְקִיד מֶלֶךְ־ בָּבֶל אֶת־ גְּדַלְיָהוּ וַיָּבֹאוּ אֶל־ גְּדַלְיָהוּ
Gedeliah to then-they-came Gedeliah *** Babylon king-of he-appointed that

הַמִּצְפָּה וְיִשְׁמָעֵאל בֶּן־ נְתַנְיָה וְיוֹחָנָן בֶּן־ קָרֵחַ וּשְׂרָיָה
and-Seraiah Kareah son-of and-Johanan Nethaniah son-of and-Ishmael the-Mizpah

weighed. [17]Each pillar was twenty-seven feet[w] high. The bronze capital on top of one pillar was four and a half feet[x] high and was decorated with a network and pomegranates of bronze all around. The other pillar, with its network, was similar.

[18]The commander of the guard took as prisoners Seraiah the chief priest, Zephaniah the priest next in rank and the three doorkeepers. [19]Of those still in the city, he took the officer in charge of the fighting men and five royal advisers. He also took the secretary who was chief officer in charge of conscripting the people of the land and sixty of his men who were found in the city. [20]Nebuzaradan the commander took them all and brought them to the king of Babylon at Riblah. [21]There at Riblah, in the land of Hamath, the king had them executed.

So Judah went into captivity, away from her land.

[22]Nebuchadnezzar king of Babylon appointed Gedaliah son of Ahikam, the son of Shaphan, to be over the people he had left behind in Judah. [23]When all the army officers and their men heard that the king of Babylon had appointed Gedaliah as governor, they came to Gedaliah at Mizpah—Ishmael son of Nethaniah, Johanan son of Kareah, Seraiah son of Tanhumeth the

w17 Hebrew *eighteen cubits* (about 8.1 meters)
x17 Hebrew *three cubits* (about 1.3 meters)

°17 ק אמות

בֶּן־ תַּנְחֻמֶת הַנְּטֹפָתִי וְיַאֲזַנְיָהוּ בֶּן־ הַמַּעֲכָתִי הֵמָּה
they the-Maacathite son-of and-Jaazaniah the-Netophathite Tanhumeth son-of

וְאַנְשֵׁיהֶם׃ וַיִּשָּׁבַע לָהֶם גְּדַלְיָהוּ וּלְאַנְשֵׁיהֶם
and-for-men-of-them Gedeliah for-them and-he-took-oath (24) and-men-of-them

וַיֹּאמֶר לָהֶם אַל־ תִּירְאוּ מֵעַבְדֵי הַכַּשְׂדִּים שְׁבוּ
settle! the-Chaldeans of-officials-of you-be-afraid not to-them and-he-said

בָאָרֶץ וְעִבְדוּ אֶת־ מֶלֶךְ בָּבֶל וְיִטַב לָכֶם׃
with-you and-he-will-go-well Babylon king-of *** and-serve! in-the-land

וַיְהִי ׀ בַּחֹדֶשׁ הַשְּׁבִיעִי בָּא יִשְׁמָעֵאל בֶּן־ נְתַנְיָה
Nethaniah son-of Ishmael he-came the-seventh in-the-month but-he-was (25)

בֶּן־ אֱלִישָׁמָע מִזֶּרַע הַמְּלוּכָה וַעֲשָׂרָה אֲנָשִׁים אִתּוֹ
with-him men and-ten the-royalty from-descendant-of Elishama son-of

וַיַּכּוּ אֶת־ גְּדַלְיָהוּ וַיָּמֹת וְאֶת־ הַיְּהוּדִים וְאֶת־
and the-Judahites and so-he-died Gedeliah *** and-they-assassinated

הַכַּשְׂדִּים אֲשֶׁר־ הָיוּ אִתּוֹ בַּמִּצְפָּה׃ וַיָּקֻמוּ כָל־
all-of and-they-rose (26) at-the-Mizpah with-him they-were who the-Chaldeans

הָעָם מִקָּטֹן וְעַד־ גָּדוֹל וְשָׂרֵי הַחֲיָלִים וַיָּבֹאוּ
and-they-fled the-armies and-officers-of great even-to from-least the-people

מִצְרַיִם כִּי יָרְאוּ מִפְּנֵי כַשְׂדִּים׃ וַיְהִי בִשְׁלֹשִׁים
in-thirty and-he-was (27) Chaldeans because-of they-feared for Egypt

וָשֶׁבַע שָׁנָה לְגָלוּת יְהוֹיָכִין מֶלֶךְ־ יְהוּדָה בִּשְׁנֵים עָשָׂר חֹדֶשׁ
month ten in-two Judah king-of Jehoiachin of-being-exiled year and-seven

בְּעֶשְׂרִים וְשִׁבְעָה לַחֹדֶשׁ נָשָׂא אֱוִיל מְרֹדַךְ מֶלֶךְ בָּבֶל
Babylon king-of Merodach Evil he-released of-the-month and-seven on-twenty

בִּשְׁנַת מָלְכוֹ אֶת־ רֹאשׁ יְהוֹיָכִין מֶלֶךְ־ יְהוּדָה
Judah king-of Jehoiachin head-of *** to-become-king-him in-year-of

מִבֵּית כֶּלֶא׃ וַיְדַבֵּר אִתּוֹ טֹבוֹת וַיִּתֵּן אֶת־
*** and-he-gave kind-things to-him and-he-spoke (28) prison from-house-of

כִּסְאוֹ מֵעַל כִּסֵּא הַמְּלָכִים אֲשֶׁר אִתּוֹ בְּבָבֶל׃
in-Babylon with-him who the-kings seat-of higher-than seat-of-him

וְשִׁנָּא אֵת בִּגְדֵי כִלְאוֹ וְאָכַל לֶחֶם תָּמִיד
regularly food and-he-ate prison-of-him clothes-of *** so-he-put-aside (29)

לְפָנָיו כָּל־ יְמֵי חַיָּיו׃ וַאֲרֻחָתוֹ
and-allowance-of-him (30) lives-of-him days-of all-of before-him

אֲרֻחַת תָּמִיד נִתְּנָה־ לּוֹ מֵאֵת הַמֶּלֶךְ דְּבַר־ יוֹם
day matter-of the-king from to-him she-was-given regular allowance-of

בְּיוֹמוֹ כֹּל יְמֵי חַיָּו׃
life-of-him days-of all-of by-day-of-him

Netophathite, Jaazaniah the
son of the Maacathite, and
their men. 24Gedaliah took an
oath to reassure them and
their men. "Do not be afraid of
the Babylonian officials," he
said. "Settle down in the land
and serve the king of Babylon,
and it will go well with you."
25In the seventh month,
however, Ishmael son of
Nethaniah, the son of Elishama, who was of royal
blood, came with ten men and
assassinated Gedaliah and
also the men of Judah and the
Babylonians who were with
him at Mizpah. 26At this, all
the people from the least to the
greatest, together with the
army officers, fled to Egypt for
fear of the Babylonians.

Jehoiachin Released

27In the thirty-seventh year
of the exile of Jehoiachin king
of Judah, in the year Evil-Merodach[y] became king of
Babylon, he released Jehoiachin from prison on the
twenty-seventh day of the
twelfth month. 28He spoke
kindly to him and gave him a
seat of honor higher than
those of the other kings who
were with him in Babylon.
29So Jehoiachin put aside his
prison clothes and for the rest
of his life ate regularly at the
king's table. 30Day by day the
king gave Jehoiachin a regular
allowance as long as he lived.

[y]27 Also called *Amel-Marduk*